AMERICA
AS A
CIVILIZATION

Also by Max Lerner

It is Later Than You Think
Ideas are Weapons
Ideas for the Ice Age
The Mind and Faith of Justice Holmes
Public Journal
The Portable Veblen
Actions and Passions
The Unfinished Country
The Age of Overkill
Education and a Radical Humanism
Tocqueville and American Civilization
Values in Education
Ted and the Kennedy Legend

THIRTIETH ANNIVERSARY EDITION

AMERICA AS A CIVILIZATION

LIFE AND THOUGHT IN THE UNITED STATES TODAY

With a Postscript Chapter
The New America
1957—1987

Max Lerner

HENRY HOLT AND COMPANY
New York

Copyright © 1957, 1987 by Max Lerner
All rights reserved, including the right to reproduce this
book or portions thereof in any form.
Published by Henry Holt and Company, Inc.,
521 Fifth Avenue, New York, New York 10175.
Published in Canada by Fitzhenry & Whiteside Limited,
195 Allstate Parkway, Markham, Ontario L3R 4T8.

Library of Congress Cataloging-in-Publication Data
Lerner, Max, 1902–
America as a civilization.
"With a postscript chapter: The new America: 1957–1987."
Originally published: New York: Simon and Schuster, 1957.
Includes bibliographical references and index.
1. United States—Civilization. 2. National
characteristics, American. I. Title.
E169.12.L45   1987   973   87-11941
ISBN 0-8050-0531-5
ISBN 0-8050-0355-X (pbk.) (An Owl book)

First published in hardcover
by Simon and Schuster, Inc. in 1957.
First Owl Book Edition—1987

Printed in the United States of America
1   3   5   7   9   10   8   6   4   2

"On an Invitation to the United States," by Thomas Hardy, from
The Complete Poems of Thomas Hardy, edited by James Gibson (New
York: Macmillan, 1978).

Prose translation of Goethe poem is reprinted with permission of
Macmillan Publishing Company from *The American Spirit* by
Charles A. Beard and Mary R. Beard. Copyright 1942 by Macmillan Publishing Company, renewed 1970 by William Beard
and Miriam B. Vagts.

Excerpt "Oil Painting of the Artist as the Artist" from "Frescoes
for Mr. Rockefeller's City," in *New and Collected Poems 1917–
1982* by Archibald MacLeish. Copyright © 1985 by The Estate
of Archibald MacLeish. Reprinted by permission of Houghton
Mifflin Company.

"America Remembers," from *American Song* by Paul Engle, Copyright 1933 by Doubleday & Company, Inc. Reprinted by permission of the publisher.

ISBN 0-8050-0531-5 HARDBOUND
ISBN 0-8050-0355-X PAPERBACK

FOR
MICHAEL
AND HIS GENERATION

Contents

Foreword to the Thirtieth Anniversary Edition

THIS is both an old book and a new one. Several times during the decades after its publication in December 1957 I was told that by updating the statistics and noting the new research I could keep the revised book in tune with the new decades of readers. But my gut feeling resisted it. If I substituted up-to-date figures for the old ones, and took account of changing trends in American thought and character, the original analysis would (I felt) look awry at the new material, and the new material in turn would feel a stranger in the home of the old analysis. The congruity of frame and detail, I felt, was too basic to tamper with. I had never intended it as a textbook but as a discourse.

The decades passed. The original hardcover became a two-volume paperback which happily stayed in print longer than I had counted on. Times changed, and with them the detailed short-range variables of American life. But the permanences didn't, so I let the book stand.

From the start, working on it from 1945 to 1957, I tried to get at the continuities and permanences. For all their differences in angles of vision the reviewers were generous, just as my original consultants had been when I submitted sections of the book for their expert criticism. A civilization overview like this stretched the information sheath I needed, but it evoked a cooperative response from an intellectual community which at that time still had a considerable nucleus of shared values. If these special readers kept me from errors in specialized areas, my analytical and philosophical frame was my own.

Thirty years later I offer the book again with an added chapter at a time when there is probably less scholarly consensus than at the original publication. I risk the outcome because I care about the intellectual and moral dialogue on America as a civilization and want it to be an ongoing one. I offer both book and chapter to a new generation of scholars and students, but also to the common reader in whose experience of American life all overviews must be embedded.

As an Afterword chapter, "The New America: 1957–1987," I have written a longish essay for this edition, letting it stand alongside the original book in the hope that each would shed light on the other. I am indebted to discussions with my faculty associates, and students at the University of Notre Dame, where I held the Welch Chair in American Studies from 1982–1984, and at the Graduate School of Human Behavior at U.S. International University (at San Diego), where I have had the freedom and excitement of formulating the outlines of an emerging America since 1974, in my seminars on civilizational changes and continuities. I am indebted throughout to my seminar colleague, Priscilla Norton. I owe a debt also to my editor, Richard Seaver, and to my assistant, Evelyn Irsay, both of whom made everything possible and writing a joy.

Foreword

AMERICANS are beginning to turn a searchlight on themselves and their civilization, and interpret both to the world. The present study is intended as a trial essay in this direction.

I start with what the book is not—neither a history of American civilization nor a description of life today in the American regions, states, and cities. Both have been done well by a number of scholars and journalists. Nor have I written here an indictment or apologia, either a celebration of "the American way" or a lament about it. Finally, this is not a "whither, whither" book embodying the prophecy of disaster. In short, those who are looking for the historical, the descriptive, the polemic, or the apocalyptic must look elsewhere.

What I have tried, rather, is to grasp—however awkwardly—the pattern and inner meaning of contemporary American civilization and its relation to the world of today.

A personal word may not be out of place. You write a book not for the elaborate reasons you spell out but mainly because you can't help it. Whatever I have written, thought, felt in the past has converged on the grand theme of the nature and meaning of the American experience. Whenever I have tried to chip off a fragment—on American government, on liberalism, on foreign policy, on morals—I found that it lost some of its meaning when torn from the rest. Yet to attempt the subject as a whole seemed a formidable, even arrogant, task. In 1945 I finally overrode my hesitation and started the book on its present scale. It has been more than a decade in the writing.

No American, perhaps no one alive today, can pretend to view American civilization with an anthropological detachment. The "anthropological attitude" (Kroeber) and the "sense of cultural shock" (Benedict) come from seeing values in a culture almost wholly disparate from your own. No American can achieve detachment in studying America, and I doubt whether even a European or Asian can. Paraphrasing Lord Acton, one might say that the only detached student of American civilization would be a dead one, since he would no longer care. The best you can do to achieve perspective is to keep a certain emotional distance from your

*subject. When the subject is your own people and civilization it is hard
to keep the distance. Your hopes and fears for America manage to break
through and color the analysis.*

*Obviously any book about America published at a time of interna-
tional discord and seething world revolution is bound to be interpreted
within this frame of planetary turmoil, and the question will inevitably
be asked whether this book is "for" or "against" America, whether it is
a rosy and euphoric picture seen in a haze of promise or an unsparing
indictment.*

*I have tried to avoid both these sins—for an American the sin of com-
placency and the sin of self-hatred. I love my country and my culture,
but it is no service to them, nor to the creed of democracy, to gloss over
the rough facts of American life. Similarly, much have I traveled in the
realms of Europe and Asia—and even in the realms of Marx and Veblen
—and if there is a single count in the anti-American indictment I have
not at some point confronted, it has not been through lack of diligence
or realism. But it would be no service to the most committed critics of
America to give them a distorted picture of American civilization only
in order to nourish their distaste. Let the great world debate about
America go on as it will and must: the task I set for myself is intended
to have no strategic relation to it.*

*America is by any standard a towering technology and culture, with
economic, military, and political power, the only rival power-mass being
Russia. Wherever you find so much vitality packed tightly in a segment
of human society, it is evidence of a striking convergence of history, environment, biological stock, psychological traits, institutional patterns,
collective will and drive. When such a combination catches fire in the
world's imagination and polarizes the emotional energies of men—
whether for love or hate—you have a memorable civilization.*

*In dealing with something so provocative it is easy to be waylaid by
the transient and miss the enduring. I have tried to remember that political struggles and economic programs wither and grow stale, the controversies which fill the pages of today's press become jangled images
tomorrow, and party leaders end up as dimly remembered steel-plate
engravings in the history books. America is not only changes and chances.
It is also permanence.*

*That is why the questions I ask about Americans are those one would
have to ask about the people of any great civilization. What are their
traditions, biological stock, environments? How do they make a living,*

govern themselves, handle the inevitable problems of power and freedom? How are they divided into ethnic and class groupings? What are
they like in their deep and enduring strains? What is their life history
like, in its characteristic phases from birth to death? How do they court,
marry, bring up and educate children? How do they work, play, and express their creativeness in art and literature? What are the connective
and organizing principles that hold their civilization together? What
gods do they worship, what beliefs hold them in thrall or give them
strength, what attitudes do they own up to, what convictions animate
them, what culture patterns do they move in, what dreams are they
moved by, what myths run through their being, what incentives propel
them, what fears restrain them, what forms of power invest their striving, what tensions and divisions tear them apart, what sense of society
cements them?

What, in short, is it that makes America not "a congeries of possessors
and pursuers," of individual wills and greeds and collective power, but
a civilization?*

M. L.

* For acknowledgments of my indebtedness in writing this book, see *Acknowledgments* and *Notes for Further Reading* at the end, p. 951 ff.

CHAPTER I

Heritage

IN WHICH we start by examining American history as folk memory and evoking the American spirit in a succession of images from the past ("The Sense of the Past"). We trace the emergence of the American heritage out of the conquest of the continent, the slavery experience, and the great migrations ("The Sources of the Heritage"), and assess the emotional impact of these migrations on the American mind ("The Slaying of the European Father"). We consider the ways in which American history has been written and the theories advanced for the greatness and power America has reached ("Why Was America a Success?"), and reconsider the Turner theory of the frontier ("American History As Extended Genesis"). Reflecting on the cult of the American tradition and the emergence of a "new conservatism" ("Tradition and the Frame of Power"), we end by focusing on some crucial elements which run through what is usually called the "American spirit" ("American Dynamism"). The chapter as a whole is an effort to evoke the American spirit by evoking its past, and to interpret the American tradition as a living heritage with changing meanings.

CHAPTER I

Heritage

1. The Sense of the Past

LIKE a person, a civilization is more than the sum of its parts. Describe a man's features, give his life history, tell where he lives and how, place him in his class or group, define his ethics and politics—and still you will not have the man himself. What slips through is his total style, quick and dead: whatever it is that makes him himself, and different from other men. Thus St. Francis had a style, and Samuel Johnson, Martin Luther, Voltaire, and Dean Swift, Alexander and Asoka, Napoleon and Goethe, Lincoln and Carnegie and Justice Holmes. History remembers this about the great men, but the rest of us remember it also about the nameless people we have known: remember the way they moved, their tricks of speech and habit, their taut or relaxed quality, the superfluous things they did and with what grace or clumsiness, what cavalry pounded through their brain, what inner battles they fought.

So it is with a civilization. When you have described its people, armies, technology, economics, politics, arts, regions and cities, class and caste, mores and morals, there is something elusive left—an inner civilization style.

In Lytton Strachey's biography, *Queen Victoria,* there is a climactic (if unhistoric) scene, with the queen lying on her deathbed as the memorable events of her life pass through her mind. A people too has its sense of the past—the remembered record of what happened, the force of the collective experience. The individual American may know little of history and is probably inarticulate about what he does know. But if (using Carl Becker's phrase) everyman is his own historian, it is because he is in some measure a sifter and selecter of his nation's past—of the quickening ideas, the hardships and heroisms, the degradation and injustices, the boisterous fables. "Everyman" will have a very different picture of the American past from that of the cultivated scholars, yet there will be something in common between them. I venture to pass some of the heritage quickly in kaleidoscopic review as it has unrolled—half myth, half fact—in the minds of many Americans from high-school age to maturity.

. . . The voyage of adventure and discovery across the far seas, *mundus novus,* the English sea dogs and the Spanish conquistadores, Cortes being

3

worshiped as a god by the Indians of the Mexicos, De Soto's body tied up in a sack and dropped into the Mississippi which he had discovered. The quest of gold and new lands for the glory of God and the enrichment of divine-right monarchs and proprietary landlords. The odyssey of the first settlers amidst scurvy, dysentery and filth in the holds of ships—an odyssey to be re-enacted by the shiploads of indentured servants, the slave ships from Africa, and in the steerage of the later immigration. The rigors of the early settlements, caught between the sea and the woods, winter and the savages. The dream of a new Jerusalem on a rockbound coast. The dark forest, the thrust into the unknown; the wild birds flying, the huge turkeys, the ospreys and eagles, the deer, the fields red with strawberries; the Indian corn and the tobacco crops; the furs of beaver, otter, muskrat, racoon.

The coming of explorer, conqueror, trader, missionary, colonizer. The painted dignity of savage chieftains on the red man's continent; the land bought of them for a few gimcracks, the twists and cunning of English land law, the despoiling of a people; the struggle of European empires for a hold on a new continent. The stockade settlements, the lonely vigils, the descent of terror out of the darkness, the scalpings and massacres, the long captivities. The Pilgrims and Puritans, little theocratic communities encroaching on the wilderness; the metaphysical passion which had crossed the oceans expressing itself in a belief in demonology and possession. The satanic apparitions, the constant living within the frame of an invisible malignant world. The idea of faith and salvation, prosperity and Heaven, filling the whole ambit of life; the interminable sermons, the droning hymns, the impassioned harangues of the revivalists.

The colonist as a Southern gentleman riding among his tobacco fields. The building and sailing of ships; the rise of manufactures, of cities, wharves and warehouses. The transplanting from England of the idea of compact; schools springing up in the unlikely wilderness—William and Mary, Harvard, Boston Latin. Lawyers marshaling their arguments not only for their clients but for the colonies, editors setting in type thunderbolts against governors and judges. Rebellious voices raised against patrician landlords and rich merchants as well as against foreign tyrannies. James Otis, in barrister's gown, arguing before the Massachusetts judges against the "writs of assistance"; young American politicians searching in the classics for "natural rights" and the fundamentals of governmental theory. The town meetings, the Burgesses, the new phenomenon of a society of planters and merchants who meant to rule themselves, and joined with artisans and farmers for that purpose. The spate of hot, angry pamphlets; "taxation without representation"; the Sons of Liberty and the committees of correspondence; the splitting of the tea chests in the solemn painted mummery at Griffin's Wharf in the quiet Boston night; the voice of a Plutarchian hero from Virginia—"Is life so dear or peace so sweet as to be purchased at the price of chains and slavery?"; the drilling of young men on the village commons, the first blood spilled by the early-morning gunfire at Lexington. Paine's words: "The blood of the slain, the weeping voice of Nature cries, ' 'Tis time to part.' " The clear, firm Declaration: "We hold these truths to be self-evident"; the huddled little "rabble in arms" shivering in winter quarters, without food or pay or hope in an unending war; "You might have tracked the army by the blood of their feet"; spies and betrayals, "the summer soldier and the sunshine patriot." The dignity and the moral strength of Washington, the bootless British victories, the guerrilla warfare in the hills from the Green Mountains to the Catawba and the Santee, the freeing of the Northwest, American diplomats asking help at European courts, the surrender at Yorktown. The new free republic on this continent.

With freedom won, the Revolutionary soldiers coming home to feeble and vulnerable times; Daniel Shays and his debt-ridden farmers; the Founding Fathers assembled at Independence Hall, the swirling debates and compromises among the men of substance; the signing of the Constitution; Franklin saying gracefully, "It is the rising, not the setting sun." Three men putting down in *The Federalist* the fundamentals of power and stability in human society. The Bill of Rights forced through at the insistence of Jefferson and his followers. Washington being rowed across New York Harbor on an Inaugural barge and riding under triumphal arches to become the first President of the United States of America. The new statesmen and the first great State Papers; a tall soldier leaving his farewell admonitions to his people; the straggling village on the Potomac that became the new Capital; Abigail Adams, as First Lady, hanging her washing to dry in the unfinished Audience Room at the White House. The struggle between aristocracy and democracy, between property and Populism; the leaders fearful of parties but powerless to prevent their rise; the fight against the Sedition Acts and the conviction of ten editors and printers; the rising tide of democratic belief, the Republic moving toward a Democracy. The "Jeffersonian Revolution"; "we are all Republicans, we are all Federalists"; the vast new accession of American earth in the Louisiana Purchase; the embargo, the young War Hawks, and "Mr. Madison's War"; the burning of Washington ("this harbor of Yankee democracy") by Admiral Cockburn; the heroism of the little American frigates in battle, "We have met the enemy, and they are ours." The young eagle nation spreading its wings in the judicial nationalism of John Marshall's decisions and the political nationalism of Monroe's challenge to the European Powers.

The triple forward movement of the frontier, the machine, and the democratic surge.

The pushing onward of the frontier lines, sporadically but with a persistent thrust toward expansion; the traders and hunters, scouts, missionaries and settlers—a nation of backwoodsmen; Lewis and Clark as the explorers of a nation's destiny; Calhoun saying in 1817, "We are greatly and rapidly—I was about to say fearfully—growing"; the armada of prairie schooners, with their human freight, crossing the mountains and plains; "a rifle, an axe, and a bag of corn." The ways of the pioneers, the rough working and drinking and playing, the cornhusking frolics, the brawling and wrestling and eye-gouging, the Yankee and backwoodsman as folk characters; "the gamecock of the wilderness," the Mike Fink and Davy Crockett legends, the tall stories, the comic boasting: "Sired by a hurricane, dam'd by an earthquake, half-brother to the cholera . . . Whoo-oop! I'm the bloodiest son of a wildcat that lives." The circuit-riding lawyers and doctors and preachers, the "old-time religion." The constant danger and constant beauty of life; the great plains, the canals, the torrential, muddy rivers, the rafts and flatboats and keelboats, and then the river steamers. The Mississippi as the grand highway of a new continent. "Remember the Alamo," "Manifest Destiny," Frémont crossing the mountains into Sacramento Valley, the gold at Sutter's Mill, the race of the clipper ships to San Francisco. The mushrooming mining camps and cowtowns, the long drive north of the Texas longhorns to the railheads, the open range turned into barbed-wire enclosures, a continent rounded out.

The new frontiers of the brain's cunning; American tinkering, the spate of inventions, the heyday of the Yankee toolmakers, the march of the machine across the American spirit; factories jostling the wharves, jutting out into the prairies; the mill girls at Lowell, child workers in mines. Cotton spreading along the Gulf plain, and Negro hands to pick the snowy harvest. The rich earth caught up in the disk plow and automatic reaper, the span of far distances shrunk by railroad ties and the telegraphic spark. Wealth untold spilling out of the land and machines and human hands.

The rise of democracy. The assertive common man, with muddy boots, stomping into the White House at Jackson's Inaugural. Old Hickory's struggle against Biddle and the Bank. Free homesteads, free schools, the whittling away of suffrage restrictions, the battle cry of States' Rights. The fall of King Caucus, the hysteria of the party convention, the rise of the political managers, the clan spirit of the Irish countryman transposed to make the ward machine run. Thoreau in Concord jail asking Emerson what he was doing outside; Melville's pursuit of Moby Dick through the whale waters; the ferment of social revolt; Dorr's Rebellion in Rhode Island; the dream of perfectibility at Brook Farm and the phalansteries; Walt Whitman on the Brooklyn Ferry glimpsing his democratic vistas.

The division of a nation into two economies and two ways of life, the tyranny of King Cotton over the mind of the Old South, the Confederate dream of a Greek republic founded on slavery on the shores of the Gulf, the shadow of slaves' chains falling across the American soul. The slave revolts and the massacres on both sides, the underground railroad, the knock in the rainy night; the heroism of Frederick Douglass and Harriet Tubman, John Brown at the arsenal at Harpers Ferry. The days of the great Senate debates, a gangling boy growing up in Illinois, "a house divided against itself cannot stand," the Presidential car transferred from one station to another at Baltimore in the quiet of the early hours. The freeing of the slaves, the draft riots, Lincoln passing long lines of hospital cots with rough jokes to hide the heart's sorrow; the scene at Gettysburg, "the world will little note nor long remember"; the burning bales of cotton in Southern ports, brothers killing brothers in the Battle of the Wilderness, Sherman's march to the sea; two soldiers at Appomattox. "With malice toward none," the fateful course of Booth's bullet, the tragic mask of death, "when lilacs last in the dooryard bloom'd." The grim, stony faces of the whites in Southern legislatures, the carpetbaggers, the bewildered freedmen, terror-riders in the Southern darkness, the tragic heritage of civil conflict.

The corruptions of the "Gilded Age," the buying and selling of the American promise. The rise of the business giant: "industrial statesman" or "robber baron"? The new empires of finance, the gushing streams of profit from oil, steel, railroads, lumber; the strenuous ascent to fortune; power sitting on top of a heap of money. The cult of size and magnificence, the gleaming confidence of the self-made man, the brownstone fronts on Fifth Avenue, "society" at Newport. The alternation of boom and bust; the Populist upsurge, the Anarchist bomb and the ordeal of Altgeld, young Billy Bryan from the River Platte, the obsession of Henry George with the single tax, Bellamy's dream of a socialist utopia, the scientific politics of Mark Hanna. The swarming of immigrants to the promised land, "your tired, your poor, your huddled masses, yearning to breathe free." Sam Gompers reading to a shopful of cigar-makers; the flare-ups of violence, the sputtering of dynamite across the land. The victorious imperialists coming back from "Mr. Hearst's war" to be annihilated by Mr. Dooley and Mark Twain. The rising energies of the quest for social justice; the Roughrider jousting both at the "muckrakers" and at the "malefactors of great wealth," Holmes on the Supreme Court impaling a dogma on a phrase, Brandeis as "the People's Attorney," Thorstein Veblen's corroding polysyllables, T.R.'s "New Nationalism," Woodrow Wilson's "New Freedom."

America taking its place as a world power. The long shadow of Sarajevo; parades, embarkations, high hopes; American blood and wealth flowing into Europe, turning the tide of war; a former Princeton profes-

sor landing on European shores, cheered by European throngs, to sit in
the mirrored halls of Versailles as the innocent arbiter of world order. A
spent President, stricken on his train in the West; the killing of the
League of Nations—a masque of death. Sacco and Vanzetti and the radical hunts; the illusion of "normalcy" in a world without landmarks; the
closing of the "golden door" against the immigrant; the greed and slackness of Teapot Dome; "Silent Cal" Coolidge saying that "the business of
America is business." The Babylonianism of American life in the twenties; the movie cathedrals, black-veiled women swooning over Valentino's
grave, greed and violence spilling over into rackets and hijacking, the
alchemy of getting something for nothing, the tumbling walls of a stock-
market Jericho. The "battle of Anacostia Flats," the trek across the Dust
Bowl, the "Grapes of Wrath," the shutting of the banks, the bread lines
and unemployment. A paralyzed President lighting again the fires of the
American will; "the only thing we have to fear is fear itself"; the Blue
Eagle and the other symbols of a collective effort; the battle over the
New Deal; "we have only just begun to fight"; the achievement of the
TVA, the soil of democracy still rich at the grass roots.

The new monster shapes across the world, America too stricken with
its own maladies to care, then rising like a Gulliver lumberingly to its
full height. The shattered hulks at Pearl Harbor: "a day that will live in
infamy." The fighting and death on foreign soil; the memories of great
battlefields of the world wars—the village of Saint-Mihiel, the sun-
beaten rock of Corregidor, the volcanic sand of Iwo Jima, the desert at
Kasserine Pass, the rubble at Monte Cassino, the shattered fir trees of
Hurtgen Forest, the landings at Omaha Beach and Tarawa, the crossing
of Remagen Bridge, the rains and the mud at Guadalcanal. The American soldier, wandering like Odysseus over the far places of the world,
always turning by a sure instinct back to the home of his remembrance.
A haggard man in a blue cloak posing for pictures at Yalta. The news
from Warm Springs, the people mourning in the streets. A huddle of
scientists waiting for a blast in a trench at Los Alamos, the fateful plane
over Hiroshima. The precarious infancy of the UN, the soldier in the
White House struggling with problems of peace. The power and the
challenge and the anxiety forever and ever. . . .

The troubled reader will say, "But this is not history; it is imagism."
He will be right. It is a history of the American *imago*, a memorandum
on American history couched not in terms of forces, causes, or events but
of images picked from the national tradition. What it recalls is not "eras"
and "factors" but dramatic moments, crisis situations, sometimes only
stereotyped episodes and hackneyed slogans. It rests on the premise that
memories help to shape the style of a people as they do of a person.

Yet the charge has often been made that Americans, unlike the history-saturated European or Asiatic peoples, are a people without a history. To be historyless is presumably to lack tradition and texture, complex motivation, nuances of the spirit. It is to be, not an old gnarled tree with its roots deep in the rich soil of the past, but a row of young saplings planted in haste and standing surface-deep against a lorn sky. Much of this charge is compressed in Thomas Hardy's answer when he was invited to visit America:

> *I shrink to seek a modern coast*
> *Whose riper times have yet to be;*
> *Where the new regions claim them free*
> *From that long drip of human tears*
> *Which people old in tragedy*
> *Have left upon the centuried years.*

Hardy, who was sensitive to the style of his own European civilization, proved himself insensitive to the very different style of the American. Goethe, writing a century earlier in 1827 on the eve of the Jacksonian era, felt a greater sympathy for the republic whose memories had scarcely begun to accumulate. As he suggests, the American experience is happily free from the Old World sense of the past, which clusters around great landed families, Junkerism, aristocracy, and what Spengler later called *"Blut und Boden."** And Hegel joined with him when he said that

> * Amerika, du hast es besser
> Als unser Kontinent, der alte,
> Du hast keine verfallenen Schlosser
> Und keine Basalte.
>
> Dich stort nicht im Innern
> Zu lebendiger Zeit
> Unnutzes Errinern
> Und vergeblicher Streit.
>
> Benutzt die Gegenwart mit Gluck!
> Und wenn nun eure Kinder dichten,
> Bewahre sie ein gut' Geschick
> Vor Ritter-, Rauber-und Gespenstergeschichten.

I take this from Charles and Mary Beard's *The American Spirit* (1942), pp. 147-8. Freely translated, it might read:

> America, thou farest better
> Than our own continent, the old one,
> Thou hast no crumbling castles,
> No basalt wreckage.
>
> Thou art not shaken in this hour of life
> By useless memories and futile strife.
>
> Take the Present with joy,
> And when thy children write their songs
> May good luck guard them well
> From tales of knights, robbers, and ghosts.

"America is the land of the future where, in the ages that lie before us, the burden of the world's history shall reveal itself."*

America has not, of course, achieved the mellowness of long continuities, nor has it been inbred long enough to fashion many ethnic uniformities. But it has been a crossroads for the sweep of cultural battles in the Western world, just as surely as the tablelands of the Eurasian plateau were a geographical crossroads for the sweep of invasion and conquest. The nomadism that made the rovers of the Asiatic grasslands "land sailors" (in the picturesque phrase of Sir John Maynard) was transmuted, in the American instance, into the social wayfaring that we call American mobility. The American tradition has grown by movement, not by sitting.

There was a period in American life when Americans—perhaps ashamed of their raw, booming growth, and convinced they were historyless—tried to atone for it by reverence for Old World sites. But that phase is over, as evidenced by Archibald MacLeish's answer to such an unhappy Miniver Cheevy:

> The Cinquecento is nothing at all like Nome
> Or Natchez or Wounded Knee or the Shenandoah;
>
> Your vulgarity Tennessee; your violence Texas
> The rocks under your fields Ohio Connecticut;
>
> Your clay Missouri your clay; you have driven him out;
> You have shadowed his life Appalachians purple mountains
>
> There is much too much of your flowing Mississippi;
> He prefers a tidier stream with a terrace for trippers and
>
> Cypresses mentioned in Horace or Henry James:
> He prefers a country where everything carries the name of
>
> Countess or real king or an actual palace . . .
>
> (From "Frescoes for Mr. Rockefeller's City")

The American sense of the past is not a fumbling for ancestors or a nostalgia for ruins. But the fact that Americans have an assurance about their future does not exclude a pride about their past—a past whose roots (as we shall see) reach deep and spread widely.

* From the *Philosophy of History*, first given as lectures in 1822, published after his death.

2. *The Sources of the Heritage*

AMERICA WAS BORN out of the first stages of the breakup of Europe, and helped the process of breakup. As a colonizing and imperial continent, Europe gave largely of its strength and heritage to the civilization which was destined to replace it in power and vitality. The richest resource of a civilization is the people themselves, and the most important fact about a people is the life force carried along from its cultural origins and crossed, blended, and transmuted with others in a developing civilization.

Generalizations about the "American tradition" are difficult because there are as many subtraditions as there were national and ethnic groups that came to America, and each has left a heritage. Usually the writers on American immigration have in mind only the white immigrants, largely the European whites. Actually there were four great separable migration families that moved to the American continent. The first was probably from Asia—that of the men who formed the strain of the American Indians. The second was from the British Isles and western Europe. The third was from Africa—the Negro strain. The fourth was from Mediterranean, central, and eastern Europe, from Asia, from Latin America and everywhere else—the polyglot ethnic strain.

In a long section of De Tocqueville,* there is a remarkable study in the contact and clash of three of these ethnic cultures in the America of his own day—the Indian, the Negro, and the European. De Tocqueville describes the extermination of the first by the predacity of the conquerors, the degradation of the second by slavery, and the effects of both in turn on the third, who were the possessors and pursuers.

How long ago the men who were to become the American Indians first came over from Asia, probably across the Bering Strait, is still in dispute. Estimates vary from two or three thousand years to twenty-five thousand. Nor is it clear whether there was a single migration or as many as five or six. Today most of the Indians both of North and South America live in such squalor that it is hard to see them as the heirs of the cultural splendor of the past. Yet there is little question that in their crops, hunts, wars, and celebrations, their language and dance, myths, rituals, magic and gods, their kinship systems, social organization, law and government, symbolism, art and decoration, the Indian cultures were not simply those of "painted savages." Whether it was the highly polished Mayan and Aztec cultures of Mexico and Guatemala, or the Inca culture of Peru, or

* *Democracy in America,* "On the Present and Probable Future Condition of the Three Races That Inherit the Territory of the United States," Bradley ed. (Anchor Books), Vol. 1, Ch. XVIII, pp. 343-452.

that of the Plains Indians in North America, they made up an impressive network of civilizations.

Impressive, that is, except in their power of defense against the men of the West. Their first response to the conquistadores and in the Caribbean area was gentle and even receptive. For a breathless moment the Indian may have felt that the white man was Quetzalcoatl, the liberating hero whose return he was expecting; but the illusion vanished and he saw the Spaniards for what they were: treasure-hunters, conquerors, enslavers. They took the land without compunction, seized the wealth of the temples and palaces, shackled the Indians throughout New Spain with a form of land tenure—the encomienda—that was in effect a system of forced labor. There followed bloody resistance and insurrection, bloodily put down. The barbarism of the conquest aroused a barbarism of the conquered, which proved true as well for the Plains Indians of North America, where the English and French joined the Spanish as conquerors.

But for all their fierceness when aroused, the Indians were like spindrift before the great tides of European immigration and settlement and the powerful movement northward and westward. They were helpless against such weapons of civilization as gunfire and alcohol, European land systems and speculators, traders and treaty-makers, force and fraud, tuberculosis and measles. They became the victims of a cruel cold war whose story no American historian has been able to relate with pride. It is a story of implacable pressure on one side and of bitterly resentful yielding on the other. In the U.S. they were finally assigned to reservations, their culture all but wiped out. There is a biting irony in De Tocqueville's closing paragraph:

> The Spaniards were unable to exterminate the Indian race by those unparalleled atrocities which brand them with indelible shame, nor did even succeed in wholly depriving it of its rights; but the Americans of the United States have accomplished this twofold purpose with singular felicity; tranquilly, legally, philanthropically, without shedding blood, and without violating a single great principle of morality in the eyes of the world. It is impossible to destroy men with more respect for humanity.

It would be hard to imagine two cultures more cross-grained and less likely to mix than the Indian and European. On the one hand there was the culture of the western European conquerors, which already showed signs of what was to become a technical, rationalist, highly mobile and acquisitive society. On the other there was the symbolic, nonrational, ritualist, passive culture of the Indians. One was dynamic, and had either to conquer or be conquered. The other could not achieve the first or suffer the second.

The methods of settlement revealed something of the outlook and inner conflicts of the colonizing Powers. The Spanish, their own economic life weakened by their religious policies, needed the New World's wealth and tried to get it too quickly. Their leaders were often brave and sometimes brilliant men, but they made implacable enemies of the Indians, using up their labor power ruthlessly but shaping no institutions to fit the needs of the New World. Otherwise they left a strong heritage behind, of language and blood and religion, and if they had been able to consolidate their foothold on the American Continent and keep the later British settlements out, the whole political and social history of America would have been different.

The British came to America carrying with them high principles of morality, religious freedom, and the rule of law. Unable to give scope to their expansive thrust (as the Spaniards did) in the name of religion, they suppressed it, and the dammed-up aggressions found another outlet. They came to identify God, freedom, and acquisitiveness with the image of the continent they were seeking to possess. If there had been room for the Indian in such a scheme, they would have included him. The Indian might have made an effort to absorb the culture of the Europeans, might have adopted wholly the settled ways of agriculture and industry, learned new techniques as well as a new language and a new religion, accepted work as a means both to earthly accumulation and Divine Grace, and stripped himself of the values which linked him with the inner social structure of family, village-community, and tribe. But even when some of the tribes made the effort, as with the Cherokees in Georgia, it didn't work. On one side there was a burning resentment at being thrust out of land and hunting grounds, on the other a haste at staking out and possessing a continent. The whole policy of Indian removal and reservations in the Southern territory was aimed at opening the Cotton Kingdom for the Southern slaveholder. Take the Puritan assurance of an inner rightness of purpose, plus the 100 per-centism of the Yankee spirit of "go" and "get," plus the land hunger of the pioneer and the profit hunger of the land speculator, plus the dynamism of the "westward course of empire" and the doctrine of America's "Manifest Destiny"—add these and you get the fateful formula of the doom of the Indian culture.

When the Indians held out against selling their land for almost nothing the whites solemnly made treaties with them and gaily broke them. When the Indians learned to combine for a stand, as with Pontiac and Osceola, the whites used their superior technology and overwhelmed them. Leaders like Washington and Marshall felt a sense of shame. But Washington's attack on the land speculators was ignored, and when Chief Justice Marshall rendered his decision in *Worcester v. Georgia* (1832) confirming the right of the Cherokees as "a distinct community, occupying its own territory . . . in which the laws of Georgia can have no force," and reserving Indian treaty relations to the Federal government, Jackson's reported answer, "John Marshall has made his decision— now let him enforce it," showed (even if the remark itself was legendary) the ruthless purpose inherent in the New Order that was arising. This New Order disposed of the hope of Indian survival as an autonomous subculture within the larger culture.

Yet the Indians left their mark on the conquerors. It reaches beyond the crops they gave America, beyond the wonderful place names and the heritage of woodlore and woodcraft, much of which became part of the growing-up years of American boys. The real mark was the image the Indian left of himself.

The early Americans, not as deeply impressed by the "noble savage" image as the French Romantic writers, could not idealize the Indian when he was an ever-present enemy. Every people needs a symbol of hostility and even savagery to round out the picture of the hardships of its beginnings and to bolster the boastings of its heroism and virility. The tales of sudden descent of Indians on white villages became part of American memory—the burnings and pillagings, the swing of the tomahawk, the transporting of victims into captivity, the babies with their skulls bashed against the trees, the burning at the stake, the burial alive to the most grisly accompaniments of torture. It is now clear that much of this savagery was real, but much also was legendary, born of the overwrought imagination of contemporaries. For the Puritans and their descendants the image of the Indian filled a psychic need as a graphic representation of the hard pilgrimage in this world and the terror in the next—a sort of native background for an American *Pilgrim's Progress*.

Just when the Indian himself was at the point of being destroyed, a new image of him was forming in the mind of the white. Fenimore Cooper's generation found his portrayal of the Indian not only romantically appealing but psychologically valid. While he idealized the young Indian braves, he drew "bad" as well as "good" Indians. What he said was that heroes and villains were to be found among them pretty much as among the whites. If Cooper relied mainly on printed sources, George Catlin spent years traveling among the Indians and painted them from life—Red Jacket, the great orator of the Senecas, and the Seminole Chief, Osceola, in his imprisonment in the Carolinas. We laugh at his depicting them as Greek heroes, but recent scholarly studies show the Indian chieftains to have had inner serenity and a kind of statesmanship as well as courage. "My God," Daniel Webster exclaimed when he saw Catlin's paintings, "I was blind to all this red majesty and beauty and mystery that we are trampling down." Francis Parkman, in his original journals of the trip on which *The Oregon Trail* was based, also saw integrity and sawdust in Indians and whites alike. Parkman described himself as the historian of "the American forest and the American Indian at the period when both received their final doom." By the time he got to them the Indians had become badly disintegrated and lived "not much better than brutes," but the whites on the frontier were also "a race of boors, about as uncouth, mean, and stupid as the hogs they seem chiefly to delight in." The post-Parkman generations belatedly tried to do justice, and perhaps more, to the personality and culture of the Indian. In the regional literature of the West and Southwest his figure has loomed larger than the historical reality, invoking a culture that became a heroic symbol after its death.

In "The Redskin and the Paleface," D. H. Lawrence saw an America "haunted by the Indian." If he was right, then the sense of guilt that overtook some Americans brought a new romanticism of the Indian which went deeper than that of Montaigne or Chateaubriand, Cooper or Catlin or Parkman. John Collier and other champions of the Indians pointed out that, harried and decimated as they were, their "group-hoods, languages, religions, culture systems, symbolisms and emotional attitudes toward the self and the world continued to live on." He finds a central secret of this continuity in the "passion and reverence for human personality and for the web of life and the earth which the American Indians have tended as a central, sacred fire since before the Stone Age." There is a measure of truth in this, despite the pathos of applying it to the straggling, impoverished remnants of a people, living in isolation, with tribal councils that no longer function. There has been a recent tendency to return to the sources of Indian feeling and the Indian outlook as to a road not taken but missed somehow in the scramble to make America a success.

Failing to tame the race they found peopling the continent and unable to keep white indentured labor in subjection or make it pay, the European colonizers brought in from another continent a race more easily managed because "they came in chains." The Spanish first brought them from Africa to their West Indies colony to replace the dwindling supply of Indian labor when the encomienda system began to break down. In defeating the Spanish sea power the Elizabethan adventurers enabled Britain eventually to take over the lucrative slave trade as a source of the prosperity of its ports and as one of the foundations of its expanding capitalist power. Later the Americans organized the slave trade on a large scale, and much of American prosperity rested on the crops and industries which depended on Negro labor.

The Negroes who came to America as a commodity had been captured by other Negroes in raids on the West African coast or traded to an ex-

panding white market by warring tribal chieftains. They were chained
and crowded into the hulls of the ships, both for economy and to break
their spirits, and set to work on the plantations of the New World. The
plantation system, which extended from the Southern United States
through the whole Caribbean and Latin-American area, was linked with
slave labor because large-scale agriculture could better afford the high
initial cost of slaves and supply the necessary supervision. When the first
census was taken in 1790, there were 757,000 Negroes, nine out of ten of
them slaves. The African slave trade became illegal in 1808, and slaves
were the more valued as property because they could no longer be im-
ported.

In a sense, slavery was a way of life for both races. For the small elite
of white planters in the South it made possible a life passed in the tall-
columned "Great Houses" built in the classic Greek style, with feudal
paternalism at its core. But it was also a life of intermittent fear of slave
rebellion, and of efforts to rationalize the obvious evil of the "peculiar
institution" of slavery. For the Negroes it was not always (as some Southern historians have rediscovered) a life of bloodhounds and Simon Le-
grees. There were, of course, the terrible burdens of slave life, as one
reads about them in Solomon Northrop's account of a slave's workday
or Frederick Douglass's description of the bleak succession of intolerable
days in the field, dawn to dark, in every weather. All labor was hard in
rural and early industrial America, and sometimes the Northern white
worker said he was worse off than the Southern slave. But the Abolitionists who saw slavery in the image of its worst examples had hold of a
deep truth: the cancer of slavery, as Avery Craven has put it, was in the
idea of slavery itself—of one man owning another—and in the fact that
there was nothing to keep the worst type of white from owning and exploiting those who were better men than himself. The slave died young.
His women were often taken sexually by the overseer and the master's
sons, whether out of passion or for sport, as the record of racial mixture
abundantly shows. Yet since slaves were valuable property they were
usually treated with some care, and a rough affection often developed on
both sides. Discipline was maintained; if the slave protested he was
whipped; if he sought to escape he was tracked down. He lived in ignorance but in a bare kind of comfort. While most of the churches admitted him to membership and the Quakers championed his cause, too
many Christian churchgoers considered him outside the scope of their
charity, compassion, and militancy.

Slavery as a human institution had many faces: it differed depending
on the state, the crop, the plantation, the master. Yet its common pattern
was intolerable. There were periodic slave-labor strikes and local upris-
ings in which the Negroes fought against hopeless odds. The one known

as Nat Turner's Rebellion in 1831, was led by a Virginia slave locally known as "the Preacher" who had visions like Joan of Arc and saw himself destined to bring it to pass that "the first shall be last and the last shall be first." His venture led to perhaps a hundred deaths on both sides, but it showed how little life mattered in a feudal domain when weighed against freedom and despair.

Eventually the slaves were freed, at the expense of a Civil War. The heritage of slavery lay heavily on the whites in their fratricidal struggle and afterward in their abiding sense of guilt. The Negro also carried a heritage of embitterment. He had to pay a painful price for his freedom, grasping at it with unrealistic eagerness only to find that liberation could not liberate so long as the former oppressors kept their power. So he was hurtled from his first dream of freedom back into the terror of Reconstruction days. He found he had to achieve everything again from scratch—to fight disfranchisement and his own ignorance, and poverty, disease, economic and sexual exploitation, the bleakness of segregation and the atmosphere of terror. At first some of the better-educated whites were ready to join with the Negro in the venture of forming a tolerable working community of both races. And the Populist movement, under leaders like Tom Watson, took the first steps to unite Negroes and whites on an equal basis in a common struggle against the economic and political exploitation of both races. For a brief interval, between the late 1870s and the 1890s, there was a flash of hope that the two races could live side by side without segregation. But it was not sustained. C. Vann Woodward, in his books on the post-Civil War South, has brilliantly traced the history both of the hope and of this failure and of the new alliance that came into being under the banner of the former Populist leaders, between the lower-class whites who wanted someone still lower to look down upon and the master group for whom every gain in Negro status was a reminder of the humiliation of Civil War defeat and who were bent on irredentist revenge. The result was the erratic course of segregation—the "strange career of Jim Crow."

Through every possible means—through direct and indirect segregation, through a racist theory of Negro inferiority and the social power of white supremacy, through propaganda and terror—pressures were exerted on the Negro to accept his traditional position. For a time his leaders acquiesced, but in the end a new and more militant leadership arose which demanded equal rights for the Negro. Confronted by a people whose docility had bounds, who—even though they came from a more primitive culture—learned quickly, the Southern whites felt that their whole way of life was endangered and came close to building a kind of garrison society.

The Negro showed himself to be a good borrower and facile adapter

to a form of life that had for centuries grown in a different direction
from his own. He took over much of the class and prestige hierarchy of
the whites, and the respectability and middle-class qualities. Nevertheless he also showed a good deal of cultural resistance and tenacity. He
proved buoyant in the face of every hardship. Even in the South he
steadily asserted and won a measure of civil rights, wrested a better education, gained a foothold in politics. Throughout the nation he made an
irresistible bid for equality. He was helped by two world wars, the march
of industrialism, the higher living standards of the Negroes, their massed
purchasing power, and the supremacy of Federal law on matters of civil
rights, even in such local concerns as schooling and transportation.

Out of the sharpness of the change from African tribalism to American slavery, and out of the suffering and sorrow of the Negro, came a
characteristic blend of elements in his outlook. It was an amalgam of
ecstatic supernaturalism, submission to fate, a belief in luck, a humorous
acceptance of the contradictions of life, a buoyant gaiety mingled with
sadness, and—from the sense of alienation—a dark strain of violence.

The religion of the Negro came close to the primitivism of the early
Christian church, when religion was the creed of the slave and the perse-
cuted. With a literalism born of plantation experience rather than of
the inner torments of conscience, Hell became an arena of fire and torture and damnation, with the Devil as Simon Legree. Jordan and
Canaan and the Promised Land took on concreteness. Heaven became a
refuge from oppression and a surcease from sorrow, as well as a reward
for faith. Jesus became a force to be invoked by a propitiatory magic—a
Man of Sorrows who was understood with a peculiar intimacy by those
who had experienced so many of their own. God the Father became the
head of a tribal patriarchate whose serenity was untouched by the turmoil of the world below. These religious attitudes, born of Negro life in
the ante-bellum South, persisted among Negroes throughout the nation
long after the end of the Civil War. In America a force which reinvig-
orated the lagging religious consciousness was bound to ramify beyond
religion itself to the culture as a whole. Thus the religion of the Negroes
took its place, along with New England Calvinism and frontier revivalism, as one of the crucial influences on the American religious consciousness—not in the sense of influencing Christian ritual or theology but in
investing again with a naïve wonder the early strivings of Christian
faith.

The beat of Negro life found its way not only into the religious "Spirituals," in which the Negro sometimes adapted old Baptist and Methodist revival songs, but also into the work songs of the plantation and logging camp and railroad, the "blues," and the more violent dance rhythms
of American jazz. For all the somberness of the Negro's slave life he

maintained an irrepressible gaiety that broke the mold of New England dourness and the high-flown gallantry of Southern feudal society. In the training of the Southern "belle" and "beau," the Negro "mammy" became a symbol of maternal warmth which persisted long beyond the slave society. The American Negro expressed in his rhythms, in his belief in magic, and in his relaxed, noncompetitive sense some of the irrationals of living that were later to form a sharp contrast to the rigidities of science and the machine. Unlike the European heritage (except for the case of the European peasant), the Negro heritage was prescientific, pre-industrial, outside the whole scope of Western culture. In the contact of European and African cultures in America something striking was bound to happen to the new amalgam. The quality of American music, dance, literature, theater, religion, today is evidence that it did.*

The migration that is usually called prescriptively "American" is that of the explorers, conquerors, and settlers from western Europe, especially from the British Isles. Statistically the British influence has not been decisive. Out of a total immigration of some thirty-five million, not more than five million Englishmen came to America. But they came early so that the portion of the population with a strain of British blood now, in addition to the British cultural inheritance, is much greater than the 10 per cent or 15 per cent that the British contributed to the immigration itself. Even more important, the impact came in the formative years of colonial growth and the history of the Republic, and it did much to shape the basic American attitudes and institutions.

It might have turned out differently. In the years of discovery and exploration, Spain and France rather than Britain were the Great Powers of Europe. Had either or both of them held on to their colonies, the United States might have become another Latin America or French Canada. But the Spanish hold was weak, largely because of Indian hostility and Spain's inner weakness and its defeats in Europe. In the crucial and protracted struggle (described so well by Parkman) between the French and British for the control of North America, the French too had to yield. Their imperial energies were distracted in the Caribbean, in India, and in Europe; internally they were split by religious and civil wars. The Spanish and French empires were on the downward sweep of their arc of power, the British with their rising commercial and industrial strength were on the upward sweep. Whenever the Spanish and French had colonized in the New World they left behind, in Parkman's phrasing, a people "bereft of civil liberty" and burdened by "a weight

* For a further treatment of the place of the Negro in American life, see Ch. VII, Sec. 6, "The Negro in America"; also Ch. X, Sec. 1, "God and the Churches," and Ch. XI, Sec. 7, "Jazz As American Idiom."

of ecclesiastical tutelage." For America the stakes of conflict lay in the question of whether the United States would become primarily feudal, Catholic, hierarchic, and authoritarian, or industrial, Protestant, capitalistic, and libertarian. It is in the choice of these great historical alternatives that the British triumph was decisive and the British influence beyond any statistical calculus.

The core of the language is English, although the native elements added to it have given it an "American" character. American law grew out of, and is still largely rooted in, the English common law. American political institutions and ideas—including representative government, the limited state, the right of revolt, the stress on individualism, the tradition of civil liberties—came largely from the British. They were an organic part of the American mind because they grew out of the political struggles in England during the Tudor-Stuart period, when America was still part of the British Empire. The American Revolution itself made the Americans more British, since they were fighting for the "true British" order and heritage that were (they felt) being lost in the mother country. American technology took its methods and ideas from the British Industrial Revolution until the Americans outstripped their teachers. The American belief in the sanctity of property and contract was derived from the British. The pluralism of the American Protestant religious sects, the emphasis on individual Bible reading and on freedom of worship, are largely British in inspiration. So also are the small-town pattern, the complexity of local government, the private ("public" in England) schools, the colleges, the charities and philanthropies, the whole network of voluntary associations, the corporations and trade-unions. The literary heritage is mainly British. So is the press, reaching back to Defoe and Cobbett. Until the end of the nineteenth century, when the German influence became strong, the contacts of American scientists and scholars were, with some important exceptions, British. In painting, sculpture, architecture, the British influence was strong until the French strains made themselves felt toward the turn of the twentieth century.

One special phase of this heritage was Puritanism. Although there is a temptation to believe it was a native American product, actually (as Perry Miller pointed out) nine tenths of what we associate with Puritanism was British. The Puritan qualities were intense, inverted, crotchety, rather than judicious or humanist. There was a tautness about the Puritans that came from their sense of living under tension and of applying pressure all down the line in order to take by storm God's grace and strength. The wilderness itself along with the Indian dangers made the "good fight" more real, and the New World with its ever-present strangeness kept the wonder-working Providence ever busy. As children of the whole Judaeo-Christian culture the Puritans considered human nature vile and kept an eye on the next world, but the other eye was kept lustily on the enterprises of this world. Their heritage accounts for much in the American combination of the visionary and the pragmatic, the righteous and the profitable. Not only New England but the Old South as well took its fashions, its education, its books and ideas, its values, even its snobbisms, from Great Britain. The two great aristocracies America has had—the intellectual aristocracy of New England and the planter aristocracy of the South—derive from the two phases of British society at the time of American colonial growth which the Americans came to think of (in somewhat mythical terms) as those of the Puritans and the Cavaliers.

I have put the case for the British heritage so strongly because it has been played down recently by the "cultural pluralists," in recoil from the "Anglo-Saxon" cult of the turn of the century and the still earlier colonialism of American thought which played up everything British. But Britain's role in the shaping of the American tradition was that of a carrier for European thought and life as a whole. If the leaders of American life in the early days of the Republic were "true-born Englishmen" they were also good Europeans, anxious to weave into the pattern of their new venture every strand of European striving. The intellectual generation that framed the Declaration and Constitution, and wrote and read *The Federalist,* was heir to the culture of the Greek and Italian Renaissance, the Reformation, the *philosophes,* and later of the French Revolution itself. The new republicans of America looked to the political history of Greece and Rome for their models of republican virtue. Early American architecture derived from the pure classicism of the French as well as from Palladio's Renaissance style, American educational ideals came from the progressive teaching of Rousseau and Pestalozzi, and American theological controversies—especially in the era of the Transcendentalists—were carried on in the murky atmosphere of Göttingen and other centers of German romanticism.*

The last of the shaping sources of the American tradition was so diversified that it can only be called the polyglot heritage. In addition to the British, the Scotch-Irish, the French Huguenots, the early German settlers from the Palatine and the later Germans who left behind the abortive German revolutions of 1848, many other strains came to America. There were Irish Catholics, driven by famine and an inner restlessness; there were Norwegians, Swedes and Danes, Hungarians, Austrians, Bohemians and Moravians, Spaniards and Portuguese; there

* For a further discussion, especially of the impact of Puritanism, see Ch. X, Sec. 1, "God and the Churches," and Sec. 2, "American Thought: the Angle of Vision." For the influence of English law and politics, see Ch. VI, especially Sec. 8, "Law and Justice." For the English language, see Ch. XI, Sec. 3, "Heroes, Legends, and Speech."

were Swiss, Italians, Serbs, Greeks, and Armenians; there were Russian and Polish peasants, Lithuanians and Finns; there were Jews, hoping that America would be the last stop in their history of wandering; there were Mexicans and Canadians, crossing not a sea but only a border; there were Latin Americans; there were Chinese, Japanese, Filipinos.

The speech of America became a medley of tongues from every language family, each helping to give form to the emerging American language. The dance of America took its shape not only from the African jungle but also from the folk rhythms of the Central Europeans and the Slavs and from the pampas of Latin America. The choral societies and *Männerverbände* of Central Europe were transplanted to Midwestern cities; the cookery of the French, the Italians, the Hungarians, the Swedes, entered as ingredients in the American menu. The vendettas of Sicily and the tong warfare of China were re-enacted on American streets. The political heterodoxies of German *émigré* Marxists and the religious heterodoxies of innumerable sects and prophets of true believers found room for community testing on the Midwestern plains; the political skills of the Irish found expression in new American cities, while the intellectual and business skills of the Jews reasserted themselves in the new favoring climate.

Thus it became part of the American tradition to be an amalgam of many traditions, even while there were pressures to select one of them (the British–West European) as *the* "American" one. The shaping forces of American society, and of its outlook and thought, grew unimaginably. To the heritage of the Indian and Negro cultural strains, of British institutional life, of the Greco-Roman and Judaeo-Christian world, of French revolutionary doctrine and artistic life, of German romanticism and the political and religious consciousness of the 1848 immigration, there were added the whole Mediterranean world, the Slavic, the Celtic-Catholic, the Hispanic-American, the Arab-Moslem, the Oriental. Each immigrant group contributed whatever elements of its tradition were absorbable by the American heritage, while in turn it absorbed the elements it found.*

In Augustan Rome the Emperor asked the poet Virgil to write an epic that would expound and consolidate the Roman tradition. But an American Virgil, commanded similarly to celebrate the American tradition, would find the task overpowering. For it would mean tracing the course of numberless rivers of thought and influence as they flowed into the central ocean of an American tradition which is still in the making.

* On the polyglot tradition, see Ch. III, Sec. 1, "Is There an American Stock?" and Sec. 2, "The Immigrant Experience"; also Ch. VII, Sec. 5, "The Minority Situation."

3. The Slaying of the European Father

THE PEOPLE WHO CAME to the American shores felt intensely about the American experience because for each of them America was the wall broken down, door broken open. Some, like the Negroes, came against their will and in chains. But as for the rest, whether they came for land or economic opportunity or freedom, they came because of the past denials in their lives. It was their pre-American experience that gave point to their life in America. The earlier memories were, of course, not wholly negative. The new setting gave the bitter memories of deprivation a chance to mellow, and it often brought to the fore a gentle nostalgia for the old culture which fused with the patriotic feeling for the new.

Thus the bundles of Old World memories, jostling each other in the New World, have enriched the American tradition. America was the place where the old memories found a new meaning. Every item of experience in the New World was packed with a heightened tension, every event was projected into a past more contrasting and into a future more exacting than in any other culture, thus forming the American image in the immigrant mind.

Although many of the later immigrants were doubtless passive, coming to America mainly because of the unsettlement of Europe, the notion of the "American promise"—of America as a cornucopia of well-being and freedom—was to some degree imbedded in their mind from the first settlers to the latest. The earliest image of the American promise was widely spread by documents like Columbus's Letter of 1493 and the *mundus novus* attributed to Amerigo Vespucci, with its picture of sensuality as well as danger. The more authentic early writings depicted an America of rich soil, where a man had room to move. In the age of capitalism the image of America became one of a land of business opportunity where an able man could start at the bottom and reach the top. Throughout, from the Spanish quest of El Dorado to the twentieth-century folklore of Sicilian and Slavic villages, the myth persisted of America as the land of untold riches where everyone dressed in finery and the paving blocks were of gold.

Whatever the reality, these myths were among the powerful forces that stirred the European mind. The dominant literary themes of Europe have often reached outside Europe: the imaginary voyage, the noble savage, the Byronic hero eating his heart out in some mountain fastness, the splendor of the exotic Orient or Africa. But in the European folk mind the myth of golden America has far outshone all these liter-

ary themes of the elite. The popular mind made the transition from
Utopia to an actual democracy and from aiming at the moon to aiming
at America. There is no other civilization in whose life history promise
has played so great a part, nor one whose promise has meant so much
to the older civilizations.

But being built on a promise, American civilization was open to questions about the degree of its fulfillment. National self-criticism had been
strong from Thoreau and Theodore Parker to Whitman, but it mounted
after the Civil War with the ending of the frontier, the dominance of
the money mentality, the awakening of labor protest, and the havoc of
recurrent economic breakdown. "America was promises," wrote Archibald MacLeish in the 1930s, and his choice of tense summed up the
temper of American self-criticism. Yet what interests a student of American civilization is less the lack of fullness in the fulfillment than the
persistence of the promise. The theme of promise has been America's
great "social myth," using the term in the sense of an imaginative idea
which—whatever its truth—induces men to feel and act. Santayana once
spoke of the "metaphysical passion" which moved men to cross the seas
to America to set up a new civilization. He was right. For all the scorn
of metaphysics that you will find in American writing, the metaphysic
of promise has been as crucial an element in the American civilization
as the metaphysic of Christianity in the civilization of Europe from St.
Augustine to Thomas Aquinas.

The medieval metaphysic was one of renunciation and otherworldli-
ness. It dominated European thought until the new science, discoveries,
and wealth undercut it. With the Commercial Revolution and the unsettling effects of the Renaissance and Reformation, a new temper was
shaped. Men sought the Golden Age not in a primitive past or murky
future but here on earth and now. In fact, the quest for America was
the quest at once for gold and the Golden Age. Thus was the foundation laid for the metaphysic of secular promise. Even in its imperial
phase of the struggle of great power systems it had its roots in the
Protestant ethic and in the humanist and secular energies loosed by the
Renaissance. The promise of American life had its way prepared by the
humanism of Europe, and the energies of American life had their origin
in the awakened energies of Europe.

This has been largely obscured in the literature of American revolt,
in which Europe was something broken away from and left behind.
You get this theme in De Crèvecoeur, with his talk of the wholly "new"
American; in Jefferson, with his recoil from the dynastic blood-feuds of
the European despotisms; and you get it in Emerson's speech at Man-

chester in the midst of the 1847 depression, with which he closes his
English Traits:

> If the courage of England goes with the chances of a commercial crisis, I
> will go back to the capes of Massachusetts and my own Indian stream, and
> say to my countrymen, the old race are all gone, and the elasticity and hope
> of mankind must henceforth remain on the Allegheny ranges, or nowhere.

But while Americans rejected Europe, the act of rejection was also
one of carry-over, and the act of revolt was itself an expression of the
European consciousness. Thus Jefferson avowed that in drawing up the
Declaration of Independence he had aimed at no originality but had
sought only "to place before mankind the common sense of the subject";
after tracing the varied sources of European thought from which Jefferson had drawn, Julian Boyd remarks that "for a people who were
to embrace many races and many creeds, nothing could have been more
appropriate than that the act of renouncing the ties of consanguinity
should have drawn its philosophical justification from traditions common to all." Without taking over the European heritage the Americans
could not have revolted against Europe. The ships that crossed the Atlantic to America carried with them not only the European economy but
also European aspirations and the European system of thought. The
revolutionary elements in that system of thought had begun to show
themselves before the settlement of America. In fact, the rise of American civilization was the product both of revolution and dissolution in
Europe.

In America the vigorous European elements were brought into play
as against the exhausted ones. It was free enterprise arrayed against
mercantilism, *laissez faire* against cameralism, individualism against
hierarchy, natural rights against monarchy, popular nationalism against
the dynastic regimes, social mobility against caste, the pioneering spirit
against the status quo. For before the American dream there was the
European dream. Sometimes internal conflicts are resolved by revolution within, sometimes by the bursting out into colonization and revolution without. If the settlement of America helped drain off Europe's
revolutionary energies, the revolution in America gave expression to
those energies. The new world of which Europe had so long dreamed
came to fruition under American skies. The European dream made
America possible: and the American experience gave the European
dream concreteness.

This was the America-Europe nexus. Why then the rejection of Europe so chronic in the American tradition? An answer is suggested by
the theme which runs through Frazer's *The Golden Bough*—the tribal

killing of the sacrificial king, or (as we may generalize it) the symbolic
slaying of the father. The motive for slaying, one may hazard, was to
ward off evil by establishing the separateness of the tribe from the king,
much as an adolescent has to disown a parent to assert himself as a
person in his own right. Taking the suggestion of the Swiss-Italian theorist Roberto Michels that every nation has two dominant myths—the
myth of origin and the myth of mission—America's rejection of Europe
and the rebellion against the father may be seen as part of its mythology.

Was the strength of the rejection due partly to the feelings of inferiority in a culture which for almost two centuries was colonial?—plus the
bitterness of a revolutionary war?—plus the cockiness of success and the
rapid strides toward power on the part of a once derided people?—
plus a metaphysic of promise which demanded that the sources of the
promise be as home-grown as its prospects were glorious? Yet there remains the paradox that the Americans who led in the rejection of Europe were themselves intellectuals deeply indebted to European books
and ideas.

There is the example of Jefferson, whose passion for freedom was
rooted in the classical and English philosophers and whose feeling for
the independent American farmer had been foreshadowed by the emphasis of the Physiocrats. As for his opponents, John Adams's doctrine
of mixed government went back to the English constitutional tradition,
and Alexander Hamilton expressed better than the European thinkers
themselves the fears of the possessors about the naked will of the people.
Inveighing against European monarchies and social despotism, Jefferson
made political capital for the Republicans by fixing the stigma of a
monarchist Europe on the Federalists. Hamilton, on his side, by inveighing against European revolutionary terrorists, lumped with them
the author of the *Letter to Mazzei*. Each used Europe as a weapon in
his political battles.

The use of these symbols was strengthened by the continued inpouring
of immigration. The big anti-immigrant movements of American history—the Native Americans and Know-Nothings of the 1840s and 1850s,
the Sand-Lot party in California in the 1870s which set off the Exclusion bills, the American Protective Association in the Midwest, and the
revived Ku Klux Klan after World War I—were related to the raw energies of a new capitalist democracy and the personal and social tensions of living in a fiercely competitive society. In a nation made up
of successive layers of immigrants there was a marginal prestige in having left Europe earlier and a marginal stigma in having left it later.
Each new batch, feeling its "Americanism" challenged, found itself blatantly claiming to be more American than the others. This led to a
mounting xenophobia, an overrapid drive toward "assimilation," and

an effort to equate "radical" and "alien" and use them almost inter-
changeably.*

This psychic necessity for rejecting Europe has affected the whole
spectrum of American social thinking. It is true that there is an underlying self-confidence in American thought. Yet for his self-respect the
young American intellectual of today is led to reject ideas for social
change far less radical than the radical democracy of Channing and
Wendell Phillips, of Henry Demarest Lloyd and Edward Bellamy and
Lincoln Steffens, on the ground that they are "European" and "Marxian." In his spiritual isolation the middle-class American seems to suffer from a sense of encirclement and to identify with a "European" or
"foreign" source whatever ills he feels he is subject to. Some of the
major *grands peurs* to which American men of property have been subject have been dramatized in these terms, and the more easily dramatized
because the rejection of Europe preceded even the Socialist scares created
by the European revolutions of the 1840s or the Paris Commune of 1870.
Finally, because a sense of encirclement fortifies a policy of isolationism,
the considerations of national interest which until recently led to such a
foreign policy found psychological bolstering here.

To be sure, the best American thinkers suffered from the sense that
they were missing something by their separation from Europe. Emerson
preached self-reliance to Americans, yet he was mature enough to know
that self-reliance excluded fear of Europe as well as abasement before
it; his relations with Carlyle and the other British men of letters were
relations between men who had something to say to each other. But
other American writers have veered between an overassertive nativism
and a votive dependence. From Henry James in the old London houses
that drew him so, to the literary proconsuls of the 1940s and 1950s in
Paris and Rome, American writers went to Europe seeking some quality
—aesthetic sensitivity, a freer expressiveness in living, old traditions,
a sense of community, dedication to artistic discipline—which the cruder
energies of the American civilization had not provided.

The sharp change in the American attitude toward Europe came with
the world wars. Once it became clear that Europe was no longer the
father demanding obedience and exerting his authority but an endangered
civilization needing help, America's response changed. It broke through
the isolationist sheath to aid western Europe in two great wars, and
afterward it helped to rebuild Europe's economic strength. Yet even
here Americans had to dress up their aid in the ideological garment of
a struggle against tyranny and authoritarianism. You ended by helping

* For a further discussion, see Ch. III, Sec. 2, "The Immigrant Experience," and
Ch. VII, Sec. 5, "The Minority Situation."

the father you had rebelled against, but you did it by continuing to slay another potential authority-image.

Thus did Americans compensate for the sacrificial slaying of the father; and thus did they continue, in the act of compensation, to maintain their connection with their image of themselves as free and rebellious spirits.*

4. Why Was America a Success?

THE VERSIONS A CULTURE has of its own strength and success are as important parts of its tradition as the versions it has of its origins or mission. Some of the early historians believed they saw the hand of God operating exclusively in American history and did not trouble to inquire why He should have shown so special a solicitude for this particular breed of His children. Not counting the inevitable drivel about the superior virtues of Anglo-Saxonism, there were also a few accepted historians (Bancroft, Fiske, Mahan come to mind) who wrote of Americans as a Chosen People in the Biblical sense of one through whose history some Higher Power works out an inscrutable design for the whole human race. There was also a tendency to guard the unblemished reputation of the revolutionary heroes and give more than life-size stature to the Founding Fathers. But the recent studies of Franklin, Washington, Jefferson, Hamilton, Adams, and Madison view them with their frailties as well as their basic greatness.

Stronger than the impulse to see America as a Chosen People is the impulse to see it as a unique historic experience. The idea of American "exceptionalism" is valid if you take it in the sense that America has its own civilization pattern, which does not follow the pattern of others and is not linked by any inevitable destiny to their doom. This does not cut America off from the universal experience of other civilizations, nor does it make America immune to the age-old forces that have seen other civilizations rise and flourish, decay and die. It does, however, stress the ways in which America has been favored by geography and historical circumstance. One view of the geographical theory underscores the expanse of continent, another the expanse of oceans. The continental version points out that America has been blessed with a richness of resources—soil, forest, water power, coal, minerals—as few other nations. The oceanic version points to the stretch of the Atlantic and the Pacific which enabled America to develop, especially in its formative pe-

---

* For a further discussion of American metaphysical assumptions, see Ch. X, Sec. 2, "American Thought: the Angle of Vision." For the ideas and emotions underlying American foreign policy, see Ch. XII.

riod, far from the wars and dynastic struggles of other nations. Thus one may say that the tutelary divinities of land and water watched over America's destinies.

Another variant of the theory of exceptionalism is the argument from pluralism—that American greatness derives from its special blend of ethnic, religious, and linguistic strains. This is the view that America was a success because it was not a nation but (in Walt Whitman's phrase) "a nation of nations." As DeWitt Clinton, the New York politician, put it as early as 1814: "Perhaps our mingled descent from various nations may have a benign influence upon genius. . . . The extraordinary characters which the United States have produced may be, in some measure, ascribed to the mixed blood of so many nations flowing in our veins." A later writer spoke of the processes of Nature as always tending "to enrich the whole by this electrical and enlivening relation between the parts." Randolph Bourne, who reflected the intellectual currents of the period before World War I, also spoke of the "trans-national" character of the culture. Here again, by the denial of a narrow ethnic view, America expressed its sense of its own uniqueness: for the crossing of so many strains presumably produced a richer and stronger new strain, the American as the New Man. Or if he was not new, there was at least in him the densest distillation of universal humanity, and in that sense too America was unique.

Even when American thinkers seemed to use other explanations of American success, the notion of exceptionalism often showed through the slits of the mask. This was true of those who saw American history as illustrating "the principle of freedom" (in George Bancroft's phrase), or the later radical democrats who made a cult of the common man and saw him shaping a unique civilization under unique conditions of freedom. For them, as for many other commentators on America, the theme of American uniqueness has been (in Rush Welter's words) "a fact transcending any particular explanation, yet evidenced by their proliferation."*

Of the American institutions singled out for the riddle of American success, the three that have received most attention are the Constitution, individualist capitalism, and the frontier.

For a century and a half the worship of the Constitution has been part of American traditional thought and emotion. It may have taken root as a way of giving Americans the sense of their place in the sun, after the struggle for freedom. It continued in the latter part of the nineteenth century as a way of fighting radical legislation and the "im-

* For a further discussion of the problem of the uniqueness of America, see Ch. II, Sec. 4, "American Exceptionalism."

ported European philosophies." Today it counts most as a symbol of the nontotalitarian organization of human living—especially important, as Clinton Rossiter has noted, for a people who lack a large store of inherited symbols of a mystical nature. Even among those skeptical of spread-eagle patriotism, there is a sober sense that the American political genius has here added something of its own to the tradition of government.

To be sure, the creative elements of the American political contribution are to be found outside as well as inside the Constitution. The party system, judicial review of legislation, the flexibility of Presidential power, the government of atomic energy, the whole administrative arm of the government—none of these are explicit in the Constitution but have grown up outside it. Yet in the popular mind they are lumped together under the Constitutional symbol. What was perhaps least to be expected was the record of the Supreme Court, in the last two decades, in refusing to make the symbol too rigid. The healthy conflict of opinion between the Justices is a sign that all of them, conservatives and liberals alike, regard the Constitution not as a sacred text but as an instrument of government, however much they may differ on how it is to be used wisely.

There is still, of course, the temptation to pay homage to a sacred document, unchanging amidst the tides and storms of the world. The document is thereby assigned an efficacy in itself which it can have only when it is seen as a living Constitution, interpreted flexibly and with a generosity of social purpose by men who are human beings and have biographies and political creeds. As an object of cult worship the Constitution becomes all too easy an explanation of American greatness and has thereby at times become an obstacle to the dynamism of the American experience.*

One of the least noted changes in the undercurrent of American attitudes has been the merging of the Constitution with the idea-of-progress strain in American thought. As the technical achievement of America became clearer in the 1870s and 1880s, the idea of progress was linked with the unfolding of the productive power of the machine and the human energies released by it. These in turn were seen to depend on capitalism, which by still another remove rested on the initiative of individual enterprise and the Constitutional guarantees of individual freedom. Thus the answer increasingly given to the riddle of American success was one linked with the institution of individualist capitalism.

The European theorist on whom the American champions of individualist capitalism most relied was Herbert Spencer. It was to turn his

* For a further discussion of the Constitution and constitutionalism, see Ch. VI, Sec. 9. "Keepers of the Covenant."

theory topsy-turvy that Thorstein Veblen wrote his *Theory of the Leisure Class;* and a quarter century later Veblen rounded out his thinking in *Absentee Ownership and Business Enterprise: The Case of America* (1923), which was an indictment of the whole capitalist thesis. Ironically, one of Veblen's teachers at Carleton College was John Bates Clark, one of his Yale teachers was William Graham Sumner, and his teacher and friend both at Cornell and Chicago was J. Laurence Laughlin. These three were the militant defenders of capitalist individualism at the turn of the century. Sumner's defense of the moral aspects of individualism and *laissez faire* paved the way for the economic individualism of the dominant school of American economic theory. The fruits of their view may be found in the speeches made at any convention of the N.A.M., in the institutional advertising of any corporation, and in the columns and editorials of almost any American newspaper.

This view is attractive as an explanation of American dynamism, since it runs in terms of the role of freedom in the release of men's energies. It offers the individual an unlimited field for careerism and enrichment and yet ties these up with the social interest, giving the twentieth-century American the feeling, at once complacent and revolutionary, of the eighteenth-century European when Adam Smith told him that each man, by pursuing his self-interest, helps the common good. It has on its side the massive facts of American material wealth and high living standards and is linked with the emphasis on the limited state and the contempt for bureaucrats.

But the champions of individualist capitalism have not gone unchallenged. Foreign observers like Harold Laski and Americans like Robert S. Lynd and C. Wright Mills have assigned it a corrosive role in American development, stressing the impact of its acquisitiveness, planlessness, and moral blindness on democratic institutions. The anticapitalist emphasis was in a sense foreshadowed by the agrarian antiprivilege thinking of John Taylor of Carolina, one of Jefferson's lieutenants, and by the similar protest of the Populist and reformist thinkers not so much against capitalism itself as against corrupt wealth and the inequalities of American life. The anticapitalist thinkers of the first half of our century have pointed to the concentration of economic power, the increasing pressures on small business, the recurring boom-bust cycles of inflation and unemployment, the waste, the jungle of competitive greeds, the desert stretches of frustration and relative poverty alongside the high living standards. The doubt they raise is whether big-scale capitalism was responsible for the prosperity of America or was itself a by-product of the margin of waste afforded by America's immense resources and geographic position. They point to the capitalist experience of other countries, with its frustrated energies and increasingly bitter social struggles, as an indication that the creative phase of American capitalism is past and the future will be that of an Iron Age.

Like other forms of determinism in America, this one has had rough going. "The theory of economic determinism," wrote the youthful and cocky Charles Beard in 1913, "has not been tried out in American history, and until it is tried out it cannot be found wanting." He later retreated from this position and denied that he had ever quite meant to try it out, yet the boldness of *An Economic Interpretation of the Constitution* left its mark on the teaching and writing of American history. His major work, with Mary Beard, on *The Rise of American Civilization* continued to stress the economic factor as the revolutionary shaping force in American development. Somewhat before Beard, but almost contemporary with him, Thorstein Veblen worked out more systematically an interpretation of society and opinion in America that (while not an economic determinism) stressed the conflict of the technological and pecuniary factors—"the making of goods and the making of money" —rather than the intangibles of the national character and destiny. And Brooks Adams, Henry's brother, starting from very different premises, developed an even more vigorous economic interpretation of his own— partly geographical (the determinism of changing trade routes), partly that of economic and administrative concentration (the "law of civilization and decay").

Thus there was a historical moment in America—somewhere between the rise of Populism and the New Deal—when the twin doctrines of capitalist apologetic and anticapitalist indictment fought it out, although under a bewildering variety of verbal disguises. Veblen insisted on an impersonal explanation, using his theory of the impersonality of the machine process and bringing within its incidence the whole structure of social thought as well. Beard was influenced not only by Veblen and Brooks Adams but also by James Madison, and was fond of quoting the famous Number Ten of *The Federalist,* where Madison analyzed the growth of party factions in terms of universal conflicts of class interest. But whether Madisonian or Marxian, Veblenian, Adamsian or Beardian, this emphasis has been attacked as too impersonal and too determinist—sometimes by the very same people who accept the impersonal market determinism of the "immutable" laws of neoclassical economics.

In its most effective form the anticapitalist indictment in America charges that capitalism turned its back on earlier American experience. Certainly the *laissez-faire* emphasis of capitalism was a latter-day one: state economic action was common and unchallenged before the Civil War. It was the continental resources and the favoring historical conditions of America (so this theory goes) that gave capitalism its start, but once started it ran berserk, so that the changes it brought over American life have betrayed the original meaning of the American Revolution. This was the favorite thesis of the intellectuals in the Populist and social-reform era. It was J. Allen Smith's thesis, and that of Smith's more famous disciple, Vernon L. Parrington. It was the thesis of Henry Demarest Lloyd and of Lincoln Steffens, of Edward Bellamy and of William Dean Howells. And in a different form it underlies the attack on capitalism by the Southern Agrarians of the 1920s and 1930s.

Answering these charges, a more sophisticated form of capitalist thinking has emerged which recognizes that *laissez-faire* capitalism no longer exists and that the giant corporation has made capitalist individualism archaic. In *U.S.A.: The Permanent Revolution,* Russell Davenport argued for the double thesis of American uniqueness and universalism. He saw American capitalism as the unique and history-chosen guardian of the universal values of freedom and abundance, holding it to be America's peculiar mission to guard these values for the rest of the world. He felt that the recent changes in capitalism—which have spread the ownership of corporate wealth and made ordinary people the participants in capitalism—have made it a "popular" or "welfare" capitalism, still holding the secret to American dynamism: in fact, so continuously revolutionary in its consequences that the American experience alone deserves the phrase Trotsky sought to apply to Communist dynamism— the "permanent revolution." Something of the same view may be found stated, with greater learning and more qualifications, in Adolf Berle's *American Capitalist Revolution.*

I shall be returning to an examination of these ideas in my chapter on the American economy.* Here I want only to say that American capitalism has been both overpraised and overindicted; that it is neither the Plumed Knight nor the monstrous Robber Barony it has been depicted; that it is responsible neither for all the blessings nor all the ills of American society; and that it cannot be brandished as the single key either to American greatness or American infamy. On no other phase of the American tradition has discussion shown the quality of excess it has shown on the nature of the American economy and its leadership. If Beard, Parrington, and Matthew Josephson in the 1920s and 1930s oversimplified the relation between economic power and stratification and the state of American civilization, the razzle-dazzle chromium-plated laudators of American capitalism in the 1950s were even more at fault in assuming that they had solved the secret of perpetual motion for American wealth and prosperity, that economic mergers, corporate cannibalism, stock dispersion, and the automatic factory would nail

* Ch. V, "Capitalist Economy and Business Civilization."

down the gifts of the gods on the American land, and that the power and the glory would go on forever and ever.

One of the most interesting efforts to explain American success was the Turner theory of the moving frontier. While Frederick J. Turner put his theory in terms of frontier democracy as well as frontier individualism, it has been used subtly to bolster the argument from individualism—and therefore from *laissez-faire* capitalism—as the source of America's greatness. Charles Beard asked acidly why Sumner's theory of individualism in economics was quickly challenged and destroyed by the progressive economists while Turner's similar theory of individualism in history got no such response from the historians. Turner has since been challenged, yet the query was a valid one. One answer is that while Sumner's argument was couched in universal terms—and Clark and Laughlin after him froze it into the eternal laws of economics —Turner's theory focused on the uniqueness of the American experience even while he gave it the force of historic law.

Turner's theory—that the characteristic American institutions were born out of the American forest and were shaped by America's characteristic frontier experience—was in one sense a pessimistic formulation, since Turner knew that the frontier was closing even while he wrote, and the closed frontier presumably meant the decline of opportunity and of democratic vigor. Yet its strong impact was positive and derived from confirming Americans in the feeling of their uniqueness, the sense of being not part of a universal equation but a fresh experiment in history. Henry Nash Smith has pointed out that Turner was in effect a poet dealing with the stuff of legend—the myth of America as the "garden of the world." What he wrote was thus part of the metaphysic of American promise and shed some light for Americans on how it happened that a people endowed as others of God's children were endowed could nevertheless create so special and successful a culture. It weakened the potential hold either of a Marxist theory of the iron laws of capitalist development and doom, or a theory of a racial elite which other peoples had found consolatory. Instead it gave Americans a theory of the shaping of their institutions and character which ran in naturalistic terms of the frontier as a process yet made them almost as elect as if they had been born of the Sun God or been given some special Aryan dispensation.

With its nostalgic evocation of a frontier America and its code of agrarian-democratic values, the Turner theory gave to highly urbanized twentieth-century Americans the flavor of the soil. Turner had broken with his teacher, Herbert Baxter Adams, who had traced American democracy from the barbarian tribes in the German forests: yet Turner, in a sense, transplanted the Teutonic forest to the American scene. "American democracy," he wrote, "was born of no theorist's dream. . . . It came out of the American forest, and it gained strength each time it touched a new frontier." This philosophy enabled the dwellers of the city to equate themselves with the dying yet romantic figure of the cabin farmer. They were able to live in a very unfrontierlike way and still regard themselves as frontiersmen, to develop massive corporate organizations while speaking of the individual entrepreneur, and to build up a Big Government with a far-flung imperium while still cherishing in politics the cult of the log cabin and the whistle-stop, back-platform campaign speech.

Most of all, Turner's appeal lay in the fact that while he talked in terms of individualism (what John Dewey called the "old individualism") the traits in America whose psychological sources he was seeking were the traits of democracy. This is what made him attractive to New Dealers and conservatives alike. Where Sumner and his followers had tried to show why the inequalities of an unequal society were inevitable, Turner tried to explain how Americans, despite their actual social inequalities, continued to believe in the idea of equality. To have a theory like this, which combined the pride of individualism *and* the cult of democracy, was a satisfying experience because it resolved the nation's inner split and made it whole.

Yet with all these blandishments, it could not have had its impact without a core of validity. Turner had a deep insight into the conditions under which the crucial American institutions were shaped. To this insight we now turn.

5. *American History As Extended Genesis*

AMERICA AS A DREAM of riches has become so familiar a world image that we almost forget how hard the American environment was at its start. From the first attempted settlement of the "lost colony" at Roanoke and the privations at Jamestown and Massachusetts Bay, through the opening of the last strip of frontier, the "challenge of hard ground" has come up afresh across the larger span of America's history.

Almost every civilization has its genesis under hard conditions, and it is during this formative period when new things are happening that a people's institutions and national character take shape. Sometimes catastrophe overtakes them early, and then comes either the darkness of the end or else the catastrophe serves to bring a rebirth of creativeness. Sometimes a process of social revolution may renew the lagging energies or break the log jam of the dammed-up ones. But in most in-

stances, after the springtime of great creativeness, a civilization settles
down to live on the accumulated capital of its achievement, loses its
sense of newness and power, grows rigid. It becomes the hulk of what
men once dreamed it and hugs its past instead of fashioning its future.
It becomes, in Eliot's phrase, an "old man in a dry season."

Although America is still a relatively young civilization, the sense of
beginnings in it has been a protracted one. Viewing the life history of
American civilization as a whole, it is clear that never in history has a
civilization risen to world power in so short a span (even the rise of
Rome took longer, and Russia goes back for its origins to the Middle
Ages) and never has the larger portion of that span been so permeated
by a sense of new beginnings. Even before the thin strip of Atlantic
colonies had achieved their freedom and a degree of unity, American
settlement had already begun to move inland and make inroads on the
continental interior. Every new gain in national consciousness and in
wealth and power on the part of the settled regions was paralleled by
a deeper penetration into the unsettled ones and the opening of new
reaches for the national imagination. From the Jamestown settlement
to the present, the span of American history has been some 350 years.
The conventional date for the end of the frontier as a continuous line
of settlement is in the 1890s, although much land continued to be
homesteaded for some time after. Thus about 300 of the 350 were years
of continued genesis. During those three centuries there was never a time
when somewhere in America settlements of men and women were not
starting anew, wrestling with their natural environment and hewing
out of the wilderness a new community, a new feeling of achievement,
new profits, prosperity, and power.

This brings us back to Turner and the role of the moving frontier
in keeping alive American individualism and democracy. Translate
the history of the moving frontier into terms of the civilization process
and it becomes the history of an extended genesis. When we think in
terms of the comparative life histories of civilizations, questions come
up which Turner's theory, limited as it was to the American experience
(Walter Prescott Webb has extended it admirably in his *Great Frontier*),
did not even raise. Toynbee, for example, propounds as a "law" of history that "geographical expansion produces social retardation." This
runs headlong into the American experience. Yet one may say instead
that in and of itself there is no social magic in the expansion of frontier
settlement, as the history of other cultures has shown. Even Turner saw
that the first result of the frontier was reduction to a more primitive condition: by diluting the intensity of the cultural experience it may actually have the retarding effect Toynbee describes.

America has not been the only civilization which retained a large, thinly settled frontier area over a long time span. It has also been true, to pick random examples, of Russia, Australia, Canada, Argentina, Brazil. It is true of any big continental stretch which has unsettled land in an expanse stretching beyond the settled population centers. Yet in none of these cases, despite some similarities that Turner noted, were the social results of frontier settlement comparable to the American. Why? What was crucially lacking in their experience and present in the American that may account for the difference?

Here Turner's analysis must be stretched. With his agrarian emphasis he tended to focus on the periphery of new settlement. Despite some later indications of his broader view after the famous first essay on the significance of the frontier, he took little account of the pattern as a whole which included the center and the lines of influence between center and periphery. Along with the ferment of a moving frontier there was the ferment of democratization and industrial development in the area of early settlement. What Russia, Australia, and the other instances of frontier settlement lacked, and the American instance had, was a major industrial and capitalist revolution taking place at the same time as the frontier settlement and linked with it, and an extension of the democratic idea linked with both.

This triple line of new development, or extended genesis, meant that American life was being transformed vertically in the original centers of settlement at the same time that it was being extended horizontally in the new areas. Thus there was a double process of dynamism in operation, the vertical and horizontal. In other words, while the march of geographical settlement was necessary to the extended genesis, it would not in itself have been adequate. To move into the wilderness with the intent of creating fresh settlements means that you refresh and keep alive whatever it is you take with you. But you must have something to take. The sense of renewal of the frontiersmen came not only from facing a natural environment with directness but from never losing contact with the sources of mechanical and governmental transformation that gave Americans their commanding control over the environment as a whole.

If the Jacksonian period is seen as a great watershed of American development, when the ferment of new energies was most evident both to Americans and to foreign observers, the triple source of the new strength is fairly clear. There was, first, the moving frontier itself. Jackson was a man of the frontier, representing its quickness of perception, freshness of experience, habit of decisive action. Second, there was the movement of the American economy, which (to parallel the moving frontier) we may call the "moving technology." The inventiveness and self-reliance that were necessary qualities on the frontier were also necessary in the Eastern towns and cities among the new "mechanics," the toolmakers, the mill and foundry managers, the businessmen.

In the third area—that of government and political ideas—the freshness of thinking and sturdiness of assertion that had shown themselves since the Founding Fathers were strengthened in the Jacksonian era. That period saw the emergence of a coalition of frontier farmers, urban workingmen, businessmen, and intellectuals who expressed the common outlook of both groups and who gave direction to their energies. George Bancroft and Orestes Brownson were New Englanders, as were Emerson, Thoreau, Alcott, and the whole Concord group, who stood aside from the Jacksonian movement and were basically Whigs. Jacksonians like Leggett, Bryant, Godwin, Greeley, Vethake, were New Yorkers and Pennsylvanians. Both groups were Easterners and formed part of the "American Renaissance" which furnished the intellectual setting for the frontier movement.

Every idea tends to move toward its limits, by cumulative force and by the extension of its inner logic. That happened to the democratic idea which moved ahead as if by some inner propulsion. Groups sprang up to work for abolitionism, prison reform, and equality for women, for trade-unionism, utopian community schemes, popular control of banking and financial power. Few of these were wholly native, and few but had their origins or parallels in Europe. Yet they serve to illustrate that along with the "moving frontier" and the "moving technology" there was something like a "moving democratic idea."

America had, in short, a major industrial and capitalist revolution and a major political and intellectual revolution alongside the revolution of frontier settlement and linked with it. American life was being transformed vertically at the same time that it was being extended horizontally, and the dynamism of each fed and was fed by the dynamism of the other. On one level Americans continued to wrestle directly with the natural environment, while on another level they contrived machines that gave them (despite the complaints of workers and intellectuals) the exhilaration of a commanding mechanical mastery over Nature. They were at once Prometheus and Dr. Faustus, and each role nourished their feeling of creativeness and their conviction of mission.

Thus, while the adherents of the Turner thesis are right to stress the fresher democratic energies of the West, there was a truer sense in which both West and East drew from the same source. For the Eastern businessman, however conservative, long retained the unquenchable *élan* of discovery; while the Western frontiersman, however progressive, never lost the Lockean sense that by mixing with his labor the domain he was hewing out of the forest he was creating a new property for himself. Somewhere the noble savage met the Alchemist. Somewhere Davy Crockett became Andrew Carnegie. And somewhere both elements were tempered by the passion of a Jackson and a Taney in subduing the power of the Bank of the United States. Where these three strains met and fused, at that point America was made, and the traits which make up its national character were roughly determined.

Under other conditions the expansion of the frontier could have taken on something like the Australian pattern—a permanent metropolis plus a permanent hinterland. But the constant growth of trade and manufacturing, the opening of new markets at home as well as abroad, the advancing state of the industrial arts, the continuing alertness both of American management and American labor—all these made certain that the hinterland was steadily absorbed by the moving industrialism, and the moving democracy went (although against great resistance and at a lagging pace) along with both.

With this clue we can understand two principal facets of the American character. Self-reliance, courage, alertness, obstinate endurance, friendliness, a democratic informality, are traits that emerged from the continuous cycles of land settlement. A sharp and shrewd aggressiveness, a willingness to take chances, an organizing capacity, a genius with machines, a sense of bigness and of power, an assumption of destiny, are traits that emerged from industrialism and the capital markets of the metropolis. The two sets of traits were fused in the national character because the two strands of development were interwoven in the crucial phases of American history. David Potter has put it well by saying that the moving frontier was one phase of the larger situation of opportunity and abundance which has marked the Americans as a "people of plenty."

6. Tradition and the Frame of Power

THE NEWNESS OF THE American tradition is one of the facts that gives it unity. America is the only great nation of modern times whose history is also the history of the three shaping forces of the modern Western world—*industrialism* as a technology, *capitalism* as a way of organizing it, and *democracy* as a way of running both. The American tradition, woven from these elements, took on their dynamism.

The first English, French, and Dutch settlers brought with them the knowledge of crafts and manufactures which had come out of the early phase of the Industrial Revolution. The year in which American independence was declared—1776—was also the year of the invention of

the steam engine and the publication of the most important manifesto
of the spirit of capitalist enterprise, Adam Smith's *Wealth of Nations*—
a fact which may stand as a symbol of the relation of all three shaping
forces. The matrix of the American democratic idea lay in the span
between the Cromwellian Revolution and the French Revolution, and
while it suffered a sea change when it came over to American shores, it
was recognizably democratic by the time the new Republic was formed.
There was only a brief span in the American national life that could
be termed predemocratic, preindustrial, or precapitalist. As Louis
Hartz has pointed out, the American tradition included no dominating
feudal regime needing to be overthrown.

One must contrast this with the history of peoples whose origins
reach much further back—the English, the French, the Mediterranean,
the pre-Soviet Russian. Their traditions were already well established
by the time the trinity of industrialism, capitalism, and democracy
came to the world stage. They had to absorb them and play down whatever elements in the trinity did not fit into their tradition. These were
the conservative cultures. There is another kind of contrast between
the case of America and the Communist cultures of present-day Russia,
eastern Europe, China, and southeast Asia. They had to rediscover their
national traditions and absorb them into their new ideologies, playing
down whatever in the tradition did not jibe with the new structure of
power and the new system of class relations.

America, on the other hand, has not had to play down drastically
either the new forces because of its tradition or its tradition because of
the new forces. As a result there has been a continuity between the
elements that make up the contemporary industrial-capitalist-democratic
culture. It is a continuity between the remembered national past and the
living present—one that has been so organic as to be perilously deceptive, and lulls the unwary observer into the illusion that the heritage
does not even exist and that America is "traditionless" as well as "historyless." The exception, of course, is the case of the South, where
slavery and the tragic Civil War defeat broke the continuity of history
much as feudalism and revolution did in Europe. This may explain
why the South has had so tragic a sense of destructiveness and has been
so conscious of its history.

But for the nation as a whole the continuity of history and tradition
is one reason for the activism of Americans. They do not think of
themselves—to use John Dollard's phrase—as "the passive porters of a
cultural tradition." They have made their tradition as well as their
culture in the same act.

One important fact must be added. America, one of the youngest of the great civilizations of the world, is one of the oldest and most continuous of the social systems. Three and a half centuries is a short time as the span of a civilization goes, but it is a long time as the span of uninterrupted social power goes.

Of the important peoples today the French had their Revolution shortly after the Americans, but a series of catastrophes in three successive wars wiped out much of the staying power of the ruling class and brought a chronic instability of regimes. The Germans had a frustrated social revolution in 1918 and a Fascist one in 1933 for which they had to pay heavily in social chaos. After several abortive attempts, the Russians had their Communist revolution in 1917, changing the base of class power; and their subsequent leadership of the world Communist movement has made them underline the newness of their social system. The modern Chinese had one revolution in 1911 and, after a protracted civil war, a successful Communist revolution in 1948-49. India, after winning its freedom by a revolution of passive resistance, launched a mixed economy with Socialist elements; the same is true to differing degrees of Burma, Israel, Indonesia. Of the Latin-American nations, Brazil and Argentina are typical in having broken away from European rule by revolution, which in turn was followed by a series of internal revolts and military coups. Even in Britain, where the system of capitalist power has lasted longer than anywhere except America, the pressures toward a Socialist economy and society have been stronger than anything in the American experience.

Not only has there been in America an unbroken succession of national administrations without violence, but all of them—whether Federalist or Jeffersonian, Whig or Jacksonian, conservative Republican or New Deal—have stayed within roughly the same broad frame of capitalist power. In this sense one may say (perhaps with too much flipness) that the system of class power has remained unchanged from the days of Cotton Mather to those of the Cotton Exchange, from General Washington to General Eisenhower and General Motors, from Hamilton and Biddle to Alcoa and Du Pont. The revolution against England was accompanied, to be sure, by a social revolution in the sense that the feudal residues which had not been left behind in transit from Europe were wiped out. But when we speak of the American Revolution as a "social revolution," we must not forget that while it was antimercantilist and (in the sense above) antifeudal, it was not anticapitalist. It did not aim at ousting one class from power and replacing it with another. Its language carried a far-reaching revolutionary potential in the social sense too. But while it embodied the emerging social thought of its day, it was followed by a Constitution which limited the potential revolutionary majority, and which protected funded property, landed property, slave property, and business property. The frame of capitalist power was built within that scheme of thought and protection.

American history has, of course, had its major party battles, in the era of Jefferson, Jackson, Cleveland, Wilson, and Franklin Roosevelt—party battles which were notable because they also marked conflicts of class interest and shifts of class power. Yet it remains true that these battles were staged within roughly the same frame of power. Whatever the differences between Federalists and Jeffersonians, Whigs and Jacksonians, Republicans and Populists, Old Guard and New Deal, they were differences within a common frame of social structure and capitalist assumptions. Only in the Civil War was there a struggle between two economic and social systems, and the victory of one over the other. But Louis Hartz quite rightly observes that even the "great conservative reaction" of George Fitzhugh "died without impact on the mind of a nation." The liberal capitalist system of action, thought, and power remained in possession of the field.*

What is the nature of this frame of power and the sources of its tenacity? A system of individualist small enterprise has been replaced largely by corporate capitalism, the individual's freedom has been limited by Big Government and the "private governments" of Big Business and Big Labor, and a system of economic incentives and controls once useful in expanding the frontiers and exploiting the resources of a continent has had to adapt itself to meet the pace of a changing technology. Yet the hope for the career open to talents is still active in the American heart, and social mobility remains a reality in the vast middle reaches of the American class pyramid, even if at the top and bottom it continues relatively rigid.

With a civilization as with a person, the wealth and power it possesses count for less than the animating idea that possesses it. The American social system, when it was young, was filled with a great hope and an animating dream. But youth is never recapturable, and it is often indecent to protract it. A time comes when it is less important to be young than to be whole. No civilization can too long tolerate a cleavage between the professing rhetoric of its tradition and the possessive force of its frame of power.

The anthropologists point out that cultures are both fulfilling and frustrating. A functional view of any society will show that its priesthood, its system of magic, its family institution, its ways of ownership and of leadership, operate as they do because they fulfill some strong drive in those who make up the society. If you take the view of a cultural

* For a further discussion of the American social system as a system of capitalist assumptions, see Ch. V and Ch. VII.

anthropologist, you will see the other side of the functional shield: how repressive the major institutions are to the individuals in the society, damming their energies, stifling their creativeness, splitting their purposes. The fact is that cultures are bundles of conflicting and even contradictory tendencies. A living culture, however much it may strive to resolve its contradictions, retains the clashes of purpose, the overlappings, and the sense of paradox of any living and growing organism.

Nowhere is this truer than in a culture like the American. The conservatives emphasize how stable the American tradition has been, and they are right. It has been open to change through the methods of majority will checked by minority right and power. It has achieved a variety of fulfillments for the dreams and ambitions of a variety of people. It has thus channeled off the energies which, in less flexible and more impoverished systems, have led to the European type of class struggles and to radical shifts of class power.

But the spokesmen of the possessing groups forget that the American tradition was shaped as part of a revolutionary quest for the good life. Some of them want to use it now as a sedative against the fretful, sleepless night of the modern world. They are like children who use any tool or plaything as a way of expressing their anxieties, a weapon with which to subdue the recalcitrant object before them. That is why the symbols of the heritage which the conservatives stress are the due-process concept, the weak state, the checks and divisions within the governmental powers, the system of federalism which divides power between the central government and the states and thus offers loopholes for escape from controls, the fear of bureaucracy, the belittling of "politics," the boast of classlessness, the stress on "Americanism" as opposed to "foreign" influences. And that is why the values they stress are those of order, inequality, and the authority of the past, as against change, the guarantee of social minima, and the claims of the future. That is also, finally, why the figures they invoke in the American tradition are those of John Adams, Daniel Webster, and John Calhoun.

Usually this version of the tradition avoids the symbols of revolution, as though the conservative spokesmen felt that the fact of change in the world around them could be exorcised by silence about their own revolutionary past. Latterly there has been an effort to make the "free-enterprise system" the center and sum of the American tradition. This obviously seeks to capitalize on the emotional value of the symbols of freedom when invoked in the cause of power, but it forgets that free enterprise was itself the product of a revolutionary movement, and that in the era of Jackson it was one of the slogans of the liberals. What happened later in history was that "free enterprise" became the slogan of big enterprise, and the "free-enterprise economy" came to link the civil liberties tradition with the economic power of a class. Behind the symbol of these freedoms is that of the Constitution itself, which guarantees them. Thus the equation becomes "Constitution equals Freedoms equals Free-Enterprise System," and by easy stages a system of economic power becomes invested with the sanctity of the Constitution itself. In this sense the trappings of the tradition have become the shrewd ceremonial of the insecure spirit of the possessing classes.

Unlike the Europeans, Americans have never turned traditionalism into a major political and social philosophy and a party movement. In Great Britain the Tory thinkers and politicians built a great Conservative movement. But the history of the Continent has been disfigured by a peculiar amalgam of literary interpretation, religious passion, and reactionary mysticism such as one finds in clerical writers like Bonald and De Maistre, in the "integral nationalism" school of Maurras, or in the "Prussian Socialism" of Spengler, not to speak of the racist writers. These European theories sought to convert traditionalism into an intellectual system which could serve as the base for a popular political movement. Since they had to work in a milieu of sharp class consciousness they sometimes directed their appeal to the declassed intellectuals, sometimes to the insecure middle class that wanted to identify with the faded feudal values of the past, sometimes even (as with the racists) to the formless mass of the lower classes.

There have been no similar roots for a traditionalist movement in America. The closest approach to a philosophy of traditionalism in America has been in the romantic cult of the section-as-nation in Calhoun's thought and George Fitzhugh's, in the glorifying of a "natural aristocracy" and the parading of democratic disasters by antimajoritarian writers like Irving Babbitt and Paul Elmer More, and in the jealous guardianship of the property tradition in the interests of business by a series of champions from Daniel Webster through Robert A. Taft. More recently Russell Kirk and a few other writers tried to evoke a "new conservatism" from a nostalgic hankering for the values of tradition, loyalty, power, and order. Their passion fluttered the academic dovecots for a passing moment, as the Southern agrarians had done in the 1920s. In a more moderate vein, writers like Clinton Rossiter, August Heckscher, and Peter Viereck tried to chart out a very different kind of "New Conservative" traditionalism: they had made their peace with the New-Deal-as-history and with modern American society, but they put more store by the centuries of past experience than by the urgencies of the present. Yet no political movements and no theorist and political leader of the stature of Calhoun emerged to convert these varied fumblings into something meaningful and powerful.

It is worth noting that when American traditionalists seek an intellectual authority on which to build, many of them turn to Burke, Disraeli, and Winston Churchill, attracted by the tradition of an aristocracy which had cohesion and perspective and kept itself free of contact with the parvenu mercantile class. A few are now willing to invoke as patron saints the spokesmen of American business and property—John Adams and Marshall, Hamilton and Webster, Grant and Choate and Mark Hanna, William Graham Sumner and Andrew Carnegie, J. P. Morgan, John D. Rockefeller, and Elihu Root. In the British case there were at least two ordered elites—the Lords Spiritual who were invested with spiritual sanctions in a state-supported Church, and the Lords Temporal who were a landed aristocracy with inherited status—neither of which the American case possesses. Nor does America possess the aristocratic arbiters of the Continent who dictated conduct and morals for the rest of the population. Thus in the anxious quest for some cementing force for a Good Society, the American traditionalists find themselves tempted to go outside the American tradition.

Another trouble with the chronic invokers of the conservative American tradition is that there is a deep split between the intellectuals of the group who shape the conservative philosophies and the political leaders who shape the conservative policies. With leaders like Theodore Roosevelt and Wendell Willkie the conservative intellectuals found common ground, as they did with judges like Charles Evans Hughes and administrators like Frederick Stimson. But the kind of teamplay the liberal intellectuals achieved with the politicians under Roosevelt's New Deal and Truman's Fair Deal, or the sympathy the "eggheads" found with Adlai Stevenson and with the large number of liberal Democratic Senators, is one for which the conservative intellectuals hanker fruitlessly. Disdaining the optimism, the cult of progress, the reliance on man's rationality, and the easy clichés of many of the liberals, and recoiling from the primitivism of the new radical Right (a more powerful movement than that of the "new conservatives") they find themselves rootless and homeless.

They feel thus also because they have no major tradition in American history to fall back upon. The doctrine of elites chosen by Divine Right to rule others, the pessimist doctrines of human sin and depravity, the fear of rapid change, the image of a hierarchical society in which each man knows and holds to the privileges and duties that attach to his place—these represent a minor, not a major, strain in the American tradition. The main current of the tradition, including even some of the Federalist and Whig figures as well as Jeffersonian, Jacksonian, and New Deal, is Lockean, optimist. libertarian, antihierarchical, fluid, dynamic.

There can be no better proof of this than a hard look at the strongest oligarchy America has had—that of the business and managerial group. I call it an oligarchy rather than an aristocracy, as De Tocqueville did, because birth and inheritance play less of a role in it than energy and resourcefulness. "Fame and success," said Samuel E. Morison, "await one who will make a fresh distillation of our entire history with the conservative tradition acting as a leaven." He was calling, in short, for someone who would take the Beards' *Rise of American Civilization* and turn it upside down, or who would follow up on the cry of Henry Cabot Lodge and Albert Beveridge that "the Democrats are always wrong."

Someday some young conservative historian will perhaps do it. Or, even better, he may follow the suggestion of Elisha Douglas that the Puritan tradition led to a "secularized Puritanism" which found expression in the tradition of stewardship by an elite of wisdom, virtue, and education. If he emphasizes the later business conservatism—that of acquisition rather than values—he will find that the tradition of American business is drastically different from the aristocracies and oligarchies of Europe: that it is based on Locke's conception both of property and of civil government, that it is buoyantly optimistic, that it out-liberals the liberals in its belief in progress, that its passion is not for order but for production and profit records, that it cares less for hierarchy than for power, that it is always in revolution because it is always being churned up in its goals and methods by technological changes which in large measure it begets, that its morality rarely rises above the moral standards of the rest of the society, that its creed is not integrity but acquisitiveness, not moderation but go-gettism and dynamism.

In any event it would be healthy for American conservatives to reappraise the elements in the American tradition that attract them most, including a fresh look at the leadership qualities and administrative ability of George Washington, the brilliance of John Adams and John Randolph, the nation-building genius of Hamilton and Marshall, the innate moderation of Lincoln, and even (as Richard Hofstadter points out) the conservative core in men like Theodore Roosevelt and Woodrow Wilson. It would be productive for them to follow the lead of historians like Nevins and Hacker and make an effort to refurbish the reputations of the "Robber Barons"* and to see the big business corporation as one of the organic units of American history. They would find that there are an endless number of points at which the major liberal and minor conservative strands in the American tradition converge and are interwoven, that the American welfare corporation offers them a

* For a discussion of the Nevins thesis on business history, see Ch. V, Sec. 2, "The Rise and Decline of the Titan."

better base to build on than the European aristocracies, that the best products of the American aristocracy from Jefferson to Franklin Roosevelt to Adlai Stevenson and Averell Harriman have found their self-expression in leading mass progressive movements, and that the ideas of dynamism and of welfare (the welfare corporation, welfare trade-union, welfare state) are common elements that run through American history, whether viewed by conservatives or liberals.*

Americans will not respond to a stick-in-the-mud creed of traditionalism that cherishes the past as a way of shutting out the facts and tasks of the present. The American spirit is inclusive rather than exclusive, optimistic rather than fear-ridden, dynamic rather than obsessed with order and hierarchy.

7. American Dynamism

THUS THE BROADEST and most inclusive approach to the American tradition would put the emphasis on its dynamism. This makes the tradition something other than a thin apologia for a "democratic totalitarianism" that would break with history, or an effort to cover oligarchical power with the trappings of the American past. American dynamism has been gradualist, continuous, persistent. It has always transcended the past in the process of incorporating it. As Nietzsche put it: "The verdict of the past is always an oracle: only as architects of the future, as knowers of the present, will you understand it." American history vindicates this insight into the nature of a dynamic civilization.

This dynamism cannot be chastely selective, with its elements chosen or rejected on the basis of class outlook and political belief. Some seek the dynamism of America only in the history of the democratic idea, others only in the history of American property and capitalism. Some seek it only on the farm or frontier, or only in the factory, only at the grass roots or only in the city, only in the quest for profits or only in the crusade against the profit system, only in American world leadership or only in the struggles on the domestic front. Some seek it only in literature and art and the works of the American elite mind, and others only in popular culture.

The fact is that the American experience has operated in every area. There has been the dynamism of the pioneer and the mechanic, the independent farmer and the trade-union worker; of the toolmaker, the inventor, the financier. There has been the dynamism of the "company men"—the managers, the factory organizers, the salesmen who have

* See also the treatment of conservatism, radicalism, and liberalism in Ch. X, Sec. 2, "American Thought: the Angle of Vision."

made the irrepressible practical imagination of Americans world-
famous. There has been the dynamism of the engineering mind, whether
in technology or in the "social engineering" of law or public health,
social work or social legislation. There has been the dynamism of the
pamphleteer, the political leader, the intellectual who saw with clarity
and wrote with courage, the government administrator who worked
on blueprints for river-valley development and the charting of new
patterns for community life. There has been the dynamism of the men
of business power whose resourcefulness and single-mindedness gave
them economic mastery in a political democracy; and there has been
also the dynamism of the insurgent movements of mass democracy, the
successive and irresistible pulsations of a democratic will that has
challenged the oligarchs and set limits to their power.

There is an often quoted passage in the letter Walt Whitman sent to
Emerson with *Leaves of Grass:* "Master, I am a man who has perfect
faith. Master, we have not come through centuries, caste, heroisms,
fables, to halt in this land today." One could not find a better summary
of American dynamism.

What crucial elements in the American experience gave it this
quality? There was the fact of a fresh start, with rich resources, by
men who carried with them a passion for freedom and an aversion
to authoritarianism. There was the vast expanse of a continent, lending
a largeness of outlook to those who lived on it. There was the richness
of racial and ethnic mixture which is part of a larger pluralism in American life—a pluralism not only of stock but of regional environments, of
Federal political units, of economic forms, and of religious sects. There
was a system of opportunity that gave scope to the energies of its young
people and managed tolerably to give work its opportunity, aspiration
its outlet, talent its stimulus, and ability its reward. There was an optimistic view of American prospects and a tough concreteness of outlook that judged ideas and values by their results. There was, finally,
the idea of equality which, in spite of economic obstructions, educational discriminations, and the distorting hatreds of racism, was kept
alive as the ruling passion of American life.

These—the expanse of space, the mixture of race, the pluralism of
region and religion, the fresh start, the release of energies, the access
to opportunity, the optimism and pragmatism of a society in motion,
the passion for equality—were the crucial shaping forces of the American
heritage.

Throughout American history new forces have been at work transforming the specific shapes the heritage has taken. One can trace four

periods which were the seedbeds of what is most viable in the American tradition.

The first was the period of revolution and consolidation, from the 1770s through 1800, when the American people went beyond discontent to revolution and beyond revolution to national unity. The second was the period of the 1830s and 1840s, when a frontier exuberance combined with a developing industrialism, an emerging workers' movement, a full consciousness of nationality, a radical democratic impulse, and a literary Renaissance to produce the classic ("Jacksonian") phase of a democracy's early strength. The third was the period roughly from 1890 to 1910, when capitalist industrialism reached its high point before it became a corporate bureaucracy, when the great waves of immigration brought new energies to American shores, when rural ways of thought were merged with new urban ways of life to produce the characteristic American middle-class amalgam, when the sweep of Populism set new sights for Americans and the cry for "reform" and "social justice" renewed the equalitarian impulse.

The fourth is the contemporary period of the "Big Change" in American society which concerns us in this study, starting with the New Deal in 1933 and continuing through the turbulent years of the war and the postwar period. This was a quarter century during which Americans transformed their family structure, population growth, suburbs, energy resources, mechanization, corporations, trade-unions, class structure, and mass media almost beyond recognition. It was the period of sprouting babies and autos, of atomic energy for war and peace, of the automatic factory, of the new middle classes, of crowded universities, of TV elections, of stock-market boom and high taxes and skyrocketing incomes which everyone lived beyond. It was also a period when Americans discovered that they could surmount the sharpest economic crises and build a viable economy regardless of the labels of "socialist" or "capitalist," and that their democratic destiny could be fulfilled only in a world framework.

This does not mean that the elements of the earlier tradition were wholly left behind. Perhaps because of their English heritage, perhaps because Americans learned through everyday experience the meaning of St. Paul's injunction, "Prove all things and hold fast to that which is good," their dynamism has been a gradualist one. Individualism—the most vaunted and celebrated of American attitudes—no longer exists in its classic economic form, but the individual's welfare remains for most the test of social striving: Americans understand that while the social means must be collective the end product must be the fulfillment of the individual life. The same sort of change, to take another example has taken place in traditional antistatism: the idea of a weak state was necessarily replaced by one that can govern in a turbulent world, but Americans retain their suspicion of concentrated power, whether in government, corporation, or trade-union. Though they know power must be there to be exercised, they insist on administering it wherever possible within a frame of safeguards and within an autonomous unit.

When I make dynamism so central in American tradition I am aware that it is a concept which carries its dangers. Walter P. Webb has traced the origins of modern Western dynamism to the boom effects of the opening of the New World frontiers upon the "metropolis" of the settled areas. The eighteenth and nineteenth centuries were the centuries of the Great Hope in the Western world, when progress was taken for granted, anything was possible, and nothing was excluded from human goals. In the end this *élan* led in Europe and Asia to the totalitarian view that nothing was excluded from human means either. History became, in Hitler's terms, "the art of the impossible"—a phrase which turned out to include the techniques of genocide. Recoiling from these prospects, American thought has recently tended toward the pessimist view of human nature expressed by Reinhold Niebuhr. As sensitive a political thinker as Walter Lippmann, who had once flirted with Socialism and called for "mastery" rather than "drift," now took over the Oriental conception of society as governed by a set of moral imperatives which were the "mandate of Heaven."

However persuasive these anxieties, they did not express the energies of the American spirit, which remained generally dynamic. True, there have been stretches, especially during depressions or in periods of danger for internal freedom, when large numbers of Americans were assailed by doubts about the reality of the America they had believed in. Yet even in crisis or stagnation most Americans persisted in their image of America as an unfinished country in which history was the art of the possible, but in which the possible, by experience, seemed to stretch farther than anywhere else. That is why they have continued —rightly or wrongly—to see their own country as a model which other peoples are bound in the end to follow.

Since the beginning there have been two crucial images in the American mind. One is that of the self-reliant craftsman, whether pioneer, farmer, or mechanic—the man who could make something of the American resources, apply his strength and skill to Nature's abundance, fashion new tools and machines, imagine and carry through new constructions. Without taking himself overseriously, the American has generally regarded the great engineering, business, and governmental tasks as jobs to be done, agenda for the craftsman.

The second has been an image from the American environment: that of a vast continent to be discovered, explored, cleared, built up, populated, energized; which has not excluded the image of a continent to be rifled, despoiled, much of it wasted, for there has been an enormous margin of waste. Scott Fitzgerald has called this continental image "the last and greatest of all human dreams; for a transitory enchanted moment man must have held his breath in the presence of this continent, compelled into an aesthetic contemplation he neither understood nor desired, face to face for the last time in history with something commensurate to his capacity for wonder."

But not, I think, for the last time. Part of the American heritage is the spirit that hates a cribbed confinement. In a world whose dimensions have shrunk so that the urgencies of possible breakdown and world suicide have come closing in like the walls in "The Pit and the Pendulum," the American will not tolerate the fate of being boxed in, like a trapped rat. He will somehow break free, even if the new independence he must win is an independence from vested power groups within and the threat of world anarchy without, even if the new federalism he must help construct is that of an expanse of diverse social systems held within the frame of an open world society.*

* For the further development of this theme, see Ch. XII, Sec. 3, "National Interest and an Open World."

CHAPTER II

The Idea of American Civilization

IN WHICH, after having looked at the meaning of American history, we take a look at the central idea of the book—the idea that America is best seen as a total civilization pattern—and grapple with some of the difficulties involved in it. In the process the reader is taken on some excursions to explore the terrain of cultural anthropology, the newer psychologies, and the philosophy of history, seeking clues to the "Figure in the Carpet." We pay our respects to the condescensions of Spengler and Toynbee, among others ("Is America a Civilization?") and try to draw a portrait—the portrait of the American as the "Archetypal Man of the West" who has focused the characteristic energies of the modern world. We review what the leading foreign and American commentators have done in trying to isolate what gives America whatever distinctiveness it has ("American Exceptionalism"), and end by pointing out that there is no single key to the "American spirit" or the "American character," but a pattern of polar and often conflicting impulses ("Single Key—or Polar Pattern?").

The reader is warned that the going is hard here and the ground treacherous. He may want to move rapidly and lightly over it and perhaps return to it after he has read Chapter IX, "Character and Society," or at the end of the book.

The Idea of American Civilization

1. Figure in the Carpet

SOME of my readers, reflecting on the title I have given this book, may ask why I choose to call America a civilization, and whether Americans or any other highly technological people are in reality "civilized." This may be prompted by the prevailing view that in a world which may run amuck with nuclear weapons man has himself become a prehistoric monster scuttling across the floor of primitive seas, and his civilization a grim kind of joke.

The trouble with the term *civilization* is that it has been badly mauled and its meaning twisted. Sometimes it is used to mean that a particular society is urbane and mature, relatively free of the irrational Serpent in the rational Garden of Eden. In that sense there has never been a truly civilized people except in the literature of the imaginary voyages and the Utopian romances. There is a second sense in which politicians and editorial writers use the term as a "we or they" bludgeon against the enemy, whether in war or cold war. We have so often heard that "civilization is at stake" in the outcome of some struggle, martial or diplomatic, that we may well wish the wretched term disposed of forever. This is how Mark Twain felt about Western civilization at the time of the Boer War, when he said, "My idea of our civilization is that it is a shabby poor thing and full of cruelties, vanities, arrogancies, meannesses, and hypocrisies. As for the word, I hate the sound of it, for it conveys a lie; and as for the thing itself, I wish it was in Hell, where it belongs." But he hastens to add: "*Provided* we could get something better in the place of it. . . . Poor as it is it is better than real savagery." These inner tortures of Mark Twain, so much like the splits in intellectuals today, are further evidence that *civilization* as a concept must be extricated from emotional distortions and used objectively.

America as a democracy has had its impact on the world, and from Alexis de Tocqueville to Harold Laski most of the foreign observers have written about it from that angle. But while democracy is still America's most important idea and ideal, it is no longer—as it was in De Tocqueville's time or even in Bryce's—a novelty to be explained to the world or an experiment whose implications need to be spelled out. We must shift the focus of study from the master idea of democracy to a more inclusive and meaningful one. Anyone using democracy as the be-all and end-all of America, as the final test of everything in the culture, is bound to emerge (as Laski did in *The American Democracy*) with an irretrievable fault line between the rhetoric of democracy and the actualities of American life. We tend to forget that, by the world at large, America is being assessed not just as a democracy but in its total impact as a civilization.

Thus one can begin to shift the focus of American analysis from democracy only, from capitalism only, from a standardized and materialist machine civilization only, from popular culture only, or from foreign policy only, to the total American civilization pattern.

Fortunately the social sciences have reached the stage where such a shift of focus has become possible. We have moved beyond both political man and economic man, and beyond both the political and economic segments of the culture. Just as the new approaches to psychology and philosophy are helping us study the total person, so anthropology and social theory in its broadest sense are helping us understand the total culture, and the studies "on the growing edge" of the social sciences are focusing on the relation of culture and personality. Much of the meaningful recent work has been done on this "edge"—on the borders between the established disciplines, or by people using the techniques of several of them who have contributed major insights to make the study of the whole American civilization pattern possible.

The first is the culture concept, largely derived from the anthropologists who discovered that every people, no matter how primitive, had an organic culture. What they found was that a primitive people had its literature, even if only a body of folklore; had its science, even if only a system of magic; had its religion, even if only the worship and propitiation of idols; had its moral and legal system, even if only a set of tribal customs and sanctions. By observing the results of the contact of "higher" and "lower" cultures, our generation has learned what happens when a primitive people is "helped" or "uplifted" by one of the imperial peoples. The effect of such culture contacts on the American Indians or on the South Sea peoples is well known in Western literature. But its full meaning was not clear until the French sociologist Durkheim developed the concept of "anomie"—the collapse of traditional norms and values in a culture or a segment of it; and until anthropologists like Malinowski and Radcliffe-Brown developed a "functional" approach to the traits of primitive cultures. What emerged from their work, and especially from that of Ruth Benedict and

Margaret Mead, was the key idea that cultures are organic patterns to be treated as living wholes. This does not mean that such practices as child sacrifice or the disfigurement of women are justified by any function they may perform after they have been pushed beyond the point of value to the culture. But it does mean that institutions cannot be lifted out and displaced or replaced without jolting the rest, and must be set in the perspective of the whole culture before their meaning can be understood.

It only needed a reverse twist to turn this idea of the organic primitive culture back again to the contemporary nonprimitive ones. The insights that the anthropologists gained in studying the Eskimos, Bantu, or Melanesians illumined American and European societies too. The "anthropology of modern life" involved a fresh look at contemporary cultures as organic patterns, each with unique and characteristic features, yet each using certain social methods and fulfilling certain life purposes common to all human societies. The recent "cross-cultural" studies have sought to find common denominators between cultures, but the deeper truth is the wholeness of each culture in itself, primitive and modern alike.

Inevitably modern psychiatry got into the picture, to furnish the second major insight, and theorists argued hotly about the relative merits of the "psychological" and the "cultural" approaches. But the search for the roots of personality disturbances was bound to lead beyond the individual life history to the culture as a whole. Students and practitioners alike found that they could not understand the total person without setting him in the total culture and seeing the relation of his needs and burdens to the common drives and purposes within the culture. This search for the conditions of individual mental health led logically to a quest for the roots of cultural unhealth and dislocation. In the area of child-raising and the dislocations of family life, in the persistent outcroppings of juvenile delinquency, in the study of sexual behavior, of religion, and of economic competition, we have not only learned things about the social conditioning of the individual's inner life but indirectly about the culture as a whole.

The historians too—especially those who are philosophers of history —have provided the third major insight through their study of whole civilizations and of their rhythms of growth and decline. Arnold Toynbee studied "societies" or "civilizations" with certain tidal uniformities of rise and decay. His predecessor, Oswald Spengler, had seen the Egyptian, classical, Chinese, and Western societies in semibiological terms, tracing their rise and fall as one might trace the life history of plants. Both of them had at least one truth by the tail: the cultures men live in are not filing cases or collections of bits and pieces but organic wholes to be studied as such in the fluctuations of their energies and fortunes, in their actions and passions, their norms, institutions, striving, failure and achievement. The enduring work of these philosophers of history may prove to lie less in their discovery of any "laws" of history than in their dogged assumption that civilizations like western Europe, Russia, Islam, India, China, America, had a life to live and a death to endure, each with a heart and will and personality of its own. The philosophers of history may thus be seen as poets trying to find ways to present through symbols the inner-civilization style of historical peoples.

But no civilization pattern can be grasped as a whole unless the figure-in-the-carpet is somehow traced. The philosopher tries to do it by uncovering basic symbolic ways of life. Nietzsche, for example, used his studies in the origins of Greek tragedy to develop the idea of the Dionysian and Apollonian civilization styles. Spengler, who learned as much from Nietzsche as he did from Goethe, took the Faustus symbol as the key to modern Western man. Toynbee, who learned from both as also from Jung and the theologians, saw the figure-in-the-carpet as embodying the racial and cultural unconscious and therefore the whole buried history of social and emotional experience. Less concerned than Spengler with assigning a principle and name to each of the great civilizations, Toynbee looked for recurring patterns of behavior in all of them which would uncover the persistent riddle of rise and fall—and he emerged mainly with a bundle of poetic and religious insights.

2. Is America a Civilization?

WHERE DOES AMERICA fit into this picture? Almost without exception the great theories of history find no room for any concept of America as a civilization in its own right.

Since Spengler's purpose was to show the West on the downward arc of the life-history curve, he placed the West of his own day at a point on the arc parallel to where the Roman world was in the days of the shattering Imperial wars. In both cases (as Spengler saw it) the springtime creativeness of the folk-mind had dried up, the roots and traditions of the land had been replaced by the rootlessness of "megalopolis," the early class system of aristocracy, clergy, and peasants had been pushed aside first by a middle class with its money materialism and then by a proletariat, and the world struggle had set the stage for the emergence of a world empire under a succession of Caesars.

Given this scheme, one might expect Spengler to have been struck by its terrifying relevance to the case of America, yet he himself hesitated to make it explicit. His American disciples (see E. F. Dakin, *Today and History*) went the whole way, seeing America as the only possible Rome of today, fated to produce its Caesars and to thrust at a world imperium. But in Spengler's thinking the role of Rome was to be played by the Germans. Writing between World Wars I and II, he was still unable to see America as much more than a truncated morphological specimen that didn't quite fit into his theory of the rhythms of culture and civilization. America for Spengler was a derivative civilization—only an offshoot, perhaps an excrescence, of the West.

Toynbee too made summary shrift of America as a civilization. In his bold image of the "cliff-hangers," to describe man's painful pilgrimage through six thousand years of human history, he lists only five civilizations (out of nineteen or twenty-one) as still active—the Western, orthodox Christian, Islamic, Hindu, and Far Eastern civilizations. Since his units were broadly delimited by religion, geography, technology, he included in Western civilization the world shaped at once by Roman and Protestant Christianity and by the techniques of modern industrialism. His discussions of America are of a nation-state on the margin of this civilization, an arid late-comer in the history of Western Christian industrial society—affected with all the latter-day scars and curses of that society without many discernible graces to offset them.

In taking issue with Spengler and Toynbee, I am not arguing for a chauvinist view of America as the source and center of Western civilization. But it is worth asking whether we must deal with America always as a fragment of a larger civilization unit whose creative center is assigned elsewhere. It is unfair even to Europe to make something called the "West" the great isolable unit: for as the initiative in technology and in economic and military power shifts steadily across the Atlantic, there is danger of Europe's being dismissed as only a tributary of American civilization. Malraux rightly argues for the concept of "European man," although he recognizes the ties of Europe with America; similarly, recognizing the ties of America with Europe, one can argue for America as a civilization.

For good or ill, America is what it is—a culture in its own right, with many characteristic lines of power and meaning of its own, ranking with Greece and Rome as one of the great distinctive civilizations of history.

Actually the American historians have been working in practice on a premise which the social thinkers were unwilling to admit in theory. Charles and Mary Beard, in their classic history *The Rise of American Civilization,* used the term "civilization" quite deliberately for the whole emerging pattern of thought, action, and aspiration. As they wrote later, "No idea, such as democracy, liberty, or the American way of life, expresses the American spirit so coherently, comprehensively, or systematically as does the idea of civilization."

I must pause here for a note on the meaning of several crucial terms as I shall be using them. I use the idea of American civilization as the master theme of this book instead of "democracy" (De Tocqueville, Laski) or "commonwealth" (Bryce), which are too narrowly political; or "character" (Gorer, Riesman), which refers too directly to personality structure. There remain the broad terms, "culture" and "society," which have a body of common meaning with "civilization." Spengler called the earlier seasonal phases of germination and bloom "culture," and the season of dry winter-hardening "civilization"; but that was his own peculiar scheme. Some American social thinkers use "civilization" for the total institutional *means* whereby a people seeks to achieve the *ends* which are implied in "culture." This is suggestive, yet means and ends, institutions and values, frame and content, are always connected in a two-way relation: it is difficult to say that the courthouse in which a marriage is licensed or a criminal tried is part of American civilization, but that the marriage beliefs or the legal system belong to American culture.

America is at once *culture* and *civilization,* and *society* as well. The terms refer to different aspects of the same whole rather than to different segments of it. "Culture" has been used by anthropologists since E. B. Tylor's famous definition of it: "that complex whole which includes knowledge, belief, art, morals, law, custom, and any other capabilities and habits acquired by man as a member of society." More recently, in the sense defined by Kluckhohn and Kelly as "a historically derived system of explicit and implicit designs for living which tend to be shared by all or specially designated members of a group," it has become the key term of the social sciences. I use it to mean the *matrix* of American living, the stuff of life that is transmitted, learned, and relearned, with the stress on the "designs for living"—the norms and beliefs and all the curious and twisted shapes they take. I use "society" to put the emphasis elsewhere: on the common structure of American living, on the group units within which it clusters (family, club, gang, neighborhood, town, suburb, army, school, church), and on the relations between them. Thus "society" refers to the total group and institutional framework, and the processes of living together and being knit together within it as *socii* or members of the same commonalty.

I use "civilization" as my broadest concept. When a culture—which is the set of blueprints for a society—has grown highly complex and has cut a wide swath in history and in the minds of men, one looks for a term more highly charged with the overtones of these meanings.

"Civilization" is such a term. One thinks of the civilizations of Greece and Rome, of China and Britain, of the Aztec-Mayan civilization, of India, of Renaissance Italy, of Spain and France, of Russia and America. They differ from the archaic cultures of, let us say, the Bushmen or Pygmies or the Andaman Islanders because each of them at some phase of its history has been a great going concern leaving a deep imprint on the human consciousness, a scar on men's minds. They had a way of life and a world view that have become deeply part of human experience.

I believe this to be true of America. It is likely that historians will look back on American life and see it—with its truths and errors, its callownesses and obsessions and insights, its childishness and its power —as one of the memorable civilizations of history. Whoever wants to convey this sense of the total pattern and total impact in canvassing the actions and strivings and passions of America may well fall back on the idea of American civilization.

3. Archetypal Man of the West

COMMENTATORS ON AMERICAN TRAITS delight in quoting De Crève-coeur's classic remark that "the American is a new man who acts on new principles." One should add that while the American was a *novus homo* when De Crèvecoeur wrote his *Letters from an American Farmer* toward the end of the eighteenth century, he is no longer so in the mid-twentieth. He is no longer an experiment: he has been proved a success, by every standard of wealth, glitter, prestige, freedom, and power. Wherever history pours fresh molten metal, in industrial achievement, living standards, and political freedom, inevitably it makes him at least in part the mold. The American has become the "New World man" —the archetypal man of the West.

For an American to write thus may seem too boastful, yet I try to write it as if I were not American but a detached observer noting a new phenomenon. Americans are not loved in the world today, although they deeply desire affection. In the countries of color there is a good deal of suspicion of them, and even some hatred. In the older civilizations of Europe there is a kind of patronizing contempt which passes for anti-Americanism. Throughout the world there is a fear of the current American stress on arms and money. Yet it remains true that the principal imperialism the American exercises is the imperialism of attraction. If he is not admired, he is envied; and even his enemies and rivals pay him the homage of imitation. People throughout the world turn almost as by a tropism to the American image. To be American is no longer to be only a nationality. It has become, along with Communism and in rivalry with it, a key pattern of action and values.

So summary a conquest of the world's imagination, never before achieved without arms and colonization, is proof of an inner harmony between America and the modern spirit. It is because of this harmony that America has acted as a suction force, drawing from everywhere people attuned to its basic modes of life. The migration to America, from the start, of capital and of human labor and talent, was followed by the migration from America of capital, talent, economic and military strength. Both migrations, to and from America, have multiplied its influence. Having absorbed the world's strength to form its own, America has been fusing its own strength with the world's.

There has been from the start a marriage of true minds between the American and the type-man of the modern era, the New World man. To the question, wonderfully put in 1782 by De Crèvecoeur in his *American Farmer,* "What then is the American, this new man?" De Tocqueville sought an answer on his visit in the 1830s. The greatness of his book lay at least partly in its portrayal of a young civilization in which incipient European forces could reach their climactic form. In America the main trends of tendency that were dammed up in Europe itself were to find expression. As Robert Payne has put it, "America is Europe with all the walls down." Although I have insisted that America is a definable civilization in itself, it first emerged as an offshoot from the larger entity of the West which was seeking a New World form. The American is thus the concentrated embodiment of Western man, more sharply delineated, developed under more urgent conditions, but with most of the essential traits present.

Consider some of these traits. I am trying here to describe, not the American alone, but a type which has cropped up all over Europe as well since the Reformation and the rise of science.*

He is mobile, restless. He has largely broken with status and moves more freely than Old World man moved up and down the ladder of wealth and class rank, as he moved over large areas, conquering space. He rifles the sciences as he opens up the continents, quenchless in his thirst for experience. He is this-worldly and not otherworldly, with a

---

* I have in mind, although I have not strictly followed, some of the delineations of modern Western man by Mumford, Huizinga, Toynbee, Ortega y Gasset, Alfonso Reyes. The best recent treatment is in Lewis Mumford, *The Transformations of Man* (1956), appearing after this book was finished. It gives remarkable portraits of Old World Man, New World Man, and the monstrous "Post-Historic Man" which is a projection of tendencies present in both American and Russian civilization. I deal with these tendencies, and with both the portent and promise of the future in Ch. XII, "America As a World Power," especially Sec. 7, "The Destiny of a Civilization."

sharp sense of time and its uses: the objects of his ambition are secular rather than sacred. Accustomed to thinking in terms of the attainable, he is optimistic, with a belief in progress and a respect for technical skills and material success. He is *homo faber,* stamping his imprint on products and on machines that make products and on machines that run machines, and increasingly in the same spirit on art and ideas. He believes in whatever can be touched, grasped, measured. He is a technical man, whose absorption is not with *to what good* but with *how.* He is non-ascetic, with a taste for comfort and a belief that the means, if not the goal, of life are found in a higher living standard.

He is *l'homme moyen sensuel,* not too finicky in his sexual life about caste or class lines or about rigid standards of virtue. Hungering for a sense of personal worth, he is torn between the materialisms he can achieve and the feeling of wholeness which eludes him. He has a disquieting sense that the old gods too have eluded him and wonders when the new ones will arrive. Yet, unlike men of previous ages, it is not salvation he is after, nor virtue, nor saintliness, nor beauty, nor status. He is an amoral man of energy, mastery, and power. Above all else, he is a man for whom the walls have been broken down. He is the double figure in Marlowe, of Tamerlane and Dr. Faustus, the one sweeping like a footloose barbarian across the plains to overleap the barriers of earlier civilizations, the other breaking the taboos against knowledge and experience, even at the cost of his soul.

For this modern man the world has not yet become one world, and as the contemporary tensions attest, some time will elapse before it does. Yet what is likely to count in this direction is less the outlook of the diplomats than of the new geographers who complete the work of the cartographers of the Renaissance. Being technical men, they turn the globe around every possible way, but basically theirs is the airman's view for whom political boundaries are minor, and the heavens arch over them to be pierced and the earth stretches out to be engirded by flight. For the airman, racial boundaries do not exist either: what he sees from the air is not the color of men but how well the fields are laid out and irrigated and cultivated, what has been done in uncovering and using Nature's resources, what chimneys and spires are the witnesses of industry and culture, what clusters of community life there are in villages, cities, metropolitan areas. This was the glimpse that Wendell Willkie had—that despite divergences of economic systems, of race and color and language and social structure, the world is compassable, interdependent, organic.

Thus the great themes of the Renaissance and Reformation are fulfilled in the American as the archetypal modern man—the discovery of new areas, the charting of the skies, the lure of power, the realization of self in works, the magic of science, the consciousness of the individual, the sense of the unity of history. These are the themes that have left their mark on modern man. Perceiving this, Wyndham Lewis said of America that "the logic of the geographical position and history of the U.S. leads . . . to the ultimate formation of a society that will not be as other societies, but an epitome of all societies." He had in mind specifically the ethnic pluralism and democratic inclusiveness of America which hold the world in microcosm. It is this trans-national character of American society which, despite the surviving American tribalisms, makes it congruous with the strivings of other peoples. The same applies to the structure of the American personality, which is mobile, ethnically diverse, energy-charged, amoral, optimistic, genial, technic-minded, power-oriented. The question is not whether these traits are admirable or lovable but whether they polarized the energies of much of the world—as they do.

4. American Exceptionalism

THE PORTRAIT OF American—and New World—man I have just drawn is not meant to be an idealized one. It has shadows as well as lights. And it poses a riddle of both logic and history: logically, how we can speak of the American as the "archetypal" man of the modern world and at the same time assert that American civilization is a pattern within itself, whole and unique; historically, how America has developed out of the common conditions of the modern world, yet developed with such an acceleration of energy and power; and whether the future arc of its development is likely to recapitulate the course of experience of European and Asiatic civilizations.

I do not underestimate the difficulties of this riddle. That is why I am little inclined to see America within any of the rather grandiose schemes of historical determinism, whose real value is to suggest lines of study and not to close them. The seduction of historical parallels should not lure us away from studying America as a civilization pattern in itself—its tensions, its lines of development, its weaknesses and strengths. The learning of Vico and Hegel, of Marx, of Spengler and Toynbee, of Sorokin, would still leave unexplained the unlikely genesis of America, its rapid rise to power, the contrast of its outer image and its inner qualities, its materialism and idealism, its isolationism and leadership role. Whether such a civilization will survive or is doomed will depend less on grand historical "laws" than upon how Americans grapple with their problems and use their characteristic resources and energies.

If I do not subscribe to the cry of "America is doomed," neither am I

pleading for the distorted version of "American exceptionalism" which
has been the pious theme of spread-eagle theorists seeking to depict
America as immune from the forces of history and the laws of life. This
version of exceptionalism is easily used as an idea weapon in the anti-
democratic struggle, as Schlesinger shows in citing the attack on the efforts to organize trade-unions in the Jacksonian period. Ever since then
the cry that "America is different" has been an unfailing answer to any
challenge that might disturb the structure of existing power, and the
carriers of the challenge have been regarded as "un-American," "alien,"
and therefore "subversive."

But these distortions should not blind us to the valid elements in the
theory of exceptionalism. The fact is that while American civilization is
not immune to the surging beat of world forces, it has developed its own
characteristic institutions, traits, and social conditions within the larger
frame. America represents, as I have stressed above, the naked embodiment of the most dynamic elements of modern Western history. What
this implies is that exceptionalism *includes* an acceptance of the European ties and does not reject them. The idea of American exceptionalism and the idea of American integration into the broader Western pattern are not mutually exclusive but are polar facets of the same field of
energy. When you speak of American uniqueness, you must speak also
in the same framework about the European diversity. It is in this sense
of what is *characteristically American* that I use the idea of exceptionalism.

A rapid listing of some of the outstanding books on America will show
that almost every commentator has fixed on some unique elements in it.
De Tocqueville saw the whole of American life as a new form of society which he called *democracy*. Charles Dickens had never seen anything to equal American money-mad materialism. Bryce was impressed
with the uniqueness of the Federal system and the party system. Whitman, castigating American corruption, nevertheless glimpsed democratic
vistas beyond them more stirring than ever before in history. Henry and
Brooks Adams saw the degradation of the democratic dogma stretched
further in America than anywhere else in the democratic world. Thorstein Veblen, who felt that American capitalism had been carried to a
unique degree of power, concentration, and finesse, did a series of studies
in absentee ownership showing how business enterprise in modern times
had taken characteristic forms in the case of America—developing such
home-grown products as the country town, the independent farmer, the
captain of industry, the technology of physics and chemistry.

Herbert Croly found a peculiar "promise" in American life he found nowhere else. Waldo Frank, in his "rediscovery" of America, found equally a characteristically excessive power and excessive childishness in the American mind. D. H. Lawrence found in "classical" American literature a mixture of the primitive and the bourgeois, in the clash of which he located the characteristic split in the American soul. H. L. Mencken, studying the one feature of American life which might have been expected to follow the pattern of its English parent—its speech—found elements of originality in it so marked as to make it a separate American language. André Siegfried, explaining America in the 1920s and again in the 1950s, saw its peculiar problems in the clash between the "Anglo-Saxon tradition" and the later immigrant strains; but he also asserted that America was a new civilization that had left the European far behind. Robert and Helen Lynd, in their two *Middletown* studies, wryly found the distillation of American thinking in the "Middletown spirit"—a body of folk-belief that set Americans off from any other culture. Margaret Mead saw the core of the American character in the distinctive effects of the authority-and-freedom pattern on the interaction of the sexes and the growing-up process within the family. D. W. Brogan saw an interrelation between the paradoxes within the American political system and within the national character. Geoffrey Gorer, arguing that the child in America is conditioned to seek love and success above all else, deduced from it a different but still characteristic American personality pattern. Wyndham Lewis saw in the ethnic mixtures of the American stock, and their ways of living together, the seeds of "cosmic man."

David Riesman explored the American character in terms of its increasing submission to the tyranny of opinion and the failure of the individual to heal his loneliness in the crowd. David M. Potter saw the Americans as a "people of plenty" and the crucial traits of the American character as arising from situations of abundance and opportunity. Daniel Boorstin saw the genius of American politics in the American's habit of taking his own premises and values for granted as "givens," not to be thought about. Louis Hartz saw the specific character of an institution as shaped by the fact that Americans never had an old feudal order to destroy by revolutionary overturn, as the Europeans did.

I do not mean to imply that each of these writers was an adherent of the theory of American exceptionalism. I do say that these important studies of the whole or some segment of American life use, as a practical matter, the working hypothesis of an American character and culture which are set off distinctively from others in history and in the contemporary world.

5. National Character and the Civilization Pattern

THE CONVENIENT WAY to deal with the problem of national character is to list a people's traits, presenting them as "American traits," the "American mind," or the "American spirit."* Some of the commentators enumerate the traits mechanically, as if it were a question of a grocery list or a warehouse inventory of odds-and-ends items. One trouble with this method of delineating character by enumeration is that the lists tend to cancel each other out. Lee Coleman, culling the lists of American traits from the available commentaries on America, found he could spot the exact opposite in some other list. Thus Americans are generous and niggardly, sympathetic and unfeeling, idealistic and cynical, visionary and practical—which leaves us with the conclusion, true but not novel, that Americans are bewilderingly human. Another difficulty is that the traits change over the generations. Compare the Garden of Eden picture of American traits in De Crèvecoeur at the end of the eighteenth century with De Tocqueville's for the late 1830s and 1840s, Bryce's contemporary picture for the 1880s and 1890s, or (retrospectively) Commager's *The American Mind* for the same period.

There are, however, certain salient traits which commentators attribute to the American in every period: Coleman finds that these are the

* Among the listings in recent books, I may cite Hacker, *The Shaping of the American Tradition* (religious freedom, enterprise freedom, the weak state, equality of opportunity, a strong middle class, responsibility under the law, the separation of powers, grass roots decentralization, and pressure-group politics); Davis, Bredemeier, and Levy, *Modern American Society*, in a final listing by the editors of the "American Value System" (ethical equality, equal opportunity, free competition, separation and balance of interests, public education, freedom of expression, tolerance, and individualism); Laski, *The American Democracy*, in the opening chapter on the "American Spirit" (future-looking, dynamism, worship of bigness, sense of destiny, fluidity of classes, pioneer spirit, individualism, antistatism, versatility, empiricism and the priority of the practical, zeal for careers and wealth, self-help and self-interest, gospel of hard work, sense of property). Robin M. Williams, Jr., *American Society*, lists fifteen "major value orientations": stress on achievement and success; stress on activity and work; a tendency to see the world in moral terms; humanitarianism; stress on efficiency and practicality; belief in progress; valuing of material comfort; avowal and (to an extent) practice of equality; ditto for freedom; emphasis on external conformity; belief in science and in secular rationality; stress on nationalism and patriotism; stress on democracy; cult of the individual personality, and its value and dignity; belief in racism and group superiority. Commager's *American Mind* gives an interesting list of traits characterizing the American mind in the 1890s. The enumeration of elements of the "American Creed" in Myrdal's *The American Dilemma* has become classic.

For collections of trait descriptions of America by travelers, see Commager, *America in Perspective*; Nevins, *America Through British Eyes*; and Handlin, *This Was America*.

tendency to club together or "join" in associations, the belief in democracy, the belief in equality, individual freedom, "direct action" in disregard of law, stress on local government, practicality, prosperity and material well-being, Puritanism, the influence of religion, uniformity and conformity.

It is hard to define the American national character by listing traits or even "value clusters," mainly because there are difficulties inherent in the idea of national character itself. Many writers are wary of it because it has been used cynically in war and power struggles to blacken the enemy symbol or sustain the conceit of a God-given or history-given national superiority. Caught between the Fascist theorists who have used it to bolster their doctrine of racist purity and pollution, and the Marxist theorists who reject it for placing too little stress on class interest and class militancy, the idea of national character has become a thorny and controversial one.

While it is risky to attribute a national character to any people, as if its qualities and destiny could be ripped out of the living body of history, it is also true that nations are realities, that their cultures develop along different paths, and that the world inside the heads of their people is a characteristic world. Much of the chauvinist and racist treachery of the term can be avoided if it is remembered that national character is a doctrine not of blood but of culture. It consists of a body of values, social habits, attitudes, traits held in common by most members of the culture. Thus the psychological field of action, thought, and emotion into which an American is born differs not only from the Russian or Chinese but even from that of an Englishman.

Traditionally, national character has been used as a semi-literary rule-of-thumb to differentiate one nationality type from another or give impressionistic force to generalization about a whole people. One of the classics here is Emerson's *English Traits,* which is witness that literary insight may be worth more than all the paraphernalia of recent social science. Yet the new anthropological and psychiatric techniques did mark a turning point in the approach to national character. First they were applied to the study of primitive personality structure, and then to psychological warfare in World War II. The psychiatrists knew from their experience that diagnosis and therapy vary with individuals of differing character types, and that these character types apply not only to neurotics and psychotics but to presumably normal persons. At the same time the anthropologists, studying contemporary primitive groups, found that each culture has its own pattern, within which there are also several different variants of character and personality. In World War II, before the military strategists could lay their plans for an assault on the enemy mind, they had to know what the enemy mind was like—hence the American studies of the Germans and Japanese, in which the theory of national character was tested in the crucible of life-and-death action. Thus the war studies converged with the work of the psychiatrists and anthropologists to form a new strain, one whose by-product has been an effort to apply the same techniques to contemporary America.

This strain of inquiry now makes possible a new way of getting at what has usually been called the "American character" or the "American spirit." It is not a disembodied presence in the sky or some mystical force inherent in race or history. Neither is it the body of folk-belief that Americans derive from their mass media and their whole cultural environment. It is best sought at the point where cultural norms in America shape personality and character, and where in turn the human material and the energies of Americans leave their impact on the fabric of the culture.

I may cite as an example of this process the way children are brought up in America, how their personalities are shaped by the emotional atmosphere of the family and the structure of authority and freedom within it, how the whole tone of growing up is set by the inordinate concentration on the child, the pervasive influence of the new big-audience media, the seeping in of the cultural values of success, prestige, and security, and the clash between permissive and restrictive codes as it is reflected in the child's mind. One can find similar examples in what is happening to the American character and spirit today as a result of suburban living, or the conditions of work and incentive within the new corporate structures, or the wave of "do-it-yourself" amateurism which has come as a recoil from the trend toward complete mechanization, or the sense of encirclement that leads to a stress on "loyalty" and "security," or the virtual ending of immigration, or the emergence of new elites and a complex, far-reaching middle class. These are only a few instances of how the energies of the individual American are channeled by characteristic cultural conditions of training and living, shaping certain common character traits for whole groups of individuals and weaving them into the fabric of the civilization.

This does not mean that, by some necromantic determinism, every little American who is born alive comes out stamped with exactly the same traits or propensities. There are in-groups, out-groups, and marginal groups; there are regional, class, and ethnic variations; there is a bewildering variety of individual personality patterns and traits. Yet the central stream of tendency remains, and with it the shaping interrelations of American personality and culture.

What are some of the ways of uncovering this interrelation? One way is a study of mental disorders, asking, as the psychiatrists do, what are the characteristic sources of personality breakdown—what it is that makes Americans crack up when and as they do? To answer this means to get some insight into the strains under which men live in America, the expectations the culture sets up in them as against the satisfactions it places within their reach, the norms of conduct and thought it seeks to enforce, the fault lines and frustrations that develop within them. Another way is to ask what personality types can be most clearly discerned among Americans, and what modes of life and striving within the culture account for the impulse toward those personality types. A third is to ask what life goals the Americans set up for themselves and what they make a cult of and are obsessed with, making sure to distinguish between the conscious and irrational levels of their striving.

One can dig deeper, perhaps, and seek some hidden dimension of the American character which symbolizes the basic American life view. Thus F. S. C. Northrop (*The Meeting of East and West*) takes the deepest thing about any civilization to be its metaphysic—its assumptions and beliefs about the constitution of the unseen universe, and he suggests that it was the reception by America of the atomistic metaphysics of Locke and Hume which has influenced the individualism and fragmentation of American life. Thus also Charles W. Morris (*Six Ways of Life*) attempts an approach through symbolic value systems. He lists the crucial systems in history as the Dionysian (surrender to the instinctual life), the Buddhist (annihilation of self for serenity), the Christian (purifying of self for spiritual values), the Mohammedan (merging of self in a holy war against the enemies of the true way), the Apollonian (conserving of traditional values), and the Promethean (conquest and organization of the environment by science and technology). He sees American civilization as primarily Promethean, but with elements of the Christian and the Apollonian, pointing out that the Promethean strain puts the emphasis on the instrumental, that the Apollonian has hardened into a Toryism of the spirit which could mean a static civilization, and that the Christian strain has had to be subordinated when it has conflicted with the more dominant elements of the civilization. I cite this suggestive scheme to illustrate how the study of the great world myths can shed light on what Americans are like and what they live by.

Since most of this is speculative, American observers have tried to approach their own civilization by the very different and more modest road of community surveys and cross-section area studies—of "Middletown," "Jonesville," "Yankeetown," "Elmtown," "Southern Town," "Plainville." What these studies offer is a degree of verification for certain theoretical leads, or of doubt cast upon others; they can show the extent to which the members of the American culture verbalize the articles in the American creed, and how they see themselves (and others) in the class system and the success-and-rating system of their time. But the community studies can never be broader or deeper than the issues they pose, nor more imaginative than the questions they raise.

Discussions of national character sometimes remind you of one of Cagliostro's magical spells or the incantatory hokum of a side-show barker telling the virtues of some nostrum. There is no talismanic quality in any of the newer approaches to national character. The hard work of giving contour to the mass of known material on American civilization cannot be dispensed with. The insights of the psychiatrists and anthropologists are all to the good, if they do not overstress some single symbolic key to the national character. The method of Gorer, for example, as used in the Gorer-Rickman study, *The People of Great Russia,* has been sharply satirized as the "swaddling theory" because it takes the infantile experience of the Russian peasant child, who was closely swaddled in the early months of his life, as a pre-verbal emotional conditioning to the rage, guilt, and violent alternations of emotion in the Russian as an adult. In *The American People,* Gorer put stress on the cult of the mother, the rejection of the father, the child's craving for affection, and the fear of loneliness, and again saw them as clue—if not cause—to the national character. A good deal depends on how hard the thesis is pushed. If we take it not as a verified truth but as impressionistic lead for further research and analysis, it is all to the good. The course of wisdom is to recognize the limits of any study of personality traits and to see the whole of the national character as one phase of the total civilization pattern.

6. Single Key—or Polar Pattern?

THE QUESTION THEN arises whether there is some single organizing principle in this civilization pattern, some key that unlocks all the doors. For generations Western thinkers have been haunted by the dream of finding the single factor that shapes all else in its image. It might be Hegel or Spencer, Marx or Sorel, Spengler, Freud or Jung, Veblen, Henry George, Brooks Adams or Henry Adams, but it was always a form of cabala. I can offer the reader no single talisman to the secret of American civilization.

The temptation is great to seek it. Following the lead of Marx or Veblen, one might stress the march of technology and the system of business power, and build all the rest on that. After Laski's *American Democracy,* which applied that method unsparingly to the analysis of contemporary America, such an approach would yield sharply decreasing returns.

While Laski's theme is democracy, as with De Tocqueville and Bryce, it is the subject of the book only as a corpse is the subject of a murder mystery. The real theme is the system of capitalist power and its business civilization: between these and democracy Laski depicts a bitter feud. Democracy in Laski's study is a little like the hero of Clifford Odets's early play, *Waiting for Lefty:* the stage is set for the hero, everyone measures his life and aspirations by him, but he never shows up because he has fallen victim to the forces of greed and reaction. Obviously economic power and class structure are important themes in the American civilization pattern, and I shall dwell a good deal on them. But an analysis which makes them the sole key distorts a good deal and misses many of the most dramatic recent changes in American life.

Laski's approach, like Veblen's, marked a recoil from the school of political idealism, which seemed to make political institutions and ideas the end and beginning and everything in the middle. In one sense De Tocqueville belonged to that tradition, since he started with the idea of democracy and traced its ramifications through phase after phase of American life. But De Tocqueville set an example of breadth of view which could not be matched by the later students of America, even someone with the insight of Bryce, whose approach was more narrowly through the political institutions of *The American Commonwealth,* while De Tocqueville's traced out imaginatively the political and moral ramifications of the democratic idea. Bryce, moreover, had lost much of the sense of wonder and excitement one finds in De Tocqueville about the revolutionary implications of democracy and was more interested in how the political actuality had worked out. In both cases, however, the organizing principle is political.

Another approach lays the key stress on psychological and moral values. It gives primacy to beliefs and attitudes, and the creative force of religion and ideas, and derives the technology and economic achievement of America from them rather than the other way round. The unacknowledged assumption is that the way to understand America is to start with the human psyche in its American form and with its whole intellectual and moral world. One finds this approach, with mystical overtones, in Waldo Frank's *Rediscovery of America;* one finds it, with religious overtones in Toynbee and Niebuhr; one finds it, in its more direct psychological form, in the writing of the young American scholars today who are exploring the relation of culture and personality.

My own view is that both economic man and psychological man—the materialist emphasis and the individualist emphasis—are each stripped of meaning without the other. The problem of social analysis is only partially illumined by the search for causes. In much of our thinking, causation is giving way to relation and interaction. "America is this," says one observer of American life. "America is that," says another. It is likely that America is both, because America is a highly polarized field of meaning, but that neither can be fully understood except in relation to the other and to the whole intricate civilization pattern. The study of American civilization becomes thus the study of the polar pattern itself, not a search for some single key that will unlock causation. It is largely a question of what you focus upon, and against what background. The problem of American interpretation is best seen in a figure-ground perspective: but what will be figure and what will be ground will vary with the purpose at hand.

Thus my concern will be neither with the material world alone nor with the moral-psychological world alone, but with the interplay between them. If there is a figure-ground relation in American civilization it must be sought in the relation between power and ideas, science and conscience, the revolutionary machine and the conservative crust of tradition, mass production and social creativeness, individualist values and collective action, capitalist economics and democratic freedom, class structure and the image of prestige and success in the American mind, elite power and the popular arts, the growth of military power and the persistence of civilian control, the fact of an American imperium and the image of an open constitutional world.

One may see in these polar impulses the proof that American life is deeply split. One may prefer to see them as contradictory parts of a bewildering puzzle. Or one may see them as signs of an effort, on a grander scale than ever in history, to resolve the conflicting impulses that are to be found in every civilization but each of which occurs here with a strength and tenacity scarcely witnessed elsewhere.

CHAPTER III

People and Place

IN WHICH we take a preliminary look at the two basic ingredients of American civilization, the continent itself and the people who live on it—that is to say, the natural resources and the human resources of America. We broach first the dangerous question ("Is There an American Stock?") of biology and ethnic types, with the emphasis on the plasticity of the human material in America. We then explore how this myriad of stocks, drawn from every corner of the earth ("The Immigrant Experience"), living under conditions of extreme mobility ("People in Motion") in a myriad of natural environments, having at their disposal the richest possible resources ("The American Earth"), use and exploit those resources. We trace the elusive pattern of how fast they are born, how long they live, and how much vitality there is in the graphs of their population growth ("Population Profile"); how healthy they are, what their characteristic food habits are and their dwellings, how well they take care of their human material ("The Sinews of Welfare"). Taking another look at them from a different angle of vision we ask what basic ways of life they have molded out of the fusion of people and place—the life of the farmer, the life of the small town (both of them waning), and the life of the city and the suburb (both of them marking the line of current and future growth). Finally, we try still another angle of vision and see how the fusion of people and place has worked out to produce the regional ways of life and thought in New England and on the East Coast, in the Midwest, in the South and Southwest, in the Rocky Mountain region and on the Pacific Coast.

The reader is warned that this will be a long chapter because it deals with the rich diversities of the American people and their continent. Without getting a picture of these diversities the general analysis in the chapters that follow will be oversimplified and distorted.

CHAPTER III

People and Place

1. Is There an American Stock?

EVERY traveler in the tropics comes away with an unforgettable sense of the pervasive jungle enclosing him. America's jungle is its ethnic environment of a myriad of peoples. In such a tropical luxuriance every ethnic type is present, everything grows fast and intertwines with everything else, anything is ethnically possible.

The best vantage points for observing the variety of American ethnic strains are on a subway in New York or a San Francisco street or at an Army induction center. Each is a broad channel through which the human material of America streams. Every people in Europe, most of the varied stocks of European and Asian Russia; peoples from Israel and the Arabs of the Middle East; peoples from China and Southeast Asia, from the Philippines, Hawaii, Australia, from the farthest reaches of India, from Liberia and Nigeria, from the Gold Coast and the Ivory Coast, from Kaffirland and the Witwatersrand, from every country in South and Central America, from every Caribbean island, from British and French Canada, from Greenland and Iceland—there is scarcely a stock on the ethnic map of the world that is not represented in America.

Let me make my use of terms clear. I use "stock" rather than "race," and "ethnic" rather than "racial," because in both cases I mean something in which race is only one ingredient. I have in mind a compound of influences from race, nationality, language, religion, region or subregion—any recognizable strain which not only by its common descent but by its length of living on the same soil, under the same sky, and in the same community has formed a relatively stable biopsychological and cultural type.

Is any one of these ethnic stocks more "American" than the others? To say of someone that "he is of American stock" has come to mean that he is white, probably Protestant and of Anglo-Saxon descent, and that his forebears emigrated to America some generations back. But there is little of solace here for the distinction-hunters. In most civilizations the conquering stock has tried to set itself off on the one hand from the conquered natives, on the other from the newcomers who may want to get in on the power and the glory. In America this has been difficult on several scores: the natives were too few and were so ruth-

lessly stripped of land, home, and livelihood that the deed trailed little
glory behind it. If "American stock" is to mean descent from those who
were most immediately in on the kill, the leaders of the Great Predation, it would carry a guilt of which many would be gladly rid. The
real conquest of America was not a military conquest, to deck out a
boast that the strength of killers flows in one's blood: it was a conquest
of forest and plain, of mountain and valley and river, of new technologies and new social forms; and in it every wave of immigrants took
part. Although the largest single group came from the British Isles,
there was no one stock that pre-empted the glory of settling America:
even in the early decades of the Republic, there was a variety of stocks
shaping the amalgam of "this new man, the American." Finally, the
leveling force of the democratic idea has resulted in a crossbreeding and
mingling of stocks which have made the task of the racial purist a hopeless one.

   This effort to pre-empt the term "American" for a single strain out
of many, and exclude from it all the others, is a familiar device in the
technique of prescriptive prestige. Whatever meaning it may have in
the case of a more inbred and homogeneous people, in America it is
meaningless. Yet there are some who recoil from racism but regard the
length of settlement as a crucial distinguishing mark. "Wouldn't European stocks which have been here longer," a friend writes me, "be more
'American' than the recent ones? Isn't a Lowell or a Roosevelt, for example, likely to be more 'American' than my Chinese laundryman's
son?" By the test of time the most "American" stocks would be the American Indians, the descendants of the Pilgrims, and the descendants of
the early Negro slaves—which is not exactly what was meant. The idea
that European stocks are more "American" not by the fact of long settlement but by the fact of being European (West European, not Mediterranean or Slavic), is an idea easy to succumb to. Its strength derives
from the fact that the English, Scottish, French Huguenot, and Dutch
influences are interwoven with early American history. It is easier and
more natural to think of a Lowell or Roosevelt as American than of a
recent Chinese immigrant or a descendant of an early Indian or Negro family, but this is because the West Europeans have run the show
in America since early times and have therefore made the rules and set
the admission price. They feel more at home and have made others feel
less at home.

   Our thinking will be clearer if we say that there are three levels of
meaning attached to "American": the links of family and stock with
American history over time; the equal or unequal claims to rights and
privileges under the law; the sense of commitment to American life.
Only on the first level does the question of stock enter, however irra-

tionally. On the second level there can be no discrimination between a Lowell or Roosevelt and the Chinese laundryman's son. On the third level the problem is one of individuals, not of stock: Americans belonging to the newer stocks may be as committed to the obligations and meanings of the American experience as the older ones, and many have enriched it greatly.

Yet in the world's most notable ethnic democracy there remains a hierarchy of prestige depending partly on stock—black, yellow, brown, and red at the bottom, white Protestant, West European on top, with the lines between the rest drawn partly in terms of closeness to Colonial descent, partly of geographic closeness to the British center of origin of the early settlements. A roughly chronological chart of the sequence of waves of immigration—English, Dutch, German, Scotch-Irish, French, Scandinavian, Irish, Mediterranean, Jewish, Balkan, Slavic, Mexican and Latin American, Filipino, Middle Eastern, Oriental—would correspond roughly to the descending scale of prestige in the ethnic hierarchy. The big divergences are that the Indians, who came first, are not at the top but toward the bottom of the pyramid; and the Negroes, who were brought over early, are not near the top but at the very bottom. On the prestige chart of the ethnic hierarchy, one could superimpose a residence map showing which stocks are distributed in slum areas, in tolerable living quarters, in middle-class districts, in residential areas. Over that one could draw an occupational chart of the functions to which the ethnic groups have been more or less specialized.

This is fluid, but the correspondences are roughly there. Making allowance for the constant breaking of the mold and the emergence of many Negroes as doctors, lawyers, teachers, ministers, businessmen, it remains true that in the South the Negroes have done and still do the heavy labor in the fields, and everywhere the dirty jobs in the factories and on the roads and wharves, in digging ditches and laying tracks and building tunnels, while their women are domestics. The Chinese, Filipinos, and Puerto Ricans are also still specialized to do domestic and routine jobs. The Mexicans (or "Spanish-speaking Americans") work at sweated labor in the factories of the Southwest and as migratory workers on the farms of the Southwest and California. The Poles, Czechs, Magyars, and Slovaks are in the coal mines of Pennsylvania, West Virginia, and Illinois, in the steel mills and at the open-hearth furnaces of Gary and Pittsburgh and Buffalo. The Scandinavians are farmers in the Midwest and loggers in the lumber camps. The Irish of the later immigration are policemen, saloonkeepers, and bartenders in New York and Boston, but also day laborers and building-trades workers, transport workers, longshoremen. The Italians and the Jews work in the garment trades of New York and the other Eastern centers; the Italians are also barbers and shoeshine boys and musicians, and they work the truck gardens in New Jersey and the vineyards of California, as do the Japanese; while the Jews move from the sweatshops into the small trades and the middlemen functions, and into medicine, law, dentistry, teaching, and the entertainment world.

But in the fluid life of America, the specialization does not stick. Cutting across the ethnic occupation map is the fact that it is the new arrivals of most stocks who do the menial and dirty work and drift to the peripheral occupations, while the earlier and resourceful ones break out of their cultural molds, buy farms and houses, get university training, attain skills, and move up to become members of the middle class. The epithets do often stick—"Wop," "Dago," "Sheeny," "Kike," "Nigger," "Norske," "Mick," "Spick," "Polack," "Hunkie," "Bohunk," "Chink," "Jap," "wetback," "greaser"—betraying a class and xenophobe animus as well as a racist one.

Sometimes, in overcompensation for this prevalent animus, one is tempted to ask whether we can in fact distinguish stock from stock, or whether there are not simply *individuals* in a rich and bewildering variety?

It is true that the differences between the stocks are not clear-cut, that one could find within one of them—say the Jews—wider differences of physiognomy, height, bone structure, skull structure, temperament, than between particular Jews on the one hand and particular Italians or Irish or Portuguese or Syrians on the other. It is also true that ethnic differences do not carry with them the differences of superiority or inferiority that the racists ascribe to them. Although there are no supermen in America, there are Americans who hunger for a cult of the blond Anglo-Saxon gods; although there are no sub-men in America, there are whites who cling to their color out of a panic sense of emptiness and who pant to assign Negroes or Puerto Ricans or Mexicans or Chinese to the category of inferior men. There are no Americans who belong to radically different branches of the human family, in the sense that their blood is of a different genus, or that some are closer to apes and others closer to gods, some born to work and others to lord it over them. There is not even an ethnically pure group in America (unless we speak of ethnic sub-pockets like the Hutterites from Russia who settled in South Dakota and have been almost completely endogamous) for at this point in history the chromosomes of any group contain also some genes from most of the others.

Yet it would be foolish to deny the reality of ethnic stocks in America and the differences between them. Those who came to America came from relatively stable ethnic groups. They brought with them obvious physical hereditary differences and habits of life that set them off from the others, and the social hostility they encountered often made them huddle together in more or less isolated ethnic communities. Many of them thus retained and even froze their sense of separateness, while others kept themselves open to every influence from other groups, including interbreeding. If we recognize that there is no stigma to membership in any one of the ethnic stocks of America the whole question of stock can be taken with realism and without passion.

The fact is that America is more than an agglomerate of individuals jumbled in hopeless confusion. America is a myriad of stocks, each with some identity maintained from the earliest to the latest migration. What gives America its biological richness is that it is a mingling of ethnic strains. What gives America its cultural richness is that it is a mingling of traditions and temperaments. Unless the stocks had brought an identity of their own, it would be meaningless to talk of their mingling. Unless those identities were changed and dissolved in the process, shaped and reshaped, caught up in the ever-flowing stream of the life of all of them together, it would be meaningless to talk of America.

Does the unlimited crossbreeding of ethnic stocks hurt or help the quality of American life? True, there are some valid objections to be raised against unlimited crossbreeding. In the process of mixture, the groups with the higher birth rate will predominate, biologically and culturally, and while a high birth rate may be one of the indices of vitality, the crucial question is that of the quality of the individuals and cultures which are crossed. There is, however, a double and contradictory line of reasoning in the "pure America" argument. One is that the more recent immigrants are clannish, refuse to intermarry, and should therefore be kept out. The other is that they will flood into the country and overwhelm and corrupt the "native" stock by the weight of numbers and birth rate and by interbreeding. One argument rests on the theory that they do not mix, the other on the theory that they mix all too much. I suspect that logic is less important here than emotion—the emotions of invidiousness, guilt, pride, and fear that dominate the thinking of the "pure America" group.

On biological grounds alone, if these emotions can be ruled out, the central argument for an exclusive concept of American stock is the argument that unlimited crossbreeding will mean the mongrelization of America. Even reputable writers seem to have been made panicky by the possible biological and cultural corruption of pure Anglo-Saxonism by the Negroes, Asians, Slavs, Jews, and Mediterranean peoples. If mongrelization has any meaning, it assumes a "pure" (but nonexistent) stock thinned out and corrupted by unlimited crossbreeding. The fear of mongrelization is the fear of strange blood and ways on the part of groups that believe their economic and social supremacy threatened by outsiders, and fix upon the racial invaders as the enemy.

This fear reaches nightmare proportions in the Southern states, where the governing group has sought to protect its "white supremacy" by a set of state miscegenation laws. States like Mississippi and Georgia, in a triumph of paranoia, enacted laws making any marriage felonious and void if it involves a white person and one with an "ascertainable trace" of African, West Indian, Asian Indian, or Mongolian blood. One of the wider aspects of the miscegenation laws, if they are regarded in terms of any rational threat of mongrelization, is that they are found in the North as well as the South, and that in eight of the states covered by them the Negroes against whom they are directed form less than 1 per cent of the population.

This is not to deny the reality of crossbreeding in America. But there can be no question of mongrelization because there is no norm of purity. Each ethnic strain, in the process of crossbreeding, "corrupts" the other; each dilutes and enriches the other. The fact is that crossbreeding is in itself neither good nor bad. Its chief effect is to increase variations at both ends of the curve of inherited traits: in other words, we may dilute the quality of what is transmitted as a result of the vast interchange of genes, but we may also get more geniuses on the top level. The range of potentials is widened in both directions. Everything depends, as I have said, on the individuals and cultures entering into the mixture. The characteristic ethnic quality of America is the outcome of the mingling of stocks and traditions on a scale unparalleled in history. Although some cultural historians maintain that the dilution of native stock is followed by cultural decadence, the example of the Italian city-states, Spain, Holland, Britain, and now Russia and India as well as America indicates that the most vigorous phase may come at the height of the mingling of many stocks. The greater danger lies in closing the gates.

No stock, once it has come to America, remains what it was. Each breeds away from type, both by the influence of the new physical environment and by the fact of intermingling. Every stock, by its migration, breaks with its past environment and enters a new one. Continued migration from one American region to another and mobility from one class and therefore one set of living standards to another continue the process of environmental reconditioning. How substantial the changes may be was shown in 1912 in the classic study by Franz Boas, *Changes in Bodily Form of Descendants of Immigrants.* Despite the prevailing view that skull measurements are an unchanging racial characteristic, Boas showed that the skull indices of the children of Jewish and Italian immigrants differed appreciably from those of the parents. This is environmental change away from ethnic type, whether due to diet, living standards, climate, or other factors in the natural and cultural environment. Boas was dealing with the physical factor that one would expect to be most resistant to change. What applied to skull changes would apply more easily to psychic and cultural changes; and what applied under the influence of environmental and standard-of-living change would apply more easily as the result of biological mixture.

I find a surprising misreading of Boas's meaning in Arnold Toynbee's *Study of History* (Vol. I, 220-1), which argues that Boas is, like his opponents, an adherent of race thinking. Boas writes that his study is suggestive "because it shows that not even those characteristics of a race which have proved to be most permanent in their old home remain the same under the new surroundings; and we are compelled to conclude that when these features of the body change, the whole bodily and mental make-up of the immigrants may change." Toynbee gathers from this "what is the fundamental postulate of all race theories: that is, the postulate that physical and psychical characteristics are correlated." But this is to miss the meaning of the phrase *"may change,"* which carries with it an emphasis on the plasticity of *both* the cultural-psychic and the physical traits under environmental pressure. The whole point of racist thinking is that there is no such plasticity but that a given set of inherent physical traits of a superior or inferior caste carries with it a rigid set of psychic traits of a similarly superior or inferior caste. Boas proved the plasticity (although he felt it was a limited one) and rejected the moral hierarchy. The racists assert the moral hierarchy and reject the plasticity.

The process of plasticity has been described in Paul Engle's *America Remembers.*

> *The ancient features of the type were changed*
> *Under a different sun, in a clearer air*
> *That entered the lungs like wine, the swarthy face*
> *Paled, cheekbones lifted and narrowed, hair*
> *Straightened and faded, and the body moved*
> *With a lighter step, the toes springy, the eyes*
> *Eager as a bird's, and every man*
> *Had a coiled spring in his nerves that drove him*
> *In a restless fury of life.*
>
> *The bloods mingled*
> *Madly* . . . . (Who knows
> What strange multi-fathered child will come
> Out of the nervous travail of these bloods
> To fashion in a new world continent
> A newer breed of men?)

Given conditions making for rapid change, the question thus put is the question of how far the plasticity of the American stock is likely to lead. Clearly, every ethnic stock in America, unless it is caught and isolated in some eddy of the American stream, is breeding away from type. But is it breeding toward a new form of its own type, where it will be more or less stabilized? Or is the process of change a continuing and cumulative one resulting in the emergence of an inclusive new ethnic type, like a loose sort of tent to cover the existing types which will survive yet be transformed?

The probabilities point to something less defined than either of these. We do not yet know what ethnic future lies ahead for America, since genetics is changing its insights and outlook so rapidly. Earnest Hooton, a physical anthropologist who liked to make bold forays into the future, predicted that "the stubby, bone-and-muscle Mr. Americas of to-day" are doomed to disappear or to be "reduced to the ranks of the institutionalized malefactors." They will be replaced (said Hooton) by a more "attenuated" body build, "taller and more gangling than ever, with big feet, horse faces, and deformed dental arches"; the women "less busty and buttocky than those of our generation." There are other guesses of the future stock, some of them less unattractive. But their common premise is that a new ethnic entity is forming which will carry with it the multiform freightage of all past generations, but in which there will also be some central cast of temperament, physique, and lineament that crops up more and more frequently.

This does not mean that the old stocks will disappear or that America will become ethnically uniform. The processes of heredity and their interplay with the physical and cultural environment are too complex to allow for uniformity. The gene variants of so heterogeneous a population as the American are fantastically large in number, and the potential directions of American stock are great. This is the first great instance in history where ethnic abundance has combined with so great a freedom in marriage, to produce an unimaginable ethnic future.

If then we ask again, "Is there an American stock?" the answer must be that there are many stocks in America—more than have ever been gathered together before within a national unit; that none of them, whatever its claims and arrogance, is more American than the others, and none, whatever its sense of inferiority, less American; that each is different from what it was in its area of ethnic origin—each touched and changed by the alchemy of the American environment, by the fact of living and mingling with all the others on the American continent. America has become a great biological and psychological laboratory, whose experiments may issue in undreamed-of results. In all the stocks there has been, whether obviously or subtly, a breeding away from type; there has also been, subtly rather than obviously, slowly, ever so slowly, and yet unmistakably, a breeding *toward* new types that have not yet emerged.

When they emerge they will be the creature of America, not America *their* creature. Yet as we watch the yeast working in the ever-re-created human material of America, can we doubt that the determiners of a not unimaginable American future are at work here? "There is but one victory that I know is sure," wrote Saint-Exupéry, "and that is the victory that is lodged in the energy of the seed." Given what we know about American stock, we must take this to mean the victory not of the seed's rigidity but of its plasticity.

2. *The Immigrant Experience*

FOR CENTURIES THE STRENGTH and richness of America have been swelled by the great tides of immigration from Europe, with the sources moving roughly from the British Isles to western Europe and the Scandinavian countries, to the Mediterranean countries, to the Slavic countries. In 1790 America had fewer than four million people, of whom three quarters of a million were Negroes: 82 per cent of the total white population was English. For the next forty years, until 1830, immigrants were slow in coming. In the 1830s the "Atlantic Migration" quickened, first with Irish countrymen, then with German farmers and artisans, and then with land-hungry Scandinavians. In the early 1880s came a greater wave of the "new" immigration—"new" in the double sense that they were no longer from western and northern Europe but from eastern and southern Europe, and that they were more likely to settle in the big cities and work in the mines and mills and factories than on the land.

A few figures tell a dramatic story. From 1800 to 1914 some fifty million people left Europe, of whom almost thirty-five million came to the United States. In the century and a half from 1800 to 1950 some forty million newcomers moved to the United States, 85 per cent of them from Europe, 11 per cent from other countries in the American hemisphere, 3 per cent from Asian countries, and 2 per cent from the rest of the world. In the single peak decade of 1904-1914, ten million came, and in the peak year of 1907 more than a million and a quarter.

As the convulsions of tyranny, war, and famine shook the world, and as the "opportunity line" thinned out in the Old World and grew bolder in the New, millions of people came spilling down the sluiceways to America, and an almost manic quality seemed to infect immigration. It was fed by the steamship companies, who sent out agents to recruit immigrants and depict the glories and grandeurs of the new star of the West; and it was aided by the increasing cheapness of transportation. But even without these stimulants the migration would have taken place. America-as-magnet exercised a hypnotic force strong enough to draw millions to the shores of promise.

It was, in the main, the peasants who came, from Ireland, from Germany, from the Scandinavian countries, from Italy, from Russia and Poland, from the Balkans. There were many others who came from the cities too—artisans without jobs, ruined shopkeepers, political *émigrés,* intellectuals who had failed to make their way and who were to establish "Latin farms" (as they were called with gentle derision) in America. But mostly the families who came had lived on the land, and the land had been unable to sustain them. The plots were too small and the village community ways were too traditionally set to yield to the new agricultural techniques. Debt was a humiliating master to serve, and poverty a bleak companion. When famine began to nibble on the margins of your life, and your little plot of land was foreclosed and you found yourself dispossessed, you began to feel the narrowing confines of your village intolerable. Ridden by the weight of feudal and clerical tradition, with no hope left for yourself and no promise to hold out to your children, what was more natural than to surrender to the image of a country where land could still be had and a man could keep moving until he had found a challenge to his strength and boundless possibilities for his young? "The rich stay in Europe," De Crèvecoeur had written much earlier, "it is only the middling and the poor that emigrate."

There was always a bitter spell of waiting and enduring between dislocation from the old home and settlement in the new. There were the weary vigils at lodging houses along the wharves in the seaport cities of Europe until passage was arranged with some broker and the ship finally sailed. The steerage quarters, oversold through greed, were often cold, crowded, dirty, disease-ridden, rat-infested. In the darkness the long nights and days differed little from each other. Scanty provisions and bad water made scurvy, dysentery, and "ship's fever" lethal adversaries. When the ship arrived the immigrant found himself, dazed and bewildered, in a world with which his traditional peasant qualities could not cope. He had to get work immediately—work of any kind, at any pay, with whatever hours and conditions—in order to sustain life; he became thus a ready prey for exploiting employers, swindling fellow countrymen, greedy moneylenders. Sometimes he settled in the first big city he came to, huddling in a ghetto with his countrymen; sometimes he was able to push on into the interior and take up a piece of land or serve his apprenticeship as a "hired man"—again, usually, near others of his own ethnic stock. In both cases he needed first to convert his work and skill into capital: for years after his arrival, thus, he had to save and scrimp, living on almost nothing, so that he could get a real start in a store or restaurant or on a farm or as a small entrepreneur.

For years, perhaps for the rest of their lives, many of these immigrants were to remain (as Oscar Handlin has so movingly described in *The Uprooted*) alienated men—alienated from the culture they had left and from the one that had not yet wholly welcomed them and that they did not understand, and alienated finally from themselves. The old patterned ways of the village community, however galling, formed a path of stability, where a man knew what was expected of him. The new ways of the buzzing big American cities and the quickly growing farm villages were bewildering. The immigrant became an object, caught within forces over which he had no mastery, having to convert his strength on the market into dollars with which he could get what he needed for life.

The tight family of the peasant community or of the Jewish tradition was subjected to the strains and dislocations of the new society; often it was fatally split, although those that survived found that the ties of cohesiveness were strengthened by the fact of their members having to face together an alien world. Most tragic of all, the immigrants often found that their own children—adapting more easily to the new ways, caught up in the new rhythms, accepting the new life goals, and eager to merge themselves with the new environment—drifted away and became alienated from their parents. Perhaps in order to wipe out the cleavage between themselves and their new fellows, they saw their father and mother through the eyes of the "Americans" and came to think of them as outsiders and strangers—in short, as objects. The circle of alienation was completed.

The immigrant experience was thus somber and tragic. Yet it would be a mistake to see it thus without adding that it was also one of excitement and ferment. Millions of the immigrants, after giving their strength to the new country, died with a sense of failure and frustration. But many more millions survived their ordeal, became men of influence in their communities, and lived to see the fulfillment of the American promise in their own lives doubly fulfilled in the lives of their children. "Everything tended to regenerate them," De Crèvecoeur wrote of his fellow immigrants, "new laws, a new mode of living, a new social system; here they are become men: in Europe they were so many useless plants, wanting vegetable mold, and refreshing showers. They withered and were mowed down by want, hunger, and war; but now by the power of transplantation, like all other plants, they have taken root and flourished!" One doubts whether this lyric description, written at the end of the eighteenth century, would have been accepted as a faithful one a century later; yet it described a process which would have meaning for many through the whole course of the immigrant experience and even more meaning for the second and third generations, who reaped the harvest of the transplanting of their fathers without having had to suffer the ordeal.

Yet there was also something in the ordeal that enriched the immigrant and his new country. He may have deemed himself a failure in the old village and helpless on the crossing, and he may have begun to doubt his manliness after every defeat. But one thing that could never be stripped from him was the immediacy of his experience: whatever he had achieved had been due to himself and his own efforts. The experience of the immigrants recapitulated the early American pioneer hardships, in many ways on harder terms, since the difficulties they encountered were those of a jungle society rather than a jungle wilderness. It added a dimension of tragic depth which American life needed: even in its most tragic phases it furnished a ferment of vitality which re-created the American experience in every decade. There was much in the American mind that tended to become fixed and conformist. The immigrant experience hurled itself against this with insistent eagerness, kindling a warmth that thawed out much of the glacial rigidity. In recent years, with the gates almost closed, there have been fewer new immigrants to keep the regenerative process going.

The immigrants eventually found their place in the American economy, each new layer that came from below pushing up the earlier arrivals to the next stratum. But the economy also felt the impact of the immigration which provided a labor force for a rapidly expanding industrialism. Whatever one may say of the importance of American natural resources, the richest resource was man power: without the immigrants America could not have found quickly enough the man power to build the railroads, mine the coal, man the open-hearth steel furnaces, and run the machines. Moreover, while most of the immigrants were pushed into the unskilled, backbreaking jobs, enough of them were skilled—carrying over techniques from a European industrialism which had made an earlier start—so that the Great Migration was not only one of people but of talents, skills, and cultural traditions. The increase of immigration also meant more consumers as well as more producers. The new machines cut production costs and prices, yet the steadily mounting millions of consumers kept big profits flowing back into industry. And since the immigrants started on so little, their living standards kept steadily improving, and the home market grew not by arithmetical but by geometrical progression.

The immigrant's obsession with rising living standards was something he gave to American life as well as something he took from it. He was a man in a hurry, not only to make money but to show he had made it, not only to sow the crop of his labor and ingenuity but to reap the harvest of his success. The stories of the "self-made man" that caught the American imagination were in many cases the Horatio Alger rags-to-riches stories of immigrant boys who rose to the top of the heap. Their business methods were little different from the methods of the earlier Americans, but since they were so avid for results the legend grew that they were distinctively unscrupulous, and there was often a cleft between the world of "respectable" (i.e., "nativist") business and "immigrant" business. Certainly there was a febrile intensity about the immigrant that was part of his world of wonder: he was the small boy with his nose pressed against the shopwindow whose sweets were out of his reach unless he could come in with a fistful of coins. He was full of wonder at the miracles of science and mechanical inventions, at the headlong course of progress, at the dizzying peaks of wealth and power. He was full of a sense of promise and possibility which renewed the pioneer spark.

When the promise faltered and the possibility ran into the sands, he could express his bitterness through labor or radical movements which started as the protest of some ethnic stock and broadened out into a dissident splinter group or even a third-party movement. But the political impact of the immigrant was felt as much in the machine politics of the big city as in the dissenting politics of the Middle West. The boss politics of Boston, Philadelphia, New York, Chicago, St. Louis, was an interchange of the loyalties of the lonely immigrants, who needed a very personal kind of help in their encounters with jobs and the law, for the protection of the men who had become sophisticated and knew the power of the massed immigrant vote.

The first-generation immigrant, whether he was on a farm or in a big city, was likely to live out his life on the margin of the new society, and from there he sent coursing through much of the culture the current of his hope, his loneliness, his individuality. It was his son, the second-generation immigrant, who was lampooned by the novelists as one driven either to imitate or to outdo the "native Americans" at their own game. He was the Sammy of Budd Schulberg's *What Makes Sammy Run?* and the Harry Bogen of Jerome Weidman's *I Can Get It for You Wholesale*. He acted as if some "equalizer" had been built into him, driving him to excesses of energy or (as in cases less noted by the novelists) to excesses of protective coloration.

The third-generation immigrant was caught in a paradox. On the one hand the continuing pressures from the world of those whose ancestors were accepted as the nation's ancestors turned him toward stability and conformism, and thus further away from his links with the immigrant experience. On the other hand Marcus Hansen pointed out in a notable essay that "what the son wishes to forget the grandson wishes to remember," and that the third-generation immigrant, no longer ashamed of his cultural ancestry, has had the courage to embrace it. Both tendencies may be found in the grandchildren and great-grandchildren of the immigrant, struggling for mastery; but I am convinced that what Hansen noted will prove the stronger.

A great change came over American attitudes toward immigration after World War I and led to the racist discrimination of the quota legislation of 1921 and 1924. Actually the movement for restrictive legislation started before the turn of the century, almost with the start of the Great Wave of the new immigration. Every people is "ethnocentric," which is a way of saying it is the sun around which the earth and moon and stars revolve; and this is particularly true of the way the dominant group feels. The Americans of English descent—whether New England Yankees or transplanted Yankees in the Middle West—felt that their old dominance had been undercut by the hordes of strange new arrivals; nurtured in the democratic dogma, some of the best of them were deeply troubled and split in their emotions. The Southern whites, trying to keep the South "a white man's country" and therefore fearful of the Negroes who surrounded them, turned their fears into a more general suspicion of "foreigners." The reserve army of labor, which meant so much to the businessman because it gave him the human material for industrial expansion, seemed a threat to many labor leaders who feared the competition of cheap labor. Some of the intellectuals of the Progressive Era, anxious about the continuity of the native tradition, turned strongly anti-immigrant. Others were influenced by European theories of racial superiority and inferiority and found "scientific" buttressing for their purist fears about what Madison Grant called "the passing of the great race."

An alliance of Yankees, Southerners, trade-unionists, Progressive intellectuals, racist theorists, population purists, and professional xenophobes made headway in convincing the descendants of the earlier immigrants that the later immigration was dangerous and should be severely restricted. They scared them with images of criminality, radicalism, and Oriental cunning, with examples drawn from the Mafia and the Black Hand, from the Haymarket anarchists and the Jewish peddlers who became international bankers. They succeeded in frightening fearful Americans who thought the country of their fathers would be made unfit for their children by newcomers who sold themselves cheap, pulled down wage standards, read dangerous books, lived like pigs, and bred like rabbits.

Certainly there was a shift in the meaning of the whole immigrant experience, on the part of both the hosts and the newcomers. Writing in the 1880s, James Bryce noted that "the intellectual and moral atmosphere into which the settlers from Europe come has more power to assimilate them than their race qualities have to change it." He thus paid tribute to the transforming power of the American environment and defended the immigrant against the charge of being a corrupting serpent in an American Eden. Yet even as he wrote, a change was coming over the American scene. To be an immigrant in the earlier years was to be part of an experience in the making. You didn't feel unwanted or a misfit, nor did you have to feel ashamed of your cultural origin. But after the Civil War, with the triumph of industrialism, America became the country where miracles were in full swing and where entrance was an admission to the miracle-making. As an immigrant coming to something no longer experimental but already tested and created, you were suspect of trying to cash in on a good thing. As a combined entrance fee and expiation, you were crowded into slums, forced to do the dirty and poorly paid jobs, made to feel an outsider.

The "natives" began to ask how these gate-crashers dared be so different from them. "If a few million members of the Alpine, Mediterranean, and Semitic races are poured among us," wrote the novelist Kenneth Roberts, "the result must inevitably be a hybrid race of people as worthless and futile as the good-for-nothing mongrels of Central America and southeastern Europe." There were so many "mongrels" pouring in; they looked strange, swarmed everywhere, were too loud; they came from a Europe thick with revolutionary conspiracy to an America where the possessors were becoming insecure. Besides, there was always in the background the monstrous (and fascinating) sexual threat that the purity of America's blood would be polluted by miscegenation with the swarthy foreigners.

Thus the later phase of immigration corroded the generous energies of the earlier America. The Israel Zangwill vision of America as a "melting pot"—a crucible into which poured metals from every country while "the great alchemist melts and fuses them with his purging flame"—was greeted with enthusiasm, but it was a dangerous metaphor since it implied that all the immigrant strains must be purified by being assimilated with something more "American." In World War I the fear cropped up of the "hyphenated American" who was not being melted, fused, and purged rapidly enough. The "Red scare" that followed the war was directed against the foreign-born and, like the even more intense furor after World War II, it reinforced the whole agonizing doubt about the nature of American identity. Some Americans found in it a sadistic outlet for their aggression; many others fell prey to intellectual and emotional confusion. The quota formula embodied in the 1921 Immigration Act was thought up by a well-intentioned China missionary who saw in the quota system a way of merging the restrictions upon Oriental immigration with more general ones and thus in effect denying their existence. In the 1924 law the base year on which the quota for each country was fixed (the "national origins provision") was pushed back in order to minimize the number of Mediterranean and East European entries. It was hard for Europeans to fathom a democratic philosophy which admitted only 3,000 French and 5,000 Italians a year, as against roughly 25,000 Germans and 65,000 British.

Immigration restriction thus became deliberately discriminatory and racist, remaining thus through the McCarran-Walter Law of 1952 to the present day. The "Golden Door" of Emma Lazarus was swung all but shut. Where, in 1900, 13 per cent of Americans were foreign-born, in 1950 only 7 per cent, in 1960 the percentage will be negligible. The irony of the exclusionist policy was that since it could not be applied to Puerto Rico (which was part of territorial America) the exclusionists had to tolerate the influx of Puerto Ricans, who were very different from their ideal type. If the purpose of immigration policy was to ensure a stable admittance of, say, 250,000 immigrants a year, this could have been achieved more rationally by setting that figure and admitting them either in the order of their application acceptance or in terms of whether they possessed the needed skills. The fight to relax the harshness of the immigration laws and their administration is still carried on but halfheartedly, as if no one believed any longer that the trend could be reversed, since (whatever the intellectuals may think) the anti-alien component in Congress and the constituencies is still strong.

Even before the door was closed the impact of the narrowing attitudes had made itself felt in the minds of the immigrants themselves. Having caught the fever of the rush to America, they were overeager and overtense. Everything in them was heightened: the love of freedom, the urge to "make good," the vulnerability to scorn, the anxiety to belong. The structure of the immigrant family was corroded, and the pride of belief in the traditions which had been brought across the seas was shaken.

The immigrant found himself caught between two ghettos. One was the outer ghetto of economic and social discrimination imposed upon him. The other was the inner ghetto which came from his feverish ef-forts to meet this assault either by wearing the badges and aping the ways of the new culture, thus rejecting his own family and ethnic tra-dition, or by an equal overemphasis on retreat within the shell of the old culture, taking the form of an ethnic chauvinism. There was thus a double process of overcompensation at work—that of an anxious assimilationism and that of a belligerent ethnic orthodoxy. In both cases it was a response to hostility and an expression of alienation. The success stories of individual immigrants do not belie this but rather confirm it. Most of the immigrant-boy-to-tycoon success stories are about men who found the transition from one culture to another too precipi-tous to be bridged without a single-minded effort that left its effects on the personality.

The "melting pot" phase of American thinking about the immigrants was happily short-lived. Today there are few serious writers and think-ers who do not see through the fallacy of viewing American culture as a kind of manufacturing process which stamps out cultural diversities and turns complex human material into a monolithic Great Stone Face. To be sure, the flow of new immigrants has become the merest trickle (since 1940 it has averaged not much over 100,000 a year), and the issue is therefore how the second and third and later generations are to guide their lives. Among the newer immigrant groups the current of think-ing that has triumphed is the one set in motion by Randolph Bourne and Horace Kallen—the idea of a "cultural pluralism" in which the ethnic groups cherish their own traditions while refusing to isolate them-selves from the larger culture.

The problem for the recent newcomers and their children, as indeed for all Americans, is to hold several cultures in organic suspension, weaving each in with the other in a process without which American society as we know it could not have been formed. The question is not whether the older traditions are to change; for change, with a measure of absorption, is inevitable. The real problem is to make certain that the pace of change is not destructively rapid and that it does not in-volve a flight from the rootedness of one's fathers which leaves the sons and grandsons with no base on which to make the transition. The dif-ference is one of mood and value as well as tempo. It is the difference between *assimilation,* which is a one-way drive that attaches no value to what is left behind and marked for extinction, and *integration,* which is a two-way circuit, where the new national consciousness adds a new

dimension to the older ethnic tradition, and the older tradition adds
emotional depth and rootedness to the new cultural product.*

3. People in Motion

AMERICANS HAVE ALWAYS been voyagers. After crossing the ocean to find
the America of their dreams, the settlers paddled, steamed, and carried
freight down its network of great rivers and built canals to connect
them. They proved to be good land sailors across the "sea of grass" on
their prairie schooners. They built graceful clipper ships that sailed
the world's seas, making America a great trading nation. They sped
on iron wheels along the railway roadbeds and then on rubber wheels
along the macadam automobile highways. Finally they became air
voyagers: a successor to the sea and the land, the air now became the
element in which they expressed their will to conquer.

"Americans are always moving on" was the opening line of Stephen
Benét's unfinished heroic poem of the westward migrations. Much of
American literature has been dominated by this theme of restless movement on land or river or sea. Of the historical writings, there is Turner's
work on the frontier and Parkman's on the *Oregon Trail,* along with
such minor classics as Morison's *Maritime History of Massachusetts,*
Webb's *The Great Plains,* and De Voto's *Across the Wide Missouri.*
Melville's *Moby Dick,* like his South Seas romances, would have been
impossible except in a maritime as well as a Puritan civilization, where
the moral quest for the principle of good and evil could naturally be
presented in the story of a pursuit over the high seas. Mark Twain's
Life on the Mississippi is an American novel of the apprentice years,
expressive of the turbulence and power of the greatest of America's
rivers. The majestic highway of Western life in Mark Twain's time, it
was a virile world of swarming passengers, profane ship captains,
tobacco-spitting, gambling, steamer races, bursting boilers, salty language, and tall stories—the perfect school of experience for a young
man with a feeling for America and the knack of literary portraiture.
Mark Twain's greatest novel, *Huckleberry Finn,* was also borne along,
now drowsily, now tumultuously, on the current of the Mississippi. A
series of books on the "Rivers of America," crowded with historic incident, has shown how interwoven America's waterways were with the
whole course of its history; yet in each case the rivers have in recent
years lost most of their importance.

* For a further discussion, see Ch. I, Sec. 3, "The Slaying of the European Father,"
and Ch. VII, Sec. 5, "The Minority Situation," where I stress not the issues of demography (as here) but the social situation of minority groups in America.

In our own time, except for Faulkner's novels and a few others like Steinbeck's *Grapes of Wrath*, the immediate natural environment has ceased to carry the symbolic themes of the writers. The violence of American life is now expressed not in the impact of the physical environment but in the jungle warfare of human living; not in the voyage across the ocean or down a river, nor in Ahab's quest for the White Whale, but in the detective hunt for the murderer whose victim is unreal and crime fantastic, and for the solution which leaves all of life's problems unsolved.

The idea of Nature, as it has been expressed in American commentary, has two aspects—that of restless mobility, as emphasized by Turner and his followers, and that of attachment to place, as emphasized by the regionalists and traditionalists. To understand America one must see them as facets of each other—a double beat of migration and the sense of place. The wanderings of Americans are due less to an innate restlessness or to the poverty of the land, as with nomadic peoples, than to a quest for opportunity. When the beat of migration has fulfilled itself, it may be expected that the same intensity which informed it will be transformed into attachment to place.

There have been three types of American migration—the transoceanic migrations, the migration to new frontiers, and those internal crisscrossings which may be called reshuffling migrations and which are basically migrations to the city and the suburbs.

The classical migration to the Western frontiers was not a planned migration in the sense in which the great dislocations of peoples on today's map are the result of the deliberate acts and policies of government. It was perhaps the last spontaneous great migration in history. Yet, looking back, one can trace a systematic progress, zone by zone, as if a campaign had been mapped out in advance; and a regular succession, wave after wave, of explorers followed by fur traders, followed by mountain men, ranchers, and miners, followed finally by farmers equipped with seed, cattle, and implements. The later stages of this classical westward movement, which crossed the Great Plains and the mountain fastnesses of the Rockies and occupied the rich areas of the Pacific Northwest and California, were filled with violence and greed as well as heroism. The hardships along the Oregon Trail, the struggle to capture the fur trade, and finally the Gold Rush to California present, in heightened form, the Faustian spirit of the classical Great Migration. Not more than one out of twenty of those who took part in the Gold Rush found anything like success, yet we have forgotten the failures and remember only the big prizes. Whole states and a whole region yielded quantities of their best young people in the "Yankee exodus" out of New England. Even after free land was no longer available, the internal reshuffling of population went on, and one may speak of a Great Trail of the past century which in its own way has been as profound in its effects as that of the classical westward movement, if less systematic in its progress.

Each road that led toward the dimly known target was a highway of hope. The contemporary hopes and the nostalgia of our own day have combined to shed a glow of idealization over the rough paths, the bumpy roads and turnpikes of an earlier day, and over stagecoach and "freighter," pony express and even the highwayman. With the railroads came a transportation revolution which left its own deposit of mythology, clustering around the gangs that laid the tracks and the engineers who drove the fast trains that seemed like fiery monsters and even the railroad barons such as Vanderbilt, Fiske, and Hill.

One of the recent phases of the transport revolution, based on the motorcar, has made America a civilization on wheels. By 1956 there were an estimated seventy-five million cars and trucks in America, owned by seventy million people, at least one for every family, including the poorer families; and the auto industry was geared to turn out eight million new cars a year, to take their place on almost four million miles of toll expressways, freeways, rural feeder roads, and city streets. One out of every seven Americans had a job in some phase of auto construction and service, and highway transport. By 1965 there should be close to a hundred million cars crowding the roads and streets, choking every artery.

America's motor technology, while it has not produced the feverish internal mobility, has made it possible. Long before he is old enough to get a driver's license the American boy, particularly in the small town and the suburb, has been holding the wheel and become conscious of himself as a potential driver. The American girl measures a male partly, at least, in terms of the kind of car he drives. Wage-earner families who live in slums—especially Negro workers—often own cars that are better than their living quarters, and a glance at the bumper-to-bumper congestion on auto roads on week ends will show that many Americans spend almost as much time in their cars as in their homes. Autos are no longer a luxury for an American elite; they have become a living-standard compulsive for the American masses. They fill a psychic need more important even than adequate housing or education or health, and form the crucial test of whether your living standards make you an accepted member of the community. The car is a house on wheels, used for daily chores, family outings and week ends, shopping, visits, business, and (by the youngsters) for "petting."

This house on wheels has developed in the past half century from a fussy, crotchety, unreliable contraption to a miracle of engineering which starts easily, shifts automatically, drives smoothly at high rates of speed, develops enormous power (although it is often driven by women and even elderly people), and comes in various shades and combinations of color to suit every taste and sometimes even to match the clothes of the owner's wife or daughter. It can be paid for on the installment plan, but it becomes quickly obsolete and is "turned in" and replaced frequently by a new one or by a better "secondhand" one. A congeries of revolutions were needed—in manufacture, quick-drying paint, macadam roads, engine power, car design, mass production, and the assembly line—to produce the end product of the American car. It congests the cities and the roads, and in the hands of the amateurs, the "hot rod" enthusiasts, and the neurotics it becomes a lethal instrument of grisly death and decimates the population. It has made the filling station, the parkway, the four-lane highway, the quick-service roadside hot-dog stand or restaurant, the "motel," the used-car lot, the trailer camp, the giant freight truck, the motor bus, the parking lot, the shopping center, the Friday-to-Sunday traffic jam, and the urban parking maze the most obtrusive features of the American landscape. It has made necessary a continual renewing of road construction, which has laid across the country a labyrinthine network of auto and truck roads, some of them toll turnpike roads financed by private bondowners, the rest financed by Federal and state funds, all of them as essential to the poor as to the rich. It has brought about a counter-railroad revolution, making freight traffic and daily travel independent of the railroad station and the commuter train, shifting factory sites and farm values, and spawning new suburbs where the family disperses every morning and reassembles every evening via the automobile. And it has made the seaside or mountain holiday and the fishing and camping vacation the routine adventure of the middle classes and even of workers' families.

The new Air Age, whose impact is just beginning to be felt, has further heightened the mobility of Americans. The sprawling airports, with the gleaming giant birds swooping in and out of them, are a portent of a time when distances will lose all meaning. Already the congestion of the airways is creating a traffic problem in the American skies much like the congestion of auto traffic. Yet the private family plane is unlikely to replace the family car, even though it may make the use of the car less obsessive. What the Air Age has done has been to make the faraway vacation possible for the boss's secretary as well as for the boss.

In the mid-1950s at least sixty million Americans left their homes for some kind of annual vacation, many of them going halfway across the Continent, some of them halfway across the world. Some go to the

mountain streams of the Northeast or Northwest or to Canada for fishing, some to Florida or California for the sun, some to the resorts or
the beach shacks or trailer colonies, some to Mexico or South America
for its atmosphere, many to Europe for its traditions and glamour, and
some simply hit the highways to get a look at the country. Tourism has
become one of America's big industries, involving expenditures of close
to twenty billion a year. Almost every wage-earner gets an annual
vacation with pay and gets away from job and home by air, train, boat,
car, or bus. The trend is toward longer vacations and therefore longer
trips. However, the recent changes in life span and the quest for personal
fulfillment have filled the world's capitals with middle-class and middle-
aged Americans whose children have grown up and who are spending
their years of leisure or "retirement" wandering over the world, armed
with dictionaries, tourist guides, traveler's checks, and an insatiable
hunger to see, hear, and feel. It is as if the impact of a machine civilization on the nerve centers of Americans had produced a constant mobility, whether out of boredom, curiosity, or an expressive sense of
freedom, which makes the great migrations of American history seem
fragmentary by comparison.

More embracing than this mobility of tourism is the restless movement from job to job and from home to home. Inside the same city
there are constant residence changes with changing jobs and social
status. Inside the same state there is a growing movement from farm
and small town to the city, and from the core city to the suburban fringes
of the larger metropolitan or cluster city. A government study of
migrant families in 1937 showed that in an industrial center like Detroit,
drawing constantly on new labor sources, four out of five people had
not lived in the same dwelling for five years. This was an extreme case,
yet it is estimated that in the decade from the mid-1940s to the mid-
1950s one out of five Americans changed homes in any one year, and in
the big cities the proportions might run higher.

The crucial phase of this phenomenon of Americans on the move is
the movement from state to state. During wars and periods of intense
arms rivalry there is a flow of workers to the defense industry areas. This
has been accompanied by a steady migration of Negroes, during and
after the world wars, from the Southern states to the big cities of the
Northeast and the Middle West, like Philadelphia, New York, Pittsburgh, Detroit, Chicago, St. Louis, and Kansas City. In addition there
has been an over-all shift of American population, along with the movement of industry, to the South, the Southwest, and the Pacific Coast,
especially to Florida, Texas, California, Oregon, and Washington. In
the single decade from 1940 to 1950 the population of California in-

creased by 50 per cent, that of Oregon by 40 per cent, that of Washington by 37 per cent.

The center of American population, where presumably the whole American plane balances in an equilibrium, moved steadily westward and slightly southward until in 1950 it was in southeast Illinois. The great boom industries of automobiles, shipyards, and aviation also moved West and South. The result was a rapid increase in the proportion of native Americans living outside the state of their birth, the current figure being around 25 per cent. In the West Coast states, where the rate of population increase has been highest, the proportion is highest: in California, at mid-century, more than two out of three were born in another state.*

What gives impetus to these waves of internal migration? Industrial workers followed the shifting currents that have determined the location of industries, moving wherever new industries opened up or where their skills could command the highest wages. Farm workers with no land of their own, or small farmers whose land had been wiped out by erosion, moved with the seasonal crops—rarely settling down, creating a permanent underlying population of migratory workers. Whole industries were uprooted, either because some boom played itself out or else to get closer to better markets or a cheaper labor force. One of the results was those "ghost towns" that are especially melancholy on the American landscape because they seem like skeletons at a rich man's feast.

But in the main the internal migrations are opportunity-and-advancement migrations. They are made not out of land hunger or the quest of freedom, as was true of the original migrations from abroad, but out of the pursuit of better chances for business and profits, for work and wages, for climate, schools, living conditions. Impalpable though it may seem as a motive, one reason for America's physical mobility is its social mobility: the lack of stable class lines and of a massive traditional past makes men's feet wander. As De Tocqueville saw clearly in his classic chapter, "Why Americans Are So Restless in the Midst of Their Prosperity," the American remains restless until he has done his best to look for the place, the job, the environing physical setting and social climate in which he wants to live out his life.

Through this search for place and vocation he comes as close to finding himself as he is ever likely to come. This is the experimental part of his life. These ventures in fortune and in change of locale are, in a sense, more truly the American educational system than the schools themselves. One of the truisms about American college graduates, for example, is that their best life training comes in the decade after college

* For a further discussion of migration shifts in terms of trends in population distribution, see Sec. 5, "Human Resources: Population Profile."

when the sequence of the jobs they pick up as they roam the nation reads like an eighteenth-century picaresque novel. The 1950 census showed that, from 1947 to 1950, 28 per cent of the 18-34 age group changed homes in any one year, but only 10 per cent of the age group after 45. The most mobile groups were the professional and semiprofessional ones—young couples and single men among the doctors, engineers, and technicians—who also took the biggest jumps across the continent. Increasingly also, regardless of search or choice, the big corporations have sent their young minor executives and technicians to take up jobs and homes in branch plants and offices across the country, moving them periodically for experience or promotion and creating a new category of American transients.

It does not follow that the migrating Americans find what they are looking for. In any deep sense many of them perhaps don't. But to move is one way of breaking the fear of being caught. The feeling an American dreads most is that of being "stuck"—held fast in the mud of an environment where everything seems stagnant. In many areas of Europe and the Far East this has been men's destiny for centuries, but to an American it seems a violation of everything he has felt about life. The sensation of being trapped is the ultimate indignity. So he moves. And his moving keeps alive his sense of social possibility, the belief that something can happen; and as long as something can happen all is not lost.

This hope and the accompanying mood of adventure are a clue to the impact the internal migrations have had on the American character. They serve to explain why each new frontier, and especially the Far Western one, has been romanticized in the folk imagination. Buffalo Bill, Kit Carson and the other Indian Scouts, General Custer, the "silver kings" of the Comstock lode, and even "badmen" like Billy the Kid have become type figures of a tradition which has run itself out in the "Westerns," the movies, and the pulp fiction. Yet they are part of an idealizing strain which has a deep beat of impulse and of which the Turner thesis itself was a kind of expression.

How crucial a need the internal migrations serve for Americans was shown after the end of World War II, when a great surge of population resettlement carried millions of Americans westward in an unplanned and uncontrolled movement that seemed almost tropismatic. Through the shifting of established industries and the opening of new war industries, the war was the spur to the reshuffling of the population. Its effect was especially great on the young veterans, many of whom found themselves training on the West Coast or shifting from there to the Pacific combat area. They saw places they had never seen, with a different physical and social landscape, and they liked what they saw. At

the war's end they took their young wives and found work there. In a
single decade Oregon's population increased by almost 40 per cent and
California's by more than 50 per cent. Many of the migrants came from
the prairie states, where the land had been ravaged by erosion and over-
grazing and where opportunity seemed at an end. Many were young
Negro veterans who swelled the Negro population of San Francisco,
Seattle, and Portland. They brought new ways of thinking to normally
conservative areas and changed the political landscape of the states that
became their new homes.

Yet the continuing strain of rebirth in all these migrations is evident
enough. The function served in the days of the classical migration, by
160 acres of open land available for the taking (to be sure, after the railroads and speculators had carved out their share), is now served by the
shift in industrial location. The young veterans went west not because it
was the West but because they found opportunities in new industries located near new sources of power and new markets. One of the consequences of the idealization of the agrarian society of the frontier was to
make it harder for American social thought to deal with industrial reality. The fact is that for most Americans the movement of social opportunity has to keep pace with the movement of industries and the building of power plants to harness hydroelectric energy. To explain why
Americans move around as they do today, one would need a theory
which took account of the relation between job opportunities, industrial
location, the determination not to get stuck, the cultural images of the
areas of growth, and the yearning for a home in which one can settle
down and get a sense of place.

It is not easy to achieve a sense of place in a culture that is always
tearing everything up by the roots, but it is none the less important. In
a big country you run the risk of feeling lost, in a new country you run
the risk of being anonymous, and the sense of place is a way of riveting
yourself down. For those who cannot achieve distinction by amassing
money or power or prestige, the attachment to place becomes one way of
salvaging the individual identity.

The sense of place is one form of the sense of belonging. Sometimes
the attachment to the soil, linked with a clear position in the social
hierarchy, is the most positive value a society can offer. This was true in
Europe in the Middle Ages, and in the pre-Civil War South in America.
But the breakup of European feudal society showed that men may want
a sense of belonging more satisfying than the sense of place when it carries nothing else with it. The settlement of America came from the
uprooting of the rooted precapitalist European society which led to the
long voyages across the seas. Out of this uprooting came a desire to strike

new roots. But the new roots could not be just any piece of land or any job in any locality. They had to satisfy what men were coming to demand of life in the new social climate of opportunity. In the case of America every value gets attached to this quest for fulfillment. Thus, paradoxically, even the American sense of place is a dynamic one.

Much of it is also nostalgic. When two Americans discover that they come from the same place, a spark is lit between them. And when an American finds that you have not heard of the place his family came from there is a sense of loss and almost of shock. It is not only that Plainville is thereby denied as if it had never existed but that the whole rich private experience that clusters about it is also denied. Thus the American feels doubly isolated. To be insensitive to these local associations of his is to strip him of a portion of his personality. The dangers of a dynamic society are that they lead to a whittling down of those accretions which the sense of place gives to the personality. When you move from the place where you were known to one where you must make your way, you cling all the more to the memories of place. Thus in the wake of the Yankee migration, "New England societies" were scattered through New York and the Middle West, as far as California. In the bewilderment that comes with the change of scale, pace, and tension, and the supplanting of face-to-face relations by impersonal ones, the place names and place memories that recall the simpler past have a powerful appeal. This was why Thomas Wolfe, moving from Asheville to New York, wove a sense of place into the web of time and memory with his haunting evocation in *Look Homeward, Angel*—"a stone, a leaf, an unfound door"—to express both his longing and his feeling of being lost.

This sense of the past as a sense of place is not restricted to the rural memories. During the great period of city-building, from the 1870s to the 1890s, the town or city took over some of the affection associated with the frontier farmstead and village. It took on a personality pattern that stuck in the memory: the layout of the main streets, the residential section, Shantytown where the Negroes and the foreign slum-folk lived; the schools, dance places, movie houses, night amusement spots; the fancy districts which had about them the tang of the forbidden. In a novel like Booth Tarkington's *The Magnificent Ambersons* one gets something of this retrospective affection. Among these scenes one lived, with these one grew up, these one remembered long afterward, setting down the memories in stories and novels or in those sentimentalized autobiographies or parental biographies in which Americans delight.

The retrospective loyalties, however, form only one of the main strands in the fiber of the American sense of place. The other is the contemporary pride of belonging to a vivid, growing entity—the pride of boosterism, if you will. There is something fiercely assertive about coming from Brooklyn or St. Paul, Kansas City or San Francisco, Maine or Oregon. A novel of manners or a Broadway comedy about Americans would scarcely run true to form if it did not have a character called "Tex" who holds forth with a genial persistence on the glories of the Lone Star State. There is an almost pathetic eagerness to find identification with the characteristic grandeurs and delights of your place, whatever it be, and to draw from the stature you give it at least a cubit to add to your own stature and security.

4. Natural Resources: the American Earth

THE LOVE OF PLACE was the earliest loyalty brought to the American shores. The settlers came from countries of their own where they had loved the familiar land and skies and hills. The American landscape was strange, untidy, uncompassable; the continent was wild, of grand proportions, with a luxuriance of plant and animal life that struck all the early explorers who brought with them "the eye of discovery."

There was the stretch of the Great Forest sweeping from the Atlantic dunes with few breaks to the deep interior, and then the stretch of the Great Plains and the long-grass prairie lands across the Ohio and Mississippi and Missouri to the foothills of the Rockies, and then the short-grass grazing lands and the mountains and deserts to the fertile valleys of the Pacific Coast, with another expanse of Great Forest northward along the coast. It was a land riven by mountain chains, from the Appalachian range in the East to the Sierra in the West, scarred by canyons, watered by broad and tumultuous rivers, with a climate that spanned all the intervals, from the frost of the North Country in the Great Lakes region and the Far Northwest of the fur trappers to the mesas and tablelands of the Southwest, the bayous of Louisiana, and the tropical everglades and swamps of Florida. It was filled, when the settlers first found it, with a fecund vegetation and wildlife: buffalo herds, deer, elk and bears, wild pigeons and geese, alligators and catfish, cod, sturgeon and salmon; with dense canebrake and coarse slough grass and needle grass and bluegrass and stands of prairie dropseed and tall-growing saw-tooth sunflower. And there were the trees: fir and spruce, maple and birch and elm, chestnut, hickory, and the always incredible sequoias, and that aristocrat of all American trees—the great white pine.

For the settlers who had come from the tidy landscapes of Europe, it was not a wholly comfortable sight and it had a touch of the frightening. But it was the right kind of stage-set for the theme and proportions of the mighty drama to be enacted on it, perhaps contrived for that purpose by a Providential scenic designer with an eye for symbolism. It was as if this myriad of landscapes swept up into one was ordained to harbor a myriad of stocks which were in time to be welded into a single nation. Thus the later expansionist cry of "Manifest Destiny," which was to rise from millions of throats as the nation pushed westward, was not only a shibboleth of jingoism but almost a tropism of the American earth, part of the inner logic of a landscape too big to be limited by the historical accidents of settlement and sovereignty. The wild and lush landscape seemed to offer to the eighteenth-century mind, which personified Nature with a capital N, a charter to build on the far-stretched continent a new social system swept clean of privilege, caste, and inequity, to be governed by "the laws of Nature and of Nature's God." This charter proved, for generations of Americans, a pathway to the unchecked exploiting of untapped resources and undreamed-of wealth and power.

It is in this indirect sense, rather than that of direct conditioning, that the American landscape has helped shape the American national character. I use the term "landscape," of course, not only in the decorative and aesthetic sense but as the total physical environment in its relation to human living. It is roughly true that habitat tends to shape habit, although we don't know just how or how much. Some recent students have tried to show how the "mighty Russian plain," with its vast stretches, its extremes of protracted winter cold and intense summer heat, has carved the Russian people into a profile of intense extremes of revolutionary violence and docile endurance. Valid or not, such an approach would be unfruitful for the Americans, who are comparative newcomers and on whom the influence of earth, sky, and climate has not operated over centuries. That is why (although I am well aware of its dangers) I prefer to stress the indirect role of the American landscape as a bold setting for a venture in social construction. This had a subtle but no less powerful influence on American ideas. The environmental silhouette of the landscape bears some relation to the cultural silhouette of American attitudes. On a continent of great richness of regional variation it has been happily difficult to break down political recalcitrance and achieve complete centralization. Where Nature shows such extremes, it is not surprising that the image of an equilibrium should have come from Newtonian thought in Europe with great force into the American Constitution and political system. And where the environment offered a hard challenge to settlement, the Darwinian idea of the survival of the fittest found a fertile social soil and helped shape a competitive social system.

But the great theme of the American earth is the theme of its rich resources and how the Americans have used and abused them—not what the land has done to the people but what the people have done to the land. In a money culture it is difficult to keep clear the distinction between symbolic wealth and the real wealth of the nation. America has been fortunate in the abundance, diversity, quality, and distribution of its real wealth—not only the soil, climate, water, and wildlife but the minerals stored under the earth, the fossil-fuel energy of coal and oil, the natural gas, the hydroelectric energy, the rare minerals entering into atomic energy.

In any calculus of the world's resources—immediate, reserve, and potential—America leads the procession of the nations, with even the Soviet Union following at a distance. America was estimated (1950) to have 30 per cent of the world's harnessed water power and to produce 42 per cent of the world's total electrical power from all sources—about 430 billion kilowatt hours (western Europe produced 25 per cent, the Soviet Union 8 per cent). It used 60 per cent of the world's total petroleum production and 25 per cent of its total coal production; its per-capita use of electrical energy from all sources increased from 455 kilowatt-hours in 1924 to 3,000 kilowatt-hours in 1954, and its per-capita use of total mechanical energy was roughly like that derived from burning eight tons of coal for every person. This was six times the per-capita average for the rest of the world, 160 times the per-capita use of energy in Asia (not including Japan), eight times what Japan used, and more than triple what Europe used.

The picture of American fossil fuel reserves and future supplies and uses of industrial energy is a complex one. A 1938 survey showed America as having an estimated 3,200 billion tons of coal of all grades in reserve, out of 7,300 billion tons for the world. America had more than half the bituminous reserves of the world but a small portion of the anthracite. Some have talked much too optimistically of a 2,000- to 3,000-year supply of coal for America, but this overlooks the fact that probably only a tenth of the reserves may be economically minable, and it assumes present levels of energy consumption, which is an untenable assumption. As population and living standards go up, as the quantity and quality of fossil fuels go down, there will be greater demands on a lessened supply, and greater energy will be required to get at the available further energy. America produces almost two billion barrels of oil a year and uses seven billion; its estimated oil reserves are some fifty-five billion barrels, a ninth of the world's oil reserves. Unless the new geophysicists spot still undiscovered oil domes, the American reserves will not last beyond 1980, but new processes of converting coal, natural gas, and shale oil into liquid fuel are likely to become feasible. America in 1950 had a proved reserve of 180 trillion cubic feet of natural gas, which was about fifty times its rate of use, but by 1960 the annual volume siphoned off into pipelines and distributed over the country was likely to double, and, increasingly, chemicals as well as liquid fuels were being manufactured from natural gas close to the site of the reserves. America also had zinc, lead, bauxite, tin, tungsten, and molybdenum, although the reserves of all of these were precarious. It had limestone and aluminum clays and brown lead ores from which new processes will be able to extract new uses.

The great event that lies ahead in the use of American mineral and energy resources is the shift to new sources of supply, new kinds of energy, new modes of conversion. Harrison Brown, writing about American mineral consumption, points out that there is an annual per-capita flow of 1,260 pounds of steel through production lines, with eight tons of steel in per-capita use, and both amounts steadily rising. There are sharply diminishing reserves of iron, aluminum, copper, sulphur, and the ore seams have to be followed deep underground. The prospects are that these ores will have to be extracted from ordinary rock, and the energy for extracting them will be atomic energy. The supplies of the great energy sources—coal, petroleum, natural gas—are finite and exhaustible, and their place is likely to be taken by atomic and solar power. The uranium and thorium needed for atomic energy can, if necessary, be extracted from the plentiful granite. As Brown puts it, "the basic raw materials for the industries of the future will be sea water, air, ordinary rock, sedimentary deposits of limestone and phosphate rock, and sunlight." Thus, while in a sense America is becoming a "have-not" nation, increasingly dependent on foreign imports for crucial minerals, its resources, under the conditions of an expanding technology, may prove enough to fill its reasonable needs.

As for the soil and what grows on it, the American endowment is great. Of its 1.9 billion acres of land, nearly a fifth (400 million) is used for crops, about a half (900 million) for pasture and grazing, and less than a third (600 million) is farm woodland and forest. Despite the denuding of the Great Forest, there are still big timber stands on the Pacific Coast, in California, Washington, and especially Oregon. There are nine-feet-high cornfields in Iowa and a vast stretch of wheatland on the Great Plains from Texas through Minnesota. There are the cotton and tobacco fields of the South and the lush valleys of the Pacific slope. America has all but conquered the problem of mass hunger that plagued men through history. There were many areas in the world where the soil was better cared for than in America, and where intensive cultivation made the yield higher. But with their skills of science and machinery the Americans applied (in the Keynesian phrase) a different kind of "multiplier"—other than sheer human toil—to the fertility of the soil itself. Thus the United States became the granary and breadbasket for many areas of the world where feudal land tenure, ignorance of soil techniques, and lack of capital equipment allowed the good arable land to go wretchedly unused.

For more than a century after the founding of the Republic there was a complacent assumption that Nature's plenty need not be guarded and would resist forever the withering hand of time and man. Americans have had a self-confidence and self-admiration on the score of their resources that few other peoples could match. The record of civilization runs against the hope that Americans will learn where others have not. In Asia, Africa, and the Mediterranean areas there is the story of the using up and disintegration of the environment as a productive system. One thinks of the "classical deserts" of North Africa and the Middle East, where (as Ritchie Calder puts it) "some fifteen civilizations, cultures, or empires foundered in the dust of their own creation." Overdramatically, one may speak of the protracted large-scale plundering of the American earth and ask who were the plunderers.

The answer may be found in a combination of land hunger, greed, haste, and planlessness. Many of the settlers came from areas in Europe where land was cramped, holdings small, and the laws of succession rigid. The yield of the American grasslands and forestland when first tamed by the plow was richer than human dream. The early settlers felled the big trees, cutting over and burning over the forest, "deadening" the ever-larger clearings. Leaving badly damaged soil behind, they kept moving westward to virgin soil. On much of this American farmers have kept the yield high by crop rotation and the skillful replacement of the soil's properties. But there are also millions of acres where the methods used were those of ruthless "soil-mining," as if the soil were a repository of fossil fuels to be extracted from it and then good-by. The single-crop system of wheat, corn, and cotton impoverished the land, the complex bundle of organic processes that held the plains together was broken, and the denuded earth was left exposed to dust storms that blew it away and floods that washed the richness of the topsoil down into the rivers and seas. It has been estimated that three of the nine inches of topsoil that the American Continent possessed in Colonial times have been destroyed, most of it since the Civil War.

What happened to the wheat and corn lands happened also to the cattle lands. The opening of the great grazing plains caught the world's imagination, and to many in Europe the American cowboy with his horse and lasso and six-shooter became the type figure symbolizing the derring-do of the American. But deterioration set in with the great livestock boom that followed the Civil War. The Western lands were overstocked and overgrazed by cattle and sheep, until now their grazing capacity is less than half of what it was; erosion by wind and water set in;

dust storms came, and droughts, and "deserts on the march." The valley bottoms of the Southwest were gutted by erosion, with thousands of arroyos cut into them. The result is that the grazing areas of the West are today the slowest areas of population growth, and the young people are abandoning them.

Perhaps the most tragic phase was the devastation of the forests. America lost nine tenths of its timber to insects, forest fires, and—most of all—ruthless cutting. A good chunk of the mythology of America, and some of the folk heroes like Paul Bunyan, came out of the lumber camps and logging. But after the romance had tarnished there remained only the pathos of the predaceous. The lumber barons stripped the land of its trees with a fervor that made huge timber fortunes and then moved on to virgin timber. With the forests gone and the hills cut away, the land was despoiled of its strength, floods and drought followed, and the small farmer had to move on with the moving deserts. Paul Bunyan was succeeded by the "Okies" and by Steinbeck's Joads. In 1918 Americans were cutting almost six trees for every one that was replanted, and the denuding reached right up to the last frontier of the Oregon timber stand. The more responsible companies are now treating trees like crops, to be farmed and replaced, but there are still "gyppo" outfits that "cut out and run," never replanting what they have destroyed. To make it worse, the cattlemen are moving up on the trees, seeking to take over for "private enterprise" the grazing lands of the national forests, situated on the high-country watersheds.

Thus the hunger for land and profits and the blind application of *laissez faire* in an area where it makes no sense have left little room either for a reverence toward the American earth or a wisdom about its long-range use. Some daemonic force seemed to be driving Americans on to despoil the land and its resources. Mark Twain's *Gilded Age* depicted caustically the interweaving of public lands, legislative bribery, and real-estate promotion in the post-Civil War days. The dramatic "land-rush" episodes of the *Cimmaron* novels and the technicolor movies have blotted out the uncomfortable fact that the lion's share of the public lands went in handouts and bounties to the railroad companies and were otherwise caught up in speculation. The speculative spirit, applied to the wheat crops, was the theme of Frank Norris's highly dramatic novels, *The Pit* and *The Octopus,* which were not too far from the truth in describing the soil's product and the fate of growers and consumers alike as the playthings of the commodity exchanges and the railroads.

In the case of the oil lands, which furnish the power for America's motor civilization, the history of the industry has also been one of get-and-grab-and-squeeze-dry. The "rule of capture," carried over by analogy from a legal system adapted to a hunting economy, gave the oil to whatever producer pumped it first out of the ground. Each oilman thus had to run his well at maximum to drain off as much as possible from the common underground reservoir, and to meet this piracy of oil-stripping his neighbors had to build offset wells. The result was a ghastly waste, as well as competitive overproduction, with only a 10 per cent recovery of oil in the early years. Eventually a "proration" system was worked out between groups of owners under government regulation, but not before the oil supplies had spouted much of their richness into the sky.

An ironic later phase in the natural history of the American land expressed the hunger for "real estate" to be "developed" and "turned over" at a quick profit. The extreme symbol of this was the Florida land boom of the 1920s, when the drive to use the land not for its products but for quick speculative riches reached manic and even comic proportions. At the end of the boom all involved found themselves stripped of the paper empires they had dreamed up, with their grandiose real-estate developments memorialized only by a few street signs and billboards still standing in the surrounding emptiness, promising urban glories to come. Incidentally, many of them did come in time, in the more moderate and sustained boom of the 1940s and 1950s.

The story of the gold lands is similarly symbolic. When California gold was discovered the "gold rush" was a dramatic sign of the whole feverish effort to scoop riches out of the earth. The gold flowed into circulation and served as base for a pyramid of credit and capital such as no economy has ever built. American investments and the favorable American trade balance, like a lodestone, drew most of the remaining gold from the rest of the world to be stored again, by a fateful cycle of return, in the American earth.

The profile of the use of American resources is actually much more of a mixed picture than this suggests. To the theme of past plunder and exploitation must be added the theme of the present efforts at conservation and the accelerated discovery of new energy sources. Americans are adept at using up very fast the resources that cannot be restored and at developing new ones. It was not until the turn of the twentieth century, with Theodore Roosevelt and Gifford Pinchot, and later with George W. Norris and Franklin Roosevelt, that the conservationists tried to make Americans aware of the effects of years of haste, waste, and ruthlessness. Recently the conservation movement has entered a new phase: not only to prevent the abuse of resources but to realize their full potential. The problems of conserving the soil are being grappled with, especially through contour farming, terracing, strip cropping, irrigation, crop rotation, and the planting of tree shelter belts. Beyond that is the larger planning of conservation by approaching an entire watershed as a unit.

But the canker of heedlessness and greed has not been rooted out. One of the prime facts about natural resources in America, unlike the case in most other cultures, is that they are for the most part privately owned and exploited. The America of the mid-1950s seems largely to have forgotten the experience of the post-Civil War years and to be un-doing much of the work of the New Deal years. Caught up in a com-placent confidence that America had found the secret to the best use of its resources, and that private owners deserved the rich prizes because they made the best use of them for the public benefit, Congress and the state legislatures gave generously out of the national largess. The for-mula usually involved the transfer of resources from Federal to state con-trol or to private associations of producers. Thus the rich offshore oil deposits, especially off the coast of Louisiana, Texas, and California, and much of the grazing land in the public domain were transferred to the states, which in turn made them available to private exploitation. The transfer of the oil deposits was not achieved without a bitter political fight and a Congressional act that overrode the Supreme Court decisions, but huge sums were at stake and big interests involved, and the outcome could not be doubted. The control of the grazing lands came into the hands of cattlemen's associations that were in effect private "guilds"— para-political organizations which were able to outmaneuver the politi-cal bureaucrats when they could not win them over. In the case of hydroelectric power there was a rollback of the New Deal effort to build giant dams under public auspices, to furnish power to private and municipal consumers, and under the impact of the Hoover Commission reports even the great achievement of the TVA was not regarded as wholly immune to this rollback.

Water has done more than any other element to force on the Ameri-can a unitary approach to his environment and its resources. If Jean Brunhes was right, that "every human enterprise is a mixture of a little bit of humanity, a little bit of soil, and a little bit of water," it is the water that has proved most difficult. It forms—with droughts, erosion, and floods—an indivisible water complex. The rains, with no trees or vegetation to hold them in the earth, grow into floods. The eroded soil, washed away by torrents, flows down in millions of tons along the rivers, becoming silt, clogging up the river channels, creating new floods. But the flood-control programs have to compete for Federal funds with programs for irrigation and reclamation. To top it off, there is the problem of water scarcity. With the falling water tables and mounting industrial water demands, areas like Southern California, the Texas Panhandle, the Southwestern states, Illinois, New Jersey, and New York have been threatened by periodic water famines. The legal problem of who gets how much of what water is available has led to a water imperialism, with protracted wars between communities and sometimes whole states for the control of the watersheds of the great rivers, and with attempted water grabs by those who have been called the "Water-Seekers."

It has become clear that the best answer to this bundle of water problems is to approach it as a unit. It is to consider the whole river-valley area enclosed and interlaced by the waters as an entity demanding social and engineering solutions which involve the land and the people, agriculture and hydroelectric power and industry, as parts of the indivisible water complex. Not that every American river and river basin is like every other. Their individual forms are unique and each must be studied for its uniqueness, as the Water Resources Policy Commission did in its study of ten American river basins. But the pattern of interrelations is inescapable. It applies to the Columbia Basin, to the Missouri and the Tennessee, to the Central Valley of California, to the Rio Grande and the Colorado, to the Connecticut and the Potomac, to the Alabama-Coosa and the Ohio Basin.

The interrelations are those between an exacting, if also a munificent, natural environment and the conditions of an industrial civilization in an Age of Power. Put in another way, they are the relations between the natural and social landscapes of the American continent. Americans have put the concept into practice in the functioning of the TVA, an American invention which is being adapted to river-basin regions in India and the Middle East. A central feature of the TVA is the multiple-purpose dam—for flood control, irrigation, land reclamation, and the generating of hydroelectric power. Not surprisingly, the extension of the TVA idea to the other American river-basin areas was bitterly fought by the power companies and their legislative champions. Eventually the multiple-purpose dam and the single-river-basin approach carry a force which will be hard to resist, since the irrepressible logic of the Power Age will prove stronger even than the power empires. The new industries that mark out the line of industrial growth—aviation, chemicals, light metals, alloys, electronics, atomic energy—are insatiable consumers of power. To meet their demands, and at the same time to meet the problems of the whole river basin and its needs, is one of the new imperatives of American life, going beyond party politics and the ideology of either private or government enterprise. Whether it is the Norris Dam that is involved, or Shasta or Grand Coulee or Hell's

Canyon, they are not likely to be wished away or cramped into crippling economic forms.

To do so would be like a man-made forging of Nature's authentic signature. Nor would it make political sense to the most conservative groups in American life—the farmer and the small businessman, who are among the new customers for the power generated by the multi-purpose dam. For rural families in the TVA area or the Pacific Northwest, cheaply available electricity means the farm revolution, the kitchen revolution, and the communications revolution—that is to say, a generator, a deep-freeze, and a TV set. For the small businessman, as has been shown in the Tennessee Valley, it means community purchasing power for his products. The TVA has given new meaning to the idea of a region and of regional planning by keeping alive the interrelatedness of the region's needs, sinews, and potential growth.

I stress the exploring of future potentials here rather than the conserving of past resources. What we count as resources changes with the changing industrial arts. Americans have been of a twofold mind on the question of their natural resources. They neglected and wasted them, perhaps with the comforting conviction that "the ravens will provide"; and when they discovered the extent of their waste they grew panicky and gave themselves to an intense conservation movement. At the same time they are basically future-minded, dwelling not so much on the Great Estate they have inherited as on continuing inventories and forecasts of "needs and resources." Along with being future-minded and potential-minded, Americans are abundance-minded, as befitting (in Potter's phrase) a "people of plenty." Despite acute periodic attacks of guilt and panic, they have never taken seriously either the doctrine of closed space or the doctrine of exhausted resources. Even their haste and their predations against Nature were part of their basic optimism: men who are continually in motion and hope to transform themselves and their fortunes are unlikely to balk at defacing and transforming their environment.

A half century ago Henry Adams saw the coming of "the new American—the child of incalculable coal power, chemical power, electric power, and radiating energy, as well as of new forces yet undetermined," and predicted that he would be "a sort of God compared with any former creature of nature." For all his pessimism and his pose as an archaism in a new society, Adams and his "law of acceleration" in history expressed as well as foretold the crescendo of energy development. In 150 years America has increased perhaps fifty or sixty times its percapita energy production from fossil fuels and water power, as compared with the America of 1800, which was mainly a consumer of wood fuel

—and the process continues. The Paley Commission of 1952 reported that since World War I the U.S. had swallowed up larger quantities of mineral fuels and of most metals than had been used in the whole span of world history. But the expanding skills of scientists also enabled them to discover synthetics, plastics, and electronics, and to open up a new dimension in the peaceful potentials of atomic energy. There was, of course, still one area of great vulnerability in the armor of resources within which America was encased. It was its dependence on foreign sources of supply for many of its strategic raw materials, such as tin and arsenic, manganese, zinc, bauxite, titanium. But this was a weakness only in the event of another world war—which in itself would destroy the whole fragile frame of technology, transport, and industry which gives American resources their meaning. The other area of vulnerability—the danger that population growth will outrun resources —was real enough, but it applied less to America than to the crowded and underdeveloped areas of the world.

America has the resources for its present and future needs, if it has the will to use them fully and the social imagination to use them equitably. What it is in danger of forgetting is that, whether in an industrial or agrarian society, in an age of giant power or of forest clearings, the web between man and his environment is broken only at his peril. The final issue goes beyond the waste or conservation of resources. It is the issue of basic attitude. Whether through land hunger or riches hunger the frontiersman rifled and used up as he went, was always in a hurry, dreamed of empires. The speculators, city-builders and empire-builders followed in his track, and the scientist kept pace with them, promising to think up new synthetic products when the old resources were used up. Despite the influence of the natural environment on the American mind, what was lacking in every case was a reverence for Nature.

Naturalists speak of the "hydrologic cycle" by which rain is imprisoned in the soil, drained into the rivers and oceans, returned to the atmosphere, and once more released for human use. They speak also of the "biotic cycle," the similar web and sequence of the growth of plant life and its use by man, and the return of its waste products and chemical properties to the soil to become once more parts of the cycle of organic growth. But encompassing both there is the balance of nature and man, by which man is sustained by the environment but only on condition that he should not murderously waste his Great Estate but "dress it and keep it." When the American loses the reverence for the American earth to which he is bound he loses more than his resources. He loses his meaning and his capacity to sustain a great civilization with its curious and ephemeral network of ways.

5. Human Resources: Population Profile

OBSERVERS WHO TRAVELED across the American Continent in the mid-1950s were usually impressed by two quantitative things they saw—the number of automobiles and TV sets, and the number of babies. The notable fact here is that a materialist America, which might have been expected to choose higher living standards rather than larger families, defied the diagnosticians and chose both. Characteristically the Americans themselves spoke of their "baby boom" as if it were little different from a housing boom or a boom in uranium stocks. Yet beneath the flipness of the phrase the "baby boom" half revealed and half concealed a dramatic revolution that overturned many accepted ideas and expectations about American population trends.

To students of civilization there are certain indices of its vitality. Borrowing and broadening an early English phrase that was restricted to a census, we may speak of these as a Domesday inventory of a people in its crucial demographic phases: its numbers, its birth rate, its death rate, its population growth, its average life span, its family size, its age distribution, its occupational and educational composition, its physical and psychic health, and the food, housing, and welfare of its people. Of these the crucial ones are the birth rate, the death rate, and population growth. The bugbear of the historians of civilization has long been the static society, or "stationary state."

Not surprisingly, most Americans share this view and get uneasy when there are signs of the slowing up of their population growth. Like some other Western peoples, they feel that a decrease in the rate of growth is somhow bad and an increase somehow good. Partly this may be an expression of the cult of numbers. But it is also a recognition that civilizations are organic and that when their inner sources of population strength dry up there will be a drying up of their national energies. History furnishes instances of peoples that failed to reproduce themselves, either because their birth rate was too low or their death rate too high. Hence the anxiety evoked by scholars in the 1930s and 1940s who talked about a "population cycle" in the history of every civilization and made projections for America showing the arc of population growth flattening out between 1950 and 1975. When the 1950 and 1955 figures stubbornly refused to follow the projections and took a sharp upturn, there was a general sense of relief, rightly or wrongly, among those who felt it to be a vindication of America's inner strength and an affirmation of the future. Instead of the population cycle determining the arc of the American life force, it turned out that the life force had something to do with shaping the population cycle.

Some of the earlier commentators on America had proved sounder prophets. Writing as "Poor Richard" in the 1780s, Benjamin Franklin addressed a prospectus to immigrants in the form of "Information to Those Who Would Remove to America": "From the salubrity of the air," he wrote, "the healthiness of the climate, and plenty of good provisions, and the encouragement to early marriages and by the certainty of subsistence in cultivating the earth, the increase of inhabitants by natural generation is very rapid in America, and becomes still more so by the accession of strangers." Franklin was justified by history: the upward curve of population came not only from immigration but also because marriages were early, the opening of new land put a premium on large families to supply labor, the economy of plenty made them possible, and the new immigration was largely of men and women in the childbearing age group.

Writing in the late 1830s, a half century later, Alexis de Tocqueville made a bold prediction of American population growth. "The time will come," he wrote at the end of the first volume of *Democracy in America*, "when 150 millions of men will be living in North America, equal in condition, the progeny of one race, owing their origin to the same cause, and preserving the same civilization, the same language, the same religion, the same habits, the same manners, imbued with the same opinions, propagated under the same forms. The rest is uncertain, but this is certain: and it is a fact new to the world—a fact fraught with such portentous consequences as to baffle the efforts even of the imagination." The 1950 census figures showed De Tocqueville's prophecy amply fulfilled. By 1957 the figures reached 170 million and were growing.

At one point there was strong evidence of a slackening of pace, when the fertility rate showed a marked decline between 1920 and 1940. The twenties and thirties were crucial years for America. Economic collapse, coming abruptly after top-pitch prosperity, produced a crisis of faith in the American experience. There was increased knowledge and use of contraception, and the size of the family unit dwindled. A study by Dennis Wrong showed that the "differential fertility" between the educated upper-income groups and the lower-income groups had been narrowing since 1910, and narrowed sharply during the Depression of the thirties. Thus the rationalistic approach to childbearing was reaching even the lower-income groups. In the "competition between consumers goods and children," as one writer put it, the children seemed to be losing out. From 1925 to 1945 there was considerable agreement that a long-range trend was in process and that the curve of growth would continue to flatten out: the Census estimate as late as 1946 was that a peak of 165 million would be reached in 1990. All the signs pointed to what some of the demographers called an "incipient decline" of the growth potential of American population.

Surprisingly, the fertility rates increased sharply after 1940, and by 1945 the increase was clear enough to cause a shift in the estimates. After reaching a low of 16.6 per thousand in 1933—the depth of the Great Depression—the birth rate moved to 17.9 in 1940 and reached a high of 25.8 in 1947. From 2.3 million births in 1933, the number rose to 3.9 million in 1947 and exceeded 4 million in 1954 and 1955. The population, which had been 130 million in 1940, grew by 35 million in fifteen years without much help from immigration.

I emphasize this episode because it is a commentary on the danger of approaching a living civilization mechanically. The scientists figured, quite understandably, that the decrease in the American death rate had pretty much reached its limits, that the doors of immigration were closed, and that the declining trajectory of the birth rate was clearly demarked. But while one can confidently study things, it is harder to mark out a path for the aberrant and incalculable ways of people. The scientists were right in saying that as people move from rural areas into the city their birth rate falls; that as women get jobs and careers and find something other to do than bearing and rearing children, it falls further; that as living standards rise they crowd out babies. But the sequel proved them wrong, because they had failed to look at an important factor. Commenting in 1954 on a paper by Joseph S. Davis (who had seen the new trend earlier than most), Frank W. Notestein looked back at the miscalculations of his fellow craftsmen: "Too much attention was paid to more than a century of experience with declining birth rates. . . . Too little consideration was given to the possibility that the processes of family formation, which had hitherto shown remarkable stability, might change with unexpected speed."

What this comes to is that American life purposes and attitudes are still in flux, as restless as the migrant movements of the people themselves. Population growth depends on the relation between fertility and mortality rates. America had made great strides in decreasing infant mortality, but for a while it seemed to run into a declining birth rate. There is a plausible explanation for the reversal of this decline in the war years, since girls preferred to marry and start their babies before their men went off to battle. The deferment of fathers helped, and so did the chance of young married veterans to go to college on the G.I. Bill of Rights at government expense. Yet the trend continued even after the end of the war. And while it is true that American family formation changed in the late 1930s and the 1940s, behind this change was a more fundamental change in values and in the images of self which American men and women had.

I have said that the stark contrast between the prosperity of the twenties and the economic collapse of the thirties produced a crisis of faith in young Americans. This crisis was somehow met and mastered in the New Deal years and those of the defense boom and full employment that followed, with results that started to show themselves in 1940. The decrease in mortality rates was a matter of science, but the increase in birth rates, at a time when birth control was readily available to most, was a matter of faith in living. Having babies is always a form of risk in giving hostages to fortune, and in modern "rational" societies it is not undertaken without a faith in the future to which the hostages are committed. With the restoration of employment and income, and the emergence of more leisure in a setting of suburban living, young Americans took an attitude toward babies baffling to everyone but themselves. They grew old-fashioned about babies and family size just when everyone was expecting them to be very modern and very cynical. As for the young wife, she belongs to a generation of women who have decided to have their children first and to think of using their talents in a career on the side or after the children are grown. The danger of a declining birth rate was a strategic one in the upper-middle and professional classes, and among the artistic and intellectual groups, since their standards and attitudes tended in time to permeate the other classes. Since 1940 there has been a marked increase in fertility rates in these crucial groups.

I have spoken of the changing image of the self as a clue to the riddle of why Americans breed as fast or as slow as they do. This is a solemn way of saying what young Americans mean when they say "it's fun" to marry young, to have babies instead of going childless (the demand for children for adoption is evidence of a feeling of pang about the childless family), to have two children instead of one or three instead of two, to buy a house in a suburb and get a car and raise a family, to put down roots, to be a "man in a gray flannel suit" who faces his responsibilities, to be the woman who meets his train in a station wagon with the children. "It's fun" even for the higher educational and living-standard groups, perhaps especially for them, since they live on a sharper edge of the search for happiness in life. To guess how these images of self—which are formed by converging lines of tendency from every part of the culture—will turn out a generation hence is to guess about the future climate of hope or despair, and what atomic energy and the automatic factory and office will do to employment, and what the ever-expanding scope of leisure and the rising living standards will do to the fertility rate.

The story of the American mortality rate is as important in population growth and composition as that of the birth rate, although it has offered less difficulty for analysis and projection. In the century from 1850 to 1950 the American population increased more than sixfold, partly because of the high immigration factor through the 1920s but mainly because of a decreasing death rate, especially since 1900, that responded to better medical care and advances in diet, clothing, housing, living standards, and public health. In America, as elsewhere in the world picture in recent centuries, the mortality rate was a more dynamic factor in population growth than was the birth rate. An American mortality rate that was 17.2 per thousand in 1900 decreased to 12 in 1920 and to 9.6 per thousand in 1950. The reduction of infant mortality changed drastically what had been for centuries the "natural" profile of age composition, increasing the number of those who reached the reproducing age, thus providing an unprecedented growth potential. The mortality reductions have been dramatic for women in childbirth (6.47 per 1,000 live births in 1927 to 0.76 in 1951), for babies in the year after birth (from a death rate of 65 out of every 1,000 in 1927 to 29 in 1951), and in general for all Americans (less so for Negroes) below forty-five. There have also been decreases in the mortality rates for those above sixty. If there are to be further reductions, they will have to come chiefly in the middle years, between forty-five and sixty, through an attack on the tension diseases which hit Americans in those years.

There remains to draw a profile of the recent changes in the make-up and distribution of the American population. In increasing the life span, the new medical techniques and the declining death rate have swelled America's population profile at both ends of the age-group distribution. A child at birth now has a far better chance of growing up (95 per cent reach at least the age of fifteen); a man or woman reaching sixty-five has a better chance of hanging on tenaciously. In the single decade from 1940 to 1950, the number of children under ten increased by almost 40 per cent, as compared with a total population increase of less than 15 per cent. In 1950 there were twenty-six million Americans over fifty-five—an increase of 30 per cent in a decade. The number over sixty-five grew from three million in 1900 (4 per cent of the population) to thirteen million in 1952 (over 8 per cent), and the likelihood is that it will reach 10 per cent in a generation. In the past half century, while the population doubled, the number over sixty-five increased fourfold.

These two trends—the conserving of children and the prolonging of life—have had effects on America that go beyond the crowding of maternity hospitals and school facilities, the craze for Hopalong Cassidy, space cadets, and Davy Crockett, and the development of geriatrics as a major branch of medicine. They have given America the paradoxical aspect of being a nation at once of the young and the elderly. And they have changed much of American thinking by changing the life expectancy. In the half century after 1900 the expectancy of an American male increased by twenty-one years; in the fourteen years from 1937 to 1951 it went up from sixty to sixty-eight and a half years. Imperceptibly the shift is producing changed attitudes toward older people and toward the pace of life: since a longer life is accessible to more people, there is a slowing down of pace in order to woo it and achieve it. There are even a number of American thinkers who are saying boldly that the problem of death can be conquered.

There are, of course, laments over America's becoming a country for the old. The median age rose by almost ten years in seventy-five years, from 20.9 in 1880 to a little over thirty in the early 1950s; since then it has declined a bit because of the continuing flood of births. But one wonders why a relatively high median age is thought undesirable, and what there is so special about a low one. The youthfulness of a population may be purchased by early death as well as by birth: it has meant historically in any culture that life was brief and pathetic, with little technological or medical development. In Asia, a newly born child is less likely to reach the age of fifteen than he would be in America to reach sixty-five. The extension of life expectancy gives the individual a chance to fulfill his promise; it gives the culture a large proportion of people who can spend their productive years in work. As for the Americans no longer being a "young" people, the answer is that words are culturally conditioned, and the population changes have also changed the meaning of "young" and "old." The span of youth in America has been stretched into the late forties, and the span of middle age into the late sixties, where the margin of old age now begins. Only in industry is it still hard for a man or woman over forty-five to get a job, but even there the old ways of thinking are beginning to yield.*

I have spoken† of the recent population shifts between states and regions, and between rural and urban areas. In these shifts the movements of migration are generally more important than birth rates. The seven fastest-growing states in the decade of the forties—California, Arizona, Florida, Nevada, Oregon, Washington, and Maryland—had greater increases from migration than from births. The four states that lost population—Mississippi, Arkansas, North Dakota, Oklahoma—had high birth rates but suffered the greatest migration loss. In general, if it were only a matter of birth and death figures, the Southern states would be the fastest-growing ones: the birth rate of the Negroes and of the "poor whites" is high. But except for states like Florida, many of

* For a further discussion of the older age groups in America, and the problems of aging, see Ch. VIII, Sec. 7, "The Middle and End of the Journey."
† See Sec. 3, "People in Motion."

the young people—white as well as Negro—are leaving the South, and the movement West continues. The freedom of internal migration makes it possible for population to adjust itself flexibly between the areas of high birth rate and low economic opportunity and those of low birth rate and high economic opportunity.

There is an important population shift away from the farms and small towns to the cities, and a shift in turn from the big cities to the suburbs on their periphery. The net result for the big-city cores, except in the areas of population boom, showed only minor gains. But on the margins of the big cities, where mass-produced houses could be bought with all the equipment of the "kitchen revolution," where autos brought people to their city jobs and recreation, and TV sets filled their leisure time at home, the population grew lushly. There was a double recoil against the stagnation of the farm and small town and against the rootless and frenetic quality of big-city living. Americans launched not a back-to-the-farm movement, as in the days of the Roman Principate, but a movement forward to the conditions under which they could have the best of both worlds.*

There has been a steady decline in the proportion of the foreign-born in the American population. By 1955 it included not much over 6 per cent of the people: the time is close when only a small fraction of Americans will have been born on foreign soil, and when the percentage of foreign-born in the South in 1955 (about 1½ per cent) will apply throughout the nation.

Before 1950 there were more men than women in America, mainly because immigration was weighted toward males and because of the high mortality of mothers in childbirth. Since 1950 the sex ratio has shifted, not only with immigration changes and the cutting of maternal mortality, but also because American women now outlive men by a bigger margin then ever. After forty-five the tension diseases hit men harder, and their wives survive to inherit the earth. As one waspish comment has it, the U.S. is becoming a "gerontomatriarchy," a society ruled by aging females.

The large American labor force—that is, the large numbers in the age groups available for running and managing the machines—has made possible the fact that with only 6 per cent of the world's population America is responsible for almost one half of the world's output of goods. The Americans "gainfully employed" in 1956 reached over seventy million, and the estimate for 1975 ran to between eighty-five and ninety-five million. The proportion of women in the work force, especially married women, is growing. The work week was reduced an average of 5 per cent every decade since 1870, and in the mid-1950s it

* For a further discussion, see Sec. 10, "The Suburban Revolution."

was about forty hours, with estimates that by 1975, under the impact of the almost automatic factory and the electronically controlled clerical offices, it would be thirty hours or even twenty-five. The striking fact is that the decreased work week has been possible without a drop in productivity: better health, less fatigue, and better chances for education have thus far made up for the reductions.

If these sentences read like a patriotic paean to American growth I don't intend them thus. The real wealth of a nation in human resources is less one of the quantity than of the quality of the population —and I propose to deal with that aspect in the next section. But the rate of American population growth has thus far not outrun either the energy resources or the productive capacity of industry and agriculture, or the available living space. The dangers of population growth as rapid as the American are that it will outrun the capacity of the agricultural and industrial plant to sustain it, especially since America now for the first time consumes more raw materials than it produces, and also because the per-capita demands on raw materials have kept increasing.

Hence there were a number of American students of resources and population in the mid-1950s who regarded the "baby boom" with horror, convinced that America might breed itself out of its potential wealth and strength and living standards through a failure to plan and a devotion to the cult of numbers. They admitted that the density of American population was still relatively small, and that it was possible in principle to support on the American continent a population of even a billion. But they argued that in such an America the living standard would fall, diet would have to be standardized in synthetic form, the complexities and hazards of daily living would be multiplied, and the trend toward totalitarianism would grow almost irresistible. Added to the Malthusian arguments there was also the aesthetic plea —the sense of distaste at the prospect of the empty spaces swarming with people, and the huge cities spilling even more cancerously over the countryside. There are a growing number of demands from scholars for the formulation of an American "population policy."

I am not arguing here against "family planning," which has the merit of leaving the question of population control where it belongs —with the joint common decision of the parents. But I find it hard to drum up much enthusiasm for an over-all "national population policy," which assumes that there is an "ideal" population size for America, and that this should be reached by a deliberate population policy. To give the decision to the government implies that we know or can know what an "optimum" population is and how to enforce it on the private decisions of people. Of that I am skeptical. The American immigration laws since 1921 have assumed such a knowledge, but it would be hard to claim that they have added to either the richness or quality of American life. If I am asked whether I see an American population growing steadily for the calculable future, I answer "Why not?" Much of the dynamic quality of American life is derived from this central dynamism of continued population growth, which in turn means new housing, new schools, new living sites, new roads and transport, a bigger home market, a larger labor force, higher productivity.

When nations have had population policies in the past, it has been either to encourage births because of a fear of stagnation (the Roman Empire, France) or a desire for war strength (prewar Japan, prewar Italy, the Soviet Union), or to discourage overrapid population growth because of crowding, famines, and diseases (India, present-day Japan, Ceylon, Puerto Rico). Sweden has adopted the most · thoroughgoing population policy of all, with the goal of increasing the birth rate in order to avert a threatened national decline because of loss of numbers. But the United States no longer needs to fear either a declining population and cultural suicide or a runaway population that it will be unable to support adequately. Thus far its economy has grown stronger with increasing numbers instead of being strained by them. Thus far also the most tribalist forces of the community have been directed against continued large-scale immigration, and their hostility to "alien" ethnic groups has been—at least outwardly—based on the fear of their high birth rate. The healthier American forces have not worried overmuch about eugenic considerations or about overcrowding of the continent, because they have felt confidence in the capacity of the nation to absorb future growth as it has absorbed past growth. The fear of totalitarianism is a genuine one, and there is point to the argument that population pressure increases the danger. Yet this is only a minor factor: if totalitarianism comes to America, it will be for other and more cogent reasons than the pressure of numbers.

It is most unlikely, however, that America will have to cope with the problems of overpopulation in the near future. While there has been a recent increase in birth rates, and the death rates continue to fall, the increased knowledge of birth control is likely to keep the population in check, and the rising curve is bound to lose its momentum in time. Despite the fears of both population suicide and population runaway, the trends are likely to continue to be healthy ones, and the decisions on population policy will be made by individual families in the light of their life purposes and life expectations within the frame of increasing knowledge.

6. The Sinews of Welfare:
Health, Food, Dwelling, Security

THE CULT OF NUMBERS is meaningless when applied to a population, unless linked with a concern for the life quality of the people. I talk of the quality of their life rather than of innate capacity because it is idle to argue whether Americans have degenerated in innate capacity: even if one could prove they had, any eugenics program imposed by an external authority to breed them better would be unthinkable. The best we can ask about the people in a culture is this: given its human beings there, do they have what is necessary for decent human living? Does the culture make available to them the sinews of welfare?

I use "sinews of welfare" here to mean the degree of well-being in terms of basic life needs that the culture enables the American people to achieve—on health and medical services, on food, clothing, shelter, on education and security. I include only the broad areas of need for both the person and the personality, on the assumption that there are minimum standards in each area (however elusive and hard to formulate) which the culture is required to provide for its people, at the peril of being judged a failure in human terms.

The American pursuit of health, plenty, leisure, security, and happiness is so well known and there is such an overspill of goods and resources that it may seem futile to inquire about the sinews of welfare. If it were only the question of minimum standards—in the sense, say, in which the term is used by students of nutrition to mean the bare margin for maintaining health—the American record would be unquestioned not only in food but in every phase of welfare. But if we go beyond minimum nutrition and talk of optimum nutrition—beyond which no diet additions would do much for health, whatever they might do for the palate and the sense of luxury—then the American sinews of welfare need revaluing on that plane. The American national product and living standards form a blade whose temper cuts away sharply all the old conceptions of subsistence living. Yet once such a standard is set, the inadequacies are shown up all the more clearly. When Franklin Roosevelt made his famous speech about "one third of a nation" being "ill-housed, ill-clad, ill-nourished," he was saying how intolerable it was that this should be true in a land of plenty.

This paradox shows up clearly in the area of health. Judged by the number and skill of their doctors, the organization of hospitals, the thoroughness of medical research, the quality of diagnosis and therapy, the array of modern machines, appliances, and available drugs, and the conquest of diseases that for centuries had scourged mankind, the Americans do well in this area. "To have lived through a revolution," wrote Sir William Osler in 1913, "to have seen a new birth of science, a new dispensation of health, reorganized medical schools, remodeled hospitals, a new outlook for humanity, is not given to every generation." And Laurence J. Henderson referred to the same revolution when he said that somewhere around 1911 the progress of medicine in America made it possible to say that "a random patient with a random disease consulting a physician at random stood better than a 50-50 chance of benefiting from the encounter."

Americans have for a half century been living in an age and land of medical miracles. They have stood in awe of these miracles, have at times resented and resisted them, but have ended by laying claim to their full benefit for all. The experience of World War II, when the whole matchless armory of American medicine, surgery, and dentistry were put at the disposal of the humblest private from Mississippi or Oklahoma, proved decisive in bringing these claims to the surface. Access to medical care came to be considered a kind of Constitutional right for all Americans, a new imperative of our time. What had once been deemed the province of the rich became a necessity for all classes, and economists soon took to surveying America's health "needs" on the assumption that their fulfillment was a prescriptive right. This assumption—even more than the medical miracles—capped the revolution in health.

Yet the dismal fact is that all this fabulous armory of skills and contrivances, which vanquished many of the dread infectious diseases, transformed childbirth, and made the human body a terrain for brilliant research, has not produced a healthy population. For one thing there is the differential health picture in South Carolina as compared with Connecticut, or in rural as against urban areas, or in the slum and low-income groups as compared with the middle classes. For another, there is the mental health picture, with ten million Americans (one out of sixteen) counted mentally ill, with a million and a half of them psychotics, with as many filled beds in mental hospitals as in all others combined.

Finally there is the dramatic evidence of the draft rejection figures —evidence from an unintended mammoth inventory of the health of young Americans, mainly from eighteen through their twenties. Of the first two million men drafted for the armed services in 1940-41, 50 per cent were rejected for either physical or mental disturbances; at the end of World War II the figure had fallen to 33 per cent, but mainly because the standards were lowered; in the period 1948-52 the rejections were 45 per cent; at the start of the Korean War they rose to 58 per cent, but at the end they dropped again to 33 per cent. The figures ought not to be used uncritically: it is true that a man may be rejected by the Army for bad eyesight or hearing or other physical disabilities, or as a "psychoneurotic," and still function well at his job or even live a long life. It is also true that when the figures for volunteers were included, the percentage of rejections fell. It might be argued finally that the American armed services held to higher standards of physical fitness because—given the large pool of man power in the military age groups— they could afford to. Yet the figures are at best bad enough in a nation and era of great medical progress. What makes them worse is the estimate that a large proportion were correctable, which means that they fell in classes where medical care was economically out of reach, or in backward communities where doctors were too few and hospital facilities inadequate. The figures on chronic diseases heighten the shadows in the American health picture. One of six Americans suffers from some chronic illness, and from six to seven million of them suffer seriously, including the victims of arthritis, hypertension, arteriosclerosis, cerebral palsy, and muscular dystrophy.

These figures have spurred the efforts at multiple screening, early diagnosis and preventive treatment of sickness, at campaigns for public-health education, and at the painstaking task of rehabilitation. They have also brought up the constant question of the scarcity of doctors. In 1955 there were 225,000 doctors in the U.S., or one for every 720 people. The problem was not one of attracting too few young men but of discouraging many of them for the wrong reasons (for example, religious and racist bias) and of not having enough schools with enough funds to meet the need for doctors. Federal grants for scholarship aid were rejected on the ground that they might put the schools in a strait jacket, although the similar potential corruption of Federal research funds was cheerfully risked. While Federal funds were refused, industry subvention—regarded as safe—was not forthcoming.

The greater difficulty thus far, however, has been the high cost of medical care, especially for the lower middle classes who fall between the free public facilities and the expensive private ones. A five-dollar office call, a ten-dollar house call, a fancy surgery fee, a sky-high fee for specialized consultants, additional fees for X rays, and the cost of expensive medicines exhaust a modest family income. Only rarely was this the fault of the doctors, most of whom were hard-working and devoted men. In a lush and byzantine economy it was idle to expect them to practice ascetic renunciation. The efforts to provide a system of compulsory health insurance, largely with Federal funds, were fought bitterly by the American Medical Association as "socialized medicine."

The A.M.A. hierarchy, while it complained of being too frequently a target for abuse, was not wholly innocent in heart; it was skillful in marshaling political pressures against the provision of medical security and forgot that while the medical profession is a sector of private enterprise, it is more deeply affected with a public interest than any profession except warfare and teaching.

Willy-nilly the achievement of medical security is on its way: through a system of voluntary group insurance for hospitalization and (to some extent) for doctor's fees, which provides at least partial coverage for more than half the people; through agreement with working teams of doctors, whether on a prepaid plan covering all ailments or on a fee-for-service basis; and through employer-union agreements providing for sickness benefits and medical care. In New York State the employer-financed health and welfare plans cover three quarters of those covered by state unemployment insurance. Yet with all these mushrooming plans there are still some Americans left out: a million families, for example. spent half their income on medical bills in "catastrophic" cases. America has lagged behind Great Britain and the Scandinavian countries in the social organization of medical facilities. The tragic episode, in 1955, of the initial bungling in preparing the Salk anti-polio vaccine while the Canadian government carried through successfully in the same circumstances, is an instance of how the cult of private enterprise in medicine hobbles American public-health measures.

But the statement by the Committee on the Cost of Medical Care in 1932—that "human life in the U.S. is being wasted as recklessly, as surely, in times of peace as in times of war"—is far less true now. In a generation the gridiron intermeshing of voluntary group plans, doctor's medical groups, industry health and welfare plans, Federal care of veterans, and Federal and state support of medical services in other forms, is bound to be all but complete.

This still leaves the question of how diseases fare in America. Here the striking fact has been the shifting pattern of national diseases, which sheds an intense light on the nature of the culture. Since 1900, deaths from pneumonia, TB, diarrhea, bronchitis, influenza, appendicitis, rheumatic fever, and syphilis have been steeply cut. In their place, since men remain mortal, have come other great killers –heart disease, the high-tension circulatory diseases including cerebral hemorrhage and arteriosclerosis, cancer, and death by violence. The heart and circulation diseases in 1953 accounted for 54 per cent of the deaths, and cancer an additional 15 per cent—together almost 70 per cent, or seven out of ten deaths. Other diseases that came to the forefront in American statistics as cripplers and disablers were mental illnesses (nine million cases in 1953), arthritis and rheumatic diseases (cerebral palsy, epilepsy, multiple sclerosis, Parkinson's Disease). One must add, as special categories of mental illness, at least 60,000 narcotics addicts, and almost 4,000,000 "problem drinkers," of whom close to a million are chronic alcoholics. One should also add that six or seven of every ten Americans suffer from headaches, and that 40 per cent of the cases of draft rejection or medical discharge after induction in World War II were cases of psychopathic personality, mental deficiency, drug addiction, or homosexuality.

One could counter this by arguing that "health" must be defined not just anatomically but functionally, that many Americans manage to live with their chronic illnesses, and that the sharp recent decreases in the death rate and increases in the life span carry with them inevitably the fact of the diseases of aging. But the paradoxical fact remains that Americans are suffering from the diseases accompanying the very dynamism which has done so much to vanquish disease. It would be too pat to say that the leading diseases in America are characteristic of the current tension of living, and that deaths in auto and industrial accidents, coronaries, hardened arteries, cerebral hemorrhages, and stomach ulcers—if not cancer—bear the hallmark "Made in America." Yet there would be a core of truth in it. Someone called the 1920s and 1930s the "aspirin age": if so, the 1940s and 1950s should be called the "sleeping-pill age," the "coronary age," the "tranquilizer age," or the "age of the fifty-minute hour." Pointing out that Americans have met and mastered the killer infections, have lengthened the life span, and must now cope with the chronic and degenerative diseases, Alan Gregg writes that "we have traded mortality for morbidity." Americans have tracked down the spoor of germs and bacilli only to confess themselves thus far powerless before the runaway cell, the strained and lesioned heart, the out-of-kilter ganglia of the nervous system, the disarranged sexual impulses, and the disturbed psyche that casts a pall of anxiety over worried days and sleepless nights—when it does not go berserk with frustrations and fears.

The character of the diseases of American middle age was dramatically illustrated by President Eisenhower's two attacks in 1955-56—one coronary, the other gastrointestinal. The fact that for months the whole American people focused its attention on charts and diagrams of the President's internal organs and the details of his bodily functioning was the result of more than political interest: it was an index of the concern of Americans with their own health. Every middle-aged and aging male saw himself reflected in the President. In making public some data on the functioning of the President's bowels Dr. Paul Dudley White explained that Americans had become "bowel-conscious." When his doctors made their optimistic announcements about the President's life chances, they were echoing the title one American writer used for a book, *Thank God for My Heart Attack,* which was a commentary on the American belief that the real killer is thoughtless drive and tension, and that to "take it easy" is the road to health.

By an interesting irony the doctors, medical administrators, and researchers responsible for the achievements of American health are often themselves the victims of the pace of American life, and die early of tension diseases. There is a restless quality about the attitudes of Americans toward health and disease. They are oversold on medical advances and expect to read about new medical miracles in every issue of *Time* and *Reader's Digest.* They are overeager about the "wonder drug" antibiotics and rely so much on the efficacy of penicillin (in the decade 1945-55 they consumed 3,000 tons, or 3,000 trillion units), the various mycins, cortisone, and ACTH, that bodily resistances against them have developed. They respond quickly to new drugs and pills—to barbiturates for sleeping, and other pills for staying awake, and "tranquilizers," drugs for calming down. Similarly the staffs in mental hospitals overuse electrical and insulin shock therapy: everywhere there is an eagerness to handle mass diseases on a mass basis and find a short cut to a cure.

In the public-health field American medical organizers have developed the institution of the "drive"—against heart disease, against cancer, against cerebral palsy—partly to raise funds for research, partly to make the people conscious of the "dread killers," with all the statistics about the casualties, the man hours lost, and how much the dead would have added to the national income had they lived. As a result, the people battered now by one "drive," now by another, become not only conscious of but anxious about disease. While the medical advances have led to a lengthening of the life span, they have also produced a nation of medical worriers about the ills of the flesh and the mind who follow every diet fad, take reducing pills or tranquilizer drugs, count their pulse beats and cherish their blood-pressure charts, vex themselves about not being able to stop smoking, meditate Narcissuslike on their kidneys and colon, and fill the bathroom medicine cabinet with an assortment of prescription bottles and "packaged remedies" (patent medicines) which keep huge industries solvent.

Foreign observers have noted that all American doctors want to "do research," and that the American medical schools—perhaps the best in the world—spend less time on transmitting what is known about medicine than in pointing out what is still unknown. This is an aspect of the theme of dynamism I have stressed in the American tradition. While there has been some swingback to the general practitioner and a considerable nostalgia for the old-fashioned "country doctor," the long-range trend is in two directions: toward further specialization, which will mean that no doctor looks at the whole patient and that doctors will increasingly become members of "teams"; and toward new institutional forms of medical care. Since, with rising medical costs and despite voluntary group insurance, good medical care is still out of the reach of many workers and especially the ethnic minorities, the trend toward corporate health plans and trade-union projects will increase. American medicine will have escaped the government but not the twin giants of the corporation and trade-union, which will become the new employers of medical and research talent. All of which is understandable, since the genius of American medicine has all along been an organizing genius.*

Next to his health the American is most concerned about his security —including even the people who are sternly set against the "creeping Socialism" of a "welfare state." Several generations behind the European and Commonwealth experience in these matters, because the individualist momentum carried them further before they could make a start on social-security plans, the Americans are tardily taking the same steps— but in their own way. The idea of a complete system of governmental security frightened some substantial citizens because they thought (probably wrongly) that it would play havoc with the powerful institution of the private insurance company, whose interests ramify into every area of industry, banking, and investment. Thus the private-enterprise core of the American security system has been left intact, and to it has been added a system of Federal old-age and survivors insurance, and state unemployment insurance, with contributions levied on both worker and employer. There is also a system of Federal grants-in-aid to the states for the blind and disabled, for old-age assistance, and for child care.

At the start all this was held revolutionary: now it is accepted almost as a commonplace, even when Republicans rule the White House and Congress. The recent extensions of the original system of old-age and survivors insurance have included domestics and white-collar workers but still exclude the migratory workers. Unemployment insurance is still inadequate: it must ultimately be extended to include every gainfully employed person, including the self-employed, so that no one becomes a casualty of the pathos of dependence. Another important development has been the assumption of responsibility for one segment of security by the corporation and the trade-union, through welfare funds, fringe benefits, and (most recently) the movement for the guaranteed annual wage. It is these growths that are rounding out the American security system.

* For further discussion of mental health, see Ch. IX, Sec. 8, "Life Goals and the Pursuit of Happiness."

Since the area of security necessarily involved the emergence of a welfare state to carry part of the burden and responsibility, storms and turbulences have raged around it ever since the turn of the twentieth century. It has been the arena of the great reform movements of America, and administrative efforts of Democratic and liberal Republican administrations alike have had to meet resistance of interest groups. The period between 1900 and World War I saw the founding of a myriad of organizations aimed at attacking national problems of welfare on a national scale—child labor, mental hygiene, public health, the protection of children, labor legislation. The New Deal period consolidated what the earlier period had begun and launched new programs that resulted in the great Social Security Act of 1935, which was extended a number of times in the next two decades. Yet the fault lines in the system were at mid-century still glaring. There is no system of compulsory health insurance, nor any provisions that give everyone access to medical care without a means test. There is little that applies the principles of social insurance to the risks of disability and illness as well as of old-age dependence. There is no protection for the families of those who become disabled by factors unrelated to their jobs.

The individualist strain in American thinking raised resistance to this trend from the early days when the New England humanitarian movements provoked Emerson into his classic outburst: "I tell thee, thou foolish philanthropist, that I grudge the dollar, the dime, the cent I give to such men as do not belong to me and to whom I do not belong," and led him to speak contemptuously of "alms for sots." Yet it was not the philanthropic impulse alone but the spur of need and emergency that led to the growth of the welfare network. The catastrophe of the Great Depression was a psychic shock, dramatizing the erratic course of Fortune's wheel which might claim as victim even the patently secure and leaving the fear of insecurity as a continuing residue in the American mind. This led to the corollary that people with troubles are the concern of all —the common concern of the commonwealth. With World War II and the Korean War there came the understanding that the ill and incapacitated, the mentally unfit and the badly educated, the products of slum housing and submarginal incomes, were a drain on the available national man power; and measures were admitted through the back door of war needs that would have been kept waiting at the front door of human fellow feeling. Yet despite Emerson's words and the derisive contemporary epithets applied to "do-gooders" and "bleeding hearts," the fellow feeling is there and is as abundantly part of the American human and cultural cast as of any other in history. Every era of free-swinging heady advance in technical and economic achievement brings with it the paradoxical double attitude of a ruthless scorn for the misfits and failures and a sense of men's interdependence with men.

Just as there is a seamless web in American welfare needs, so there is one in the response to them—although not in the sense that Americans respond to them as a whole. They have responded piecemeal and in irregular fashion to the need for workmen's compensation, unemployment benefits, old-age insurance, subsidized low-cost housing, health insurance, corporate-sponsored welfare funds, the annual wage. Their relatedness is rarely grasped except by the professional students of the problem. The American response has been consistent in a different sense: what has emerged in each area of welfare is the acceptance of the principle of responsibility but with the least challenge to private enterprise, the least burden on the tax structure, and the greatest reliance on the voluntary principle. The broad formula has been for the government to set a floor below which security and welfare cannot fall, to use government funds for the more clamant forms of social insurance but to let the others go, to give the states the widest possible discretion, to steer away from centralized authority and administration, to rely wherever possible on forms of group insurance, to work through private companies (as in workmen's compensation) even when the state provides the funds, to underwrite the private risks (as in housing), to make ampler provision for soldiers and veterans than for civilians, to put the burden of expanding the programs upon continued popular pressures.

The chances are strong, given American dynamism, that these pressures will continue. The coverage of welfare protection is still incomplete and in some cases pathetically so; the insurance benefits are still low, allowing for only a portion of the normal income deriving from the job, thus incurring the danger that inadequacies of food, housing, education, and psychic security in the lives of the children will be handed on for several generations. The financing of security is either left to the individual's means in private insurance, savings, stock holdings, or the group plans, or rests on a payroll tax which is regressive because proportionately it bears more heavily on the lower incomes.

These point to the remaining agenda of welfare: yet despite what remains to be done, America has grappled with the problem of security, sometimes with an inventiveness that has added to the European experience instead of merely imitating it. And in doing so it has passed through a revolution in action, thought, and feeling which makes its welfare structure wholly different from the America of the 1920s which most European commentators still take as their prevailing image.

What about the habitations of the American inhabitants? In anthropological terms a tribe needs shelter, in social terms a community needs housing, in psychological terms a family needs a home. The statisticians speak of the number of dwelling units that Americans have, whether they be flats, apartments, "row houses," or estates. The test of welfare here is not only whether people have somewhere to lay their head but whether the place is clean or disease-ridden, spacious or congested, beautiful or dreary and ugly. American abundance is such that the minimal needs of "adequate" shelter no longer express the true criteria of what the society does with the means at its disposal.

It is no longer true of mid-century America that one third of it is "ill-housed." There has been a flattening out of the curve of housing at both extremes of the income scale: the purple imperial mansions of the Vanderbilts and other multimillionaires of the turn of the century are no longer considered good taste, and even the top crust lives more simply on its estates; and the slums, while still scarring the face of the country, are slowly—all too slowly—being razed and used as sites for low-cost housing projects. The big housing bulge comes at the middle of the income scale, where millions of housing units have been built in our time.

America has been the scene of a housing "revolution" similar to the medical and social-security "revolutions," but coming at a different time. During the reform decades before World War I, when so many associations were cropping up to deal with the inadequacies of American society, there was also a movement for tenement reform, to get rid of the firetraps and clean up the pesthouses, and frame and enforce the "multiple dwelling" laws. But the New Deal in the mid-thirties raised the sights of the whole housing movement, with federally subsidized large-scale housing projects that started the clearing of the city slums and revived the lagging housing industry. Adequate shelter had become a pressing welfare need for millions of Americans, and the method the New Deal used was to appropriate money to local housing authorities, to work through private construction firms, and to build tall apartment houses and row-house projects. Generally they increased the density of the population in the same area but were "decent, safe, and sanitary" (in the phrase of the U.S. Housing Act), with some green space around them. The life-insurance companies took their cue from the Federal government and built Stuyvesant Towns of their own. The Resettlement Administration built a few Greenbelt Towns—garden cities for government and white-collar workers. During World War II the process continued in the war-industry centers, because it had been learned that people wouldn't pick up and move, or work productively, without minimum housing of some sort. After the war there was a splurge of too hastily and shoddily built housing for young veterans and their families. And then the housing boom began in earnest: in a decade, during the Truman and Eisenhower regimes, ten million dwelling units went up, rehousing from thirty-five to forty million people at an average cost of $10,000 and a total one of 100 billion, and housing became the biggest industry in the nation.

Drawing the profile of contemporary housing, one would start with the derelict areas such as those in Chicago's South Side or the Puerto Rican ghetto in New York—the 9 per cent of decrepit American dwelling units that are rated as "dilapidated" dwellings and tell the deterioration story of the big city cores, the small-city "shanty towns," and the small-town houses "on the other side of the tracks"—littered, tattered bedlams which are cold in winter and unbearable in summer, with few bathrooms, rat-infested, sheltering mainly unskilled workers or the people who live on relief or part-time jobs or old-age pensions. One would go on to the more tolerable tenements and to the "row houses" like those of Baltimore and Philadelphia, where skilled workers and white-collar families live wall to wall in constricted and standardized monotony; then to the towering monolithic canyons of low- and middle-income urban building projects I have described—some still segregated, others having made the first breaks in the segregation taboo; then to the myriad crowded beehive individual houses that blanket the suburban areas, where you get five or six rooms plus a garage and can pick one of five standardized colors and styles, and have a back yard that juts into your neighbor's, and be near a shopping center; then to the more spacious "homes" in the "residential sections" of the richer suburbs or the more expensive "developments," Tudor or Spanish Moorish or California ranch house, set in synthetic "villages"; then finally to the "house on the hill" and the lavish estates of the parvenu millionaires and the quieter ones of those who have wealth-over-time.

There is no common denominator for all these forms. But of the newer ones it can be said that they embody a feeble attempt at individuality within a cellular framework of standardization. In the years immediately following World War II it was thought that prefabricated houses might break the housing bottleneck, but they struck several snags, including the jungle of building restrictions and trade-union hostility in the building trades. Then came the idea, associated with the Levitts, that instead of bringing housing to the factory, the solution was to apply factory methods to the building lot, using a small number of basic designs with minor variations and getting mass-production savings by large-scale purchasing of materials and by a basic plumbing and kitchen core, with TV sets and access to community pools and playgrounds thrown in as added lures.

Following this pattern, the splurge of "community developments" on the outskirts of cities has become the dominant feature of the American landscape. The costs, while reduced by large-scale building and the cheapness of land outside the cities, are still high. Because of archaic building codes and union practices, a committee of architects and builders has estimated that too much cement, lumber, steel, and piping are

used; the housing "revolution" is still not a technological one. Yet standardization is the price paid for what has been achieved. More and more
middle-class Americans were coming to live in houses as constricted in
standardized forms as the Fords, Plymouths, and Buicks that were
parked outside their doors. Like the cars also, the houses were bought on
credit; to do this their owners plunged, not without some misgivings,
into mortgaged debt: the stigma that had once attached to the family
mortgage no longer applied. Americans unashamedly were out to purchase "gracious living" on the installment plan, and a continuously rising housing market wiped out most of the mistakes.

The new houses were not only standardized: they were also mechanized. The oil burner, the deep-freeze, the dishwasher, and the laundry
equipment operated on the principle of the automatic feedback; there
were toasters, mixers, pressure cookers, electric stoves, and garbage dis-
posers to take much of the burden from kitchen work; there was a TV
set and an automatic record turner. All this mechanized complexity
went along with both the high cost of building and the scarcity of domestics in the labor market, so that income groups which once ran their
households with several servants now were servantless, except for an occasional baby-sitter. To accomplish this it was necessary to simplify the
layout of the house. The parlor, living room, and dining room were
compressed into a single all-purpose room; in some cases, even the
kitchen became a subdivision of the room. This was the extreme point
reached by the trend toward the small house. The opposite trend was
toward privacy. Compared with the European house the American had
space enough to enable parents and children to sleep in separate rooms;
given the small size of the American family, this often meant in middle-
class families that each child had a room of his own. This was the principle of cellular housing—of individual cells for individual units—carried to its logical extreme.

As with the social-security system, the Americans have tried to carry
through the housing revolution with a minimum of socialization and a
maximum of private enterprise and profit. Yet the impressive fact was
the degree of Federal intervention in housing that was taken for granted
by Democrats and Republicans alike. The housing business was not only
a large-scale operation but also a thoroughly "mixed" enterprise. The
Federal government subsidized public housing, slum clearance, redevelopment and renewal of slum areas: it also took over most of the risk
for "private" housing. More than four million of the ten million houses
of the 1945-55 decade were financed with mortgages guaranteed by either
the Federal Housing Administration (FHA) or the Veterans Administration (VA). In some metropolitan areas the proportion was as high as
75 per cent. The kind of suburban subdivision I have mentioned above

—which formed the core of the suburban revolution—was essentially the creature of the FHA mortgage-insurance system, which began in 1934 as an emergency measure and then grew to be a more permanently established feature on the housing scene than public housing itself. The fact that between half and two thirds of American homes were occupied by their owners was largely due to this kind of Federal intervention-through-underwriting. Despite its involving Federal action it was palatable to the banks, insurance companies, and private builders (and was extended under the Eisenhower Administration) because it guaranteed them against losses and spurred their business and profits.

Thus the "housing Socialism" (even Senator Robert A. Taft was accused of being a Socialist because he backed this program) amounted actually to a socializing of business losses and an underwriting of business profits. As such it has met with scorn from European Socialists—yet for America it seemed to work. Actually there were very few losses for the government to assume, although another Depression might tell a different story. More important was the fact that as mortgage underwriters the Federal government had to establish the basic standards and conditions that controlled private construction. At one point the FHA forced builders applying for mortgage funds in certain areas of mixed ethnic groups to write restrictive covenants into their deeds. Yet the Federal power can be turned in a quite different direction, and a committee of housing officials headed by Catherine Bauer has recommended an affirmative program for eliminating racist bias in housing. Following the Supreme Court decision in the school segregation cases, the Court was likely sooner or later to rule against discrimination in housing built with Federal aid. When this happens there will be a good deal of turmoil in the politics of housing. But in the long run the impossible situation of what Charles Abrams has called "forbidden neighbors" in housing is bound to be eliminated.*

The most elementary ingredient of welfare—food—is one that most Americans take most for granted, although next to shelter, food takes the largest cut (thirty-one cents) out of the consumer's dollar. The impulse of countries with traditions of famine is to save every crumb because someday the food may not be there. In America the food is almost always there in abundance. Even for the immigrant the question was not whether there would be food but how to buy it; later the question became *what kind* of food to choose from abundance. There have been times, especially in war, when a combination of war needs and maldis-

* For further analyses of American dwelling, see Sec. 9, "City Lights and Shadows," and Sec. 10, "The Suburban Revolution," in this chapter. See also Ch. VIII, Sec. 2, "The Family As Going Concern," for the American home. And for building and architecture, see Ch. XI, Sec. 8, "Building, Design, and the Arts."

tribution undercut the sense of plenty. In 1941, for example, a poll showed that one of every two Americans wanted more to eat than he could get. But the surveys by the Food and Agriculture Organization of the UN show the diet of the United States since World War II to be at the extreme of the world food scale, averaging 3,200 calories a day per person, with 1,800 pounds of food intake a year and a high protein diet, while an Asian area like Java is at the other extreme (2,000 calories, largely rice, with 800 pounds food intake and a low protein diet). The diet differences are so great that a fifteen-year-old boy of Asian immigrant parents in the United States, living on an American diet, is likely to be four inches taller than a boy of the same age in Asia living on the lesser diet.

In the past quarter century, especially since World War II, American food habits changed drastically. The change was best signalized by two ideas—that of the "balanced diet" and that of prepared ready-to-eat foods that defy time and space, being both freezable and compressible.

The idea of a balanced diet came from the nutrition studies, which started with the chemical elements the body needs and translated them into terms of available foods. But the food-education program would not have come home to the mass of people without the Army experience of World War II which introduced millions of young men to new food emphases. Soldiers from mountain and farm areas who had grown up on corn pone, fried pork, hot biscuit, and potatoes learned the uses of leafy vegetables, orange juice, and milk. The heavy reliance on grains and breads shifted to meats and fish for large sections of the population who had eaten little of either; the reliance on fats and carbohydrates also shifted; the protein content of the diet increased; the words "proteins," "calories," and "vitamins" came into everyday use. The measure of the change was shown by the fact that vigorous American males—at college and in Army camps—were not ashamed to drink milk: while some called this a sign of the American male's dependence on his mother, the less tortured conclusion is simply that Americans became nutrition-conscious. The seamier side of this impulse was in the health-food faddism, the anxious counting of calories, the compulsive weighing, the multiplication of trick diets, and the obsession of Americans—especially women— with "reducing" as a standard both of beauty and will power, the outward sign of an inner grace.

Americans overeat badly, as one might expect in a country where immigrant origins and memories linger among people who are "upward mobile"; they overdrink badly, as one might expect where there is so much stress on happiness and so much frustration in its pursuit. There is no country in the world where obesity is so much of a problem (many rank it as the most serious of American diseases) yet where people are so constantly aware of the danger. It was largely this fear, plus the fear of dental decay, that caused a drop of three pounds in the per-capita candy consumption in the decade from 1945 to 1955. The American child is fattened like some heifer meant for sacrifice; the American female starts to "reduce" as a young matron or even sooner as an adolescent, and the American male at middle age. The life cycle is traced in the taking on and sloughing off of poundage.

But this nutrition-consciousness was less true of America in the 1950s than it was in the 1930s and 1940s. It had become embodied and absorbed in institutional food planning—in the school, church, university, factory, hospital, Army—where so many meals were served. The newer trend was toward new experimentalism about food as taste. The ethnic pluralism of America proved on this score both a problem and a treasure house. It was a problem because of the large number of food backgrounds that were brought to mingle in an American city. The cafeteria, for example, developed largely as a way of breaking a menu down into individual units which could be reassembled by each person according to his own traditions and taste. It was thus an ingenious device for individualism in food habits and is rapidly spreading over the world. But the myriad of ethnic traditions also added a culinary richness to American life which merged with the myriad of regional cooking traditions.

The Puritans had seen food as part of a life measured out in duty, effort, and reward, and the later immigrant, in a similar spirit, had taught his children to finish whatever was on the plate. But there was another American strain too, rooted in Virginia, the Carolinas, and Louisiana, which went with Southern plantation largess and the arts of Negro cooking. Having little truck with health, nutrition, calories, vitamins, or a balanced diet, it saw eating as pleasure rather than duty, and it gave scope not only for individual taste in eating but for individual expressiveness in cooking and preparing meals. The American soldiers and travelers abroad, who had discovered how much love could be squandered by Parisians, Florentines, and Viennese upon wines, sauces, salads, and condiments, came back to rediscover the glories of their own ethnic and regional cooking traditions.

For such people the old delicatessen store and the new supermarket, with their array of treasures, furnished more provocation to stir the patriot blood than all the loyalty hunts of the 1940s and 1950s. Cooking became an art for millions of dedicated amateurs, men as well as women. They were further prodded into doing their own cooking by the virtual disappearance of domestic servants, and they were encouraged by one of the great events of contemporary America—the rise of "convenience foods" (frozen, processed, packaged, "prepared mixes") and the perfection of the home "deep-freezes." To some extent these were a phase of

America-in-a-hurry, and often the prepared foods were too synthetic and the refined foods (as in the case of bread) had important materials refined out of them.

In general, American cooking still leaves much to be desired, and not only for the gourmets. The average American cooking tastes are perhaps best evidenced by the luncheon menus at a Childs restaurant or a Howard Johnson road stand. It has been observed that even when its income increases an American family's food habits are the last to feel the effects of the change. But for a growing number of Americans the new technology of food restored taste as an adventure, added a ceremonial element to it, brought in informal cookbooks and conversation about food, and rounded out the "eating revolution" which had begun with the shift of diets.

It is not yet clear whether this changed approach will have much impact on the emotional meanings with which Americans ordinarily invest food. Since the formation of eating habits forms part of the "socializing" of the child, food has come to be the center of a pattern of emotional tensions between parent and child, involving a system of rewards and punishments and the granting and withholding of love. Mostly these tensions operate between mother and child, although latterly the father is likely also to take part in the wrangles over feeding: the mother, however, is the marketer, the selecter of diets, the judge of what is "good" or "bad" for the child, the arbiter of table manners and habits. It is she who uses cajolery, scolding, punishment, in her unflagging effort to build a strong and healthy child.

The result is too often that the process of eating becomes invested with anxiety or hostility, with the child's submission to authority or the adolescent's assertion of independence. Certain foods take on excessive symbolic value within the family context, leading sometimes to neurotic disorders and psychosomatic diseases. It is just possible that the newer tendency of the adults to enjoy food in a relaxed way may also over the generations serve to relax the parent-child tensions: where the basic attitude is hedonist rather than Puritan, the obsession with food-as-duty for both mother and child is likely to lessen.

There are more genial food obsessions, coming less directly from the family and more generally from the culture, that will probably endure. Certain foods, by nostalgic memories of childhood and the home place, have become evocatively American—wheatcakes and sirup, baked beans, fried chicken, sirloin steak, the Thanksgiving and Christmas turkey dinner, baked potato, blueberry pie or peach cobbler. To these should be added the almost compulsive American drinks—hot steaming coffee, Bourbon whisky, ice-cream soda, and the various "cola" drinks. I single these out as the contemporary symbols, but George Stewart is right in

emphasizing that there are two drinks rarely mentioned but more characteristically American than any of them—milk (somehow regarded
and highly publicized as healthful) and ice water for drinking, neither
of which has as much vogue in other cultures. Human beings cherish
the symbolic, and Americans traveling abroad or returning from a war
are likely to be haunted by these short cuts to a sense of longing and
belonging. Yet these stereotypes tend to obscure the bigger fact of the
myriad richness of American dishes and cooking.

7. The Way of the Farmer

WITH ALL THE MARVELS of science in increasing energy sources and food
abundance it is easy to forget that the final source of food is the land,
and that the way of life on the land is the way of the farmer. This is
not because of any deficiency of sentiment. Ever since Jefferson's dream
of a society of free farmers, Americans have idealized the rural way of
life, even while it was being displaced by the urban—perhaps exactly
because it was being displaced. Many of the men in *Who's Who* come
from farm backgrounds. It is not only the disproportionate political
strength of the rural areas that gives farm-aid and crop-support programs an easy passage through Congress but also the folk-belief that
the farmers form the nation's backbone and that there is somehow a
healing grace and an elixir of sturdiness and integrity in contact with
the soil which are not to be derived from contact with city pavements.

The way of the farmer, enthroned in American sentiment, has fared
erratically in American reality. Until seventy-five years ago America
was predominantly an agricultural economy, an agrarian polity, and a
rural society. It is no longer any of the three. Fewer than twenty-two
million, or only 13½ per cent of the population, lived on and from the
land in 1955, as contrasted with 25 per cent in 1930. Even while
frontier lands were still accessible the proportion of farmers to the total
working force kept dropping. Around 1825 three fourths of the gainfully
employed Americans were on the farm; around 1875 the proportion was
one half; in 1955 the farmers and farm workers comprised fewer than
seven million out of sixty-five million Americans with gainful jobs, or
less than 11 per cent. Of these seven million, three million are farm
workers, either hired men on small- and medium-sized farms, sharecroppers, or migratory workers on the large corporation farms of the
West and Southwest. This leaves only some four million in the category
of the independent farmer on the family-size farm. One should further
subtract from this figure the "one-mule" cotton farmer and those still
clinging to impoverished and eroded land and earning only the meager-

est of submarginal livings from it. It was estimated in 1955 that between 800,000 and 1,750,000 farm families were unable to earn a decent living on the land and would be better off if they were shifted to industry.

All this has been part of what Gilbert Burck, writing in *Fortune,* has called the "magnificent decline" of American agriculture. The quantitative decline is clear enough. In a quarter century, from 1930 to 1955, the number of farms shrank from 6,300,000 to 5,200,000, with the likelihood that they would continue to shrink as the submarginal farms were pushed out. It was estimated that in another quarter century, by 1980, the 13½ per cent of the American people living on farms in 1955 would have become 8 per cent, and extended far enough the curve would end in a small, professionalized group of firms running a highly mechanized and productive farm industry much as any other industry is run in America.

The "magnificent" element in the decline of American agriculture is to be found in the productivity gains. The break-through came late in the 1930s, largely because of the basic research on plant genetics, hybridization, and crossbreeding which has been done for years under the schools of agriculture and came to fruition under the New Deal; it was given impetus by World War II, and it reached its pitch in the decade from 1945 to 1955. In the latter year 37 per cent less farm man power produced 54 per cent more than in 1930, and farm productivity had increased 110 per cent in only a quarter century. The acreage remained relatively stable, and the man hours decreased. What then made the difference? The answer lies in science and industrialization— in new forms of fertilizer, new hybrid breeds of corn, new ways of feeding hogs, new insecticides and pest controls, new methods of irrigation, new machinery, new capital investment, new techniques of business (cost accounting) management.

What has happened is that the sweep of the business spirit and of the machine has caught up the whole enterprise of farming and transformed it in the image of industrial enterprise. Far from being an overnight growth, mechanization has been a fact of American agriculture from the start. American farmers carried their initial crops and livestock over from Europe and made brilliant adaptations of them to the conditions of their own climate and soil. Scientific farming started in Europe and its techniques were used in England long before they were used in America. But the farm machinery, as embodied in the work of Whitney, McCormick, and Case, was America's own invention. The motorizing of the farm through the reaper, the threshing machine, the combine harvester, the multi-row cultivator, and the cotton picker was largely the product of necessity, since there was plenty of land in a new country but a scarcity of labor. In Europe, where land was scarce and population crowded, the standard of progress was productivity per acre: it is still true that the intensive European agriculture gets an extremely high per-acre yield—but with a large expenditure of man power. In America the standard of progress has been productivity per man hour.

In recent years, however, the conquests of American farm machinery have been unparalleled. In 1935, American farms had a million tractors; in 1955 they had 4,500,000, along with 2,500,000 trucks, almost a million combines, and three quarters of a million milking machines. The "motor revolution" was followed by an electrical revolution: in 1955 at least nine out of ten farms had electric power, as a result of the far-sighted thinking of the founders of the Rural Electrification Administration—Morris L. Cooke and John Carmody, and the creative work of the electric co-operatives. Corn pickers in Iowa, haystackers in Montana, combines in the wheat country of Washington, potato harvesters on Long Island, citrus sprayers in Florida, cotton pickers in the South —these were the typical expressions of an investment of close to twenty billion dollars in farm machinery. On a California corporate farm the "big-time growers" level the soil with bulldozers, spray it from airplanes, irrigate it with deep-well pumps, and get a yield of cotton per man hour undreamed of in agricultural history. In the same spirit the hogs are fed by a nutrition calculus on a production-line basis, and the beef cattle are fattened with female sex hormones.

This has been called the coming of "automation" to the farm, which is inaccurate since human labor is still the indispensable factor in farming. Yet the march of mechanization on the farm is clear. A complex cotton-picking machine in 1955 did the work formerly done by sixty or seventy men. The small farmer, who cannot afford to operate on a scale to encompass it, is becoming an archaism. The average size of the American farm in 1955 was 215 acres, and if the submarginal farms were not counted it was much higher. About two million American farms, grossing $2,500 a year, formed the heart of the farm operations. The bigger farmer, able to invest in machinery, has shaken his spear across the land. Were Thomas Jefferson to come back, with his dream of a small-scale agrarian America, he would turn in dismay from what would seem to him a monster of technocracy—man-hour productivity, chemical and hormone science, production-line efficiency, high capital investment, and motor and electrical mechanization.

Thus the machine and its camp followers have gone far to transform the way of the farmer. His relation to science, industrialism, and business power has changed. The lines of energy now flow from the center, once represented by the small independent farmer, toward the big farmer and the corporate farm, with its massive, impersonal organization: yet one cannot ignore the less characteristic submarginal farmer, the sharecropper on tired soil, the migratory hired field worker.

The independent farmer as the "masterless man" has dwindled in importance. He may still be found growing corn in Kansas and steers and hogs in Iowa, potatoes in Maine or on Long Island, or grazing cattle in Wyoming. His wife is peerless at baking pies and putting up preserves, which she now does in an electrically equipped kitchen; his children belong to the 4-H clubs (Head, Heart, Hands, Health), raise blue-ribbon fair winners of their own, play basketball at high school, attend land-grant universities, drive cars and tractors, and study science; he is usually a Republican (except in periods of steeply falling prices), a churchgoer, a moviegoer, a TV set owner, a book-club subscriber, reader of *Life, Time, Newsweek, Look,* and the *Reader's Digest,* a member of the Farm Bureau or the Grange, a political power in his community. Yet he is not, as he was in Jefferson's or Jackson's time or even Bryan's, the bulwark of the American community.

In looking at the splendid efficiency of the best American farming, it is easy to forget how much of it rides on the backs of humble, anonymous men. In California, for example, there were over a half million farm workers; through the whole Southwest (although their number was recently reduced) there were still swarms of Mexican-American "wetbacks," or illegals, who swam the Rio Grande at night, turning the border into a sieve, and had to be rounded up periodically and deported by airlift; and there were many contract workers, some of whom settled down as American citizens, while some came and returned each year. In California's San Joaquin and Imperial valleys the corporate farms, which were once described by Carey McWilliams as "factories in the field," have improved considerably in their condition; yet their workers are not included in Federal security and social legislation, are still paid submarginal wages, and buy their food from company commissaries.

In the South also it would be hard to talk of the "independent farmer." The South suffered in the past from being a one-crop region, where Cotton was King until very recently, when agriculture became more diversified. With other countries now growing cotton, America's share of the world market decreased sharply, and the pressures were toward efficiency. In the Mississippi Delta, in Texas, in some areas of Alabama, cotton growing was mechanized on a large scale, feasible only for the "plantation farms" or for those with capital to invest or for co-operatives banding together to buy farm machinery. The small cotton grower of the South, a victim of high labor cost on the unmechanized one-mule farm, and of the boll weevil and debt, is on the way out. On the eroded soil only the wretched living standards of the submarginal croppers and subsistence farmers and on the good soil only the mechanized and large-scale farms are now possible.

I do not mean to give the impression of backwardness on the American soil. Compare the American farmer with the Malayan or Indonesian peasant—impoverished, sick, undernourished, badly housed and clothed, a prey to the usurer, without incentive, tilling land he does not own—and the contrast is dramatic. Take the family-size farm in the mixed-farming areas of Ohio, Wisconsin, Minnesota, Illinois, and in the corn-wheat-hog and prime-beef areas of Kansas, Iowa, Nebraska, and the Dakotas, and compare it with the European peasantry that exasperated Karl Marx into talking of "rural idiocy" and of the farmer as a primitive "troglodyte": again the contrast is dramatic.

Yet every system of agriculture pays its own kind of social price for the methods it uses. In the late nineteenth century much of American farming was a kind of soil mining which stripped the land while it made production cheap. (Incidentally, by undercutting the more highly priced British agriculture of the time and selling their food cheaply in England, the Americans almost killed British farming.) At present the highly organized and rationalized nature of American farming carries with it a different kind of social price. The acreage under cultivation has remained steady while the number of farms and farmers has decreased. The traditional "hired man," who was close to the farmer's family, is disappearing and is being displaced by migrants and machine tenders in the fields and in the dairy. Landlessness has become a reality: there are the landless croppers and tenants, the landless Negroes, the landless seasonal workers. The reach of landlessness grows in direct proportion to the reach of mechanization. California, for example, where agriculture developed late and as part of the machine era, shows the clearest cleavage between the controllers of the mechanized corporate farms and the landless casual laborers whose situation is worse than that of the machine tenders in the factories because they have no unions, are not protected by social legislation, and lack access to the leisure activities and the popular culture of urban life.

One may grow unduly sentimental about the disappearance of the Jeffersonian image of the farmer on his soil, and of the old family-size farm that was not part of the machine technology. "The truth is," wrote Louis Bromfield, "that farming as a way of life is infinitely more pleasurable and satisfactory when it is planned, scientific, specialized, mechanized, and stripped of the long hours and the drudgery of the old-fashioned, obsolete pattern of the frontier or general farm." This has always been the case for agricultural rationalization. Yet it cannot obscure the fact that the old love of the soil has been replaced by a fetishism of output, efficiency, and cost accounting. This is already evident in the arguments of the efficiency-minded agricultural experts who say that the small, "inadequate" farmer will simply have to get off the land. What applies now to the small farmer is bound in time to apply to the middle-sized farmer. The logic of this latter-day advance of capitalism upon the land is as unyielding as in the case of the historical enclosure movements. The fact that the victims of the large-scale expulsion from the land are being absorbed in industry does not make it any less an expulsion.

There is a striking paradox at the heart of the relation between farming and the American capitalist economy. On the one hand farming has become thoroughly mechanized and industrialized and has thus become part of the larger wide-flung economy: the farmer, purchasing chemicals and machinery on a large scale and applying them to the land, has become largely a processor. On the other hand, farming is the only large sector of the economy—apart from national defense—that is subsidized and thus stands apart from the rest of the economy.

There are two basic reasons for this dependent state. One is the limited expansionism of the demand for farm products. Even with the "eating revolution" and the new habits of the American worker in consuming meats and dairy products, the rise in living standards does not mean a proportionate rise in food consumption. What is true of the home market for industry—that lower production cost has led to larger demand, the rise of new industries, and the indefinite expansion of old ones—is thus not true of farming. The second factor is that farm prices are fluctuating prices, and historically the fluctuations have been violent and the farmer has been at their mercy. In high-price periods, especially war periods, the American farmer historically gave way to his land hunger, and in an expansionist spree he mortgaged himself to buy up more land and nourish his pride of ownership. In low-price periods he was wiped out.

That is one reason why the "farm problem" was finally stabilized by making the farmer in a sense the ward of the state—by price support, parity payments, crop restriction, acreage control, "soil bank," and government purchase and storing of the farmer's surplus so that he would not again be the victim of the price fluctuations of the free-enterprise system. Another reason was the failure of farm income to keep pace either with the advance of the national income as a whole or with industrial prices. In 1929 the farmer's share of the national income was 7 per cent; in 1954 it had fallen to 4 per cent. Roughly it doubled in that period, but the national income increased fourfold. The position of the marginal farmer made the situation worse. By the 1950 census figures, over a million and a half farm families had a cash income of less than $1,000 a year, mostly on eroded or poor soil, or on sandy soil on the coastal plain, or on tiny tracts in the South. Even the national average farm income was less than $4,000 per farm—which was low when compared with nonfarm income in America, although very high when compared with farmers in other countries.

The farmer used his massive political strength—far disproportionate to his numbers—to get government price supports which would balance these inequities and give his income some stability. Although the original policies of price support developed out of the New Deal, no Republican administration has dared abandon them. In 1955 there was a seven-billion-dollar surplus of farm products under government price support. The granaries and storage space were full to bursting. The efforts to ease the problem by finding foreign markets were necessarily limited by the adverse effect of dumping policies on American foreign relations. The efforts at acreage reduction were also futile, since they were easily evaded, and the productivity was rising higher than the acreage decrease.

There has been a good deal of discussion of the American "rural mind," but it is hard to talk of it as if it were a single entity. The "mind" of the Arena Imperial Company is different from that of an Iowa corn farmer, which in turn is different from that of a Maine potato farmer, or an Alabama "red-neck" or Georgia "cracker" or "wool hat," and all in turn are different from the mind of an Arkansas Negro cropper, a Rio Grande Valley wetback, or a Jamaican or Puerto Rican contract laborer on the Eastern truck garden or tobacco farms. The mind of a corn-belt farmer is different from that of a cotton-belt farmer, a wheat-belt farmer, a Wisconsin or Pennsylvania or New York dairy farmer, a Rocky Mountain range cattle grazer or sheep grazer, a Florida or California citrus grower. Economic, sectional, ethnic, and class variations, not to speak of individual differences, cut across the conditionings of the farm life itself.

Are there common elements forming what may still be called the farmer's outlook? Veblen thought it was precapitalist and "animistic," due to the farmer's having been by-passed by the technology—and therefore by the psychology—of the machine; that the farmer was conservative because he dealt with a physical environment he could neither calculate nor control, and that he was therefore more inclined to a belief in the magical aspects of social institutions than the industrial worker whose animism had been rubbed away by habituation to the machine.

The trouble with this view—aside from its ignoring of the later machine revolution on the farm—is that it turns the facts of American history on their head. It was the farmers who were associated with the historical American movements of political protest and dissent. From Shays' Rebellion to the twenty-four-hour violence of the farm-holiday movement of the Great Depression, earlier American radicalism was largely agrarian. This radicalism may have been an assertive opposition to the business power the farmers saw challenging them, and their Populism from Bryan's time to La Follette's may have been a last stand against the monopolists who had taken over both the economy and the government. Agrarian radicalism always had in it a strong sense of property and traditionalism: the Populists wanted more to recapture an imaginary agricultural independence than to create new conditions. It was also a radicalism which found room for a heavy component of isolationism and anti-Semitism, as the currents of thought showed in the late 1930s. But it would be hard in any event to maintain Veblen's thesis of the farmer's conservatism in American history.

What was the source of this radicalism and why did it all but disappear? The core of the farmer's attitude has been a fierce individualism. As individualism became more and more linked with the anti-interventionist antibureaucratic doctrines of Republican conservatism, the farmers became the great conservative force of America. The Granger Revolt, the Farmers' Alliance, the Farmer-Labor parties, the Non-Partisan leagues, the Populist and Progressive groups whose center was in the agricultural states of the Middle West, were largely ironed out of the American political picture. The "sons of the wild jackass" who used to come to Congress from the Midwestern states are no more. This does not mean the Republicans can always count on the "farm vote." The elections for a twenty-year period, from 1932 through 1952, showed that the farmer shops around for price supports. But his basic conservatism of outlook survived the New Deal and Fair Deal. Strikingly, this change from agrarian radicalism to agrarian conservatism became more pronounced with the mechanization of agriculture. In the case of the farmers, Veblen's "discipline of the machine" has worked in an inverse way. It would be more to the point to say that the farmer grew more conservative as his living standard rose.

The farmer's individualism had its roots in the fact that, except for the corporate farms and the co-ops, the farmer has to wrestle with soil and climate, bugs and boll weevils, chemistry and hormones, largely by himself. It is not that he deals (in Veblen's terms) with "magic" but that whatever he deals with he has to deal with as an individual enterpriser: the directness of effort and reward, the Lockean sense of property as whatever a man has acquired by mixing his sweat with the soil, are as nakedly manifested in the family farm as in small-scale business enterprise. This has made both of them areas of individualism.

In one respect the American farmer differs from farmers all over the world. He is not a village-dweller. In India, for example, three quarters of the population lives in the traditional farm village. The European village-community might conceivably have been transferred to America and for a time in New England—while the dangers from the Indians were still felt—the farmers huddled together. But except for the Mormon settlements in Utah and the village culture of the Spanish-speaking groups in the Southwest, the way of the American farmer is to live on his farm homestead and leave the village and town to the traders, farm-implement dealers, grain and feed dealers, storekeepers, mill-workers, and service groups. The decisive historical moment here came in the settlement of the Middle West. The Homestead Acts required residence on the land to support the title: the typical homestead was a "quarter section" of 160 acres, which meant that the farmers lived scattered over the land, separated by far distances, with a one-room schoolhouse for their children and a small church set in the open country for their worship. The difficulties of transport kept the farm community within the distance of the "team haul." The result was a fierce localism which laid its stress on local autonomy, a fear of statism, an isolated way of life that led to isolationism in outlook. The farmer's relation to the town was one of hostility: it was the relation of a producer to the middleman who bought his products cheap, and the storekeepers who sold him other products dear; it was the relation of the debtor to the banker, the creditor, the mortgage-holder. This increased his individualism, his isolationism, his burning sense of grievance.

Life has changed for the independent farmer, whether in the Midwest or elsewhere. He has come into a new relation to the standardizing forces of American culture and has become part of the communications revolution. The automobile, the radio, movies, and TV have brought him out of his isolation; he does his shopping and trading less in the farm village and more in the larger industrial center where he can get spare parts for his machinery and the newest fashions for his wife and daughters. His one-room schoolhouse has become a consolidated school located in the trade center to which his children ride daily on a school bus; his land is no longer heavily mortgaged; his crops are price-supported by the Federal government, and in raising them he gets the help of government technicians. The work of a farmer is still hard, heavy work, and the risks of weather and market fluctuations are still real risks. But as farming has become a subsidized sector of the economy, and the security of the farmer one of the tasks of the welfare state, his antistatism is shown up as an anachronism. Nevertheless as a traditional "agin-er," it is still as logical for him to be "agin" the state which subsidized him as it was for him to be "agin" the system of business power which organized the home-market and world-market demand for his products.

In most areas of the world the rural population is custom-bound. In the United States custom has largely loosened its hold, and the farmer is battered by all the dislocating forces of contemporary life. What used to be called the "rural community" has been churned up and is to be found across the country in various stages of disorganization. There has been a steady movement away from the land. The farmer's daughter who has been to the university moves to the towns and cities for marriage or a career; the farmer's son who has gone to an agricultural college sometimes stays to manage the farm, sometimes is drawn away by the more powerful suction force of city life. The slack is taken up by bigger farm units and by corporate management.

The pull of the farm has not vanished: every year there are young Americans who would like to take up farming as a way of life, but the only available government land is the small tracts of Western public lands newly reclaimed by irrigation, and the waiting list for each is a long one. A more important trend is that of the man with a career in the city who likes to farm as a supplementary way of life (much like the English gentleman of the eighteenth and nineteenth centuries) and can afford the investment it requires—and in many cases writes the loss off against his high-bracket income tax. He is another example of how the farmer's way has been swept up into the powerful sway of the pecuniary culture of America.

8. The Decline of the Small Town

THE AMERICAN PLACE started with small population units, rapidly grew to big ones, and has ever since been under the double tension of moving from the small unit to the big one and at the same time moving from the center of the bigger unit outward toward the rim. Traditionally the small town has been held to embody the American spirit better than the larger frame. De Tocqueville affirmed that the township as a unit both of government and of living had preceded the state and nation in America and was more important than either. In New England the township has lasted over three hundred years, and while it has been battered by heavy pressures from state, nation, and economy, it still retains traces of the two goods that Americans have always seen in it—

the friendliness of face-to-face relations and the concern about the town's affairs felt by all its citizens.

De Tocqueville had a reason of his own for his tub-thumping about the New England township—his hatred for French centralization, which made a person "a kind of settler, indifferent to the fate of the spot which he inhabits. The greatest changes are effected there without his concurrence. . . . The condition of his village, the police of his street, the repairs of the church or parsonage, do not concern him; for he looks upon all these things as unconnected with himself and as the property of a powerful stranger whom he calls the government." He saw American town government as the ideal contrast to this lugubrious picture. For all his bias he was nonetheless right about the "provincial independence" of the American small town and the fierce identification of even its poorest citizens with the disputes and rivalries that raged about its affairs. This intensity still prevails in many New England towns, governed by three "Selectmen," who draw up annual budgets that are examined, item for item, by the entire citizenry sitting in the primary democracy of the town meeting. In the early days of the Republic the small town was the tap spring of the revolutionary spirit and of cultural strength. There were few Presidents from Lincoln and Grant to Truman and Eisenhower who were not the products of small-town culture. During most of American history, until the turn of the twentieth century, it was the basic community form for most Americans.

But the growing point of American life is scarcely to be found in the small town today. Latterly the important lines of growth have been elsewhere. It is partly that all the small units in American life are having to wage a losing fight—not only the small town but the small farm, the small business firm, the small college, even the neighborhood within the big city. Somewhere between the turn of the century and the New Deal the small town felt the withering touch of the Great Artifact that we call American society, and in the quarter century between 1930 and 1955 the decisive turn was made, away from small-town life. The currents of American energy moved around and beyond the small towns, leaving them isolated, demoralized, with their young people leaving them behind like abandoned ghost towns.

What happened was that the small town lost its economic and cultural base. Partly this happened in the areas most badly scarred by soil erosion, where the destruction of the rural hinterland stripped away the substance of small-town existence. But actually this was a marginal force. Everywhere, even in the most prosperous areas, the small town was undercut by the big changes in American life—the auto and super-highway, the supermarket and the market center, the mail-order house,

the radio and TV, the growth of national advertising, the mechanization of farming—so that it turned its face directly to the centers of technology. It was the city and the suburb—the cluster-city complex—that
became the focus of working and living, consuming and leisure. "None
of the kids ever come back here to live after they've gone away to
school," said an older man from Shannon Center, Iowa, which had lost
almost half its population in the 1940s. The young people go on to find
jobs in factories or businesses far from where they grew up, or they go
away to college or technical school and get the kind of training for
which the small town, with its limited opportunities, simply cannot
offer a demand.

I have been talking here of an entity hard to define, especially in
drawing a line between the small town and the city. The Census Bureau
calls any community of over 2,500 people "urban," and for 1950 showed
some 3,000 communities in America with a population between 1,000
and 2,500; more than 3,000 with a population from 2,500 to 10,000;
and 3,800 with a population between 2,500 and 25,000. One might put
the dividing line at around 10,000 or 15,000 people, but it would be
an arbitrary line.

The test is at what point the town grows too big to make life compassable. The value of small-town living lies in the face-to-face relations
that it makes possible throughout the community. One might say that
a small town ceases to be one as soon as someone who has lived in it a
number of years finds unfamiliar faces as he walks down the street and
is not moved to discover who they are and how they got there. For in
a small town it is the unfamiliar that is remarkable, just as in a big
city the memorable experience is to meet in a random walk through
the streets someone you know. It has occurred to more than one observer that if a big-city inhabitant were to respond to all the people
he meets to the same degree as a small-town inhabitant, he would end
as a raving lunatic.

One notes that most of the communities in the spate of recent surveys
(the Newburyport of Lloyd Warner's *Yankee City,* the Morris of his
Democracy in Jonesville, the Natchez of John Dollard's *Caste and Class
in a Southern Town,* the Grafton of Granville Hicks's *Small Town*)
were about towns of less than 25,000. Muncie of the *Middletown*
studies by Robert and Helen Lynd (38,000 at the time of the first study,
48,000 at the second) was somewhat larger. Each study was an effort
to catch the distillation of American life through a microscopic analysis
of a cross section of it. Clearly, the small town lends itself most easily
to this kind of inductive study because it is small enough to grasp. But
I doubt the symbolic value it is intended to have for America as a whole.

What the studies are discovering is the America of an earlier generation. The changes operative in the growth centers of American life are reflected in distorted form in the small town, like the shadows in Plato's cave.

The idea that the small town is the seed ground of what is characteristically American has not been restricted to its glorifiers or to the survey-makers. It may be found in so hostile a critic as Thorstein Veblen, in his classic essay on "The Country Town" (*Absentee Ownership in America*). He wrote as an agrarian radical of the Scandinavian Midwest, resenting the Yankee merchants and bankers who had come from New England to take over the Great Plains. He saw in the country town the roots of the capitalist attitude—the "predatory" and "prehensile" spirit of American business enterprise, middleman rather than producer, quick to discern a profit, greedy to grasp it, tenacious in holding on to it. It was ruthless evaluation yet not without its insight. A history of American industry will show how many of the men who came to the top of the heap spent their formative years in the small town and in many instances got their business start there. But even when Veblen wrote in the mid-1920s the small town was ceasing to be the focus of the capitalist spirit.

The fact that the small town is dwindling in importance makes Americans idealize it all the more. The phrase "small town" has come itself to carry a double layer of meaning, at once sentimental and condescending. There is still a belief that democracy is more idyllic at the "grass roots," that the business spirit is purer, that the middle class is more intensely middling. There is also a feeling that by the fact of being small the small town somehow escapes the corruptions of life in the city and the dominant contagions that infest the more glittering places. History, geography, and economics gave each American town some distinctive traits of style that are imbedded in the mind, and the memory of this style is all the more marked because of the nostalgia felt, in a largely urban America, for what seems the lost serenity of small-town childhoods.

This was probably part of the basis for the "Renaissance" of the small town at mid-century, just when its decay and the movement of population from it were most marked. There was a return to it emotionally, if not intellectually, as a repository of the older and more traditional values. A number of writers, advertising men, newspapermen, and artists dreamed of forsaking the competitive tensions of New York, Chicago, or Hollywood to settle down in a small town and find the abandoned "heart of America." In the university centers some of the professors made heroic efforts to revive the energies of the small town and recapture its control for the people, much as the Russian *Narodniki* at the turn of the century dreamed of "going to the people" and finding among them new strength with which to grapple with the tasks of social revolution and reconstruction.

The question few of them faced was why the small town had declined and been rejected by the younger people. One might have expected the face-to-face quality of its living and the strong personal ties it afforded to have served as an attraction to young families settling down to a tranquil and satisfying way of life. But this reckons without the counterforce of recoil from the torpor and tyranny of the small town. The best clue to this counterforce showed up in the literature of the 1910s and 1920s—in the portrait of Spoon River in Edgar Lee Masters' poems, in the Gopher Prairie of Sinclair Lewis's *Main Street*, in the bitter narratives of Sherwood Anderson and Theodore Dreiser. As early as 1882 Ed Howe had laid bare the meanness and sterility of small-town life in *The Story of a Country Town*. All these writers depicted mercilessly the provincialism of small-town life, the stifling constraints, the sense of stagnation that came from living in a closed room. It is unlikely that the forces of American conformism were more cruelly displayed anywhere than in the heavy hand that the small town habitually laid on the man or woman who too rashly broke the moral code. Just as heavy was the hand one laid on one's own rebel impulses. The record at once of the outer social tyranny and the inner repression may be read in the stony faces of Grant Wood's provincials.

Even the efforts at "reform" were part of the mood of disillusionment. Carol Kennicott, who tried to bring culture to Gopher Prairie, was in the line of succession of the women who had founded the Minerva Clubs, the Ladies' History Clubs, and the Ladies' Library Associations of Sioux Falls, S.D., and Weeping Waters, Neb., and Sleepy Eye, Minn., seeking to bring culture to the moving frontier. Yet while Carol was not new, she expressed a change of mood. Sinclair Lewis, like Masters, Dreiser, and Anderson, drew for much of his creativeness upon his smoldering rebellion against the "lassitude and futility" of Gopher Prairie. Its Main Street, he wrote, "is the continuation of Main Streets everywhere." And he added, with his heavy satiric underscoring, "Main Street is the climax of civilization"—although it is worth adding that in his later novels Lewis reversed his position and took back his satire. His fellow townsmen were meanwhile content with Main Street. "Somehow Harry Lewis didn't like it here," was the way one of his boyhood friends from Sauk Center put it many years later. But this was no crotchet of Lewis's: it was true of other writers and artists. The city revolution had brought with it a widening of horizons and a dislocation of social ties. The sensitive ones who were left behind felt cheated of life.

A number of critics, including T. S. Eliot, have linked creative achievement with the face-to-face relations possible in a small community. This may be so, but in the United States the poets and novelists of the period wrote as they did not because they had ties with the small town but because they were breaking their ties. The creatively releasing force for them was the sense of breaking through the encrusted mold of custom. The very smallness of the small town gave them compassable symbols of grievance and hatred, and it dramatized both the clash between the small town and the Great Society and also the sense of breakthrough. Even in the 1950s many young men writing their first novels chose the macrocosm of some small town to depict, as in *Sironia, Texas*. But in a sense the 1920s saw "the last of the provincials," as Maxwell Geismar put it, and the great writing moved away from the small town and its life to the city and its suburbs and the outside world.

What happened to the small town was not only that the big social changes undercut it and swirled around it, leaving it isolated, but they also drained it of its store of power. The power of America today is to be found largely with the business and community leaders of the city, who initiate policies for corporate empires, trade-unions, national pressure groups, and big-audience media. Knowing this, we tend to forget that in an earlier America the decisions that expressed the American will were largely made by small-town lawyers, bankers, merchants, editors. As merchandizing, transport, and recreation shifted, the locus of power shifted. The town could no longer perform most of its functions alone—roadbuilding, relief, education, taxation, public works—and it came to depend on subsidies from the Federal and state governments. As the power diminished, however, the intensity of the feuds and rivalries did not always subside, and the small town sometimes offered the unreal spectacle of an intensified struggle over dwindling stakes of power.

To the outward eye, the town of the 1950s, with its church spires, its Town Hall, its Main Street stores, its bank, its weekly newspaper, seemed what it always was. But its decay was unmistakable, taking the form of a displacement of its power and a disorganization of its traditional ways of life. Charles Francis Adams had seen it generations earlier, in his poetic description (in *Three Episodes of Massachusetts History*) of the disappearance of the New England village. Even the close controls which the code-makers of the town once exerted on its moral standards had to be relaxed in the face of the general moral confusion.

George Homans pointed out, in commenting on a study of the social disorganization of "Hilltown"—a Massachusetts farming town of about 1,000 people—that a town clerk who absconded with community funds was no longer dealt with draconically as in similar cases in the past, that girls being dated were expected to "come across" sexually, and that virginity before marriage was no longer stressed or counted upon. Few would argue today that the condition of mental health in the small town is better than in the city, or that there is less alcoholism or a better family situation. Nor can one any longer underplay the seamier sides of American localism—the heartbreaking inertia, the presence of corruption and greed even at the grass roots. Human meanness and human generosity are widely distributed in a culture, and the pursuit of the cultural life goals goes on with little reference to the unit of living. There may be greater tranquillity in the small town but no more happiness; there are face-to-face relations but no deeper understanding of the human situation; there is a more compassable universe to grasp, physically and socially, but in reality it is no less bewildering.

If I have been unsparing here in dealing with the legend of small-town superiority, I do not mean to belittle the enduring although lesser place the small town is likely to have in American life. The growth of a highly urban and mechanized Great Society has by-passed not only the town itself but also some of the values with which it was historically linked. Emerson's Concord, Lincoln's Springfield, William Allen White's Emporia, Truman's Independence, and Eisenhower's Abilene must have borne along on their current a way of life strong enough to shape the men they produced. Some of America's towns, especially in New England and in the prosperous areas of the Middle West, are still conscious of being the carriers of a tradition and a philosophy. When Harry Truman, commenting on the problem of juvenile delinquency, wrote that "our children need fewer gadgets and more chores," he was expressing a recognizable small-town philosophy—the direct, no-nonsense, keep-life-simple philosophy of small-town mores. Truman's own personality—informal, downright, salty, with its strong sense of task, its stress on personal loyalties and obligations, its rejection of cant, its shrewd assessment of men and issues, and its built-in moral code—is the distillation of what is healthiest and most pungent in the surviving values of small-town culture. Although most small-town politicians (and much of American politics still derives from the small town) would shy away from Truman's identification with majority aspirations and minority causes, with labor interests and civil liberties and Negro civil rights, enough of them are enough like Truman to make a fusion of urban and small-town values conceivable. If the small town is wholly sacrificed there will be sacrificed along with it some continuity of face-to-face relations, an awareness of identity, a striving to be part of a compassable whole, a sense of counting for something and being recognized as a person and not a cipher.

A number of recent American writings indicate that the nostalgia for the small town need not be construed as directed toward the town itself: it is rather a "quest for community" (as Robert Nisbet puts it)— a nostalgia for a compassable and integral living unit. The critical question is not whether the small town can be rehabilitated in the image of its earlier strength and growth—for clearly it cannot—but whether American life will be able to evolve any other integral community to replace it. This is what I call the problem of place in America, and unless it is somehow resolved, American life will become more jangled and fragmented than it is, and American personality will continue to be unquiet and unfulfilled.

If the small town survives at all in a future America, it will have to survive within this frame and on a new economic base—not as the minor metropolis of a farming area, or as a mill town or mining town, but as a fusion of farming and industrial life along with the residential spill-over from the city and the suburb. I shall deal with both these forms in what follows, but it is worth saying here that neither the mammoth city nor the dormitory suburb is as it stands an adequate solution of the problem of place in America. Neither is the small town as it stands. But it can diversify its economic base, especially with the trend toward decentralizing industry. With the new modes of transport it can reach even the distant big city easily—for work or recreation, school, medical facilities, or friends. And it can build a way of life which forms a continuity with the small town of the past but without its cluttering accompaniments of provincialism and torpor.

9. City Lights and Shadows

AMERICA WAS FORMED in its present mold in the process of city building, and it is still true—even in the era of the suburban revolution—that wherever American places are being shaped anew the new forms irrepressibly move toward becoming cities. While making goods and making money, the American has become in the process a city maker as well.

Lewis Mumford, in his *Culture of Cities*, has traced with learning and passion the historical rise of the city as shelter, fortress, industrial center, mechanical way of life—the stages toward "Megalopolis." In every civilization the rise of the big city has been a by-product of technical and industrial development. This has been true not only in

Europe, whose cities grew big earlier than America's and whose population density is higher, but also in Asia, where the recent upsurge of
population and the ferment of new forces have raised the size of the
big cities staggeringly high. It is truer of the American city, however,
that the rise of megalopolis has meant the accumulation not only of
masses of people but of masses of power. The growth of the American
city has gone along with—and been the product of—revolutions in production, motive power, transport, communications. Every transformation in the economy, including the rise of new industries and the
changes from roads to canals to railroads to autos and aviation, and
from steam to gasoline to electric and atomic power, has further complicated the web of city life. Yet the changes move inexorably, and as
they occur they keep transforming the outer sky line and the inner structure and life of the city. Every new step in technology tends to destroy
the inner forms of the cities on which they rest and which have made
them possible, and on their ruins new forms arise.

The statistical growth line is by now familiar enough. In 1790 when
the American nation first emerged it had no cities, large or small, that
could compare with the glory of European cities. There were a few
small "cities in the wilderness"—three between 10,000 and 25,000, two
over 25,000, none as large as 50,000. Not until 1820 did New York
have 100,000 and not until 1880 did it have a million people. By 1955
it had over eight million, five other cities were over a million, and
twenty ranged from New York's vast mass to the roughly half million
of Cincinnati, Seattle, and Kansas City. There were 106 cities of over
100,000. Putting the figures differently, the urban population by Census Bureau definition (those living in places of over 2,500) increased
between 1940 and 1950 from around seventy-five million to around
eighty-nine million, the latter figure representing almost two thirds
(64 per cent) of the total population; in the Northeast the proportion
was some 80 per cent, in the West 70 per cent, in the South 50 per cent.
Add to this the fact that much of the nonfarming rural population is
really urban, in the sense that it lives on the outskirts of metropolitan
areas, with city jobs and values, and the urban percentage then goes as
high as 80 to 82 per cent for the whole nation. Taking a still different
approach, and using 25,000 to 100,000 as the range for a small- and
middle-sized city, there were seventeen million Americans living in 378
such cities in 1950, while there were forty-four million living in cities
of over 100,000—some sixty-one million in all living in cities of over
25,000.

Each of these cities has a character and style of its own. New York
and Boston are proud of their role as intellectual centers, but Chicago,

"hog-butcher of the world," was the scene of a literary Renaissance in the early decades of the century and later became an educational center. A number of cities—San Francisco, New Orleans, Charleston—have a sure sense of their style and picturesqueness as carriers of a history-laden or exotic tradition, but Boston, Philadelphia, and Baltimore would make rival claims on that score. Some cities in turn are proud of their recent growth as boom towns—Los Angeles, Detroit, Houston, Dallas, Seattle, Portland; and in America the claim to boom is more swaggering than the claim to tradition. Most American cities owe their growth to industry and transport, yet Washington is what it is because it is the nation's capital; Los Angeles, the movie center of America, is also in an area of oil production and owed its original boom to the silver mining of the Sierras.

Emphasizing this, there is a danger of forgetting the strength of the agricultural hinterland out of which many of the American cities grew. They got their start as marketing centers for the products of the surrounding areas: Chicago and Kansas City became shipping centers for the steers of Texas and the Far West. But Pittsburgh and Cleveland owe most of their growth to iron and steel, and Detroit is the automobile center of America. Miami is the center of the vacationing and leisure industries, although recently it has been developing light industries less seasonal and precarious. In the East, cities like Boston, New York, Philadelphia, Charleston, and Atlanta got their start as strategic ports and others rose because they were at the convergence of the great trails and rivers or dominated high ground as forts. There are instances where a city of promising growth remained small while another grew into a metropolis, mainly because in laying out transcontinental railroads the line by-passed one and went through another. Thus many of the Western cities without natural location on rivers are mainly the result of the accident of transportation history, often aided by political pressure, land speculation, and outright bribery.

At some point in its history every American city has been a "boom" city, meaning the sudden spurt of growth when a particular city exerts a suction force upon people looking for opportunity, jobs, profits. Often this spurt of growth takes on a motive force of its own and threatens to run away with the city, outstripping its productive base. The great example of a synthetic boom was that of Florida in the 1920s when blueprint cities were staked out, with water systems, lighting systems, and even community centers. Some later boomed again, and successfully; others remained as derelict reminders that a city cannot be wholly the creation of hope, hysteria, and paper profits. Even in the Paradise of real-estate values a city responds to organic laws of growth. When that growth has a valid base the initial boom will be succeeded by others in mounting succession. The original Chicago boom was that of a stockyard and railroad center; its later phases were those of farm-machinery manufacture, grain and commodity exchanges and speculation, and then war research and production. In Los Angeles a silver-mining boom was succeeded by an oil boom, a movie boom, and a war boom. In Houston and Dallas the booms were chiefly those of oil, real estate, and war industries. A smaller city like Norfolk grew originally as a port and then achieved a shipbuilding boom during World War II.

But the story of city growth is not summed up in the strategy of industrial location. Once the cities were established they exerted a suction force on many diverse groups. Until World War I the city magnet drew immigrants from Europe and boys and girls from farms and small towns. In the forties and fifties it drew Negroes from the South and (in the case of New York) Puerto Rican immigrants. In most cases the trinity of motifs was comfort, opportunity, glamour.

The comfort motif was the answer a later generation gave to the harshness of frontier life that earlier generations had encountered. It was especially important for American women, who had found the frontier settlements bleak and welcomed the restoration of European comfort to the American situation. The middle class carried this motif further, and the calculated comfort of American heating, the American bathroom, and the garishness of the American hotel became symbols of "materialism" which the rest of the world first ridiculed, then envied and imitated.

Related to it is the glamour of city life. In the 1880s the magazine illustrations called it the "lure of the city." They depicted a country lad lying on a hillock, gazing longingly into the distance toward the towers and spires of the city. The mass city—Chicago, Detroit, Minneapolis, Cleveland, Pittsburgh, Boston, New York—was what the young men yearned for. It was their City of God. As for the young women, they turned toward the freedom and blandishments of the city and its romantic possibilities. It was in the cities that the young people hoped to find the excitement and fulfillment which the dynamism of their culture made them ask of life. Where people clustered together there was a greater choice of people, a chance to show one's beauty and wit to advantage, a chance for dress and gaiety, sexual adventure, love and marriage. The glamour of city life was part of the impulse back of the great migration from country to city in the past seventy-five years.

The greatest of the trinity of motifs was the idea of limitless opportunities for the young, strong, and able. Often the mass city proved to be a jungle in which many were destroyed and the survivors brutal-

ized. But those who build a temple to the idols of success do not inquire too closely about the burdens of the sacrifices.

As a result of city living, Americans are becoming a people whose
earliest memories are less apt to be of the farm or village or the main
street of a small town than of pavements and movies, and swimming at
the docks, and running in gangs, and "going downtown." They have
had to get accustomed to the jangle of city sounds striking on the nerve
centers, to new ways of dodging city traffic or of waiting it out patiently,
to the complexity and pavements of the "asphalt jungle."

Why do they stand it? The answer is that many don't, hence· the
Great Exodus to the suburbs. For those who do, the city has become
more than a convenience: it is a necessity. This is true for workers who
must be near factories, railroad yards, and offices; for businessmen who
must be near their markets and customers; for writers and artists, advertisers, workers in the big media, who must be near the centers of the
nation's life.

The city is no longer a mode of comfort, as it was in its earlier
phases. In some ways it has become the acme of discomfort—congested,
traffic-stalled, smog-filled, shut out from sunlight, with scarcely space for
breathing and no feel of soil beneath one's feet and no sense of the
rhythm of the seasons. Any subway rider during the rush hours in New
York can testify that city life has rigors challenging the frontier. This
ascesis is made endurable (at least for the eggheads) because of the excitement of theaters, concerts, night clubs, restaurants, sports events, universities, art schools, which only the city can furnish and for which even
the big media and the modern arts of mass reproduction are no substitutes. Beyond these amenities the core attraction of the city as a way
of life is tension, movement, opportunity, and a swarming kind of
warmth. A recent survey of Detroit, into which waves of workers have
swept from farms and small towns, shows that most of them do not
share the fashionable despair about city living. They like living in
Detroit. It is as if there were an unlocalized yearning for what is big in
size, dense in numbers, varied in type and stock of people, mobile, responsive. The cities are fed by this restlessness and grow through it.

Thus the American city as a way of life is the product not only of
technical and economic factors but also of loneliness. It is here that
the byzantine aspect of American city culture becomes important. What
is involved is not only the quest for liquor and night clubs, late hours,
sexual excitement and sexual opportunity. These are the more obvious
garments of a Faustian hunger and an almost pathetic fear of being
left out of things. The city is at once the product and symbol of human
alienation and the longed-for antidote against it. It is the sum of all

the signatures that a restless spirit has left on a people sensitive to experience. "This city," as E. B. White put it in a prose hymn to New York which is the distillation of the urban mood, "this mischievous and marvelous monument which not to look upon would be like death."

So dedicated an attachment does not exclude a sense of the realities of city life. White has said that there are three New Yorks—that of the natives, which gives continuity to the life of the city; that of the commuters, who use the city for business during the day and for evening forays but live in the suburbs; that of the migrants—the polyglot invaders from Europe, Africa and Asia, and from Puerto Rico nearer to home, and the youngsters coming from the Midwest to make a career and discover a universe. To some extent other cities are streaked with the same strata. The big cities offer a greater variation of ethnic stock and a heavier emphasis on the professional and intellectual classes. But otherwise any American city contains, in replica, much the same pyramid of class and mass, of wealth and poverty, of conspicuous consumption and heartbreaking scrimping that American life as a whole contains. The difference is that in a city the contrasts are heightened because there are greater extremes at both ends and because the whole is brought within the compass of a single area.

At one end of the scale the big cities furnish the frame of American wealth and power. They provide the banking and financial mechanisms for the rest of the country, the centers of communication, the starting points of advertising, publications, and salesmanship. This does not mean that they are unproductive, since every big city owed its rise to some crucial relation to the American productive economy. But what the city adds as its own is the pecuniary frame of American society. This is where the money is, this is where the credit structure rests, and with the money and credit go the power and the glory.

Big cities are centers of absentee power, often holding the small ones in fief. In a medium city like Elmira, N.Y., for example, only a few of the big plants on which income and employment depend are locally owned. The others are subsidiaries of corporations with home offices in New York, Pittsburgh, Detroit. In Elmira even labor has an absentee structure of authority, because the national labor contracts on which the Elmira contracts are modeled are signed elsewhere, after negotiations that are carried on at conferences elsewhere. This absenteeism of ownership and control is especially true of the South and Far West, which are linked with control centers in the East and Midwest. A big city like Atlanta and a small city like Decatur, Ala. (pop. 25,000), bid anxiously against other cities for plants which will be the subsidiaries of absentee corporations. The chief function of chambers of commerce is to sell the city as a potential location for new industry. Newspapers, banks, mayors, and city administrations join forces to lure industry to the city. A corporation looking for a Southern plant close to cheap power will get bids from perhaps a score of cities offering hydroelectric power, cheap labor power, low taxes, and political favors. Once the city has the plant, it is dependent on a massive impersonal corporation that makes its decisions within the frame not of local conditions but of its whole empire. Face-to-face relations in the everyday area of job life become impossible. And when the corporation abandons the plant for a cheaper or more favorable spot, the effect on workers and merchants is devastating.

Although the gods whom it must propitiate for its destiny are not local deities but the gods of "business conditions," each city has its sense of welfare and catastrophe. The usual "community feeling" is a hopped-up, synthetic semihysteria called "boosterism." To be a "booster" is to sing your city's praises, push its wares, and defend its good name against defamers. It is an item in a spurious mythology of city promotion, tending to cancel out against the synthetic mythologies of the other cities. But at a time of general joblessness, the false front falls away and people feel caught in a common plight. The plants close down, the pay envelopes shrink, you buy on credit and face the threat of eviction notices. In such crises, or in the event of hurricane or flood disaster, the city discovers itself not just as a chance collection of atoms but as a whole whose parts are members of each other.

Despite the fond conviction abroad that all American cities look alike, each has its own characteristic architecture, its own sky line, its own style of building and of living, its own mood. Each has also its natural history, passing through a series of phases at each of which its characteristic style changed. Philadelphia and Boston, once the great political and cultural capitals of America, are now a mixture of the provincial and the ethnically pluralist. Several cities that started in a somewhat lurid fashion as centers of promiscuous frontier gambling and scarlet sex—such as San Francisco, Cincinnati, New Orleans—are now almost as respectable as their sister cities. From some cities, like Indianapolis, the stamp of rural provincialism is hard to efface. But others—Chicago, Cleveland, Cincinnati, Minneapolis, Kansas City, Louisville, Houston, Dallas—to which lecturers and theater troupes and concert companies used to come only as an act of condescension or uplift have become centers of regional culture.

Compared with the slow growth of the great cities of Europe, the American cities seemed to shoot up overnight. There were several turning points at which the efforts made to plan their growth might have taken hold and become a permanent part of the American scheme. For a time in the colonial America of Charleston, Annapolis, and Williamsburg some ideas of spacious planning were set in motion, but the Revolution interrupted them. After the emergence of the nation there were city plans in the air on a grand scale—not only for the Washington of Major L'Enfant but also for Boston and Philadelphia, and for the new frontier cities of Buffalo, Cleveland, and Detroit. But except in Washington and Savannah they came to little, largely because most cities were growing too fast to allow for the luxury of planned squares and open spaces at the city core, or for broad avenues fanning out on a radial pattern with houses well set back and with space between them. A New York study, which rejected such planning in favor of a cheaper and quicker gridiron pattern divided into uniform rectangles and subdivided with building lots, was later described by Edith Wharton as the expression of "a society of prosperous businessmen who have no desire to row against the current."

Once again, at the turn of the twentieth century, there was a Renaissance of city planning, sparked by the apprenticeship of American architects in Paris and by the Chicago Exposition of 1893. But while it yielded an influential Chicago plan and an attempt to put a beautiful façade on cities from coast to coast, under men like Daniel Burnham, Frederick Olmstead, and Charles McKim, the inertia of haphazard city growth was too great to arrest. What was called the City Beautiful movement caught the imagination and pride of American architects. It was a movement that dealt with state capitols, civic centers, universities, churches, and even railroad stations; eventually, inspired by the garden-city movement of England, it also left its impact on the layout of suburbs. Yet essentially its weakness was that it focused on boulevards and parks for the rich and did little about wider sidewalks and better quarters for the poor. "It had a lot of democratic phrases," writes William Wheaton, "but little democratic action."

A hundred years had elapsed between the city-planning movement at the turn of the nineteenth century and the one at the turn of the twentieth. Not only had vested interests become encrusted but so had habits of building, thinking, living. They were held fast by a century of custom and by greed and speed and the mistaken *laissez faire* that carried over from the realm of moneymaking into the realm of beauty, utility, and orderly growth. Still to follow were remarkable feats of city engineering and the building of skyscrapers, auto parkways, and thruways. But as for city planning, the movement was renewed so heartbreakingly late that it was no match for the strength of real-estate groups and the down-to-earth sense of the "practical" men. The American cities had already established their basic pattern of growth. By the time the Depression had stripped away the burnished surface of the cities and revealed the blight beneath, and governmental housing projects were started under the New Deal and new city planning commissions established, they could do little except operate within the accomplished fact of city history.

The core of that accomplished fact was planlessness. Most American cities had risen helter-skelter, wherever some convenience of location might place them or some rapacity push them. They grew up thus— grim and unlovely; often wrongly situated for health, huddling against tracks and wharves, clustered around railroad stations, stockyards, chemical factories, and power plants, with the scars of congested slums on them; swept by fires, vulnerable to epidemics, cradled often in low-lying areas periodically ravaged by floods; their air poisoned with smoke and polluted from the slag of the furnaces: sprawling and crowded aggregates that grew by haphazard and piled-up wealth and excitement but offered large segments of their people a mode of living which was neither spacious nor gracious, with neither plan nor meaning.

To say the cities were without plan does not mean that their growth lacked any discernible principle. A group of thoughtful students of city development have tried ingeniously to uncover a theory by which planless growth unfolded in various cities according to somewhat similar patterns. It became clear, for example, that many cities had a central core—the downtown business and shopping district, with hotels, banks, theaters, movie houses, office buildings, and the City Hall; and that around this core the other areas were to be found—the warehouses, railroad yards, factories; the wholesale and light-manufacturing districts; the blighted area with slums, rooming houses, and tenements (some of them once residences but later abandoned); the better low-cost houses of the skilled workers living near their work and the middle-class homes and apartment houses; the heavy manufacturing district; sometimes an outlying business district; the "residential" area of bigger houses, set off from the street with trees and space around them; finally the suburban ring of commuters, including residential and industrial suburbs and comprising high and low incomes alike.

At first it was thought that the districts grouped themselves around the core in widening concentric zones, with the expansive energy pushing from the center outward. Then with the coming of modern transport, a radial sector theory depicted the city as growing outward from the center along the lines of automobile and bus transportation, always away from low-lying, blighted, and dead-end areas toward higher and open country. Finally, to take account of the complex and bewildering growth of metropolitan cities, the theorists developed the idea of the multiple-nuclei city which grows around a number of cores.

Obviously all this was theorizing after the fact, and the naked fact was that the growth of the American city followed profitability and transport. The real arbiters of city growth were the railroad (which often pre-empted some of the best open space), auto traffic, and the real-estate promoter. It is these forces that dictated the shape of city growth far more than any city plan. To some this may seem evidence that American cities have grown organically rather than by some synthetic design, but haphazard growth is not organic. It is possible to provide for informal as well as formal features of growth, for variety as well as regularity, but the essential thing is to allow scope for both by taking thought.

In its layout the city tends to reflect the life history of its movements of immigration. The history of Brooklyn, for example, was that of successive migrations of Dutch, British, New Englanders, Irish, Jews, Italians, Negroes, Scandinavians, East Europeans, Syrians, Puerto Ricans, and even a colony of Mohawk Indians. They form a polyglot gridiron across the face of the city, with enough distinctness so that each section has its ethnic core and gives each neighborhood a sense of ethnic identity. This is why it has been said that in New York every street becomes a village, every area of ten or a dozen blocks becomes a neighborhood.

One of the results of the failure to take thought is the American city slum. Every big city has its slum area. Tolstoy's famous sentence—that all happy families are alike but every unhappy family is unhappy in its own way—applies inversely to cities: their gleaming and burnished streets belong uniquely to the city itself, but there is a deadly sameness about most slum areas. It is the universal quality of the scabrous areas where poverty and disease, delinquency and prostitution, walk together. The pattern of ethnic ghettos and race violence that has scarred some cities with blood and hate—among them Chicago, St. Louis, Detroit—comes out of elements that have a haunting similarity. The Negro slums in Atlanta do not differ much from those of Memphis, Birmingham, or Jacksonville. The Polish slums in Detroit, Buffalo, and Chicago are similar. The Mexican-American slums in San Antonio are worse than in Denver, but it is a difference of degree rather than of kind, and it is paralleled by the Barrio in New York City where the newly arrived Puerto Rican immigrants cluster.

William Bolitho once called the slums of Glasgow the "cancer of Empire," a phrase even better for the American slums, which are the blight on the gaudy flowers of American prosperity and power. The first buildings meant to house workers and immigrant families in the big Eastern cities were put up in the 1830s. They were followed by a dreary line of successors, each uglier and more macabre than what it replaced, with a greater population density and a blanker separation from the living needs of the time. They usually provided a higher profit return than the better housing units and were a continuing temptation to the exploiting of human helplessness. "I rent to the people no one else will take," said a Philadelphia "firetrap" landlord in 1956. Some of the slum houses were multiple dwellings encased in the old "balloon frame"; others were "three-decker" wooden tenements or rotting brown-stones; still others were railroad flats stretching out endlessly in the "dumb-bell tenements," with windows looking out into narrow side courts; or they were five- and six-story walk-up tenements.

The 1940 Census revealed that in fact one third of American dwellings were substandard. As late as 1948 the head of the St. Louis Chamber of Commerce said that 30 per cent of the quarter million dwelling units in the city lacked bath and toilet; in 1950 it was possible for Alfred Roth, a Swiss architect teaching in St. Louis, to say of its slums: "I've been many times in the slums of London. I've seen the damaged areas of western Europe. But never in my life have I seen anything like this." Families everywhere lived doubled up and looked often into sunless shafts. Periodically the newspapers of Chicago or St. Louis or New York sent reporters out to survey the slums. They found a jungle of garbage cans spilling over, people living in dark basements, back yards, and vacant lots, with kids playing among tin cans and broken bottles, decaying dock areas and trash-laden river fronts, children growing up to delinquency. Along with the neighborliness that the poor never lose, they would also find hustlers and jackals, and amidst the overcrowding they might (if they were acute enough) find a dimension of loneliness and terror that no tenement law could isolate or prohibit. This is the aspect of city life that Nelson Algren's novels depicted, even in the 1950s.

No account of the mass city can exclude the pathos of life for the millions who don't get the prizes, the mean and scrubby struggle for a few scraps from the table of plenty, the wreckage of derelicts cast up by the unyielding tides of city struggle, the manic perversions and crimes, the organized preying on women, the conscription of children into vice. An American city shows to the defeated a different face from the one it shows the conquerors. With the slums come the vice areas, acknowledged and unacknowledged—those of brothels, "boarding houses," cheap hotels, saloons; those of narcotics addicts, whores, and pimps. It is for them that the Biblical words run true: "So shall thy poverty come as a robber, and thy want as an armed man."

What makes the slums ominous is that they represent a blight which, to a lesser degree, infects larger areas of the city as the restless movement of population shifts from one to another neighborhood. Land values in any particular segment of a big city are either moving up or down; neighborhoods are either gaining in prestige or getting "run down." Once they start to deteriorate the process moves with cumulative swiftness: the ethnic "undesirables" begin to make inroads, panic sets in, and soon the whole character of the area has shifted. As the new transition zones are swept by the crosswinds of ethnic struggle, the schools express some of the tension, and street fights break out. The exodus may be to other neighborhoods or it may be wholly out of the city to the suburbs. The vitality of neighborhood and city is drained.

Decay and blight have occurred, of course, in every phase of the city's cycle of growth. In the past they have been followed by renewal, where the old was continually displaced by the new. But the city today is asked to find the energies for renewal exactly when it is faced with pyramiding costs of government, throttling traffic, mounting crime, and a drain on its more prosperous and educated population (it is largely the lower income groups who remain because they have nowhere else to go). As its people join the Great Exodus to live in the suburbs, they remain as users of the city's services and facilities, but they are no longer taxed for them, getting a "free ride": thus far the efforts to combine the city and its suburbs into a single tax-and-governmental unit, to share the costs, burdens, and services of government in the metropolitan community, have failed. The suburbanite swells the throng who seek entrance to the city by car every morning and exit at night, clogging bridges, tunnels, and thruways, congesting the streets, snarling the traffic. Ironically those who live in the city all week join the monster auto rally on week ends, eager to get away for a day or two, and spending hours in traffic jams on the way out of the city and back.

Thus the mass city, which came into its present stature as a by-product of the revolutions in transport, finds itself being choked by the millions of artifacts the auto industry has created. The city seems to have become mainly a temporary stopover place for men and families in motion—which may explain why so many of the efforts at city replanning are geared to its traffic problems and its auto arteries. It is true that the network of roads leading, let us say, out of New York and Newark to the New Jersey Turnpike, was not only an engineering achievement but (seen from the air) of breathtaking beauty of design. But to rebuild cities mainly around road design and traffic clearance was to make man an adjunct of his creature, the automobile, and to lose sight of him as a human being needing roots in a living community. It meant undoing thousands of years of human evolution since the discovery of the wheel and making man the servant of the wheel, incomplete without it.

The American city is being replanned and rebuilt, but in what form, and with how much forethought, and with what image in mind of man and his needs? As the city core decays one would think it would not be too hard to buy up the deteriorated property and start afresh, with living quarters embodying what we know about the kind of work life and leisure life that will be within reach of the American family in the latter half of the century. But this is to reckon without the tenacity of vested institutions and habits of thought. The New Deal set in motion a sequence of housing projects that did more for slum clearance in a decade than had been done in a century. But the houses thus built had at least the same population density as the razed slums they displaced; and often they were built without adequate provision for neighborhood schools, churches, or markets or for pooled facilities for supervised play —which led Lewis Mumford to quote a sentence Patrick Geddes wrote in 1915: "Slum, semi-slum, and super-slum: to this has come the evolution of our cities."

The bleak, efficient, multi-story, barracklike apartment houses that are likely more and more to dominate the sky line of the big American cities are the expressions of the industrial organism, and their parallels will in time be found in the Communist societies of Moscow and Peiping as well as in capitalist New York. This is the skeletal frame within which industrial man is encasing himself, and here again the American has not so much created a distinctive pattern of man but foreshadowed the direction that industrial man is taking.

The new urban personality which is emerging in America is the product of the machine—but also of a good deal more. The machine aspects of city living are obvious enough. Who can forget the swift tunneling of the machine-as-subway in the earth, the scurrying of the machine-as-automobile over its surface, the exacting regularity of the machine-as-traffic-light, the droning of the machine-as-television, the stream of print emerging from the machine-as-press, the silent power and precision of the machine-as-dynamo? Who can escape the tempo of the mass city—hurrying to work, to appointments, to crises, to pleasure, to tragedy?

Yet what gives the city its character as living is not the tempo or discipline of the machine but the effort to reach for values beyond it. The youngster becomes a member of the city gang, partly at least because the gang gives him a chance for a sense of belonging and feudal allegiance. Similarly with mechanized sports and amusements in the big city. Prize fighters pummel each other like gladiators before thousands; baseball contests are commercial events staged on schedule, with team standings calculated down to the fourth decimal point; movies and TV project the same *imago* on thousands of screens to the accompaniment of millions of fluttering pulses; choruses of dancing girls tap out their rhythms in night clubs with machinelike precision. Yet the big fact about all of them is not that they are mechanical, which is true enough, but that they furnish channels for mass emotion which relieve the tension of machine living.

Within this frame the city has developed a type of American character different from the type that De Crèvecoeur, De Tocqueville, or even Bryce depicted. It is less conditioned to the soil and the seasons, less religious, more skeptical about motives and chary of being "played for a sucker," less illusioned in the sense in which illusions—about friendship, work, sex, love, and God—provide an internal sustaining force for the personality. It has been psychologically hardened by innumerable brief encounters—in public schools, on subways and busses, in restaurants, in the course of shopping—which would become intolerable if one did not sheathe oneself against them with a constricted response. It is precocious about money matters and sex, since so many city people grow up in crowded quarters where few things are concealed from them. It is stoical in the face of hardship and the man-made catastrophes of economic life. It is not "urbane" except in the small groups in which one can afford to be generous, but it is much more likely to strip the jungle life of the city down to the nakedness of the human animal. It economizes time with an almost manic earnestness during the hours of business, only to waste it with equally manic intensity during the hours of pleasure and recreation. It lays stress (within limits) on individual traits of personality, on uniqueness in dress and sophistication in taste, on awareness, on the dramatic impact that the individual makes in his brief meetings with others. It has replaced fear by anxiety, and the concern about danger from elemental forces with a vague concern about security, safety, and the opinions of others.

What this means is that city living has carried men and women ever further away from their instinctual endowment. The city is not the root of the planlessness, the tensions, and the conformism of American life, but it is the envelope that encloses them. Or, to change the figure, the city is the battleground of the values of the culture.

In addition to its slums every city has its vice area and its crime problem. Whenever some vice inquiry has caught national attention or a newspaper puts on pressure or a city reform administration gets to power, the police force develops a spurt of energy. At such times there are "roundups" of petty criminals, prostitutes, or even the usual lodging-house population, and sometimes the more scabrous criminals also are kept moving and forced to seek other hunting grounds. But reform administrations are short-lived, and the ties between vice and politics, and between "rackets" and the respectable business elements of the city, are too close to be easily broken. In many cities the dynasty of political bosses started with the saloonkeeper who knew the weaknesses and tragedies of the slum people and built his political empire on the exchange of loyalty for favors. At a later stage in the dynasty, the boss may have become a contractor, dealing by a Providential coincidence with the very materials the city needed for its public works. There is scarcely a big American city whose administration is not at least marginally involved in this trinity of crime, political corruption, and business favors.

The city "machine" got its name because it operated with an impersonal efficiency to retain in power a group of political professionals who claim to know how to "deliver the vote." City crime is also mechanized, and the gangs, rackets, and shakedown outfits operate on a nation-wide plane. Yet in the case of both politics and crime the machine aspects can be overplayed. The political machine was usually run by a highly personal "boss" who gave a dramatic color to big-city corruption, as in the old days of Boss Croker in New York or more recently Boss Crump in Memphis or Boss Curley in Boston (it is Curley who is the protagonist of Edwin O'Connor's novel, *The Last Hurrah*). The function of the machine was to keep a firm hold on blocs of cohesive ethnic voters and thus capitalize on the inertia of the rest of the public. The relation of the political professionals to the ethnic blocs was mainly an emotional one of exchange of loyalties. The outward mechanism of the political machine conceals this inner structure of almost feudal allegiance—a structure of hierarchy, fealty to the overlords, and subinfeudation. Similarly the criminal machine reaches on the one side to the feudal gangsters, who are held together by greed and loyalty, and on the other side to the business community. The racket kings, levying their toll on the victims, are lawless versions of the "barons of the bags" who levy their toll on competitors and consumers.

But the problems of city government have now reached beyond crime and corruption. The big city generated administrative tasks which were never foreseen in the earlier years of American political thinking. Since the country was rural for most of its history, its political institutions were intended for small governmental units. The Founding Fathers could not have dreamed of a metropolitan unit like New York City, or of the web that it would spread from Westchester to Jersey City. The budget of New York City is higher than that of most state governments, and its administrative task is second only to that of the Federal government. It must run a huge police system, a school system that has to deal with Irish and Jewish children, Negroes and Puerto Ricans; it must run its subways through a Transit Authority, direct its bridge traffic through a Tri-Boro Bridge Authority, solve its harbor, truck, and air-line terminal problems through a Port Authority; it must run a network of public hospitals and clinics, a penal and prison system; it must deal with juvenile delinquency, run a set of magistrate's courts, and take care of the indigent who are "on welfare."

At best this involves an array of administrative services that can be only loosely held together. American cities have groped at once for the kind of technical civil service to be found in the Federal government, and for the kind of political leadership for which the American Presidency is the symbol. The city-manager movement, combined with the focusing of political leadership on the mayor, may convert city government into something a good deal better than what James Bryce lamented in his *American Commonwealth*.

The big fact about the mass city is that it has become so massive as to burst its bounds. It has become a "runaway city." New York, Cleveland, and Chicago each now contains a set of "satellite cities," which have developed their own civic pride and striven to become autonomous units within the larger metropolis. Yet the more difficult development has been that of the suburban communities which are functionally part of the metropolitan city but do not share its financial or administrative burdens. Like the single metropolitan area from Westchester to Jersey City, there are similar stretches through the industrial centers of Connecticut and Massachusetts, and around Buffalo, Pittsburgh, Chicago, and Los Angeles, where workers in chemical, automobile, and airplane factories cluster in a central city and in suburban communities that stretch for hundreds of miles in a continuous stream. These aggregates are not so much cities in the old sense but provinces in a larger industrial empire.

A number of American architects and planners have had a vision of how these monstrous masses can be kept within limits, the central cities renewed and replanned, the fringe growths contained, the whole turned into a set of decentralized communities each with an integrated pattern of work, residence, and recreation inside the far-flung larger frame. It is a moving vision, yet it would be surprising if Americans who had tolerated a planless past of the cities were to be converted—even under the spur of need—to a drawing-board-planned future.

In one area there are signs of concerted action—that of urban renewal. By 1955 there were 250 cities involved somehow in this effort, some to a minor degree, a number in a major way. They were starting to tear down the deteriorated parts of the central areas and rebuild them; they were taking steps to rehabilitate the indifferent areas; they were growing alert to the need for conserving the healthy ones. Except in cases like Pittsburgh and St. Louis, it was still being done without imaginative boldness, on a scale of cost suitable to the past and not to the staggering resources of the present. Yet the big fact was the emergence of the conviction that governments have a responsibility for city redevelopment.

Under the New Deal there was for the first time a clear recognition that the big metropolitan cities could not survive without Federal subsidies for crucial tasks, like housing, health, and unemployment relief, which affect the national interest. The countertendency was to follow the doctrine of states' rights and to give both the burden and the power to state governments. Since these state governments tend to be dominated by the rural members of their legislatures, the big cities fought this trend, feeling that their relationship should be directly with the Federal government.

The fact is* that the growth of the metropolitan city has destroyed the base of the earlier version of federalism. A new equilibrium must be achieved between not just the center and the rim but between a whole new set of nuclear centers in the form of metropolitan cities as well as in Washington, and their rim in the rurally-oriented state capitals. Hence a new alliance is emerging between city needs and Federal aid, to break the old dependence on the states. While Republican administrations are more reluctant than Democratic ones to push this alliance, they have recognized and continued Federal aid to private housing construction, to public housing, to slum clearance and the relocation of slum families, to community facilities like water and sewage. This aid, in turn, has spurred more comprehensive city replanning, and to feed the hope that in a generation or two the older city areas will be recast, the problems of the new runaway city will be grappled with, and both will become fitter places in which to live, work, and play.

I have talked entirely here of the city in peacetime. But after 1945 the atomic shadow darkened a good deal of city planning. The American mass city and the industrial stretch of the greater metropolitan city form an unparalleled target for atomic and radiation destruction. One answer has been that of the dispersal of the industrial concentration in the cities, so that the target would be more scattered. Actually, some kind of dispersal and decentralization has been taking place. Industries have tended to move out of the city itself to be nearer their source of labor supply in the suburbs. Department stores have established suburban branches. Retail stores have grouped themselves into shopping centers in suburban neighborhoods. But what this dispersal has done, desirable as it has been, has been to form a more or less solid line of industrial and popu-

* See Ch. VI, Sec. 5, "Power and Equilibrium."

lation growth. It has burst the boundaries of the mass city, but it has not solved the problem of its survival in atomic war. The vulnerable areas still exist, but they have been stretched thinner. The "city panic" has not been wholly removed from the minds of millions of city and suburban dwellers, and it may be revived.

The firmest answer has been given by those who say that dispersal and burrowing in the ground may save lives but that they will not save civilization; that the city grew out of the expansive energies of America and that if the city does not survive a suicidal war the civilization itself may perish. The destinies of the two are intertwined, and the best way to save both is by the kind of affirmation from which the cities originally drew their strength.*

10. The Suburban Revolution

AN AIR VIEW OF America in the mid-1950s compared with one a decade earlier would show a wholly different picture of people and place. Where once there had been open spaces between the farms, towns, and big cities, one would now find an almost continuous line of settlement and population. This line stretched from Massachusetts to North Carolina, from Chicago to Detroit and Buffalo and then to Pittsburgh, and from San Francisco to the Mexican border. The formerly open spaces were being rapidly filled in; the movement of population was out of the small towns and the cities into the unsettled areas between them; it was not only a decentralizing movement but also an interstitial one. Its product was the suburb and the greater cluster city.

The emergence of the suburb as the characteristic form of American place, supplanting as well as supplementing the city, has been so rapid, with consequences so far-reaching, as to be revolutionary. The drift out of the cities had started in the 1920s, when discussion of the "metropolitan community" began; it was seen then as a city of wards and boroughs with a *hinterland* of small towns to which the rich had been retreating since the late nineteenth century. But at the turn of the century the railroad commuter appeared, shuttling between job and home, and in the 1920s, in the era of the automobile, he was joined by the car commuter. In the Depression years of the 1930s the movement marked time. After World War II it began again at an intense pace, with the building of ranch-house "developments" and apartment courts in the "dormitory" or "bedroom" suburbs. In the 1950s it speeded up still more, with whole new communities growing up where once there had been meadow and

* For a further discussion of city, from the standpoint of building, architecture, and planning, see Ch. XI, Sec. 8, "Building, Design, and the Arts."

scrub brush and potato fields, and with department-store branches and shopping centers breaking the downtown city's marketing monopoly.

The suburbs ceased to be either a hinterland for the city or its dormitories: each suburb became a center of a community life of its own but connected with the city by complex strands. Something had come into American life that was not there before. It was a new kind of relation between people and place—not just an overgrown or runaway city but a living-complex that resulted when the city reached out to form the suburbs and the suburbs reached back to transform the city and at the same time create a hinterland of their own; and all three—city and suburban nuclei and hinterland—became entangled with other forms like them in a sprawling, complex pattern that I call the cluster city.

By using one kind of definition of the suburbanite (one who works in the city, lives where there is more space, and can afford to commute between the two), it was estimated that in 1953 there were thirty million suburbanites in America, and that the great increase (from twenty-one to thirty million) came since 1947. Of these, eleven million lived in the older suburbs within the limits of the metropolitan city, and nineteen million in politically independent newer ones outside. Using another definition that would include the ring of settlement on the fringe of the suburbs, usually more distant from the city ("semi-suburban" or "exurban"), the figure was forty-two million.

By the 1950s suburban living was no longer confined mainly to the Northeast, Great Lakes, and Far Western regions but had come to include the Southeast, Southwest, and Plains regions as well; in every area except parts of the Deep South (it was to be found in Florida) it was the form of American living that was coming into the ascendant. In two decades, between 1934 and 1954, the suburbs grew by 75 per cent while the total population grew by 25 per cent. Between 1940 and 1954 people living in 168 "standard metropolitan" central cities increased by 14 per cent, those in the suburban rings around the cities increased by 35 per cent, and those living in the semi-suburban rural rings around the suburbs increased by 41 per cent. Thus the drift was a double one—from the city (and small towns) to the suburbs, and from the suburb-cities to the sparser settled areas around their rim and fringes. The prospects were that the trend would continue until the suburbs had generated suburbs of their own, and most Americans lived in a continuous semi-urban and semisuburban line of cluster cities.

The meaning of what was happening was that America was resettling itself, wherever it could, looking for open spaces and "grass for the children to walk on," and better schools, and a garage for the car, and a closer-knit community. As the automobile was brought within the reach of most, and TV carried urban culture into every home, the suburbs could afford to stretch further away from the metropolitan center. The "garden city" or "satellite town" which Ebenezer Howard first envisaged in England took a very different form in the American suburb, not so clearly planned or laid out, nor so definitely separated from the central city by open spaces. Nor was this the rationalized metropolis of Le Corbusier. Americans were too much in a hurry to wait for a plan or for rationality, and too bent on profit to waste any open spaces. Even in getting away from the cities they made use of the city principle of maximizing ground rent.

The whole process was a kind of development by sprawl. Young married people preferred moving to where they could bring up children and tinker around the house. If they didn't have enough money to buy a house in the suburbs, they could get a low-down-payment, long-amortization loan under the FHA and later the VA provisions, from private funds but insured by the Federal government. High building costs led them naturally to the real-estate "developments" that bought up cheap land outside the cities, built houses on a mass scale, and sold them on easy terms. The rapid mobility of their jobs in corporate organizations (as in the armed services, the younger men were moved about freely from corporate branch to branch) required them to find ready-made communities where they could strike roots easily and leave them without too much pang, and could quickly resell the houses they had bought. Thus the suburb as an institution moved into the vacuum of the American home place left by the decline of the small town, the unlivability and decay of the city, the sheer statistical pressure of population, and the fluidity of the corporate managers, junior executives, and technicians who came to the suburb to live.

I have spoken of the suburbs as growing by sprawl. Despite all the publicity clatter about "planned communities," they did not (except for a few instances) grow by plan. One must understand here the nature of the real-estate "development" which was the carrier of suburban growth. To "develop" a community meant to buy a tract of open ground, clear it of brush and trees, level its hills and straighten its curves, install utilities, build roads, subdivide the space into building lots, set up a number of basic "model" houses to serve as choices for prospective buyers, apply factory-on-the-site methods of construction, and come away with a good profit. In a few cases (the "Levittowns" on Long Island and in Pennsylvania, of which William J. Levitt was the moving figure, or Drexelbrook near Philadelphia, or Parkmerced near San Francisco, or Park Forest outside Chicago whose mover and shaper was Philip Klutznick) the planning went further. Community recreation and activity centers were built. Land was provided for schools and churches, which the home-

owners had somehow to build and subsidize; and in a few instances a
village government was set in motion.

But mostly the planning never went beyond the real-estate necessities.
The bulldozing of the area to make construction costs easier also resulted in stripping the terrain of much of its beauty and naturalness.
The sinking of hundreds of thousands of cesspools was the despair of
public-health officials. Rarely was provision made for open areas in the
center which could serve as the core of the communities of the future,
such as the Greek and Italian cities and the New England town, but
which most American cities lack. In too many instances the greed to sell
every acre of land for building meant there was nothing left for parks;
the expectation that everything would be park meant that no one made
provision that anything should be park. As suburb spilled over into
suburb, like cars bumper to bumper on the week-end treks, few open
spaces were left between them to give the community a natural setting.
Inside the suburb the spacious shaded avenues that gave their character
to Southern cities were rarely laid out.

As the new incursions of population came in, new problems of zoning
arose which had not been anticipated, and caused political wrangling.
Ironically also those who had fled from the traffic congestion of the city
found new traffic and parking problems springing up like dragon's
teeth in the suburb. The schools could not keep pace with the increased
demand for them, since the suburb rarely had industries to carry the
main tax burden as they did in the city and even the rural school districts. (In Park Forest the development company provided land for the
schools, with subsidies for their operation—but this was unusual.) As a
real-estate development the suburb grew as a residence area, and the
absence of factory smoke and grime was one of its attractions. But in
time the suburban dwellers and planners were to learn that a community must embody a balance between industry and residence, as it must
also have variety and surprise in its outward aspect, and a balance of
age and class groups, of ethnic groups, of innovation and tradition.

Most of these the suburb lacked. It was too new, too raw, too uniform in look, too homogeneous in composition, too hurried in construction. It arose with frantic haste to meet the needs of the new
middle classes and the new era of mass leisure. The fault did not lie
with those who took part in the Great Exodus: they were responding
to the pressures behind them and to their hopes for a way of life for
their children. It lay rather with the leaders and officials who failed
to provide ways of planning and control to regulate the growing suburb.
This suburb recapitulated in a few decades the problems that most
cities had encountered over the centuries. What it chiefly showed was
that the Americans had learned little and forgotten little from their

experience; that the lacks and defects which critics of American life had been at pains to point out had not cut deep into the consciousness of most Americans; and that when they were given a chance at a fresh start, this was how they did it.

The shift to the new suburbs also meant a shift in class composition. The suburbs used to be the residential areas for wealthy businessmen, bankers, and lawyers who wanted the manorial touch. But now the "rich" suburbs, like Bronxville (near New York) and Winnetka (near Chicago) or the Quogue that Fitzgerald celebrated in his *Great Gatsby* (it was set in what he called West Egg, on Long Island), have been outstripped by others. There were the rented or purchased homes in the big "developments," like the Levittowns and the Park Forests, which were filled by professional people and by technicians and junior executives of the big corporations; there were the suburbs of skilled workers, usually mushrooming around aviation plants and other defense industries that had to be built in open territory or near power sources, as in the Buffalo–Niagara Falls area; there were even trailer courts for retired middle-class couples as well as for war workers.

Geographically one could speak of the *inner* suburbs (nestling near the cities), and the *outer* suburbs (at a commuting distance). One would have to add *exurbia* (the "country") which A. C. Spectorsky explored and placed on the American map—the Eastern rural area (including Fairfield County in Connecticut, Bucks County in Pennsylvania, Rockland County in New York) of week-enders, gentlemen farmers, and either the artistic or prosperous who didn't have to go to the city regularly. But the scheme was too neat, and class composition meant more than geographic distance.

Suburban America was mainly middle-class America. It was recognized as such by the builders who laid out the houses at middle-class prices for middle-class incomes and living, and also by the department stores and chain stores which hastened to set up suburban branches. In fact, there are some who discuss the American suburbia largely as a business market which came into being as a prosperous middle-class appendage to the new marketing methods. But the truth was that the new middle class, comprising corporate and government bureaucrats, advertising and sales executives, technicians, professional people, and white-collar workers represented the growing point of the American class system. Anxious to live under better conditions than the crowded apartments in violence-ridden neighborhoods of the city, they sought "warmer" living in communities which would be within striking distance of the cultural services of the metropolis. It gave them the sense of status that was crucial to their self-respect. It enabled them to have the best of both worlds—of the big city and the small town.

Thus the suburban movement was an effort of the new middle classes to find a garment for their living that would express outwardly the changes that had already taken place inwardly in their image of themselves and in their relation to their society. They no longer wished to be identified with the "city masses," nor could they stand the anonymity of urban life where the lonely are terribly lonely and no one knows anybody else who happens to live in the same big apartment house. They were the transients, living in an era of transiency, and therefore they were all the more seized by the panic of temporariness: thus they wanted a home of their own, whose mortgage they could at least in part pay off, with whose lawn and garden they could mix their sweat, and where they could putter in a toolshed or garden and have a garage with a car of their own that could carry them away from it all. This was class in action—that is to say, a class personality assumed in the act of striking new roots for itself.

So the would-be suburbanite picked his plot and his house type and got his homeowners' loan, and made a down payment. He moved his belongings to a row of Cape Cod or "ranch-type" or "split-level" houses. His wife furnished it to look like the layouts in *House Beautiful* and she shopped in supermarkets, highway stores, and shopping centers where she could park and get everything at once. She filled the house with the latest kitchen appliances, and there was a TV set in the living room. There were rows of middle-priced sedans and hard-top convertibles lining the block which were as interchangeable and standardized as the houses, deep-freezes, TV sets, magazines, processed foods, and permanent waves that a community survey would reveal. Husband and wife wore casual clothes which gave them a sense of release from the "rat race" of competitive dressing, while giving them also a leisure-class "country" feeling. They did without domestic help, except for an occasional baby-sitter or cleaning woman; they mowed and manicured their own lawns, cooked their own meals, and with the aid of self-help manuals they did for themselves on a variety of chores where outside expert help was too costly. The husband was in the city most of the day, and an intensive father from the time he came home from work until the children went to bed. It was calculated that in a lifetime, as a commuter, he traveled a half million miles (twenty times around the world) between home and office. But the reason he endured perpetual motion was that he might occupy that secure spot in the center of his tornado— in this case, the middle-class status of suburbanite.

As a way of life it defied all the traditional claptrap about American individualism. It was largely standardized and to a surprising degree collectivized. The intensive study of suburbia included in William H. Whyte, Jr.'s *The Organization Man* depicts brilliantly the emerging way of life today which may become the dominant way of life tomorrow. The suburbanites found new roots for their lives in a new sense of neighborhood which was closer than anything in previous American experience except college dormitories or fraternities or the communal settlements of the early nineteenth century. The neighbors in the same apartment court dropped in on one another with casual intimacy, rarely bothering to knock. Not only did the doors within houses tend to disappear (for economy, and to give a sense of space) but the outside doors ceased to have much function, and picture windows took their place. Newcomers were expected to become "outgoing" and to "join the gang"; introversion was frowned upon, and the society of ex-introverts was like the society of ex-sinners. There was intensive "joining" in club work and community participation, including greatly increased church membership, and there were daily morning get-togethers of the women in *Kaffeeklatsches*. There was little chance for the contemplative life. Privacy became "clandestine," in the sense that those who sought it did so apologetically. "Keeping up with the Joneses" was considered a form of exhibitionism; instead of "conspicuous consumption" the rule became "inconspicuous consumption," so that no one would embarrass anyone else. There were car pools for shuttling children to school and back; there was almost communal use of bicycles, books, and baby toys; there was an enforced intimacy, so that everyone's life was known to everyone, and no one had to face his problems alone. In Whyte's phrase, the suburbanites were "imprisoned in brotherhood."

This kind of living has some elements of the co-operativeness-in-crisis of the American frontier, some elements of Army life, and some of Socialist collectivism. The thinkers who celebrate the mystique of the organic community as against the atomistic individual may shudder a bit when they study the American "package suburb" as the flowering of the community impulse under conditions of American standardization. What made the standardization even bleaker was the uniformity of age, income, and class outlook. In their early stages these suburbs tended to comprise mainly young married couples (there were no bachelors and few chances for unmarried girls), with an average income of between $6,000 and $7,000, with children below ten (the childless couple was an anomaly, as were old people), and with a strikingly similar class outlook that was at once tolerant, mobile, hard-working, ambitious, and hopeful for the future.

But it would be a mistake to call it an entirely one-class society, except in the sense that so much of the new America is middle class. The big suburban "development" was not nearly as selective as the earlier and smaller suburbs had been. It had to appeal to a mass market, and so it accepted Catholics and Jews as well as Protestants (while drawing the line at the Negro), clerical and technical as well as professional groups, blue collar as well as white collar—taking all of them into the same neighborhood. The common denominators were income, age, and reliability. It was a democracy of a kind, on a broader spectrum of inclusion than was true of the "residential" and "restricted" neighborhoods in the cities and the earlier suburbs. Yet its exclusion of Negroes, mainly for fear that they would cheapen real-estate values, showed how limited a democratic dream it still was, and how the same dependence on the market that released it from some of the fetters of prejudice kept it fettered in others.

Suburban society was deeply involved with the mobile elements of the American class system. As a man moved from production line to foreman to shop superintendent or from salesman to division manager to sales manager, he would also move from one type of suburb to another. As the family income went up by stages the family moved from court apartment to ranch house and learned new ways of behavior, new standards of tastes, and met new circles of friends to keep pace with its rise. To some extent even the "lower-class" family could find its suburban niche—that of the plumber or carpenter, for example, which could live in the middle-class neighborhood to which the family income admitted it, even though the occupational level was that of the worker. But these gradations were roughly inside the broad limits of the middle class, and there was little of the sense of class crossing, class transcendence or class betrayal that one found in a less homogeneous society. The extremes of income were in the central city, not in the metropolitan rings.

I don't mean that Suburbia, U.S.A., is a conformist society. Its outer aspects are standardized and its ways of life tend to be uniform; yet this is different from conformism. The social intimacy that prevails in the suburb is partly a quest for roots, partly (as I have said) a flight from the temporariness and the loneliness of American life. To some extent it is also an effort to mitigate the bleakness of spending one's life within the confines of the same corporate "organization" and in pursuit of the same technical or sales proficiency. The chance to be intimate with people of different faiths and backgrounds, to share with them the experience of building a new community, and to take part in group action is an appealing one to those who have absorbed the cultural ideals and stereotypes of America. It would not be easy to impose conformity from without upon the suburbanites: but the conformity that comes from mutual accessibility and a yearning for group "belongingness" needs no outside pressures because the impulses from within are leveling ones. There were some observers who feared that this was the kind of society which the "organization man" would ultimately create in the image of his corporate ideal—a one-neighborhood, one-gang, one-class, one-perspective society.

There was substance to the fears. When Erich Fromm, among other writers, singled out the herd aspect of suburbia for attack he was adding a new facet to his escape-from-freedom thesis. But when, in his *Sane Society*, he added a vision of the way out which was strikingly similar to the Fourierist communities of the nineteenth century, he ignored the fact that it is precisely in the suburb where you would find a kind of new Fourierism. The defect of individualism is isolation, the defect of community living is standardization and conformism.

Meanwhile few of the suburbanites had such fears or reflections. Instead they had a stir of excitement in them because they had a widening of horizons and an accession of experience. What G. M. Trevelyan said of the English middle class in the eighteenth century might apply equally to this segment of the new American middle class in the mid-1950s: "Meanwhile the hour was theirs and it was golden."

But the golden hour was streaked with dross and was bound in time to pass. A one-class community like the new suburb was a community without a labor supply, and hence without an industrial base. The balanced community is not to be achieved without paying a price. The price is that of refusing to withdraw from the diversity and bustle of American life, but of embodying some of its noise and grime along with its energies. The parents in most American suburbs were certain they wanted only "the best" for their children in the way of schools, yet they were usually unwilling to subsidize that "best" by including taxable industries in their communities—even on the assumption that they could attract them if they tried. Often they rezoned the suburbs in order to keep out "undesirable" income groups and then wondered why their schools, thus cut off from a cross segment of an American life, proved to be aseptic and sterile. In the long run the suburb would have to turn by an inevitable tropism toward the centers of industrial life and find links with those centers.

There was also the question of the relation between the home and the job. The ideal of town planners was that a man would be able to walk to work and walk home after work. But when the reality of the suburb came, the journey to work was dependent on the automobile and became in most cases a traffic struggle every morning and evening. The newer trend involved a migration of a good deal of the commercial and industrial activities out of the central city into the suburban and metropolitan areas, so that large numbers of suburban dwellers ceased to be Central City commuters but found their jobs on the rim, closer to home. If these trends continued there was a good chance that the industrial and residential zones would be intermingled in the complex pattern, as was already true of the northern New Jersey area in the mid-1950s.

This meant a loose, sprawling cluster city, spreading out across the landscape, still depending on the automobile, but with job-home patterns now running both ways instead of only one. Unexpectedly it came closer to Frank Lloyd Wright's Broadacre City than to the comfortable and segregated "new towns" about which the English and American planners had dreamed. When I said earlier that the trend toward suburban America would continue I did not mean that the suburbs, growing in numbers and importance, would be self-contained, insulated entities. The phase of dispersal from the city was bound to be transformed into a phase of reintegration of the city and suburb in some pattern.

To take New York as an instance, it was clear that the five boroughs were reaching out across state barriers and forming—along with the suburbs in a larger industrial-residential complex—a vast cluster city. Its extent could scarcely be calculated because its boundaries spread out in an octopus pattern. In the 1950s it had reached fifteen million people, perhaps more; by 1975 it would have passed twenty million people— larger than many sovereign countries. The migration to the suburbs changed the character of the central city too, leaving it an "underdeveloped area" which needed rebuilding and renewal, and leaving it also an area of steep class contrasts, with a diminishing middle class to mediate the abrupt differences between the rich town-house families and the low-income groups, often Negro and polyglot.

But neither the city nor the suburbs could survive by themselves: I have described what the new suburban way of life meant and the functions it filled; the city continued to serve its own constellation of functions, in industry and finance, in fashions, in recreation and the arts, in intellectual stir. Together the city-suburb complex would have to discover some new form of a cluster community government, which would require creativeness if it was to hurdle all the obstacles of law, habit, and convention. Yet whatever happened to the cluster community as a whole, the suburb was destined to be a permanent part of it, not as a hinterland to the city but as an equal among equals.

All this was being accomplished by Americans at considerable social and aesthetic costs. The cluster city, filling in the interstices that had once existed between cities, was consuming open space voraciously. There was often the kind of ugliness in the landscape that made a British writer, watching the same thing happening on his own countryside, call it a "subtopia." Yet here as elsewhere the Americans were accomplishing a transformation in their way of living which, despite its improvised quality, was an exciting response to their new needs and conditions of life. They were doing it in their own way. They did not follow the British lead of the "new towns" approach, although a number of the cities that were being planned for government and industrial workers around the centers of atomic experiment and power were "new towns." Nor did they follow the earlier American architectural dream of a landscape dotted with "Greenbelts." To the extent that a balanced community was emerging—which was doubtful—it represented a balance not within the central city nor within the new suburb, but between the larger frame of the cluster city.

It looked as if Americans were achieving this only through a chance combination of pressures and changes. If there was an internal logic in the improvisation it was the logic to be found in the rest of the American pattern.*

11. *Regions: the Fusion of People and Place*

THE IMPULSE TOWARD forming living units that cut across governmental boundary lines—of which the trans-urban city is an instance—runs throughout American history. Despite the need for speaking of an "America" and thus making it seem unitary, it is clearly not a single and homogeneous entity. America has not one signature but many. It is divided formally into forty-eight states, and while their boundaries don't bound anything in particular, most of the states have over the years developed their local prides, prejudices, and personalities. Less artificial are the aggregates of states called "sections," each of which Turner described as being fashioned in "the faint image of a European nation." Sections, like states, are the counters on the political chessboard. A realistic party leader must reckon with sectional appeals in campaigns, sectional pressures inside his party, sectional blocs in Congress.

But the more meaningful divisions are the fusions of people **and** place, of environment, stock, economics, dialect, history, consciousness, and ways of life, which are called "regions" and "subregions." The section may be the region in its political aspect, but it has divisive overtones, while the region has cohesive ones. The region may be the unplanned outgrowth of a historic process; its unity may, as in the case of the river-valley developments, be reinforced by engineering and regional planning. But always it operates as a compassable fragment of an otherwise unwieldy American whole. For the continental expanse of America is too big to crowd into the ambit of the individual life,

* For further discussion of the impact of the suburban revolution, see Ch. VI on American politics and Ch. VIII on the American family and life cycle.

while the town or city may be too particular to satisfy the reaching for meaning. The region is somewhere "between the village and the continent." What it does—and the subregion too—is to act as a counterforce against both the standardizing and atomizing forces of American life.

By its nature the outlines of the region are elusive. The most frequent usage (no two lists will agree) is to speak of New England, the Middle-Atlantic region, the Upper South, the Deep South, the Southwest, the Midwest, the Great Lakes region, the Rocky Mountain region, the Far West, and the Pacific Northwest. These are at once geographic, economic, and cultural units. There are also agricultural groupings which cut across them: the type-farming regions such as the Cotton Belt, the Wheat Belt, the Range Livestock area, the Dairy area, the Western Specialty Crop area.

The larger regional units are in turn broken up into subregions. One type is built around the river valley or river basin as a nucleus —the Tennessee, Missouri, Arkansas, Mississippi, Columbia, Ohio, Connecticut, Shenandoah, Wabash, Santa Fe, Red, Colorado, Sacramento, Salinas. Since a number of these are the sites of flood-control and hydroelectric dams, they are sometimes called "technical regions." One could make a somewhat similar regional map for the mountain areas, including not only the Rockies and the Appalachians but also the White Mountains, the Green Mountains, the Berkshires, the Blue Ridge, the Ozarks. The titles of the volumes in the "American Folkways" series suggest the type of subregion involved: "Lakes Country," "Blue Ridge Country," "North Star Country," "Palmetto Country," "Deep Delta Country," "Ozark Country," "Mormon Country," "Short Grass Country," "Snowshoe Country," "Golden Gate Country," "Desert Country," "Piñon Country," and "Panhandle Country." The picturesque calendar of such subregions could stretch almost endlessly. For a region is a cultural unit within a frame; in some areas the frame may be mountains or river basin or lakes, delta or bayou or desert; in others it may be the type of crop grown there; in still others the decisive element may be the enforced isolation or the uniformity of stock and tradition. The components may vary, but to form a region or subregion there must be a roughly homogeneous physical environment and a roughly homogeneous economic unity which together serve as a frame for community living and a common history and consciousness.

These regional cultures are the carriers of American diversity. If the stock of America is made up of a myriad of peoples, the regions of America form a myriad of environments. This pluralism is one of the facts that gives Americans their impulse to cohesion, in pulling together the diverse strands of their universe.

Often this leads to antagonisms which must be accepted as part of the balance-sheet of regionalism. There is usually an urban-agrarian hostility, which may pit downstate Illinois against Chicago, or upstate New York against New York City. One can almost always premise a struggle of hinterland against metropolis. Sometimes the same region or even state may include several subregions whose way of thinking is different because their ethnic strains and traditional ways of living are different. The Salinas Valley area of California is sharply different from the Southern California region. The political history of Louisiana would not be what it is without the hostility between the English-Protestant culture of the hills and the French culture of the bayous. The red-soil, red-neck, red-gallus hill region of the Georgia crackers is a different South from that of industrialized Atlanta.

American thinkers of the 1930s and 1940s were wary of regional loyalties that cut across class lines, and they tended to deny reality to the "regional mind," whether of the South or Middle West, New England or the Pacific Coast. Influenced by the class emphasis in Veblen and Beard, they saw regional and subregional cultures as part of the backwash of the stream of history, a residue of pre-industrial cultural attitudes.

The result was to leave regionalism largely to the traditionalists, especially among the Southern writers. The Southern Agrarians of the 1920s sought to turn it into a conservative economic and political program and a literary principle and used it as a weapon against the pragmatic humanitarianism of the North. Another school of Southern regionalism, centering at the University of North Carolina, was more academic and liberal. It is interesting that regionalism, both as an intellectual system and as a literary movement, flourished best in the South, with an almost metaphysical intensity of passion. No doubt it was because the great issues of slavery, the Civil War, and Reconstruction drove a wedge between the South and the rest of the nation. These, along with the caste system, ruralism, evangelicism, and the low standard of living, forced Southern writers to re-evaluate their identity and to seek the connection between their art and thought and the nature of the South as a culture.

If we ask what the nature of American regionalism is, the clues to the answer must come from an examination of each of the regions.

There is no single New England mind. How should there be, since there are obvious differences between the up-north Maine Yankee, whether potato farmer or shipyard worker or fisherman, and the industrial workers of the Housatonic and Connecticut valleys; between the old aristocracy of Boston's State Street and Harvard Yard and the political leaders of the newer Irish immigration; between the Vermont and New Hampshire Yankee farmers and the owners of big mansions and big wealth in Newport or Greenwich; even between the French-Catholic immigration in the mill towns of New Hampshire and Vermont and the Irish-Catholic and Italian-Catholic immigration in Massachusetts, Connecticut, and Rhode Island? But whatever new materials have been poured into the old mold, the mold itself has not broken. There are some who doubt the survival of the Yankee in the land of his origin. Yet if New England has a regional culture style I should still call it that of the Yankee—spare, austere, shrewd, Calvinist, individualist, with a ramrod down his back, tenacious of his dissents as he is confident in his affirmations.

At its best this tradition has produced a great line of American writers and thinkers. Its early divines, including the greatest of them, Jonathan Edwards, had a fanaticism about them, but it was a complex and self-torturing one and it imposed even greater rigors on oneself than it demanded of others. The New England temperament is a little like the climate, ranging from temperate to severe but always with the tang of sharpness in it; and a little also like the soil, where a farmer can make a living if he works hard—but even in the early days he did not have the richness of the Midwest earth at his command.

Although the "Last Puritan" presumably has vanished, and George Apley only now and then is seen at the dining and supper clubs of Beacon Hill and Louisburg Square, there is still a controlled strength in the New England mind at its best, coming out of its Puritan heritage and nourished by soil, climate, and history. From the intense commitment of Calvinism came the movements of Transcendentalism and abolitionism, the radical-equalitarian rebellions of Shays and Dorr, the anarchist doctrine of Josiah Tucker. There is a continuing craggy skepticism in New England which counterbalances the Utopians and Messianists. From Thoreau to Calvin Coolidge, its philosophy has been astringent and its humor closer to Britain than to the folk tales of the Southern mountains or the tall yarns of the lumber camps of the Northwest. Emerson could write *English Traits* because there was a good deal of Old England that survived in New England, including a species of Stonehenge that may still be found in the rocky Maine setting or with the tight-lipped Vermont farmer or the State Street banker.

If Justice Holmes was a "Yankee strayed from Olympus," his combination of intellectual aloofness with the shrewdness of the common experience is central to the New England outlook. One finds it in Lowell's *Biglow Papers*, in the Yankee shipbuilders who—however exotic the seas they sailed—never lost their sense of the New England shore, in the spare adjectiveless poetry of Robert Frost. One finds it in the Adamses, who were men of property and substance at the same time that they explored statesmanship, abolitionism, diplomacy, medieval cathedrals, the history of trade routes, and the laws of energy in human history. The great New England families—Adams, Lowell, Peabody, Holmes—were as close as America ever came to an intellectual aristocracy. They kept reaffirming their right to their lineage by an energy that sought productive outlets.

Yet the specific political contributions of New England came in the realm not of oligarchy but of democracy—that of the congregation and the town meeting. Or better, it was a peculiar amalgam of oligarchy and democracy. Nowhere else do you get the Calvinist individualism on which the mercantile, textile, and financial fortunes were built, along with the radicalism that flourished in the atmosphere of dissent. It is the tradition of the dissenters that is New England's greatest tradition. "Resistance to something," Henry Adams wrote, "was the law of New England's nature. The boy looked out on the world with the instinct of resistance; for . . . generations his predecessors had viewed the world as chiefly a thing to be reformed, filled with evil forces to be abolished. . . . The New Englander, whether boy or man, in a long struggle with a stingy or hostile universe, had learned also to love the pleasure of hating; his joys were few." This self-portrait suggests the dream New England had of itself—a dream that flaunts its austerity as if it were chosen as the elect of a spare and stony universe by contrast with the materialist indulgence elsewhere. The idea of a hardy elect has at times led to a rock-ribbed Republicanism, at others to radicalism, but it is disdainful of an easy conformism.

Latterly New England found its textile industries moving South or West, its wharves idle, its former financial supremacy stripped away. Its economists, asking what had happened to the famed "Yankee ingenuity," were spurred to make regional surveys looking toward an economic Renaissance. Partly New England industry, with a lagging technology, had to pay the "penalty of taking the lead"; partly it suffered because of its stubborn resistance to Federal hydroelectric projects. The old theocracy of the Puritan divines was overcome, but a new Catholic population with a cohesive attachment to its Church made a bid for power. The sense of bewilderment which Henry Adams had expressed at the confident industrialism that was breaking up his inherited world was replaced by an almost resigned acceptance of the New Order of society.

Yet with the passing of the traditional New England mind, American thought and expression lost a source of brooding intensity. The novels of Hawthorne expressed Americans in tragic life more probingly than any others, and the somewhat prosaic satire of a Marquand did not replace them. Nor was the Day-of-Doom self-analysis of a Cotton Mather or a Jonathan Edwards adequately replaced by the statistical survey of the mind of "Yankee City." The burden of the dark strain of American literature passed to the writers of the Deep South who used it to express a different agony of conscience from that of New England —less a sense of original sin and inevitable doom than the stain of guiit.

Some of New England's traits came in for good-natured caricature, like the hub-of-the-universe illusions gathered in Cleveland Amory's *Proper Bostonians*. When one Beacon Hill lady was chided for her failure to travel she asked, "Why should I travel when I'm already there?" Another, when asked where the ladies of Boston got their hats, said simply, "Our hats? Why, we *have* our hats." The New England scientist, Agassiz, reported that "New England is the oldest spot on the earth's surface." Many Americans of other regions resented the New England pride of past—the bland assumption that Boston was "Athens, with culture," and that New England had achieved a monopoly of that commodity. In the amiable ribbing of the Brahmins and Beacon Street and the "institution men" with their eccentric habits and unruffled ways, it is good to have Perry Miller remind us that historical New England was filled with passions and conflicts, and that the stable elite society did not tell the whole story. New Englanders risked their lives for Abolitionism and in strike riots, they spread themselves all over America in the "Yankee Exodus," they dared to fight the land-grabbers and monopolists, they became the conscience of every community they settled. Their willingness to wear themselves to the bone for the glory of God and 10 per cent on their investment gives point to Van Wyck Brooks's remark that the New Englander was an amalgam of the Puritan and the freebooter. The freebooter was indeed strong in him, yet in the process he built much and felt intensely, and no other region can so securely claim to have been the matrix of the American mind.

The New England mind and social structure were in part transplanted to the Midwest. But in place of the stony, niggardly New England soil there were rich prairies, and in place of the New England village there were far-flung homesteads. As New England's Puritanism crossed the continent it became evangelistic and Fundamentalist, and the mentality of Calvinism gave way to the mentality of what Mencken joyously called the "Bible Belt." As for political attitudes, the difference between the Adams family of Massachusetts and the Taft family of Ohio is an index of the difference between New England and Midwest conservatism. The first had the flair of aristocracy in it and a devotion to dissent even

while it affirmed orthodoxy. But Midwest conservatism—that of Mc-
Kinley and Hanna, of Harding and the Tafts—was that of the small-
town and business middle class, with a lack of imaginativeness a little
suggestive of the flatness and bareness of the landscape. The Midwest radicalism became largely agrarian and Populist—the radicalism of farmers in
protest against absentee wealth, and of ethnic minorities like the
Scandinavians and Germans against the home-grown groups. Actually
there have been two Midwests: the area of Ohio, Indiana, Illinois, and
Michigan which in the past proved the stronghold of conservatism,
while that of Missouri, Minnesota, and Wisconsin was the area of an
agrarian radicalism. Ohio played the role of "mother of Presidents"
for the Republicans, while the Populist states were the cradle of reformist stirrings. In the mid-1950s Minnesota and Michigan alone continued the radical tradition of the past.

The political picture that was true in the days of Hanna and Bryan,
of Altgeld and the La Follettes, is no longer true at mid-century. The intensity of Midwest radicalism has dimmed, and Midwest isolationism—
which has been ethnic as well as geographical, but the single political
trait most readily associated with the region—was buried at Pearl
Harbor, although its ghost still stubbornly and spasmodically walks
the battlements of foreign policy. The Midwest which gave birth to the
Republican party is still usually Republican by a margin but never
by a wholly safe one. Giant industry, the mass city and the shift of balance to ethnic groups geared to industrial pursuits, like Negroes, Poles,
Czechs, and Irish, have destroyed the political picture of a predominantly agrarian region. The comment that might have been made
in the 1920s and 1930s—that the industrialism of the Midwest was more
primitive in its social outlook than that of the East—would not hold in
the mid-1950s: the Midwest pattern of heavy industry, consumer-goods
industry, processing, distribution, and finance gave scope to every
business energy, so that whatever sense of economic provincialism the
Midwest had cherished no longer retained a valid base. It was true
that political primitives like Senator Joseph McCarthy still cropped
up in the Midwest, as they did in the South, spurred by a similar deep
animosity toward the East. But, at least in McCarthy's case, they proved
a national rather than a regional phenomenon.

The danger of persisting regional labels, as I have suggested, is best
shown in the phrase "Midwest isolationism." The fear and dislike of
anything "foreign" and "radical" was to be found in the South as well
as the Midwest; but while in the South it fused ruralism and the caste
system with the tradition of the martial virtues, in the Midwest it fed
a distrust of the dimly known, turbulent world beyond American shores
and expressed itself in the impulse to have no truck with that world.

The sturdy symbol of that "isolationism" was Senator Robert A. Taft; yet before his death he had come to accept much of the Eisenhower foreign policy, as indeed he had absorbed a considerable measure of public intervention in housing and health. There had also been a more radical Midwest isolationist strain than Taft's—the Jeffersonian "continentalism" of Charles A. Beard, which held that America could work out its democratic destiny on a continental scale if it were not beset by foreign troubles and could deal with its problems in peace. Both these strains of thinking met and crossed in the interior of America. Both were made archaic by atomic weapons and the intercontinental missile.

Graham Hutton, an Englishman who in his *Midwest at Noon* laid bare the Midwest mind with more success than most other foreign visitors, thought it could be partly explained in terms of a climate of radical intensities, one which has almost no spring or fall but follows a stretch of summer heat with a stretch of winter cold. I have cited earlier Veblen's effort to explain it through the linkage between the prehensile tenacity of the mercantile and business mind with the social climate of the small town. The Lynds, in their study of Muncie, Indiana (*Middletown*), and Warner in his study of Morris, Illinois (*Democracy in Jonesville*), stressed in different ways the dominance of middle-class values in the communities they surveyed. Their premise was that while the whole of American culture is middle class, the Midwest reveals the American social structure and mentality more sharply than the other regions. It has been difficult for anyone—whether novelist, poet, traveler, or sociologist—to write about the Midwest without assuming that any light cast upon it would somehow light up the whole of the American character. It has long held a special niche in the American consciousness as being more crucially "American" than the rest of the country.

This has been the image that Midwesterners have held about themselves. They have seen the East as the seat of a stodgy plutocracy, the South as caught in the stagnant pool of a past grandeur, the Far West as a still unformed fledgling region. But they have seen their own region as at once solid and hustling, carrying the best of both the conservative and progressive worlds. This idyllic feeling which Midwesterners themselves and outside observers have had about the region is a perilous one, since the idealization is bound to wear off and give way to disillusionment. A strain of this double feeling runs through much of the Midwestern literature. As the gap between the middle-class myth and the realities of middle-class experience became clearer, the disillusioned strain in the literature grew stronger. Dreiser expressed his rebellion against the sexual Puritanism of the Midwest, daring to draw Nietzschean figures against the flatness of the conventional folk. Sherwood

Anderson's *Winesburg, Ohio* portrays the rancorous inner struggles of the spirit which portended that the Midwest dream was near its end. The *Spoon River* of Edgar Lee Masters depicted the descendants of the pioneers as having betrayed their spirit, "with so much of the old strength gone,/And the old faith gone,/And the old mastery of life gone,/And the old courage gone."

But Masters and his fellows were too quick to write the epitaph of the region. The shrewd constructiveness that built new industrial empires did not end with Henry Ford and could still be found in steel and rubber, machine tools, aviation, and electronics. The inventive genius of the Wright Brothers did not wholly disappear. The architectural daring of Louis Sullivan and Frank Lloyd Wright, which transformed the sky line and landscape of America, found successors among the architects of Chicago and Detroit. The folk quality that produced the "yarns" and tall tales carried over in Sandburg. In politics, a Missourian called Harry Truman illustrated again the Jacksonian premise that an uncommon common man can stretch his qualities to meet the demands of great political office; a Kansas soldier called Dwight Eisenhower tried fitfully to restore some of the fading energies of Republican leadership; and two lawyers called Wendell Willkie and Adlai Stevenson, one from Indiana and one from Illinois, both them political failures, gave a new pungency to the American political tradition.

It is better to approach the Midwest without either idealizing it as the "heart of America" or overreacting to it as a Chamber of Horrors of American middle-class Babbittry. The truth is that the Midwest has been the crossroads of American experience in more than a geographic sense and has therefore absorbed both the strengths and weaknesses of that experience. There are some who feel that it never was a region in a true sense and is not one now: that it has no geographic, economic, ethnic, or cultural unity. Certainly it is today less a region than, let us say, the Deep South or the Southwest, the Far West, or even New England. Its qualities have been fused and absorbed with the generalized qualities of America as a whole.

Actually the Midwest went through a series of phases in its relation to the rest of the country. There was a phase when it was the frontier, and a wild one too; then there was a phase when it was the most quickly growing segment of American industrial and city life; but in the mid-1950s it was no longer either frontier or a laboratory of overnight growth. In fact, its very name as a region—the Midwest—no longer suited it, since to the real Westerners it seems part of the East.

It had become the American Midlands or Mid-country. It was Middle America. As such it was still a geographic and cultural crossroads, but the institutional forces that swept through it were new ones. The historian will underscore the fact that the shaping of the Midwest did much to shape the whole of America--in the nature of its small town and its city alike, in its political attitudes, in its friendliness toward people and its hostility to new ideas, in its rapid class mobility. The shaping role of the Midwestern frontier is well known. Almost equally well known is the decisive part that the Midwest played in the Civil War, which may even be viewed as a struggle between North and South to control the future development of the Midwestern area. The speed with which industrial profits were plowed back into industry by Midwestern businessmen gave the whole of American industrial growth much of its stamp of feverishness.

But the outlines of the America which was emerging in the mid-1950s were also largely identifiable with the outlines of the newly emerging Middle America. There was the renewed cult of the businessman, who had as warm a place in President Eisenhower's heart as in President Grant's. There was the same profusion of wealth and gadgetry and the same confusion about life purposes. If you looked at the most marked traits in Middle America today—the drift toward conformism, the sense of loneliness, the emphasis on middle-class habits of living and thought, new patterns of suburban living, the informal neighborliness of people, the intolerance of strange-sounding ideas, the chaos of moral standards, the influx of educational and leisure opportunities, the uses of popular culture—you would also see the most marked traits of the whole of American culture. Thus if New England was the matrix of the elite culture of America, the Midwest was the crossroads of its popular culture.

Unlike New England it never had a stable social elite, nor did it have one at mid-century. Its folk hero was the businessman, but the circulation of this elite was too rapid ever to give it stability as a shaping group. Its prime characteristic, like that of America as a whole, is that it has been always in flux, a more or less faithful barometer of the cultural climate surrounding it. Other Americans have both idealized it and condescended to it, but it has gone ahead at its own pace and toward its own goals. It has been too much in a hurry to care much about beauty, it has lacked grace, it has been a prey to some of the worst intolerances in American life, and it is today the locus of the "organization man." But for better or worse it carries with it a good deal of the meaning and future of America. If Middle America is unattractive and undigestible to anyone experiencing or studying it, then he had better conclude that this is true of America as a whole.

What is usually called the South is in reality three subregional cultures—the Deep South, the Upper South (a border strip of states), and

the Southwest. The Deep South is the region where the one-crop system
has lingered, where agriculture is still important, and where the Negroes
either outnumber the whites (in the Black Belt counties) or are still
numerous enough to sustain the Great Fear. Roughly this area includes
Georgia, Alabama, Mississippi, South Carolina, Louisiana, and Florida,
while the Virginias, North Carolina, Kentucky, and Tennessee are in
the border strip of the Upper South, and Texas, Oklahoma, and
Arkansas may be seen as part of another border strip adjoining the
Southwest. For most Americans all three areas form part of a going
regional unity they call "the South."

Most of the characteristic traits of the Southern mind are a heritage
from the past. The old aristocracy dreamed of the South as an autonomous nation—a Greek republic rising proudly from the cotton
fields and savannas, built firmly on the economic base of the plantation
system and the social base of slavery. The imaginative flame of this
dream burned intensely in the political theory of Calhoun and Fitzhugh, and their followers saw the South as a separate culture, conscious of its destiny. But the Civil War and the Reconstruction destroyed the old aristocracy and undercut the plantation system. The
South paid a terrible price for the war, in a whole young generation
that was killed off, in economic ruin, in the memory of armed occupation and corruption, in hatred.

The "new South" that Henry Grady evoked in the 1880s, and which
has been three quarters of a century in coming, is still turned toward
the past, with a nostalgia for its lost glamour and glory, a hatred of the
Northern absentee owners whom it identifies with the conquering
enemy, and a sense of guilt about slavery which is interwoven with a
fear of the encircling Negro population. The South is the only region
in America tied together not by its common consciousness of present
growth and future potentials but by its past, not by what it can achieve
or build but by what it cherishes and fears. Its sense of destiny has been
carried over but has become mainly a tenacious clutching of past
enmities and ideals.

I do not mean to imply that there is a single Southern mentality or
a one-class system in the South. One may validly ask, when the South
is discussed, "Whose South?" Is it the South of the Negro field hand or
share tenant, or the South of the white textile-mill worker, or the
South of the cotton farmer, or the South of the new sales and distributive middle class, or the South of the Coca-Cola or insurance-
company executive, or the South of the universities at Chapel Hill,
Charlottesville, Memphis, Austin, Norman, and Fayetteville, or the
South of pastors or labor organizers or newspapermen who take daily
risks in challenging the prevailing prejudices around them? This is only

to say the South is changing so rapidly that it is almost as fragmented in its attitudes and its classes as other regions are, and that a phrase like "the South" necessarily conceals far more complexity than the unity it premises.

The class cleavage is not, however, wholly recent. There was a cleavage in the Old South between the planter-aristocrats and the democratic farmers: the former lived in the world of Sir Walter Scott, Lord Byron, and Carlyle, imitating the ways of life and thought of the British rural gentry, and were often aristocrats of only one generation; while the latter were rough and boisterous and Jacksonian. The Civil War defeat changed the picture by forcing the classes into a more cohesive mold. But as the result of Reconstruction a new class emerged —that of the educated and well-to-do "Redeemers" like Gordon, Grady, and Watterson, who aimed at moderation and adopted the cunning of the fox in place of the suicidal courage of the lion. They worked closely with Northern capitalists, and C. Vann Woodward has documented the secret deals they made with the Republicans, one of which led to the election of President Hayes as the price for a *laissez-faire* solution of the Reconstruction problem. When the whites of the lower economic groups rebelled against their power, the rebellion took the form of Southern Populism, and its leaders were men like Tom Watson and Ben Tillman.

There was a continuity between the Jacksonian Democrats of the prewar South and the Populists of Watson's day, but by an ironic twist of history the political and economic militancy of the Populists turned into the most illiberal racism. The later figure of Huey Long partook of some of the same mixture of radicalism and totalitarianism, although he was the least racist of the Southern demagogues. Both Watson and Long remain in the Southern memory as half-mythical figures around whom legendry clusters. Their Populism was mainly negative, consisting of an antagonism to the business and finance of the North. Their radicalism sprang out of resentment, and it was not too hard for events to turn it (in Watson's case) into racist demagoguery and (in Long's case) into a cynical Fascist demagoguery. Watson used a behind-the-scenes power to make and break governors of Georgia for a decade; Long held absolute power over his Louisiana empire. The careers of both, and of their successors, are part of the penalty the South has had to pay for the bitter memories of its defeat. The role once played by the Jacksonian Democrats of the South has now been taken over not by the Populists but by the Southern liberal Democrats—in the newspapers, the universities, the courts, the legislatures, and local governments, the embattled movements for a humanist approach to race and a modernist approach to economics.

Social changes are coming fast to the region which used to be called "Dixie," with connotations of Arcadian quaintness and charm. A common folk saying had it that "cotton is going West, cattle are coming East, Negroes are going North, Yankees are coming South, money is coming in." In twenty years, between 1930 and 1950, the South's population employed in agriculture went down from 5.5 million to 3.2 million. Shaken by the Depression, the New Deal, and World War II, by mechanized agriculture and the migration of Negroes, the South changed so drastically that in the mid-1950s a liberal Southerner could write an "Epitaph on Dixie."

The old agrarian South is no longer agrarian but has become substantially industrialized. Offering power sites and cheaper labor, Southern cities have bid for factories moving from the North. A new middle class has risen which has lost much of its nostalgia for the faded glories of the old aristocracy. The type-figure of the South is no longer the plantation farmer or the courthouse politician but the member of the local chamber of commerce. In the 1950 figures the South (counting Texas) had seven metropolitan cities of over a half million people—Houston, New Orleans, Atlanta, Dallas, Louisville, Birmingham, and San Antonio, with Miami and Memphis crowding them closely. Even suburban life—that expression of the modern American condition—has invaded the South. With the new middle class has come a breakup in the one-party system of the once "Solid South." The migration of industry, especially textile mills, also brought with it efforts to unionize the workers. To the extent that these efforts succeed, they change the consciousness of the "poor whites" and make them less amenable as dupes of racist demagoguery.

A movement for civil rights under Federal authority cut across the states'-rights complex which had sustained the Southern sense of autonomy, and Supreme Court decisions of a far-reaching character gave young Southern Negroes at least a fighting chance at normal education, stripped of the hypocrisy of the "separate but equal" doctrine. The long tenure of the Democrats in national power from 1932 to 1952 gave a number of Southern Senators and Congressmen experience at the helm of national affairs. In the Supreme Court decisions of Justice Hugo L. Black something new emerged from the South—a strain of radical democracy with its source in the Southern Populist tradition, crossed with New Deal conceptions, wholly dissociated from racist bigotry. Coming out of the red clay of Alabama, it had about it a hard, sunbaked quality which gave it a regional uniqueness. The era of Virginian political creativeness (Virginia had produced Jefferson, Madison, Monroe, John Taylor, and Edmund Randolph) was over, and the locus of Southern political ferment shifted to industrialized border states like Kentucky and Tennessee and to Georgia and Alabama in the Deep South.

It was in the Deep South that, for weal or woe, one of the planetary battles of the American experience was being fought out. There was an intransigent quality about this struggle, reminiscent of the "old-time religion" with which Southern culture is saturated (Calvinism was the only import from New England which the South welcomed in the period just before the Civil War). The South has an unmistakable culture style of its own which shows itself even more clearly in its periods of stress than in its moments of easy grace. Watch a jury at a Southern trial, or loiterers on the steps of a courthouse, or young people at a Southern college dance, or a crowd at a small-town Southern political meeting, or sheriffs in action at a Southern plant where a strike is taking place, or a marketing center on a Saturday night, and the traits of the Southern culture style come through. Power takes a more naked form in the South than in any other region; political passions are more primitive; all the colors are primary colors. The White Citizens' Councils that arose in the Deep South to meet the challenge of desegregated schools distilled the potential violence of the tradition that reached back beyond the early days of the Klan. Equally, the liberalism of the South was a home-grown regional liberalism, deeply steeped in religious consciousness and imbued with a sense of mission. It took more courage in the mid-1950s to be a genuine liberal in the South than in any other part of America. And it was harder to maintain a middle ground there than anywhere else.

The new South, emerging under the driving force of rapid social change, had to pay the price for the swiftness of the change. Under the double impact of industrial transformation and Negro militancy, the single-mindedness of the South was crumbling, and despite the flurry of strong feeling during the school desegregation fight it was unlikely ever again to achieve the certitude about its cause that it had in the Civil War and in Reconstruction. As it moved away from its economic colonialism and its single-party system, it had to confront responsibilities and tasks that could not be resolved by the old defensive slogans.

Some signs of maturity were not lacking. Floyd Hunter's study of "decision-making" and the local power structure in "Regional City" showed a cross section of community living that mirrored the power struggles in the country as a whole, along with the specifically Southern ones. Even the class structure of the South, which had traditionally been far more rigid than in any other region, showed signs of loosening. The five-class layers—Negroes, poor whites, middle class, residues of the old aristocracy (sometimes still powerful, more often considerably frayed), and the old aristocratic class—were more clearly stratified than in the class system elsewhere in America, but they were unmistakably in flux. There were Negroes moving into the middle class, there were poor whites in the trade-union movement, members of the old aristocracy were having to become absorbed in the middle class under threat of sinking down further, and the movement into the high-income groups was bewilderingly rapid. The rise in the general income level in the South was faster in the quarter century from 1930 to 1955 than anywhere else in the nation.

Out of this ferment came a burst of creativeness in Southern writing that placed it with the best American writing of our time. In fact, the "Southern renaissance" parallels the Midwestern literary movement of the early twentieth century and the Renaissance of the New England "Golden Day." From Ellen Glasgow through Thomas Wolfe to William Faulkner and Eudora Welty, in Robert Penn Warren and in Tennessee Williams, Southern writers reflected the deep internal stirrings produced by regional conflict and change. Something of the same sort happened in the Midwest when Dreiser, Sherwood Anderson, and Sinclair Lewis expressed the heightened awareness that came from watching their world being transformed from an agrarian and small-town world into a city world of industrialism and of revolution in moral standards. In the case of Southern writers, one feels that while they are being pushed reluctantly into the future they are forced into a similar heightened awareness of their regional past, and of the moral and psychological transformation being wrought around them. To push the parallel further, New England's literary renaissance also took place during the period when the coming of industrialism compelled New England's writers and thinkers to re-evaluate their Calvinist tradition and the nature of the human personality that was being threatened by the changes.

It is not unusual for a literary and artistic flowering to come just when the outlines of the culture are changing radically and when something that seemed eternally stable is disappearing forever. It is this pang of loss which has jolted Southern writers into an intense awareness of the Southern place and of the time dimension, so that it is not unusual for them to write on several time levels, shuttling from one to another. The tragic enactments of the Southern scene since the Civil War, juxtaposed against the turbulence of contemporary change, produced a violence of mood and interior action which fascinated foreign as well as American critics. Faulkner's novels bear somewhat the same relation to the guilt and pride of the South that Hawthorne's novels bore to the guilt and pride of Puritan New England. Faulkner's career was an agonized effort to re-create in symbolic terms the life history of the Southern consciousness and the emotional structure of the status system. But he has been more than a regional writer, because in the process he has reached to the universal values of the human condition. The same has been true of the novels of Robert Penn Warren, particularly *All the King's Men,* which dealt with the Huey Long theme. It was true in a different sense of Thomas Wolfe's turbulent lashings, like a Polyphemus among his sheep. One may guess that Wolfe's classic search for his father was a search for a principle of authority, all the more intense because of his break with the culture and values of the Old South. The South as a region has shown an almost compulsive hold upon the minds of its writers, far beyond any other American region. It seems to demand either celebration or rejection, and those who write in it must write about it.

Yet it is an interesting fact that the greatest contemporary Southern writers are not social realists like Lillian Smith, whose *Strange Fruit* indicts the system of caste and the heritage of hate for producing emotional blockages and stunting the growth process for Negroes and whites alike. It is as if the social reality of the South were a Medusa head turning those who confront it with too much directness into stone. The novelists and playwrights I have mentioned, from Faulkner and Warren, Wolfe, Eudora Welty, and Tennessee Williams, preferred to deal with it by indirection, through allegory and symbolism and an antinaturalist style. Their world was drenched with a sense of sin and the fall from grace which was at once religious and classical. To a lesser degree they reproduced the great flowering of literature in Czarist Russia at the time of Turgenev and Dostoevski, who also dealt in a non-naturalist fashion with a feudal society that was passing forever.

While the themes and moods of the Southern writers derive from the passing of the Old South, the turbulence in their writing reflects the turbulence of the contemporary South. The persisting problems of poverty and race relations have not vanished, even though they have been allayed by both economic and political advance. While the population ratio of Negroes to whites diminished with Negro migration, there were still states—Mississippi, Alabama, Georgia, South Carolina— where the whites had a sense of being encircled by Negroes. This produced a garrison mentality which often expressed itself in a hatred of "foreigners" and "radicals" as well as of Negroes and Northerners. The political uses of this hatred were all too apparent in stirring up popular passions to maintain the mold of segregation and caste. There was also a curious attraction-repulsion pattern in the relation of Southern white to Negro, which John Dollard and others explored, based on the conflict between a long-standing physical proximity and sexual attraction and the rigorous requirements of White Supremacy.

I have not meant in this regional portrait to exclude the elements of grace in Southern living which persist side by side with its violence and sadism. The reason why the cultural flowering of the South has taken the form of literary expression is because the South has traditionally had a verbal grace, which goes back beyond the Southern orators, journalists, and political thinkers to the English romantic school on which the Old South was nurtured. The military tradition—the Southern plantation owners lived almost literally on horseback—also persists, and the South from Virginia to Texas still furnishes the core of military enlistments and of the officer group in the Army and Air Force.

The memory of this distinctive way of life tempts some Southern leaders into the delusion that the South can maintain a condition of nullification of Federal law and semi-secession from the Federal Union. The South remembers the history in which it is steeped: it remembers that in the slavery crisis it stubbornly refused to retreat and preferred the havoc of war, and in the Reconstruction crisis it held its ground until the Northern radicals and the carpetbaggers were beaten. It may feel that in this third great crisis of civil rights and desegregation it can maintain autonomy with equal success. It forgets, what Vann Woodward has tried to point out, that segregation is not an ancient Southern institution, and that Jim Crow laws are relatively recent, dating in their vigor only back to the turn of the century. Thus curiously a history-obsessed culture nourishes an unhistorical delusion.

This delusion may help explain why the South, which has produced novelists and dramatists, poets, and literary critics of the first rank, has not produced a political or social thinker of note (I put Justice Black in the category of legal thinkers) since the days of Calhoun. To think greatly on a political and social level requires confronting your problems directly, which is almost impossible in the Southern atmosphere today; the social fictions which have to be maintained are creative soil for fiction and poetry but not for political thinking and the life of ideas. For some time the intellectual process in the South has been not a dialogue but a monologue: the arts of persuasion have found their ground pre-empted by the arts of rhetoric and force. The irony is that when the condition of semi-secession is resolved, and the South once more is absorbed into the social structure and the political mores of the rest of the nation, it may also lose the literary creativeness and the regional culture style that give it its distinctive stamp today.*

* For further treatment of the South and its problems, see Ch. I, Sec. 2, "The Sources of the Heritage," and Ch. VII, Sec. 6, "The Negro in America"; also the section on Civil Liberties in Ch. VI, Sec. 10. For a further discussion of the American novel, see Ch. XI, Sec. 2.

The Southwest is caught between the culture of the Southern staple crops and the culture of the Great Plains, the Great Desert, and the Great Mountains. It shades off in one direction to the single-crop system and the White Supremacy of the Deep South, in another to the wheatlands of the prairie Midwest, in still another to the cattle-grazing lands of the mountain states. Its own economic base is in the oil and cattle lands and the new industries of Texas and Oklahoma, and the tourism and irrigated farming of New Mexico, Arizona, and Southern California. From the South it gets some share of its intensity along with a leisurely grace; it owes a good deal to the Indian whose land it stripped from him but who left behind a heritage of art and spirit, and something also to the old Spanish culture and its mission architecture; from the adjacent Great Plains and mountain states, as well as from its own cattle lands and desert, it gets a sense of space and magnificence. In the blend it is achieving a regional culture of its own, not yet clearly formed but in the making.

It is today one of the fastest-growing areas of American economic expansion and therefore re-creates the "American spirit" of boom, recalling the booster optimism that the Midwest had in its years of early growth. The capitalist of Dallas, Houston, and Los Angeles is close in spirit to the capitalist of Chicago and Cleveland a quarter century ago. Some of the fabulously wealthy men of contemporary America are to be found among the Texas oil kings who rule over complicated domains of corporate wealth and whose oil fortunes—added to the real-estate and cattle fortunes—make the bonanza mentality dominant in the Southwest. Its mood is still that of the great American myth: that anything is possible and will probably happen.

Individualism in the old freebooter sense has probably found its last foothold here. It expresses itself in the intransigence with which big corporations have fought public utility and power regulations; its great victory came when Congress by-passed the Supreme Court and turned the rich tideland oil deposits over to private exploitation under state control. There are few areas in the country in which labor remains as unorganized as it does in this region, partly because of the inferior status of the Spanish-speaking migrant and wetback farm workers, partly because the role of the frontier in weakening labor militancy is being re-enacted on the quasi-frontier of the Southwest.

It is the incongruous mixture of historic frontier and booming industrialism that gives the Southwest its dramatic contrasts. The graceful culture of the Navajos, the Hopi, and the Zuñi suffered from the invasion of industrialism, leaving the area a happy hunting ground for ethnological expeditions. A lusty folklore gathered around the cattle and coyotes of the great Texas plains, and a body of legend was built on the cowboys and rustlers in badman territory. But the type-figures of the South-western past—the Indian, the Spanish conquistador and Jesuit, the cattle rustler, the gambler, the cowboy—have been replaced by cattle and oil kings, real-estate speculators, large-scale corporate farms, Army airfields and aviation factories, luxury hotels that serve as gambling resorts, giant conservation projects and hydroelectric dams.

As the newest frontier, the American Southwest may (in the Turner tradition) lay claim to being the seedbed of a rawer and more vigorous democracy—but it does not follow. A reversion to earlier forms of na-tional experience is not necessarily a renewal of national vitality: it may be only a treadmill retraversing of the past or a throwback to an earlier form of social organization, under conditions not present in the original frontier experience, and may prove disintegrating.

The case of Texas presents this puzzle along with several others. Texas is the most cussed and discussed, demeaned and explained, cele-brated and orated state in the Union. Much effort has been spent to ra-tionalize why Texans are what they are—and to decide what it is exactly that they are. Its key word is scale: the magnitudes of place and capital-ism have converged, so that everything in Texas is bigger than else-where. Texans spoke louder, more confidently, and more boisterously than most other Americans. They had the sureness of a Golden Era. Money was quick in the making and ostentatious in the spending. A close student of Texas estimated in the 1950s that there were 400 millionaires in Houston alone. Many of them had started as farm boys or cowhands; they grew rich from oil and boom, and from tax provisions that gave oil-men a generous untaxed annual "depletion allowance" for their oil wells. When wealth came many of them were unprepared to use or spend it. The garish display of Rolls Royces, diamonds, minks and vicuñas, and the lavish spending outdid the vulgarities of America in its Gilded Age and of the new super-rich in Chicago at the turn of the century. The strong streak of anti-intellectualism (even a Texas newspaperman boasted that Texas had produced no poets) may have derived from the fact that there was no elite tradition, as there was in the South and in New England, to serve as a frame for business and frontier energies. The political emotions were also raw ones; wealth and power came so quickly that the tolerances which a successful democracy requires had less chance to develop than they had in the other centers of business power. Texas grew rich before it came of age, and its years of confidence came ahead of its years of maturity.

There was also another Southwest—that of the Spanish and Indian country, where a modern industrial culture has been built on an old Spanish one, and that in turn on a still earlier Indian culture. This Southwest had a wholly different rhythm of life from the boom Southwest of Texas and Oklahoma: it had neither oil tankers nor skyscrapers; the pace of life was slower and lazier; the impassivity of the Indian, the passion of Spanish Catholicism, and the grandeur of mesa, mountain, and desert, had left their mark on it. To writers as diverse as D. H. Lawrence, Mary Austin, Edmund Wilson and J. B. Priestley and Jacquetta Hawkes its appeal was prehistoric and mystical, and the same appeal has drawn colonies of artists to it.

There are equally dramatic contrasts and contradictions in the Far West, which still retains the Gold Rush psychology of its early days and has, like the Southwest, the feeling that anything is possible. It has a natural grandeur of scene which, in both the Rocky Mountain and the Pacific Coast regions, surpasses anything in America. The canyons, the high grazing lands, the deposits of ferrous and precious metals, the great stands of timber, are witness to the largess of Nature in this area.

There are, of course, marked differences of topography between the Rocky Mountain region, which is high and dry and rugged, and the Pacific Coast, where the soil is rich and the vegetation lush. There are similar contrasts in the economic mood and structure of the two regions. The Rocky Mountain region is largely still a captive economy whose great mines and other resources are under absentee ownership, so that the region is largely colonial to the corporate empires of the East and the Midwest. The story of the Anaconda Copper Company not only dominates the history of Montana but is also symbolic of the exploitation of the whole region. I have spoken earlier of the movement of population away from the eroded grazing soil of the livestock areas to industrial centers. The great hope of the region is that land reclamation will arrest this trend, that hydroelectric dams will harness the power of the region and invite new industry, and that the new requirements of an age of atomic energy will revive the prosperity of an area which depends on the metals deep under ground.

The economic mood of the Pacific Coast region is a dramatically different one. It has grown so rapidly in population, industry, and prosperity that there has been a kind of "law of combined development" operating: all the stages through which the East and Midwest had passed have been foreshortened on the Pacific Coast and quickened as in a rapid-motion movie. The rich resources of the plains, valleys, and forests were brought into the market at a time when industrial techniques were already highly developed and the power and mastery of the machine were at their summit. The result is an amalgam of frontier roughness along with capitalist power and anticapitalist attitudes of an extreme sort. The industrial prizes opened up to the American industrial system came relatively late in the social and class development of

American society, so that they became the stakes of a more bitter industrial-labor conflict than elsewhere in the nation. In this respect the social and political climate of the Pacific Coast resembles that of Texas, both areas representing the combination of frontier boom and industrial power. In both areas also there is a friendliness toward easy folkways of behavior along with an extreme intolerance of dissenting thought. One might say of both these regions that in their hurry to get rich quick they skipped some of the stages in the slower industrial and political development of the East and Midwest, and skipped also some of the discipline of democratic experience which they had painfully to endure.

One striking difference may be noted in the intellectual climate of the two boom areas: where Texas was undistinguished in literature, the written word runs through the whole course of California history. Bret Harte, Mark Twain (really a Midwesterner, but he got his start in journalism in the Western mining towns and on the California frontier), John Muir, Ambrose Bierce, Jack London, Frank Norris, Robinson Jeffers, John Steinbeck, all attest to the literary vigor which the region drew as much from its ardent society as from its natural environment.

There remains to speak of "the East," or the Middle-Atlantic region —a strip of Atlantic seaboard states caught between New England and the South, between the ocean and the Great Lakes. Beyond Pittsburgh and Buffalo you are in the Midwest, beyond Washington you are in the South, beyond Long Island you are in New England. All up and down this stretch you find an almost unbroken line of industrial plants, metropolitan cities, old and new suburbs. Here are the centers of manufacturing, trade, finance, advertising, and of much of the intellectual and political life of the nation. Having been dominant in American life since the beginning of the nation and grown accustomed to dominance, the Middle-Atlantic region is not moved by the striving for a place in the American sun, which has given the other areas much of their consciousness of regional identity. Polyglot in ethnic composition, cosmopolitan in attitude, highly urban and industrial, these states are not usually regarded as a genuine region. They have less of a consciousness of the natural environment, less feeling than the South, Midwest, and Far West have of their regional destiny in fighting against the distant centers of power—because they *are* the centers of power. Facing in one direction toward Europe, in the other toward the interior of the country, they have a sense of centrality that has kept a feeling of separate regional identity from growing, as it has also saved them from (or denied them) the smoldering grievances and resentments of the interior.

The heart of this area is, of course, New York itself. New York City and its suburbs form a "regional city" in themselves. The familiar warning that "New York is not America" is doubtless true, but neither is any other regional culture. The fact that this obvious proposition has to be asserted is more than an index of the common hostilities to New York: it shows the extent to which New York's culture has impinged on the imagination of America and the world.

New York has a double heritage—that of the old Dutch aristocracy, now supplanted by the aristocracy of finance, talent, and "café society," and the intellectual heritage of western Europe toward which it faces. It has fused, adapted, and transformed that heritage, and used it as a base for a cosmopolitan culture which is nonetheless American because it results from the enormous suction force it has exerted on the world. Its ethnically diverse population is drawn from every corner of the world and from every region and subregion of America. Latterly the currents of population in and out of New York have changed its character, making it largely Catholic, Jewish, Negro, and Puerto Rican. But this is to see it residentially. As a working entity, or as a regional city, it reaches into the surrounding counties and states and retains millions who still work in it and use it as the center of their energies although they make their homes elsewhere.

Its lodestone strength continues. The constant stream of young people who come to New York to make their careers brings with it a continual refreshing of the American image. And if New York gets its productive forces from the nation, as is so often asserted, then the finished products—art and the theater, radio and TV, newspapers, magazines, advertising, books, ideas, managerial patterns, trade-union techniques, intellectual movements—make their way all over the nation. It is because of this power and fertility that New York is suspected, feared, and not a little hated by the rest of America. The greatest bitterness comes from the South, Midwest, and Southwest, sometimes from a defensive feeling of cultural difference or newness, sometimes expressing historic conflicts or current frustrations. But one must add that part of this hostility is repayment for the attacks on Midwest "provincialism" and Southern "White Supremacy" made by the liberal intellectuals of New York and the East.

It must be clear that regionalism is not so much a "movement" as a fact—one of the massive facts about America. It embodies the pluralism of the American environments and cultures. Where there have been regional movements they have been largely afterthoughts. What the regional movements have been able to do has been to make Americans more conscious of their regional heritage, prouder of their characteristic diversities, more aware of the material they offer for literature and art, of their folklore and folkways. There is always a danger, of course, that people will go on from the self-conscious to the cultist. But the centralizing and standardizing forces of American life are so insistent that the merely cultist and archaic has no chance for survival against them. Only the tough-fibered regional energies can make the fight, and thus far they have done pretty well.

It is possible, of course, to overestimate the importance and endurance of regional differences. American change moves at two levels and by two clocks, one being the changes common to the nation, the other those peculiar to the region and locality. The regional changes are the wheel within the larger national wheel, and many are trivial and many ephemeral. But it is no superstition to see them as essential parts of the total pattern of diversity. Foreigners who have never been to America are likely to have a single image of it, like a monstrous monolith hewn out of undifferentiated rock. The hardest thing to understand about America, even for many Americans, is that it contains diversities as well as uniformities of speech, dress, consciousness, pace and ways of living, patterns of thought, modes of character. From the white pine and blue water of Maine to the big redwoods and the ocean coast line of California, from the subzero frosts of the upper Great Lakes to the King Ranch and the Galveston docks in Texas, America eludes the single formula that its praisers and damners would force upon it. This does not mean that it is a snatch-batch of unrelated local traits and vagaries, but that it is richly diversified within its unmistakable and frightening uniformities, and the abbreviated symbol of some of these diversities is the region.

The standardizing trend is stronger in America now than it has ever been. It is largely a by-product of American technology. The regional differences are obviously diminishing. Hartford, Atlanta, Wilmington, Akron, Dallas, Denver, and Seattle have more in common than they had a quarter century ago, and this is even truer of the suburbs around them and the small towns that dot them. Any research team, studying their ways of life and thought, would find them largely made up of interchangeable parts. There is a swift and striking erosion of regionalism taking place, especially in the older regions like New England and the South where the consciousness of region goes back for centuries. The regional concept persists even after the regional reality has begun to give way and the differentiations are losing their sharpness of outline.

A distinction may be useful here between what relates to society, or the social structure, and what relates to the culture or the community ways. In their structure as a society—in their business and labor trends, their machines and machine living, their class directions, in transport, in distributive systems, in their use of the big media, in advertising and salesmanship, in consumers' goods and processed foods—the regions are being fused into a national standardized pattern. It is this pattern that one sees in magazines and movies and on TV. But in whatever concerns group life, race relations and attitudes, legal customs, architecture and building, walk and talk, song and dance, the arts, the pace of living, in the use of leisure (except for the big media), in the life of the mind, in prejudices and loves and hates, in the way people grow up and die and the way they feel about the place where they live, the regions still retain or are capable of autonomous creativeness. The process of erosion goes on here too but less swiftly than in the more external social forms that are being standardized.

Take as an instance the musical idiom known as "jazz," which is regarded throughout the world as characteristically American. It was a local creation, coming out of the life of Negroes in New Orleans, out of the marching songs at their funerals and the honky-tonks of Bourbon Street. Gathering strands from the idioms of Africa and the Caribbean, it developed in New Orleans until it achieved its own form; then it was joined by similar forms that developed in St. Louis and Harlem, came into the stream of national life, and ceased to be merely a regional idiom. Something of the same may be said of the folk tales and ballads of the Ozarks, the badman legends of the Far West, the architectural style of mission and pueblo and ranch house of the Southwest, the writing of a small group of Mississippians, the cooking of the Deep South, the religious revivalism of the Midwest, the passion for dissent of New England, the openness of New York to winds of doctrine from every quarter.

Is this regional creativeness coming to an end? I have talked with New Orleans writers who tell me that the walls of regional insulation there have broken down, that Bourbon Street is a playground for visiting tired businessmen from the East and Midwest, and the Mardi Gras has become synthetic. They say that the big media and the big money have destroyed the sense of regional and folk uniqueness from which the creative impulses came, and that nothing as fresh or delightful as jazz will ever be born again, whether in New Orleans or St. Louis or anywhere else. There is a streak of truth in this, and a sad one. I should add that when one of my friends who spoke thus had a chance to leave New Orleans and get at the big media and the big money in New York, he preferred to work and write where he felt at home. There would seem to be a persisting autonomous element that is still regional.

We shall probably never know what historic combination of circumstances and talents produced New Orleans jazz or New England dissent, just as we shall never know the secret of individual creativeness. In this sense the regional culture—the fusion of place, people, and tradition—is a primary datum of American life. In the course of American history, now one region and now another has acted for a time as the principal carrier of cultural creativeness and has had a formative role in shaping the national character. Just when it has seemed that this vein of gold was running out in one region it has turned out that elsewhere another deposit has been gathering, secretly and slowly, richer than any Comstock Lode that ever brought its lucky exploiters to the heights of Nob Hill.

I do not say, as some do, that only the regional culture can keep America from being ironed out into a flat conformist country. The champions of regionalism conveniently forget that the region may harbor a rigorous cultural tyranny. The region is a force against national patterns of standardization, but there is a difference between standardization, which has to do with the outward life, and conformity or nonconformity of spirit. Since the region is a more compassable unit of living, it may also, like the small town, be a more compassable unit for enforcing conformity.

One cannot expect of the regional culture that it should save America from the anthill society. Only the autonomous impulses of the unlegislated individual, working in small groups with others like himself, conscious of the larger directions of American life and of his place in them, owning loyalties of a richly diverse kind yet remaining a person within these loyalties, can perform that difficult role. What the region can do, in its more limited way, is to serve as a buffer between the individual and the impersonal forces shaping national life. In that role the best that American regional cultures can hope for is to find a healthy balance between insulation and accessibility.

CHAPTER IV

The Culture of Science
and the Machine

IN WHICH we examine how modern science and its machines have fared under the conditions of American life and what contributions Americans have made to both. We trace the relations between power as it is expressed throughout American life and power as it shows itself in the characteristic sciences (Sec. 1, "The Enormous Laboratory: Science and Power"), and we ask how much the climate of a free society in America is crucial to the growth of science and its fruits (Sec. 2, "Science in an Open Society").

Tracing the series of industrial revolutions that have given America the sense of being in a "permanent revolution," we examine the technician and pose the probably insoluble question of whether he (and the scientist too) can be "neutral" when faced with the choices of what shall be done with his science and machines (Sec. 3, "Big Technology and Neutral Technicians"). Shifting to the worker and looking at the same scene from his vantage point, we analyze the factory as a society, ask what has happened to work as a calling, what incentives spur the best kind of work, and what lies ahead for the worker in a society where his machine-tending role is diminishing. We stop for a glimpse into the future of "automation" and the almost workerless industrial plant and office (Sec. 4, "Work and the Automatic Factory").

Shifting now to the consumer, we look at the array of commodities that America creates daily, ask what life values they serve and how they can serve them best, and trace the effect of plenty upon American thinking (Sec. 5, "The Wilderness of Commodities"). Finally we tackle the moot question of the "standardization" of American life by the machine and examine how a humanist culture can best be developed not only in spite of but through the machine as instrument (Sec. 6, "The Culture of Machine Living").

The Culture of Science and the Machine

1. The Enormous Laboratory: Science and Power

AMERICA is a civilization founded on science and rooted in its achievements. Without science the whole ribbed frame of American technology, and with it American power, would have been impossible. America itself was born at the beginning of the great age of European science. Back of the flowering modern technology were the long centuries when the seed grew silently in the earth. The same expansive forces that produced the intellectual discoveries of that *saeculum mirabile* of European science—the seventeenth century—produced the American settlements as well. Europe reached out intellectually, as it reached out physically, for new frontiers. In England, the history of the Royal Society paralleled that of the plantation companies. The whole atmosphere surrounding the settlement and peopling of America was an atmosphere of scientific beginnings. Except in a climate of innovation the American experiment would have been impossible; conversely, it was in the intensely innovating social climate of America that invention was bound to flourish.

To be sure, science as the heir of centuries of intellectual development needed something better than a wilderness to grow in. It needed universities, intellectual exchange, and the leisure for idle curiosity; it needed also a consciousness of national strength which did not come until the era of Jackson. Mitchell Wilson has pointed out that during the first half century of the nation's history American invention was sparse and imitative, and American science lagged behind that of Europe. There were hopes that invention would flourish, but by 1834 (when the present patent law was passed) there were only a little more than 1,200 patents on file. The great burst of inventiveness began in the following period. But once started on its career, American science had a few crucial things in its favor. It had the whole body of Europe's science to use as an unlimited drawing account; yet it had also the advantage of distance—the extra margin of freedom from the grooves of conventional thinking which often hemmed in the European scientists.

An amusing example may be found, even in the earlier period, in Benjamin Franklin's career as a scientist. Franklin is one of the important world names in electricity. He began to putter with it when an English friend sent him some rudimentary equipment with a few hints on how to use it. Without European science he could not have started; but once started he worked with a sense of excitement and in an atmosphere of intense popular interest. So much was he on his own that when he wrote his friends in Europe about his experiments, he didn't know whether the terms he had newly coined for what he observed were the first. With the growth of his fame as a scientist his European friends sent him the literature containing the orthodox vocabulary and the traditional ideas on electricity. "As he learned from books, rather than his own investigations," says Franklin's editor, I. Bernard Cohen, "he ceased to have a free, unfettered mind. As he became more and more familiar with the literature of electricity, he made fewer and fewer discoveries until finally he made no more." Franklin's discoveries were discussed in the Royal Society, which when asked to protect a powder magazine from the effects of lightning recommended the Franklin lightning rod, with pointed conductors. One committee member dissented, insisting on blunt conductors (or "knobs") instead of "points." He continued to attack Franklin without success—until the Revolutionary War, when George III intervened and ordered "blunt" conductors for the Royal Palace. When the head of the Royal Society refused to reverse the committee's recommendation on the Franklin rod, the King forced his resignation.

One may take this delightful story as a somewhat distorted allegory of the conditions of science in Europe and America. I do not mean to overstate the favoring conditions of American scientific work or to give an inflated impression of its achievement in its early phase. Such early scientists of note as Joseph Henry and Draper did work that stood out like mountain peaks from the general flatness of the amateur work around them, much of which repeated what had already been done in Europe with greater subtlety. The lack of contact with other working scientists, which gave a few men of genius a chance at originality, also cut many others off from the access to other working scientists without which they could get no stimulation. Yet there were important institutional hindrances from which American science was free. It could pursue the laws of Nature without troubling about the laws of monarchies; it could work in an atmosphere in which it did not have to cope with a codified body of religious taboos or with a church rooted in state power; it did not have to reckon with either priestly or aristocratic castes. It was free to follow its impulse and develop the resources of a continent. In that impulse were tied together the main threads of the American mind—its Puritan emphasis on work, its sense of newness and confidence, its technical skill, its energy, its sense of the "go" of things.

But American achievement has been less in pure than in applied science—that is, in invention and technology. When an American today thinks of science, he is likely to think of test tubes and laboratories, of such end-product inventions as atom bombs or antibiotics, guided missiles, proximity fuses, or the latest process for cracking oil. The great scientific revolution of the seventeenth and eighteenth centuries had already taken place by the time America became a going concern. A raw country could not quickly develop an intellectual tradition out of which emerges the giant figure of an Aristotle or Euclid, a Galileo, a Newton or Darwin or Mendel, a Faraday or Einstein. The names that keep cropping up in the American histories, biographies, and current scientific literature are distinguished enough: Franklin himself; Joseph Henry, a physicist who made some remarkable discoveries in electricity and magnetism; Nathaniel Bowditch, mathematician and "Practical Navigator"; Audubon, ornithologist; Simon Newcomb, astronomer; Benjamin Silliman, chemist; Asa Gray, botanist; Willard Gibbs, physicist; Holmes and Morton, who did much for childbirth and anesthesia; John W. Draper, Thomas A. Edison, and George Eastman, the trio whose connected work did much for the modern sciences of communication. The list could be lengthened with names like Millikan, Langmuir and Gilbert Lewis, with G. W. Hill and Birkhoff in mathematics, with Julian Schwinger, I. I. Rabi, and Robert Oppenheimer in physics (I omit those who developed as scientists abroad and came to America as refugees), with Urey in chemistry, T. H. Morgan and H. J. Muller in genetics, W. B. Cannon in the theory of homeostasis, and names like Hale, Boade, Hubble, and Shapley in astrophysics. To these must be added a galaxy of contemporary names linked with radio, television, electronics, automation, and atomic energy.

It is a rich and diversified list and disproves any idea that Americans do not carry their share of the burden of scientific research and thinking. Yet of the whole list, there is only one—Gibbs—who would clearly be recognized as a theoretical scientist of the highest world rank, standing apart from the productive laboratory experimenters, scientific organizers and classifiers, distinguished teachers, and brilliant inventors. Much of the enormous laboratory of modern American scientific power rests on the laws of chemical energetics that Gibbs discovered. The processes of separating metals from their ores, refining petroleum, fixing nitrogen, synthesizing rubber, and many other operations make use of

Gibbs's "phase rule" and other formulas. Yet even in Gibbs's case his great theoretical work in physics and chemistry was carried on under a blanket of indifference on the part of the universities, the industrialists, and the public. Even the European scientists failed to see the meaning of his work. When, in 1876, Clerk Maxwell gave a lengthy analysis and appreciation of it before a European audience, he got little response.

The American achievement in the atomic era may seem to disprove the scarcity of great American theoretical work. Yet the theoretical groundwork for atomic fission was laid in Europe, and the achievements at Hanford, Chicago, Los Alamos, and Oak Ridge are based on the revolution in theoretical physics begun with Einstein's 1905 paper in Germany and with the work of Heisenberg, Born, De Broglie, Schroedinger, and Dirac, which overturned the ideas about time, space, mass, and length. The theoretical discoveries were the result of world-wide knowledge, but it was America that took over the knowledge, organized it, underwrote it, and thus got out in front. The achievement of the Americans was a triumph of engineering and of hospitality in giving harbor to scientists like Einstein, Fermi, and Szilard who had fled from tyranny. The Americans achieved what they did through the division and distribution of the research, the fitting of the findings into a pattern, the construction of plants, machinery, and machine tools, the combination of economic power with wealth and inventiveness, and with an experimental and empiric cast of mind.

Heine once said that while England ruled the seas, Germany ruled the clouds, and his jibe at the vaporous metaphysical broodings of his countrymen has been echoed by others. For great theoretical work in science, Americans, boasting that their feet are always on the ground, have not been in the clouds enough. It is this feet-on-the-ground compulsion that has kept American genius largely limited to applied science and engineering. The strain of empiricism runs through the whole of the history of the American mind. Americans find their ideas in things: they understand generalizations in terms of the operations involved in using them. The segment of the European philosophic heritage they took over was in the main the British segment, which ran less in terms of absolutes than the others; and the portion of the British segment that influenced them most was the thinking of Hume and Locke, who distilled the empiricism of the British tradition. It is also characteristic of American science that its most brilliant theorist in the philosophy of science was Charles S. Peirce, the founder of the Pragmatic school, for whom the "meaning of a statement" lay in the effects which the belief in it has on human behavior. This strain of thinking helps make a civilization a technological one, using scientific theories to the hilt but not generating great new ones. The place of science in American civilization is thus closely linked with the characteristic cast of the American mind.

The question about a civilization is not whether it uses science but how it uses science, what contributions it makes to it, what sciences are closest to its temper and civilization style. While the Greeks did important work in astronomy and physics, the characteristic Greek sciences were botany, zoology, biology, and mathematics, as befitted a people absorbed with the individual, the category, and their relations. The characteristic sciences of American technology turned out to be chemistry and physics, electronics and radiation, as befits a people absorbed with energy and speed, communication and power. In both cases the sciences are a key to the crucial civilization traits. In one case they are mainly the life sciences and the sciences of order, in the other the sciences of energy and power.

Spengler had at least a half-truth by the tail when, writing in his *Decline of the West* on the Faustian and Apollonian nature conceptions, he said that "force is the mechanical Nature-picture of Western man. . . . The primary ideas of this physics stood firm long before the first physicist was born." While this notion—that the science type in any civilization exists long before the science—has an element of poetry, it cannot be ignored. Veblen brushed the same problem in the 1920s when he linked the American "technology of physics and chemistry" (radiation and electronics had not yet emerged) with "absentee ownership" by and of corporations. And if you push absentee ownership and corporate power still further back, you get the "natural rights" of property.

Here, I think, we reach a significant relationship. The American conceptions of science went hand in hand with the American conceptions of nature: the Declaration of Independence, with its theory of the natural rights of the individual, was the forerunner of the great upsurge of American energy which led to the technological triumphs of the nineteenth century. The Federalist Papers are in themselves a microcosm of the forces in the American mind that were to shape the uses of science: on the one hand an equilibrium-politics, on the other a drive on purely pragmatic grounds to establish the principle of a central authority with the power to govern essential for survival. The two may seem inconsistent to the critical student of today, and their inconsistency has been shown in the creaking of the American governmental machine: yet the important fact is that they were both part of the eighteenth-century American mind, and the sense of natural law in the equilibrium principle coexisted with the empirical power sense in the principle of central authority.

These two—the sense of natural law and a power empiricism—have been the formative forces in American science and technology, as they have been in American political science and economics. The "reception" that the Americans gave the principles of John Locke, as Walton Hamilton has analyzed it and Merle Curti has traced it, is another instance of the transforming drive in the American civilization: for the Locke that emerged from American thinking on property was very different from the Locke that came into it from the English. It is in the nature of a civilization's "genius" that whatever material it borrows from others it transforms in its own image. When John Locke came out of the American transforming machine his name was Andrew Carnegie and Henry Ford. The Declaration of Independence became the "due process" decisions of the Supreme Court; Tom Paine's flaming pamphlet on natural law became the comfortable doctrines that bolstered property interests; the American idea of Nature turned into corporate ownership, and its servant was the technology of chemistry and physics. The congruity between American science and the driving spirit of American political and economic development was the congruity of *élan* and energy. The geography and resources of America invited a physics of force, and the role of Nature in American political thinking reflected it and prepared the ground for it. Out of the sciences of force came American technology and the machine process; and they in turn cast their spell back upon science.

This capacity for transforming science into technology, which accounts for so much of the success of American power, is not one to be taken for granted. The Greeks, for example, played a greater role in the history of scientific theory than the Americans. They took the great step from myth to science, just as Europeans in the seventeeth century took the final step in separating science from religion. Centuries before the Christian era there were thinkers in Thrace and Athens, in Sicily and on the coast of Asia Minor, who did basic thinking about biology and mathematics, about the nature of the world and the constitution of matter, upon which later centuries were built. At the height of the Greek achievement a Stagirite called Aristotle was able to synthesize what the Greeks knew of Nature and its workings into a system more comprehensive than any mind before or since. Yet Greek science, although it continued its achievements as science for several centuries after Aristotle, never took the crucial step from science to technology. To be sure, the Alexandrian world in the later Greek era had an impressive number of mechanical contrivances described by Hero, like the endless chain, the compound pulley, and the crane for lifting, some of which they put to practical use. Yet it remained true that Greek technology, however you measure its achievement, never explored and applied more than a small fraction of what Greek science might have made possible. It did not run machines, relieve labor of its burdens, increase man's productive capacity greatly, build a powerful industrial civilization. Why?

The clues to the Greek failure in technology may shed some light on the American success in it. Partly they lie in what may be called the slave syndrome. There is a British school of historians, including Benjamin Farrington and V. Gordon Childe, who look to the slave system for the explanation of the arrested Greek development. They have pushed their thesis too hard in applying it to science, for it is obvious that the slave-based society of the Greek city-states was well developed by Plato's time, yet Greek science went on growing for several centuries in the work of Euclid, Archimedes, and others. But the heart of the matter is less in the failure of science to develop fully than in its failure to make the transition to technology. The thinking of the Greeks was done by free men and citizens; the work was done by foreigners and slaves. Where there is a contempt for work and trade and the sweat they entail, there is a separation from the sources of experience and Nature, and a blindness to those imperatives of practice that shape innovation. The American scientist or technician, no matter how famous and whether he works at industrial research or at a university, does not cut himself off from these sources of experience. Less a creator of world views than the ancient Greek or modern European scientist, he has been a discoverer of new ways of pushing old and new things to completion.

There have, of course, been other explanations of the failure of Greek science to develop into technology. One scholar suggests that the Greeks in the Hellenistic period were developing an experimental technique, but that the invasion of the Roman "barbarians" from the Italian peninsula cut it off before it had a chance to flower. Another scholar contends that it was because the Greek ideal of life, in its stress on the public place and its underemphasis on the home, had no interest in raising living standards, and therefore no zeal for technology. Neither of these is inconsistent with the approach that stresses slavery. Even if the Roman barbarians had never come, Greek society could never have developed a revolutionary technology. Greek science developed to no small extent out of the reflectiveness possible in a leisure-class society sustained by a moral and political individualism, with a civic ideal of life. But in the context of slavery and of the leisure-class contempt for work, it could not go much beyond science and was arrested before it carried its insights over into technology.

The atmosphere of America was less favorable for the reflective than for the dynamic aspects of science; the emphasis was not on philosophy and the shaping of new world views but on experience and the mastery of the environment. The achievements in technology thus outran the creativeness in pure science.

If the South had triumphed in the Civil War (and the reason it did not was that the North had developed a technology) and had gone on to spread its "peculiar institution"—the slave syndrome—over the whole of America, the same paralysis might have befallen American technology that befell the Greek and Hellenistic. Calhoun and Jefferson Davis dreamed of a Greek slave-based Republic, and with a Southern victory the American ruling class might have lived more gracefully but less efficiently than the business elite has done. The Civil War was thus more than a moral or Constitutional struggle: exactly because it was fought over moral and Constitutional issues it was also a crisis in technological history.

Having triumphed over the plantocracy of the South, the business class went on to the conquest of a continent and the economic empire of the world. Whatever else might be said of it after the Civil War, it was hospitable to the science underlying the technological changes that had given it power. For only technology could master the needed domain for these rulers: strip the forests, open the land, build the railroads, pick the cotton, thrash the wheat, harness the energy. In Europe the business class had to fight an unremitting struggle for centuries against the political rulers and the social aristocracy: only in England and Germany did it win; especially in Germany, where Bismarck built a technological welfare state in alliance with the army. In America the sway of the business class was undisputed. It lavished its gifts on science (although not always wisely) through research funds and big laboratories, because science in turn opened a cornucopia of profits. It whipped technology on because every discovery of new techniques and processes meant the cutting of costs, the opening of new areas of investment, the reaching of new heights of productivity. America became the Enormous Laboratory.

2. Science in an Open Society

OUT OF THIS laboratory have poured whole new industries: electric power, aviation, the telephone, radio and TV, movies, antibiotic drugs, aluminum and other light metals, electronics, radar, isotopes, X rays and radiation therapy. The bulk of the newer arms produced in the war-geared economy of our generation comes from processes unknown, perhaps even undreamed of, in the 1920s. The people in closest contact with them must reckon with continuous obsolescence; they live within universes that must be renewed in constantly shortening cycles. The scientific revolution out of which the new industries and techniques came is itself scarcely a half century old. The earlier work in quantum mechanics, cosmic rays, the neutron and meson, and the overturning of the classical concepts of mass and measurement led to an era of scientific changes that present a challenge to a science civilization like the American. Having become an Enormous Laboratory, America had the task of maintaining its industrial and military primacy against any rival constellation.

A great scientific civilization depends on two imperatives: the mutation outcroppings of scientific genius, and the pervasiveness of the scientific outlook. Assuming a fair share of the first, there must be a favorable climate in which the insights demanded by the modern scientific revolution can flower. The young Einstein, pondering the question of the speed of light and the errant behavior of the planet Mercury, could not have reached his solution by empiricism alone. He reached it by undercutting the assumption of classical physics, seeing the universe as a series of observations by a scientist who is himself part of the frame.

The revolution in science jolted young American physicists loose from empiricism. It also jolted American industry and the government into subsidies of scientific research so extensive that one must speak of General Electric or Du Pont Chemical or General Dynamics as the new Maecenases of young talent in science. They are ready to foot the bill for theoretical research. Yet the empirical shadow of the Enormous Workshop continues to fall on the Enormous Laboratory. It is hard for a culture to rid itself of its encrusted habits of thought, even in a universe in which God emerges as the Great Mathematician rather than as the Great Artificer. The whole organized—perhaps overorganized—material civilization of America, so different from the reflective and the metaphysical, brings America closer to the symbol of Osiris than of Isis. Amidst the research endowment, science clubs, and the new bureaucracy of the vast science enterprise of America, there is a danger of losing sight of the quality that Einstein had along with Newton and Harvey: a basic simplicity of approach that cut through the clutter of intellectual and scientific bric-a-brac. Despite some brilliant and mature teaching of science in the universities, many American students are trained less in the ways of "idle curiosity" than of the technician who sees a job to be done and sets about doing it. Benjamin Franklin, who did his best scientific work in the spirit of free curiosity, left a different kind of heritage too: for the Franklin mixture was made up of equal parts of the Puritan doctrine of work, Poor Richard's bourgeois doc-

trine of thrift and profit, and the tinkering with new gadgets. It was a
utilitarian heritage for practical men.

The scientific discovery, we have come to understand, is likely to
start with the inspired hunch and end with the culminating calculation. But in a technological culture, intellectual production is viewed
very much in the image of mass production and the factory belt line.
The subsidizing of inspired hunches is obviously hard: it requires both
risk and faith, and in a utilitarian culture the pressures on the young
scientist to prove his mettle by "delivering the goods" come from
within, yet are a reflection of the pressures from the culture as a whole.
Conant has defined science not (as Karl Pearson did) as a classification
of facts but as a series of conceptual schemes linked with observation
and experiment both before and after, and has made a plea to encourage
these "conceptual schemes" by emphasizing not the belt line or the job
but the person. He has asked universities and industrial concerns to
subsidize not the project but the scientist.

Rarely have they done so. Industrial research produces many inventions and gadgets but few scientists of top importance, and while industry and government together in the mid-1950s spent over four and
a half billion dollars a year on research and employed some 400,000
scientists and engineers at it, little of the money or energy went into
fundamental research as distinguished from empirical inventions. It is
true that some of the industry research men contribute first-rate papers
to professional journals, and that industrial raids on university faculties are often returned in a two-way process. Yet my general statement
must stand. This may seem surprising in the light of America's industrial leadership and its reputation for working miracles in the solution
of technical problems. But in his study, *The Organization Man,* W. H.
Whyte, Jr., examines the record of industry with the result I have given.
He makes a crucial distinction between empirical research, which (let
us say) sets out to develop a better automobile engine or electric bulb
and does so, and fundamental research, which doesn't know what it is
looking for until it stumbles upon a problem, whereupon a whole series
of new questions arise. Only two American scientists from the industrial
laboratories—Irving Langmuir and C. J. Davisson—have received Nobel
prizes, as compared with dozens from the universities. A *Fortune* study
of outstanding scientists under forty, by Francis Bello, found that all
but a small percentage of the creative younger men were in the universities rather than in the research laboratories of big industry. The days
of Langmuir, Steinmetz, and Wallace Carothers seem to be over, and
the day of the "adjusters" who are not eccentrics or troublemakers is
upon us. The emphasis of the corporate managers is upon finding people who will be "co-operative" and work as part of a "team." And the

same trend is beginning in the universities as well, where "team research" is making inroads as the dominant concept, wherever military
subsidies support the research. As a counterforce, however, the argument has been pressed that the work in atomic energy would never
have been possible without fundamental theory—but it remains to be
seen whether this truth will stick in the military mind.

It is, of course, difficult to separate the individual heroic figure in
science from the whole collective of scientific scholarship, in which the
man who makes the culminating calculation stands on the shoulders of
so many other men. But given free communication between scientists,
the concentration on the scientist himself and his inner brooding and inspired hunches is an essential one if fundamental research is to flourish.
The fear of "geniuses," felt through most of the industrial structure,
scares off a number of men who value independent thinking and cherish
their own cast of personality. But the managerial attitude is even more
corrosive for the marginal men who may decide to go into industrial
research and who develop their own inhibitions against original thinking once they find themselves in an atmosphere hostile to it.

While the corporate managers feel uneasy with scientific "geniuses,"
the community as a whole distrusts and even fears them. A survey of
New England teen-agers, reflecting probably the opinion of parents as
well, described science as an occupation fit for "queer geniuses" who
were cold and lacked moral standards. This is part of a current of anti-
intellectualism that swept in recent years not only through America but
through the whole Western world, largely as a consequence of the
atomic crisis.

Actually there is a double impulse of worship and fear in the way
Americans feel toward science. They address it as Shelley addressed
the west wind: "Destroyer and preserver; hear, oh, hear!" For the multitude, science has been a worker of miracles which they have come to
take almost for granted as part of the natural course of America's
development. This has led to a popular fetishism of science, which
Henry Adams grasped when he used the contrasting symbols of the
"virgin and the dynamo." But he failed to make the distinction between
the personal and the tribal symbols of worship. To the medieval mind
the Virgin had a personal immediacy; to the Americans the dynamo—or
the atom bomb, or streptomycin, or the electronic brain, or whatever
the current miracle symbol may be—is connected with the nation's
destiny. The American makes a cult of science as a tribal symbol, just as
he makes a cult of success as a personal symbol.

That—and the fear of which I have spoken—may be the reason why
the man of science has not yet left as deep a mark on American litera-

ture as, let us say, the journalist, the soldier, the business Titan. The closest approach to a glorifying of the research scientist as a saintlike, dedicated person was in Sinclair Lewis's *Arrowsmith*. In the popular biographies of great scientists the laboratory process was transmuted into something else: scientific research seemed most understandable to Americans as an ascetic endurance contest or a criminal manhunt or a success story—as anything, in fact, except the penetrating simplicity of intellectual insight. The other popular image of the scientist was a cross between the heritage of the Gothic romances and Wells's *The Island of Doctor Moreau*—the diabolical scientist of the horror movies or of supernatural fiction, the Svengali of the intellectual world, a sinister and lethally dangerous figure who in the end destroys himself or is shot by the F.B.I. Most familiarly and ludicrously the scientific process was dramatized by the movies in the ritual of surgeons donning the hygienic invincibility of rubber gloves before a delicate brain operation.

Something of a revolution has taken place recently in the popularizing of scientific research through magazines like the *Scientific American*, and a group of able science writers has arisen who have technical competence along with a dramatizing capacity. On another level a genre of popular science fiction has emerged, dealing less with scientists than with the projection of the scientific imagination in the Wellsian tradition, half fantasy, half prophecy. In the form of Buck Rogers and the space ship it also reached into the comic books and television. Some of the same writers who once did pulp magazine "Westerns" now turned to the frontiers of the Space Patrol. Even the G-Men of the F.B.I. were touched by the image of the scientific investigator who operates with a deadly detachment and laboratory efficiency, and science came thus to be invoked by Americans to preserve them from subversives within as well as from enemies without.

The sharpest dilemma that science posed was in its relation to the weapons of war. The Enormous Workshop became the Enormous Arsenal. Without war science and war technology America could not produce the radar and sonar, rockets, jets and jet interceptors, guided missiles, strategic bombers, short-range interceptors, submarines, atom bombs, biological and radiological weapons which, rightly or wrongly, were considered necessary for the survival of a great modern nation. Yet the whole bundle of attitudes—awe and terror and a clinging reliance—clustering around the science-created tools of war generated an atmosphere in which the free pursuit of science became more difficult.

Science depends upon open communications, both between cultures and between scientists within a culture. But in a spy-ridden, security-conscious world of the Great Powers the inevitable response of administrators to the demands of the armament race was the sanction of secrecy. The scientist working on a defense project was investigated and cross-investigated, tagged and watched. In the past this was partly true of scientists working for corporations engaged in intense competition. But in a war-geared society the political tests became the crucial ones, and the scientist was watched for entangling alliances and even for dangerous thoughts. Since the larger share of scientific research in the universities came under the defense services, with government subsidies and government supervision, the danger was that scientists would in effect have to put on uniforms. Only a small percentage of the university and industrial projects under government contract might be "secret," yet they infected the rest. Thus American science tended to become not only project-ridden (as I have put it above) but security-ridden.

Even sympathetic students of the Soviet Union, like Sidney and Beatrice Webb, point out the remarkable degree to which the Communists developed both the cult of science and the disease of orthodoxy. Their devotion to science is crippled by the taboos of Communist thinking and by the dogma of Party Truth: so much so that, while they can expect to nurture good technicians, they cannot hope to rival the theoretical discoveries of the world outside, on which they must continue to draw either by espionage or by keeping the communications open. Yet it must be added that a conservative orthodoxy is only a little better for science, because while less rigid than a Communist orthodoxy, it may in its own way have a repressive effect on science.

I am not arguing wishfully that science can function only in an open society and that it dries up wholly under totalitarianism. The experience of the Soviet Union, where important work has continued in mathematics, physics, chemistry, and astronomy, should make anyone wary of pushing the argument too far. The important fact is that the scientific enterprise in a closed society is taken over by the state, for state ends and under state stimulus and penalties. The task of recruiting young people from the schools and universities for scientific work is performed by the party and state, and the organization of scientific societies and the rewarding of scientific work is under the same auspices. In short, the pursuit of science gets encased inside a bureaucracy and an elite, much as with the officers of an army. As long as the party and state give this elite encouragement and scope for its work, the work will continue tolerably. Where political purposes cut across scientific freedom, as was the case in Soviet genetics during the Stalin era, the work of science becomes stultified. If the strength of the state falters, and along with it the belief in the state's purposes, the morale of the scientists is bound to disintegrate and their work to suffer. Thus the fortunes of science under totalitarianism tend to rise and fall with the fortunes of the state and the incentives it furnishes to its scientific servants.

This contrasts with the case of an open society where science continues its work independently of the state and its power, and where (in fact) the fortunes of the state itself may be affected by the course of scientific thinking. True, the eighteenth- and nineteenth-century situation where the language of science was still close to the language of the ordinary educated man no longer applies. Science today speaks in esoteric symbols, and even in democracies scientists are likely to form themselves into an even tighter elite. But it is one that must remain independent of the state if its best work is to continue. It depends for recruitment upon the interest and morale of the young people in the schools, and when they feel that the life of the scientist is an unfree one they are likely to move into business or the professions instead. It depends for its creativeness upon the *élan* of men whose commitment is not to the state but to science itself and the human purposes it serves. Although they are an elite they are reluctant to function as a military one.

Thus the operation of science in an open society is a productive one, but only if the society continues open. Scientific discoveries depend on overturning the orthodoxies of received doctrine: but it is difficult to sustain habits of scientific skepticism in a society in which political conformism comes to be expected. Only in an open society can scientists undercut the basic preconceptions of their own disciplines. One trouble with scrutinizing science for subversion is that there is an irreducible element of subversiveness in scientific method itself. The creativeness of the scientific outlook lies exactly in the fact that it is no respecter of taboos.

Its method is at once bold and rational. At its best it takes nothing for granted; finds no hypothesis too daring to assume or too sacred to test; finds no past conceptual scheme too established to discard if generalization based on a different scheme fits the observations better. It is tedious and painstaking, ingenious in posing problems, bold in hunches, unsparing in making verifications. It is planful in that it looks backward at old failures and forward to new solutions. It is optimist, holding that there is nothing which will not someday yield to inquiry; it is economical, preferring the simplest formulations, opposing waste and futility.

I have tried to describe science in the phrase that Max Weber used of it: *Wissenschaft als Beruf*—science as discipline or calling. To a great degree this describes the place of science in a civilization like the American. There are some who in their overzealousness for science succeed only in distorting it. One group makes a cult of scientific neutrality. It makes of science not a method for handling experience and organizing observations but an end in itself—a dedicated, superhuman, almost inhuman way of life: in Nietzsche's words, "the last, most subtle asceticism." It regards scientific culture as the only important culture today, forgetting in its overrationalism that much of what men do and think is unreasoned, arising from the promptings of the unconscious self. It shades off into another group, which expects science to remake society with a conscious rationality of purpose.

It is true to a degree that in American society there is some obstruction offered to the free play of science, or better of technology, when new inventions would threaten existing investment and profitable patent pools, or create obsolescence too quickly. But while this has often been stressed by critics of the American economy it is only marginal, as the history of the unbroken dynamism of American science testifies. What is more crucial is that science finds itself operating in a society forced to spend billions for the discovery and manufacture of tools of war, but chary of smaller expenditures for health and education. One of the paradoxes about science, in America as elsewhere in the world, is that with all its vaunted use it has not done enough to release the social imagination (the exceptions are river-valley development, city planning, public-health work) or fortify the social will; and that the most advanced scientific methods in the realm of technology sometimes may be found side by side with surviving taboos in the realm of social thought and action.

But this is scarcely to be set down as a failure of science peculiar to America. It is part of a more widespread wave of anti-intellectualism, and a failure of commitment to humanist values on the part of the peoples of the world. It shows itself in two ways: first, in the stubbornness with which men hold on to the habit of war-making and the use of science for killing. (As Bertrand Russell once put it, "Overeating is not a serious danger, but overfighting is.") Second, in their failure to give full scope to scientific inquiry and freedom to scientists. Of all the political creeds the one that seemed to embrace science most avidly was that of the Communists; in America they taunted the businessmen with fearing to encourage the scientific method lest it undercut business power, and they laid claim to a synthesis of "science and society." The Marxist tradition, in arguing for a "scientific socialism," had asserted the unbroken web of physical and social science and had gone so far as to apply the dialectic method to science itself. Yet, if anything, science proved to be more crippled by the disease of orthodoxy in the Communist societies of Russia, China, and eastern Europe than in America, and the institutions of those countries were more subject to the arbitrary shiftings of the irrational will than in the relatively open American society.

The fact was that America, itself the child and product of the eighteenth-century Enlightenment, was committed to the values of science, freedom, and rationality, which the Enlightenment taught. In a letter to a young student, written in the closing year of the eighteenth century, Jefferson identified the struggle for freedom with the struggle for science:

> Great fields are yet to be explored to which our faculties are equal, and that to an extent of which we cannot fix the limits. I join you therefore in branding as cowardly the idea that the human mind is incapable of further advances. . . . While the art of printing is left to us, science can never be retrograde; what is once acquired of real knowledge can never be lost. To preserve the freedom of the human mind then and freedom of the press, every spirit should be ready to devote itself to martyrdom. . . . That the enthusiasm which characterizes youth should lift its parricide hands against freedom and science would be such a monstrous phenomenon as I cannot place among possible things in this age and this country.

One might expect the successive eras of discovery in American science to have carried this spirit of the Enlightenment further, but it doesn't follow and it didn't wholly happen. The impulses of the Enlightenment spent themselves and were succeeded by the impulses of technological advance and economic power. While in Jefferson's day the fight for science and the fight for freedom were parts of the same fight, they came to be split away: both were still carried on, but not in relation to each other. Moreover, the interior world of the scientists changed. What they learned in each generation became for those of the next generation not so much a heritage to be cherished but a tool to be used: in other words, as soon as science achieved its successive goals it made the transition and became technology. There followed another consequence: since a technology is to be used, science was no longer an idle curiosity, or even a form of objective knowledge, but a mode of action. The final step in this sequence of logic—or illogic—has proved ironic enough: since science is a mode of action, and since the world of action belongs centrally to the men of affairs, in government, business, and the armed services, it seemed to follow that the scientist ought to be judged by the values of these men of action and by their view of the prevailing social ethic. Hence scientists came to be assailed for their failure to conform to the dominant mood and policy of the time, as happened in the classical case of the security hearings of Robert Oppenheimer in 1954. Science thus helped to set in motion some of the anti-intellectual feeling which in the end threatened the survival of the scientific spirit itself and the freedom of scientists to pursue their unknown goal.

I speak of it as an unknown goal because the traditional image of the world of the scientist as a tidy and rational world, with all the loose ends fitting together, is no longer a true image—if it ever was. It is a world of bewildering duality that even the scientists themselves do not understand. In atomic physics, for example, the classical description in terms of Newtonian mechanics seemed no longer adequate to the scientists. The same phenomenon can be described from one standpoint as a wave of light, from another as a particle of matter; and while the two cannot logically be reconciled, functionally they fit the needs of scientific action and come closest to portraying the image of the world with which the scientists must operate.

Within such a frame the old dream of Descartes, that the individual's reason could move and shape a universe, left out of account the deep springs of the irrational within man himself. Einsteinian physics brought the observer back into the physical universe from which Newton left him out; but (if I may stretch the parallel unduly) a social science which brings the irrational impulses of the human being once more into the picture of the social universe is unlikely to expect the method of science to yield a progressive mastery of the social environment. Physics has shown man himself to be the measure of his universe. He must be the measure of his social universe as well, but the methods by which he can achieve a mastery according to this measure are even more complex than the quantum theory and more elusive than the principle of uncertainty in physics.

Some recognition of this may have kept Americans reluctant to accept an emerging elite of scientists based on the theory that super-inventions must be the product of supermen. Nor is there, despite some doleful beliefs to the contrary, an emerging religion of science in America. It is true that science has done much to eat away the old structures of belief, and it is true that the old gods no longer rule over the American cosmos. But neither have the gods of science quite taken their place. So far from being wholly materialist, the scientific outlook did not prevent Dean Edmund Sinnott from speaking of "the biology of the spirit." So far from being wholly rationalist, science has led some of its most penetrating observers to a firmer belief in an unscientific religion which embodies some of the mystery that science has been unable to penetrate. To the Americans there is a duality about science, at once benign and baleful, which makes them wary of committing themselves wholly to it. They have learned that science can destroy as well as create, and they fear as well as embrace the miracles that seem to emerge from it.

Their crucial approach to science is manipulative. Compared with the Latin word *scientia* and the German *Wissenschaft,* the popular American word *know-how* distills the whole American approach, making sure to add the "how" to the "know." That is why science in America is not only a description of how things work (as it has been since Thales) but so quickly becomes a technique for making them work. It thrusts into the background the "why" of the philosophers and fails to ask the crucial question the Greeks asked: *To what end?* Science for Americans is a means toward ends never specifically delimited but taken for granted, perhaps because it is felt they are implicit in the technique itself. Thus a means which is limited to technology runs the danger of becoming a servant of the machine process.

For some Americans the potentials of science seem far darker exactly because of this failure to master the machine. It is the Destroyer that they see in science and not the Preserver. They sense that a science which came to liberate has left man not with a cosmos he can order but a vacuum from which he recoils and a predicament he cannot resolve. In the past a gloomy group of thinkers has argued from the laws of entropy that the world's energy is running down, and more recently another group has feared the destruction of the world through cosmic rays. But this sense of the seeds of destruction within the universe is not what troubles those who fear science today. They are troubled far more by what a science-created atomic cloud can do, or science-created radiological poison. In the case of some, at least, what was once the cult of science has become an antiscience panic.

Most Americans, however, with an organic optimism largely bred out of their experience of technological gains, are not troubled by these anxieties. They see science, and especially technology, as a means in the quest for an attainable good, and they feel certain that the good need never be explicitly defined but is implicit in the scientific quest. They regard the television eye and the electronic brain as proof that science has never lost the secret of mastery. They live within the realm of science and technology much as the American farmer once lived with the soil, as something close to their mood and experience. It is a medium in which they move much as they move in the air that they breathe.

Yet the gap between the scientist and the ordinary man, as they confront each other, is still an open one. The scientist is skeptical of every certainty except that of the method which makes him skeptical; he doubts everything except what enables his doubts to be productive of new formulations. He tries to rid himself of any sacred-cow beliefs in social institutions except for the open society without which he cannot breathe as a scientist. The common man, on the other hand, does seek certainties and is fearful that the scientist may destroy them. He wants a universe which is closed and comfortable, compact and finished. The universe of the scientist is still an expanding one, discontinuous and open. To keep it thus the scientist requires the willingness of an open society to let him follow his nose and give him the right to be wrong, both as scientist and as citizen.

3. Big Technology and Neutral Technicians

THE AMERICANS DID NOT develop modern machine technology first, but they have carried it furthest and shown the most marked affinity for it. The sway of the machine is less disputed in America than that of any other institution, including the science which made it possible, the capitalism which has organized its use, and the democracy governing the distribution of the power that flows from it. Unlike the democratic idea, which is assigned to the realm of what ought to be, the empire of Big Technology is an integral part of the daily living and thinking of Americans. They pride themselves on their "production miracles," much as the English used to call their islands the "workshop of the world."

The Big Technology has been for Americans what the Cross was for the Emperor Constantine: *In hoc signo vincas.* It set the pace for an impressively swift and thorough conquest of a new environment and of world leadership. The American has been a machine-intoxicated man. The love affair (it has been nothing less) between the Americans and their Big Technology has been fateful, for it has joined the impersonal power of the machine to the dynamism of the American character. As by some tropism of the spirit the Americans have followed out the logic of technology all the way. The world has seen civilizations based on diverse principles: on beauty and an equipoise of living, on other-worldliness and the reality of the supernatural, on close personal allegiance, on military prowess, on ascetic control of the self. But in each case the principle was embodied in the life and outlook of an elite group. Never before has the motive principle of a civilization spread so pervasively through all strata of its population, changing the lives of its ordinary people.

Veblen's ironic argument on the "merits of borrowing" (in *Imperial Germany and the Industrial Revolution*) is now familiar: that England, where the Industrial Revolution was first given scope, paid the "penalty for taking the lead" by falling behind in the later industrial race, and that the borrowing countries—America, Germany, Japan, Russia—forged ahead because they started on a higher technological level, without the cluttering bric-a-brac of customs and vested interests which Britain had developed. Toynbee, an Englishman himself, ruefully approaches the same problem in terms of "hosts" and "parasites," quoting J. B. S. Haldane's "A step in evolution in any animal group is followed by an evolutionary advance on the part of their parasites." (*A Study of History*, Vol. IV, p. 430.) Yet one cannot fail to notice that aside from the Americans the other "parasites" or "borrowers," whatever they be called, do not make the same effective use of their borrowings or hosts; and that the Germans, the Japanese, even the Russians still seem technologically like bright and enterprising younger brothers of the Americans, trying hard to catch up with his skills. There is more complexity in the machine achievement of America than is dreamed of in the philosophy of Veblen and Toynbee.

What I have said above about the social climate that favored the development of the borrowed science in America applies even more to the flowering of the borrowed seeds of technology. The resources, the separating ocean which at first spurred self-sufficiency and then served as a carrier of commerce, the lack of institutional hindrances, the tinkering skill of the craftsmen and the organizing skill of the managers, the lure of profit, the growing population and markets, the Promethean sense throughout of the mastery of a continent: it was in the frame of these influences that the Big Technology came into its empire in America.

This technological flowering came early in America's industrial revolution, so that even before the Civil War the movement of America toward industrial pre-eminence was already recognized in Europe: the testimony of Adam Smith and Malthus was that the American living standard even in their day was higher than the European for the consumption levels of the comparable classes. While the financial leadership of Britain was to continue until the turn of the century there was little doubt about where the industrial pre-eminence belonged. Not the least of the factors spurring America on this path was, as Ray Ginger has pointed out, the scarcity and mobility of American labor. Since labor was scarce, wages high, and the turnover great, an industry like American textiles had to introduce labor-saving devices rapidly and avail itself of what labor it could get, including unskilled female operators for the looms. It was a case of labor necessity mothering technical invention.

More than anything else, this pace of technological change is what gives America its revolutionary character today. It is idle to talk of a second or a third Industrial Revolution in America. The changes in production and motive power, in transport and communications, on the farm and in the city, in the air and on the ground and under the ground, have been so unremitting as to merit somewhat Trotsky's phrase, the "Permanent Revolution," which by a bold twist the editors of *Fortune* applied to the American technical and social scene. While the phrase is ripped out of its context of class meaning that Trotsky had intended, the vaguer idea of a continuing dynamism with far-reaching consequences still makes sense. The technological advance, through war and peace, through prosperity and slump, has been so constant as to become an element of the surrounding American atmosphere, easily taken for granted. The American is scarcely aware of the changes in the physical conditions of his living almost day to day; he takes a longer measurement of it by the span of generations when he compares his grandfather's daily life with his own, and that in turn with the life his grandchildren will live.

There have been brilliant American inventors, from the colonial craftsmen and the Yankee toolmakers, through Eli Whitney and Samuel Morse and Charles Goodyear, Thomas Edison and the Wright Brothers, to Lee De Forest, Leo Backeland, and Vladimir Zworykin. Yet the nature of the Big Technology cannot be understood in terms of the drama of the inventions; nor even in terms of the billions of energy units which the horsepower school of American technological greatness is fond of citing. For the transformations of power are only one phase of the characteristic pattern of American technology.

Item two is the use of precision machine tools, which have made possible the mass production not only of commodities but of machines themselves. Item three: the principle of interchangeable parts which allow the machine not only to be assembled but to be repaired with standardized ease. Item four: the "assembly line" or "belt line" method of processing an operation, first applied to iron and steel in the earlier foundries and to meat slaughtering in Cincinnati and Chicago, and then made famous by Ford in automobile manufacture. This has been modernized into a system of "continuous assembly," with conveyor belts and fork trucks both to feed the parts to the assembly line itself and also to take the finished product away; and with the whole factory laid out around the central assembly line, as around the heart arteries. Item five: the related principle of "automation," as applied to the process industries, especially to America's newest and greatest industrial segment, the chemical industries, in the form of the "continuous-flow" operation in chemical plants. In 1952 an entire napalm plant in Ohio required only four operators per shift, thus "missing 100 per cent automaticity by a hair," as a recent article on "The Factory of the Future" put it. Item six: the vacuum tube principle, which carries the automatic machine to its furthest reach in the "robot machines": already developed in the electronic calculators and the magnetic tape recorders, and likely to go much further in making the assembly line automatic and in revolutionizing not only the factory but the office as well.

Obviously not all of this is American. The development of precision machine tools is largely British, the use of power sources comes from the common Western technology, and some of the elements of the continuous-flow process were contributed by the German chemical industries. The roots of the whole mass-production process go back several centuries to the beginnings of the Industrial Revolution in Europe. American technology is the logical fulfillment of them.

One element the Americans have emphasized is the over-all principle that organizes all the technical elements—what used to be called "scientific management" and is still called the "managerial function." This has led to a high degree of resourcefulness and flexibility in both process and product, and the imaginative use of a technology that was available to all. Out of it has come an emphasis that would be impossible except where the principle of industrial organization is central: the focusing on productivity per man hour. This has become for Americans the measure and common denominator of all forms of technical progress. The strides in productivity were what amazed the Europeans most in the American production record; and when under the E.C.A. the Europeans expressed a desire to know more about the methods of American technology, they were asked by Paul Hoffman to send "productivity teams" to visit American factories and study their methods. This emphasis on a rising productivity has helped give Americans the self-confident *élan* which Nietzsche saw as a possible by-product of modern technology, and which accounts for much of the optimism and bounce in their character.

But where the Americans hold their foremost position most securely is in the machine skills. Whether they be those of scientist, inventor, machine-maker, engineer, factory planner and manager, or skilled worker, it is the skills that count most in a technology. In the abstraction of the "machine" we tend to forget that machines are created by human beings, organized and run by them. American technology is the collective possession, as it is the collective creation, of the American community. Individual inventors have been responsible for specific additions to the sum total of knowledge, tinkering, and experiment, but in every case they have stood on the shoulders of all their predecessors. Giedion, in his masterly summary of Western (especially American) technology, *Mechanization Takes Command* (1948), calls his book "anonymous history"—the story of what has been created by thousands of men whose names have in many cases been lost. This includes also the additional thousands whose ingeniously contrived ideas and gadgets never found practical use and are gathering dust in the files of the Patent Office, yet left some mark on the successful ones that follow them.

Today the task of the American inventor has become harder. If he is a lone wolf he must find a laboratory to work in, the capital to make his invention "practical" and "marketable," the factory to produce it, and the sales organization to sell it. The days are over when a couple of bicycle fixers called Wilbur and Orville Wright got some pointers for the wing design of their plane by watching the flight of birds and then built a foot-square windbox for a couple of dollars to test the wings for the flight across the sand dunes of Kitty Hawk. Plane designers today need a wind tunnel costing millions, capable of testing the stresses on planes under conditions of supersonic speed. Many inventions today are therefore the product of corporate employees working in corporate laboratories with corporate research funds, seeking new processes and products that can be subjected to corporate mass-production methods and marketed under a corporate patent monopoly by corporate distributive mechanisms to a vast mass market for corporate profit, with the inventor getting sometimes only his employee pay, and sometimes a small royalty payment added.

Americans call these collective skills underlying their technology, as they call technology itself, by the expressive word *know-how*. More and more there has been a transfer of this know-how from the many workers who used to tend the machines to the many machines that now need ever fewer workers to tend them. The crucial technological skills are now located in a small elite group of engineers and technicians who design the machines and lay out the continuous-process operations, and who know what to do when the machines break down. They are in the highest demand in industry, and every year the graduates of professional engineering schools are eagerly grabbed up by the corporations. The ultimate goal of this process is, of course, the Aldous Huxley nightmare of an auto factory or chemical plant with no worker on the assembly line, directed only by other machines which direct and feed themselves and need only taping by man's hand to set them on their course. The goal of complete automation may never be reached but it is always being approached more closely.

This process has not, as expected, resulted in the much mooted "technological unemployment." There have been two other results. One is the steady shifting of workers from the unskilled (the earth-lifting machines have almost wholly done away with the pick-and-shovel man) to the semiskilled, and from the semiskilled in turn to the skilled and highly skilled, or the technicians. Since the latter group remains small, the second result has been a further shift of workers out of the industrial occupations themselves into the merchandizing, distributive, and white-collar groups of the corporations, the professions, and the government and Army bureaucracies.

Thus by an ironic twist of history the American industrial mass civilization which seemed about to conscript the whole population into machine occupations is actually becoming something very different. It is emerging as a civilization with small specialized industrial groups, with a growing population of machines and a dwindling population of machine tenders, and with an ever larger portion of the population in nonindustrial (what Veblen used to call "pecuniary") occupations. Thus the reliance of industry on the workers is growing less, and its reliance on the machines themselves is growing greater.

As a consequence the competitive strategy of corporations is also shifting. It is less important now to keep wages down than to use the new machines in increasing productivity per man hour. And it is less important to be near a supply of cheap labor power than it is to have control of a patent tool, either to keep one's competitors at a disadvantage or to control the use of the patents by them and to collect royalties for their use. The Big Technology made the strategy of patent control the crucial strategy of American business; but it did not wipe out the fact that patent tools and patent rights themselves have little meaning except as broken-off segments of the collective heritage of community know-how.

Given these changes, and the changing patterns of work in America (which I shall discuss in the next section), there is a problem which has baffled students of American society, especially those who come to it from the experience of European history. Here (they argue) is a working population cut off from the soil, severed from its tools and from the idea of work as craft and calling: why does it not become the victim of revolutionary movements and demagogues? Granted that the unique conditions of American history have played hob with the idea of a self-conscious revolutionary proletariat, why has not America retraversed the experience of the Roman Empire, whose landless, rootless, tool-less population was used by adventurist leaders? Or the similar experience of Hitler's Germany?

Behind these questions there is the running theme of alienation and its political effects, which has been emphasized in the literature of Socialism and psychiatry from Marx to Erich Fromm. Most Americans, especially the industrial and white-collar classes, have been alienated from some crucial life experiences—from the soil, from independent enterprise, from the ownership of tools, from the sense of craft and the dignity of work, from the feeling of relation to the total product. One might expect this to turn the American into the "formless" man whom Nietzsche dreaded and whose emergence in the modern machine world Ortega y Gasset has described, and thus into easy material for either revolutionary or reactionary adventurers.

The catch is in the failure to see that men uprooted from one kind of social and institutional soil can become rooted in another. The loss of some of the old life values may affect the long-range survival of the culture, but what counts for the cohesion of a culture in the generations immediately ahead is whether people have (or think they have) what their culture has taught them to value. While the American has been alienated by the machine from his old role as independent farmer-artisan-entrepreneur, his culture still has a strong hold on him. The loss of a sense of independence in the productive processes has been replaced by a feeling of well-being in consumption and living standards. The pull of property, no longer in tools or productive land but in consumers' goods; the sense of power and pleasure in the means of sight and sound and movement placed at his disposal by the communications revolution; the glorying in what makes the world of drama and entertainment accessible; the whole range of popular culture; the feeling of access to new gradients of income and experience: these form the new soil in which the American has found new roots.

The values of income, consumption, status, and popular culture are a different set of values from those of soil and craft and small-scale productive property, and in that sense the whole ground tone of American civilization has changed under the Big Technology. But the point is that in their own way they are values, not emptiness or formlessness. Even more strikingly, it is the Big Technology that has raised living standards, created leisure, carried through the communications revolution, and set the conditions for the new popular culture. That is to say, it is the machine itself that has cut American industrial, white-collar, and professional workers away from the machine and has transferred their interest and life energies from the making of goods to the making of money with which to buy and enjoy the goods.

In this sense Big Technology has been a conservative rather than a revolutionary political force. This runs counter to Veblen's classic theory that the "instinct of workmanship" has been left in the trusteeship of the industrial workers and engineers, and that the unremitting "discipline of the machine process" is bound to undercut the "price system," whose values are at variance both with technology and the instinct of workmanship. Veblen worked out his thesis with an impressive and subtle detail. He even took account of the suction force of "leisure-class" (capitalist and consumption) values on the "underlying population," while contending that it is more than counterbalanced by the daily contact with the material and tangible and the daily submission to precision techniques. He read into the machine process, however, a psychological potency for inducing political skepticism which it does not seem to possess. Russia was industrialized under a Communist regime and Japan under a militarist one, yet in neither case did the introduction of Big Technology shape minds prepared to question the bases of authoritarianism. America was industrialized under capitalism, but the minds of the machine workers have been more concerned with their place in capitalist production and their share of capitalist distribution than with questioning the power and glory of the system which carried industrialism through.

In fact, under every system of power it is not the industrial or white-collar worker—subject to precision techniques or engineering or calculating techniques—who questions the basis of power but the intellectual dealing in ideas, values, and other intangibles. The machine process tends to make the mind more conservative by limiting the sense of personal reliance and the play of the imagination. To the worker accustomed to the tangibles of the machine, the intellectual who deals with ideas seems "up in the air" and therefore dangerous. The machine tender is likely to seek only relaxation from the machine's rigors and a larger share of the enjoyment which the machine's products place within his reach.

The sense of craftsmanship that was spread widely through the whole of the earlier agrarian-artisan society has, under the Big Technology, been specialized with the group of technicians. From Saint-Simon in nineteenth-century France to Veblen and James Burnham in twentieth-century America, students have written about the technicians ("engineers," "managers") as the carriers of social transformations. There was a brief moment during the Great Depression when the technocracy movement seemed to promise or threaten a social system run by what Veblen had called a "soviet of engineers," in terms of energy (ergs) rather than prices, profits, and wages. But technocracy, with its hopes and fears, was only a spluttering brief candle. Of more long-range importance is the "managerial revolution" which has brought about in every industrialized society a reshuffling of class lines and a shift of power. In America it would be farfetched to say that the technicians have taken power, but they have come to represent a fairly well-defined group with some marks of an elite.*

The technicians feel themselves the creators and guardians of the community's productive skills. Once the men who made the products had this sense of guardianship. Now it is the men who design and make the machines and machine tools, lay out the factories, and plan the industrial and plant operations. It is this monopoly of skills and sense of guardianship rather than any special status or power that give them the character of an elite.

I speak here, in the first instance, of the industrial technicians, but for some purposes we may stretch the category of "technician" and bring in the organizers and managers from other areas as well. There are problems of definition and analysis here which have sometimes led to confusion. When Burnham talked of the "managerial revolution," he included those who deal with people as well as those who deal with things, but the two are worth separating. In industry, for example, there are the engineers who deal with machines and production, and the executives who deal with people. Both groups may be called technicians and both may be called managers. But as technicians their skills are different, since one group is technically skilled in designing or directing the actual processes of production, while the other group is technically skilled in the business aspects of the corporation; as managers, one group is skilled in manipulating Nature and co-ordinating the tangible processes that result in making goods, while the other organizes the intangibles and manipulates men and their minds.

Both groups are integral to American life today, but while one has developed in the shadow of Big Technology, the other has developed in the shadow of the corporate empires. The two differ also in power terms. An "engineer" or "technician" usually holds an intermediate place in the corporate hierarchy, while the "managers" or "executives" are on the top rungs. When C. Wright Mills speaks of the "power elite" he includes the "chief executives" but omits the engineers and technicians. This illustrates a tendency on the part of some American observers, following Veblen, to stress the manipulative and power aspects of the new managerial groups, while they underplay their technical aspects. You can, of course, squeeze a good deal of irony out of the paradox that the top men in industry actually know relatively little about the technical

* I am here primarily concerned with the technician as engineer, who deals with things and materials. For the technician as businessman or "chief executive" of a corporation, see Ch. V, especially Sec. 2, "The Rise and Decline of the Titan," and Sec. 3, "The Corporate Empires." For a further discussion of political technicians, see Ch. VI, Sec. 4, "The Party System and the Voter," and Sec. 6, "The Governmental Managers," and for the military technicians, see Ch. XII, Sec. 4, "Landscape with Soldiers."

processes of production and get paid mainly for manipulating and co-ordinating men. They can therefore shift almost at will from one indus-try to another—from autos to cigarettes to electronics—and they become thereby the truly mobile men of American society.

Yet this should serve as a clue to what I am myself stressing here—the central neutrality of the technician (whether engineer, manager, or ex-ecutive), in the sense of his dissociation from passion, commitment, or value other than his own skill in execution. The very fact that an execu-tive can shift, without a break in his career, from cracker-making to radio-making is a sign of this neutrality. Equally a sign of it is the fact that since the executives don't own the business they manage, the profits and losses and risks are not their own. To be sure, they possess power and relish it, but even their power may be called a neutral one: it is a disembodied power that can be linked now with one enterprise, now with another. Not only the engineers but the executives as well thus have a kind of neutrality, in the sense of seeing themselves as executors of interests and purposes not their own. They have not taken over the governing functions, nor is there any sign that they want to or can. They have concentrated on the fact of their skills rather than on the uses to which their skills are put. The question of the *cui bono* the technician regards as beyond his own competence. With his training in specializa-tion and the division of labor, he is the more inclined to leave the values of politics to the politician, war to the general, beauty to the artist, and religion and morals to the preacher.

The role of the Neutral Technician thus casts its shadow over the whole present era. It becomes the Great Withdrawal, or—as Erich Kahler puts it—a kind of nihilism of values along with an exaltation of tech-niques. "What is the job you want done," asks the technician, "and I'll do it." Many worriers about American life have worried about commer-cialism in art and literature and thought, but often what seems a sell-out for money is as likely to be surrender to the technician's sense of neu-trality: the feeling that the technique carries its own ethic with it and that the use of technics is not to be judged by a system of ethics out-side it.

One can speak of the varieties of technical experience in America. They have obscured the fact of a unity of outlook which cuts across them, whose core is the overriding sense of technical assurance and neutrality. The engineers, corporate managers, government administra-tors and civil servants, scientists, Army officers, lawyers, writers for the movies and the radio, ad writers, public-relations men: however diverse they may be in other respects, they are all there to do a job whose shape and purposes are determined by others. Thus the Federal government workers are required by the Hatch Act to refrain from any political activity: America has gone much further than Britain, for example, in making political eunuchs of its civil service. A similar neutrality is coming to be expected of the growing centers of transport and communication. In the case of policemen, for example, even the right to join unions has been challenged. In the case of the military services the doctrine of neutrality is of great moment, since the swelling of military forces and of the war segment of the economy has given the officer class more power than ever in American history.

The episode of the dismissal of General MacArthur in 1951 illuminated the crisis of technical neutrality. On the one hand, the principle of civilian control of the military had been challenged by a great soldier in an important area of policy. On the other hand, much of MacArthur's popular support came from the implicit belief in the technical division of labor: since MacArthur was a general (it was reasoned) he ought to know about war and peace; therefore President Truman's effort to control him was civilian meddling. Which is to say, again, that the technic carries its own ethic.

The situation of the scientists sets them apart from the other technicians. Given their freedom to work, American scientists have paid little heed to what is done socially with their discoveries. Scientific detachment, which began as a shield against entangling alliances that might hamper the single-minded concentration on scientific work, became an isolating barrier. Objectivity became quietism and withdrawal, disinterestedness turned into uninterestedness, scientific method into social apathy. The scientists' pride of specialization buttressed the wall he had built between what was being fashioned in the realm of science and what was happening in the "unscientific" realm of human relations.

It took the atom bomb to shatter that wall and jolt American scientists into a sense of responsibility about the new world they had been so instrumental in shaping. Perhaps nothing short of the vision of atomic death—"the good news of damnation"—could have had such an effect. The American physicists became men who have known sin and cannot erase the memory. The sense of shock and guilt led some to turn their emphasis to the life sciences, led others into the cause of "world government," still others to a group vigil for civilian control of atomic energy and for the maintenance of an open society in the face of the "security" demands of the new war weapons. Almost alone among the technicians, the scientists grappled with the ethical consequences of technics.

A study by Meier of the political attitudes of scientists (in the *Bulletin of Atomic Scientists*) showed the engineers tending on the whole toward conservatism, the chemists toward the middle of the road, and the physicists toward the liberal and radical. Allowing for the vagueness of the political terms, the study is worth noting. It suggests that where science approaches most closely to the applied sciences (mainly engineering, since chemistry is borderline) the neutral role of the technician asserts itself; but with theoretical science, especially in physics, the scientist asks questions about the uses to which his work is put. For the work of theoretical science is not a reflection of the machines: it precedes them. It is work involving a high degree of imaginativeness and severe logic. Like other men of ideas, the scientists are not content, with Hamlet, "to eat the air, promise-crammed." Science and technology are revolutionary only in the sense that they have extended the realm of the socially possible to keep pace—although always at some remove—with the sense of the technically possible.

But turning back to the technicians, what makes their place in America so contradictory is that, despite the stretching of social possibility by technology itself, the technicians for the most part remain a guild of neutral artificers. They have brought a universe of living standards and popular culture within reach of a population from whose choices and dilemmas they have cut themselves off.

4. Work and the Automatic Factory

IN FEW RESPECTS has American culture been as radically transformed as in the relation of the machine to the industrial process, and of the worker to the machine and the job. One thinks back to Emerson's "the office of America is to liberate" and wonders how the assembly line fits into this office, and whether those who tend the machines and whose work is set to their pace have been liberated.

Many of the generalizations about work, as about other aspects of life in the Old Society of Jefferson and Jackson, and even of Lincoln and Bryan, are no longer true in the New Society. The greatest change has come about in the "gospel of work." Except for the ante-bellum South there were no Greek notions in America of work as a badge of dishonor, something belonging to a lower caste while the elite cultivates the mind or the graces of living. Freshly wrested from the frontier wilderness, the American land was a living reminder of the relation between work and survival; and as America grew in wealth it was a reminder also of the relation of work to its immediate rewards.

And to ultimate rewards also, for the religious spirit of America's Protestant sects reinforced the practical reasons for work by bringing God's reasons to bear as well. The American bourgeois spirit, which existed in its purest form where economic man met religious man, regarded idleness as sinful and the way of work as the good way. "Work

. . . while it is day," said Jesus to his disciples. "For the night cometh, when no man can work." The American moralists found other ways of saying this, but the utilitarian reasons were strongly buttressed by religious sanctions. In the whole calendar of economic virtues, from Franklin's Poor Richard and Samuel Smiles and Richard Parton to Andrew Carnegie and Henry van Dyke, work was the primal source of all the others. Even the rich who did not have to work felt uneasy when they did not, and a life of complete leisure was more likely to be regarded as parasitism in the context of the Puritan tradition than anywhere else in the capitalist world. The great folk myths of America too, which expressed the proletarian spirit as Poor Richard expressed the bourgeois spirit—the stories of Paul Bunyan and Mike Fink, of Casey Jones and John Henry—are myths of mighty workers and their work prowess.

But as the myth has it, John Henry broke his heart when he tried to compete with the monstrous strength of the steam crane. I take this as an allegory of the dehumanizing of work in consequence of Big Technology.

The gospel of hard work took long to die. There has been no American chronicler of the "condition of the working classes" to equal Engels or the Hammonds for the condition of the English. But it is clear that Blake's "dark, Satanic mills" do not apply to the factory experience of America, where labor was scarce, technical innovation moved fast, and "scientific management" had an early start. The American factories in the early nineteenth century were very different from their European counterparts; the early factory owners tried to avoid the excesses of the English and the European experience, including long hours, child labor, poor pay, and scabrous working and living conditions. Eli Whitney's factories were relatively comfortable places, with decent housing provided for the workers in the vicinity. The Lowell mills were models of comfort, and the girls who came to work in them were drawn to the work in preference to the less interesting and more menial jobs of domestic work and teaching. A few years' work at Lowell provided a young girl of good family with money enough so that she could bring a respectable dowry and a dignified background to her prospective husband. The idea behind the early American factories, as Mitchell Wilson has pointed out, was that the American worker was a dignified human being entitled to decent treatment.

The panic of 1837 changed the picture, driving many millowners and manufacturers to the wall and giving them a reason for treating the workers in a more exploitative way. The new tides of immigration, by providing a large labor force whose living standards were lower, made the situation worse. Toward the end of the century there were "sweatshops" in American garment manufacture, there was child labor, and until 1923 there was a seventy-two-hour week in the steel industry. Yet despite these changes the old Protestant-bourgeois work ethic died in America for other reasons than applied to the dirty, crowded factories and the long, exhausting hours of the English Industrial Revolution.

One might say that the old work ethic died because the work became dehumanized and joyless, but this would miss the fact that joylessness in itself might strengthen the Puritan work ethic, making work an end in itself. What did happen was that, with the growth of the big corporation, work became depersonalized; and with the change in the immigrant experience and composition, hard work became associated with the foreign-born, the Negroes, the illiterates, and the underlying social strata. The atmosphere of the Big Money and the knowledge that so much of the income comes by way of what the workers consider "easy rackets," all conspired to strip work of its incentives. In the thinking both of the corporate employers and the trade-union members work came to be expressed mainly in money terms. It was cut off from a sense of creativeness and lost much of its dignity and meaning. The idea of the dignity of work died not in the "dark, Satanic mills" but in the well-lighted, ingeniously laid out, scientifically organized assembly-line plants, and in the spacious headquarters and offices of the great American corporations. What has replaced it on the employers' side is the ethic of efficiency and profit and on the workers' side the ethic of security and success.

There is a triple process of transformation that has taken place in the American work pattern. The symbol of one phase was the white-collar worker; the removal of work, for an ever-growing section of those "gainfully employed," from industrial operations themselves to the stockroom, the fileroom, the office pool, the salesroom, the promotion and advertising office. This was part of the more general bureaucratization of economic life. The functional split in the work patterns carried with it a psychological split as well, with the white-collar worker clinging to his sense of differentiated status and of superiority to the industrial worker. The second phase of the change was the assembly line, which came to dominate an ever-larger segment of what workers were still left in contact with the industrial processes themselves. The assembly line arose because of the need for connecting isolated machines and workers: this need was precisely the point at which industry became bureaucratized. The outcry against the assembly line misses the fact that a bureaucracy is the natural and necessary outgrowth of modern technology. The third, applying to those who still worked at the stationary machines and were the "machine tenders" proper, was monotony and anonymity, the carrying of the process of subdividing industrial operations so far that the worker became himself almost an interchangeable part in a factory world of interchangeable parts.

White-collar work, assembly-line work, anonymity: these were the new work patterns which transformed the American work attitudes.

The mechanical skill and curiosity of American workers have continued unabated. In a nation of tinkerers, the American youngster as he grows up delights in taking apart and putting together whatever machines and motors he can lay his hands on. The drive to understand how and why machines work is the impulse behind much of the American talent for technology. It was this impulse that furnished much of the incentive for the early toolmakers and inventors. Nor has *homo faber* died out in America, whether in the small factory, the school machine shop, or the home basement workshop. But these are residual areas in which the old sense of craftsmanship still finds scope. It is not applied as fervently to work done for impersonal corporations and invisible employers with whom the worker has no direct relation.

Life on "the job" tends to be a joyless life, squeezed dry of any zest in work. On most jobs the frame of the day is set by the time clock. On the assembly line especially, as in the auto factory, time is the master. A worker who cannot keep pace with the speed at which the line is moving disarranges the whole process and throws the work of everyone else out of gear. He is enclosed in a space out of which he can move only by invading the working space of his neighboring worker. Hour after hour he uses the same muscles in the same motions at the same operations. Armed with his power tools for setting the parts in place and tightening them, he is himself a machine using a machine for assembling another machine. The tensions on his nervous system are great, but while he must concentrate on his work he does not become absorbed with it, since neither his creative faculties nor his imagination are caught.

The crux of craftsmanship is the satisfaction of seeing the relation between the hard and monotonous detailed work and the form and quality of the finished product. This means understanding how the details are put together: even though the craftsman may work at only one segment, he must see and understand the organization and planning of the whole. The American worker gets little chance at this. Not only does he work at only a fragment, about which he cares little, of a whole he rarely sees: he also is cut off from any participation in the planning. It was therefore (as Roger Burlingame has pointed out) entirely characteristic that—except for a few top scientists—those who worked on the atom bomb project should have been unaware of its nature. This was, to a heightened degree of deliberate secrecy, the logical expression of the anonymous place the worker has in the industrial process even when no secrecy is intended. The worker, who had been torn away from the American land by Big Technology and from the ownership of his tools by large-scale capitalism, has now been torn also from his total product and denied a chance to build his personality around the processes at which he works. The idealized profile of the worker in the dithyrambic book by Ernst Jünger, *Der Arbeiter* (1932), which made so great a stir in a Germany on the brink of National Socialism, was a portrait of the modern type-figure of power who is at once planner and creator and is impelled by a mystical demiurge to the shaping of the future world. This would strike no chord in the men who work and live in Detroit or Duluth, or in the "industrial triangle" between New York, Chicago, and St. Louis.

There is little in the American industrial or white-collar worker either of Ruskin's medieval craftsman or Jünger's romantic proletarian demiurge. His life on the job is flat and two-dimensional, contained between the wage system and the price system. As a consequence of having himself been made a means rather than an end in the work relation he has in turn made his job a means rather than an end.

This has happened even while the American corporate managers have been paying considerable attention to the worker and his morale. Where England's contribution to the arts of management was the factory system itself, and Germany's was the early introduction of social legislation, America's managerial genius showed itself in "scientific management" and "human relations in industry." From Frederick W. Taylor's early time-and-motion studies to the most recent work of Elton Mayo the aim has been a double one: to keep the worker cheerful and happy (scientific managers speak of workers' "morale"—a term otherwise reserved for the wartime mood of soldiers and civilians) and at the same time to get the highest productivity per man hour out of the worker-machine combination.

The earlier scientific managers tended to think of the factory mainly as a physical arena for efficiency operations. Their layout of plants and their organization of line-and-staff functions, departmentalizing, unit size of operations, and even the fatigue factors of the job were masterpieces of forethought. But the later managers noted anxiously that workers were sullen, resisting the best-intentioned managerial layouts and reorganizations, and that—for all the ingenuity spent in keeping them happy—they had no basic interest in their work. The emphasis therefore shifted from the factory as a managerial arena to the factory as a society.

An American factory is more complex than appears on the surface. What seems a single assembly line contains a whole network of sub-assemblies, conveyer belts, and unloading and loading systems. And

what seems a uniform group of workers is a society made up of sub-
groups, income and power hierarchies, status clusters. True, the job
has been separated from the bar, the ball game, and the TV set, and
once the worker is off the job he turns to what will recreate and re-
charge him. Yet almost half of his waking hours are spent on the job.
The factory is thus, next to the family group, the most constant society
that Americans know during the major part of their adult years. Here
friendships are formed and maintained, here a man's endurance is
measured against others. Here he seeks and gets his sense of prestige
and status, here his rivalries are centered and his hopes or heartbreak
over merit and promotion. Each man stands here in some kind of relation to an authority over him (foreman, inspector, department head,
plant superintendent, owner-boss) and in many cases to subordinates
or apprentices under him. The prestige divisions of the world outside
the factory—between ethnic and religious groups, between native and
foreign-born, between skilled and unskilled, educated and illiterate—
find here their mirror and expressions.

Thus the Big Technology has gone beyond techniques and has become a principle of social order. The earlier idea, as Roethlisberger
puts it, was that "all you have to do is produce, and human problems
will take care of themselves." But the personnel managers and their
bosses had to learn to reckon with the factory as a society. Through
pamphlets and promotion material, through special courses, through
social events organized for both the rank and file and the executives,
they tried to link the personality of the worker with the corporation.
They even reached back into the high schools, distributing literature
and films to prepare the potential employee for identifying himself
with the company.

How hungry some of the workers are for this kind of recognition of
their human quality is shown by the work of Roethlisberger and Dickson in the Hawthorne experiments, under the guidance of Elton Mayo.
In an effort to isolate the factors affecting productivity he kept shifting
one factor after another, only to find a progressive increase of productivity with each shift. One conclusion has been that the workers—semiskilled and white-collar girls—worked better because the interest shown
by the investigators in their jobs and them gave them a renewed sense
of the importance of both. Yet the problem was not so simple. In one
of the Hawthorne studies—that of the bank wiring room—there was the
same condition of the observer and his interest in the work, yet there
was no increase in productivity. Mayo himself did not seem to have
resolved this paradox, but Conrad Arensberg and others have suggested
an explanation. The bank wiring room operated inside the ordinary
channels of supervision and management; on the other hand, the girls

in the test room, as part of the experimental procedure, helped make the decisions about their own working conditions.

If this key is the valid one* it has far-reaching implications. As long as the worker is treated as a physical object, as only a factor in production, the efforts to give him recognition and status will be futile. True, he reacts positively to the Hawthorne type of experiment, which deeply affected American personnel work. But eventually the feeling of being noticed peters out, and what was once special recognition becomes the expected and routine treatment. This is why wage-incentive and profit-sharing plans work only up to a certain point. Before long the incentive situation becomes the expected situation. In the end the worker must find recognition and status in his own feeling about the work he does, and if the work is trivial and he has no hand in setting it he will never feel that he has any dignity in it. That was the importance of the bank wiring study since it showed that what the worker wants is not (like a spoiled child) only some attention but the chance of a mature person to make his own decisions and set the frame of his work.

The sympathetic interest in the worker may in the end seem only synthetic to him, because the primary relation on the job is a wage-and-profit relation. Hence the "industrial-welfare offensive" always contends with the suspicion that the corporation is using its welfare plans as a dollars-and-cents device and not as a social end. A number of observers have written skeptically of the "harmony-of-interests" premise underlying the corporate "welfare offensive," whether in the form of employee representation plans or shops' councils, company unions or corporate insurance plans; and the response of many unions to the growing shift from "practical" to "sophisticated" conservatism on the part of the corporate employers has also been skeptical. Yet many unions are going along with the trend, for the simple reason that it makes sense to the workers in human terms, as well as in dollars and cents. The "welfare corporation" is emerging as a natural corollary of the "welfare state." It must be noted, however, that whether the union's attitude is sympathetic or militant, whether the premise is class harmony or class conflict, both flow from the transformation of the work relation and the alienation of the worker from his job.

Men are lined up in the closed world of the factory as items in cost accounting, along with the machine and materials, the plant, and the distributing mechanism. Rarely is the worker used to the hilt of his capacity; it is in the failure to give him scope for his full abilities that the tragic failure of Big Technology comes. Even when the corporate job gives him a chance to develop or use responsibility, the worker is

---

* There is still considerable doubt about this. For a brilliant study of the whole problem, see Daniel Bell, *Work and Its Discontent* (1956).

unlikely to seek it. Sensing that the crucial decisions about his work are made by others, he feels no responsibility and little creativeness in it. As for the trade-unions, even when they have fought militantly for workers' rights, they have interpreted those rights narrowly, as claims to a larger share of the income from the product. The crucial fact about a job has become the money payment, and the jobs are measured against one another almost wholly in terms of money rather than of satisfaction or craftsmanship in the work. The top-level people in the trade-unions tend to concentrate on the big economic issues, leaving the problems of human relations to be worked out on the floor of the plant by the local representatives. On that immediate level there have been, as William F. Whyte has pointed out, a number of situations in which management and the union officers have succeeded in finding substitute satisfaction for the lost sense of craftsmanship. Again this has happened mainly where the worker has been drawn into some of the decisions on the technical, economic, and social problems of the plant.

In the absence of such efforts the idea of work tends to become on both sides the idea of a job—that is to say, a dollar relation rather than a human relation. The worker knows that when his responses are not as alert or his stamina as great, he will be discarded, with pension provisions if he is lucky, but that with or without them he will feel useless. If he is a Negro there will be a limited market for his ability or training. The decline from the idea of "work" to the idea of a "job" measures the falling away from the work pattern of everything except the pecuniary factor.

The job idea is an important one for Americans. In one sense it means any technical task to be finished and disposed of: war, a political campaign, a book to be read or written, a household chore, a gangster's assignment. A good executive in any area disposes of people with dispatch and then sweeps both his desk and his mind clear of encumbrances. The periods of unemployment, when for millions there were no jobs to be had, gave an added febrile value to "the job"; but it was a value deriving not from a sense of the fitness of the work but from the fear of having none at all. The job becomes mainly an earthwork thrown up against insecurity. The primary necessity is that the job continuity should not be broken; the primary question is the amount of take-home pay. The continuity of the pay envelope is the pay-off.

While the amount of pay and the degree of security are the primary questions about the job, they are not the only ones. Elmo Roper adds from his polling experience four other elements that count for the workers: whether the job overworks them, whether merit is rewarded, whether there is a chance for advancement, and whether they find the job "interesting." It is worth noting that all except the last can be translated into terms of burden and pay, even the reward of merit and the chance for advancement. The results of Roper's polling of a cross-section of Americans on their attitudes toward their jobs show two out of three (64.7 per cent) finding them "really interesting," the rest either lukewarm or apathetic. However vague the question, it is worth noting that men were more satisfied than women, whites more than Negroes, city workers more than those in small towns and on farms, professional and executive people more than wage-earners, and the prosperous (87.2 per cent) more than the poor (48 per cent).

It is not so much that the Americans are (as Mills would have it) "cheerful robots," as that they live in a twilight world between a sense of loss and a sense of resigned acceptance. The acceptance emerges clearly from the Roper figures, provided we note that it diminishes as the job decreases in pay and status. The sense of loss is not so clear. Two out of three (62 per cent) felt that they were neither "ideally" nor "miserably" adjusted to their job and company, but felt split or apathetic about it. When asked whether, in starting their working life over again, they would choose a different trade or occupation, 57 per cent answered that they would, and only one out of three (31 per cent) that they would choose the same. Just possibly this may be an expression of dynamism, but more likely it is an indictment of the work life Americans have. Many felt their mistake had been made in not getting enough education in their youth. Many also felt certain that their sons would do better than they did—again the dual expression of dynamism and a sense of loss.

To be sure, one must be wary of taking these figures at their face value. Many workers may say they are dissatisfied with their jobs because they are *supposed* to be dissatisfied: that is the self-image they have. The fact that they don't change their jobs more often, in a relatively fluid labor market, may be the effective commentary on their supposed dissatisfaction. There are frequent complaints from management that it cannot find enough workers with skill, interest, and curiosity to fill the needed foremen's jobs. There is also the fact that many workers prefer repetitive and monotonous jobs exactly because they are undemanding and do not stretch them too much. But this lack of initiative on the part of the worker may itself be the most damning of evidence of the deterioration of the whole work relation which I have described.

"Where your treasure is, there will your heart be too." To those who complain that American workers do not have their hearts in their jobs, one may suggest that they do not feel the treasure of their creativeness to be there. It is only in wartime that the American worker is asked to devote himself and his work to a larger goal than individual gain and profit. The old question of nonpecuniary incentives is raised sharply where the psychic drives of people have been split away from their work lives. The talent for organizing that Americans have shown, the time sense and the sense of timing, the ability to break a job into small parts and reassemble them into a working whole, the feeling for effective structure shown in the distributive mechanism, add up in the end to a manipulativeness of the spirit. They are an expense of genius (for the collective managerial talent of America is nothing less) in the pursuit of ends that rarely get below the surface of the personality. With all the vaunted organization of the plant and office, what is left out is a feeling of growth and fulfillment for those involved. Whether Americans are happy and expressive, and to what extent, are moot points. But what is not moot is the fact that they pursue their happiness and get their expressiveness principally away from their jobs.

In the case of a minority there is a powerful impulse for advancement which pushes them to hard work, often to extra work beyond the call of the job: but the aim here is success, not growth and development. But for most the work on the job is so monotonous that they are incapable of generating the extra energy or imagination on the job which form part of the great American work myth. It is in this sense that a technological system so magnificent at producing and distributing commodities runs the danger of flattening out the men themselves.

How much of all this has been changed by "automation," which is the latest and perhaps the culminating phase of the American technological revolution? The essence of automation is the replacement of the worker who operates the machine by the machine that operates machinery. During the earlier phases of the continuing revolution the elements of production were broken down and assigned to machines that had to be regulated and controlled by workers. In the case of automation the productive system has developed built-in mechanisms of regulation and control. Its ultimate goal is the almost workerless factory, office, and salesroom. The characteristic of the old machine was its repetitive capacity: raw materials were fed into it while it repeated the same operation endlessly, but it had to be overseen and its products had to be assembled. What is fed into the automatic machine is not raw material but *information*. The machine then operates by the principle of *feedback*, and the results are communicated to the entire process, whether it be the generation of electric power, or the mixing of chemicals, or the making of synthetic fertilizers, soaps, and detergents, or the numberless uses of telecommunication.

Since the principle involved is similar to the mechanism of the human nervous system and even of the human brain, these machines have been spoken of as "thinking" machines, and some commentators have been moved to suggest that the machine can now replace the human brain, while the brain is little more than a machine. Such an approach misses the difference between machinery and the human spirit, between the brain itself and what the brain contrives in order to rid itself of routine burdens, and it is therefore itself a symptom of the age of automation. What concerns us here, however, is not so much the fallacy that the machine can duplicate man, but the fact that the new machinery is coming to function without the men and women who used to watch over the operation of the old machines.

The old Malthusian fear—that there would be a surplus of population over the available food supplies (and therefore jobs)—has been replaced by an anxiety about whether there will be enough jobs (and therefore food supplies) to go around when the machines have taken over the empire of industry. In the mid-1950s America was still exploring the answer to this problem. But in essence it was no different a problem from the one that had faced Americans throughout their technological revolutions. There had always been anxiety about the displacement of men by machines, and in the end the machines had always created new jobs by broadening the scope of the industrial process, by creating new income and new consumer demands, and by shifting the emphasis to distributive, social-welfare, and leisure-time services. The consequences of automation were likely to be of the same sort, but to a higher degree. Americans would need a large number of technicians to plan, make, and drive the machines. They would need fewer workers in industrial production and more in meeting the leisure needs that would flow from the reduced working day. The economy was shifting from one organized around the use of natural resources and human labor to an economy organized around the use of time and the access of more people to what the culture offered.

As another consequence of automation, Americans are looking forward to the end of drudgery-on-the-job. The trivial tasks are being turned over wholly to the machines, without the need for the strained pace-setting of the assembly line and the attention it required. What remains are what Adam Abruzzi calls the "distinguished" as against the "undistinguished" jobs—the planning for what the new machines will do, the study of the situations in which they are likely to break down, the imaginative and the contemplative challenge of thinking out the total design for work and leisure of which the machines form a part. An era was opening in which the worker might again have restored to him his skill and responsibility, and the control of his working pace.

The dogma that idleness is somehow a sin was part of an age that is passing. An age of automatic machines would put a premium on leisure in which the mind would not be idle.

This has already transformed America into a nation of amateurs. If one phase of the work revolution was summed up in "automation," another was expressed in the phrase "do-it-yourself." Nourished by the fact of the vanishing domestic servant and of skyrocketing costs, "do-it-yourself" was primarily an effort to recapture in the leisure hours the sense of the wholeness of a piece of work that had been lost in the plant and office when work was transformed into the "job." The same worker who hurried away from his plant because his job offered few psychic satisfactions was likely to spend hours tinkering with carpentry, adding an attic to his house,, or painting a canvas, putting into his amateur work the emotional energy he could not express on his job. Here he could see the relation between the initial idea and the finished product; here he could follow his own pace and be his own boss. Without intending it Americans found that they were swinging back at home to the kind of work relation that had been lost somewhere in the course of building up a factory system and the job-wage nexus.

America found itself in the mid-1950s with three streams of tendency in relation to work: a factory system which was still the heart of industrialism but was losing its workers and being run by machines; a growing working population of engineers and of nonindustrial technicians, with an ever greater role for education in the further changes of the productive process; and a trend toward do-it-yourself amateurism which helped to fill the void left in work-hungry human beings by the dehumanizing of the "job."

5. *The Wilderness of Commodities*

THE WORLD of the consumer which results from American work and technology is one of profusion and variety. The consumer lives in a wilderness of commodities whose impact on the minds of Americans themselves, as on that of the world, is one of richness. American living standards are the boast of politicians and editorial writers and the target of sermons, and during the Cold War they were a main reliance in American psychological warfare against Communist systems. "No ordinary Russian," Bruce Barton told a convention of salesmen, "ever suspected such a wealth of wonderful and desirable objects exists anywhere in the world as the Sears, Roebuck catalogue presents." On a more academic level David Riesman ironically told (in "The Nylon War") how the hold of the Russian rulers was broken by a military campaign of bombarding them with millions of pairs of nylon stockings and other items from the American cornucopia. For the ordinary American the belief in the idea of progress is reinforced by the visible sign of his rising living standards. Adapting a phrase of Toynbee's, one might call this the "idolization of ephemeral enjoyments." The popular literature and culture celebrate not technology or even business and the making of money but the grandeurs and miseries of a consumer's civilization. America seems strikingly to illustrate Sorokin's category of the "sensate culture."

This has led to an indictment of Americans as "materialists," which has generally been accepted by both Americans and foreigners, by the intellectuals as well as the preachers. Recently some of the intellectuals have begun to question the indictment. "The virtue of American civilization," Mary McCarthy has ventured, "is that it is unmaterialistic. It is true that America produces and consumes more cars, more soap and bathtubs, than any other nation, but we live *among* these objects rather than *by* them."

In getting at the truth about American "materialism," we may ask what are the dominant gods in the heaven of the American as consumer?

First, there is *comfort*. Waldo Frank described it as "the violent lust for ease" on the part of the American pioneer, and it is true that after the rigors of American settlement there was an effort to cushion the rudeness of the physical environment. The pioneer had a rough life; his descendants wanted comfort—in home and travel, in hotels, cars, and planes, at the clubs, in visiting and entertainment. The Puritan made the inner *ascesis* of spirit tangible by outer denials; his descendants want neither the outer nor inner denials. Yet the persisting malaise of spirit remains, whether due to the American situation or the human condition. The more comfortless the American feels, the more he seeks to pile up physical comforts.

Next to the godliness of comfort, there is *cleanliness*. Giedion has noted how many of the American mechanical improvements have been concerned with the bathroom. The American household has a whole cleansing hierarchy, with chemical and mechanical aids to constant domestic and personal cleanliness. Every part and pore of the body has its special cleanser, disinfectant, deodorant. The most frightening surmise in the world of the fear advertisements is that you may be afflicted with the odor about which "your best friend won't tell you." Perhaps all this came from an effort to shut out the sights and smells of industrialism, perhaps from the desire to dissociate oneself from the indicia of manual labor. Some who have been struck by the constant bathing of the American—female and male alike—have even suggested that there is a relation between the obsession with cleansing and some collective and Puritanical sense of guilt. Whatever the sources, the fact is there.

Peeling away the layers of meaning in American "materialism" one comes next to *novelty:* the sheer delight in a gadget-cluttered environment, with new devices and new models constantly replacing earlier ones. The American acknowledges with a wry humor that the latest models of cars, refrigerators and bathroom fixtures, of fashions in clothes and books and ideas, do not necessarily serve the life purposes better than the previous models: yet he seems driven by a compulsion to replace them. There is, to be sure, a nostalgic affection for the days of the Stanley Steamer and other early automobile models, but with the nostalgia of yesterday there is the sense of the superiority of today.

There is, on the other hand, nothing whimsical about the American attitude toward *service.* It is the lagniappe of the bargain the American consumer makes with his machine culture, the "extra" thrown in. To get service in buying a dress, or gas for your car, or a meal in a restaurant, is to feel that your personality is recognized. To be sure, the fact is that service in crowded American restaurants or on trains and planes or at airports is often wretched: in an era of approaching automation the extra touch of concern for human sensibility may seem archaic. Yet it is exactly this function of service—as a survival of pre-machine standards in a machine age, a footnote attesting to the graces of the past—that makes it still important to the American consumer.

The comfortable, the convenient, the clean, the polished and glittering, the ingenious, the novel, the extra bit of service: these form some of the ingredients of the American "materialism." And the most marked ingredient of all, containing and encompassing all the rest, is the overwhelming measure of American consumer abundance.

It is as wide of the mark to deride this as "a Coca-Cola civilization" as it is to use the standard N.A.M. argument that this plenitude of products and gadgets is proof of America's having found the key to a good life. Actually there is a grotesque disproportion about the national values which is revealed by the direction of American spending. More is spent on cosmetics, tobacco, liquor, than on public education. The health services are relatively starved, the serious arts are sometimes neglected. And for one American family out of four or five, life is still a rat race of worry, work, and scrimping.

It remains true, however, that there are more good things available to a higher proportion of Americans than in any other society. This is not a matter of piglike, sensuous reveling in material things. The long-established image of America as a kind of golden sty is a stereotype with more envy and ignorance than truth. The vast array of available commodities has become an American way of living, but it does not follow that Americans are more likely than others to confuse living standards with life values, or mistake good things for the good life. Many Americans— like many other human beings—do live *by* things as well as *among* them. But many others know that, like the machine, the shopwindow crowded with glittering items carries no ethic with it. It does not become an end in itself except for the impoverished of spirit, who are to be found in any civilization. What is true in America is that they find it easier to disguise their impoverished spirit behind the gaudy raiments of a consumer's plenty.

A more marked element in the American situation is the drive toward competitive consumption. The "folklore of capitalism" has it that production in America is competitive and that living is co-operative. It is truer to say that competition is being crowded out of production and that its real area is now in consumption. The drive to "keep up with the Joneses"—or with the fashion magazines, the TV heroes and heroines, the movie colony, the advertising slogans—has been an undoubted spur to consumption and living standards for all classes unparalleled in history. Veblen made much of it in his satiric description of "conspicuous consumption" and "pecuniary emulation," yet he underestimated the inner drive of expanding consumption that did not depend on emulation but drew upon the pervasive hunger for commodities and material satisfactions. Erich Fromm analyzed the competitive strains in the "marketing orientation" of the personality under capitalism, but his emphasis on the "alienation" that resulted from it missed the point that Americans find a kind of wholeness in their living standard as a substitute for what they once found on the land. Riesman described the "other-directed" emphasis of the emerging American character, where less depends on what you are or even on what you enjoy than on what others think of you; but he was more interested in the impact of the popular culture than of consumption upon the national character. David Potter supplied the latter emphasis in his *People of Plenty,* where he traced the effects of consumer abundance and especially of advertising on the American personality.

On one level, competitive consumption is simply a phase of the Faustian sense of power which has shown itself throughout American history. To strive for the biggest city population, the highest office building, the largest football stadium, the most successful charity drive, the biggest national magazine circulation, the longest theater run, the most staggering book sales, is characteristic of a culture still exulting in the illusion of the illimitable. For the consumer it shows itself in the steadily enlarging dream which has brought life's necessities within the scope of most people and has made one luxury after another a necessity.

What class is the carrier of this expanding dream? Again Veblen serves as a useful measure of the distance that American living has traveled in the past half century. In his *Theory of the Leisure Class,* Veblen saw turn-of-the-century America as the climactic expression, under modern capitalist forms, of the values which were given shape by the old feudal aristocracies and which spread down to the masses. It is true that the emphasis on prowess may be found in a money culture as well as in a feudal one, and that the consumer stereotypes which Americans seek to copy were originally those of the elite. Yet this again misses at least half the point, which is that American living standards and mass-produced commodities have leveled many of the class differences. The car of the wealthy man may be a Cadillac or Chrysler, but the Oldsmobile or Plymouth or Ford of the middle and working classes may look almost as glittering and may be equally chromium-adorned. The rich woman has more dresses and more expensive ones than the suburban housewife or the secretary, but their taste is probably as good as hers. They get their styles from the same fashion magazines and often they look every bit as chic. The carrier of the consumer's dream in America is as much the middle class as the monied class or aristocracy.

The aristocracy is there—a monied aristocracy whose sons make power and whose daughters make glamour a way of life; and there is in it a luminous and magnetic force to which, as to a moon, the tides of American living standards respond. But the tides themselves are mainly middle-class tides. "Society," in the sense the term had in the days of the great mansions and the early big fortunes, no longer exists in America. The old "society" has merged with "cafe society" and the "expense-account aristocracy" and has been muted by a prevailing informality of manners, clothes, and taste. The new informality of suburban clothes is not unlike the informality of Hollywood and Palm Beach. What was not clear to Veblen and his emulators was that the new American power groups who took over the forms of past aristocracies filled them with values of their own—middle-class values; that the dog beneath the skin of the aristocratic hound was a middle-class dog; and that the copiers, however fumbling their progress in taste, were no less momentous an emergence in the history of civilization than the models had been in their day.*

The most striking fact about American consumption is that it is dominated less by a class (even the middle class) than by the tastes, fantasies,

* For a further discussion of "Society," see Ch. VII, Sec. 2, "The Seats of the Mighty," and for fashions in consumption, see Ch. IX, Sec. 3, "Manners, Taste, and Fashion."

and standards of the American woman. In American folk history the pioneer woman is the heroine of the sagas of frontier endurance; but as embodied for example in Beret, Per Hansa's wife in Rölvaag's *Giants in the Earth,* she is also the softening cultural influence in a harsh new environment, the link between the European amenities and the rough life of the frontier. In the America that emerged from its frontier phase into industrial wealth and power you could always find a female counterpart to the masculine spirit of capitalist expansion. One thinks of Undine Spragg in Edith Wharton's *Custom of the Country* who, as she listened to Elmer Moffatt tell of his business intrigues, with his

> epic recital of plot and counterplot . . . hung, a new Desdemona, on his conflict with the anthropophagi. It was of no consequence that the details and the technicalities escaped her: she knew their meaningless syllables stood for success, and what that meant was as clear as day to her. Every Wall Street term had its equivalent in the language of Fifth Avenue, and while he talked of building up railways she was building up palaces, and picturing all the multiple lives she would live in them. To have things had always seemed to her the first essential of existence, and as she listened to him the vision of the things she could have unrolled itself before her like the long triumph of the Asiatic conqueror.

Or one thinks of a later heroine, the American girl in Fitzgerald's *Tender Is the Night:*

> Nicole was the product of much ingenuity and toil. For her sake trains began their run at Chicago and traversed the round belly of the continent to California; chicle factories fumed and link belts grew link by link in factories; men mixed toothpaste in vats and drew mouthwash out of copper hogsheads; girls canned tomatoes quickly in August or worked rudely at the Five-and-Tens on Christmas Eve; half-breed Indians toiled on Brazilian coffee plantations and dreamers were muscled out of patent rights in new tractors—these were some of the people who gave a tithe to Nicole, and as the whole system swayed and thundered onward it lent a feverish bloom to such processes of hers as wholesale buying, like the flush of a fireman's face holding his own before a spreading blaze.

It is the middle-class woman and her teen-age daughter, especially in the suburbs, who are America's type consumers. To them the advertising men pay homage, for them all the blandishments of salesmanship are unrolled. It is their urge to respectability and their dreams of glamour, their psychic yearnings and fulfillments, that make the machines run. To speak of the American male dressing his wife and daughter with conspicuous extravagance is to omit woman's independent economic will and her autonomous dreams. To speak of his hiring servants to show his means and prowess is to forget that the domestic servant is a rapidly disappearing feature of the American landscape.

It would be untrue to say that the American woman's role in the culture is wholly that of the lilies of the field who toil not, yet are arrayed in glory. The middle-class woman was a household drudge before the "kitchen revolution," and the woman worker is still a factory operative or an office worker. The machine, which lightened the burdens of the one, shut the second up to work under often dreary conditions. But it also brought new levels of social experience and personal expressiveness within the reach of both, while it dangled tantalizingly before their vision still further levels that seemed always close and yet were out of reach. The American woman's creative role as consumer is a phase of her larger role as the organizer and transmitter of the culture.* It is she who decides what the house will look like, what everyone will wear (including her husband), what schools the children will attend, what books will be bought.

That is why some paths have to be cleared for her through the wilderness of commodities, and consumer reporting has become in a double sense a necessity of the American economy: on one level it guides the consumer through the maze of offerings, amidst the pitfalls of brand names, quality, durability, and value; on another level the corporation needs research on available markets and on the probable desires and responses of the buyer. Here the consumer is the target, as she is indeed the target of all the talent and ingenuity spent on merchandizing, packaging, and advertising the product. American technological skills, which have solved the problem of production by the automatic machines, are driving ever closer in the effort through advertising to make the consumer an automaton also, conditioned to give the right response to the right stimulus or slogan. Hence the cold manipulativeness of "motivational research," which seeks to lay bare the unconscious drives to which the packager and advertiser of the commodity can appeal. The cynical quality of this effort is attested by the number of novels and movies about Madison Avenue—the center of the advertising profession—and the moral recoil of bright, young advertising men from the dehumanizing task of "the hucksters."

Critics of American life have shed many tears for the powerlessness of the consumer and the formlessness of his outlook. It is true that, measured against the gigantism of corporate or trade-union power, the consumer is a puny figure. The effort to organize consumers into co-operatives has been less successful in America than in Europe. As a political pressure group the consumers are almost nonexistent, as would be clear

* For a further discussion of this, see Ch. VIII, Sec. 6, "The Ordeal of the American Woman."

from the history of any Congressional price-control measure. But viewed as a shaping force in the economy and the society as a whole, the consumer is far from negligible. It is still he—or she—who channels the productive energies and shapes much of the taste of America.

The guidance of consumer choice underscores the jungle character of the Great Market of American commodities, created by Big Technology. But the more important feature of the wilderness of commodities is not its tracklessness but its luxuriant growth and abundance, and the way in which living standards and consumer habits have been shaped in its image.

Every phase of American consumer habits is oriented to the national market. Standardized products are nationally produced, nationally distributed, and nationally advertised, and to the superficial eye they seem to play an important role in holding the national together. The American as a consumer is the target of more concentrated attention than in any other phase of his personality. There are, I have said, groups of hardworking experts in "motivational research" and "consumer depth research" whose job is to fathom "consumer psychology" so as to overcome "consumer resistance" and create "consumer demand." Americans are continually told that "the consumer is king" and that he holds the "golden key" to unlock the riddle of prosperity or depression for the entire economy. In fact, there is a school of American economic observers who go so far as to say that it is the Great Market rather than the Big Technology which is the heart of the economy, and that the "unseemly economics of opulence" (as Galbraith puts it) have provided a margin for error in economic policy and a solvent for social strains. The fiction is that consumers operate in herd fashion. Actually they represent hundreds of millions of individual decisions which comprise the Great Market, but among that multitude of decisions the experts are always on the lookout for buying trends and consumer propensities.

Certainly, once the capacity to produce a spate of commodities is given, the crucial question is whether they can be sold. From this angle of vision the consumer is central: he is more than a target; or at least he is a highly mobile and nervous one, and therefore a highly incalculable one. He tries to balance his expected income, his probable taxes, his savings (which he either has or plans for), the prices and price trends, the desirability of the available goods, and the certainty or uncertainty of the national future and his own individual one. At the end he reaches a result that could not be arrived at mechanically even by the most complex feeding of "information" into "feedback" electronic calculators. On any particular commodity or new style a shrewdly geared advertising and selling campaign may be able to win the consumer over. But in his behavior as a whole he remains incalculable—in theory the delight of the eulogists of the system, in practice their despair.

But if we look at them not in short-run but in long-run terms there are generalizations one can make about American living standards and consumption habits. It is clear that standardized products have made conspicuous consumption more difficult than in the past. It is also clear that mass production for a national market has spread to what were formerly luxury items, giving a burnished glitter to the whole realm of consumption. The spread of high-school and even college education, the war experiences of American soldiers in European countries, the new habits of tourism of the middle classes, and the extreme development and resourcefulness of the advertising arts have all contributed to narrowing the gap between the classes in their consumer habits. Marx's prediction that under capitalism the living standards of the industrial workers would fall and keep falling has been turned on its head in America. The industrial worker, as well as the middle-class self-employed person or the professional, consumes at so high a rate that he has become absorbed with the rest in the Great Market.

In a study for the National Bureau of Economic Research, Frederick C. Mills has come up with some figures which show that the national product (everything produced and sold during a year) was five times as high in the decade of the 1940s as that of the 1890s, while population doubled. Of this national product, after subtracting what was needed for customary consumer standards and for replacement of capital goods, the rest (the margin above maintenance) amounted in the decade of the 1940s to $558 billion, of which $285 billion went into increased consumption, and the rest into war goods and increased capital equipment. Thus the Americans were adding to their living standards even more than they added to their capital equipment and fed into the great maw of war. Another way of putting this is that there have been annual increases of real income in America averaging almost 2 per cent a year since 1870, and that more than half of these increases have gone into added consumption.

One might conclude, after this gleaming history of ever-higher consumption figures, that the American consumer would be approaching the satiation point. Thus far it has not happened. There is still a receding horizon for the felt needs and desires of potential purchasers. They are always seeing new things they want and thinking of new things to buy. One may say rather fliply that this is a testimony to the effects of high-pressure advertising and salesmanship: but this is to pay more homage to these highly developed arts than they can rightly claim.

Neither advertising nor salesmanship can sell what the potential purchaser is not prepared to be convinced about. The fact is that the
American as a consumer of goods and services has not yet had his hunger
sated, and that even when comparative satiation is approached at one
end of the income scale, new classes and new income groups are brought
into the Great Market from the other end of the scale.

There is little question that the American personality has had to pay
a heavy toll for the advertising now lavished on material goods, not only
in standardized habits of consumption but also in conformist habits of
thought. When the ears and mind are continually besieged by hypnotic
repetitive slogans, it is impossible that there should be no residual effect
upon the responses of the whole personality to repetition and sloganeering. It is little wonder that serious students of politics have begun to
speculate about the effect of Madison Avenue on the mind of the voter,
and serious teachers see in it the seeds of slackness and laziness in the
thinking of college students. This too is part of the price America has
had to pay for the Great Technology and the Great Market.

There are, however, some signs of the approach of what George Soule
has called "comparative satiety." That is to say, given their present living standards but also their hunger for the intangibles of reading, travel,
and personality development, more and more Americans are now likely
to choose an increase in leisure time rather than an increase in material
consumer goods. American workers have already shown that they prefer
the shorter working week, even when the longer hours would give them
even higher wages than they get. As one observes the recent American
"giveaway" shows on TV, one notes that the winners of the big cash
prizes are at least as interested in "salting away" a big chunk of them
for future leisure, travel, and enjoyment as they are for spending them
on material goods. In short, American technology—by making ever-
higher "living standards"—is now within reach of giving a new meaning
to the phrase, putting the emphasis increasingly upon greater expressiveness of life rather than on material goods.

6. The Culture of Machine Living

ANY PRINCIPLE that comes to dominate a culture can do so only by making itself part of the life processes of the people. This has happened in
the case of America, and it is one of the reasons we can speak seriously,
and not as a literary flourish, of the culture of machine living. Siegfried
Giedion points out that the machine has mechanized such fundamentals
as the soil (mechanized agriculture), bread (mechanized milling), death
(assembly-line slaughtering pens and the use of by-products by the big

meat packers), and the household (the kitchen revolution, the household-appliance revolution, mechanized laundering, and the mechanized bathroom). The analysis can be carried further. Mechanization has extended to transport (boats, trains, autos, busses, trucks, subways, planes), to living outside the home (hotels, motels, sleeping cars, "automats"), and to the basic phases of the communications revolution (newsprint, book publishing, magazines, telephone, telegraph, movies, radio, TV).

Aside from these arterial forms of American living there is also the interminable gadgetry. From the automatic vending machines to the automatic gas stations, from the gadgeted car to the gadgeted bed, America has taken on the aspect of a civilization cluttered with artifacts and filled with the mechanized bric-a-brac of machine living. The Big Technology of the mass-production industries is supplemented by the Little Technology of everyday living.

One could draw a gloomy picture of machine living in America and depict it as the Moloch swallowing the youth and resilience of American manhood. From Butler's *Erewhon* to Capek's *R.U.R.*, European thinkers have seized on the machine as the cancer of modern living. Some have even suggested that there is a daimon in Western man, and especially in the American, that is driving him to the monstrous destruction of his instinctual life and indeed of his whole civilization.

Part of the confusion flows from the failure to distinguish at least three phases of the machine culture. One is what I have just described: *machine living* as such, the use of machinery in work and in leisure and in the constant accompaniments of the day. The second is cultural *standardization,* aside from the machine, but a standardization that flows from machine production. The third is *conformism* in thought, attitude, and action. All three are parts of the empire of the machine but at varying removes and with different degrees of danger for the human spirit.

The danger in machine living itself is chiefly the danger of man's arrogance in exulting over the seemingly easy triumphs over Nature which he calls "progress," so that he cuts himself off increasingly from the organic processes of life itself. Thus with the soil: the erosion of the American earth is not, as some seem to believe, the result of the mechanization of agriculture; a farmer can use science and farm technology to the full, and he need not exhaust or destroy his soil but can replenish it, as has been shown in the TVA, which is itself a triumph of technology. But the machines have been accompanied by a greed for quick results and an irreverence for the soil which are responsible for destroying the balance between man and the environment. What is true of the soil is true of the household: the mechanized household appliances have not destroyed the home or undermined family life; rural electrification has made the farmer's wife less a drudge, and the mass production of suburban houses has given the white-collar family a better chance than it had for sun and living space. What threatens family life is not the "kitchen revolution" or the "housing revolution" but the restless malaise of the spirit, of which the machine is more product than creator.

Even in a society remarkable for its self-criticism the major American writers have not succumbed to the temptation of making the machine into a Devil. Most of the novelists have amply expressed the frustrations of American life, and some (Dreiser, Dos Passos, Farrell and Algren come to mind) have mirrored in their style the pulse beats of an urban mechanized civilization. But except for a few isolated works, like Elmer Rice's *Adding Machine* and Eugene O'Neill's *Dynamo,* the writers have refrained from the pathetic fallacy of ascribing the ills of the spirit to the diabolism of the machine. The greatest American work on technology and its consequences—Lewis Mumford's massive four-volume work starting with *Man and Technics* and ending with *The Conduct of Life*—makes the crucial distinction between what is due to the machine itself and what is due to the human institutions that guide it and determine its uses.

It is here, moving from machine living to cultural standardization, that the picture becomes bleaker. Henry Miller's phrase for its American form is "the air-conditioned nightmare." Someone with a satiric intent could do a withering take-off on the rituals of American standardization.

Most American babies (he might say) are born in standardized hospitals, with a standardized tag put around them to keep them from getting confused with other standardized products of the hospital. Many of them grow up either in uniform rows of tenements or of small-town or suburban houses. They are wheeled about in standard perambulators, shiny or shabby as may be, fed from standardized bottles with standardized nipples according to standardized formulas, and tied up with standardized diapers. In childhood they are fed standardized breakfast foods out of standardized boxes with pictures of standardized heroes on them. They are sent to monotonously similar schoolhouses, where almost uniformly standardized teachers ladle out to them standardized information out of standardized textbooks. They pick up the routine wisdom of the streets in standard slang and learn the routine terms which constrict the range of their language within dishearteningly narrow limits. They wear out standardized shoes playing standardized games, or as passive observers they follow through standardized newspaper accounts or standardized radio and TV programs the highly ritualized antics of grown-up professionals playing the same games. They devour in millions of uniform pulp comic books the prowess of standardized supermen.

As they grow older they dance to canned music from canned juke boxes, millions of them putting standard coins into standard slots to get standardized tunes sung by voices with standardized inflections of emotion. They date with standardized girls in standardized cars. They see automatons thrown on millions of the same movie and TV screens, watching stereotyped love scenes adapted from made-to-order stories in standardized magazines.

They spend the days of their years with monotonous regularity in factory, office, and shop, performing routinized operations at regular intervals. They take time out for standardized "coffee breaks" and later a quick standardized lunch, come home at night to eat processed or canned food, and read syndicated columns and comic strips. Dressed in standardized clothes they attend standardized club meetings, church services, and socials. They have standardized fun at standardized big-city conventions. They are drafted into standardized armies, and if they escape the death of mechanized warfare they die of highly uniform diseases, and to the accompaniment of routine platitudes they are buried in standardized graves and celebrated by standardized obituary notices.

Caricature? Yes, perhaps a crude one, but with a core of frightening validity in it. Every society has its routines and rituals, the primitive groups being sometimes more tyrannously restricted by convention than the industrial societies. The difference is that where the primitive is bound by the rituals of tradition and group life, the American is bound by the rituals of the machine, its products, and their distribution and consumption.

The role of the machine in this standardized living must be made clear. The machine mechanizes life, and since mass production is part of Big Technology, the machine also makes uniformity of life possible. But it does not compel such uniformity. The American who shaves with an electric razor and his wife who buys a standardized "home permanent" for her hair do not thereby have to wear a uniformly vacuous expression through the day. A newspaper that uses the press association wire stories and prints from a highly mechanized set of presses does not thereby have to take the same view of the world that every other paper takes. A novelist who uses a typewriter instead of a quill pen does not have to turn out machine-made historical romances.

The answer is that some do and some don't. What the machine and the mass-produced commodities have done has been to make conformism easier. To buy and use what everyone else does, and live and think as everyone else does, becomes a short cut involving no need for one's own thinking. Those Americans have been captured by conformist living who have been capturable by it.

Cultural stereotypes are an inherent part of all group living, and they become sharper with mass living. There have always been unthinking people leading formless, atomized lives. What has happened in America is that the economics of mass production has put a premium on uniformity, so that America produces more units of more commodities (although sometimes of fewer models) than other cultures. American salesmanship has sought out every potential buyer of a product, so that standardization makes its way by the force of the distributive mechanism into every life. Yet for the person who has a personality pattern and style of his own, standardization need not mean anything more than a set of conveniences which leave a larger margin of leisure and greater scope for creative living. "That we may be enamored by the negation brought by the machine," as Frank Lloyd Wright has put it, "may be inevitable for a time. But I like to imagine this novel negation to be only a platform underfoot to enable a greater splendor of life to be ours than any known to Greek or Roman, Goth or Moor. We should know a life beside which the life they knew would seem not only limited in scale and narrow in range but pale in richness of the color of imagination and integrity of spirit."

Which is to say that technology is the shell of American life, but a shell that need not hamper or stultify the modes of living and thinking. The real dangers of the American mode of life are not in the machine or even in standardization as much as they are in conformism. The dangers do not flow from the contrivances that men have fashioned to lighten their burdens, or from the material abundance which, if anything, should make a richer cultural life possible. They flow rather from the mimesis of the dominant and successful by the weak and mediocre, from the intolerance of diversity, and from the fear of being thought different from one's fellows. This is the essence of conformism.

It would be hard to make the connection between technology and conformism, unless one argues that men fashion their minds in the image of their surroundings, and that in a society of automatism, human beings themselves will become automatons. But this is simply not so. What relation there is between technology and conformism is far more subtle and less mystical. It is a double relation. On the one hand, as Jefferson foresaw, the simpler society of small-scale manufacture did not involve concentration of power in a small group, was not vulnerable to breakdown, and did not need drastic governmental controls; a society of big-scale industry has shown that it does. In that sense the big machines carry with them an imperative toward the directed society, which in turn—whether in war or peace—encourages conformism. On the second score, as De Tocqueville saw, a society in which there is no recognized elite group to serve as the arbiter of morals, thought, and style is bound to be a formless one in which the ordinary person seeks to heal his insecurity by attuning himself to the "tyranny of opinion" —to what others do and say and what they think of him. He is ruled by imitation and prestige rather than a sense of his own worth.

These are dangerous trends, but all of social living is dangerous. The notable fact is that in spite of its machines and standardization America has proved on balance less conformist than some other civilizations where the new technology has played less of a role. One thinks of the totalitarian experience of Italy, of Spain and Portugal, of Germany, of Russia and the East European countries, of Japan, of China. Some, like the Germans, the Japanese, and the Russian and Chinese Communists have been seized with an admiration for the machine; the others have had clerical and feudal traditions, and have lagged in industrial development. The totalitarian spirit can come to reside in a culture no matter what the shell of its technology is. There is no unvarying relation between machines and rigidity of living and thinking.

Americans have, it is true, an idolatry of production and consumption as they have an idolatry of success. But they have not idolized authority or submitted unquestioningly to human or supernatural oracles. They have had their cranks, eccentrics, and anarchists, and they still cling to individualism, even when it is being battered hard. It will take them some time before they can become "man in equipoise," balancing what science and the machine can do as against the demands of the life processes. But where they have failed, the failure has been less that of the machines they have wrought than of the very human fears, greeds, and competitive drives that have accompanied the building of a powerful culture.

It has been suggested that the American, like the Faustian, made a bargain with the Big Technology: a bargain to transform his ways of life and thought in the image of the machine, in return for the range of power and riches the machine would bring within his reach. It is a fine allegory. But truer than the Faustian bargain, with its connotations of the sale of one's soul to the Devil, is the image of Prometheus stealing fire from the gods in order to light a path of progress for men. The path is not yet clear, nor the meaning of progress, nor where it is leading: but the bold intent, the irreverence, and the secular daring have all become part of the American experience.

CHAPTER V

Capitalist Economy and Business Civilization

THIS CHAPTER examines the most bitterly attacked and ardently defended sector of American life—its economy, including both its business system and its labor unions, its wealth and poverty, its grandeurs and miseries, its theory and practice. The first approach is to catch an over-all view of the economy as a going concern, confronting its principal strengths and weaknesses (Sec. 1, "American Capitalism: Trial Balance"). We then look more closely at three of its aspects: what has happened to the businessman as entrepreneur and folk hero (Sec. 2, "The Rise and Decline of the Titan"); how the corporation has emerged as the type-form of American business enterprise, replacing the individual and family firm, and revolutionizing American business (Sec. 3, "The Corporate Empires"); and what the revolution has done to the old concepts of property (Sec. 4, "The Property Revolution"). Following the new forms of business enterprise into some of their ramifications, in advertising, salesmanship, the stock market, "public relations" (Sec. 5, "Business and Its Satellites"), we try to appraise what the business spirit has done to the noneconomic phases of American life (Sec. 6, "The Reach of the Business Spirit").

We then look at the other side of the shield—the role of labor and the trade-unions in the American economy and in the broader aspects of living, assessing the extent of labor power, the strategies it has adopted for its self-defense and preservation and for getting what it regards as its rightful share at the banquet of American life (Sec. 7, "Revolution in the Trade-Union"); we try to draw a portrait of the new trade-union leader and of the varied activities that the trade-union has assumed after its long history; and we note the characteristic way in which American labor operates in American political life and in the larger culture (Sec. 8, "Labor and American Society").

Finally, after examining how Americans live both at the top and at the bottom of the pyramid of income and wealth (Sec. 9, "Poverty and Wealth"), we draw a profile of the changes in the pattern of economic and governmental relations in America, which defies easy labeling as either "capitalism" or "Socialism" but is a unique amalgam of both (Sec. 10, "The Emerging Amalgam"). This gives us a chance again to take an over-all view and strike a final balance of the newer trends of the economy.

CHAPTER V

Capitalist Economy and
Business Civilization

1. American Capitalism: Trial Balance

GIVEN this culture of science and the machine, how about the system of American capitalism which organizes it? The appraisal of American capitalism as a going concern must be made largely in terms of a balance sheet. Whoever embraces its achievements should not flinch from acknowledging its costs; whoever condemns the costs should be candid enough to recognize the achievement.

The record of achievement is clear enough: a continuously rising curve of man-hour productivity; a high rate of capital formation; steadily rising profits which have made a corpse of the Marxist predictions about profits under capitalism; employment levels which in the mid-1950s were at their top peacetime pitch; a wilderness of available commodities and a strong "propensity to consume," reflecting the spread of high and increasing living standards even among middle- and low-income levels; a steadily increasing growth in real wages; a continuing secular increase in the national product; a production record which has provided the military production for two world wars and the current "readiness economy" for defense, while increasing the products available for civilian consumption; a capacity to take in its stride an ever-heavier tax structure without destroying freedom of economic movement and decision within the economy; a continuing sense of economic dynamism, and finally an economy with the capacity for changing its forms under pressure so that it could in the mid-1950s lay claim to being a "people's capitalism" even while being to a high degree a corporate and monopoly capitalism.

The debit side is also clear: a haste for profits which has used up too rapidly the land and resources of the continent and built unplanned cities; an economy which made heavy productive gains (especially in World War II) through the expansion of war industries and seems still to be buttressed by a government budget for arms which runs to 15 or 20 per cent of the Gross National Product; one which has lived like a fever-chart patient by constantly taking its pulse and has not been able to control firmly the periodic swings of prosperity and depression; one in which the Big Enterprise corporations create private empires chal-lenging the state itself; one in which the chances for a competitive start in the race for the Big Money are less open to small businessmen and depend more upon upward movement in a corporate bureaucracy; an economy in which, despite its production levels, much remains to be done in distributing the final product more fairly.

The observer is tempted to say (with Hamlet): "Look at this picture, and here at this one."

The defense of American capitalism runs largely in broad abstrac-tions like "the American system" or "the free-enterprise economy," or in epithets like "serfdom" or "totalitarian" applied to noncapitalist systems. Underlying these catchwords are some basic arguments. One is the *argument from incentive:* that men's brains and energy work best when they have no hampering restrictions, and when they see an immediacy of relation between effort and reward. The second is the *argument from a free market:* that an economy runs best as the result of millions of individual decisions made through the operations of a free production, wage and price system; that when it goes off kilter, it can generally set itself right again by individual adjustments within a frame of government spurs and checks; and that even government regu-lation is best accomplished by the indirect methods of inducements and pressures on the free market, rather than the direct method of planning and control. The third is the *argument from managerial efficiency:* that the corporate managerial group is recruited from the men with the best skills, who deal with the problems of industrial production more flexi-bly than a governmental bureaucracy could.

The arguments, though vulnerable, are basically valid. True, the free market no longer exists in anything like its historic form, and Big En-terprise and the giant corporation, with prices largely reached by ad-ministrative decision, have in part taken its place. Yet the economy has developed its own distinctive forms of freedom, and the decisions reached in it are still freer than in a cartelized or largely government-directed economy. The system of profit and property incentives has been transformed in the giant corporation; yet new incentives have emerged that keep the corporate managers alert and drive the productive system on. The argument from corporate efficiency has much in its favor, pro-vided we do not forget that a corporate bureaucracy has a strong inner impulse toward conformism of spirit and, like government bureaucra-cies, runs the danger of stagnation.

Some corollaries of these doctrines that emerge in the capitalist apolo-gia are more open to question: the argument that the big corporations and their managers administer their power *as a trust* for the people as a whole; and the argument that there is a *harmony of interests* which ties labor and the farmers to business prosperity and therefore business decisions. While most Americans are too realistic to accept the view that Big Property is being held in trust for them, they do not resent the power of the possessing groups because they hope themselves some-day to be secure enough to "take it easy." As for the harmony of inter-ests, they may have some skepticism about it, yet they have never been caught by the European idea that class cleavages must deepen until the whole system breaks.

The real problems of capitalism, however, are not the doctrinal strug-gles but the operational strains—the periodic breakdowns, the sense of insecurity, the shadow of monopoly, the dependence upon war expendi-tures, the question of distributive justice. The American economy, be-cause of its power and prosperity, has become the last, best hope of free economies in the world. But by the same token the issues of its capacity for survival, its social costs, and its impact on the human spirit have called in question the nature and survival value of the system of capitalism itself.

What are the elements of American capitalism as a going concern, distinguishing it from other going systems? It is customary to say that capitalism is organized as a "private-enterprise system," for private (in-dividual or corporate) profit, with the resulting rewards protected by the state as private property. This is valid enough, except for the fact that far-reaching changes have taken place in the structure and func-tioning of American capitalism. The profit incentive, for example, does not operate in corporate management as it used to operate in individual enterprise, since ownership and management have split apart: it still holds, however, if it is rephrased as the drive within the manager to make the best possible profit record for the corporation. The idea of private property has also suffered a change, since industrial ownership is now widely scattered in the form of stock ownership, some of the stocks being owned by trust funds, investment trusts, other corporations, life insurance companies, and even trade-unions. The earlier picture of capitalism as a competitive system has also had to be changed. To some extent competition has been inhibited by price agreements and "oligopoly"—the control of an industry by a handful of big corporations competing only partly in price and mainly in packaging, advertising, and brand names, as in meat packing, automobiles, or cigarettes. Yet the impressive fact about the American economy is the extent to which it has effectively resisted the monopoly tendencies. The concept of big-ness is not the same as the concept of monopoly, and something that can fairly be called competition is still a power regulator of the economy.

The core of capitalism then is still present. It is in essence concerned with decision-making within a profit-competitive framework. Under communism the decisions are made by a small group of political functionaries assigned to strategic industrial posts. Under democratic socialism they are made by technicians operating largely within government corporations, responsible ultimately to the people. Under American capitalism the decisions on production, pricing, advertising, and sales policies are private decisions—that is to say, they are made by individual businessmen or heads of small corporations, whether they be producers, middlemen, or retailers, and in the case of big corporations they are made by the managers to whom the power of decision is delegated by the stockholders; the decisions on wages and labor policy are generally made through collective bargaining by the managers and trade-union leaders. Obviously there are restrictions placed on these decisions by price and wage legislation, sometimes by priorities and the allocation of scarce materials in a defense economy. But within these limits the decisions are linked with ownership and management, and they are made always with a view to profit and in competition with other enterprises. At the other end of the capitalist process there are millions of decisions made by the consumer: production and investment policies are guided not by governmental decisions or by what might be considered socially necessary production but in the light of consumers' decisions about how they will spend their money and for what.

Thus at one end American capitalism is guided by decisions made by businessmen, managers, and trade-union leaders, at the other end by consumer decisions. This decision-making operates within a frame in which there are strong surviving elements of private property, private and corporate profits, and competition.

In assessing American capitalism as a going concern, one important test is the test of *productivity*. Here American capitalism shows the most impressive facet of its record. Socialists might argue that, given the resources of America and the accidents of its history, some other system of organization, ownership, and power could have attained the same productivity with a better distribution of the products. This is one of those iffy questions that will never be resolved. On the other hand it is hard to sustain the claim that the creative force in the American record of increased productivity is the capitalist entrepreneur and manager, and he alone. Science, technology, the legal and governmental framework, and the skill of the worker—all belong in the larger pattern along with the supplier of risk capital and the business organizer. Yet the American record of an increase of productivity running between 2 per cent and 3 per cent a year must be counted one of the over-all achievements of capitalism. Nor has this production record been only a matter of technology and resources. The drive toward productivity has also been due to the elements within the social structure which have invested the whole productive process with the *élan* of freedom. This is as true today as it was a century ago, as John Sawyer has shown, basing himself on the accounts of European travelers in America in the 1840s and 1850s.

All this brings us to the question of *incentive*, which is more troublesome. Those who contend that profit alone has furnished the effective incentive for industrial production must plead guilty to a lower view of human motive than applies even in an imperfect world. The fact is that the managerial function in the big corporation has been performed through incentives quite different from those of ownership profits or dividends, and more closely related to competitive performance and pride in a job well done. Through a complex mingling of profit, salary, bonus, and craftsmanship incentives, capitalism as a going concern has enlisted considerable talents in the processes of production and selling; and it has plowed back into increased production a steady portion (recently around 7 per cent) of the national product, keeping the process of capital formation an active and growing one.

It is on the test of *stability* that American capitalism is most vulnerable. American economic thought is crisscrossed by conflicts of opinion about the underlying causes of the periodic swings and breakdowns of the system, resulting in cycles of prosperity and recession, boom and depression. There are still die-hard critics of the system who believe that boom and bust are inherent in the system and will never yield to anything short of full-scale socialism. There are also True Believers of another stripe who feel, as their forerunners felt in the boom days of the 1920s, that Americans have somehow found the golden key to perpetual prosperity.

Aside from these two groups there is fairly general agreement, however, that, while the swings in the "business cycle" may not yet have been mastered, American business, labor, and government leaders have learned to detect the danger signals and put in motion some preventive measures, and have learned also—once the cycle is on its way—how to cut the length and severity of the downward swing and cushion its impact. In the mid-1950s there was an upsurge of conviction that the cycle had to a large extent been mastered and need never again operate drastically. The bitter experience after 1929 taught the nation's leaders how to use "counter-cyclical" measures in the form of tax and fiscal policies, rediscounting rates, Federal expenditures for defense and public works, state and Federal programs for building roads, schoolhouses, and hospitals. The President's Council of Economic Advisers, working with a committee of Congress, is now accepted under Republican as well as Democratic administrations. Its reports, carefully studied in business, labor, and government circles, are in effect an embryonic form of corrective and preventive planning. The government's massive role in a war-geared "readiness economy" has also given it a leverage in guiding, checking, and stimulating business activity and as such it is a form of indirect planning.

America has thus characteristically used an indirect approach to the control of the swings of business activity, aiming at stability without embracing a direct program of planning and without transferring the crucial decisions from the corporate managers and the consumers to government managers. The specter of Depression is, of course, always present. At the close of World War II there were widespread prophecies of economic catastrophe, yet the real danger proved to be not mass unemployment but inflation, not a paralysis of production but a boom induced by high demand and sustained by the armament race. This mood has lasted into the mid-1950s. Obviously there is a serious problem in the steady inflationary movement of American prices, year after year, largely due to the pressure of rising consumer demand, with its tragic effect in wiping out much of the substance and meaning of savings. Yet, while Americans are still far from solving the basic problem of boom and bust, they have at least a heightened awareness of what is involved and are willing to take decisive action. There are few economists who would accept the European notion, seemingly as widespread among scholars as among the people, that American capitalism will once again in the calculable future be as helpless as it was in the years following 1929.

On the test of *security and insecurity* American capitalism has made steady if reluctant progress. So far from interfering with prosperity, it is now accepted that effective, well-administered insurance programs make the economy more stable as well as adding to personal security. Every person must confront the tragic elements in life, but the pathetic elements can be whittled down by common action. To the degree that America has become a welfare state it is not because of effeminacy or the importation of "foreign" ideas, but of practical grappling with a deeply felt need to make the individual fate more secure.

Judged by another test—that of *income spread and distribution*—the going economy has in the past evoked strong self-criticism from American writers, if not from the economists. Especially in the decade before World War I, and in the 1920s and 1930s, they unsparingly subjected the economy to the test of equity. The extremes of wealth and poverty, the discrepancies between the Babylonian living at the top of the pyramid and the scrimping and degradation at its base, became staples of the American self-portrait. There was a time when the prospects of the future for many Americans seemed precarious. Any European or Asian who thinks that Americans need to be prodded about this should read the almost unparalleled record in which sensitive Americans have made their own indictment of their own vaunted system. But the note of self-criticism has recently grown fainter because of the overwhelming evidence of American living standards. These have improved all through the class system as productivity has increased and the trade-unions have been able to claim a share of it for their members. The problem of poverty in America is now circumscribed within the lower fourth of the population.

One could argue, of course, that the depressed groups in backward areas in other countries are far worse off than this lower fourth in America. This would be sound if American living standards were judged by productivity in other areas of the world, but they must be judged by American productivity. In every economy, as Sumner put it, "there are dinners without appetites at one end of the table, and appetites without dinners at the other." The American economy as a production miracle has evoked life claims in America not roused in the underdeveloped economies: what would be a full meal elsewhere is a skimpy one at the table of the American business system.*

The final test of a going economy is the *creativeness* it evokes and makes possible. Few systems in history have attracted so much talent and put it to use, and in no other economy have men's business abilities been so continuously tapped. The problem is not whether the economy gives scope to creativeness, but what kind of creativeness it gives scope to. The question asked is always whether a new idea or a new insight is "practical"—that is, whether it can be translated into dollar-and-cents terms. The creativeness that is not vendible is likely to be ignored and to wither. Yet within this pecuniary framework there has been broader scope for the creation of use values and life values than the critics of the money calculus have been ready to admit.

This then would be a rough trial balance of American capitalism as a going concern: that it has done brilliantly in productivity and national product; that it has done less well with the swings of the business cycle and with boom and bust, but that substantial steps have been taken to meet this; that its greatest weakness on this score lies in the dependence of the recent prosperity on the war-geared economy;† that its growth in the areas of concentrated economic power has been at

* For a fuller development of this theme, see Sec. 9, "Poverty and Wealth."

† The relation of American capitalism to war expenditures is too complex to be dealt with in this summary. For a further discussion, see Sec. 10, "The Emerging Amalgam."

the expense of small business; that in its income distribution it is a good deal better than its opponents would admit but not nearly as good as its apologists claim, good enough to retain the faith of those who are fulfilled by it but not good enough to exact the loyalty of those who feel left out; that it allows for creativeness but within a limited sense of that word; that as a whole it is an economy which has wrested from the world its envy along with a grudging respect, but not its imitation.

2. *The Rise and Decline of the Titan*

"THE TYCOON IS DEAD" was the way *Fortune,* the best spokesman for the American business mind, phrased the basic change that has come over the structure of American business. In what sense was this true?

Every civilization has its characteristic flowering in some civilization type, the *persona* of the social mask on which the ordinary man in the civilization models himself. In the Athenian civilization the *persona* was the leisure-class citizen with a turn for art and philosophy; with the Jews it was the lawgiver-prophet, in the Roman Empire the soldier-administrator, in the Middle Ages the cleric dreaming of sainthood, in the Chinese civilization the mandarin-scholar, in the Indian the ascetic, in the Italian Renaissance the patron-*condottiere,* at the height of French power the courtier, at the height of British power the merchant-adventurer and empire builder; in German and Japanese history it was the elite soldier of the *Junker* and *samurai* classes, with the Communists today it is the worker-commissar.

The *persona* of the American civilization has been the businessman— the "Titan," as Dreiser called him; the "Tycoon," as *Fortune* called him. Where other civilization types have pursued wisdom, beauty, sanctity, military glory, predacity, asceticism, the businessman pursues the magnitudes of profit with a similar single-minded drive. When confronted in business by appeals to nonpecuniary values, his comment is likely to be that he is not in business for his health. "The business of America," as Calvin Coolidge put it, "is business." The survivors in the fierce competitive struggle were those who most clearly embodied the businessman's single-mindedness of purpose. They were men like "Jupiter" Morgan, Vanderbilt, Jay Gould, Daniel Drew, John D. Rockefeller, Jay Cooke, "Bet-a-Million" Gates, Andrew Carnegie, Charles T. Yerkes, Solomon Guggenheim, Henry Ford, Irénée Du Pont. Some have been honest according to the standards of business honesty, some have not hesitated to use force, guile, and bribery. All have been unsentimental and hard in business, even when they have been pious in the church, devoted in the home, and softhearted in friendship.

The business spirit was not indigenous to America. It grew out of the history of European capitalism, and by the time of the American Revolution it had already found expression in Italy, England, and Holland. During the first half century of American national life the American business spirit lagged behind the European. While there were land speculators, a shipbuilding and commercial group, an incipient factory system, and (as John Taylor used to put it) an "aristocracy of paper and credit," the type-figure of America well into the Jacksonian era was the farmer-turned-artisan or the artisan-turned-farmer.

De Tocqueville gave only the briefest mention to the new "aristocracy of manufactures" in America, although his few pages are perceptive. He noted that "the number of large fortunes there is small, and capital is still scarce," and called America "a nation which contains, so to speak, no rich men"—compared, that is, with the great fortunes and landed families of Europe. Yet even in this early stage De Tocqueville saw that "the Americans carry their businesslike qualities and their trading passions" into all their pursuits, including farming. In other words, he saw the beginnings of that business civilization which has almost obscured every other aspect of American life. When he wrote, there was as yet no consciousness of American businessmen as a class. Yet he saw that the best talents were being attracted to business pursuits, and that the gap between employer and workers was widening.

When Charles Dickens made his second journey through America several decades later he found a hard materialist spirit everywhere. The events of the next quarter century burst the bounds of confinement which De Tocqueville had seen around the business spirit. The spread of a railway network in the 1850s, the triumph of Northern capitalism over the Southern plantation system in the 1860s, the rise of investment banking and the process of rapid capital formation in the 1870s, the trust movement of the 1880s, the harvests of money and power reaped from the Big Technology throughout this period: all these combined to make of America a Paradise for the new business fortunes and a stamping ground for the business spirit.

The result was the emergence of the Big Money and the Big Businessman. In a single decade between the election of McKinley and the Panic of 1907—the decade of the great "consolidations"—there were Harriman and Hill building railroad fortunes as well as railroads, with Harriman dreaming of a world railroad empire, like some daring Sidonia such as Disraeli had imagined; out of the steel industry were forged the fortunes of Gary, Schwab, Gates, Carnegie, Morgan; oil spouted forth a whole tribe of Rockefellers; farm machinery clattered away like the roaring of a McCormick; street railways, with their clinking nickels, built the fortunes of Widener, Whitney, Ryan, Yerkes. The armies of finance wheeled and maneuvered, attacked and retreated.

There was a time when the Titan was treated with unctuous servility. In the 1870s James Parton, a sort of American Samuel Smiles, had edited a volume of Sketches of Men of Progress, and the chapter by the Reverend Mr. McClintock on Daniel Drew had spoken of his "affording an example of industry, energy, and business talents of the highest order, combined with a sense of personal honor and unimpeachable integrity. . . . May he be long spared to enjoy the fruits of his industry, and to share in advancing the kingdom of Christ on earth, not merely by his Christian use of the large wealth of which God has made him steward, but also . . . by his living example of peaceful but active piety." Alas, Charles Francis Adams and Henry Adams, in their *Chapters of Erie*, gave a different picture of Drew, as well as of Gould and Vanderbilt, as men who cheated and tricked one another, acquired railroads and wrecked them, built paper structures of securities and unloaded them on a gullible public. By the turn of the century, after the work of the muckrakers, the mood of the press and the reading public became more realistic. By the time of the first World War the Titan had caught the imagination of the novelists as well as the populace, and for the press and magazines he became a legendary figure in a manner different from the sugar-loaf legends of the early admirers.

Americans needed no fire-breathing imperialist swaggerers to express their sense of national importance. The Titan was all the symbol they needed. Wherever he went there was a planetary turmoil and a sense of construction, and the big money poured around him. Even when the muckrakers excoriated him for corrupting legislatures, buying up city governments, and betraying the original democratic premise, they left little doubt that their target was indeed a Titan. The magazine readers glimpsed the outlines of the heroic in the subjects of the biographical exposés and felt more envy than indignation.

Some of this may be found in the novelists as well. Mark Twain, himself a businessman and absorbed in money-making schemes, wrote a blistering indictment in *The Gilded Age* of the methods by which the big fortunes were built up. William Dean Howells was torn between an admiration for honest businessmen like Silas Lapham and the anger against the men of "the Accumulation" which he set down in *A Traveler from Altruria*. Henry James recoiled from trade yet, like Scott Fitzgerald after him, he was obsessed with money and its aura. In the James tradition the Edith Wharton novels come to life, in *The House* of *Mirth* and *The Custom of the Country,* when she deals with her money-driven women, her female counterparts of single-minded business-men. The muckrakers themselves, as they dug around in the archives of business methods and corporate finance, were moved by a complex *odi et amo* feeling about their subjects. Even the novelists who attacked the Titan most drastically, like Frank Norris and Theodore Dreiser, were (as Kenneth Lynn has pointed out in the *Dream of Success*) covertly admirers of his greatness and sharers of his values.

Dreiser's portrait of Frank Algernon Cowperwood—which he took from Charles Tyson Yerkes, the Philadelphia and Chicago traction king—shows most clearly the combined fascination-and-recoil which, until the Great Depression, most Americans felt for the power and the ruthless drive of the business Titans. Dreiser did his studies of Cow-perwood-Yerkes while he was brooding over the Darwinian doctrine that the survivors must be the fittest, and over the beyond-good-and-evil and will-to-power ideas of Nietzsche. The term he used for Cowper-wood—"the Titan"—was a Lucretian image, implying that these men who operated far above the groundlings and held themselves superior to human law were not so much immoral as amoral. He wrote about Cowperwood with the sympathy of an Indiana boy out of the Mid-western climate of striving and dreaming from which so many of the business Titans came. Plebeian that he was, he was himself half in love with the symbol of the plebeian-turned-plutocrat that he portrayed. He shows Cowperwood growing up in Philadelphia like a boy with his nose pressed against a shopwindow, looking in at the wealth that spells power and is crowned by the need of beauty. The class lines in such a society had to be sharp, yet not too sharp; resistant enough to apply the spur to the hungering youthful will, yet mobile enough so that one could master them. The process of mastery involved for Cowperwood a term in a Philadelphia jail, the betrayal of his friends, the corruption of city councils and legislatures, the destruction of those closest to him. Yet he lived out his willed dream, and as he did so his prowess and predacity hardened. He piled up wealth and power, crushed the men who stood in his way, combined with those he could not crush; he won a mastery over women as well—especially *their* women—the daughters of those who had been the symbols of his dream of success and the ob-stacles in his path. In the end he failed and got religion (in the third volume of the trilogy, *The Stoic*), but this was an afterthought of the later Dreiser.

As Dreiser and many others saw him, the Titan was half conqueror, half child. He had a daring vision and made reckless use of his resources to gain his ends; he had a quick sense for estimating and using people and an ability to see his lucky chance and grasp it. Yet with all this, there was a restless search for novelty, as with a child; a love of big things because they are big, almost as if his great projects had become only toys. There was in him a joy in the creation of means but an obtuseness about ends. Most of all, there was a quality of tenacious single-mindedness of purpose which was preindustrial in the American character, and the symbolic theme of Captain Ahab's unrelenting pursuit of the whale of *Moby Dick*.

There is one division which cuts across most of the Titans of the earlier prewar era of America—the split between the Puritan and the magnifico. J. Pierpont Morgan, the greatest of all the Titans, was a magnifico in the sense that he operated on a scale of magnificence. So also were Hill, Gates, Gould, several of the early Du Ponts, and Yerkes himself. There was a lustiness and a grandeur of scope in their private as in their business lives. They bet and gambled, lived conspicuously, gave parties, sailed yachts, were seen in the European capitals; there were legends of the stables of women they kept; they built palatial homes and crammed them with art treasures rifled from the museums and collections of Europe. There was a native optimism in them; in business as in private life they were "bullish"; their motto was Morgan's "never sell America short"; their fortunes were made on the upward arc of an expanding American economy. They saw far enough ahead to see the expansion and contributed to it their boldness and their measure of vision.

There was another strain, however, represented by Daniel Drew, the Rockefellers, Henry Ford: not the strain of magnificence but of the taut Puritan qualities. These men came out of the small towns and remained at home in small-town America. They were abstemious, churchgoing, taught Sunday-school classes. They spent little on themselves, and what they did they spent quietly. Like Rockefeller, they handed out shiny dimes; like Ford, they plowed everything back into the business. They had the eccentricities in which men can indulge when they sit on top of a pyramid of power. They were apt to be gloomy men and presented a stern visage to the world, at once unsmiling and unrelenting. Yet they were probably closer than the magnificos to the theological roots of capitalism: the demonstration of virtue through success, the doctrine of calling, the gospel of work and thrift.

Together these two strains condense the appeal of business enterprise as a way of life. To the middle-class mind the appeal is to the Puritan virtues of austerity and acquisitiveness, to the Faustian spirit of the imaginative it is that of movers and shakers and of empire builders. One stresses efficacy in the sight of God, the other power in the sight of man. One moves step by step, the other by bold leaps. One is the accumulative spirit, the other the gambling spirit. One operates best in the realm of production and managerial organization, the other in the realm of promotion and finance. Neither is complete without the other, and while in every Titan one or the other had predominated, no Titan has lacked elements of both. Their combined appeal has been powerful since even the groundlings, who could not live the life of the Titan, could identify themselves with his economic efficacy and share vicariously in his magnitudes.

As De Tocqueville noted even before the Civil War, the old European sense that there was something degrading about business quickly vanished in America, and the talented young people turned to business pursuits. The legend of the Titan attracted them almost as much as the Big Money itself. For while the formal goal of business enterprise is profit, the psychic rewards of the businessman's way of life came to consist as much in the pursuit of power as in the accumulation of money. There was a sense of risk and excitement in Big Enterprise. And while it was possible for many of the businessmen to pursue profit and power with a meanness of spirit and impoverished intellectual and emotional resources, this was not true of the outstanding figures. Unlike the worker chained to the machine, and the small businessman embittered by his struggle with his competitors and workers, the Titan often showed himself to have a spacious and creative mind.

Something happened to the Titan in the two decades after World War I. Before that time the indictment against him had stressed the enormity of his power, the charge being that he used it to betray the early ideals of the Republic. John Chamberlain has suggested that the reason for the persistent "belittling" of the Big Businessman by American novelists was their rebellion against their fathers and their search for a different kind of father symbol on the Left. Sometimes this was so, but I suspect that most of them wrote what they wrote out of the disillusionment that overcame them at the chasm between the Jeffersonian dream of a spacious and egalitarian American democracy, and the actual power of Big Business. They were protesting against the wasteland of American moral and cultural life between the time of Grant's Presidency and that of Wilson.

What happened in the Great Depression changed the image of the Titan more drastically. Big Business of the 1920s, certain that it had found the secret of perpetual prosperity, claimed the right to the policy-making decisions not only in the economy but in the government. But the economic collapse of 1929 resulted in a disillusionment with the Titan: the Big Money of the boom of the 1920s came clamoring to the

White House for extreme unction in the 1930s. Those who had seemed to be the "Lords of Creation" were stripped of a good deal of their stature and grandeur.

The businessman began to lose stature even before the Great Depression. After Dreiser's Cowperwood, Sinclair Lewis's Babbitt was a letdown. Babbitt is the biggest real-estate dealer in the minor universe of Zenith, Ohio, whose life revolves around his house, car, service clubs, lodge, and church; who mouths platitudes about business ethics but sees nothing wrong in pulling a real-estate squeeze play on a small butcher: Babbitt is no Titan, neither a great creator nor a great destroyer, but the fag end of business enterprise as a way of life. Lewis did what was in some ways a moving portrait of him, yet gave him none of the quiet dignity and sense of craftsmanship that Howells gave the painting-firm hero of *The Rise of Silas Lapham:* and the shift from the portrait of the 1890s marks the running down of a tradition.

Some of the other novelists showed an even sharper disenchantment. *U.S.A.,* the novel trilogy by John Dos Passos, applies to fiction some of the elements of Veblen's savage critique of American business enterprise. Charlie Anderson, who plays an important role in *The Big Money,* is the embodiment of constructive drives which have been corrupted by the manic passions of promotion. In a less intentional way Scott Fitzgerald's *The Great Gatsby*—the buccaneer who was part phony promoter, part racketeer, the man seemingly from nowhere whose shimmering appearance is woven out of the cloudless fabric of nothing— is also a figure of disenchantment. In Thomas Wolfe's *You Can't Go Home Again* the head of the "Company" is obsessed with finding new advertising slogans; and Wolfe portrays the squeezing of every sales executive in the lower rank by the one above him in the panicky sales hierarchy of the "Company." The emphasis was shifting from the figure of production and finance to that of promotion and sales, from the man who made the goods to the man who knew the magic of extracting something from nothing; from the major legendary figures like Morgan to the minor legends of the rising sales curve and the "hucksters" of the advertising legions. The portrait of business reached its furthest remove from the Titan in the description, in Faulkner's *The Hamlet* and *The Town,* of the locust invasion of his Mississippi county by the swarming Snopes family, which moved with mercantile ardor into all the crevices left by the crack-up of precapitalist Southern society.

But the crucial transformation of the Titan was wrought not so much by the Great Depression, nor by the invasion of the groundlings, but by the corporation. The type-figure who carved out the great industrial empires was almost submerged in the impersonality of the corporate form. In every area of life the winning of power has always required bolder and more vigorous talents than its consolidation. In the new and highly specialized technology, experts took over every phase of the corporation's activity—engineering, financing, production, promotion, advertising, salesmanship, personnel relations. In place of the heroic adventurism of the Titans came a group of "managerial skills" that required talent and judgment in the art of management but seemed earth-creeping by comparison. The increasing division of labor built up business hierarchies in which the aggressive mind of the Titan was less at home than the corporate bureaucratic mind. Once the regime of high-salaried managers was created it took on a life of its own, crowding out the life of the Titan. He ceased to be the giant in whose shadow the business institutions were shaped and became himself the shadow of the institution, taking his stature from the corporation. The corporation as instrument grew in importance while the men wielding it shrank. Those who were once considered barbarian invaders now became absorbed in the structure of the power they themselves created. The conquerors were conquered.

Does this mean that the Titan "reformed"? The big fact about the "Robber Barons" (the phrase was Matthew Josephson's) was not their personal ethics, although to a moralistic generation of reformers it may have seemed so. When Commodore Vanderbilt made his famous "public be damned" remark he was expressing a generalized sense of swaggering power. In broad perspective the ethics of the Big Businessmen were, taken as a group, no worse than the ethics of any other historical group of conquerors. Comparing how America was industrialized with the methods by which Germany, Japan, and Russia were later industrialized, the American record seems like a Sunday picnic or a huddle of innocents. Even the worst of the Robber Barons—men like Gould, Fisk, and Yerkes—were men of virtue compared with the Gauleiter and commissars who performed a similar task in their own countries. The real point is not that the Titan has "reformed," for he was never truly evil. It is rather that he has grown less colorful, less swaggering, more sophisticated; he has had to take his place in a bureaucracy in which his predecessors would have felt stifled; he has had to cope with the regulatory demands of a welfare state and the power of a labor movement; he has had to worry less about his competitors than about "business conditions," domestic and world politics, advertising, consumer demand, and the securities market. He must always feel the pulse of public opinion and be wary of alienating it. Wherever he goes he is accompanied by survey makers, "human-relations" technicians, public-opinion analysts, public-relations experts.

Once known primarily as a man of action (*furor Americanus* is what Aldous Huxley called the American cult of action), the businessman still remains that. But the areas of significant action have changed. They are no longer concerned with the crushing of competitors, the piling up of big fortunes, and the carving out of family dynastic power. The old competitive system has been replaced by a system of "imperfect competition" in which the corporations compete with one another less in prices than in brands and in "products"—that is, in alternative materials for achieving the same results. As for the big fortunes, a more drastic tax system than any continental European can envisage has made them archaic. The heads of the corporate empires no longer get their sense of fulfillment from personal accumulation, nor is their prime quality that of acquisitiveness. They are still movers and shakers, but for a different reason than before. The new Titan is still the creator and consolidator of corporate structures, the guiding mind of monopolies and cartels, the organizer of business "peak-associations." The men who run Metropolitan Life or General Motors, General Electric or U.S. Steel, Alcoa or A.T.&T., are men of power not because of their great fortunes or talents but because they have powerful instruments at their command. They have control of enormous blocks of investment and power. For income-tax purposes the new Titans allow the corporate profits to remain inside the corporation and then declare stock dividends. They create "charitable trusts" as legal fictions, and "foundations" as ways of escaping the ax of the inheritance tax. But where they once sought profit, they now seek the retention of the power over their capital investments. Their prime concern is the figure they can cut in America and the world as proconsuls administering their huge aggregates of power.

This requires and has developed a new personality profile for the Titan—that of a corporate statesman. He reads more than he used to, goes to college, makes speeches and statements (alas, too many and too platitudinous), is seen at public conferences. His suavity is more evident than his ruthlessness. He knows something of the workings of the economy and the government, and of world affairs. I am speaking, of course, not of the run-of-mill corporate vice-president, nor of the sales manager or advertising manager who may be only a contemporary Babbitt, but of the small group of sophisticated holders of business power who embody business creativeness. He has even had to take a hand in developing the idea of the welfare state itself, as Wendell Willkie did; or administering its controls over business, as Charles E. Wilson did; or in supervising the American economic aid to Europe, as Paul Hoffman did.

The Big Businessman has had to come up squarely against the problems of the survival of the economy and the organization of a transformed society. This new type of businessman—represented, for example, by the members of the Committee for Economic Development —is still not accepted by the mediocre but stubborn men who remember the old catchwords of the free-market economy and strike out blindly against any innovating doctrine. These men act sometimes like the defenders of a besieged city, a League of Frightened Men who in their panic are bent on searching out heresy in their own ranks. Once the new businessman makes clear his premise that the productivity which is the source of profits is more important than any particular profit, that an expanding economy may require the co-operative action of the welfare corporation and the welfare state, he runs the danger of being branded as a maverick and cast out of the herd.

The image of the old Titan still remains in the popular mind and colors the dreams that the young men dream. But the effective figure is a new one, in a new setting, the result of the complex and powerful transforming process of the past half century of American society.

It may be significant that no one has yet found a name for him that will stick, as "Titan" and "Tycoon" did to his predecessor. He is often called a "business statesman" by those who stand in awe of him and feel there must be some appellation of a dignity that parallels his massive business power—also sometimes his wealth. Such men as Alfred Sloan, Charles E. Wilson, and Harlow Curtice of General Motors are considered a cut above the old-fashioned, profit-seeking, money-grasping Titans. As a result they have been called on to speak as oracles not only on industrial matters but on the welfare of the nation, and sometimes have convinced themselves (often with public approval) that the country is only an enlarged image of the company and that they have the right to make decisions about what is good for both.

Perhaps the simplest name for them is what their employees tend to call them—"Mr. Big"—carrying with it a half affectionate, half scornful set of overtones. In conversation the ordinary American will say of one of these new corporate moguls that he is the "head" of such-and-such a corporate empire. These are indeed the "head men" of American life, and what gives the name some aptness is that it refers less to the stature or personality of the man himself than to his position at the head of a hierarchy of function and power. When one head man goes, another arrives to take his place. What is crucial, as in the hierarchy of the Middle Ages, is not so much the individual as the status. In fact, a number of writers have noted that these American head men are emerging as corporate seigneurs, and that their position and power have much in common with the frame of medieval society.

Yet what strikes the popular mind is their power and ruthlessness as they contend for place with the most modern of weapons—promotion schemes, mergers, corporate reorganizations. During the 1950s, a new type of novel about the businessman emerged, in which the problems of authority and ethical codes were posed. In Cameron Hawley's *Executive Suite* the tradition set up by the corporate founder, which seemed archaic to the new managerial group, finally triumphed, and with it the idea that the heart of corporate enterprise is what it can do for the workers, the community, and the values of craftsmanship. In the same author's *Cash McCall* there is a skillful delineation of the new Napoleons of corporate finance who march and wheel their chess pieces across the board without much concern for what any particular corporation is producing: here again, once the ethical problem has been posed, it is resolved (as in the case of religious conversion) by a saving insight into the productive values that transcend the merely financial ones. In a TV and movie story called *Patterns* the resolution is not so simple: the "head man" is depicted in almost Nietzschean terms as driven by an urge to stretch himself and his associates to the utmost of their powers, beyond the human. But Nietzsche never foresaw that in the American case the effort to reach to the godlike would apply to the creation not of the Superman but of Super-corporation. And the hero of this story, while seeing the evil and ruthlessness of the head man, is himself at the end half caught up in his fervor and asks only for a chance to be more ruthless himself and to make a victim of the man who has made victims of others—all in the name of the Corporation.

3. The Corporate Empires

IT IS TIME to take a closer look at the corporation as a social contrivance. A discerning anthropologist, studying characteristic American inventions such as the dating pattern, the success system, and judicial review, might seize on the corporation as the most important of all. Reaching into every area of life, it has become the instrument by which Americans organize any project demanding group effort, impersonality, continuity beyond the individual life, and limited liability. It is striking that a highly individualist people should accept a transformation of its life wrought by so impersonal a social invention.

Much ingenuity has been invested in the corporation as a mechanism. The refinements of corporate law and finance, of corporate liaisons and marriages, of corporate dissolution and reorganization, have absorbed some of the most resourceful talents of the American legal and financial elites. In the planning of corporate strategies there have been field marshals of genius and Napoleons of dazzling megalomania. Some, like Samuel Insull, came to grief; others received for their exploits the admiration of the members of the corporate fraternity. But in the main the corporate form is what it is today in America because of the patient labors of thousands of talented but largely unknown men who have been drawn to their work, by some obscure impulsion, as beavers to the construction of their dams.

The early American corporations were wards of the state, chartered only in rare cases and supervised by the state in every phase of their operation. When a group of men received a charter to build a railroad or canal, or run a toll bridge, or organize a college, the assumption was that the state was grudgingly signing away one of its inherent functions, retaining the responsibility of supervision. The corporation thus began as a state instrument, to be kept within the ambit of the state power. But such was the dynamism of American business enterprise within it that it ran away with the original intention. It helped gather vast blocs of capital by subdividing and dispersing business ownership and collecting the savings and hopes of many. By consolidating a number of enterprises and tapping the profits from their combined future growth, it anticipated these future profits and expressed them in the immediate market value of stocks. The corporate form thus suited a business spirit which sought always to capitalize the future, and in turn it created the stock market as a way of mirroring men's shifting calculations about future earnings and values.

In these ways the corporation built vast power blocs whose size and impersonality daunted the Populist thinkers of the turn of the century. Henry Demarest Lloyd felt that the "Wealth" whose concentration it made possible was destroying the "Commonwealth." Frank Norris called it the "Octopus" and portrayed in his novels how its impersonal power blasted personal lives and hopes. The generation of muckrakers called the alliance of corporation and political machine the "System," and Steffens described it by resorting to the mystical "It." William Dean Howells, writing in his Socialist phase in *A Traveler from Altruria*, called corporate power the "Accumulation," and reflected with sadness that "by a logic irresistible and inexorable, the Accumulation *was*, and we were *not*." If American social critics today are no longer so colorful in their epithets, it is because they have come to accept the corporate form as a fact. Like Adolph Berle, they recognize it as embracing a crucial phase of "the twentieth-century capitalist revolution" and are concerned mainly with realistic ways of keeping its power within bounds, as well as being curious about the direction in which it will move and grow.

These corporate power blocs make possible the industrial concentration which was for a time the subject of repeated government investigations—the Report of the Industrial Commissions in 1904, the Pujo investigation a decade later in 1913, and the TNEC (Temporary National Economic Committee) inquiry two decades later in the 1930s. In the 1940s and 1950s there were fewer occasions and less impetus for such critical investigations—a sign not only of friendlier Administrations but, even more, of an acceptance of the dominating position of a handful of corporations in whose shadow the rest live.

A Federal Trade Commission study in 1947 showed that of some one hundred thousand corporations in America, 113 had assets of $100 million and over. Twelve of them ran into billions of dollars in their holdings. The most recent figures, at the end of the 1940s, show that 135 corporations own 45 per cent of the industrial assets of the nation, and that a few hundred men, in eight or ten loosely allied financial groups, control assets of over $100 billion. The picture in particular industries is similarly revealing. Out of twenty-six major manufacturing fields there were nineteen in which at least 60 per cent of the industry was controlled by six or fewer corporations, and thirteen in which at least 60 per cent was controlled by three or fewer. Heading the list were aluminum, tin, linoleum, copper, cigarettes, liquor, plumbing supplies, rubber tires, office equipment, automobiles, farm machinery, and meat products.

The trend toward the big corporate unit is partly explained by low production and distribution costs. The big corporations are in a real sense the children of competition. In the fierce struggle for survival and profits the pay-off is in efficiency, and those who triumph in the competitive struggle quite naturally drive their rivals to the wall, where they are willing to be bought out. This is especially true in the case of brand competition, as with automobiles, in an era where economic success depends on the psychic contagion among buyers as much as it does on the quality or utility of the product itself. It has long been known, of course, that the best producing units vary in size and are frequently a good deal smaller than the cancerous size of the giant corporation. "If God had intended us to have anything as large as the U.S. Steel Corporation," said Justice Brandeis in developing his idea of "the curse of bigness," "he would have given us the brains to run it well." But the persistent question is: "How big is too big?" American businessmen know that the steel industry, once the leader in technological advance, has fallen behind such newer industries as aviation, chemicals, and the electrical industries. Even in the relatively new industries, the size of the corporate unit extends well beyond the daily direct knowledge of any managerial officials. A corporation like General Motors has been compelled to split up its empire into more or less autonomous producing units, in order to prevent the spread of elephantiasis.

Thus one may venture that corporate bigness has as much to do with the strategic capture of power as with possible efficiencies of production. Current technology involves outlays so huge that only the big producers find them compassable: the big firms, moreover, can spend more on advertising campaigns and put a bigger and more aggressive sales force into the field. The corporate power bloc has command of raw materials often not available to its smaller competitors, especially in an armament economy, when procurement officials are hurried and harassed, and give the priority allocations as well as the contracts to the big firms. Because of its research laboratories and its ability to buy up promising inventions, it has command of patents and processes with which it can freeze others out of the market. It can attract scientists, engineers, technicians; it can set up elaborate marketing and advertising structures; it can surround itself with the artfulness of "public relations." It can control a big enough portion of the market so that its voice is heard loud and clear in the price agreements which are becoming standard practice in the corporate field. It can apply pressures to the government itself, by lobbies in the capitals and by its influence over party managers, candidates, and local machinery.

Thus the advantages of corporate bigness may come after the fact, not before. Corporations, by the very fact of their bigness, may achieve a strategic power that sometimes makes it unnecessary for them to pursue efficiencies which can cut costs. They become tired and unwilling to take risks, and in some cases grow backward in their response to technological change.

As I have noted above in speaking of the corporate head men as feudal seigneurs, the corporation which started as a legal device has ended by carving out an imperium for itself. John Dewey saw how far this had gone, and in an early essay called "The United States, Inc." he spoke of "the corporateness of society." W. J. Ghent, one of the turn-of-the-century critics of corporate capitalism, called it "the New Feudalism," which seemed an apt term for a system in which the feudal lords owed formal allegiance to the central political authorities yet retained their own domains of power.

The corporations have become, in a sense, private governments. Their decisions influence the size and distribution of the national product, the channeling of investment, the levels of employment and purchasing capacity of the workers. In effect they levy taxes on the consumer and make alliances with foreign corporations in cartel agreements. Operating basically for private purposes, with public consequences secondary, they can (as I have noted) crowd out competitors, divide the market, keep profits high, determine price levels and production volume. The picture of prices fixed in the free play of the market needs to be modified today: in a number of the mass-production industries corporate prices tend to be set "administratively," by the action of a small number of corporations, with an eye to costs, profits, volume of sales, and what the traffic will bear. This is modified somewhat by the fact that while the prices are set administratively—say by the auto companies— the retail dealer makes adjustments to a variable market through discounts and by varying the turn-in allowance for the old car. This should not, however, obscure the fact that the functions I have described affect the public interest deeply, yet they are being carried out by holders of corporate power who are not chosen by the people, responsible to them, or replaceable by them.

The defenders of corporate power sometimes make the mistake of denying its scope, picturing the American economy still in terms of the legendary capitalism of a market system of competing small enterprises. The better course is to admit the power of the corporate empires and assess its sources and uses. Adolf Berle, whose long and intimate knowledge of the corporate world demands respect, agrees that "the corporate empire wants all the commercial power it can get," but adds that "it has little instinct for going beyond that. Its political adventures are primarily to safeguard its commercial position. It has somehow got itself into a situation where it is held responsible for a great deal more than that—and is painfully trying to understand how it got there and what to do." Berle and other observers also contend that a new kind of statesmanship is developing in the corporation, with a sense of restraint and of responsibility for the public consequences of the private managerial decisions. Certainly the corporate ethos has changed since the 1920s, although innovation in business practices has not kept the same pace as innovation in technology and managerial organization. The disturbing fact is that, in the absence of strong outer controls over corporate practices, reliance must be placed on inner controls: and thus far the corporation has not developed built-in controls that restrain its behavior. It relies instead on a rising level of business education (the Harvard School of Business Administration is like nothing else in the world and has profoundly influenced the idea and performance of the managerial function) and on self-criticism within the corporate community, both of which may prove a frail line in time of acute economic stress.

The sharp question that might be put by the defenders of the corporate empires is: What was the historical alternative? Without the

corporate form America could probably not have developed industrialism so rapidly or on so large a scale, nor could it have accumulated
capital and plowed it back into industry as dramatically as it did. An
economy of small firms was possible in Jackson's day but scarcely in ours.
One alternative was national ownership with big-scale enterprise under
government trusts. But this would have raised even more far-reaching
issues of power than the corporate empires have done. Whatever group
owns or runs the economic plant of a country has enormous power
vested in it; that holds true also of the group that runs the trade-unions
and even more of the group that runs the government. If the same group
holds power in all three of these areas there is scarcely a crack possible
in the combined monolith of power. What can be said of the American
corporation as a power bloc is that, while it may sometimes control
and even cow specific officials or agencies of the government, it is not
in itself the government. Along with the other power institutions it
presents on the American landscape a plurality of power groupings
which are the better for their dispersal.

The Big Corporation, Big Unionism, and Big Government live in an
uneasy ménage in America, with no one of them able to crush the
others. A new constitutional structure of industry and government is
emerging, with a new separation of powers that is more relevant for
contemporary America than the classical separation of governmental
powers. The corporation and the union have tacitly agreed roughly on
the boundary lines beyond which neither interferes with the other,
while there is a common area between these boundaries where they
bargain collectively; and the government has agreed roughly on the
limits beyond which it will not interfere with either the corporation or
union, nor will they in turn seek to overthrow it. But this delimitation
of provinces should not obscure the fact that the corporate system as a
whole has immense weight with every American government, nor the
fact that the corporate empires have revolutionized the price system,
profit system, and property system, so that the actualities of American
business power bear little relation to the golden legendary profile of
capitalism.

There has been a recent tendency to depict the American economy as
a "people's capitalism." The ownership of America's industrial plant has
been diffused. In the 1950s A.T.&T., which carried stock dispersion furthest as a matter of policy, reported 1,307,000 owners (roughly one out
of every fifty American families), of whom a quarter million were company employees. General Motors had 482,000 stockholders, and Westing-
house Electric had 111,000. In all, seven and a half million Americans
owned stock in corporations, many of them in the companies they worked

for, especially through union-employer pension funds. This has given the corporations some roots in popular acceptance. Yet most of the stockholders owned only a few shares: 60 per cent of the shares in the 200 largest industrial corporations, according to the classic Berle and Means study, *The Modern Corporation and Private Property,* were owned by 1 per cent of the stockholders. For all the companies listed on the exchanges, stockholders of over $10,000 (4 per cent of the number of stockholders) owned 60 per cent of the stocks. In the Berle-Means figures, 90 per cent of American stockholders in 1937 had incomes of less than $5,000 a year. Along with the diffusion of ownership there has also been a transformation of it. The old owner-manager no longer exists in any significant sense and has been replaced by a managerial elite that acts as deputy for the owners, whether their holdings be diffused or highly concentrated.

The striking fact here—pointed out by Veblen, developed by W. Z. Ripley, and elaborated on a major scale by Berle and Means—is that while the corporation has diffused industrial ownership, it has concentrated control and split one from the other. When an institution is as important as the corporation, its internal structure becomes of moment for the society. Berle and Means studying the 200 largest industrial corporations, found that in 88 per cent of them control was held by a small group of men: either by a management group (44 per cent) or by some legal device such as a voting trust or a holding company (21 per cent), or by a bloc of minority stockholders (23 per cent). Only in 5 per cent of them—10 of the 200 corporations—was the control in the hands of the stockholders who held a majority of the stock.

This makes a legend of the classical theory that capitalism works because private ownership is spurred to creative acts of business enterprise by the prospect of private profits. What it shows is that a new corporate managerial oligarchy has emerged which stands between ownership and the profit incentive. Ownership has had a wedge driven around it in three directions: it has been split from profit and therefore incentive, from management and therefore from direct contact with the operations of the business, and from control and therefore from the major decisions.

This three-way split has been revolutionary. It has meant that "private enterprise" and "private property" have lost much of their former meaning as effective forces. The groups that had stakes of public interest in the control of the major decisions in the economy—the owners, the workers, the consumers, the government—have been largely left out of the control. A group of "insiders" who are not the principal parties of interest have taken over the control. What seems to have happened is that the corporation, by diffusing private ownership so widely, created a vacuum of control; and by increasing the scale of business operations so greatly, it created a management bureaucracy. While everyone was looking elsewhere—at the struggles between labor and capital, between business and government, between big and small business—the corporate bureaucracy was quick to move into the vacuum of control.

But to say that the new corporate managerial group is also the controlling group is to oversimplify a complex situation. The controlling group has no sharp boundaries. The top officers of management form part of it; others in it may represent the owners of substantial but minority blocs of stock, or investment trusts that subscribe to new stock issues and thus supply risk capital, or bankers and lawyers who may have had a hand in forming or reorganizing the corporation or who hold proxies for their stockholder customers. The problem of locating control is further complicated by the bewildering network of intercorporate relations: the fact that the same men are directors in a number of corporations, that corporations hold blocs of stock in other corporations, that "holding companies" are formed to control the stock in a number of corporations. The structure of the Du Pont industrial empire may serve as one illustration of this complexity. The Du Pont Company began in munitions, expanded after World War I in automobiles, rubber, and other peacetime products. It controls both General Motors and U.S. Rubber; it ramifies into a number of satellite companies in chemicals and synthetic products. Its own stock is held by the Christiana Company, which is a holding company controlled by the Du Ponts and their friends; and at the top of the pyramid of control is the Delaware Company, an even more restricted holding company controlled by the inner circle of the Du Pont family.

Family holdings play a great role in the Du Pont empire, as they still do in the Ford empire, even after the Ford family turned the bulk of its stock over to the Ford Foundation. A number of the smaller corporations are still family-owned and also owner-managed. There are also some famous financial families, like the Rockefellers, which continue to be active in business and especially in the segment of it where their family fortune was originally made. Yet this is not typical of most of the big corporations, where the stockholding is diffused and the managerial group exercises control. The breakup of "family capitalism" in America has been far sharper than in Europe. What is left of it in the corporate form is only a fragmentary residue. In the realm of social structure this represents the counterpart of the transfer of power from the owners to the managers.

What can be clearly said of corporate control is that it is rarely wielded by the majority of stockholders, but rather by powerful overlapping oligarchies of managers and insiders. There have been a few efforts by small stockholders' committees to appear at stockholders' meetings and demand democratic procedure, but they have been ineffectual. A wistfully written sketch in *The New Yorker* by a small stockholder who took it into his head to assert his rights and attend a Du Pont meeting at Wilmington brings out satirically the lights and shadows of the grotesquely unimportant status of the ordinary "owner" of a corporation who comes to hear the report of his "employees."

It is difficult to know where to place corporate responsibility, since the corporation is an amorphous entity whose core is hard to locate. As the editors of *Fortune* put it, "The control of the typical big corporation is now in the hands of 'managers' who do not own it, and its ownership is in the hands of stockholders who do not influence its behavior. The corporation has become a disembodied, almost self-sufficient, socially 'illegitimate' force." Ironically this anonymous force achieved a number of exemptions and immunities from public regulation, both state and Federal, by claiming to be a "person" within the meaning of the due-process clause of the Fifth and Fourteenth Amendments. The story of how the Fourteenth Amendment was transformed—from a shield of the new Negro citizens against discriminatory treatment into a shield of corporate power against public regulation—is an absorbing study in American legal and intellectual history. Some of the earlier students of constitutional history treated the episode as an example of a "conspiracy" by corporate power; but the conspiracy premise proved unnecessary, the truth being that the corporate symbols exercised a hold on the legislative and judicial mind, which personalized the corporation even while the corporation was depersonalizing business enterprises.

In fact, the new corporate capitalism, which is in one sense a "popular capitalism" is in another a new and peculiarly American collectivism— a form of business syndicalism. If one were to generalize the traits of collectivism, they might run as follows: the crowding out of the "private" principle in enterprise by an authoritarian principle (not necessarily governmental); the whittling away of private property and of the profit incentive; the separation between the formal and real loci of power; the transfer of decisions from an open or "free" market to an administrative group (not necessarily governmental); the steady enlargement of the administrative units, and their pre-emption of a monopoly position; their control by a self-perpetuating bureaucratic elite, and their removal from popular responsibility.

The structure of corporate capitalism fits pretty well into this generalized pattern of collectivism. The "owners" have been relegated to the role of investors; the separation of ownership from control, along with the factor of steep taxes, has obscured the profit incentive; "private property," the "free market," and the "price system" have been changed in meaning. What remains of the profit stimulus, the sanctities of con-trol-by-property, and the free-enterprise system must all be viewed within the framework of a corporate managerial group. The "iron law of oligarchy," which Michels saw operating in every power structure, has not left corporate capitalism exempt: the positions of power in the new elite are filled by men who wear the badges of success and can recognize them on the faces and records of the younger men coming up; the man-agerial elite is not a closed one, and it is highly competitive, yet there are intangibles that give a man entrance to it or can exclude him from it as surely as from the German imperial officers corps. For all its indi-vidualistic slogans, the business class in America has effectively substi-tuted its own form of collectivism for the old individualism.

But although this collectivism has power and has shown a genius for production and marketing, it has not often shown the very quality of "statesmanship" which the champions of corporate capitalism claim for it. While the corporation has a mastery over its internal affairs, the cor-porate economy as a whole does not possess a self-regulating principle which can keep it going in social health and prosperity. It cannot create by itself the structure of order in which the multiple processes of far-flung enterprises are kept within a rational framework. Its failure has rested not on a lack of organizing ability, as its achievements in admin-istrative intermeshing and legal finesse attest, but on the fact that an administrative mechanism intended for one sector of the economy can-not organize the whole, and one intended for conflict and the conquest of power is not equally useful for co-operation and order. Hence the need for a gridiron pattern of governmental, legal, and trade-union controls added to the inner controls that are being built into corporate practice. Through this pattern of voluntary decisions and institutional control a number of the problems that had plagued American capital-ism—including some of the problems of the business cycle, inflation, un-employment, insecurity, and labor conflict—have been made more man-ageable.

Nor did a corporate General Staff emerge, as it did in other capitalist structures, as an instrument of social power. The trade-association move-ment proved useful in the effort at price-fixing and restriction of pro-duction, chiefly by the smaller firms, but its defect was its emphasis on freezing rather than expanding the economy. The next logical step was the formation of "peak associations" (after the German usage, *Spitz-genossenschaften*), as with the National Chamber of Commerce and no-tably the National Association of Manufacturers. Here too the rigidify-ing process set in. Alfred Cleveland's study of the N.A.M. for the period 1933-1946 showed that 125 corporations, making up less than 1 per cent of the membership, divided among them almost nine tenths of the executive committee posts and two thirds of the directors' posts of the organization; during the same period, the Cleveland study shows, the N.A.M. policies were mainly negative, being concentrated on opposing labor, taxes, and governmental restriction. The efforts of government to use the corporate form that had been so successful in business, and to develop the government corporation as entrepreneur (as with the TVA) have also been bitterly opposed by the business associations in the name of the "American way." Legislatively they have been effective as lobbies and pressure groups; politically they have operated to fight the "creeping Socialism" of the Democrats and maintain orthodoxy within Republican ranks; ideologically they have conducted "educational" campaigns in the schools, churches, and women's clubs.

But this effort has not added up either to the hopes of its organizers or the fears of some of the critics of corporation trends. The "law of centralization and decay," as formulated by Brooks Adams, has operated in corporate collectivism at least on the score of centralization, but the signs of decay are still murky. The more exacting believers in economic determinism argued in the 1930s and 1940s that the American corporate economy, with its peak associations, monopolies, and cartels, was taking the road that business power took in Italy, Germany, and Japan. Robert Brady, writing in the 1940s in *Business As a System of Power,* saw the N.A.M. as acting no differently from the Zaibatsu, the Federation of British Industries, and the German cartels, but this proved wide of the mark both as description and as prediction. Actually the experience of German business in aiding the rise of Nazism remains a scorching memory to American businessmen, who know that they would be engulfed by the totalitarian wave they invoked. Corporate collectivism has shown few signs of moving into the phase of the corporate state, although what would happen in the event of another world war cannot be foretold. It seems more inclined to digest the lessons of the boom-and-bust cycles of the past, to accept—however reluctantly—the necessary minimum of taxation and government intervention, and meanwhile to bask in the sunshine of big profits and rising prestige. American corporate capitalism shares a good measure of the pliable temper of American life as a whole. Even the corporate empires have shown little inclination either to form themselves into a monolithic common front or to raise up demagogues, supposedly to rid them of their enemies, as in a Fascist state.

How can one explain the failure of the American corporate empires to take possession of the whole society, as many observers predicted they would do, and turn the commonwealth into a corporate state? According to Marxist theory this should have happened some time back. In the first decade of the century Jack London foresaw, in *The Iron Heel,* the emergence of an oppressive power that would trample upon American society. As late as the TNEC study of *The Structure of the American Economy* there was a surviving emphasis upon the enormous power of the business corporation. At that time a number of American liberal critics, writing in the shadow of Marxism and with the heavy sense of the march of the corporate empires weighing upon them, wrote at times as if it had already in fact happened, and as if "monopoly Fascism" had already taken possession of America or was about to do so.

There are several important facts about the corporate empires to be kept in mind. One is their nonpolitical character. Even with the decline of the profit-ownership incentive, the great spur in corporate activity is still that of profit and productive achievement rather than political power. This absorption—and quite properly—is with economic aims, not primarily political. As a result, what has developed is not a corporate totalitarianism but more like a corporate syndicalism, using "syndicalism" in the sense of a concentration of power for the purposes of economic action.

Another fact is that the decisions in a corporate economy are decentralized. The classical economic theory of decisions made by small individual enterprisers, with Adam Smith's "hand of God" watching over them, is obviously no longer true—if it ever was. Yet even with the big corporations doing most of the decision-making, it is still true that each of them does it as a going economic concern, instead of its being done at the governmental centers as part of a planning process. As Galbraith puts it, "Even where the concentration of control over industry is relatively great, the final authority over production decisions is held at a comparatively large number of points." Given the high and complex living standards of the Americans, centralized decisions would be almost impossible. In a period of serious inflation they become necessary, especially on questions of price and wage ceilings, and governmental intervention moves in: even when they are necessary they make the economic process clumsy.

Finally, the corporate empires continue to struggle with one another. Using Galbraith's suggestive phrase again, the older concept of competition among a host of individual producers or sellers has now been replaced (since competition has in many senses vanished) by the concept of "countervailing power." There is a struggle inside the corporate hierarchy between the Big Corporation and Big Distribution, chiefly in the form of the chain stores and the mail-order houses; there is a struggle also between Big Agriculture, which exercises considerable political pressures, and the Big Corporation; add to that the struggle between Big Unionism and all of them; and add finally the struggle between all of them and Big Government.

In this sense there is a pull and tension within the American economy which lessens the power of monopoly capitalism itself. The drive toward centralization of power has affected not only the industrial producers but the farmers, the workers, the distributors, and the government itself. What gives the economy its freedom is no longer the "free market" in the old sense but the tug of war between power groups whose swollen strength has burst the bounds of the free market. It is the great paradox of the American economy that it escapes totalitarianism by the fact of a continuing titanic struggle of vast imperial units within itself. It follows, therefore, that the growth of monopolies and mergers, dangerous as they are because all concentrated power is dangerous, has not in itself destroyed American freedom.

It may be this kind of unconscious insight that has led Americans to allow the growth of monopolies at the same time that their logical minds have led them to put antimonopoly laws on the statute books and to make feeble efforts at enforcing them. It follows also that, given the growth of monopoly capitalism, the emergence of the powerful trade-unions has been not a menace but an element of economic and social health, as one of the great counterbalancing forces. It follows similarly that the power of the chain stores and of the agricultural bloc has operated further toward holding this balance. And, finally, the bigness of the government and its network of regulatory measures—dangerous as they are in themselves—have operated to keep the other power concentrations from destroying one another and the public welfare in the process.

Thus corporate business in America does not have anything like the political power that is sometimes ascribed to it, especially by those who are still influenced by foreign parallels. Yet in a curious way business has a good deal more power than its defenders will admit. It comes largely through default. In a mass-consumption economy of high living standards there is inevitably a de-emphasis of political struggle: the issues as between classes and interest groups grow less sharp than they were in the period before World War I or in the 1920s and 1930s. While the economy itself is maintained in something like an equilibrium by the confronting of the "Bigs," the only forces that can swing considerable power are the corporations and the trade-unions. As between the two, the corporations have more money, control the destinies of more people, and can influence the stereotypes of thinking of the whole population. They therefore tend to be the top dog, even though they may not be themselves aware of having clearly political aims and drives.

4. The Property Revolution

In SPITE OF America's role as the chief residual defender of the system of private property in its pristine purity, the position of property in America is neither private nor pure. In a dynamic economy like the American the bundle of legal claims called "property" never remains stable: a change in technical processes, a shift in consumption habits, a new invention in technology or managerial practice, a depression or a war, may give new value to claims hitherto ignored or diminish others hitherto cherished.

Property is not a simple or single right. It has become a property-complex—a tangle of ideas, emotions, and attitudes, as well as of legal and economic practices. As such it has been drastically transformed in the era of Big Technology and the corporate empires. According to the more naïve version of the business legend, private property has always been the American "way of life" and always will be. This has lost much of its meaning. For those who possess property, in the sense of substantial stockholdings and investments, it is mainly a symbol of status for the present and security for the future. For the rest, who may have homes and automobiles but are propertyless in the sense of industrial holdings, it is something they hope to acquire for themselves or their children: this hope, along with the things in their own life that they value and enjoy, serves to link them with the holders of property and power. The forms of property have changed, but the emotions and loyalties it evokes go back deep into the American past.

The American ideas about property were deeply influenced by a trio of English thinkers—Locke, Blackstone, and Herbert Spencer—but it was the structure of American society up until the end of the nineteenth century that gave substance to their theories. The components of the property idea—that a man had a right to the things with which he had mixed his sweat, that his property was linked with his craft and job and therefore with his personality, that you could no more deprive him of his property than of his freedom and individuality, that in fact his individuality was linked with the property which made him self-sufficient and self-reliant, and that he could do what he wished with the property that was his—these elements of the property idea had force in a social setting where almost every man owned a piece of land or hoped to save enough on his job to start a small business. In the America of the farmer and the owner-enterpriser, private property was a way of organizing not only the economy but also the personality.

This was reinforced by the underlying theological premises of the

Christian idea.* The Christian allegory of death and resurrection—the sacrifice for a principle sacred to the personality—gave a militant edge to the crusade for property, which was so closely tied with the personality. The roots of individualism in the Calvinist idea of calling and election gave further strength to the secular insignia of success in vocation. The theological premises of St. Augustine's *City of God* and of Bunyan's *Grace Abounding* combined in America to give property the aura of grace. In the moral and emotional climate of the earlier America, entrance into the Heavenly City required that one be shrived of poverty and invested with property. The clinching element of the property idea was the doctrine of natural rights, by which private property came to be accepted as inalienable from the person, part of "the laws of Nature and of Nature's God" that predated human society and therefore could not be changed by human enactment. This theology of the property idea helped the possessors to hold on to their power and invested their position with the support of popular conviction. In a society that regarded property as grace, business enterprise had strong roots in the general allegiance.

But as the conditions of property changed, with Big Technology and the corporate empires, the gap between the property idea and the social reality widened, until property of the old sort—family-owned and owner-managed—became a kind of residual legend, still clung to even when it was stripped of all but a lingering historical memory. Industrial property became centralized, family ownership waned, the corporate form pushed aside the others, the size of the property unit shifted—and America, which had once been a society mainly of small property owners, became a society not only of the Big Technology and the Big Corporation but also of Big Property.

Small Property still exists in the form of small farms, small businesses, and tiny shops, but the independent farmer is a dwindling fraction of the population, the small manufacturer is being crowded by the great corporations, and the little merchant finds himself precariously caught in an economy of big department stores, chain stores, mail-order firms, and discount houses. In the division of the nation among big property, small property, and the unpropertied, big property is increasing in power, small property is increasing in numbers (there were over five million nonfarm enterprises in the mid-1950s, an increase of over a million in a quarter century) but shrinking in power, while the unpropertied are growing in numbers despite the wider diffusion of stock ownership and are as powerless as the unpropertied have always been everywhere.

Before the world wars there still seemed a chance to have the issue

* The argument given too sketchily here is discussed further as the freedom-property complex, in Ch. X, Sec. 2, "American Thought: the Angle of Vision."

fought out between Big and Small Property, and the great names of the Progressive Era—Wilson and Brandeis, La Follette and Norris, J. Allen Smith and Parrington and Beard—were the men who, even in the face of the challenge from the corporate empires, clung to the Jefferson-Jackson-Lincoln conception of an America of small property. It was this issue which furnished one of the great stakes of the social struggle for several generations. The struggle was lost by Small Property, mainly because it was waged not only against the corporate empires but also against their Big Technology, which was even harder to beat. In this struggle the impersonal Big Corporation had the advantage of putting on its enemy's uniform, garbing itself in the emotion-laden insignia of the idea of individualist property that had been shaped in an era of petty trade, small handicraft, and family ownership and operation, and was being invoked to sanction the triumph of the corporation and its new managerial elite.

I do not write of Big Property here as if it were always evil and monopolist, and of Small Property as if it were always good. Neither is necessarily true. The American worship of magnitudes, even when turned upside down to become a cult of the small, still remains an obsession with numbers. The monopoly power—defined as the power to manipulate price and output by being strategically placed to do so—may apply to both big and small corporations that are thus strategically placed, although it is more likely to apply to the big ones. In the ever-greater market of a high-level, mass-production economy the increase in corporate size is bound to keep pace with the growth in the size of the market. The American economy has shown a striking capacity for maintaining its freedom of energy even while changing and seemingly rigidifying its forms.

Two examples may serve to underscore this. One is in the area of competition: to a striking degree price competition in the mass-production industries has been replaced by brand and product competition; for example, technological innovation has made glass, rubber, steel, aluminum, and plastics compete with one another in many industrial and domestic uses. The second example is in the insurance companies, the investment trusts, and the pension funds. During the 1950s it was estimated that at least 80 per cent of all the new venture capital which was supplied to the organized capital market came through these big institutional investors. In a sense it may be said that they act as trustees for the savings and holdings of the ordinary American—a new kind of trusteeship which differs from the vaunted trusteeship of the Big Corporation itself. To the extent that these institutional investors safeguard the property interests of the small man, Small Property may be said to have re-emerged in the investment market even after it had to give way in production itself.

It would be wrong to say that the corporate empires entrenched private property, but even more wrong to say that they destroyed it. A better way is to say that the modern corporation "smashed the property atom," breaking it into constituent particles and reassigning them. The bond owner now gets one kind of return; the stockholder gets another; the large-minority-bloc stockholders have a hand in corporate decisions, sharing control with the managers, while the small stockholders who may together represent the majority ownership get their dividends but have little power of control except as their interests in the profits and security of their holdings are the concern of the big institutional investors I have discussed. The worker, who once had the hope of becoming a property owner by starting a business, still makes a stab at it in many cases but with a high rate of business failures. His realistic chance of owning property rests on becoming himself a small stockholder. For a fitful moment, during the "sitdown strikes" of 1936 and 1937, there was talk of the worker's property right in his job, but this did too much violence to the whole property tradition, which was emotionally linked with owners and not workers.

What the corporate revolution did was not to strip the propertied class of its power but to extend the reach of that class and change property relations within it. Where the owner had once controlled his own industrial property and capital and received profit from his own management and risk, he still got the profits in the form of dividends, but the decisions and control on which they were based were now bureaucratized, being shifted to the managerial group.

The processes of corporate investment have also suffered a drastic change. A recent analysis of the formation of capital from 1919 to 1947 shows the following: in that period the American capital accumulation was 770 billion dollars; 34 per cent (262 billion) was undistributed profits of the corporations themselves and was plowed back; 40 per cent (310 billion) was in the form of bank credit, used for capital expansion; 26 per cent (198 billion) was individual savings—that is, the savings of the risk-taker in the classical sense. But when the last figure is broken down, one finds that most of it went into savings banks or life insurance or durable consumers' goods which count as personal capital; some of it went into corporate bonds, paying a set return. Only a little more than 3 per cent of the individual savings went into corporate stocks. In 1948, in a year when the national income was 225 billion, only a billion dollars went into new corporate stock, common and preferred.

This means that the big corporation no longer goes out into the market looking for savings. It plows back its own profits. This was foreshadowed decades ago: Charles M. Schwab, the steel industrialist, when asked in 1923 what the future of American industry would be, answered, "Why won't it be in the future as in the past, all the money you make and more put back into the business?" A few recent figures indicate that business has followed his advice. In 1929 the American corporations re-invested 20 per cent of their profits; in 1950 they reinvested 70 per cent.

There are many reasons for this high rate of corporate self-financing. With huge profits, high government taxes, and the desire of the man-agers to show corporate growth as an index of their own managerial skill and achievement, the corporation has become almost self-sufficient, even in terms of its capital formation. Its new bond flotations are largely taken up by savings banks and insurance companies. This has led to the suggestion that most of the corporate capital today is in a sense "con-scripted capital," either plowed back by corporate administrative deci-sion, or invested for individuals by banks and insurance companies, or taken by the government in taxes and invested in public works pro-grams and armament industries. Even more important is the decline of the investment banker. Compare his role in the merger movement of the 1890s and 1900s with his lesser role today, and the change becomes dramatic. There has long been a conviction that whoever controls the money market controls the corporate empires, and that whoever controls credit possesses the crucial power. This conviction was the basis for the economic thinking of Louis D. Brandeis about "other peoples' money" and for a whole series of Federal investigations of the "Money Trust." It was also the core idea of the European conceptions of American "finance capitalism" from Lenin through Hilferding to the lesser Marxists of to-day. This is far less true now, given the new trend of corporate self-financing which keeps the economy moving. The American economy during the past half century or longer has shifted from finance capital-ism to corporate capitalism.

The consequences of all this for the property idea are far-reaching. It is hard to use the individualist "natural rights" defense of corporate power and talk of the managerial elite mixing their sweat with the soil or with their tools. As for the question of profits and power as a reward for business skills, what has happened is that the profits in the form of dividends go to the stockholders who have to show few business skills except shrewdness in knowing when to buy or sell stocks, while power without profits has gone to those who show the managerial skills.

As for the idea of risk-taking, one of the stock themes of business-minded editorial writers was that risk capital was the life blood of the economy, and that the welfare state might destroy it. But the reality is that risk capital has changed its form and nature. Like the profit motive in business, it was a carry-over from the era of small business enterprise into the Era of the Sure Thing. There is still risk in corporate enterprise. In their measured and ponderous way, corporations do take risks and often very great ones. But the capital they use is not individual entrepreneur capital, and the managers do not take risks with their own money. Nevertheless they have a sense that the corporate capital that they are risking is theirs, that it might otherwise be used for dividends or for strengthening their working funds, and that their own prestige as managers depends upon risking it wisely. In addition there is the generalized risk of violent fluctuations in the economy as a whole, due to the business cycle: the Great Depression confiscated more business values, running into the tens of billions, than the New Deal could ever have done, and when President Eisenhower suffered a heart attack, the loss in corporate values by stock-market quotations was immense.

With its two main underpinnings removed—the profit incentive and the reward for risk—what remains of the original theory of private property? Not much, it must be admitted: the original theory needs drastic overhauling, yet the social reality of private property is still a force in the American economy. Private property has not been abolished, either by Big Government or the Big Corporation: it has taken new forms. It is still private in the sense that it is not statist, but it has ceased to be individualist and has become corporate, institutional, and managerial. The incentives of the owners of Big Property are no longer profit-from-skill but have become profit-from-dividends, security for life, and if possible a "killing" on the stock market.

As for the incentive of the managers, some of them get options on blocs of stock at a low price as part of their salaries and to that extent are corporate owners also. Their salary range is broad: some may get less than $25,000 a year, others more than a quarter million (the highest salaries are in tobacco, liquor, cosmetics, drugs, movies, and broadcasting), and many of them get extra "bonuses," but only a handful are in the millionaire income class. Nonetheless as a group they belong to the big-income class and consider themselves part of Big Property. They know that each quarter they must show a good profits record, along with a good production and sales-volume record and a good labor-relations record.

They are usually able men, college graduates from the Midwest or the Northeast who "get along with people," wear the right clothes, have the right friends, and possess "agreeable" personalities. They work hard, carrying their work home with them at night, are reluctant to retire, and have great pride in their craft. They may be spurred on by the pace of technical advance behind which they dare not lag, or by shifts in the market situation with which they must keep up; but their important incentives are pride, prestige, and self-expression in their work. While they may have few competitors in their own industry, the corporate rivalry is usually intense. Sometimes it is a gamelike rivalry, as with the General Motors–Ford struggle to show which of them will be Number One in the small-car market. Sometimes, as with the automobile manufacturers in the lesser companies, it is a grimmer question of whether they will be pushed out of the market altogether. The cannibalism among corporations is as great as among the tribes in the Congo jungle, although it operates with the sanction of law as well as corporate tribal practice.

One of the great spurs, for both owners and managers, is the sense of power flowing from the massive capital whose investment they organize. This includes the indirect power over legislators, government administrators, and the communications industries, which the possessors of big investments and the dispensers of big advertising can count on. The managers associate themselves with Big Property and have become its agents. A Regent has become King, but he rules in the old regal fashion, in the interests of the dynasty. The freedom to do what one will with property, which is still claimed by the corporate regents as it was once by the individualist business kings, is still the watchword of the champions of corporate "private property"; and the property fears of the managers express themselves as strongly in opposition to "dangerous" ideas at home and abroad as those of the owners ever did.

One change in attitude has, however, taken place. The managers of the big corporations are likely to have a broader vision of the economy as a whole and its place in the world than the individual small businessmen, who are close to the competitive struggle and feel embittered both by their labor difficulties and by the big chunk of their income which the government takes in taxes. No Poujadist movement has arisen among American shopkeepers and small businessmen, as it did in France in the mid-1950s, yet there is a discernible narrowness of outlook in the small sectors of the American economy as well.

There remains to speak of the property ideas of the propertyless. The path to property in the earlier America was either through small landholding, usually on the advancing frontier, or by starting a small firm and making it larger, finally building it into a great established business and even a family fortune. The path to property now is more likely to be by the carving out of a career in the managerial hierarchy. Those who are not managers may shift from one occupation to another, or from industrial worker to white collar or professional, but they remain unpropertied.

Yet it would be wrong to conclude that the property idea has no

hold on them. No dogmatically Socialist appeal has ever had much success with them in America, and they have consistently refused to take
on the class-conscious bitterness assigned to them by the Marxist writers.
However great the gap between the corporate reality and the theory
of private property, the propertyless still assign the production record
of America and their own increased living standards to the regime of
private property. It may be "folklore," but folklore has a way of retaining its hold on the people. They are willing to consider the masters
of corporate property the trustees of the private-property system until
such time as they themselves or their children (for hope has never died
in their hearts) will break into the charmed circle. They are resigned
to Big Property not because they believe in some "harmony of interests," or think there is no conflict between top dog and bottom dog,
but because each in his heart hopes still to be a top dog and therefore
tends to identify with him. Even American unionism, as Hoxie long
ago pointed out, is a property-minded "business unionism."

But I do not want to emphasize too much the identification with the
Big Property group. Most of the propertyless are so only when judged
in terms of industrial capital or land. Their real concern is with their
personal property: a "home," even if it has a mortgage; a car, even an
old one; some savings, even if inflation is depleting them; clothes and
fashions; a TV set and kitchen appliances; a job, which to most Americans is *theirs* and therefore has property aspects; perhaps even a few
shares of stock; and the hope someday of "taking it easy" and "retiring,"
on a different scale from the rich corporate owner and manager, but
in much the same spirit of being invested with property as grace.

5. Business and Its Satellites

LIKE ANY imperial force, the corporate empires have opened hitherto
untapped areas of American life and added to their domain a whole
array of satellite activities. Even the barest profile of the business pattern in mid-twentieth-century America shows it unlike anything De
Tocqueville or Bryce dreamed of and unlike the picture of American
business in even so late a study as Harold Laski's *American Democracy,*
which depicted a doomed figure of business enterprise in the sickroom
of capitalism. There is no doom and no sickroom. One should not underestimate the swaggering sense of power of the Big Corporation in
the "New Age of Confidence" of American business. It is the confident
behavior of a conqueror, not the delusional behavior of a victim.

In the galaxy of the satellites one starts with the accountants who are
in charge of the anatomy of corporate enterprise and who chart the

pecuniary position of tax avoidance without too openly committing evasion, and the lawyers who snarl and unsnarl the legal relations with other corporate empires or the government.

Take the long-drawn-out litigation of the antitrust suits against the nation's investment bankers or the Giannini banking chain or the Du Pont empire or the A & P chain or U.S. Steel; add intramural suits like that of Kaiser-Fraser against Cyrus Eaton of Cleveland, or the color television patent rivalry of R.C.A. and C.B.S.; add the internal battles for corporate control between rival groups of stockholders, as in the cases of Montgomery Ward, the N.Y. Central, and the Penn-Texas Co.; add new corporate creations and reorganizations; add the intricacies of calculating plant and machinery obsolescence for tax purposes, or allowances for plant expansion in the case of conversion to an armament economy; add charitable trusts, family foundations, and other devices; add transactions between the semiautonomous branches of the same corporate empire: the sum becomes a complex of activities that can be carried on only by a general staff of legal and financial trouble shooters. In Newton's universe, it has been said, God became a mathematician. In the Newtonian universe of the Big Corporation the mathematical roles of accountant, tax expert, and legal technician gave their possessors the status, if not of gods, then at least of demigods.

Then there are the statisticians, economic analysts, and survey makers. The Big Corporation is continually sensitive to the world outlook, the business outlook, the stock market, the raw material markets, the labor market, the "Washington scene," the political outlook, and the market analyses and motivational research for its own products. The alert corporate executive must either develop broad perspectives himself or get good expert advice, or both. He reads the newsletters with the "inside" of the Washington and world scene. He relies on one survey after another: in fact, this trend has even reached into the movies and the mass magazines, which can scarcely take a step without first finding out by a survey sampling of reader opinion or audience reaction what the consequences are likely to be. Thus the business executive finds his attention focused on an array of barometers.

The stock-market barometer is one of these, both for the executive and for the large massive investors. The struggle of "bulls" and "bears" has become an American form of bread-and-circuses. In the boom of the late 1920s there was a scramble for speculative profits by clerks, schoolteachers, millhands, industrial workers. Again and again they were slaughtered by "insiders," like the Meehan-Raskob-Durant-Chrysler pool in 1929 which bid up R.C.A. stock and unloaded it on the unwary outsiders for a profit of over five million. The great market crash of

1929 has become part of the folklore of America, an image of tangled ticker tape, desperate men, and ruined lives, ruefully remembered by a burned generation of amateur speculators. The Securities Exchange Commission (SEC), one of the features of reformed capitalism-on-probation, bans the cruder forms of mayhem practiced on the small-scale investor, yet for twenty years after Black Friday the sound investors stayed away from all except the bluest of blue-chip common stock and preferred bonds. The Stock Exchange finally took to advertising to persuade the public to "come back in," and some of the Exchange firms held classes to educate investors, especially the women.

More important, however, was the fact of a continuing inflationary trend after World War II, based on staggering profits and dividends, the emergence of new industries, government buying in a war-geared economy, and rising living standards. During the whole postwar decade of 1946-1956 a series of bull markets, punctuated by periodic downward bearish swoops, kept the financial and investors community in a state of almost constant buoyancy of mood, finding new devotees for the "New Era" theory of market analysis—that stock buyers should be bullish because in the New Era stock values were based on the American future itself. Some analysts asserted that an inflationary trend had become permanent in the economy; and institutional funds—savings banks, life insurance, pension funds, and private trusts—began buying common stock. In 1952 a Brookings study found 6,500,000 Americans in the stock market, holding 30,300,000 shares in stock issues traded on the organized exchanges and over the counter. In the mid-1950s the figures were even higher.

Actually the history of the market, whose daily ups and downs are read on commuters' trains and club cars like the Koran by the Moslem faithful, has shown violent fluctuations over the course of the years, resulting in what business circles know as "brokers' blood pressure" and the ulcer-diet, milk-and-cracker menus in the restaurants near the Exchange. Stock speculation—the "exchange of present money for an expectation of future money"—expresses the impatient desire of many Americans to get rick quick—at least quicker than the normal process of work and savings will allow—and thus provide security for the future and some of the luxuries which have become necessities. It also gives scope to the risk element that is being crowded out of the society, and it has a special appeal for those who lead humdrum lives on rarely fluctuating incomes. The peaks, troughs, and plateaus of the market, as shown on plotted charts, are for them the only landscape worth watching. For them the tons of market-analysis literature are produced, most of it not much better than palmistry or astrology. A study by the Cowles Commission, of the predictive success of the forecasters over the span of two generations, shows that they did no better than the guessers in a random card game. Even the famed Dow-Jones theory, of watching the monthly averages of industrial and railroad stocks and betting that a distinct trend will continue rather than change, has been described as a kind of primitive weather forecasting.

Some of the stock-market professionals, in Bernard Baruch's words, have had to study "the whole history and background of the market and all the principal companies whose stocks are on the board, as carefully as a medical student studies anatomy" and have needed "the cool nerve of a great gambler, the sixth sense of a clairvoyant, and the courage of a lion." They have made fortunes, often by selling "short" or getting out at the right time. But the mass of the people has generally shown a talent for being perversely wrong.

There is also the large, undramatic group of real investors, who are less concerned with short-range fluctuations than with long-range trends, who have a basic confidence in continued corporate prosperity and wish to share in it. Stocks enable them to become the "owners" of the majority stock of corporations, although they are like the passive spectators of mass sports and cannot control what takes place in the ring or field. They get a stake in the success and survival of the corporate system itself, which is one of the strongest psychological facts about the hold of business on the American mind. Yet even for those who do not invest, the market has continued to be a register of hopes and fears for the economy. In terms of ethnology, the fluctuating market has become the totem of the business civilization, which has moved away from the fetishism of the commodity to the fetishism of "business conditions."

A more crucial form of business magic is salesmanship. There has been a well-marked transformation of the art of the older personal seller, who either owned his own shop or had a group of customers whom he knew well, into an impersonal although synthetically "personalized" salesmanship. In an economy of the Big Technology and the Big Corporation, it is not surprising that Americans have developed Big Merchandising. One of the lessons American businessmen have learned during the last twenty years is a paradoxical one: while mass production makes mass distribution necessary, it is even truer to say that mass distribution makes mass production possible. And salesmanship is the key art of the whole structure of mass distribution.

In this sense it is the core activity of the American economy, with technology, production, and financing all subsidiary to it. A business magazine described it as "the biggest man-made force to keep the economy going. When it falters . . . recession follows." Even though competition has been drastically modified within any one mass-production industry, there is still brand and product competition and—most of all —the need to keep the machine going. The role of productivity is to set the pace: where machines are pouring out so much commodity volume, and the high profits are being plowed back into the new technology, the problem is to continue unloading the products on the consumers. As a result, the sales manager is in some way the key figure of the American corporation—more so than the engineer, the production manager, or even the financial executive. The new corporation presidents often rise to their posts because of their work as sales managers. What should have been "finance capitalism"—according to the Marxist gospel—has become a sales economy instead, and capitalism has enacted a Copernican revolution in which all the other planets are now found to be revolving around the central sun of selling.

The salesman may operate in the shop itself or "on the road"—that is, selling to shops, department-store buyers, manufacturers; he may operate on an international level, like Grover Whalen, who "sold" the World's Fair to foreign governments, or James A. Farley, who made Coca-Cola a symbol of American business enterprise all over Europe, or Paul Hoffman, who rose from Studebaker salesman to Marshall Plan Administrator. On every level American business has developed salesmanship into the "art of planned persuasion." The elements of this art are the right kind of packaging (this is notably true in cosmetics, which stress seductive and glamorous mystery, and automobiles, which stress chromium-plated razzle-dazzle); systems of installment buying and consumer financing; an effective sales "theme," sales "line," or sales "angle" (the "line" of the insurance salesman has become part of American folklore); and the stress on the personality of the salesman or salesgirl, whose "smile behind the counter is commercialized lure" and who have become part of the "personality market," where the skills are skills in selling people rather than producing things. One of the less attractive by-products of the stress on salesmanship has been the development of personality courses, charm schools, and a popular literature of self-improvement that teaches the art of manipulating people.

But this kind of manipulative face-to-face salesmanship is itself giving way to the absentee selling through advertising in national media of press, magazines, radio, and television. Like the corporation, advertising was not invented by the Americans but it has been carried furthest and is most at home within the American frame. The go-getting temper which used to be associated with the personal salesman has been transferred to advertising copy, the singing commercials on the radio, and the "selling pitch" on television. Their purpose is not so much the immediate selling of the product as the creation of a favorable climate within which either the sale becomes easy or the customer is induced to ask for the product himself.

Much of the thinking of American corporate executives is devoted to the refinements of the exact nuance to be conveyed in the advertising. A whole new industry—that of the advertising agencies, their account men, their idea men, their layout people and artists, their professional models—has arisen to extol the merits and suggest the glamour of particular commodity brands. Without such national advertising the mass-circulation magazine would have to find a different revenue base, and radio and television—at least in their present form—would wither on the vine. A literature and a cultural folklore have been built around the "hucksters"—their techniques, personality patterns, ulcers, and consciences. Where a generation ago young college men whose sole capital was their boldness and quick wits and ready charm tended to go into stockbroking, they now go into the advertising agencies. With a febrile intensity they aim at what television advertising circles call the "relaxed sell" and the "hard sell." Their craft has had a more than transient effect upon the vocabulary of the business world. "Want to mark yourself as a comer in the advertising field?" asks W. H. Whyte, Jr., in *Is Anybody Listening?* "Speak, then, of fun stories, sweet guys, the hard sell, straw men you set up to back into, and points you can hang your hat on. For each field you will find a subglossary, and, common to all of them, such universal terms as 'play it by ear,' 'the pitch,' 'the deal,' and the many expressions built on the suffix 'wise.' ('Budget-wise, Al, the pitch shapes up like this . . .')"

Advertising does more than help sell the products on which business is built: it has also provided a special kind of language for the people as a whole. Even before American children learn the language of the primer and the schoolroom they mimic the language of the commercials on TV, and of the world of comic little Disneylike men and animated packages that accompany the commercials. Even more important, as David Potter has noted, is the fact that advertising speaks in highly charged symbolic terms and surrounds Americans with a universe of images of plenty. This conditions them to the act of purchase, but it also conditions them to a view of the American economy as a cornucopia abounding in good things. Periodically there used to be attacks from the Left upon advertising as an institution: it is a proof of the efficacy of advertising that these attacks have died down. Either the critics have concluded that the whole venture is futile or they have themselves ended by being "sold" on the object of their attack.

"Public relations" is the youngest of the corporate satellites and brings with it into the corporate world a spanking brashness and an appetite for power. The theory behind public relations is that a corporation is judged not only by the products it turns out but by the total impression it leaves on public opinion. "Today's business formula," we are told, "is: make a product the public wants . . . and an impression the public likes." In a sense, it was the New Deal which created the corporate public-relations industry. When Roosevelt spoke of "driving the money-changers out of the temple," he received so impressive a popular backing that the corporations were jolted into looking around for help. They had been driven, they felt, into a gilded doghouse. They were determined to get out and never to re-enter. They have paid handsomely the "public-relations counsel," "publicity consultants," and others who would dry-clean their public wash and give them a general valet service so as always to appear in public at their best.

Some of the shrewdest and most imaginative brains of the business world have moved into the orbit of this corporate satellite. They help write the speeches of the big corporate executives, cushion the impact of bad news on the public (as with aviation accidents or disasters in the chemical industries), issue public statements for them, see that they are on the right public committees, and—most of all—try to get the right kind of stories "planted" and the wrong kind excluded from the mass-communication media which may represent life or death in the race for markets and profits. Their techniques are based on an unsentimental assessment of the hidden springs of belief, gullibility, and action in men. As an approach not only to business but to the whole of life this mentality has come to be known as the "Madison Avenue" mind, thus adding another symbolic street to Wall Street in the demonology of business. The skills of public-relations men have been taken over into politics, where they are used for the "build-up" of your own candidate and the destruction of his opponent. If anyone in America today has access to the experience which would enable him to write a new grammar of power, reclothing Machiavelli's *Prince* in more modern dress, it is the sophisticated, resourceful, amoral public-relations man.

Sitting at the center, served by these satellite activities, is the corporate executive himself. What was once a somewhat haphazard set of business offices clustering around the executive has now been transformed into a mechanized central office, with hierarchies of secretaries and sub-secretaries, with dictaphones and typist pools. In American life the industrialization of the office has been only less important than the mechanization of the kitchen. But even with new electronic machines, the sense of movement and stir which make the job of the corporate executive exciting is unlikely to be eliminated by mechanization. Sometimes he is in the top ranks of the new middle class, with strong links to the owners of big blocks of minority stock; sometimes he is himself a member of the new elite. Generally he has come up the ladder through service in the sales force or advertising, or less frequently as an engineering technician. Chester I. Barnard, himself a manager who has written searchingly on his fellow managers, lists the crucial qualities of a business executive—in a descending order—as "vitality and endurance; decisiveness; persuasiveness; responsibility; and intellectual capacity."

Much of metropolitan life has been molded by the working day and the recreations of the corporate executive: the conservative but well-tailored clothes, the long and usually liquid expense-account lunch at which "deals" are made, the institution of the cocktail hour at the end of a tense day, the gobbledygook of interoffice memoranda, the rise of a bureaucratic jargon rivaling that of a governmental bureaucracy, the athletic clubs with swimming pools and squash courts for keeping fit, the elaborate layouts and paraphernalia for "businessmen's golf," the amenities of the club car on the commuters' trains, the heavy consumption of alcohol as a necessary stimulant, the emphasis in the theater upon musical comedies, the growth of the night club as entertainment and as industry.

This is the "executive life," as *Fortune* calls it. It has its costs, including the fifty-five- or sixty-hour week, the tension about "decision making," the agonies of promotion and firing, the characteristic executive diseases of ulcerated colitis, rheumatoid arthritis, asthma, and hypertension. It even has a characteristic "executive crack-up," which sometimes comes just after or just before success is achieved, and indicates how saturated with anxieties and conflicts the executive life can be. But it also has its triumphs and its sense of achievement. This, more than anything else, is what America has come to stand for in the deep secret images of the young Americans.

6. The Reach of the Business Spirit

BEYOND THESE central and satellite activities of business the reach of the commercial spirit penetrates into every area of American culture. The business principle has sometimes been confused with the machine principle. The latter is used to dispense with human labor and make possible standardized and large-scale production, while the business principle focuses on market sale for profit. It puts the making of money ahead of other craft and civilization values, gives primacy to the cultural and personal traits which lead to that end, and tends to apply money values even to the human personality.

America has often been called a business civilization, but the term is too sweeping. One cannot say that the business principle is the only one operating in American culture. In some areas—religion, education, the arts, the family—it exerts only an incipient influence. But even where it has not become decisive, there has been a creeping imperialism of business over the other domains of life.

The business principle has given a synthetic cohesion to the far-flung diversity of American life. Before the Civil War it could genuinely be said that American culture was a loose collection of principalities— those of politics, of farming and industry, of religion, of literature and art and the press—tied together mainly by a pride of pioneering and a sense of the emerging national strength, and some belief in the democratic idea. The advance of business power and values weakened the hold of the democratic idea, while translating both the pioneering sense and the nationalist pride into the boom terms of growing industrial power and profit.

In the realm of politics, the political boss has come to run his domain (the "machine") very much as an industrial boss (businessman or corporate manager) runs his. Unifying both of them is the principle of organization—the setting up of a regularly functioning structure to achieve certain ends. The difference is that where the businessman delivers commodities for profit, the politician delivers votes for power. An American may speak of belonging to an "organization" and refer to being a functionary in either a corporation or a political machine. The political "organization" has taken over much of the corporate structure. It is true that in its origins the party system in America preceded business enterprise, and its first brilliant innovator, Aaron Burr, used the Army as model. But the new model is the corporation, with the voters in the role of the owner-stockholders, the national committeemen in the role of the corporate directors, and the professional politicians in the role of the corporate managers, who are in theory the trustees and employees of the owners but in fact the decision-makers and power-wielders.

In America, as everywhere, politics has been vulnerable to bribery. Yet it is a paradox of a business civilization that there has been notably less political corruption in America than in many precapitalist societies such as in Asia, the Middle East, and South America, or even some of the Latin societies of Europe. Perhaps this is exactly because of the importance of business: for those to whom money is all-important there are in America (as in no other culture) more direct channels open to the money-making energies than through the circuitous routes of the political career and political power. Political corruption is most rampant in the cultures where for many men it is the only road to wealth and status; in America it is only one of many.

Yet the business spirit, which directly carries along in its torrential course so many of the talents and energies of men into money-making, also breaks down some of the moral barriers that had been built into the conscience for generations. The big temptation in the era of the expanding frontier was land speculation. In the era of an expanding capitalism the temptations lie less in speculation than in the sale of political influence to businessmen intent on getting some of the Big Money, by crucially placed governmental subalterns who don't see why they too should not get their cut. As in the post-Civil War days of Grant and Conkling, or the post-World War days of Harding and Daugherty, the torrents of fresh business energy which open new opportunities for big profits also carry away with them much of the terrain of social conscience. In this sense it is not the periods of business decay but the periods of business expansion and vitality which play havoc with moral principles, because they fix men's aims at the attainable goals of the Big Money.

This is true of the sins of commission within business which Edwin Sutherland analyzed as a special type of "white-collar crime." It is also true of its sins of omission. Discussing the failure of the great respectable banking firms to warn American investors against the worthless German and South American bonds in the 1920s, Herbert Pell wrote, "There is not a Morgan partner who would not give a yell to frighten ducks off a pond if he saw that they were being approached by a couple of fat hunters with pump guns. Apparently they do not extend the same protection to gulls."

There has been a growing American conviction that there is hidden gold in the Washington hills. The Wall Street legend thus merges with the Washington legend (witness Blair Bolles's *How to Get Rich in Washington*), but there is a core of truth in the legendry of both. Of the two great types of corruption in the American Federal government, it is hard to say that the efforts of small businessmen to get tax favors by gifts of mink coats or deep-freezers and to pick up arms contracts by bribery are worse than the efforts of the big corporations to get the kind of tax exemption that will save them tens of millions, or the lavish distribution of checks and the faking of pressure telegrams by corporations who want to get a tidelands-oil or a natural-gas bill through Congress. Where the impact of business has been most destructive for morality has been perhaps less in its open corruption than in the incalculable prestige that business success and power have in the eyes of city magistrates, county judges, state legislators, Congressmen, Federal administrators.

Business methods and values have also reached the national political parties, which have increasingly drawn upon the big advertising agencies for the conduct of their campaigns; public-relations firms are coming not only to advise the political managers but sometimes to replace them in the effective conduct of the campaign. The slogans that have proved successful in preparing the public mind for the sale of a deodorant, a breakfast food, or a mouthwash are also counted on to be successful in "selling" a candidate and his cause. Political campaign slogans may be tested beforehand as carefully as the advertising slogans in business sales campaigns, and the question of whether a "hard sell" or a "relaxed" one will be used may be the subject of earnest discussion among party directors who resemble a corporate board of directors.

Even crime and racketeering in America have taken over some of the organizational structure of business. Just as they have learned in some cases to assume the disguise of trade-unions, they have also a line of command and an administrative organization not crucially different from that of the corporation. To many of these criminal groups business enterprise is (in Veblen's tongue-in-cheek phrase) the "art of getting something for nothing"—which is what it seems to any greedy adventurist spirit brooding on the chance to get a "free ride" into riches. Actually, however, the racketeer imitates only the outer organization of business and has little relation to the business spirit itself. For while business flourishes by the widest publicity, what the racketeer sells is illicit; the motive for paying him is immunity from the violence to follow if the payment is not made. Racketeering is the precapitalist feudal spirit, using the techniques and structures of business enterprise and thriving because business has spread throughout America the dream of the easy-money bonanza.

Until recently, at least, the appeal of business has been as a way of making money, not as a way of life. Sensitive people have rejected the way of life but then been lured by the money; hence the split in the American attitude toward business, which has been most marked where the tradition of an educated elite has been strongest. The Adams family, for example, showed both a cultivated understanding and a cultivated fear of the new and pushing type of business activity. Writing in *The Education*, Henry Adams expressed the melancholy sense that for all the processes of civilization that had gone to make him, he was unfit to survive in the world that business values were fashioning. Brooks Adams, living as a *rentier* from corporate securities, was able to dissect pitilessly the social sources of his income, all the time ransacking history to explain the emergence of this new form of centralized power to which he owed the leisure he had for ransacking history. The third brother, Charles Francis Adams, was a railroad president who wrote with shriveling contempt for the narrowness of outlook and the niggardliness of spirit of business as a way of life. Henry James, for all his preoccupation with money and what it could buy, always pushed the question of its sources into the background and felt slightly soiled by them. He was most at home with a businessman like the hero of *The Golden Bowl,* spending in Europe the fortune he had made in America, a Maecenas who knew what he wanted and went after it with the practiced assurance that betokened the habitual conqueror. The secret that Sir Joseph Duveen discovered about American businessmen, which made his fortune as an art salesman, was that they gloried in their power over the things that money commanded but hungered for the symbols of the life values that went beyond money. Throughout the history of the business spirit, the monied men have used business first as a way of making the Big Kill, then turned to philanthropy or the life of the patron, travel, or hobbies as a way of making a life.

The business spirit, then, has not in itself been regarded as a nourishing one but as a means to bring a good life within reach. For that reason perhaps it has exerted an attraction for the young men of talent who in other civilizations might have gone into government, the Army, or the priesthood, into literature or the arts or the study of philosophy, into science or the professions. Even those in government service have, when successful, been tempted to turn their knowledge to the service of the corporation: if they have worked in the Treasury Department on taxes, or as economists in government bureaus, they can command good salaries as consultants or executives in business. If they have been good newspapermen they are eagerly recruited for public-relations jobs in the corporate world. And the corporations have learned to go directly to the colleges in recruiting young men of talent who are rarely able to resist the offer of an immediate job as against the uncertainties of a career in the arts or professions.

Even for those who stay outside business, there is a strong drive to conduct themselves in a "businesslike" way. The trade-union movement in America has been largely, as Hoxie first described it, "business-unionism," expressing the competing claims to income of the corporate employees as part of the larger structure of the business economy itself. In education the school administrator and the university president have tended to act as corporate executives. Even in the churches the temptation is to be "practical" in administering vast properties rather than unworldly in pursuing the values of the spirit. In the newspaper and magazine fields the pressure is toward building big power aggregates that can command writing talent and the reader market and get a big share of national advertising: the magazine or big newspaper is likely to make its more blatant public boasts not so much about its newsgathering or its crusading spirit as about its circulation and advertising gains. In radio and television the art forms are subsidiary to the selling of time to the business sponsors. In moviemaking, the final art product has to run the gantlet of box-office appeal, and the Hollywood values of inflated salaries and skyrocketing careers are a kind of caricature of the corporate executives. In literature the emphasis has shifted to the products that can be marketed to a mass audience, notably crime and detection thrillers.

In fact, it may turn out that the business spirit will leave its most enduring imprint on the adjoining provinces of literature and entertainment, government and opinion: for these are the areas in which capital investment counts least and personality and talent still can carve out empires. They are the last Klondikes of venture skills, which are even more important in the history of business than venture capital. The lure of the acquisitive impulse, wedded to talent and ideas, produces a powerful amalgam.

It is customary to speak of this as the "commercializing" of art and opinion. But the process is more complex. The crux of it is that the dominant activity of any civilization colors the prevailing notions of what is effective or futile in the exercise of men's talents. In a business civilization the stamp of effectiveness is placed on whatever can be exchanged in the personality market for money and success; the stamp of ineffectuality is placed on whatever talent is not vendible, whatever cannot move to a maximum degree into the channels where it is capitalized and reaches a mass market with all the accruing rewards. Thus the business spirit, itself incapable of yielding nourishing life values, has become for Americans the prime gateway to a way of life, with few questions asked about what you find when you have gone through the gates.

When one inquires what may account for the "domination effect" of the business spirit, the answer lies partly in the attractiveness of the big rewards and the big market, partly in the admiration felt for the men who have shown that they can run things best, partly in the pragmatic strain of a culture which accepts whatever is practical and successful as the valid and pays it the flattery of mimicry.

The final tribute to the domination effect of the business spirit is the extent to which the phases of the human personality are measured in its terms. In a seminal analysis of types of character structure that bear aptly on American life, Fromm has spoken of the "marketing orientation" as one that is crowding out much else in the business society. There is little question that the marketable personality is becoming the dominant one, even in areas outside business. Courtesy and charm come to be valued not for themselves but because they pay off in salesmanship; clothes must be worn well to make an impression on a prospective customer or employer; the "dreamer type" of person is dangerous because he will estrange those who seek alertness. America itself, in the impact it makes on other peoples in the struggle for world leadership, must "sell" itself and its ideas; and the clinching argument used even by liberal intellectuals against the denial of civil rights of Negroes and other minority groups is that it will interfere with such international "selling" and acceptance.

This then is what seems to have happened in the American business economy. The more strictly technical problems of production and scarcity, of income distribution, of bigness in the sense distinct from monopoly, even of the business cycle, are fairly on the way to being resolved. But the bureaucratization of life through the new managerial structures in business, the trade-union, the government, and the corrupting reach of marketing values and the money spirit are being extended through the whole culture. The real problems of the business culture are thus less the technical and strictly economic problems than the moral and psychological ones.

Yet to say, as some foreign observers and American critics have said, that only money talks in America is to vulgarize the impact of the business spirit. Other values than the acquisitive find a place in American life, and often they triumph; and other qualities than the money-making qualities blossom. But even when they do triumph, it is only after they have been measured and defended against the money values and the vendible qualities. That they survive is the final tribute to their hardihood, and when they do survive—in literature and the arts, in human relations, in religion and education and government, in the armed services, in the professions, perhaps even in business itself—they have a greater strength than in those cultures where they do not have to measure themselves so searchingly against the domination effect of the business spirit.*

* For a further discussion of the impact of markets, money, and commercialism on the American spirit, see Ch. IX, Sec. 8, "Life Goals and the Pursuit of Happiness," and Ch. XI, Sec. 9, "Artist and Audience in a Democratic Culture."

7. *Revolution in the Trade-Union*

THE "SPLITTING of the property atom" could not help carry along with it a splitting of the labor atom. There has been a far-reaching growth of labor's power and a change in its place in American society. Labor's position in the mid-1950s was diametrically different from its position at the time of the Homestead and Pullman strikes in the 1890s, or even under Harding and Hoover. This does not mean that labor dominates the economy, as implied in Sumner H. Slichter's description of America as a "laboristic economy" rather than a capitalistic one. At the heart of the economy is the network of decentralized choices by corporations, businessmen, and consumers. Yet it is also true that there is a corresponding network of labor decisions giving a massive power to the trade-unions.

Actually the corporations and trade-unions represent two galactic systems of almost sovereign power. Each has its managerial government, each its autonomous realm in which it is supreme, each is connected with its sister stars in the galaxy by loose ties of common interest and outlook. While the two systems are often locked in struggle, they are part of the same firmament in the same universe. That is why the discussion of American labor cannot be separated from a discussion of the growth of the corporation and the sweep of the business principle. American business and labor are rival empires, sometimes friendly, sometimes hostile, fighting for similar stakes, aiming at roughly similar goals, with jealously divergent power drives and interests inside the same set of cultural values.

This is why American labor did not start its mature phase until the growth of the American Federation of Labor under Gompers. The pre-history of labor before that time, with all its valorous chapters of struggle, represented a fumbling for a stable and characteristic form. In the deepest sense the trade-union arose out of the same impulse for social freedom and struggle as the American Revolution itself. From its origins there were strong influences in the American labor movement which kept it from abandoning the main stream of American experience. Labor power was scarce, land was plentiful, jobs were fewer than the men available for them, and the way was open for apprentices and mechanics, artisans and mill hands, to move on into farms or enterprises of their own. Under these conditions it was hard for any specific labor movement to take root, whether class-conscious or job-conscious. The "working-men's associations" of the 1830s fought for free schools and other reforms and were a major element in the triumph of Jacksonian democracy. The free-workers' associations later fought also for the freedom of the Negro plantation labor of the South, formed the mass core of the abolitionist societies, and flocked into the Republican party to join with the commercial class and the New West in electing Lincoln. Thus the early phases of American labor were not the "failures" that later labor leaders have sometimes called them: they assisted in the triumph of democracy, much as European labor did in its heroic age.

When the time for growth came, and for a redefinition of labor's tasks in a democratic society, there was a double impulse: to focus on the American radical tradition in politics and society and join with men of good will in all classes to revive it; or to focus on the broad upward movement of American living standards and act in concentrated fashion by every vocational means to gain some of its benefits for labor.

Neither impulse was crotchety, each was "organic" to one of the main drives of American life. The first impulse expressed itself through the Knights of Labor, a class-wide, politically conscious movement affiliated with nonlabor reform groups, as a response to the political unrest which swept the country when the vision of a nation of small farmers and artisans was shattered by the rise of corporate power. But the Knights were too sprawling in their organization, and they made the mistake of aiming at political power before establishing a strong economic base. Under Gompers the A.F. of L. sought to rechart labor's course, devoting itself to a job-conscious, wage-and-hour unionism, restricting its political activity to lobbies and pressures, and at election time to the policy of "rewarding labor's friends and punishing labor's enemies." Thus labor had its period of conscience-searching as between the decision to challenge corporate power drastically and the decision to bargain with the corporations for a larger share of income.

It might be said that the leaders of organized labor in the 1880s made the unheroic choice by concentrating on the strategic power of the skilled workers rather than deciding to organize the unskilled. Certainly their task would have been more dangerous had they chosen to stand with the unskilled and the new immigrant workers. But they faced a difficult situation: public opinion was unsympathetic, the state legislatures and the Supreme Court were hostile, and the employers fought every form of organization. The question in such a situation was what kind of labor organization could survive and achieve stability. Where there was a high labor turnover among millions of unskilled immigrants, anxious to secure any work at any wage, it was hard to attain stability. It was among the skilled workers, who would keep an interest in their craft and who could not easily be replaced by newcomers and "scabs," that the effective organizing work could be done. This was the choice that Gompers and his young colleagues of the new labor movement made, with a devotion to the hard, pragmatic task they had cut out for themselves.

Another chance at creating industrial unionism came after World War I, when labor turnover had decreased with the disappearance of the frontier and the slowing down of immigration. But another anti-labor offensive, joined to a Red scare, headed off this chance as well. The industrial unions that had emerged suffered severe defeats in the 1920s, particularly in coal, textile, and clothing. The result was that the A.F. of L. was driven into becoming narrower than it had to be, while the "revolutionary unions" of Wobblies, bindlestiffs, and new-stock intelligentsia who sought to counterbalance it were driven into becoming more extreme and frenetic than the American occasion justified.

Once victorious, the job-conscious philosophy of Gompers and the A.F. of L. was never wholly displaced. A number of today's labor leaders were apprenticed to Socialist theory but dropped it when they came to lead a mass labor movement. The unions worked for goals set by the job, within a social framework which they sought to use and improve but not transform. Even the C.I.O. (Congress of Industrial Organizations) —which came into being when the A.F. of L. failed to expand from skilled crafts to a militant, industry-wide organization—has, in the process of breaking with the Gompers tradition, actually carried out the full logic of the Gompers philosophy by willing the necessary changes in organization and tactics for the effective protection of the job. It was Gompers who remained the great type-figure of American labor leadership.

The characteristic theory of American labor behavior—the Commons-Perlman, or "Wisconsin School," theory—aimed to show how the Gompers philosophy and tactic fitted in with the American national psychology and social system, and why it was the only plan for action under which American labor could have survived. Holding that American trade-unions are soundest when built around the protection of the job, the theory goes back (as Philip Taft points out) to the worker's "consciousness of scarcity" and of limited opportunity. Until the sense of limitation and scarcity arose, and while the frontier was still open and vital jobs had not been pre-empted, no strong trade-union movement could be formed. When workers looked forward to being farmers and capitalists they were unlikely to take their stand together as workers. It needed the end of the frontier, the inpouring waves of immigration, and a partial saturation of job opportunities before the unions could generate any propulsive force. It also needed the rise of the new corporate employers, many of whom used their power to pay low wages, locked their workers out in times of unemployment, penalized the more militant ones, and were unconcerned about what happened to their labor force when they grow sick or old or were mangled in accidents. The aim of job-conscious trade-unions was to band the workers together in order to keep them from being crushed by this new juggernaut. Neither the method nor philosophy was that of class struggle, but the intent was certainly class survival as a necessary step for the security and dignity of the individual worker.

This theory must not be taken as valid for the whole course of American labor history: it applies to only one phase of it. With the later rise of the C.I.O. in the 1930s and the reassessment of political action by the A.F. of L., the Commons-Perlman theory was also re-evaluated. There was a consensus that it illumined the period it described, but that it needed modification when applied to the present and future of American labor. Gompers saw clearly that the trade-union in America, in its phase of major growth, had to be an integral part both of the capitalist psychology and of the democratic process. The break with the European tradition of feudal rank kept the American worker from accepting the paternalism either of a tyrannical employer or of a tyrannical government. Since he saw himself as the "masterless man" he did not feel the resentments of the class struggle at whose root is a master-ridden proletariat trying to unseat its masters. Gripped by the property idea the American worker, who found he could no longer move with ease from his job to business independence, developed in its place a sense of property-in-the-job. To "have a good job" came to mean that the worker had a stake in the future worth protecting in common action with others.

Also worth fighting for. An element of violence ran like a red strand through a century of American labor experience, from the "Molly Maguires" in the Pennsylvania coal fields, through the Homestead steel strike, the Pullman railroad strike, the copper mine bloodshed, the dynamitings by West Coast "Wobblies," the violence of the Lawrence, Passaic, and Gastonia strikes in textiles, the "sitdown" strikes in the auto industry, the Herrin massacre in Illinois, and the ghastly violence of the Little Steel massacre of 1937. We may note here, incidentally, that in the past twenty years there have been no comparable incidents of bloodshed.

The hardheaded pragmatic unionism of American labor has often been decried as unheroic, perhaps because it has not talked in swaggering terms of revolutionary overthrow of state power. But it is naïve to think that the revealing Gompers trilogy of symbols—"pure and simple" unionism, "here and now" purposes, "more and more" as the stakes of conflict—excludes a heroic struggle to secure them. Along with the "pork-choppers," the swivel-chair bureaucrats, the "walking delegates," the racketeering union leaders, and the fatty degeneration in some segments of American labor life, there was a militancy in others which secured for American labor a new leadership among the world's free trade-unions. It was not only the corporate empires and their corporate managers that the unions had to meet but also a hostile Congress and state legislatures, an often hostile set of Federal and local courts, a network of "citizens' committees," a number of company policies, hired thugs, bravados, and "deputy sheriffs." Finally, they had against them the overwhelming weight of the press, the almost solid phalanx of the academies and even of the churches. Most of all, they had the hostility of farmers and lower-middle-class Americans, fearful of labor's economic power and its strike weapon. While these hostile attitudes, and also labor's fighting mood, have diminished in the contemporary generation, the tradition on both sides is still remembered.

Yet this bitter day-to-day struggle, even with the violence on both sides, has been carried on within a framework of ultimate consent. No matter how long-drawn-out the strikes, the aim after settlement has been the resumption of work; no matter how drastic the resistance to the organizing drive, the unions have in the end been recognized, not liquidated, by the force of the state.

The greatest achievement of the trade-unions in the economy as a whole has been that they have made possible the government of industry by constitutional means. If the massive corporate empires had been the sole survivors and had bargained with only the individual worker, and if collective bargaining had continued to be viewed as a conspiracy against the antitrust laws, there could have been anarchy or tyranny in American industry. Instead the weight of the big trade-union was invoked by the workers as a counterbalance for the weight of the big corporation, to achieve (as Justice Holmes put it in his dissent in *Coppage v. Kansas*) "that equality of bargaining power from which freedom of contract begins."

The classical theory of Anglo-American economics saw industrial order as the product of an equilibrium between individuals in the market, and from this individualist concept the economists evolved their elaborate justifications for antiunionism, strike breaking, and court injunctions. But with the growth of the corporate empires the conditions of the market were transformed. An equilibrium was still possible but it had to be an equilibrium between competing collectives, with the bargaining strength of the trade-union matching that of the corporation. In this sense the unions have not only raised living standards for their own workers and protected their jobs, but they have also helped give balance to the American capitalist economy.

A change of phase passed over American labor with the coming of the Great Depression of 1929 and the New Deal in the 1930s, although we are still too close to this phase to see its full outlines. The strength of the Gompers A.F. of L. tradition lay in focusing on the workers, who had group cohesiveness and bargaining power and could therefore be held together effectively even in the face of court injunctions, company police, state militia, jail sentences, and hostile middle-class opinion. Its weaknesses had become clear by the end of the 1920s. One symptom was the fact that for the first time in its history the A.F. of L. lost rather than gained members during a period of prosperity. Nor could it break through its limits of membership (somewhere around three and a half million) without organizing whole new industries, skilled and unskilled alike, which meant breaking away from the craft-union principle and experimenting with industrial unionism. The A.F. of L. did include some industrial unions, but their effectiveness had not been proved: the main issue was that the A.F. of L. leadership was itself part of the craft unions and thus conditioned by its whole life history to resist organization on an industrial basis. Moreover, with the Gompers concentration on trade-union action as against broader political action, there was no clear way for the unions to act in the national political arena to counteract the strategy of corporate power and also to organize a legislative attack upon national economic insecurity.

The process of labor's awakening to its past weaknesses and its future opportunities extended from the early days of the New Deal and its NRA (National Recovery Act) around 1934 well into the war years of the 1940s. In this decade something like a revolution took place in the trade-unions. During its early phase the leadership was assumed not by organized labor itself but by a mixed group of intellectuals, social workers, and politicians who felt that they needed a stronger labor movement to restore the balance between the corporations and their workers, and build a Big Unionism alongside the Big Corporation. The New Dealers found that they needed a strong labor movement also to give a new vitality of bargaining and purchasing power to the depressed economy. But they could not get the labor base they needed without in a sense creating a new frame for the trade-union movement. That was why the New Deal became, as the quip put it at the time, a "government in search of a labor movement."

Eventually labor responded to this stimulus by forming the C.I.O. in 1938: it symbolized, under the leadership of John L. Lewis, Philip Murray, and Sidney Hillman, better than anything else the meaning and spirit of the new phase of labor history. Labor discovered, less as a matter of dogma than as part of the harsh crucible of the Depression itself, that it could survive best in its era of trial by becoming part of the Great Coalition around the New Deal. The concepts of industrial unionism, social security, labor's stake in the total economy, the relation of corporate power and practices to the breakdowns in the economy as a whole, and the need to gain access to governmental power in order to achieve equality of bargaining: these constituted at once principles of the C.I.O. and also of the New Deal. The alliance between the two was never a formal one, nor did Roosevelt make the mistake of working politically with only one segment of the labor movement. The New Deal secured a mass following; the labor movement achieved a National Labor Relations Act which gave it a new charter of growth, and a structure of minimum-wage and social-security laws to fill out the charter. Thus was formed a working partnership between the American labor movement and the principle of welfare democracy which was to affect the history of more than one American generation.

For a time the resulting growth of the labor movement was remarkable. Membership figures for all unions moved from a low of less than three million in 1933 to over four million in 1936, over seven million in 1937, almost nine million in 1940, ten and a half million in 1941, fifteen and a half million by 1947, and seventeen million in the mid-1950s. Industries like steel and autos, which had been citadels of antiunionism, furnished the sinews of labor growth. The trade-union leaders found themselves not only sitting in the councils of the Federal Administration but they also made labor a force in the government of cities and towns where it had formerly been only tolerated. Pittsburgh and Detroit, for example, were transformed politically as well as industrially and culturally. There was in time, of course, a countermovement culminating in the Taft-Hartley Act, which chipped away labor's gains and set a pattern of restrictive action. A number of states followed, in the decade between 1945 and 1955, with harsh antiunion right-to-strike laws. Yet the counterattack could not wipe out what the original revolution had achieved.

The healthiest thing about this upheaval in labor was that it did much to heal the sense of alienation of the workers. Lacking access to governmental power and a voice in the big governmental decisions, they had necessarily felt like outsiders. But that feeling disappeared, and in its place leaders like Murray, Lewis, and Green—and later Reuther and Meany—spoke with the confidence of power. In this sense the revolution in labor deflected the potential energies of a sullen working population from more destructive revolutionary channels and became—like the New Deal—an essentially conservative force. Some revolutions shatter and destroy; others have a maturing effect even while the upheaval is in process. This one changed the character of the labor movement by bringing a change of phase, yet it did not in a broader sense break with the Gompers tradition. What it did was to develop new techniques which could achieve for its time the underlying purposes of the Gompers philosophy. For in spite of the alarms felt about labor's advances in numbers and strength, the basic idea remains of a democratic labor movement operating within a capitalist welfare economy, making possible a constitutional government of industry and trying to recapture for the worker his dignity as a human being.

Since the end of the New Deal the American labor movement has come to another change of phase, if a less drastic one. The impulses remolding American society as a whole have not left labor organization and thinking untouched. I have spoken earlier of automation and what it has done to the position of the unions, diminishing the number of workers engaged in industrial jobs, transferring many of the gainfully employed to white-collar and middle-class jobs where labor organizing has been least effective. The sustained prosperity of the 1940s and 1950s also had an impact on labor consciousness, making the unions less militant, muting the past accent on violence, and all but eliminating the resort to large-scale strikes. Within this new climate the A.F. of L. flourished—after 1945—more effectively than the C.I.O., which was riddled with internal strife, even to the extent of the expulsion of unions with close to a million members because of their Communist leadership.

The result was that the A.F. of L. and C.I.O succeeded in 1955 in reuniting their forces within a single organization. Of its fifteen and a half million members, only four and a half million were in the C.I.O. at the time of the merger, with the other eleven million in the A.F. of L. The total figures for American trade-unions, by the U.S. Department of Labor estimate, were seventeen million, with an added million of Canadian workers affiliated with the international unions in the United States. In 1930 organized trade-unions represented only 7 per cent of the total labor force ("gainfully employed") of the nation; in 1945 they were 22 per cent; in 1955, using the base figure of over sixty-five million gainfully employed, they were more than 25 per cent. If the farm workers, the self-employed, and the professional people are excluded from the base figure, more than one third of the labor force were members of trade-unions.

Thus the current period in labor history is one of consolidation. Since American labor has no revolutionary dynamism in the class sense, it did not follow through on the revolutionary potential which the New

Deal gains gave it. Its power to strike, especially in the arterial industries and nerve centers of American economic life, might have been used to paralyze the economy, yet it was not. Seventeen million Americans, along with their families, could have shaped a labor culture if the job relation and the trade-union had been the center of their life activity. Yet they have not done so. They could build the most powerful political labor party in the democratic world. Yet they have not.

The reason is that Americans do not think of themselves as being exclusively members of any single group. A steel or automobile worker, a clerical worker, or a carpenter is not only a trade-unionist. He is also a homeowner, a stock investor, a Democrat or Republican, a Mason or Elk, a Presbyterian or Methodist or Baptist, a resident of Cleveland, Detroit, or Glendale. He may come from a farm family, and his children may be moving into the corporate managerial group or into one of the professions. He does not inherit from his father or transmit to his children a "working-class psychology." Nor is he likely to be content as a member of a labor party which seems to take him out of the main stream of American political life. In fact, he sometimes resents the efforts of his union leaders to lecture him on how and for whom to vote. His loyalties are not single but multiple. All the numberless pulls of American life operate upon him, so that—while remaining a strong trade-unionist—he is also many other things in the act of being an American. This multiloyalty character has been partly due to his freedom from the feudal restrictions on the right of association which plagued the European worker; partly it has been due to the pluralist richness of American life and its expanding life chances. It may thus shed some light on the great question of why American society never developed in a more class-conscious direction.*

The fight for higher wages and shorter hours still goes on through American unions, especially the drive for a four-day week and a five-hour day, to cope with the impact of automation. But it has had a receding emphasis as the living standards of the workers have gone up and their life needs have moved in many directions. There has been a transfer of union interest from wage-and-hour demands to so-called "indirect wage increases," "fringe benefits," pension funds, holiday and vacation provisions, health centers, and welfare setups. There has also been a movement toward the guaranteed annual wage, already achieved in several industries and likely to be fought for in others, since the industrial worker is moving toward the status of a salaried employee instead of a wage earner. The annual wage will probably never be wholly achieved and will have especially hard going in the small-scale industries, but it

* For a further discussion of this theme, see Ch. VII, Sec. 4, "Class Profile of the Worker."

has already brought a substantial improvement in unemployment compensation.

In league with the welfare state and the welfare corporation, labor is turning to the welfare union. The constructiveness shown in the garment industries a generation ago when Hillman and Dubinsky saw that the bankruptcy of marginal employers would throw men out of work and depress labor standards, and therefore set up business clinics to revamp their managerial methods, is still operative. Studies by the National Planning Association show scores of "participating plans" scattered through industry, in which there is a creative approach on both sides to the problem of recurring grievance cases. In mining, in steel, in autos, in garments and textiles, and in dozens of other industries, both sides have worked out joint pension and welfare schemes which focus on the worker as a person. A new "industrial sociology" has grown up which recognizes tardily that the worker is a human being and the factory is a small society or subculture. While there are elements in it of what Daniel Bell has called "cow sociology," in the effort to make the workers contented in order the better to milk their productive power, there is also a wariness of making productivity the final goal, and a genuine feeling that the cultural disintegration and emptiness of the worker's life are enemies not only of productive efficiency but also of the health of the culture itself. Some conservatives may welcome this development in the hope of using it to deflect trade-union militancy. Yet the union leaders who have taken the longest steps toward a welfare unionism are exactly those who had shown the most effective record of bargaining gains for their men, and have not hesitated to use the costly weapon of the strike when there was no other recourse.

We may trace currently four main trends in the character of American unionism. One is the new interest in Administration policies in Washington, especially those that defeat wage gains through inflation, making the struggle for further wage increases a tortured spiral. The second is an interest in world affairs, to keep alive abroad the idea of free trade-unions, and to help achieve a world stability without which the American worker's struggle for a good life would be meaningless. The third was foreshadowed by the General Motors strike of 1948, when Walter Reuther demanded "a look at the books" in order to assess the truth of the corporation's contention that it could not grant the union's demand without a price increase for its products. This was summarily rejected as an invasion of managerial decision and the privacy of managerial secrets, techniques, and accounts, and it has made no headway since. Yet the growth of administrative agencies for mediation, through fact-finding and public disclosure, means inevitably a greater publicity of both corporate and union affairs. Finally, there has been a trend, still minor but increasing, toward the union as entrepreneur.

The growth of the big union empires has meant also the growth of big union funds, both from dues and from pension and welfare contributions. It is hard to estimate what disposable funds the unions have at their command, since recent guesses about union assets range from one to four billion dollars. More important than the assets is the variety of new activities in which the great trade-unions have a stake: banks, stores, consumers' co-operatives, housing, health and vacation resorts, hospitals, radio and movie projects, schools and staff-training institutes. Thus far the unions have invested their funds chiefly in government securities, but it is interesting to speculate on what will happen when they (as well as their members) invest in corporate stock issues—a logical development since such investment would be a dividend for labor's own continuing contributions to productivity.

I have not meant to suggest that all was well in the mid-1950s on the horizon of American labor. There was still widespread suspicion of its aims and methods in the population as a whole, and there were pockets of active hostility in the South, where every known method was being used to keep out union organizers. The organizing power of labor did not keep up with its bargaining power: that is to say, the national unions were able to win higher wages and benefits for their members, yet they were unable to organize areas and industries that continued to resist them. Moreover, no one could tell whether a break in the expansion of American industrial life might not come to interrupt union progress or hurl it back.

But the fact remains that the American unions have become entangled in the growth, ramifications, and destiny of capitalism to a degree that would have been undreamed of not only by Terence Powderly but even by Gompers. They have not abandoned their militancy, but it operates within a framework more meaningful under American conditions than the wasteful bloodshed at Homestead or Herrin or the Memorial Day massacre at South Chicago.

8. Labor and American Society

THE REAL REVOLUTION in American labor has been the impulse to see the worker not just as a union member or a ward of the welfare state, and certainly not as a serf in the hierarchy of corporate power, but as industrial man who is part of his society.* To many Americans the organized

* This section should be read along with Ch. IV, Sec. 4, "Work and the Automatic Factory," and Ch. VII, Sec. 4, "Class Profile of the Worker."

workers in their new and massive strength have appeared like a horde of barbarians attempting to storm the gates of capitalist power. Actually, however, they have been neither barbarians coming from without, as with the Roman Empire, nor a disinherited and uprooted inner proletariat. They have emerged not from the disintegration of America but from the logic of its unfolding; nor are they a group of aliens and exiles forced by their rootlessness to create a "higher religion." They are, on the contrary, the core of American experience.

A double charge has been leveled against labor in American society. As a member of a monopoly group the worker is accused of clogging the channels of the free market and imposing his tyrannical power upon the rest of the economy. But he is also seen as a revolutionary who by the nature of his demands operates to destroy the price system.

If American trade-unions aim to become monopolies, it is only in the sense of aiming to concentrate their power beyond question. That is why they drive toward the closed shop (the union shop is a different matter) and the checkoff, and insist upon controlling the sources of the labor supply. They have learned from experience that the lack of labor unity leads to labor weakness in a showdown. Unions, moreover, sell nothing but seek to set the conditions under which their members can sell their labor advantageously. And there is point to Thurman Arnold's distinction between collective bargaining monopolies in labor and restrictive monopolies as such. Where a union, in collusion with an employer, conspires to get gravy for both at the expense of the consumer, a restrictive monopoly exists. Where "featherbedding" practices are followed, and the union seeks to fight technical advance even at the price of slowing down production, again a restrictive monopoly exists. But collective bargaining under a unified leadership need not (any more than the large-scale corporation) itself be a deadening force. This is true even when the union has a monopoly over the sources of the labor supply, forcing those who benefit from the gains of trade-unionism to take on the responsibilities of membership.

More serious is the impact of the union on the price system. It is Lindblom's thesis that American unions are revolutionary not because of any class ideology but because of the inherent upward thrust of higher wage demands on the whole price system. Since the market mechanism (the argument goes) imposes some limit on profits, the continued upward revision of wage levels can result eventually only in price inflation, or in forcing marginal producers out of the market and therefore into unemployment.

What is valid here is the fact that the unimpeded pressure of union demands would eat away profits and make business enterprise intolerable. But equally, the unimpeded pressure of business power, in the absence of a counteracting union power, would eat away wage levels, make labor a poorly paid commodity, injure consumer buying power, and thus again make business enterprise intolerable. To deny the workers their share, either in higher wages or a lighter work week, is to deny that the factors making for the increased productive capacity of labor-plus-machine are broadly social factors, such as research, invention, communication, mass distribution, rather than narrowly managerial factors in any one plant or industry. It is to treat labor as only a factor in production, calculated coldly by the managerial group, rather than as a crucial human resource in the economy and society. In this sense unions are an organic part of the capitalist economy: capitalism would destroy itself without them, and if they did not exist it would be necessary to invent them. It is true that Lindblom tries to keep ethical values out of his analysis: maybe workers should get higher wages (he says), and maybe they deserve to, but their fair gains may be subversive of the price system by inducing inflation or unemployment. The trouble with this view is that thus far the inflation in America has been induced by high demand rather than high wages, although the latter may prove true in the future. Even more, the trouble with the thesis is its static quality: it assumes profits as given and sees them whittled away gradually by wage gains, whereas the fact is in America that both profits and wages have kept rising because both come out of the dynamism of science and technology.

To those who cling to the badges of status and respectability the fear of labor persists. The crises of large-scale strikes and the constant irritation of small ones have widened the gap between the worker and the considerable middle-class group fearful of labor's power and designs. American labor is learning that strikes incur not only economic costs but also heavy opinion costs in the splitting away of "neutral" middle-class support. It has learned that antilabor legislation usually comes in the wake of a strike wave. It has also digested the lessons of European experience in which the sense of constant industrial paralysis and labor crisis was one of the effective weapons of the Fascist adventurers in lighting the fires of antilabor hatred.

The problem of the strike weapon goes beyond the relation of labor and the middle class. No society can survive if its economy can be repeatedly and successfully paralyzed. In that sense there is something of the Syndicalist philosophy of direct action inherent in every strike, however responsible, and in every trade-union, however conservative. Yet to resolve the problem by suppressing the right to strike is to make an auto-da-fé of the democratic process: a society does not grow strong by lopping off its problems but by transcending them within a larger framework of action and power. Some way of limiting the strike weapon makes sense clearly in the area of atomic energy and the munitions industries, as also in the police and public-service municipal departments. But with the increasing role of the government as employer and the banning of strikes involving government workers of every kind, the withering away of the strike weapon could mean the replacement of corporate and union monopolies by the far more dangerous monopoly of government, combining at once political and economic power.

This is not to say that the trade-union imperium is always a democratic one. Unions like those of the teamsters, carpenters, musicians, coal miners, and building trades made only a minimal attempt at internal democracy. At their best they were run by a benevolent paternalism, as with the miners and the musicians; at their worst there were unions like the teamsters of Dave Beck, which became part of the shadowy underworld of racketeering, captured by a mercenary for whatever he could shake down from workers and employers alike, the instrument for his private dream of enriching himself at their expense. Yet these dictatorial and racketeering unions, taken together, formed only the margin of labor organization. It would be curious if labor were wholly free from the scars of corruption, venality, and the easy-money, something-for-nothing creed. Most American trade-unions are guided by honest, hard-working men, trying to achieve for their followers a measure of security and continuity of work, caught between rising living costs and the dangers and costliness of the strike weapon. The greatest threat to internal union democracy would emerge in most unions with a break in the successful pattern of trade-union activity.

The big internal fact about the American labor federations is their loose and autonomous character. Labor power is scattered among about 200 international unions and some 75,000 local unions, which are covered by more than 125,000 collective bargaining agreements; nineteen of the international unions have more than 1,000 locals each. The heads of the international soon discover—as the government does—that an important local may be a little sovereignty in itself. Increasingly, power in the unions has moved from the local toward the center, yet the process cannot stretch too far without destroying the roots of consent which give a trade-union its strength. Labor autocracies still exist, and a labor baron like John L. Lewis held absolute power for a long span: yet he did so only by convincing his men that he could help them raise their living standards and better their safety and welfare. When he tried to influence their voting in Presidential elections, as in 1940 and 1944, against the clear evidence of what the New Deal had done to help them, his paternalism did not save him from failure.

The trade-union has become, like the corporation, a vast administrative organization, with a large technical staff, and with representatives sitting in on governmental commissions and international agencies. The new trade-union officials are part of the managerial elite that came into being with the growth of economic collectives. From recent studies the American union leader today emerges as younger and better educated than the earlier leaders, more likely to come from the lower middle class, more alert to national and world events. He follows the technological changes in his industry, is hardheaded and astute in his relations not only with corporate but also with the government managerial groups, and is adroit in politics. He is well paid, has a staff and an expense account, has quarters in union offices that sometimes rival in splendor those of the corporation, lives in good hotels, travels by plane; yet his rewards are not primarily financial and he finds himself fulfilled rather in terms of power and of loyalty to a group with whom he feels tied.

I do not intend this as an uncritical portrait. There are many locals and their leaders who practice Jim Crow in their own unions, although impressive progress has been made recently in this area. Men with long labor experience have documented the charge that unions tend to become monolithic and to make policy at the top. Union leaders have had to develop toughness not only in the fight against antilabor forces from the outside but also against Communist attempts to capture and hold power from within. Greater than the danger of ruthlessness is that of bureaucracy, with a tendency toward settling down to a mediocre level of officialdom. In a number of instances this has happened. Yet a group of British trade-union leaders, after a study of American unionism in 1952, reported that the American unions were more concerned than the British with raising the efficiency of submarginal plants, that they used bolder methods in publicity and educational work and were readier to accept the results of scientific management.

In the light of these strides, the question remains why American labor has not established its own party and made a bid for political power. The answer the unions give is that they have not had to, since they have been able to achieve their ends without it. They have not had to overthrow a feudal social structure and introduce the methods of political democracy. They do not think in European terms of Socialism as state ownership or government operation of industry. Gompers deliberately turned his back on the intellectuals who led the working class up to his time, insisting that union leaders—however brilliant—should come from the ranks. The tradition has continued, and Robert Ferguson may be right in suggesting that it helps explain the pragmatic bent of the American union leaders. They feel they made greater concrete

strides in two decades under Roosevelt and Truman, without nationalization and without a separate labor party, than British labor made from
Keir Hardie to Ramsay MacDonald.

These men may be right or wrong, but they are not *novi homines*
hungering for wealth and power and admission to the ruling groups.
Neither do they work from the deep resentment which Nietzsche saw
operative in European revolutionary movements, with an itch for shear-
ing the rich. Their aim is to get a welfare democracy which will establish adequate controls for an economy-as-a-going-concern, a juster order
to increase the national income, and common action to keep life from
being wretched, insecure, and pathetic for the mass of people.

To achieve this, American labor has become an active political as
well as economic force. Thus far it has operated within the current two-
party system, trying to hold the balance of power between the parties, or
to increase the power of its voice inside the councils of the Democratic
party. The unions refuse to form their own party until they are convinced that the major ones have both become hostile. Meanwhile they
are an extraordinarily effective political force. They have in their favor
the big fact that it is easier to organize men politically for common action when you have first organized them economically. They have also
the fact that to workers pressing for social legislation and for safeguards
to collective bargaining, government is not a distant and abstract affair
but something quite concrete. They have finally the *élan* of common
action and of knowing what they want.

But American union leaders are still considered interlopers in the
political field, special pleaders for a single-interest group. Americans
who have only recently come to swallow, and have not yet digested, the
idea that collective bargaining is not treason are likely for some time to
view labor political action as a compact with the Devil and an agreement with Hell. The legislatures and Courts will continue to block
union efforts to raise campaign funds from member contributions. Although the strongest political group in the nation, labor is still a politi-
can outsider. The prevailing attitude in the major parties is that, like a
mastiff, it must be kept tolerably content, but under no circumstance
admitted into the house.

The final question about the American worker is the question of what
kind of life he leads, how much his work means to him, and what its
effect is upon his play and leisure. The "human-relations" approach has
revealed the pathetic extent to which the worker responds to any show
of managerial interest in him as a human being. The stress in this new
approach is how to explore the worker's personality so that he will get
satisfaction out of his work and do effective work, contributing to a

harmony within the plant. The danger is that the worker will come to be regarded merely as an object of psychological manipulation; yet some impressive results have been achieved in this sphere, and the best unions have lost their suspicion of these efforts.

The doughtier champions of the trade-union believe it has contributed much to re-establish the dignity and pride of craftsmanship, yet one may be skeptical. Given the obsession with the protection of the job, with work rules and seniority, with absence of discrimination, with wages and hours and fringe benefits, the creativeness of the work itself has been lost sight of. Seeing in the economic world only the drive for profits and dividends, for power and efficiency, the worker finds his own drive becoming one for wages and job protection rather than an interest and joy in the work itself. The trade-union would do well to make the performance of the job in its fullest sense the core of the worker's responsibilities. But it can do so only when it feels confident and secure enough in its acceptance by the people.

However, here, as elsewhere in American society, the emphasis has shifted from the satisfactions of the producer to those of the consumer. What keeps the worker going is what the job makes possible for him, the commodities he can buy, the new social experience that has come with the communications revolution, the chances for retiring with some security while he can still enjoy the evening of his life. These are not heroic objectives, but they are part of the whole expansive movement of the American economy. Engels wrote in 1882 from England to Karl Kautsky: "There is no workers' party here, there are only Conservatives and Liberal-Radicals, and the workers merrily share the feast of England's monopoly of the world market and the Colonies." The American workers have a different kind of feast of world power to share, but they are aware of being caught up in a stream of flowing abundance, and as long as the economy continues to expand in that fashion they will be part of its pattern and its values.

9. Poverty and Wealth

EVEN AT THE PITCH of prosperity, American life does not lack its pathos of privation. This is the darker side of the crescent moon.* Americans like to call those on whom the dreary burdens of privation fall the "underprivileged groups." It is in itself a revealing periphrasis, its premise being that these are not the dispossessed or disinherited, or the ex-

---

* This section should be read along with sections 1 and 10 of this chapter, where the problem of poverty is placed in its setting along with other phases of the going economy; see also Ch. III, Sec. 6, "The Sinews of Welfare," and Ch. VII, Sec. 2, "The Seats of the Mighty."

ploited, or the insulted and injured, but merely some who have got less than others of the gravy of life.

Franklin Roosevelt, who was less unctuous, spoke of them in his Second Inaugural in 1937 with a classic directness. He saw them "trying to live on incomes so meager that the pall of family disaster hangs over them day by day," living "under conditions labeled indecent by a so-called polite society half a century ago . . . lacking the means to buy the products of farm and factory. . . . I see one third of a nation ill-housed, ill-clad, ill-nourished."

The situation has changed considerably since Roosevelt spoke, but the spread between what Disraeli called the "two nations" is still there. A Senate committee made a study of the 1948 income figures which showed that a fourth of the American families (9,600,000) had incomes below $2,000 a year, or about $38 a week. Many were farm families, a large number were in the charge of old people, in others a widow was wage earner or the head of the family had been disabled. In many cases the worker was too unskilled to command a decent wage and could get no education to improve his lot. Of the nonfarm families in the poverty group, one out of five were Negroes.

Given the 1948 price levels, $2,000 a year for a family was on the margin of subsistence and well below the conservative budgets for minimum decent family living. One out of every ten American families was below the $1,000-a-year mark, which means wretched poverty. Senator Sparkman's subcommittee asked some social work agencies to find out how American families managed to make ends meet on less than $2,000 a year. In a study of 100 such families it was found that they went almost entirely meatless and fruitless, ate mainly starchy foods, cut down on tobacco, could afford no milk except for babies, bought day-old bread and second-hand clothing, and lived in crowded, light-deprived slums. One need not underscore what this means in terms of disease, ignorance, crime, cultural impoverishment, and the waste of ability and life potential through the denial of opportunity.

A decade of prosperity had cut the Roosevelt "one third of a nation" to one fourth in 1948. Since that time the decrease has continued, although at a slower rate. Comparing the 1948 figures with the 1954 figures, the number of families with income of under $2,000 dropped from 9,600,000 to 8,300,000—meaning that they decreased from 25 per cent to 20 per cent, or from one fourth to one fifth of the nation. However, the price inflation made these figures less meaningful: when prices were adjusted, the drop was only from 9,600,000 to 9,400,000. This was taking place, moreover, at a time when the rise in income and living standards at the upper half of the national scale was steady and substantial.

The over-all family income figures in America portray a nation of rising prosperity. The U.S. Commerce Department figures for mid-1955 gave an average family income of $5,600 a year, with an average for nonfarm families of $6,393 a year. The Census Bureau figures were lower but applied to a somewhat earlier period; the Commerce Department figures were more descriptive of the trend of mounting prosperity and inflated prices. Even the lowest estimates gave the average family income in 1955 at $4,200 a year. But the more significant figures were those showing the increased income of Americans during the years of the postwar boom. In 1948, 21 per cent of the American families (over 8,000,000) had an income of over $5,000; in 1954 the percentage had risen to 30 per cent (12,700,000 families), with allowance for price increases. Similarly, in 1947, 5 per cent of the American families had incomes of $7,500 and over, accounting for 23 per cent of the nation's income; in 1954, 11 per cent had similar incomes, accounting for 31 per cent of the nation's income. Perhaps the most dramatic figure of all had to do with incomes between $5,000 and $10,000 a year. In 1947, 11 per cent of the American families were in this range, totaling 22 per cent of the nation's income; in 1954, 35 per cent were in the $5,000 to $10,000 range, totaling 42 per cent of the nation's income. There could be no doubt that the large middle class of Americans, as well as the elite groups, were living well in the mid-1950s.

Yet these rising living standards, along with high productivity and full employment—the three idols of liberal economic striving—proved to be compatible with a hard residuum of poverty. In a breakdown of the income changes between 1935-36 and 1948, Dewey Anderson estimated that, after making allowance for price changes, only 4 per cent of the sixty-nine-billion-dollar increase in national income went to the lowest fifth of the population, less than 20 per cent went to the lowest two fifths, while more than 36 per cent went to the top fifth. Just the increase in itself for the top fifth was almost equal to the entire income of the bottom two fifths of the population in 1948, and four times the total income of the lowest fifth. The income of the lowest fifth in the earlier period was one thirteenth that of the top fifth, and in the later period, one twelfth, indicating that the income spread was decreasing only slightly, while the living standards of all groups were going up.

The 1954 figures on the incomes of American families varied depending on the source of the figures. According to the Office of Business Economics 10 per cent of the families had incomes of less than $2,000 a year, and 20 per cent less than $3,000. The Federal Reserve figures were 15 per cent under $2,000 and 26 per cent under $3,000; the Census Bureau figures were 20 per cent under $2,000 and 32 per cent under $3,000. The OBE figures showed 50 per cent over $5,000, while the Federal Reserve showed 43 per cent and the Census Bureau 37 per cent.

Some deny that poverty in America is mainly due to a faulty distribution of America's vast national income. They argue that it is a matter of
productivity. Yet a rise in general productivity is not likely to do much
for sharecroppers, migratory workers, Negroes who are kept out of a
living wage through discrimination in industry and in education, older
men who are ousted from good jobs, disabled men waiting for a chance
at rehabilitation. An increase in productivity means a greater national
income and prosperity. But into what channels the prosperity flows,
whether it goes mainly into salaried income or corporate dividends,
whether it is diffused or concentrated, whether it is siphoned off mainly
into the top income levels or is used to allay the cruder inequalities in
income distribution: these are the important questions. To ignore the
distributive aspect is to assume that new productivity will somehow drip
down from the top to the bottom.

Thus, in terms of income, as in terms of economic power, there is still
an inequality pyramid in America which the recent years of income expansion have not substantially leveled out. The standard of living for the
lowest fourth of the population, difficult enough in itself because of the
price inflation, was psychologically more difficult because it was measured against the backdrop of vast luxury expenditures. In a typical boom
year (1949) Americans spent $37 million on horse and dog races and $233
million on pari-mutuel betting; spent $8.5 billion for alcoholic drinks,
more than a half billion for taxis, and $22 billion for clothes and jewelry.
The poverty at the bottom of the pyramid was the harder to bear because
of the lush living not only at the top (this has been true throughout history) but even in the middle-income groups.

Thus it is that the income distribution in America is tangled up with
paradoxes. Compared with the corresponding groups in Southeast Asia
or the Near East, Africa or South America, Russia or China, or even
Italy or Greece, the living standards of the lower fourth of America are
relatively good. The distance between a maharaja and a starving Indian
villager is not paralleled in America, since most of the corporate managers live unobtrusively, without the ostentation of the feudal princes,
plowing their profits back or consolidating them in vast corporate holdings. There is nothing in America quite like the poverty of peasants in
Haiti or the southern Mexican provinces, or the villagers of India and
the fellaheen of Egypt. Americans have never become deadened to poverty, nor have they accepted disease and high infant mortality as the
visitation of Providence.

The striking fact about wealth in America is that its range goes far
beyond anything known in the history of the world's great fortunes.
Robert Heilbroner, who has freshly surveyed the "great acquisitors of
history," points out that Jacob Fugger in early modern times accumu-

lated $75 million in his lifetime, that John D. Rockefeller left an estate of less than $900 million, but that General Motors' income before taxes in the year 1955 alone was $2.5 billion, and its income after taxes almost $1.2 billion. From 1945 to 1955 corporate business in America averaged $34 billion in profits annually before taxes, and half of that after taxes. Even more striking is the fact that in the top income brackets in 1952, with incomes of a million dollars or over, more than 45 per cent of the total incomes came from dividends, and another 45 per cent from capital gains, estates, and trusts, while only 1½ per cent came from salaries. The very rich in America, one must conclude with Heilbroner, "are not money-makers but money-receivers." The figures are only slightly different for the incomes between $½ million and $1 million. The proportion of earned to unearned income in the $100,000 to $500,000 bracket is roughly 40 to 53 per cent, and it is not until the $50,000-$100,000 bracket that they become 63 to 33 per cent. The last two brackets are roughly the corporate managers; the top two are the wealthy *rentiers* living on income from past accumulation.

The paradoxes of wealth and poverty in America stretch further than these dramatic figures. One may say that, unlike Asia and Africa, poverty is not organic to the American economic system. With all the glaring inequalities of life in India or Iran, Italy or China, the poverty of the impoverished is part of the poverty of the country as a whole. In the backward economies of Asia and Africa or even some of the once prosperous economies of western Europe, there is now not enough national income to go around. The important fact about the American economy is that there is. One would not have to cut much into the high corporate profits or into lush living at the top and the ample comfort in the middle brackets to wipe out the poverty of the lower fifth, who make less than $2,000 a year. The rich need not be much less rich for the poor to be very much less poor. The poverty of America, in fact, is almost entirely outside the economic sphere proper. An analysis of the families in the income groups below $2,000 and $3,000 shows that it is largely the poverty of anti-Negro discrimination, of exclusion from adequate education, of physical or psychological handicap. It is also, in the case of the marginal farmer or marginal petty trader, the poverty of noncapitalist enterprise. The economy of the corporate empires has little room for it. America is the first civilization in history that has at its command the means for the total abolition of poverty.

Given the nature of the hard core of poverty, the natural answer has been a welfare democracy, with its steep tax structure, its minimum-wage laws, and its growing network of social-security benefits. America has not moved so far or so fast in this direction as Britain and the

Scandinavian countries, which are far less able to carry the load. This is due mainly to the swaggering American sense that in a dynamic economy a mounting productivity will absorb all social ills; that those who fall by the way are lazy or weak; and that the concern about economic security is a debilitating trait in any culture. So ingrained has this been in the American mind that even the victims of the Great Depression used to take themselves at the valuation of the possessors and wonder whether the fault might not, after all, be their own. It is this outlook that has made "relief" so vulnerable a target for those who decried the retreat from the ancient virtues.

It is a hard thing to be a poor man in any culture, but hardest to be a poor man in a rich culture. It is equally hard to be a helpless man in a power culture that has not lost the ideals of the "masterless man." The effect of poverty on the human personality in America makes it as wasting as it is wasteful, as withering as it is needless. The people at the bottom of the pyramid spend so much of their waking hours thinking about how to make ends meet that they have little energy left for the available stir that fills American life, and none for recreation, clubs, or the cultural resources to which most Americans now have access. Worst of all, they feel alienated from the rest of the culture, with no subculture of their own (like the proletarian culture of France or Italy) to give them comfort or a sense of cohesion.

In more static societies the underlying population has learned to accept its lot as a kind of fatality; in societies with a permanent proletariat, there is a proletarian consciousness which may offer some nourishment, so that poverty has a kind of psychic balance sheet. But in a rich consumers' civilization, with abundance so pervasively present, those who are caught in scarcity feel themselves not only the despised and rejected but come to despise themselves. They are the outsiders to whom the culture gives only denials, who lose their sense of confidence, and who in many cases do not even have the consolations of a traditional, deeply felt religion.

Their only hope is that by some secular miracle what they have missed will somehow be achieved by a child who will win the big prizes and thus get into the swim of the Golden River.

10. The Emerging Amalgam

DURING THE 1930s and 1940s the Great Debate in America, aside from foreign policy, was on the relation of business and government—or, as J. S. Mill put it, "the province of government" in the economy. Much of this Great Debate moved out of the economic sphere itself and by the 1950s had become political polemics. Under both major parties the government pushed very far into what was once considered "free enterprise," and both business and labor have come to accept government's new role. As the political capital of America, Washington has become a polar center of business power to rival New York. In the war economies and "readiness economies" of the past generation, the once accepted lines of demarcation between free enterprise and government control have little meaning. Some of the biggest of the big corporations are one-customer enterprises, doing most of their work for the government and depending for their profits and existence on government contracts. On the other hand, the crucial decisions within the government on questions of priorities, allocations of scarce materials, distribution of plants, and price control are made by men identified all their lives with corporate systems. Even in the case of industries not directly involved in armaments, the scale of taxation, the control of credit and of investment, and government fiscal policies have played havoc with the old terms of "free enterprise" and "Socialism."

What is emerging in America is a new amalgam of the old elements, so welded together that they are scarcely recognizable in the final product. There are still clearly private sectors of the economy, and there are also clearly public sectors. But the trend is away from both, toward the new amalgam in which the private sector is a form of business collectivism and the public sector is a form of state capitalism.

Another way of putting the trend is to note that the old boundaries between the "private corporation" and the "welfare state" are no longer as clear as they were. The needs of continuous large-scale industrial employment, without the cost of violence and bitterness, have led many corporations to adopt welfare plans for health insurance, recreation, employee housing, retirement pensions and annuities. Thus a welfare corporation has taken its place alongside the welfare trade-union and the welfare state. Together they form a welfare democracy. There are still sharp differences about how the financial burdens shall be distributed between them, but only the dinosaur right wing of conservatism challenges the goal itself.

The main area of conflict is still the choice of techniques for organizing a stable economy. While placing stress on lower taxes, the encouragement of investment, and the minimum possible regulation by government agencies, a business group like the Committee for Economic Development shows how far the more liberal corporate managers are willing to go in accepting the amalgam itself. The emphasis of the American Keynesians is upon tax policies, credit controls, government-subsidized construction, and a periodic assessment of over-all trends and over-all needs.

In these terms the American economy is today an example neither of pure "capitalism" (as so many Europeans and Asians still seem to think) nor of "creeping Socialism" (as some of the more frightened American Tories seent to think). It is becoming a mixed economy, with large areas of freedom and varied techniques of regulation, control, and some forms of planning. Those who fear that a mixed economy is the "road to serfdom"—a halfway house toward totalitarianism —are worried about this trend. Still others wonder whether so pluralistic an economy may not lead to chaos, whether a "hybrid" economic system does not distill all the worst elements of public and private ownership without any of their merits, and whether an economic "house divided against itself" can stand.

American history since 1933 is such as to calm the doubters on at least several of these scores. The experience since the start of the New Deal has been that of dynamic economic growth. That is why the crises of European economies are not relevant to the case of America. With its immense resources and its capital accumulation, and with a national income of close to $400 billion a year, America does not have to make the cruel choice the Europeans still have to make between immediate living needs and capital equipment. The steadily rising expenditures for social services and for armaments have still left room for higher profit levels, greater capital formation, improved wage scales and living standards. This may seem to be a mathematical impossibility, but with full use of labor, resources, and machinery, the expanding national product can take much in its stride that was once considered burdensome.

The arms phase of the new amalgam raises the question of whether the continuing economic dynamism of America would be possible without arms expenditures, and whether an economy geared to war production for a generation can make the change-over to a peace economy without serious disruption. Most American economists say yes to this, pointing to the New Deal, which used a nonmilitary public-works program to considerable effect, and to the early years after World War II when the American economy prospered in a period of demobilization and against the Cassandralike forebodings of heavy unemployment. A "mature" economy, which has exhausted its capacity for rapid spontaneous growth, could not use the stimulus of war production to produce enough for the purposes of life as well as of death. But by the growth of such new industries as radio and television, antibiotics, the electrical industries, commercial aviation, and the non-armament phases of the chemical industries, the American economy has shown that it is far from "mature" in this sense. It is capable of growth from within—from the convergence of great resources, capital formation, technology, labor skills, and consumer standards.

The only doubt about this argument is less economic than political. In the extreme emergency of economic crisis, as in 1933-36, it proved politically possible for Congress to vote a large peacetime public-works program. But afterward both the Roosevelt and Truman Administrations found it more difficult: there was always the Congressional fear that the taxes and expenditures for peacetime uses would extend "Socialism." The Eisenhower Administration left its public-works program for a new network of highways largely to state rather than Federal subsidy. Every administration finds that it is easier to get billions for defense than millions for Federal hydroelectric projects and river-valley developments. The Republicans felt that they had taken important steps under President Eisenhower to convert the economy to peacetime production and charged the Democrats with a dependence upon war expenditures for prosperity. This was an interesting reversal of the usual European situation where it is the conservatives who are under attack for relying on a war economy and the Left which takes the position that capitalism is doomed without war. But it should be remembered that the antiwar tradition in America has been mainly isolationist and Republican, and that Senator Taft opposed foreign interventionism largely on the ground of its weakening effect on the economy. The liberal Democratic economists counterattacked in the mid-1950s with the confident assertion that only a bold program of a full-employment economy could be counted upon to effect the conversion.

In economic terms the expansion through arms expenditures operates much as would any other—by a kind of investment and managerial conscription. One of the weaknesses of a "normal" capitalism is that periodically there is "oversaving," which is a way of saying that there is both underinvestment and underconsumption. In an arms economy, which is accompanied by a much higher tax rate than would otherwise be politically feasible, the high taxes cut into the savings, and the corporations—to keep expanding—have to use large blocs of their income for investment and expansion. The government does not use the taxes for investment in the private sector but as expenditures which nonetheless increase employment, thereby increasing further the capacity to consume. In this sense an arms economy keeps the economic energies flowing, but the energies must first be there: it can never be a substitute for them. It also conscripts for the purpose of the new state capitalism the managerial abilities of the best minds in the corporate bureaucracy, who would be hostile to a state capitalism un-

der conditions that invoked their class bitterness rather than their patriotism.

With all this extension of the tax structure and government spending, the American economy continues to develop within pluralistic
forms. American industry has no single pattern of operation or of
power. What applies to autos or cigarettes does not apply to textiles
or coal, and none of them in turn applies to magnesium or the chemical industries. A by-product of the TNEC inquiry in the mid-1930s was
the evidence it gave of a kind of inventory of capitalist industrial
action, showing the plurality of procedures by which the various segments of American industry operated. Even if a form of Socialism
were to arise in America, it would have to reckon with such pluralistic
material and be an extremely sophisticated Socialism. On the other
hand, the TNEC reports also showed the similarity of the larger pattern of power under the dissimilar surfaces of industrial production,
pricing, and distribution. From this at least some Americans may conclude that with the proper knowledge—and perhaps even with much of
the same managerial talent—what a private corporation can do can
also be done by a government corporation, such as those already existing in hydroelectric power in the Tennessee and Columbia valleys,
and to some extent in atomic power. If such a new Socialism were to
emerge, it would have to discard the dogma that sees nationalization
as a grand and simple plan and apply the same pragmatic approach
to the government corporations that is now applied to the private
corporations.

For the present at least, however, the economic direction of America
is not toward state Socialism, even in the form of the government
corporation. It is toward the extension of the New Deal as an amalgam
of state capitalism and business collectivism. This is becoming clearer
in those industries which get their contracts from the government,
have their supplies allocated by the government, are allowed to write
off generous obsolescence at government expense for plants built at
government behest, and pay heavy chunks of their profits to the government in the form of taxes, which are then plowed back into the appropriations that make the contracts possible. It is shown also within
the structure of the corporation itself, where profit and private property have lost their old relations to business enterprise, and a new
managerial form of business collectivism has risen to replace the old
economic individualism.

Insofar as this complex economy is subject to planning, it is obviously different from the kind envisaged by Democratic Socialist

theory, or practiced in such mild Socialisms as the British or Scandinavian, and it is of course drastically different from that of the Communist economies. Using the distinction between direct and indirect planning, the basic planning element in the American economy is indirect. That is to say, instead of nationalization or codes of regulation and control by government administrators, the planning is mainly by pressures, nudges, and prods. The Keynesian revolution in economic theory has largely taken over American economic policy. An excellent system of national income accounting has been developed, and an over-all survey is made periodically, presumably for the President by his Council of Economic Advisers, but actually for the whole of industry and the fraternity of economists. These and many other surveys made by corporations, foundations, and professional business analysts are studied by the whole community, and a rough consensus is always in process about what must be done to avert too-violent swings of the business cycle. The "indirect planning" controls can then be put into operation: tax policies, government bond flotation programs, Federal Reserve interest policies, armament or other public-work programs, installment selling control, credit control, price-control and wage-control policies.

These indirect methods involve a loss of speed and precision of movement, especially since many of the measures depend on Congressional action, which tends strongly to be hostile toward any efforts at economic control. Above all, it must be understood that the effectiveness of the methods depends largely on influencing corporate and trade-union policies, and must be achieved by persuasion rather than coercion. This feature of American planning, which is anathema to the dogmatic Socialists, is exactly what recommends it to the new American liberalism. For whatever may be lost in the process of this kind of planning, what is gained is a degree of spontaneous energy in the economy as a whole, a sense of freedom of movement which is the principal element in American economic dynamism. There is a clinging so far as possible to decentralized decision, a degree of devotion to economic pursuits through the spur of managerial effectiveness and private success that is hard to achieve through direct planning and impossible to achieve by coercion.

Thus America is evolving a *tertium quid* between an unmanaged capitalism and a tightly planned and managed Socialism: a loosely planned and indirectly controlled progressive capitalism, whose big prizes continue to go to the rich, but which keeps a prosperous economy going for the nation as a whole; which is sprawling, wasteful, still unjust in its distribution, Byzantine in its extravagance, precipitous in the differences between the big rewards and the mean existences; but which is nevertheless still in the process of growth, with undiminished bursting energies, already touching a $400 billion national product, and capable in time of organizing the economic life of 300 million people or more.

The long-debated question of the survival power of such an economy has been basically resolved, but not without lingering anxiety. Not an anxiety about the inherent strength and staying power of the economy and its capacity for growth, but about the ways in which it achieves stability. America is today the only great economy capable of large-scale export of capital: even the Russians cannot rival it in this respect. If we can speak of the "imperialism" of the American economy, it is in this sense of capital export: a very different type of imperialism from the classic type which sought to pump capital from the colonies into the nation instead of exporting it. But American foreign economic aid has largely aimed at helping other economies enough to keep them from moving toward communism. Its capital exports have thus had a political purpose, like its own internal arms economy. And they raise a similar question of how long they can continue without either military explosion or internal business contraction.

But this prospect is more of a logical dilemma than an actual one. By the same logic the American economy should have been doomed long ago, during the Great Depression. In this sense the turning point in the history of the American economy came with the New Deal, which tried to transform as much of the economy as was necessary to save the whole of it, along with the political, social, and moral system that went with it. While the New Deal was full of blunders and improvisations, it did hit on corrective measures which restored the vitality that had seemed wholly lost. The final pattern included a set of governmental strategies to guard against the plague of boom-and-bust cycles which had blighted the economy; to keep small business from being crowded out; to keep the bigness of the Big Corporation within controllable bounds, by holding-company legislation and anti-trust prosecutions; to set up a system of social security and deal with the more blatant forms of social misery; to equalize the bargaining power of trade-unions as against the big corporations; to lift the living standards and the purchasing power of groups whose lack of buying capacity had formerly dragged the economy down; to use fiscal controls and public-works programs as ways of preventing oversaving and of filling in the gaps left by private enterprise; to push production levels toward the full potentials of the national plant.

Thus America has moved under the prodding of necessity toward enlarged sectors of public action in the economy. In terms of dogma

Americans have looked askance at every step in the process. Some have called it "creeping Socialism" and worse. But under the spur of the Great Depression and of two world wars, and with the thrust of the traditional democratic welfare impulse, the economy has kept moving in this direction in spite of name-calling. The historic impulse of Americans has been to cling to the private sectors wherever they can and move toward the public sector only where they must.

There is no danger within the American psychology that Americans will embrace a subservience to the state out of dogmatic enthusiasm. The greater danger lies in the fact that the big power structures in America are the aggregates of corporate power; that they function very much as governments function; that more than ever they control the agencies of public opinion and influence the direction of education and belief; and that, given the necessary extensions of the public sector, they may prefer a continuing arms economy to the alternative of successive New Deals.

By way of summing up, and striking a final balance of the nature and operation of the American economy, several observations must be added.

The first is that the whole profile of what used to be called "economic problems" has changed. The strictly economic issues—those of production and productivity, of the distributive mechanisms, even to some extent the issue of the size of the economic unit and the division of the national product—have increasingly become technical problems and have been pushed into the background. What may be called the political, psychological, and moral issues of the economy have come into the foreground, and the anxiety that an observer must still feel about the economy must more and more be directed to them.

The American economy of today is not the same one that Veblen attacked at the turn of the century and John Bates Clark defended, nor is it even the same that the TNEC described and analyzed in its path-breaking survey at the end of the 1930s. There are few more remarkable stories in the history of social institutions than the way in which the American economy transformed itself and its problems in the era of the Big Technology and the Big Market.

The problem of scarcity, for example, which is so dominant a problem in other economies, has practically ceased to exist for Americans. A dramatic illustration is the decreasing number of Americans who are involved with production itself, in the sense of coming into contact with the soil or other natural resources, or even in the manufacture of basic subsistence goods. There is a style or flavor to an economy as to other segments of a culture. A vivid feature of the

American economic style is the rise of the tertiary industries, which go beyond farming and manufacture to form a distributive and service sector of the economy.

This is bound to have an impact on the psychological climate of the culture. It means the end of economic man, in the primitive sense of having to confront the eternal environment in constant struggle. It also means that the American lives and strives more derivatively than he once did, without the sense of immediacy that came from contact with the soil and from the skills of craftsmen and artisans. Perhaps a fairer way to put it is to say that the basic economic skills and arts have not vanished or become less real to the people themselves but have changed in form. The production arts—those of *homo faber*—apply to ever fewer people, and for them they are becoming highly technical and professional. For more and more Americans the economic skills have become either the engineering skills or else the middleman skills of salesmanship, advertising, distribution, and servicing.

The ordinary American has come to assume that somehow the "goods" will be there for the economy as a whole. He doesn't have to produce them or worry about them. His job and worries are either to think about the machines that will produce them and how to keep them from breaking down, or else to run around seeing people, or sit in his office or shop while they come to see him, or push pieces of typed paper around, or see that things or people get from one place to another in an orderly fashion, or think up slogans, or devise little selling tricks that will get the sales volume of one brand of car or detergent or one model of dress ahead of the others. Even the earlier economic virtues have been transformed: thrift, industriousness, tenacity, daring, have given way to efficiency, technical expertness, the ability to handle people ("human relations"), organizational adjustment and loyalty, and a high degree of mobility.

The result is a pervasive air of unreality that encompasses the economy. It is as if everyone were involved in the intermediate and satellite processes and by-products instead of in the products themselves. The American knows that he makes *his* living but has little sense of how this fits into the collective means of livelihood for others and for the society as a whole. Little wonder then that he finds it hard to identify himself with the plight of the underdeveloped economies in Asia and Africa, whose problems are so unlike those of his own economy.

The debate on the concentration and diffusion of economic power in America has largely taken the place of the older debates on centralism and federalism in government. The same dualism which runs through American attitudes in many segments of life is dramatically present in the attitude toward bigness and monopoly in economic life. As with science, the feeling about corporate bigness contains elements both of fear and attraction, of the impulse to leave it alone and the impulse toward control. In fact, this mixed attitude does not merely separate conservatives from liberals, and Hamiltonians from Jeffersonians, but it is to be found as a dual strain in every American. Lewis Galantière has put it well: "Just as every Frenchman may be said to be at one and the same time a child of monarchial authoritarianism (Richelieu, Louis XIV, Napoleon) and of Republican individualism (the Revolution of 1789), so every American contains within him the seed of Hamiltonian mercantilism and the seed of Jeffersonian agrarianism with its distrust of the merchant. Americans have encouraged unbridled business enterprise as Hamiltonians; they have been suspicious of it as Jeffersonians."

This being so, one may say that the new amalgam of economic freedom and economic control which I have described is more expressive of the American economic mind and temper than any other system could be. To put it concretely, there is a free money market but if it shows any sign of going berserk there are Federal Reserve controls to check it; there is a system of free farmers, but if their income falls too badly there are government parity payments and other subsidies to bolster it; there is free profit-making and profit-taking, but in order to perform the functions which keep them free the government takes a big bite of them in taxes; there is a free labor and talent market, but to make sure that it does not end in wretchedness there is also a governmental social-security setup; there are thousands of small firms that supply General Motors, but there is also General Motors in all its magnitude; there is wide stock dispersal of A.T.&T. and other such corporations, but there is also a tight managerial control on the conduct of their operations. If this amalgam did not already exist it would be necessary for Americans to invent it.

One of the results of the debate about business bigness has been the emergence of a "New Enlightenment" in economic thought, led notably by J. M. Clark, M. A. Adelman, Peter F. Drucker, and (in his later phase) David E. Lilienthal. Their contention, in essence, is that Americans have paid too much attention to the advantages of smallness in the business unit and free-market competition; that there are forms of business bigness which do not involve the evils of monopoly power, and that there are new forms of competition which achieve the same results as the older ones. Clark used the test of "workable competition"—not whether competition is free but whether the gains resulting from the advantages of corporate bigness, in the form of lower costs, higher wages, industrial peace, greater innovation, and more funds for research, are passed on to the consumer and the worker.

There is obviously a good deal of force to this view. Certainly there have been consumer advantages flowing from the emergence of the big automobile companies, the big food chains, and the great manufacturers of new synthetics. Nor can it be doubted that bigness must be separated from monopoly: some big corporations are not in a monopoly position but simply express the increased size of the market, while some small corporations are strategically located to exercise monopoly power. Yet it is wishful to say that because there have been social advantages from bigness, therefore the anxieties about it may be dismissed. What is happening is that the emerging amalgam has found still another form in which to express itself, that of an amalgam of competitive and monopolistic practices which defies any neat statement by the economists and adds to the pluralistic character of the American economy. It appears to be achieving some of the results that its defenders acclaim while pushing very close to some of the dangers that its critics deplore. Despite the prevailing degree of industrial oligopoly, the performance of the American economy has been a brilliant one. Yet the price that has been paid is a growing amount of vertical integration, a tendency to pass on to the consumer not only reduced costs but also the increased prices flowing from wage settlements between the Big Corporation and Big Unionism, and the power of corporate bigness to put pressure on government itself and exact conformity from its managers and technicians.

I have mentioned the doctrine of "countervailing power" which Galbraith has introduced into the economic vocabulary. This has tended to reassure a number of liberals who might otherwise have continued to fight against the trend toward bigness. The picture they get is one of "bilateral monopoly," in which the concentrated power of the corporation and the union balance each other; of inter-industry competition, where glass bottles are challenged by tin cans and they in turn by paper containers; and of an industry-government equilibrium in which the corporate power over price and output is balanced by the power of the Federal agencies to regulate and control them and by the position of the Federal government as a powerful (sometimes the only) purchaser of what the corporation is selling. But Walter Adams has shown bitingly that the corporate-union bilateral monopoly tends to end in "escalator" arrangements by which the consumer is exploited by both sides; that inter-industry competition often means only that the older monopolies enter the field of the newer product (for example, the current mergers of motion-picture chains with TV networks, or the entrance of big newspapers into the broadcasting field); and that the government agencies which are supposed to regulate the big corporations often end up by having their personnel diluted and replaced to make them more amenable to corporate pressures, while the government as the big or only purchaser of corporate products often finds the purchase contracts being written by military or civilian officials who had been connected with the industry involved.

Historically, however, the Galbraith approach has shed considerable light on some of the factors that have kept the American economy relatively stable since the Great Depression. A good part of the basis for this stability is to be found in the operation of countervailing power which has prevented any of the "Bigs" from pursuing their own interests and accumulating their own power without thought of the economic picture as a whole. There is, of course, a danger that this explanation may become a new kind of Newtonianism, with a built-in self-regulating mechanism operating between the "Bigs." Yet as a rough rule-of-thumb it is historically true that the pulls and pressures of these mastodons of business, labor, farming, distribution, and government have done much to give balance to the economy.

In themselves they could not have achieved this, but their balancing force has been aided by the fact that Americans have learned a good deal about countercyclical measures. Here again there is an emerging amalgam of measures taken at a number of levels and by a number of agencies: the periodic corporate surveys of resources, labor supply, the business market, capital expansion, and technological change; the similar surveys made on a larger scale by the Treasury, the Bureau of the Budget, and the Federal Reserve Board, and the readiness of these agencies to act through fiscal controls whenever there are danger signals; the techniques of striking a national economic trial balance periodically by the Council of Economic Advisers, which I have already discussed. All of these in turn operate inside a price system which, whatever the inroads that have been made upon it by elements of closure, is still fluid enough to adjust itself to the actions taken by these groups and agencies. It may be said that, so far as the technical and economic problems are concerned, Americans now have adequate knowledge about how to stabilize their economy: the real question is whether they have the political wisdom and the moral courage to take the necessary measures.

This leads to the most difficult question of all. If an organism is to have a healthy and stable growth, there must be a direction toward which that growth moves. One of the greatest defects of the American economic system is that, while it has undergone revolutionary changes in almost every phase and area, it lacks a sense of direction. As long as the economy was moving away from scarcity, expansion was itself a goal, and there was an internalized drive toward the "bigger and better." But Americans have learned to be skeptical of the "bigger" in and for itself. As for the "better," an acquisitive society has few ways of measuring it. For years "prosperity"—general and personal—was the aim of the American economy. America now has prosperity and is likely, unless there is a world catastrophe, to maintain it for decades at least. But where does it go from prosperity?

In wholly planned economies there are external criteria imposed by political leaders and power elites. But America has wisely kept away from fusing its economic and political leadership. As for its power elite, which is mainly in corporate enterprise, the neutrality of the technicians which I have described in the previous chapter operates to a great extent for the corporate managers as well. To be sure, there is a continuing *élan* in the economy which is largely due, as Peter Drucker points out, to the vertical mobility which corporate enterprise makes possible for very large numbers of its employees. And there is an additional *élan* in the new products, the new services, and the new leisure which the American economic achievement has made possible. Yet again it must be asked: what kinds of products, what kinds of services, and leisure for what?

The only possible answer, here as elsewhere in American life, is that in the absence of an aristocracy to answer these questions authoritatively for Americans, the answers are left to the decisions of millions of people—consumers, workers, small businessmen, farmers, corporate managers, union leaders, government policy-makers. The important fact about these decisions is, of course, a negative one: they are not imposed from without. This is why there is so much waste in American life. If Veblen had been right and if there really had been a deeply rooted leisure class in America on which to base a theory, there would have been far more direction than there is on the side of standards of consumption and living. Since there is no such direction, it is left to the millions.

Americans have a faith that four million or seven million decision-making points (the figures refer to the total number of enterprises and the number of nonfarm enterprises) are better than just a few. But they are better not because they are quantitatively greater, but only if they are free decisions and if a principle of taste and welfare informs them. One may ask how free they are when one remembers that General Motors buys six billion dollars' worth of products a year from twenty-one thousand "primary" suppliers. How much initiative and self-reliance is left to the little fish that cluster around the big fish? Similarly, there are millions of technically trained men who supply skill, ideas, and research to the economy. Yet, as I have noted, they have to do their work and make their individual decisions within a bureaucratic framework which evokes only a limited initiative and a diminishing daring and accents the less admirable qualities of manipulation and success. I speak of the limited initiative: this becomes clear when you compare even the most generous big corporation with the typical exciting story of earlier business enterprise—that of the obscure man with an idea who throws his whole life into making a product, carves out a small business until it makes its mark and becomes nationally known, and has the satisfaction of constructive achievement.

CHAPTER VI

The Political System

———————

IN WHICH we examine the curious but effective ways that Americans have of governing—and misgoverning—themselves. Starting with the American "political style"—the belittling of politics, the contempt for the politician, the refusal to take politics in a "grand" fashion, yet also the political daring and practical experimentalism—we ask what basic contributions Americans have made to the arts of government in a free society (Sec. 1, "The Style and Genius of American Politics"). We then take a closer look at the concept of democracy (Sec. 2, "The Democratic Idea") in its double sense of republican constitutionalism and the "leaves of grass" belief in the common man, asking how and why this idea has been frustrated so often in American history.

There follows an analysis of the most powerful office in the free world—the American Presidency—and the sources of its strength in the relation of the President to the people (Sec. 3, "Presidency and Demos"). We then examine the most difficult and elusive phase of the American political system—the operation of the parties, the conduct of American voters, the ethnic and class bases of American political behavior, and the shifting lines of party growth (Sec. 4, "The Party System and the Voter"). This leads into the problem of how the power massed within the American political system operates, how it is concentrated and dispersed, and what its consequences are: the principal themes being the question of majorities and minorities, of power at the center and power at the rim (centralism as against grass-roots localism), and the equilibrium which the American political system has succeeded in maintaining amidst its tensions and conflicts (Sec. 5, "Power and Equilibrium"). This, in turn, leads into the problem of the day-to-day operation of the American government in a managerial age, the growth of bureaucracy, and how Americans have coped with the dangers of stagnation, red tape, and arbitrary power (Sec. 6, "The Governmental Managers").

The final cluster of topics deals with American law and freedom. We examine first the Congressional lawmakers, noting how the legislative function has been limited and transformed, and how the "watchdog" or investigative function has grown (Sec. 7, "Tribunes of the People"). We then turn to the nature and operation of the legal system and the American attitude toward law (Sec. 8, "Law and Justice"). This leads into a discussion of the Constitution, and of its guardians and interpreters—the U.S. Supreme Court, along with an analysis of how the Court has performed its tasks of interpretation, including the political aspects of the legal process (Sec. 9, "Keepers of the Covenant"). Finally we examine (Sec. 10, "The Struggle for Civil Liberties") the status of civil liberties in America, the hazards to which they have been exposed and the jeopardy in which they have recently found themselves. We note the great issues over which the struggle for civil liberties has raged—segregation and desegregation, the treatment of domestic Communism, the government security programs, the impact of investigating bodies on the freedom of the individual, the tenure and loyalty of teachers, the censorship of reading matter, the use and limits of wire tapping, the place of the alien in American law, the emergence of a "radical Right" as a new fact in American popular attitudes toward civil liberties. We end by noting the ways in which America is seeking to restore the strength of its great civil-liberties tradition.

CHAPTER VI

The Political System

1. The Style and Genius of American Politics

EVERY civilization has a government of some sort, but each differs from the others in the way it organizes and conducts its political life—its mode and style of "politics." Jakob Burckhardt, writing on the *Italian Renaissance*, noted that the men of the Renaissance made even the state a "work of art." The Americans make their state, as they make their armies and corporations, a vast organizational achievement: they speak of "the business of government." To the sound middle-class American the most telling complaint against any administration is that it has been wasteful of the "taxpayer's money." On the local level, politics is often regarded as a "racket"—that is, a cushioned berth where you can make a quick and easy dollar. And viewed in terms of spectator sports in a competitive society, politics is also seen as a vast competitive contest, played for the big stakes of office and power, but nonetheless a game: "the great game of politics."

But the observer will be misled if he concludes from this that Americans view government solely through the eyes of economic man. Here is another instance of the polarity of the American character. With his ruling passion for freedom, the American is contemptuous of any government; he says, with Emerson, that "all states are corrupt." Yet since the days when Jackson had his clash with the big banking groups, the "strong" Presidents and administrations which used the power of government effectively, whatever their party or program, have received a popular accolade as well as the verdict of history. The attitude of the American toward political power is a curiously dual one. They hem in their state governors, for example, with a jungle of restrictions; they seek to balance the power of every official with another official; they maintain bicameral legislatures that are clearly archaic; they multiply agencies and offices, from the Federal to the local, instead of adding new powers to those of the old agencies. No people ever had less reason to fear the arbitrary abuse of governmental power, yet Americans have been traditionally reluctant to yield power, and they still tend to deflate it. In time of crisis, however, they view power in a practical and undogmatic way. In every great emergency of the national existence they have yielded their government and leadership the necessary power for meeting it, whether the crisis be civil war, the danger of inner economic collapse, or the tragic burdens of world war in an industrial age.

Yet while managing the problems of political power with tolerable success, they have also found it necessary to be antistate and antipolitician. The traditional American antistatism (or better, "anti-government," since Americans use "state" not as a political but as a geographic expression) has stopped just short of anarchism, although Henry Thoreau and Benjamin Tucker show that a part of the American tradition crossed that line. The American anarchist strain is not, like the Italian or Spanish, mixed with syndicalism or with a peasant hostility toward the tax-gatherers; nor is it, like the Russian, mixed with a revolutionary aim. It flows rather from the tradition of individual self-reliance. The American, especially in rural America, felt he could get along by himself, and that the mastodon power of the government threatened the conduct of his life: in urban America this antistatism has been somewhat diluted by the mingling of ethnic strains, the multiplication of new tasks for government, and the turmoil of life. Yet even in rural America and even in the South today, where antistatism remains strongest, the attitude toward government has been a split one—positive when its help is needed, resentful when it seems to interfere.

Compared with the genuine if ambivalent antistatism of the individual, the element of *laissez faire* in American thinking—the antistatism of the corporation—seems spurious. American business has not refused to accept state authority when it has taken the form of subventions, tariffs, or subsidies. *Laissez faire* has been therefore an opportunist antistatism, that of the corporation as a power form rivaling the state. It has found an echo in the American mind largely because the formative years of American political thinking were the years of revolt against British power, and back of that the period of British revolt against their own absolute monarchies; so that the corporate spokesmen had a convenient chance to clothe their cause in the intellectual garments of the struggle against Tudor and Stuart absolutism. Thus the anarchist and the rebel latent in every American have joined hands with corporate power to proclaim that "the government is best which governs least." Or, as someone put it, the American motto is "In God we trust; in government we mistrust."

The most characteristic trait of the American political style thus became the belittling of politics; and with it the professionalizing of the politician. The American is prone to suspect every government he elects. Nose-thumbing has become his traditional gesture not only of contempt for the politician but, even more, of the freedom to express contempt, to show that Americans have a corrosive skepticism about those whom they have presumably chosen to govern them. The darling of the newspaper caricaturists has for decades been the bloated, gorilla-faced, cigar-in-mouth fellow with an inevitable be-watch-chained paunch. In the political zoology of the American mind he combines the qualities of swine and fox, feeding greedily at the public trough, plotting cunningly to win and hold power. In recent years his primacy in the caricatures has been challenged only by the bureaucrat—the only word in English, as Harold Ickes put it, that can be hissed although there is not a sibilant in it.

Thus the politician and bureaucrat are fair game for every shaft, the sacrificial kings to whom the Americans grant power but whom they reserve the right to stone to death. The poorest, meanest, most misery-ridden fellow—the town drunk perhaps, the farm ne'er-do-well, or the city derelict—can say anything, no matter how scurvy, about a man in public office. Not only does he have the legal right, but it performs a therapeutic function for him: it shows who is boss, whose is the ultimate power, thus giving him an outlet for his frustrations and consoling him for the disparity in power and income between himself and his target.*

This belittling of politics is partly responsible for the abandonment of politics to the professional politician. What you despise and attack you do not engage in or give your life to. This has meant a break with the Jacksonian doctrine of rotation in office, which was based on the belief that there are no mysteries in governing, just common sense, integrity, and a devotion to the public good, and that any able citizen can therefore do it; and which was itself a way of rationalizing the spoils system, and for taking politics away from the elite of ability and education. In the rise of the big city, and its strata of new immigrants who were largely illiterate and were grateful for aid and guidance, the professional politician found his métier and gathered both money and power from it.

A vicious circle came into being: the contempt for politics as predation made the Americans shrink from the task of government; but the more they left a vacuum into which the professional politician moved, the more violently they recoiled from the result. Most of the able young people turned their talents to business and the professions,

* For a further discussion of political power, see Sec. 5, "Power and Equilibrium"; for the bureaucracy, see Sec. 6, "The Governmental Managers"; for the professional politician, see Sec. 4, "The Party System and the Voter."

where the great rewards loomed; and in many cases to the armed forces, perhaps because war represented the only nonpecuniary calling with glamour and prestige attached to it. The arts of government, which the Greeks had deemed the noblest arts within human competence, came to be considered defiling and defacing. In recent years a growing awareness of this gap between politics and creative talent has spread among the colleges and has served to counteract the tendency. This awareness was especially evident after World War II among the young veterans who came back to complete their studies under the G.I. subsidies and brought a new current of realistic intelligence into politics.

Where the professionals operate, however, is not in public office itself but behind it. The officeholders—the mayors and governors, the state legislators, the whole array of county and state administrative officials, even the Congressmen themselves—are men of varying ability and integrity who may hold office for a few years and then go back to their private business. The threads of continuity in the skein of power are furnished not by them but by the party managers, the men who make a lifetime career of manipulation and alliances and have become masters of the "deal" and the "fix." They swing the whole vast structure of patronage, political profit, and power, using apathy as their medium and the party machinery as their leverage. The fact that there is no career tradition in officeholding itself, as in England, means that there is a gap between politics and the best creative talent of the country. It is what gives the professional political managers their chance to use their own talents. As Lincoln Steffens discovered in years of interviewing them, and many other newspapermen have confirmed, they are likely to be men who combine an ancient cunning with a massive will and the freshest energies of a new country.

I have spoken of the political apathy of a large portion of the American people. But this is part of a pattern which includes also streaks of "good government" reformism and considerable emotional and political invective. The history of American political campaigns is studded with outbursts of political passion, rough-and-tumble tactics of political combat, hyperbolic professions of patriotism, and the assignment of diabolical traits and motives to one's opponents. The deflationary gap between this verbal extremism and the actual continuities of power in the hands of professionals is likely to produce a kind of despair which leads to apathy, so that American politics offers to observers the aspect of violent alternations between activity and quiescence, and between moralism and cynicism. This is true of foreign policy as well, with its alternations between isolationism and a crusading fervor.

On every showdown, however, what comes into the foreground of the pattern is the deep pragmatic strain of American political behavior: not moral doctrine and dogma, for which there is considerable scorn in the anti-intellectualism of a "practical" people, but a grappling with whatever needs to be done—and doing it. There is little doctrinal commitment in American politics. The party combats do not take place in ideological terms but rather in the assessment of personalities and what they are likely to do. The growth in the independent nonparty votes is a sign that this is increasing rather than decreasing. Unlike the Europeans, the Americans have had no "grand" political theory; they rarely talk of the "state" or even of "government," but rather of *the* government" and "the Administration." It is almost as if there were a fear of principles because they might lead to commitments from which it would be difficult to extricate oneself. This does not, of course, prevent the rise of waves of fanatical feeling and the suppression of unpopular ideas, which have swept the nation, especially after wars. Yet America has never enthroned fanaticism in national power. It has thus far managed to avoid following an authoritarian national leader or subscribing to any party-line "truth."

One of the great political documents, which is worth study for the light it sheds on the American political style, is the series of commentaries on the Constitution which have come down as *The Federalist*. The three collaborators—Hamilton, Jay, and Madison—were of different political leanings and were to play very different roles later, yet their preferences on politics were submerged in their common assumptions about the art of government. They had read widely and deeply, had studied the new political science of their day, and were skillful in conscripting the beliefs and experience of antiquity to the purposes of the new venture in government. Yet they were not closet students but men who focused on the idea-in-action. They had a sense of the perilousness of the social fabric and at the same time of the tenacity of social habits, yet even as conservatives (which all of them were in varying degree) they had a bold capacity for political innovation. They were among the early realists who, long before Marx, saw the meaning of what we have come to call class structure and class conflict in relation to politics, yet they never lost their overriding sense of the national interest. As practical psychologists they knew about the elements of the irrational in men, which they called the "political passions"; and accordingly they sought to set limits to the power of government and were jealous of possible tyrannies in the name of the majority. Yet, though they elaborated on the checks and balances in a "mixed government" of separated powers, the state they were trying to create was an affirmative state, with more power at the center than any Republic had ever possessed, to perform the jobs of taxation, defense, and the control of the vital processes of the nation. What they sought was a government "energetic" enough, in the terms of their own day, "to preserve the Union."

In their combination of practical daring, along with conservative techniques for setting a brake on the underlying radicalism of the whole experiment, these men—like the whole group that framed the Constitution—expressed the American political genius not only of their own day but of the later centuries as well. The Americans have had to govern a vast territorial expanse, hold together diverse ethnic and sectional and economic groups, and organize a rapidly mounting mass of wealth and power. How well they have done it will long be argued, but that they have done it at all—and still survived as a tolerably free society—is no mean achievement for their system of government.

The American governmental system, in practice rather than in theory, has made some notable contributions to the arts of government. The outstanding ones are *federalism* as a working equilibrium; the clinging to the rule of law, especially through the technique of *judicial review* by both state and Federal courts; the *Constitutional convention* as a way of formulating and revising the fundamental law; the *two-party system* as a method for insuring the freedom of political opposition and for organizing power and its transfer; *Presidential government* as opposed to parliamentarianism, and Presidential leadership and responsibility as against the unstable shiftings of cabinet government; and the creation of *semi-independent administrative agencies* to carry out the burdens of democratic control of industry under conditions of modern technology.

I put these in terms of political techniques and institutions largely because the Americans themselves, with their bent for mechanism, think of them in those terms. One could argue that the rule of law (although not judicial review) and the party system were both derived from British experience, and that to a lesser extent this holds true of the administrative agencies as well. Yet the question is not only one of originality but of the final stamp. The Americans have not pushed their innovating drive nearly so far in the realm of government as in the realm of industrial technology. One may note that while they continue to imitate the Founding Fathers, the Founding Fathers imitated no one but struck out on their own. The political genius of America has not been one of doctrine but of a practical bent for political contrivances and management, and for the adjustment of old forms to new conditions. It is rarely that a nation, in the course of almost two centuries of constitutional history, is able to maintain—in the face of the changes and chances of growth and power—its essential ability to balance the conflicting drives of property and democracy, of majority power and individual freedom.

It is in this bent that the American political genius best shows itself: the combined pattern of a persisting *belief in majority rule and the democratic idea,* along with a clinging to *civil liberties and the image of a free society;* and at the same time a pragmatic approach to power and administration, showing itself in the *arts of equilibrium* between the strong pulls from every direction, and the use of Presidential leadership and other techniques in order to achieve *effective government.*

The basic instruments of the American government were shaped in an agrarian era, for the needs of a small-scale agrarian society. But it would be unwise to conclude that they are hopelessly dated in a large-scale industrial society, and that the old machinery should be scrapped and perhaps some of the old ideas as well, like democracy and civil liberties. There has been a tendency in American social thought to consider the "social lag" as a crime against progress and humanity; and many may wonder whether a bundle of institutions and practices, set in a Constitutional code long ago and changing only when change was forced upon them by haphazard event, can have greatness.

Yet, on reflection, there is nothing wrong with the "lag" of the old institutions and ideas, provided they had a valid meaning to start with. In the field of government, unlike industrial technology, basic ideas and techniques may be as old as Aristotle and still embody a permanent truth. Although the American Constitution is a written one, there has been room in it for the changes compelled by growth and time. While the Constitution is procedurally conservative, it does not operate in a substantive way to keep forever any particular economic, political, or social beliefs. It may prove as useful in protecting a liberal policy from reactionary assaults as it has been in the past in protecting the *laissez-faire* dogmas of economic conservatism. Americans have shown something of the British knack for making day-to-day changes in practice and then letting the customary practices become the acknowledged "usages" of government. That is why Americans have never taken seriously the various projects for a thorough "modernizing" of their government, to make it more logical or orderly. They have let well enough alone. It was Lord Bryce who is reported to have said that "Providence has under its special care children, idiots, and the United States of America." Which may be another way of saying that, given the industrial development and power of America, even a halting, stumbling, and outdated political system can be a success. America has had the Midas touch; everything that a rich nation touches turns to gold.

With this Midas touch there has been a sense of political brashness which has irritated foreign observers, and a lack of self-restraint that has shown itself in periodic political witch hunts, in a Congress whose utterances have sometimes made American political figures seem more stupid than they are, and in a press whose more sensational outbursts have at times reached manic levels. This has led many observers, especially Europeans, to conclude that the American political style lacks balance and is immature. In fact, the charge of immaturity is the one most frequently leveled at Americans. This is partly true and may be set down to the zest of a still growing society, although in periods of anti-Communist hysteria one is tempted to call it rather the paranoia of a declining one. But I would argue that the imbalance is largely in the outward aspects. As with much else in their life, Americans like their politics pugnacious. They operate through what Lubell calls "democracy as arena." Despite the outward violence and even childishness of word and manner there is often a balancing mechanism at work.

2. *The Democratic Idea**

"I LOVE LIBERTY," John Randolph of Roanoke once exclaimed, "and I hate equality." America is a democracy, but the inner tension that has always existed between the two poles of the democratic idea was never more passionately described than in Randolph's sentence. There are two major meanings—or better, a double aspect of meaning—of the idea of democracy. In one aspect it is free or constitutional government, a going system for assuring the safeguards within which the will of the people can express itself. In this phase—set off the more sharply because of the rise of the new totalitarianisms—the emphasis is on the natural rights of the individual and the limited powers of government, on the separation of powers, on civil liberties, on the rule of law, and the protection of freedom and property against the arbitrary encroachments of the state.

In its second aspect the democratic idea is egalitarian. In this phase it emphasizes the rule of the majority. It presents the spectacle of a demos unbound, a whole people striving however imperfectly to make social equality a premise of government. It shifts the emphasis from the narrowly political—from the ballot and the constitutional guarantees—to the economy and the class system. It stresses the conditions for putting within the reach of the ordinary man the opportunities of education and the making of a living, regardless of his confessional faith, his ethnic

* I deal with the democratic idea here as the ideological phase of American government. For its place in American thought, and an analysis of American conservatism, radicalism, and liberalism, see Ch. X, Sec. 2, "American Thought: the Angle of Vision."

group, and his social level. It carries with it that essential self-respect and refusal to truckle which formed the frontier fact of Jackson's time, that "every man is as good as any other—and a damned sight better." It is democracy defined as the institutions through which, and the social and moral context in which, the collective will can best be organized for the life purposes inherent in all human striving. It is the image that moved Whitman to his glimpses of democratic vistas, and Sandburg to set down the tall tales and the affirmations of "The People, Yes."

The recent American experiences in the context of world events have made it clear that in neither of these phases can democracy stand by itself, whether as constitutional government or popular government, "property rights" or "human rights," antistatism or welfare state. These are not different and self-sufficient "brands" of democracy, to be purchased from the shopwindows of history according to the taste, tradition, or means of a people; nor, to take the other extreme, are they merely semantic quibblings—verbal variations of the same democratic reality. They are polar ideas within the same field; or, to vary the figure, they are currents in the same stream of historic tendency. They are complementary aspects of how political communities in our time have tried to answer the central problems of power, welfare, freedom, and creativeness. They are parts of each other, each of them either barren or dangerous unless set in the context of the other. The recent experience of Europe has shown that constitutional government without popular government may end in the bread lines or in a *coup d'état,* in inner economic or political collapse—or both. It has also shown that a mass democracy (or "people's democracy") without the safeguards of freedom may end in the concentration camp or the slave labor camp.

Throughout the history of the American experience there has been a planetary struggle between the two aspects of the democratic idea. But it has not been primarily a doctrinal struggle, nor waged in academic cloisters. The battles have been waged between parties, sections, classes, pressure groups, using the opposing concepts of "aristocracy" and "people," of "republic" and "democracy," of "conservatism" and "progressivism," of "minority rights" and "majority rule" as symbolic abbreviations for their interests and outlook and aspirations.

The split reaches back into the history of European philosophy and social thought, from which the American democratic idea derived—to the struggle between the thinking of Harrington, Locke, and Montesquieu and that of the English Levelers and Rousseau, between the capitalist liberalism of the new propertied classes and the hydraulic pressure exerted by the mass aspirations still unexpressed in middle-class liberal thought, however revolutionary it was at the time. One of the difficulties in reading Parrington's *Main Currents in American*

Thought, whose first volume traces some of these conflicts in the European background as projected into the early period of the Republic, is that he writes as if it were a choice between democracy and antidemocracy. Actually it was a battle for position between two crucial, interlocked phases of the democratic idea. The correspondence, for example, between Jefferson and his circle shows how closely the early American leaders followed European thought, and how freely they drew from both the currents I have mentioned.

This was true of the authors of *The Federalist* as well, who showed a strategic skill in meeting objections to the Constitution that came from both the Right and Left, and with that skill, a knack for blending the two strains of the democratic idea. To the charge that the Constitution was a revolutionary *coup d'état,* their answer was the residual sovereignty in the people themselves to change an instrument of government inadequate for them. To those who feared a strong central government, their answer was the need for effective national power at the center in order to avert ineffectuality and chaos. By a masterful distinction they argued that the new power would be *federal* in its extent (that is, divided between two spheres and leaving an area of state power to balance the central power) but *national* in its functioning (that is, the national government would have power to act in the sphere where the states could not act effectively). To those who felt that a "mixed government," with separated powers and a system of checks and balances, was too timid an expedient in a revolutionary age, their answer was the classic one of the corruption and ambition of political leaders and the need for a rule of law to guard the people against their own worst impulses. Thus the Founding Fathers sought always not so much (as Beard felt, and J. Allen Smith before him) to guard the rights of the property owners alone, or to give unchecked rein to revolutionary impulse, but to find an equilibrium between the charged tensions of the democratic idea.

Thus, at the very beginning of American government, the two basic drives in it had already shown themselves: the government had to be strong enough to be effective and revolutionary enough to give the people the power they had been denied as colonists; but it also had to be safe against a too-rapid or far-reaching extension of the Revolution. The Hamilton group was intent on creating a going governmental concern so that property and the commercial interests could flourish in safety. The Jefferson group wanted to make certain that the people's liberties and the agrarian interest were protected by a Bill of Rights, and that the dead hand of the past did not smother a full life for even the lowliest American freeman. Each caught a glimpse of the needs of a future America, but, as in a stereoscope, both were needed to bring the picture in focus.

The question has often been raised whether the American political system should be called "democracy" or "republic," the latter being a neutral term without the equalitarian major premise of the democratic dogma. This is not merely a closet controversy carried on by scholars: it crops up in editorials and newspaper columns and in heated Congressional debates. It seems to be the whimsical notion of the "republic" school of thought that "democracy" should be dropped from the American political vocabulary. They call it a word which (despite Jefferson and the Jacksonians, De Tocqueville, Bryan and Woodrow Wilson) didn't become popular in America until Georgi Dimitrov used it at a Comintern meeting, and which is today tainted beyond redress by the "People's Democracies" of eastern Europe.

This would surrender to world Communism a concept as American as cherry cobbler. The revealing fact in the whole debate is that the stress on "republic" is on the strategy of weakening the majority will by the action of pressure groups and the corporate spokesmen in Congress and the press. Behind it is the fear that "democracy" makes too dangerous a commitment to the participation of Negroes and Jews, recent immigrants and low-income groups, in both the guarantees of civil rights and the shaping of social decisions, and the fear also (as old as the Cromwellian debates or even Aristotle) that "democracy" leads to "Socialism." There is an irony in this animus against the term, in a civilization that has become a world symbol as the most powerful carrier of the democratic idea.

A historical graph of American political development would show an alternation between the principle of constitutional democracy ("republic") and that of majority action and passion ("democracy"). Once the Constitution was a success and the new frame of government accepted by all, the emphasis was on constitutional government. Hamilton's Report on Manufactures, the Report on Credit, and the protectionist writings of the school of economists headed by Mathew Carey laid the political and intellectual basis for building an industrialized economy; and the series of brilliant decisions by John Marshall, mainly on the contract clause and the commerce power of the Federal government, served to link the rising system of capitalism with the doctrines of constitutional nationalism. But Marshall's absence of principle in the case of *Fletcher v. Peck,* when land speculation and legislative corruption were sanctioned in the zeal to establish the sacredness of contracts and the legal doctrine of vested interests, also showed the canker in the flower even while it was in bloom. John Taylor of Carolina spoke witheringly of the "aristocracy of paper and credit" that was pushing for Marshall's constitutional conceptions.

This raises the issue of what clash there is between the democratic idea and capitalist power. It was Harold Laski's major thesis that capitalism and democracy had met in the American experiment at the convergence of two lines of historical tendency, but that they were partners in an uneasy marriage of convenience rather than of true affinity. Actually, whatever clash there is between capitalism and democracy—and it is real enough—is a phase of a larger and more relevant struggle between what we may call the "dominant minority" and the "popular majority." In the correspondence of Jefferson and his friends and in the whole literature of the Jeffersonian period, this was phrased as a struggle between "aristocracy" and "democracy." Jefferson equated the aristocratic principle with that of a disbelief in man's inherent capacity for self-government. "We are told," he wrote, "that men cannot govern themselves. Can they then govern others?" His most passionate phrasing of the indictment of the principles of a dominant minority came in his classic comment that no select group of men had been born, "booted and spurred, to ride mankind."

It is true that the first group which came into American history well equipped to play the role of a dominant minority was the business class and its champions among the lawyers and political leaders. Before the rise of industry there was none equipped to take the part that a social and political aristocracy had taken in British and European life. When Fisher Ames talked of the government of "the wise, the rich, and the good" he was trying to put into American terms the principle of an elite which had no strong roots in the American soil, and which— even in the great days of Hamilton and John Adams—was too amorphous to be more than the tag end of the European tradition. To be sure, in the colonial days there was considerable frontier hostility to the commercial and business groups who were overrepresented in the legislatures and in other positions of power. But the American Revolution was not a social revolution in the European sense largely because it did not have to be one, since there was no feudal tradition and no entrenched American aristocracy to overthrow. It was the absence of such a cohesive elite which made possible the victory of Jeffersonianism in the "revolution of 1800" and the continuing power of the "Virginia dynasty" in the first quarter of the nineteenth century. By the time of the feud between the Biddle and Jackson-Taney forces over banking power, it had become clear that a new minority group was taking charge, but it had not yet found a credo.

This was the time when Ralph Waldo Emerson wrote sadly:

Of the two great parties, which at this hour almost share the nation between them, I should say that one has the best cause, and the other contains the best men. . . . They (of the radical party) have not at heart the ends which give the name of democracy what hope and virtue are in it. The spirit of our American radicalism is destructive and aimless. . . . On the other side, the conservative party, composed of the most moderate, able, and cultivated part of the population, is timid, and merely defensive of property. It vindicates no right, it aspires to no real good, it brands no crime, it proposes no generous policy; it does not build, nor write, nor cherish the arts, nor foster religion, nor establish schools, nor encourage science, nor emancipate the slave, nor befriend the poor, or the Indian, or the immigrant. ("Politics," in *Essays: Second Series*)

If his judgment of Jacksonian democracy was (as historians see it now) too negative, Emerson was right in seeing that the conservatives had not found a fighting faith. When the Civil War came, the challenge of the plantation-owning military caste and its allies was met by a new party which—even while it kept strong continuity with the Whigs— broke with them by equating the interests of free labor and free capitalism with the interests of the nation.

But the equalitarian impulse of Lincoln, as well as of Greeley and the Abolitionists, trickled away in the Reconstruction period. The business organizers who became the new dominant minority were more swaggering and assured than any other before their time. The old Radical opposition had been disorganized by war and Reconstruction, and a new opposition had not yet come into being. The new dominant minority developed within its business organizations the habit of command: they were the "bosses" and they ran the machines in their economic empire. What more natural than that they should transfer that habit of command and operate through "bosses" and "machines" in the political empire as well, on the theory that those who own the country should run it? The far-reaching transfer of business organizing skills to politics was symbolized by Mark Hanna. How impressive was the achievement of Hanna and his class may be judged from the fact that the fusion of Populist passion with the Democratic forces under Bryan in the 1896 campaign had all the features of a sweeping and irresistible mass movement. That it was whittled away, fragmented, and finally beaten by a combination of external events and good political generalship by the Republicans underlined what capitalist power at its most efficient can do within the democratic framework.

The struggle between the capitalist power group and the popular majority has thus far been kept well within the framework of a larger national interest. It is true that business forces have not hesitated to break the fabric of political legality itself, as evidenced by the dramatic instance of the 1876 elections when a corrupt deal was worked out between the Northern Republicans (including the railroad interests) and the White Supremacists of the South, to "throw" the crucial Southern electors from Tilden to Hayes. Nevertheless the American picture has been very different from that of the European, in the sense that there has been at least a minimum consensus between the opposing forces, and the victories for the popular majority have not met with violence from the other side, but have been accepted. This was true of Woodrow Wilson's "New Freedom" as it was later true of the "New Deal" and the "Fair Deal" of the Roosevelt and Truman administrations.

There is an interweaving of these two impulses in American life beyond any hope of disentanglement. There are few members of the power groups who have not been at some point infected by the democratic idea; and even more certainly, there are few Americans who have not been touched by the property ideology. The split between capitalism and democracy is thus less a class conflict than a split within every American.

Is this likely to be a fatal split for Americans? There is no reason why it must be, unless the organization of an effective majority will become too difficult to meet the crisis of democratic life. Since effective democracy involves the organization of will, it is extremely vulnerable to the operation of minority pressures and power. The path of the democratic idea has therefore often been a *via dolorosa,* and the record of democratic action a Heartbreak House.

If a program is marked for destruction, one path open is a direct assault in the area of public attitude, where the dominant minority has a massive influence in the opinion industries. If they lose there, they can turn their energies to the prevention of a majority for the measure in either house of Congress, using to their advantage the committee system, the rules of parliamentary delay and filibuster, the high-pressure operation of lobbies, and the fact that Congressional representation is badly skewed to favor the rural conservative constituencies as against the urban liberal ones. If they lose there, they can fall back—as they did for a half century from the 1880s to the Roosevelt era—on the protection of the judicial power as interpreted by a property-minded Supreme Court. If they lose there, they can concentrate on weakening the administrative enforcement of the measure or even capturing the administrative machinery and its personnel. And always they have the chance, by their immense wealth and power, of capturing the party machinery and dictating the choice of candidates in both the major parties. In short, the battle for an affirmative democratic program is like an action in which

one army, in order to win, has to take every one of a succession of fortified places, while the other army has only to win and hold one such
fortified place, even though it loses all the rest.

The reader may well say that this somber view does not square with
the achievement of the New Deal, the great social gains in the quarter
century after 1932, and the gradual Republican acceptance of many
features of a welfare democracy. I should answer that this shows another
side of the democratic process—the potential of social achievement under a strong leadership like Franklin Roosevelt's. The task of the
dominant minority is always hardest in the area of the Presidency,
where the focusing of popular attention on a single dramatic struggle,
with personal symbols to express the social forces involved, gives mass
democracy a chance to organize its resources. Under the Eisenhower
Administration a working alliance of Democrats and liberal Republicans was able to put through a more enlightened legislative program
than in any Republican period since Theodore Roosevelt. Yet under
both Truman and Eisenhower the Congressional investigating committees incited and expressed some of the popular passions corrupted by
an era of military anxiety and world fear. To balance this there has
been a change in the role of the judicial power. From the eighties to the
New Deal constitutional crisis, the judiciary formed the last line of defense against liberal movements of opinion; but in the recent postwar
period it again became, to an encouraging extent, a sword to achieve
civil rights for Negroes and a shield (often, alas, too frail) against the
hatreds engaged in the hunt for "dangerous thoughts."*

The political history of American democracy has thus been an alternation of social achievement and frustration or a battlefield where freedom and reaction have fought a continuing seesaw engagement. To the
economically and ethnically depressed groups it may be difficult to
maintain so detached a view of the democratic process. The fact is that
for them the homage paid in America to the democratic idea has at
times seemed an empty thing. The psychologists have found that the
human personality is brilliantly resourceful in the kind of compart-
mental thinking in which the mind isolates contradictory ideas from
each other. As the depressed groups of American life have learned to
their sorrow, a culture can do the same in the separation of democratic
rhetoric and practice.

Yet there is little that is surprising in the failure of American life to
achieve wholly the original democratic aspiration. Democracy is a
heartbreakingly difficult as well as a dangerous enterprise. The effort to
combine the principle of constitutional protection along with that of

* For a further discussion of the Presidency, Congress, and the judiciary, see the
relevant sections of this chapter that follow.

the organized majority will is bound to lead to strains and contradictions. The tragic results of the Rousseau-Marxist principle of "people's democracies," which has swept over half the world, have led to a reassertion of emphasis in America on constitutional democracy. The Communist regimes, whatever else they may be, are a travesty rather than a fulfillment of the democratic idea: actually they are an amalgam of apostolic religious fervor and the lust for power of a new elite group, along with some mystique of "the people" thrown in. This amalgam, which has been well called "totalitarian democracy," almost wholly excludes the rule of law and the tolerance of a political opposition. Thus it is the image of individual freedom, along with that of technological abundance, which America stresses.

With this emphasis some Americans are in danger of forgetting that the effective dynamism of the democratic idea, throughout the nineteenth century and through most of the first half of the twentieth, has been expressed by what George Santayana has called the "natural democracy" or "leaves-of-grass democracy"—the idea of equality of opportunity and of the basic fraternity of men within it. It is the image of America as a society not equal but potentially equal—an open society whose twin ideas are equal access and the dignity of the person. The equalitarian idea is, of course, subject to corruption as well, yet the corruptions in American history have been due less to flirtations with Marxist movements than to whatever racist and antilibertarian passions seemed at any time to prove useful to the dominant minority.

I have spoken of the seesaw of achievement and frustration within the framework of freedom. The frustrations have been part of the enormous difficulties of a democracy operating within a system of corporate dominance and of political machinery suited to the deadlock. The achievement, in turn, has time after time broken through the deadlock and the integuments of power, especially at times of economic crisis when the forces seeking to establish an affirmative welfare state have had a chance to move ahead. When they have done so it has been by thrusting toward the principles set forth in the Declaration of Independence: that the primary purpose of government is to protect the natural (that is, indestructible) rights of the people; that the crux of government is to discover the consent of the governed through the electoral process; and that the people, as the possessors of the ultimate power, must pass final judgment on what the men in power have done and have a right to change them. The social cost that has had to be paid for the maintenance of these natural rights in the free democratic arena has at times seemed great, yet it can never be too great, nor can it be paid and the account closed, since to maintain freedom is to maintain the machinery for social change.

To round out the meaning of American democracy, a third factor must now be added to that of individual freedom and of mass participation in the democratic process. It is the element of a moral sensitivity to the tragic human experience. America has the potential for this in the fact that one of the great sources of its democratic thinking is the Biblical tradition of Puritanism, including both the Old Testament passion for justice and the Christian allegory of love. And America which has thus far used its genius for equilibrium by balancing the demands of individual freedom and majority will may find it a harder task to balance the struggle for world power with the moral sensitivity it will need to save its democratic soul.

3. Presidency and Demos

ONE OF THE MIRACLES of American government is how it has managed, with its creaking machinery and its capacity for deadlock, to respond to emergencies. Part of the answer may be in a deceptively hidden dynamism which at the moment of crisis gathers its reserves of strength and comes crashing through. The most crucial governmental agency which shows this elasticity for change and mastery is the American Presidency. But given the net of obstructions confining an attempt to organize the national will, only the stronger and more skillful Presidents have been able successfully to break it. This is one way of defining the task of Presidential leadership.

In its present status as a great industrial and world power, Americans have learned the truth of the remark that modern democratic government is "just one damn crisis after another." That is why the center of gravity of American political life has moved from the other two branches over to the Executive power; and the system which in the early phase of the Republic was called "Congressional government," and in the *laissez-faire* decades of the late nineteenth century "government by judiciary," must now be called "Presidential government."

For a man of deep convictions, the process of getting nominated for the Presidency is itself a major feat: for to be "available" in the eyes of the political managers a man must as a rule be basically "safe" and moderate, however militant outwardly. The life of every pre-Convention candidate thus becomes a heroic wrestling match between conscience and canniness. Of those who proved "strong" Presidents, Jackson came into his first term on the wave of a mass revolt in his party, Lincoln and Franklin Roosevelt both seemed relatively mild men before election and only showed their strength later, Theodore Roosevelt became President when McKinley was assassinated, and Wilson received the nomination only after the bitterest fight in the Convention and then only with Bryan's help. Wendell Willkie was nominated in 1940 when the Republicans wanted someone not an isolationist who could run against Roosevelt; in 1944 he was passed over partly because he had been beaten but also because in the intervening years he had too clearly shown his deep liberalism and a set of internationalist convictions that made him enemies. Very often a man whom the Convention delegates support strongly, like Senator Bricker in 1940 and Senator Taft in 1952, fails of the nomination because the managers read the public-opinion polls (especially from the urban "key" states) and conclude that he could not be elected. The conditions for reaching the Presidency are so haphazard and opportunist that the way is too often open for a genial, mediocre man who means well, commands a popular following, and will not be too intractable.

But while the tradition has been against men of committed views and creative holders of the office, the most important trait of the American Presidency is that its mantle of office seems to have the magic of shrinking or expanding to the potential stature of the wearer. It has room enough for a big man to fill it out; a small man can make it seem small enough to fit him. It has been held by a Buchanan and a Lincoln, a Harding and a Roosevelt alike.

Apart from the textbook discussions of the President's constitutional powers, there is little question that the actual powers of the office have grown. There has, of course, been an ebb and flow of Presidential power depending on the aggressiveness of the incumbent. But the secular trend—despite the massive powers that Jefferson and Lincoln exercised—has been unmistakable. There are some commentators who are melancholy because they feel (wrongly, I think) that the growth of Presidential power has been largely at the expense of states' rights and the separation of powers. Others ask where in the Constitution one can find specific grants of some of the many powers the recent Presidents have assumed. The usual answer to the latter is that the Presidency operates not on a grant of specific powers but on the comprehensive executive power, which includes all the residual powers demanded by effective government and not specifically denied by the letter and spirit of the Constitution. Another answer is Theodore Roosevelt's famous "stewardship" theory, which depicts the President as holding these residual powers in stewardship for the people.

The tendency has been to take a functional rather than legalistic view of the Presidential office. There are things which none of the branches of government have explicit power to do, and which the states cannot do adequately, but which must nevertheless get done. There are conflicts to be resolved shrewdly by someone with the skill and prestige to overcome obstacles. There are crises to be met by someone who can muster the drive and find the power to meet them, and who will answer for how well or badly they are met. There are policies to be shaped by a group for whose decisions a single man will take the responsibility.

Even with this functional view of the office, the elastic doctrine of Presidential power lends itself obviously to abuse as well as use. President Franklin D. Roosevelt's threat of "packing" the Supreme Court in order to compel resignations and give him a chance for new appointments was widely attacked at the time as a dictatorial move. His "destroyers-for-bases deal" with Great Britain before America entered the war rested on a notably elastic opinion of its constitutionality from his Attorney General. President Truman, who was considered less "strong" a President than Roosevelt, also had three major encounters with the limits of Presidential power: once when he tried to break a national railroad strike by the threat of enrolling the railroad workers in the Army, again when he committed a large American Army to Europe (and later to Korea, in the U.N. "police action") without any state of war, and finally when he sought to resolve a steel industry lockout-and-strike by taking over the steel mills until a settlement should be reached, on the plea of a military emergency but without specific statutory power. He was checked on the first, was successful on the second (which illustrates that the real elasticity of Presidential power lies in foreign policy), and on the third he was sharply rebuked in a historic Supreme Court decision which held itself narrowly to the immediate issues but raised questions about the scope of the theory of implied powers.

The fact is that the whole question of Presidential power is enmeshed in a faulty idea of how the Presidency is related to the sources of its power. The Constitution, under the Court's interpretation, provides the channel through which the President's powers flow; but the power itself derives from the President's relations to the events around him and to the minds and purposes of the people whom these events affect. These are in truth the sources of the Presidential power. There are, it is usually said, two Constitutions, not one: the written document and the unwritten usages. Actually the more meaningful second Constitution is to be found not in the usages but in the outlines of economic power and interests, of religious convictions, of ethnic loyalties, of rural and urban thinking, of attitudes toward war and peace, with all of which the President must reckon as exactingly as he reckons with the written Constitution.

It might be better to say that the *authority* of a President is even more important than his *power*, because it is the authority that shapes and decides what the power shall be. I use "authority" in the sense of the President's habitual command of popular consent. The sources of the President's authority are subjective—flowing from his personality, his political style, his conduct of the office, his impact on the people— rather than being objective and forever imbedded in a constitutional document. If he has grasp, contagion, political artistry, and a mastery of his purposes and methods, then he will carry authority no matter what powers he claims or forsakes, and his authority will work magic to bolster the claims he stakes out. If, on the other hand, he is like John Adams or Herbert Hoover and fails to carry authority, then even a limited view of the Presidential power will get him into trouble, and even a clear grant of power will prove ineffectual.

The President has not only massive powers and authority; he has also massive burdens that weigh him down. The Presidency eats men. The demands on the incumbent are at once imperative and paradoxical.

Once elected,* a President must manage to unify the nation which has been temporarily split by the election ("We are all Federalists, we are all Republicans," Jefferson said in his First Inaugural), yet not abandon the program he has been elected to carry out. He must be national leader without ceasing to be party leader, and party leader without alienating the factions into which every party splits. He must frame a legislative program without seeming to deprive Congress of its exclusive control over legislation and get it through Congress without seeming to drive it. He must head up a vast and sprawling administrative system of whose workings he can know only the tiniest fraction, yet whenever anything goes wrong he must stand accountable to the people for every detail. He must select, recruit, and hold administrative talent on the basis of merit, while "playing ball" within the patronage structure. He must co-ordinate the workings of the thousands of interlocking cogs of the governmental machine, yet somehow find a space for creative concentration on great issues. He is by the Constitution the sole organ of foreign policy in a peacetime Great Power, and in time of war or "cold war" he is Commander in Chief of a powerful military machine and head of a vast war economy. He must express and carry through the people's wishes, yet he must function as Educator in Chief, helping them to formulate their wishes and organize their opinion. He must be a symbol of the world's greatest democracy—its vigor, its effectiveness, its potentials—and, as a symbol, remote; yet he must also have the human immediacy which gives the ordinary American the sense that he is not lost and that he has someone to speak and act for him. He must be all things to all men, yet also a bold leader hewing out a path in a single direction. In short, he must be Pooh-Bah and St. George at once.

* For a discussion of Presidential nomination, campaign, and election, see Sec. 4, "The Party System and the Voter."

Obviously only a comic-strip Superman could combine all these qualities. Actually the Presidential function is filled at any one time not by one man but by a number of men. Except at the top level, even most of the major decisions are made from day to day by a group of men each of whom serves as his alter ego in some area of policy. When a new President is elected, the commentators are as likely to turn their klieg lights on the "men around the President" as on the President himself.

No President can avoid the formation of juntas around him—insiders who are bound to have a vague conspiratorial air to the outsiders. Sometimes such a junta is actually sinister, as with the "Daugherty gang" who ran the White House under Harding; others only seem so to opposing groups within the President's own party and to the opposition party. Thus Roosevelt had his "Brain Trust," Truman his "cronies," Eisenhower his "Regency" group. Actually there are circles within circles of influence and power radiating out of the White House. To take the Eisenhower Administration as an example: there was a formal Cabinet to which the President delegated his powers over each decision-making and administrative area; there was the National Security Council, which possessed immense power and included the Secretary of State and several of the President's crucial advisers; there was an inner Cabinet group, in which the Secretaries of the Treasury, of State, and the Attorney General played the principal roles; there was an inner White House Staff group, led by Chief of Staff Sherman Adams and Press Secretary Hagerty; there was an inner Congressional group, consisting of several trusted leaders of both Houses along with the staff liaison people who served as links with Congress; and there was an inner group of the President's close friends—the "Regency" group—including leading political and business figures, who advised him from the start on crucial matters and kept a supervision over affairs on the two occasions of his serious illness.

I must add that since the President is Chief Executive, the question of what kind of executive he is is an important one. Given his military experience, Eisenhower operated in the White House also with a line-and-staff organization, leaving most matters for decision to the men in charge of the respective areas, and leaning heavily upon his Chief of Staff. His tendency was to lay down the general line of policy and then stay out of things, even relatively important things, until real trouble arose, when he came back into the picture with his power and authority to clear up the trouble. Truman, at the other extreme, arose early every day, worked intensively, had his finger on all important matters, was chary of too-inclusive delegations of power, swept his desk clean, and was ready the next morning to begin again briskly. Compared with both of them, Roosevelt was a sloppy administrator who might delegate overlapping areas of power to several of his lieutenants and could not keep his own hand and mind out of any of the areas: as he was his own Secretary of State, so he was his own Secretary of the Treasury and his own military strategy staff.

There is room for a number of types of the executive mind in the Presidency. But what is crucial in every case is that the President should avoid at one extreme the danger of so much delegation that he loses contact with the processes and temper of his administration, and at the other extreme the danger of becoming so preoccupied with details that he loses sight of his grand goals and strategies, and has no time or energy left for reflection on them.

In the end the Presidency is thus a one-man job, and that one man cannot escape either the burden of or the accounting for it. The inventory of the tasks of the Presidential office is a reminder at once of how capacious and exacting it is. Even more, it defines where the center of gravity of the office is—in the special relation of the President to the American demos.

That is why the people's instinct, in reviewing the history of the Presidency, has been not so much to ask whether Presidents have been "liberal" or "conservative," men of thought or men of action, but whether they have been "strong" or "weak" Presidents. The strength or weakness with which they have exercised their functions has been partly a matter of their own character structure and inner drive, partly of the philosophy with which they have approached their office, but to a great extent the result of the tensions which they have had to face. A man of seemingly ordinary capacities, like Harry S. Truman, showed how the Presidency stretches a man as well as eats men, and how great is its capacity to educate the man who holds it.

Even the strongest of Presidents learns that the Presidential office is the veriest Gehenna unless the people make it tolerable; that whatever powers any particular President seeks to assume, it is the ultimate power of the people that grants or checks them; and that a President is helpless except insofar as he can win the people's confidence. This relation between leader and demos is at the heart of the organization of the American political will.

Arthur M. Schlesinger, Sr., polling a number of American commentators, found that the six "great Presidents" were Lincoln, Washington, Franklin Roosevelt, Wilson, Jefferson, and Jackson, in that order. I should agree with Clinton Rossiter in adding Theodore Roosevelt to the list. Yet the notable theories of political leadership, especially the theory of "charismatic" leadership and of leadership as vocation as developed by Max Weber, apply much more to European leadership politics than to American Presidential politics. When the American thinks of his government, he thinks first of the President as its symbol. But while the President is often cursed extravagantly, he is rarely praised extravagantly. This is what Kenneth Burke has called the "debunking of the chosen symbol." Except in a rare instance like that of Eisenhower, the symbol is there to do a job under pitilessly critical examination, not to be followed blindly and adoringly. However sacred Americans may consider the Constitution itself and its judicial guardians, the bent is toward the deflation of authority in individuals.

Partly this derives from the American skepticism of all political power; partly too from the structure of authority in the American family and school system, where the emphasis is not on paternal power but on the development of individual self-reliance; partly too from a market system of *caveat emptor* in which the individual keeps himself continually on guard against being made a "sucker" from a too-unwary eagerness. Whatever the psychic sources, however, the fact is that Americans as a nation have rarely shown a sustained capacity for clinging to a political father. The only important exceptions were Washington ("the father of his country"), Lincoln (seen as "Father Abraham," although mainly in retrospect), and Franklin Roosevelt, who was a father symbol in a time of depression and world war, and then mainly for the minority groups and the underprivileged and excluded. To these must be added the figure of the soldier-as-man-of-peace, in the person of Dwight Eisenhower, whose father image was at once authoritative, kindly, and carefully kept above the party battle (although he was a shrewd politician) and who rounded out his image, as American fathers so often do, by incurring a heart attack and having an intestinal operation. But the records of the Presidential office show torrents of popular and partisan abuse of men like Adams, Jefferson, Madison, Jackson, Lincoln, Johnson, Cleveland, Theodore Roosevelt, Wilson, Franklin Roosevelt, and Truman—usually on the score that they were tyrants and dictators. A nation that has never recognized political masters needs to reassure itself continually that it is not falling under one.

The leadership qualities of Franklin Roosevelt and Dwight Eisenhower deserve special scrutiny because their common and contrasting qualities illumine the nature of "charismatic" leadership in the Presidency. James M. Burns, by calling his study of Roosevelt *The Lion and the Fox*, placed him in the tradition of Machiavellian strategy, and there is little question that Roosevelt used imaginative daring and pugnacity along with the cunning of maneuver. Both qualities led him deep into party politics, where he fought the unfaithful within (he was one of the few Presidents who tried to purge

Congressional leaders of his own party) and smote the heathen without.

Eisenhower had less both of the lion and the fox: he was not savage in attack, but usually soft-spoken; and he affected the style of staying outside political involvement and keeping above the party battles. His total political style was thus an unusual one among American Presidents. He was not an intellectual, like Wilson or Jefferson; nor a lusty exponent of the strenuous life, like Theodore Roosevelt; nor a dour Puritan, like Coolidge; nor an introvert, like Lincoln, with a flair for jokes and an undercurrent of tragedy. He was the soldier-statesman, combining the two qualities more strikingly than anyone before him since Washington. If he had some of the fuzzy outlines of another soldier-President, Ulysses Grant, who never quite learned what had happened to him when he fell among the businessmen and politicians, he was far less of an amateur in politics than he liked to seem. He knew the political uses of the genial, warming smile, of folksiness, and of the earnest moralizing little sermons with which he sprinkled his press conferences. He understood the deep American impulse toward the belittling of politics, and by seeming to avoid partisanship he could win more converts to his cause than the most partisan leader. He came at a time when Americans wanted peace desperately, after a war and a cold war, and his political style as a soldier who knew war and could therefore bring peace exactly fitted the felt psychological needs of his time. He was widely supported during his first term both within his own party and among the Democrats on issues of war and peace, particularly when he met the Russian leaders at Geneva. The genial conflict-avoiding bent of Eisenhower and his reliance on the decision-making of the men around him weakened his second term, and were of some danger to the Presidential position: increasingly Eisenhower himself became an image—and a very popular one—while the burdens of the office were more dispersed than they had been before. While the Democrats used the slogan of a "part-time Presidency" in the campaign, this dispersal of the duties and powers of the office was not wholly due to the President's illness but was integral to his personality and his political style.

Yet this is unlikely to recur often in the future. The greater probability is that the burdens of the office will increase, and that the American President will, as in the past, have to win everything the hard way. He will have to meet the problems and opposition of Congress, his Party, the judiciary, the press, the power of Big Labor and the Big Corporation, the rivalry and jealousy of sections and classes. Presidential government thus becomes an obstacle race, and the Great President the Great Hurdler.

In this context the fear that a President will abuse his powers, while real enough, is only one phase of the danger. The other phase is that all but the stoutest of heart, the firmest of will, and the most passionate of conviction will give up the struggle long before they have achieved their objective. It is only widespread popular support that will enable any President to clear his hurdles. Unless the people are with him all the way he cannot carry through his program. His last chance of having the people with him is at a time of grave social crisis and in a national emergency, and then only if he is a consummate tactician. The Presidential office is like a field headquarters, which operates best in the heat of critical battle. But the fact that it has come through well in every period of crisis is proof that in an age of disintegration, democratic government is not too fossilized and inflexible to survive.

The President combines within himself the double function of reigning and ruling. Using Walter Bagehot's idea that every government must have a "dignified" element in it, this element in America is divided between the Presidency and the Supreme Court. Of the two, the President is more subject to vituperative attack but by that token more constantly present in the minds of the people. He occupies the center of the national stage. He is a "republican king." As with the British monarch, his daily life and acts are constantly under scrutiny, and his personality style (along with that of his wife) sets a pattern which is more or less consciously imitated by millions of Americans. The fact that Woodrow Wilson read detective stories, that Franklin Roosevelt collected stamps, that Eleanor Roosevelt worked hard at welfare problems and international affairs, that Dwight Eisenhower was an ardent golf amateur, and that Mamie Eisenhower wore bangs and had a gracious manner left an impact upon the reading, stamp-collecting, and golf-playing habits of American men and on the life style of American women. A President's smile or frown or look of anxiety, when reproduced in the press, may influence the stock market and the action of foreign governments, but even more the habitual demeanor of Americans whose image is formed in the Presidential mirror.

There is also another kind of Presidential image—the composite picture that the people keep in their minds of the traits a President ought to have. For example, he ought to come from a small town rather than a big city, since the tradition of a superior virtue and strength in such origins has survived the decline of the small town itself. He is likely to be of West European family origin—English, Scottish, Dutch, Swiss, German, or some mixture of them. No American President has yet derived from Scandinavian, Latin, East European, or Slavic origins. He is likely to come from one of the big states with a heavy electoral vote which can help swing him into the Presidency. He has always been a Protestant, but since the Civil War he has never been identified with a Southern state—a serious limitation, given the political talent that the South has shown throughout its history. He is most likely to be a lawyer by profession and a politician by passion. If the Presidential aspirant is either a businessman or a labor leader, the chances are heavy against him. He must have managed to preserve an integrity of family life and (except in a few instances) avoided any public disclosure of violation of the sexual mores of his culture. Thus far no divorced man has ever been elected President, although the nomination of Adlai Stevenson in 1952 and again in 1956 despite this limitation may be a sign that the taboo is being eroded.

Like the corporation, the Presidency has been caught up in the managerial transformation of American life. In one sense it can be said that the President is himself a "manager"—in foreign relations, in war and peace, in economic affairs, in the daily functioning of the government. But it would be truer to say that the President has become a kind of Chairman of the Board, while the real managers operate the day-to-day affairs of the government and even make substantial policy decisions. When President Eisenhower had a heart attack in 1955 the national government went on functioning much as it had done before: there was an "inner group" operating under Sherman Adams, who was in effect the President of the corporate managerial nucleus, and who never burdened the Chairman of the Board with anything except crisis problems and top policy-making decisions. The effect of this is to bring the President into the decision-making picture only when and where something goes badly wrong, and only when broad new policy needs to be formed. The President thus becomes basically a conciliator between opposing factions within his administration, a resolver of crises, a god from the machine stepping out of the sky to restore order from chaos. This may help explain why the dignity and distance of the Presidential office are maintained even in the most constant struggle and bitterness of the daily political arena. Eisenhower, for example, was rarely branded with the stigma of what his underlings did. Under other Presidents as well, notably Franklin Roosevelt, the underlings who were unlucky enough to threaten the image which the administration wished to preserve in the popular mind have often had to be sacrificed.

Given this position, the President must rely on the people he picks to carry on the daily work of the government. He operates under the written Constitution as defined by the courts; but, even more, he operates under an unwritten Constitution, composed of a body of executive orders which are drawn up by the Presidential assistants and are based often only on the fact that some previous President had done something of the sort. The process of Constitution-making thus resides in the Presidency far more than in Congress and rivals the similar process in the Supreme Court. As a distributor of power, the President not only bestows his blessings on a large number of lucky individuals who come in for the political prizes and flock to Washington when their man has won: he also blesses a particular class or segment of the population. Under Roosevelt's New Deal the intellectuals got a chance at power; under both Roosevelt and Truman the labor groups were similarly cut in; under Eisenhower a large number of corporate executives, major and minor, eagerly found their place in the Washington power hierarchy.

But even with the maximum degree of delegation of Presidential duties to staff and advisers, the Presidency remains a tense and crushing office, and is likely to take its toll in the future as in the past. This has made the problem of Presidential succession, in the event of death or disabling illness, more crucial. The likelihood is that Americans will be more aware of the importance of the Vice-President in the Presidential succession, and that the Throttlebottom type of Vice-President is on his way out.

4. The Party System and the Voter

SECOND ONLY TO THE development of Presidential government has been that of party government. The deriding of party government is a favorite American sport, and at times the disillusionment with it reaches the proportions of despair; yet few Americans would change their party system for any other. They feel about it a little as Emerson felt about some of the workaday features of his own time, including the party caucus: "Banks and tariffs, the newspaper and caucus . . . are flat and dull to dull people, but rest on the same foundations of wonder as the town of Troy and the temple of Delphos." The skeptic might say that the party system in America is indeed a "foundation of wonder," since it provides the invisible underpinning for the visible government and therefore allows the respectable show of formal decisions to be buttressed by transactions which are more effectively hidden.

Americans think of parties largely in national terms, and it is true that the national party organizations become sharply focused every four years as the Presidential elections approach. In fact, the party system has been defined as a loose aggregation of local machines that come together for the stakes of power embodied in the Presidency. Yet it is an error to view the party system primarily on the level of the national committees, and thus give too much emphasis to the Presidential stakes. The tough fabric of the party is to be found in the persistent and continuing bread-and-butter efforts to elect Senators, Congressmen, governors and other state officials, sheriffs, county attorneys, and the wide, bewildering array of administrative and judicial posts which form the jungle of American local politics. When it is remembered that there are more than a million elected officials in the United States, not to speak of the vast number of appointed ones who form the basis of the patronage system, it will be clear that the party organization which seeks to elect and appoint them constitutes the frame and musculature of American government. The relation between the local organizations and the national committees is one of mutual gain and loyalty. The party that wins can dispense patronage to the local party workers who have helped in the victory. In turn the local bosses are expected to be faithful to the national candidates at the party conventions and to "deliver" the votes in the national elections. The national organization in turn is expected to bolster the prestige of the state and local candidates and to give direction to what would otherwise be a chaos of local campaigns.

It would be too cynical to say that the only thing holding parties together is patronage and office. The party system, while resting on these, is actually a way of transmitting the broad ideas and philosophy of government from the Presidential and national leaders on top to every corner of the country, and of transmitting in turn the sentiments and impulses from every locality to the state and national capitals and to the top candidates and officials. If in terms of power it furnishes, as I have said, the frame and musculature of government, then in terms of the communication it forms the circulatory system for the ideas and convictions that animate government.

The parties have played a great functional role in American history. It is ironic that this should have been exactly the phase of the American governmental system which the framers of the Constitution were most anxious to restrain, regarding them as dangerous and fearing (as James Madison did) the rise of "factions" that would split the new society as they had once filled the Roman and Greek states with bloodshed. Yet a hundred years later it was exactly the part of the American government to which Bryce, in his *American Commonwealth,* paid most attention and for that reason got a warm review from a rising young professor of politics at Princeton called Woodrow Wilson. The vast, sprawling conglomerate of American life—with its sectional, ethnic, and religious pluralism, its welter of local governments, and its rural-urban hostilities—required some unifying thongs to hold it together. On the other hand, the stiffness of the political machinery and the diffusion of authority which always tended toward deadlock required some kind of oil to keep the creaking machinery going. The party system has helped to furnish something of both: the resiliency and the cohesion, the springs to absorb shocks and the thongs to hold the sprawling aggregate together, the oil and the cement. It has given American democracy a rough kind of politically functioning unity without the social cost that the unity of a single-party totalitarian system would have involved.

The "price of union," in Herbert Agar's phrase, has nonetheless had to be paid. That price has been the series of compromises with both political principle and doctrinal symmetry which have made American history the despair of the ideologists, and also of observers who have tried to see them in the image of the European doctrinal parties. It has also been at least a partial surrender of the heritage of the Founding Fathers to those whom Gerald Johnson has called the "Founding Uncles"—the masters and manipulators of machine politics. Although they are regarded as the black sheep of the family and are always linked with "partisan" politics, their actual role has been to temper the sharpness of conflict which, with more doctrinally committed men, could have proved intolerable. The party system has thus channeled the emotional and polemic energies that have struggled for mastery of the nation's destiny; it has—with the great exception of the Civil War—made it possible to avoid outright violence in the transfer of power from one majority to another. Viewing American history from the angle of parties, one might even say that the Civil War became inevitable when the party system broke down and when the Democratic party, which had still held the sections together loosely, was split in two.

One thing should be added about the party boss and his machine.* They too have not been immune to the changes that have swept American society. These changes—the ending of the big flow of immigration, the shift in class lines, the sustained pitch of prosperity, the emergence of the welfare state, the mobility of population, the rise of TV as the principal mode of reaching the voters—have played havoc with the textbook and newspaper cartoon figure of the boss. The old-time boss, who was gruffly illiterate, who used strong-arm methods, who recruited his stalwarts from the docks and saloons, who got his share of the gravy of city contracts, who took care of trouble in the families of his constitutents and sent them Christmas baskets, has given way to a very different kind of figure. One need only cite as examples the current or recent figures of David Lawrence of Pittsburgh, Carmine De

* For a discussion of the boss and machine in the context of urban culture, see Ch. III, Sec. 9, "City Lights and Shadows."

Sapio of New York City, James A. Finnegan of Philadelphia, and Jake Arvey and Richard Daley of Chicago, to get a flavor of the change. The new boss is likely to be highly literate; he still has a feel for tight-knit organization but has learned the methods of using surveys and polls before making any important moves; he works closely with the network of Washington agencies; he is still responsive to the needs and outlook of the minority ethnic groups which form the core of his voters, but he talks in terms of public welfare and often of national issues; on the floor of the national conventions he is interviewed on TV and delights in the image he presents as a kingmaker; rarely any longer does he reach out for some stumblebum to put into office as a front for his machine: he is far more likely to pick a liberal candidate with prestige, intellect, and glamour for the large mass of voters; while he gives this candidate a chance at office and power, the candidate in turn gives him respectability and the feeling of taking part in a meaningful political movement.

I do not mean to prettify the darker elements of the picture of political power and acquisitiveness. One can still find the alliance between the political and criminal underworlds which is part of the pathology of American life. In almost any sizable American city one can start with the gambling syndicates, the bookies, the slot machines, and the "numbers racket," and draw a line to the police and administrative officials with the reasonable expectation that somewhere along the line "protection money" will be flowing freely. On the Federal level one can start with the officials awarding public-works and defense contracts, or administering the tax laws or some phase of business regulation, and draw a line to substantial corporations and "fly-by-night" firms, and somewhere along the line one will find "kick-backs," "influence peddling," and those "conflicts of interest" which arise when a government official also has a stake in a particular business firm and its profits. Any political party long in power becomes slack in its moral standards. Any political party long out of power becomes hungry for the fleshpots. Often party lines are wholly erased, and the political machine in power "cuts in" the mercenaries of the political machine out of power.

While Americans continue to denounce corruption, they also continue to practice it. It must be obvious that such features of American life as the "fix," the "shakedown," "protection," the "pay-off," and the "racket" go deeper than the nature of local politics itself. They express a moral slackness not limited to politics but reaching into business and labor and the operative codes of what you can "get by with." The role of the local party system in this pattern is clear: by creating what Elihu Root called an "invisible government" behind the formal one, and a class of political hangers-on who live in the twilight world between the lawful and the lawless, it makes the moral breakdown easier and institutionalizes the gap between profession and behavior.

The scar left on American life by this corruption is not a negligible one. It is one of the factors that contribute to the recurring moods of political despair. The gap between the moral rhetoric of American life and the periodic revelations of what actually happens in politics and business is enough finally to desensitize the citizen and produce in him a despair of ever getting any reform accomplished. This despair leads the voter, however mistakenly, to lump the minor frailties of a "reform" candidate with the major larcenies and treacheries of the boss-dictated machine nominee. It is one of the facts of American political life that local reform administrations are rarely sustained, and that the waves of new political resolve which periodically sweep over the American conscience somehow get dissipated, leaving behind only echoes of the surge and thunder of the reformers.

A balanced picture of the local political organizations would take account of the corruption, the alternations of reform and despair, the residues of the old ethnic "machines," and the emergence of a new type of boss or "leader" who could better be described as a "manager," since he has become part of the new technical forces that organize so many sectors of American life. The drive for power is a crucial element in the motivation of these managers, but there are others as well: personal ambition, the hunger for prestige and respectability, the pull and excitement of the political "game," the eagerness for community standing on the part of members of ethnic minorities who can find such standing only in politics, the desire to be associated with the national party leaders and to appear in public with the great men on their campaign visits. This is a medley of motivations, at once petty and powerful, but one must take account of all of them or run the danger of simplifying one of the complex facts of American life.

The role of the party system is no slight achievement. What it seems is that American parties should be viewed not so much in terms of the grandeurs of statesmanship or the miseries of corrupt political machines, as of the moderating and mediating brokerage role which for better or worse both Presidents and machine bosses perform. They are brokers between the shifting desires and pressure intensities of the diverse opinion blocs that make up the "public," and the twists and turns of action by the men and agencies that make up the "government."

The brokerage function of the party system does not diminish the role of "public opinion" in America but serves to define its important place in politics. Americans are as torn in their attitude toward "public opinion" as they are toward most of their shibboleths: they both defy and despise it. They think of it mystically as a "brooding Omnipresence in the sky" which somehow decides on a shifting variety of "issues," and whose decisions are as final and as divinely inspired as the Ark of the Covenant. They are repeatedly told that "public opinion" requires this or that course of action. But it has often turned out that the "opinion" thus invoked is either a protective mantle for the interests of a small minority, or a passionate majority hatred, or an idea with which a large number of the people are obsessed. Following in the track of Graham Wallas, Walter Lippmann wrote at the beginning of the 1920s the classic American analysis of "public opinion" as a bundle of emotional stereotypes, deeply irrational and unverified, which have often been the creation of the very editors and political spokesmen who have invoked them. As a result, some Americans find themselves fitfully scorning the deity with feet of clay at whose shrine other Americans worship.

This double projection is reflected in the attitude toward the public-opinion polls, the sample tests taken of popular attitudes on political and social issues of the day. For a time Americans followed their ups and downs like anxious relatives watching the fever chart at the bedside of the patient, trusting it as a reliable and even infallible guide. But critical voices were raised to point out that this continued pulse-taking was not only treacherous but in itself symptomatic. The failure of the pollsters to predict the outcome of the 1948 Presidential election, when Dewey snatched defeat from the jaws of victory and Truman found himself elected although he was the only man who believed he would be, marked the turning point of popular disillusionment about polling. Yet even the disillusionment was focused on the wrong aspects of the polls— on the statistical percentage of error which might make them unreliable in a close election, rather than on the impossibility of reducing to count and measure in advance so complex and emotionally intricate an entity as a people's feeling about its own tangled problems and institutions.

The polls are important, however, as a sign of increasing mechanization in the process of political choice in America. This mechanization, which has transformed other areas of American life, has affected Presidential elections as well. While the local campaign oratory and the whistle-stop tours still linger and retain a real function, there is a widespread feeling that they are archaic survivals from a past that will never be retrieved. The press association wires, and more recently the radio and TV, have made political campaigning a massive, large-scale affair which is directed from the center and through which all parts of the nation are reached instantaneously. The appeals of the candidates get to the most remote areas, and the responses are checked and charted on a week-to-week graph by the "pollsters," whose fortunes rise and fall with the degree of accuracy of their predictions. This mechanizing process tends to reduce the voter to an item in a statistical calculation, and a digit in a vast radio or TV audience.

As part of the same process, elections have tended to become more and more like a business sales campaign, with the voter playing the role of a potential buyer to whom a commodity must be "sold." At this point, politics merges with the larger arts of salesmanship, packaging, and publicity. The history of American Presidential elections can be partly written as the history of slogans which expressed the felt needs of the time and jibed exactly with the mood of a particular moment. It is not that the slogans themselves, in their repetition, won or lost the elections, but that they were symbols for the interests and emotions which did. The campaign planners chart out their strategy much as they might chart a national sales campaign for their commodity. In both cases they call in the aid of the crack advertising agencies and public-relations firms. And as they test the effects of each tactic on the fever chart of the poll samplings, they shift emphasis and slogans, thus finding new wrappers in which to package the commodity they are seeking to sell to the voter.

What is most dangerous about this mechanization of politics is that it threatens to dehumanize the political process itself, which is at heart a human process. When the American corporation sells its product to a mass audience, using radio and television to capture attention, its great fear is that the program may alienate potential buyers in some ethnic, religious, or sectional group. Something of that sort happens in political campaigns. A smart candidate will evade any issue which might bring him into head-on conflict with a sizable organized group of voters. Since there are few issues that are "safe" in this sense, the trend is for the campaigner to speak in blurred generalities, except when he is appealing to a specific voting bloc or interest group and bidding for their support against his rival. The mechanization of the voter ends up in the dehydration of the candidate and of the issues.

I have described these trends toward mechanization as forcibly as possible, yet I do not believe that they will prevail and occupy the whole field, or even that they represent the larger truth about American electoral choice. It is a mistake to overemphasize the theme of mechanism in American politics. It is dangerous to assume that the American voter is a puppet, either propelled by drives of class and group interest or manipulated by professional politicians and public-relations experts. In addition to this mechanistic fallacy, as it may be called, there is a parallel tendency to depict American political parties as monstrously efficient autonomous machines, giant Tweedledums and Tweedledees which operate apart from the voters, using them cynically every four years but themselves beyond capture and control. Both these fallacies underrate the common run of American as a willing and valuing human being. They make him a passive entity, a globule who is acted upon but never acts, who is chosen but never chooses, who is led but does not shape his leadership, who is counted but does not confound his counters.

This conception of the voter is especially dear to those who find his changing behavior baffling and fear to face the fact of genuine differences between the political parties on the issues of great moment, and who therefore prefer the picture of puppets easily manipulated. One might point out that if the politicians manipulate the voters, the voters also manipulate their politicians by casting the political leader relentlessly in the role they want him to play and making a candidate a symbol of their feelings and drives regardless of how he may himself feel. In every election the leader catches the contagion of his followers just as surely as they catch his. If the voters are sometimes manipulated men, the leaders are often driven men.

But the strains of irrationalism may themselves be overstated. The fact is that, however irrational the stereotypes by which the herd does its herd thinking, politics for Americans is not only a puppet show. To some extent it is a question of whether they will have jobs or be unemployed, whether they will be able to survive as small businessmen, what they will get in their pay envelopes or for their farm products, what will happen to their unions, what will be the destiny of their kin in countries abroad, whether there will be peace or war for their sons and husbands, what measure of civil rights they will achieve and to what extent their freedoms of speech, thought, and religious worship will be protected.

Thus the image of cigar-smoking politicians sitting in a smoke-filled room, deciding the destinies of the parties and the nation, is not adequate for American politics. It is not even adequate for the party conventions that nominate the candidates. It is true that state conventions do designate the party's choice for Senators and Congressmen, and for governor and other state offices, are often (although by no means always) rubber-stamp affairs which confirm decisions already reached by the party managers. But a national convention is something very different. There are rarely any managers who can control the national party: the chairman of the National Committee is likely to be a technician, usually chosen by the titular party leader and filling a caretaker role between conventions; his value to the party is imperiled if he identifies himself too closely with any one candidate or segment of the party before the convention has made its choice. The convention itself turns into a battle between rival party "wings" and between the rival candidates for nomination, their managers, and the heads of the already committed state delegations. It is a battle whose initial skirmishes are fought in state primaries and party huddles long before the convention assembles; its techniques are usually those of making exaggerated claims of the candidate's strength, appeal, and prospects and minimizing those of his rivals; its tactics are intricate, devious, and so often carried on through commitments and "deals" behind the scenes that the TV audience (which has become an immense one in recent years) often misses the decisive elements of the battle while focusing on the overt drama of the speeches from the rostrum and the demonstrations from the floor; its final outcome may not be known for certain until a close roll call, when the delegations have already been polled but ask at the end to change their votes, either to nose out a victory at the finish line or to "get on the band wagon" when victory for one candidate seems inevitable.

There has been a movement to abandon the convention because it lends itself to manipulation by the managers and to shift the choice of candidates to state primaries which will be binding on the delegations. But I doubt whether this either will or should take place. The people would be denied the crucial thing about a national party convention: the fact that it is often genuinely an arena, although sometimes only a fake one; that it is in a sense a preliminary nation-wide election held inside the party, in which national rather than local issues can be canvassed, and the candidates can have an intense light focused on their personalities, their skill and maneuver, their candor or cunning of character, and their capacity to express the surging emotions of the time and therefore to attract votes. Manipulation does not always work. It often happens that a candidate for the party nomination will come to the convention with a number of state delegations safely sewed up, perhaps with a plurality of delegates, yet lose the nomination because the consensus of the delegates is that he cannot win the election. It also happens, as with the Republican nomination of Lincoln in 1860 and of Wendell Willkie in 1940, that several rival candidates are in deadlock and the convention decides on a third who had not been in the running ("dark horse") because the delegates hope that the qualities which give him a fresh appeal to them may appeal to the voters as well.

I do not say that politics in America is in any sense deeply ideological. It is differentiated from European politics exactly by its nonideological quality. There has always been an organic optimism in American society which Europe today lacks and which communicates itself to the party system. Equally, the lack of rigidity within the American social system is paralleled by a lack of rigidity within the party system. Just as America remains a relatively open society, so it contains a relatively open party system. The difference between Democrats and Republicans, while it is more than the difference between Tweedledum and Tweedledee, is not such as to split the society itself or invite civil conflict. The Democrats move, at most, toward a welfare state: the Republicans

try to minimize some of the trends toward state power which the Democrats accept; yet the idea of welfare democracy has been so strongly established since the New Deal that it would be a reckless party or candidate who would now dare repudiate it. The choices between the two
are usually substantial choices but not desperate ones. There is vituperation which runs rampant during American Presidential elections, and
there is a constant stream of criticism of the Administration which may
seem to most Europeans to verge on violence. Yet the violence is wholly
verbal, and the vituperation is likely to be personal rather than ideological. Because there is an atmosphere of economic and social hope, the
American voter still feels that he can make his choices.

These choices are not between dogmas or doctrines. They are mainly
the choices between particular men, who are the symbols of a political
direction more or less clearly discerned. The program itself—despite
"party platforms" and "planks"—is less important than the personal
symbol. That is why, especially in the back country regions of America,
candidates make their appeal to the voters in a histrionic fashion. It
is not unusual, in the Deep South or in Texas or in the mountain or
Pacific states, for a candidate to campaign by dressing up in costume,
with a familiar symbol of red suspenders or a coonskin cap or with the
help of a hillbilly band. It is truer of Americans than of others that
they can afford this kind of happy-go-lucky cynicism. They can afford
to take politics less seriously than those peoples who live closer to the
margin of survival. Yet, as I have suggested, one can easily be misled by
this surface tomfoolery. American politics are a politics of ingrained
attitude rather than of doctrine, yet the attitudes are based on a clear
sense of interest and on social realities.

Since these social realities have been transformed by the currents of
change in the past quarter century the party system has also been transformed. Utopians of the Left and Right on the margin of both major
parties have long yearned either for some new and gleaming third party
that would clear up all the confusions or for a realignment of elements
within the two parties that would make one of them clearly "liberal"
and the other clearly "conservative." Yet this has not happened nor is
it likely to. Instead there have been political changes in both parties
and in Congress that have left party lines as blurred as ever but, as
Lubell has shown, more *nationalized* and more responsive to the deep
social changes in American life and culture.

In the earlier pages I have discussed some of these changes, and in the
pages to follow I shall deal with others. Among the most notable are
what has happened to the city and the suburbs, to the ethnic and religious groups in America, to labor, to the middle classes, and to class

mobility, to the internal population migrations, to the rural areas and the small towns, to the thinking of Americans on war and cold war and on world power and civil liberties. Party politics are the most sensitive barometer of the changes taking place in the mood and thinking of Americans. It would be surprising if American party politics had not registered these far-reaching changes by a party transformation which —while its evidences are more or less hidden—is as real as the suburban revolution or the technological one.

We must remember that the party system is more than an organization for power and spoils. It is an arena in which not only sectional and regional differences but also ethnic, religious, and class forces converge and battle it out. Traditionally the sectional divisions have thrown the "Solid South" into the Democratic column, while New England and the Middle West have been considered safely Republican. The ethnic vote generally found the Irish and (after the Smith candidacy of 1928) the Italian Catholics in the Democratic party, while the Midwestern Germans and Scandinavians and the Northern Negroes were in the Republican party. Recent events have changed the picture. With the New Deal the Negroes became more identified with the Democrats, as did the Jews (later both, especially the Negroes, began to swing back). The migration of Negroes from the South to the Northern cities opened them to the fluctuations of prosperity and depression, made them more sensitive to the struggle for civil rights, as well as placing them in a position to do something about it through their votes. In the cities they and other migrants from the farms and hills of the South and Midwest found themselves allied with second- and third-generation immigrants whose families had come from Europe before the gates were closed and settled down mainly in the big cities. The double movement of migration to the cities—from abroad and from within the nation—created the material for an ethnically conscious urban population.

It was Franklin Roosevelt's success in mustering these minority groups within the Democratic party under the big city machines, and allying them with labor, the Solid South, and to some extent the farmers, that produced the Great Coalition on which the Democrats relied for two decades. The Democratic leaders were more alert to the mood and needs of these groups and offered them greater hospitality than the Republicans. But there was a deeper reason for their success: these city groups were largely of the working class and the lower middle class, open to the ravages of unemployment, dependent upon government action to protect their interests, ready material for arguments on behalf of the welfare state. The Great Depression, by precipitating trends inherent in American politics even before Roosevelt, led to the Great Coalition.

More complex was the role of the suburbs and the new middle class in the party revolution. The movement from farm and small town to city was accompanied (as we have seen) by the movement from city to suburb. With mounting prosperity and living standards the children and grandchildren of the immigrants left the cities in search of a better life and a better social status. The new middle class, settling in the suburbs, was drawn largely from the ethnic groups that were part of the New Deal coalition. In some cases they changed their politics along with their mode of life, despite Adlai Stevenson's injunction to "vote Democrat so that you can live like Republicans." But, while the meaning of the voting shifts in the suburbs is still under study, the chances are that a number of newer suburban dwellers retained their political allegiance even with their new mode of life, so that the traditional Republican strength of the older suburbs was infiltrated by the Democratic newcomers.

The role of the middle class proved to be a very different one in the case of the South, where the course of industrialization brought a new strain of white-collar, small-business, and "organization-man" thinking into what had once been solidly sectional. For the South this middle class was an almost wholly new phenomenon, with values much more closely related to the thinking of the corporate bureaucracy and its satellites throughout the country than to the more strictly Southern concerns. Hence a new Republican strain in the South, especially in states like Florida, Texas, Virginia, and Georgia, which took the lead in industrialization. The trend toward a two-party South was unmistakable, and by the mid-1950s the Southern cities were almost on a two-party basis; yet the rural areas were still overwhelmingly Democratic, and there was still some doubt as to whether and when the South would achieve a two-party system. There could be little doubt that the once solid South would in time become a two-party South. To be sure, industrialism also brought with it a new population of industrial workers, who would normally share the Democratic preference of the trade-unions. But the drive for trade-union organization in the South lagged badly behind the new middle-class consciousness.

The role of labor and the farmer in party politics underwent changes throughout the nation. As the industrial workers grew more confident of their place in American life, and as they won most of their objectives in wages and union security, their political militancy tended to fade. While the leaders of the new labor federation were still generally part of the Democratic coalition, they knew they could not count on a solid political support from the trade-union members. The 1952 Eisenhower victory, which would have been impossible if the Republicans had not cut substantially into the labor vote, was proof that American workers do not vote wholly along class lines. But the obverse has happened in the last decade to American farmers. The farm price support program, inaugurated by the New Deal, caused normally Republican farm areas in Iowa or Minnesota to vote Democratic in several elections from 1936 through 1948. Even the traditional isolationism of the German and Scandinavian ethnic groups among the farmers (these groups usually vote on issues of war, peace, and foreign policy) could not reverse this trend. The farmer tended to vote his crops, his crop prices, and his crop parity supports as he had been doing for some time, and the vote might easily go to either party, depending on its promises and performance; but the normal tendency of the rural areas still remained Republican: they are conservative chiefly because most of the other welfare-state issues, except for the issue of farm subsidies, grow out of urban and suburban needs and outlook.

Even with a declining farm population and a lesser role for the farmer in the economy, there is no more important cleavage in American politics than the split between the rural and city forces. This is true in state even more than in national politics, as witness New York, Ohio, Wisconsin, Illinois, and Indiana, where the city-farm split reflects the division between the two major parties. Within many state governments a similar city-farm division is reflected in the tug of war between the governor and the legislature. The strength of the farm groups clearly does not lie in their numbers as voters but in their strangle hold on the legislatures, both state and national, which they retain through the failure to redraw Congressional district lines, through the seniority rule on Congressional committees, and through the "county unit" rule in a number of states where small rural population units are counted equal with heavy urban concentrations. The more than 70 per cent of Americans classified as urban pay well over 90 per cent of the taxes and elect only 20 per cent of the representatives to state legislatures. It follows that overrepresentation of the rural and small-town areas means underrepresentation of the city groups, including the racial and religious minorities and the worker and middle-class groups. It will usually be found that the divisions in Congress between the rural and the urban states or districts have more impact on the Congressional votes than the party divisions themselves.

It has been suggested, notably by Lubell, that the fluctuations of party fortunes are cyclical rather than immediate. Certainly the history of American Presidential elections would seem to bear this out, as witness the long tenure of the Republicans from Lincoln through Hoover, with the sole Democratic interruptions by Cleveland and Wilson; similarly one could trace a Democratic cycle from 1932 to 1952, broken by the Eisenhower victory. To speak of a cyclical swing is to restate the idea that party politics respond to long-range changes inside the society and the culture. But where these changes are as tangled and cross-grained as they have recently been in American life, each of the major parties is bound to be affected by them within itself. The partnership of the race-conscious South and the minority-conscious big cities is bound to be an uneasy one, although probably not an impossible one for the Democrats to maintain. Even within the ethnic minorities the political ties are often difficult to sustain: there is friction between Catholics and Jews inside the Democratic party, as indeed there is friction in a few big-city machines between the Irish and Italian political leaders. The cold war has further split the political unity of the Catholics, a number of whom have responded to Republican attacks upon the "softness" of Democratic administrations both in foreign policy and in domestic "security" and "loyalty" cases. As for the Republicans, they too have suffered serious internal splits. On the one hand there are the Eastern and big-city Republicans who feel that the best conservatism is that of consolidating the gains made by the welfare state without letting them get out of hand and become revolutionary in a destructive way. On the other hand there are the Republicans of the Midwestern power centers who are convinced that voters wanting a welfare state will vote Democratic rather than Republican, and who therefore move toward a more drastic conservative position.

Given these party shifts and internal strains, it seems academic for American political thinkers to call for stronger discipline inside the parties. This internal battle will inevitably be fought out because it is only a reflection of the deep clash of forces outside both parties, within the social system. One can speak of party discipline on some particular issue, up to the point where the issue becomes so important that it will break the party before it is itself broken. The way of politicians on such matters is to avoid both discipline and conflict and avert disaster by evading the whole issue, at least outwardly. This is a solution of a sort, but it is scarcely consistent with either ideological clarity or any meaningful party discipline. How the party strategists handle such problems as those of Southern consciousness and Negro rights, or those of Catholic and Jewish consciousness, may prove the decisive difference between party victory and defeat. Obviously any sizable minority which feels strongly enough its sectional or religious or ethnic interests becomes a balance-of-power group, staying as long as possible away from party commitments, knowing its strength and determined to exact concessions through that strength.

To add to the complexity of the picture, there has been increasing talk of the "independent" vote and a growing tendency of both parties to appeal to this vote by speaking in "moderate" language. It may have been the vote of the sizable group of voters uncommitted to either of the two major parties that threw the pollsters into confusion in 1948. Certainly it is the independent voter, once called "Mugwump," who keeps the party system from becoming rigidified and maintains the margin of free choice within it which makes it a living instrument. He prides himself on the mobility of his allegiance and on the fact that he cannot be taken for granted. It gives him the virtuous feeling of being outside the political machine, above the muck and corruption of party politics, committed to principle rather than to party. Yet it is still unclear whether the strength of this "independent" bloc will increase or diminish.

Instead of speaking of a big bloc of uncommitted voters outside the parties, it is more relevant to speak of shifting groups of voters inside the parties who are inclined to abandon them on one issue or another but will probably return when the issue is no longer a strong one. In practice the appeal to the growing number of these voters has meant at once a sharper appeal to the voting blocs cutting across the parties and an emphasis on the personality of the candidate. Eisenhower was able to win in 1952 and 1956 because he expressed the vague feelings of many voters who were caught between the parties and who responded to his earnest contention that he was a "dynamic conservative" or a "conservative progressive," a mixture of terms which meant that he preferred not to make a choice between more clear-cut sets of political principles.

This looseness has its limitations. William Allen White contended that there were four parties in America—the Liberal Republicans, the Tory Republicans, the Bryan and (later) New Deal Democrats, and the Southern Democrats. In Hoover's Administration the "sons of the wild jackass" led a Republican revolt which embarrassed the main body of conservative strength within the party. Under the Roosevelt and Truman administrations the President has had to contend with an adverse coalition of Republicans and Tory Democrats which played hob with Administration programs. Since Congress is organized on the committee system, where the shift of one member to the opposing side can make the decisive difference, this hostile coalition made the whole domestic program of the Fair Deal an ineffectual one. Hence the tendency among American political thinkers to emphasize the need for internal party discipline if the party is to maintain its identity. The problem, as throughout politics, is to find the balance between the "iron law of oligarchy" which makes all structures too rigid internally and the anarchic tendencies which make it difficult to hold any structure together for any length of time. For the present the American party system suffers more severely from anarchy than from rigidity. Yet over the decades it has managed to perform its function of canalizing without violence the energies and loyalties of Americans of diverse national origins, and of achieving a measure of political unity without imprinting on it the totalitarian stamp.

The idea of a two-party system is more crucial to keep alive now, when it is being challenged by single-party totalitarianisms, than it has ever been. Both the major parties in American politics owed their origins to movements of popular radicalism—the Democratic party having been firmly established by the Jacksonian revolution on the Jeffersonian cadre, and the Republican party having come to birth out of the anti-slavery libertarianism and free-land equalitarianism of the 1850s. The history of third party movements in America is the history of lost causes, some of whose energy, ideas, and programs were eventually absorbed by the major parties. Third parties, when they have been dangerous enough, have caused the major parties to shift their position. But to be wholly successful, a third party has had to displace the weaker of the major parties and become itself a second party. This happened when the Whigs replaced the Federalists, when the Democrats replaced the Democratic-Republicans, and when the Republicans replaced the Whigs. But in the case of the Populists, the Progressive party of La Follette, and the Socialists, the typical experience has been that of an open larceny of their platforms by the existing party system. Each of the major parties in turn is full of contradictions; but of the two, the Republicans still present a more nearly consistent adherence to business and corporate views, while the Democrats more nearly express the aspirations of the classes and minorities still struggling to find their place in the sun.

While party lines are shifting and will continue to shift, they are unlikely to add up to any drastic party realignment, least of all to the emergence of a new party like the British Labor party, with a new class base. The American parties will continue to absorb new energies and new points of view while remaining a two-party system. The line of party growth in the calculable future may possibly involve the absorption by the Republicans of a number of Democratic conservatives, and by the Democrats of Republican liberals. Yet the stronger signs point to the ever-growing strength of labor political action within the Democratic party, the fashioning of a sharper philosophy and strategy of planning and socialization, the continued absorption of a philosophy of welfare action by the Republicans, and the organization of the economically and politically lagging South. The long-term trend seems to be a consistent, if hesitant and intermittent, movement of both parties further toward the liberal direction—unless a war catastrophe changes the whole national as well as party picture.

5. Power and Equilibrium

I HAVE SPOKEN of the Presidency as the force that shapes the national mood and direction, and of the party as the frame that holds the polity together and keeps it functioning. But the central fact of any political system is power, and its gravest danger is that the contending power pressures will disrupt it by their intensity, or else dominate it if they become too concentrated. How has the American system met this problem? And how has it dealt with the related problem of the division of power between the central government and the states, between power at the center and power at the rim?

Power in America cannot be understood by looking only at the governmental structure. American historians and social thinkers have sometimes overvalued and sometimes undervalued the role of political power in the American story, depending on their own angle of vision and their theory of history and human nature. The conservatives, secure in their economic power, have stressed the dangers of the political. The liberals have inveighed against economic power, while counting on the political most heavily for modes of change and reform. The radicals have stressed economic power because of their class approach to history, while (as shown in the case of Veblen and Beard) they have grossly undervalued political power and its use as an instrument for change.

Mostly, however, the run-of-the-mill American has shown a healthy concern for all phases of power: as a practical matter he has pursued purchasing power, admiring intensely its accumulation in the hands of the rich. While focusing his political interest on the Presidency as the core and symbol of the government, he has been wary of the Federal power and its administrative arm as too complicated for the mind to grasp. He has been suspicious of trade-union power and church power even more than of corporate power, and suspicious also of military power—at least until the period of the world wars and cold wars.

Recent American history has witnessed important changes in the distribution of power. There has been a shift from Congressional to Presidential and administrative power, a shift from formal policy-making to budget-making power which often has carried policy-making with it, a shift from local and state power to Federal power. Similarly there has been a shift of power from the churches, the universities, and the lawyers to the Big Press and the opinion industries, from the farmers and small-industry groups to the big corporate industries, from the owners to the managers of industry, from civilians to the military.

The fact about American power, as about so many other phases of

American life, is that it is plural and fluid. It is many-faceted rather than uniform; it is dispersed among a number of groups; it has shifted geographically and in its class distribution. There has been, to be sure, a steady movement toward concentration in every form of power. Yet the agencies of power have multiplied, as witness the growing distribution of economic power among the corporation, the trade-union, and the government.

Since the beginning of the nation the whole American atmosphere has been saturated with power—technological, economic, political, religious, military, financial. From the cop and the precinct boss to the foreman and trade-union leader and corporate executive, from sergeant to general, from bureau clerk to President, the sense of power has been pervasive in the American experience, and the sense of the limits of power has also been constantly present. In contrast with aristocratic or military societies, America has had no elite groups of birth or status trained to the exercise of power. There has been enough diffusion to give the nation as a whole the chance to revel in the feeling of abundant power. The Americans as a nation have been relatively parvenus in its use and have therefore distrusted its users, but what is remarkable is that this nation of parvenus has not carried the abuse of power further than it has.

The reason may perhaps be found in a distinction drawn by Santayana between *power* as a generative force and *domination* as a frustrating and destructive one. The atmosphere in which American life has developed has been one of a continued expansiveness which has kept America relatively free of the frustrations of power that more constricted cultures have incurred. This offers a clue to the fact that while there has often been corruption in American political life, there has never been a serious attempt at dictatorship. The dangers of tyranny are greatest in a society where power has never been widely diffused. As Santayana again points out, in a comment on Lord Acton's great epigram on power, only those unaccustomed to power are corrupted by it. While Santayana means it to be an argument for aristocratic societies and against popular democracies, it has actually worked differently in America, where the corruption is likely to be in the lure of the Big Money rather than of absolute political power.

This raises the question of what De Tocqueville stressed and Aristotle foresaw long before him—the dangers of a majority tyranny on the one hand and on the other the servility of the democratic mob to a demagogue-dictator. As one of the great innovations of world history, majority rule powerfully attracted De Tocqueville and other commentators to the American experiment while it raised in their minds profound doubts and fears. These doubts and fears have a real base, as shown by the popular hysterias that have swept over American opinion. Yet the power of the demagogue-dictator has worked itself out to a grim sequel not in America, where mob rule had been most anticipated and feared, but in Germany, Italy, Russia, China, and the "People's democracies" of eastern Europe.

What was wrong with the calculations of the fearers and predictors? Partly they failed to reckon with the strength of the constitutional tradition, but mainly they failed to take into account the pluralist character of power in America—its many loci, its widespread diffusion in one form or another, the heterogeneous quality of American society, and the talent for equilibrium it has shown.

The tyranny of the mob is a very real tyranny. It shows itself notably in America in periods after wars, when tensions have come to the breaking point, and on the brink of war, when the cult of the nation-state gives an opportunity to the loyalty hunters and the professional accusers. Yet it would be hard to point to any period in American history and say, "Here is where the majority ran riot in America and trampled upon freedom."* A close student of American power is more apt to study not the majority but the minorities—the lobbies, the pressure groups, the sectional interests, the corporate and trade-union leaders, the heads of the Congressional investigations. Even in the case of the loyalty hunts and the search for "subversives," the effective stimulus has not been majority hysteria but a cold campaign by pressure groups in the hunt for some particular quarry. A new feature on the landscape of American power is the "veto group," which pretends to act in the name of the majority but actually terrorizes it.

To understand the American pressure groups, one must understand that to move a huge and unwieldy mass, such as the American leviathan, you have to push very hard. The strength and variety of these pressure groups, the brazenness of their lobbyists, the vast sums they have spent on propaganda, their use of techniques as diverse as the corruption of government officials on the one hand and large-scale direct mailing on the other hand: these have often been described. The number of registered lobbyists in Washington, not taking account of those who operate under cover, exceeds the number of Congressmen. They are paid more than the President and the Supreme Court justices, and they have the big money at their disposal. There is little doubt that they influence legislation, in many cases help draft the laws; they are especially active in a war economy where big contracts are at stake; they

---

* For further discussion of this theme, see Sec. 10 of this chapter, "The Struggle for Civil Liberties"; also Ch. IX, Sec. 4, "Varieties of American Character."

often succeed in reaching and sometimes even supplying strategic members of the government.

The political theorists of the early twentieth century, including some Americans, used to write a good deal about guilds and hanker for a society in which a network of them would hold the power and perform the functions of government. In a sense there is a network of American pressure groups—from the farm bloc, the trade-unions, the churches militant, the ethnic groups and the patriotic societies down to protective associations for birds and historic shrines—that form a kind of *guildism* in American life. Sometimes they are merely a nuisance with which Congressmen and bureaucrats have learned to deal, sometimes they represent permanent group interests which they do not allow the legislators and administrators to forget. Always they express the individual's sense that he is powerless alone in so huge a society and must therefore band with others to exert pressure; they also express the principle of the right of free association gone berserk. Alongside this guildism there is also what has been called a *clientelism* that has developed in America, meaning that when a man has some particular interest at stake and wants to exert his power to protect or advance it, he turns as a client to a professional influence technician who knows—for a fee or a percentage—how to get what, where, when, and from whom.

I doubt whether any of these—interest groups, pressure groups or veto groups, guildism or clientelism, lobbyists or per-centers—will undermine the American Republic. Just as the tyranny of the majority in American life has been overrated, so also more recently has the destructiveness of minorities. Both have been facets of the effort to balance the principle of popular sovereignty with the fact of a richly diverse and pluralistic society. America's enemies nourished the hope of a nation so fragmented that it would succumb to a concerted attack, whether by arms or propaganda. The hope has proved wrong. So have the fears of those who felt that it was ripe for tyranny.

One can read in American history, with all its travail, an impressive capacity for the balancing and accommodation of interests. This has worked out best in the problem of the powers of the nation and the states. The authors of *The Federalist,* who first grappled with the problem systematically, saw beyond the abstract question of the distribution of authority-in-the-members as against authority-at-the-center. For them, as for most of the delegates at the Constitutional Convention, the term "federalism" had the accent on the central power, whereas today it has the accent on the power of the members. For them it was not so much a problem of judicious balancing as it was one of political survival itself.

They had to settle first the question of whether there would be a unified nation, and then the practical political question of whether they dared dispense with the states. The answer to the first was that a nation was a necessity, to the second that the states had to be retained. From that point on it was a question of the means of working out a dual system. It must be said for the framers of the Constitution that they contrived intricate but effective means. It was in the same pragmatic spirit that the great names in the history of federalist thinking worked —Justices Marshall, Taney, and Waite Presidents Lincoln and Franklin Roosevelt.

For the moving force behind the increasing centralism of power in America one must, of course, look to the expanding technology. In 1787, while the Constitutional Convention was in session in Philadelphia, its members are said to have watched a demonstration of John Fitch's steamboat on the Delaware. The symbolism seems ironic, yet the constitutional framers had a strong enough feel for the realities of power to provide a framework even for the steamboat and its latter-day tribe of children. The same forces that led to welfare-state controls, and to the gigantism both of business and labor, led by the same logic to a steady growth in governmental centralism—"federalism" in the sense in which Hamilton and Madison used it. There is a peculiar futility in inveighing against only one of the leviathans of American life—that of government—without recognizing that it has come into being to balance the other leviathans.

There is a curious tenacity in the fallacy which sees the states as the champions of individual liberties and the United States as their enemy. The States' Rights doctrine has had a number of diverse champions: the Jeffersonians, the Federalists at the time of the Hartford Convention, the Southern Democrats, the Republicans who feared national social legislation. It was used by both the White Supremacy and the corporate groups to maintain an area of immunity from Federal control and keep the political power in the hands of state and local units, which are more amenable to pressures. This was the tactic employed in the struggle over the offshore submerged ("tidelands") oil deposits, which the Supreme Court held to be the property of the Federal government but which Congress by special legislation handed over to the states in 1953. Sometimes a "No Man's Land," in Franklin Roosevelt's phrase, has been created in between the unexercised state power and the forbidden Federal power. In general the appeal to States' Rights has been made whenever it was to the advantage of any party, section, or group to make it, with little regard for doctrinal consistency.

There is, I grant, a strong argument in favor of power on the rim and against power at the center. It is one to which the modern generations, with their sense of loss and alienation from the soil, are particularly open. There are many evidences of the grass-roots virility which is celebrated in American political oratory and editorials. Yet a student of American thought must learn to be wary of a fetishism of the grass roots. Aside from the greater safety from gigantism that decentralized decision offers, there is no inner healing power within the local governmental units that is denied to the central ones. In fact, the local governments which impressed De Tocqueville had become by James Bryce's time so corrupt that he called them "the one conspicuous failure of the United States," while Andrew D. White wrote that "with very few exceptions, the city governments of the United States are the worst in Christendom—the most expensive, the most inefficient, and the most corrupt."

These comments on American city government were made before the turn of the century. Since then there have been successive waves of municipal reform, the crucial improvement coming through the application of the technical managerial approach to city government. Perhaps because the larger unit draws on better talent and gets greater public attention, it still remains true, however, that the quality of government is better on the national than on the state level, and better on the state than on the city and county level. Nor should it be forgotten that the local unit is more vulnerable to the nonpolitical forms of power which may seek to dominate it. Thus there are some American cities which are "owned" by an interlocking directorate of business interests —perhaps the railroad company, the insurance company, the banks, the newspapers, the radio station, the local mill or factory.*

But these are marginal and somewhat moralistic considerations. Since the Civil War the steady movement toward power at the center has come as a result of felt needs rather than reasoned preferences or logical doctrines. Lincoln found it necessary to assert the Federal government's power not only as against the seceded states but also as against the governors of the loyal ones, who tried to fight the war as the heads of autonomous little empires. With the growth of an industrial network cutting across state lines, Justice Waite asserted the power of Congress under the "commerce clause," which was an important instrument for effective control of interstate business. With the Great Depression the breakdown of local finances led to a system of direct Federal aid to local units which transformed the whole power gridiron. Finally, in both the world wars, the needs of military power and of the war economy played hob with the traditional lines between governmental units.

* For an earlier discussion of city government, see Ch. III, Sec. 9, "City Lights and Shadows."

The building of a new defense plant at Willow Run in World War II, for example, gave rise to a new community which cut across the various township and county authorities who could not cope with the new housing, health, schooling, and policing problems except under central direction.

Yet it is characteristic of the American temper that after each extension of the Federal power, a new equilibrium is struck at the higher level. Hence the "new federalism" of the present generation, which runs toward the return of power to the local units. On questions like flood control, the co-operation of states with Federal agencies has been hard to get. A number of states have entered into interstate compacts on the allocation of common water resources. The Supreme Court has asserted the power of Federal control over trade wars between states but has interpreted state powers broadly in most other cases, including restrictive "right to work" laws and loyalty tests. Competition between Federal, state, and local governments for the tax dollar has grown sharper every year. On the other hand, there has been a working agreement for co-operation between Federal and state agencies regulating corporate securities, power companies, and communication utilities. Even where the Federal power is complete, as in the case of wartime rationing and the military draft, care is taken to put the administrative tasks in the hands of local groups who know their neighbors. And in the case of the Tennessee Valley Authority the seminal principle has been developed of decentralizing administration even where power has had to be centralized.

The spirit of the new Federal-state equilibrium can perhaps be best expressed by paraphrasing Lincoln's classic theme: Does it follow that a governmental system centralized enough to escape fragmentation must be so centralized as to destroy the spirit of local initiative? The American answer has been No. Nor should one conclude from the trend toward centralized power in America that it has carried everything before it in its triumphant career. America is still a highly complex and unwieldy system of crisscrossing governmental lines, a little as if there were forty-eight nations carved out on the state level, along with twenty or thirty small ones within each state on the city level. In fact, F. J. Turner's comment on the operation of sectionalism—that it converted American internal history into a struggle between nations—is still largely true, but it goes beyond sectionalism to the whole distribution of power.

The debate on the question of power at the center as against power at the rim continues with considerable vigor among American observers mainly because there is still some leeway in the allocation of power, and in many legislative and administrative instances the choices are still open. Hence the appeal to history and to the logic of American government. In assessing this appeal there can be little question that there are built-in controls in the Constitution itself which favor state and local power and close the issue in many cases. For example, the role of the states in selecting the President, through the Electoral College or (if there is no majority) through the House voting in state units, cannot be ignored. Neither can the Senate's great role in legislation and foreign policy, which is also based on the equal representation of the states; nor the fact that states decide the qualifications of voters (hence the effective disfranchisement of Negroes in the South for generations) and also control Congressional districting within broad limits set by Congress (hence the overrepresentation of the rural areas). How strong is this drive of the political mechanism toward state power is shown by another fact: much of the function of judicial review has been to be vigilant about the constant intrusions of state action into the realm of the national government. In a number of areas, as in the management of land and water resources, the crisscrossing of a double Federal system of jurisdictions and agencies has led to a jungle of decisions which only the expert can penetrate.

There are obvious weaknesses in any system which places too much power either directly at the center or on the extreme rim. The American system has escaped the weakness of a highly centralized prefecture setup, as in France, but it has not wholly escaped the weakening influence of extreme local power. Wherever these local units have tried to take on important functions on their own, there has been an evident lack of skill, financial means, and local initiative, which has been one of the principal factors in the expansion of Federal power. At the municipality level the immense number of units (there are some 120,000 in the United States), their lack of an effective tax base, and their failure to get home rule in many instances have underscored the weakness of local initiative.

What has been developing instead is an intermediate layer of government, through which the states, bolstered by Federal funds, have assumed many local and even national functions. The national government, through technical aid, through financial grants and tax offsets made conditional upon the states' living up to certain standards, has in effect pushed the states into adopting welfare programs, school-building programs, employee merit systems, inheritance taxes, and road-construction projects. The result has been that the states have become vehicles of what conservatives might call "creeping Socialism" if it were not state action rather than Federal action that was involved. For example, in the mid-1950s they spent nearly $4 billion on health and welfare activities, which was almost twice as much as the expenditure of the national government.

In an era of world struggle the American federative principle has taken on a deeper meaning than ever in its history. I do not refer here to the easy parallelism between the situation that faced the Constitutional Fathers and the one that now faces the world leaders. I mean, rather, that each of the Great Powers recently on the world scene has had to grapple with its own Federal problem. The Germans did it badly at home, which may partly account for their failure in terms of empire. The British did it well in their empire since the Durham Report but did not apply the principle in time to their Asian and Middle East dependencies. Both the Russians and the Americans, today locked in mortal stuggle, have served an apprenticeship in the Federal principle—the Russians, under Lenin, in seeking to hold the Czarist power together after the Revolution, and the Americans as I have described above.

The capacity for Federal relationships may decide how successfully each of the two rival empires will be able to hold its forces together and associate new ones to them. After a successful use of the principle of national autonomy under Lenin, largely under the stress of compulsion in consolidating the Revolution and minimizing civil conflict, the Russians too easily allowed themselves to attempt a resolution of the Federal problem by the overrigid use of Communist party discipline as a tying device between the supposedly autonomous but actually satellite units. America has not made the same mistake at home. The reason may be that, except for the final power of decision in the Supreme Court between the conflicting claims of Federal and local governments, American federalism has few tying mechanisms. A number of tying devices have, however, been developed through the guild professionalism of the technicians who operate in the welfare areas. Thus health officials, engineers, social workers, agricultural workers, the forestry service, and others have cut across the various strata of governmental jurisdiction in attacking particular problems. The deepest strength of federalism lies thus in the habits of mind developed in the course of settling the practical problems of the distribution of authority.

Thus the pluralist, pragmatist, and federalist character of American politics has compelled it to develop the arts of compromise and to achieve an equilibrium of conflicting powers in motion. Yet the fact is that Americans did not always succeed in settling their conflicts of authority or escape disaster. At one point the frame of both federalism and the party system could not contain the tensions, and the result was a Civil War. To be sure, America was not alone in its tensions, and the quarter century between 1840 and 1865, which saw the gathering forces and the explosion in America, witnessed in Europe also a series of bitter class conflicts and revolutions. The contemporary writings of Marx and Engels on the American Civil War interpret it as part of this world revolutionary surge toward freedom. Yet Lincoln saw it more realistically as a challenge to national unity—that is, to the traditional Federal balance. At the time of the Gettysburg Address he was using the Federal power to ride herd on the state governors who challenged it. "Government, of, by, and for the people" under American conditions could not dispense with an adequate degree of unity at the center.

The doctrinal struggle involved in the Civil War was Calhoun's doctrine of the "concurrent majorities"—actually a doctrine of minority power through veto—as arrayed against Lincoln's doctrine of national unity. Lincoln won, and by that fact the sovereignty of the minority was squeezed out of the American system: since the Federal system allows for autonomy enough in the constituent parts and at the rim, along with enough effective power at the center, it was unnecessary to make a fetish of the minority's veto power. It is this knack for framing their crucial problems in terms of equilibrium ("both/and") rather than of doctrinal struggle to the death ("either/or") which has helped Americans give continuity and survival to their history.

This is illustrated by the relative absence of class struggle in America. Actually the power of the contending classes, both of business and of labor, has been greater than in most European countries which have shown more class conflict. But Americans have perforce learned the arts of balancing their classes in the equilibrium as they have learned to balance their sections. This is true not only of the economy but of the society as a whole. The gigantism that has afflicted American life could long ago have destroyed it had not some sort of balance been achieved between the contending forms of bigness. Thus America developed not only Big Government but also Big Business, Big Labor, Big Distribution, the Big Press, the Big Church, and the Big Army. No one of these is monolithic: each of them in turn is a tangle of conflicting forces, and each in turn has had to achieve an equilibrium within itself. Thus the American system of power has become like a system of nebulae held together by reciprocal tensions in inter-galactic space.

But, unlike the nebulae of the physical universe, the dangers of disrupting the equilibrium are a constant concern. It is not only the traditional fear that one of the Bigs may overshadow and finally annex the others, and with them the principle of freedom, or that a combination of them might become imperialist and destroy the equilibrium. There is also the danger of a fetishism of the equilibrium principle itself, which could give each of the new forces the veto power that Calhoun once sought for each of the sections. Because of the problem of reaching a consensus among the giant structures that dominate American society, a number of "veto groups" have emerged—minorities with a strategic position, whose psychic intensity takes advantage of the equilibrium and draws a confining line around the diversity of American life. The problem of reaching a consensus has always been hard in America, yet it has always had to be solved. Otherwise government would be deadlocked and society stagnant, and the carving out of a line of direction for American growth would be frustrated.

6. The Governmental Managers

WHEN A CONSENSUS is reached, who converts it into a policy and carries it out? The formal and logical answer would be the President. Yet obviously one man, even with the help of his Cabinet and his closest advisers, cannot run a government and a nation in a technical age. Increasingly in the last century a bureaucracy has emerged, operating under the President and Cabinet but with a wide margin of responsibility for the day-to-day conduct of affairs. This has meant a transfer of the locus of power which has been little short of a revolution in governmental technology.

The men who run this governmental machine are, in effect, the managers of government. They are not the rulers of America in the sense of making the strategic over-all policy decisions, which are made, rather, by the President, his advisers, the leaders of both parties in Congress, and the leaders of industry and labor. It is these men on top who are there to make the policy decisions, and not their subordinates in the bureaucracies. Americans recognize this, in the newspapers or political debates or in ordinary speech, when they speak of "the Administration," by which they mean the immediate managers, the President, his Cabinet, and the Congressional leaders of his party. By using the term they put their finger on the essential fact. If the substance of power is located at the point where the big gaps in decision-making are filled in by day-to-day administration, then it is true that the administrators are the new men of power.

This is not a truth restricted to America or its government. Balzac saw the danger when he called the French bureaucracy a "great power wielded by pygmies." It applies equally to the corporations, trade-unions, armed forces, and even the churches and universities. We have seen in earlier chapters how far the bureaucratization of industry has been carried. It has been carried just as far in the government. In fact, there is a peculiar irony in the attacks made on government bureaucrats by the men who speak for "industry" but who are themselves simply another group of bureaucrats. The irony lies in the fact that American business enterprise has had an enormous impact on the forms and shape of American government enterprise. What first made a government bureaucracy necessary was the spate of scientific inventions which in turn created a vast industrial organization that needed regulation from without as well as order from within.

The government has also taken over from business enterprise its key ideas of scientific management, of classification of jobs, of the continuity of staff regardless of the changes of policy on top, of the distribution of function, of a hierarchy of prestige and power, of a set of fiscal controls, and of the idea of planning itself. It has taken from business also its standards of operation: what the American demands of a government bureau above all else is that its operations should be "businesslike." Finally, the newly emerging "government corporations" (like the TVA), which represent the probable form of any future quasi-collectivism in America, are simply business corporations run by a governmental bureaucracy, although the fact that they are being run for the general welfare rather than for private profit sets a different tone to their operation.*

Thus American government has grown a "fourth branch" to add to the three branches expressly provided for in the Constitution. There is a prevailing fear in the American mind that the fourth branch will grow so fast that it will shut off the light and nourishment from the other three. But it must not be forgotten that this fourth branch also has deep roots in American history, as shown by Leonard White's series of volumes viewing American governmental history in terms of the administrative process and seeing the men of the Revolution and of the Jefferson-Madison and Jackson periods primarily as administrators. In the early decades of American industrialism there was a heavy growth of regulatory laws in the state and local governments, so that the idea of *laissez faire* did not become dominant until later, after the triumph of the Northern business group in the Civil War. Even in the 1870s and 1880s a new base came to be laid for government regulation of railroad rates, of business practices, and of banking. But it was the two world wars and the New Deal which did most to insure the triumph of the new men of administrative power. The American Federal bureaucracy is the child of crisis and has fed and grown on crisis.

Despite the prevailing American opinion, bureaucracy is not linked

---

* For an earlier formulation of this theme, from the viewpoint of economics rather than administration, see Ch. V, Sec. 10, "The Emerging Amalgam."

with any radical idea of governmental function or of social policy. The British and Continental experience has shown that bureaucracies are needed under any philosophy of government; and, in fact, that even conservative governments cannot dispense with the regulatory state. Only in America has the term "welfare state" as a term of invective come to imply a form of Socialism imposed on the people by "left-wingers." The growth of a Federal bureaucracy can be charted through both Republican and Democratic administrations, but its great spurts of growth have come in Democratic administrations from Woodrow Wilson on. The efforts to grapple with the problems raised by the Great Depression, the two world wars, and the cold war, came largely under Democratic administrations; and there can be little question that they fitted in with the Jeffersonian purposes (although not with the Jeffersonian means) of the Democratic tradition.

Yet if we take Herbert Croly's definition of a welfare state as one which reaches for Jeffersonian ends through Hamiltonian means, and remember that the centralization of Federal power was closer to the Republican tradition while the doctrine of States' Rights was closer to the Democratic, it becomes clear that the technology of the new state power is politically neutral. For better or worse, every administration will have to use it. Each party can seek to maximize or minimize it and use it for one or another set of social purposes. But a bureaucracy knows no party lines. Its inherent nature is to professionalize the process of government, to achieve continuity of administration through all the changes in party power, to bring expertness to the technical problems of government, and to effect a fusion of legislative, executive, and judicial powers wherever necessary despite the formal separation of those powers.

It was an insight of Brooks Adams that all revolutions have followed on the breakdown of bureaucracies and have in turn depended for the consolidation of their power on the creation of new bureaucracies. But one must add that administrative breakdown and reconstruction are in turn the consequences of forces at deeper levels within the culture. This was true in the case of the Nazi revolution under Hitler after the breakdown of the Weimar bureaucracy, as it was also true of the Communist revolution under Lenin after the breakdown of the Czarist bureaucracy. In both cases the revolutionaries were quick to forge a new "steel frame of power" under a system of gauleiter and commissars.

This lights up the crucial difference between a democratic and a totalitarian bureaucracy. In the totalitarian case the bureaucracy is the servant of the party and its leaders, is built on the party cadres, and is responsible only to the party leaders who are also the state rulers. In the democratic case the bureaucracy is largely recruited by civil service, except for the top policy-making posts in which party patronage enters strongly, but the succession from one party to another is accomplished without violence. The bureaucracy has a continuity regardless of party changes and is accountable to the Constitution and the people under the "rule of law."

Every bureaucracy reflects thus the basic social organization and power structure of the society whose governmental business it administers. It is in itself neither ogre nor Messiah, neither a road to serfdom nor a way of salvation, but it can be used both destructively and creatively, depending on the inner social impulses and on the direction given them by the policy-makers at the top. That it can be an instrument of tyranny has been abundantly shown. But in a free society it can be kept free, as shown by both the experience of the Labor and semi-Socialist governments of western Europe and the less developed welfare state of America.

What was most creative about the New Deal period was less its economic or social philosophies, which were fuzzy, than the administrative strategies developed to meet specific emergencies. Their obvious result was the multiplication both of *ad hoc* bureaucratic agencies and a heavy new burden of taxation. Yet the withering barrage of criticism directed against the tax-fed bureaucrats stressed only the obvious negative aspects—the red tape, the routineering, the stuffiness and self-importance of men with power attaching to their office, the frequent cases of sheer incapacity for the job.

There has been a too animistic quality in the attacks, as if some whim of power or some demonic malevolence had brought the bureaucrats into being. What is missed is the fact that the welfare state, with its bureaucratic base, came in America as a response to the felt urgencies of modern industrial society. There was the need of setting a floor under economic insecurity; there were clashes of interest groups, which required the intervention of the government as umpire and as equalizer of unequal bargaining conditions. There were new industrial practices which had to be regulated if chaos was to be prevented; there were concentrations of economic power which had to be kept in check, lest they lead to the growth of a state within a state; and there were actual failures of functioning in various segments of the economy which brought the government in as entrepreneur and investor. Added to all these were the war economy and war services which could be run only through the state.*

The failure to meet these needs would have led to democratic disintegration. In this sense the "wonderland of bureaucracy" and the

---

* For an earlier discussion of the welfare state, see Ch. V, Sec. 10, "The Emerging Amalgam."

much derided "alphabetical agencies" and "Brain Trusts" of the New Deal were contrivances that kept the democratic idea vital in the face of overriding crisis. The new administrative corps was given the power to do what Congress and the Judiciary by themselves—and even the Executive by itself—could not do. Much of the appeal which America has for nontotalitarian peoples elsewhere comes not only from a going business system but even more from a going democracy, and the fact that both have been bureaucratized does not diminish the power of the appeal.

This does not exclude the real dangers presented by the new men of power if they are not checked. Every form of power can become cancerous and eat up the other forms. This has not happened in the American experience mainly because the bureaucracy is the servant of the whole state rather than being linked with a single-party system, and also because of the strong tradition of judicial review. The courts, it is true, have hesitated to set aside any administrative finding if it has some factual basis. They have, that is to say, refused to supplant the administrative agencies as fact-finders. But they have on the whole guarded against the invasion of the freedom and privacy of the individual by arbitrary administrative action, glimpsing the shadow of a police state in such arbitrariness. And they have insisted that where legislative power has been "delegated" by Congress to an agency, the delegation must be something other than what Justice Cardozo called a "vagrant roving commission." I suspect that the widespread American distrust of administrative agencies comes not so much from what they have done to the liberties of the people but from what they might do—that is to say, not from the American historical record but from a deep impulse in American political thinking. This impulse in turn has been bolstered by the experience of totalitarian systems and by the fear on the part of the possessing classes that a strong and independent bureaucracy might prove a leverage for social change and might prevent them from staffing the administration's key posts with their own people when they came to power.

The popular feeling about government bureaucrats combines mistrust, dislike, and contempt with a degree of fear. It may be found both in Congress and in the popular mind. The reasons for it are many, but they converge on the same deep current of feeling. To start with, Americans are suspicious of any kind of elite, and the bureaucrats come closer to looking and behaving like an elite than do the professional politicians in Congress or in other government posts. Ever since the Jacksonian doctrine that any man is equipped to learn and perform the tasks of government, Americans have clung to the notion that a trained corps of government servants is somehow a challenge to Americanism. There is also the strong feeling that bureaucrats are in a protected position when they are under civil service or have stayed in a government job so long as to pre-empt it. Behind this is the belief that every American should be compelled to prove himself from time to time in some market place: hence the classic charge that the bureaucrat has never had "to meet a pay roll or deliver a precinct." The run-of-the-mill American, who has to struggle in the labor or business market, feels that the men at the Washington desks have latched on to an easy thing and won't let go. Moreover, they are seen as people who spend the taxpayers' money but don't have to pay for it themselves. It is felt that somehow they are responsible for the burden of high taxes on the ordinary citizen, and that they spend it mainly for such un-American purposes as governmental planning. Much of the propaganda against bureaucracies exploits and bolsters these hostilities.

The fears involved in them have thus far proved baseless. But there are other dangers with much more substance. These are the dangers not so much of tyranny as of lack of creativeness, not so much from the leviathan of power as from the slough of stagnation. The haphazard gathering of a "Brain Trust" under the New Deal was at the start an emergency device and had to be institutionalized. The hewers of wood under the top bureaucrats inevitably became almost immovable parts of a civil-service system whose gods are not ardor and creativeness but seniority and stagnation.

The crucial problem of an administrative group is that of the recruiting of talent from the best brains and energies of the culture. This talent cannot be restricted to any single class or political outlook. Each party in power finds that it must take men, even in the policy-shaping posts, who are not wholly sympathetic with its basic aims. The problem of educating them is almost insoluble, since narrow technical capacity without a broad education can throttle the imagination, while education without technical competence and experience can lead to costly and largely academic forays. Moreover, even when they are trained, the administrative officials do not remain long in the government service. They are lured away by higher salaries and by offers from corporate groups or from private professional firms for which their government experience has made them valuable. It is the mediocre who tend to remain, and this trend—exactly the opposite of Vilfredo Pareto's "circulation of the elites"—is reinforced in American life by the fact that the best brains and energies are usually drawn off into business or are frightened away from government by the "security checks" and the "loyalty" investigations. There is a marginal difference of efficiency between the run of the government bureaus and the run of corporate enterprise which is largely due to the differences in the kind of talent available to each.

This is, however, not an inevitable affliction of government, as was shown in many New Deal agencies, which caught the imagination of young men. What the New Deal was able to do was to attract a new type of government servant who was an amalgam of the lawyer, the economist, the engineer, and the administrator. He had to fight the tradition of spoils and patronage, he had to learn how to get along with Congress, and often his relations with the corporate bureaucrats became intolerable. Yet he added something to the flavor of democratic government. As the original impulse weakened, the quality of the administrative groups also weakened. With the cold war came the deadly ideological ("security") purges of the government services, necessary only in a few cases where men of doubtful loyalty held sensitive posts, and resulting in the other cases in a destructive effect on the quality of the whole governmental process. Where the Grand Inquisitors entered, the margin of freedom necessary for creative thinking was squeezed out.* There has been therefore a steady diminution of the quality of American administration, both at home and in the far-flung foreign services, which forms a serious problem of effectiveness and prestige.

Obviously there are considerable dangers in allowing the civil service to be kept in a constant state of political anxiety, since it places a premium on the survival only of the conformist. Yet I do not wholly share the distress of C. Wright Mills at the American failure to make bureaucracy more rigid, or at the large number of "outsiders" in the upper ranks of the bureaucracy, among the 1,500 "keymen" who hold the policy-making posts. One cannot take the German bureaucracy of Max Weber's day and impose it as a model upon the American situation of today. German society was one of authority, hierarchy, strict order, with an educated class that was still limited. American society is fluid, with widespread education, with a passionate bent against hierarchy, with a high sense of the personal rather than impersonal values. Quite naturally Americans share the belief that each new President has the right to bring in his own "outsiders" (Roosevelt and Eisenhower both did it) in order to carry out the principles of his regime. The Germans felt that the task of government was to transform extraordinary problems into routine tasks and tie them together with neat co-ordination. The Americans do this in industry and do it well; but they regard human relations as quite another sphere, and government as part of human relations. Peter Blau has pointed out that the German ideal of

* For the "security" cases, see Sec 10 of this chapter, "The Struggle for Civil Liberties."

an official who, in Weber's words, meets the public "in a spirit of formalistic impersonality, *'sine ira et studio,'* without hatred or passion, and hence without affection or enthusiasm," simply does not apply in the welfare agencies that form a growing segment of American state and Federal services, where contacts with clients are a major part of the satisfaction of the job.

It is also characteristic of Americans that a bureaucracy, once established, seems to them constantly in need of renewal and reorganization: hence the periodic plans of redrawing the blueprints of government, including that of the Committee on Administrative Management set up in 1936 under the New Deal and, more recently, the Hoover Commission. But the interesting fact about the voluminous reports of the latter was their stress on two highly American themes: first, the cutting away of waste, duplication, and surplus expenditures and man power; second, the plea for giving the President a clearer line of command and more control of his own establishment. Even in coming a long way from the Jacksonian doctrines of rotation in office and party spoils, Americans still clung to the notion of flexibility and change in administration. What Jackson was driving at, in his own rather primitive way, was a continuing method of reorganizing the government services and giving the new policies a group of devoted executives. Whatever Americans may feel about property in the economic realm, they have never come to feel that there are property rights in government jobs.

Herbert Luethy, writing about French parliamentary institutions and bureaucracy, has said that "France is not ruled but administered, and it is her apparent political instability which guarantees the stability and permanence of her administration." Almost the opposite is true of America. It is administered, to be sure, but primarily it is governed within a frame of major political decisions. Its impressive degree of political stability gives it the luxury at times of playing hob with its bureaucracy. Americans will, of course, have to settle down and become more sober and mature about their administrative tasks. They do not lack money, yet in their money economy the lower ranks of the bureaucrats are shabbily paid, reflecting the low esteem in which they are held in the culture. They are lopsided in their distribution: out of two and a half million civilian Federal employees, half of them are in the defense establishment and most of the others in the Post Office, the Veterans Administration, the Treasury, and Agriculture; the number of welfare employees is growing but is still only a small fraction of the whole. The professional career services are still in an early state of development: in the areas where they were strong during the security and patronage raids of the 1950s, the resistance proved most effective.

Most of all, they need to get away from the idea that a government servant cannot also be a person in his own right. There is a distinction to be drawn between political neutrality, without which a bureaucracy becomes chaotic, and the nullification of personality. A man can be politically detached yet also be excited by the professional idea he is seeking to fulfill, and have a sense of meaningful teamwork in an important task. Without that sense the whole work languishes, including even the formalized parts of it. Yet it will be difficult to achieve and maintain such a work spirit as long as the popular distrust and contempt for the bureaucrats continues. To overcome it will require considerably more political leadership on the part of the President, the parties, and the press than is likely to be forthcoming soon.

7. Tribunes of the People

THERE ARE TWO main agencies of the American government which have been entrusted by history and tradition with the safeguarding of individual rights and interests, whether against the governmental managers or any other force. They are the Supreme Court and Congress—one because it is the carrier of legal due process, the other because it is the representative assembly. In theory the whole of America is representative government, and each branch of it in one way or another represents the people in the sense of being government of and for the people. Yet traditionally there is one branch, Congress, which is considered to represent them most clearly and directly. Its members are chosen by state or locality and feel themselves to be part of "the folks back home." They are thus the American version of the Roman "tribunes of the people."

The idea of a separate representative tribunal is a master idea of Western parliamentary history, which Americans have inherited and to which they have given their own slant. It fits in with the American's distrust of government: one might say too glibly that a Congressman is sent to Washington not so much to *do anything* but to see that his constituents are not *done in* by "the Government." It fits in also with American localism: he is not sent to represent the national interest but only a geographical and local segment. Congress reflects many of the sectional, political, economic, religious, and ethnic antagonisms within the vast body of American life—which does not mean, however, that it is a true mirror of America.

Actually the representative idea has not worked out exactly as anticipated. The President, elected not by a single locality but by all the people and able to take a commanding view of their moods, emotions, and interests, has come to represent them as "the President of all the people." But the power structure in Congress is set up to reward those who come from "safe" districts (for the Democrats, the rural South; for the Republicans, the rural Midwest and New England) and to give disproportionate representation, especially in the Senate, to such economic interests as wool, silver, oil, natural gas, as well as the corn, hog, and dairy farmers.

Congress has become a problem child of the American governmental family. It is noisy, volatile, vulnerable to pressure groups and lobbies, often parochial in its outlook, jealous of its prerogatives, insecure about its position, implacable in its vendettas, bewildered by its mounting tasks. It has lost its reputation for great debate, has become intractable to party leadership and discipline and incapable of disciplining itself, and in recent generations it has developed fewer examples of the great leadership it once possessed. It seems less capable than ever of forming a steady majority which can carry through a planned and reasoned program of legislation. Only in the closing weeks of the session, under the hard driving of administration managers working with the majority and sometimes the minority leaders, does a legislative program get pushed through, with far too much carelessness and haste.

This has not prevented the persistence of a kind of folklore of Congress which gives it deep roots in the public mind. The people think of it at once as supreme legislator and supreme watchdog. In his legislative role the Congressman dresses himself up as the lawgiver, a seer who lays claim to his oracular role because he feels closer to the people at the "grass roots" than anyone else in "the Government." But he has also hewn out the image of himself as the eternally vigilant guardian of the people's interests as against the tyranny of the "Administration" —or, as he used to be called, "the palladium of the people's liberties." He sees himself as the sole watchdog of those liberties, and it is scarcely conceivable to him that the President or a Cabinet member or the head of an administrative agency might have an equal solicitude for freedom and an equal competence in judging how it is to be preserved.

Congress did not dream up these two roles. Its model was the British Parliament. The framers of the American Constitution followed the thinking of Montesquieu and Voltaire, who bungled the description of the actual role of the British Parliament in the eighteenth century and evolved the idea of three separated powers of government. The striking fact about the British system is that it fuses the legislative and executive powers in a single body, which is the Cabinet acting as part of the Parliament, and enables a majority to carry through a majority program. But in the American scheme Congress has clung to the idea of its sole guardianship of the legislative power and its monopoly of the watchdog function. Its model in British experience has been that of the Tudor and Stuart periods, when Parliament carried on a continuing battle with a series of absolute monarchs for the very life of the representative system. Once that battle was decided the British Parliament moved on to its present form, but the Tudor and Stuart image remained imbedded in the folklore of the American people and the glory image which the American Congressman has of himself.

It is not an unqualified image and has its paradoxes. The same American who cheers Congress because it is "agin" the Administration may find it hard to recall his own Congressman's name. The same American people who regard Congress as their watchdog are likely to breathe more freely when Congress has adjourned and the watchdog has gone home. All of which points to a gap between the folklore of Congress and the realities of the world in which Congress must function.

Actually there has been a sharp decline in the prestige and stature of Congress, corresponding to a decline in its policy-making functions. The operation of Congress in the technical age of physics and chemistry and electronics puts an enormous burden on an average man—which most Congressmen are. When you add to the burdens of modern technology the burdens of a world of competing imperial powers and clashing idea systems, it is no wonder that a Congressman's days become for him days of wrath, and his tenure a time of troubles which he must think of renewing before he is well launched on it. He feels himself (in Housman's phrase) "a stranger and afraid in a world he never made." As a result he tends to seek security in a redoubled militancy against the "Administration" or sometimes the "Interests," and in the solacing role of a Grand Inquisitor.

In the early decades of the new age of technology Congress shifted its emphasis from that of a debating body to a network of committees. The number of committees multiplied alarmingly, and periodically Congress sought to reorganize itself and cut away the unnecessary committee tissue. Yet here it ran into another difficulty—the system of seniority which gives the powerful committee chairmanships to those Congressmen who have outsat their colleagues, either because they are safe and silent men or, more likely, because they come from one-party constituencies like the Democratic South or the Republican Midwest, the safely Democratic "down state" big cities or the safely Republican "upstate" districts. The committee chairmen are therefore in many instances arrogant and reactionary old men, elected without much opposition and often from states (as in the South) where only a small segment of the people exercises the franchise. To match the dead hand of the seniority rule in committee, there is the paralyzing hand of the filibuster and unlimited debate on the floor of the Senate. Finally there is a lack of co-operative action between the two Congressional bodies and a lack of party discipline and coherence in both, which make Congress a battlefield of shifting blocs and coalitions inside the party structure, but manage nevertheless to create a working coalition hostile to the incumbent Administration.

The result is often government by deadlock. One may argue whether the deadlock comes because of governmental mechanisms or because the people, in their distrust of all government, want it that way—but the fact is there. Every President, after a brief honeymoon period, has had the experience of losing control over his own Congressional majority—if he had it to start with. The burden of linking the Executive with Congress falls on the operation of the party system, but that in turn is raked by a crossfire of sectional, doctrinal, economic, and personal disputes. The achievement of Franklin Roosevelt in keeping a tolerable degree of party unity within Congress during most of his first term on a program of drastic New Deal reform is almost unexampled, and was possible only because of the combination of deep crisis and skillful leadership. Something of the same sort happens also in wartime when external danger unifies Congress along with the nation. But the normal relation of Congress and the Executive is, as with many modern marriages, that of an exasperated cold war punctuated by periods of intermittent agreement.

To some extent the Presidents have themselves been responsible for this hostility. The burdens of the Presidency in a technical age are greater even than the burdens of Congress, and the vast administrative machinery by which the Executive must act is often cumbersome, arrogant, and in the worst sense bureaucratic. The Congressman who tries to get some action out of an administrative bureau is likely to feel like a rat imprisoned in a cage crisscrossed with red tape. He sees all around him waste and extravagance, and often the inexpertness of those who profess to be experts. His fury and contempt toward the "bureaucrats" may start as a commodity for home consumption by his constituents, but it runs the danger in the end of becoming habitual. He finds them men who, he feels, could never get elected to any post but hold their offices by patronage or civil service; and men, moreover, whose ideas seem to him outrageously different from the ideas of the "folks back home." He feels called upon to attack, investigate, and expose them. They in turn live in continual fear of his power and in unremitting contempt of his ignorance.

One can, of course, overstate this mutual hostility. There is considerable day-to-day co-operation between the bureaucrats in "the agencies" and the people "on the Hill." There are innumerable friendly ties between the two branches of the government, and even considerable "back-scratching" whereby favors as well as amenities are exchanged. Much of the hostility is an outward show by the Congressman for the benefit of his constituents and by the bureaucrat for the benefit of his colleagues. Yet the underlying strain is there, mainly because the Congressional leaders and the Executive have come in recent years to represent antagonistic social forces. For the past twenty years, since 1938, there has been a continuing alliance of some firmness between rural Southern Democrats and rural Midwest and New England conservative Republicans. This alliance has cut across both parties and has operated with an indifference toward the shades of party liberalism represented by Roosevelt, Truman, and Eisenhower.

What makes it worse from the Congressman's standpoint is, as I have noted, that much of the legislative initiative has in recent decades shifted from Congress to the Executive. This is mainly because of the technical complexity of the legislation, with which the administrative agencies are better able to cope because they are more specialized in it, but partly also for two other reasons: the increasing use of the President's veto, which gives him a chance to exercise a restraining hand on legislation; and his press conferences, which give him a leverage for directing its course. In these areas the Congressional committees sit almost constantly to consider and scrutinize the legislative proposals that actually come from the President or his advisers or one of the administrative agencies. The fact that the big expenditures are mostly in the areas of Presidential initiative makes Congress the more skeptical of them. In the mid-1930s, before the Hitler crisis in Europe became intense, the total House report on foreign aid called for an appropriation of not more than $100,000; in the recent annual budgets this has run into the billions.

Congressmen understand this and are resigned to it, yet they resent the dominating role of the Executive in foreign policy and several times have rebelled against the lines of State Department direction. In 1948 Congress forced on the Executive the China Aid Act, which changed the whole emphasis of Far Eastern policy; in 1950 it replaced a Korean aid measure with a Formosan one. In the same year it forced a big loan to Spain, incorporating it in the ECA Act and changing the emphasis of American policy toward Spain. Much of the major domestic legislation which liberals have to some degree fought—the Taft-Hartley, McCarran Immigration, Internal Security, and Tidelands Oil acts, and the Natural Gas Amendment—came by Congressional rather than Executive initiative. The same was true of the much needed Legislative Reorganization Act of 1946. Congress has been far from inactive legislatively and has fought hard to resist the inevitable loss of its legislative function in many technical areas.

More recently Congress and the President have attempted to work out a going system of co-operation in legislative policy. This is especially important on budgetary appropriations, on atomic energy, and on foreign policy, all of which have required not only a high degree of technical competence which Congress cannot alone command but also a continuing measure of liaison between the two branches. The problems of atomic energy and of foreign policy involve issues of national life and death which can scarcely be left to the mercies of deadlock. In these areas the President takes Congressional leaders into his confidence, using them as a kind of Privy Council with whom he consults before making his major proposals. During the periods of war and cold-war crisis this was supplemented by a "bipartisan" foreign policy, latterly again abandoned, which was often more rhetorical than real, but set an important precedent for future periods of crisis.

From the Congressional standpoint the galling fact about Presidential power is that it keeps eating into every new area of decision-making functions, and that in the area of foreign policy the President is the "sole organ" of foreign relations. The great Holmes decision in *Holland v. Missouri* extended almost indefinitely the powers of the President to legislate, in effect, through treaty-making and through Executive agreements. Even more, the swift pace of necessary tactical movement in the diplomatic and economic struggle for the world has meant that the President and Secretary of State often present Congress and the country with a series of *faits accomplis,* leaving Congress bothered and bewildered if not bewitched. The surprising support for the "Bricker Amendment," which sought to cripple the Presidential power over treaties and Executive agreements to an archaic degree, was largely an expression of the frustration of Congress and its suspicion of the Administration's foreign policy.

While both the Budget Bureau and the Atomic Energy Commission retain important ties with Congress, there are other bodies with crucial decision-making functions which are more dissociated from it. One is the National Security Council, made up chiefly of the defense, foreign policy, and psychological-warfare leaders, sitting in solemn council with the President. The other is the Central Intelligence Agency, which has charge of espionage and counterespionage abroad. These two groups, acting with the Atomic Energy Commission, have more to do with the shaping of the life-and-death decisions for the nation than any combination of Congressional committees.

What has been happening to Congress, in the large perspective, is that while its legislative responsibilities have grown more complex than ever and its burdens more demanding, the axis of policy-making initiative—even on legislative matters—has increasingly shifted to the Administration leaders and the bureaucracy. Congress has not lost its legislative function, but in comparison with the rate of increase of Executive power and involvements, it has been difficult for Congressional members not to feel that they are being passed by. Add this to the bipartisan conservative alliance that I have mentioned, largely rural, and one can understand the dogged resistance Congress has shown to new measures of a welfare democracy (except for farm legislation), to new legislative action meant to bolster Negro rights, to "internationalism" in the sense of foreign aid and diplomatic involvement, and to the maintenance of the liberties of the mind. Ralph Waldo Emerson had the notion that Congress was a safety valve for letting off the national steam: "A Congress [he wrote] is a standing insurrection and escapes the violence of accumulated grievances." History has shown instead a persistent, almost built-in, combativeness in Congress which seems to accumulate grievances. The traditional mistrust of the Executive, which Congress has always shared, has been sharpened by the new assertions of Presidential power—especially in foreign policy—which have come with the growth of the Presidential office.

Partly as compensation for its sense of loss and chagrin, partly because of the era of wars and cold wars, Congress has expanded its supervisory activities and shifted its attention to its role of a watchdog. The dramatic Congressional committees have now become the investigating committees. It is still true that the positions of power and prestige are those on the Rules Committee, the Foreign Relations Committee, the Appropriations Committee, or the Military Affairs Committee, and the able and experienced men aim at those. Yet the recognition of long and devoted service in these crucial posts may not be what paves the way to political advancement. Much of the drama of Congress is now centered in Congressional investigations, where a talented or demagogic Congressman can play the inquisitorial role, get the newspaper headlines, reach the people through radio and television, and become a household name. The committees serve not only as approaches to the spotlight but also as ways of resolving the terrible frustrations of a Congressman's life in giving him a sense of effectiveness and fulfillment.

The history of Congressional investigations in America* goes back a long way, and even further back there is a body of law and tradition in English history meant to protect the rights of the person in the inquisitorial process, some of which was taken over by the American Bill of Rights. The recent rash of Congressional investigations was thus in no sense new, although their pace and scope were transformed. It would not be hard to make out a strong case for the Congressional investigating power as a whole. The Federal bureaucracy has taken on vast and new powers, yet the bureaucratic wheels grind with terrible slowness, whether it be a passport application that is involved or a claim urged upon the Veterans Administration, or an application for a housing loan, or a labor contract. This not only adds to the Congressional load of private legislation and to the errand duties of a Congressman, but it also prods him into a sharper scrutiny of the bureaucratic maze. When he makes it, he finds how difficult it is to place responsibility for bureaucratic action, to find out where the blunders were made, where the buck was passed, where the corruption took place, and where—and here is where the anxieties of the cold war entered—the subversion may have taken place. Congress may thus feel that if it is to exercise its proper surveillance of the bureaucrats, gain access to their secrets, and fix responsibility, its members must turn themselves more than ever into glorified public personifications of the "private eye."

But the fact is that thus far the recent investigations raised many more problems than they solved. To the evils of government by deadlock they added the evils of government by inquisition. They often filled an important function in digging up necessary information that would otherwise have remained obscure or hidden, as in the case of the crusades by Norris and La Follette, or the railroad investigations under Senator Wheeler, or the investigation of defense contracts which placed a Senator called Harry Truman on the path to the Presidency. But the Congressional committee is not ideally suited to the task of detection of wrongdoing or the digging up of hidden items, as for example are the Moreland commissioners of New York State, or the Royal commissions of inquiry in the British system. Much depends on the kind of committee counsel and investigating staff that is chosen and the spirit that animates them, much also on the restraint and judgment of the leading members of the committee. During the 1945-55 decade the inquiries became decreasingly a pursuit of the facts and increasingly crusading inquiries or politically inspired; too often the committee chairman or counsel was out to "get" someone or prove a predetermined thesis, and too often a single committee member sat with the counsel

* For a further discussion, see Sec. 10, "The Struggle for Civil Liberties."

and questioned witnesses, while his colleagues were busy elsewhere. Similarly, while the British commissions cannot argue their case in the press until they have submitted their reports, the Congressional committee aimed for the headlines just as soon as it had a lead, thus making the press an integral part of the Congressional investigative process. Men and ideas found themselves condemned in the headlines long before the public had a chance to learn the facts.

This danger of prejudgment was greatest in the committee hearings themselves. Although in theory the investigations preceded any resort to the courts, the fact is that they became in effect prosecutions before tribunals which not only brought the charges but also sat in judgment on them. They had the power to summon witnesses, to compel attendance, to cite for contempt or for perjury. They have not developed procedural safeguards to protect the individual in the face of this punitive power, as the American courts have done. The record of the House Committee on Un-American Activities, and of the Senate (McCarran and Eastland) Subcommittee on Internal Security, was one that deeply troubled many Congressmen who did not believe in the Divine right of the Congressional inquisitors. These latter years were doubtless the years of growing pains for this new Congressional function, and a number of suggestions were made for a code of safeguards of individual rights. In the meantime a number of Congressmen were able to throw their weight around and organize what came close to being a reign of terror over the State Department, the other administrative officials, and men outside the government in professions like the movies, the theater, and the radio whose livelihood depended on their not becoming "controversial" figures.

Thus, if the Congressman had in the past tended to think of himself as a watchdog, his new role was that of the hound of heaven, divinely appointed to track down the sinners and execute the Lord's vengeance on them. This is the most crucial transformation that has taken place recently in both the power and the function of Congress. It turned that body into what Lippmann described as "a band of orators, investigators, prosecuting attorneys, and objectors." It afflicted Congress with a kind of broadcasting neurosis, in which it felt fulfilled only when it was exhorting the people to rise in wrath against the desecrators of the Temple. Thus this tribunal which was intended to represent and mirror public opinion set itself the primary task of arousing public opinion. It goes without saying that this consumes energy, time, and attention and has not done much to help the legislative process itself. That is still as clogged as ever, with hundreds of bills thrown into the Congressional hopper on the first day that Congress convenes, and thousands more

piling up as the session goes on. As a result, the Congress that has
normally operated by deadlock and obstruction now operates also by
inflammation.

What I have said here applies to the mechanism itself and to some of
the more volatile or more embittered figures who set the tone by which
it functions. Their grievances against the Administration, or some
agency or member of it, are likely to make them the more complacent
to suggestions from interest groups which share their hostility and can
play upon their injured self-esteem and rankling sense of inferiority.
Despite the instances of efforts at outright corruption, scattered through
the annals of Congress, bribery is marginal. The men who become
spokesmen for the farm, labor, or veterans' blocs, or for the real estate or
oil or natural gas or aviation lobbies, do not need to be bribed: they
succumb more easily to flattery, calculation of electoral advantage, and
a sense of identification with the interests of those groups.

Most Congressmen are neither heroes nor villains but well-meaning
men caught in an almost impossible job. Half the Congressman's time
is spent on trivial inquiries for his constituents, the other half in a desperate effort to keep up with the heavy volume of mail, with committee
assignments which are multiple and far too burdensome, and in an anxious absorption with personal political tactic and fence-mending. The
Congressman thus becomes in part a glorified errand boy, in part a vest-
pocket Talleyrand.

He is subject to harrowing pressures from every side to shape his conduct to the parallelogram of forces brought to bear upon him. Since
there is little of a cohesive and disciplined party system to take the responsibility for the decisions of the individual member as in England,
the Congressman must carry almost the whole responsibility himself
and is left to be buffeted by all the forces loose in his world. Given so
exposed a position, he tends to follow the line that the press takes, which
is generally the line taken also by the corporate groups, the veterans'
groups, and perhaps the labor and church groups in his community:
this means that he follows the stereotypes of his culture. When this involves a clash with his moral values, the result is either a corrosion of
those values or exposure to political defeat. When it involves a clash
with the majority of his constituency, he is likely to escape their
vengeance by falling deeper into the embrace of powerful individuals
in the community who can protect him.

But the chances are not strong that the Congressman will feel any
anguish of mind or conflict of conscience. "The French deputy," writes
Herbert Luethy, "is . . . able to have his heart on the left and his

wallet on the right without their coming into conflict." The American Congressman is likely to wear both of them somewhere Right of Center. He will probably have his roots in the mentality of the small town and of the lower middle class in it. He may be a lawyer of moderate income, or engaged in a small business, or an editor, or a cog in one of the new corporate bureaucracies. His thinking is likely to be that of the interest groups with which he has spent his life. He will prefer the steady support of those groups to the unreliable and sporadic enthusiasm or wrath of the lower income groups. In short, he would rather have a steady job as Congressman than be a Spartacus. Some have charged Congress with being either delinquent or defective, and others have felt that it could do no wrong. But the fact is that Congress is neither an assembly of gods nor a pack of rascals but a fairly accurate mirror of the strengths, weaknesses, and tensions of American middle-class life, and the average Congressman is only an ordinary man under extraordinary pressures.

What makes the situation tragic is that Congress does get good human material. There is a creative minority in Congress, as elsewhere in American life, and there is a steady stream of men who come to Washington with a sense of freshness and even of mission. But Congress has ceased to be the main channel through which the political energies of America flow. It is no longer the arena of great debate, except in times of sharp crisis, and even then the Presidential role is the decisive one. The steady stream of demands for the "reform" of Congress has led to several Reorganization Acts, notably one in 1946. These have tried to limit the errand-boy functions of the Congressman, help him with expert consultants, diminish the number of committees, give him a chance for some reflection and creative thinking without which no man can grow in stature. But they have had only limited effectiveness, largely for the reasons I have set down in this section.

The procedural reforms can help the Congressman but they cannot resolve the basic dilemma of Congress. It is the dilemma of a body which still has, at least in theory, the control both over the purse and over the sword, both over appropriations and over the declaration of war; but which in effect finds that the decision over great events in a complex industrial society and a world in turmoil has passed to the President and to his experts, to the bureaucrats and generals and technicians. Caught in this dilemma, Congress has been groping for some new place in American life. The investigating committee has seemed a natural handle to grasp, but in its frustration Congress has used it like a group of violent men wreaking their sense of powerlessness on the nation. It remains to be seen whether Congress will be able to use it with greater restraint and combine the legitimate watchdog function with that steady and critical sifting of the great issues of the time, for which it was originally intended, instead of the trivia and details, which too often occupy its attention.

8. Law and Justice

AMERICAN LAW HAD its roots in the method and body of the common law which the American colonists brought over with them from England. There was still a chance in the seventeenth century that the new settlements, especially since they resented the British judges, might develop their own system of law. But in the eighteenth century the English common law, which had served as a weapon in Parliament's struggle against the absolute monarchy, began to be taken over as a colonial weapon in the struggle for freedom. The great argument against the Writs of Assistance, delivered in 1761 before English judges in a Massachusetts court by James Otis, was an argument for freedom taken directly out of the common law tradition and the Parliamentary struggles. Once the political recourse to the English common law was fixed, it fixed also the dominance of the common law in the American legal system. Those who went to British legal thinkers to find arguments for freedom remained to absorb their approach to law.

The process was by no means inevitable, and there was always a chance that America would make a fresh start in law as in other areas: as late as the 1830s, writes Roscoe Pound, "it was still not wholly settled that we should receive the common law." The fact that this finally happened was due mainly to the influence of the great American judges and treatise writers of the pre-Civil War generation, like Kent, Story, Shaw, and Gibson. With the rise of a business economy the new American business class was glad to have an instrument like the common law, fashioned out of the experience of British life, ready at hand for dealing with the problems of commercial litigation and justice. The lines of conflict in the struggle that raged around the common law through the first half of the nineteenth century were drawn between a largely conservative group who were attracted by the spirit of the English property institutions which the common law embodied and a liberal opposition which feared a judge-made, piecemeal law and felt that Americans could organize a better and more rational system, closer to their own experience.

The common law, however, was the victor. The result has been an American legal system which has a continuity with the English much like the continuity of the American language with the English. There are local variants in usage, but the frame and tradition are the same. A

legal system has emerged embodying a number of master ideas interwoven with those of politics, economics, society, and the American
mind.

The first is that of experience as a guide to legal growth and therefore
to justice. "The life of the law," said a young lawyer called Oliver
Wendell Holmes, Jr., in the opening chapter of his book *The Common
Law*, "has not been in logic. It has been in experience." He went on to
talk of the "felt needs of the time," as the later Holmes—then a Supreme
Court Justice—was to talk of the "hydraulic pressures" exerted on a
decision by the practices, beliefs, and attitudes of the community. In
recent years Holmes has been sharply criticized, especially by a moralist
and natural-law school which feels that he exposed American law too
nakedly to the animal appetites of society and the empiricism of the
chance atom. But he best represented the tradition of American legal
thinking, just as his friend William James best represented the spirit of
American philosophy and social theory. Reading the famous Holmes-
Pollock letters, one sees both the common ground and the differences between the British and American legal attitudes.

The idea of the primacy of experience carried with it the idea of the
pluralism and the diversity of that experience. America embraced the
common-law tradition largely because it offered room at the joints.
Just as the cult of experience is a recoil from the rigidity of the Continental concepts of reason, so the cult of the case method in law is a
recoil from the rigidity of Continental concepts of codified law derived
from a fount of revealed wisdom. The idea of each case as a new bundle
of experience, to be measured against other cases, fits into the American's conviction of the uniqueness of his own experience. It fits in also
with a culture of diverse jurisdictions, of state and local governments,
of regions and subregions, of plural religious sects and ethnic groups.
The common law appealed to the English at the time of Edward IV
largely because it brought unity into the diversity of feudal life. It appealed to Americans because it kept American growth from being
cramped within rigid codes and fixed principles. Every body of law
contains both a core of stability and a line of change: but if the English stress the element of precedent, which is that of tradition, the
Americans stress the dynamism by which the lawyer and judge are able
to fashion new law out of new social experience.

The battle of legal doctrines in America was fought out in the conflict between natural-law and common-law ideas. At first the two
worked together: in the spirit of the common law the early American
lawyers appealed to the "inalienable rights of Englishmen," as Jefferson was to base the American claim for independent nationality on "the

laws of Nature and of Nature's God."* But later the natural-law doctrines, linked with an appeal to a "higher law" than statutes and other man-made laws, came to be used in a different way and for quite other ends. They were used to entrench statutes that sought to bolster the rights of the possessing groups, or to invalidate those that might undercut those rights. Thus natural law, like the common law itself, played at once a revolutionary and a conservative role in American legal thinking. To achieve continued growth, American law had to break away from the mechanical conceptions which had grown up around it, having their origin in the natural-law and "higher-law" doctrines but taking the form of rigid notions of legal principle. In the hands of unimaginative men this mechanical jurisprudence became a "slot-machine" theory of the law, by which a case was measured against a legal principle much as a nickel might be dropped into a slot, and the judgment was held to come tumbling out ready-made.

In contrast to this, the "revolt against formalism" (as Morton White has called it) reasserted the original spirit and intent of the common-law tradition. Professors Ames and Langdell expressed this revolt in the case method of legal study, through which several generations of lawyers were trained by studying not the "law-in-books" but the "law-in-action" in concrete situations. Justice Holmes was skeptical of all absolutisms: "There is in all men," he wrote, "a demand for the superlative, so much so that the poor devil who has no other way of reaching it attains it by getting drunk." He expressed this skepticism by a gentlemanly Darwinism, in which legal rules and decisions merely summed up the balance of conflicting interests, desires, and power forces at any time, with the judge standing by as umpire, discounting his own preferences. Justice Brandeis, more of a legal and social activist, expressed the revolt in a characteristic type of decision (originally the "Brandeis brief") which sought to keep the law abreast of social progress and found in history, economics, and statistics the envelope of social reality within which the meaning of a case was contained. Pound gave it the name of "sociological jurisprudence" and showed eruditely how it fitted into the history and spirit of the Anglo-American common law, which he made almost into a cult. Justice Cardozo viewed the "nature of the judicial process" from inside the judge's mind, describing how at best a judge must weigh considerations of precedent and change, history and contemporary pressures, private rights and public policy. Jerome Frank and Thurman Arnold called for a philosophy of "legal realism" which described judges, lawyers, and litigants as quite fallible human beings,

---

* For a further discussion of natural law and other themes considered in this section, see Ch. X, Sec. 2, "American Thought: the Angle of Vision."

and took account of how law impinged on American life not at the lofty levels of constitutional law and philosophy, but at the everyday level of business maneuvers and human entanglements.

In an interesting chapter on the legal profession, in his *American Democracy*, Harold Laski attacked the case method, accusing it of fragmentizing the American legal mind and of leading to the evasion of the social logic of the American class structure. Certainly, by dispensing with general propositions, it has offered a way of avoiding embarrassing political or economic commitments on the part of teachers and judges. Nor has it always escaped formalism, which has found its way into American law by an intricate network of jurisdictional and procedural rules. The mind of the typical lawyer tends to be atomistic and procedural, concerned with the proper forms and safeguards and with keeping his client out of trouble, and resourceful mainly in the legal means for accomplishing the limited objectives set for him. This is what has made the American lawyer so crucial a technician in the scope and growth of corporate power. But it has also led to his partial replacement by the "public-relations" expert, who stresses the irrationals of human conduct rather than the formalisms of legal action. A growing number of businessmen, tired of the expensive delays and intricacies of litigation, have had to include in their contracts a clause for the arbitration of differences. Yet the case-method approach, used along with social and documentary material, has helped keep American law from the paralyzing abstractions that plagued the more logical legal systems.

Three great foreign observers—Burke, De Tocqueville, and Bryce— noted successively how legal-minded the Americans were. Largely they have remained so. Their early interest in the law may have been due to its usefulness in providing intellectual weapons for the revolutionary struggle and the early days of nationhood, just as Gandhi went to London to study law and young Asians and Africans in our own time have turned to Marxist theory to fortify their national liberation movements. Later the law was crucial because it served as one of the two main elements of continuity, along with religion, in holding together a societyin-the-making. Among such a people the relation of law to the lines of social force was bound to continue as a meaningful one.

To start with, American law has been strongly individualist in its emphasis, which has sometimes been explained as the expression of Puritanism and the frontier spirit. Yet in many ways the Puritans cared less about the freedom of the individual than about his control by society; and as for the frontier spirit, its influence was great but only as part of a larger complex. In speaking of legal individualism, we must remember that the protection of the individual's freedom did not end the matter: just as important, perhaps even more so in an acquisitive society, was the protection of his right to improve his lot and enrich himself as a man of property, and the security of that property once it had been amassed. Hence the crucial areas of private law in America were contract (with labor law as merely a subheading of contract law), torts (with emphasis upon the intrusions upon a man's possessions), and equity (with emphasis upon the adaptation of the law to changing economic conditions, and the creation of new property rights not recognized in the formal and established law).

The realm of contract is of particular interest because of the role it has played in bridging the gap between private and constitutional law in America. It was only a step from the use of law in making private bargains and acquisitions secure to its use in fending off interference in the relations between a corporation and its employees. When, for example, New York passed an act at the turn of the century providing for a ten-hour day and sixty-hour week in bakeries in order to protect the health of the workers, the Supreme Court, in the famous case of *Lochner v. New York* (1905), struck it down on the ground that it violated the sanctity of contract. This was the occasion for the notable phrase that Justice Holmes used in his dissent: "The Fourteenth Amendment does not enact Mr. Herbert Spencer's *Social Statics.*" The doctrine of liberty of contract was similarly used to invalidate statutes that tried to regulate collective bargaining between employers and employees, just as the common-law doctrine of "master and servant" and the rule of "contributory negligence" were used to leave the worker helpless in industrial accidents until the state compensation laws were finally accepted after a long struggle.

I have been speaking here of contract and related themes in the realm of public as well as private law: but the whole point is that the boundary between the two in America has been not nearly as sharp as is sometimes assumed; one of the master devices used by the lawyers and judges has been to take over the doctrines of private law, which developed in an English society of agriculture, small enterprise, and petty trade, and apply it to the area of public law, where giant business units were seeking to fashion a system of order according to their own interests and their own likes.

Something of the same sort happened in the field of equity. Originally it was intended in England as a way by which the new mercantile class sought to evade the burdens and loosen the rigidities of the still largely feudal phases of the common law. It developed as a "court of conscience" under a separate system of judges (chancellors), and with its own set of doctrines (such as the trust) and its own writs and injunctions. The American tendency has been, except in a few states, to use the same set of courts for both law and equity, but the doctrines and procedures of equity have had a far-reaching effect in the area of business, labor, and property. The management of inheritance and estates, through probate courts, has lent itself to the pressures and corruption of those who have large interests at stake in the inheritance of considerable fortunes. The "trust," once intended in England in order to make land law more flexible, became in America a device for the crushing of competition, the concentration of industrial power, and the pyramiding of corporate control in the hands of a small percentage of the ownership. The injunction, once meant as a way of giving relief through equity before an intolerable situation could become a *fait accompli,* came to be used in America by pliant judges as a way of paralyzing trade-union strike action. The device of equity receivership has been used in the case of looted or badly run railroads and other enterprises as a mode of effecting corporate reorganizations, and some of the most ingenious of American legal dodges have developed in this field, to the profit if not the glory of the American legal profession.

Thus it is that law in a business society develops in the direction required by the power of the dominant business groups. This is as true of American private law, as I have suggested in exploring only two or three areas of it, as it is in public law.* It is within this context that the individualism of American law takes on meaning by accomplishing two ends—that of treating the corporation as an individual personality and that of isolating the ordinary individual from the group action by which he seeks to protect himself in an age of mastodons. Some of the exacting studies of particular judges, like Carl Swisher on Taney, Charles Fairman on Miller, and Leonard Levy on Shaw, portray the harsh and rigorous individualism that pervaded virtually every area of law, private and public alike, during the era of economic *laissez faire.* The hero of American law, as Levy suggests, was the property-owning, liberty-loving, self-reliant, "reasonable" man, and if the giant corporation was recast by the law in the image of this man, it had its reasons for doing so. One should add that he was also the hero of American society, whether celebrated by Jefferson as the freehold farmer, by Hamilton as the town merchant, by Jackson and Frémont as the frontiersman, or by a string of people from Carnegie and McKinley to the current business writers as the independent businessman. There is a remarkable likeness between the American image of the ordinary man and the com-

* For a discussion of the relation of public and constitutional law to American society, see Sec. 9, "Keepers of the Covenant."

mon law's accepted ideal of the American, intended to be used as a standard on which to base legal judgment.

Despite this glamorized ideal, however, the attitudes of Americans toward their legal system are likely to vary from one class to another. For the top income groups the law is an instrument for security and a technology placed at the service of money and power. For the middle class the object is a law-and-order stability, and the law is valued by how effectively it copes with crime, corruption, and class disputes, particularly strike violence. For the trade-unions the law seems very close to a class monopoly, especially in the use of the court injunction to break strikes, and the strength of the state militias when thrown on the side of the corporate employers. For the lowest classes the law is trouble, and its officials are trouble whenever they are encountered. The legal technologies developed largely to meet the needs of the business groups, especially in corporate and tax law and procedure; but the dynamism of legal change has responded to the grievances and protests of the lower-income groups, and new law has emerged when the "sense of injustice" (in Cahn's phrase) has been sharpest.

If there were an American Montesquieu, seeking the "spirit of the laws" in American life, what salient themes and features would he pick? He would, I think, find American law cluttered and individualistic, a "wilderness of single instances"; in the main, uncodified; embodying many of the moralisms and taboos of the American mind in the past, yet changing slowly with changing needs; based on precedent, yet allowing for considerable leeway; for that reason, relatively unpredictable, especially in the "borderline cases" that form the delight of the lawyer; secular, being based on no divinely inspired and revealed source, nor on the original wisdom of some great "lawgiver"; careful of property rights and skillful in using old precedents of individual liberty for the purpose of consolidating new structures of corporate power; matter-of-fact, neither demanding nor receiving reverence, since it is meant for and administered by ordinary men.

The decisions most discussed in the law journals are those in the higher reaches of the legal system—in constitutional and administrative law, in the problems of Federal procedure and jurisdiction, and in the cases involving the rights of the person. Yet the impact of law upon ordinary Americans is most marked in the large areas of private law, like contracts and torts, and in the lower reaches of "courthouse law," both criminal and civil, where the American has his minor brushes and major encounters with the law. Here he forms the image of it that he carries around with him.

While power in America is widely diffused, as I have noted in an earlier section, legal force is the monopoly of the government alone: there are no nongovernmental tribunals (except for the defense services, which are an arm of the government) with the power to punish through the deprivations of freedom. The dramatic expression of the government monopoly of force is the criminal law. From the most sordid and banal cases of routine pickpocketing and prostitution in the police courts to the most sensational murder cases, the criminal law gives to the lives of bored and lonely Americans some fillip of distraction.

The administration of American criminal justice has been often scored as inefficient, corrupt, and archaic, and all three charges are probably true, but again probably no truer than of past eras and other societies. The supervision of criminal justice is mainly in the hands of the local authorities; the Federal courts handle crimes under Federal jurisdiction but try to minimize the appeals from local and state jurisdictions. A lawbreaker is tracked down by local police, prosecuted by a local district attorney and defended by a local lawyer, tried in a local courthouse in a trial reported prominently in the local press, convicted or cleared by a local jury, sentenced by a local judge, and shut up in a local or state prison. At every point there is a good deal of bungling, prejudice, poor judgment, or corruption. Yet on the whole there is a widespread feeling that the results are tolerably good and that the frailties of the whole process are a reflection of the frailties of the society in which it takes place.

The four symbols of "the law" for Americans are the policeman, the district attorney, the judge and jury, and the lawyer.

The encounters with the "cop" are part of American folklore, especially in the traffic violations which are the everyday concern of a motor civilization. The American is not overly impressed by police authority, considering the police officer as a badly paid job holder, not above being "fixed" by a bribe. The police, in turn, are assigned to dangerous and brutalizing tasks, especially in big cities where they must cope with lawless hoodlums spreading "terror in the streets"; and they are exposed to the temptations of petty bribery and the Big Money. An "honest cop," accordingly is considered by the cynics much rarer than he actually is. The fact is that police administration has its pathology, but that American cities from California to New York have been learning to use the new technologies of police science, as used for example by August Vollmer, the police chief of Berkeley, California, with motorized squads, a system of signal calls and radio communication, technically competent crime detection and identification, and a community-wide approach to juvenile delinquency and crime prevention.

The rise of a modern police system came very late in American cities: even with over 300,000 people, New York had only a "citizens' watch"; many cities had bloody riots that the ward constables and watch were helpless to handle, and not until 1844 was the first permanent police department set up in New York. In more than a century since then the connection of the police with vice and racketeering graft has been often spread on the record, from the Lexow Investigation of the 1890s to the Kefauver Committee a half century later. Steffens wrote his *Shame of the Cities* about corruption at the turn of the century, yet when Albert Deutsch made the rounds of much the same cities in the 1950s after the pivotal work of exposure by the Kefauver Committee hearings, while he still found corruption he also found skill and professional standards, and he concluded that few communities would tolerate for a moment the depths of police degradation that Steffens described.

Even more important than the problem of police honesty is that of equal justice under the law at the police and prosecutor level. It is hard, for example, to be a Negro in the South—in Birmingham or Biloxi—and expect human or just treatment at the hands of the local police. But it is almost equally hard for a Negro in Harlem, Chicago, or Detroit, or a labor organizer in almost any Southern or Midwest town, or a recent immigrant speaking with a telltale accent, to get equal treatment with others. Instances of police use of "third-degree" methods are common enough to have received recognition by the appeals courts. The inherent violence of modern life finds outlet both in the lawlessness of lawbreakers and the counter-lawlessness of some of the guardians of the law, especially when used against obscure and illiterate men. The Wickersham Report in the 1930s documented the use by police of the "third-degree" methods of secret pretrial examination to extort confessions, and the studies of crime reporters indicate that the practice persists.

Moving several layers up from the cops, the system of electing judges, district attorneys, county prosecutors, and the surrogates who administer estates and supervise bankruptcy proceedings, makes the administration of justice part of the machinery of political influence and power. Often these are regarded as plums in the cake of political patronage; and the theme of the crooked D.A., or one who is outwitted by the defense attorney, is a constant one in the movies and the crime stories. But so also is the D.A. who sets out to "clean up" the lawlessness of powerful criminals and politicians, and as a heroic figure is sought out for mayor, governor, or even President.

The prosecutor is the dominant figure of criminal law. If he has a flair for publicity he can leave ruined lives and reputations behind him on the road to political preferment. But he has also a vast discretionary power which allows him to decide what indictments to present to the Grand Jury, what lesser pleas to accept, what cases to bring to trial. The impact of the market on American law is shown in the bargaining process by which most of the business of a district attorney in the big cities is transacted: only one case out of fifteen in a city like New York is ever brought to trial, the rest being settled in pretrial negotiations through the D.A.'s office. This is a "marketing orientation" with a vengeance. As for the trial itself, the theory behind it is that of truth-by-combat. American justice has experimented with new psychological devices like the "lie detector," but it still clings chiefly to the adversary method of getting at the truth—one well suited to the popular American conditioning to games. Unlike the Continental system, the judge sits as referee instead of as inquisitor until the verdict is reached, when he becomes the vessel of punishment; the witnesses are the immediate targets; the real players are the battery of counsel; and the jury of one's peers weighs the evidence to reach its decision.

The jury system has latterly been under attack, mainly on the grounds that most jurymen are irritated with the burden of jury duty, that they are bored with the cases and incompetent to see through the tactics of lawyer and prosecutor or resist their blandishments, that in a press-dominated trial they are easily prejudiced and become the dupes of emotional manipulation. Descriptively this is not far of the mark. But the American as juror is part of the same equalitarian experiment that includes the American as husband or father, wife or mother, the American as voter, the American as consumer. The jury system is one of the remaining survivals of the Jacksonian idea that there is nothing over the head of the common man for which he cannot use his native intelligence. The purpose of the jury system is to elicit the common experience of men and bring it to bear on the problem of guilt and innocence. However well or badly it achieves this, it also performs the function of training the juror—and along with him the large body of newspaper readers— in the weighing of the human heart. Americans commit more misdemeanors than felonies, more crimes of fraud than of force, more offenses against property than against the person: but in every case there must be a scrutiny of motive.

To say that the juror usually does it badly is beside the point. He is probably no more easily duped as juror than the same man is in politics or love or family relations or the wilderness of commodities. If an open society is to survive, he must learn to find his way in each of these areas. To play God with a man's life or his freedom in the deliberations of a jury room may be more dramatic than to shape the destiny of a child in the nursery or of a whole nation in the polling booth, but it is no more important. In each case it is a God-playing role which cannot be delegated to an elite that claims to know best what is good for the rabble.

This may be related to the fact that Americans have become a nation of amateur sleuths. The "whodunit" is likely to thrive under democratic systems, as in both England and America, where legal judgments are not delivered by authoritarian tribunals but where the rules of evidence are rigorously applied. With the modern American press the evidence is sifted not only by the jury but (in notorious cases) by the whole locality or even the nation. From being a nation of jurymen it is only a step to being a nation of detectives. The "private eye," who shows up the complacency or stupidity of police officials and D.A.s, becomes a vicarious symbol of the revenge that every reader takes for his brushes with the law. The improbability of the murderer's identity in the whodunits (he is rarely the person to whom the evidence points) is a reflection of the premises of the law of evidence in a democracy. A basic assumption of American law is that a man is held innocent until he is shown to be guilty. It shocks an American to discover that an innocent man has spent years in jail before the evidence turns up that proves the mistake or the "frame." The jury system brings to bear on the evidence the non-expert flexibility of everyday experience; courtroom procedure brings to bear the accumulated wisdom of centuries spent in the guarding of a person's rights; but the whodunit brings to bear on the evidence the combined reader role of being at once detective and rebel. Since in a democracy "everyman is his own historian," everyman is also his own sleuth and his own judge and jury, and his triumph is that of showing up the authoritarian fable. American legal attitudes are to their marrow antiauthoritarian. That America is a government "of laws and not of men" is even more strikingly proved in the wish fulfillments of the whodunits than in the formal vindications of judicial review.

It need scarcely be added that the American attitude toward the courts is not always one of reverence. The exception is the higher courts, especially the Supreme Court. The lower ones, from the local magistrates and police courts up, command little respect. Unlike the Continent, there is no specialized training for the judicial profession as such. The judges come up from the ranks of lawyers and go back to legal practice when their terms are up or when they find a judge's salary inadequate. This preserves a circulation of talents and prevents the judges from being cut off from the realities of legal practice and procedure. But it is hard to respect "the dignity of the Court" when it is presided over by a man whom you knew only yesterday as your legal competitor and perhaps even inferior, since it is not always the lawyers of ability and integrity who achieve the judicial robes. The "contempt of court" procedures in America are less rigorously invoked than in the English courts, and the newspapers are given greater latitude in comment on a case before or during trial, especially in the more sensational criminal cases on which their circulation often depends. It is only recently that emphasis has been placed on the role of both prosecutor and defense attorney as officers of the Court. thus giving the judge greater control over court behavior. In his social position in the community, the judge has, however, the advantage even over the rich and successful lawyers; and in the South especially, the early tradition that arms and the law were the two professions of gentlemen, and that the able lawyer who became a judge was also the repository of learning and influence, has carried over to the present day.

De Tocqueville's famous chapter on the place of the lawyers in American society may seem an anachronism now, but it is not hard to see why they played so great a role in American history. In a new country, with claims and rights in flux and the distribution of authority still to be shaped, lawyers were needed to set lines of division and organize the local will. Since the feudal baron and the manorial lord no longer existed, and the clergyman and schoolteacher did not have the required prestige and worldliness, the lawyer emerged as the ideal amalgam of learning and practicality. He took his seat in the state assemblies and the national Congress, and with his knowledge of the drafting and interpretation of laws he became indispensable. As the country grew, the mounting needs of business enterprise and especially of corporate organization and reorganization gave further importance to the lawyers, who were now needed to tell the new ruling group what they could or could not do legally.

The role of the lawyer began to change. Whatever his failings, the early lawyer had a secular mental discipline that was almost the only one available in public affairs and had learned law as part of the arts of statecraft. The frontier lawyer and the circuit-riding judge had the vigor revealed in the later careers of men as divergent in social views as Justices Field and Miller of the Supreme Court. But when, after the Civil War, the big corporate interests began to move into the seats of power, disintegration set in. The lawyer became a hired man—the "Great Mouthpiece" for the corporations or for the marginal local bosses and racketeers.

With the turn of the century, men like Holmes, Brandeis, and Hughes made efforts to bring lawyers to a consciousness of the public responsibility of their profession. Holmes especially spoke of the chance that lawyers had to "study the law greatly" and to "wreak themselves" upon their subject by seeing "the relation between their fact and the frame of the universe." Brandeis spent his great talents on reform causes and became known as "the People's Attorney." The law schools and law journals subjected legal decisions to an intense scrutiny, setting standards for judicial decisions. The legal historians began to emphasize the brilliant names in the history of the American legal profession, from Marshall and Story to Stimson, Hughes, and Stone. The constitutional scholars became aware of the extent to which the lawyers, in their briefs and arguments, shaped the course of the law—sometimes even more creatively than the judges because they gave the judges their cues.

Yet one had to remain skeptical of whether a profession so tied to the holders of power could free itself and become autonomous. The big Wall Street legal firms tended to become "law factories," organized much like the big industrial corporations which they represented. In the struggles between labor and the corporations, the trade-unions proved powerful enough to develop their own competent legal staffs as well as their own research organizations. But the real test of law as a public service profession came after World War II, when the challenge to civil liberties found few members of the bar with the courage to risk their economic prospects by defending unpopular causes and hated men. The lawyers had moved a long way since the time when John Adams defended the British commander charged with the massacre of American patriots on Boston Common. The American attitudes toward the lawyer are hard to define. His social position varies with his success and wealth, but is likely to be a good deal higher than on the European Continent, and similar to that of a businessman or corporate executive. Yet the distrust of him persists.

Thurman Arnold pointed up the paradox of Americans' calling for law enforcement at the same time that they multiply the laws beyond the point of enforceability and violate them from day to day. This may be less an American trait than the very human one of wanting, in the sphere of the law as elsewhere, both to eat one's cake and have it. In all societies, formal codes are set up which go largely unheeded because their rigid enforcement would cripple the practical needs of social life and violate the insistent impulses of man's nature.

The Americans have sought to solve the problem by alternations of neglect and enforcement, as shown by their traffic regulations, their disastrous Prohibition experiment, their gambling and betting laws, their vice and narcotics laws. They have moved between the twin beats of complacency and conscience, cynicism and Puritanism, silence and crackdown. There will be long periods of "patterned evasion" of the legal norms through corruption and the "Big Fix." Then there will be a "crime wave" or some other index of alarm, followed by the inevitable crackdown on racketeers, "vice kings," fee-splitters, "ambulance-chasers," narcotics peddlers and addicts, gamblers, bookies, prostitutes, gang warriors, traffic violators, or just vagrants and bums. In this crackdown the police, prosecutors, judges, press, clergy, and politicians tumble over one another in an hysteria of legal enforcement, feeling at once virtuous and inwardly silly. Then a vast apathy will blanket the community, and the silence will be as before.

If this were not similar to other polarities in American life, one would be tempted to speak of it—with its alternating fits of elation and gloomy quiescence—as a sign of a manic-depressive personality. But it is more sensible to trace this pattern back to the Puritan attitudes, with their combination of moralism and practicality; or to cite the experience of frontier law, as shown in the California Gold Rush days, when the new communities had long spells of complacent laxity of law and in morals, followed by a reckless vigilantism. Behind the law-and-order crackdown there remains even in the modern period more than a trace of lawlessness and vigilantism. Judge Learned Hand, speaking of a roundup of vagrants and petty criminals listed on the police blotters by Grover Whalen when he was Police Commissioner, and the general approval of press and citizenry, pointed out that any of these men would bridle at the thought that someone should be punished at official whim without evidence of guilt: "they are loyal to our institutions in the abstract, but they do not mean to take them too seriously in application." One suspects that the law-and-order obsession of the American is fed by a sense of guilt about his own circumventions of the law, and by his increasing insecurity in a world in which the old codes no longer seem adequate. The enforcement crackdowns are thus related to the psychic and emotional sources from which come also the periodic raids on civil liberties.

There are other forms of patterned evasion. There is the deliberate circumvention of the law in tax evasion, or in the sabotaging of safety inspection codes. There are the cases where, as in divorce law, the legal norms take too rigorous a view of social needs, as by the paradoxical "rule of collusion" that no divorce will be granted where both husband and wife are anxious to have it. Here the American practice is the tacit legal violation of the law through uncontested divorce actions in fictitious jurisdictions. Finally there are the areas of legal distortion through archaism, as in the law governing sex offenses, where the punishment of "statutory rape" or of "sodomy" takes an approach to human behavior based on the Hebraic-Puritan theological tradition, without taking into account the insights of psychology.

While American law is a loosely fitting coat, draping the figure of American life too haphazardly at some points while pinching too tightly at others, the Americans find it a fair approximation and have learned to live with it. They might even feel uncomfortable with too snug a fit. They take their system of law a little as the French or Italians take their system of Catholicism—observing most of its rituals, living up to few of its precepts, but clinging to it nonetheless with a tenacious if genial infidelity.

I have spoken of the particularism, the pragmatism, and the matter-of-factness of the American legal system, of the relation of the great areas of private law to American property and class attitudes, of the spirit and temper of American criminal law, of the policeman, prosecutor, judge, and lawyer as symbols of the administration of justice, of the somewhat schizoid attitude Americans take toward law enforcement, and of the loose but operative fit between the law and the social realities.

Another instance of the affinity of the spirit of American law and of American life is in the unpredictability of both. One of the major aims of all legal systems is to achieve the maximum security and stability through predictability. Where the law is codified and handed down by authoritarian tribunals as part of a centralized system of justice, the predictability of judgments is great but there is likely to be little dynamism in the society. In America the opposite is true. Justice Holmes once defined law as quite simply "the prediction of what the courts will do in a given case." Or, as he put it, the law is "the hypostasis of a prophecy"—which is to say that it is a gamble. The "bad man" gambles on what he can get away with; the law is the croupier playing for the house against him.

This element of risk in law, which might prove too costly in a less dynamic society, fitted the mood of the Americans as long as the element of risk was strong in their society as well. The large number of state jurisdictions, each with its own line of precedents on disputed points of law, added to the confusion and the unpredictability. One reason perhaps why the litigiousness of Americans is not as great as in some other social systems, despite a "litigation neurosis" to be found in certain personality types, has been that litigation is expensive and risky, and the delays long. What American society has always wanted—and American law as well—is to get the disagreements settled and to move on.

Yet not without at least a backward glance at the moral base of the legal decisions and solutions. American law, like English, focuses not on abstract right and wrong but on specific acts within a frame of traditional moral codes. But these codes are not always clear enough to resolve the question of whether the moral claims as between plaintiff and defendant should be translated into legal penalty and award. In a perceptive classification and review of the typical problems of the "moral decision" in the context of American law and society, Edmond Cahn notes the cases of injury to trespassing children at play, of sexual relationships, of the conduct of husband and wife in family disintegration, of honesty or deceit in business, of spite offenses against property, of tax cheating, of the impulse to rescue the unfortunate, of suicide and death.

Lecky pointed out that in an industrial civilization like England the needs of commerce and business put a premium upon honesty and truth-telling which did not apply in the preindustrial labor cultures. He called this "industrial veracity." This is even truer of American life, where the fabric of business would crumble if fraud were permitted to grow rampant and the law did not enforce at least a minimum of compliance with honesty. Given the fluid character of American family life and sexual mores, the same applies in those areas. To be sure, at no time in American life has there been a greater impulse to rethink questions of moral behavior than in the past quarter century, and at no time has there been a sharper challenge to the traditional codes, especially from psychology and psychiatry. It is in the American law journals and psychiatric publications that the question of the moral responsibility for crime on the part of a mentally unbalanced person was being most hotly debated: an effort was made to displace McNaghten's Rule—whether the accused knew that what he was doing was wrong—with one which (as in the decision in the Durham case) allows for the newly revealed subtleties of mental disturbance. Yet one may doubt whether this effort will wholly succeed.

With all the turbulence of shifting moral standards, American thinking is too deeply rooted in the idea of the individual's rights ever to become very relaxed about his obligations which form the other side of the shield. It is too concerned with the fullness of human personality ever to move away from the idea of individual responsibility. The forces that shaped American law in a frontier society, and then in a capitalist society, will continue to shape and reshape it in a society of abundance and welfare, where the collisions that occur have their greatest meaning in the quest for personal expression.

9. Keepers of the Covenant

AT THE APEX of the American legal system stands the Supreme Court as interpreter of the Constitution. Walter Bagehot said that every government must contain something of the "dignified" or "majestic" principle, rooted in men's emotions and in what we should today call the irra-

tional mind. Its purpose is to give government a cohesive force outlast-
ing the temporary political changes. This element is enshrined in the
Constitution, and amidst all the turbulences of history the Constitution
as eidolon has remained a fixture in the American mind.

The fact that the Constitution is a written charter, lending itself thus
to idolization; that it grew out of the War for Independence, has lasted
since the beginning of the nation's history, and survived even a bloody
Civil War; that within its framework America has risen to wealth and
world power; that it has not been shattered by the tensions of the major
depressions and wars; that under it American freedoms have not been
extinguished, although they have at times been severely limited; that it
has been the object of imitation by other peoples: these are some of the
facts that have fed the Constitution cult. But beyond all these there is
the human need for roots, which finds expression by clinging to some
strong symbol of allegiance.

The symbol of the Constitution has fulfilled this need. It has been invoked by the Americans of earlier immigrant origins—the "native"
Americans—and equally by the newer Americans who have worshiped it
the more eagerly because they found in it the symbol of what makes
Americans equal before the law. Amidst the change and decay of human
circumstance the Constitution—presumably framed in wisdom, maintained by courage, and proved by time—must have seemed to almost all
Americans the great fact which changeth not and therefore abideth.

Nevertheless, if one analyzes the imagery of belief it has embodied,
this unvarying symbol has had a changing content. The Constitution
started as a *compact*—whether of the states or of the people is still disputed. Later the Civil War burned it into the consciousness of Americans as a *symbol of indestructible union*. Later still, when the Supreme
Court interpreted some of the constitutional doctrines in a way to invalidate legislation, the Constitution became in the popular mind
mainly *a set of limitations* on the power of government. Only after the
Supreme Court crisis under the New Deal did it clearly emerge as an
instrument of government, capable of being used in the people's interests, flexible enough to be a living Constitution in a living society. Recently, under the tensions that have beset civil liberties everywhere, the
Constitution has come to be stressed as *a code of freedom:* a set of guarantees of human freedom and a symbol of vigilance against the arbitrary
use of man's power over man.

Since the Constitution is America's covenant, its guardians are the
keepers of the covenant and therefore touched with its divinity. As the
tenders of the sacred flame, the justices of the Supreme Court cannot
help playing the role of a sacerdotal group. By reason of its technical
function every priesthood exercises a political power: since they alone

are privy to the mysteries on which the destiny of the tribe depends, the priests must be consulted on what is permissible and what is taboo in tribal policy—a veto power which filters every major political decision and is thus a form of decision-making even when the Court deliberately refrains from exercising its power.

The American Constitution started without a specific grant to its judicial priesthood of this taboo power ("judicial review"), although the explicit grant was debated at the Constitutional Convention and the evidence is that it was at least implicitly intended. But early in the Supreme Court's history Chief Justice John Marshall boldly asserted the power of the Court to decide the constitutionality of an act of Congress: the claim lay dormant for some time but was resumed in the mid-nineteenth century after it had been applied in many cases to the acts of state legislatures. While there was a bitter challenge to this power by the Jeffersonians and their constitutional theorist, John Taylor, and debate flared up anew with the Dred Scott decision, the income-tax cases, and other crises in constitutional history, the Court's assertion of judicial review was never effectively resisted.

The reasons are clear enough. It fitted well with the needs of a Federal system: the strongest argument for judicial review is the chaos that would flow from unresolved clashes between states and national government. It fitted with the fears the big corporations later felt in the face of rising movements for social legislation. Finally it fitted with the psychic hunger of Americans for a symbol of ultimate guardianship of their rights under the law. Holmes said of John Marshall that his greatness lay in the place he held in "the campaign of history"—the "fact that he was *there*." The role he served was as a crucial link between nationalism, constitutionalism, and a rising commercial system. In its exercise of the power of judicial review the Supreme Court has been one of the chief elements in the planetary struggle for power within the economy and the social structure.

One may stretch the term (as I have suggested earlier) and say that there are two Constitutions in America—one the formal Constitution as interpreted by the Federal judiciary, the second the structure of power within American society. With the triumph of the business system after the Civil War, the chief energies of the Court—especially in the period from 1885 to the Depression of 1929—were directed toward making the legal Constitution fit with the structure of economic power, thus bringing the two Constitutions into line. The purpose was to exempt the business groups from hampering legislative and administrative controls by both state and Federal governments. "There are certain fundamental social and economic laws," said Justice Sutherland two years before he was appointed to the Court, "beyond the right of official control." He was clearly a fit person to effect the legal encrustation of *laissez faire*. It showed again that public law in a capitalist state, perhaps even more than private law, tends to take the shape demanded by the protection of the dominant property interests.

But the business groups had to pay a costly price for this temporary victory. To gain the victory the Court had to distort traditional and established constitutional doctrine; to take the Fourteenth Amendment, framed to protect Negroes against discrimination by Southern states after the Civil War, and use it to ward off regulatory legislation from business corporations; to stretch the meaning of "person," as I have mentioned, to include the corporation; and to stretch the meaning of "due process" from the guarantee of normal judicial procedures to the tabooing of reformist legislation.

Once this was done, however, the door was opened wide to the use of the Constitution as a living instrument for the needs of a living society. The game of adapting constitutional doctrines could be played by a Miller, a Brandeis, a Black, and a Douglas as well as by a Field and a Sutherland. If there could be a constitutional theology of profits and property there could be a counter-theology as well. The Devil could learn to quote this particular Scripture. The pressure of labor and the farmers and of reform movements could become more clamorous, if less well financed, than the pressure of corporate interests. Whenever a conservative Court showed an inclination to stand pat against legislation that seemed to meet the felt needs of the day, the liberal groups had the ready answer of pointing to the free-and-easy handling of judicial concepts by conservative majorities when it suited their interests. A Constitution whose amending process is notable for its brass-bound rigidity showed surprising qualities of flexibility without formal amendment. As "Mr. Dooley" put it, with a certain sophistication about the implications of judicial review: "Whether or not trade follows the flag, one thing is clear: the Supreme Court follows the election returns." The seeming detachment of the Court from political struggles was illusory. The Supreme Court bench was the quiet spot in the center of a tornado.

The great crisis of the Supreme Court's role in American society came with the New Deal's challenge to the conservative Court majority. For almost three quarters of a century the Court had operated as a bottleneck of social policy; but the Great Depression of the thirties, bringing the need for a program adequate to meet it, broke the bottleneck. Thus the economic crisis brought along a constitutional crisis. Its first phase was the refusal of the Court majority to admit that a social program with which they disagreed could be constitutional, its second phase the effort of President Roosevelt's "court-packing plan" to secularize the judicial priesthood. The Roosevelt plan was beaten, but not until the third phase, when the priesthood had clearly shown it was ready to withdraw the taboo it had invoked.

Out of this came the present equilibrium of the Supreme Court as a power institution. The power of judicial review remains, and along with it much of the sanctity of the keepers of the Covenant. The "dignified" principle that encases the Constitution has happily not been broken. On the other hand, the Court's power to frustrate future movements which may seek to organize the national will in meeting an emergency, as the New Deal did, is no longer likely to go unchallenged.

"I may not know much about law," wrote Theodore Roosevelt in 1912, "but I do know how one can put the fear of God into judges." He was talking of the movement for the popular recall of judges. But such movements have lost their appeal, mainly because judges and lawyers and much of lay opinion have come to understand that judicial interpretation is flexible enough to make the crude device of recall unnecessary. Americans have learned some of the facts of life about the workings of the judicial process. They no longer believe so readily that judicial decisions are babies brought by constitutional storks. They know something of the pain and wrack of the whole adventure of social organization, with its deep-rooted problems and its difficult solutions, out of which new constitutional interpretations emerge and old ones are modified.

It need no longer be argued vehemently that there is a political cast to many Supreme Court appointments, but the argument is often greatly oversimplified. Certainly the Supreme Court has never been "democratic" in the sense that appointments are meant to represent a cross section of the nation. Nor is the Court democratic in the mechanically responsive sense of changing with the shifting waves of popular opinion: one of the reasons for giving the judges life tenure and putting them beyond the reach of political and popular vindictiveness was to fashion a judicial independence without which any effort to interpret the basic frame of constitutional principle as principle would be a sham. There can be too much flexibility in judicial interpretation, as well as too little, especially if the flexibility is dictated by opportunism and is a surrender to the passions of the moment.

The great appointments have been those of farsighted men who could grow on the bench into judicial statesmanship. Sometimes, as in the appointment of Holmes by President Theodore Roosevelt, these choices were made on the mistaken assumption that the judge would go along with the political policy of the President (after the Holmes dissent in the Northern Securities case, T. R. is reported to have cried, "I could carve out of a banana a man with more backbone."). In other instances the political purpose of the appointment is well known and is carried out, as when Jackson appointed Taney or when Truman appointed Vinson. Sometimes a judge has started his judicial career inauspiciously, as with Hugo Black's admission of early membership in the Ku Klux Klan, and grown to judicial greatness. Sometimes a series of remarkably able appointees have been followed by a series of mediocrities, as with the general level of President Truman's appointments (Burton, Vinson, Clark, and Minton) when compared with the general level of the Roosevelt appointments (Black, Reed, Frankfurter, Murphy, Douglas, Jackson, and Rutledge). Sometimes, as with Stone and Cardozo, the unmistakable sentiment of the whole legal profession has made the choice of a particular man inevitable.

Yet on the whole it has been true of membership on the Supreme Court, as of the Presidential office, that the garments of office have expanded or shrunk with the dimensions of the wearer. Some of the great judges, like Marshall appointed by Adams, Harlan appointed by Hayes, Stone appointed by Coolidge, Hughes appointed by Taft and reappointed by Hoover, and Warren appointed by Eisenhower, might well have made greater Presidents than the Presidents who appointed them. It is true that no member of the Court has ever been elected to the Presidency, although Hughes came close and Taft reversed the process. On the whole, however, it has been a healthy tradition that the Court should not be considered a pathway to Presidential office. The very fact that the Court does have decision-making power of vast political consequence makes it even more important for the justices to be invulnerable to the charge of playing for political advantage. It takes great courage to fill the role of final constitutional arbiter with an eye to the enduring lines of national growth and greatness, rather than of any particular group, pressure, or power.

It is not necessary for biographers wholly to unclothe the judges in order to disrobe them and show the street clothes under their traditional vestments of office. A Supreme Court judge is a human being, which means that he is a thinking and valuing animal, with emotions about his fellow human beings and often very decided convictions about the processes of government. Their earlier careers—as corporate and utility lawyers, as governors and Senators, as attorney generals or heads of administrative agencies, as law school teachers, as crusading reformers—are usually a pretty good indication of the kind of judges they will make. To take an instance almost at random, of a mediocre judge who was nevertheless as Chief Justice an efficient presider over the Court: Melville W. Fuller was a Northern Democrat who had been a prosperous business lawyer; he had opposed both Abolition and Secession, had disapproved of the Fourteenth Amendment, and had been a vehement champion of the doctrine of "hard money." It was not too hard to foretell that he would vote to hold the Federal Income Tax of 1894 unconstitutional.

Or to take a more eminent instance: after the experience of the nation with Taft as President it was not hard to project his career into the Supreme Court and predict that he would make a highly political judge. Taft later boasted that during one term as President he had been lucky to have six Supreme Court appointments to make, while his successor Woodrow Wilson could make only three in two terms. One of those three, McReynolds, who had shown social fervor as attorney general, turned the tables on the guessers and became a conservative (although still unpredictable) justice. But Taft regarded the other two, Brandeis and Clarke, as "of socialistic tendency"—and it might be added that the leaders of the legal profession and the holders of economic power agreed with him about Brandeis, as witness the massive effort to kill his nomination, first in the Senate Judiciary Committee and then in the vote on the floor. Taft saw shrewdly that one of the high stakes of the 1920 election was the fact that four of the justices had passed the retiring age and would probably have to be replaced. "There is no greater domestic issue," he said about the 1920 campaign, "than the maintenance of the Supreme Court as the bulwark to enforce the guarantee that no man shall be deprived of his property without due process of law." Harding's election underscored the political realism of Taft's view, for in three years there were four new appointments, including Taft himself, Sutherland, Butler, and Sanford; these four joined three other conservatives to form a bloc of seven who consistently outvoted and isolated Holmes and Brandeis. When Taft met his colleagues as Chief Justice he told them in conference, "I have been appointed to reverse a few decisions," and (he wrote later), "I looked right at old man Holmes when I said it." Even after Coolidge had appointed Stone, who seemed at first relatively "safe" but developed into a fearlessly independent member of the Court, there was still a minority of only three at best on crucial cases. When Hoover appointed Cardozo the potential minority became four, but his appointment of Roberts and Hughes kept the majority safe. It was this political approach to Court appointments which evoked the drastic and equally political counterapproach of the Franklin Roosevelt court-packing proposal, and later his deliberately political appointments of New Dealers to the Court.

I have given some detailed scrutiny here to the appointments in one period of the Court's history, but the same would be true of the earlier periods to a much higher degree. During the whole stretch of Republican Presidential power from 1860 to 1912 (except for Cleveland's terms) the proportion of property-minded, business-minded, and corporate-minded judges who reached the Court was, needless to say, very high. The striking fact is that great judges do manage to emerge from this process—men like Marshall, Taney, Miller, Harlan, Holmes, Hughes, Brandeis, Stone, Cardozo, Black, Frankfurter, Douglas, Warren. (There were also judges like Van Devanter, who was a brilliant craftsman although a reactionary one and unable to write.) It would be hard to find a governing group in any society to match these men in talent, character, vision, and statesmanship. They have proved a fit corollary to the gallery of great Presidents.

The task of the Chief Justice is especially difficult, since he must keep the Court as cohesive as possible, iron out differences that need not be aired, avoid too-public splits, assign the writing of the majority opinion (here he can exercise a subtle influence of great importance), and set the whole intellectual tone of the Court. Marshall, Hughes, Stone, perhaps Vinson, and certainly Warren lived up notably to the dimensions of this great office. The case of Stone, which can be read in meticulous detail in Mason's biography, is especially interesting. He was appointed Attorney General to sweeten the stench left by Harding's Daugherty; he campaigned for Coolidge with speeches that were stilted and stuffed-shirtish; he performed his job as Attorney General with distinction, yet when he was appointed to the Court a few liberal Senators, like Norris, who were distrustful of his having had the Morgan bank as a client, opposed his confirmation. "I have always been sorry," said Stone later, "that I didn't have the Morgan House for my clients more than I did." And Norris, in 1941, voted to confirm him as Chief Justice: Stone had shown that capacity to rise above his earlier conditioning which is the saving quality of greatness in a judge.

One of the problems of the Court has been the overwhelming pressure of judicial business. In 1925 Congress reorganized the Court's work, and later changes were made in the same direction so that the Court would not have to remedy the wrongs of every litigant on appeal, but could choose the cases involving important principles of constitutional interpretation. The real question has always been what approach the Court would adopt to these principles.

The traditional "great split" between the liberal and conservative views of the Court's function, which Franklin Roosevelt phrased in popular terms as a split between those who cared about "property rights" and those who cared about "human rights," still retains a good deal of its meaning. But the livelier controversy in recent years, which split the liberal camp itself, was the conflict between the school of social "activism" or "dynamism" and that of "judicial self-limitation" or "self-restraint." Both schools of judges went beyond the earlier pretense that there is something fixed and known, which is called "the law" and which judges make known to the people. They recognized what Charles E. Hughes meant when he said that "we live under a Constitution, but the Constitution is what the Supreme Court says it is." He gave the simplest possible definition of what has come to be called "judicial supremacy." The two schools differed, however, in the method by which they could best live up to their task of interpreting constitutional powers, rights, and immunities.

The "self-limitation" school, deriving largely from Justice Holmes and notably championed by Justices Frankfurter and Jackson, rested on Holmes's insistence that the judges should minimize their role, stay out of the social struggles as far as possible, accept state and Federal legislation unless clearly outside the powers of the legislatures, and decide cases on technical and procedural grounds where possible in order to avoid committing the Constitution to principles that may later prove mischievous. The philosophy of the school was well expressed by Justice Stone in the agricultural controls case, when he warned his colleagues that "the only restraint we have is our self-restraint." Ultimately it is based on the premise that judicial supremacy can become a form of tyranny, that judges are frail and ought to discipline their sentiments, that all of government and human life is a fragile process, and that a Court is wisest when it raises as few broad controversial issues of principle as possible.

One difficulty here of course is that even the decision to use self-restraint is an exercise of judicial power, and even a judge like Robert H. Jackson, who carried this principle far in most of his judicial opinions, broke it on something like the case of the religious liberties of the Jehovah's Witnesses. Another difficulty is that the principle of staying away from principles, and of narrowing every constitutional issue to the minimum one compatible with the immediate facts, can become a bleak function for the judicial process. The danger of the doctrine of judicial restraint is that it becomes judicial abdication. Still another danger, as I note below, is that when it is applied to the problems of legislative or administrative interference with civil liberties, it leaves the field of action open to arrogant or frightened and sometimes hysterical legislative majorities, acting often under the pressure of intense minorities in the population.

The "activist" school, championed by Justices Black and Douglas, was derived largely from Justice Brandeis and held that the Supreme Court has a positive role to play not only in guarding civil liberties but in setting a legal frame for the quest of a greater measure of economic and social democracy. This approach was strengthened by the philosophy of the New Deal and the appointments that Franklin Roosevelt made to the Court. At base it represents an instrumental approach to the judicial process. It candidly makes a distinction between the protection of individual freedom and the progress of economic and social advance. In the latter case it is willing to go along with legislative majorities and administrative action on the theory that these broad issues have been hammered out under long public debate and represent the response to the needs of the time. But in the case of civil liberties, where freedoms of long standing may be threatened by emotional new doctrines expressed through hasty majorities, it holds that the role of the Court is that of acting to protect the old freedoms against the new dangers. The field of administrative law is especially important because of its rapid recent growth: in this field the school of judicial restraint is unlikely to go beyond the findings of facts by administrative agencies and restricts itself to questions of law; the activist school, on the other hand, will review findings of fact if it suspects that they conceal an instance of arbitrary power by the agency. Just as the weakness of judicial self-restraint is that it may become a form of abdication, so the weakness of judicial activism is that it may become a form of arbitrary intervention by the Court itself into the other areas of government and into state action.

The period of the "cold war" during the decade after 1945 presented the Court with one of its great testing periods. The Court at first faltered. The classic distinction between belief and action was blurred, and the Court accepted the dubious notion that if a number of people "conspired" or "organized" to "advocate" subversion, Congress should legislate for their punishment. Once the gate was thus opened, some very dangerous freightage managed to get through. But it should be added that at the end of the 1945-1955 period the Court grew firmer. In 1957 came the climactic decision in the case of the California Communists under the Smith Act. Speaking through Justice Harlan, the Court defined "organize" strictly to mean the creation (not continuance) of an organization, and in defining "advocacy" it made incitement to action—rather than mere belief—the test for the juries to pass on. In the Watkins Case, Chief Justice Warren cut down the cancerous growth of the Congressional investigating power, held that a Congressional inquiry must be "in furtherance of a legitimate task of Congress" (adding "Who can define the meaning of 'un-American'?"), and reminded the Congressional committees that "there is no Congressional power to expose for the sake of exposure." It was clear that the Supreme Court had finally ridden out the cold-war crisis and had put into broad legal terms the calmer judgment of the majority of the American people.

There has been considerable recent discussion of whether the Supreme Court is a democratic or an undemocratic instrument of government.

The stronger view would seem that it is democratic in its response to the larger fluctuations of public opinion, and its accessibility to changing Presidential regimes. One should add, however, that for long stretches, especially from the 1880s to the 1930s, it lagged behind the best legal and judicial opinion. In essence what this means is that the Court is part of the changes and chances of its time, and also part of the power structure in the society as a whole. It was this quality, of being part of the power structure, that made the social thinkers of the 1930s and 1940s attack it as "undemocratic." On balance one may say that the Court is part of American democracy, but that it serves as a tempering influence both upon social and economic advance and also upon attacks on the freedom of the person.

The best type of judge is one who maintains the kind of skepticism of ideas which Holmes had, and has the saving impulse to restrain his own power that Stone had, but believes that even within this frame of skepticism and restraint the Court has both the duty and opportunity to make judicial action square with a social humanism of the kind Brandeis strove for. This means that there can be no single formula for the judicial process, and that the judge cannot escape the infinitely difficult task of weighing his intellectual caution and skepticism against his social boldness and his moral faith in human possibility.

One of the best instances of how a great Court acted in some such spirit, under a great Chief Justice, was the unanimous decision in the school segregation cases, written by Chief Justice Warren. It represented a break from the turn-of-the-century segregation decisions, and it broke with them sharply and boldly, without any apparatus of protective citation and without the hypocrisy of trying to "distinguish" so that an actual judicial change would seem to be no change at all. In this sense it was a political decision, yet not in the narrow spirit of being a partisan one. North and South alike, Republicans and Democrats on the Court, joined in it because it aimed to sum up the conscience and progress of the nation in the area of civil rights, and because it boldly completed a long line of decisions that had been moving in the same direction. It went outside traditional legal categories by taking notice of studies by psychologists and sociologists which showed that separate and segregated schools could not be "equal" because the fact of their separateness was the fact that left a scar on the minds of the schoolchildren, Negro and white alike. Yet it was a decision reached not in haste but only after long deliberation; and it directed that the states and the local school districts carry it out "with all deliberate speed."

In this sense the Court has an important role as a national educator, trying to set standards of social control taken from the best levels of thought and asking the nation as a whole to measure itself by those standards. It cannot ever place itself in the vanguard of social thought, since its job is to distill what has already been thought and done and translate it into legal norms. But neither does it have to wait forever, until the bold has been frustrated and destroyed or until the novel has become archaic. Its task is a creative one in the sense that it must recognize when the action and thinking of popular majorities is valid for the long term, and when it is dangerous, must seize upon the thinking of the creative minority to hold it up as a standard for the majority to follow. No Court that could do this in a sustained way has yet been put together in Supreme Court history, but it is a not impossible ideal.

10. The Struggle for Civil Liberties

THE AREA IN WHICH the Federal courts have performed their most crucial work of guarding the polity is that of civil liberties, and the shield of freedom has been the Bill of Rights. Watching from Paris while the battle over the Constitution was being waged at home, Jefferson wrote that the necessary guarantees were "freedom of religion, freedom of the press, freedom from monopolies, freedom from unlawful imprisonment, freedom from a permanent military, and a trial by jury." And again, "A Bill of Rights is what the people are entitled to against every government on earth." They got one, in the form of the first ten amendments to the Constitution. Along with other constitutional provisions, including the Fourteenth Amendment, they represent both substance and symbol of American freedom—although the commitment to them by majorities and minorities has often been notably weak in practice.

The most elusive word in the political vocabulary, "freedom" is also one of the most important in the American consciousness. It is the first image the American invokes when he counts the blessings of his state. The inheritor of the English and French revolutions, as well as of his own, he has gazed so long into the pool of freedom that he has fallen half in love with his own reflection in it. He may be at the base of the income pyramid or a segregated Negro in the South, yet whatever his place in the social system, he sets store by freedom: it gives him a yardstick to measure his deprivation and a hope that he can remedy it. The historical record shows that the denials of freedom are part of the scar tissue of American culture and not its principle of growth and being.

In the triad of American "liberal capitalist democracy," the "liberal" component has generally meant the freedom to make your own decisions in your political and personal life. There are many constraints that the American does not regard as the denial of freedom. The conditions of his job, the rules of his union, the rigors of business fluctuations, the tyrannies of the community, and the prejudices of his fellow men may in fact represent harsh constraints on him. Yet he does not consider them violations of his freedom because they come as the fabric of his everyday life, and not as encroachment by anyone in authority. He is prepared to accept the informal but not the formal constraints, those from within the culture but not those from political authority.

To be cramped by someone who has power or superior position in a graded official hierarchy—that is counted the real denial of freedom. For example, the Great Depression of the 1930s wiped out billions in property values and income, reduced many to pauperism, saddled others with burdens it took a lifetime to discharge: yet it was not held to have diminished American freedom. The real threat was held to be the structure of bureaucracy built to cope with the periodic economic breakdowns. The spirit of this thinking shows up in the story of the Negro, living in squalor and precariousness, who was asked what he had gained by exchanging the security of slavery for poverty in freedom, and who answered, "There's something about the *looseness* of this here freedom that I like."

The obvious defect of this conception is its negativism. It stresses freedom *from* the powers and principalities of organized government, but not freedom *for* the creative phases of living. It derives from the whole freedom constellation of the eighteenth century, which saw a simple and natural plan of self-regulating human life, complete with an economic and political theory, a psychology and a metaphysics, and which asked only that the government keep its hands off and leave it alone. It underscored *let live* but forgot that in the jungle of the industrial culture *let live* without *help live* can be morally empty.

Yet there are few civilizations in history in which freedom has flourished as it has in America. What explains it?

There have been three principal explanations—the environmental, the political, the economic. The environmentalists say that the isolation of America, cut off by oceans for centuries from the wars and embroilments of Europe and Asia, kept it from standing armies and internal crises, and therefore free. They say also that the continuing availability of frontier land gave an outlet to energies that might otherwise have clashed in civil conflicts. The economic explanation holds that the core of American freedom is the free-enterprise economy, on the theory that free markets make free men, that political and social freedoms could not have been preserved without freedom of investment and the job. The political explanation stresses the separation of powers, the limited state, and the *laissez-faire* tradition.

The environmental theories, with their core of truth, fail to note that geography is only part of a larger social environment, that the span of distance America had from the European centers was less important than the spaciousness of American institutions and their distance from European feudalism. Similarly, the economic approach must be seen as part of the economic expansionism of American life. During one phase of American history *laissez faire* played an important and releasing role; but later experience showed that a mixed economy was a better base for freedom, since one of the great threats to it is economic breakdown.

Finally there is the political argument from the separation of powers. But there are other forms of it more crucial than the traditional splitting of the three political areas of power: the separation of economic from political power, the separation of church from state power, the separation of military from civilian power, and the separation of majority passions from the power of the law. This seems the more productive approach.

American freedom has been largely interstitial, located in the crevices between necessary power systems. It is protected by the fact that the men who run the economy do not always run the country—and also the other way around. It is also protected by the fact that the men of religion, who shape and organize the supernatural beliefs of Americans, cannot use the power of the government to make their creed exclusive—and also the other way around, in the fact that the government cannot interfere with freedom of worship. Further, it is protected by the fact that those who can send men to death in war are themselves held to account by civilian authority—and again (the other way around) in the fact that the political leaders cannot make themselves military heroes and go off on adventures of glory. It is strengthened by the fact that there is an independent judiciary which need not, although it sometimes does, respond to temporary waves of popular hatred against particular groups—and (the other way around) by the tradition of judicial nonparticipation in the tensions of political life.

Thus freedom may be seen partly as a function of the way power is distributed, separated, and diffused in a society. Americans tend to think of the government as the prime enemy of freedom, and see the history of freedom in America as the story of a Manichaean struggle between the angels of (individualist) light and the hosts of (governmental) darkness. But governmental power is only one form of social power. Wherever power is concentrated, whether in a government bureaucracy, a corporate combine, a big trade-union, a military staff, a powerful opinion empire, or a church organization disciplined to action, those who care about freedom must find ways of isolating that power, keeping it from combining with other power clusters, and holding it to account and responsibility.

But this effort to hold power accountable, which may sometimes involve attempts to break it up in its concentrated form, may itself endanger freedom by rousing latent social hostilities. With its lusty energies American life has always had a considerable violence potential which has flared into actual violence when a challenge has been offered to the continuance of some power structure. For concentrated power, whatever its form, is never so dangerous as when it feels itself in danger. A number of the movements chipping away at the civil-liberties tradition have come from power groups that felt their status to be in jeopardy. This was true of the Federalists who passed the Alien and Sedition Acts; of the White Supremacy movement in the postwar South, using night riders to terrorize and disfranchise Negroes; of the Oriental Exclusion Acts, supported both by the landowners and the trade-unionists of the West Coast; of the vigilantist violence used against labor organizers in communities where the police are tied in with the holders of economic power, and where even the churches sanction the fusion.

The history of a people is, from one angle, the story of the seesawing acquisition and relinquishment of power by a number of competing and intermeshed groups. But to relinquish power is never pleasant. Sometimes it may lead to an almost paranoid fear of encirclement. Franklin Roosevelt expressed a double-edged truth when he listed "freedom from fear" as one of the Four Freedoms. It is a truth because freedom from fear, rightly understood, can assure all the other freedoms. It is double-edged because the effort to achieve freedom from fear of the threats and challenges of foreign powers, and of subversion within, involves a military posture for the entire nation which itself breeds further fears and therefore dangers to freedom. One of the great difficulties is to distinguish between the fears which have a basis in reality and those which are anxieties and hallucinations.

Every great crisis in civil liberties contains a mixture of fears of both sorts. After World War I there was a wave of raids and deportations; it arose from the uneasy feeling that the Russian Revolution had caused a shift in the world balance of power and spawned a fanatic faith threatening American survival. After World War II there was another wave of assaults on civil liberties. It had a number of interrelated phases: the Smith Act prosecution of Communist leaders, the security purges of government officials, the Congressional investigations of "Reds" and "subversives" in government agencies and in colleges and universities, the sharp restrictions on foreign travel, the security surveillance of scientists, the scrutiny of the associates and even the families of men in the armed services, the widespread use of wiretapping in the effort to get evidence on political suspects, the heaping up of dossiers which were often filled with trivial and hearsay material, the setting up (under the McCarran Act of 1950) of emergency detention camps for political suspects, the grant of unprecedented power to put together an "Attorney General's list" of subversive organizations which in effect served as a measuring stick for loyalty, the deportation of aliens as political undesirables, the blacklisting of movie, radio, and TV performers, the use of anonymous evidence against "security" suspects who had no chance to confront their accusers, the dismissal of political unreliables from presumably sensitive posts in private industry, and group pressures within small communities against suspected books and individuals in a movement that came to be called "cultural vigilantism."

There was a stronger base for fear of external danger in this later period than after World War I, since the challenge of Kremlin expansionism was real and the conspiratorial nature of Communism had been made amply clear. Most Americans learned enough about the techniques of Communist penetration, espionage, and propaganda to know the reality of the designs against them. Yet along with the recognition of real threats, there was also a mixture of neurotic fears and fantasies. Inevitably the vast power struggle and arms race awakened popular passions, and the crisis was all the sharper because the old fears of a welfare state were merged with the new fears of Communist penetration.

A "security syndrome" brought into active eruption many of the hatreds smoldering below the surface. The accusations against "subversives" sometimes had a factual base but were often a loose and enveloping cover for racist, religious, xenophobian, political, and economic hostilities. Despite its prosperity, American life generated enough frustrations to clamor for expression in the often unconsciously disguised catchwords of "loyalty," "security," and "Americanism." A segment of the American population which had always been potentially strong now found a target for its sense of grievance and its malaise. Seymour Lipset's concept of "status politics" came into use to express the extreme political positions taken by those who were fearful of the security of their status in American life, and a new "Radical Right" emerged to challenge the Left with an equal fervor and with an inverted form of some of the old Leftist dogmas.

In a searching analysis of the history of American civil liberties John Roche has concluded that the idea of a Golden Age of freedom in the past and of a later expulsion from Eden is an illusory one, and that the record has actually been one of advance. To test this the two periods of postwar crises are worth comparing. The actual dangers from the outside—from Communist world power and its conspiratorial organization —were greater in the later than in the earlier periods, and the Communist organization within the United States was more substantial and tight-knit, although Communist strength within America could easily be overestimated. The turnover of membership within the party was high, the residue of indoctrination slight, and the anti-Communist bitterness of former members considerable. In the early 1930s the Communists had made some headway among intellectuals, artists, and students, comparable to their hold on these groups in some continental countries, but by the 1950s this hold had vanished, and Communist leadership was reduced to an intellectually ragged group without distinction or prestige. Moreover, the fear of internal unrest which had plagued the American mind in 1919, especially with respect to the labor movement, had all but vanished in the prosperity and stability of the 1950s.

Yet there were three sharp differences between the periods that made the later one more dangerous. The first was that the methods used in the suppression of civil liberties were less blatant: the 1919 method was one of arrests, criminal trials, and deportations; the later methods included Congressional investigations, destructive publicity, purges, blacklists, and indirect pressures. Second, the resistance to them was more fragmented than it had been in the earlier period, partly because the fears were more complex and widespread, partly because there were greater divisions and disunity among liberals. These divisions in turn were the result of a thirty-year history of Communist treachery and ruthlessness within the United States as well as the shock of liberal disillusionment with the nature and methods of Kremlin power. Third, the popular unrest in the earlier period was considerable, fed by the fact that the new Communist creed coming out of Russia still seemed an idealistic one and made an appeal to a union movement still feeling its way and a group of intellectuals stirred by the great events of the time. This was not true in the later period. The fact that there was so little base in popular unrest for the structure of repressive measures was itself one of the dangerous facts about it, since it underscored its synthetic quality.

The one new factor in the American situation, missing in the earlier period, was the fact of atomic weapons at a time when America and Russia were locked in a struggle for world power. This was the major premise of the Great Fear, underlying each of the minor premises of the particular case involved. Many Americans, battered by a swift succession of bewildering events and by the repeated accusations against "disloyal" government servants, came to feel a sullen, brooding sense of secret dangers lying in wait for them in an era of incalculable death. While only a few of the accusations were against scientists who could deliver atomic secrets to Russia, the cases of the Rosenbergs, Sobell, and Gross were enough to precipitate the fears, and every new accusation—no matter how trivial, far-fetched, or baseless—took on a sinister meaning in the context of the possible betrayal of the new secrets. To add to this "torment of secrecy," as Edward Shils aptly called it, the new situation gave many people a chance to express a delayed reaction of hostility to the New Deal and its works. The two trials of Alger Hiss, linked in the minds of most people with the "bright young men" of the New Deal, seemed a symbol of a generation of betrayal.

In the minds of many, as Eric Goldman spelled it out in detail in a survey of the 1945-55 decade, this was the "Great Conspiracy." It mattered not that the secrets which counted were secrets of Nature that could not be guarded, to which every community of scientists had access; nor did it matter that not a single one of the thousands of "security cases" in Washington involved any charge of sedition, or that the whole notorious Fort Monmouth investigation failed to uncover a spy or even a Communist. What counted was not the facts but the fears, not the actual dangers of the betrayal of secrets but the trumped-up dangers shouted through the microphones. It was the publicity-conscious politicians who were most obsessed with secrecy. Shils noted that the British, less anxious about their security problem, had more concern for the privacy of the person, while the secrecy-conscious Americans reveled in a Roman holiday of publicity.

This was the American mood in the inquisitional years of the early 1950s that came to be called the era of "McCarthyism" after its principal symbol, and caused a good deal of apprehension abroad. One may overemphasize what Justice Douglas called the "black curtain of fear": there was much double-think by liberals who assumed that none of the accusations could be true and that the accusers were always self-interested and hysterical. There was also considerable double-think by ex-Communists and ex-fellow-travelers who (as Mary McCarthy put it) "carried with them into the democratic camp the emergency mentality of totalitarianism," viewing "the mass of ordinary people . . . as so much plasticine to be molded into a harder form through constant indoctrination."

In time the American political and intellectual leaders, groping between these destructive alternatives, found the way of sanity. Without flinching from the Medusa head of Communist reality, they refused to be panicked into surrendering hard-won American freedoms as their response. One of the striking developments was the emergence eventually of an articulate resistance, made up of men of diverse political viewpoints—a liberal Senator like Lehman, a conservative Senator like Flanders, commentators like Edward R. Murrow and Elmer Davis, a newspaper editor like James Wechsler, a New England Republican lawyer like Joseph Welch—around whom a demoralized public consensus could re-form its ranks and regain a sense of perspective. The Army-

McCarthy hearings were the turning point in this process because they confronted the highly emotional symbol of anti-Communism with the older and more deeply rooted symbol of national defense, and stripped away from McCarthy the outward show of nationalism to reveal underneath an anarchic thrust toward power which would have wrecked the civil-liberties tradition.

The judiciary played a role in this process. After a period of hesitation while the Federal courts agonized over finding some standard by which to delimit the area of permitted speech, the Supreme Court had to grapple openly with the problem in the *Dennis* case. Writing the decision on the Circuit Court level, Judge Learned Hand said the courts would have to decide "whether the gravity of the evil, discounted by its improbability, justifies such invasion of free speech as is necessary to avoid the danger." Despite the involved phrasing of this formula, what it said was clear enough: that the more serious the internal danger, the more justifiable is the governmental action to suppress freedom of speech.

What it did, in effect, was to change the Holmesian formula of "clear and present danger" into "clear and *probable* danger." Chief Justice Vinson adopted this approach in his opinion for the Court, but he spoke for only four of the justices in the 6-2 split. But in 1957 a reconstituted Court, headed by Chief Justice Warren, narrowed the application of the Smith Act by holding that the "abstract doctrine" of believing in the violent overthrow of existing institutions was not enough to convict a man. The essential distinction, wrote Justice Harlan, was between belief and incitement to action. This still left a blurred margin between the two, within which a judge and jury bent on sending political trouble-makers to jail could find ample means for their intent. There remained, moreover, the old question of how dangerous the incitement had to be to the Republic before it could eat away the First Amendment's protection of a man's political beliefs. On this question of the immediacy of the danger and the time element involved, Justice Brandeis' formula in *Whitney v. California* still seemed the best approach, although the Supreme Court has never adopted it. The test that Brandeis used was whether there was still any time left to carry on the process of public education in counteracting the error and evil of the propaganda that the government was seeking to suppress. This was a later version of Jefferson's belief that a democracy need not fear "to tolerate error so long as reason is free to combat it."

From this angle the hunt for dangerous thoughts made little sense in an America which continued both through war and postwar years in a strong and stable condition. Such an America could afford to dispense with the trappings of loyalty oaths for teachers, the widespread use of professional informers, and the harrying of political opponents, however misguided. It could afford the luxury of allowing freedom of expression even for those who would themselves deny freedom if they were in power, and even to a disciplined and subservient Communist party whose leaders were undoubtedly involved in a network of conspiratorial action. The crucial distinction between action and doctrine, including "conspiracy to teach" the doctrine, was one that Americans persisted in making, although it was beclouded by the tensions of the early 1950s. When the McCarran Senate Subcommittee and the Justice Department sought to press a perjury indictment against a writer and scholar, in the Lattimore case, because he had helped shape a viewpoint toward Asian policy which was widely repudiated later, Judge Luther Youngdahl sharply reasserted in a memorable opinion an American's right to be wrong.

Of the problems of legal and political theory with which Americans struggled in their civil-liberties crisis, one of the most perplexing concerned the problem of self-incrimination in testimony before Congressional investigating committees. The protection of the right to remain silent, which is part of the guarantee against self-incrimination in the Fifth Amendment, came out of a long history of struggle both in England and America. Interestingly enough this guarantee was first established in English law to protect persons accused of (and often guilty of) the religious and political crimes of heresy, schism, and sedition. Once the precedent had been set for them it was extended to common felons as well, in the area of criminal law. The religious and political cases, mainly involving Puritan dissenters in England and in America as well, were the trail blazers; the others followed. If Tudor and Stuart England had recognized freedom of religion, speech, assembly, and press, no explicit right against self-incrimination would have developed because none would have been needed.

Similarly, when the political climate in postwar America became harsh, whether for "heretics" or "conspirators," and when Congress and the courts narrowed the area of freedom of expression, they sought refuge in the Fifth Amendment ("stood on the Fifth"). It became clear that many Communists availed themselves of the constitutional protection as a way of evading damaging disclosures, along with non-Communists who used it because they found it distasteful to name names. The temptation was strong to brush aside the irritating obstacle presented by this guarantee, in the urgent drive to smash the Communist movement and its strength. The resort to the Fifth soon took on a public stigma, and while the government could do little except to pass "immunity statutes," private colleges and private industry usually rid themselves of anyone who took this stand. Yet on the whole the saner course—that of clinging to the constitutional safeguard, even at the cost of giving a tactical advantage to the enemies of democracy—was likely to prevail.

A balance sheet of civil liberties in the mid-1950s would stand somewhat as follows. Freedom of worship for all was established beyond any danger of being dislodged. The right of private parochial instruction was also established, but the doctrine of the separation of church and state was being challenged by the movement for religious instruction in the public schools. The area of freedom of speech was still in flux, and that of the freedom to stay silent was becoming clarified. The right of political association was shaky so far as the Communist party was concerned. The "right to knowledge and the free use thereof," involving freedom of teaching and research as well as of press, movies, and publication, was threatened less by the government than by organized citizen boycotts which extended to bookstores, libraries, theaters, and movie houses giving hospitality to a suspected writer or artist. The ban against wiretapping in Federal court cases still held firm. The rights of aliens in immigration and deportation cases did not get much recognition from the courts, but the safeguards of administrative procedural fairness were being strengthened there as well as in the passport cases involving the right of a citizen to travel. The struggle for the right of franchise for Negroes received a setback because of Southern bitterness over the school integration cases, but it was bound to be won; the same applied to the right of equal opportunity in education, travel, housing, and other areas, where it was the Supreme Court rather than Congress which represented the great line of advance.*

Despite many confusions on the question of freedom and security, there was a persistent belief that freedom is an unbroken web whose strands are interdependent, and that if it is arbitrarily broken at any point it becomes more breakable at all the others. Benjamin Franklin summed it up with his usual pungency: "those who would give up essential liberty to purchase a little temporary safety, deserve neither liberty nor safety." The real aim of the hunters of dangerous thoughts was less to protect national safety than to secure general conformity. In pursuit of that aim they were willing to endanger public freedom and veto the individual life. But the stakes of the civil-liberties crisis did not end in minority rights. Even more important was the process of genuine majority rule. The basis of the whole theory of the democratic will is that the people will have alternative courses of action between which they can make a choice. This is what Holmes meant in his famous dissent in the Abrams case in 1919 when he spoke of "the power of the

---

* For a further discussion of the struggle for Negro rights, see Ch. VII, Sec. 6, "The Negro in America."

thought to get itself accepted in the competition of the market." Unless alternative policies can be freely presented, the majority will becomes truncated and ultimately meaningless. Again we return to the Brandeis conception of democracy as a prolonged conversation among the people in which various groups seek to carry on a process of competitive education and persuasion.

There was one element in the American civil-liberties situation in the 1950s, that of its world impact, which had not applied to the same degree earlier. America was engaged in a competitive struggle for survival, waged against a totalitarian movement of world scope which could exploit every instance of American hypocrisy about democratic freedoms. A glaring instance of suppression of freedom, a case of lynching, or a "legal" jury murder of a Negro in a Southern state which the Federal government felt powerless to punish, was immediately telegraphed around the world and used to undermine American prestige. The most powerful weapon that America had in the struggle of ideas was the image of a free society. Whenever the enemies of civil liberties inside America tarnished that image they weakened American power and safety far more than could the shabby and pathetic cadres of Communist propaganda inside the nation.

The great force that has thus far broken the shock of the periodic assaults on freedom from within American life has been the civil-liberties tradition—the historical commitment of Americans to the public protection of the freedom of the individual person. Its roots go deep into the history of American thought and attitudes.

We may start with the Puritan (and generally Protestant) emphasis on the importance of the individual conscience. Beyond that there was the teaching, from the religious tradition, of the intensity of sacrifice for individual conscience and for the ideal of justice and equality. Broadening out still further, there was the emphasis on the individual personality and its sanctity, resting on the tradition of natural rights, the religious belief that each person has a soul, and the premise of potential individual creativeness. Add to this the property complex which has put a premium on the value of individual effort and its relation to reward, and the success complex which has linked freedom with the sense of competitive worth and the impulse for self-improvement.

Round it off with the two basic American attitudes toward freedom as an ingredient in the social process. One is the pragmatic attitude expressed in Holmes's phrase about the competition of ideas, which is a more astringent way of putting Milton's ". . . who ever knew Truth put to the worse, in a free and open encounter?" It says in effect that the idea which survives may not be necessarily the truth, but what better way does a society have for choosing the ideas it will live by? The second is the belief that the individual personality is more productive if it functions in freedom than if it must obey someone else's authoritarian behest. Put all these together, and in the convergence of intellectual, emotional, and institutional factors you get the strength of the American freedom constellation.

It is not the possession of any single group in American life, nor can it be left to the sole guardianship of any group—not even of the Supreme Court. The labor groups care about freedom of collective bargaining and freedom from strike-breaking violence, yet they may themselves be scornful of the civil rights of Negro workers whom some unions still exclude. The business managers are concerned about their freedom from government controls, yet American history is filled with the denials of freedom by employers to workers who sought to organize. Liberals claim the civil-liberties tradition as their own, yet some of the staunchest defenders of civil liberties have been conservatives, from John Adams through men like Charles E. Hughes and Henry L. Stimson. Some who have called themselves conservatives have forgotten that the civil-liberties tradition is the most precious heritage to conserve; some who have called themselves "liberals" have been known to run from the defense of freedom as soon as the firing became hot; while, in a different grain of "liberalism," there have been some so bemused by the "world revolution" of Communism that they did not face with realism the nature of the Communist threat to freedom.

In all the instances of faltering, the weakness that breaches the defense of the civil-liberties tradition is the lack of genuine commitment to freedom. This is sometimes the result of a poverty of moral generosity, sometimes the failure of imaginative insight into the plight of others and its meaning for the civilization as a whole. In the end it reduces itself to a contempt for the sovereignty of another's personality. Freedom is an inherent part of the development of personality. Wherever freedom is diminished for anyone, the personality—however noble or ignoble, intelligent or doltish—is thereby diminished. The diminution affects not only the personality deprived of freedom but others as well. For freedom is indivisible. What is disturbing to the student of contemporary America is not only the number of infringements of freedom but the fact that so few Americans who were not themselves targets rallied early or spontaneously to the support of the victims. Equally disturbing is the fact that many of the continuing threats to freedom come not from government action but from private boycotts.

For a clue we must go back again to the nature of freedom as the American conceives it. He sees it as the right of an individual against hostile forces outside—usually the government. But the individual is helpless to defend himself against the attacks on him, especially in an age of publicity when accusations made before a Congressional committee or by a speech on the floor of Congress or a resolution of a veterans' group gain wide circulation. He can be secure only if the group—committed by the social duty of defending his rights even as against itself —protects him against assaults until he is proved guilty of overt action or covert conspiracy involving sedition or treason. The test, of course, must be the law itself, operating through judicial procedures and not through some extrajudicial procedures or emergency measure.

Some of the critics of America abroad have cited these recent invasions of civil liberties as proof that the whole American concern for freedom is hypocritical. The charges do not sit well with cultures where the power of party and state spells the moral annihilation of the individual, and where the total fusion of diverse powers crushes the liberties of the person. Many Americans have not understood, however, that the reality of the totalitarian threat furnishes no adequate reason for betraying the whole career of freedom in America. The measures which seem to be dictated by the urgency of danger are in fact as badly calculated to meet the real threats to security within the nation as they are to advance the democratic cause in the rivalry for world position outside. The conditions of living in a contemporary industrial society are likely to produce, as Erich Fromm has pointed out, a fear of freedom and an impulse to escape from its burdens. But they are the burdens of self-government and of moral decision, and they cannot be escaped. Those who sell Americans short on the capacity to survive as a free people ignore the perilous but great career of American freedom that disproves their calculation.*

* For a discussion of related phases of the problem of freedom, see Ch. IV, Sec. 2, "Science in an Open Society"; Ch. VII, Sec. 5, "The Minority Situation," and Sec. 6, "The Negro in America"; Ch. IX, Sec. 4, "Varieties of American Character"; Ch. X, Sec. 2, "American Thought: the Angle of Vision"; Ch. XII, Sec. 4, "Landscape with Soldiers."

CHAPTER VII

Class and Status in America

IN WHICH we look at the American system of class and status, asking what the modes and structures of power are in America and the modes of access to that power; also how Americans rank each other and themselves, in what kind of hierarchies, how much it means to them, how mobile and how rigid the classes are, and how they conform or conflict with the prevailing beliefs in the American mind.

After an initial over-all view, trying to sift fact from fiction about the American class system (Sec. 1, "The Open-Class Society"), we study more closely the three main strata of power and status in American life—the ruling groups, old and new (Sec. 2, "The Seats of the Mighty"), the complex emerging forms of the middle classes (Sec. 3, "The New Middle Classes"), and the workers (Sec. 4, "Class Profile of the Worker"). For each of the three we ask how cohesive or loose are the ties of the members with each other, and their bonds of common feeling and action, what are the current shaping forces that determine their power and standing, how they feel about their own position, and about the other classes. And always we ask what the struggle to achieve and maintain their desired status does to the mind and personality of the Americans in each class.

We ask somewhat the same questions about the out-groups in American life—the ethnic minority groups (Sec. 5, "The Minority Situation") and especially the situation of the Negro (Sec. 6, "The Negro in America"). We examine the extent and direction of racist feeling and discriminatory practices in America, and strike a trial balance of what has been happening in the past quarter century to the Negro and his struggle to free himself from the humiliations of Jim Crow and achieve an equal and common life with other Americans. In these sections on American stratification we are dealing less with class than with status—that is, systems of prestige and standing, and with the evidences of the breaking up of the only phase of American life that might be termed a system of caste.

We end by approaching the problem of class and status in a democracy from two angles of vision. First we inquire into the nature of the badges of belonging in America—the outward insignia of status and the inner satisfactions and scars of being accepted or being excluded (Sec. 7, "The Badges of Belonging"). Second, we test the idea that a genuine class struggle is in process in American life (Sec. 8, "The Democratic Class Struggle"), but that it has few of the features that Marxism ascribes to the class struggle, since it is focused on individual attainment of income and rank and power through individual effort rather than on the image and consciousness of collective struggle, and also because it takes place within an open-class system by methods characteristic of such a system.

CHAPTER VII

Class and Status in America

1. The Open-Class Society

AMERICA was in conception a classless society. Behind its settlement and growth was a heritage partly borrowed from revolutionary Europe, partly shaped by the American experiment. It included four related elements: hatred of privilege, the religion of equality, open channels of opportunity, and rewards based on achievement and not on birth or rank.

This was the image of a classless American society. No man was to get a better or worse start than another; each was to have the same chance to show the stuff he was made of—to begin and end as a man; none was to bare his head or bend his knee to another by reason of birth, rank, or vested power; each was to be judged by what he was and could do. In the phrase that Jefferson picked up and adapted from an English rebel, "the mass of mankind has not been born with saddles on their backs, nor a favored few booted and spurred, ready to ride them legitimately by the grace of God." This is what he had meant in the Declaration of Independence, by his assertion that "all men are created equal": not that there were no individual differences between men, but that no man-made differences of class, caste, and subjection were to be added to those that nature had made.

One gets here a picture of a society with no depressed and subject classes and without aristocracies of blood, race, or position. The only élites recognized were those of ability and achievement. In the hierarchies of European society it was blood that talked; in America it was to be achievement and success that talked. The difference between the two meant a difference in the *élan* of the society. For blood and rank are given facts which a man has himself done nothing to achieve and cannot undo. Thus a society of blood leads among the privileged to an indifference about effort and among the pariahs to a hopelessness about reward. But a society where achievement talks, and where the marks of worth can be acquired as they can also be dissipated and lost, is by its nature a society shot through with effort and suffused with hope. Even when it is a plutocracy its top members are *novi homines,* and where all the members of an elite are *novi homines* none of them are. The fact of being "self-made" men is their signature of honor. The place of the

Great Estates is taken in America by the Great Fortunes. But unlike an estate, which is the result of status, a fortune is held by Americans to be the result of will and skill. Some can lose it, others acquire it. "From shirt sleeves to shirt sleeves in three generations" is part of the American myth.

Thus the American image of a classless society is one with a minimum of resentments, with few class tensions to rip it apart, without menace for the future, and with unlimited hope because of almost unlimited social mobility. There is an idyllic quality in this image, as in Eden before the Fall. It is not, however, the ideal of a stagnant society but of a freewheeling, perhaps even a freebooting, society.

As such it is part of the Great Folklore of America. This does not mean that it is all moonshine. It has a strong basis in American social reality. But it also has accumulated a distinct folklore, which is uncritically accepted by a large body of American opinion and often used as propaganda. In fact, the great reliance of the corporate propaganda in America is on the symbols of the free economy and the classless society. "I have heard thirty sets of lectures in defense of the Christian religion," a Scottish professor once said, "and, thank God, I'm a Christian still." After reading all the corporate defenses of the American "classless" society, it is only the saving remnant of sanity that allows one to hold on to the belief in the American open-class system.

The trouble with the class image of American folklore is that it rests on doctrines which tend to close the class system rather than to keep it open. The theory of "natural selection" assumes that a man who gets rewarded must therefore have deserved the reward. Yet it does not follow that the animal who survives in the jungle has proved anything more than his power for survival. To say that an able man ought to be rewarded is not the same as to say that those who are rewarded are therefore the ablest, and those excluded from the prizes must be dolts and weaklings. This distortion has led to a crass apologia for the existing distribution of income and economic power.

Similarly, even in a society with rapid social mobility not everyone can move upward. Beyond the expansion and dynamism of any society, it is inevitable that if some move upward others must be replaced and move downward. This process of downward mobility, or of declassing, mars the perfection of the legend of American classlessness.

One consequence of the Great Folklore is what may be called the Great Hunger. In any society in which the people have a great deal of freedom, they want more. Where privilege is minimized, it is belligerently hated. "This never dying, ever kindling hatred," De Tocqueville called it, "which sets a democratic people against the smallest privilege." Americans have, by the very fact of a high degree of equal opportunity, formed the habit of making ever-greater individual claims on their culture. It is a hunger, as De Tocqueville saw, that "grows by what it feeds on"—the material out of which a psychic dynamism has developed to match the economic dynamism. The American has been encouraged by this psychic dynamism to expect that it will fulfill his legitimate life demands. More than by anything else he is moved by a hatred of privilege and a passion for equal opportunity which is the true "permanent American Revolution."

The Great Hunger sets its face against privilege and against hierarchy of any kind. It is the stuff on which much of the infinite hopefulness of American life feeds—the hope for a chance to get at the goods in American life and at the good life in America. Yet bitterness also feeds on it. The struggle for civil rights, for example, would not be possible without the Great Hunger. Every advance in the legal status and social opportunities of Negroes is seen as a steppingstone to another advance, and if it is blocked the bitterness is intense. There can be no end to the dynamism which seeks a continually better job, income, and social position in the community.

The meaning of "classless" in American usage is different from the European. It does not, in the American ideal, mean an absence of rank, class power, or prestige. More exactly it means a class system that is casteless and therefore characterized by great mobility and interpenetration between classes. American thinkers since Madison and John Taylor have been preoccupied with the economic basis not only of politics but of social prestige and position as well. Ward, Sumner, Small, Giddings, Veblen, Cooley, Ross—all the first-rate sociologists—had to grapple with the problem of class and based much of their thinking on it. When therefore the Americans speak of their "classless society" they do not mean it in the Marxist sense but are rather answering the Marxist challenge. What they mean is better expressed by the phrase "open-class society."

How classless is this society? Only in the sense that the class formations in it are fluid, that mobility is the rule rather than the exception, and that class change is impressively obtainable. The most striking trait of the American class system is what the theorists call "vertical social mobility," the rate of movement up and down the ladder of income and social prestige, which has probably been greater in America than in any historical civilization. Partly this came about because of the break with the relatively closed class system of Europe, partly because there was a continent waiting to be opened and exploited. The idea of rigid and untraversable class lines is not a plant that grows well on wind-swept plains spanning long distances. It is more likely to flourish where the horizons are cramped and the margin of life is meager. Even in the big American cities the same dynamism which expressed itself on the plains was transmitted into a restless, unremitting movement of men and ideas that accompanies the movement from one income and prestige rung to another.

There are evidences that the class reality of America is moving steadily away from the image of the classless ideal. Compared with this image and with the intensely fluid character of the class system on the frontier, some scholars say, there has been a creeping closure of mobility. If this were true it would be disquieting to those who believe that the heart of the American social system lies in continuing mobility and in the access of all to opportunity. One would not argue this position from the spread in the distribution of income, wealth, and power, drastic as that spread is. The ladder of mobility, along which are stretched the rungs of income and position, has always been long enough to reach from the extremes of luxury down to the extremes of privation. The rich have grown richer in the last generation of Americans, but the poor have not grown poorer: in fact, many of them have become tolerably comfortable.

A study by Anderson and Davidson in California of the groups at the bottom of the ladder during the Great Depression showed a considerable shift of job and occupation as between father and son, but overwhelmingly inside the same larger class; and it showed also, as might be expected, a shift away from the number of small businessmen toward the professional, white-collar, and semiskilled occupations. Finally a recent study by Form showed that seven out of ten manual workers had started as such and remained where they had started, and that the same applied to eight out of ten white-collar workers. Mills reports that nine out of ten wage workers were wage workers at the time of their marriage and had never moved beyond, that none of the well-to-do professional men or big businessmen in the community he studied had come from wage-earner's or lower white-collar worker's backgrounds. On the other hand, the Mills study also showed that two out of three foremen had started as wage workers, and four out of five small businessmen had also risen from the lower ranks. Nor is the income spread in itself conclusive, since it has in the past existed alongside very extensive mobility. Actually the rise of living standards at the bottom and the impact of heavy taxation at the top are tending to diminish the spread, although for many Americans the steep disparities will remain as the never forgotten denial of the genuineness of the open-class system.

A similar debate has raged on the question of whether mobility has slowed down and rigidity has increased in the class layers at the top and at the bottom. A number of recent studies show pretty well the nature of this trend. In the 1920s a classic study of the class origins of business leaders by Taussig and Joslyn showed that half of them were sons of business leaders, although in the previous generations the big business-men had come from the farms and small towns, from clerks and sales-men and small business families. The adherents of the view that Ameri-can class is growing more rigid hold that in each succeeding genera-tion there has been a tighter closure of the top control positions in big enterprise as the capital required to start or sustain them has grown ever larger, keeping many of the sons of the rich in the charmed circle by the fact of their wealth and inheritance and shutting most of the others out.

One criticism of this viewpoint is that it assumes a classless or wholly open-class society in earlier America to start with, from which present-day America is moving with ever-greater class rigidity. It is a case of Eden and the Fall. Yet the original picture needs revision. America did not start with a relatively classless society, nor is it moving rapidly to a class society. In the America of the Puritans and the Cavaliers there were classes which were marked off as distinct styles of life, even though the aspect of power may not have been as important as it is in America today. Perry Miller has shown that even the Puritans, after their first years of settlement in the New World, made their peace with class dis-tinctions and even gave them a blessing, although they supported the principle of open access to all positions for the believers. In Southern society, as well as that of Philadelphia and New York in early times, the idea of the gentleman had considerable strength, although again it had more to do with a mode of life than a structure of power. The famous essay by James Madison, which appeared as Number Ten of *The Federalist* papers, showed a consciousness on the part of intellectuals of the existence of economic power and interest groupings on which class distinctions as well as political "fractions" could be based. The often crotchety and radical, but nevertheless meaningful, pamphleteers of the Age of Jackson, as Arthur Schlesinger, Jr., has depicted them, could not have written and spoken as they did in a society without class distinctions.

It would be truer to say that the movement in America has not been from classlessness to class or from an open to a more rigid class system but from relatively clear divisions and modes of life to a situation where the divisions have become more blurred, the stratification has become more subtle with shadings that are imprecise and elusive, and the modes of life have tended to converge in a large category of middle-class living.

The changes in the American class system have involved increases in mobility and in rigidity in different areas and at different times, but it would be a mistake to view those changes outside the larger framework which gives them meaning. The greatest mobility is from the lower strata, particularly the industrial wage earners, up into the ranks of the salespeople, clerical workers, foremen, small businessmen, and the lower corporate managerial group. The mobility of American life in this middle area is probably greater than in any comparable society, and there is a steady stream of movement up into the middle class and within it from one stratum to another. But it is still hard to rise from the very lowest ranks of the unskilled and depressed class at the bottom of the income pyramid, although the diffusion of education has begun to reach even to that stratum and promises in time to make it relatively mobile. While the great mobility has been the movement into the middle classes, the rigidity should not be overestimated. It is still true that some of the bottom dogs are able to break away, although it requires will and ability.

The most difficult question has to do with mobility at the top of the pyramid. What has been happening to the channels of access to top income, wealth, power, and prestige? Here we must distinguish between two trends. One is the continuity of class, by which a son inherits the enormous advantage of his father's position. The other is the constant creation of new managerial elites who occupy the strategic operative positions in big business, and who often come from below.

Actually there was more upward and downward mobility in the top class positions in the America of the mid-1950s than appears from studies like Taussig's which were done a generation earlier. A study in 1955 by Warner and Abegglen, focused upon the top ranks of the new managerial elite, gave a different picture and showed that the trend noted by Taussig was being reversed. It was still possible for young men starting in technical or sales positions in the corporate bureaucracy to move into executive positions. And the Warner study shows that a considerable number of them came from families that had not been in big business—either farmers or workers, professional people or small business.

Another study, however, a *Fortune* study of "The Executive Life," which drew its material from the 900 top management executives, shows that in one respect the Taussig picture still continues to be true. The fathers of 43 per cent of these men came from business occupations, while 15 per cent came from the professions. In the case of almost 26 per cent of the top executives studied, their fathers had been either the founders or the executives of corporations. In very few of the cases did the fathers come from nonbusiness and lower-income ranks: less than 13 per cent of them were farmers, and less than 8 per cent were workers. What is even more striking is the fact that the figures for the fathers of executives who were under fifty years of age showed an even lower percentage: only 11 per cent were farmers and 2½ per cent were workers. In short, conclude the editors of *Fortune,* new members of the nine hundred are tending to come increasingly from economically comfortable families. And they go on to comment that the struggle of impoverished forebears to fight their way to better living standards is no longer the heritage of the manager of the big corporation. He is more likely to come from a "tranquil family"—that is, while he may still have bettered himself compared with his father, the struggle has not been a sharp one, nor has the mobility been as marked as in earlier generations.

The transfer of education, skills, and relative economic comfort enables the new generations to live in ease and inherit also the jobs of their fathers or jobs comparable to them; but unless they show a good portion of the ability of the parents they are less likely to remain in the strategic posts. New men keep coming up, and while they do not become the owners or build great fortunes, they are recognized as part of the top class stratum. Thus, what occurs at the top is more a rigidification of income than one of business operation or power. This may explain why American society has not had to pay a heavy price thus far for its recent rigidity. It has escaped paying the price either of stagnation at the top or of revolutionary class conflict at the bottom.

To draw the profile of the American social strata is more elusive than almost anything else in American life. American society is still in the continual process of being formed and re-formed, and there are still few signs that it is settling down long enough for the observer to delineate the structure of the social hierarchy and the lines of division within it. It may well be many years before one can formulate a coherent theory of power and class in America.

In analyzing the nature of the American class system we must separate the question of the modes of power that define a man's strategic place in relation to his fellows from the modes of access to higher positions that are open to those below; and we must distinguish both of them in turn from the modes of status or prestige which define how a man looks in the eyes of his fellows and, by reflection, in the mirror of his self-image.

In terms of power, there has been a broad shift in the past three generations from industrial ownership to stock income and managerial position in the corporations, the trade-unions, and to some extent in the government; in the middle classes there has been a corresponding shift from small middle-class property to the new middle-class skilled occupations and professions, many of them in the tertiary service areas of the economy. In terms of access and mobility, American society seems to have countered every tendency toward closure by opening up new channels in other areas of effort. Thus it would be difficult to say, despite the growth of monopoly tendencies in the economy, that the actual or potential degree of mobility has declined in America since the nineteenth century. In some areas it is even possible that it has increased. The chances of moving into a commanding position in the economy as a businessman in control of his own business have become, of course, considerably less. But the independent entrepreneur has, as I have emphasized, become far less the type-figure he was in an earlier economy; and the chances of rising to top managerial positions, through apprenticeships in every phase of the company's activities, are still open to young men of the middle classes as well as the ruling class, although they are slimmer for the sons of workers and farmers. As for movement from those groups into the intermediate ones of power and income, the channels are still open except for the poet at the very base of the pyramid, which the impulses of ferment and change through the whole society take longer to reach.

What I have said about the increasing closure of the top power and income positions to the sons of workers and farmers may offer a clue to the character of the newly emerging class system. Men make their way up to the top less because of inherited wealth (although that is still an appreciable factor) and less because of technical and specialized skills: more and more the qualities called for are the generalized skills of making men work together in a "team," of "keeping everybody happy," of riding out crises, of "making contacts" and "being in on deals," of being alert to new developments in technology, marketing, advertising, and public relations, and being hospitable enough to the new ideas so that the company doesn't "get into a rut." This is another way of saying that education and brains are not enough in themselves to insure movement to the top; they are more important in the more technical aspects, such as science, engineering, market analysis, and corporate law. The more generalized skills are related to a style of personality, and this "personality market" is open only to those who have been conditioned to it by the mode of their education and the range of their "contacts." This may suggest why the boys from the lower classes and the lower middle class, and particularly from the minority ethnic groups, are less apt to rise to these positions than their fellows from the strata above.

As for the modes of status and prestige, some considerable degree of income and power is necessary for them, but there is no one-for-one correspondence between the two categories. There are top income groups in American life who elicit prestige within their own area of action—in their own industrial or professional or political circles—but have not achieved the same community standing as families of lesser income who have had the badges of status over a number of generations. At a lower stratum the white-collar occupations may carry a better status in the community than higher incomes which derive from skilled labor or from the petty trades.

I speak here of the levels of prestige and status, but not of their security. One of the striking facts about the whole American status system is exactly its high degree of *insecurity*. This is understandable in a society of such rapid change and movement, where the social image of a man and his own image of himself are interlocked, and where both of them derive not only from the objective facts of his income and strategic position in life but from a whole array of intangibles as well. This is one of the points at which the American picture of mobility differs most sharply from, let us say, that of the Russians. Some studies done at the Research Center for Russian Studies, at Harvard University, estimate that the likelihood of vertical mobility is about the same in the two societies—a striking fact when you consider how recent the Russian Revolution is and how profound were the changes that it sought to achieve in the society. But in the Russian case the insecurity of prestige and status changes mainly with political factors inside the regime; in the American case the political factors are of slight importance, and the array of intangibles is crucial.

2. The Seats of the Mighty

THE CREATION OF new elites, as Pareto saw, is the product of the circulation of talents. In that sense the American ruling groups are part of the picture of class mobility, rather than of the rigidification of caste at the top. America has had a series of aristocracies, although it has overwhelmingly rejected the aristocratic ideal. The men of religion who governed some of the original New England colonies formed elites in the quite literal sense, for they considered themselves the "elect" of God, and they shut out the unbelievers and the nonbelongers not only by class taboo but by the flaming sword of everlasting damnation. They represented status-by-religious-belief; accordingly they did not last in American life, since they performed no function linked with personal success or national survival.

The American Revolution, which was to a degree also a social revolution, swept away the beginnings of the second aristocracy of America—the landed aristocracy—along with all the cluttering accompaniments of British land law. To some of the conservative thinkers this removed the basis for government, as John Adams put it, by "the rich, the well-born, and the able." But their thinking ran against the American grain. Only in the South, with its prewar plantation economy and its linking of prestige with hereditary land and gentlemanly leisure, was there an economic base for an aristocracy of land and blood. It was demolished in the Civil War, and its pitiful residues in the frayed gentility of the postwar South turned inward into the bitterness of a frustrated elite. It is the memory of this aristocratic tradition and the nostalgia for it that have produced some of America's best writing.

There have been some other aristocracies in American life, as in the effort to build an aristocracy of prior immigration among the F.F.V.s ("First Families of Virginia") or the descendants of the Dutch patroon families in New York. And in New England there lingered deep into the nineteenth century the only vital aristocracy of culture and education, linked to some extent with family, that America has had—that of Concord, Brook Farm, Cambridge, and Beacon Street in Boston. While all these aristocracies had an effect on the taste and intellectual life of America they were only marginal to the structure of class as power.

In this sense of power the place of the aristocracies was taken in America by a plutocracy unparalleled in any prior culture, including the Roman Empire at its height, or the Italian merchant princes and the Dutch capitalists, or even England at the peak of its nineteenth-century commercial and industrial power. But because it had not been attached to land, blood, and dynasty, it was more fluid than the feudal and even commercial aristocracies, and gave access to some of the most resourceful talents. Its hallmark has been not nobility but mobility, not family dynasty but individual dynamism. De Tocqueville was struck by the fact "that amongst the Americans all honest callings are honorable," and that the contempt which the European aristocracies felt for "labor with a view to profit" had no place in American life. The fact that the field was left clear for the business ruling group enabled America to avoid the conflict which every western European country had experienced between capitalism and the authoritarian tradition. America did not have on one side the eagerness of the parvenu, nor on the other the condescension of the nobility. Nor was there the steady infiltration by the commercial class into the landed aristocracy—the conquest of blood and honor by money—which colored the thinking and politics of both Germany and England.

The American business class became the pivotal elite of the country because in an acquisitive society there was no other to challenge it. It had no time or taste to govern politically, as the European aristocracies did. It had not yet learned how to use its leisure. It pursued business not only for the profit in it but also, as De Tocqueville saw, "for the love of the constant excitement occasioned by that pursuit." It was attracted by magnitudes and got a sense of confidence in itself by its constant relation to those magnitudes. It did not care much about the people it employed: "the object is not to govern that population but to use it." And at the end of his classic chapters discussing the new business group, De Tocqueville wrote: "The manufacturing aristocracy which is growing up under our eyes is one of the harshest which ever existed in the world; but at the same time it is one of the most confined and least dangerous. Nevertheless the friends of democracy should keep their eyes anxiously fixed in this direction; for if ever a permanent inequality of conditions and aristocracy again penetrate into the world, it may be predicted that this is the channel by which they will enter."

De Tocqueville's brilliant insight has been confirmed by a century of history. Yet the "permanent aristocracy" which he foresaw does not accurately describe the American rich, since they too are somewhat subject to downward mobility and very much to the upthrust from below. And if De Tocqueville overestimated the rigidity this class would assume he underestimated its cohesion as a class. "To say the truth," he wrote, "though there are rich men, the class of rich men does not exist; for these rich individuals have no feelings or purposes in common, no mutual traditions or mutual hopes; there are therefore members, but no body." Not more than a quarter century after he wrote this, his generalization was contradicted by the bitterness with which the "rich men" resisted the new union organizing drives. In their labor relations, as in their pressures on government, the ruling business groups acted more consistently as a self-conscious class than any other groups, even including labor; the Marxist thesis of class-consciousness applied more aptly to them than to any American proletariat. In recent generations also the business elite has learned how to shift some of its energies to the arts of government, how to use its wealth and leisure as patrons of the arts, and how to live with a degree of imagination which the earlier business pirates did not share.

Much has been written about how the steep taxes and the diffusion of wealth have diminished with "great American fortunes," about which Gustavus Myers once wrote; yet the facts are against this view. In a careful study of the admittedly incomplete and shaky data on the "very rich" —whom he defines as men with fortunes of thirty million dollars and over—C. Wright Mills examined the top ninety in the generations of 1900, 1925 (the top ninety-five), and 1950. In each group there was one in the billionaire class (Rockefeller in 1900, Ford in 1925, and Hunt, and perhaps Cullen, in 1950); there were three in the first two generations with $300 million and over, and six in 1950; in each generation a fifth of the group were in the $100-million-and-over group. The geographical shift of the sources of wealth away from the East is shown by the fact that of the richest ten in the 1950 group, five were Texans, and of the richest ninety there were nine Texans. Despite the inheritance and income taxes and the loud outcries against governmental interference with the accumulation of wealth, the acquisitors in the mid-1950s in America were still active in acquiring wealth and still able to hold on to it.

To this group of the top rich, and cutting across it, there should be added another—the big-income group. The profile one gets of American wealth from this angle of vision—not the accumulated fortunes but the continuing annual income—is a striking one. There were in all, in the mid-1950s, fewer than 14,000 persons with declared incomes of $100,000 a year and over. Of these, roughly 11,500 had incomes of between $100,000 and a quarter of a million dollars a year; 1,383 had incomes of between a quarter and a half million; 379 had incomes of from a half million to a million; and 120 a million or more. The notable fact here was that this group of 14,000 (Mills calls them the "corporate rich") got roughly two thirds of their income from corporate dividends and capital gains, and from estates and trusts, while the remaining third came from corporate salaries, direct business profits, and professional services. The "unearned" income was thus double the "earned." There were, moreover, known methods in corporate and income-tax law for excluding or concealing income for taxable purposes, or for declaring income at a minimum taxable rate—including "capital gains," "depletion allowances" in oil and mineral incomes, and tax-free municipal bonds. Given these methods and also the tax-free family foundations, the amount that the top-rich Americans were able to keep for expenditure and accumulation was considerable and ranked with any high-income, big-fortune ruling group in the world.*

The question of access to the seats of the mighty—to these positions of the top rich and the corporate rich—sheds light on the American class structure. Studying his 275 "top-rich" multimillionaires, Mills found that access to the accumulation of these big fortunes was being restricted to an ever-smaller group. In the 1900 generation 39 per cent came from lower-class families; in the 1925 group it had sunk to 12 per cent; and in the 1950 to 9 per cent. The proportion coming from the middle classes remained relatively stable—between 20 and 30 per cent. The proportion coming from the upper class was 39 per cent in the 1900 group, 56 per cent in 1925, and 68 per cent in 1950. Almost nine out of ten of those

---

* On the business leaders of America, see Ch. V, Sec. 2, "The Rise and Decline of the Titan." On the inequalities of wealth and income, see Ch. V, Sec. 9, "Poverty and Wealth."

who came from upper-class families inherited fortunes of at least a half million dollars, and there can be little question that they found their path toward wealth, power, and status eased by the fact of the wealth, power, and status that were transmitted to them. Of Mills's whole group, roughly one out of three had to make his way to his position of wealth and power: the other two either rose in firms which were owned or controlled by their families or else got their wealth by the fabulous increase in the value of stocks during the past generation.

W. Lloyd Warner, studying the corporate decision-makers rather than the top rich, found that the problem of access to their positions of power and income yielded quite different results. He took the 8,000 business leaders who held "the highest positions in the largest companies in all types of American enterprise." He made a basic division between the "birth elite" and the "mobile elite" and found that the numbers in each were roughly even: 52 per cent of his 8,000 business leaders were "born to business," while 48 per cent "moved into business"; actually, the degree of mobility of access was greater than these figures show, since of those "born to business" only 23 per cent came from families that belonged to the birth elite, while the others came from families that had had to achieve their position. Mills found that the typical road of advance among the top rich was, in one way or another, to come into command of some strategic position, to have a sufficient sum to take advantage of it, to make the "big jump"—and then to pile up an "accumulation of advantages," partly by skill and partly by exploiting the position achieved through the big jump. Warner, on the other hand, found that the "royal road" to business leadership (and the income wealth and power going with it) was higher education, which is available in America to middle-class as well as upper-class groups.

Looking at the whole problem of rigidity as against mobility in the elites of top wealth and top corporate jobs, several generalizations are possible. So far as the very big fortunes are concerned, the process of rigidification has set in, and it is difficult for men to move all the way from the very bottom of the pyramid to the very top; yet they can still move from a little below the middle of it to the top. Looking at the top income group, it is also hard for a member of the submerged group, or even of the working class or the independent farmer group, to get to them; yet mobility still takes place from the middle classes to the top income. Looking at the small number of top executive posts in business, the rigidity is considerably less and mobility greater: men can move into them along the road of education, energy, and resourcefulness; although it is still true that those who come from families that have possessed such power over one or more generations find the going much easier. But if we broaden the range of our vision to take in the whole group of

8,000 business executives who held the high posts throughout the industrial structure, Warner's conclusion jibes well with the empirical experience of most Americans: the possibility of moving into these posts from the middle and lower ranks is still decidedly open. Warner's results were the more striking because he compared them with a similar study of access to posts of business leadership made a quarter century earlier by Taussig and Joslyn, which I have discussed above. He found that mobility has increased rather than lessened.

This leads to some general reflections on the nature of access to the elites in an open-class society. The important fact about those who have a differential advantage is that what is transmitted to them is not just wealth or income but a chance to show their ability which they might not have got otherwise; but unless some measure of ability is there, they will in time be pushed out of decision-making posts and become *rentiers* living on dividends and interest. What is transmitted then is not just money but the chance to make more; not just power but the chance to increase it; but both depend upon maintaining a level of ability. For those without the differential advantage of birth and opportunity, the meaningful channels of access are not those that lead to the big fortunes and income but to comfortable wealth and income. While the top berths may be pre-empted, those just below are still fairly open. Those that are most open have to do less with piling up big wealth and income than with the decision-making power in the managerial posts. Here the American business elite is still fluid—perhaps more so than ever in its history after the earliest beginning.

One difficulty with much of the research that studies the biographies of the members of the American ruling group and tries to treat them statistically or by questionnaires—and this applies both to Mills and Warner—is that such a method must omit the factors of personality, will, and even genius. By its inherent nature an elite is made up of selected men; it does not therefore lend itself easily to statistical uniformity. It is true that there are "insiders" and "outsiders" among those trying to make their way upward into the positions of power. This is underscored by the fact that the channels of success are growing less specialized, and that they have more to do with "personality" in a broad sense, and with the blurred contours of personal relations. This is where the "insider" has the "inside track." Yet here again, unless he has the qualities to exploit his advantage and maintain it, he can be passed (especially on a rough track) by someone coming from far behind with zeal and resourcefulness, and sweeping around and beyond him.

It must be added, however, that the new people, who come up from the lower middle classes, usually do not have final control over corporate decisions even though they are in the managerial posts. That decisive and final control often remains in the hands of those who, by the fact of being a birth elite and having money and power over generations, have the prestige that adds weight to their functional qualities and equities within the corporation. To that extent one can still regard this group as *the* ruling group. Yet those who rule from week to week, from day to day, and from year to year, ruling interstitially (as it were), between crisis decisions of others, are largely a new elite, and they bring a new point of view.

Somewhere in between an aristocracy of blood and land and a power elite of acquired wealth there is the domain that the American newspapers call "Society." Wealth alone does not open the portals of this domain, as a number of rich men and their wives have ruefully learned in studying the "Social Register." Birth and family are the key to entrance, although a number have declassed themselves by marrying below their station, and there is a question of how long the birth and family continue to exercise their spell without the added witchery of wealth. In communities such as the old New England cities, only the "old families" hold the top social positions. The "new families," while they may belong to the plutocracy and command much greater wealth, do not carry the same charismatic quality.

There was a period in American life when "Society" meant, however, a good deal more than it does today—the period of the great Fifth Avenue mansions, the estates at Newport, and the consciously modest houses of Louisburg Square. Henry James's *The American Scene*, written after a tour of the watering places and Society centers, is a brilliant evocation of these evidences of a way of life which even then was beginning to crack and which today—in the remains of the Vanderbilt mansion at Newport or the great hotels at Saratoga Springs—are studied as monuments of a past era. What has happened is not that there is less money to spend—actually the very rich families have far more—but that it is no longer fashionable for the elite of wealth to swagger in the old way of "conspicuous consumption." The more established it has become as the top social stratum, the more sophisticated does it become in expressing its dominance. It is the radiant moon toward which all the other tides of American life are drawn. There are still particular focal points at which it gathers, from Nob Hill in San Francisco to Aiken and its "horsy set," and from the east shore of Maryland and the Hamptons on Long Island to Sun Valley in the Rockies. Yet these are playgrounds which one finds ever harder to differentiate in their outer trappings from the playgrounds of the upper middle class or of the "New Families," and the consciousness of the social elite exists more in the valuation placed on them by the rest of the community than in any differential social display.

The rise of an upper class of newly rich families has transformed the upper American social status, both in small and large cities, and has introduced a ferment of new moral standards. The earlier America had a number of cities, each of which boasted its "old families" and its inner circles of blood and standing. The emphasis was upon kinship, intermarriage, landownership (especially in the South), and wealth over time. These local "social sets" not only dominated the more intimate social life of the city, making decisions about who belonged or did not belong: they were also the people who made decisions about economic and political power. But increasingly this local "society" has been subordinated to the power groups and social sets of the big metropolitan centers, where celebrities cluster and the Social Register operates, and men make decisions affecting the whole nation. In most cases the "country club" groups of the small city link their aspirations and dreams with the society of the big urban centers and especially of the night-club and "café society" groups.

The fact is that there is no longer a single "400" as there used to be but a whole constellation of "social sets" which interlock and overlap, some of them more exacting than others about their membership and their moral standards. As class lines became more fluid there was an epidemic of "Cinderella marriages," with an invasion of pretty and ambitious girls from across the tracks into the once jealously guarded inner circles, and a dilution of the birth elite of the old families with this new blood. The aristocracy of taste and manners got blurred around the edges. Moreover, with the spread of wealth in the days of the Big Money, and with the incursions of the income tax, it became more difficult to distinguish between the real social set and the phony one on the basis of money and spending power alone. Where so many were rich it became harder for the rich-over-time to hold their distinction or their sense of assurance. The breakdown of status lines accompanied a breakdown of standards. Whenever the newspapers featured some sensational murder or other scandal in the "social set" the nation had a chance to look behind the façade and to see the rather pathetic lives and loves inside. Any authority that the wealthy and well born might have exercised in the past over the standards of the lower-status groups was thus corroded.

The Big City social sets have themselves been transformed. The older upper class still furnishes the great names, but a new upper class has forced its way in, with a surer sense of what it wants and with the power to get it. Hungry for recognition and status, it has opened the gates to "celebrities" whose social origins would have shocked the dowagers and patriarchs of the earlier inner circles. As a result, "society" in the Henry James and Edith Wharton sense no longer dominates American rank and taste, except residually in those lingering social centers that Cleveland Amory called the "last resorts." It has been replaced by the arbiters of "café society" and Hollywood—a group of talented and attractive young men and women who are the celebrities of the Big Media and have proved the revolutionary element in the new situation. In many cases their members are parvenus whose love life is carried on in public, whose morals are fluid, whose education is dubious, and whose financial position is momentarily thriving but insecure. What they have that is decisive is their public éclat. Their pictures appear in every newspaper in order to give it the febrile vitality that Americans call "glamour." Their exploits are dutifully chronicled, their frailties are exposed, their marriages and divorces become headline news, and a whole new set of scandal magazines has cashed in on the business of laying bare their infractions of the moral code.

It would seem strange that, in the face of this kind of image, the linkage would persist between society and the celebrities. Yet each gets from the other something it seems to need: the society groups get the infusion of new vigor, and the gods and goddesses of the Big Media get the feeling of being linked with wealth and power. A list of those who are given priority at the Cub Room of the Stork Club or at Twenty-One has taken the place of Burke's Peerage and the Social Register. The list of the "ten best-dressed women" may have been thought up originally as a public-relations stunt for American tailors, but it became part of the folklore not only of fashion but of glamour and social standing. Inevitably the newspaper and picture layouts of the magazines have replaced the records of birth and lineage as the focus of social attention. The avoidance of publicity by the great families is a thing of the past. Where once no reporters or photographers were allowed at the great balls and parties, a "Society function" scarcely counts as such now unless it has been reported and photographed and the gradations of social rank have been recorded under klieg lights. What counts in American status is thus not money alone—not even primarily—but closeness to the sources of power, publicity, and popular success.*

The Big Media constitutes a different kind of elite as well—the power elite of opinion-molders and taste-shapers whose symbol has become "Madison Avenue," where the offices of the broadcasting chains, the advertising agencies, and the public-relations firms cluster. This is a differ-

* For a further discussion of American "Society," see Ch. IX, Sec. 3, "Manners, Taste, and Fashion."

ent kind of power from that of the top executives of the corporate managerial group, and different also from the elite of Great Fortunes and Big Income. The power they represent does not flow from their control over strategic decisions but from their capacity to shape the stereotypes and mold the tastes of the opinion public and buying public who are reached by the Big Media. Americans set a good deal of store by "public opinion" and are conscious of its transient quality and its fickleness. The elite of Madison Avenue are the high priests who are considered to have a magic way with the changing moods of the public. It is they who advise the politicians about how to sway voters in elections, they who guide the big corporate executives in their "public relations," they who have to worry about the private lives of celebrities, they who do the "motivational research" on which sales policies and advertising campaigns are based. They are the new symbol manipulators of the American power structure, the new "invisible government," the "hidden persuaders"—and therefore themselves a symbolic target of a good deal of popular resentment. Some of them reach the top posts in their organizations because of their verbal facility and their capacity to manipulate symbols. Others have the same generalized ability to co-ordinate these skills and the same impact of personality which marks the successful top executive in the corporate managerial group.*

There is, finally, the new elite of the officers of the Armed Services. I shall have occasion to deal later† with the role of the military in relation to American government, foreign policy, and freedom: what concerns me here is its relation to the class system. It is the only one of the strata of American society which does not depend on the operation of the market for its valuation but has developed a sense of dedication and an *esprit de corps* linked with patriotism, discipline, and the arts of killing. It comes thus closer to forming a caste, despite its rotation of rank and its very high recruitment of new abilities, than any other elite.

Even more important, the vast increase in the Armed Services means that the experience of caste is transmitted for at least several years to every young American male and many of the women. Since it is a totalitarian society, with an iron hierarchy of rank, obedience, and deference, this experience may habituate future generations to a new kind of subservience hitherto unknown in American life, and to a concern with what their "station" in life is rather than their inner worth. Yet in several respects this long-range trend has been qualified in more

---

* For the opinion-molders as a force in the economy, see Ch. V, Sec. 5, "Business and Its Satellites"; for their role in elections and in party politics, see Ch. VI, Sec. 4, "The Party System and the Voter."

† For the role of the military, see Ch. XII, Sec. 4, "Landscape with Soldiers," where the power of the generals and admirals over decisions is further discussed.

immediate terms. Many young Americans, after their Army caste experience, suffer a violent revulsion against it, as witness James Jones's *From Here to Eternity* and other recent novels of the seamy side of Army life.

But the totalitarian rigor of the Army makes it also a great leveler. The Negroes especially have recently found in its ranks a break in the Southern tradition of segregation, a tapping of new experience, and the chance to learn new mechanized skills which enable them to move out of the depressed class of sharecroppers, field hands, and mill workers into the skilled trades. Finally, the "G.I. Bill" has opened for millions of young Americans who have survived the battles a chance for vocational training and higher education under government subsidy, which comes at just the right time when they have measured their capacity and are mature enough to know where they want to go. In this sense the Army experience has brought new stir and mobility into the American class system, even while it promises to exercise in the long run a deadening effect upon a sense of initiative and the resistance to authority.

If we ask then who are the Americans who sit in the seats of the mighty, the answer must be that there is no single "ruling class" in America—well defined, articulated, conscious of its role and power. There is, to be sure, an upper class, in the sense of a top-rich and big-income stratum for whom leisure is at once habit and burden, which is the recipient of privilege and (to a limited extent) the shaper of ideal living patterns and an imitated life style. But such an upper class is different from a ruling class, whose essence is power over the behavior and destiny of others that flows from its strategic control of production and its decision-making in industry. The conditions of American society, which is geared by its history and mood to accept innovation, where the base of economic power is constantly shifting under the force of social mobility, and where pluralism and ferment pervade the whole, are not such as to favor either the emergence or the encrustation of a unitary ruling class.

Robert Lynd has argued, in an incisive criticism of the work of Mills and others, that the concept of "elites" (or even of some "power elite") as a substitute for the class concept is an illusory one, and that even in America there is a dominant class which is the center and source of the meaningful community power, and of which the various elites are only branches or tributaries. There is force in this view, in two senses. First, it is in the nature of power that it feeds on itself; economic power, whether or not it "determines" other forms of power, casts its shadow on them, so that there is at least a *prima facie* assumption that the holders of economic power will also have a strong hold on political elections, on decisions that affect war and peace, on education and religion, on the world of opinion, ideas, and the arts, and on social standing and values. Second, there is a common attraction that the holders of power have for one another, and a community of viewpoint ("class conscious-ness" is one way of putting it) which they inherit and perpetuate: this is especially true at a time of common danger, when they feel the *novi homines* or the trade-unions hard at their heels.

But my own tendency throughout this book is to approach America in terms of its nature as a richly pluralistic society. The pluralisms I find in American stock and regions, in American loyalties, in the American character structure, in religion and the sects, in political and economic life, I find also in the class system and even in the ruling groups.

Within the frame of this pluralism there are what may be called *power and prestige clusters,* which include the social elite ("Society"), the intellectual elite, the big-wealth and big-income elite, the top church leaders, the opinion-industry elite (press, radio, TV, movies, advertising agencies, public-relations men), the government managerial elite, the corporate managerial elite, the labor managerial elite, the military elite. Merely to list them thus conveys a sense of what I have said in my discussion of power in American life—that the whole of American so-ciety is power-saturated.*

But to say that there are many such clusters of power, prestige, and privilege does not mean that all are equally powerful, or that their powers balance each other out of existence. Quite clearly there are some power clusters which are more pervasive and dominant than the rest. The four fairly obvious ones are the corporate executives ("Big Business," "Wall Street," to use the popular symbols), the political decision-makers (again, in popular usage, "the Administration," "the Hill," "the White House"), the military leaders ("the brass hats," "the Pentagon"), and the opinion-shapers ("Madison Avenue"). I mention the popular designa-tions of these groups because on the question of power the instinct of the "man on the street" is likely to be closer to the truth than that of polemicists, students, and apologists. The interesting thing about the American popular consciousness is that it does not fix on a single and central power symbol but on a number of them.

Mills, in speaking of his "power elite," combines the first three of the four elites I have mentioned, in a kind of coalition of elites to form a cen-tral one. But, as Lynd points out, he does not assign primacy to any one of them. I should myself say that there have been shifting constellations of these power clusters in American history, and that at each period one of them has had primacy over the others. At the present time, at the height of the role of a business economy in a business culture, it is natural for the corporate executives to be the dominant elite. But this

* See Ch. VI, Sec. 5, "Power and Equilibrium."

does not exclude or minimize the importance of the others, especially (in an age of nuclear science) the military elite.

This is very far from the key image, in Marxist theory, of the ruling capitalist class as engaged in a naked warfare, including the force and violence that war uses, the hostilities on which it feeds, the bitterness it engenders, the survivors who emerge from its ordeal as victor or victim. In the view of Max Weber, there is a different key image of the elites, taken from that of the German governmental bureaucracy and the German army of the Weimar period, which were highly organized around the principle of professional competence and distinction and of a certain life style. Neither of these applies in the American case, where the image of naked warfare holds only for the underworld and among the racketeers on its margin, as it holds also *inside* the corporate world and in the top positions of the Big Media. As for the bureaucratic image, it is true that each of the four elites I have mentioned is a bureaucracy of a kind; but it would be truer to say that the power group uses the bureaucracy yet stands above it and apart from it, unfettered by its orderliness and its routineering.

Mills makes a good deal of the interchangeability of leaders in the three elites that form his "Power Elite." It is certainly clear that the same kind of person and the same kinds of talents will make good in each of his elites, and that there is even a kind of understanding by which the members of each "co-opt" men of their own kind to work with them and succeed them. But one need not conclude from this that there is a rigidity or even a cohesiveness within the elites that unifies them. In fact, the more important conclusion would stress the element of mobility rather than of rigidity. The striking thing about the elites in American society is their continuing mobility. This applies to the high government posts (despite the exclusions on ideological grounds at the time of the McCarthy hunt for dangerous ideas), to the military posts (as witness Eisenhower, Marshall, Ridgway, Bradley, Gruenther, and others), to the Madison Avenue opinion-makers, to the corporate executives who form the most important of the elites.

This still leaves open the question of whether there is a unifying element—other than mobility—that holds the elites together in the shifting constellations I have mentioned. They are not just Dantean circles in an upper-class Hell, but neither are they tied together by some historic determinism. If there is some common substance I should look for it in the ethos of the society and the tension between the power of the elites and the prevailing social values—to which the elites, however amoral they may seem, are not wholly immune. The curious fact about the elites in American life is not that they corrupt democracy or destroy it but that they are part of the continuing dialectic of what may be called the democratic class struggle.

3. The New Middle Classes

THE EMERGENCE OF a strong, broadly inclusive middle class is the characteristic class achievement of America. Where the pivot class of other civilizations has been some aristocracy, merchant class, or peasantry, the culture carriers of America are the middle classes. Earlier in American history they comprised the independent farmers, the small businessmen and shopkeepers, the professions, and the middlemen. But in the last two generations there has been a revolutionary occupational shift away from agriculture and even manufacturing—away, that is, from the extractive and industrial jobs—to the distributive phases of the economy, the white-collar jobs, the bureaucracies in government, industry, the trade-unions, and the public services like schools and hospitals. This has broken up the old class structure and thrust a new one into being: a new one in which, while the power elites still have the power and the working class has remained relatively stable, the growing points of American life have become a variety of middle-class occupations.

I have already discussed the result of this shift in the creation of a powerful group of technicians, managers, and business and governmental bureaucrats.* Even more important is the emergence of the new white-collar groups, including salesmen and sales girls, office workers, advertisers, middlemen, and the talent professions. The older middle classes, including the farmers, shopkeepers, and small businessmen, have diminished in their relative importance in the middle-class constellation; the newer ones have given the whole constellation less a productive and commercial than a technical and white-collar character. They form a loose collection of occupational strata, probably more anxiety-ridden than the rest of the culture, dominated by the drive to distinguish themselves from the working class, uncohesive, held together by no common bond except the fact that they are caught in a kind of Purgatory between the Hell of the poor and weak and the Heaven of the rich and powerful. Yet they have thus far managed to give stability to American society and to form a massive chain of social experience which links the changes in America's technological revolutions with the changes in the consumer's revolution, and which gives American society its characteristic stamp. When an American speaks of the "common man," it is these classes that he refers to along with the industrial workers.

A somewhat similar shift took place in English society in the eighteenth and nineteenth centuries, when England ceased to be a nation of

---

* See Ch. IV, Sec. 3, "Big Technology and Neutral Technicians," Ch. V, Sec. 3, "The Corporate Empires," Ch. VI, Sec. 6, "The Governmental Managers."

yeomen and became "a nation of shopkeepers," even more than one of factory and mill workers. Engels complained in his letters to Marx that in mid-nineteenth-century English society even the workers had become bourgeois. And it is clear enough to the sharp observer today that even British Socialism, under the Labor party, is largely a middle-class Socialism. Yet the American middle classes are not a duplication or imitation of British experience. The "shopkeepers" have in America diminished in importance as the big chains have crowded them out. The solid British citizen who rose every morning in a London suburb and went to the "City" in frayed frock coat and bowler hat, with rolled-up umbrella, and returned every evening to his newspaper and garden, was only in externals the forerunner and prototype of the American white-collar employee. He was the residue of the diminished middle-class strength of an England which had once been a great middle-class society and not—as in America—the cutting point of new class formations and transformations.

The new white-collar middle classes of America have emerged as a result of new modes of mass production and specialization, new routines of organizing, new techniques of salesmanship and advertising, and Big Distribution. They are therefore the product of American dynamism fully as much as the elites of big-business ownership or the corporate managers, whose *élan* and confidence take them out of the scope of the white-collar classes, although technically they belong with them. Grim as is the class profile of the white-collar people in such an analysis as Wright Mills's *White Collar,* it must not be forgotten that they are the outgrowths of an expanding economy and a society of rapid movement.

So rapid—in fact, for some time so unnoticed—that the new middle classes emerged on the American scene almost unobtrusively, with no cataclysmic revolutionary clangor and no fanfare of messianic change. Yet the transformation they have brought goes beyond anything else in the American class system. The middle classes as a whole made up 6 per cent of the labor force in 1870 and 25 per cent in 1940; roughly two thirds of them are office and sales people. In the early 1800s, Mills points out, four fifths of the Americans were self-employed or in some way "entrepreneurs"; in 1870 there were only one third; in the 1940s only one fifth were self-employed. Since 1870 the number of the self-employed in America has increased by only 135 per cent; the wage workers by 255 per cent; but the salaried employees have increased 1600 per cent, until they now form more than half of all the gainfully employed and four fifths of the wage receivers in the economy. America has become a salaried rather than a profit-making or wage-earning society. For a time the greatest increases were among the corporate and governmental civil-service people, the professions, and the sales people, but recently the office workers and clerical staffs have outstripped them.

What holds this loose collection of new social strata together? Objectively it is the fact that none of them owns the enterprises for which they work: that is to say, they are as propertyless as the industrial workers, except for those who may be speculating or investing in the stock market as part of their effort to become secure or rich, which is irrelevant to their jobs as such. The other fact is that they all receive salaries rather than wages, have no heavy manual labor to perform, don't get their hands dirty, and wear their street clothes to work. Like the industrial workers, they are employed by business units over which they have no control and in which they have no property shares or stakes. Unlike the industrial workers, however, they do not think of themselves as belonging to the working class but are oriented toward the values of their employers; they are only marginally unionized (only 16 per cent of them were in unions at mid-century, compared with 44 per cent of the industrial workers, and many of their unions have renounced the ultimate weapon of the strike) and they get most of their psychic satisfaction through the consumer's and Big Media culture to which their income and status give them access.

To deepen the shadows in the picture, especially as Mills draws it with bold and dramatic strokes, even this differential prestige is being stripped from them. In the 1890s the average white-collar pay was double that of the wage workers; today the margin between the two is very slight, and in many cases the skilled industrial jobs are higher paid than the white-collar jobs; tomorrow the margin may swing in the direction of the worker's average pay. The biggest factor in the fluidity of American classes—namely, the spread of access to college education and technical training—may be digging the grave of white-collar distinction, for as the market for college graduates gets saturated the differential salary a college education can get grows ever slimmer. The day may be approaching when the prestige of wearing a white collar may disappear because everyone does.

This then is a possible portrait of the new middle classes, from the managerial employees and the "idea men" in the talent professions at the top to the file clerks and sales girls at the bottom: a formless cluster of groups, torn from the land and from productive property, with nothing to sell except their skills, their personality, their eagerness to be secure, their subservience and silence. Since they must act as the personal eyes, ears, hands, and brains of impersonal corporations they are no longer the "masterless" men of an earlier America: they must always wear the public mask of their occupation; to be marketable they must shape themselves to a personality pattern of efficiency, smoothness, sales vigor or charm or deference—which is what is expected and what will be paid for. They end by not knowing themselves, all the more fearful because they have no core of self-knowledge and no collective consciousness that leads them to act with their fellows, caught in a "status panic." The only fact that gives them cohesiveness is that together they hold the middle position in the occupational hierarchy and the prestige scale of American society.

One can paint this kind of picture which dooms them forever beyond redemption to their peculiar Purgatory. Yet, as with many oversharp analytic schemes, this one misses some of the realities of a changing America. You can look at the picture as a deterioration story when compared with a Jeffersonian or Jacksonian society of independent farmers, self-employed artisans, and self-reliant small businessmen. But you can also look at it from another angle, in terms of the upward movement of depressed and minority groups, of Negroes and Catholics and Jews, of the sons and daughters of industrial workers, thrusting their way into occupations that give them the badges of belonging to a middle-class society and therefore the standing for which they have hungered.

The same Irish Catholic worker's family that watches one son go into the priesthood may see another move up the corporate ladder from the sales force to the lower managerial group, and get an equal sense of prestige from both. The Italian or Jew whose son becomes a college teacher, a writer, a lawyer, or surgeon may have the feeling that America has been good to him and has put the stamp of success upon his migration from Europe. Their striving may be riddled with social illusion, their values may be borrowed, but if these are illusions they belong to a social position that is fought for with eagerness: its psychic satisfactions belong to them and not to others, and both the illusions and the satisfactions furnish the social cement that helps hold them and the society together. Many of the men and women who work in the bureaucratic posts of government or corporation or trade-union, who become teachers or script writers or TV performers, who play in the jazz bands, who turn out advertising copy, who stand trimly at the counters of the big department stores or travel about as buyers for them, who work as inspectors and sales engineers for the public utilities, who preach the sermons or write the books and magazine articles, who staff the newspapers or run the political parties of America—many of these men are far less aware of the tragedy of their plight, the emptiness of their values, or the slipping security of their prestige than the stern observer who measures them by the standards of a simpler technology and of a society as it was before the property atom was split and before the Big Media emerged.

There are three tests we may apply to a class system: how well it fills the psychic hungers as well as the objective needs of the people; how much stability it gives to the social structure; and how much fluidity it gives to it. Judged by these tests, the new middle classes are imperfect on each but don't come off too badly on any. To most of their members they offer to some degree the "career open to talent" and the sense of upward movement on the income and prestige scale, or at least the sense of not being outsiders. As for stability, I do not deny the possibility that the new middle classes may in a time of stress turn against the industrial and union workers from whom they distinguish themselves and become the dupes of a totalitarian leadership, much as happened when the middle classes of the Weimar Republic turned in panic to the Nazis: but I doubt that it is inevitable or even likely. The German middle classes were mainly the bureaucracies of a stratified society, in which the career open to talent had never strongly taken root, and in which deference was traditional and authority habitually accepted. They were also part of a defeated society which had, at least for a time, lost its power of expansion and was caught in political paralysis and inflation disaster.

As for the test of fluidity, the perception of Max Weber laid bare the outlines of the "three hierarchies" of the social structure, and he saw that the middle class was caught in an "iron cage" between the two others. The difference between the situation of the German and American middle classes is found exactly in this symbolism of the iron cage. German middle-class society was at once too rigid and too amorphous. When economic disaster came there was no underpinning that could save the middle classes from being wiped out by inflation and thrown into the arms of the Nazi adventurers by political hysteria. The new American middle classes are so diverse that while some of them suffer the scars of the chances and changes of economic life, they have never all been affected at once. They are far less rigid and more fluid than the German classes which Weber described, possessing a flexible capacity to adjust themselves to economic transformations which—more than anything else—gives the American class structure the resilience it has.

The fact is that no class structure ever offers a solution to social problems except in the Marxist canon, and it ought not to be judged by the test of whether or not it does. Toynbee has said that the two big rocks on which every civilization has foundered have been war and class. In each civilization there has been the choice between a frozen class system, managed and manipulated from above, and a mobile one; among the mobile ones there have been those which have moved from crisis to crisis through the mechanism of class struggle, always sharpening class distinctions and aligning the people in one camp or another without any intermediate middle ground; and there have been, on the other hand, the class systems which have always sought a moving equilibrium to give the society some stability. The American class system belongs with the latter. It does not—as no class system by its very nature can—make people happy or creative, rooted or alienated, powerful or weak, active or apathetic. All that it can hope to do is to organize the differentials of life choices and life chances with a maximum of access to opportunity and social experience and a minimum of the riving social tensions.

Seen in this frame, the American middle-class society is an operative effort to distribute power and prestige, opportunity and social experience, among the major sectors of the American population which comprise neither the owners of industrial power nor their challengers, neither the powerful nor the embittered, neither elites nor proletarians. By the very nature of the social function they perform, the middle classes cannot be the great militant or assertive force of American life. They are mediators and twilight people, and the most that can be asked is that they should occupy their middle positions with a tolerable measure of social energy and personal fulfillment. Unless a society is dominated by a single class, or is caught in the lethal struggle of two armed class camps until one or the other becomes the dominant one, only a middle-class society can furnish the pattern of a class equilibrium. Obviously the economic and technical changes of the society will be most strongly transmitted to these middle classes, which have received the shock of the changes, cushioned them, transformed them into new forms of social energy.

A middle class which is frozen or is caught in an iron cage has, by this token, ceased to perform its broadly mediating function, and it is doomed along with the society to which it belongs. But in recent American generations the dynamic movement that so swiftly and silently brought the new middle classes onto the stage of American history may also usher them out and bring new forms of class power, prestige, and experience in their place. Where change is so constant and active the strength of the class system is to be measured not in terms of the stability of any particular class formations, nor the happiness or security of the individuals who form it, but by the fact of the change itself. The dynamism that has produced the present middle-class formations in America can produce others as well. This is the growing point of American social experience, and these are the shock absorbers of American social change.

Thus America has become a great historical experiment in a shifting middle-class society. The middle classes do not hold the power of government or rule the economy; they do rule the culture, set the tone of consumption, serve as the crucial audience for the Big Media. They are in this sense the pivot class of America. It is they who read the books and the "slick" magazines, and see the plays and movies with just enough of a cultural veneer to make them palatable and give them gloss. They do not have either the burdens or satisfactions of manual labor, nor the daring that comes from large-scale enterprise. They are middling folk with middling goals, caring for comfort, a competence, and security. Although they still pride themselves on their individualism, they have lost much of the old individualistic stress on hard work and self-denial. They are not out for the old virtues but for some new, relatively safe gamble, whatever it may be. The feel for the safe gamble is the key to their conformism, politically and culturally. They look up to the high places of big business that they hope to reach and down at the lowly places of the workers that they wish to avoid.

Yet I am stretching this too far if I imply that these are barren leaves on a barren tree. Much as it may pain some of the intellectual elite to say so, it is often the middle-class people who dream the dreams, see the visions, and push forward the new formulations that make a people great. The paradox is that out of the middle classes have come some of the most creative talents of America, including the movement for governmental reform and for collective international action. Even the New Deal was as much a movement of the middle class as it was of labor: it first had to shape itself as a movement of middle-class reform and then it went out to find a labor movement which would furnish it a base of mass action.

Like Toynbee, De Tocqueville felt that no civilization could survive unless it resolved the problem of class; his own conviction was that only a middle-class society could sustain political and social democracy. Since then the analysis of thinkers like Veblen, and more recently Laski, Lynd, and Mills, has argued the opposite: that in the key struggle between capitalism and democracy, the middle classes more or less consciously serve the cause of capitalism and are therefore dangerous to democracy. The trouble with this argument is that noncapitalist societies, with very little of a middle class, notably those of eastern Europe and of Asia, have been drawn more strongly than the middle-class societies to totalitarianism and have become managed societies, linked not with democracy but with its antithesis.

De Tocqueville's argument also needs rethinking. The middle classes he knew in the America of his travels were very different from those of today. They were the middle classes of masterless men—farmers always seeking new land, self-employed artisans and mechanics, shopkeepers, small-town editors and lawyers, small businessmen. The independent middle class with which he linked the fortunes of democracy has grown less independent, less secure, more complex. There is no certain democratic health in it as there is no certain democratic destruction.

An effort must be made to distinguish between types of middle-class experience—between the corporate bureaucracies, for example, and such professions as teachers, writers, scientists; between the middle classes with crucial skills which keep them in social demand and those whose living standards become indistinguishable from the average workers; between those who have risen from the ranks and those who, starting at the top, have become declassed; between those, like the technicians and some of the sales and advertising and distributive people, who are the product of economic expansion and those who are caught in a back eddy of history. The fact that they are neither proprietors nor workers defines their outer boundaries but sheds no light on the social functions or the creative force of the groups which are the growing point of American society.

The more functional middle-class groups, especially when they have moved up the class scale, have an *élan* too, which flows from the feeling of not being frozen in a permanent lower class, and therefore of seeing the possibilities of life ahead. Thus the middle classes are not automatons, nor merely the hollow men. When politicians and parties have sought to use them by manipulating them politically, they have sometimes succeeded, but just as often they have been disappointed in finding that their material was not as pliable as they had thought. The middle class has done much to mute the jangling sharpness of American competitive tensions and blur the class divisions. It has had to pay the psychic cost of such a role. It is the most vulnerable, perhaps, of the American social strata, and as permeable by fears, hates, and frustrations as the depressed classes or the rat-race executives and the top rich. Nevertheless it exerts a mediating force, at once flexible and massive, fluid and resistant, which has helped keep American society from the class agonies that others have experienced.

4. Class Profile of the Worker

UNLIKE THE MIDDLE classes, the American working class is neither the pivot of the culture nor its mediating force, nor is it so vulnerable to the shifting tides of change and opinion.* Yet here too there have been far-reaching changes since the days of Jefferson and Jackson, especially in the last half century.

The American working class disappointed both its champions and its enemies by proving less revolutionary than the former had expected and less docile than the latter had hoped. Unlike the working classes in more clearly stratified societies, it has never shown any of the marks of a permanent proletariat. Nor has it, on the other hand, wholly submitted to the process of *enbourgeoisement* which defeated the hopes of European trade-union organizers who had counted on the continued militancy of their working class. The American workers have been militant enough, but only in trade-union terms, and not in the ideology or politics of revolution. They have shown little proletarian potential and have persisted in refusing to isolate themselves from the main currents of American life. But they have also refused to be absorbed by the other classes and have maintained a sturdiness of viewpoint which makes them neither subservient nor class-embittered. This is part of the anomaly of the American working class.

As with other classes in American society, the dominant historical drive among the workers has been that of fluidity. From the start they saw in America vistas of possibility that were denied to the permanent proletariats of Europe, caught in the iron mesh of a system of status. As early as the Jacksonian period, however, the shadows began to fall on the American workers. Part of the radicalism of the "Workingmen's Associations" and of the Knights of Labor came from the effort to keep the sluices of opportunity open—by fighting off centralized banking and corporate power and by demanding full educational facilities for their sons which would enable them to compete for the prizes of an opening continent. At mid-century the workers, to keep from getting caught as a class, had to rely upon cheap government land; but the process of getting to the frontier with a family required in itself a considerable capital outlay, which in turn became an inhibiting factor. By the 1870s it had become clear to some of the farsighted leaders of the workers that unless they could keep the class system fluid by fighting the new power groups, it would imprison them. Hence the militancy of the Knights of

---

* See Ch. V, Sec. 7 and Sec. 8, for the history and role of trade-unions and the position of the working force as a whole in the social structure, and Ch. IV, Sec. 4, for the transformations within the factory culture itself and within the concepts of work and the job.

Labor, which reached for weapons of political organization as well as economic and sought alliance with farmer and middle-class groups outside the labor movement. When that effort failed, and the job-conscious unionism of the A.F. of L. took the stage, it spelled the end of one phase in the class development of the American workers. They did not become a proletariat in the sense of becoming hopeless or em-bittered. But they emerged with a definite consciousness of their com-mon interests, geared to the job rather than to social transformation, yet nonetheless aware of their need for cohesiveness as a class in the struggle with the massed power of the employers.

This phase of class conflict in America has sometimes been slurred over in the eagerness to prove that America is a classless society. There were debt struggles in America as there were in Rome, but in the American case they were between the farmers and the mortgage com-panies. There were struggles over access to markets, sometimes between farm shippers and the railroads discriminating against them, more often between small businessmen and big monopolies. Yet the class militancy of the farmers and small businessmen largely ebbed away, with the one becoming wards of the government and the other feudatories of the big corporations. The militancy that continued has been in the conflicts over wages and work and life conditions for the workers. Their antago-nists have been not only the big corporate managers but even more the small entrepreneurs who have encountered the workers in the face-to-face struggles of collective bargaining, strikes, and lockouts. Since they have been the most direct antagonists the class bitterness between them has been the greatest. This has tended, as I have suggested earlier, to iso-late the working class from the middle classes and has imposed upon it the burden of taking on another antagonist along with corporate power.

The class militancy of American workers has not been, therefore, the product of a taste for violence or of the dogma of social change. The magnetic attraction of middle-class and elite values has operated strongly on the workers; often their leaders have been drawn off and lost to them because of that attraction; and the rank and file would have preferred to be absorbed in the rest of American society. The con-tinuance of the workers' militancy has been largely due to the business-men and the corporate managers who have shown themselves most tenacious of their power, as they have been most resourceful in their use of every means of resistance to union organization and demands. They have used their control of press and propaganda, their vast eco-nomic power, and—when pushed hard—even violence itself. How far this had gone beyond sporadic instances was shown in a *Harvard Law Re-view* article commenting on the National Labor Relations Act (1936) by Professor (now Judge) Calvert Magruder. "Away with yellow dogs, company unions, black lists, deputy sheriffs in the pay of employers, barricades, tear gas, machine guns, vigilante outrages, espionage, and all that miserable brood of union-smashing detective agencies." It was an epitaph on a phase of the labor-management class struggle that was never to return in full force.

For the American worker to be a worker—that is to say, to belong to the working class—is an act of involuntary association, but one sealed in the fire of historic struggle. The antagonism and coercions are not what he would have wished, since his whole pull is toward acceptance in the community, away from proletarian consciousness. Yet, given his refusal to be placed below the salt and given also the tenacity of the Big Business owners in resisting his claims, the antagonisms have been inescapable. The worker has suffered scars and met defeats, and he has also tasted of victory. He has learned a little about the "prowess order" in American society, and what goes with the status of the bottom dogs as of the top dogs.

In the process he has caught a glimpse of the power he can exercise in common action with his fellows. He has refrained from exercising that full power—at once economic, political, and social—despite the fervent prayers and upbraidings of side-line coaches who want him to act for the salvation of society. He acts, however, according to the laws of his own being within the American frame—peaceful when he can be, violent when he must, an economic man most of the time, a political man in the great crises, an individualist when he can indulge himself in that luxury, but acting with class solidarity when he can do no other. As a result of the struggle, some traits in him have become desensitized, others sharpened; on the whole a democratic dynamism has come out of it, since the worker's fulfillment of at least a good portion of his life claims upon the culture is a condition of vitality in a people's society.

To a desolating degree these life claims remain unfulfilled. The worker often leaves school as a child, to keep the family vessel from foundering, and he never gets back to equip himself with the needed skills for advancing out of his job. Often a worker who has started with eager hopes for thrusting his way up has wound up with the job he had at the start. The hope for advancement becomes a youthful memory, and he accedes to the quenching of his hopes and the drab limits of his uneventful historyless life career. Thus forces which in other cultures expressed themselves in a permanently depressed proletarian class have in America been transmuted into defeated life claims and "deadened choices" for a segment of the unskilled and semiskilled workers—and perhaps even some of the skilled workers and lower white-collar groups.

Why then has not the American worker asserted his resentments more strongly? The German scholar, Werner Sombart, put this question at the turn of the century in a book called *Why Is There No Socialism in the U.S.?* The two Lynd studies of "Middletown," which are powerful attempts to trace the logic of class relations in America, suggest that he has been bemused by the mass media which the business class controls and the legendry it has fashioned, and has forgotten his own interests, allowing his militancy to be absorbed in "the Middletown spirit."

Yet at least three additional factors should be mentioned. One is the democratizing influence of public education, which is free and universal for all social classes through the public high schools and which can be had at a minimal cost in the city and state universities. Even the private universities have increasingly been opening their doors, through scholarships and subsidies, to the sons and daughters of workers. What I have said above, about the working-class child having to leave school to help support the family, is happily true only of an ever-decreasing segment of the workers. Second, there is the democratizing effect of mass consumption, which has meant that the worker and his family now have access to many of the things from which they were formerly cut off. Third, there is the persistent hope that the worker's children will "do better" than the parents did, with respect to a job and education and the class into which they will marry. I must add that in terms of both mass education and mass consumption the real problem for the worker has been not that of being able to cut across class lines but of finding in the new norms to which he has penetrated some content with richness enough to nourish his personality. Generally these norms have been filled with the values of the middle classes, for which the worker has hungered because they have been alien to his experience, yet which have often left him with the frustrated sense of achieving less than he had hoped for.

There has been considerable evidence since the Lynds that subjectively the workers think of themselves in middle-class terms and yearn for a middle-class status. In 1940 a *Fortune* poll found that 79 per cent of the American people called themselves "middle class" rather than "lower class," and a Gallup poll found the percentage to be 87 per cent. But a Princeton study by Richard Centers, which put the question differently, got very different results. Centers asked a sampling of Americans whether they belonged to the "upper," "middle," "working," or "lower" class. This time 51 per cent put themselves in the "working class," and 43 per cent in the "middle class."

While there are serious doubts about what any of the attitude studies really show, the shift in percentages between these studies is striking.

The American worker does not think of himself as part of a permanent underlying proletariat. He refuses therefore to put himself in the "lower class." He will bow subserviently to no man. But he is not ashamed of his role as worker, and when confronted with "middle class" and "working class" as a designation, he chooses the latter. Although in income terms he belongs below the middle of the hierarchy, he does not feel an outsider in his culture. His whole striving has been to shun proletarianism and seek equality of status with other common men, whether they be in the middle or working class, yet not to give up his militancy as a worker and not to hesitate about calling himself one.

The three crucial indices of class are power, income, and status. In terms of power the American worker as an individual does not have the formal economic and social power that the corporate owners and managers have, in the sense that he cannot strategically shape the behavior and destiny of others. Yet acting collectively in the trade-union the workers do have a vast power over the destinies of the economy as a whole, and, whether they choose to exercise it or not, it gives them a feeling of assurance. In terms of income, the worker's purchasing power and living standards have risen steadily, although not as rapidly as the wealth of the owners, and in many cases are higher than those of the lower white-collar groups. In terms of his social standing in the community, however, the worker does not have the badges of social rank that the middle class has. In this area of status and prestige he tends to imitate not, as Veblen thought, the prowess and ostentation of the businessmen in the "leisure class," but the comforts and living standards of the middle class: he hopes to have his daughters marry into it and his sons move up into the professional, technical, managerial, or small-business ranks, while his wife moves into its churches and clubs. This is a slow process, but it is taking place in America, especially for the upper income ranks of the working class. The middle classes have become, in status terms, a compassable goal for the working class while it retains its own identity and solidarity on the job.

Thus, when Europeans ask why there has been so little "proletarian potential" among the American workers, the answer is the multiple one I have suggested. It runs in terms of education, mass consumption, the Big Media, the fact of high living standards and income, the constant movement into the middle-class status, the sense of hope for the future of the next generation. The greater democratic atmosphere of social intercourse in America has shorn membership in the working class of much of the social stigma that it has carried elsewhere. The outlets offered for democratic political activity, where the worker has the same vote as the employer and is protected by the same legal right, have a similar effect. But above all, there has been a steady increase in the productivity of American workers, unequaled in world history. The role that was formerly played by continued access to free land, in cutting down a sense of class inferiority and class bitterness in the worker, was later played by the continuing rise of the productivity curve due to technological advance. It is notable that there is no exactly parallel word in the European languages for the sense in which Americans use "productivity."

In fact, technology had at least as much to do as the much mooted frontier with shaping the profile of the class system in America. The task has been to transmute a substantial part of the productivity gains into higher real wages and lower hours for the workers, which has been the task of a job-conscious, astutely led, tenacious trade-unionism. The result of all these influences together has been to drain off the "proletarian potential," which is to say, the revolutionary energy of the American worker.

While he has functioned on the economic level with class solidarity, the worker has been drawn on the social level toward the values of the middle class which he often rivals in his income. His reading, sports, amusements, hobbies, heroes, are the same as those of the white-collar classes, the small merchants, the professional people, the businessmen. He is caught in the contradiction that while his political and economic attitudes recognize his class identity and are an expression of it, he persistently refuses to give up his belief in a fluid class system. Thus is created the great class anomaly of American society—that of the worker who acts militantly as one, but whose leanings and dreams are toward the values of the middle class.

5. The Minority Situation*

EVERY NATION, seen realistically, is several nations, and in every historic civilization, stock and race—as well as class—have been the traditional lines of cleavage. In America, where the class lines have been blurred by social mobility and where most of the society is middle class, the more stubborn cleavage lines have proved to be race, color, religion, and the social hierarchy of ethnic and national stocks. Visitors to America, especially from Europe and Latin America, have for generations been puzzled by the ordeal by contempt to which the American

* I have already touched on this theme in Ch. III, Sec. 1, "Is There an American Stock?" and Sec. 2, "The Immigrant Experience," both of which deal with the composition of the American people. I deal here with the social situation of the ethnic minorities in relation to the majority.

ethnic minorities have been subjected. The Negro, Chinese, Japanese, Mexican, Filipino, Italian, Jew, Catholic, the foreign born (and to some extent the second generation) of almost any stock have found to varying degrees that their standing and acceptance depend less upon themselves as persons than upon the labels attached to them.

It is difficult to get at accurate figures on the size of minority groups, partly because of definition and partly because the census figures are lacking. But G. E. Simpson and J. M. Yinger have made some calculations that are worth setting down. They indicate that as of 1950 there were fifteen million Negroes in America, one half million other non-whites, two million Mexican Americans, ten million foreign-born whites, and five million Jews. Allowing for overlappings, they estimate that thirty million Americans, or a little less than one fifth of the total population in 1950, belonged to one or another of these minority groups. This was a smaller percentage than forty years earlier, in 1910, when the Negroes and the foreign born formed more than a quarter of the total number of people.

Thus the trend has been toward a more homogeneous population. This is especially true of the foreign born, whose proportion to the total has been decreasing since 1910 and whose actual numbers have also been falling since 1930. If we move beyond the foreign born to the second generation, there were in 1950 somewhere around twenty million "of foreign or mixed parentage." When added to the thirty million figure above, we get over fifty million Americans—roughly one third of the nation—who could be said to belong to the minority groups or to feel the impact of the current attitudes toward minorities. In their sum they form a system of not very disguised lower status. They have again in varying degrees become the targets of socially sanctioned hatred, contempt, and fear upon the part of the majority. They occupy the lower positions in what has become a hierarchy of belonging and alienation which can scarcely be squared with the clangor of American ideals, the professions of churchmen, or the pronouncements of political spokesmen.

This hierarchical pattern is not, except for some state laws and ordinances in the South, embodied in statute or legal decision, but more dangerously in the practices of everyday living and the emotions of everyday thinking. To assign it to the crude energies of a lusty, growing nation—a kind of sowing of cultural wild oats by an otherwise generous and equalitarian people—contains a core of truth, however bitter the rind may be. One of the paradoxes of American life has been the simultaneous passion for equality among "insiders" and the almost equally passionate rejection of the "outsider." This is, in effect, a kind of American tribalism expressing itself through a system of upper caste and pariahs—grudgingly recognized, accompanied by a sense of agonized guilt, inveighed against by some of the "best people," yet nonetheless practiced.

Amidst the varieties of racist experience represented here, one may trace the main lines of the historical graph by which the "outsiders" were isolated from the culture. As long as America's greatest need was for more manpower to clear and settle the land and build the industrial plant, men of all nations and creeds were accepted, if not welcomed, by the earliest arrivals. From the beginning there were stereotypes imposed upon the more marginal immigrants. As was perhaps natural, the members of each new wave of immigration were assigned the lowliest tasks, the longest hours of work, the poorest and dirtiest living quarters. The basic pattern was, however, for the immigrants of each new influx to be in time absorbed by the rest, yielding the role of strangeness in turn to the still later comers. Most of them moved up the hierarchical ladder, while those who followed grasped eagerly the lowly places that had been relinquished. But during this period the discriminations were (so to speak) objective: it was taken as a fact of life in the New World that the earlier arrivals got the favored positions; what prejudice existed was more against immigrants as such than against any particular groups, although even in the 1840s the Irish immigrant was a favorite target of abuse.

The entering wedge of a new order of prejudice came with the racism developed by the struggle between North and South. The first Negroes, even when they came as indentured servants, were not regarded by the other Americans as a separate order of mankind. The whites who had come as indentured servants, and even those who had come as convicts, were later absorbed, and their descendants are today merged with the rest. But the cotton gin, and with it the development of large-scale methods of cotton growing on the Southern plantation system, made necessary the importing of a whole population of cheap black slave labor, recruited from the easy sources of African supply. Since the Southern spokesmen could not square this with their democratic or Christian ideals of the brotherhood of man, they developed a doctrine to justify the ways of the master race to the subject race—a doctrine of the biological superiority of one and inferiority of the other. This effort to create a permanent legal and social caste system clashed not only with the American ideals of equality but also with the efforts of the other sections to keep the society open for free labor and investment. The North won, with its belief in free labor and an open-class system; yet in the South the bitterness of defeat and the postwar urge to keep freed slaves in subjection served to harden the mold of racist doctrine.

Its consequences to the American mentality were not restricted to the South. In the free West, which had joined with the antislavery cause, movements developed after the Civil War for the exclusion of Chinese immigration, again on grounds of a biological racism. The peopling of the continent grew less pressing, and the scarcity of man power was less felt. New currents of thought came in from Europe— those of Gobineau and Alfred Schultz, and later of Wagner and Houston Chamberlain; in America there was a response in the racist writings of Lothrop Stoddard and Madison Grant. As Oscar Handlin has noted, the liberal thinkers were not guiltless on racism and immigration: the Populist campaign (sometimes with anti-Jewish overtones) against "Wall Street," the campaign of Gompers and the A.F. of L. against Chinese immigration, and the writings of Edward A. Ross and John R. Commons (and later of H. P. Fairchild) were all the more influential because they were known liberals on other scores. Immigration policy grew tighter, and with the passage of the quota laws racism came of age in America.* Not only did caste thinking develop on color lines, but America in effect declared officially that the stocks of eastern Europe, the Mediterranean countries, and Asia were less welcome as permanent residents than the supposedly "Aryan" stock of northern Europe and the British Isles. The revival of the Ku Klux Klan in the twenties and the spread of anti-Semitic forgeries like the "Protocols" gave a new dimension of hatred and violence to the prejudices of previous generations. With the Great Depression, the anxieties of survival and status were deepened for millions of Americans who were ready to turn their frustrations on the vulnerable groups. The rise of Nazi power in Europe, and the spread of Rosenberg-Goebbels propaganda by the Bund and other organizations, completed the graph.

The sources on which racism had fed and grown strong were deeply related: some of the same domestic tensions which led to the closing of the immigration gates led also to inner economic and political struggles, as in the Depression and the New Deal, which in turn served as arenas for deepened racial and religious hatreds. The impact of world struggles was also felt, as witness the internment of the Japanese in California in World War II and the efforts both of anti-Semites and of Communists to turn some of the atom-spy episodes involving persons who happened to be Jews to the purposes of their own propaganda.

One could tell the story of minority-group Americans in a very different fashion, turning the seamier side inside and displaying some of the less gloomy aspects: that the whole minority experience in America has been a successful one; that, except in the South, no local

* For a fuller discussion, see Ch. III, Sec. 2, "The Immigrant Experience."

prejudices have been translated directly into law; that, again excepting the South, no political candidate or party since the Know-Nothings has run successfully on a platform of racism; that these irrational prejudices, which form the chief outlet for social tensions and frustrations, have resulted in remarkably little violence; that mingling of majority and minority groups in the Armed Services during World War II resulted in considerable erosion of racism; that statutes like the Ives-Quinn Law in New York helped whittle away discrimination in employment, without coercion and with little publicity; that recent Supreme Court decisions, especially in housing, transportation, and education, show the secular trend of constitutional law; that the political party on which the racist Southerners depend for their power is the same party that won five successive Presidential elections in the span of a quarter century by a coalition which included labor, anti-racist liberals, and the minority groups; that the prejudice against Negroes, Orientals, Catholics, Jews, and the various national minorities has been steadily decreasing; that when Hitler relied on American racist discords to pave the way for victory, he calculated badly; that the similar reliance of the Communists, using very different techniques of propaganda, is also based on a miscalculation.

While each item in this defense is valid, their sum still leaves standing the massive fact of a "divided America." To a degree the class inequities and the ethnic discriminations in American life are both subject to erosion by mobility, which, however slow it may be, makes the open-class system one of hope. But I doubt that it makes a status system open enough to stand alongside the open-class system. If there were still the kind of open-caste system there was for a time, when only the most recent immigrants were made the targets of stereotyped ridicule and discrimination, that too would be tolerable. But in the case of Negroes and Jews, and to some degree Catholics, Orientals, and Mexicans, the lines of division are drawn tightly. The danger, of course, lies in the idea of two Americas—one a presumably authentic America of traditional blood and ways, the other an inferior and supplementary America of second-class citizens, made up of those who do not belong to the exclusive club and who have to fight for equal access to opportunity.

It would not be hard to make out a rational defense for the philosophy which wants to keep a society from becoming too "mongrelized" or "cosmopolitan." There are social values in the tightly knit, relatively cohesive communities—Sparta and Puritan New England and Renaissance Italy come to mind—for which one can at least make out a case: values of like-mindedness about manners and morals, common assumptions, a common pace of living. Even the best of these societies have foundered on the problem of growth: to expand means to take in variant ways of life and thought. But if the choice ever existed for America —which I doubt, since from the beginning it was founded on the idea of inclusiveness, not tribalism—it exists no longer. America has moved far beyond the limits of a simple tribalism. It has so successfully absorbed diverse stocks and strains that the warnings about being overwhelmed by "mongrel" groups sound a little like the forebodings of a future in which the insect kingdom will overwhelm the human race. Even those who plead that the spirit of the immigration restriction laws is not racist argue at most for a "breathing spell" in which to consolidate the population gains, but not for discrimination against those who have become Americans.

Actually the logic of the "breathing-spell" position should lead more powerfully toward the idea of an inclusive America, in which the "foreign" parts are brought into a synthesis with the whole instead of remaining as excrescences. A civilization does change in its ways of life and thought as it absorbs elements from diverse biological stocks and cultural traditions. One can even understand the fear of the more prolific birth rate of the minorities, but since they are largely the product of lower living standards the strategy of keeping the living standards low by enclosing the minorities in walls of caste would seem self-defeating. However, this fear of being "swamped" by alien stocks and ways of thought is in itself a curious contradiction, since from earliest times the Americans welcomed accessions of individual vigor and cultural strength, from whatever ethnic source.

The rituals of expulsion and purification, which can only rest on the premise of a core stock which is alone pure and the assumption that everything else is polluting, are themselves grotesquely alien to the traditional American spirit. The individual has the right to be wrong in choosing his social associates and intimates on the basis of attraction, taste, snobbery, or conviction. Nor is there anything unhealthy about the existence of ethnic communities within the larger American community, each of them trying to hold on to elements of its group identity and in the process enriching the total culture pattern. What is unhealthy is the freezing of ethnic lines into caste lines, especially when they purport to be also dividing lines of "Americanism" and "loyalty." When these lines are congealed, so as to separate top dogs from bottom dogs, and are made tests of belonging regardless of an individual's own worth, the explanation cannot be found in the intellectual rationalizations that pass as "arguments," or even in the traits of the minority groups themselves. They must be sought in forces within the society which the racist impulses somehow mirror or express.

If we try to understand these forces and tensions, anti-Semitism in America offers a case study a little sharper than the other minority groups, although less sharp than the case of the Negroes. Until the turn of the century the problem of anti-Jewish feeling was little different from that of anti-immigrant feeling in general. In fact, one could not have found anti-Jewish movements similar to the Know-Nothings or the American Protective Association, nor were Jews anywhere in America treated as the Irish immigrants were treated by the Boston Brahmin community in the 1850s and 1860s. In common with the others, the anti-Jewish stereotypes could be expected to yield to the mellowing effects of time and mutual acquaintance. In a Bible-conscious America the Jews had one advantage over the other minorities—the affinity between Protestant militancy and the tradition of Hebraic prophecy.

If one holds, with Carey McWilliams, that anti-Semitism is "the mask of privilege" and therefore crucially related to the class struggles in a capitalist economy, then the refusal of a famous Saratoga hotel in 1871 to admit the wealthy Jewish banker J. W. Seligman becomes a symbolic turning point in the treatment of the Jews. But I should be inclined to see the incident more narrowly as part of the elite thinking of New York "Society" and its pettiness in seeking to close its gates to the parvenu Jew. To see anti-Semitism as a deliberate "diversionary issue," created by a ruling class in order to turn away the gathering anticapitalist wrath, seems somewhat too pat. In more complex terms, one can see a triple separation—at once stock (ethnic origin), recency of immigration, and religion—which made the Jew seem more of an outsider than other minorities, and a heavily Jewish city like New York more exotic and sinister to Americans from the South and the Midwest.

Thus anti-Semitism gained a cumulative force, fed even among the other immigrants themselves by the centuries-old hatreds of Europe, by echoes of Chaucer and Shakespeare and Dickens, of Oberammergau and Wagner, of the traditions of the Slavic peasant and the German bourgeois. The economic struggle contributed its competitive rivalries-turned-to-hatreds. McWilliams notes rightly that there was little outcry against the Jews from eastern Europe as long as they stayed as proletarians in the needle trades, but when they moved into the middle classes and made a bid for higher living standards and better schools, residences, and resorts, the anti-Jewish tensions mounted. Yet it was not until the era of Depression and Nazism that anti-Semitism took its place, after anti-Negro racism, as the most serious movement of ethnic hatreds in America. This was not due so much to capitalism or economic exploitation, nor to any logic in the racial doctrines themselves, but to the aggressions and frustrations of life in a rapidly changing, highly charged society. The Jews became in a sense the residuary legatees of other stored-up and unexpended hatreds.

What this has meant scarcely requires review. The planes and dimensions on which it is expressed are complex: exclusion from residential areas, resorts, and clubs; exclusion from many colleges of standing except on a rough quota basis, and dwindling admission into many professional schools, especially medical and engineering; as well as economic discrimination, in getting employment and advancement; a depressing number of anti-Semitic episodes. Obviously these forms of discrimination run from the genteel and perhaps largely unconscious, through the instances where they are used as a kind of group style in conforming to dominant habits of thought, all the way to the open incitements of fanatical professional anti-Semites. In the large they comprise an effort to isolate and segregate the Jews, and to squeeze them by pressures, gentle or otherwise, into a system of status for which they have not proved tractable material.

On any rational level there is a wild paradoxical quality in the charges made against the Jew in America. His position in business and finance makes him a target for nativist "Populist" movements, while his position in liberal and labor circles makes him the target of the Radical Right. By using the Jew as the symbol both of Bolshevism and of international finance, his enemies have managed to link him at once with the two movements that have invoked widespread hostility. They also get him coming and going on the score of his ways of living. If he seeks to embrace the ways of the larger community—in work or play, in marriage, in social intercourse—he is either repulsed as an intruder or condemned (not the least by his own people) as a fawning "assimilationist." If, either as a response to the rebuffs or out of pride in the Jewish tradition, he lives and marries and brings up children largely within his group, he is condemned as clannish and unassimilable.

A similar paradox invests the passions of the small rabble of violent anti-Semites. Although they regard themselves as part of the American majority, they speak and act more as if they were a victim minority themselves and as if the Jew somehow represented the dominant cultural profile. They see him as the center of a successful conspiracy to dominate the whole of American life—its banks and trade-unions, its government, its colleges and school system, its Big Media, its book publishing and reviewing, its judiciary and even the Supreme Court. Making a bid for the role of pursuer, they retain the mentality of the victim. They manage to bridge both roles, as Theodor Adorno has noted, by saying vaguely that "blood will flow," thus implying that it might be theirs at the hands of the Jews, and rationalizing their own role as that of counterviolence. Much of their literature and their speeches contains a sense of discovery, as if they had found "the key" which so many of the bemused and bewildered are seeking—the key not only to American salvation but to the solution of the world crisis.

Some of these racists come from the working class and some from the

wealthy strata, but most from the lower middle classes. As a result of
the new phases of American life that have cut many away from internalized codes of thought and behavior, they have developed a malaise.
Whatever the established patterns of hatred, they move to them because
they find them socially sanctioned hatreds. But in addition to a sense of
status, they also get a sense of being rebels fighting to overthrow the
reigning idols. They join the racist "crackpot" organizations, are prose-
lytized and in turn become fervent proselytizers. They become obsessive,
as much the victims of their hate as the hated ones.

In a massive collaborative study, *The Authoritarian Personality,* a
number of American social scientists, mainly with a European background (Adorno, Frenkel-Brunswik, Levinson, and others), sought light
on the personality pattern of those who succumb to racist prejudices
and become their carriers. Using various schematic scales for attitude
measurement, interviews, and projective techniques, they found racism
most pronounced in two types: in a California study of college girls they
found an insecurity that came from their need to maintain status in
their genteel, well-groomed, upper-middle-class groups. They were over-
trained for the status struggle and full of social anxieties. Another group
was made up of war veterans in Chicago, largely from the working class.
In them the violent and rebellious strains were more apparent. As
Nathan Glazer has pointed out, there is no contradiction between the
strain of nonconformism at one stratum and of conformism at another,
both entering as ingredients into the racist syndrome. Both are mani-
festations of a malaise that may take either a chip-on-the-shoulder form
or that of status anxiety. In both cases the family context and the
processes of child-rearing, rather than experience with minority groups,
seem decisive in the formation of the personality pattern. In both also
there is a haunting sense of failure in the life goals. The traits that each
individual most feared or disliked in himself were found to be projected
onto the symbol of the target victim.

Finally, the investigators found an interconnected pattern of attitudes: anti-Semitism almost always was linked with hatred of Negroes
and of other ethnic minorities. (This was proved accurate in the agitation against school integration in the South in the controversy of the
mid-1950s.) These in turn were linked with a hatred of labor, the New
Deal, and liberalism, and a tendency to use highly charged nationalist
and religious symbols in condemning them together. Thus the racist
hatreds are not to be seen as isolated prejudices but as an interconnected web of hatred whose scope, like its sources, embraces the tensions
and problems of the whole of American society.

I have used the status of the Jews as an extreme example of ethnic hostility toward a minority whose members, unlike all except a few Negroes, could "pass" if they wished—that is, could renounce their minority membership and join the majority. Strikingly very few American Jews have availed themselves of this chance. Instead there has been an alternation, almost cyclical in nature, between the urge toward assimilation with the larger culture and the urge toward a militant assertion of the identity of the subculture. These cycles of changing emphasis have probably been true of immigrant groups in general—of the Scandinavians, the Slavs, the Irish, the Italians, the Greeks, the Arabs, the Chinese and Japanese; but the conflict has been sharper in the case of the Jews, partly because they have been more articulate about it and have thrashed it out in novels, Community Center meetings, and in their newspapers and magazines. In the quarter century after the rise of Hitler to power, during which the profile of Jewish life abroad included the experience of martyrdom, the needs of the refugees, and the crises of the new Jewish state, the emphasis within the American Jewish group shifted away from assimilationism toward a sometimes overmilitant assertion of their uniqueness and separateness as a historical community.

As with other minority groups in America, this was partly a carry-over of earlier ethnic patterns, partly a response to the hostility, partly a tenacity of group survival under the great assimilative force of American life. One result has been a continuing tendency toward ethnic endogamy, not only among Negroes upon whom it is forced but also among Catholics and Jews where it is also a willed community act. It is especially true in the towns and cities where there is a heavy concentration of minority population and where they have built up a community life of their own. It is a striking fact that even in cities like New York, Chicago, Detroit, Cleveland, Philadelphia, and Buffalo, where the ethnic minorities are substantial and often together form a majority, they still retain minority attitudes. The isolating ghetto pressures, both from without and from within, build up little ethnic pockets which make for cultural diversity but which also perpetuate needless frictions and divisions, and contribute to a sense of minority isolation and (especially among Jews and Negroes) even a victim psychology. There is among Negroes a surprising amount of "passing," where pigment and conscience allow it. Like the other white ethnic groups, the Jew, to "pass," has only to become "assimilated," which is a matter of cultural conformity and absorption. Yet even the Jew who strives hardest for such absorption finds that it is not enough for him to wear his religion lightly or even discard it and break his ties of identification with his ethnic group. In many instances his offer of assimilation is not acknowledged: it is only his children and in turn their children who are finally accorded a substantial measure of acceptance. Even where the pride of Jacob has been discarded, the fear of Ahasuerus lingers.

It is a hard thing for a member of such a minority group to hold the balance even between his sensitivities about status, his temptation to overreact toward hostility and either belittle himself or hate himself or flaunt in the face of the majority the very minority traits that have been called in question, his pride in his ethnic heritage, his ties with the victims and martyrs of his tradition, his hunger amidst it all to prove himself and fuse his own experience into the larger cultural pattern. It is these crosscurrents of impulse and emotion that made the Negro or Jewish youth a stock figure in the problem novels of the 1940s and the 1950s. His quest for identity was a voyage that had to survive dangerous shoals and rapids. He had two cultures rather than only one with which somehow he had to make his peace—identifying himself with segments of both as he grew up, sifting both of them through his fears and insecurities, his hopes and strengths, accepting and rejecting, and out of it having to discover who he was. The young Negro or the young Jew who managed to come through this experience was perhaps the sturdier personality for having been through it, and he carried with him a richer freightage of family and cultural memories. But in too many cases the experience warped or broke him.

Concentrating on such problems, there is a danger of slighting the very substantial progress that American minorities have made in finding their place in the larger culture without surrendering a saving remnant of identity. The Jews themselves, for all the restrictions on them, have advanced more rapidly on the social scale than the other minorities. But the Negroes have also won an increasing measure of socially recognized as well as legal equality. To many foreign observers what is remarkable about America is not that there should be the conflicts I have recounted but that in the midst of so many tensions there should be so striking a measure of success in living together. On the score of religious freedom the Catholic and other churches have been given by the Federal courts the right to run their own parochial school systems as alternatives to the public schools; the Jehovah's Witnesses have been protected against local ordinances restraining their activities; the sects of conscientious objectors to war have been recognized as such by the draft boards. Negroes and whites, Protestants and Catholics and Jews, ethnic groups from every part of the world, live together in the big cities without violence. Even the racist syndrome itself is in one sense a response to the democratic creed: confronted with equalitarian ideals which he dare not openly reject, the embittered and frustrated person who seeks a purge for his frustrations may find refuge either in the fantasy of an elaborate Jewish or Catholic conspiracy or else in a theory of the biological inferiority and superiority of the subject and master races.

Yet America remains a house divided against itself so long as the minority groups are kept from normal access to a wide range of life choices and from the normal processes of absorption. With perhaps a fifth of the population and considerable strength as a voting force, the Catholics have in recent years effectively protected themselves against Know-Nothings of contemporary America and have achieved a degree of power in the government, especially in Congress and in some of the administrative services. The anti-Catholic crackpots who are bemused by a world "Catholic conspiracy" are still to be found, and there are also serious students who fear objectively that Protestant America will not show the strength to resist the organized pressures to make the Catholic viewpoint prevail in a number of areas in American life. Yet on the whole it can be said with some assurance that the dangerous phase of anti-Catholicism in America is a thing of the past. Lower in the scale than either Jews or Catholics are the three million Mexican Americans, who are either migratory workers or live ghetto-wise in the "colonia" of the cities of the Southwest, where they rank just above the Indians and the Negroes: provided with poorer schools, discriminated against in hiring and firing, kept out of unions, given a shabby justice by local police and court officials, largely ignored in the choices for public office.

There is a curious paradox to be found in the American attitude toward minority groups, as disclosed by a recent Roper public-opinion poll. When asked whether various minorities should be given "a better break," one third of those questioned said that Negroes ought to get it, yet 79 per cent expressed a distaste for the idea of intermarriage with Negroes. The figures on the Jews were reversed: only 8 per cent thought they deserved a better break, while 50 per cent were against intermarriage. It is worth noting that the latter figure comes closer to the 40 per cent who thought the Jews had too much economic power. The response on the Catholics was 7 per cent for their deserving a better break, and 21 per cent against intermarriage. It is clear that intermarriage carries a decisive emotional freightage, since on the question of working side by side in factory or office or store and on the question of entertaining them in one's home, Jews and Catholics had evidently been pretty much accepted. The groups against whom prejudice persisted here were the Chinese, Filipinos, and Mexicans, and especially the Negroes. Two out of five Americans prefer not to work with Negroes, and more than half do not want them in their homes. Thus there is a hierarchy of sensitivity in the attitudes toward minority groups, ranging from the casual contacts of everyday life, through work and social intercourse, to the intimacies of family relation.

Whatever may be the current state of ethnic prejudices, it is never the "majority" that holds them. Except in the attitudes toward the Negroes, the majority of Americans hold—at least on a conscious level —enlightened views. In the wake of the Nazi excesses, a relativist concept of race has become widespread, and increasingly in the scholarly literature the older idea of a correlation between biological stocks and such traits as intelligence, disease, and criminality has been discarded. The kind of "cultural pluralism" which Horace Kallen and Randolph Bourne championed has become a staple of American writing and teaching. The carriers of racism are intense individuals who represent only the minority forces in American life.

Yet by their intensity, and by appealing to traits and tendencies on the level of the often unconscious and irrational elements in the majority, they have been able to exercise a disproportionate influence on American behavior. No Negro, for example, has ever gone beyond the House of Representatives in an elective office; none since Reconstruction days has ever been chosen in state-wide elections either as governor or Senator. Negroes have recently been appointed to the Federal courts, but none has reached the Supreme Court. Jews and Catholics have been governors and Senators, held Cabinet posts, and have even sat on the Supreme Court, where among the Catholics (Taney, White, Butler, Murphy, and Brennan) and the Jews (Brandeis, Cardozo, and Frankfurter) there have been some who have made judicial history. No Jew has ever been nominated for the Presidency, and in the one instance where a Catholic ran he was greeted by a revealing campaign of bigotry. Nevertheless, Senator Kennedy came close to getting the Democratic Vice-Presidential nomination in 1956, in a setting that made the Southern delegates paradoxically his most ardent supporters—which must be taken as a revolutionary turning point in the American attitudes toward Catholics. For a Jew, even a converted one, to head up the American imperial power as Disraeli headed up the British or Blum and Mendès-France the French, would still seem to most Americans politically unthinkable. To choose either a Jew or Catholic for the highest symbolic post in the nation would seem like choosing an outsider, and a political party which ventured such a candidacy would be challenging an encrusted tradition.

This is one of the things that sticks in the craw of the ethnic minorities. It has been suggested that ethnic pluralism breaks up some of the rigidities of the class system, and there is truth in it, but what counts for the minorities is that they have one additional hurdle—and often a steep one—in the competition for life's goods. What they resent is not just the prejudice but the closure of the otherwise open-class system in their case, just as what the Negroes especially resent, even more than racial hostility, is the lingering rigidity of caste in a society whose every fiber otherwise cries out against it. More than anything else, this accounts for the persistence of fairly cohesive voting of minority groups in political elections. It would be exaggerated to say that they vote as "blocs," yet in practice the politicians go on the assumption that the blocs do exist, and make their appeals accordingly in the campaigns. Usually the minority groups vote not so much their interests as their fears, their insecurities, their resentments, and the eagerness of their hopes.

These hopes must not be left out of the total picture. The central fact remains the vast assimilative force of American life. In a sense the xenophobic and racist hatreds are a response to it—a form of protest by the more backward and primitive elements against the onrushing pace of this force, an effort by embittered men and women to stay the strength of the current which is bearing them out to a chartless sea. In a sense also the elements of hope and affirmation in the lives even of the victims of hostility are also a response to it, for they sense that even the victories of their enemies are victories in a rear-guard action. The assimilative force of American life is more powerful than the logic of the liberal arguments, more powerful than the specialized sense in which "assimilation" is used, more powerful even than the economic and voting strengths exerted by the minorities. For it is intrinsic to American growth and experience, and as such it is itself a nonrational dimension which can match and overshadow the irrationalism of the racist impulse.

6. *The Negro in America*

I WANT TO deal separately with the case of the Negro in America because there is nothing in the experience of the other minority groups quite like it. The Negroes are the real outsiders of American life, and their situation is not one of disguised caste but almost nakedly of a pariah caste, kept in subjection by law, social custom, terrorism, and fear, at its worst in the South but even in the North anything but a thing of beauty. The "Negro problem" is a "white problem" as well: it is at once the ugliest scar on the American conscience and its gadfly. In terms of America's class system it presents the hierarchies of class in heightened and more rigid form, with (until recent years) relatively little of its mobility and sense of hope.

The case of the Negro can be spelled out in the relation between race, class, and caste. On race one can only say that it is a reality whose precise definition has defied generations of study. The Negroes form a more sharply defined ethnic group than most in American life. Coming as they did from the isolated and primitive life of African tribalism, their cultural heritage differed drastically from the culture to which they were brought. But even with the strongest differences in pigmentation and in cultural heritage, one misses from the factual picture of race any clear-cut evidences of superiority and inferiority.

In the jungle of American physical diversity, as I have said earlier, any notions of ethnic "purity" or prescriptive ethnic superiority become incongruous. Among the more recent theorists, Cox has defined race as any population with a large "penetrance" of a particular genetic trait, and the UNESCO statement defines it in closely similar terms. In this sense the Negroes form a race. But even when you single out pigmentation from all the other genetic traits, there are still a bewilderingly large number of color gradations and combinations in America that would defy a corps of skilled ethnologists: the varieties of black, white, yellow, red, mulatto, quadroon, octaroon, almost white, "passing," Creole, Indian-white, Indian-Negro, Caribbean-Latin, Hawaiian-Filipino-Chinese mixtures. Where the culture is, like the American, made up of human material from many ethnic groups that were crossbred to start with, and where it has carried the biological and cultural crossbreeding so far, the stalking of ethnic purity has an ironic irrelevance, and to base social caste on it becomes a cruel fantasy. The richness of ethnic composition that makes America a microcosm of the larger world transforms racism into a bad joke. It was the American school of anthropologists, headed by Franz Boas, that did most to lay bare the absurdities of racist thinking, even before the Nazi theorists had raised the absurdity to a political dogma.

The roots of American racism are to be found partly in the tragic history of both blacks and whites in the South.* Slavery itself, the "peculiar institution" of the South, was a way of life for both peoples. But once the Negroes got their freedom, their progress toward equality—however slow—could not be stopped. Partly this has been due to their own quality of tenacity—the asset side of that necessary obsessiveness with their plight which has been (as Kardiner puts it) the "mark of oppression." Less noted, but no less striking, is the role played by certain phases of the same American society which for many of the em-

* For an earlier discussion of the Negro strain and influence in America, see Ch. I, Sec. 2, "The Sources of the Heritage." For the problem of Negro and white in the Southern regional mind, see Ch. III, Sec. 11, "Regions: the Fusion of People and Place."

bittered Negroes seemed the chief actor in the whole diabolic drama.

To see this clearly one must start with the situation of the "New Negro"—new, that is, since World War I. The beginning of this phase came with the great migrations, north and west from the South. The Negro migrated for the best of possible reasons: because life in the South became intolerable, because he glimpsed the horizons of freedom elsewhere, but mainly because America was a society of restless, mobile striving. The two world wars gave them the chance they wanted, jobs in the North, money flowing so richly that some of it trickled into Negro pay envelopes in St. Louis, Detroit, Chicago, Pittsburgh, New York. From 1915 to 1920, 50,000 Negroes moved into Chicago; by 1938 there were 150,000 Negroes in the slums of Detroit, along with the lower-class whites and the mountain people who also migrated to the new auto center—all of them, white and black alike, drawn by unparalleled wages like the highly publicized five dollars a day that Henry Ford was paying. "It was kind of crowded on McComb Street," Joe Louis recalls. "It was kind of crowded there, but the house had toilets indoors and electric lights. Down in Alabama we had outhouses and kerosene lamps." In the two years from 1940 to 1942, 60,000 Negroes came to work in Detroit.

The combination of the New Deal and the Second World War gave the Negro struggle another fillip. The Northern Negro, who suffered terribly in the Depression (the first to be fired, the last to be hired), found jobs again. In the Armed Services he finally won a measure of equality: Jim Crow in the business of death was too grim a jest to be tolerable. But mostly what the Negro found in the era of the New Deal and Fair Deal was a new confidence in his collective power. For the first time, along with the other ethnic groups and the unions, he found himself part of a coalition forming the base of a victorious political party. For the first time he had the bargaining strength that went along with a decisive balance-of-power vote in crucial states.

His settlement in the big Northern cities had a double consequence. In immediate terms it meant the creation of new ghettos. In New York's Harlem the crowding of Negroes is worse than in Atlanta, and the spatial separation of blacks and whites is perhaps greater. In Chicago's South Side, which holds 250,000 of Chicago's 400,000 Negroes, in Detroit's East Side (called bitterly "Paradise Valley"), in St. Louis and Kansas City and Pittsburgh, in Philadelphia's "inner city" crowded with 300,000 Negroes, in the hideous clustering Negro shacks that scar Washington, the Negro ghettos are the worst slums in America—dingy, crowded, dive-dotted, whore-patrolled, disease-ridden. The Negro migrations were a bonanza for the owners of the tenements and cold-water

flats in the areas where they settled and within which they were circumscribed: it was a landlord's market, and they could extort higher rents
for the sleazy ghetto quarters than had to be paid for a clean, well-
lighted space outside the ghetto.

When the Negroes tried to break out of their cage the real-estate
boards—in a panic lest a leak in the segregation dike might mean an
inundating Negro mass movement into white residential areas and suburbs—"covenanted" the houses. Behind the real-estate boards with their
profit fears were the status fears of the white middle classes. Even under
Federal housing aid the FHA accepted the "local real-estate reaction"
as a standard for decision and refused to insure most mixed housing
projects. After the Supreme Court had held the covenants unconstitutional, some of the white-collar Negro families sought to move into
"white" areas, but too often they were met by terror. When the Clarks,
for example, moved from the Chicago slums to an apartment in near-by
Cicero, ironically it was another minority ethnic group, the Czechs, who
loomed large in the group that stoned and burned them out.

Recent studies, challenging the idea that there can be no interracial
housing because of the encrusted attitudes of hostility, have stood the
idea on its head. For example, a 1950 study by Deutsch and Collins,
comparing integrated public-housing projects in New York with segregated projects in Newark, showed that the fact of living more closely
together leads to greater friendliness and tolerance between the Negro
and white groups, and that it even has a healthy impact on relations
inside the white groups themselves and produces a more closely knit
community as a whole. As a result the Newark policy was changed, and
the segregation elements were eliminated—again with healthy results.
There have been similar experiences on the job in factories and work-
shops, in department-store selling, and most strikingly in the defense
forces, where every step toward eliminating segregation made the next
step possible by breaking down hostile attitudes on both sides.

The same concentration of the Negroes in the large Northern cities
which spread panic fears of mass inundation, also helped them as a
political and economic force. Since they bunched themselves in their
jobs and living quarters, they bunched their votes as well. As Henry Lee
Moon has pointed out, this has meant a decisive Negro vote which gives
them not only the balance of power in the state elections of New York,
Illinois, Michigan, Ohio, and Pennsylvania, but also may at times give
them the same kind of marginal power in swinging Presidential elections. It is this power which revived the movement for Federal civil-
rights legislation, and in turn caused the urban Negro to be wooed by
both major parties. In terms of economic force, it meant that much of

the fifteen billion dollars the Negroes spent annually in the American market was also concentrated, giving them a considerable economic pressure force against discrimination.

An even more powerful weapon the Negroes have had has been that of the law. In the South more than in the North, but in both areas, the machinery of police and law enforcement has operated unequally, protecting the Negroes least, bearing down on them most heavily. Yet their greatest advance has been achieved through the instrument of the law. They have waged an unrelenting fight for legal equality, knowing that the law on the statute books or in the court decisions may not settle things in practice but does set a frame. On the issue of voting without burdensome poll taxes, on getting free of housing covenants, on breaking out of Jim Crow schools for their children, on access to law and medical schools, on travel across state lines, on hotel accommodations and restaurant service, on parks and swimming pools and hospitals, and on equality of job opportunities, they have fought with a tenacity which has enraged their enemies all the more because they have known that this force, once set in motion, was irresistible.

Recent Federal Court decisions in the Sweatt, Henderson, McLaren, Seipuel, and Clarendon cases must be seen as forerunners of the final victories to come. The great decision in the school segregation cases in 1954 represented a climactic point in a long series of earlier constitutional battles. They were hard-gained and dearly paid victories, and sometimes the pace seemed heartbreakingly slow both to the Negroes and their allies, South and North. Yet the debate has been about the wisdom, validity, and workability of legal action. Particular Court decisions have been attacked, but even the most extreme of the Negro's opponents have not dared deny them in principle the right to make use of the legal weapon.

I have spoken of political, economic, and legal action. More powerful than any of them, and what gives them their momentum, is the American conscience. It has had a sorry enough state of facts to operate on. I cite a few dramatic figures from the report of the President's Commission on Civil Rights, which had a striking impact on later events. The average annual income for Negro families in 1947 was a little over $1,000 compared with three times as much for whites. Forty per cent of the whites had incomes of over $2,000, but only 11 per cent of the Negroes. Twenty-two per cent of the whites were below $1,000, and 75 per cent of the Negroes. In the segregated Southern states, where nine of the fifteen million Negroes lived, the value of the school plant used for the Negro children was $52 per child compared with $224 for a white child, and the amount spent every year for a Negro child's schooling was $57 compared with $104 for a white child. In 1900, before the Jim Crow laws became hardened, a Negro in Washington, D.C., could enter any hospital; by 1950 there were only two that admitted them. Throughout the South there was not a "white" hospital which would admit a sick Negro or a "white" church that would allow him to pray to the God of all races. Until 1950 the only chance for a Negro in the Navy was as a mess attendant, and in the Army as part of the segregated transport units; since that time the color walls have been broken down with increasing success. No Negro in the South could break the laws and traditions of segregation when he went to work on a bus, or wanted to eat lunch or dinner in a restaurant, when he tried to travel on a train, when he wanted to see a movie or a play. In most Southern cities no Negro would dare park his car in front of the post office without running the risk of being considered "an uppity nigger," nor would he dare walk late at night in the white section of the town. The life expectancy of a Negro child in the South was eight years less than that of one born white. And from birth to death the Negro lived in constant tension and insecurity, walking always in the shadow of uncertainty and fear.

It is this image which spurred the American conscience, and that conscience in turn goaded Americans of all kinds into action. While there are still poll-tax states in the South, the Negro votes in growing numbers in every Southern state, and while there have been efforts at intimidation there has been a reluctant acceptance of the fact of the Negro as voter. His children have forced their way into a number of Southern colleges, with several thousand Negro students squeezing their way through the college gates, and the siege of the professional schools now is in full swing. The 1955 case of Autherine Lucy, in Alabama, represented a temporary setback in this steady advance, but no one believed it would long hold back the tide. Even the "separate but equal" doctrine, fatefully enshrined in *Plessy v. Ferguson* in the 1890s, finally crumbled sixty years later, and a unanimous Supreme Court under Chief Justice Warren held that "separate" (segregated) schooling could not by its nature be equal because it stunts the whole growth process of the child. Southern legal resourcefulness, of course, was able to invent new strategies of state action ("interposition") to evade and nullify the Supreme Court decision. The movement of Southern resistance, especially in the smaller towns where the White Citizens' Councils made effective use of the weapon of economic boycott, was bitter and protracted. Yet all along the line white supremacy was waging a losing battle.

Thus it has been the context of American society and the "American creed" that has reduced the walls of the caste system. The American economy, with its impersonal relations in the market of buying and selling, gave the Negroes a new bargaining power. So also has the American political system, with its formal principle of counting each head once no matter what the pigment of the face, and its reliance on an equilibrium of pressure groups. The American legal system, with its tradition of growth to meet the changing demands of a changing society, gave the Negro a slow and belated but irresistible measure of justice. Even American social science, especially sociology and psychology, were drawn into the constitutional struggle and played the great role in the reversal of *Plessy v. Ferguson*. The dynamic quality of American life allowed the Negro to shift from section to section, from sharecropper farm to auto and airplane factory and steel mill. It raised his income and living standards, in the South as in the North, gave him entrance into the trade-unions in spite of the persisting hostility of many of the union leaders. The emergence of new big-audience media enabled him to break through the walls of his ghetto, and radio and TV sets brought even into the dingy living rooms the spaciousness of a world hitherto denied to them.

Even in the South the economic, political, and educational levees are being broken by the rising waters. Until the Great Resistance after the schools decision the white students in Southern colleges were increasingly demanding the entrance of Negro students. In Northern colleges there were sporadic revolts against the system of segregated fraternities. The Negro can no longer be treated as the child, savage, or beast—which were the stereotypes applied to him ever since he came out of the holds of the slave ships. The classic statement of Lincoln about a "house divided" has proved true, in a sense which he may himself never have foreseen: not that the moral principle makes it impossible for such a house to stand, but that the laws of action in the society as a whole are bound to break down the enclaves inside it which defy the principle by which the society lives. Just as the American class system rejects a permanent proletariat, so it rejects a permanent pariah class buttressed by a caste system.

It has been argued that the erosion wearing away the soil of Negro segregation came not from the society of a liberal capitalist democracy itself, and from its economy, its law, and its conscience, but primarily from the changes wrought by two world wars, and from the needs of a permanent "readiness economy" during the cold war. Those who hold this view call this a process of "negative democratization," which comes because the ruling groups in the society need the Negro for their own

purposes and must yield him his rights out of self-interest rather than
out of conscience. This is an ungenerous view which would deny that
any reform is ever achieved except by force or any privilege ever
relinquished except through selfishness. It denies any sort of creativeness within American society except one flowing negatively from the
power struggle. It is true that the progress in civil rights for Negroes
came partly through their own bargaining strength and partly through
the self-interest of the whites, but that progress could never have been
achieved except through the operation of law and public opinion and
the impulsion of the idea of equality. Without these even the needs
of war and cold war would have been powerless to achieve the same
ends. Strikingly, the South, which has met the advance of Negro civil
rights with the greatest resistance, has also been the region most committed to military pursuits and the idea of total war.*

There remains, even among those prodded by conscience, the unyielding issue of "social equality." As noted in the preceding section, many of
the majority group, who when polled felt that the Negroes ought to get
a "better break," recoiled from the image of Negro-White intermarriage.
Actually, there has been very little of it even in those Northern states
where the law allows it: only five out of every 10,000 marriages—or
one twentieth of 1 per cent—represent a crossing of the color lines. Yet
in twenty-nine states there were drastic laws against miscegenation,
carrying in some cases the penalty of imprisonment. Even more oppressive are the sexual taboos in the Southern states. Although the
promiscuity of whites with Negro women has long been recognized as
the perquisite of a master race, the Negro boy who dared court a white
girl in the South would expiate his effrontery only by death.

Under the slave system the most terrible punishments were reserved
for cases of "rape," and the intensity of feeling on this issue has scarcely
subsided since then. White supremacy in the South has always used
lynching as the ultimate sanction against the defilement of white blood.
While these lynchings have steadily decreased (the Tuskegee figures
show that the five-year period from 1900 to 1905 averaged 105 lynchings
a year, while the 1945 to 1950 period averaged three, and then practically ceased), the Southern courts have operated on a double standard
of justice in applying the laws against rape: most of the prosecutions
are against Negroes, and even where whites are brought to trial they are
not given the death penalty that is visited upon the Negroes.

Modern psychiatry, especially in the trail-blazing study by John
Dollard, *Caste and Class in a Southern Town*, takes the view that the

* For a discussion of civil liberties, as distinguished from Negro civil rights, see
Ch. VI, Sec. 10, "The Struggle for Civil Liberties."

deepest roots of Southern hostility on the Negro problem are sexual: that the male Southerner brought up by a Negro "mammy" finds the Negro woman his abiding sexual symbol, and that the Southern woman is at once attracted and repelled by the sexual vitality of the Negro. Certainly there is a complexity to race relations in the South which is better expressed in the nuances of a novel like E. M. Forster's *A Passage to India* than in the thunderous simplicities of the denunciations on both sides. Lillian Smith, writing about her own Southern upbringing in *Killers of the Dream,* underscores the terrible blight which the treatment of the Negro has left on the white family, with the wife set on an impossible pedestal of "purity" and cut off from her own children, and the husband ridden by guilt about breaking the taboos he himself has set up. Yet the whole question of "social equality," aside from these psychoanalytic probings, is largely a straw issue. The bounds of class and status have proved strong enough to prevent intermarriage not only between Negroes and whites but even between the class extremes within the social system of the whites themselves. The Negro does not ask (because no one could ask) any kind of Force Bill to compel intimate social relationships which the whites are unwilling to engage in—or at least acknowledge. All that he asks, as Robert Carr has put it, is "freedom to enter the main stream of American life."

The most tragic fact about the long effort to maintain the Negro caste system is that it has left its scars upon whites and blacks alike. The effect on Southern whites, at once in economic and psychic terms, can scarcely be calculated. To keep nine million people in poverty—and in ignorance, so that they will not get ideas that will make them unruly —impoverishes the economy itself and forms a drag both on the market and on technical development. It means a social system riddled with formal taboos and with furtive violations of them. It means a constant sense of living, as a white garrison, in the midst of a hostile surrounding Negro population, with alternating moods of anxiety and aggression. It means, finally, an obsessive concentration on a single theme of racist exclusiveness which has for many Southerners become more deeply their religion than religion itself. This obsession, bred into the children from infancy through adolescence and maintained in the adults by the constant agitation of politicians and press, keeps many Southerners of good will from seeing that fair treatment of Negroes would improve the lot of the whites as well. The fears of the elite groups, who resist the organization of Negro labor and want to keep their cotton profits high and their domestic labor cheap, do not express the interests of the South as a whole. Yet the obsessiveness continues, making the efforts of the militant Southern liberals and even of the Southern moderates one of the most difficult in the American experience. It takes courage to be a liberal in the South.

The greatest psychic cost for the Southern white is the constant sense of guilt, accompanying the constant feeling of being misunderstood. There are, of course, psychic consolations. The greatest of them is the sense of power in the elite itself, and among the poor whites the feeling that no matter how low you sink on the status scale there is always a Negro whose status is below yours. Yet this is a shabby compensation for the frustrations and aggressions that life offers the Southern whites. For them the "Negro question" is a twisted folk bias that permeates every phase of their consciousness—religion, sex, family life, the economy, education, the legal system, and literature. The only gainer has been literature itself, which, in the agonies of the Southern novelist and playwright, has found an inverted tragic strain which gives their work an emotional dimension not found in other regions.

If the psychic burden on the Southern white is heavy, the burden on the Negro is intolerable. The stereotype which describes the Negro as a carefree child singing and dancing his way through life, unmindful of his scars, is a pitifully partial one. The American Negro inherits most of the tensions of the white culture, and to its heavy load he adds his own. So much of his everyday energy has to be expended in a constant struggle against discrimination and taboos, a constant anxiety, a constant need for making choices and uncertainty as to what to expect from people and situations. "There is no time in the life of the Negro," say Kardiner and Ovesey, "that he is not actively in contact with the caste situation." These two men had a series of long interviews with a cross section sampling of Northern Negroes. Their psychological profile of the Negro is one of self-hatred, depression, emotional instability, frustration, because the goals of the whites which he has accepted are for him unattainable.

This portrait is obviously overdrawn, and to get a more balanced view one must set it against the equally overdrawn folk picture of the Negro as a happy and carefree savage. Yet of the two the psychiatric profile is the more relevant to the tensions of the Negro's life. The cruel paradox of that life is that even the success of the Negroes—I should say especially the success—in wresting gains in living standards and freedom from the white society makes life more difficult psychically for him. For it is the Negroes moving up on the social scale who encounter the sharpest doubts as to their status. At one end is the inverted psychic security of being wholly a subject caste and knowing therefore where you stand; at the other end is the security of complete equality with the whites; it is the area between the two which exacts the heaviest psychic toll.

The Negroes have developed social and economic class lines of their own within their own hierarchies. A new Negro elite has arisen—"black millionaires" (as the Negro magazine *Ebony* puts it with a curious pride) who "travel by Cadillac," send their daughters to debutante parties, and despise their own caste inferiors almost as much as the whites do. There is also a new Negro middle class, the "black *bourgeoisie*," as Frazier has called them, that is riddled with the same status fears as the white middle class: "No self-respecting Negro [again I quote *Ebony*] would smoke a cheap cigarette." Frazier's theme is that the Negro middle class, caught between a status it rejects and one it has not achieved, has been reduced to a *nothingness* of values and identity. The Negroes have also developed their own remedial measures: the racist Garveyism of the 1920s and the messianic Communism of the 1930s have lost ground, but an intense nationalism persists whose excesses are the product of the racism and fanaticism of the whites. They find themselves caught, as every struggling caste is caught, within a compulsive frame which shrinks the horizons of the world at large until it encompasses only the world of their own grievances, sufferings, strivings.

Yet the striking fact is not that a Negro population, striving to free itself and enter fully into the stream of majority life, finds its effort a terrible ordeal but the fact that the effort is made and that it is succeeding. The striking fact again is not that 12,000 light-skinned Negroes disappear every year from their ethnic ranks—"pass" into the white world —but rather the fact that so many who could pass choose to remain Negroes. It is an affirmation of the worth of being an American without surrendering your ethnic heritage. And on the side of the whites the remarkable fact is not continued hostility but the irresistible force of acceptance.

Under the impact of this acceptance, the Negroes themselves grow more relaxed. Roi Ottley offers as evidence a recent trip of his through Europe and the Middle East, as described in *No Green Pastures*. Among the Negroes in Europe he found that the American Negroes were considered an aristocracy with the highest living standards and the great symbolic leaders of the race. Since 1900 a half million Negro immigrants have come to America, despite its caste system, and today there would be few Negroes elsewhere who would not welcome the chance—despite the realistic understanding of what the ordeal of life would be. Here again one confronts the overmastering fact about American society—its mobility and stir. They count for more than the fears and anxieties that carry over from the breaking of the chains of caste, and they alone are making it possible for the chains to be broken.

7. The Badges of Belonging

THIS THEN IS the picture of the over-all stratification of American society—the open-class system, with its mobile and rigid elements; the ruling groups of the wealthy and powerful; the new middle classes, vulnerable and uprooted, yet with a sense of well-being that defies all predicted dooms; the working class, tenacious of its gains, job-conscious, with none of the marks of a permanent proletariat; the minority ethnic groups whose peculiar status cuts across the class strata; the Negroes, whose history marks them for the role of a depressed caste but who have enlisted all the force of American dynamism to break through their constrictions.

Any assessment of the American class system must ask two sets of final questions: how are the class distinctions mirrored in the minds of Americans, and transmitted and transmuted into their daily lives? And what is the nature of the competitive struggle for status in the American open-class system? To these questions this and the following section are addressed.

The writers who shy away from the harsher phases of the class system lag behind the ordinary American whom they study. He recognizes pretty well the objective facts of class: that "money talks" more frequently than merit or grace; that income and what it can buy give a man access to power and privilege, from which the moneyless are cut off; that class power is not only command over commodities but command over obedience—the ability to decide what shall happen to those who depend on you for livelihood; that for the classes toward the bottom of the hierarchy, and for their children, the chances for scope and expressiveness of living are less than for those toward the top.

It is remarkable that he has cherished few rankling resentments. Class consciousness, in the sense of hostility at the service of the conscious understanding of the class role in history, is almost absent from the American scene. It does exist in the secondary sense of divergent class attitudes on the issues of the day. But the characteristic form it takes is that of a subjective rating system. "How does he rate?" may apply to any aspect of a man's personality, or to his technical credit rating, but mostly it refers—not necessarily with any snobbish overtones—to the community's valuation of his income, wealth, power, standing, repute.

This process of rating oneself and others is, consciously or not, a constant part of daily life. It has often been noted and satirized by the critics of American life as "keeping up with the Joneses." Veblen, using his most barbed phrases, called it "invidious distinction" and "pecuniary emulation." A nonmoralizing view would see, however, how closely it meshes into a society possessing high mobility. When people in a class system are in constant movement they are likely to reassess constantly one another's position and their own. How healthy this process is depends on the kind of qualities chosen for rating, and whether it is a single factor (like income or the size of one's house) abstracted from the whole. Even at its best there is a vicious-circle quality about the rating system: those who have prestige receive even greater deference because of it; those who have power assume even greater authority; those who lack them are further shorn of what little they have. This is a rigidifying process, and often a cruel one. Yet it is at once the price of mobility and the product of effort. When it becomes a form of closure of the channels of opportunity it is most destructive. Taken as a whole, it is part of the valuing process which is integral to life in society—a way by which every individual puts out antennae to feel where he is in relation to others.

It should be clear then why the characteristic school among contemporary American class studies should be that of Lloyd Warner, which tends to slight a man's objective power over others as it also minimizes the actual conflicts of class interest, and which makes his class position depend so strongly on the community's valuation of him. Similarly, the dominant school in the study of human relations in industry is that of Mayo and Roethlisberger, which minimizes the inherent relation of mastery and dependence where men work for other men and holds that frictions can be lessened and production increased by fortifying esteem and self-esteem in the factory-as-society.

The impetus to the Warner community studies, as earlier in the Lynd studies of "Middletown," came from anthropology and is linked with the American passion for the inductive method. The Warner class concept is almost wholly statistical: it finds and charts the position of a man on the graph of social standing according to a number of indices of community rating. Instead of starting with the European theories of class structure and class conflict, the students of American society prefer to start, as businessmen do, with a factual survey. Obviously they do bring to it an intellectual scheme which perhaps unconsciously shapes what they find. Obviously also a good deal depends on how much of a cross section of America their sample community is, whether it be Muncie, Ind. (the "Middletown" of the Lynds), or Newburyport, Mass., and Grundy County, Ill. (the "Yankee City" and "Jonesville" of Warner), or Burlington, Vt. (which Elin Anderson studied in *We Americans*), or the Illinois town studied by Hollingshead in *Elmtown's Youth*, or the Southern communities that John Dollard, Allison Davis, and Hortense Powdermaker wrote about. These are all small towns or cities, chosen as such to be compassable for study, but they do not tell us much about the class experience of big cities, which is likely to be at once more mobile in some phases and more extreme in class contrasts. Nor do they make allowance for regional characteristics: the Midwestern town is likely to look eastward for its patterns of living, while the Eastern towns are more self-sufficient; in the Deep South and New England the class lines are more set and the elite groups more firmly established than elsewhere; and very few of the surveys deal with the Far West. Yet with all these caveats the community surveys have heaped up considerable evidence on the nature of American society, which is particularly valuable on the class system because most of them made class cleavages and strata the focus of their analysis.

The survey team (it has been waspishly described in Marquand's novel, *Point of No Return*, set in his home town of Newburyport) moves into a community with letters of introduction, gets acquainted, settles into the community life, and observes how people talk of one another. Class is a local reality in every community, with local designations for each of the classes. Warner found the "old families" at the top of the pyramid, with wealth inherited over time, living in the old mansions "on the Hill," the arbiters of manners, taste, and social distinction. Just below them in the upper class he found the "new families," with more recently acquired wealth, the heads of the corporations and Chambers of Commerce, the "country club set" who often associated with the "old families" and were *in* but not *of* their class. In the middle classes he found toward the top the "comfortably situated" and "highly respected" men, substantial, self-made, either small-business or professional men or members of the corporate managerial group, living in the suburbs, belonging to social clubs and the good churches. Below them in turn are the salaried people of the lower middle class—the store managers, white-collar workers, little shopkeepers, salesmen, who make up the most fluid and rapidly growing phase of the American "common man." Then there was the upper layer of the lower class—the skilled industrial workers, "poor but honest," who work for wages, belong to unions, are unlikely to belong to clubs but are members of the poorer churches, drive small cars, and have clean-looking small houses or "flats" on the "other side of the tracks." Finally there was the bottom layer of the lower class—the unskilled workers, the Negroes, the Puerto Ricans or Portuguese or Mexicans, who live in run-down houses or in the slums or in trailer camps on the outskirts of the town, the "ne'er-do-wells" who "don't belong" and are often unemployed and on relief.

In developing this six-class system (upper-upper, lower-upper, upper-middle, lower-middle, upper-lower, lower-lower) Warner and his associates relied mainly on criteria that correlate roughly with the economic indices of occupation and income but rest principally on prestige (who is above, who below), associations, clubs and cliques (who goes with whom, who belongs to what), family standing, taste in spending, and the veneer and trappings of life. In Newburyport he found 3 per cent in the top two classes, 39 per cent in the middle two, and 58 per cent in the bottom ones. He recognized the fact of continual movement between the classes, but what he observed and described were the divergent privileges, prestige, and standing of a stratified system of status whose individual members may change but which does not itself change as a system. With the American talent for reducing abstractions to a statistical rating scheme, he worked out an Index of Status Characteristics (I.S.C.) to guide his staff interviewers, with a point scale assigned to four objective facts about a person: his type of home, his neighborhood, his occupation, and his income source (more important than income size). To this he added the results of the Evaluated Participation (E.P.) scale, or the ranking assigned to a person by the community, especially those toward the top who run a community and preside over it and therefore ought to know it.

One may ridicule the pseudo-precision of ranking the sons of Mary and the sons of Martha, but it is hard to laugh off its reality. One gets a similar picture, more sweepingly drawn, in Hollingshead's Elmtown study, which found a five-class system: the top class, with money and family; the upper middle class, still based on money, family, and marriage into both; the lower middle class, with good steady jobs, who form the America of the "common man"; the factory workers and clerks who "live right but never get anywhere"; and the bottom class of the unskilled and unrooted who "aren't worth a damn and don't give a damn."

The image that people have of a man's class standing and his image of himself are important facts about him. An influential element of the class system is what is in people's minds, in rating their fellows and judging between those who belong and those who don't. Even wealth and income are not in America the ultimate badges of belonging: they are currency to be converted in time into the "right kind" of associations and thus into the "right kind" of manners, clothes, behavior, in which each person shapes himself to the model of the class to which he aspires. Although this has phases of snobbism and conformity, it cannot be dismissed thus. It is the point of all the straining and striving, the ambition, agony, and ruthlessness of competitive living from the bottom rungs of the class ladder right up to the top ones. And, to round out the circle, Americans also know that social standing is in turn a key to further income and job advancement: that by getting into the "right crowd" they get access to those who have power, and thus get a trial for their talents or a hearing for their plans. Thus there is a continuous circuit by which money is converted into prestige and power, which in turn are converted into money, and so on.

Most Americans recognize these facts of their class life. While there has been a drastic shift of people from one set of occupations to another in the past generation, the rule-of-thumb ratings of the occupation have not changed appreciably. It depends on how much skill each occupation requires, what income it affords, how much authority and power over others it carries, the standing and respectability it affords in the community. Thus the American combines a realistic sense of the objective facts of class power and income along with the subjective factors of prestige and position.

There are elements of American life which still cut across the class divisions and give it the rough kind of social equality that De Tocqueville noted. People work together in the factories and on the farms, shop together in the markets, worship together in the churches, compete in and attend the same games and sports events, read the same papers and magazines, vote in the same booths. Except for the Southern Negroes, they ride in the same trains and busses, go to the same movies and theaters, send their children to the same schools; and even the Southern Negroes have increasingly been winning equal access to these areas. Americans of all classes buy and drive the same cars, watch the same TV programs, eat the same packaged foods. In a standardized economy there is a leveling effect produced by the wide diffusion of standardized goods. Add the fact that gas stations, recreation and amusement centers, transport systems, automatic vendors, and professional services are available pretty much to all on an impersonal market. Add also the free public services—parks, swimming pools, band concerts, public dances, libraries —where at least technically no distinctions of class or caste are allowed.

Yet every American knows the breaches in the observance of these ideals, as he knows also the extent to which social equality has been eroded by the crystallized system of class ranking. The divisive effects of this system and the social expression of class differences are manifested in everyday life.

They bear hardest on the children. There is no double-class system in the American schools, as there is in the British, although the emergence of a network of private schools augurs the start of one. The real double-class system is to be found in the lingering residues of segregated schools in white-supremacy areas. Yet even in the school systems that admit children of all classes and races, there are gerrymandering devices by which children of similar class or ethnic origin are assigned to the same schools. And where a class cross section exists inside the school, children from families who "belong" tend to segregate those who do not by a tacit understanding which they derive from their elders and from the social atmosphere. Children from the higher income levels develop ways of acting, thinking, feeling, that keep them apart from their fellows. Recent studies of the youth in Midwestern public elementary and high schools (Warner and Havighurst, *Who Shall Be Educated?* and Hollingshead, *Elmtown's Youth*) found evidence of "cliques" and "sets" that form in the school system on class levels, with the insiders feeling a snobbish satisfaction and the outsiders experiencing heartbreak. They suggest that popularity depends partly on the insignia of class membership, and that whoever strives for it pays a heavy psychic price. There are few places where the pathos of social imitation is more striking than in the American school system.

The schools are at once agencies of class equality (for many children there are no other means for breaking across class lines) and agencies of class conditioning. When schoolchildren are asked to name those who are "clean," "good looking," and "always having a good time," they usually choose the children from the upper social levels and ascribe the negative qualities to children from the lower ones. While there is little sense of class or ethnic differences at the start of schooling, by the time a child has reached ten (fifth grade), he has become "socialized" and his preferences are marked. Thus the roots of class superiority and ethnic hatreds lie less in propaganda than in social training through one's peer groups. This is, of course, especially marked in the South, where the Federal courts found that the training in segregation demonstrably hurt the personality growth of the children of both groups. But even in a nonsegregated high school in the North, Hollingshead found that school disciplines involving both rewards and punishments (high grades, failures, and disciplinary measures) bear more heavily on the children of the lower strata and are skewed in favor of the upper; and Allison Davis found that the values which the teachers underscore and which run through their teaching as unquestioned assumptions are middle-class values. Thus the lower-level children learn early the gap between their actual status and the desirable ideal.

This insulation of the classes is carried beyond school through life: in food habits, etiquette, reading tastes, health opportunities, courtship and sex habits, marriage, divorce, taste exchange, clubs, lodges, even churches. In every phase of social expression the badges of belonging separate one class from another and pervade subtly the whole expression of personality. There are, of course, wheels within wheels—the big wheel run by the fate of class, and the little wheels run by the grace or talent of a particular person. But the picture of social distinction, seen in terms of differential life chances and life conditioning, is nonetheless roughly true.

Much of the stream of energy is turned into the channels of social acceptance. Life in every community is lived with a yearning eye cast toward the class above. Middle-class families scrimp to send their children to private schools and good colleges, at least long enough for them to make the right kind of "contacts" and be out of reach of the wrong kind. Some are steered toward careers that will bring money and success, while the vigil of protecting daughters from giving their hearts too cheaply to an unrewarding love gives the American middle-class parent that air of watchful anxiety and dissatisfaction that the novelists have noted. In the lower classes there is the steady hope that education will turn out to be a means for improving the social position of the children, and the wild hope for the occasional Cinderella marriage of the daughter of a Slav steelworker to the heir of an oil fortune, or of the rise of a girl sprung from a seedy music-hall troupe to become the Love goddess of the Hollywood screen and a familiar of the "International Set." But there is also the constant anxiety among the "moral poor" of the lower middle class that the son or daughter will slip down into the ranks of delinquency and crime.

This burden of class watchfulness is not a light one, no matter what the class is. To go to the right schools, to attend the right dances and parties, to belong to the right churches, to be accepted in the right social and country clubs, to be a "potentate" in a lodge, to drive the right make and model of car, to wear the right clothes and have the right manners, to have your daughter (at certain social levels) "introduced" to "society" and presented at the cotillion, to have your son spend his military service in the officer corps and not as a lowly private: these become for their appropriate class members matters not of choice or opportunity but a social necessity. The burden of these obligations, and the psychic tension of keeping intact the margin that distinguishes you from your inferiors or of overcoming the margin that separates you from your superiors, can become not only exacting but destructive. It is an all the greater burden in an open-class system because the chances of advance upward and the dangers of incursion from below are real. In a society of more or less permanent and crystallized classes, grown too rigid for redress, the anxieties of the psychic class vigil are likely to be less. In the pursuit of American status the pursuers are also pursued.

I have mentioned several areas of life in which one finds important differences among the classes in behavior and attitude. The cleavage can be extended into almost every area. We have seen that you can make rough predictions of voting behavior in politics, depending on whether the voter belongs to the trade-union or managerial groups, whether he is an urban Catholic or a rural Protestant, whether he is of Midwestern German or Scandinavian descent or a Southern cotton farmer or a Jew in one of the new talent professions. The children of these various groups will usually take over the political attitudes of the parents, which reflect their social stratification: the child of a Detroit auto worker's family or of a TV writer in Hollywood is likely to vote and think differently from the child of a General Motors executive.

There will be differences also in the stability of a Negro or Irish slum family when compared with that of a middle-class Protestant family. There are recognized class differences in fertility, depending on the differential choices made between more children and, let us say, better education and life chances for fewer: although I have pointed out in an earlier chapter that some of these differences have been badly blurred in the recent population trends. There is a different life expectation at birth between Negroes and whites, and lower and upper classes. There are, as the Kinsey studies have shown, differences in sexual behavior—especially in the case of American males—as between the lower and upper educational groups: the street-corner adolescents in the city slums have a different profile of sexual activity and a different set of sexual attitudes from the adolescents in an Ivy League college. In courtship and in marriage the prestige of a middle-class or upper-class girl of "native" stock is far higher than that of a working-class girl or one from a minority ethnic group. There are important class differences in the class composition of the various religious sects—between, let us say, the Catholics and the Episcopalians, the Baptists and the Jews, although in recent years the differences have become more blurred, and all the major sects are reaching a higher percentage of people in the lower classes than they did and spreading out into the whole class range. Even in the case of mental illness, there are likely to be differences in neurotic and psychotic behavior among the various income and occupational groups, with a higher rate of mental disturbance and breakdown, as well as of hospital commitment, in the low-income groups as compared with the upper ones.

These again are some of the badges of belonging and they serve not only to differentiate one income and prestige group from another but also to explain why the upper groups try to insulate themselves from too much encroachment and the lower ones strive to push their way up. But the class insulation does not always have its impetus from above. Sometimes it comes from below. I have noted the prides and resentments that cause some of the minority ethnic groups to impose a taboo on intermarriage. Observers of the social structure in New England point out how little the new immigrant groups intermarry with the earlier stocks, but also how little they intermarry even with each other. The crossing of national origin lines is not frequent, and when religious barriers are added, the crossing of both becomes for many families an inconsolable infraction of the code. The class lines are not the only ones that count. For an impoverished Catholic to marry a rich Jew, or for a Jewish middle-class boy to marry the daughter of the Protestant banking family in the town, might in both cases be considered a catastrophe, despite the class advance. The latter situation is treated movingly in Norman Katkov's novel, *Eagle at My Eyes,* which has a Midwest setting but might happen anywhere.

The force of class-bound marriage, added to the force of race-bound and religion-bound marriage, makes the system of social distinction a gridiron instead of a set of stratified layers. Whatever the freedom of social relations—including sexual relations—before marriage, the act of marriage itself becomes the testing ground of group cohesion. For it is through the exclusions and inclusions of marriage that the class-ethnic system becomes the transmitter of stored experience, and through it also that the cohesion or exclusiveness of the group is broken down and its experience changed and enriched.

It is in this area of conflict between the insulation of the old class experience and the vitality of the new that the American novelists of manners have found their best themes. Since the elite of the "old families" is strongest in the old established regions of the South and New England, the anxieties of status are most searchingly explored in the fiction of these areas. Hardly a Southern novel or play is written in America which does not deal with the theme of a family of high standing that has lost its money but holds on fiercely to its sense of distinction. Faulkner, who has carried this theme to its highest pitch, deals therefore (as Irving Howe points out) not so much with *class* as with *clan.* The setting of these Southern families in the larger frame of rapid American class mobility, and therefore of rapid disintegration, is what gives Southern writing its added dimension of the "nerve of failure" in the sense of courage in the face of doom. In the case of New England, Marquand has almost pre-empted the theme of a young aristocrat pulled by the attraction of sexual vitality and the exotic toward the plebeian strength of some "outsider," but choosing in the end the ties of class and tradition: but on this level Marquand is only Edith Wharton and William Dean Howells rewritten, diluted, and given modern instances. Yet so crucial is the understanding eye and ear of the novelist that Marquand's insights into the nuances of the social hierarchy of Newburyport, in his *Point of No Return,* form a necessary supplement to the factual picture that Warner gives of the class structure of the same town.

It is more difficult, both for novelist and sociologist, to chart the gradations and resistances of class mobility in the big cities. Class differences
in the cities are more impersonal in their daily expression. The occupational shift has been greater there, and most relationships are the
more casual ones of the market, business, and the professions rather
than of intimacy over time. This diminishes some of the subtle cruelty
and anxiety of class gradations in small-town America; and while it has
all the faults of a depersonalized life, this depersonalizing—in the flow
of city living—may make the cleavages of class more tolerable for those
below, just as the glamour of city living makes wealth itself more re-
splendent and the miseries of city living make the distance from extreme
wealth to extreme poverty more desolating.

Yet this holds out hope for those who do not relish the prospect of
a class-encased American society. The important class differences are
not so much the rural-urban ones as those between communities of
economic growth and those of economic decline. The sway of cliques
and respectability, the tyranny of the "old families," and the rigidities
of caste are more likely to be found in static areas from which the
younger and more vigorous are moving out, while the less class-bound
situations are in areas of the greatest economic stir and therefore social
mobility. A rapidly expanding economy is thus, in spite of the power
it piles up at the top and the groups it uproots from their old skills,
the best insurance against the meannesses of class distinction, which
fester most wherever energy is turned inward toward social introspec-
tion rather than outward toward social growth.

I have used marriage as an example mainly of class insulation in
American society, but this is only a partial view. Compared with other
class societies, marriage in America crosses class and caste lines so frequently as to create the continuing mixture of stocks I have described
earlier (the estimate in the mid-1950s was of 300,000 marriages a year
crossing religious lines alone) and also so frequently as to raise the
problems of divergent class conditionings between the generations in
child-rearing. The ethnic and class differences that apply to marriage
apply also to divorce. It has often been remarked that there are three
class levels in American divorce methods: the rich can afford to go to
Reno or Florida; the middle classes stay in their home states and resort
to courts where they must often commit perjury to fulfill the requirements of the state law; and the lower class falls back on desertion, which
has been called the "poor man's divorce."

These distinctive badges of class membership help explain also some
of the phases of the changing American personality. Instead of the

static injunction to "learn your station in life" and stay within it, there is the constantly haunting question "Do I belong?" The decisive answer rarely is forthcoming, since every move upward on the class scale is an invitation to another, so that the sense of satisfying your status hungers and of feeling secure in your standing is rarely achieved. This may be expressed in terms of a class-personality cycle: a man's income and power go to determine his social standing, which in turn determines how others value his personality and even how he values it himself; these valuations help mold the personality, pushing it to orient itself toward income and power, and the cycle starts again. The end result is at once a drive toward success, a recoil from failure, and a hunger for security. Many who celebrate a mobile class system deplore these qualities of the American personality, forgetting that they are qualities that are bound to accompany the mobility. You cannot have at the same time the freedom and fluidity of an open society and the values of security that go with a closed one.

The serious aspect of the dilemma is how the personality can grapple with the terrible sense of failure, and of being left behind in the race. Most observers of American society are aware of the pathos of social distance and the neuroses of frustration that come in the wake of failure. Some of them have stressed the individual's need to adjust himself to his place in the system, and they have defended the TV "soap opera" and "daytime radio serial" as a mode of consoling working-class and lower-middle-class women for their sense of failure. It is not so much that these people console themselves with the Big Media: rather they derive from them a set of fresh impressions and enjoyments, however trite to the sophisticated, which serve as substitutes for continued class advance.

The real warpings must be sought in the constant tendency to see every phase of life through the lenses of advancement. Thus education is viewed almost solely as a step toward a new social ranking, which it often is, and rarely for its effect on the personality. This applies often to clothes and fashions, to marriage, to clubs; in fact, much of the American's life is focused on the fulfillment of status hopes.

Thus far the emphasis in the American system of class and social distinction has been on mobility. The question that follows logically is: mobility for what life purposes? I shall deal with this question of American life purposes in the next chapter. There remains, however, to put the second question posed at the beginning of this section: To what extent does the American open society offer the individual access to social opportunity, and therefore a base for the American folk belief in his society?

8. The Democratic Class Struggle

"No WESTERN SOCIETY," writes A. J. P. Taylor, "will ever again tolerate great extremes of rewards." The American extremes have in recent years been somewhat lessened by the steeply graduated tax structure at one end and the shrinking of the poverty group at the other. A big spread remains both in wealth and income between the top and bottom dogs, yet it is not the crucial inequality, either in America or in any other democratic class society. It would be truer to say that no society will ever again tolerate the large-scale damming of aspiration and hope on the part of the plain people. This danger the American class system has thus far averted.

This is why it has been for Americans, in Popper's phrase, an "open society." But how open is this open society? I have reviewed the mobilities and rigidities of American class, the changes in the alignment of classes, the nature of the caste strata, the way in which class distinctions are expressed in the differentials of thinking and action. It remains to point out that the crux of the openness of an open society is the degree of access it affords to the opportunities of life.

This is the "religion of equality" of America—not equality of reward or of social standing but of access. It is roof, center, and underpinning of whatever "classlessness" there is in American society. Nor is this, like other religious feelings, a mystical or dedicated one. The Puritan conscience, which once kept watch over the growing inequalities to keep them in bound, no longer operates to the same degree. In its place has come a hard empirical feeling that sharp inequalities make very little sense. The margin of tolerance has narrowed for whatever shuts the door against the life chances for any boy or girl. To be sure, this is qualified by the new status vigil that gives many Americans a sense of satisfaction at the status discomfiture of those below them, as well as anxiety about their own status. But this satisfaction has little to feed on if the position of the depressed classes is due to their never having had a chance. Just as the American's demand for class advancement for himself is unsparingly concrete, growing by what it feeds on, so he will refuse to tolerate a caste setup which puts unpassable obstructions in the way of a reasonable chance at making a living and a life.

This suggests a functional definition of class for Americans—a stratum with similar economic opportunities, similar access to education, health, courtship, and the other major elements that fit a man for the voyage of life. Thus, to dam up equal opportunity for travel or recreation, for holidays and leisure, for the acquirements of taste and the refinements of manner, is only secondary to damming up the equal opportunity for schooling, nourishing food, housing, medical attention, and job chances. The principle of equal access embraces not only physical fitness and vocational skills but preparation for all the major social experiences that mean the growth and health of the personality. Seen in this frame, the idea of class is neither narrowly economic in the Marxist sense of income and power nor narrowly subjective in the Warner sense of prestige and status, but is broadened to include the total strategic situation of the personality in the culture—the sum of the chances he gets at life and the preconditionings to life which flow not from his heredity or personality but from his location in the society. If the deadened life chances of the worker who gets stuck in his groove or the caste exclusions of the Negro from the main stream are seen in these terms, then the doctrine of equal opportunity becomes a decisive fact about the society rather than what Justice Holmes once called "a fiction intended to beautify what is disagreeable to the sufferers." Given such access, the class system then becomes itself a means toward continued class mobility within it and uncovers the truth of Woodrow Wilson's "I believe in democracy because it releases the energies of every human being."

This may also suggest a fresh way of seeing the meaning of the class conflicts in American history—as phases of a democratic class struggle whose purpose was never (as in other contexts) the extermination of the other classes, nor even always class domination, but the effort of the majority to achieve access to the means of a good life from which the shifts of technology and of economic power were cutting it off. It is clear enough that this was true of the Jeffersonian revolution of small farmers and planters and artisans against the landed and funded wealth and the shipping interests; it was equally true of the new farmer class of the West and the new artisan class of the cities when they swept Jackson into power. How characteristic it was, then, for the Jeffersonians to emphasize, as a set of means for their class struggle, the freeing of land tenure from feudal restrictions, and guarantees of religious freedom, and the establishment of colleges where a democratic elite could be trained. How characteristic also that the Jacksonians should have fought so hard to broaden the base of the franchise, to outlaw imprisonment for debt, to establish a free school system for all, to keep the financial power of the new banking group from blocking a fluid currency and credit, and to keep the new business groups from achieving monopoly through their corporate charters. Each of these measures was aimed at destroying the obstructions to what Joseph Blau has called "the enterprise of freedom . . . and freedom of enterprise." A class of journalists, lawyers, skilled artisans, and small farmers was struggling with a class of merchants, *rentiers,* businessmen, and clergy to keep class closure from setting in.

This analysis could be extended through the major class conflicts of American history that were to follow, from the struggle between the landowning and slave-working class and that of free workers and businessmen in the pre-Civil War period to the struggle of the New Deal coalition of small shopkeepers, trade-union workers, ethnic minorities, small farmers, and professional classes to build a welfare economy. In every phase of the New Deal program the struggle ran in terms of class interests, but always with a view to blasting away the obstructions that corporate power and a rigidified class system had placed in the path of class mobility. Throughout their history, in this kind of democratic class struggle, Americans have used not only the methods of trade-union and economic action but also of pressure politics, bloc voting, and other forms of interest-group political action. This kind of political action has been at once a form of the democratic class struggle and a solvent of class frictions that might otherwise have resulted in violence.

Why such a result has not occurred is one of those miracles of the class system which, like all secular miracles, may be subject to explanation. It has not been due to the lack of class resentment or the absence of sharply divergent class attitudes. The richest prizes and most desirable strategic positions in the economy have been pre-empted by the big corporations and all but frozen by the legal maintenance of privilege. The insecurities of the market, where a whole family's destiny depends on the earner's capacity to sell his skills or products and buy his materials and means of living within what he gets, have further sharpened class attitudes. America is a class society in the sense that its people fall into more or less well-defined income groups, living-standard groups, and status groups, although the lines between them are blurred. Those within each group are affected much the same way by the same ups-and-downs of prosperity and depression, employment boom or recession, inflation or deflation, or by tax laws and social legislation. Although they do not always think together, they do tend to act, lobby, and vote together for their common ends, especially when an emerging leadership makes them conscious of the identity of their interests.

Recent attitude studies—those by Arthur Kornhauser and by Richard Centers are most striking—have documented the differentials of political and economic opinion as between the occupation groups in the class system. This cracks the veneer of hypocrisy about class attitudes, but it could scarcely have been a surprise. There is as great a social distance between a South Side Negro and the head of the Chicago *Tribune,* between a Southern white sharecropper and the top managers of the absentee-owned new industries of the South, and between a fitfully employed unskilled worker in Wilmington or Newark and the directors of great chemical corporations, as there was in Rome between a landless soldier and a Crassus, or in feudal England between a noble and his lowest retainer. The great difference between these earlier societies and the American is that the Americans in the lower classes—and certainly in the middle ones—have (in Max Weber's phrase) a "culturally induced discontent" which flows from the aspirations of the culture and is based on the actual experience of actual class mobility. It is this disaffection-linked-with-hope which sets the tone of American class life. The classes have a roughly common plight, common vulnerabilities, common prospects, but they have also common levels of what Werner Sombart called "ascent aspiration." The democratic class struggle is sparked as much by the aspiration as by the disaffection. Together they explain why the lower classes think liberally in many of their political attitudes and vote New Deal, yet cling to a belief in the open society and retain the hope that their children will do better than they did.

This sheds light on the Great Paradox of the American class system. It has two phases: first, although political and economic attitudes differ sharply between the upper and lower classes, those below reject the notion that they are there permanently; second, despite the often big gap between the encouraged claims of each class, especially the lower ones, and the limited fulfillment possible in any one generation, there is neither great class tension nor loss of cultural hope. It sheds light also on the relaxed quality—along with the militancy—of the American class situation: the sense of "taking it easy" which has been the despair of the class-obsessed radicals. I do not account for this, as Russell Davenport does, as "a social partnership that only the craziest optimist would have dared foretell." The term "social partnership" elides the elements of class difference and class struggle, but it is true that the struggle is carried on within a framework of mobility and hope.

Much of this may be a form of folk belief, and writers like Robert Lynd have bitingly asked students of American society to shape their class doctrines to social reality rather than to this folk belief. There is value in such prodding, but it ignores the fact that folk belief is in itself an important phase of social reality, especially when the belief finds considerable support in past experience. There is a distinction between folk belief and folk fable, as there is between a social myth concocted and sustained by propaganda techniques and one rooted in a people's history and in the genius of their institutions. You cannot dismiss the American folk belief about class as untrue on the ground that its truth is mainly a psychological one. It does distill the American experience with class as sifted through the popular mind over the generations. Obviously there is a deep surge of feeling coming up from below, merging with and strengthening the inherent cultural optimism of America. There is in it an inextinguishable hopefulness that keeps corporate power and the hierarchy of social distinction from breeding that despair which is the matrix of class revolution. What is bred in the American situation is quite a different thing—not the resentment of the rebellious but the pathos of the excluded, and the unremitting anxiety under which life in any status system is lived.

Yet even taking account of the pathos and anxiety, the dominant tone is hope. It is based on a number of trends: on the expanding college attendance, especially for the children of the working class and the lower middle class; on the movement to the suburbs, which has added to the buoyancy of the class system by giving a people largely torn from the land and from home-owning a new sense of roots and a new stake in community living; the growth and social acceptance of the trade-unions, which have brought the bargaining power of the working class to its height; the new Mass Media, especially TV, which have reduced the sense of class isolation and opened vistas of experience for all to feed on; the fact that 70 per cent of the American population is in the areas where upward mobility still operates, so that in almost three out of four American families the sense of social possibility and the upward pressure on the levels of aspiration are still operative; finally, on the history of the New Deal and its successor administrations which have proved that government action can help remove the obstructions that stand in the way of the immediate upward goals attainable for many. In other words, at the base of the folk belief is the fact that the recent experience of most of the strata of the class system has kept their members from feeling caught in the trap of a closed class.

Big gaps still remain. If they did not, what I have described as the Great Paradox of the class system would be no paradox. But neither is it a blind alley. In a frame of hopefulness even the class gaps perform the function of spurring individuals to greater effort and providing strength to the failing individual incentives of the economy. As long as the immediate goals continue to seem and be compassable they spur whole classes to span the distance that lies between. If in delineating American life we are to borrow anything from the Marxist armory of class concepts, let it not be that of a classless society, which is as false in the American as in the Russian context, but the concept of class struggle, which goes back before Marx to the early American political writers and takes on a special meaning when it is placed in a frame of democracy.

CHAPTER VIII

Life Cycle of the American

WE MOVE away here from American technology, economy, government and class structure, and shift our attention to the growth of the American personality. We trace what happens to the American in the course of his life cycle from birth to death, focusing on the interactions between the developing personality and the pervasive culture at each of the turning points of the individual's life (Sec. 1, "The Personality in the Culture"). It is here that we take stock of the American family, noting its flux and transformations and seeing it as the primary laboratory for the forming of personality and the basic attitudes on authority, freedom, and individual expressiveness (Sec. 2, "The Family As Going Concern"). We look into the cultural anxieties involved in the cult of the child, and the recent reassertions of the parental role (Sec. 3, "Children and Parents"). We trace the process of growing up and coming of age in America as one of finding models to identify with and roles to play, of earning one's spurs, and finally finding one's identity (Sec. 4, "Growing Up in America"). We go on to the courtship years, with their "dating" and "pairing" patterns, and look into the American attitudes toward love, and the failures and successes of marriage in America (Sec. 5, "Courtship, Love, and Marriage"). We then turn to the situation of the American woman, at once the most vaunted and least fulfilled of the American cultural products. We analyze the roles the culture assigns to her, the rebelliousness she has engaged in, the social revolutions that have transformed her situation, the multiple lives she leads and the deaths she dies, the dilemmas she still has to face, and how she is confronting them (Sec. 6, "The Ordeal of the American Woman"). We carry the American on into the middle years of his life, noting the changes taking place in reorienting toward middle age in the light of the lengthened age span and the changing conditions of leisure, but not omitting the desolate spaces on the landscape. And we end with the new American in a new conception of old age and its possibilities, and with American attitudes to the eternal but un-American fact of death (Sec. 7, "The Middle and End of the Journey").

CHAPTER VIII

Life Cycle of the American

1. The Personality in the Culture

ONE way to get at the quality of a culture is to ask how the human personality fares in it through the life cycle. In the more primitive folk societies, where there was a close collective concern with magical and religious rituals, and where a member's relation to his tribe and the tribe's relation to the supernatural world were almost blended into one, the society intervened ceremonially in the life cycle of the individual. The Belgian anthropologist Van Gennep has used the term "rites of passage" for the ritual transition points at which the individual is inducted into the succession of crucial life experiences.

Like other modern cultures, Americans have almost lost the impulse to magical ceremonial. What survives of that impulse is found in a few desultory religious services at birth, puberty, marriage, and death, when the occasion is restricted to family and friends rather than celebrated by the community as a whole. Yet from cradle to grave the community does come in with its norms and codes, if not with its ceremonies, to shape the stages of the life cycle. In one sense the true American ceremonials are not the rites of passage but the rituals of the scientists and doctors. As James Klee has said, the Salk polio vaccine may be a more important ceremony to them than Confirmation.

In every civilization the life cycle is culture-bound. One may say that the life history of the American is the unfolding of the person in the culture, and equally the condensation of the culture-in-the-person. There are some truisms here that tend to be forgotten: that people make their culture, as their culture makes them; that no culture can rise in its quality above the kind of human material developed in it; but equally that the final test of a culture lies in the quality of the setting it provides for the individual personality to form itself.

There is a risk of overstating the importance of the particular culture, and how unique a stamp it can place on its human material. The phases of the life history are much the same in every culture: birth, the forming of infant habits of eating, talking, walking; child growth to adolescence; the onset of puberty; adornment and courtship that come with sexual awakening; the induction into the community and its adult patterns; betrothal, marriage and procreation, starting another life cycle; child-rearing; the assumption of the economic burdens of family and the civic and religious duties of the community in the maturity of one's powers; the middle years and the sexual climacterics; sickness and the decline of physical powers; old age, with its dependency; death.

But if the invariables of human life make the life cycle itself pretty much a constant in its skeletal structure, they have to be filled in by the history of the culture and the biography of the individual, leaving room for the interplay of "culture" and "personality." John Dollard emphasized how powerful the culture is in shaping ahead of time what will happen to the individual: "All the facts we can predict about the organism . . . will define the culture into which it comes. Such facts can include the kind of clothes it will wear, the language it will speak, its theological ideas, its characteristic occupation, in some cases who its husband or wife is bound to be, how it can be insulted, what it will regard as wealth, what its theory of personality growth will be. . . . These and hundreds of other items are or may be standardized before the birth of the individual and be transmitted to the organism with mechanical certainty."

These cultural shaping forces, although lying below the surface of the individual life, are powerful in their effects. Even in America, with its stress on the uniqueness of the individual, the strong common elements that place diverse personalities in similar cultural molds are undeniably present. Sometimes it is the role in a subculture that is more important than the culture: the life of a Mississippi Negro sharecropper will in most respects differ from that of a Du Pont, but it will parallel the life of other Negro sharecroppers, just as Du Pont's will parallel the lives of other families who have enjoyed wealth and power over a long time.

In some respects the culture or subculture will act through some short cut that eases the individual's growth, as for example through formalities of language, manners, or moral codes. In other ways it will act through controls that circumscribe the individual's expression, as through rigid standards he must live up to and taboos he dare not violate. Anatole France had such cultural burdens in mind when he said that every child born into civilization is born with a beard. Changing the figure, the journey of the personality in any culture is like walking under water, or struggling past heavy obstacles in an enveloping dream.

How much control does American society, compared with others, exercise over the individual? It is usually said that American society is "restrictive" rather than "permissive," but this applies mainly to the control of sexual relations. On premarital intercourse, especially for girls, and on homosexual relations, Americans are severely restrictive in their formal codes, but a good deal less so in their operative ones. On the other hand, on the child's behavior in the household, on discipline in the school, on the freedom of the individual to move about physically and to cross social lines, on freedom to change and exchange opinions, and especially on its refusal to demand deference to any priestly, magical, parental, or governmental authority, American society is among the most permissive in history.

Since these two extremes are found in the same society, it is useless to apply either term to it. One finds here again an instance of the polar nature of American life. But this fact is in itself important in assessing the impact of the culture on the personality, for it means that the American goes through life meeting not one but a number of varying degrees of pressure or permissiveness. He is like a diver changing quickly from one sea level to another: if it doesn't make him bleed profusely or kill him, he emerges more able than most people to adapt himself to contrasting changes. But most of all, the contrast of tight pressures and permissive freedoms must seem confusing to the young American and produce in him a sense both of being boxed in and of being left bewilderingly alone.

The same problem may be put in terms of how purposive American life is. The formal codes are mainly negative, in the shape of taboos. The positive goals for individual striving are never imposed or enforced as such by the community. The individual is seemingly allowed the utmost latitude in making his own choices—choosing his interests as he grows up, his companions and friends, his job and career, his mate, the size of his family, the color of his opinions, his recreations and hobbies, his books, his tastes, his residence. This degree of freedom of choice leads some observers to count America as the most permissive of societies. Yet there is some constriction under this deceptive aspect of extreme freedom. From birth to death there are pressures molding the individual in the direction of "what is expected." The major and minor goals for individual striving—to succeed, to have a job, not to waste time, to do and not to dream—are pounded into him. The fact of his freedom of choice makes it more imperative for him to choose rightly, not aimlessly or heretically. Thus again he is torn between seeming freedom and the persistent process of social molding.

Such a society has little patience with the "marginal man." I have been discussing here the person-in-the-culture, but every society develops also the man-out-of-the-culture. There are some, for example, which make a place for the-homosexual even while they recognize his divergence: they give him a social function to perform for which he is temperamentally fitted. There are probably few societies in which as much divergence for the man-out-of-the-culture is allowed as in the American, yet few also in which there is so much anxiety to hide that fact. The poet, the exotic, the dilettante, the political and social rebel, the Thoreau-like idler, the aesthete, the saint, the devotee of one crotchety "cause" after another: all of them are allowed to live without molestation, and even the sexual deviants are harried less by the penalties of law than by the censure of their shocked neighbors. All that Americans ask of their people on the margin of the culture is for them to pursue their eccentricities privately. They provide them with a reluctant neglect, but only rarely do they relax the obvious and continuous disapproval of what clashes so deeply with the main currents of community energy.

In discussing cultural patterns, Ruth Benedict has noted the problem of continuities and discontinuities in the cycle of the generations. In folk societies where occupations are stable, and even in most of the European societies from which the Americans came, a boy or a girl grew up in the calling, the crafts, the ways of life and thought, of ancestral generations. These continuities have been broken by the drastic geographical movement, the occupational shift, and the social mobility of Americans. It is rarer than in the past for children to grow up and raise their families in the homes, or even in the towns or neighborhoods, where they were born—or on a similar level of living standards. As a result the crucial process of social education, of inducting the growing child into the ways it is expected to follow, is carried on mainly not in the primary group of the family but in the larger society-as-a-whole.

This is especially true of sexual education. In some primitive groups, as Margaret Mead has noted, the child is brought early into contact with the later sexual role it will have. The girl, for example, is encouraged to think of herself sensuously as a coming mother, and by observing and imitating she prepares herself for her role. In the American case the taboos upon premarital sex make such imitation and preparation more difficult, so that the continuity of the cycle of generations is broken. Each generation makes its start afresh, learning through trial and error, in a new city and a new setting with new attitudes toward parental and child relationships. For most the effort of self-reliance is too great, and they try to learn from the current tastes, fashions, and taboos of the larger community, so that the result is almost as constricted as in the traditional societies.

The image thus received from the legislators of emotional development and the arbiters of character is never wholly stereotyped or clear. But there are assumptions in the culture by which the growing person learns to judge his effectiveness. These are the more powerful because they are never codified but are taught by the indirection of what is taken for granted. It is assumed that the child will "do well"—that he will be part of the main currents of play in the nursery or early primary grades, and not stay on the margin; that he will be "popular" in high school and a "leader" in college; that he will be a "success" at his job or career and in gathering his portion of the world's goods; that when he gets into emotional difficulty he must become "adjusted"; and, most of all, that he will strive to be "happy."

Although happiness is an elusive intangible, the individual is assumed to be more or less indifferent to the whole cluster of other intangibles— the sense of wonder and mystery, the sense of honor not because it is the "best policy" but as its own end, the awareness of beauty, the dedication to what will not pay off. He is not expected to tap successive layers of his personality, except in a competitive situation—at sports, or in some heroically demanding piece of work which is regarded as a "character builder" ("the Army will make a man of you"), and where he is praised for drawing upon his reserves of strength and will. He finds little value placed upon growth through suffering, nor (despite the Christian base and overtones of the culture) is he likely to learn that it is by a series of deaths that men have reached fulfillment in life. It is assumed that personality growth pretty much takes care of itself as a by-product of the pursuit of the immediate goals.*

Such a scheme of assumptions leaves the American without much sense of wonder at the successive phases of the individual's life history. Primitive groups, by contrast, are so close to the life-cycle experiences that they celebrate it in ritual drama and build their great folk myths around its stages. In the case of the generic mythical hero, one finds him achieving his effects by some exaggeration or inversion of the usual human role. Thus, as Joseph Campbell has developed the theme in *The Hero with a Thousand Faces,* the hero is likely to be born of a goddess or at least of royalty and not a human being; abandoned on some mountaintop or left floating among the bulrushes in the river; suckled by a wild animal, perhaps a wolf; discovered as a foundling and brought up in isolation in the extremes either of poverty or of nobility; courting and winning the beloved one through the ordeal of danger; mating, by the fateful inversion of incest, with mother or sister; slaying his father; wrestling with demons and living out a life of penitence on the desert or in the mountains; in the end founding a new religion or nation.

The American folk myths are of a different type. Their exaggerations and distortions are more likely to be applied to feats of work prowess, or rollicking boasts of superhuman effectiveness, or life in a mythical

* For more on American cultural goals, see especially Ch. IX, Sec. 8, "Life Goals and the Pursuit of Happiness."

paradise of splendor, or the Superman feats of magical science.* Thus the popular imagination is torn away from the great transitions of the life cycle, which are conceived as burdens somehow to be borne, and it is fixed upon the more abstract goals of the society.

In the process the sense of wonder is replaced by anxieties and tensions. Malinowski, in his studies of the Trobriand Island culture, held that the rituals of primitive life fulfill the deep psychic needs of the person. He cited the anxiety felt by the husband and relatives of a woman in childbirth and later by the parents of the newly born child, and saw the community birth rites as a response to these anxieties. But A. R. Radcliffe-Brown, who had studied the Andaman Islanders with equal care, shrewdly pointed out that in some instances the rite is not a response to the anxiety but itself creates it. The best way of putting it is probably the way that G. C. Homans uses: that in the group life of every society there is a circular process of creating and satisfying needs, so that the same primitive rituals which are a response to the tensions and anxieties of the life cycle also help to bring them into being. The whole elaborate hierarchy of customs and codes in America is partly a response to the tensions of a new industrial culture and the anxieties it begets, but also the existence of the customs and codes helps create the tensions and anxieties.

In the life history the individual American may, however, take part in a great drama of cultural transformation, especially if he is a second- or third-generation member of an immigrant family. His life expectations and aspirations change, his notion of means and ends changes, his whole personality style changes. Anyone reading Handlin's *The Uprooted* cannot help feeling that he has witnessed the broad sweep of a ritual drama in which millions of new Americans and their children and grandchildren have had a role. Much of it, to be sure, is adaptive and imitative rather than creative, but the creativeness is not lacking. This is one of the great typical interactions between culture and personality in America. And if, in the case of many of the immigrant cultures, the rites of passage have tended to wilt in the new social climate of America, it is because the intensity of the cultural transformations has overshadowed the sense of regular life transitions brought over from another cultural world.

One of the striking facts about the American scene, however, is the absence of a ritual drama except in the sense I have described, and even the unofficial extrusion from the culture of the artist-dramatist. He is marginal to the culture and moves on the periphery of it. Among the primitives the ritual drama was a means toward the defining of tribal

* For a discussion of American folk myths, see Ch. XI, Sec. 3, "Heroes, Legends, and Speech." For children's literature, see Ch. VIII, Sec. 3, "Children and Parents."

tradition and the discovery of individual identity: since it has diminished in America, the task of the·discovery of identity becomes correspondingly harder.

Yet the process of discovery does go on and is perhaps the crucial phase of the interaction of culture and personality. As he grows up the young American finds himself and develops his sense of identity partly, at least, by identifying with aspects of his culture—with the heroes of its competitive sports, with its figures of glamour in the Big Media, with the image of swift movement in a convertible or a plane, or equally swift success in the rise to the top of one's field, with the discoveries of scientists, the building feats of engineers, the swagger of the newspaperman, or the solid achievements of the executive life.

American social scientists have recently talked a good deal of "role-taking" in this process of the discovery of identity, and it is true* that the growing-up process runs largely in terms of experimental probing of the roles of wooer and wooed, pupil and teacher, son and daughter, husband and wife, soldier, adventurer, man of substance. Yet surely this fragmentizes the whole process far too much, breaking the total personality up into separable phases which are never in actual fact separated from each other. The process of self-discovery is one that keeps taking place of, by, and for the total person. The dynamics of this process lie hidden in the recesses of personality itself, which the Freudians think of at least partly in terms of a dark battlefield swept by confused alarms of struggle and flight, but which some of the more recent American psychologists have interpreted also in terms of a more expansive feeling of creativeness.

The difficulties arise, of course, with the question of whether the individual absorbs and identifies with all the phases of his culture, meretricious as well as healthy, repressive as well as releasing, in the process of his growth toward maturity. Much of the confusion of the inner life of the American derives exactly from the terrible burden of making a selection of what one will identify with, and thus having to sit in a kind of judgment on the culture—which one cannot do without having already arrived at a sense of one's identity. This is the vicious spiral that the individual runs into in any culture: that he is infected with its confusions and contradictions unless he can detach himself from them, yet by the fact that in most cases he cannot, he is pervaded by them and adds to them. It is usually the innovator and the marginal man of the culture who achieves enough of a detachment from it to help it to clarify itself and grow more creative. One is likely to forget, in the stress on the identity and growth of the individual, that the culture too has an

* See Sec. 4, "Growing Up in America."

identity, that it has continuities, that it is faced with the chances and the problems of growth, and that the kind of culture which serves as a frame for the individual's life may make all the difference in deciding whether that life is to be stunted or expressive.

In his cultural frame the American has shown a resilience of mood and a variety of temperament. The end product of the life process is not the cultural type but the individual himself in all his multiple forms. American society does not encourage individual diversity where it conflicts with the standards of an often ruthless peer group or community. Yet individualist tradition has managed to break through even these layers of conformity. American society is both overorganized in some areas and underorganized in others, but it allows ample room at the joints for individual development. The real question is not whether particular divergences are allowed, but whether the whole social climate is one in which the impulses to know yourself and to be yourself can grow strongly.*

Let us now see how this climate operates and how these impulses fare through the stages of the American life history.

2. The Family As Going Concern

THE AMERICAN FAMILY has been caricatured both by American and foreign observers, and in one sense it is a caricature of itself, since it always seems to be parading its excesses. In the more dramatic and distorted version the American family is an anarchic collection of delinquent adolescents, spoiled cacophonous brats, a domineering wife, and a harassed, two-timing husband, their discords frequently aired in divorce courts and tabloids, the whole of it watched by Dr. Spock for baby care, Dr. Gesell for child growth, and Dr. Kinsey for the record of erotic successes and failures.

On a less caricatured level the picture is still somber enough. Americans tend to marry young and run into divorce problems often, have small families whose size they seek to control, give their children unparalleled freedom; they marry romantically for love and are often disillusioned, experiment a good deal sexually, and then in most cases they remarry for love or money, pleasure or companionship; the husband tends to be absent, the wife unhappy, and both to be sexually unfulfilled. There are many broken families, insecure children, possessive mothers; the family seems uprooted and unstable, scarcely performing

---

* On the problem of conformity, see Ch. IX, Sec. 4, "Varieties of American Character." On codes, see generally Ch. IX, especially Secs. 5, 6, and 7, and Ch. X, Sec. 1, "God and the Churches."

its traditional functions; and the instability of the family seems both to express and intensify the general sense of cultural disintegration.

I have put the indictment as strongly as I can, yet anyone except the special pleaders and Juvenals will see that it is overdrawn. With all its weaknesses and excesses the American family is a going concern reflecting less the disintegration of the culture than its mobility and genius for innovation. For that reason it is a pain to moralists, traditionalists, religious absolutists, bourgeois-baiting Marxists, and professional cultural pessimists. If the American family system is sick, then the class system must also be sick, and the whole economy, the democratic idea, the passion for equality, the striving for happiness, and the belief that there can be free choice and a future of hope. For it is on these that the American family is founded. You may feel varying degrees of approval or disapproval of the American institutions and ideas I have listed, but the point is that the American family is part of the totality and reflects its virtues as well as weaknesses.

The elements of the traditional family that took root in the American soil have largely been stripped of their function. In the Europe from which the American stocks came, the father was the unquestioned head of the family, since he was the ruler of his farm or had a clear status in society; in America he is unlikely to have an economic domain of his own to rule or a sharply defined social position. His sons leave him to carve out careers of their own, just as he left his own parents; his daughters follow their husbands and set up families of their own. He no longer tills the soil as he did: the large New England or Midwest farm family, which was the product both of overflowing pioneer energies and the need for family labor, is no longer the rule. Thus the traditional family —large, three-generation, patriarchal, attached to the land, closely integrated in performing the collective economic functions of farm homestead or small shop or family business—has almost gone out of the picture. It is more likely to be small, two generation, mobile, whole-family-centered, equalitarian. The family no longer performs to the same degree the old functions of economic production, religious cohesion, kinship continuity, educational and cultural transmission.

But this does not mean that the American family has found nothing to replace what it has given up of these functions. No longer a production unit, it has become a more demanding consumption unit, based on the earning power of both husband and wife and the spending power and tastes especially of the wife and daughters. It is still a residence unit, even when it is highly mobile. No longer an educational and religious entity, it is becoming a more broadly cultural one. It seeks to supplement the traditional bondage to father or husband by free decisions

among its members. It tries to make companionship and common interests rather than social duties its psychological basis. It is cemented, if at
all, by the pursuit of happiness rather than the exercise of authority.*

I have no alack and alas for this. The oldest function of any family,
that of producing and caring for children, it still performs. The relation between husband and wife, between parents and children, between
brothers and sisters, is less traditionally regulated than it was. But who
will say that bonds of kinship maintained in a spirit of free commitment, with a continuous inquiry about their meaning, are any less
strong for that fact? Given the necessary elements of obligation and tradition, the American has fashioned anew the features of his family institutions, as he does everything else about him—his clothes, income,
technology, production, government, class system, laws, occupations,
ideas, and opinions. The result may seem chaotic, but only because it is
also revolutionary.

The American family is "nuclear," by which is meant that it is not
the old "organic" or "extended" family and has come further from the
clan than is true in any other culture. Certainly it is sharply different
from the Moslem family with its man-centered polygamy and its depressed caste for women; or the Indian "joint family," run by the elder
women; or the Chinese father-son family axis, run for and by the old
men; or the continental family based on the marriage of convenience
and still father-oriented; or the various concubinage systems; or the
Soviet family, in which the parental or filial roles, whether of power,
obedience, or affection, have been largely diluted by a state which has
tried to distill away for itself the essence of all these roles. Along the
path of its development the American family shed in-laws, grandparents, cousins, aunts, and retainers; it handed over production to the factory and office, religion to the churches, the administration of justice to
the courts, formal education to the schools, medical attention to the
hospitals, and it has even begun to hand over some of the basic life decisions to the psychotherapist. It has been stripped down to the spare
frame of being marriage-centered and child-fulfilled.

Actually there are at least five definable family types in the American
culture. Four are still largely traditional. First, the rural family (in the
Midwest or New England), which still is large, where the children still
do field and household chores and do not usually disperse when they
come of age and get married. The second is the "old family" unit, especially in the elites where there has been wealth over time, considerable
pride of standing, and little geographical mobility, so that the old ideal

* I am, of course, giving a generalized portrait. The precise picture presents a good
many overlappings.

of the "Great House" of the Southern plantation or the "family on the hill" in New England still holds. The third is the family of second- and third-generation immigrants, especially Slavic, Mediterranean, Irish, and Jewish, with residual traditional elements: it shows instances at once of great cohesiveness (largely because of the carry-over of the old ways and the old urgency for holding together in a strange and changing social environment) and of a persisting break between the generations. The fourth is the Negro family, shaped by the plantation heritage caste conditions in the South, great geographical and social mobility in the North, and a high desertion rate: the father is often absentee, the mother has a factory job or lives out in domestic service, and the children are often raised by grandparents in a truncated three-generation family.

The fifth type is the middle-class, big-city, small-town, or suburban family, which is the dominant American form. The father is a somewhat transient figure and the mother a pervasive one. This new archetypal family may best be described in terms of the social changes that brought it into being. One was geographical dispersal, the constant physical and occupational mobility of Americans that flings them around over the face of the land in constantly shifting internal migrations in search of jobs and opportunity. Another was the technical revolution that turned America from a farming society into an urban and suburban one and made it possible for women to become machine tenders or to take their place in a vast clerical and office hierarchy. Aided by a "sexual revolution" and a "kitchen revolution," the American woman of the upper and middle classes (not the lower ones) achieved the kind of freedom from household chores which the slave system gave the wives and daughters of the plantation owners of the Old South. Operating on all these changes has been a ceaseless equalitarian impulse, whittling away the subordination of wives to husbands and of children to parents, and making romantic love and free marriage choice the center of the family relationship.

There are several levels on which the dominant American family type can be analyzed: its structure of authority; its inner emotional climate, and how it mediates between its members and the world of outer social experience; how stable and viable it is; how it brings up children. To the first three of these I now turn. The fourth will be discussed in the next section.

One of the things that has struck European travelers and observers sharply has been the comparative difference in the authority of the fathers. Busy at job or office, the American father cannot exercise the continuous direction required in the patriarchal family. His authority is still recognized in theory, and usually he is the court of last resort on questions of discipline. But he is no longer backed up by a religious sanction of his paramount authority, nor does he have the will to assert it. On daily matters his wife is his deputy, and under the absentee sovereignty of the husband the deputy becomes king—only to give up her authority on week ends to the husband or at times to the children themselves. Thus the libertarian tradition is reinforced by the changes in the inner authority structure of the family. The children think in terms of claims and rights, more than of duties and obedience. Their world is not that of deference to authority but of "talking back" to parents and bargaining to exact a set of rewards for their surrender to family rules on food habits, manners, and behavior.

This portrait of the child-centered anarchy of the family is again overdrawn. In effective families there is little of that tyranny of the weaker which has caused the family to be described as the "dictatorship of the sickest member." The rules are made together, to be followed together. Money saved up is not something to be scrambled for by competing children, but it is used for trips and treats for the family as a whole. Family rituals which meet with strong objection from any of the members are likely to wither away, nor can the authority of the parents alone sustain them if they lose their meaning for the children. There are, to be sure, constant opportunities for neurotic distortions of the emotional structure of the family. For reasons inherent in their own personalities the unconscious bias of one or both parents may be toward one child or against another, and a child may grow up as a "golden boy" or as a family scapegoat. The rivalry of the children for affection and concessions makes the shaping of family decisions difficult in the extreme.* More difficulty is introduced by the fact that comparisons are continually being made with rules and decisions in other families. Yet, however faltering the process is, the decisions are part of what may roughly be called a democratic family process.

The resulting democracy is vulnerable, as all democratic structures are. The attacks on the American family on the ground of its dissolution of authoritarianism are a good deal like similar attacks on American political democracy. The family is more vulnerable, of course, because it must bear the heavy burden of making its democracy function. This burden is placed on a large number of small family units, many of them broken and disorganized, with ignorant, confused, neurotic, or dissolute parents. They often make a mess of bringing up children in a framework of affection and responsibility. In the society as a whole the failure of some persons to live up to the democratic burdens, through ignorance

---

* For more on the emotional structure of the family, as expressed in the parent-child relation, see Sec. 3, "Children and Parents."

or frustration, may be balanced by the greater maturity of others. But exactly because the family is the primary group, no other family can do much to rescue it. Thus it sinks or swims depending on whether its members can make a go of the co-operative venture. If they fail, the authority structure becomes tyrannical, possessive, or anarchic.

It is often said that because of the individualist authority structure of the American family a political dictatorship is impossible in America. If this is true it is not because of any carrying over of the rebellion principle from the family into the political sphere. Actually it is the over-possessive, domineering parents, in insecure family situations, who are more likely to create in their children the drive to search for a father or to displace him with another. What links the family structure with democratic political habits is a two-way relation: only in a democratic political milieu could the family have thrown off the burdens of arbitrary authority and sought equality for its members; and—even more crucial—the process of coping with the problems of government-by-consent in the primary social group, through joint rule-making and rule-observing, makes the family an unparalleled laboratory for government-by-consent in the larger political sphere. Children and parents trained in such a joint effort are unlikely to become cogs in an authoritarian machine or find their fulfillment in following a leader blindly—although the evidences of conformism in recent American political attitudes show how much the family is itself caught in the cultural pressures.

The nostalgic amusement and archaic flavor, as if from a museum piece, which American readers and theatergoers got from Clarence Day's *Life with Father*—a patriarchal father who claimed a religious sanction for his authority—attested the span that the American family has traveled in the intervening generations. The current folklore which shows Father at the other end of the authority scale—having to squeeze his way into a family bathroom pre-empted in the rising hours by an aggressive group of children, or manipulated by children and wife in the "Bringing Up Father" comics—is a genial recognition of the loss of his power. Yet the satire is gentle, for the American father has accepted his diminished authority partly because his work takes so much of his time and energy, partly because his role fits into the spirit of his society as a whole.

In comparing the American family with that in authoritarian societies, the difference between them is striking. The authority structure of the pre-Nazi German family spilled over into the rest of German society. Under the Nazis the influence ran the other way, and the *Führer-prinzip* in society reinforced the position of the father. But there was a degree to which the German family remained, as Max Horkheimer put it, a "shelter against the mass-society" of the Nazis, which was why the Hitler regime had to "reconstruct" it, for even with its authority principle it did not go far enough in the discipline of the Nazi virtues. It may be noted that recent studies of the German family indicate that the father is losing his authority and coming closer to the American image. In the Soviet system the Communist party has tried to reinforce the authority structure within the family after the model of the same structure within the state. The Latin-American family has recently been throwing off both the dominance of the church and the tyranny of the father; and the anticlerical movements in Latin-American countries have developed alongside the steady penetration of the society by the image of the free-choosing American family structure. In fact, there is every evidence that Western nations are quite generally following the American lead in family development, just as America carried further the tendencies already present in European society.

The concern of the American family is with raising and socializing the child. At the heart of the recent family changes in America is a hedonic revolution which asserts that life can be pleasurable, that the size of the family can be planned and the sequence of children spaced, that bearing them need not be a curse, nor raising them a burden, that happiness can be found for both partners in a freely willed marriage and freely willed children, that family decisions should be made largely with a view to preparing the children for a good life. I stress the children as the focus of the nuclear family, and their rearing and socializing as its chief function. Yet part of the hedonic revolution is the growing belief that there can be a life for husband and wife alike even after the children are raised. With the average age at marriage for the woman somewhere at twenty, the childbearing cycle may be completed for her before thirty, and the last child has outgrown dependency before she has passed her mid-forties. This gives her a chance, at the prime of middle age, to turn back to her earlier interests and assume new ones, as it also gives the husband a chance to ease up on his work and tensions—if he knows how.

In the early years of family building, however, the whole focus is on children and home, at least for the woman. His job and career strivings allow the husband little scope for continuous attention to his family. He becomes a residual father, and his wife what Geoffrey Gorer has called the "encapsulated mother."

The American mother is not only the organizer of consumption and spending but also the one who reads books and magazines and studies the mysteries of child psychology: she thus becomes the child's rearer, cajoler, censor. Her ways are less authoritarian than manipulative. She is a matriarch not in exercising firm power but in managing the family.

Since she is the chief socializing agent—along with the usually female schoolteacher—the American boy comes to identify moral codes with women, and thus either to think of them as "sissy stuff" or else to associate the sexual life with an impossible goal of purity. If she proves too possessive the result is shown in the psychiatric records of battle-shock cases in World War II, when the boys from mother-sheltered families found the transition to the realities of an all-male world too sharp. In the cases where she is the dominant adult the boy may find it hard to establish his own later role, having no effective masculine model. The daughter may seek a strong father symbol in her future husband, or come to think of him as an object for the exercise of her own power. What Philip Wylie has termed "Momism" in America may be, as he suggests, an overcompensation for the boy's rebellion against a mother-dominated home life. Or it may be a nostalgic harking back to the idyllic days of mother and home from which the grown man regrets having moved so far.

An idyl the "home" is, at least in later memory. It is the most lyrical of American symbols. It may mean a sharecropper's hut, a tumbledown shack near the railroad tracks, an estate at Newport or on Long Island or the east coast of Maryland, a company house in a mining or steel town in West Virginia, a government housing project in Detroit, a Lake Shore Drive mansion near Chicago, a movie star's estate-cum-swimming-pool at Beverly Hills. But generally the image is that of the middle-class suburban or small-town home, with memories of pies eaten in the kitchen, and a radio or TV set in the living room, a tool shed, a bicycle to ride to school, perhaps (in the earlier days) a swimming hole and sand-lot baseball games.

The fact that America has been so mobile makes this home idyl the more evocative. Until the suburban revolution most Americans grew up in crowded city quarters, which meant that the home idyl, with its small-town and semirural associations, became for the culture all the more a figure of the Golden Age. It is not nostalgia alone that moves Americans but the longing for a social unit to stand firm in the wrack of a dissolving world.

The young people, as they sit courting, spin their dreams around the "dream home," and they turn the pages of the apartment and house-for-sale ads and the magazines embodying the latest architectural plans and interiors. They want the home for the comforts it gives them but also because it sets a seal on the marriage, provides a frame within which children can grow up, gives the family a clear standing in the community, and certifies in a tangible way the ideals of security and permanence for which Americans hunger. This attachment to the home underlies the vast housing boom that developed after World War II, and which has been discussed in an earlier chapter. It also inclines Americans to associate a number of social ills, especially juvenile delinquency, with bad housing—a mode of interpretation that has a core of truth but also carries with it a favorite American thesis in linking the nature of the home neighborhood with character formation.*

I am thus more than a bit skeptical of the predictions of decay and doom freely made for the American family. It is true that its kinship ties are not as strong as, for example, the father-son ties in China, nor does it perform so well as the extended family the function of transmitting the social heritage from one generation to the next. The strength of such ties varies in every society with the rate of social mobility. Those who care about an America in which the channels of social movement are not closed can scarcely quarrel with its consequences for the family.

As for the rising divorce rate, it may show not so much a disbelief in marriage as an intent to take seriously the American premise that a marriage is held together by love and common interests. The steadily rising rate of remarriage after divorce shows that Americans still believe in marriage even after a disastrous experience with it. The stability of these post-divorce marriages does not differ markedly from that of first marriages. As for the children, many of them learn to get along even after the family ties have been broken, and after the remarriage of one of their parents they again become parts of a whole family. The worst consequences of broken families are in the cases where they lead to neglect of the children or brutality toward them, but family life even without divorce has its seamier side in the same social strata. The evidence of psychotherapy is that it may be even worse for children to grow up in families where the bonds are held together despite the unremitting hatred, unhappiness, and sadism of the parents.

One image that we shall have to discard after studying the recent divorce figures is the romantic image of the lower-class family as stable, integrated, and happy, while the middle-class family is divorce-ridden and neurotic. This is simply not borne out by the facts. Actually, as William J. Goode has shown, there is an inverse relation between class and divorce, the lower-class families having higher divorce rates and the middle- and upper-class families lower ones. The factors behind this are complex. It is probably true that there is more effective sexual understanding between husband and wife at the lower income strata than at the upper ones. But it is equally true that the economic strains at the

* For an earlier discussion of house and home in America, see Ch. III, Sec. 6, "The Sinews of Welfare."

lower strata express themselves in family conflict which often disguises their origin and becomes a nagging relationship making marriage intolerable. The easier economic means at the higher-class levels will often enable a marriage to survive that could not have outlived privation. Similarly, there is a broader network of social involvement at the upper levels, in leisure, recreation, and "going out," which can make life tolerable for both husband and wife even with an unsatisfactory marriage. It is possible that divorce was originally an upper-class institution which has been taken over into the lower strata and carried further, but it is more probable that family instability has changed its form among the lower strata: where once it found an outlet in desertion and protracted separation, it now finds divorce a simpler solution. I do not deny here the reality of the objective facts on the increase of divorce, but I suggest that they do not tell the whole story.

In any event, the middle-class family cannot be caricatured any longer as an unstable and neurotic chaos. It carries the burden of family changes in the culture as a whole, being usually in the vanguard. This was true of the growth of sexual experimenting, especially by the American woman, and the practice of contraceptives. The widespread acceptance of such "birth control" led to considerable anxiety about population decline and childlessness, as in the case of the Roman Empire. But again the evidence points the other way. Certainly the first effect of "family planning" is to cut down the birth rate, with the family income going into higher living standards and better education for fewer children. But the next phase is quite different—the raising of the birth rate when young parents, especially among the better-educated classes, find that the psychic satisfaction of having children is greater than extra house furnishings or clothes without them.*

The greatest strengths of the family system must be sought among those parents who have made a willed choice to stay together because they find their deepest expressiveness in family life. This expressiveness is again part of the much ridiculed American search for happiness. It is a search which goes beyond the sexual partnership itself and even beyond the marriage relation, finding its fulfillment in the pattern of children, home, community status, and warmth of human relationship which together form the family.†

* For more on divorce, see Sec. 5, "Courtship, Love, and Marriage." For the larger aspects of the birth rate and family planning, see Ch. III, Sec. 5, "Human Resources: Population Profile."

† For a fuller discussion of some of the material of this section, see Sec. 5, "Courtship, Love, and Marriage," Sec. 6, "The Ordeal of the American Woman," and also Ch. IX, Sec. 7, "Society and Sexual Expression," and Sec. 8, "Life Goals and the Pursuit of Happiness."

3. Children and Parents

THE CHILD BORN into an American home has a better chance of survival and health (as does also its mother) than in the comparable social classes of most other societies: the American record ranks roughly with the best on these scores, including New Zealand, Australia, and Holland. The death rate in infant births was cut in a single generation from 64.6 per 1,000 births in 1930 to 29.2 per 1,000 births in 1950. Katharine Lenroot noted that in the sixteen-year span of her tenure as head of the Federal Children's Bureau the maternity death rate dropped from almost sixty per 10,000 live births in 1934 to seven per 10,000 in 1950.* In the mid-1950s a large corps of psychiatrists, welfare workers, graduate students, and volunteers was scattered around the nation, hidden behind screens in child clinics, hovering over the children in nursery or playground, stalking them from one activity to another, all busily studying child behavior, taking action photos and movies, making countless records, running the results through electronic sorting machines, and presenting conclusions on conflict, co-operation, competition, aggression, and frustration among children with an alluring if illusory mathematical precision. If research funds and statistical surveys could purchase understanding of the great mystery under the heavens—the way of a child with an adult, of an adult with a child, and of a child with itself inside its own universe—Americans would today be certain of having penetrated that mystery.

But they are not. While the American child's chances of survival, health, and economic competence are good, his chances are not equally good for growing into an emotionally mature adult, with a stable personality, a sense of identity, and the capacity for living a productive life.

The defect does not lie in science or social rationality. The problems of underdeveloped countries, where the birth rate outruns current living standards, do not apply to America. Birth control and birth spacing as part of a family life plan, although still not officially accepted among Catholics (many American Catholics probably accept it in practice in some form), have become the rule for most American families. To a considerable extent the blighted areas of child life still exist in America: malnutrition, slum living, squalid housing, substandard schooling, family neglect, teen-age prostitution, and narcotics addiction. Some cities use their budget for less relevant items and leave the schools overcrowded and the diagnostic clinics and child-health centers under-

* See also Ch. III, Sec. 5, "Human Resources: Population Profile."

staffed. As for child labor, there are still two or three million children under seventeen employed during the year, many of them during school hours. But the factory children and the "climbing boys" of eighteenth- and nineteenth-century England, or even the child-labor situation in America at the turn of the century, find no parallel in America today. The problem of the American child is less that of the poor and exploited than of the comfortable and even the pampered. The blight is not one of economic privation but of emotional deprivation.

Americans today sometimes idealize the life of the child in colonial and early agrarian America. Actually there was a struggle of parents and children with the hobgoblins of Original Sin, a continuing war with the Devil, and an adamant effort by parents and clergy to repair the child's ignorance and willfulness by catechisms and prepare him early for the trials and duties of life and the deliverance of death. It is easy to note in the history books the recorded successes of this method of child-rearing and to forget the obscure failures, the "lives of quiet desperation" that Thoreau saw around him, the wild outbursts of family rebellion. The early ills of excessive piety and family authority have been conveniently overlaid by the later ills of excessive materialism and family confusion. Several generations of Americans received their impression of childhood in agrarian America from Louisa May Alcott's *Little Women,* with its picture of happy domesticity and of cheerfulness in meeting the shocks of genteel poverty. But it must be remembered that the author was the daughter of Bronson Alcott, himself the child of the Enlightenment, a devotee of the ideas of Rousseau's *Émile* transplanted to the new world.

It was roughly at this time, in the 1840s, that De Tocqueville saw and described the democratic structure of the American family, the ease and equality of manners within it, and the new paths opened up in the education of girls. The one disharmonious note he reported was the assertion of independence of the sons from the father as they moved away from the family to hew out their own careers. A solvent was already at work which, through American mobility, prevented the incipient rebellion against the father's authority from becoming chronic and violent, as in Europe. The revealing documents of the American family structure are less concerned with the tyranny of the father than with the domination of the mother or the absence of any family core.

Bringing up children in America is not the product of impulse followed by neglect. If anything, the approach is too rational. Most American children (especially in the middle class, much less in the lower classes) are born only after a careful calculation of whether their parents can afford them, both in "initial investment" and "upkeep." There is heart-searching about whether the child will get a good education.

will live in a "good neighborhood," will meet the "right people." Under highly skilled medical attention the children are put through a process of "factory childbirth" in a hospital, with a speed and detachment that make American birth the most sanitary in the world but also the most impersonal. During the early months every energy is focused on a rational schedule of bathing and feeding the child, and on the other rituals of a highly sterilized regime. Studies of a number of cases of autism (or extreme withdrawal) among children found that the parents usually were members of the educated middle and professional classes who had shown the children no emotional abandon and had given them no feeling of sensual contact. In these extreme instances the children, as a psychiatric study put it, were "kept neatly in a refrigerator that didn't defrost."

The entire family plan, especially on the middle-class level, centers around the child. It is dressed up, coddled, socialized early. In an effort to set the stage for what Margaret Mead calls the "expected childhood experience," the parents sometimes squeeze themselves dry of spontaneous emotion. They watch the stages of the child's growth against the statistical norms of Gesell or (on a lower-class level) the traditional folklore of expected growth. They brood over the moot questions of child-rearing: the child's thumb-sucking, the choice of feeding and the time for weaning, its toilet training, its bed-wetting, its temper tantrums; and later its speech and reading difficulties, lying, stealing. An agonized parental debate is always in process: is the child too timid or too brash, is he a "sissy" or a bully, does he withdraw or does he "show off," does he eat like a little pig or is he too finicky? Does he suffer as an only child or is he the victim of "sibling rivalry"? Is discipline too stern or too permissive? Does he need most (as an earlier generation put it) "the Bible and the birch rod," or a psychotherapist or psychiatric social worker with some "play therapy"?

It is evident that in no other culture has there been so pervasive a cultural anxiety about the rearing of children. Here is another instance, as noted above, where in meeting anxieties a culture manages to create and intensify them. In a culture with rising living standards, smaller families, a "kitchen revolution," greater leisure for women, uprooting from the land, physical and social mobility, and universal schooling, there came also the stirrings of self-criticism in the rearing of children. As Stendler has put it, along with the excitement about railroad reform and antitrust reform in the first decade of the century, there was bound to be excitement about baby reform too. We might add that in the 1920s, along with the sexual revolution and the kitchen revolution, one had to expect the baby revolution. G. Stanley Hall had already in the 1880s started lecturing about "child development," emphasizing the changing physical structures and attitudes of the child. He was followed by reverberations from Europe of the work of Freud and his followers. But in America the impact of John B. Watson's behaviorism preceded the full force of Freudianism. Watson taught that except for the primary impulses of fear, rage, and hunger the child came into the world a *tabula rasa* on which the parents and culture could write what they wished. This put a heavy burden of anxiety on the parents, made all the more onerous by the Behaviorist injunction to the parents to decide on routines for the child, treating it like any other object of conditioning, but otherwise to restrain themselves and leave it alone, not encumbering it with the irrelevancy of pampering love.

The Freudian period proved even more fertile of anxieties. The parents were taught that childhood is the fateful molder of the later personality, with the Oedipus romance as its decisive crisis. This was followed by the revelation that the first five years, those discussed in Freud's *Three Essays on Infantile Sexuality,* were the crucial ones, and that afterward everything was closed; then the determining period was narrowed to the first two years, before the formation of language; then the first year, before weaning; and finally, the first six months, with some schools pushing back even further into the intra-uterine period and the trauma of birth. Americans had moved all the way from the Puritan view of the life history as a battlefield on which the virtues were pitted against the Devil to the post-Freudian view of the formation of "destiny in the nursery."

If the fate of the personality was sealed in the earliest phase of childhood, it became crucial to learn what the experts advised on child-rearing. The debate raged around issues like "schedule" as against "demand" feeding, permissiveness as against limit-setting, *laissez faire* as against early socializing, ego-strengthening protection as against the rude preparation of the child for the realities of adult life, "pouring love" into the child as against the exercise of discipline and control. In these debates material was drawn from troubled, delinquent, and even psychotic children, including extreme cases of withdrawal and regression, and from the life histories of schizophrenics, and was applied with admonitory overtones to something like forty million normal children under the age of fifteen. Easy guides for infant care and child-rearing flooded the book market; parents flocked to meetings where psychiatrists discussed "penis envy" and "sibling rivalry"; a whole new vocabulary containing the gobbledygook of child care was added to the American language, and a new technology came into being, to be ranged alongside the other technologies of the machine age.

As with all technologies, it had its roster of "authorities" on whom the conscientious parent leaned. Like every group of experts dealing with life, death, and salvation, this one too became a priesthood, whose oracles were studied for their cryptic meanings. Even when the liberation movement got under way at the turn of the 1940s, the Declarations of Independence from the experts invariably appealed to other experts: "the authorities agree," Americans were told, that little definite and scientific data is known on which to base the sway of the authorities in the nursery and home. Thus the priesthood was invoked to place its stamp of approval upon the secular revolt against the priesthood.

But it was a healthy skepticism that came to change the cultural climate in which parents lived. They had oscillated between fads, alternately repressing and expressing their parental longings and rages, until their natural confidence reasserted itself and the recoil swung them back to the attitudes of the 1890s, when parents had worried less and mixed their permissiveness with a measure of discipline. The snake was coiled full circle, tail in mouth. A residual reliance on the authorities still continued, except that the parents now listened to the experts who tried to repair their basic confidence in themselves. Studies were now made of groups of "normal" and "healthy" children, emerging with the discovery that they had been reared and disciplined with a variety of techniques, but whichever technique it was, had been applied with consistency. Parents began to relax their anxieties and trust their instincts. So sensitive a barometer of the new moods as Lewis Mumford, in his *Conduct of Life,* stated the problem of the growth of personality as one of the "increase of effective love," with the real problem being "how to make ourselves capable of love and ready to receive love." Not only had the cycle come full swing but a new one had started, its anxieties centered not on the fateful early events inside the child's psyche but on the dehumanizing of all personality—adult and child alike.

This is not, of course, wholly new. Much of the anxiety directed toward the child had always sprung from the insecurity of the parents about themselves and their society. Some child experts speak of the "good child in the bad culture," as if what happens to a child is always the result of bad cultural situations and pressures, and never of its own predispositions. One finds the same premise, in more ironic form, in Brock Chisholm's foreboding that despite all the care lavished on children they "may turn out to be the same kind of people we are." This conception of the child as a Noble Little Savage possessed of an artless innocence which is corrupted and distorted by civilization, and also the attitude that the child is always the victim, the adult always the guilty fumbler, bumbler, meddler, and destroyer, are part of the cult of the American child. The other strands in the cult are that the child must be "understood" instead of being allowed to become a functioning part of a functioning family and community; that he must be continually "adjusted," (which seems curious if it is true that his fate is sealed early); that the culture and the future are founded on him; that he will have it better in a better future and will himself *make* the future better. Thus the American overvaluation of the child is compounded of equal parts of guilt, anxious concern, and cultural hope.

There is evidence that this portrait is heavily weighted toward the middle-class family and is less true of the working-class one. Certainly there are differences of family and childhood experience that measure differences in income strata, class, residence, prestige, and ethnic derivation. What is true of a child brought up in a Back Bay house in Boston, or a Park Avenue apartment in New York, or a suburb outside of Chicago or Los Angeles will not be true of one brought up in a Kansas City slum or a California migrant camp or a Negro quarter in Detroit. In *The Father of the Man,* Allison Davis and Robert Havighurst studied child-rearing in different income strata in the Chicago area and found a greater freedom and less tension in the attitude of slum mothers to their children than of middle-class mothers.

Throughout the nation the class posture is a distinctly different one: where middle-class parents are restrictive—on sex, cleanliness, toilet training—the working-class parents tend to be permissive; where middle-class parents are permissive—on talking back, on discipline—the working-class parents tend to be restrictive. The working-class mother never quite caught up with the reliance on experts, nor could she afford the psychotherapists and play therapy. There were enough troubled and sick-minded children coming out of the lower classes, especially from the economically deprived strata and from the Negro and Puerto Rican ghettos, to cause a delinquency problem; but the roots of the delinquency—the alcoholism of parents, family disintegration, the resentment at a lower social status for the ethnic group, the eagerness to overcome the economic and ethnic gap by short cuts—were different from the roots of the middle-class cases of delinquency, which were more likely to be overpossessiveness and overprotection. The feeling of the working-class mother about her children was less one of anxiety, guilt, and overconcentration than the sense that they were something of a burden and that housework had become a bore, and the wish to get away for a while to the movies or a TV audience-participation show. Living on a thin economic margin, moreover, the working-class children had a necessary role in the family as helpers in a common struggle, and in the large families the older children had the added function of caring for the younger ones. In the case of middle-class children there was little of this functional sense: instead of finding their useful place in the family, the children tended to feel that the family existed for them, and too often the parents failed to disabuse them.

It is possible to see the general American overconcentration on the child as marking a phase in American social and class history. Many writers seem to put the blame for what we may call the child panic on the psychologists and psychiatrists. But the deeper source lay in the rapid social mobility and the consequent emotional insecurity of the families that were pushing up into the middle and upper classes. Of the millions of American families which moved into these classes in the years between 1915 and 1955, many had come from farms and small towns, many others were of immigrant stock—most of them second generation, some third. Having achieved income and position, and seeing limitless vistas ahead, they hoped their children would keep moving upward and fulfill the dreams they had themselves fallen short of. In many cases they had broken their ties with their own parents or felt that the old experience would not apply to the new situation, and so they had no traditional rules for bringing up their children. It was into this vacuum that the "experts" and "authorities" had moved.

Seen thus, the focusing on the child was a stage in America's total development, but in a period of constant movement into the middle class it took its character largely from the emotional problems of that class. Yet when compared with corresponding classes in other cultures, even the rural and working classes shared it, since all of them shared the culture's emphasis on success and happiness and the belief that if you took the right path you could achieve both. In a more traditional culture the stress on raising children might have been on the mastery of the tradition in a mold of civic discipline. In a more materialist culture (i.e., one in which material achievement was harder and therefore counted more deeply) the amassing of money at any psychic cost would have been stressed. But the dreams that American parents dreamed for their children were those of mobility (success, partly in money terms, mainly in terms of education and prestige) and happiness. In the past two or three generations the emphasis in the perspectives of parents for their children shifted from material well-being to psychic well-being. The main concern was to give the child a good start in life and to protect him against the social jungle outside the family until he could "adjust" to the demands it would make on him. If he was "badly adjusted" he would prove a failure in "popularity" and happiness. The ultimate disaster might strike him—a "nervous breakdown."

The trouble here was that the parents became cultural surrogates for the child, building for him a substitute world not always relevant to the problems of emotional maturity, offering him an emotional diet that fell short of what he was capable of absorbing. An example was the children's stories and the difference between the kind that parent and school fed them and the kind for which they themselves reached out. The orthodox children's literature in America presented a pastel, two-dimensional world in which only cute or trivial things happened, with surface experiences and unreal emotions. Even the great children's myths that have carried over from other cultures—like the Grimm and Andersen fables—became suspect to modern parents, perhaps because they reached too far to the deeply emotional folk experiences of the human family. There was a quality of primitive terror in these experiences, and American parents avoided them as the Medusa head that might turn the fragile child to stone. Even the Bible stories came out prettified. As for native American children's literature, except for the Br'er Rabbit versions of the widely dispersed "coal-tar baby" myth and the Paul Bunyan "tall stories," America produced little to compare with the continental cultures, where the peasant families made the child part of their own imaginative world. The world of Mark Twain's boyhood America, with its cave and hidden treasure, its tramps and drunken fathers, its raft on the Mississippi, has not been paralleled by any contemporary creations of the same imaginative power. The American child sought a substitute for these in the culture heroes of the popular arts—of baseball, the prize-fight ring, the TV screen. He also reached out, with a perversity that was the despair of his parents, to the heroes of the comic strip and the comic books, to the masks of evil and terror and Superman derring-do which might heighten the anxieties in him, but which managed to take the place in the child's imagination that nothing else had filled.*

If the parent tries to be the culture surrogate for the child, the child is often the emotion surrogate for the parent. American living, for all its outward gusto, is emotionally unexpressive. To the American the emotional richness of Latins, for example, seems wayward and explosive. It is not that he maintains an emotional passivity, like the Orientals or the native Indians of his own continent. It is rather that the combination of success hunting and sexual repression often starves the emotions. All the frustrated hopes of men and women who have come to adulthood without fulfilling their dreams and drives are poured into the child's upbringing, which becomes a means of vicarious living or reliving for the parents. They seek to fashion the child into their own cherished image, using him eagerly to fill the emotional void in their own lives.

* For folk tales and legends in American life, see Ch. XI, Sec. 3, "Heroes, Legends, and Speech"; also Ch. VIII, Sec. 1, "The Personality in the Culture."

It may be said in paradox that the American parents, and especially the mother, do not begin to live emotionally until the child's rearing gives them function. So deeply felt is this need that a black market for the adoption of illegitimate children usually operates, children often being "placed" in families before they are born, at prices reaching into thousands of dollars. Since Americans start with an intensely romantic ideal of love and courtship, and then find they must live realistically in their marriages, they transfer their romantic fixation to the child, thus preserving their belief in the miracle of love-into-happiness. The child, on his part, instead of developing affectionate relationships with a variety and succession of adults, finds himself often fixing on a particular one. In a small "nuclear" family, often isolated from the outside world, having to narrow his whole emotional life in his earlier years to the compass of his family and depend on it for emotional security, his alternatives are few. This means, as Arnold Green has noted, a "capture" or "personality absorption" of the child by the family, often by one parent. Depending on whether parent or child is dominant, it may be regarded on the parent's side as a love imperialism, and on the child's as a form of juvenile blackmail.

In either event the tyrannies of love are substituted for the less exacting relations of affection, friendliness, and respect. When the parents believe they must mute their own personalities in their anxiety about the ego of the child, the result is a deference vacuum. It is underscored in the case of second-generation immigrant children, where there is a cultural break between the generations, while little in the new culture teaches respect for Old World values. It is also true in situations of rapid social mobility, where parents of humble class origin seek to rear their children on upper-class living standards, or where college sons and daughters recoil from the trade sources of family wealth. Finally it is underlined by the influence of the Big Media, which displace the father-hero with the TV, sports, and other popular culture heroes. The more deference the parents pay the child, the less deference they get from him.

In the already child-centered American family this deference vacuum often brings the family close to a child-centered anarchy. This is not because of indifference or lack of love: the attachments are often intensely demanding. In the American variant of the Oedipal "family romance," with a crisscrossing of the mother's concentration on the son and the father's on the daughter, the emphasis is not on the child's moving toward maturity but on the "staying young" of the parent to remain attractive to the child. This is one reason for the extreme American emphasis on youth. As Jean Cocteau put it petulantly on one of his New York visits, "Everyone in America seems so youthful. They all drink milk, as though they were still near their mothers."

If I have stressed here the cultural anxiety about children, I have not meant to imply that American family life is merely ridden with burdens and drenched in anxieties. In the traditional paternalistic families of Europe, Asia, and Latin America, children were almost without rights except what the head of the family granted them. In the recoil the American family has replaced children-without-rights by children-with-too-many-claims, and the transition to a freer structure of family authority has been attended by pains and near chaos. Yet the effort to replace the bonds of one-sided authority by those of mutual consent has meant a social gain. The crucial experimental element has given a new meaning to the child's role in the culture. In no other culture has the rearing of children been so earnestly approached as a problem to be solved, not in terms of conscious purpose or choice but because it grows out of the whole configuration of American life.

Fortunately, in the mid-1950s there were signs that the child panic, as one might call it, was relaxing, and that the cult of the child was giving way to a new perspective which sees both parents and children as worth attention from each other. The popular child experts, like Benjamin Spock, were those who counseled parents to go back to their instincts and rely on common sense. There was a trend toward firmer discipline and a reassertion of the personality of the parents.

But the problem reached deeper than merely that of freedom of discipline, *laissez faire* or authority. At its core is the question of how young children can best be given an effective start on the road toward growing up, without too many crippling limitations. There were things about this process that Americans had not yet learned, but which they were equipped by many of their traits to understand.

One was the idea that parents educate their children less by what they say than by what they are in their totality—by their body stance, their muscle tensions, their rhythm of life, their anxieties or repose, their fears or courage. If this is true, then it follows that effective love —so necessary for healthy emotional growth—cannot be transmitted to a child by a parent who sets no limits on him and who clearly does not value himself. A child must learn how to deal with freedom as a reality principle, which means that he must learn the nature of the limits staked out for him in the primary group of the family, and the reason for them. He will thus more confidently discover the area within which he can make his own choices, more effectively than if he were confronted by either tyrannical or too indulgent parents. As he finds both his limits and his freedom, he will feel that the parents have helped him find them and will take it as a mark of their concern and love for him.

This is linked with another idea—that of the effective model and the sense of identity. During the early years when the child forms his crucial image of himself and of his future role, he may miss the firm model of a self-respecting adult and encounter instead the anxiously wooing parent who pours love into him, exacts it in return by a love imperialism, demands always that the child prove himself worthy of love, and makes the granting or withholding of love the guerdon or punishment of the child's behavior. With this blurred model, the child is bound to fumble in his efforts to discover his identity. Parents who have lost their own identity in their anxiety about their child cannot expect thus to help him find his. Similarly those who live in the shadow of their children—who sacrifice so that their children can spend, or stunt their own lives in order to live in the right neighborhood for their children, or hold a loveless marriage together "for the sake of the children"—cannot complain if their children get a distorted view of personality.

Finally there is the idea of the child's having a functional place in the family. One of the losses in the passing of the large, rural, traditional family was the loss of function for the children. But there are utilities to be rendered, functions to be performed, and crises to be met in the family type of every era, and this applies as much to the new American family as it did to the old. When the child helps to perform these utilities, fulfill these functions, and meet these crises he learns to fuse responsibility with freedom. At the same time he will be measuring himself against brothers and sisters, and other children of his age outside the family; and he should encounter as many adults as possible so that he may have a choice of models broad enough to give him the freedom to find his own identity and individuality.*

4. Growing Up in America

THE GROWING UP years are not easy in America because the choices to be made are so many and the securely prescribed areas of conduct relatively few. I shall deal in this section not so much with the biological

---

* See also, on the family and mental health, Ch. IX, Sec. 8, "Life Goals and the Pursuit of Happiness"; on the problems of TV and "comic books" for children, Ch. XI, Sec. 2b, "The Reading Revolution," and Sec. 6, "Radio and TV: the World in the Home." On the folk heroes of the American child, see Ch. XI, Sec. 3, "Heroes, Legends, and Speech," and Sec. 4, "Spectator and Amateur Sports."

universals involved in growing up as with the interplay of the biological, the emotional, and the cultural in the American frame.

In his early years the child is mainly concerned with the discovery of his body and its functions, and with his emotional relations to his parents and family. He "catches on" to social experience as well, but it is largely filtered and mediated, as if by osmosis, through the envelope of the family. As the child grows into adolescent, and the adolescent in turn into the young adult, the agencies by which his personality and character are shaped broaden out from family to community, from immediate kin to the whole social milieu. These are the years of the "latency period" in the Freudian description, when little is really latent, followed by the period of puberty and its immediate consequences. They are the years when the young American, bursting with discoveries and searching always for new experience, reaches outward from the family to the peer groups of school and "camp," to street gangs, cliques and clubs, sand-lot and water-front sports, dating and dressing, odd jobs, summer adventures, college, and military service.

The American family does not let go of him early but tries to hold on as long as possible, recognizing his need for self-reliance but anxious to protect him and eager to enjoy him. Unlike the British, it does not push the boy abruptly into the "public school," where he is away from home and wholly on his own, subjected to the cruel rules and taboos of his fellows. It allows the boy or girl to make the break away from home by easier stages—at first in the "summer camp," whose use is growing among middle-class parents, then perhaps in a private boarding school (still confined to the upper income groups), finally (for the boys) in the Army. This blending of home and away-from-home experience is one of the things Americans are learning to do best, although one must remember the large number of still overprotective parents who cling to the child, and the equally large number of working-class parents who let him drift off into a job of his own as soon as he has passed school age or been in a trade school. There are also the middle-class parents who send him off very early to a military academy or school on the convenient theory that he will learn independence and discipline but actually to shift to someone else the burden of the decisions about his rearing.

On the formal level the qualities he is taught, both in the family and the peer groups, are those that will fit him best into the competitive race: to be resourceful, industrious, persuasive, friendly, popular, an easy mixer, strong of purpose, inventive, self-reliant. The emphasis in a mobile society built on immigration is on outdoing your parents—getting a better education, marrying into a better social stratum, making more money, living in a better neighborhood and with higher living standards. The traits stressed are those of packaging your abilities in the best salesman's fashion, and of a constant quality of *push*. These traits, inculcated and renewed in each generation, take on a cumulative strength in the culture. They leave little room for the withdrawn and reflective personality, who may be detached from the competitive struggle. In fact, when American parents or teachers find these traits in a boy, they may regard them as signs that he is "badly adjusted" and in need of therapy.

Some American scientists, like W. H. Sheldon, see the physical constitution as shaping temperament and even character, and a number of biologists stress the "built-in" mechanisms which set the frame for all growth. Yet there is little of determinist thinking in the attitude of most Americans toward the growing-up years. The pluralism of stocks, the high living standards, and the strides in medicine, all tend to disarrange any preconceived frames of physical growth for Americans and put the stress on will. Similarly, the stress in popular thinking about personality and career is not on the limits but on the potentials of development. "Be a king in your dreams," said Andrew Carnegie to the young American. "Say to yourself, 'My place is on the top.'"

Thus the young American grows up to see life as a cornucopia spilling its plenty into the lap of those who are there to take it. Within the limits of his family's income, and sometimes beyond it, there are few things denied to the growing son and daughter. Their attention is focused on what they can *get*, first out of their parents, then out of life. The growing girl learns to get clothes and gifts from her father and later from her husband. The boy fixes his attention on a succession of artifacts, from a toy gun and an electric train to a car, preferably a convertible. Their levels of aspiration stretch to infinity. Often the parents are blamed for this pliancy and indulgence, yet it is also true that the culture, with its sense of plenty, contains the same principle of infinite possibility. It tells the boy that if only he wants something hard enough, even the Presidency of the nation, he can achieve it. This spurs his striving but it also sets unrealizable goals, since his capacities may not equal the tasks he sets himself, or his class and status handicaps may be too crippling. Thus he misses the sense of security which one gets from the compassable. No limits are set to his goals, and often he reaches for incompatible sets of goals. Rarely does he learn the tolerance of deprivation or the recognition of limits which are a matter of course in less dynamic cultures and which exact a lesser psychic toll than the sense of infinite possibility.

Such an oceanic sense of possibility has its elements of strength for the boy or girl in growth. The feeling of impasse that so many of the youth of Europe have, in cul-de-sac economies where the job chances are narrow and they feel they must break through doors shut against them, does not crop up often in America. It is hope and not hopelessness that runs like a repeated chord through the growing-up years. They are the years in which heroisms are dreamed, tight-lipped resolutions made, values first crudely formulated. The emotional life awakens in all its tumbling confusion, the imagination ranges far, the lights and shadows of the moral life are accented, the shapes of good and evil take on their most intense forms. Anything is possible, and everything is fraught with far-reaching meanings. There is a sense of limitless potentials, of obstacles to be overcome by a surpassing display of energy and talent. At home, as in school, the archetypal prizes held up are the big ones and the stories told are the success stories. There is a constant demand for vitality, in season and out, regardless of whether it is charged with meaning. The emotional dangers that the young American runs are not those of apathy or despair but of anxiety about success or failure. He finds it hard to keep from wondering whether he is swift and strong enough to win in so exacting a race. Even within the minority ethnic groups, with their residual sense of status restrictions, the young American feels the pressure to succeed within the standards of the minority mold, or even to break out of it—especially to break out of it. And if he fails he cannot assign the failure to his goals or society but only to himself.

Growing up with the assumption that he will "make his mark" and "knock them dead," he is rarely allowed to forget that he lives in an expanding civilization in which he must accomplish "bigger and better" things. Just as he is enveloped by the sounds of cars, trains, planes, so the symbols investing his life are those of speed and movement, violence and power—the symbols of competitive drive. They don't have to be preached to him: they come through the culture-in-action. He picks them out of the air—from how his family behaves, from what his teachers and schoolmates say and what he reads and hears, from the men and careers held up to him for emulation.

Asked for more than he feels he can fulfill, he comes in turn to ask more of his family and milieu than they can fulfill, with a resulting insecurity and bleakness of mood. He turns to his age peers to find with them the expressiveness and sense of kinship not to be found among their elders. Their families may be too distraught to pay much attention, or too protectively concerned with providing for their children's outward wants to be able to gauge their inner nature with wisdom. An adult society, with churches that seem distant and "preachy" and with spinster-staffed schools that seem only an extension of the nursery, offers little that exacts loyalty or heroism from young people who are hungry for both. Their hunger arises from the fact that when they are torn away from the primary ties to their parents there is no corresponding growth in their confidence of their own strength. They yearn for the sense of belonging which will restore those primary ties, and they attach them now to agencies of their own peers.

Into this vacuum come the teen-age activities, some of which amuse the elders, while others worry them. Among the first are the hero worship of the gods of popular culture, the love affair with the TV screen, the calf-love obsessions that turn the teen-agers "girl crazy" or "boy crazy," the jazz or jive madness that "sends" them. Less amusing are the "hot-rod" frenzies in which they court mechanized suicide, the escapades of bored baby-sitters that break into the headlines, or the sexual antics of the high-school "non-virgin" clubs which shock parents and teachers without jolting them into an understanding of their emotional sources.

There is a passage in Thomas Wolfe's *You Can't Go Home Again* describing "the desolate emptiness of city youth—those straggling bands of boys of sixteen or eighteen that one can always see at night or on a holiday, going along a street, filling the air with raucous jargon and senseless cries, each trying to outdo the others with joyless catcalls and mirthless quips and jokes which are so feeble, so stupidly inane, that one hears them with strong mixed feelings of pity and shame." Wolfe asks "what has happened to the spontaneous gaiety of youth," and answers that these youngsters "are without innocence, born old and stale and dull and empty . . . suckled on darkness, and weaned on violence and noise." In his *Studs Lonigan* novel sequence James Farrell shows similarly the social violence and cultural emptiness which condition the emotional bleakness of a boy's life on the city streets.

Yet in his formative years the city boy, especially from the working class, learns more—bad and good—from the gang than from any other group except the family. The gang is a group on the margin between rebellion and crime, forming a clannish community in play and war against parents, elders, teachers, police, and rival gangs. Sometimes it is a harmless effort of normal youngsters in a disturbed and impressionable life phase to huddle together for human warmth, sometimes it is a desperate attempt to channel floating aggressions. The gang brings into the emotional vacuum of the boy's life a structure of authority which makes demands on loyalty, on spartanism in the face of adversity, even on honor and heroism of a sort; above all, on a sense of acting together. That is where the boy learns crudely and even brutally the mystery of sex, the warmth of friendship, and the heady sense of prestige gained not through class position but through strength and natural leadership. It is ironic that the lack of effective codes in the larger society should leave the gang codes as the only substitutes: or perhaps these are only negative parallels of the middle-class codes from which the boys (most of them coming from the lower classes) feel themselves shut out as from an Eden; and so they turn the Eden upside down into a Hell. But even the gang codes prove tawdry and worse as the gangs move over the margin into the pathology of violence and rape and crime.

Not many young Americans follow them that far. But most of them look back to the adventures of their all-male peer groups as their time of expressiveness. It may be that the gang gatherings on city street corners, the loitering counter at small-town drugstores, and the cross-roads taverns in the rural areas where you smoke and buy cokes and play the juke boxes are for American boys the playing fields of Eton.*

What is true of the gang for the urban working class is also true of college for the educated classes. It is remembered as the Golden Age of their lives. It has relatively few economic pressures and is the last phase of growing up, just before the boy breaks wholly from the tutelage of family and local community and goes off on his own. It makes its demands in terms of prowess, popularity, and prestige: intellectual content in most American colleges is secondary to friendships, fraternities, "contacts," "bull sessions," sports, and the furious crossfire of campus politics and extracurricular activities. The boy can wreak some of his strongest drives on college life, including heroisms and hero cults, fierce intellectual loyalty, combativeness, the sense of honor, the straining of nerve and will for a cause which at the time seems real enough to evoke an effort beyond the human. In most college novels, as in Scott Fitzgerald's *This Side of Paradise*, there is always an Amory Blaine—a grown man who goes back nostalgically to the time at college when he caught a forward pass and wooed a beautiful girl. They may be mock battles and mock victories, a preparation for something that in the end fails to come off. But here too, as with the gangs, the later remembrance of these rivalries and loyalties reveals them as an outlet for youthful energies that the growing boy does not otherwise express.†

What happens in the process of growing up in America is an emphasis on the individual that results in a feeling of separateness with-

---

* For more on the teen-age gangs, see Ch. III, Sec. 9, "City Lights and Shadows," and Ch. IX, Sec. 5, "The Disorders of a Society."

† For the college as a sub-culture, see Ch. X, Sec. 3, "The Higher and Lower Learning."

out the quality of distinctiveness. The growing boy (or girl) is taught by the whole cultural environment to assert his individual self, and the way he is expected to find himself is by breaking his ties with his family and rebelling against parents, teachers, neighborhood. In the process he wrenches himself free of bonds and codes, only to find himself isolated from what had given him security. He comes to miss most the sense of belonging, or relatedness, to the "primary ties." Much of the feeling of loneliness in the growing-up years comes from this sense of loss and isolation, and the yearning to recapture the primary ties from which he has been too sharply separated.

In the families where there is close contact between parents and children, in a freewheeling, affectionate atmosphere, these ties can be recaptured adequately enough to tide the child over until he has made ends meet in his personality struggle and is on the threshold of adulthood. It is true that the old cohesive relations, which families had when they did their work together and had to stick together, have largely been lost. But with the new leisure there is a chance for families to spend vacations together, go on automobile trips together, watch and discuss the media programs together, talk and play together. This does something, if not enough, to alleviate the sense of isolation. It is in the families where this closeness of relationship does not exist that the yearning to belong is left unsatisfied. They may be families where both parents are at work, or where the father is hardly ever at home, or where alcoholism or grinding poverty or lovelessness creates a destructive vacuum. At the other extreme they may be families which, even with a high living standard and an outward show of affection, are emotionally empty. It is from the families at both these extremes that most of the cases of failure in the growing-up process come.

I must add the factor of discrepancy between class perspectives. Most commentators on American life have moved away from discussion of class experience and class conditioning. Yet much of the human material that comes to grief in American society will be found in the working class, in the case of youngsters brought up in working-class families and working-class neighborhoods but surrounded everywhere by middle-class and leisure values. That is to say, their subculture is a working-class subculture, while the larger culture is a middle-class culture. Their whole sensate world of striving and their glory dreams are middle-class strivings and middle-class dreams. Yet they find themselves shut out of the world they long for, much as Adam and Eve (as I have suggested above) were shut out of Eden after the Fall by a flaming sword.*

* For an elaboration of this theme, with respect to the "mutiny of the young," see Ch. IX, Sec. 5, "The Disorders of a Society."

Thus the "opportunity line" which exists for young people in America, given its rapid class mobility, is accompanied by an insecurity line—or better, by an isolation line. There is scarcely a culture in the world where the longing to belong in the growing-up years is as intense, and where the failure to satisfy it is as destructive of the potentials of personality.

When a culture trains young people there is much that it tries to train out of them. Growing up thus becomes not only a process of *inculcation* of the socially approved virtues, but—shall we say—of *exculcation* of the socially disapproved ones as well. Thus there is a need of exculcating the primitive sense of equality with which children start. In the early years before the social norms begin to harden, as I have noted above, the children of every stock and religion play together: only later does the society teach them what is expected of them. Lillian Smith, in her novel *Strange Fruit*, pictures a beating a young Negro mother gives her small son when he has dared dispute something with a white boy: she must show him that his mortal life is in peril if he does not observe the man-made fence between him and those who hold supremacy. And from the side of the whites, Miss Smith has told how "the mother who taught me what I know of tenderness and love and compassion taught me also the bleak rituals of keeping Negroes in their places—which could be applied to other minority groups as well." The mingling of status groups becomes less frequent as the child moves through the grades into high school and college, and goes dating and dancing and week-ending. The growing-up process in America involves the loss of the social innocence with which children start.

Similarly, the growing boy is taught to develop mainly his vendible talents. "I couldn't stand Asheville now," Thomas Wolfe wrote in one of his remarkable letters to his family from college. "I couldn't stand the silly little grins on the silly little drugstore faces. I couldn't stand the silly little questions of 'What're you doing now?'—and the silly little 'oh' and the silly little silence that follows when you say you are writing."

For all except the strongest-willed youngster (and Wolfe was one) the cult of the vendible means the exculcation of other talents and impulses. Neither family nor school can protect him against these tyrannies of the culture: for are they not themselves caught up in the same tyrannies? So they discourage "woolgathering" and "daydreaming," which lead nowhere, get you into mischief, don't pay off as action and business do. Rarely is a protective sheath thrown around the contemplative impulses that are as crucial in the growth of personality as the impulses to action. Rarely is there support for the brooding exploration of the whole enriching range of emotional life in a culture as complex and paradoxical as the American. In the end the children become themselves the taboo-enforcing censors, and anyone violating their canons of orthodoxy is an outsider, a "square," a "goon."

This is reinforced on the side of the parents by the pressure to "mix well" and be "popular"—but within socially acceptable groups. The impulse toward popularity flows at once from the cult of success and the shaky self-image of its devotee. It narrows the complex realm of personal relations to the art of manipulation. Tragically, it cuts the child from his fellows just at the phase where such a severance is most destructive to him. For the tissue of human connections cannot be reduced to the manuals of popularity. Which may explain why, in the most glittering of cultures, so many Americans are scarred—as Fitzgerald's Jay Gatsby was all through his years—with the sense of having lost what they have so insistently been taught to capture.

To strive for popularity, yet to feel alone and unwanted; to hunger for use, yet to go unused; to carry the sense of comradeship like a burning city in your heart, yet to have to extinguish it in order to keep your position in the hierarchy; to replace the idle impulse and the brooding intensity by the attitudes of Faustian power, of violence, of speed and aggrandizement: for all too many youngsters this is what growing up comes to mean.

Aside from what the society tries to inculcate into him or exculcate from him the growing child has a double task of preparation: for making a living and for making a life—one, the problem of finding a career; the other, that of finding himself. In the case of the girl—except in the instances where she is in earnest about a career—the two preparations are merged into the preparation for marriage, which is viewed as both a living and a life. With the boy the pressures are to give primacy to making a living, so that he finds himself thrust into choosing the job or career for which he must train before he has gone far enough in his emotional unfolding to have much basis for choice. The result is often a gnawing conflict between what is expected of him and what he finds welling up within himself, rebelling against the plans for him.

Both processes—of finding himself and finding his vocation—involve the boy's spur-winning. He measures himself against the strength of his age peers, of his older brothers, even his father. A time comes when his father notes proudly that the son has caught up with him in stature and strength, and even towers over him. He has a "paper route," mows lawns, shovels the snow off sidewalks, does odd jobs after school; in the summer he perhaps overestimates his age to pick up some quick money in a factory or at the shipyard. He saves his money carefully to buy some prized possession, with the calculation of a junior capitalist. He starts learning the trades, skills, tactics out of which competence and success will later come. In American society his expected growth as a person takes largely the form of the kinds of spur-winning that lead into a career and into business habits. And the way he is assessed by his elders and assesses himself is also in those terms.

The American theory is that a boy "chooses" his job or career. For many, however, the choice is narrowly restricted. Sometimes the limited choice of jobs, especially on the lower-class level, is frustrating and embittering. Sometimes, however, it may be a saving fact physically, since it does not burden the boy with the sense of inadequacy which a middle-class boy has when he finds few choices where there are supposed to be many and comes to blame himself. To avoid this self-doubt he may be more precipitous than is good for him as a person. The process John Milton described, of seeking what was to become his epical life work—"long choosing, the beginning late"—is a luxury that most Americans deny themselves. Even at college American students (like German university students as well) are anxious to choose the courses that will lead directly into their chosen career and thus give them a start in the competitive race. Only a good deal later do some of them come to understand the cost that the personality had to pay for their career haste. But in a culture so nervously paced and so poised for the big killing, any other choice is difficult.

On some scores it is easier in the American case than in others. There is not the same need to rebel against a tyrannical father, or the same galling sense of being caught in a blind alley with no chance either to develop or show one's abilities. On other scores it is harder. The boy (or girl) comes to biological maturity a good while before either of them comes to emotional maturity. The society—permissive in so many other respects, restrictive in this—cracks down on sexual expression before marriage. In the case of the boy, the military draft has recently become an organic part of the life cycle: while the sexual taboos are relaxed for military personnel, the all-male society and the severe discipline of the Army conflict; and the need to postpone both career and marriage during the most crucial years is a chafing one.

From the parents' behavior and their responses to his own the child forms the crucial image of himself. He has a need to understand and emulate his father's job, as the girl has a need to play house, but a job at "the office" is a hard one for the boy to use as an effective model, and often the substance of the job slips out of the child's mind and all that remains with which he can identify himself is its aura of respectability or power. In an earlier society, where the struggle with nature and the conquest of animals had meaning, the boy's spur-winning might take the form of the hunt or the fishing expedition. Americans today who read Faulkner's long story, "The Bear," or Hemingway's *The Old Man and the Sea,* find it hard to attach much meaning to the hunt for the killer bear or the apprenticeship of a boy to an old fisherman, since it has no parallel in their own experience; yet they are drawn to such stories because of this vacuum in their growing up.

Their own spur-winning experiences are likely to follow more closely the pattern of the American boyhood in *Tom Sawyer* and *Huckleberry Finn,* with the swimming hole, the fence-painting, the treasure hunt, the bloodcurdling oaths of gang secrecy, the cult of male separateness from females. One of the striking facts of this Mark Twain tradition of boyhood is its emphasis on both the "badness" and the maleness of boys. Every American boy is expected, as he grows toward his teens, to be intractable about soap and water, to look (whatever his family's means) like a ragged and tattered waif, to resist the blandishments of school and teachers, to be awkward with little girls and flee their advances, and to regard any dancing class or other frippery as a conspiracy of the Devil. This tradition of the good-bad boy is one the elders cherish as part of their recognition that the American household and school are governed by a regiment of women, and its antifeminine bias (included in the anti-"sissy" complex) is the price they pay for continuing that government. From the boy's side, however, it is part of the necessity for breaking away from this domination and of finding who he is.

In the process his reading helps him, and it is notable that he seeks out the reading about bad men (the old frontier and bandits have given way to whodunits) and science fiction. In the city life that has replaced the farm and frontier, spur-winning gives new forms to the old activities—learning how to smoke and swear, hearing about sexual exploits, showing athletic prowess, taking part in school pranks and escapades. One can view this as the impact of crowded city life on the boy, but it is better to view it as part of the quest for identity. "Who am I?" the boys asks, and his answer is first given in terms of being part of a male peer group.

Then in the teens comes the further process of awakening identity, in which he splits himself from even his earlier boys' groups. He is breaking away from the ways of a child but has not yet learned the ways of an adult. He goes to parties and dances, he needs spending money, he works and saves in order to learn his own nature: for it is his own job, his own car, his own girl, that he now wants. Even in his courtship he is perhaps less concerned with erotic aims than either Freudians or Americans generally suppose and more concerned with that ceaseless problem of probing and parrying by which adolescents of both sexes come to discover their identity. They want their own sense of rightness, grope for their own codes. This is where they come to feel most split away from their elders, and that struggle between the generations which the parents find so intolerable an ordeal emerges most sharply. In fact, the two generations become almost subcultures, the younger one finding both its goal and its modes of expression within the new social situations more readily than the older one.

It is in the teens, unhappy as they are because of this struggle and the difficult quest for identity, that all the new wealth and excitement of social experience in America impinge on the young people. They experiment with adult modes of consumption, learn the terrifying ways of speed and travel, enter into the kingdom of the Big Media. They are able to move about the country, trying themselves in a variety of occupations. The typical American first novel, for example, is likely to be a novel of these apprentice years, and every first novelist puts on his dust jacket the calendar of his job and migratory experiences, just as he is likely to focus his story around his boyhood, with its trials and triumphs. The critics may continue to call for a novel of manners or of mission, but the kind the American first writes is either a novel of adolescent unhappiness or one of the tribulations of early life and loves, and at the end of it the hero has finally discovered who he is.

I have not meant to say earlier that America crushes every diversity and irons out the nonconformers. The adolescent finds ways of evading many of the cultural pressures and often grows adept in the process of finding his own growth pattern in spite of them. Success and power and competitiveness are not the only American growth goals, even though they are the principal ones. For they are only one aspect of the individualist ideal. The other is self-fulfillment, and the young Americans (sometimes a minority) who learn how to know themselves are on the way to learning how to become themselves.

They develop, in the process, a life style which they partly shape and which partly is shaped for them, inside the frame of their work, their class, their locale, their culture. They have first to find some models on which to mold the personality through imitation: they find them in their parents, older brothers and sisters, teachers, age peers. Out of these and out of the personality images presented to them in the culture as a whole they form an ideal image of self toward which they probe experimentally as they play one role after another, fitting each of them on for size and looks in the mirror of others as well as of themselves.

But in this copying and playing of roles a dangerous clash takes place

—the clash between what I want to call the *cultural image* of self and the *identity image* of self. The cultural image is the one borrowed and imposed from without, and inevitably it tends toward conformity. The identity image is one that emerges from the quest for a distinctive self-hood and is the product of a continual interplay between the individual's need and whatever measure of cultural elements he is able to absorb in growing up. The clash is always there because there has been no culture in history in which the individual has been able to ignore the cultural demands and pressures. But where it is too great the result is alienation on the one hand, or else an overreceptiveness to the cultural pressures in order to resolve it, or else some form of breakdown. Yet there are unmistakable evidences that the child growing up in America is learning to make the resolution tolerably well. When he does, there is a richness of the final personality style which is itself both the index and product of the difficulties encountered in the process of growing up.

5. *Courtship, Love, and Marriage*

LOVE COMES IN the American's life cycle as the harbinger of life's fulfillment, with a violence of expectation characteristic of a culture built on promise. "Love is sweeping the country" ran a tune in *Of Thee I Sing*—the Kaufman-Gershwin musical which was a satirical take-off on star-spangled politics and on the national pastime of being in love with love. More than any other people, Americans believe in love and make a cult of it, lose themselves in it and feel lost in it. Every French schoolboy, it has been said, dreams of becoming a *flaneur*, happy in his numerous erotic affairs. The young American schoolboy is more likely in his daydreams to see himself the sole and successful wooer of a creature who combines Hollywood contours with the steadfastness of Penelope; and the young American girl is eager for a handsome young man who will be coveted by her rivals but will cherish only her forever. They expect obstacles in their quest: how could there be victory in the scheme of romantic love if there were no obstacles to be overcome? But they expect also to triumph over them, as witness the moot Hollywood formula: boy-meets-girl, boy-loves-girl, boy-wins-girl. If the girl whom the American middle-class or working-class boy is likely to meet has not always the long-limbed, busty perfection of the "pin-up" girls or the prize winners in the annual "Miss America" contest, the courtship is nonetheless carried on within a frame of idealization and is suffused with a springtime eagerness.

The roots of this need for love go back to the emotional structure of the American family. The child, asked constantly whether he loves and assured he is loved, learns that love can be a weapon in the emotional power struggle of the family, to be granted as reward or withheld as punishment. Thus he comes to test the success of his relations with the outside world by whether he is accepted and loved, and is more swayed by a panicky fear of deprivation than by the expectation of love and bounty. By becoming an early life goal, love is made part of the calculus of failure and success.

The emphasis on parent-child love yields, in the life history, to the later romantic love, and perhaps some of the psychic mechanisms are carried over from one to the other but with a strongly different emphasis. The romantic ideal came into the Western tradition from the Middle Ages, when it emerged as passionate love. Denis de Rougemont, its most learned and astringent historian, traces it intricately back to the Cathar heresy, which held that the Devil had intervened to complete God's work. The current of passionate love came into the main stream of Western sensibility through the "medieval courts of love," the love lyrics of the Troubadours and Minnesingers, and the Tristram-Iseult story.

It is pretty clear that this ideal of passionate love came as a reaction against the anti-erotic strain in Christianity and the cult of virginity, and that it was a convenient literary way of providing a cover for the new erotic energies of European society. It started as an aristocratic and feudal idea, but it flourished best in the middle-class societies of Europe, giving rise to the European novel and drama. It reached its most intense form, however, in American culture, with its novels about romantic love, its slick-paper magazine stories, its Hollywood formula movies, its radio "daytime serials." Neither the heritage of guilt left by the Puritan tradition nor the mechanization of American life—the two great enemies of romantic love—has succeeded in destroying it. The Puritan heritage, with its *Scarlet Letter* pattern of shame and secrecy and its furtive pleasures stolen in the face of harsh community punishment, led to a recoil which actually strengthened the hold of the romantic cult. As for mechanization, love in the American machine age is still, in its ardor and intensity, closer to the old romantic tradition than it is, let us say, to the new Puritanism of another machine culture—that of Soviet Russia.

The crux of romantic love, in this larger Western and American frame, lies in two elements: the conviction of uniqueness and the submission to fatality. Behind the quest for the love partner is the premise that there can be for each person only the exactly right "one person." Love in America is thus an intensely individualist emotion in an intensely individualist society. The fatality idea, on the other hand ("falling in love"), is a deposit left from earlier societies where star-crossed lovers drank love potions and thereby committed themselves to the destiny of their love. It is true, of course, that the romantic ideal of the ordinary American is borrowed not from the Tristram-Iseult theme and the Arthurian cycle but from Hollywood; yet the Hollywood image, in turn, is taken from the fiction writers whose obsessive theme reaches far back. What the Tristram-Iseult legend has shed in its sea change is its death sequel and its tragic overtones. Instead of committing himself to death, the American lover surrenders to the irrationals of his passion, but the target is life and happiness.

Thus the American has taken over a medieval theme and has shaped it to the temper of his society, combining the strain of fatality out of an earlier era with the strain of uniqueness out of his own. The American stamp, however, has become so dominant that even the fatality emerges largely as uniqueness.

One reason the American is obsessed with romantic love is that it is the only socially acceptable secular escape from the iron individualistic prison of himself. It is one of the few instances in which the philosophy of free will is swept away by a sense of submission and fatality. Here is the point in the life cycle of the American when he ceases to play God in his own universe, losing himself in a passion of surprising power and in the play of forces that for once seem to be not of his own choosing but to possess an awesome inexorable quality. The surrender of the American to love has about it for the moment an appearance of completeness not frequently found in other cultures. In each great Henry James novel—*The Portrait of a Lady, The Ambassadors, The Golden Bowl*—the sophisticated detachment about love comes from the foreign partner to the match, the sense of love as compelling and absolute comes from the American. There are suggestions in James that this may be because the American brings to whatever he touches a fresh and generous energy that contrasts with the somewhat jaded feeling of the European. It is more likely, however, that the impulsion comes not from surplus energy but from the loneliness of the American and his impulse to escape from it into a secure harbor where he can find the absolute of love with his loved one.

This overvaluing of love is reflected in contemporary American fiction. The creative novels dealing with love take it seriously as the great business of youth—in many cases as the only lasting life value. But one must add that it is also a literature compounded of violence, disillusionment, and frustration. In Dos Passos's documentary trilogy of American society, *USA,* the characters (mainly on the make) use love as a commodity of exchange, and are incapable of anything but its hollowest forms. Ring Lardner's short stories (as in "The Love Nest") lay bare the heartlessness behind the show of heart. In Faulkner the symbols of love are often associated with the violence of incest and rape. In Farrell the *Studs Lonigan* worthies gang up on a girl in a drunken brawl and use her in succession. O'Hara portrays with compassion, in *Appointment in Samarra* and *10 North Frederick,* and with more violence and disillusionment in *Butterfield 8* and *A Rage to Live,* the defeat and dissipation of the generous impulses of love. Even in Hemingway, whom two generations have found deeply moving, the symbol in *The Sun Also Rises* is that of a mutilated incapacity for love, in *A Farewell to Arms* it is the cup dashed from thirsty lips, in *Across the River and into the Trees* it is that of a mingled ritual of war and eroticism. I cite these almost at random, not as an accurate transcription of the operative force of love in American society but because the reflections of American attitudes in the minds of sensitive and creative writers, however transmuted, are an index of what people believe about themselves.

In an acquisitive society, moreover, love somehow is charged with the power and violence of the acquisitive drive. It is as if the two circuits had become crossed, and the way Americans feel about money and success had got tangled up with the way they feel about love. There can scarcely help being some continuity between economic success and erotic success in a culture where both are viewed as forms of prowess. Consciously or not, the American carries over into his erotic life the drives of his economic life. This is especially true since the days of courtship are also those in which the adolescent is preparing to make a start in his career or in the Armed Services. On the threshold of manhood, he is concerned about proving his strength to himself and to the world. With a sketchy sex education, casually acquired through the family or distorted in transmission by the "gang," he is often a prey to feelings of inadequacy and guilt. In such instances he cultivates love not as a creative relationship between like-minded people but as a testing ground for his virility. Courtship becomes a matter of personal success in a quest whose goal is that of proving oneself. In marriage also the man who is a hardheaded competitive businessman or corporate executive outside comes home to play the role of tender husband and father. Money talks during the day, but love is expected to dominate the evening and night. These shifts from one mode of personality to another make it hard for many Americans to discover their sense of themselves on which the art of love depends. The sense of loneliness, the hunger for fulfillment, and the search for identity become tangled with the compulsion to power.

For Americans, courtship is localized in the later adolescent years. By the age of seventeen, when the American boy is likely to be a high-school senior, he is (at least quantitatively) somewhere near the threshold of his sexual powers; and at eighteen the pattern of his later sexual behavior has been pretty well foreshadowed.* Thus the five or six years after seventeen, when the boy and girl seek a mate, are also (at least for the boy) the years of fully awakened sexual interest and activity when both partners are looking for the new personal experiences and sexual adventures. This double purpose and the crisscrossing pattern of biological drives, social pressures, moral intuitions, and inner anxieties make these years at once troubled and eager. These are the years of "dating," of dancing and driving together, of "necking" and "petting," of "going steady" or "playing the field." However constricting they may seem to the young people themselves, they are years of great freedom, if one compares the American culture with most others. Since an American strives to marry for love this involves a far greater variety of courtship experiences than where marriage is arranged or moves in highly traditional grooves or is severely held within class lines. The American conception of love-as-encounter is possible only in a society of relative physical and class mobility and the free mingling of the sexes.

There are considerable class differences in courtship practices, ranging from encounters on campuses, at proms, house parties, and "deb" parties and night clubs at the top levels, through movies, "church socials," and bathing beaches or resorts at the middle levels, to amusement parks and taverns at the low-income levels. "Pickups" are likely to be somewhat casual on the lower level, sophisticated on the top ones, most frowned upon in the middle classes.

Yet what all the classes have in common is the institution of "dating," which foreign observers regard as strikingly American while the Americans themselves take it for granted. To "have a date" is the raw material of courtship; to date the same partner a number of times is a sign of being smitten; to change dates frequently is, on the other hand, a token of being heart-free; for a girl to be "dated up" is proof of being "popular," and (as on any market) the high rate of demand enhances the value of the commodity. Thus, in what Willard Waller has called the "rating-dating system," there is a reciprocal valuation process by which dates are made on the basis of popularity and sexual attraction, but both sexual attraction and popularity increase wi.h the number of desirable dates each partner has.

What has interested students of American society even more than the rating system is the ritual of granting and withholding favors. The boy is expected to make advances, to boast of his prowess and conquests, to exult over each step of kissing, "necking," "petting," and to aim at the

---

* For a further discussion of sexual behavior during courtship and marriage, see Ch. IX, Sec. 7, "Society and Sexual Expression."

ultimate sexual surrender. The girl is expected to yield just enough to keep her partner interested, yet to withhold the final sexual boon. Put in this way American courtship seems loveless and joyless, a calculated exercise in prestige and self-satisfaction. It has been ironically described as such, particularly by observers with an anthropological training, who view it as they might the rituals of a primitive tribe. Geoffrey Gorer has called it a "competitive game of chess," and Margaret Mead has defined a successful date as one "on which there is no petting at all, but merely a battle of wits, of verbal parrying, while the boy convinces the girl that he is so popular that he has the courage to ask for anything, and the girl convinces the boy that she is so popular that she has to give nothing." Compare with this the more common view, shared chiefly by anxious parents and teachers, that young Americans even of the high-school age are teen-age Casanovas and Liliths, experts at seducing and being seduced, members of "non-virgin clubs," practitioners of the wildest promiscuity, little monsters who are wise in the ways of contraceptives and old before they have grown mature.

Each of these divergent pictures has enough core of truth to make it believable. The violence of some of the adolescent sex behavior is the result of rebellion against home and school repressions, and embodies an effort to use sex as a weapon of power or as a way of buying personality acceptance. The mechanical elements of much of the dating complex—at once loveless and sexless—go along with any ritualized behavior.

But it would be a mistake to consider this a meaningless ritual. Much of dating involves the effort of each partner to find his identity—to discover the limits of acceptance and rejection, to exchange experience with an age peer who shares his problems and perplexities, to explore the corners of another's personality, and therefore of one's own. Both the boy and girl know the human and social costs of too easy a conquest. Their "necking" seeks to avoid the emotional entanglements of a liaison, without complete abstention. It is their way of setting limits for themselves and mediating between the conflicting pulls of the biological impulse and the social code. Dating is thus a way of welding in courtship the need for marriage choice with the impulse to experiment. Obviously this requires at best a high degree of skill, and what some have viewed as heartless calculation in a mechanized society may be seen better as the diplomacy and statecraft of courtship, including power politics, strategic maneuver, cold war, and the peace that passeth understanding.

The attacks on dating and the defenses of it have both lagged behind the actual institutional change. The dating pattern, without being replaced, is being supplemented by a petting-and-pairing pattern which is really a form of early, steady, and sustained dating. Those acquainted with American college life have observed the growing tendency of sexual inhibitions to break down at the last moment, especially for girls seeking emotional security and the knowledge that they are desired. "Necking" has been to some extent replaced by what Kinsey called "petting to climax." In fact, this is the most marked of the very few changes in the pattern of overt sexual behavior in American life since the "sexual revolution" of the 1920s. Kinsey's figures show that by the age of twenty almost half the college-level boys have taken part in such petting, while this applies to less than a fourth of the grade-school-level boys at that age, and that the frequency on the college level is three times as great. The same study shows also less frequent intercourse as part of dating than on the grade-school level. Assuming that the college-level partners set standards of courtship which are followed by the others at a time removed, one may hazard that young Americans are seeking a way of expressing their sexual drive while maintaining technically the community forms and the sense of limits.

There seems also to be a growing tendency of daters to "pair off" very early and for extended periods. Dating in the strict sense of rapidly shifting fencing matches is being replaced by the "steady dating" where a boy and girl stress continuity rather than experiment. The "pairs" may last during a whole college year, or even during most of the four years; more and more frequently they are found even in the early high-school years and may stretch on after college, during the years when the boy is in a professional school or trying himself at a job. Usually, though not always, they lead to formal "engagements." What they represent is something distinctly this side of the experimental "companionate marriage" which was so moot an issue in Judge Ben Lindsey's time; it is a semi-companionate of two young people who have no living quarters together and who may restrict themselves (often they do not) to "deep petting" with both its satisfactions and frustrations, but who nevertheless are together almost constantly and are recognized as a "couple" by their friends. Especially in the early high-school years the result may be precocious sexual involvement (which is the basis for the stand that the Catholic Church has taken against it in parochial schools), or it may often become an *égoïsme à deux* which narrows social experience long before the marriage itself. Yet often also it is a working compromise between the necessity of postponing marriage and the wish for a constant compatible partner. It must be seen as another expression of the craving for psychological security among the younger Americans.*

I have spoken above of the debt of American romantic love to the medieval ideal. The great difference is, of course, that in medieval cul-

* For more on moral codes and the succession of the generations, see Ch. IX, Sec. 6, "Morals in Revolution."

ture romantic love was a frill to embroider the institution of chivalry and a make-believe ritual under whose cover the women of the knightly order could get release from the bleakness of medieval marriage. It had its being outside the marriage vows and was in fact hostile to the marriage institution, which was a product of caste and church and which excluded romantic love. But in the American case romantic love looks to marriage as its fulfillment. Pouring so much into courtship and expecting so much of marriage, Americans find themselves frequently disillusioned, as witness not only the divorce figures but the disgruntlement and smoldering conflict in many of the ménages that hold together. The slick-paper love stories generally end with orange blossoms and wedding bells: beyond that, all is silence; but American novels about marriage are usually problem novels. It is not that the path of love is smooth in the courtship novels: by its nature it cannot be, for romantic love feeds on obstacles; but in marriage, the love obstacle turns into conflict, frustration, and often a sense of desolation. In courtship the obstacles arise from an outside source—family interference, religious or class differences, economic difficulties—and the lovers face them together; but in marriage the obstacles become conflicts *between* the former lovers inside the marriage relation, and the feeling of facing them together is dissipated.

This may explain why Americans associate the idea of romantic love only with the premarriage years: afterward they are likely to speak of love ironically as of a deflated ideal or of a pleasant but foolish dream. The young wife has perhaps had in her mind an idyl of marital suburbia acquired from magazine fiction and the movies. The husband finds perhaps that his earlier image of his wife as June Allyson in an apron is jarred by the reality of crying babies, economic worries and tensions that make sexual understanding difficult. The result is the well-known marital "letdown." Yet it is characteristic of Americans that neither husband nor wife wholly discards the romantic ideal. The wife continues as its principal carrier, reading the novels and poems, seeing the movies, continuing the daydreams of a not-impossible-he. The husband, with more preoccupations outside the home, may plunge into his job, haunt his club or lodge, or find on "back streets" the concealed liaison which suggests that he has not abandoned the love ideal. More often perhaps than the critics are willing to admit, the partners resolve their conflicts and find a depth of epic quality in love-as-marriage that they did not find in the lyrical love-as-encounter. In other cases a merely tolerable working solution is reached, with a grudging working arrangement inside the marriage tie and sexual adventure outside, or else with frustration and neuroticism as the steep cost of the maintenance of the tie. More and more frequently divorce is the outcome. But the rate of remarriage among the divorced is so high as to suggest that Americans get divorced not because of disillusionment with marriage itself but because they believe in it deeply enough to want to be part of a successful going concern rather than a bankrupt failure.

It is idle to urge Americans, as recent moralists and "marriage counselors" have done, to abandon the ideal of romantic love and base marriage upon more rational and stable concerns. In a much discussed polemic novel, *Marjorie Morningstar,* Herman Wouk has his heroine turn away from her illusions about romantic love to a safer, more secure and more rational marriage that fits better with the traditions and way of life of her Jewish ethnic group. Certainly the novel expressed a current counter-trend to the great Western myth of fatality and uniqueness in love. But it is something of a misnomer to speak of the "cult" of romantic love in America. It would be better to call it part of the folk belief, which hangs on tenaciously in the American mind even when there is so much to shake the faith in it, very much as the belief in a wholly open-class system hangs on. In fact, there is some relationship between them. The American believes in romantic love not only because of the mystique of fatality but also because of the sense of choice and possibility it carries. What both partners hope to get from a love marriage is happiness; and while at any time it seems that only one person can bestow it, the finding of that one person is an act of free will appropriate in an open-class society, to be tried again if it fails.

Obviously the freedom of marriage choice is also largely myth, at least for many. There are class limits, income limits, race limits, the accidents of geographic and ethnic closeness. You may dream of a rich, handsome, and gallant corporate executive who will swoop down to woo you, but you actually marry the boy down the street, whose mother knows your mother and who gives you his high-school fraternity pin to wear. Only the very attractive and successful have anything like a large range of choice. Many young men, in their awkwardness and fear and their income limits, settle for something less than Helen of Troy. For many middle-class and lower-class women, who don't want work or a career of their own, or are fearful they will lose their value on the marriage market, marriage becomes a way of finding a means of support and getting status in the group. Sometimes money becomes important enough to cut across the field of choice, as with Lily Bart in Edith Wharton's *House of Mirth.* Lily Bart will not marry merely for money if it will demean her socially, but she has been brought up to the view that a marriage of love *without* money is an intolerable fate: thus her values are conventional values, not money values as such, but under the conventions there is a money base.

There is also another and deeper sense in which marriage choice is not free: even in the most romantic matches the American is likely to seek out the partner who is selected not by his conscious choice but by stronger unconscious currents which flow from his character structure and his early life history. What applies to courtship applies also to the years after marriage, as attested by a symposium published in the mid-1950s on *Neurotic Interaction in Marriage,* in which a number of psychiatric writers point out that two neurotic partners may out of their unconscious drives make life intolerable for each other or—by some Freudian destiny—may luckily find that their neuroses intermesh.

Since Edith Wharton's day Americans have increasingly made happiness the test as well as the goal of marriage. Were I to say that this has been a movement from the romantic to the hedonic ideal, I should be distorting both of them somewhat, since the romantic ideal in the American setting always had an element of pleasure in it, and the quest for happiness does not end with the libidinal pleasure principle. Yet it would be at least a half truth. The American wants happiness out of marriage, and he believes in a love marriage not because he makes a cult of love but because he thinks there can be no happiness when love is wholly lacking. This leaves Americans vulnerable to the charge sometimes made, that marriage is but a joining of two *egotisms*—a mutual orgasm pact between two self-centered individuals, maintained not until death do them part but only as long as desire remains fresh.

But this is unfair. Marriage in America is no more to be summed up as a transient pleasure pact than as a permanent maintenance pact. In part, it has elements of both. But mainly it is an earnest partnership quest: on the part of the man, for someone with whom he can achieve self-expression and build an effective going concern; on the part of the woman, for self-expression through children, a home and the status it brings, and the figure she can cut in her group. These are human goals but not ignoble. And in their restlessness they express the dynamism and mobility of American society.

A study by Geoffrey Gorer (*Exploring English Character*) concludes that an English husband wants his wife to be a good housekeeper, an understanding and faithful person, and a good cook—in that order. The English wife wants her husband to show understanding, a sense of humor, moral qualities, fidelity and generosity. There is little stress on beauty and attractiveness, on financial ability, on sexual qualities: only in the prosperous classes does the question of sexual compatibility in marriage assume any importance. By contrast a successful American marriage is closely linked with love, with financial competence, with continuing elements of attractiveness, and with sexual compatibility and fulfillment. Thus the British marriage criteria have to do more with personality factors and with making everyday life smoother, while the American criteria (as I have suggested above) are at once more romantic and hedonic.

The American situation has its drawbacks. American husbands and wives develop anxiety about whether they fulfill each other's expectations. Young married people read the popular sex and marriage manuals, both to prepare themselves and to overcome whatever difficulties they may encounter. Often the manuals are helpful in dispelling ignorance and fear, sometimes they produce more anxiety than they allay. American husbands and wives tend to worry overmuch about their sexual adequacy and performance, just as they worry overmuch about bringing up their children. But these mark the growing pains in a rapidly shifting cultural pattern—a sign that Americans have not yet found themselves in their happiness society and wonder whether they are getting out of marriage everything they should be getting.

Nor do they complain about sexual incompatibility just because they make sexual gratification an end in itself. If they did they would seek for gratification outside, as husbands did in European cultures for centuries, when prostitution served to bolster the institution of "respectable marriage." The reason this is less true in America (professional prostitution has grown less important in America) is because they feel that sexual response is crucial for love and for personal expressiveness, and that both are integral to marriage as a going concern. The American husband does not pose as the family boss, as his grandfather did; and he wants much more out of marriage than the sense of power and authority. Similarly, the American wife is coming to feel that marriage is a joining of partners, each of whom is a person in his own right. Both of them see a chance to enjoy life and find personal expressiveness, and they don't want to be left out.

This unwillingness to be left behind and cheated out of important life experiences is assuming importance in the minds of Americans whether in or out of marriage. It may be the negative phase of the happiness quest, but it is not negligible. It is too easy to see American life wholly in terms of power and glamour and the sexual experimenting of *avant-garde* intellectuals. One thinks of Sherwood Anderson's novels and of the stories in his *Winesburg, Ohio,* and the record they offer of the hunger of obscure people for a sense of connection. America is, at least in part, millions of such obscure lives, seeking at least one event that will transform the humdrum into the meaningful. That is why Nathanael West, in his novel *Miss Lonelyhearts,* chose as the central symbol for his novel a newspaper hack who runs an "Advice to the Lovelorn" column and—still possessing a capacity for empathy—suffers every day the crucifixions of the agonized letters he gets. More often these columns, which are an established part of the American press, are saccharine in content, and sometimes cynical in their conventional values, advising the questioner not only to forgive her *fiancé* or understand her husband, but sometimes to resort to callous strategies in holding him. For all the vaunted camaraderie at the service of American life, the individual has a sense of isolation. It is the fear of loneliness which also helps account for the high rate of remarriage after divorce, and for the forlorn men and women who join "Lonely Hearts Clubs" because they recoil from evenings spent alone and want someone to talk to.

Despite the fears of marriage decline commonly expressed by commentators and moralists, the marriage rate in America has not shown signs of falling away, as in the often invoked case of the Roman Empire. While population increased 14½ per cent in the decade of the 1940s, the number of married couples increased almost 24 per cent. With all the cultural forces (the rise in living-standard imperatives, the longer span of professional and technical training for careers, the required period of military service) pushing in the direction of marriage postponement, the "propensity to marry young" seems if anything to have more than held its ground. The median age at which American girls marry has dropped to 20.4 years; the husband is likely to be only two or three years older. Some moralists have attacked this as a sign that the American girl doesn't want to work and is eager to be taken care of as early as possible; others interpret it to reveal an eager sexuality on the part of both that cannot wait to be fulfilled. But, as I have noted, the Kinsey figures and the growth of the "pairing-off" pattern show that the sexual impulse is not wholly unfulfilled even before marriage, and the increase of married mothers holding jobs to supplement the family income shows that they are not entirely lazy.

The propulsive force leading to early marriages must be sought elsewhere. In both cases the clue is the pursuit of happiness. For the woman it is likely to lie in a home, children, and social status, for in the woman's case—far more than in the man's—marriage is the determiner of status. For the male the impulse to marriage is not—as Freud suggested, with his eye on the European social structure—to emulate the image of the father's family authority. For the American male it is rather the desire to be part of a family which is a going social unit, with a wife who is a good homemaker, a good mother, a good hostess, and wears clothes well; and on her part, with a husband who has a good job, is respected in the community, is a good father, and has a circle of friends with whom the couple can "spend the evening." Both partners are told often enough that the marriage may fail, but they take the risk because for them the stakes are crucial.

The hazards of marriage in America are real enough. The boy and girl about to be married are constantly advised to make sure of their ground. A pamphlet intended for high-school and college students lists —among the "test of love"—the test of the "electric spark," of "time," of "separation," of "companionship," of "crisis situations." But, with all the warnings, mate selection (as I have suggested above) is more likely to reflect hidden and unconscious drives. It is part of the new folklore of American marriage counseling that the best marriages are those based upon what has been called the "myth of common interests," and that husband and wife ought to concern themselves with the same range of interests and friends. Yet this is to stress the rational approach in an area in which the demands of the irrational cannot be overlooked. In marriage, as in love, it is the covert drives rather than the overt rationalizations that are commanding. The sense of the uniqueness of the loved one is likely to be a recognition of the striking extent to which he (or she) meets one's psychic hungers, which in turn are the unconscious product of the whole buried life experience. When these psychic needs and values dovetail and supplement each other there is a "meeting of true minds"; when they clash or are irrelevant to each other the result is conflict or vacuum. A successful marriage must thus manage to meet not only the conscious purposes and life goals of the two partners tolerably well but also their unconscious drives.

The probing of marriage failure in America has been intensive. The principal causes usually listed are incompatible temperaments, loss of attraction of the partners for each other, infidelity, money worries, and quarrels. The statisticians have even charted the most dangerous years of a marriage, when divorces are most likely to come. But it is a mistake to think that these tensions arise wholly from the marriage relation itself. They reach further back to the life cycle of the partners, each of whom is likely to reproduce in his marriage role the characteristics he developed during childhood and adolescence in the emotional structure of his family. They reach back also to the society itself—its economic demands, its tense rhythms, its stress on glamour and security, on sensuality and power and success. One thinks here of John O'Hara's best fictional portrait—that of Julian English in *Appointment in Samarra,* beset by economic difficulties which help turn his sexual life into barren and violent gesturing, until the fear of losing both his business and his wife's love breaks up his marriage and drives him toward a tragic suicide. Thus the marriage relation has to bear the total burdens of the personality and the society.

There are no people in the world who make greater demands upon marriage than Americans do, since they lay greater exactions upon it and also expect greater psychic satisfactions from it. They do not make the necessarily right demands, but whether right or wrong, they don't settle easily for a small fraction. Again the comparison with the Gorer study of the English may shed some light. The English husband and wife don't ask for the stars plus sexual fulfillment; they don't restlessly demand happiness, nor do they worry so much about extramarital errancy. The difference between the two situations may be the difference between a more established society which has resigned itself to a limited economy and a diminished place in the frame of world power and a more swaggering society with an expanding economy and a feeling of unlimited life chances.

Yet alongside this earnest quest for happiness one may find in American culture a bitter folklore on the tribulations of marriage. There is a mythology of comic-strip quality dealing with the bored husband and the bridge-playing wife, the hardened husband who pays the bills for the many hats his wife buys, the tired husband who comes home from the office and doesn't take his wife's conversational gambit seriously, the husband with a roving eye and wife with a prim policewoman's vigilance, the husband who talks ironically of his wife as "my better half" and "my ball and chain," the husband and wife who are engaged in a cold war of extinction and survival. This cruel public banter reveals a good deal more than it intends. The ritualistic buffoonery of a people is likely to convey in its overtones more than a hint of the accumulated frustrations and aggressions that are to be found along with the swagger and the power.

The more serious concern is with the problem of marriage fidelity and infidelity. I shall deal later* with some recent findings on extramarital sexual behavior in America. What is of interest here is the paradox of a culture in which sexual infidelity has become extensive but is not taken lightly, and is a matter of great anxiety and concern. This again is part of the experimental pattern of American marriage, in which the evasion of moral standards is not a matter of moral disintegration but of a quest for personal fulfillment within a shifting frame of morality. As with most other problems, Americans tend to view infidelity as a question of mental health, usually as part of the crisis of the middle-aged male in his search for sexual reassurance. The psychiatrist is likely to say that it is only the compulsive types of infidelity that present a serious problem, since their compulsiveness makes them self-destructive—and therefore destructive of others as well, and of the whole family pattern. In other words, instead of thinking of infidelity

* See Ch. IX, Sec. 7, "Society and Sexual Expression."

as a rigid moral category Americans tend to think of it in terms of what it does to the personality and to the web of relationships. Yet this does not mean, again, that Americans take it lightly. When it is dealt with in an American novel, unlike a French novel, it is treated as a crisis matter, where the failure to resolve it leads to the destruction of the personality. This is also the way American novelists treat the problem of incompatibility within marriage, with an emphasis on the emptiness it leaves inside the personalities of both partners.

Judged in terms of viability, a large number of American marriages are failures. The high and steadily increasing divorce rates* have given great concern to commentators who regard it as the sign and proof of the disintegration of American culture which will make it topple as the Roman Empire did. Some writers have compared divorce with bereavement and the divorce trauma with the trauma of the mourning period. As William Goode puts it (*After Divorce*), they think thus because they tend to feel that divorced people ought to suffer for breaking up the romantic American image of marriage. Studies like Goode's, based on field interviews in Detroit in 1948, should lead to some revaluations of long-standing American myths about divorce.

Foremost among these is the tendency to attribute divorce to the willfulness that comes from wealth and materialism, seeing it as a special middle-class disease which is rampant among the spoiled and neurotic who can afford it, while the simple lives of the working-class folk are presumed to be less riddled by it. No doubt there is some relation between the laxity of divorce standards and the laxity induced by American creature comforts and material values. But divorce in America is not the prerogative of the rich. The available studies show that there has been an inverse relation between class membership and the divorce rate: that the service and white-collar groups and the unskilled labor groups show a higher divorce rate than the skilled labor, professional, and managerial groups. Thus the divorce rate is higher among the lower-income classes and is lower as the income rises.

The reasons are complex. Partly they are economic: when it is hard to make ends meet in family maintenance, the irritations pile up and the clashes of personality are heightened; similarly, a comfortable economic margin may make many irritations tolerable. Moreover, a wife in the upper-income groups may find that there is a wide gap between her living standards within marriage and her living standards as a divorced woman (this does not take account of the mounting alimony figures), while a working-class wife may find that she can do almost as

---

* I have already touched on the subject of divorce in my discussion of the family: see Sec. 2, "The Family As Going Concern."

well with a job of her own as with a ne'er-do-well husband. The evidence shows, at any rate, that divorce is not due merely to the self-indulgence of the rich or of the Hollywood elite whose marital difficulties enliven the press headlines and the weekly picture magazines. It is true that studies of families during the Depression years show a shifting of divorce figures with the changes in the business cycle, with a lower rate in the "hard times": the grimness of economic reality presumably pulls the marriage together and dispels fancied hurts and secondary grievances. But a closer study, by Mirra Komarovsky, shows that the Depression strengthened certain types of families but weakened others. Thus, economic pressures, whether in good or bad times, are rarely to be seen as final causes of the breakup of marriage or of its strengthening: they are important mainly as they express themselves in the psychological postures of the two partners toward each other. It may be true that marriage is largely a maintenance contract, but it has a psychological as well as economic structure. It is the shift in American attitudes, rather than the materialism or prosperity of the economy, that accounts for the changes in the marriage institution.

The question of the divorce trauma is an elusive one, and certainly no one will underrate the impact of anxiety, sleeplessness, and heartache. But the evidence fails to back up the belief that divorce in America is shattering to the personality. Goode found that once the final separation was achieved, even before formal court action, the psychic shock tended to lessen, and when dating began again the post-divorce adjustment was on the way. While the statistics are not wholly clear, most divorced persons (as I have said earlier) pay marriage the homage of trying again, and in many cases they make a success of it where it had been a failure before. This is not to say that the divorce experience improves the stability of marriage. The figures show that a marriage is more likely to break up if one or both of the partners have been married before than if they have not. Yet it remains true that for the divorced woman her second marriage is likely to prove more stable than her first.

The greatest anxiety that Americans show about divorce is about the children of divorced parents. There is no question that they suffer in divorce—not necessarily from the divorce itself but from the conflict it involves and from the separation from one of the parents, generally the father, since American courts, by a curious quirk of gallantry and a tenacious belief in mother love, almost invariably award the children to the mother. Yet the mothers who remarry report their belief that the lives of the children are better than they were before the divorce, when they were the victims of an atmosphere of lovelessness and conflict.

The important shift in American attitudes about marriage has been the tendency to believe more deeply in the possibilities of finding marital fulfillment. This carries with it an experimental feeling toward marriage, with divorce seen no longer as a final disaster but as a temporary setback in a continuing quest. What is relied upon to hold the marriage together is not the religious and social prohibition of divorce, or even the extreme legal difficulties placed in its path in some American states (notably New York), but the feeling of inner unity that expresses itself in the sense of a going concern. In its deepest currents of feeling the American consciousness is now more apt to condemn a marriage entered into or continued without love, than even a love relationship outside of marriage. A Soviet professor recently charged that "bourgeois marriages are mere business matches in which love gets dirty and trampled." This was even wider of the mark than most Communist utterances on Western societies. The burden of concern that Americans feel about marriage has been shifting away from the economic toward the psychological, from the maintenance contract toward the pursuit of happiness. The whole question of sexual activity, which was once considered a phase of moral codes alone and only incidental to the marriage relation, is now viewed as an integral part of it, and sexual fulfillment has become one of the prime tests of marital happiness.

In fact, it is here that American marriage has developed a new area of vulnerability. With the quest for happiness, as with the fight for social equality, great expectations feed on themselves, and every new gain means a more critical view of the gap that remains between reality and promise. The high divorce rate does not necessarily mean that there is more unhappiness than there was in American marriages, but only that there is less propensity to accept unhappiness as part of the eternal frame of things which cannot be mended. Americans have become more watchful of unhappiness and more clamant in their demand for an expressive life. This means a far greater emphasis than ever upon sexual fulfillment, whether in or out of marriage; it means a sharper conflict than ever between moral codes and operative behavior; and it means, for that reason, a resort to the marriage counselor, the psychotherapist, and the pastor as well as to the divorce courts.

The changing patterns of attitude and behavior on marriage have thrown the courts into confusion, as the "crazy quilt" of divorce decisions testifies. They have also thrown the older moral standards into confusion. Premarital intercourse and adultery tend to be regarded as only venial sins: the mortal sin is coming to be considered the lack of a productive life. Someone has remarked that, given the different pace at which the partners may develop, marriage is a "mutual mobility wager." What has happened to the American attitude toward marriage, as it has happened to the family and society as a whole, is a growing earnestness about making the whole pattern work without sacrificing the values of individual independence and fulfillment. The emphasis here is not just on the self-indulgent individual but on an effective partnership. A viable marriage has come to depend on whether the two partners keep pace with each other in their sexual rhythms, their attitudes toward children, their awareness of the world, their structure of values, and whether they "work at" the marriage in the sense of putting their creativeness into it.

6. The Ordeal of the American Woman

RARELY IN HISTORIC civilizations have women been as free, expressive, and powerful as in America: yet rarely also has the burden of being a woman, and trying to be a fulfilled one, been as heavy to carry. That is one of the many paradoxes which characterize the social role of the American woman. Everything in American life seems to conspire to make her a glittering, bedecked, and almost pampered creature, yet also one bedeviled by a dilemma that reflects the split both within herself and her culture. She is torn between trying to vie with men in jobs, careers, business, and government, and at the same time find her identity as wife, mother, and woman. The tussle between them accounts in great measure for the ambiguous place she holds in American society and for the frustrations and neuroses commonly associated with her.

The growing-up years of the girl differ from those of the boy. She is welcomed less enthusiastically: to the low-income families she brings consuming rather than earning power, to the middle-class families she presents the problem of being married off. She is shunted away from the "gang" in which her brothers are accepted and must exchange giggly and self-conscious confidences with "girl friends." She feels left out. Yet she is carefully tended and decorated, taught how to wear clothes by her mother, pampered and worshiped by her father, and given by both a greater degree of independence than in most contemporary cultures. It is, however, less independence than her brother gets: one of the consequences of her training is that her sheltering as a girl by her own family makes her more dependent on her husband after marriage.

She is more closely watched than her brother, by the family of which she is part, by the community outside, and by the censor inside her. Since she is considered the frailer vessel, she must be shielded; since she is to marry well, she must be marriageable; she must be careful not to cheapen herself, not be "talked about," to encase herself in the triple armor of inaccessibility. A small town or suburb, where everyone knows everyone and where the Puritan heritage in morals still lingers, is especially stifling for her. As a result, many a small-town girl seeks the blessed anonymity of the big city. Yet even there she is plagued by her dilemma: with one side of her she wants an adventurous and exciting life, but another voice tells her that she lives in a culture where few women can make a go of it on their own, and where therefore she must find the marriageable male who will invest her with security and status. As for the city girl, especially in the minority ethnic groups, she too is encased in a protective armor of what is "expected" of her.

This means the narrowing of her range of absorptions until they focus mainly on what makes her feminine and desirable. The American male, who specialized in the lamp of power, has left the lamp of beauty to the female. In fact, America's greatest work of art may well turn out to be the American woman, from sixteen to fifty, whether stenographer or society belle, shopgirl or movie queen. She is known the world over for her pertness, her spirit, and her looks, for the contours of her figure, the smartness of her clothes, and the vitality of her person. Some of this derives from the image left by the spread of American movies, but mostly it is the deposit left by her place in her culture. Simone de Beauvoir has said, "One is not born a woman. One becomes it . . . by the ensemble of civilization."

The American woman, who must accept the assumptions of romantic love and also those of the merchandising economy in which the sale depends on the packaging, channels her pent-up energies largely into dress and decoration. She finds here an expressiveness and feeling of power that are not balked as they are in other channels. She finds available in the economy around her an array of fabrics, colors, furs, jewels, cosmetics, and even in the middle and lower income groups she finds copies of expensive items scaled down (almost) to her ability to pay. In decorating and beautifying herself she discovers a talismanic admiration, "dates," popularity, and the right kind of husband, all of which are counted as signs of female success. As she grows older, some of her hopes fade, her jauntiness wilts, and she must work harder to contrive lesser effects, but the task itself she dares never relax.

Out of this arises what the advertising copywriters call the "American look," on the premise that the American woman does have a *different* total look from that of the Roman woman, Chinese, British, Latin, or Russian. It is hard to distinguish the reality from the *imago*, which the movie magazines, TV, the advertisements, and the "pin-ups" have projected, representing the American male's dream symbol. In some ways the image is almost a Petty or Varga caricature, with shapely silk-clad legs longer than the torso, with small waist, narrow hips, long neck, swollen breasts, pert features, dilated and inviting eyes, blond or red hair, sinuous body, and an expression at once vacuous and sophisticated, helpless and predatory. In actual statistical measurement and look the average American woman falls short of this dream, as the range of motley sizes and shapes in women's clothing testifies. Yet the cultural ideal is often approximated in height and slenderness, ankles and legs and contours, and even where it is not its hold is tyrannous.

The effort to approximate it has absorbed generations of skill and concentration, the suiting of techniques to taste and to the prevailing modes and moods. I shall discuss later* the shifting codes of fashion that have governed the cycles of American taste in women's dress and profile from the crinoline-and-stays period, to the Gibson girl, to the inter-wars flapper, to the current norm I have tried to describe. Within these larger and baffling cycles there are the whims and tyranny of the short-run changes in fashion on which whole industries may be built and by which they may be ruined. For the Goddess of the Right Thing is an exacting one. She demands specialized clothes for city and week end, for work and play, school and church, for beach, ski resort, mountain re-sort, for the seasons and sub-seasons, for evening and afternoon, for the shopping trips themselves—so that by an endless circuit one must dress correctly in sallying out to buy the things which will dress one correctly. She demands also the matching of the elements of the en-semble and the accessories, including hats, hair-do, shoes, stockings, handbags, gloves, jewelry, and furs. On the level of the Big Money this Byzantine profusion is, of course, achieved without much difficulty. Where it hurts is in the middle and low income groups, but even there —by smart buying of low-priced "copies"—one manages to respond to the unrelenting demands.

Being "smart" means, for the American woman, staying within the frame of fashion but adding her own individual touches. Her skirt length must be neither too long nor too short, her suit cut must be in style, her hairdo must not depart too far from the fashion magazines. All this involves an array of handbooks of fashion, from the expensive fashion arbiters like *Vogue* and *Harper's Bazaar,* through *Charm* and *Seventeen,* down to the picture weeklies and even the cheap movie magazines: in fact, the movies themselves serve many women as tips for clothes. The editors of the fashion magazines have become female Napoleons ruling their domains. Yet even they can rule only by giving their subjects room for individual creativeness. The lipstick, compact,

* See Ch. IX, Sec. 3, "Manners, Taste, and Fashion."

hatbox, shopping list, become part of a freemasonry which give scope to the most impassioned rivalries, out of which come the artistries of a minor art, perhaps, but one carried on at a fever pitch.

The arts of advertising and salesmanship lose no chance for encouraging this rivalry. If the American woman were in danger of forgetting a moment about clothes and cosmetics, lingerie and nylons and "foundation garments," deodorants and perfumes, the advertisers make sure the lapse is brief. "It is our job," said the head of a trade association of women's retail stores, "to make women unhappy with what they have in the way of apparel and to make them think it is obsolete." From every side there are focused on her the cozenings and admonishments of advertising, using every technique from open seduction to concealed terror. The models are languorous, the images sensuous, the language tactile and erotic.

Yet for all the tyrannies and blandishments with which she is surrounded, the American woman remains the center of the constellation. Are we wrong in sensing some of the qualities she thus expresses: *triumph* ("see the richness of my setting"), *boredom* ("what's new? what's different? what's a bit shocking?"), *craftsmanship* ("I'm an artist, and I am my own work of art"), and *seductiveness* ("take me—I'm trim and smart and the slightest bit expensive, but that's all the more reason for taking me").

The miracle is that with all this world of make-believe she has not succumbed wholly to its tyrannies. She has kept a measure of independence, wrecking many a big investment built on the premise that she would follow the command decrees of the great designers and clothes manufacturers. Even in the elite arts of dress and decoration, steeped in the vocabulary of exclusiveness, the democratic note has been sounded ever more insistently. The language of the fashion magazines and the advertising copy has increasingly become that of a democratic snobbery —an exclusiveness that includes shopgirl and stenographer along with debutante and young Park Avenue matron. Mail-order fashions, patterns for those who do their own clothes, mass-production models that are a triumph of cheapness and taste, "home permanents" that have cut into the role of the beauty shops—these are part of the great paradox of the American woman as artist and artifact.

I have already discussed* the strategic role of the American woman as organizer of consumption. But her economic function is only part of her larger social one, shaped by a series of changes so drastic that

* See Ch. IV, Sec. 5, "The Wilderness of Commodities."

they are usually spoken of as "revolutions." The most continuous American revolutionary is the American woman.

First there was the *suffrage revolution,* as part of the long, hard-fought movement for equal rights in which a succession of strong-minded women, in the face of jeers and humiliation, broke into previously barred professions and won the right to an equal education with men, to speak in public, to vote for and hold office. Second, there was the *sexual revolution,* directed against the double standard of morality and aimed to gain for women some of the same privileges of sexual expressiveness as the men had. Coming in the wake of the equal-rights movement, it was a phase at once of the revolt against Puritanism and of the dislocations caused by the first World War. Related to the revolution of morals was, third, the *revolution of manners,* with women shedding their cumbersome garments and adopting form-fitting clothes and revealing swim suits and shorts, taking part in sports, driving cars and even piloting planes, serving in wartime as WACS and WAVES, smoking cigarettes and drinking in public. Fourth, there was the *kitchen revolution,* with mechanized kitchens and canned and prepared foods giving some women greater leisure and enabling others to get industrial and clerical jobs. Finally there was the *job revolution,* which transformed the American working force as it also transformed women's role in the economy. In 1920 there were eight million women holding jobs; in 1955 there were more than twenty-seven million, comprising over 30 per cent of the labor force. For the first time in American history, married women outnumber single women in paying jobs, although most of the women in clerical and professional jobs are single.

One can see these "revolutions" as a succession of liberating movements. They have come in semicyclical form, each of them with a recoil at the end which overlaps with the start of another cycle of liberation. They have come as part of a double thrust of aspiration, with the American women trying to be equal to the men and therefore like them, yet also to be themselves and find their own identities.

On one score the American woman has not had to struggle for her economic position. While there are no hard figures, the usual estimates are that women control up to 70 per cent of America's wealth, that they have 60 per cent of the savings accounts and are the beneficiaries of 70 per cent of the insurance policies, that they represent more than half the stockholders in the big gilt-edge corporations, that they own close to half of the nation's homes, and that at least three quarters of the nation's purchasing power is funneled through them. The catch is that women hold their purchasing power largely as wives and have acquired their wealth mainly as widows: economically they are disbursing agents, not principals. Or as one unmarried woman has put it with some acerbity: women have trust funds, stocks, and real estate, mainly "because their husbands die early, of overwork for these economic parasites." Not only do American women live longer than men, but many rich Americans who marry for a second time marry younger women who outlive them by a number of years.

But it does not follow, as some would have it, that this has turned America into a matriarchate, or that the American women are idlers who spend their husbands' salaries or clip interest coupons. The real control even of the wealth of wealthy women is in the hands of male trustees, lawyers, and bankers. Few women are directors of big corporations, just as there are few who form government policies. As for the women in industry, most of them work for a living or to supplement a family income too low for decency. Thus American women, like men, are divided between an elite arrayed in glory and a majority who must work for what they get; and even the minority of women who are powerful in their ownership of wealth are functionless with respect to their wealth, because they lack the strategic control of it.

During the first quarter of the present century the American woman strove for equal rights with men: having achieved them, she has spent the second quarter wondering about the result. The struggle for the vote, for the right to hold and transfer property in her own name and to have legal control of her income, to go to the same colleges and professional schools as men, engaged the stubborn and persistent energies of a succession of woman leaders, from Emma Willard, Mary Lyon, Fanny Wright, Margaret Fuller, Elizabeth Stanton, Catherine Beecher, Lydia Child, Jane Swisshelm, to Jane Addams, Carrie Chapman Catt, and Eleanor Roosevelt. There were career women all through the nineteenth century, but the gap was great; in the twentieth it was narrowed. The boos and cheers that greeted the suffrage parades in the early twenties seem quaint now, when there have been women mayors and Senators, UN delegates, and even Cabinet officers, along with judges, doctors, scientists, commentators, novelists, playwrights, war correspondents. To be sure, a few of the "equal-rights" militants still resent the protective social legislation for women, on the ground that to single them out for protection is to doom them to a subordinate role.

But there can be no question of the glowing victories won in the successive cycles of emancipation. In theory, in law, and to a great extent in fact, the American woman has the freedom to compete with men on equal terms: but psychically and socially she is caught in a society still dominated by masculine power and standards. That is her dilemma.

What disturbs her most is a doubt that what she wants most is her rights. However important the legal and economic struggle, it has brought no ease to her unquiet spirit and her turmoil of mind, and so her heart is not in it.

I do not mean to underplay her effect in humanizing the rigors of a society bent on power and acquisitiveness. The great achievements in the history of American reform movements—in civil service, prison reform, labor and social-security legislation, temperance, social case work, settlement houses, slum clearance and housing, public health and movements for international organization—have owed their patience, passion, and compassion to women. These women may often have acted the Lady Bountiful, and sometimes laid themselves open to derision as caricatures in the Helen Hokinson style. But they have been moved—as Helen Keller and Julia Lathrop were moved, Jane Addams and Lillian Wald—by the defeated and embittered lives of obscure people, and they often showed a capacity to see the world through their eyes. Partly this was because their energies, dammed up by the denial to them of careers normally open to men, overflowed into social protest and swept the men along as well. It was Maria Lowell who inflamed and sustained the antislavery radicalism of James Russell Lowell in the *Biglow Papers*. And no small part of the great role Eleanor Roosevelt played in history was to help keep the power aspects of the New Deal in perspective within the human aspects.

Kept out of the full stream of American power expression, the women often had a capacity few men develop to insulate themselves against the ruthlessness of an expanding young nation. Although Hawthorne was contemptuous of the "damned mob of scribbling women," Henry Adams later said grudgingly, "I suspect that women are the only readers—five to one—and that one's audience must be created among them." It is the view of most American college teachers that the girl students keep alive the flame of the liberal-arts education. American music and literature depend largely upon women for an audience.

In a society tending to grow more militarized, American women blunt the sharpness of the obsession with arms and power. Discussing the history of the Spartan state, Arnold Toynbee points out that the men were caught in the rigidity of overspecialization to arms, and only the women in the end could adapt themselves to changing conditions, winning thus the moral superiority over the men and even the political and economic control. This was not the last time in history that men's concentration on power stripped them of their flexibility and gave the women a moral edge on them. But it may also be true, as Stanley Diamond suggests, that in every culture the woman's concentration on child-rearing and the family provides her with a kind of built-in insulation against cultural shocks which hit men when they are deprived of their traditional social roles. Among the Jews of East European origin, for example, torn from the shelter of the "shtetel" (small town) and its culture, the women emerged as sources of family strength and as the practical tacticians in the new competitive struggle of the big American city.

One aspect of the history of ideas is worth noting here. The cycles of women's emancipation came relatively late in American history. Thus American woman's intellectual and social coming of age, and her alertness to the vanguard ideas of her time, came recently enough so that she was able to equip herself with a less obsolete set of ideas than her husband or brother. This does not mean that American women have been consistently more "liberal" than the men; actually women have tended in party terms to divide pretty much as the men have. Often their desire for the security of the family has ranged them against radical political programs; but by the same token they have been more vulnerable to human values, and in each of the major parties have tended to gravitate toward the liberal wing. Unlike the women of continental Europe and Latin America, they have not been swayed politically by the church authority which in those cultures has made the political role of women a conservative one.

However important the humanizing role of the American woman, her creative achievements at the top level have not matched those of the men. There have been good novelists (Edith Wharton, Ellen Glasgow, Willa Cather), poets (Emily Dickinson, Edna Millay, Elinor Wylie), short-story writers (Katherine Anne Porter, Eudora Welty), dramatists (Lillian Hellman), dancers (Martha Graham). But except perhaps for Emily Dickinson none has seemed to break through to the furthest reaches of achievement. They have been good craftsmen, as Jane Austen and George Eliot were in England, and have shown sensitivity, taste, and insight. But the woman who gets a good start in a career or in writing and the arts seems to falter before the goal is reached. The writers I have mentioned have not shown the sustained strength of, let us say, Hawthorne, Melville, Mark Twain, Henry James, Faulkner, Dreiser. One quality that women seem to lack, in a masculine culture like the American, is staying power. They would have to possess greater self-confidence than they do and be free from the psychic constrictions that come from trying to lead their lives on several levels at once.

But this merely shifts the analysis and poses the question of whether there may not be certain modes of creating that are closer to the feminine temperament and for which the dominant cultural drives in

America offer little scope. One could, for example, conceive of an American woman novelist who might be another Henry James, but not of one who would be another Melville, Dreiser, Hemingway, or Faulkner. We would have to conclude that the main drives in American culture are creatively less assessable and congenial to women than to men, and that the "creative component" in women finds less hospitality within the American cultural frame. For the dominant energies of American culture are power-saturated, violence-ridden, filled with pursuits and triumphs, so that the creative woman finds herself cut off from them and less expressive within them. Hence she turns to the novel of manners, to the short story, to the dance, in all of which she can either operate as a marginal commentator on the American scene or express her own form of protest against it.

This does not mean that the American woman belongs, as several writers have put it, to the "lost sex." She is no more "lost" than her husband or her brother, except that she finds it harder to perform her variety of social roles without feeling the full weight of the cultural contradictions that bear down on her. Like men, she has suffered a loss of function in losing the productive place she once had in the frontier and farm home; nor has she been able to replace it with a sense of new power over the environment, as the men have largely done. But it is a distortion to think of her as suffering badly from a lack of function.

If anything, she is bedeviled by too many functions. She leads simultaneously a multiplicity of lives, playing at once the role of sexual partner, mother, home manager, hostess, nurse, shopper, figure of glamour, supervisor of the children's schooling and play and trips, culture audience and culture carrier, clubwoman, and often worker or careerist. Of the two sexes, it is the man who is specialized to making a living or money, or working at whatever productive job he is doing; the woman, remaining unspecialized, becomes the converging point for all the pressures of the culture. The usual portrait in the foreign commentaries, picturing the American woman as idle, wasteful, and pampered, is not one she will herself recognize. If she has lost some of the stamina of her slightly mythical pioneer grandmother, she has had to take on jobs and problems that her ancestors never dreamed of. She is prized and bedecked as never before, is freer of a tyrannical husband than ever, is equal to him before the law, and has had opened to her a range of opportunities and activities that no civilization before has ever offered to a woman. Margaret Mead's studies have made clear the range and malleability of women's interests and capacities in a variety of cultures: she has added the significant comment that even in the cultures where women do the things we regard in ours as men's prerogative, prestige continues to attach to whatever it is the men do. Thus the relation between prestige and sex status cannot be ignored. Yet what the American woman has already accomplished in a masculine culture and the multiple tasks she assumes and performs show that there is no biologically fated block against her achievement or her happiness.

The crux of it lies neither in the biological nor economic disabilities of women but in their sense of being caught between a man's world which they have no real will to achieve and a world of their own in which they find it hard to be fulfilled. Thus Thurber's famous drawings of the "war between the sexes" (where but in America could so savage a conception, so furiously executed, strike so deep a response?) do not reach that most tragic theme, which is the war within women's own hearts. When Walt Whitman exhorted women "to give up toys and fictions and launch forth, as men do, amid real, independent, stormy life," he was thinking—as were many of his contemporaries—of the wrong kind of equalitarianism. The American woman did it, thinking she was doing it to show she was as good as the man. In the sense that she achieved a new kind of freedom of action for herself and the whole family structure, the movement for equal rights and jobs was a fruitful one. Yet the bobbed hair, the latchkey of her own, the cigarette, the cocktail, the ballot, the pay envelope, proved to be symbols of a quest not so much for equality as for identity. Much of her energy may have been motivated, as the more waspish critics have suggested, by envy of the man, and some of it by a hard-driving emulative rivalry which displaced much of her frustration. But she has primarily aimed at discovering who she is, as a woman and as a person.

She has been kept from finding herself mainly because all her cultural conditioning—in the setting of American equalitarianism and the American economy—has been at once to compete with the man and to manipulate him. As she grows up, her preparation is to find the right man for marriage and marry him before her attractiveness and bargaining power have been diminished. What resources she will bring to the marriage are left to the chance of the individual instance. The whole duty of parents is held to be that of teaching their daughters the code of what girls do and don't do, dressing them to the extent of the family means (and sometimes beyond), giving them accomplishments and schooling, and marrying them off well. As to what will happen after marriage, it is assumed that the sum of her wisdom will be to have children (not too many) and look after them, furnish a house or apartment, keep her looks and figure, build a circle of friends, and prevent her husband's attention from wandering too much. The question "Are you happy?" is more often addressed to the woman than to the man and has come to have almost a technical meaning in the American cultural context, as if to say, "Are you content with your domestic arrangements, and are you getting along pretty well with your husband and children?"

What women become is thus largely what they are expected to become by the standards of a culture in which the male is held to be the prized quarry and the female the lucky or luckless hunter. The ultimate disaster for women is to miss out on getting a husband. In college courses on "Marriage and the Family," readings are included on how and when to make the best use of the opportunities for meeting men; and the newspaper "Woman's Page" often runs a series of tips to unmarried women which take much of their predatory quality from the culture; it is the method of salesmanship and business aggressiveness transposed to the area of personal relations. "You're going a bit far, Miss Blanchard" is the heading of a Thurber cartoon showing a weakly protesting male as the woman carries his helpless body to the waiting couch. But the unhappiness of the unmarried woman is less the cultural problem of America than the unhappiness of the married one. To have caught up with the prized quarry, and then to find that the excitement of the chase is over and there is only a sense of emptiness left, is too common an experience to be set down as a matter of individual unhappiness.

This applies, of course, not only to the woman but to her husband as well. There are mutual antagonisms, rivalries, fears, recriminations. Sometimes the only important thing the two of them have in common is the sense of emptiness. The husband may feel that the wife does not give herself sexually to him in a satisfying surrender. The wife in her turn may feel that after marriage the husband forgets how to woo with either ardor or imaginativeness. The psychic casualties are drastic—not only in the heavy incidence of frigidity among American women and (to a lesser extent) of impotence among the men, but on both sides the feeling that life and happiness are passing them by.

The unhappy wife has become a characteristic American culture type. She may feel that what her husband expects of her is trivial and trivializing. In the low-income groups she spends her best energies as the heroic family economist, but not always with a sense that the heroism leads anywhere. In the upper income groups she is often forced back into the erotic dream world of plays, movies, and novels, into psychoanalysis, even into astrology and spiritualism and all the thousand ways by which a discontented woman expresses the autumn of her discontent. Where psychoanalysts are too expensive, there is no less need for help: a recent American study of "where people take their troubles" has revealed the quackeries and charlatanisms that shoot up like weeds out of this psychic need. The classic studies by G. V. Hamilton and Katherine Davis show to what extent women of all income groups feel themselves sexually unsatisfied, and a number of recent studies—including the insights offered by the Kinsey volume on women—evidence the fact that a substantial percentage of American women find fitful sexual adventures in extramarital relations.* This sense of being emotionally unfulfilled, along with the sense of being socially unused and functionless, combine to create what Pearl Buck has called the "tinderbox woman" in America.

Nor has it helped the unhappy woman to know that she has become the focus of the system of consumption and adornment, the moon that radiates the shimmering surface of American life. What she wants is not to be treated like a well-dressed toy or called "Baby" but to be a person in her own right, with an emotional and intellectual life that makes her a person. As a brainless charmer, who needs to be protected and who learns to manipulate her protector and provider, or—in recoil from that —as the determined careerist who demands the chance to show she equals the male on every level, the American woman finds herself in a blind alley.

One key to her plight is the freezing of models and roles for the behavior of the sexes in the culture. There is an idealized model for both male and female at which each has been culturally conditioned to aim, as an image of oneself and also as an image of one's desired partner. These cultural models may have little relation to the real life goals of the person. As Margaret Mead has suggested, a woman may have a low level of sexual vitality and a slow life rhythm, and a man may in his own terms be of the same type, yet instead of finding happiness in each other, each is bludgeoned by the demands of the culture into aiming at a model of sexual vitality and aggressiveness which may represent the exactly wrong mate.

A similar freezing of roles applies to the whole life cycle of the woman. In girlhood she is brought up to measure her effectiveness by the standards of popularity and success. In her late teens, on the eve of marriage, she becomes the overvalued darling of the culture on whom concentrated attention is lavished, but what she is valued for is her youth and good looks and not any talent she may have or any function she will fill as wife and mother. Once married and started on her childbearing, she is transferred from one frozen role to another, this time as presiding spirit over the home, where she may feel isolated or crowded; the spotlight is shifted from her, but she takes on a series of tasks for which her education has scarcely prepared her. Where the social role of her hus-

* For a discussion of the sexual patterns of American women, see Ch. IX, Sec. 7, "Society and Sexual Expression."

band is that of a man growing to the height of his powers, the ideal of a mature woman is strangely absent in American thinking; from the time she passes the peak of the socially fixed ideal of youthful beauty she feels herself on the downward slope, and much of her psychic energy goes into fighting off her anxieties on this score. When her children have grown up and left the home, she tries again to pick up the old threads of her life, but she no longer has the self-assurance of her youth, nor is she likely to have built up a real competence in any field: she marks time until she is frozen again in the role of an elderly lady whose life is filled by grandchildren and good works.

There are signs, however, that these rigid social roles are being relaxed and more fluid ones are taking their place. There are as yet no signs of a clear direction in which the American woman is moving. But if she is to discover her identity, she must start by basing her belief in herself on her womanliness rather than on the movement for feminism. Margaret Mead has pointed out that the biological life cycle of the woman has certain well-marked phases from menarche through the birth of her children to her menopause; that in these stages of her life cycle, as in her basic bodily rhythms, she can feel secure in her womanhood and does not have to assert her potency as the male does. Similarly, while the multiple roles that she must play in life are bewildering, she can fulfill them without distraction if she knows that her central role is that of a woman.

America has realized better than any other society the vision of Mary Wollstonecraft's *Vindication of the Rights of Women:* yet equal rights do not mean an interchangeable identity with men but scope to lead a diversified life while remaining a woman. In this spirit the American woman is groping for a synthesis of her functions in her home, her community, and her job. Her central function, however, remains that of creating a life style for herself and for the home in which she is life creator and life sustainer. She is learning that she need not lose functions simply because she has talents and because she aims at a productive life which will develop her interests and her inner resources. In using these talents she will not follow what the man does simply because of his prestige in a masculine society, but will seek through them to fulfill her own life style.

7. The Middle and End of the Journey

THE MOST DIFFICULT years in American life are the middle years, when the first bleak intimation comes to a man that he has fallen short of the standards of the culture and his own life goals. He may find that the success he strove for either has not been achieved or has offered little satisfaction, that the tensions of living have left him depleted, and that the pot of gold at the end of the rainbow looks tarnished and insubstantial. The middle years ought to be the pay-off years in the American scheme—the reward for the work and saving and competitive striving. There is a good deal in the recent Kansas City study, covering people in the age span from forty to seventy, which indicates that they are indeed the pay-off years. But there is also evidence that they are years filled with intimations of mortality and with anxiety about the future.

I have spoken of how the American woman, with her children grown up and away, is faced with the problem of picking up again the severed threads of life and finding new interests to fill the emptiness. Something of the same is true of her husband, except that he continues to be absorbed by his job or business. But the mounting crises of life come for both of them in these years: of declining sexual powers for men and the menopause for women, of anxieties about health, of the prospects of loneliness, and of economic and psychological insecurity, of having to face the inner self and finding there perhaps poverty of spirit and failure to grow. These are parts of the life cycle, in any culture, but in the American their impact is greater because the original promise is greater.

Americans live in a rapidly changing culture but, since all their changes tend to be equated with changes for the bigger and better, they are reluctant to face the fact of change in their own bodies and personalities—at least, changes that might be for the worse. Middle age is the time when the individual must recognize that while he lives in an expanding society he is being passed by others in terms of promise and career, and perhaps being by-passed by life itself. His problem is to find a universe of possibility that is not restricted to the shrinking compass of his own skin. In the case of a man he may make a final attempt to break out of that compass, sexually and emotionally, in what Edmund Bergler called "the revolt of the middle-aged man." A woman's restlessness and revolt are likely to take less concrete form, and—especially when her children are grown—are directed into channels of club and community work. In recent years the extension of the life span and the spread of leisure time have intensified the problem of middle age by presenting Americans with the question of what they will do with their leisure during the middle years; but the new leisure has itself also offered a potential solution to the problem in the form of tours and vacations, part-time jobs, voluntary jobs, and the various new life interests that may result.

All this applies even more strongly to the group that Americans call the "aging." I have spoken of the American cult of youth, especially of the growing boy and of the girl on the threshold of marriage, and later of the successful young executive. There is, as I have noted, no pride in the mature woman, and little even in the mature man except to the extent that he may have reached success and power. If Americans in the middle years of the journey, passing over into the later ones, do not accept and value themselves it is partly because they sense that the culture does not value them.

This is linked with the American time conception. The American is usually held up as Exhibit I of the time sense of Western man. Note, however, that he thinks of time mainly in precision terms—the regular reiterations that are like equally spaced pegs on which the net can be hung which meshes together the parts of his world. He has little sense, such as one gets, for example, in Thomas Mann's *Magic Mountain,* of the relativity of time and its changing pace and emotional density. Time, to the American, means make-haste-and-get-to-your-appointment; one minute slips into another and all are part of a democracy of equal quality. There is no cumulation in the succession, no leaving of residues. The movement of time is on a flat plane, so that the passage of time may mean "progress" or growth in magnitudes, but it does mean a three-dimensional qualitative development and growth.

Given this time conception, it is natural for the culture to treat the old like the fag end of what was once good material. It requires a different sort of time conception to see that a man who has ceased to be a hustler may have deepened thereby, and that the urgencies may have given way to something of greater value. The most flattering thing you can say to an older American is that he "doesn't look his age" and "doesn't act his age"—as if it were the most damning thing in the world to look old. There is little of calm self-acceptance among the old, of the building of the resources which give inner serenity and compel an outer acceptance.

There is correspondingly little cultural valuing of old people. One finds nothing like the Japanese reverence for ancestors or the valuation the Chinese set on the qualities of the old. Since the American has been taught that success belongs to push and youth, it is hard to revere those who no longer possess either. One can be fond of them, tolerate them, take reluctant care of them, speak whimsically of their crotchetyness and frailties; but these are far from the genuine homage of heart and mind. To build a code of conduct toward the old requires not only personal kindliness but generations of the practice of values from which the old are not excluded—of which indeed they are the summation. The cement of the filial relation crumbles. Where there are few codes of honor, it is difficult to build a code that will pay honor to the old.

Every culture has what may be called a style of aging, as it has a style of growing up and a style of maturity. The style of aging in America is not a graceful one. It is filled with constant efforts to fight off anxieties, until one encounters what Martin Gumpert has called the "shock of aging"—the sharp recognition (usually associated with disease) that one is "done for," and the final loss of confidence that comes with it. There come then, as Albrecht and Havighurst have put it, the "insults" that assail the aging person—the loss of physical attractiveness, the loss of life partners and friends through death, the loss of status, the loss of useful and respected roles in the family and culture, and the final insult of being imprisoned in a body which is the shell of its earlier self.

The two-generation nuclear American family, usually constricted in living space, has little room for the old people, nor does it allow them any participating role. In a society of rapid change the gap in outlook between the generations is too great to leave the older people any sense of their function in transmitting the mores of the culture. They retire from business or are arbitrarily retired from their jobs. Absorbed as they have been with making money, making a living, or running a household, they are unprepared for the burden of leisure, and helpless when the family web has been broken. They are left almost functionless, with no status and no sense of being useful. What remains for them? To become spectators, in a culture that values only participants and puts a premium on action; to crowd into the lodges and fraternal orders, the bridge clubs, the women's clubs; to go to church regularly, watch censoriously over what others are doing, dwell increasingly on the compensations in a future life for the shortcomings of this one; to tinker with doctors, drugs, and patent medicines, to worry about failing health and alien ideas and subversive influences; to be anxious, to nurse fears, to find scapegoats.

These are the most conservative years of the life cycle. Instead of bringing political revaluation and opening the mind to new influences, the years of disillusion make even more tenacious the hold on what seems so precarious. Property, possessions, status and superiority, prejudices and stereotypes never seem so important as when all else seems to be slipping away. A culture is made up of people living by different clocks, each age group with bundles of habituations formed in a different period, each with different sets of conditionings and different outlooks on the future. The American population trends make it increasingly a nation of aging people, with corresponding attitudes.

In increasing the life span* the new medical techniques and the declining death rate have increased the proportion of the population in the later age groups. By the 1955 figures there were twenty-nine million Americans over the age of fifty-five, an increase of 45 per cent over the

---

* For an earlier discussion, see Ch. III, Sec. 5, "Human Resources: Population Profile."

1950 figures. In 1900 there were three million Americans who were sixty-five and over, forming 4 per cent of the population; in 1955 they had grown to fourteen million, forming 8½ per cent; the Census Bureau estimates for 1975 were almost twenty-one million, forming more than 10 per cent of the population. Thus the old people constitute the most rapidly growing portion of the American population. During the half century since 1900, when the total population doubled, the number of people sixty-five years and over nearly quadrupled. Much of this increase is due not only to the new techniques for prolonging life in the old years but to the drastic cutting down of mortality at birth and in infancy. The current American emphasis on medical and psychological advances in "gerontology" promises to prolong the life span further, thus intensifying the trends and problems of an aging population.

There has been a growing recognition of these problems, and, characteristically, Americans have bestirred themselves to cope with them. Although there was a lag in introducing social-security legislation, compared with what had been done earlier in Britain and Germany, the pace of advance has recently been swift, and Republican administrations have confirmed what the New Deal began. The Social Security Act was passed in 1935, and twenty years later, by 1955, the benefits paid out under it totaled thirty-four billion dollars, of which the old-age benefits were sixteen. The demand for greater benefits continued, however, and social-security coverage was extended to new groups, while there were residues of the movements for old-age pensions—like the "Townsend Clubs"—which had flourished in the 1930s.* But the greatest advance was made as the result of trade-union action, especially in the steel, coal, automobile, and garment industries, where pension plans incorporating and extending the government benefits were made part of the "fringe benefits" of the collective-bargaining contracts.

The problem of "retirement" has occupied a good deal of attention in America recently. It has two aspects: for most Americans it is a problem of discriminatory barriers against the employment of the aged; for a smaller but increasing number it is a problem of finding new interests after leaving their business pursuits.

One of the facts about American industrial organization is its haphazard and ruthless waste of human resources and potentials. The industrial machine demands the young. When a worker has reached fifty —sometimes even at forty-five—it is rarely that he continues in demand. Where possible, except in wartime, he is brusquely cast aside and replaced by a younger man. Even in the corporations, in the top business posts, the older men are pushed up into do-nothing positions in order to

* For the problem of social security, see Ch. III, Sec. 6, "The Sinews of Welfare."

make room for "young blood." The result is a reserve army of productive capacity which is kept largely unused and unpaid. In 30 per cent of the cases where the head of the family was sixty-five or over, the mid-1950s figures showed the family income to be less than $1,000 a year; in more than half it was less than $2,000. There were still six million workers—almost one out of ten among the gainfully employed—who were not covered by a retirement program of any kind, while only seven million were covered by industrial pension plans. The odds against a worker of over forty-five finding a new job were something like six to one. In some of the Utopian schemes, like Bellamy's *Looking Backward,* the state was to underwrite the leisure of every citizen after the age of forty-five. In the American case one might say grimly that for many there is a similar "Inca Plan"—but one of enforced retirement, where the underwriting of leisure is absent or very skimpy. The resulting effects on the self-respect and the attitudes of the older people are disastrous.

Americans generally use the term "retirement" to apply to people in the middle and upper income range who have given up their business or work, and whose children are grown up and married off. Retirement in this sense is one of the great cultural dreams. Since it involves a sort of "means test" for distributing latter-day leisure, it works for only a small minority. They may be living on insurance or annuities or on savings invested in stocks, and in some cases on pensions. They may either have given up their business or work or may be tapering off. For them the symbolic paradise has become Florida or California, where they dream of spending their time in the sun, gossiping or visiting, listening to the radio or watching TV, pursuing their hobbies.

For a period the idea of complete retirement had great appeal for those who could afford it, and the doctors recommended it as a way of prolonging life, especially since the greatest killers among the chronic diseases in America are heart disease and hypertension. But more recently the old people discovered that to be functionless, even with comfort and leisure, is to eat out your heart. Away from your old haunts and interests you are lost; and you find yourself more miserable out of harness than in harness. "Retirement" becomes in this sense mainly a design for self-indulgent dotage ridden by loneliness. The students of geriatrics now emphasize that the problem for old people is not to drop their work but to slow its pace, rechannel their energies and fuse them with broader interests. The trouble here is the question of whether strong enough psychic resources have been stored up to make the latter years a time of harvest and not of emptiness.

I have not taken account here of the differences in the aging process by reasons of class, occupation, region, ethnic group—and sex as well. To start with the last: the American woman, who is culturally expected and conditioned to be "well preserved" at fifty-five or later, takes aging with a more calculated deliberateness (although not with less anxiety) than her husband or brother. In a sense she has to face the "shock of aging" much earlier than he, since the cultural ideal of youthfulness applies more stringently to women than to men. Even at thirty-five she is beginning to look back at her mirror with awakening doubts, and in her forties and fifties they reach a crescendo of anxiety. By sixty she has encased herself in an habitual wariness about the aspect she presents to the world, her family, and herself. Being thus gradually conditioned to adjust herself to aging, she is likely to suffer fewer scars than the American male, who rushes headlong into a seemingly indefinite future, playing the role of the alert young executive until he is brought up sharply by an abrupt awareness of bodily and psychic changes.

The differences in the aging process between classes, occupations, regions, and ethnic groups still remain to be studied. But there is enough material to suggest that aging hits the working class harder than the professionals, artists, or business executives. One might also speculate that it leaves more psychic casualties in the rural areas and small towns than in urban centers, on the theory that the older person can find more stimulation in city surroundings and is not thrown back on himself too bleakly. But we also know that there can be a terrible loneliness for the old in cities as well—a loneliness which is enhanced by the fact that there is so much vitality all around them. The whole problem still awaits study. But we do know that the lonely American is all the more lonely when he is old.

The most difficult question is the degree to which an individual's ties with the culture enable him to weather the inner storms of aging. In a suggestive typology Riesman ventures the guess that there are three types of reaction to aging—the "autonomous," the "adjusted," and the "anomic." At one end of the scale there are people who find sources of self-renewal as their physical capacities shrink, and they move beyond their accustomed limits to discover new levels at which they can function productively. At the other end there are people without a sense of identity, who crumble under the encroachments of age. In between them Riesman places the "adjusted" who are kept going in the later years by their ties with the culture, getting their resistance to the inroads of age not from their own inner strength but from the cultural roles they have learned to maintain. In the case of some ethnic groups, as with Negroes and Old World orthodox Jews, the ties are not so much with the larger American culture as with the immediate ethnic subculture, and the result is likely to be something more than merely "adjustment": it is rather an inner harmony between the personality and culture which enables the life cycle to fulfill itself without much strain and without the "transcending" quality which the "autonomous" must have.

I may have given here a picture of aging in America with too few lights and too many shadows. The response of Americans to the aging process is varied. It may run all the way from hurt vanity or resigned acceptance to the creative tapping of new resources; their feelings range from anxiety or panic to a mellow affirmation. An attitude study of people over sixty-five in a small Midwestern city showed 17 per cent of them checking the statement "My life is so enjoyable that I almost wish it could go on forever"; another 20 per cent checked "These are the best years of my life"; and another 40 per cent checked "My life is still busy and useful." This would indicate that three out of four elderly Americans have come to terms with the fact of aging. The obvious difficulty with these figures is that old people are likely to draw a veil over their sense of isolation and failure, and to show by a cheery response to such questions that they are taking their burdens with courage. Robert Havighurst, who has been close to the research and interviews in this field, believes that "the age period from sixty to seventy-five is just as happy as any other age period for Americans, and is actually a good deal happier than the period of adolescence." This does not jibe with my own impressions, nor with what we know about the strong major currents that flow through the life history of the American; yet it is good to have this counteremphasis to balance the prevailing pessimism about this period of American life.

How any particular individual will respond is likely to depend more on his whole psychic history than on any category in which he may be placed in a typology. If Americans do not grow old gracefully it is not because of any failure of awareness of the problem. They try earnestly and self-consciously to meet it, yet it is also a harder task for them. For old age is the time when, as Martin Gumpert put it, "fewer and fewer things are done for the first time, and more and more things are done for the last time"—and American culture is the kind that places its premium on firsts rather than on finalities, and on challenge rather than acceptance.

Much of the American anxiety about old age is a flight from the reality of death. One of the striking qualities of the American character is the unwillingness to face either the fact or meaning of death. In the more somber tradition of American literature, reaching from Hawthorne and Melville and Poe to Faulkner and Hemingway, one finds a tragic depth that belies the surface thinness of the ordinary American death attitudes. By an effort of the imagination the great writers faced problems which the culture in action is reluctant to face—the fact of death, its mystery, and its place in the back-and-forth shuttling of the eternal recurrence. The unblinking confrontation of death in Greek times, the elaborate theological patterns woven around it in the Middle Ages, the ritual celebration of it in the rich peasant cultures of Latin and Slavic Europe or in primitive cultures: these are difficult to find in American life, except among the Negroes or where immigration and its cultural transfers may have left some colorful residues of death customs within some of the ethnic groups.

Whether through fear of the emotional depths or because of a drying up of the sluices of religious intensity, the American avoids dwelling on death or even coming to terms with it: he finds it morbid and recoils from it, surrounding it with word avoidance (Americans never die, but "pass away") and various taboos of speech and practice. A "funeral parlor" is decorated to look like a bank; everything in a funeral ceremony is done in hushed tones, as if it were something furtive, to be concealed from the world; there is so much emphasis on being dignified that the ceremony often loses its quality of dignity. In some of the primitive cultures there is difficulty in understanding the causes of death: it seems puzzling and even unintelligible. Living in a scientific culture, Americans have a ready enough explanation of how it comes, yet they show little capacity to come to terms with the fact of death itself and with the grief that accompanies it. "We jubilate over birth and dance at weddings," writes Margaret Mead, "but more and more hustle the dead off the scene without ceremony, without an opportunity for young and old to realize that death is as much a fact of life as is birth." And (one may add) even in its hurry and brevity the last stage of an American's life—the last occasion of his relation to his society—is as standardized as the rest.

Americans repress closely the emotional drives concerned with death and sorrow—so closely that what the psychiatrists call the "grief work," in Erich Lindeman's phrase, is given little scope. It is true that the death of a husband or father leaves a great void in the American family, and that widowhood is a difficult state to bear, especially when the widow—who is generally left with adequate insurance and other economic resources—is left without the psychic resources to live her own life self-sufficiently. (The mid-century figures show nine out of every 100 families in America broken by widowhood.) But however intense the personal grief may be, there are cultural pressures to put an end to it, to keep it from interfering with the survivors' effectiveness, and to recapture one's "peace of mind." Because the great values of American culture are all associated with the power and pulsing of life, there is felt to be no point in dwelling on the values that transcend life and reach into death, nor any profit in trying to see the everyday values take on a new meaning in the withering perspective of death.

In almost every culture there is a fear of death, yet the fear may carry along a fascinated absorption. But in America there is little of this fascination. The recoil from death betrays in itself a lack of sensitivity toward its implications for the spirit. One reason why Hemingway's *The Old Man and the Sea* came from outside the culture (Hemingway wrote it in the setting of the Cuban fishing villages) was its celebration of old age and its heroisms. There had been little in American literature about the dignity of old age, as there is little also (except in the war novels) about the grace of dying. As for suicide, although it has lost some of the fierceness of the taboos that were thrown around it by medieval Christianity, it is still regarded as the act of an unhinged mind and the final insult to a culture which underscores effectiveness in life. It is not, as it has been in some other societies, a culturally recognized way out of the human dilemma; nor would it be easy to imagine an American thinker writing the kind of philosophic defense of suicide one finds among the French existentialists. Conversely there is little in American philosophical speculation that deals with the theme of immortality. American culture cuts away the sensitivity to death and grief, to suicide and immortality, emphasizing the here-and-now as it emphasizes youth and action.*

And so, from birth to death, "from the cradle to the grave," the life cycle of the American.

* For a further discussion of the American time scale and time perspective and the American attitudes toward death, see Ch. XII, Sec. 7, "The Destiny of a Civilization."

CHAPTER IX

Character and Society

WE DEAL here with a variety of themes, all of them relating in some way to the wholeness and fragmentation of American life, to the codes by which Americans live or which they break, and to the relation between the structure of American society and the lineaments of the American character. First we stand back a bit and ask what elements of cohesion there are that hold America together, and what it uses for a social cement in the absence of the traditional cementing forces of the great societies in the past. In the process we inquire into the curious fact of the lonely American amidst all the bustle and swagger and power, and the alienated American in a society that sets so much store by the quality of community (Sec. 1, "The Cement of a Society"). This brings us to the associative impulse which has made America a nation of joiners (Sec. 2, "The Joiners"). And this in turn leads to the emergence of new standards and codes in manners, taste, dress (Sec. 3, "Manners, Taste, and Fashion"). From the discussion of these nuances in American behavior we take a sweeping look at the whole gallery of emerging American character types, noting that there is no single new "American character" but rather a plurality of diverse and conflicting personality trends that take shape in a number of new character portraits (Sec. 4, "Varieties of American Character").

We turn then to face the Gorgon head of all discussions of the American social structure—the question of the forces of disorganization in American society, and we ask whether the "cracks in the cement" mean that the whole structure is disintegrating, or whether they mark the excesses of the same tensions and strivings that give America some of its qualities of strength (Sec. 5, "The Disorders of a Society"). We continue with the theme of changes in American codes, grappling with the convulsive changes in moral codes and standards, and concluding that as the older ones are transformed newer ones take their place (Sec. 6, "Morals in Revolution"). On the question of sexual morality we note the gap between the American obsession with sex and the sexually repressive codes, and examine the stratagems of "patterned evasion" of the formal standards (Sec. 7, "Society and Sexual Expression"). Finally we look at what these strivings are, in the form of basic life goals that move Americans to their actions and passions (Sec. 8, "Life Goals and the Pursuit of Happiness").

CHAPTER IX

Character and Society

1. The Cement of a Society

WHAT holds America together? A democracy, De Tocqueville wrote, cannot function without a religion and a philosophy. Which is to say that while every civilization needs some principle to hold it together, a democracy has a special problem of cohesion. Paradoxically, it may be easier to hold a people together through inequities sanctioned by tradition, religion, or monarchical authority than through the equality that is always questioning itself and being questioned. To the extent that American culture is tangled and various, diverse in ethnic tradition and geography, free of recognized social hierarchies, obsessed with the individual and his rights, averse to the claims of social duties, it is a wonder that it holds together at all. The paradox is that so atomistic a civilization should have found so effectively the stuff of cohesion.

In any tribal culture there is always the clannish differentiation of the "we" from the "they" to serve as a cohesive force. But more important are the ties of institutions and ideas. The Greeks had pride in their city-states, yet Plato suggested myths for the ruling Guardians to instill into the underlying population. The Romans had a conquering zeal and a sense of historic destiny to link them, yet they also used an imperial religion to which both Machiavelli in his *Discourses on Livy* and Gibbon in his *Decline and Fall* assigned an important role in the Empire's fortunes. The Japanese used the Emperor God. The medieval world stressed a universal church and a system of feudal statutes and personal allegiance; and the Catholic societies of Europe and Latin America have relied on the residues of these and on the close-knit rural communities tied by honor, loyalty, and social obedience. In feudal China and in India the cement used has been a caste system, again fused with religious traditions. England relied on a social aristocracy, an established Church, the Monarchy, and the rule of law. The French since 1789 have used their revolutionary tradition and their attachment to the native soil. Russia has a myth of hostile encirclement, plus a messianic belief in the invincible march of Communism, plus a surviving if incongruous mystique of "Holy Russia."

The American case has been different. None of the cementing forces which have held together these other societies—feudal hierarchy, caste, aristocracy, monarchy, state Church, religious or revolutionary mystique —has counted for much in America, with the exception of an idea like Manifest Destiny. Nor has authoritarianism taken hold, whether military or clerical. When the new American society broke with that of the Old World, the break was not only with the outer ties of dependence but also (to a lesser extent) with the inner ties that held the old society together.

What many American settlers did have, to start with, was a deep religious feeling and the sense of social commitment that came with it. They had in addition the sense of a new community being hewn out on a new continent, with the world's eyes on its course, and the belief in equal opportunity. Returning to De Tocqueville's remark, that a democracy cannot survive without a religion and a philosophy, the Americans had as their stuff of cohesion the religion of free worship and the philosophy of equality.*

A philosophy and a religion cannot operate effectively, however, unless they are at harmony with current practices. We have seen the nature of the atomizing forces which came into American society. The diverse immigration and the mingling of races and religions meant group differences in ways of thought and living, and tensions pulling apart the society. The operation of competitive capitalism brought with it the coldness of a business spirit which measured men as items in a market economy. The expansion of American power meant the assumption of new political burdens in the world and exposure to new influences. To a great extent the old codes and the old consensus based on them dissolved. Americans were confronted with the most difficult task that a society ever has to face—that of finding organic continuities to keep its life from being pulverized.

One can argue, as F. S. C. Northrop has done, that the atomizing principle was present even in early American thought; that it had been taken over from John Locke's theory of ideas, which saw reality as only a collection of atomic sense data, and which saw society similarly as a loose collection of atomic individuals. Northrop points out that the British based their own polity on Thomas Hooker, who conceived of the Church of England as an organic society of individuals whose individuality was absorbed in the common mystical body. But this leaves open the question of why the thinking of Locke and Hume, rather than of Hooker, had so strong an appeal for Americans. Perhaps it was be-

* For religion in America, see Ch. X, Sec. 1, "God and the Churches." For the philosophy of equality, see Ch. VI, Sec. 2, "The Democratic Idea," and Ch. X, Sec. 2, "American Thought: the Angle of Vision."

cause their thinking was congruous with the surging strength of the new economy and the competitive spirit and with the force of business materialism. It is idyllic to believe that whatever breakdown there has been of faith and morals is a recent event in American life, part of a cataclysm sweeping away the original system of faith and morals. The fact is that these were already broken with the later advances of science, the machine, and the market economy.

Nor were they peculiar to America. Karl Polanyi, studying English economics and social history at the turn of the nineteenth century, noted that the automatic market mechanism became the principle for organizing not only the economy but also the society—although the automatic market was constantly haunted by reform movements, Chartism, and a variety of religious cults. The older controls of British society, which Edmund Burke had celebrated, were replaced by the free-market-as-control, and the mutual responsibilities between society and its members were replaced by *laissez-faire*-plus-the-poor-laws. Using Polanyi's term, this was the "Great Transformation." Something of the same transformation took place in American life in the 1840s and 1850s, when the landless industrial worker first became a permanent part of American life; and in the decades after the Civil War, when the market economy came to be accepted as the principal regulator not only of the economic but also of the social and moral order. As Mr. Featherstone put it in one of Thomas Love Peacock's novels, "Every man for himself, sir, and God for us all." Again it must be noted that in America, as in England, the automatic market was haunted by Fourierism, Transcendentalism, and reform movements. Yet the religion of freedom and the philosophy of equality were steadily transformed into the creed of the automatic market, whose religion was individualism and whose philosophy was the competitive and acquisitive spirit.

A drastic critic of American society could draw a quite terrifying picture of the dominant role of money in effecting outward ties without any inner ones. From birth to death the centrifugal pull of money values is felt. There is little equality in the surroundings of birth: in the hospital wards there is a hierarchy of solicitude for mother and child depending on income. In school there is a similar gradation in the way children are dressed and the homes they come from which shapes the child's attitude toward other children. The child learns quickly the gulf between those who have everything assured and those who have to struggle for them. In the years of growth the conditions that make for an expanding personality must be paid for—leisure from work in the early years when work can be oppressive, adequate medical care, the chance for recreation and travel, access to sun and sea, music and art and books. In adult life the principles of business operate, and even friendships are overridden by the principle that "business is not philanthropy." In his job life the worker often comes to feel that the corporation is not a benevolent father, and in turn he gives his work grudgingly and without enthusiasm. Those who care about honor and love, about fighting for causes that yield no return and spending themselves for people with whom they have only the bonds of a common humanity, are called "idealists," "do-gooders," and "eggheads." In old age those who can no longer pay their way are forgotten. And even in death they are hurried away silently into an obscure grave.

This may be overstressed. The nonpecuniary values of generosity and honor, friendship and comradeship and love, workmanship and creativeness, are present to a high degree in American life. The whole force of American literature supports them. It is also true that Americans can be as sentimental as any people in the world. Yet aside from personal sentiment the pressures of the culture run the other way. A market economy means a market society, in which the great crime is to be "taken in," and the great virtue to be tough and illusionless. This means resisting the pitfalls of fellow feeling and breaking whatever it is that ties person to person in the web of a common plight. The nightmare of American life is to be left dependent and helpless—a greater nightmare than failing to help others when they need help. The result is the desensitized man whose language is the wisecrack and whose armor is cynicism.

It is interesting that the characteristic American contribution to psychiatry should have been Harry Stack Sullivan's concept of "interpersonal relations." It is, of course, true that in the last analysis a society is composed of persons, and in such a sense all social relations are interpersonal. Yet this misses the big fact that—without assuming any actual social organization above persons—a society is more than the sum of the individual atoms in it. There is a whole web of symbols and going concerns that weaves together the lives of people, and the greatest of these is the notion of society itself. The American emphasis, however, is individualist and atomist. It gives rise, for example, to such a characteristic popular myth as the feeling that the social services undertaken by government are a rape of the public treasury by incompetents who have fallen behind in the battle of life and that all collective effort is a betrayal of the laws of life. This jungle attitude is coupled often with a moral neutrality which makes the "innocent bystander" keep hands off even when he sees someone victimized, lest he become too involved. The conditionings of American life are to flee needless entanglements and vulnerabilities ("Don't stick your neck out," "Don't be a sucker"). This vacuum of the passions of fellow feeling is the most desolating measure of what Nietzsche in another context called the "pathos of distance."

How to bridge that distance has been a constant problem for American humanism. Since most Americans fear the role of playing Santa Claus to countries in need, the internationalists have had to argue that every dollar lent or granted abroad is an act not of generosity but of national self-interest in fighting the nation's enemies. The same appeal to self-interest is made by those who plead for the civil liberties of minority groups: "If you let it happen to them it will in the end happen to you." In one of the movies about anti-Semitism, there is an eloquent speech by the hero-detective to a hillbilly soldier from Tennessee, saying that unless he takes to heart the brutal slaying of a Jew, the irrational madness might spread until Catholics become the victims, then Protestants, then redheaded men, and perhaps even men from Tennessee. Thus the argument is one of skin-saving rather than belonging to an organic social whole or being implicated in a common human plight: and while it is true that skin-saving is an impulse that goes back to a fundamental human selfishness, a cohesive society can never be securely founded upon it. If the depersonalized quality I have mentioned were the whole truth about America, it would be hard to explain—in the face of all the fragmentizing pulls—how American society has managed to hold together as it has.

In negative terms, the answer lies partly in the tradition of toleration which is one facet of *laissez faire*. Given the pluralism of American life and the bewildering array of group differences, the agreement to disagree is an important force in avoiding tensions and conflicts. Americans have learned a toleration of ethnic and religious differences (although not of personal nonconformism) which amounts to a kind of mutual insulation. Even the ghettos—the closely packed ethnic communities of Irish, Italians, Jews, Puerto Ricans, Germans, Czechs, Negroes, Chinese—play an important part in this insulation. They are little islands or enclaves, and as such they may seem to fragmentize American life further. But actually they are the natural response of like-minded persons who find themselves a minority in a culture still strange to them; and until the new generations can take their place in the main stream of American striving, these little back eddies serve to minimize the turbulent conflicts of group differences. For a sensitive observer, like Alistair Cooke, the remarkable thing about life in New York City is not that there are tensions among the ethnic groups that make it up but that they manage to live together with an almost unparalleled absence of conflict. In time the ghettos are themselves atomized, and as they break under the disruptive force of standardized ways of living, the danger is not one of too slow but of too rapid absorption of the American subcultures. They are one form of insulation against the violence of change which would annihilate the identity of the individual within his group.*

Something of the same process may be found even in the market society. The relations of purchase and sale, of work in big corporations, of standardized consumption, and of large-scale advertising are depersonalized relations. Yet in fact there is a saving quality that many observers may miss. To take the American Negro group as an instance, despite the persistence of job and wage differentials the place where segregation begins to break down first is exactly in the market society, and the place where it holds on unyieldingly is in the intimate social relationships that are least governed by the market. It is true that in many cases the Negro's money may still fail to buy him the house he wants or an equal place in a restaurant or theater. Yet in the national market his purchasing power is eagerly sought by the makers of competing commodities, and in local retail outlets the Negro purchaser finds increasingly a freemasonry of the dollar which puts his money on an equality with the others. There is thus an impersonality about the contacts of the market place which qualifies even caste divisions and reduces the loneliness of status. Even what Riesman calls the "false personalizing" of relations between salesman and customer serves as the starting point for diminishing prejudices that had been uncritically accepted. Studies of department-store buying show that the addition of Negro or Jewish clerks helps rather than hinders the volume of sales. Thus the social changes in American life are being absorbed into American consciousness through the operation of the profit motive. Even more important is the impersonality of the job relation, which leads workers of diverse origin to work side by side in the day-to-day relations of the factory, meeting common problems and fighting against common enemies, until finally they develop the sense of fellow relation which is at the heart of any society.

The social theorists draw an important distinction, which goes back to Frederich Tonnies, between "community" or "society" (*Gemeinschaft*) and the "association" (*Gesellschaft*). It is the distinction between the close-knit unit of community living, as found mainly in traditional rural societies, and the loosely organized unit familiar to modern urban industrial living. No one would claim that the concept of "community," as it existed in a society like that of sixteenth-century Spain, based on the common traditions of land, church, and hierarchy, comes anywhere

* For an elaboration of this theme, see Ch. III, Sec. 2, "The Immigrant Experience" and Ch. VII, Sec. 5, "The Minority Situation."

near applying to American society. In its place has come a social organization created by the people of an industrial culture, fashioned (in Helen Mims's phrase) as their "master artifice." American society may stand as the characteristic expression of this master artifice. It is looser than a "community," which has a freightage of meaning that conveys inner traditional ties of long standing. But it is a good deal more than is usually conveyed in the word "association," which Americans use for specific voluntary groupings.

In fact, the "master artifice" of American society contains in it more of the affirmative element of mystique than most students have been willing to find. The avoidance of disruption and conflict and the impersonal market forces, which I have stressed above, do not in themselves hold together the fabric of a society. The real cement of society lies in the folk beliefs about it. These are not as abstract as the philosophic ideas, nor are they a religion in any formal sense. Yet they serve effectively to link people with each other and with the culture.

I have spoken above of the folk belief in the American open-class system. Just as important, in the political area, is the belief in fair play and the "rules of the game," which accounts for the difference in ideological intensity between political conflict in America and Europe. In the legal area there is the belief in law which gives the underlying groups a chance to invoke the slogan of equality before the law and prevents a society of frozen status from forming. In terms of models of living, there are the common symbols and type-figures in the realm of sports, business, movies, and television to serve as folk heroes.

This is mainly the stuff of standardization, and a valid doubt may be raised as to whether genuine social cohesion—or even (as Erich Fromm puts it) the capacity to love—is possible in a thoroughly standardized society. This doubt has been raised especially about the Big Media, on the ground that they are corrupting and disintegrating forces rather than cohesive ones. But while the media may dilute the aesthetic quality of popular culture and of the American experience, it is hard to deny their striking role in effecting communication between individuals and their society on every class and ethnic level. The fearers and doubters should reckon with the force of individualism in American life, which keeps it from becoming wholly a mass culture, valueless and normless.

The weight of this individualism, plus the impersonality of a market society, plus the insulation and later the integration of conflict groups, plus the effects of participation on the job and in the market, plus the ideal of equality before the law, plus finally the symbols and hero figures of folk belief—these have somehow added up to the cement of American society.

2. The Joiners

A STANDARD CLICHÉ about American society is that the Americans are "joiners" and "belongers." The derisive attack on the symbol of Sinclair Lewis's Babbitt, who belonged to the Elks, Boosters, and a network of other service clubs and lodges, became a stereotype of American social criticism. It is true that the associative impulse is strong in American life: no other civilization can show as many secret fraternal orders, businessmen's "service clubs," trade and occupational associations, social clubs, garden clubs, women's clubs, church clubs, theater groups, political and reform associations, veterans' groups, ethnic societies, and other clusterings of trivial or substantial importance.

When the intellectuals speak scornfully of Americans as "joiners" they usually forget to include themselves: there are more academic organizations in the United States than in the whole of Europe. They have in mind a middle-class American who may be a Shriner or an Elk, a Rotarian, a Legionnaire, a member of a country club or outing club, and at least a dozen other organizations. In the Warner studies of "Yankee City" (Newburyport) which had 17,000 people, there were over 800 associations, about 350 of them more or less permanent. Taking some random figures in the mid-1950s for illustration, the fraternal orders included in the past at least twenty million members; there were about 100,000 women's clubs; there were two million young people who belonged to the rural and small-town "4-H" clubs. At least 100 million Americans were estimated to belong to some kind of national organization.

Max Weber, the German sociologist, visited America in 1905 and spoke of these "voluntary associations" as bridging the transition between the closed hierarchical society of the Old World and the fragmented individualism of the New World, and he saw how crucial a social function these groupings perform in American life. After World War II the students of German society, looking back at the Nazi experience, thought they could trace a connection between the lesser role of such voluntary groups in Germany and the rise of totalitarianism. Their assumption was that when the associative impulse is balked, it may express itself in a more destructive way.

Certainly one of the drives behind "joining" is the integrative impulse of forming ties with like-minded people and thus finding status in the community. Americans joined associations for a number of motives: to "get ahead," to "meet people" and "make contacts," to "get something done," to learn something, to fill their lives. These drives shed some light on the human situation in America. Constantly mobile,

Americans need continuities to enable them easily to meet people, make friends, eat and drink with them, call them by their first names. The clubs and lodges help fill the need. They are at once a way of breaking up "cliques" and "sets" and at the same time forming new ones. They are a means for measuring social distance, narrowing it for those who break in and are included, lengthening it for those who are excluded. For a newcomer in a community it is hard to break the shell of the tight local social groups unless he comes with a recognized stamp from a national organization or makes his way into a local one. Once in it, he joins with the others in a critical surveillance of the next new-comer. This is a way of solving the need in any society both for clan-nishness and for social flexibility.

In the midst of constant change and turbulence, even in a mass society, the American feels alone. In a society of hierarchy, loneliness is more tolerable because each member knows his position in the hierar-chy—lower than some, higher than others, but always known. In a mo-bile, nonhierarchical society like the American, social position does not have the same meaning as in a vertical scheme of deference and author-ity. A man's status in the community is a matter of making horizontal connections, which give him his place in what would otherwise be a void. It is this social placing of an American—in church, lodge, service or women's club, eating club, Community Fund drive, veterans' group, country club, political party—that defines his social personality. Through it he gets the sense of effectiveness he does not have as a minor part of the machine process or the corporate organization. Here he can make his way as a person, by his qualities of geniality and friendliness, his ability to talk at a meeting or run it or work in a committee, his organ-izing capacities, his ardor, his public spirit. Here also he stretches him-self, as he rarely does on the job, by working with others for com-mon nonprofit ends.

Thus Americans achieve a sense of collective expression which belies the outward atomism of American life. "Not to belong to a *we* makes you lonesome," says the adolescent girl in Carson McCullers' *The Mem-ber of the Wedding*. "When you say *we*, I'm not included, and it's not fair." Since there is little emphasis in America on some mystical com-munity of religion, there is a greater hunger to belong to a "we." This was less true in the earlier history of the nation. The American rarely thought of himself as "lonely" until the twentieth century. Before that time the dominant note in his thinking was that he was a self-sufficient individual. But he is no longer sufficient unto himself. He gets a cer-tain degree of shared experience from his job at the factory or office, and from his trade-union, but he needs a good deal more from personal relations outside his job life. Margaret Mead notes that at their first meeting Americans are distant and ill at ease, but at their second they act like old friends. It is because they have had a shared experience, no matter how slight, which removes their inhibitions and makes them feel expansive because of it. Karen Horney, coming from Germany to America, was compelled to change her whole theory about the neurotic personality when she found how different were the inner sources of conflict in America from those in Germany, and how much of a role loneliness played in American conflicts.

It is a striking fact that friendships in America, especially male friendships, are not as deep as in other cultures. The American male suspects that there is something sissified about a devoted and demonstrative friendship, except between a man and woman, and then it must pass over into love, or perhaps just into sex. In their clubs and associations, however, at first in school clubs and college fraternities and later in secret lodges or women's clubs, Americans find a level of friendship that does not lay them open to the charge of being sentimental. In his clubs a man is not ashamed to call another man "brother," although outside of the lodge, the trade-union, and the church the term "brother" is used sardonically in American speech.

It is the hunger for shared experience that makes the American fear solitude as he does. More than a century ago Emerson spoke of the polar needs of "society and solitude." The days in which Americans pushed into the wilderness to find solitude are largely over. Many of them still leave the crowded cities for "the country," but their search is not so much for solitude as for greater living space and smaller and more compassable groups. Lewis Mumford has made a plea for housing arrangements that will assure each member of the family a room of his own to which he can retreat when the need for solitude comes upon him, to rediscover the shape of his personality. But for many Americans solitude is still too frightening, whether because they dare not face the dilemma of their own personality or because they recognize themselves more easily by reference to their association with others.

There are many ways of dividing American associations into broad types, none wholly satisfactory. The best one can do is to point out some dramatic contrasts between them. There are the occupational and economic groups at one end of the spectrum, geared to self-interest, and the crusading and cultural ones at the other. There are the patriotic societies of the "old Americans" and the newer ethnic societies of minority groups. There are broadly inclusive associations (political parties, trade-unions, *ad hoc* reform groups) at one end, and at the other there are highly personal groups that run all the way from high-school cliques to the adult eating clubs and the "country-club set." There are, as Warner has put it, "secular" organizations and "sacred" ones, matter-of-fact ones and highly ritualistic ones.

Some of these are more saturated with symbolism than others, yet all of them in one way or another deal in symbols and take their appeal from them. The symbolic complexity of American life is largely expressed in these clubs, lodges, and associations, which fulfill to the hilt what Durkheim long ago laid down as the essence of religious groupings—"collective representation." The degree of ritual varies, being very high in the case of Masonic lodges and church groups and less so in the case of *ad hoc* reform groups. Yet the symbolism and the ritual are present, explicitly or implicitly, in all of them.

Behind the urge toward "joining" is the sense of the mysterious and exotic. To belong to a secret order and be initiated into its rites, to be part of a "Temple" with a fancy Oriental name, to parade in the streets of Los Angeles, Chicago, or New York dressed in an Arab fez and burnoose, to have high-sounding titles of potentates of various ranks in a hierarchy: all this has appeal in a nonhierarchical society from which much of the secrecy and mystery of life has been squeezed out. The fraternal groups flourish best in the small towns of the Middle West: the drearier the cultural wasteland of the small town, the greater the appeal of the exotic. Americans have an ambivalent attitude toward secrecy: they want everything out in the open, yet they delight in the secrecy of fraternal groups, as Tom Sawyer's gang of boys in Mark Twain's books did, and as the cellar clubs and the boys' gangs in the big-city slums still do. Much of the appeal of the Ku Klux Klan lies in this mysterious flim-flammery, at once sadistic and grimly prankish. In many ways the American male of adult years is an arrested small boy, playing with dollars and power as he did once with toys or in gangs, and matching the violence of his recreation to the intensity of his loneliness.

This is especially clear in the veterans' groups, like the American Legion or the Veterans of Foreign Wars, which banded together not only for bonuses and other lobbying purposes but through a nostalgia for the ultimate shared experience of killing and facing death. Under the form of vigilant patriotism they are an effort to recapture the adventure of youth and death in a life that seems humdrum by contrast with the memories of war and derring-do. Since they have the self-assurance of being patriots and hunters of subversives, they come to feel that they have earned a license for license. Their political views take on something of the same cast as their prankishness at conventions, and there is a peculiar irony in the spectacle of drunken and boisterous middle-aged men whose leaders deliver solemn speeches about saving the nation. Curiously, some of the men who are pursued by these Hounds of God got themselves into trouble originally by reason of the same proclivity to become joiners, sponsoring a series of liberal and Leftist letterheads through a mixed impulse of gregariousness and reformist action.

For many American women, the women's club fills the emotional void of middle age, helping in the fight against loneliness and boredom. For others it means a chance to act as culture surrogates for their husbands, who are too busy to keep up with the trends in literature, the arts, or the community services. Americans have learned to take the clubwomen with a kindly bantering acceptance, much as in the Helen Hokinson caricatures. The jokes about the ladies' club lecture circuits cannot conceal a measure of pride on the part of a new nation in having wives with leisure enough to spend on veneer, like garden clubs, reading and discussion clubs, parent-teacher associations, and child-study clubs. In every American community the lecture forums, Little Theater groups, concerts and symphonies and poetry readings are in the custody of little groups of devoted people—men as well as women—who combine the sense of community service with a feeling of membership in a cultural elite.

These cultural groups are part of the array of *ad hoc* organizations which Americans form for every conceivable purpose. Some of them are meddlers and priers, seeking to impose their will upon the society by hunting other Americans down and boycotting and censoring their activities; others are formed to combat them with equal militancy. There are vigilante groups and civil liberties groups; there are radical, conservative, liberal, reactionary, and crackpot groups. Each of the three great religious communities—Protestant, Catholic, and Jewish—has its own welfare, charity, social, recreational, social work, and reformist clubs. In fact, the Negroes as well as the newer minority ethnic groups have a more intense participation in associational life than the "old Americans": it is their way of retaining their cohesiveness and morale in the face of the pressures of the majority culture. Cutting across the religious and ethnic divisions are Community Chest drives, hospital societies, private schools, settlement house and welfare groups, and groups built around every conceivable hobby. They go back in their impulse to the idea of self-help, and many of them combine the pressure group with self-interest and "do-goodism." To some degree they embody the fanatical energy drive that has transformed the face of American life.

It is through these associations that Americans avoid the excesses both of state worship and of complete individualism. It is in them, and not in the geographical locality, that the sense of community comes closest to being achieved. Through them also the idea of neighborhood has been re-created in America: for in most American cities the neighbors next door, who may be fellow tenants or fellow houseowners, have little else in common. The real common interests are shared by people working in the same industry or profession, sending their children to the same school, belonging to the same welfare organization or club, fighting for the same causes. Sometimes this involves "sets" and "cliques" which form from the encrustation of shared experience; sometimes it involves common membership in leisure-and-recreation groups whose chief tie is an interchange of taste and experience. But through the sum of these ways the American manages to achieve a functional set of social relations with like-minded people, the core of which is not propinquity of place but community of interests, vocation, preferences, and tastes.

The propensity to join is not new in America. It goes back to the ladies' reading clubs and other cultural groups which spread on the moving frontier and softened some of its rigors, and which were the forerunners of the parent-teacher associations and the civic and forum groups of today. The jungle of voluntary associations was already dense enough for De Tocqueville to note that "in no country in the world has the principle of association been . . . more unsparingly applied to a multitude of different objects than in America." The permissiveness of the state, the openness of an open society, the newness of the surroundings, the need for interweaving people from diverse ethnic groups—or, conversely, of their huddling together inside the ethnic tent until they could be assimilated—all these shaping forces were present from the start. What came later was the breaking up of the rural and small-town life of America and the massing in impersonal cities, bringing a dislocation that strengthened the impulse to join like-minded people.

Yet here again one runs a danger in generalizing about Americans as a nation. There are phases of class and status that must be taken into account. There has been a tendency to believe that because Babbitt was a joiner all joiners and belongers must therefore be Babbitts and must come from the middle classes. But the studies show a different picture. Warner found in Newburyport a direct correlation between the height of the class level and the propensity to join associations. Using his own six class categories (two uppers, two middles, and two lowers), he found that 72 per cent of the people in the upper classes belonged to associations, 64 per cent in the upper middle, 49 per cent in the lower middle, and 39 per cent and 22 per cent in the two lowers respectively.

Moreover, each of the classes tended to join different kinds of groups, for somewhat different purposes, and each of them had a different "style" of behavior within them. The elites used the associations chiefly as instruments for the strategic manipulation of the life of the community—through their control of the country clubs, the eating and discussion clubs, the civic associations, the fund-raising drives. Even when they belonged to such middle-class groups as the women's clubs or the businessmen's service clubs, they brought with them a prestige which enabled them to run the show, and sometimes they used their social power as a form of blackmail in extracting larger civic contributions from the parvenu groups. The middle classes used the associations largely as a way of improving their social status and for training themselves in articulateness and leadership. For the lower classes the emphasis was mainly upon church activities. Actually, the figures for their participation in club life would be even lower if it were not for the fact that a large proportion were in the minority ethnic groups and belonged therefore to their ethnic societies. The lower-class "old American" has very few associational ties.

An added word as to why the "low-status" people (as a number of studies have shown) belong to relatively few associations: partly it is because the nature of their work leaves them less time, partly because they lack the needed money for membership, partly because their interests and perspectives are more limited. With more limited life chances there is a corresponding shrinkage of participation in community experience through the associations. In fact, the Lynds found in their *Middletown* studies that the low-income and low-status groups made few visits except in their immediate neighborhood, formed few ties outside it, and had few friendships: their contacts of a more intimate sort were with their "own kin." Thus the low-status groups in America tend to become isolated, and their isolation is all the greater because they are part of a culture in which everybody else "belongs." I have spoken of the differences in class style. One of the striking differences is that the club activities of the lower and middle classes tend to be more symbolic, emotional, and ritualistic: those of the upper classes are more rationalist, with greater emphasis on speeches and discussions.

There are certain common elements, however, in the whole range of associational life. Members are expected to be "active." They belong to committees, take part in campaigns, try to get publicity for their activities in the local press, lay a good deal of stress on fund-raising (especially in the case of the women's groups), and engage in a kind of gift exchange by a reciprocity of contributions which Warner compares to the potlatches of some of the American Indian tribes. A good deal of American humor has concerned itself with club life, including Robert Benchley's classic film on "The Treasurer's Report." But club and com-

mittee work has also meant a training in democratic forms and procedures and an instrument for integrating the community.

Some commentators have guessed that Americans are intense joiners
because they need some way of alleviating the tensions and anxieties that
arise in their competitive living—which would account for the large
number of philanthropic, service, and reformist organizations. Certainly
the ritual of the fraternal associations may be an answer to the humdrum character of the daily tasks, and the sense of brotherliness and of
service may be a way of allaying the accumulated hostilities and guilt
feelings. E. D. Chapple, using an anthropological approach to the theory
of associations, suggests that a person who has suffered a serious disturbance may get relocated either by some form of ritual (the *rites of passage* mentioned above) or by changes in his "tangent relations," which
he achieves by activity in clubs and associations. This is a technical and
roundabout way of saying that the American propensity to join meets
a need of the personality and mediates disturbances within that personality, and that keeping busy in association work is one way of meeting,
avoiding, or channeling tensions within oneself. Yet this seems a negative and partial approach. Like other human beings, Americans don't
do things just to avoid trouble or allay guilt. In a deeper and more affirmative sense the joining impulse is part of the expansion of personality, even while it may often help to create some of the insecurities it
seeks to allay.

This jibes with what I said above about class differences in community participation. If joining were only an answer to inner tensions, then
the low-status groups would be fully as active as the middle classes, or
even more so: yet they are much less active. Their lesser activity derives
from their lesser income, lesser education, narrower perspectives and life
chances. The urge to associate is thus linked with the expansion of perspective and personality, at least in the intermediate stage, since there is
plenty of evidence that a highly developed personality tends in the end
to seek solitude. But solitude is different from isolation. Another bit of
evidence is to be found in the trend toward suburban living. The theory
has been that the impersonality of the big city breeds associations. Yet
recent experience shows that when people move from the mass city to
the more compassable suburb, their participation in club and association life increases deeply. Again this indicates that the American is a
joiner because he feels the freedom to expand, to fill out a personality-
on-the-make, and he has an inner need to find outer symbols of the fact
that he belongs to his culture and has not been left behind by it.

The clubs and associations which he joins do not, however, simplify
his life but make it more crowded and complex. The demands on his

time and participation multiply. The "new leisure," which is in itself the product of mechanization and the shorter working week, is getting filled in with the beehive activities of common ventures. Keeping up with club work has become one of the new imperatives of middle-class life. What makes it worse for a small group is that the range of leadership is a constricted one, and the most difficult tasks fall upon a few. America has become overorganized and association-saturated. Yet it may be worth the cost since the associations serve as filaments to tie people together in a community of interests less accidental and casual than it may seem.

Such filaments reach across the continent, so that periodically Americans gather in "conventions" of every sort, which serve formally as legislative bodies but actually as ways of tightening the ties of interest by face-to-face encounters. It may be a convention of a political party or of a trade-union or trade association, sales representatives of a big national corporation, scientists or scholars, church groups, or women's clubs, Shriners or Elks or Legionnaires. In the case of a big national organization as many as 100,000 people may descend upon the convention city to stay for a week, although usually it means only a few hundred or few thousand. They outdo one another in antics and pranks; they swarm over the hotels, sustaining the hotel industry, bars, night clubs, and call girls. In the case of conventions called by big corporations or trade associations, the purpose is to build morale and give a personal touch to an otherwise impersonal organization. The dominant note is that of "greeterism," in which the managers and inside groups seek to make the "visiting firemen" feel at home.

But changes have come over American conventions, as over the whole institution of "joining." The "service clubs" such as Kiwanis and Rotarians—a combination of Big Brother, Good Neighbor, and Greeter—are regarded with some amusement even among their own circles. The world of Babbitt exists in perfect form only in the pages of Sinclair Lewis and in the "Americana" items enshrined in the faded issues of Mencken's *American Mercury*. Even the antics of veterans' groups and fraternal orders are coming to be regarded with boredom and annoyance. The emphasis is shifting from adolescent hoopla to the concerns of particular interest and taste groups. Even in the conventions, as Raoul Denney has pointed out, the "greeters" are becoming "meeters"; and the techniques of "participating" sessions, in which work experiences are exchanged, have reached the trade association and corporate meetings.

Yet with all this sobering current of change, Americans as joiners have not wholly lost the *élan* which has made their associational impulse a cross between promotion, interchange of ideas, and the exorcising of loneliness through modern saturnalia.

3. *Manners, Taste, and Fashion*

THE HURLY-BURLY I have been describing, of clubs, "greeters," and "meeters," would be impossible in an aristocratic society where the mi-nutiae and *elegantiae* of conventional behavior are part of its being. Ob-viously they are not unimportant in the American living scheme, as witness the question-and-answer columns in the newspapers, the eti-quette books by Emily Post and Amy Vanderbilt, and the anxiety with which stenographers and salesgirls, adolescents and young wives, study "the right thing" to do. The difference is that the aping of one's social superiors in America takes other and more meaningful forms than the aping of their manners. The imitation is directed rather at their busi-ness ways, their genteel ferocities and their modes of consumption. Be-sides, there are today no established arbiters of American manners and taste, as there were in English and French society of the seventeenth and eighteenth centuries, so that the compendia codify diffused popular usage rather than class edicts.

Despite Veblen's satire about how the underlying population apes the leisure class, what sets the emotional tone in America is not so much *imitation* as *striving:* not the aping of the behavior of superiors but the straining to catch up with their living standards. Where a society is in rapid movement, class differences are not sharp or stable, and manners become fluid. Their function becomes not so much that of setting off groups from one another as of merging them. That is why De Tocque-ville spoke of the "democratic manners" of the Americans of his day. He was writing for an audience of nineteenth-century Europeans who valued *la politesse* as a mode of class expression; and he was struck by the fact that manners in America crisscrossed the class strata, expressing neither deference nor condescension but the easy give-and-take of equals.

This was truest, of course, in the frontier communities that De Toc-queville visited, as it continued to comprise a large constituent of the democratic spirit of the frontier: manners counted not as etiquette—what was "correct"—but as a valuing of the person by others. The earli-est American books of etiquette (as Arthur M. Schlesinger, Sr., has shown in his little book, *Learning How to Behave*) dealt with the theme of deference to rank; and in the South these books continued to present the way of life of the English landed gentry and "the chivalry." After the Civil War the rise of the newly rich in the North brought with it a new solicitude about manners on the part of those who wished to gloss over their class origins.

The contemporary foreign travelers, who can now be read as ama-teur anthropologists of American behavior, were impressed with the gap in manners between the Americans and the Europeans. Mrs. Trollope especially, in her famous book on *Domestic Manners of the Americans* (1832), wrote about the American people, "I do not like their principles, I do not like their manners, I do not like their opinions." She was shocked at the male habits of tobacco chewing and spitting, at the execrable theater behavior of both sexes, at the silent bolting of food in public eating places, and at the rudeness both of women and children. Anthony Trollope, trying to heal the wounds his mother's book had caused, was able to add very little in the 1870s that could correct her picture of the 1830s. He agreed with her about the American "lower orders" who did not know their position, yet he had a grudging admiration for people who scorned subservient manners and demanded respect for what they were as persons. The comments of Charles Dickens on the materialism of American life and the grossness of manners that flowed from it are now classic. Yet despite the strictures of these travelers who came from a more rigidly stratified society, De Tocqueville's judgment that American manners were on the rough side but had the ease of an equalitarian society seems to give a better perspective.

After World War I, when leisure was spreading among the new middle classes, the problem of good manners took a new form—that of correct etiquette. Books of etiquette were marketed by artful advertisements presenting embarrassing moments, with the caption "What's Wrong with This Picture?" The 1930s were filled with "fear ads" showing the discomfiture of a well-meaning young American who didn't know the right thing to do. Peter Arno caricatured this whole literature of fear in a cartoon which showed a bride resting her wrong arm on her father's hand, the caption reading, "A Laugh Went Through the Congregation." But while the sophisticates laughed, a million copies of Lillian Eichler's *Book of Etiquette* and an equal number of Emily Post's *Etiquette* were sold in the quarter century between 1920 and 1945.

In an essay on Emily Post, Edmund Wilson has pointed out that her world of the 1920s is peopled by "characters" like those of La Bruyère: Mr. and Mrs. Worldly, the Gildings of Golden Hall, Mr. and Mrs. Kindhart, Mrs. Littlehouse, Mr. and Mrs. Oldname, and Mr. Richard Vulgar. The archetypal life that Emily Post had in mind was that of the Oldnames, who lived not lavishly or ostentatiously but in a style that was (as Wilson puts it) "costly and glossy, smart, self-conscious" and always with the perfection of taste which made every piece of furniture and every item of clothing "priceless." The America of today has moved away from this impossible norm. The new books of etiquette, like Amy Vanderbilt's, are written on the assumption that "it is no longer smart to be stuffy," that the mannerly American housewife may be running a servantless apartment, mingling with Catholics and Jews and needing to know their customs, and that she may even herself be a "new citizen." Yet the need to know the "correct thing" in every situation is still an insistent one in a mobile society in which the codes are difficult even to formulate. This is especially true since so many Americans came from cultures whose patterns of behavior were different from the American, so that they had to strip themselves of one pattern and take on a new one.

With the expanding life of the middle-class American in a consumer's civilization, new rules are necessary for dress and manners, entertaining, social letter writing, conversation, bringing up children, speaking before a club audience, travel abroad. The vogue of the cocktail party, night club, football, or World Series baseball games, "dinner and the theater," country week ends, summer vacations, has raised new conventional anxieties, from what to wear at the cocktail party to the "etiquette of the road." But the manners, fashions, and tastes of a society of widespread leisure, which govern its minutiae of social relations, are different in character and function from those of a society where leisure is sharply stratified by class.

These codes are not needed in a democracy, as they are in an aristocracy, to hold the society together, but to clarify the confusions that arise from class mobility and diverse ethnic origins. In the South, where status is more rigid, manners have always been much more formalized: visits, dances, dueling (in the earlier days), even conversation, were governed by a highly developed ritual. To a lesser degree this was true of New England society, and it is notable that the "novel of manners" flourished mainly in the regional literature of the South and New England. Both on the frontier and in the big cities the rigors of manners were dissolved: but even the frontier developed its own codes of rough-and-ready social relations, and in the early mining days of California there was a punctilio of violence. Thus "democratic manners" do not mean that codes are discarded but that the same etiquette and the same freedoms apply to all classes; as a result, the classes develop an ease of manner toward one another not found in more rigid societies. But this ease is not without its own anxieties. Especially among the white-collar classes and the parvenu rich, there is a malaise which reflects a fluidity of social movement without fixed standards of social behavior.

Each society infused its codes of etiquette with the characteristic tone and overtones set by its dominant ideals. The ideals in America are neither those of chivalry and status nor those of the aristocratic *noblesse oblige*. They are the ideals of making your way, of being popular and charming, of being a success. Etiquette books and columns are read in America largely as part of the "how to" literature. The problem in knowing the correct thing is not to fix your station but to avoid discomfiture and learn how to be popular and charming. The dominant drive is social acceptance.*

In societies with codes of good manners, there is likely to be good conversation, which at its best contains ritual elements. American conversation, while it has a ceremonial of its own based on the radio gag writer with his routinized "wisecracks," is not good conversation. On every class level it is built around much the same staples—gags about marriage and sex, banter about sports and parties, offers to bet someone on practically anything, jokes about politics and corruption, shop talk about business or office, women's talk about clothes and shopping, family persiflage, scandal about figures in the headlines, ripostes about "dates" and attractiveness. Thus conversation in America is fragmented and stereotyped, tending to copy the talk on TV and in the movies. An evening of conversation becomes a succession of stories, jokes, retorts, and discontinuous comment, where little is sustained and nothing explored. It is not so much a probing of personality or an exchange of ideas as a discharge of nervous energy.

Conversation thus holds a mirror up to popular culture and not to the life of intellectuals or artists. Even in popular culture it does not today parallel the traditional "tall stories" of the frontier or the "Southern conversation" which was a ritual prelude of every visit in Southern families of breeding, just as it marks a break from the conversation at the dinner tables of the New England Brahmins. But a society must be judged by its ideals, and the conversational ideal of the London of Samuel Johnson and Alexander Pope or the Paris of the great literary salons is not that of America. There is a racy quality in the Broadway characters of Damon Runyon, so cherished as an American image by British intellectuals, and there is a vitality in the rapid-fire dialogue of the American suspense thrillers which is admired by French intellectuals. But they have little relation either to the cultural ideals or reality of American everyday convention. Similarly, letter writing, which was one of the great arts of a stratified society in the days before the communications revolution, is practically an extinct one in America. The published letters of Henry Adams and of Justice Holmes—graceful, barbed, learned, wide-ranging—are unlikely to be duplicated among the literary men of today who don't have to write letters since they can phone or fly, or are too busy for leisurely correspondence, or have a ready financial market for whatever flows from their typewriters.

The problems of taste are more important to most Americans than those of conversation. Like etiquette, taste is a new empire brought

* For a discussion of "Society," see Ch. VII, Sec. 2, "The Seats of the Mighty."

within the reach of lower- and middle-class groups by the spread of leisure. The violent attacks on American mass culture should not obscure the role of leisure in breaking the old fences which used to shut millions of people from the elite standards of appreciation and taste. There are great popular audiences in America for good concert and recorded music, as well as a new mass audience of perhaps a hundred million readers for books in popular reprints—most of them trashy but some on a level which never had a mass audience before:* on questions of food and cooking, of household furnishings, of dress, of the choice of schools and colleges, of vacation places, of movies and plays, of methods of child-rearing, there is a constant "taste exchange." This has been true in other societies on the upper-class levels. But there has never been so wide a range of choice for so many people, nor so demanding a task in making the choice.

The standards of taste in America have been decried repeatedly by those who feel that Americans neither like the right things nor know what they do like and why. This is not wholly the product of recent commercialism. Even in Emerson's and Hawthorne's time the superficial and gracile "Zenobias" and "Cleopatras" that American sculptors fashioned on their trips to Europe became the rage among a public that found prestige in the appreciation of classical themes; and the flaccid Hiram Powers statue of *The Greek Slave* was admired at exhibitions and became, in miniature copies, a standard embellishment of the American home. In the new American society there was a collapse of the taste standards of the European societies from which Americans had come. The principle of social equality made impossible the European idea that the lower classes were to derive their tastes from those above who acted as arbiters. Most Americans prided themselves on having become liberated from their bondage to aristocracies, in matters of taste as well as in matters of politics. "You are in a country," wrote the novelist James Fenimore Cooper to the sculptor Horatio Greenough, "in which every man swaggers and talks, knowledge or no knowledge; brains or no brains; taste or no taste. They are all *ex nato* connoisseurs, politicians, religionists, and every man's equal and all men's betters." Inevitably the large new middle class that became dominant in America failed to show the requirements of taste found in a society clearly divided between patrician and commoner, or one in which the crucial relation was between patron and artist.

Yet it was not for want of trying. American women filled their houses in the 1850s with bric-a-brac, knickknacks, and *bibelots*. American husbands dreamed of building houses which looked like Greek temples.

* For a further discussion of this theme, see Ch. XI, Sec. 2b, "The Reading Revolution."

James Jackson Jarves, who was an art critic and collector in the 1850s and 1860s, wrote that "it has become the mode to have taste." Jarves and his family had lived in Florence, and many people since him have measured American taste by the standards of that great Italian city. Obviously American taste could not touch the height of Florentine society in the Renaissance, and there were many depths of vulgarity that it did touch. Yet the taste it fashioned was its own, set not by the arbitrary standards of a specialized group but by energies within the whole of American society. Edith Wharton believed that if the taste of the rich could be elevated, this would seep down and reform the taste of the rest of American society. Other writers and critics have fondly hoped that the taste of an intellectual elite could perform the same function. But they have all been proved wrong.

I shall return* to the problems of taste posed by a Big Media culture where the artist does his work for a mass market, and where new designs are mechanically reproduced in millions of copies. What I am concerned with here is the codes that shape American taste, and the pressure toward conformism in taste as in morals and personality.

It is true of most cultures that the popular taste is derived from the high-income upper class, and to an extent this has become true of America as well. But where America is different is in the fact that its middle classes have access to much the same goods that its top rich possess. Thus both good and bad taste are diffused through the whole society instead of being specialized to particular classes. The work of designers of some distinction is brought into millions of homes. Even when it gets there through imitation rather than through genuine taste, it may often succeed in molding taste. As a result the stuffy ornateness of much of nineteenth-century living, especially in American home interiors, is being replaced by designs and fabrics more closely related to the needs of American living.

There is an obvious leveling-out process going on in American taste. The eccentrics who gave flavor to eighteenth- and nineteenth-century American life find fewer counterparts in the mid-twentieth century. The grotesquely bad taste of the frontier society, or of the immigrant and working-class culture of big cities, had at least an element of lustiness, and the same is true of the lavish extravagance of plutocratic society from the end of the Civil War through the 1920s, which has been often caricatured by American satirists. The great danger in this area is not that Americans will accept conformism—as they tend to do in matters of opinion—but that the middle-class impulse toward "good taste" tends in itself toward the anemic. As Louis Kronenberger has

* See Ch. XI, Sec. 8, "Building, Design, and the Arts."

put it, the nerve-grating, teeth-on-edge qualities of American life come not from a people that is "overbred" (as in aristocratic societies) but from one that is "overburdened." This is another way of saying that taste is not a dominant cultural ideal in America, as it is in more stratified societies. The dominant ideals are prestige, security, and success. It is they that produce the strain and tension and cause the psychic burdens to mount. They, as well as the taste, are part of the price that a society of rapid mobility has to pay.

American taste has moved through successive layers and transformations, as through the phases of a cocoon. Russell Lynes, writing the history of the *Tastemakers,* speaks of the three broad eras of "public taste," "private taste," and "corporate taste." While one may argue whether this is not too neat a categorizing of history, there is little question that all three are present as elements shaping American taste today. The combined anarchy-plus-tyranny of democratic taste is still a reality in a mass-production society; so also is the new role of the corporations acting as Maecenases, and the tax-deductible efforts of the private collectors; so too is the autonomous taste of the individual who uses what is usable from the domains of public and machine-made taste, yet is bold in forming his own judgments and tenacious in holding to them against the current.

All of which does not mean that there are no leaders in fashioning taste, even in a democracy. The vogue of a sculptor like John Rogers, an architect like Richard M. Hunt, or an interior designer like Elsie de Wolfe in past phases of American taste has given way to the vogue of new "tastemakers" like Loewy, Dreyfuss, and Bel Geddes in the domain of industrial design. The plush-and-crystal crazes of past periods, expressed in the garish hotels, river boats, and Pullmans that were advertised as "palaces for the people," have become muted in contemporary America, where there is a fear of being too loud, and where glitter-and-gold seem too reminiscent of the parvenu decade. Ostentation has become unfashionable. Yet it would be too early to predict that the aesthetic energies of so rich a civilization will remain leashed very long.

The most striking taste development in America is the emergence of a consciousness of strata of taste which parallels to some extent the class stratification. The now classic division between "highbrows," "lowbrows," and "middlebrows" is an expression of prestige levels, not in the area of economic or social position but in the areas of dress, speech, reading, and preferences in art. Lynes has rightly pointed out that in this area there is a different kind of power politics from the one that applies in class stratification as such. There is a working alliance between highbrows and lowbrows, in the sense that the high-

brows value the folk impulses of the lowbrows and take over such popular preferences as the taste for comics and jazz. Very different from
both is the taste of the middlebrows, toward whom the highbrows feel
a condescension, and who in turn fear to be confused with the lowbrow. When one adds the distinction currently being made between
the taste of the "upper middlebrows" and that of the "lower middlebrows," and between the "old highbrows" and the "new highbrows,"
the whole picture takes on some of the quality of Warner's six-level
scheme of class stratification.

What is involved here is that the middle class, which has come to
dominate the rest of the culture, has found forceful challenges in the
realm of taste and feels isolated between the snobbery of the highbrow intellectuals and the vulgar energies of popular culture. Yet this
is in itself evidence that there are no class tyrannies in American taste,
and that the whole process of social change is still fluid enough to
allow for the upward movement of popular culture from below, and
the downward movement of critical taste standards from above. The
middlebrow is caught between the two currents, yet he does not long
remain the middlebrow. Nothing is more rapid in American life than
the changes in taste which form part of the same ferment as the
changes within the social order itself.

In dress as in other living standards, the lines of distinction between
the wealthy and the middle class have been almost wiped out in America.
This is not due to a redistribution of income: the buying capacity at the
top levels is still many times what is available at the middle and lower
levels. Nor is it the product of the willed simplification of technology
which shows itself in the industries of women's clothes as elsewhere. To
make big profits American designers have had to break through the
luxury trade, to tap new middle-class and mass markets. To do so they
have reduced the number of their basic models and distributed widely
"copies" of the work of the great designers of Paris and New York. The
differences are still there—in quality of fabric, in detailed work of finish,
in the time differential before new models are available for mass distribution. Yet a degree of smartness and taste is achieved even with cheap
fabrics and in factory-made designs, and they have also speeded up
changes in fashion.

Few societies in history have been as fashion conscious as the American, and there have been few in which styles and clothes have changed
so often.* Students of human society know that changing fashions are

* For an earlier discussion of fashions, as they affect the social role of American
women, see Ch. VIII, Sec. 6, "The Ordeal of the American Woman." For dress as living
standard, see Ch. IV, Sec. 5, "The Wilderness of Commodities."

an index of the pace of social change within the society: in the great Oriental civilizations, which were closed societies for centuries, there was little change in styles of clothing, whether for women or men; the stability of dress expressed the stability of status. In the class societies of the West, notably the French and British since the Industrial Revolution, changing dress fashions expressed the changing class relations, and the Victorian middle classes dressed as differently from those of the seventeenth and eighteenth centuries as the Europeans of today when compared with the Victorians. In the American case, however, women's fashions have changed more rapidly than can be accounted for by shifting class relations. Skirts rise and fall in length with a baffling periodicity; the female figure is first constricted in corset and hobble skirts, then flattened out into a shapeless tubular frock which gives it freedom as within a flour sack, then blossoms forth in the seductive outlines of the "glamour girl." "New Look" follows "New Look," revolutions and counterrevolutions in fashions succeed each other with bewildering rapidity, especially when the dress industries are in need of rescue.

America produced in Thorstein Veblen's writings one of the seminal theories of the relation of dress to society. He saw "dress as the expression of the pecuniary culture," especially in setting off those who don't have to work from those who do. He saw the modern woman as a prime exhibit of "conspicuous waste" and "pecuniary emulation" on the part of her husband, to impress the underlings. *The Theory of the Leisure Class* was written at a time of corseted and restricted women's dress and of garish display by the captains of industry. It explained a good deal about women's clothes in America, but not enough. For Veblen's theory is far less applicable to the American case than to any other of the Western societies. The fact is that American fashions are neither set by the "leisure class" in the sense of the capitalist elite nor could they be sustained by that elite. It is the upper middle class, including the girls of the college generation and the young matrons of the professional and small-business class, who are the carriers of fashion change. They vie with the women of wealth in showing that they can be as smart and modish on a much smaller outlay; and the women in the lower middle class, pushing up the ladder of mobility, vie in turn with them. As Quentin Bell has put it, "The society which produces changing fashions must itself be changing," and the transformation of the middle class has constituted the crucial class change in America. But American women are likely to wear their clothes not so much to impress the class below, nor even to ape the class above, as to show their distinction and individuality on their own class level. Dressing becomes for them at once an expression of status and a form of creativeness.

Efforts have been made to trace the changing profile of the American woman through the shifting male attitudes toward women and the shifting responses of the women. Some of these theories have focused on the impact of a war, the premise being that in war and postwar periods the male feels heroic and wants his women to be feminine and seductive. Thus the Gibson girl of the turn of the century is seen as a response to the Spanish-American War in her elegance of dress, her emphasis on feminine hips and bust, and her ankles peeping out from yards of skirt. The profile of the American woman in the era of the suffragette and of the militant feminists was reflected in the hobble skirts and the sheath gown. After World War I, the pendular swing was once more toward the sultry femininity of the "vamp." But during the rest of the 1920s the women, with their knee-length skirts and their concealed or flattened bust and hips, again took on a boyish and sexless look. In the 1930s and 1940s Hollywood emerged as the archetype of fashions, with Jean Harlow and Rita Hayworth as the "love goddesses" toward whom the world of women's creations moved. Toward the middle 1950s there was a struggle going on between the forces tending toward a return to the "Dark Ages" of the tubular, shapeless figure and those emphasizing the natural attractions of the female.

This theory, typically formulated by Winthrop Sargent in a *Life* series, has the merit of reckoning with the currents that govern the emotional life of the woman and are therefore reflected in her dress and adornment. Since fashions, like fads, contain much of the element of recoil that springs from the boredom of the repetitive, a cyclical theory can be maintained with only a measure of distortion. Yet it leaves out of account the long secular trend in American fashions, which has steadily drawn away from the cumbersome garments to the freer ones and from the concealing to the revealing ones. Again, as part of the long secular trend, each of the "vamp" or "glamour" phases is a step further toward the cult of legs and breasts that expresses American sensuality. With its sleek and shining quality of the "siren look," it adds the elements of danger, expressiveness, and accessibility to the sensual cult. Again, each of the "Dark Ages" counterrevolutions toward the masculine and assertive in women's dress and attitudes falls ever shorter of the goal of women's revolt. In the mid-1950s there were efforts at reviving the fashions of 1900 and 1920, but they were tongue-in-cheek affairs, largely by college girls whose freshness of looks and mold of figure allowed them to "get away" with almost anything, and who underscored Quentin Bell's suggestion that the American woman adds "conspicuous outrage" to Veblen's other categories of conspicuous display.

Moving steadily, despite occasional retrogressions, toward freedom of dress, the American woman, however, fails to be a free agent. She responds to the tribal compulsions that move in waves of tendency.

Simone de Beauvoir calls the world of women an "immanent" one, and Gina Lombroso has suggested that women tend to fix their sentiments not on ideas but on objects, deifying them and using them as symbols. If this is true generally, it would be doubly true of a civilization in which women live among a wealth of objects and means of adornment. The American woman lives in the ever-recurring hope that a change in her silhouette can achieve the miracle of a change in her life cycle or life destiny. Emerson quotes a lady as saying, even in his day, that a "sense of being perfectly well dressed gives a feeling of inward tranquillity which Religion is powerless to bestow." But is it always tranquillity? Obsessive interest in fashions is more likely nowadays to be a response to boredom or frustration, or to a failure of life goals. Thus the woman is the more ready to accept the gyrations of fashion because she half hopes they will compensate for what she has missed in life.

The great designers know this: if clothes help unhappy women to forget, then the way to sell new clothes is to force them to remember. "We must accelerate obsolescence," one businessman said. Another told his trade colleagues in 1948, when the "New Look" had swept the country, "We must have a New Look every year. It is our job to make women unhappy with what they have. You might call us the merchants of unhappiness." American designers have arisen to challenge the Parisian empires of Balenciaga, Dior, and Fath. New synthetic fabrics on the market have added novelties of texture to those of design and have placed both within the reach of lower-middle-class women. The art of dressing up and photographing models to bring out their height and slimness and the sculptured grace of their characteristic skull formations has been carried to a degree of perfection never achieved elsewhere. The dress industries have only a limited power to create fashions, but they can prod them.

The creative role is in the culture and in the woman herself. If women are birds of plumage, American women have a special assurance in the knowledge that the resources of the consumer's culture are at their command. College girls at the height of their social valuation are especially resourceful in dress, since they are pretty enough to take risks. They ransack the centuries and vocations for ideas, using jockey caps and the British soldier's tam-o'-shanter, ranchman's overalls, Peruvian Indian capes, Indian moccasins, American army jackets. They use every available fabric from the finest silks to fish netting and potato sacking. From hairdo down to shoes, they seek novelty and turn everything that strikes their attention to decorative uses. Yet these individual variations are within the frame of the larger fashion cycles, which are, at bottom, tribal compulsions.

As for men's clothes, they are equally subject to tribal compulsions, but in a quite different sense. While the conventions dictate constant change of style, design, and material for women, so that last year's fashion is as archaic as some monster of the Reptilian Age, the conventions dictate much the same men's clothing year after year. There are some exceptions to this, notably the "sports" garb of Miami and Hollywood, where a certain garishness is held modish; the "sharp" styles of the man-around-Broadway, as also the Harlem dandy; and the Texas-Western style copied from the ranch boss or ranch hand, with cowboy boots and ten-gallon hat. But for the rest there is the "standard business suit" or "N.A.M." garb, in blue or brown or gray, which has varied little for a half century. The great dividing line in clothes is between the work clothes of the manual and the white-collar occupations. The difference in clothes look between a corporation executive and his salesman or advertising copywriter is very little, except for the quality of the fabric and the cut of the suit. The difference between both of them and the railway or steel worker or elevator operator is much greater.

There is little valuation in America of the dandy, except in extremely limited cosmopolitan circles: there is no one in American life who takes the place of the French dandies of the eighteenth century, partly because Americans regard one who has no visible occupation as a wastrel, partly also because there is a fear of overdecorated male finery and refinements of taste in men's clothes lest one be suspected of a homosexual bent. Only recently, especially in the suburbs and at the resorts, has the American male broken away from his traditional drabness and ventured into experimental colors and styles. But here too it is the middle class, not the elite, that has been the innovator.

The possessors of power in America feel at once fearful of fripperies of dress and contemptuous of them. Their wives, who must express the decorative impulse for the husbands as well and who must win and hold their affection, are absorbed with fashions and clothes. In both cases it is the code that governs, but in the case of the woman there is greater scope for expressiveness within the code and greater need for it, since it must help fill the haunting sense of being unused.

4. Varieties of American Character

DESPITE THE simplified versions of the "American character" that fill the commentaries on American life, it is in reality diverse and multiple.* This is a product of the geographic variety, the crisscrossing ethnic strains and cultural traditions, and the intermeshing forces and

* For a preliminary statement of the problem of the American character, see Ch. II, Sec. 5, "National Character and the Civilization Pattern." See also Ch. VIII, Sec. 1, "The Personality in the Culture."

counterforces in a changing American society. The crucial fact is that there is no single pattern that can be called the "American character," nor is there a neat set of categories into which the American personality fits. Riesman, who developed a striking set of character types for America in *The Lonely Crowd*, stressed the ambiguities within each and the fact that any individual American contains elements of all. When he brought together a series of interviews and case studies of particular contemporary Americans, in his *Faces in the Crowd*, he found that they eluded his categories. Each personality is a battleground of forces sweeping from every direction of the cultural landscape.

Whatever makes America a relatively open society makes it also more mobile in developing a potpourri of personality traits. The plasticity I have noted in American ethnic types is also present in the personality patterns. I do not mean that American personality is less rigid than personality in other cultures: it may actually in many instances be more rigid. But the mobility which gives Americans access to new forms of leisure and experience exposes them also to the new postures of personality that go with unaccustomed modes of life.

Seventeenth-century England produced a number of books on *Characters* depicting English society through the typical personality patterns of the era. Trying something of the same sort for contemporary America, the first fact one encounters is the slighter emphasis on a number of character types that stand out elsewhere in Western society: to be sure, they are to be found in America as well, but they are not characteristically American. One thinks of the scholar, the aesthete, the priest or "parson," the "aristocratic" Army officer, the revolutionary student, the civil servant, the male schoolteacher, the marriage broker, the courtesan, the mystic, the saint. Anyone familiar with European literature will recognize these characters as stock literary types and therefore as social types. Each of them represents a point of convergence for character and society. Anyone familiar with American literature will know that it contains stock portraits of its own which express social types. I want to use these traditional types as backdrops and stress some of the social roles that are new and still in process of formation.

Thus there is the *fixer*, who seems an organic product of a society in which the middleman function eats away the productive one. He may be public-relations man or influence peddler; he may get your traffic fine settled, or he may be able—whatever the commodity—to "get it for you wholesale." He is contemptuous of those who take the formal rules seriously; he knows how to cut corners—financial, political, administrative, or moral. At best there is something of the iconoclast in him, an unfooled quality far removed from the European personality types that always obey authority. At worst he becomes what the English call a "spiv" or cultural procurer.

Related to the fixer is the *inside dopester,* as Riesman has termed him. He is oriented not so much toward getting things fixed as toward being "in the know" and "wised up" about things that innocents take at face value. He is not disillusioned because he has never allowed himself the luxury of illusions. In the 1920s and 1930s he consumed the literature of "debunking"; in the current era he knows everything that takes place in the financial centers of Wall Street, the political centers of Capitol Hill, and the communications centers of Madison Avenue—yet among all the things he knows there is little he believes in. His skepticism is not the wisdom which deflates pretentiousness but that of the rejecting man who knows ahead of time that there is "nothing in it" whatever the "it" may be. In short, he is "hep."

Another link leads to the *neutral* man. He expresses the devaluing tendency in a culture that tries to avoid commitments. Fearful of being caught in the crosscurrents of conflict that may endanger his safety or status, he has a horror of what he calls "controversial figures"—and anyone becomes "controversial" if he is attacked. As the fixer and the inside dopester are the products of a middleman's society, so the neutral man is the product of a technological one. The technician's detachment from everything except effective results becomes—in the realm of character—an ethical vacuum that strips the results of much of their meaning.

From the neutral man to the *conformist* is a short step. Although he is not neutral—in fact, he may be militantly partisan—his partisanship is on the side of the big battalions. He lives in terror of being caught in a minority where his insecurity will be conspicuous. He gains a sense of stature by joining the dominant group, as he gains security by making himself indistinguishable from that group. Anxious to efface any unique traits of his own, he exacts conformity from others. He fears ideas whose newness means they are not yet accepted, but once they are firmly established he fights for them with a courage born of the knowledge that there is no danger in championing them. He hates foreigners and immigrants. When he talks of the "American way," he sees a world in which other cultures have become replicas of his own.

It is often hard to distinguish the conformist from the *routineer.* Essentially he is a man in uniform, sometimes literally, always symbolically. The big public-service corporations—railroads, air lines, public utilities—require their employees to wear uniforms that will imprint a common image of the enterprise as a whole. City employees, such as policemen and firemen, wear uniforms. Gas station attendants, hotel clerks, bellhops, must similarly keep their appearance within prescribed limits. Even the sales force in big department stores or the typists and stenographers in big corporations tend toward the same uniformity. There are very few young Americans who are likely to escape the uniform of the Armed Services. With the uniform goes an urge toward pride of status and a routineering habit of mind. There is the confidence that comes of belonging to a large organization and sharing symbolically in its bigness and power. There is a sense of security in having grooves within which to move. This is true on every level of corporate business enterprise, from the white-collar employee to "the man in the gray flannel suit," although it stops short of the top executives who create the uniforms instead of wearing them. Even outside the government and corporate bureaus there are signs of American life becoming bureaucratized, in a stress on forms and routines, on "going through channels."

Unlike the conformist or routineer, the *status seeker* may possess a resourceful energy and even originality, but he directs these qualities toward gaining status. What he wants is a secure niche in a society whose men are constantly being pulled upward or trodden down. Scott Fitzgerald has portrayed a heartbreaking case history of this character type in *The Great Gatsby*, whose charm and energy are invested fruitlessly in an effort to achieve social position. The novels of J. P. Marquand are embroideries of a similar theme, narrated through the mind of one who already has status and is confronted by the risk of losing it. At various social levels the status seeker becomes a "joiner" of associations which give him symbolic standing.

The foregoing personality types are, in one way or another, forms of what Erich Fromm has called the "marketing orientation." Their chief concern is with what is vendible, what can be quickly marshaled and exchanged for valuable commodities. I do not mean this as a stigma on the American society which is built around the market. It was inevitable that when the exchange of commodities for money—which in turn will buy more commodities—became the focus of social energies, the logical final step would be to make man himself a vendible commodity. Marx had an insight into this when he spoke of the "fetishism of commodities" in his era, pointing out that the commodity (especially money) is personalized and becomes a fetish, while human labor becomes a commodity. Were he writing today he might stress that it is not labor only which is up for sale but also love and the whole human personality. He was so preoccupied with class exploitation that he failed to see the *vendible personality* as a fixture on every class level, so that even the ruling groups themselves become its victim. What this character type seeks is not so much the money into which it can turn its talents as the assurance—which the money partly offers—that by being in demand it is an effective personality. In a society where the measures of value become increasingly external, the vendible personality strives to be in demand so that it can be sure of its identity—sure, in short, that it exists.*

The vendible personality has aspects of the hollow, but it contains little that is destructive. That quality lies rather with another facet of American life, the *authoritarian personality*. One of the historical functions of the free market and the open society was to break up the authoritarian mold of the society of status which preceded it. But the Devil cannot be driven out with a pitchfork. The authoritarian bent reasserted itself in American life as did the drive toward status and security. On every class level at mid-century one found signs of a cocksure intolerance which expresses the "true believer" who does not hesitate to impose his belief on others by an imperialism of will. A number of American psychologists, who had learned something about the classic Fascist and Communist personality patterns in Central Europe, made extensive studies of the same personality types in the American context (*The Authoritarian Personality*, by T. W. Adorno and others) and found the essential pattern present, although it took a specifically American form under American conditions.

As pioneers in the Big Media, Americans are also sensitive to the authority of the media. As a result, the *publicity seeker* became an organic part of a society in which the Big Media are crucial in achieving status. He gets a glow from seeing his "name and face" in the papers. He will often work hard in organizations mainly to become an officer, and he reaches the summit of his dreams when his picture is taken with a visiting celebrity. In the small town he may be in the church-and-club set, and in the big city in the café-society set, but always he does what he does in order to be seen doing it. He is happiest in the goldfish bowl of the public eye. The surrender of privacy which has been a marked trend in recent American life is for him no sacrifice but an assurance that he is "in the swim."

Another aspect of the whittling away of privacy is the emergence of the *informer-confessor* as a recognizable character type. In the earlier days of evangelistic religion the confessor came forward and bore witness to having been saved from the flames of Hell. In latter-day America (I am speaking of the avid confessor, not the reluctant one) he bares his political past with a virtuous sense of having achieved salvation after sin. He exposes others who worked with him in the past, either to save the nation or his skin, or to compel them to save their own souls.

The confessor impulse is not confined to former Communists or even to politics. The obverse side of the confessor-informer is the *voyeur*, who

* See also Ch. V, Sec. 6, "The Reach of the Business Spirit," and Ch. XI, Sec. 9, "Artist and Audience in a Democratic Culture."

craves a glimpse into the private lives of others, especially the noted and notorious. A by-product of the Kinsey interviews was an epidemic of fake "investigators" who got a thrill out of interviewing women on their sex lives—and in a remarkable number of instances the women were willing to tell all to men they had never before seen. Social workers have also encountered this confessional urge; and it is obvious that part of psychiatric treatment is the chance it offers for baring the soul, however painful the process. This helps account for the American vogue of the gossip columnist and the gossip magazines, several of whom have built a following and a structure of power unparalleled in other societies. By catching the great with their guard down, the ordinary man is reassured that they are of the same human condition as he.

The Age of Anxiety has also seen the emergence of the *fearer-pursuer*. He is convinced that he is encircled by enemies; at the same time he is a hunter for dangerous thoughts. He can combine these two seemingly contradictory sets of traits because each serves as psychic source and reinforcement of the other. The paranoiacs who feel themselves surrounded by conspirators are likely to become the Hounds of God in hunting them down; those in turn who spend their lives in a sustained quest for subversives are likely to feel themselves caught, like the Emperor Jones, in the jungle of their own anxieties. To breathe they require the constant euphoria of the chase, alternating with the shivers of conspiratorial fear. This personality pattern is also closely related to that of the debunker, since it thrives on the conviction that the institutions of a capitalist democracy are window dressing behind which a secret enemy—Communist, Fascist, Liberal, Wall Street, or Jewish—is carrying on his machinations.*

I have mentioned the vendible personality and the authoritarian one. Two other broad character types need to be added to them. One is the *adjusting* personality—and, as a counterweight to it, what Peter Viereck has called the "unadjusted man." The loss of clear life goals,† the fragmentizing of the mind, the feeling of being part of a going concern too vast for any one individual to resist, have all contributed to the outer and inner pressures of the American to "adjust." This is a different matter from selling oneself in a talent and personality market, as it is also different from wreaking oneself on others or surrendering to an authoritarian hero.

The adjusting man may have little of the authoritarian animus within

* For aspects of the authoritarian personality in action, see Ch. VI, Sec. 10, "The Struggle for Civil Liberties," Ch. VII, Sec. 5, "The Minority Situation," and Sec. 6, "The Negro in America."

† See Sec. 8, "Life Goals and the Pursuit of Happiness."

him and little of the aggressive drives of salesmanship. He just wants to merge into his social landscape, to offer as little exposed and vulnerable surface as possible to the storms of life, to take his place in the scheme of society with a minimum of effort and an economy of psychic hurt. This applies to his political behavior, as it applies also to his behavior on his job, in his neighborhood, in his family, among his friends, and in his social set. There is an aspect by which the American "common man," who seemed so vigorous and assertive a figure from the Age of Jackson to the New Deal Era, has become merely the "little man," who asserts only his urge not to assert himself.

If these portraits of social roles that have emerged during the past half century in America seem to have unnecessary shadows and even smudges, it is because the stormy experience of a half century of social dislocation and change, war and cold war, is bound to take its psychic toll from the personality. It would be strange if this experience had not produced far-reaching changes in the American personality pattern. But one could set up a similar gallery of portraits and roles, done in very different colors, that would express the other side of the American personality pattern and might be as faithful to the varieties of American character.

I have mentioned the *unadjusted man.* He is, of course, the *rebel* American whose life history stretches all the way from the Revolution to the present moment. He may be the highly sensitive and socially conscious American, derisively called "bleeding heart," who has not lost the antennae of fellow feeling and who suffers every ordeal or injustice and deprivation to which others are subject. He may be the *libertarian* who has broken away from the illusions of revolutionary theories born in very different cultural milieus and is all the more stubborn in defending the freedoms of his tradition. He may be the writer or artist who uses irony as well as indignation as his weapon and who stays in his own society to fight it out, unlike his predecessor who went to Rome or the Left Bank of Paris. He may, however, find a different kind of solution, not in civic battle but in retirement to the realm of the private life, where he can be an amateur of the arts and of thought and release his imagination by making his own personality into a work of art. Or he may be the *committed* American, whether the roots of his commitment be religious or aesthetic or moral, who survives the wrack of change because his primary drive is to be part of something meaningful which transcends himself, without ceasing to be himself. I might add that the very use of the phrase "unadjusted American," with its negative reference, is itself a sign that the personality types within this broad category of the marginal American have not yet found themselves within their new setting.

I have left to the end a personality type which may reach closest to the heart of the American experience. For want of a better term I call him the *operational* American. Again he falls into a number of subtypes. He may be the *engineer-businessman* of broad perspectives, whose pride is that of construction and who thinks in terms of welfare. He may be the *organizing* American, able to translate dreams from a blueprint stage into reality. He may be the *commanding* American who adds energy to whatever situation he finds himself in and carries with him always the prospects of achievement. He may be the *footloose* American who roams through the new empires carved out by his technology, with a generosity of outlook that few conquerors have had. But the generic trait of all of them is the creative impulse that takes its characteristic shape through the urge to get a job well done, so as to release rather than constrict the spirit.

No one of these portraits is more than a facet of the complex multiple personality that we call "American." What makes the new American of inexhaustible interest is that he can be interpreted by every observer so as to bear out his own bias. Much depends on the accident of the particular moment of history at which the composite portrait is drawn. I know, of course, that all these personality patterns have changed as they have responded to contemporary changes in the social situation, and that they will continue to change. It is a risky business therefore to set down these temporary frames of personality as if they were permanent. But it is a risk that must be taken. For even if the particular social roles and character types are transitory, the larger patterns that I have sought to sketch out will probably survive.

5. The Disorders of a Society

WHETHER OR NOT every punishment should be made to fit the crime, it is pretty clear that most crimes and disorders fit their culture. To those who take pride in the normalities of the "American way" it may come as something of a shock to consider that it is exactly the excess of that same "American way"—the norm gone beserk—which represents the disorganization and pathology of the culture.

Every society has its characteristic types and styles of disorganization, its inner nature being illumined by the breakdowns of its codes. Thus where postwar Europe had its black markets, America had its rackets; where other societies are riddled with widespread illegitimacy of birth, America has the problem of illegal abortions; where other societies have their legalized prostitution districts, America bans them but has the call-girl trade and the adolescent "amateurs"; where other societies may encourage childhood thievery and marauding adventures, America is deeply concerned about its fourteen- to sixteen-year-old delinquents; where crimes against the person prevail elsewhere, in America the characteristic crimes are against property, and particularly the white-collar crimes of business and professional groups.

Americans are likely to worry most about juvenile delinquency. This is because of the sense that the young people are the foundation of the American future, and if they are corrupted, then the future becomes blank. Boys of fourteen and over who pilfer and steal, and girls of the same age who show "ungovernable behavior" or become sexual delinquents, pour through the juvenile courts in increasing numbers. The problem is not usually in their intelligence but in the conditions under which they grow up. The spate of statistical studies and life history "documentaries" shows them to come from "delinquency areas" where several subcultures are in conflict, and from homes whose emotional and moral atmosphere is unhealthy.

There are recurrent waves of guilt about these facts that periodically sweep over American society. The denunciation of slums and poverty gets the best responses when they are depicted not as ills in themselves, ugly and debasing, but as the breeding ground of child delinquency. The studies of rejected and unloved children leave their mark on the American mind less because the lack of love mutilates the personality than because it makes vulnerable material for delinquency. There are citizens' committees, surveys, conferences on juvenile delinquency. The newspapers dutifully record the solemn, scolding speeches, the moralists moralize, and the denouncers denounce. Usually there is a cry for more "recreation facilities" (recreation has been called the "nostrum of the citizens' committees"), which sheds light on the guilt feeling Americans have about delinquency. In contrast with the original image of immigrants who saw America as a wonderful playground, they have been compelled by the condition of the children to think of it as a condemned playground.

A persisting question is whether the volume of delinquency has actually increased during the past two decades or whether there is merely greater sensitivity to the problem and a more intense fixation upon it. The official figures show an actual and dramatic increase. Focusing on the ten- to seventeen-year-old, and taking as a base the estimate of annual delinquency at the rate of 1 per cent of the young people in this age group before World War II (between 170,000 and 200,000 children), the figures for the mid-1950s were just about double, meaning an annual rate of 2 per cent (around 385,000). If we add the children who are picked up by the police without having their cases brought before the courts, the total figure becomes roughly a million; and, according to the estimate of the Federal Children's Bureau for 1953, the probable total figure for 1960 is likely to be a million and a half. If, finally, we add the figures of children involved in dependency and neglect cases, which are the breeding grounds for delinquency, the official delinquency estimates are increased by 25 per cent.

The crisis moment in the life of a child in his encounters with the law comes at the age of fifteen to sixteen, a fact that underscores the relation between delinquency and the sexual and psychic problems of adolescence. The 1952 figures showed boys outnumbering girls about five to one in delinquency cases—a not very surprising fact when you consider the different demands that the culture makes upon growing boys and girls and the different roles it assigns them. The attitude of the society is a good deal more permissive toward the growing boy ("boys will be boys") and a good deal more solicitous in the parental control of the adolescent girl, especially in lower-class families. One should add that just as the society is more permissive about the code of the growing boy, it is more lenient in punishing his infractions of the code; in the case of the girl, there is a far higher percentage of referral to social agencies and commitment to correctional institutions. While delinquency is still centered largely in cities, the rate in rural areas is rising rapidly. Yet the basic problem remains one of the rejection of the children of minority groups by the larger culture. The normlessness which underlies what has been called the "mutiny of the young" finds more intense expression in those groups which have not made the transition to a new milieu and which feel themselves excluded from it.*

The human harvest of these seeds of disorder may be found in the ominous "statistical profile" of crime in America. At mid-century there were about fifteen million arrests annually in those cities where the statistics are fairly regular—a figure which represents only a fraction of the total offenses committed. Most of the arrests are for larcenies, burglaries, auto thefts, and other offenses against property. In only one case out of twenty does the offense result in imprisonment. In the case of white-collar crimes, involving business cheating, embezzling, illegal stock-market manipulation, tax evasion, defective merchandise, the proportion of offenses discovered to the total number committed is even smaller.

Despite a long history of prison reform and the relatively high standards of administration in Federal prisons, the condition of American prisons is still backward in most states, especially in the South, where the chain gangs are used to get cheap labor for public works and where

* For an earlier discussion of the adolescent gang, see Ch. VIII, Sec. 4, "Growing Up in America."

race feeling is added to the usual inhumanity between captor and captive. In most prisons the inmates are still kept shut up in cell blocks, given largely meaningless labor, and cut off from the responsibility which alone can restore a man to a productive life. In a society which stresses sex they are also cut off from normal heterosexual relations, so that prisons fortify and even breed homosexual tendencies. A few voices are now asserting that "prisoners are people too," and experiments are being made in informal prison farms where the men can come closer to normal patterns of daily living and have their confidence in humanity restored.

But the individual criminal dwindles in importance before "rackets" and "syndicates." The racket is a pattern of extortion and tribute which urban brigands levy on night clubs, shopkeepers, bars, manufacturers, trade-unions, waterfront companies, and truckers, under threat of despoiling their goods or premises and even death. The syndicate is a business combine with a feudal structure of authority, organized to exploit activities beyond the law or on its margin—gambling, betting, slot machines, houses of prostitution, "call-girl" services, and narcotics.*

These activities are not as marginal to American life as they are to American law. One trait on which the rackets and syndicates build is the belief in luck, which is deeply ingrained in a culture that underlines the big prizes. There is widespread betting on sports events—on horse racing, prize fighting, baseball, basketball, football. Slot machines are the center of rural and roadside taverns as well as of urban bars and luxury clubs. One of the purest forms of the belief in luck is the "numbers" or "policy" game, in which bets are placed on what numbers may turn up each day in officially published reports, such as Federal Reserve Bank statements. The crowds gathered around New York's newsstands for early editions of the morning tabloids are probably more interested in getting the racing results and the "numbers" pay-off than in the international news. The annual "take" from slot machines has been estimated at two billion dollars. The income from "policy" betting in Chicago alone, largely in the Negro areas, is estimated at fifty million dollars, most of it in nickels, dimes, and quarters. In such low-income Negro areas, "policy" may mean destitution for thousands of families—and wealth for the few men who organize and run it as a big business. For the gambling industry as a whole, including bookmaking, legalized or pari-mutuel betting, the "numbers" game, "policy," slot machines, and lotteries, the annual business has been calculated at fifteen billion dollars, involving an industry that ranks in gross sales with such major American industries as chemicals.

* For the "racket" and the "fix" in the context of American politics, see Ch. VI, Sec. 4, "The Party System and the Voter."

To protect these industries against the uneasy conscience of the community, an alliance is sometimes formed between the syndicates and rackets on the one hand, and on the other the political bosses, machine politicians, police-force officials, wire and phone services, trade-unions, and seemingly respectable business concerns that operate as "fronts." It was this alliance which was the principal target of inquiry by the Kefauver Committee in 1951 and the McClellan Committee in 1957. The importance of these inquiries, as also earlier of the writings of Lincoln Steffens and the muckrakers, was that they made the American people aware of the tie-up between lawlessness, politics and the marginal aspects of business and trade-unionism. What they saw did violence to their cherished belief not only in law and order but in the healthy organization of their society. A few men went to jail, a few local administrators and labor leaders were thrust out of office, new Federal tax laws made the "bookie" profession a good deal more dangerous—but the basic pattern of the rackets and syndicates went on.

America today, as in the past, presents the picture both of a lawless society and an overlegislated one. In some of the earlier societies the reliance was less upon detailed legal norms and penalties than upon custom and the sanctions of community opinion. But America is the type-society of the West in which little is left to loose community action, and the characteristic way of dealing with crime is to set down definite statements of legal transgressions and punishments. Nevertheless, Americans consider crime a problem they cannot master, which will continue to grow because it is an outcropping of some inner disease of their society. Recognizing this, they also recoil from it, thus displacing on the criminal their own guilt and powerlessness—which may help explain why the treatment of crime has lagged. To feel mastery over the environment, over things and money, and yet to feel baffled by so elementary a fact as crime, has become a source of frustration.*

Like the belief in luck, the habit of strong drink is something Americans worry about while many of them continue to practice it. The frontiersmen prided themselves on their drinking excesses: the isolation of life, along with its rigors, led to a plentiful consumption of homemade spirits. For the plantation leisure class of the Old South, heavy drinking was at once an antidote to boredom and the mark of hospitality for the landed gentry. Among the miners and cattle ranchers of the Far West, the frontier saloon was an outlet for the turbulence of new and lawless settlements. All these strands of social inheritance may still be found in American drinking, yet while the old reasons for heavy drinking no

* For the concept of the criminal in American law, see Ch. VI, Sec. 8, "Law and Justice."

longer apply in the urbanized indoor society, the drinking remains. The new reasons for drinking are probably more closely connected with the driving tempo of life in America and the anxieties, frustrations, and aggressions it engenders. It should be added, however, that the practice of "local option" means that a large part of the nation is legally "dry," and what drinking there is must be done in private homes or by subterfuge. The heavy drinking is to be found in the Eastern centers, on the West Coast (California leads the nation in alcoholism), and in the centers of new wealth and social change, like Texas.

Not the least of America's mores are woven around the night club, the roadhouse, the public bar—and the private bar at home. Just as betting and gambling take on emotional overtones from the ritualized competitiveness of American sports, so liquor in the night hours and night spots takes on sexual overtones from the orgiastic arts of "hot music" and sexually revealing "revues" and "floor shows." The sexual revolution of the 1920s removed the restraints against drinking by women; except in the small towns, where the older mores prevail, women will be found drinking in public restaurants and bars, or at private parties at the "cocktail hour," which is as basic a national institution as afternoon tea for the British or the Continental *apéritif*. So crucial did the consumption of alcohol become in America that the Prohibition episode came closer to dividing the nation into two camps than anything since the Civil War, and the cleavage between "wets" and "drys" became a struggle between Guelphs and Ghibellines. Much of the network of rackets and syndicates goes back to these Prohibition days: so strong was the feeling against "law enforcement" that the American attitude toward the Prohibition agents in the 1920s was very like that of a Resistance movement toward an army of occupation.

Distinguishing between "social drinkers" and compulsive ones, there were some forty or fifty million of the former and about two and a half million of the latter, of whom at least a half million were confirmed alcoholics. While these figures seem large, the problem of alcoholism in America is not as serious as in European countries like Sweden and Germany. In their efforts to deal with alcoholism, Americans characteristically resorted to the device of a club, "Alcoholics Anonymous," whose members supported one another in their efforts to refrain from drinking. As for narcotics addiction, the narcotics traffic increased after World War II, and the vigilance against it tightened. About a fifth of the fifty or sixty thousand drug addicts were teen-agers, mainly from the metropolitan centers and especially the Negro areas. The smoking of "reefers" (marijuana) was more widespread among teen-agers than drug addiction: its danger lay in its leading so often to heroin or morphine.

To these items of social pathology we must add organized prostitution, illegal abortion, homosexuality in its more compulsive forms, and sexual offenses—especially against children—which were often in the headlines and roused intense popular anger.*

These are all departures from the dominant norms of cultural health. Some of them, like crime, are deliberate attacks upon the norms; others, like delinquency, alcoholism, drug addiction, and prostitution, are forms of failure in living up to the norm. In some instances, as with homosexuals, or heavy drinkers who are not alcoholics, or those migrant and homeless men who are unemployed and who cluster in the flophouses, it is a question of being on the margin of the norms. In the case of mental defectives (which Americans tend to push away without much discussion except when there are drives to sterilize them by law) and in the case of sexual psychopaths, we are dealing with the clearly pathological. Some forms of disorganization fall under none of these categories, but—like many cases of suicide, for example—flow from normlessness, or the failure of any kind of values to take hold of the individual.

Americans are concerned and baffled about these phases of their society. Having found that many of their problems yield to technology and organization, they feel ordinarily that their way of life ought to move toward purpose and contain solutions. Yet in the norm-breaking and normless behavior we have discussed they find a spectacle to shake their belief in their own institutions. They see the social breakdowns as symptoms of the decadence and disintegration of American society as a whole. Things "fly apart at the center," reversing what Americans regard as the natural order: children grow up to become criminals, gangsters, gamblers, the face of innocence takes on the hideous mask of the narcotics addict, families are broken up by divorce, "nice girls" engage in promiscuous sex or even become professional prostitutes, the image of the clean-cut young businessman turns into that of the uncontrolled alcoholic or the compulsive homosexual, respectable citizens are revealed as white-collar criminals, and the basic activities of life are turned into rackets. Thus the Americans find the most cherished symbols of their society turned topsy-turvy.

Yet does disorganization always violate the essential spirit of the culture? Does it always mean the abnormal, pathological, anticultural? Actually the departure from norms may shed extraordinary light on the inner nature of the culture. In trying to explain why Americans are themselves deeply drawn to the gangster films which they know to be distortions of their urban life, one notes that a gangster is an American

* For sexual deviants, see Sec. 7, "Society and Sexual Expression."

"cultural hero" in whom Americans recognize a symbol of the energy of their culture. Or take American criminologists, who stress the paradox of the "rationality" of the habitual criminal, in the sense that given his twisted antisocial premises, his acts flow logically from them. What they often ignore is a different kind of rationality: that the criminal takes seriously the barely concealed premises of the culture itself. He sees easy money being made and predacity practiced, knows that the rules are constantly broken, knows that there is an internal violence in the act of exploiting the market and ravishing the environment.

Thus the forms of American disorganization arise from the more naked drives within the culture itself, with the workaday masks stripped away that have hidden the sadism and ugliness which are part of the human condition and are to be found in every culture.

In every society forces are generated that are harmful to its functioning and in the end destroy it. It would be strange if this were not happening in America as well. But those who fix upon crime and rackets, divorce, prostitution, and alcoholism as proofs of American decadence and degeneration may be fixing upon the wrong symptoms of the wrong disease. Most of the phases of social pathology I have listed are the extreme applications of principles which, in lesser degree, may be healthy. The delinquent and the criminal, so greatly feared by Americans, are not so dangerous to the social fabric as they seem to be. The point about the gangster, the racketeer, and the syndicate operator—even the housebreaker and the burglar—is not that they scorn property but that they value it enough to be ruthless in seeking short cuts for making it their own. The adolescent delinquent, in turn, in the act of rebelling against family or school or community, may be seeking the cherishing love upon which the family and other primary groups must be based.

The principles by which American culture lives are those of freedom and acquisition, and—where the two meet—the freedom of acquisition. There are always a number of people who feel themselves left out of the operation of these principles, or who are too much in a hurry to wait, or who feel resentful because others seem to start with an unfair set of principles, and who therefore seek some equalizer. Since they feel at a strategic disadvantage in the competition of life, they feel justified in ignoring the usual inhibitions and in tearing down the accepted cement of social relations. Because they use a distorted version of the cultural energies to destroy social bonds and rip apart the cohesiveness of the society, they in effect pit the culture against the society.

One may deplore these dislocating energies, but they would seem to be an inherent part of a society in which the pace of life is set by freedom, competitiveness, and acquisitiveness, and they are part of the price the society pays for those informing principles. A society less free and less dynamic—one of tradition and status, or one of totally state-directed power—may escape some of these dislocations but be beset by others. The whole impulsion of American culture is to raise hopes and claims in the individual and spur him on to fulfill the hopes and nail down the claims. At the same time it is too young a society to have developed the kind of inner discipline which—let us say, in England—can serve to inhibit the full sway of the impulsion.

Take, for example, the extreme case of the narcotics "pusher," who is even willing to corrupt children and develop the narcotics habit in them in order to make customers for his product. He represents the principle of creating a market, inherent in the market economy. In the mid-1950s he was thriving in America mainly because the severely repressive Federal narcotics laws, with constant "crackdowns" by enforcement officials, kept increasing the danger of narcotics distribution and therefore the price and profits—without reaching at all the terrible sense of isolation which underlies the use of narcotics. But he is also an example of the desensitized man in whom the principle has run wild, like cells in a cancerous growth. Or consider the case of the racketeer, who on principle recoils from the notion of earning his bread by the sweat of his brow, but who invests great resourcefulness in applying *force majeure* at the most vulnerable points of business enterprise.

The racketeer is likely to come up from the slums, reaching for quick affluence by breaking the windows of the mansion of American success rather than by entering at the door. There are studies showing how the prominence of Jews, Irish, and Italians in urban crime has swung from one immigrant group to another as each has flooded into the United States, sought to orient itself in American society, and become assimilated to it. At the beginning they are dislocated from their old culture but have not absorbed anything of the new culture except its cruder aspects; they have demons within them to assert themselves in a challenging new environment, they have few inhibiting fences around them, and they are in a hurry. The violence with which intense slum youngsters imitate the values of the culture, even while distorting them, may be seen as their own form of flattery. What they do is legally and morally wrong, but instead of being a sign of the decay of American life it may be taken almost as a sign of its vitality.

One of the clues is the dynamism of rapid social change. Racketeering crops up mostly in the areas of new business enterprise which have not yet been reduced to order or become subject to tradition, and where economic change moves more rapidly. The most serious outcroppings of violence and crime come also at the times of greatest social change, involving a rapid migration of population, the shifting of industries, the contact and clash of subcultures, the improvement of living standards, and the opening of new perspectives for which people are not yet prepared.

As a case in point we may take the known fact of the prevalence of reefer-and-dope addiction in Negro areas. This is usually explained in terms of poverty, slum living, and broken families, yet it would be easy to show the lack of drug addiction among other ethnic groups where the same conditions apply. One may guess that the rapid movement of Negroes from a depressed status to the improved status and partial freedoms of today, with new jobs and new living standards, has led also to the breaking down of old goals, while the new ones are still vague and seem inaccessible. I have noted in an earlier section that the passion for equality feeds on itself, setting the goals ever higher and making the distance from them more embittering. Drug addiction thus becomes one of the expressions of the isolation and normlessness that are the by-products of social advance, achieved under nerve-wracking stress, bitterly paid for. Where rigid status is being broken up and class lines shifting, and where a sense of social hope persists, social disorders are the tribute which the unbalanced individual pays to the naked premises of the culture.

Their real danger lies not in the pathology of cultural values but in their denial. The delinquencies and moral breakdowns which flow from the sense that only power counts and all American life is a racket are less dangerous than those which flow from the sense that nothing counts —not even the rackets. The breakdowns of family life or of sexual morality, and the crimes against property, by threatening the foundations of the American social structure, evoke counterforces in turn which solidify the social structure in its own defense. A frontal attack tends to be met by a defense in depth. Yet the disorganization which flows from the desensitizing of men, and from a lack of belief in any values, is a threat to the idea of social structure itself.

6. Morals in Revolution

ALMOST SINCE THE beginnings of their society, Americans have been as troubled about the everyday infractions of the moral codes as about the pathologies of social disorders. Their moralists are forever talking of the "moral breakdown" of their time. In few civilizations is there so constant a sense of moral crisis—to which one might remark that where there is so continuous a crisis there is no crisis at all, but only an unremitting malaise and anxiety. It is shown by the nostalgia for the "good old days"—the primitive simplicities of an agrarian society where right and wrong were clearly delimited. They have a Golden Age feeling of a lost Eden, and of the face of innocence covered over with latter-day Babylonianism.

Much of this anxiety focuses on the young. In the 1920s the American moralists were shocked at the "revolt of the younger generation," with new freedoms of smoking, drinking, petting, and premarital sex. Some saw it as the end of the world, others as a passing rebellious whim. Actually it was neither, but a phase of a continuing revolution in morals. The form it first took in the 1920s has been described by Lloyd Morris in terms of a semantic change: "The word 'neck' ceased to be a noun; abruptly became a verb; immediately lost all anatomical precision." Armed with bootleg liquor, the young and the old flaunted the codes of the bluenoses. The flapper-and-flask "lost generation" of the 1920s gave way to the "social significance" generation of the Depression and the New Deal in the 1930s, hot for certainties in political causes. This in turn gave way to what one of its members has described as the "beat generation" of the 1940s, canny and de-emotionalized, addicted to bebop, its boys dazed by wars and cold wars, its girls torn in the lonely debate whether "to sleep or not to sleep." As for the 1950s, the "beat generation" in turn has given way to what may be called a "sure-thing generation," anxious to find moorings early in an insecure society.

With every change in the nuances of rebellion and despair on the part of the young, the elders cluck-clucked and the moralists viewed with alarm. In the realm of morals Americans tend to regard man as fundamentally good and are shocked when they find men breaking the codes and turning out untamed and evil. This sense of shock has become chronic. While the moralist finds widespread evidence of the disintegration of controls over the personal vices (sex, alcohol, and gambling), his outcries against public corruption are as loud as against private immorality.

All moral codes are experiments in social control—instruments through which the family, church, school, Army, community, and state maintain their hold on the individual. As long as religion held a central place in belief and organized the lives of individuals, the codes were a corollary of religion but secondary to it. When faith in God began to slip, the Americans of the later nineteenth century tried to put secular morality in its place.* The weaker the religious bonds became, the more rigid the moral codes grew. Since they largely lost their religious sanctions, the effort to prop them up with the supports of community

---

* One should separate out the Catholics from these generalizations: what I say here applies less to them than to other religious groups. They have tried to maintain a religious rather than a secular control over morals.

opinion and secular hell-fire became more frantic. Inevitably the next step was taken—the use of legal measures through censorship, Prohibition, and the revival of old statutes against sexual offenses. America thus became an overlegislating and overmoralizing society.

Censorship is a case in point. There has been no central political censorship to seize upon ideological heresies, but there is a Legion of Decency under Catholic auspices, plus a handful of state censorship boards to watch over the moral level of films. In addition, there is a network of new unofficial groups that watch over the reading habits of their neighbors, imposing a private ban on the publication and sale of "obscene" books and magazines. These censors have built their moral case on the mushrooming growth of magazines and book reprints that blatantly display sexual drawings and photographs on their covers and deal with those who exceed the limits of obscenity. Most of the cases fall short of those limits, and the policing problem is too difficult for government machinery to handle. This has left the field open to the private groups, which try to impose their moral imperialism on the public and periodically force local booksellers to remove books and magazines (including some good ones) from sale under the threat of community boycott.

Professional moralists, from Anthony Comstock in the 1870s to the vigilantist local busybodies of the 1950s, have had little effect upon actual behavior. Americans remember that sensitive foreign observers were shocked by the widespread American habit of tobacco chewing and tobacco spitting, and that the moralists once included smoking, lipstick, theaters, and novels among the vices. Today smoking is accepted for women and adolescents, and is the base for major American industries. The recent medical research on the relation of smoking to lung cancer in males has probably done far more to inhibit American smoking than all the homilies of the churches and elders.

The turning point in the American attitude toward the moralists came with the "Great Experiment" of Prohibition. The efforts of the "women's crusade" and the Anti-Saloon League over a number of decades had finally pushed the nation into a large-scale suppression of drinking. The result, in Herbert Asbury's graphic language, was "a horde of bootleggers, rumrunners, highjackers, gangsters, racketeers, triggermen, venal judges, corrupt police, crooked politicians, and speakeasy operators, all bearing the twin symbols of the Eighteenth Amendment—the tommy-gun and the poisoned cup." This experience made Americans recoil from what Gerald Johnson has called "the illusion that you can establish morality by law," and they came to take a less Catonian view of human frailties. Its most revealing result was the light it shed on the organized evasion of the law. The "speak-easies" and "bootleg" liquor were a dramatic expression of the process of "patterned evasion" observable throughout the social system.

More subtle than individual code-breaking, patterned evasion is a collective circumventing of the codes, paying lip homage to them as codes while allowing the individual to tailor the code to his life and personality. One finds a parallel in Great Britain, where—if a law has been made archaic by social changes—the practice is not to repeal it but quietly to disregard it. There is a similar parallel in the French attitude toward the collection of taxes. American examples may be found in divorce practices as against the formal law of divorce, in "graft" and "influence peddling" as against the formal administrative procedures, in sexual promiscuity as against the codes of marriage and chastity, in white-collar crime and corporate "rigging" as against the theory of business morality. Some writers have spoken of the "structured corruption" in American society, through which the principle of "each for himself," "what's in it for me?" and "I might as well get mine" finds expression in practices socially recognized even while they are legally and morally ruled out. A notorious gangster, Willie Moretti, put it plaintively to the Kefauver Committee during its crime investigation: "Everything's a racket today. Everybody has a racket of his own. The stock market is a racket. Why don't they make everything legal?"

The answer to Moretti, of course, is that legal and moral codes have their function, setting norms for the conduct of life and fixing the direct and indirect penalties that serve as control instruments. But patterned evasion also has its function, which is to allow interstitial room for those who must deviate from the letter of the code while accepting its framework. In this sense, structured corruption and patterned evasion are the price society pays for the survival of the codes when too great a rigidity would break them. They furnish, in short, a way of living with codes without an intolerable psychic strain.

Thus to say that one cannot have one's moral cake and eat it is to reckon without code evasion. The evasion is not merely hypocrisy, although an element of hypocrisy does enter. It rests rather on a collection of social or cultural fictions, which James Woodward has termed "functional deviousness." In the clash between strong impulse or self-interest and the moral code, men may resolve the clash by giving it the homage of a stereotyped fiction, while following the impulse or self-interest which conflicts with it.

A characteristic instance is the practice of padding expense accounts for the purpose of tax deductions. Much of the luxury restaurant, bar, hotel, and night-club business in the larger American cities is based on a new "expense account aristocracy" which writes off many of the amenities of life against the "necessary expenses" of business entertainment and travel. Strictly, it breaks the legal code and is subject to fine or jail, but usually it is accepted even by the government as a convenient fiction by which the structure of heavy taxation remains while the individual is able to cushion its rigors. A distinction is often drawn between tax "evasion" and tax "avoidance": the latter stays inside the margin of legality while the former falls outside. But Justice Holmes, who believed that law expresses the operative rather than rhetorical moral practices of society, protested against this hair-splitting. He held that law enforcement has to draw a line at an arbitrary point, and that everything this side of the line must be considered legal and not simply "avoidance" of the law.

What is true of expense accounts is true also in the area of sexual adventure. In business it is true of the evasion of antitrust laws by the fictions of corporate organization and reorganization; it is true of many practices of the stock market, of the construction industry (where the codes are so cumbersome as to be nonsensical), of trade-unions. It seeps down into school and college, as shown by instances of collusive "throwing" of basketball games and "cribbing" in examinations.

The margin between immorality on one hand and patterned evasion and cultural fictions on the other is a narrow one, yet the basic dividing line is clear: the group accepts the evasions and fictions while it rejects the immorality. But even in the acceptance there is an ambivalent quality. For a nation with a Puritan tradition, there is a measure both of guilt and triumph in the stolen sweets acquired by eluding the outer and inner censors. What are the psychological sources of this evasion of norms? One can discern in the mixture the desire for freedom of action, the constrictions of small-town morality in an expanding society, the greed for profit, the impulse to "have fun," the reasoned willingness to take social risks within the community in the interests of the "pursuit of happiness."

I have left out of account the morality-breaking impulse itself. In an individualist America there have been many individuals who lived in deliberate defiance of morality. The history of American radicals who fought with this Nietzschean beyond-good-and-evil impulse against the encrusted codes, especially those who broke the rigid taboos on American women until the first World War, is a history of men and women who courted martyrdom in order to achieve social liberation. Some of them flaunted the codes in order to dramatize their archaic quality.

The story of Robert Dale Owen and Frances Wright, of Bronson Alcott and Orestes Brownson, of Josiah Warren, Stephen Pearl Andrews and Victoria Woodhull, of John Humphrey Noyes, Ezra Heywood, Benjamin Tucker and Moses Harman, is one of struggle for a society in which the hold of codes would be broken and the individual left free to enter into "natural" relationships. The invasion of Socialist thought brought with it another crop of moral debunkers who hoped to substitute the utopia of a "rational" collectivist society for the code shackles presumably imposed by the capitalist system. They did not see that they would destroy one set of codes only to replace them by another.

To measure the impact of these morality breakers upon the American mind, one may quote a sentence from Mark Twain, who was a sensitive barometer of the climate of American thought: "We have no real morals, but only artificial ones—morals created and preserved by the forced suppression of natural and healthy instincts." Mark Twain assumed here what Rousseau had assumed—that the "natural" instincts are "healthy," that man is born in innocence and freedom and only by society and its codes is he corrupted and enslaved. This was the credo of the moral reformers I have called "morality breakers." They must be distinguished from another type of "reformer"—the code fanatic like Anthony Comstock or Bishop Cannon or the small-town moralists whose task was to nail down the code provisions. Thus Twain's credo had its countercredo in these moralizers, who held that the natural instincts are corrupt and the human passions dirty, that human sin can be checked only by community vigilance and the individual's inner censor. They held that codes are broken only by willfulness or weakness, and that the answer is a system of legal and social penalties, since morality can be established by law and enforced by community scrutiny.

Caught between the morality breakers and the moralizers, the American has fumbled for a moral credo of his own. This credo takes the biological drives as neither wholly good nor wholly evil, but faces the need to reckon with them. It looks to the main chance. It is the credo of people in a hurry, striving for their quota of money, power, and "fun," snatching at what they can get while they run—although not without anxiety and guilt. To assuage their guilt and square conscience with impulse, they rely heavily on institutional evasions.

De Tocqueville in the 1830s was impressed by the strictness of American morals, which seemed far more chaste and severe than the European. He attributed the difference to freedom of marriage, the education of women, the cohesiveness of the family, the sway of religion, and the single-minded preoccupation with business which seemed to him to make life more orderly. But he also thought that once immorality set in, the equalitarian impulse in America would level the moral codes as well as the political ones, fixing them from below rather than above; in America, he notes, "no class exists which can undertake to keep society in order."

He was partly right in his analysis. American moral codes have been small-town codes, fixed in a simple agrarian society by the austere standards not of the dominant economic or social class but of the lower-middle-class "respectable" churchgoing groups. The wealthy and powerful did not shape the codes but lived largely on their margin. The business Titans whom I have called the "Puritans" shared the small-town morality, paying it at least lip service; those whom I have called the "magnificoes," like Morgan, flaunted them. Unlike the codes of manners and fashions, the moral codes are not copied from the groups with social status by those who yearn for it. The upper groups, with their mobility and prestige, manage to purchase only a degree of freedom from the codes. The shaping force of the codes is the Judaeo-Christian tradition as taken over by a Bible-reading people, who transposed the taboos from ancient Hebrew to modern American society.

The great moral revolutions in American history came with the changes in technology that gave rise to new classes—especially the white-collar and professional middle classes—and gave them access to new experience. Just as it was the old middle classes that fixed the moral standards of American life, so it was the continued flux of the new middle classes and the new elites that forced a change in the operative moral codes. Only a society with rapid social mobility can carry through so drastic a series of moral revolutions without being shattered or becoming cynical and sophisticated.

One can trace several phases in the continuing recent moral revolution in America: the revolution of morals and manners of the 1920s, the revolution in the status of women, and the continuing sexual revolution whose results are shown in the Kinsey studies. The striking fact is that they were not accompanied by the open cynicism one may find in Paris, Rome, or Vienna. Nor do Americans show the lack of self-consciousness one finds in the Scandinavian countries. Being troubled by their moral lapses, they feel neither wholly sophisticated nor wholly pure in heart. Yet they resolve their problem by continuing to observe formally codes which operatively they evade and sometimes even ignore. They use their new mores to relieve the pressure of the rigid older codes. These new mores generate a momentum of their own as they are more widely practiced—a momentum which carries them beyond the original goal of a convenient device for evasion and sets up a new norm in the form of an operative code.

As the shift from the formal to the operative codes took place, the force of the mores in American life became stronger than the force of morals. Americans are apt to denounce strong drink, inveterate gambling, and loose sexual morals—yet embrace them in practice. The formal code says a man must be temperate in drink, prudent in avoiding games of chance, continent in sex, and governed by the values of religion and honor. It says similarly that a woman must be chaste and modest. But this formal code has been replaced by an operative code which says that men and women may drink heavily provided they can "carry" their liquor and not become alcoholics; that they may gamble provided they pay their gambling debts, don't cheat, or let their families starve; that a girl may have premarital sexual relations provided she is discreet enough not to get talked about or smart enough to marry her man in the end; that husband or wife may carry flirtations even into extramarital adventures, provided it is done furtively and does not jeopardize the family; or (if they are serious love affairs) provided that they end in a divorce and a remarriage.

If these operative codes are broken, life can become intolerable in the smaller communities, and even in the cities it will be conducted only on the margin of respectability. These codes are an effort at approximating the life experience of Americans. They seek to arrive at new rules of conduct which will be more than merely the mores of the community but will prescribe for the good life in a manner not too widely separated from the mores.

What Americans are suffering is not so much a moral breakdown as (to tear a phrase from Nietzsche out of its context) a moral interregnum. One king is dead and a new one has not yet been crowned, as with the moral interregnum at the time of the Roman Empire, when the pagan codes had broken down and the Christian codes had not yet been shaped. In fact, although American writing and thinking show signs of a constant search for a new formulation, it is not even clear out of what line the new kingship will come—out of what ethos the new moral code will emerge.

Whatever the new codes emerge from, they will have to reckon with the cultural life goals. It is difficult to make the ideal of honor persuasive in college sports when it is not applied to business, labor, and politics. It is hard to preach homilies to young people who have witnessed the triumph of shams in their communities and homes. There is a popular quip that a man who steals a small sum from another is sent to jail but one who extorts a huge sum from the public—by his control over legislators, his lobbying power, or his ability to hire smart lawyers in a tax deal or a corporate reorganization—is an honored citizen and can flout the code from the top of his heap of money. Government administrators who cry out against the vices of the trusts are themselves often captured by a big corporate job. Corporate executives who cry out against union racketeering and government corruption tend to forget the role of businessmen who are in complicity with both. For every bribe taker in the government, there is a bribe giver, generally in business; for every union racketeer there is a context of collusion between a cynical employer and a cynical union official. From the defective muskets of the Civil War to the embalmed beef of the Spanish-American War, from the Teapot Dome scandals in the 1920s to the lobbying corruption of the natural-gas industry in the mid-1950s, the record of American economic and political power is not one to reinforce moral preachments against individual private infractions of the code. Thus American moral standards have had to fight a difficult battle against the mounting hypocrisy of institutions.

If the knowledge of this hypocrisy spreads it may produce a feeling of hopelessness about enforcing the codes in the case of the top power elite. Where this hopelessness exists, morality is hard to inculcate. Even the traditional control agencies—including the churches, schools, courts, and home—become infected with it. In the end the strength of a code depends less on the penalties it can threaten or the taboos it invokes than on the conditionings which produce inner restraints within the individual. He is responsive to a code only as he has a sense of belonging to the society which it helps to hold together. In America the cultural life goals—success, competition, power, prestige, security, happiness —speak more loudly than the moral codes. The indices of belonging are belongings. What gives a person status is less integrity than success; what drives him is the emulation of the possessors; what is likely to fill his thoughts is not the right way of life but new access to the goods of life.

Other people's actual values may be more effective in shaping a person's morality than the codes they preach. If public opinion frowns on stealing it frowns also on poverty and gives grudging admiration to a quick dollar made quickly. A girl who is generous with her charms may find that "the whole town is talking," but if it finds that she has no talent for interesting or holding men, its silence and its indifference to her may be more scathing than talk. A successful Hollywood starlet or TV actress is expected to move toward her goal with few scruples about the moral price she has to pay. A cynic may say about American life, as Balzac and Thackeray said about nineteenth-century European society, that the effective immorality is not code-breaking but failure.

I do not mean to leave the impression that what I have said applies equally to all Americans. There is a diversity to be found in moral beliefs and practices in American society. There are still a large number of Americans, especially in the small towns and among the stricter religious sects, who adhere pretty closely to the formal moral codes. Recent studies of American soldiers indicate that about one third of them, during World War II, did not make use of their "leaves" to let off steam and contented themselves with the operative codes of Army behavior. Moreover, in the case of many parents the anxiety or dismay over the conduct of their children is not hypocrisy but the result of a real shock because of the discrepancy between the formal and operative codes. There is a constant stream of young people coming from the small towns and villages to the large cities, where they can find an escape from the censure and censorship of their neighbors: but the older people whom they leave behind often still cling to the codes.

This brings us back to the primary truth that the source of morality in a society is the culture itself and the operative (not rhetorical) valuation that it places upon the comparative goods of life. Morals arise not from a vacuum nor from lawgivers but from the common apprehension of men, and they change as that apprehension changes. If there has been a breakdown of morals in America, its clue is in the relation of the unfolding personality to the values of acquiring, possessing, competition. These are hammered in on the growing child by movies and TV, by the press and schools, by the family itself. The cyclical recurrence of prosperity, depression, and war only serves to heighten the impact. For depression brings the disintegration of old ties; prosperity brings the heady sense of the big money; war—and there has been a war in every generation—brings both. None of these can produce deep moral belief or a stable moral code. When the moral middle classes in America bemoan the "moral breakdown," they are bemoaning something which they and their life values have largely brought about, corroding the old moral code without bringing a new one into being. That is the moral interregnum in America.

Meanwhile the reigning moral deity in America is "fun." Martha Wolfenstein has noted the role of "fun morality" as a shaping force in the operative moral code. There may be little that is novel in this morality, at least for the upper classes. The latter part of the eighteenth century was a period of intemperate pleasures; the period from the end of the Civil War to the turn of the twentieth century was one of ostentation and garish display, as noted by such chroniclers of the rich as Alva Johnston and Cleveland Amory. There is a similar garishness in the contemporary New York and Chicago night clubs, displaying dancing girls in diaphanous nylon net or in panties trimmed with mink.

The big change that took place, therefore, was in the democratization of fun. The quest for it was no longer limited to the rich but became pervasive through the whole social structure. "We had fun" or "It was lots of fun" became an almost compulsive description of a successful party. The turning point came in the moral revolution of the 1920s, whose spirit Scott Fitzgerald caught as being "like a children's party taken over by the elders." In fact, much of the emphasis on fun was a recoil from the responsibilities of adulthood in an iron age, and a recasting of the American's image of himself in the image of a gay and irresponsible child. From another viewpoint "fun morality" may mark the passing of the older belief that life in this world is of little worth and only a preparation for eternity: since the present is the only life there is to live, then why not have fun?

Thus the idea of having fun is a protest against a number of the traditional sources of morality—the Puritan conception of seemly deportment, the solemn values of the elders of the community, the ideal of purposeful work, even against the business and money pursuits which make the fun possible. It is a way of standing American life on its head, reversing its solemnities with a jesting mockery. Thus Max Eastman, in his autobiography, could speak of his moral heritage from his ancestors as "my load of virtues"—which makes the Greenwich Village revolt intelligible because the fun was a recoil from the unendurable load of virtue. Most of all, fun came for many Americans to represent an abbreviated way of expressing the sexual freedom which flowed from irresponsibility. It meant dates, parties, autos and speed, drinking, dancing, late hours, necking, and petting. It came to be an elastic word whose meaning could be stretched all the way from the wholly innocent to the delightfully culpable. In the end it took on a final ironic twist, becoming itself a social compulsive, so that the necessity for having fun became as rigid as the old Puritan taboo of it. Parties, dates, or vacations that could not be described in terms of fun had a lingering sense of failure attached to them. Instead of freeing himself from the old codes, the American was caught in a new social imperative, often a curiously joyless one. One should add here the stretching of the life span, which means that even middle-aged and elderly Americans now have far more time for fun than was possible for their parents and grandparents.

Despite the spread of relativism in many areas of American thought, it did not triumph in the sphere of morality. As each of the generations came of age, it did not discard the idea of enduring moral values but was skeptical as to whether the values it inherited were those it could live by. Americans must live in three universes—a natural or biological universe with impulses they can neither ignore nor suppress, a social universe with life goals and institutional practices of which they form part, and a moral universe with values that give life much of its meaning. As each generation breaks away from the standards of the preceding one, it is moved not only by rebellion but by an experimental impulse. It is the impulse to find the warmth of fellow feeling which it needs, or a sheath within which it can insulate itself from the harshness of contemporary life and develop its own values. Thus these rebellions express as much the effort to achieve belief as they do disillusionment.

The blinkered critics of American life see only the corruption and the sensuality, the chasing for fun, the moral breakdown: they fail to see the elements of strength behind the continuing moral revolution. American morality is not summed up by its emotional frustrations and its tongue-in-cheek code evasions. The quest for new standards is itself a sign of cultural strength. The revolutions in morals come not out of weakness or resentment but out of a ferment which pervades the society and especially the groups moving up the social ladder and getting new increments of experience. Obviously this new experience is at first disintegrating in its effect, when the individual on his new level of living gropes for a freedom of action he had never had. But out of this groping there may emerge challenger codes which will distill, as all successful codes must, the ambivalent sense of social discipline and of individual striving for emotional expression.

7. Society and Sexual Expression

THE TUMULTUOUS CHANGES that overturned the codes of moral behavior and of manners, fashions, and taste could not help affecting sexual behavior in American society. It is a truism that sex is sex the world over and has been all through the ages. But unless this is meant as a joke it would scarcely imply that anything so deeply culture-rooted and socially conditioned as the relations of the sexes would remain untouched by the storms that swept across character and society in America.

Every society imposes regulations and codes upon sexual relations, but the striking fact here is that American codes, permissive in most other areas of behavior, are more restrictive about sex. The American girl, with wide leeway in choosing friends, clothes and schools, books and magazines, movies and plays, places to go and people to see, with freedom of movement, education and opinion, is nevertheless closely watched and admonished on everything affecting sexual relations. Even the American male adult, who may be ruthless in business and is expected to be inventive and adventurous about his work, comes up against a strong taboo when he is tempted to show the same qualities in his sex life. Thus sex is locked in an anomalous position within the frame of American society. The American cannot help becoming aware of the gap between what the society formally exacts of him in this area and what it allows in almost every other. From the start sex is separated from the rest of life, surrounded with stronger (and therefore more exciting) prohibitions, banned except within the traditional forms and inside the limits of marriage.

After puberty and menarche the American boy or girl must make a choice between curbing the biological impulses or breaking the codes. In the small-town society before the sexual revolutions of the twentieth century, the choice was generally toward curbing the drives. Since World War I the choice has generally been toward evading or changing the codes. But there has been little relaxation of tensions. The figures on mental health suggest that the psychic strains of American life were at least as heavy in the mid-1950s as they were before World War I. What happened is that the forms and sources of the strain changed. Sexual life in America grew freer in breaking and evading the taboos, but conscience in the face of the codes remained, and as long as it did the evasion of the taboos remained a source of anxiety and guilt. Since freedom generates its own tensions, which grow more assertive with every new gain by freedom, every gain in sexual freedom in America has generated the appetite for further gains and has widened the gap between code and conduct.

America has become in many ways a sensual and sexual society, but with a curious blend of blatancy and deviousness. The marks of the blatancy are in evidence throughout, but especially in the advertisements, the picture magazines, the movie posters, on the covers of paperback books, in musical comedies, and on TV programs. America has come to stress sex as much as any civilization since the Roman. When the buried ruins of New York and Los Angeles are uncovered by some future Winckelmann they will show erotic pictorial images not strikingly different (allowing for the difference in American conditions) from those of Herculaneum and Pompeii. The cult of female legs and breasts will be noted by future historians as characteristic of Americans: "beauty contests" turn upon the contours of both these anatomical features; newspapers and magazine picture layouts exploit both, and the "cheesecake" of a movie starlet's legs enticingly displayed for the photographers at the airport, or the half-exposed breasts of a Hollywood love goddess who is outstanding for her natural resources are recognized publicity stunts.

But the combination of this sexual emphasis with the Puritan taboos results in a sexual furtiveness. The American movie code, for example, is rigorous about how nakedly the sexual attractions may be revealed, but the publicity agents expend great ingenuity to promise seductive delights. In the actual production of a movie a minor fortune may be spent in filming a tantalizing bathtub sequence and a king's ransom in publicizing it. Thus what is most expressive about American culture is not sex in itself but the public furtiveness in the use of the sexual appeal as a way of stimulating the senses and suggesting images of secret delight—at the same time that there are outcries against it. The culture betrays itself in the conflict between the sensual pulls and the Puritan restraints.

In a study of the "folklore of sex" Albert Ellis noted the split between the overt repudiation of sexual behavior infringing the codes and the covert acceptance and even celebration of it. He found mass media authors explicitly supporting the conventional sex attitudes while introducing sexually inciting themes and hinting admiration for those who get away with the illicit pleasures. The impulse to have one's cake and eat it, in the sexual realm as elsewhere, offers an insight into American personal relations. Undogmatic, making no fetish of principle in itself, the American follows the hedonic impulse in a happiness civilization, while he refuses openly to flaunt the accepted moral standards of the community. This is not so much hypocrisy as it is part of the pattern of accommodation to reality, which treats both conventional attitudes and the hedonic side of life as realities and tries to make the best of both worlds.

The American absorption with sex has been put under a crossfire of attack—from the Left as evidence of "capitalist decadence," from the Right as proof of the horrendous results of "atheistic materialism." Pitirim Sorokin, finding it the climactic expression of the widespread disease of the "sensate culture" of the Western World, sees American sexual freedom as leading directly to the inner collapse of Western society and the conquest of the American imperium by outer barbarians, as in the case of the Roman Empire. One of the weaknesses of the argument that sexual freedom dooms America to destruction and oblivion is that it mistakes the sources of the American absorption with sex. It derives less from sexual freedom itself than from the centuries of the Puritan heritage of repression. This applies not only to the overt and covert sensuality of American life but also to the heavy incidence of sexual neuroses, which are the product of the conflict between human drives and social goals and codes, and the internalizing of that conflict within the developing personality.

The life goals of success, hedonism, and power, and the preoccupation with magnitudes and statistics, are reflected also in American sexual behavior. Thus the characteristic American contribution to the study of sex—the work of Alfred C. Kinsey and his associates—is statistical in method and emphasizes the calculation of average and modal sexual "outlets" in a statistical sample. Kinsey was anxious to break with what he called the "philosophic" tradition in the study of sex, in which he included not only the moralists, poets, and philosophers but also the psychoanalysts and psychiatrists. Trained as a zoologist, he sought to limit himself to what could be measured and classified. Yet this expression of behaviorism in a realm reserved for sentiment and moralizing is itself characteristically American. It helps account for the popular emphasis upon the sexual calculus, which is the contemporary American successor to the Benthamite calculus of happiness. One may guess that the effort to keep track of sexual frequency became merged in the American mind with the cultural ideals of success and happiness, which came to depend partly upon the test of sexual activity.

The two volumes of Kinsey studies, however—*Sexual Behavior in the Human Male* and *Sexual Behavior in the Human Female*—met with considerable criticism. The interview method was widely attacked as unreliable in studying sexual behavior, since the subjects in their unconscious mind were likely to distort the versions they gave of their sexual record, either by boasting or by covering up. In any event (it was contended) human sexual behavior cannot be measured statistically, like an animal's: to try to study it as if it were the wingspread of the gall wasp is to miss the depth and emotional content of human sexual relations. Finally (it was argued) the frequency of the sexual "outlet" sheds little light on its morality. It became a stereotype in the Kinsey criticism to say that the frequency of sexual outlets no more makes them moral than the frequency of the common cold makes it healthy—an equating of sex with disease which in turn sheds considerable light on the heritage of Puritan repression.

In answer, Kinsey and his defenders said that he had set himself the task of studying measurable sexual behavior and not sentiments and emotions; that he left morals to the moralists, love to the poets, and the unconscious to the psychoanalysts; and that he wrote only as a biologist when he put men and women in their setting in the natural universe of the mammals. The answer had force, yet it left a core of validity in the indictment. Kinsey understandably swung the balance away from past moralizing in the direction of measurement and behaviorism. The history of all human knowledge is the record of this kind of seesawing from underemphasis to overemphasis. As a biologist, Kinsey sought the source of human sexual drives in the natural universe and in man's animal behavior—which does not mean that a person's animal behavior sums him up as a human being.

If Kinsey had one foot planted in the world of nature he had the other in the social universe, emphasizing the taboos and codes that seek to hem man in. In the spirit of Rousseau's "Man is born free yet he is everywhere in chains," Kinsey put the responsibility for repression upon the social heritage. If the American could be unshackled from the traditional moral codes (he reasoned) he could be restored to his natural and healthy state. Thus, despite his dedication to his massive work in the spirit of a detached scientist, there was a reformist element in Kinsey which sought to bring legal and social attitudes closer to the nature of human sexual drives. The weakness of his premise was the assumption that the "natural" was the healthy and that the social and moral were almost necessarily repressive. This was to take a negative view of the intricate web of social arrangements (in Freudian terms, the "superego") which not only check the biological impulses but give them dimensions of emotional and aesthetic meaning scarcely to be found among the "infra-human mammals." Kinsey failed to see that it is not only the biological drives but also man's emotional needs that are part of human nature and require fulfillment.

This does not diminish the importance of the insights derived from Kinsey's work. He found a far greater spread and variety in the forms and extent of sexual activity for both sexes than had been assumed earlier. He shed light on the sexual life history curve of American men and women. The profile of male behavior shows the adolescent, at seventeen or eighteen, to be at the threshold of his full sexual powers, while in the case of women there is a much slower development, with the peak not being reached until around the age of thirty. After that, the woman's curve of capacity levels off to a plateau which remains relatively stable often well into the fifties; by contrast, the male curve, starting earlier and rising more steeply, also declines more precipitously. Kinsey also found a greater prevalence of premarital and extramarital sexual relations than had been previously established; while the percentage of such activity was higher in the male than in the female, it was the findings on female behavior that caused the greater stir. His figures on deviant forms of sexual behavior, especially homosexuality in the male, were equally striking. Just as dramatic was his contention, based on a sample of almost 15,000 subjects of both sexes, that women respond less frequently and intensely to psychological stimuli than do the men, and that the role of the imagination in sex is therefore a more important one for the male.

In the case of the American male, the sexual life pattern he is likely to follow is, in Kinsey's view, set during his adolescence. But while this life pattern is in large measure genetically determined, the forms in which the sexual drive expresses itself are shaped by class, education, and social environment. One of Kinsey's striking conclusions was that male sexual behavior in America varies greatly with the class and educational level. He found the strongest sexual activity among the lower middle classes, who get to high school but not beyond it, while he found the lowest activity among males on the college level. More important than frequency, however, are the differences in the forms and styles of sexual behavior. "Petting" starts mainly on the college level, although it has spread to the groups on the high-school level. Premarital relations are most frequent on the grade-school and least frequent on the college level. Homosexual relations are lowest on the college level. Nudity and kissing, which are held in suspicion on the elementary-school level, are most accepted among college groups. On marital fidelity the lower educational groups start in a more vagrant mood but come increasingly to confine their relations within marriage, while on the higher educational level the relative fidelity to marriage vows is corroded and there is an increasing tendency to seek sexual adventure outside of marriage.

These class differences apply far less to the case of the American woman. Instead, Kinsey found striking differences in the sexual behavior and attitudes of women depending on the decade of their birth. This was especially true of "petting" and other forms of premarital sexual experience. Kinsey's findings served to document other evidence that a sexual revolution took place in America around the time of World War I, and that since then every successive generation of women has followed the new pattern of sexual freedom and pushed it further. In fact, Kinsey's work is best seen in the context of a continuing sequence of sexual revolutions that go back for many generations. A little more than a century ago Orestes Brownson attacked Hawthorne's *Scarlet Letter* for its blatant parading of adultery. Theodore Dreiser's novel, *The Genius,* expressed the drive toward sexual reform, although it made its hero a Nietzschean man-out-of-the-culture, whereas actually the sexual revolution came to permeate the lives of ordinary Americans. In its initial phase, its aim was to liberate the American woman from her status as a chattel of her husband and a ward of community opinion. But once started, the revolution was extended from women to men, from the young people of the 1920s to the middle-aged people of today. The latter are being told in the popular magazines—what most of them have already discovered—that sexual expression need not end with the end of youth, and that the middle years can be sexually the richer because the tensions of youth have diminished.

In the midst of changing sexual behavior, the legal codes and attitudes remained relatively rigid. Kinsey made a good deal of the point that the legal and moral codes derive from the Judaeo-Christian tradition, chiefly from the Jewish tribal laws as set down in the Old Testament, which accept only reproductive sexual relations within marriage and which were carried further by Christianity. Students of religious history have seen considerable differences between the Jewish and Christian traditions on this score, and—within Christianity—between the Catholic and Protestant traditions. Yet there can be little doubt that much of the harshness of the American legal codes toward sexual offenders is due to the harshness of the religious heritage. In spite of a good deal of recent insight into the psychogenic factors in homosexuality, all homosexual relations are still subject to severe penalty under the law. The problem of sexually obsessed psychotics who prey upon the young and defenseless is being given intensive study, and in some states there has been considerable progress toward treating these cases as problems in mental disease. Yet the problem of sexual deviants—or "perverts," as most Americans tend to call them—remains a baffling one.

The political debate early in the 1950s on the presence of "sex perverts" in the State Department and in other "sensitive" government posts opened a broader debate on homosexuality. There was an uneasy sense that it was increasing in America, due mainly to widespread social disorganization and the distorted emotional patterns within the family; yet there were no comparative historical figures to indicate the secular trend. Some students took a wholly relativist view in the debate, contending that "normality" in sexual behavior had little meaning; that homosexuals ought not to be treated as a pariah caste; and that the task of mental health was to help these deviants to live at peace with themselves and their partners so long as they did not hurt the community. There were others, however, who, without either hostility or hysteria, regarded homosexuality as a form of neurosis and therefore of unhealth, and as a departure from the heterosexual cultural norm, which was deeply interwoven with the whole web of social institutions and moral codes. This view rejected the harrying and ostracism of sexual deviants but sought—wherever possible through psychiatric aid and through preventive work within the emotional structure of the family—to cut down to a minimum the growth of homosexuality and the harshness of social attitudes toward it. Its underlying premise was that of flexibility of view within a broad frame of sexual norms. It held that sexual behavior is a matter of personal growth, deeply impelled by biological drives, taking place within a social and moral frame, and in turn affecting the style and quality of social experience as well as the basic health of the civilization.

Despite crosscurrents and counter-eddies the full sweep of the broad stream of the American sexual revolution has scarcely yet been felt. As against the legal prohibition of their sale before 1920, contraceptives have been passively accepted as a functioning part of social practice and are made widely available. Their basic rationale is the need for birth planning and family spacing in marriage, and it should be noted that American scientists have recently been at work to develop cheap and effective contraceptives for the fight against overpopulation in areas like the Caribbean and the Asian countries. Yet in the setting of American sexual behavior the new knowledge has been closely related to the sexual revolution. The same is true of the development of effective treatment of venereal diseases, removing much of the sense of menace that served as a taboo against sexual experimenting in the past.

One of the results has been a sharp decline in commercialized prostitution. I do not mean that commercial sex is not still substantially present. While the streetwalkers and the segregated districts of the big European and Asian cities are less important on the American landscape, there are still teen-age "B-girls" to be picked up at dances or bars, "call girls" who are available by phone, "kept women" who are the American form of the Old World concubines, and attractive "V-girls" who may have jobs and live on the margin of the respectable but supplement their income by selling their sexual favors to out-of-town businessmen or convention visitors in the big cities.

But the great change that has occurred is outside prostitution, in the availability of men and women alike for sexual adventure. The files of marriage counselors and of psychiatrists and psychologists are crammed with material about sexual episodes hidden in the shadows of the lives of outwardly conventional people of every class and ethnic and religious group. By comparison with the Restoration period of sexual license in England and the eighteenth-century sexual revolution in France, the new American sexual orientation is far more pervasive. In the British and French instances the sense of sexual release was felt chiefly among the upper nobility and often took the form of perversions and libertinism—as witness the erotic literature of both periods, especially in the writings of the Marquis de Sade and the licentious romances of the British. In the American case there is considerable spread through all the classes, although Arthur Hirsch is probably right in calling attention to its concentration among the "upper-cultured"—that is to say, the college-trained groups. It is part of the folklore of America that the greatest release from restraints is to be found in the Hollywood colony —as witness a novel like Norman Mailer's *The Deer Park*. Yet there are other segments of American life where sexuality is more privately conducted and is incorporated into the busy lives of hard-working executives and professional groups, without the white glare of publicity that focuses on Hollywood.

The important fact here is that a shift has taken place from the commercial to the private sexual releases outside of marriage. With the failure of the religious sanction, with the new geographic and social mobility and the gospel of personal fulfillment and happiness, a new sexual orientation has taken shape. The carrier of the revolution has been the American woman rather than the man. Recent novels present her as expecting sexual fulfillment and confronting the male with the challenge of developing a "psychological potency" which will equal hers.

On a different level Americans have had to contend with disturbing developments in the sexual behavior of adolescents. It is here that the gap between the codes on the one hand and the biological impulses and social stimulants on the other has shown itself most dramatically. The adolescent boy at seventeen finds himself in high school, probably in a classroom with an unmarried middle-aged female teacher, and watched over at home by censorious parents and neighbors. He knows that he is old enough soon to be subject to the military draft—to be given a gun and sent to the far corners of the world, perhaps even not to return. The adolescent girl, having newly discovered lipstick and grown-up clothes, living in a culture where marriages come earlier in each generation, is equally impatient of the taboos and restraints that encircle her. In both cases the adolescent is surrounded by clamorous sensual stimuli—the movies and TV, juke boxes, newspapers, and magazines. The resulting conflict between the codes and the biological and social stimuli has resulted in a considerable breakdown of community moral standards among adolescents.

The fact is, as Herbert Blumer has noted, that adult practices and attitudes in the area of sex have been pushed down increasingly to early age levels. Dating, formal dances, and petting may be found at the age of twelve or thirteen, and sometimes even earlier in the pre-adolescent age. There is constant pressure on the parents for permission to act the role of precocious adults. The power of decision about sexual behavior seems to have largely shifted from adults to adolescents and preadolescents. This has meant a strikingly earlier sexual sophistication than in the past—another instance (along with advertising, consumption, and TV) of how America is basing its society on the triumph of adolescence.

The question of how to deal with this phase of "the mutiny of the young" still baffles most Americans. Exposés of "non-virgin clubs" and sexual "orgies" among high-school students have been splashed in headlines across the nation. The community has tried to deal with the problem by periodic "cleanups" which soon subside and are forgotten. The courts have tried to deal with it by reform schools and correctional institutions, and often by severe jail penalties in the case of "statutory rape," where the girl is below the age of consent. The trouble is that in the case of premarital sexual relations, the law classifies as criminal the types of behavior that are practiced and tacitly accepted by a large part of the population. Given the gap between actual behavior and formal codes, Kinsey estimates that 85 per cent of the younger male Americans could be convicted as sex offenders. In the gap and conflict between these two forces he finds a source of much of the American sense of guilt and anxiety, which form the heavy psychic toll that Americans pay.

A curious fact is that Kinsey did not follow up this insight adequately in his work. Instead of regarding sexual deviants and sexual disturbances among both men and women as evidence of the psychic devastation wrought by sexual conflict, and instead of viewing the sexual precocity of the young as a phase of the complex interaction of instinctual, social, and moral factors, he allowed his naturalistic emphasis to triumph and refused to regard these forms of behavior as posing difficult problems for American society. While he did not explicitly make statistical frequency the test of the normal, his whole emphasis was on sexual expressiveness whatever the nature of the "outlet" and its surrounding emotional tone. There was also an element of the naïve in the premise that gave him his faith—that once the operation of the taboos is exposed and the accumulated moral hypocrisies laid bare, the hold of archaic laws, codes, and attitudes will be broken. He failed to understand that despite the fluid nature of American society there is a tenacity in the codes that is hard to break through, and their hold is all the greater because the loose and sprawling character of the society frightens most Americans and makes them cling all the harder to the challenged codes.

However vulnerable they may be, the Kinsey studies nevertheless represented a monumental advance in the understanding of American sexual behavior. The courage and candor with which they were pursued would have been impossible if the sexual revolution starting in the 1920s had not paved the way for them, but, equally, the social challenge that provoked the studies as response would not have been possible if it were not for the depth of resistance to the revolution.

The American society that Kinsey studied was in its sexual aspects half Babylonian and half Puritan. There was an explosiveness of release from the older taboos which was largely a recoil from the repressiveness of the past, especially in small-town America. But the shocked, angry reaction to the Kinsey findings, especially those in the volume on the American female, showed that the repression had not been torn out. Kinsey's own response to this hostility was a bristling one, perhaps because he was so certain that future generations would vindicate him. Even in his own day the fact that a team of responsible scientists undertook the studies and that responsible foundations financed them was a sign of growing maturity in American sexual attitudes. The size of the statistical sample, surpassing that of any previous studies, and the care with which the interviewing techniques were developed, were themselves indications that—within their limits—the studies were thorough.

It is somewhat ironic that the Kinsey studies should have been attacked as an invasion of privacy, when much of their impact was to strengthen the right of each person to his individual decisions in the area of his greatest privacy—his sexual life. It was in this sense that Kinsey, like Freud, must be counted a liberator. Not that his work can be proved in itself to have wrought much change in the actual pattern of sexual behavior: it would be truer to say that it had its effect on American attitudes and gave some scientific sanction to the underlying forces that were changing the behavior patterns. Thus Kinsey's impact was that of a kind of Guilt Killer. After all the valid criticisms have been made, it remains true that Kinsey's work has broken the taboos surrounding the last area of human behavior which had been left almost wholly unexplored. In that sense Kinsey's pioneering work was characteristic of American pioneering in the large.

Sexual revolt in America has asserted three freedoms: the freedom to break the formal codes; the freedom to diverge from the majority sexual patterns into deviant behavior; the freedom to lead a fully expressive sexual life in the pursuit of happiness. It is the last of these three which has become most meaningful in recent years. It is not revolt for its own sake, nor revolt to bait the community censors, nor to establish the rights of sexual deviation, but revolt for a healthily expressive life.

In an important sense this liberation movement differs sharply from the sexual revolts of the past. It has become in its own way a protest against the lack of standards characterizing the earlier sexual revolts. It calls for liberation from a kind of sexual anarchy which was becoming in itself a new tyranny. It emphasizes the sustained relationship as necessary to a healthy sexual life. Even while it is willing to treat sexual deviants with humanity, it does not regard them as expressing a satisfactory way of life. It is not moved by status panic or fear of conventions, since most of the people who form part of this new mood are not averse to iconoclasm in other fields and are the effective enemies of social conformism. It is less a question of the observance of codes than the fulfillment of life purposes.

Looking backward, one sees that the more rigid Puritan tradition stressed the Biblical virtues which limited sex to procreation and then led to widespread repression, hypocrisy, frustrations, and neuroses. It was challenged by a series of sexual revolts which started as far back as the 1840s and were climaxed by the great revolution of the 1920s. The extension of these forces into the 1930s and 1940s, in a world torn by social struggle and personal insecurity, led in turn to the excesses of sexual cynicism and normlessness.

If I am right, this mood too has passed its crest, and a countercurrent has set in, replacing it by an outlook far less restrictive than the Puritan. It takes more account of sexual needs both in adolescence and adulthood, and is thus permissive of experiment, especially in premarital relations. It is also more favorable to a wider range of sexual techniques. But these freedoms are all directed toward the fulfilled relation between a man and a woman as the core of a healthy society. Put in a different way, the sexual freedoms won in the last century are unlikely to be relinquished. But there is discernible an American attitude which insists upon directing these freedoms more and more into the channels of happiness. That, in turn, is being redefined not in terms of success or material goods or power, but in terms of the broad personal expressiveness which includes sexual expressiveness.

This may, of course, be somewhat wishful on my part, discerning a stream of tendency where there is only a whirlpool of crosscurrents. Americans are probably engaged in a complicated struggle in the building up of definitions as to what is permissible and truly expressive in the area of sexual behavior. There has been nothing approaching an accurate account of this struggle, with its agonies and blindnesses and earnestness, taking place on the darkling plain of the American psyche. One possible outcome may be a reversion to a new form of the Puritan codes, with new and more indirect repressions. But the more likely outcome is the newer expressiveness which I have outlined above.

8. Life Goals and the Pursuit of Happiness

THE SEARCH for personal expressiveness and happiness leads into the question of American life goals.* To find the life goals of a culture one must look for the impulses toward value that come out of the culture and take the shape of a Grand Design for living. I do not have in mind those virtues or "value clusters" which family, school, and church seek to instill into the young. They are listed in every book on American society, including such traits as freedom, democratic equality, competitiveness, thrift, honesty, loyalty, social mobility, practicality, and the

* For earlier material on American cultural goals, see Ch. VIII throughout, especially Secs. 1, 3, 4.

belief in the individual life and its worth. Together they add up to a kind of cultural superego. Yet the question is not what Americans believe they believe, but what animates them and what their main energy drives actually are.

They grow up in a quasi-individualist society, expecting great things of life, and they are disappointed if they don't achieve them. The point is that they measure their lives against these expectations mainly in terms of what the culture accepts as life goals. Robert and Helen Lynd showed with great force in their *Middletown* studies how bitter the disillusionment can be when the expectations are not matched by the outcome.

Life goals are a complex interweaving of strands from both the culture and the personality. They are given shape as stereotypes derived from the culture, but they are constantly changed and enriched by stirrings from within the personality which cannot long be denied or belied. Whether or not "human nature" can be changed, there is no question that the life goals which have shaped American striving have changed decisively. It is difficult to trace them in their changing forms, since they are never codified and are rarely made articulate.

In an idyllic vein American social historians look back to an earlier society in which the operative life goals were related to the Puritan virtues of work, pride of craftsmanship, thrift, achievement, and the fulfillment of the vocation and tasks to which one was called. To spoil this Garden of Eden view, it must be added that these virtues were from the start contaminated by those of money, materialism, and success: or, to put it differently, these life goals were all along implicit in the earlier ones and grew out of them. By the turn of the twentieth century a new pattern of life purposes emerged. Its components were *success, prestige, money, power,* and *security.* This is loosely termed the "success system," and it is true that at its core is the cult of what William James called scornfully "the Bitch Goddess, success." But it might be better to call it simply the *five-goal system,* since each of the goals has enormous pull for the American imagination and a sovereign place in the constellation as an equal among equals.

The system as a whole stresses achievement—or, in James Plant's terms, *whatness* as against *whoness*. I have tried to trace in an earlier section* the changes in American character and society that are interwoven with the acceptance of these life goals. One might say, with Lawrence K. Frank, that people on the move, geographically and socially, are bewildered about their "whoness" and look to "whatness" for security and for a definition of their personality; also that persons

* See Sec. 4, "Varieties of American Character."

who have only a blurred sense of their "whoness" turn to "whatness" as a surrogate.

To understand the importance of *success* as a goal, one must remember that for the ordinary American the test of an idea is in the end product of action, and the proof that something is valid lies in its being effective. He cares about success because he prides himself on living in an illusionless world and cannot let himself be bothered with futilities. Hence his homage is given to the best-selling book, the candidate who is elected by a "landslide," the stock speculator who makes a "killing," the play or performer that gets "rave" reviews, the general who wins the battle, the businessman at whose touch every enterprise turns to gold, the football player who catches the decisive pass or breaks away for the winning touchdown, the song on the "Hit Parade," the movie star who gets on all the magazine covers. It adds to the American's stature to be associated with a going concern.

The only disaster is failure. But even failure is tolerated if it is used as a springboard for a "comeback" which is a success underlined by a dramatic reversal. The golf player who came back after an auto smash to win all the tournaments, the faded movie star who was found to have a revived box-office appeal, the Wall Streeter who lost several fortunes only to make a new one—these are the American equivalents of Lazarus come back from the dead. I do not say that the success drive is stronger now in America than it was in William James's time: the chances are that it is somewhat weaker, not in itself but relative to some of the other components of the American system of life goals, especially prestige and security. But it is still an integral part of the larger pattern.

Prestige is at once the subjective aspect of success and its reward. To achieve success is to receive the respect and applause of one's fellows. In a society of competitive striving a man's standing in the community is measured against others by what Veblen called the "invidious" emulative bent of his fellows—the differential advantage he has over others in income and status, and the "pecuniary emulation" that he practices or of which he is the target. The sources of prestige in the socially mobile American society are less likely to be birth and family than job, income, spending habits, clothes, car, residence, club and group memberships. In his studies of stratification, Lloyd Warner makes prestige the nucleus of the class system, getting at the social rating a person has in the community by asking neighbors and friends to rank each other in the prestige hierarchy. One must agree that the drive toward prestige has done much to release American energies. But the price has been high—the hollowness of values in a system where life is lived in the mirror of how people rate you, and whether (in Arthur Miller's phrase in *Death of a Salesman*) you are not only "liked" but "well liked." Life becomes thus a joyless and derivative affair, laden with endless anxieties in an endless prestige rat race.

In a society where the traditional goals have been undercut, the goal of *money* has an alluringly tangible and massive quality. In speaking earlier of the "cement" of American society and of the changes in the American character, I noted the role and the limits of pecuniary values in a society in which most things become marketable. It is true that the American expectation is largely measured in money terms, and that the "law of the fast buck" is a powerful force in American striving. This is not uniquely American. Older civilizations, like the French, combine the values of culture with those of greed.

There is at least some evidence, especially in recent novels (which serve as telltale documentaries in such matters), that the role of money as a decisive life goal is being questioned. Americans are aware that "money talks," but they are also aware that "you can't take it with you" and that there are things that "money can't buy." That it needs constantly to be challenged is, of course, a mark of the hold of acquisitiveness on the American mind. Yet the fact is that challenger goals are emerging. Mary McCarthy has noted, speaking of American materialism, that Americans live *among* things but not *by* them: similarly, one may add that they find money necessary but not adequate in the system of life values. They agree that other values count more but add that men without money find it difficult to achieve them.

As for *power*, I have noted earlier* how it pervades every phase of American society, which is not power-starved but power-saturated. One source that feeds the power drives is the American emphasis on the life of action: the imperialism of action demands control over the actions of others. The critics of American machine society have also built a seductive theory by which machine power is projected into the human personality and generates a similar power drive in men. I suspect that it is less the machine than the bureaucracy which feeds the power impulse. For those whose lives are geared to their status in a hierarchy, power has meaning. Government bureaucrats, corporate managers, trade-union leaders, Army officers, press and radio barons, and all the minor gods and demigods of America may find in power a psychic reward they cannot find elsewhere. But except for the mutilated personalities, most people in a dynamic society are unlikely to feed and live on power alone. The "authoritarian personality" is far less dominant in America than it was in Nazi Germany or than it is today in

* See Ch. VI, Sec. 5, "Power and Equilibrium"; also Ch. VII, Sec. 2, "The Seats of the Mighty."

Communist societies or in the feudal societies of the Arab Middle East. One must remember also that a market society is less power-ridden than a wholly bureaucratic one, and a mobile society less dependent on power than one where the personality can find little fulfillment except in the strategic control of others.

The important newcomer in the five-goal system is the stress on *security*. Anyone studying the emerging personality pattern in America must note how the propensity for risk-taking has slackened, and how risk-cutting and security-seeking have come forward with a new strength. The stress on insurance is, of course, the base on which one of the biggest private industries has been built. The newer stress on "social security," especially since the Great Depression, is the base on which much of the welfare state is built.

However, it is not economic security alone but a whole psychic security syndrome that is involved. Each new generation seems less geared to risk-taking and more bent on nailing down the future beyond chance and doubt. Elmo Roper's annual polls of college graduating classes show life goals that have moved far from those of the adventurous entrepreneur, the intellectual pioneer, the social maverick. What the graduating classes envisage as the "good life" is a home, two or three children, one or two cars, and a salary of ten thousand a year. They are wary even of the harsh competitive struggle and the driving quest for success. They look mainly toward merchandising and "personnel" work ("because I like people"). As one of them put it, he didn't want to become a "big operator with blood pressure and coronary thrombosis." Instead of setting up an independent business, they aim at joining a corporate organization ("A.T.&T. might not be exciting—but there will always be an A.T.&T."). Their goal is to become "good technicians, good managers, good neighbors," to cut risk and dig in for a sure if unexciting income. To some extent this is the result of the draft experience of the young Americans, but it goes beyond that.

I do not share the anxieties of the corporate personnel managers who deplore the lack of "enterprise" among American youth. Generally what they mean by it is the lack of a sense of "push" and "go," and a passivity which does not infuse energy into the "team." For me the real tragedy lies rather in the psychic insecurity which carries with it a yearning for a secure niche in a known and orderly structure, and which thereby strips the individual of his individuality. This is true of adults as well. Polls of adults in the working class and lower middle class show that the groups which are least secure economically—Negroes, the unskilled, white-collar workers—are also the most willing to take a job at low pay if it will assure them a steady and secure income.

How much of a clash is there between this yearning for the secure life and the belief that the future holds hope and that one's children will be better off than oneself? It may be a case of trying to have the best of both emotional worlds—that of a dynamic society with its hope, always breaking continuities and making new beginnings, and that of a security society where there are few breaks and no risks. By precept and by the example of daily living, Americans teach their children both the creed of risk and the creed of security. They are torn by polar pulls in both directions. The most corrosive element in the security syndrome is its narrowing of the margin of generosity toward others. To think of your own safety means to fear involvement in the plight of the victim, lest you be tagged with the stigma of the outsider. It is to develop the yearning for the securely normal which leads to a massive conformism.

If asked to reflect on what was their main aim in life, most Americans would probably shrug the question away, since they tend to take life goals as given; but if pressed, they would probably say, "To be happy," or "To lead a happy life." If asked what they want for their children, their answer would again be happiness. As I have several times noted, America is a happiness society even more than it is a freedom society or a power society. The underlying strivings may be toward success, acquisitiveness, or power, toward prestige or security. But what validates these strivings for the American is the idea that he has a natural right to happiness.

Howard Mumford Jones has traced the web of meaning in the concept of the "pursuit of happiness" since it was introduced into American thinking in the eighteenth century. One phase came from the aristocratic idea taken over from the classical writers, who saw happiness (as Jefferson himself saw it) as a gracious way of life led by landed gentry or farmers, with leisure for contemplation and a taste for books and for science, the arts, and Nature. The second came from the Puritan idea of obeying God's laws and having a store of worldly goods to show for it. This in turn was linked with what became in the nineteenth century the core idea of a happy life—the idea of material success.

Even in nineteenth-century America the seeds were present for a conception of happiness that was to go beyond materialism and success. Emerson defined happiness as self-realization within the spiritual laws of the universe. Later in the century William James helped give it a fateful twist of meaning as the "agreement" of a man's inner life with the realities of his outer experience. James himself, as we have seen, rejected material success as a goal. Yet his "agreement" came to be translated into "adjustment," and the idea of adjustment was taken over by vocational guidance counselors, personnel experts, and scientific managers, and interpreted as making one's life effective within a society of business and money values. The "mental health" movement also for a time made adjustment its central concept, adding its own twist of meaning. It saw adjustment as whatever fits a person into his social frame to lead a useful and normal life, so that he does not feel himself a rebel and outsider. This was soon challenged by the more perceptive people in the field of mental health. The question some psychologists raised—among them Robert Lindner in his *Prescription for Rebellion* —was whether the individual does this at the cost of trimming away his own individuality and his impulses toward uniqueness. If this is true, then what William James meant as a way out of the trap of conventional values became instead a way of leveling down the jagged ends of personality. Thus "adjustment" became, along with "security," a life purpose that modified the five-goal complex but did not seriously challenge it. Under its influence the pursuit of happiness came to be defined mainly as the pursuit of conformism and the avoidance of neuroses.*

If it is true that every civilization has its characteristic culture style and social structure, it will also have its characteristic pattern of neuroses. I do not mean to assert that neurotic behavior arises from specific social strains, rather than from the underlying and perennial human situation. But there has been enough recent exploration by psychiatrists and anthropologists to enable us to draw a rough correspondence between the culture and the neurotic pattern.† The neurotic-personality-as-American may feel caught in the conflict between the stated ideals and operative drives of his society. Because of this gap he may feel guilty, anxious, and insecure, and may seek to build himself up in the mirror of other people, or may seek the elusive inner security in the feverish effort to achieve money, power, and an outer security.

The neurotic patterns of continental European societies are likely to be those of people who feel caught in a blind alley, unable to extricate themselves from the encrusted habits of their fathers and their community, desperate to make a fresh start. The characteristic American neuroses, on the other hand, are those of people who have to pay a heavy psychic price for freedom of movement and decision, and the flux of fortunes, station, and values. In a constantly shifting social situation, with a high rate of personal mobility, few Americans have an anchorage in traditional values. This may mean an intense anxiety

* For the "adjusted man" and the "unadjusted man" as contrasting American character types, see Sec. 4, "Varieties of American Character."

† I deal here with mental health and disease. For other aspects of health and disease, see Ch. III, Sec. 6, "The Sinews of Welfare."

about the changes and chances of life, and a feeling of inner emptiness.

There is an interesting difference in the nature of the "family romance" in the European and American situations. The Freudian doctrine developed in Central Europe, in an authoritarian family frame where the son grew up resenting a tyrannical father: the Oedipus relation and the repressed libidinal energy thus came to occupy a central place in the Freudian system. In the middle-class American family, where the authoritarian father has all but disappeared, the family romance is more likely to revolve around the emotional relationship between son and mother, and an overemphasis on loving and being loved. While the repression of libidinal energy has proved important in a culture that still carries some of the scars of Puritanism, the more important problem in the American personality is that of insecurity and identity—the lack of models to follow, the absence of a sense of self, and the feeling of failure in living up to one's own expectations or those of others.

It has been suggested that while the European neuroses are those of the id and the superego, the American neuroses are those of the ego. This jibes with Erik Erikson's observation that the central problem of American personality is the "quest for American identity." It is a quest that takes place in the growing-up years in every culture. But it is especially hard to find your identity in a society where the temptation is to live in the mirror image that others have of you, where the patterns of group living are still unstable and your role in the group is not clearly outlined. Thus the American yearns for unattainable goals set by the shifting standards of his group, yet he does not exact from himself the willed effort to live within his own psychic limits and resources and to be a personality in his own right. To add to the difficulty, there is the outer image of the abundance of life opportunities in American society, so that the individual feels he is falling short of his duty to exploit them and therefore is inadequate for life. He has thus the sense of starving psychically amidst psychic plenty, and hence of being cheated in life.

When William James heard Freud's lectures on the latter's visit to Clark University, he told Freud and Ernest Jones: "The future of psychology belongs to your work." James may have spoken from his interest in motivation and in nonrational beliefs such as the varieties of religious experience: he had himself had a breakdown as a young student. Yet despite his remark the characteristic psychological interest of America, which he expressed in his own work, was with normal behavior and the area of the conscious. It is true that a number of doctors —including Benjamin Rush, the elder Oliver Wendell Holmes, and

S. Weir Mitchell (all three of them writers as well)—showed sharp insights into the irrational phases of behavior. Adolf Meyer at Johns Hopkins and William Alanson White in Washington had also moved beyond neurology into psychiatry. Nor should we ignore the insights of such literary figures as Hawthorne and Melville into the realm of the unconscious. Yet the development of American psychiatry came mainly as the result of a major borrowing from Central Europe, with the importation of Freudian ideas and techniques. When President G. Stanley Hall, who had made important studies both of adolescence and senescence, invited Freud to speak at the Clark University Centenary, the impact of his visit was startling. Freud's ideas eventually found fertile soil in an American society in which new insecurities, anxieties, and tensions had arisen to assault the psyche and produce blockages in the effective functioning of personality.

What was still lacking was a trained corps of men to apply the insights to the new American experience. This was provided as a result of a great migration of Austrian and German analysts and scholars in the 1930s from Nazi persecution, among them such figures as Karen Horney, Erich Fromm, Theodor Reik, and Bruno Bettelheim. There have been few migrations of skills with such far-reaching consequences. So complete has been the transplanting of these ideas in the American soil that most foreign observers have come to identify psychoanalysis with contemporary America.

Yet the mobile, bustling, power-drenched American society of the twentieth century was drastically different from the exhausted cosmopolitan society of Vienna in the early days of Freud's career—culture-proud, highly skeptical, conscious of the shutting off of avenues of mobility and power. Such key ideas of the Freudian school as the Oedipus complex and castration fears made their appeal to a narrow group but could not hope for a wider appeal in the common-sense atmosphere of American popular thinking. The European doctrine had to find new roots in the characteristic American family structure. The conditions of American life did as much to transform Freudianism as Freudianism did to change the intellectual atmosphere of America.

One may speculate on the forms that neurotic behavior has taken in America—or what may be called the characteristic American neurotic posture. In the late nineteenth century the typical case was that of the neurasthenic upper-class woman who had convinced her family and herself of her chronic invalidism and used it to tyrannize the household. To some degree she is still a fixture on the American psychic landscape, disillusioned after an impossible romantic courtship, using the psychoanalytic couch to give her life some importance.

But new figures have come on to the scene. There is the daughter or son who, within an overprotected milieu, has been torn away from many of the life experiences which once gave the young American a sense of identity. Some psychiatrists have called the result the "Smith-Vassar" or "Harvard-Princeton" syndrome. There is the "silver cord" relation between an obsessive mother and a weak son which has blighted the lives of many young Americans and paved the way for a considerable growth of homosexuality. Add the portrait, so often met in the contemporary American novel, of the alienated young Jew or Negro who feels himself an outsider in a culture he has tried at once to fight and woo, and who carries with him the scars of the struggle. But the scars are not restricted to minority groups. There is also what Arnold Green has called "the rural Protestant in the modern metropolis," who finds that the codes developed in a small-town agrarian society do not fit the rootless conditions of urban life and is riddled with anxieties in a society without landmarks.

I have left for the end the case of the schizophrenic, which has come to engage so much of the attention of American psychotherapists. At bottom, schizophrenia marks a breakdown in communication, so that the afflicted person is unable to cope with the world of reality but lives instead on two levels which move ever further apart. There are some who believe that American culture is itself schizophrenic, split with a deep fault line which is driven between the clamorous exactions of the culture and the confused responses of the individual. Certainly schizophrenia has proved more of a problem in America than elsewhere. It may be called a home-grown psychosis, just as the diseases of tension—the heart, the circulatory system, ulcers, and colitis—have proved home-grown psychosomatic diseases. It is notable that one of the native Americans who made a great name in psychiatry was Harry Stack Sullivan, a disciple of Meyer and White, and that at the start of his career he put in long years of work at the Enoch Pratt Hospital in Baltimore with schizophrenics, for whom he seemed to have a particular empathy.

The common thread in these characteristic American neurotic and psychotic situations is the inability of the personality to find any clearly defined and culture-sanctioned patterns of ideas, conduct, and feelings which will express its deepest drives. A number of writers have described in rich detail the defensive strategies and ruses by which the neurotic personality tries to bolster itself. There is a certain fitness in this way of putting it. For it is understandable that in a power society like the American, the neurotic situation should be focused on what Harold Lasswell has called "security, income, and deference" and that it should revolve primarily around the use of the stratagems of power to relieve the sense of the inadequacy of the personality to the demands and possibilities of the culture.

Foreign commentators have often remarked that America seems to be one vast mental hospital, but no one can be more conscious of the problems of mental health in America than American observers themselves. Granted the inherent vagueness of definition that plagues statistics in this area, the psychiatric profile they give of America is a striking one. By mid-century the estimate was that 8,500,000 Americans—one out of every eighteen persons—were suffering from some form of mental illness; that in the course of his life, one out of every ten would need some kind of psychiatric care; that there are as many patients in mental hospitals as in all others combined, and an equal number who require hospitalization are crowded out; that close to a million Americans who reported for the military draft were found to be suffering from some kind of psychic difficulty.

Even with a training program for turning out more psychiatrists the magnitude of the problem goes beyond the available resources of therapy, which are geared to the intensive treatment of the few. The answer seems to lie in two directions—that of group therapy and the development of low-cost clinics, and that of preventive therapy. The latter, of course, would involve a considerable change in the prevailing life goals of the society. To avoid so drastic a change, the home-grown American modes of thinking have brought a shift of emphasis from Freudian "depth psychology" to the idea of "adjustment" within the existing social frame. Dating from the dramatic case of Clifford Beers, as a "mind that found itself," the American genius for organization mustered the resources of the new psychiatry into a Mental Health movement which developed local groups in a number of communities. It addressed itself to the problem of organizing mental health in the same deliberate way that Americans have gone about the problem of social work, factory legislation, and juvenile delinquency. It declared that its goal was not the diagnosis and treatment of mental ills—necessary as that might be—but the development of healthy minds and personalities.

For all these vexing questions the key ideas of psychoanalysis have permeated the American intellectual atmosphere. In American social science the psychological approach is more common than the economic. In the novel, theater, and movies the unraveling of hidden memories and the removal of psychological blocks to personality have become dominant themes. Popularizations of Freud and Jung have become stock literary material. A mushrooming group of popular magazines is devoted to the self-knowledge and self-improvement of salesmen, secretaries, small businessmen, corporate executives, and housewives.

The psychoanalyst and his couch have been enshrined in a legendry of popular jokes and cartoons and have become imbedded in American folklore.

Beyond the controversies and the cult, the spread of psychiatric thinking serves a long-range function in American life. Partly it measures the strength of revulsion against the repressions and denials of the instinctual life. Partly it marks a fumbling for the identity of the individual in a bewildering culture. It has served to tide America over the period between the life meanings and goals of a simpler society and the emergence of new ones. Most important, it has led to a questioning of shoddy purposes and too easily accepted conformisms within the frame of the pursuit of happiness.

CHAPTER X

Belief and Opinion

WE TURN in this chapter to the influences that shape the convictions, opinions, and attitudes of the American people and the forms they take. We start with the religious tradition, the role that religion and the churches have played in American intellectual history, and the recent varieties of religious experience (Sec. 1, "God and the Churches"). We go on to trace the history of American social thought in its main stream and its tributaries, noting how it has expressed itself politically in the three principal angles of vision—radicalism, conservatism, and liberalism (Sec. 2, "American Thought: the Angle of Vision"). We follow this by a close look at the American school system and its educational philosophy, analyzing the school as a subculture within the larger culture and as an agency for control, and moving on to a similar analysis of colleges and universities and the increasing access to them which has been made available to young Americans (Sec. 3, "The Higher and Lower Learning").

We then examine American journalism and the press, both in their inner structure of power and in their impact on the public mind (Sec. 4, "Profile of the Press"). We end with the technological changes that have produced a revolution in the opinion industries, viewing them not as "mass media" but as Big-Audience media—new forms of power in shaping opinion which cut across the classes and hold an immense potential for good and ill (Sec. 5, "Revolution in the Big Media"). This chapter restricts itself to the opinion and belief aspects of the Big Media, leaving the aesthetic and cultural aspects to the chapter that follows.

CHAPTER X

Belief and Opinion

1. God and the Churches

IS America a religious culture, shaped by men who sought freedom of worship, with God constantly present in their minds even when the Church has become formalized? Or is it a secular culture, with a "wall of separation" between Church and State, and with religion playing only a marginal role in men's daily lives? Each of these questions can be answered affirmatively, which indicates how deeply the religious ambiguity cuts into American culture. America is as secular as a culture can be where religion has played an important role in its origins and early growth and has been intertwined with the founding and meaning of the society. It is also as religious as a culture can be whose life goals are worldly and whose daily strivings revolve not around God but around man.

De Tocqueville rightly underscored the strong religious base of American life and thought, both in the older Puritan communities of New England and in the new frontier states. The Calvinist doctrine of predestination, which played a dominant role in the early colonies, was a hard and bleak doctrine fitting the mood of communities founded on the "challenge of hard ground." It called for ascetic living, but its asceticism became part of the secular world rather than the religious and led to an activism which left its mark on American history. Similarly, the earlier intolerance felt by men who had an inner sense of loneliness as they waited for a sign of God's grace was in time replaced by the doctrine of toleration.

This mixture of theocracy and secularism, of dogma and indifferentism, is one of the striking features of the American religious heritage. One finds a clue to it by noting the difference of religious climate at each important stage of American history. The colonies were settled under the stress of religious revolt, in an age of creative religious feeling; American freedom was won at the end of the eighteenth century in an age of Deism and revolutionary freethinking; the major growth of America took place during the century which followed the Jeffersonian era and which was strongly marked by scientific rationalism; in the contemporary Atomic Age there has been a revival of religious feeling under the stress of social tensions and personal insecurity. This mixture of seventeenth-century Calvinism, eighteenth-century Deism, nineteenth-century rationalism, and mid-twentieth-century anxiety may help explain some of the contradictions in the relations between God and man in America.

Religion has lost a good deal of its former hold on the American character and no longer pervades the daily content of living as it once did. Yet we must not underestimate the hold it still has. While there was an atheist strain in the writings of Tom Paine, and while atheism is still protected by Supreme Court decisions, there is less and less room for the "godless" in America, since godlessness is usually associated with Communism and depravity. America is regarded as a "Christian country," with an emphasis on "Christian" that carries it beyond the tolerant deism of the Founding Fathers who wrote of "Nature's God" with an inclusive anthropological sweep. There is no candidate for even minor political office in America today who would dare to mock religion or alienate any of the denominations. In every major speech a President is likely to include what Franklin Roosevelt used to call the "God stuff."

Yet religion plays more than a surface part in the conduct of American government. Woodrow Wilson was a Presbyterian, Franklin Roosevelt an Episcopalian, Harry Truman a Baptist, and Dwight Eisenhower grew up in Kansas among the mushrooming religious sects of the frontier, although he turned to Presbyterianism on the threshold of the White House. Examine the Presidential tenure of each and you will find features of it illumined by the particular kind of religious training he received. The religious ambiguity of American politics is further shown by the fact that every President (and Vice-President) has belonged to one of the Protestant sects, yet few pay much attention to the particular sect to which he belongs.

As the child of the Reformation, Americans took over not only its dominantly Protestant heritage but also its deep individualistic strain. Every European sect that found itself constricted or in trouble emigrated to the New World, which thus became a repository of all the distillations of Reformation thought and feeling. Since the Reformation had broken with the authority of the Church and left to the individual the meaning of the Scriptures, America became a congeries of judging individuals, each of them weighing the meaning and application of the Word. A Bible-reading people emerged, drenched in the tradition of the Old and New Testaments. This may help explain the stress on the idea of "convenant" in American thought, which Helmut Richard Niebuhr has noted. It also suggests why a people so concerned with the meaning of the Holy Writ has been the first to give a sacred character to a written Constitution but has at the same time remained a nation of amateur interpreters of the Constitution.

Two basic concepts of the Christian belief—the soul and sin—took on a new emphasis in individualist America. Each man was the judge of his own religious convictions, since his possession of an immortal soul gave each man an inner worth regardless of color, rank or station, political belief, wealth or poverty. Thus the foundation was laid in religious freedom for a political equalitarianism which no later history of privilege has been able wholly to extirpate from the American mind. But if each man had an immortal soul to save, it was because it had been steeped in sin. As a Bible-reading people, the Americans took over many of the preconceptions of the Hebraic society in which Judaism and early Christianity were rooted. Among them was the sense of individual—aside from original, or inevitable—sin, without which there could be no individual salvation.

There is a resulting ambiguity between the sin-and-salvation strain in Christian doctrine and the organic optimism of American economic and social attitudes. The Hebrew prophets, as they lamented the disintegration of Biblical society, called on each Jew to ward off God's wrath from his people by cleansing himself of his own inner guilt; the Christian allegory added to the somberness of this conception. But there have been few occasions on which Americans could believe with any conviction in an impending collapse of their social structure and their world. The sense of sin and the sense of doom were therefore importations from the Old and New Testament that somehow flowered in the American soil in spite of the worship of money and success—or perhaps exactly because of this worship, which required a compensating doctrine to ease the conscience.

The result has been an American religious tradition which is at once deeply individualist, anti-authoritarian, concerned with sin and salvation, yet secular and rationalist in its life goals, Bible-reading in its habits, with its emphasis on man's relation to his own conscience and therefore to his private religious judgment. The Americans have been salvation-minded, each believer being engrossed in his relation not to the church but to God, in Whom he was to find salvation; yet they have also formed a secular rather than a sacred or hieratic society. Since they were believing and judging individuals, they did not lean on a priesthood: even their churches were based less on the authority of a hierarchy than on lay presbyters or the congregation itself.

This conflict between secular social goals and the religious conscience has colored both the religious and the democratic experience of America. It underlay the agonized conscience of early New England, the preoccupation with God's way with man in good and evil which characterized American Fundamentalism, the fear-drenched frontier religion filled with literal-minded terrors, the Social Gospel movement; and it will be found in the latter-day movement of neo-Calvinist religious thought, with its Atomic Age setting of apocalyptic guilt and terror. For all its optimism and its cult of action and success, American culture has been overlaid with a sense of both agony and evil.

America owes much of the effectiveness of its democracy, as well as much of its dynamism, to this strain in its religious experience. I am suggesting that the fiber necessary for democracy is not the product of any particular religious doctrine but of the lonely debate within the free conscience. Democracy is the polity of individual choices and of majority consent; it can be run effectively only where there is a habituation to hard choices. Those who are certain of the simplicity of revealed truth make the initial choice of submission and do not have to make any subsequent choices; they do not furnish a fertile soil for the democratic seed. Those who expect miracles will not take the risk of dissent. Those who are sure of dogma given to them will not make the arduous effort of winning the slow and gradual victories of an always unfinished society. Finally those who suffer no conflict within the arena of their own minds will not generate the needed dynamism to transcend the conflict and resolve their conscience.

American democracy, in the sense that it is linked with private judgment and freedom of dissent, is thus also linked with the stir and turmoil of free religious choice. To be sure, the psychic toll of this conflict and dynamism is a heavy one. But the stakes have been great—nothing less than the creation and sustaining of an open society which is based on the judging and the choosing individual caught on the battleground of his own mind.

In an era when the threat to democracy is conformism of mind and stereotyping of character, one of the great counterforces is the traditional American religious nonconformism. This nonconformism had its roots, as Arthur G. Parker has put it, in "a religiously inflexible New England, with its mores forged upon the anvil of Jeremiah by the sledge of Calvin." Something of the dark intensity of this religious commitment has persisted in America until the present day. It gave American history some of its Calvinist dourness from the time of the Mathers and Jonathan Edwards to the current revivalists whose chief stock in trade is still hell-fire and brimstone. For all its optimism and its cult of action and success, American history has been overlaid with a brooding sense of agony and evil. One finds it in Hawthorne, Melville, and Poe, as also in Mark Twain and Henry James, Thomas Wolfe and Faulkner. While this strain persists, there is less danger of the flattening out of personality and of a herd-mindedness in opinion.

It is here that American religious Fundamentalism has its roots. The brand of Christianity that the earlier Americans took to their hearts was not the mildness of Jesus's teachings or the doctrine of brotherly love, but the probing of man's relation to good and evil and of God's ways to men. In the mid-eighteenth century, as Perry Miller pointed out, a deeper shadow came over American Puritanism. It remained during the century and more of frontier expansion, forming a frontier religion of the Right Way, filled with literal-minded terrors, with swift rewards and stern punishments. Its basic image was that of life as a hard pilgrimage pursued by temptations and dangers, an unrelenting quest beset with trials and testing. Much of this view has survived even into the contemporary era of diluted and sophisticated religion. Its continuing strength suggests that it fulfills a function—that of keeping alive a ferment of enthusiasm within individuals surrounded by collapsing moral standards, who face denials and frustrations in their own lives. Sometimes, as in the case of the religion of the American Negroes, there is a quality in their religious expression akin to the simplicity and creativeness of the primitive Christian church in its catacomb days. But in many other instances of enthusiastic religion the fervor lacks creativeness and represents a mechanical reassertion of faith in the face of inner fears and emptiness.

One of the striking facts about American history has been the linkage of the "religion of the fathers" with what Mencken delighted to call the "Bible Belt" mentality—a narrow view of life and morals, a belief in the literal inspiration of the Bible, and a reactionary code of political belief. The passion of the "Hot Gospel" and the archaism of the hell-fire-and-damnation religion have been put to work as a counterforce to the inherent humanism of the Christian teachings. It has enabled a number of demagogues, especially in the rural Midwest and South, to clothe their racist and reactionary appeals in Biblical references. In the big cities the tradition of Charles G. Finney and Dwight L. Moody was continued with modern publicity techniques by Billy Sunday, Aimee MacPherson, and Billy Graham. They were evidences of how broad is the gulf in American religion between the loudly committed and the deeply committed. Unlike Puritanism, which with all its excesses embodied an internalized religious conviction—the product of people who wrestled with God as Jacob did—the current evangelism is a form of religiosity externalized in a public spectacle.

The question here is not one of "liberalism" and "conservativism," whether in religion or politics, but of the inner relations between religious attitudes and democracy. There is a curious example in the Populist political movements in the South and Midwest, in which the stress on saving one's soul and preserving religious orthodoxy was linked with an anticapitalist radicalism. The type-figures were William Jennings

Bryan and Tom Watson. In them a crusading Populism was fused with a harsh Catonian moralism. The common element was the need for the salvation of the believer from the wickedness of the Cities of the Plain where both wealth and freethinking accumulate. The anticorporate strand was thus intertwined with the moralistic, and Bryan's famous Cross of Gold speech was in direct line with the crusade for Prohibition and the Scopes anti-Evolution "monkey" trial. In its characteristic latter-day form this amalgam has lost its anticorporate militancy, replaced by an antilabor, anti-Negro, and anti-Jewish emphasis. Thus in these areas religious Fundamentalism has damned minority groups along with the urban liberal intellectuals who are vaguely felt to be undermining the tribal traditions.

I take another example from the relation of Christian ideals to the American business spirit. Modern Protestantism and the modern business spirit were born out of the same historical soil. The real problem for religion came with the harshness of the acquisitive spirit. Confronted with this, the churches too often faltered, and instead of challenging business enterprise they emulated its premises, investing business power with religious sanctions. In the case of figures like Dwight Moody, Sam Jones, and Billy Sunday, Christian exhortation either became an apology for the acquisitive and competitive or gave religious confirmation to the caste system in race relations and to the status quo in industrial relations. This approach came to be vulgarized to the point where one writer depicted Jesus (*The Man Nobody Knows*) as the Great Salesman, and the campaigns for the revival of religious faith were mapped out with salesmanship strategy. In the hands of such men religion became conventionalized, status-fulfilling, and smug.

Yet, having said this, one must add to this phase of American church history the Social Gospel phase, given impetus by Washington Gladden and Walter Rauschenbusch, which dedicated the churches to a militant role in economic and social reform. Some of the best energies of the denominations, including the Methodists, Presbyterians, and Baptists—the three sects which also made the greatest headway on the frontier—were turned toward the new pathways of social action in the spirit of a Jesus who had given himself to the poor and been denounced as agitator and revolutionary. In this spirit some of the pastors of every denomination have fought for racial equality and economic justice and have explored settlement work, adult education, and psychiatric pastoral counseling. Wherever this has happened, whether with Catholics, Protestants, or Jews, it has been attacked as a secularizing of religion. It is true that it has turned the main stress of religious energy away from the supernatural to the social, from transcending the human to the serving of human needs. It is also true that such a humanist emphasis has in many in-

stances become theologically thin. It is easy for sophisticates to deride religious liberalism, to caricature the sermon-turned-book-review, to
depict the wrestling of the spirit with God in the form of the muscular
Christianity of young men in the YMCA gymnasium or in the sports
activities of settlement work. Yet it has served the function of making
religion a living part of the needs of the people and keeping it militantly alert to the furthermost stretches of social possibility.

A reaction has, however, set in against this humanist emphasis. Increasingly the young American intellectuals have been turning not to
a social religion but to a new theological intensity which is at once
radically pessimist in its premises about human nature and social possibility, and also a return to some of the old Calvinist themes. Theologians like Paul Tillich and Reinhold Niebuhr, while affirming a deep
interest in contemporary social struggles, put their chief stress on the
corruption of the human enterprise, the limits of human will and action,
the difficulties of spiritual growth as well as of social struggle in the
process of history, and the heroism called for in the "courage to be."
But the crucial division in American religion is not between funda-
mentalists and modernists, or between liberals and neo-Calvinists. It is
between active and passive belief, between those for whom religion is
commitment and those for whom it is lip service or conformist respectability. The Social Gospel and the new Calvinism have at least one trait
in common—that of seeking to bring vitality once again to the religious
commitment. Both feel the difficulty of the human situation and the
unremitting arduousness of the struggle for belief. The enemies of both
are smugness, apathy, an easy optimism, and a short-cut conformism.
The introspective religion flourishes best where man feels isolated, struggling against the eidola of secular society. The early America, with its
lonely frontier communities torn up from their European roots,
furnished such a soil. But when American society came into the full
swing of prosperity and became itself a great artifact with numberless
institutional relationships, the lonely meeting of man and God became
more difficult.
Much the same can be said of prophetic religion. Prophecy is the
product and sign of social failure, and in the American myths there is
no room for failure. Even the mid-nineteenth-century sects which used
to forecast the doom of the world at an appointed time could not survive the ridicule of their contemporaries when the time of doom came
and the end was not yet. The voice of ridicule was the voice of a culture
built on boundless hope and optimism. Even the Fourierist and other
Utopian communities of the nineteenth century were the product of
millennialism rather than of social despair. Everything in America has

seemed to conspire against pessimistic and other-worldly religions. It is hard to talk of the mysteries of Nature where science exploits it, or of compassion in a culture that flees failure, or of humility in an imperial culture that makes an idol out of wealth and power. It is hard to see how a religion of poverty can strike continuing root in the richest civilization of the world, or a religion of denial in one of the most Byzantine.

How then account for the strong pulsation in America today toward a religion which is imbued with a sense of the corruption and weakness of human institutions, and which is once again ridden with pessimism? I suggest that the revival of this impulse comes in an age of anxiety and alienation, when Americans are disillusioned with the idea of automatic progress, when the world struggle and the menace of atomic doom have become pressing anxieties, and when optimism, liberalism, and modernism have come under suspicion. But while this new mood has led some of the best elements in the churches toward new depths of religious feeling, it is part of the dilemma that history presents to American religion. The religion-creating capacity, as witness the great period in the Middle East at the time of the Roman Empire, depends on social failure and catastrophe, while the open society depends on prosperity and peace. To put it another way, the creative soil for religion is social anxiety, which may be the product or the harbinger of democratic failure.

I do not believe that such a sense of failure is likely to thrive long in the American cultural setting. The cultural strains that have given America its power and greatness are those of dynamism rather than despair. Perhaps a new religion will someday emerge from some impending world catastrophe as the religions of the Orient emerged from the collapse of the Greek and Roman worlds. But short of such an apocalyptic vision the American religious future is likely to grow out of the American past, whose chief features have been social optimism, dynamism, and a continuing equilibrium between the conflicting pulls and tensions of American society.

This may offer a clue to the creativeness of the American religious experience. It differs from the religion-creating genius which showed itself in Asia and the Middle East. Its striking characteristic lies in the luxuriant growth of religious denominations splitting off from each other amoeba-wise. Pluralist in so many other phases, the American culture is supremely pluralist in religion. Staying mainly within the broad frame of historic Christianity, Americans have explored new ways of life in new communities (from the Shakers to Father Divine) or proclaimed new particular insights (as with the Mormons, Christian Scientists, Jehovah's Witnesses) or fragmented a denomination into cults and sects. Nowhere else could William James's *Varieties of Religious Experience* have been so congenial to the cultural temper. Nowhere else did the tradition of religious dissent lead to such a spread of denominational forms—not only the broad religious divisions of Protestants, Catholics, and Jews, but also Episcopalians, Presbyterians, Methodists, Baptists, Congregationalists, Unitarians, Friends, Lutherans, Moravians, Christian Brethren, Christian Scientists, Jehovah's Witnesses, Seventh-Day Adventists, Disciples of Christ, Mormons, and the adherents of The Church of God with Signs Following After.

The sects have been derided because they split what might have been religious unity and cast themselves out of the "Eden of infallibility." Yet to attack them for this is to ask America to be other than it is, not only in religion but in every phase of its life. For the pluralism of the American churches is like the pluralism of America's regions, its diverse economic forms, its political localism, its ethnic and immigrant stocks. It is closely linked with religious freedom which, as Madison put it at the Virginia Convention of 1788, "rises from the multiplicity of sects which pervades America and which is the best and only security for religious liberty in any society." The competition of creeds has prevented Americans from erecting intolerance into a principle of government.

There is perhaps less meaning than meets the eye in the figures on the growth of American church membership. It is estimated that, as of 1954, there were ninety-seven million church members (of whom fifty-seven million were Protestant, thirty-two million Catholic, five million Jewish, the rest scattered) comprising over 60 per cent of the population, a larger percentage of the total population than at any time in the past century. This represents a "return to religion" of some sort, but what sort is far from clear. It could mean a new groping for faith as a compensation for the ugliness and danger of life. Or it might mean that in most American communities church membership is a badge of social status, and that membership in them represents safety in a conformist, churchgoing society. Clearly the traditional social nonconformism has been giving way to a conformism which accepts the power structures either as a positive good or as an evil which it would be futile to resist. It is not that the churches practice a conscious hypocrisy about Christian teachings but rather that religious doctrines have been turned into counters in a game men play to bring their consciences to terms with their universe. It is less a question of what the pastors say than the fact that they are no longer listened to; having lost the capacity for belief, they have lost also the power to instill belief.

On the question of the relation of the churches to the class composition of their membership there have been some recent changes of note.

On the whole the Protestants and Jews are more strongly represented in the upper and middle classes, while the Catholics draw more heavily upon the lower-income groups, especially among organized workers. Nevertheless the strength of Protestants in the lower class has been growing, especially since World War II. Of the Protestant sects the Methodists, Baptists, and Lutherans have their heaviest membership in the lower class and are lightly represented in the upper class, while the Presbyterians, Episcopalians, and Congregationalists show a higher proportion in the upper class and a considerably lighter one in the lower class. Yet these figures should not obscure the fact that Protestants and Jews, especially the latter, are largely middle-class groups and most typically come from business and the professions and from the white-collar and service strata of the population. The Protestants and Jews also draw from a higher educational level than the Catholics.

The church affiliations of the American Negro offer a special case. The available figures are at least a decade old (most of them come from the year 1946) and there are considerable differences between the figures given in the studies by Liston Pope and William W. Sweet; yet the main outlines of the profile of membership are fairly clear. Sweet estimates that 70 per cent of the fourteen million Negroes in 1946 belonged to churches—a higher percentage than whites. Of the nine and a half million Negro church members, more than eight million were Baptists or Methodists (Pope's figures are six million out of the almost seven million Negro church members). The studies agree that only a small fraction of the Negroes are Catholic (the number has been growing rapidly in the past decade) and, of the Protestants, only a small fraction belong to the predominantly white denominations. The striking fact about Negro church membership is the heavy emphasis upon the all-Negro denominations. This is partly due to the force of white discrimination and partly to the Negro's own desire to control the organization of his church, in which he has found the freest expression of his leadership and his emotional life. The latter fact does not relieve the white churches of their responsibility for religious jim-crowing. The estimate is that less than 1 per cent of the white congregations have any Negro members—usually only a handful—and less than one half of one per cent of the Negroes who belong to these congregations worship regularly with them.*

There remains the question of the nonchurchgoer and his religious outlook. If 40 per cent of the American population are not claimed as members by any of the denominations, this comes to some seventy million people: taking into account the exaggerated claims of a number of

* For a further discussion of the religion of the American Negro, see Ch. VII, Sec. 6, "The Negro in America."

the churches, the figure is probably considerably higher. It does not follow that they do not have religious beliefs. Abraham Lincoln refused to belong to any particular church, yet he was a deeply religious man. No doubt some of the number are atheists, a good many are agnostics, many are indifferent, many are puzzled, many may feel themselves too poor to afford church membership and its social obligations, and still others prefer to keep their religious beliefs to themselves instead of joining a church and worshiping in common with others. Since Americans are, as I have pointed out, a nation of "joiners," the substantial percentage which has stayed out of the life of the church is all the more striking. There is a current tendency to emphasize church membership, which is bound to put pressure upon the nonmembers and reduce their numbers. But it remains true that one of the articles of the democratic belief in America is the disbelief in any state church or any equation between membership in a church and membership in the American commonwealth. This distinction is crucial to the idea of religious freedom as Americans have practiced it.

The issue of religious freedom in America thus goes beyond discrimination and also beyond the pluralism of the sects, to the core principle of the separation of church and state, as embodied in the constitutional prohibition against any "establishment of religion." Given the experience of Europe as well as that of the early Puritan settlers, the generation of Madison's famous *Remonstrance* saw that an official recognition of a "religious establishment" would hamper religious freedom.

There are some polemicists who ask whether a democracy can remain indifferent to religion when its deepest faith is based on religious premises. One might answer that the official religious neutrality of the government does not imply the personal religious indifference of its members. An American President, Senator, or Supreme Court Justice may have his own explicit religious views, including President Lincoln as Protestant, Senator Lehman as Jew, or Justice Frank Murphy as Catholic. But each knew that unless he refrained from using his official power to propagate the strength of his creed, all the creeds would become entangled in a murderous war.

As Justice Rutledge stated clearly, there is a double price Americans pay for religious liberty: one is the self-restraint of the government in noninterference with a man's creed; the other is the ban on the use of governmental machinery by or for any church. That is why the Supreme Court has tried carefully to draw a line of distinction between valid aid to parochial and public schools and the kind that violates the principle of separation. Another problem that confronted the Court involved the sect of the Jehovah's Witnesses, against which a number of local ordinances were directed on the ground that house-to-house visits for the sale of their religious literature created a nuisance. The Court majority ruled against the ordinances, seeing more in these cases than the importunings of a minor religious sect—nothing less than a central principle of American religious freedom.

No creeds have had better occasion to profit from this principle than the Catholics and the Jews, living among a Protestant majority. Swelled by a great immigration from the 1840s to the 1920s, the Catholic population grew from fewer than two million in 1850 to thirty-two million in 1954. Despite some anti-Catholic movements of bigotry, they have grown in popular acceptance, community importance, and power. Nowhere in a non-Catholic society do they enjoy the freedom and prestige they have in America. The same is true of the roughly five million Jews, who—despite sporadic anti-Semitic outbursts—have flourished in the climate of American religious freedom and economic opportunity. It may be noted that no other Catholic community contributes as much to the Vatican world position as do the American Catholics, and that the American Jews form one of the two polar centers (the other being Israel) of the Jewish world community.*

In fact, while America is still dominantly Protestant, it can no longer be described as a primarily Protestant culture with Catholic and Jewish minorities: it is close to becoming (in Will Herberg's phrase) a three-religion culture. One might predict that in the latter half of the twentieth century these three religious groupings will harden rather than dissolve. They are becoming increasingly self-contained. There is, for example, greater mobility within the class system in America than among the three religions; to put it another way, an American (especially if he is a Catholic or a Jew) is less likely to marry outside his religion than outside his class. The Catholics are critical of intermarriage, pointing out that Catholics who marry outside their faith are likely to abandon that faith. The Jews, anxious to maintain their identity in the face of world hostility, have also strengthened their resistance to intermarriage. The Protestants, less unified in organization and in religious consciousness, have been slower to join this trend. It is in American politics that the trend toward a three-religion society is most clearly reflected: in a city like New York, for example, the political slates of candidates are likely to be carefully composed of representatives of the three major faiths, and as much care is given to the ingredients of this political-religious recipe as to any recipe of a gourmet —and deviation from it is as sensitively noted.

In the days of the great migrations from Europe, the immigrants brought with them to America their own religious denominational be-

---

* For a further discussion of the Catholics and Jews in the American class structure, see Ch. VII, Sec. 5, "The Minority Situation."

liefs, along with their language and customs. It was part of the American creed of freedom that while the immigrant was to assimilate "Americanism" in all other respects, he was expected to keep his religious separateness. The second generation often moved away from this religious heritage, and the third and later generations have returned to it—but in a different form. Again a phrase Herberg uses (taken from a study of intermarriage in New Haven by Ruby Jo Kennedy) is illuminating: that the descendants of the immigrants have fused their religious beliefs in a "triple melting pot." For the new generations it is important to be a Protestant, a Catholic, or a Jew "as the specific way, and increasingly perhaps as the only way, of being an American and locating oneself in American society."

This becomes then a new kind of secularism—not outside the churches, as with the seventy million Americans who are nonmembers of any denomination, but inside the churches. The best illustration of this trend is the recent movement to introduce religious teaching into the schools in the form of a stress on "spiritual values." While some Americans, alert to the danger of the erosion of the "wall of separation," have regarded this as a dangerous offensive by the religious vested interests, it may also be seen as a sign of the flattening out of religious belief. This flattening out takes the form of the conviction that religious faith is somehow "a good thing." Or, as President Eisenhower has put it, "our form of government has no sense unless it is founded in a deeply felt religious faith, and I don't care what it is."

It was part of the disquiet and disorder of the era of anxiety that Americans should be seeking some inner link between religion and democracy. One may cite the characteristic intellectual pilgrimage of Russell Davenport, who first sought the meaning of life in the "permanent revolution" of the American free economy, then tried to link it with a Republican political renaissance under Wendell Willkie, and finally left as his testament an unfinished manuscript asserting that the future of democracy and of the "dignity of man" lies in charting the still uncharted and nonrational elements of religious faith. It might be truer to say, however, that instead of finding their democratic faith in supernatural religion, Americans have tended to find their religious faith in various forms of belief about their own existence as a people. The deepest element of Lincoln's faith, as Edmund Wilson has pointed out, lay in a religious *mystique* of the national Union. If Americans have been turning toward the vague phrases about "spiritual values," it may be because their existence as a unified people is no longer threatened as it was in Lincoln's day.

There is little doubt that the American religious community is linked with democracy, but the linkage is less through "spiritual values" than in the fact of America as an open religious society. What is most striking about it in this sense is the fact that, with its multiplicity of faiths speaking as with a confusion of tongues, there have been no religious wars or massacres. You will find in American history few of those blood-encrusted crimes which in world history have been committed in the name of the only true God and the only true religious way. No other civilization offers a parallel in this respect. There has been marked bitterness between Catholics and Protestants in the struggle for political power, and between the Jews and both of them in economic rivalries. But the principle of the open society, with its rapid class mobility, its religious intermarriage, its respect for the right of religious dissent, has proved a dissolvent force both for bigotries and hostilities.

By the same token it has been corrosive not only of bigotry but also of religious intensity. An example may be cited in what has happened to the religion of American Negroes, whose church affiliations I have already discussed. It has been said that the real inheritors of the creative Christian tradition were not the Protestant descendants of the Calvinists or the powerful Catholic church but the humble and despised Negroes. To them fell the role of continuing the dynamism of frontier religion. Toynbee has written eloquently of the primitive Christianity of the American Negro as one of the few strong growths of spontaneous Christian faith in a "post-Christian era." But as the social lot of the Negroes has improved, their characteristic religion—with its buoyancy, tragedy, and myth-making imaginativeness—has been diluted. With prosperity and a measure of equality has come respectability. Today the middle-class Negro finds himself increasingly caught in the same churchgoing middle class as the white.

A note may be in order on the relation of religion and the economy. The historians of Protestant societies have stressed the doctrine of vocation and its carry-over from religious to secular uses. Given the history of American democracy, one should add another aspect—the inner relation between religious pluralism and a pluralist economy. What both have in common is the process of decision-making through the exercise of private judgment. The free-market economy, as Karl Polanyi has shown, was alien to the ethos and psychology of medieval Europe. It carried in its wake some devastating social irresponsibilities for the human costs of industrialism. But what we have not seen until recently is that the decentralized decisions involved in capitalism put the burden of decision-making on numberless individuals. True, the growth of monopoly has diminished the scope of this, but in great measure it still applies. I do not say that every small businessman or corporate manager or highly skilled worker carries the moral burden of the decision-making well. In many instances he does not. But I do say that a society in which he ceases even to make the attempt is a society in which the habit of decision-making in moral and political terms becomes also constricted. It is a striking fact that the same societies which have maintained a decentralized choice in religion have tended to maintain it also in the economy and in politics.

To those who believe, finally, that it is the religious metaphysic which alone has made American democracy possible and held it together, I would enter a qualification. It is the dissenting pluralist tradition in religion, rather than the religious orientation as such, which has been most strongly linked with American democracy. Religious dissent has carried along with it the tradition of political dissent. It has fostered the democratic idea mainly through its stress on the right of the individual to face and master his own solitariness, according to his own lights. Thus Americans have managed to remain largely a believing people (far more than has been true of other industrial cultures) without the compulsion of imposing their religious beliefs on others—or of imposing *any* religious beliefs, although they hope plaintively that every American will have a set of "spiritual values."

2. American Thought: the Angle of Vision

To MOVE from America's religious belief to its secular thought is less of a jump than may appear, since the belief became largely secularized and the thought had deep religious roots. Americans questioned their gods in the act of believing, just as they retained a substratum of almost religious belief in their political institutions, despite their refusal to build structures of theory on them.

This American aversion to intellectual system-building is striking when contrasted with continental thought. Perhaps those who felt sure they were shaping in social actuality what Jefferson called an "empire for freedom" did not hunger for empire building in the realm of the mind. Daniel Boorstin suggested, in *The Genius of American Politics*, that the reason Americans found political theory superfluous is that they accepted the "givenness" of their institutions, and where something is "given" it needs neither laborious nor subtle definition. In the European sense Americans have had little "grand theory," whether of the state, the economy, the society, the culture, Nature, or God. In the case of such towering figures as Jefferson and Lincoln in political thinking, James and Peirce in philosophy, and Veblen in social theory, one finds a rich array of fragments rather than an artfully laid out master plan. Peirce despaired of ever making his philosophical ends meet, and both Emerson and Whitman flaunted the contradictions in their thinking.

Americans have a fear of rigidifying thought. Believing that forms are empty, they have an antipathy to formal thinking which has caused them to shy away from programs of long-range social change. Thus American thought is tentative, fragmented, directed at the immediate object, and open to change at both ends.

Except for the brief period of the Puritan oligarchy, American thinkers have also been largely free of the appeal to authority and revelation. One of their dilemmas has been to square their basic nonconformism with the stability required by property, investment, and law. When property was riding highest, firm in the saddle of power, the nonconformism almost dropped out of American thought—as it did through much of the quarter century from the Civil War to the Populist revolt. American thinkers have been at their best in their antiauthoritarianism: in the dicta of Jefferson and Madison on freedom of thought, in the pamphleteering of the Jacksonians, in Calhoun's plea for a veto power by which political minorities could hold their place, in Thoreau's doctrine of "civil disobedience," in the thunderbolts of Henry Demarest Lloyd against Standard Oil, in Brooks Adams's gloomy predictions of "centralization and decay," in William James's "pluralistic universe," in Justice Holmes's "can't helps," in Veblen's polemics against "absentee owners." Even the American ruling groups, unlike those of Europe, have relied less on authoritarianism than on the prestige of success and the attraction of the Big Money.

Every generalization about American thought can be offset by a countergeneralization. Suppose you mention the lack of mystical thinkers: except for some of the early Puritan divines you will be on good ground, yet in Poe, Hawthorne, Melville, James, and Faulkner there is a remarkable power in the handling of symbolism. If you note how much of American thought has been secular and rationalist you are confronted in reply by the tradition damning the merely rational, from the divines who denied that it could encompass the mysteries of God's way to man, to the latter-day thinkers who find that the concept of a purely rational man excludes all the half-aberrant, half-heroic ways by which men belie the blueprints of their minds.

If you deny tragic depth in American thought, there are Hawthorne and Melville again to refute you; and Mark Twain, whose comic mask scarcely hides his pessimism of spirit; and Lincoln, whose tragic sense shone through the humorous anecdotes by which he tried to make the ordeal of civil war tolerable. If you say that American thought has a feet-on-the-ground realism you must correct the picture with the millennialist tracts spawned by the experimental communist settlements, and the creative Utopian classics of Bellamy, Donnelly, and Howells. Finally, if you say that American thought—like the American class system—remained pluralistic instead of single-tracked, and was hostile to any scheme of rigid determinism, a minority report would again note the determinism of Frederick Jackson Turner, of Henry and Brooks Adams, of Veblen, and Beard.

Certain historical trends, at least, are clear. American thought has moved from the Utopian and millennialist to a focusing on the calculable future, from a single-factor determinism in history to the more complex multiple-factor view, from religious to secular, from idealist to empirical, from focusing on ultimate goals to focusing on means, from absolutist to pragmatic, from radical to reformist or conservative. On some themes it has gone through cyclical alternations of mood and emphasis. But always there has been the steady beat of change in American life, carrying with it a constant change in the angle of vision of the American thinkers.

In a search for the roots of American thought the first clue is in the interrelations of religion and capitalism. The quest that led to the settlement of America, from the beginning of the seventeenth century to the middle of the twentieth, was a search at once for freedom of conscience and for the El Dorado of the Big Money. Both quests were Utopian in aiming at an ideal community; both were stubbornly practical, responding to felt needs. American social thought was thus, from the start, compounded of conscience and practicality.

The first expression of the American conscience took the form of Puritanism—the fullest amalgam of religion, economics, and politics within a single mold that Americans ever achieved.* Although the Puritan strain came to be watered down, American thought never wholly lost its preoccupation with God's design on the American Continent and with the alternate beat of conscience and acquisitiveness. This suggests a key problem in American intellectual history: how did the early absolutism of conscience turn into the pragmatism of the later period, and how have strong elements of both managed to coexist in the American mind?

A crucial link between the two was individualism. Since a man's conscience was in his own keeping, he had to allow others also to answer to theirs alone. Thus religious *laissez faire* was a strong source of American individualism. It was reinforced by the doctrine of "calling." Puritan thought was dedicated to the City of God and an unremitting enmity to the Adversary. "Calling" started as the reception of grace

* For a discussion of the place of Puritanism in American religious development, see Sec. 1, "God and the Churches." Here I deal with it in the larger American thought pattern. The same applies to individualism, freedom, property, and Natural Rights, all of which have been discussed in their own frames in earlier chapters but are here brought together for the larger frame of American thought.

which marked the commitment to God and the release from the Adversary; it grew into the economic "calling" by which a man's vocation and its accumulated fruits became an outward sign of inner grace. Americans are deeply concerned with private property not because they are made of more grasping human stuff than others but because their culture developed in a climate where a man's individuality was linked with property as a sign of grace, just as it was linked with his conscience as a witness of his identity. The individualist strain was further reinforced by the Christian allegory—the tradition of willingness to incur martyrdom for conscience.

A final link was needed before the chain of thought could be forged joining individualism to property and conscience. This was the doctrine of Natural Rights, with its origins in European thought and a life history of its own in its American locale. It gave a metaphysical basis to the civil-liberties tradition in America, which holds that freedom of thought and utterance, like freedom of worship, is rooted in the "laws of Nature and of Nature's God." Through the link of "Nature's God," much of the emotion attaching to the allegory of martyrdom as well as the doctrine of grace was carried over into the "natural order." Americans came to regard everything related to their individualism as part of that natural order—not only their rights to freedom but also their rights to property.

This freedom-property complex has dominated American thinking throughout the nation's history. It managed to combine the strongly mystical intensity of seventeenth-century thought with the deism of the eighteenth century, the world of transcendence with that of rationalism. To the deeply religious it offered the nourishment of belief, to the skeptical and rationalist it offered secular sustenance. To the nineteenth-century mind it made possible the linking of social progress with individual freedom. For the rationalists it provided a mystique by which freedom, capitalism, and individualism combined to explain the success of the American experiment.

Thus was formed a pattern woven of individualism, Puritanism, conscience, vocation, the allegory of martyrdom, the belief in natural rights, the passion for freedom, and the clinging to property. Within it there have been swings of emphasis—cycles of thought moving spirally in response to the needs and changes of American life.

In its origins, as we have seen, the dominant strain was religious and absolutist. But the sharp advance of science and the democratic impact of the frontier undercut this emphasis. As a result there was a movement toward religious tolerance, the multiplying of sects, and the undermining of authoritarianism, which set the pattern for American religious thought.

In the 1820s and 1830s new winds of doctrine blew westward from Europe in the form of German mysticism and merged with the democratic energies of Western farmers and Eastern intellectuals. The leaders of this "Transcendentalist" movement were Emerson, Brownson, and the Concord group. Strongly idealist in its philosophical roots, it contained within itself the counterpoint to Jacksonian tough-mindedness. Its historians and philosophers saw in the American experience, as in the whole religious experience, the working out of a transcendent idea of good or truth. But some of them began to identify this idea with the good of the common people, the welfare of majorities, and the truth of democracy: from which it was only a step to the reformism which made social gains, rather than a transcendent idea in history, the test of action and thought. As the seedbed for much that was to follow, this strain held within itself the beginnings of hardheaded movements for reform, along with Utopian and millennial schemes. Eventually the discordance within it grew too great to be contained within a single school, and as it burst, the fragments flew in many directions. But during its "Golden Day" its core lay in the strength which the American democratic experience gave to the fusion of German philosophical mysticism with the original intensity of American religious feeling.

Transcendentalism never took root in the formal philosophy of the academies. But it had important parallels in the "democratic vistas" of Walt Whitman, who, in his philosophic base, was idealistic (note his phrase about "the terrible doubt of appearances"). It also had a corollary in the sense of excitement about the energies of the rising nation. Between the Age of Jackson and the Age of Big Business, the driving force in American social thought was the search for a base on which these expanding national energies could build. For a time the struggle over slavery channeled the search into questions of constitutional law and political theory. Calhoun sought a theory to protect the minority rights of the South and the slave-owning property interest without breaking with the basic idea of a Federal union. As Louis Hartz has pointed out, Calhoun did not see that the logic of the Secession movement led to a cult of sections which would be nations in themselves, and which would find a fighting faith in the rightness of their own "peculiar institution." In the North there was a similar groping for an absolutism of individual freedom, which in turn did not dare envisage the cost of a civil war.

With the end of the war two opposing mystiques emerged—Whitman's "leaves of grass" democracy, and the Divine Right of Property.

Each formed a complex of religion, politics, and economics, and around them the forces of radicalism and conservatism took up their positions. It was in the universities, during the entire period from the 1820s well into the 1870s and 1880s, that conservatism found massive support: first in courses on "Mental and Moral Philosophy" which transmitted in diluted form the doctrines of the school of "Scottish Realism" and correlated Christian morality and the "Law of Nature" with *laissez faire* in business and religion; when the Scottish school was overthrown by a "Germanic invasion" of Kantian and Hegelian doctrines, the conservative view shifted its ground and took over the bloodless academic idealism, finding its supreme exponent in Josiah Royce. Just as the realists had insisted that there was no problem as between appearance and reality, so Royce proved triumphantly that all problems, including the crucial one of evil in human life, could be resolved in the larger harmonies of God and man.

When the gap between *laissez faire* and social welfare became too obvious after the Civil War, conservative thought called into play the new popular interest in the Darwinian theories. The jungle character of the economic struggle was frankly admitted, but it was justified and even glorified by Social Darwinism on the ground that Nature had decreed it. The new natural law came to be "natural selection" and the triumph of the "fit" who survived.

The stretch from the turn of the century to the New Deal saw a movement of pragmatism that reached into law, politics, history, education, business, labor, science, and even art and religion. Its seminal minds in philosophy were Peirce, James, Dewey, and Mead. In economics Veblen maintained a withering fire against the abstractions of the English classical school and the Austrian "marginal utility" school, championing a home-grown attitude that studied economic institutions in their whole life context; and Wesley Mitchell applied his insights to the study of business cycles. In law Holmes asserted that "the life of the law has not been logic: it has been experience," asking how the "reasonable man" would assess the customs of his group, and what the "bad man" would be unable to get away with; and Brandeis developed the technique of shaping the judicial judgment less to the logic chopping of "mechanical jurisprudence" than to the community experience. In history James Harvey Robinson and Charles Beard gave new vitality to the relation between social movements and the history of ideas, emphasizing the driving forces of class interest and the ways by which men rationalized these drives. In "progressive" education, Dewey stressed the growth and experience of the child as he "learns by doing."

Through these variations there ran the common thread of the "revolt against formalism" and against fixed principles or rules—that truth did not lie in absolutes or in mechanical formulas but in the whole operative context of individual growth and social action in which the idea was embedded. This movement of thought was, in a sense, the American counterpart to the Marxist and historical schools of thought in Europe which tried to apply the evolutionary process to social thinking. This intellectual base made possible, as it also expressed, the political reform movement from Theodore Roosevelt to Franklin Roosevelt.

The most recent phase of the cyclical swing has been a revolt against the pragmatic revolt. It has taken the form of an attack on the "pragmatic acquiescence," as Mumford called it, including chiefly the phases of American culture that vulgarized the meaning of pragmatism, reducing truth to whatever "works," thereby casting out other standards of value. As in religion, American intellectuals have been groping for a transcendental philosophic belief, turning against the pragmatic on the ground that it ignores the depths of the psyche and the tragic dimensions of life. To some extent this meant a rejection of the humanist matter-of-factness associated with realism in philosophy, law, economics, and politics; but as a repudiation of mass values, it was also a humanist reassertion of the role of the individual personality as against the operation of group interests and the calculus of mass welfare.

Thus the cyclical swing in the history of American thought has moved in a wide arc from the tough to the mystical, back to the pragmatic, and again to the transcendental. To some extent the cleavage between realists and pragmatists on one side and idealists and absolutists on the other has measured roughly a cleavage between the progressive and conservative forces. This parallel can be carried too far. Thoreau and Brownson, each in his own way a radical in politics, were Transcendentalists in philosophy. Veblen started as a Kantian, John Dewey as a Hegelian. The whole philosophy of conservative Big Business thinking, on the other hand, is thoroughly pragmatic.

However much it may be qualified in particular applications, the parallel does hold. The reformist appeal has generally been from social actuality to social possibility, from the facts of poverty and inequity to the potentials of a fast-moving society which can minimize both. Most liberal and radical reformers have made a habit of thinking in these terms of the socially actual and the socially possible. For the conservative, on the other hand, the absolute and the transcendental offer the advantage of being abstracted from the immediate struggles of society, hanging somewhere (as Holmes put it) as a "brooding omnipresence in the sky," never having to be brought down to earth.

Unlike the European societies where the radical movements have a Marxist intensity, in America it is the conservative movements that have carried the sharper edge. They have appealed to the absolutes of economic freedom and the sanctity of property, while the reformers and liberals (in whose minds the Marxist systems never struck deep roots) have appealed mainly to the moderate goals of progress and the common welfare. This is not to say that American political thought has been dominated by the holders of power. Even with the advantage of power on their side, the conservative thinkers have thought of themselves as fighting a rearguard action, just as the reformers seem forever to be defending civil liberties and are ridden with a sense of ineffectiveness. The trait common to both is a Promethean sense of waging an unequal battle to overthrow the reigning divinities. This may shed some light not only on the American character but on American political society, suggesting that power is distributed more diffusely in it than the contending groups are willing to admit.

I do not mean to say that American thought has always or primarily had a political angle of vision. If anything the philosophic tradition in America has been less directly concerned with politics than in Europe, although it has been more directly concerned with the ethical and other problems of society. It is worth noting that George Santayana, Spanish in descent but brought up and for a time rooted in the American intellectual soil both as student and as teacher, left his greatest mark upon American thought as a moral philosopher as well as a literary stylist. The central stream of American philosophy has probably been that of Peirce (with Chauncey Wright as a forerunner), William James, and John Dewey. Yet in the recent decades there has been a strong critical reaction against this strain, especially against Dewey. It has come not only from what may be called the philosophic "Right," which is to say Niebuhr in religion and Hutchins in education, but also from the empiricist and analytic "Left." In the philosophy of science, in the sociology of knowledge, in metaphysics and ethics, American philosophic thought has become more disciplined and exacting in its analysis: it has also become more fragmented in its concerns and more insulated than the James-Dewey tradition was from the currents of social striving. Through the European refugees from the totalitarian regimes it has also been enriched with elements of continental thought, especially from two Vienna circles—that of the Freudians in psychology and that of the "Logical Positivists" in philosophy.

Despite these new strains of thought, the great intellectual tradition in America has been close to the concerns of social reality, and the political camps have reached out and made use of the academic currents of thought whenever they could.

Of the great political angles of vision, the radical tradition has fared hardest. Its handicap at the start was the fact that the American Revolution was colonial and not social. Once it was over and British imperialism pried loose, the radicals had no enemy target left. Since there had been no social revolution they could not, like the French after 1789, fight to maintain its gains; with no dictatorships on the American scene there could be no resistance movements; with no tyrannies there could be no conspiracies of tyrannicide. Except for the limited episode of Dorr's Rebellion, there were not even—as with the Chartists in England—any grand failures of radical action to be retrieved. As a result American radicalism remained a series of sporadic and sometimes eccentric flare-ups which kept alive the equalitarian dream but had no sustained program, no continuing party, nor even a body of common doctrine.

That was why it did not serve as the intellectual Left Wing of the effective liberal movements of the nineteenth and twentieth centuries. In this sense it fell short of the role played by some of Jefferson's circle who as agrarian radicals attacked the newly rising capitalist class, but whose ideas proved usable in a later industrial era. There was also a Jacksonian Left Wing which saw the worker and farmer as protagonists in the struggle against the tyranny of money. The antislavery Left Wing was formed by abolitionist thinkers like Garrison, Wendell Phillips, and Theodore Parker, who prepared the ground for the slavery struggle, and by the Radical Republicans who laid down a devastating fire against Lincoln's compromises with the slavery issue and the South. In the 1890s Left Wing thinkers like Henry Demarest Lloyd gave form to the Populist drive against railroads and trusts which made Bryanism possible; nor could the victory of Wilson's "New Freedom" in 1912 have taken place if it were not for the novelists David Graham Phillips, Howells, and Frank Norris, the muckrakers Lincoln Steffens and Upton Sinclair, and the constitutional critic J. Allen Smith. Finally the New Deal had intellectual roots in Veblen, Beard, and Parrington, as well as the earlier Populists, and Roosevelt's Left Wing critics proved as troublesome as Lincoln's.

There were also more cantankerous intellectual movements which spent their energies in isolated radical episodes—the Fourierists and other experiments in communal living, the movement for "People's Banks" in Jackson's era, the schemes for currency reform, the blueprints for salvation through Henry George's "single tax" or other creeds, the "twenty-four-hour violence" of mass episodes from Shays' Rebellion to Coxey's Army and the Bonus marchers, the sustained violence of the IWW "Wobblies" and their Syndicalist dream of "one Big Union," the succession of third-party movements, including that of La Follette in 1924 and Wallace's in 1948. Despite their crotchety character, the radical thinkers released some of the sturdier energies of American striving. If we may take Henry George as a symbol for the rest, his Single Tax movement was in itself unworkable and sterile, yet it came from a larger intellectual context—Henry George spoke for a "reforming Darwinism" which saw the social order as the outgrowth of evolution but wanted to use it deliberately in a humanizing effort for the weak as well as the strong; and despite the failure of the Single Tax movement, it did have some effect by liberating the social imagination.

What then accounts for the final failure of the American radicals? Some clues will be found in the pace of social change and the constant sense of dynamism, the moving "triple frontier," the persistence of the open-class system. Most important is the folk belief in the going economic and social system. Labor support, without which there could be no class base for radical thought, was given not to the radicals but to the liberal reformers. The Socialist party, which was bidding for popular support as late as 1920, failed because its dogma of the future commonwealth and of "pie in the sky" seemed unreal to workers who were finding life better here and now. The Communists reached their peak of influence in the Great Depression and the early New Deal; from the late 1930s to the mid-1950s they became entangled in the net of Party conspiracy, moral betrayal, the gyrations of the Party Line, and the world adventures of the Soviet Union, and dribbled away what little remaining support they had.

The radicals could not compete with the liberal reformers in an immediate concrete program, yet they had no long-range program. They could not preach "revolution" effectively in a society where actual revolution—in the form of continuous technical and social change—was taking place all around and its products were being distributed at least tolerably well. Nor could they rally the embittered, since even the hopeless retained a shred of hope for their children's future. They could find no rich soil for their dogma in the minds of people who were turning more strongly every decade toward immediate goals and pragmatic means.

What the radicals succeeded in doing was important: they reaffirmed the equalitarian impulse by fresh challenges to swollen power, injustice, human indifference about suffering. Denouncing corruption, plutocracy, and the vested interests, they were obsessed with a dualism between the angels of light and the princes of darkness. They tried to measure American institutions against the original vision, harking back to an American Eden before the Fall. Not content to gloss over class difference and struggles, they saw that all exercise of political power involves conflict. What they did in their episodic attacks was to feel out the strength of the dominant economic minority, testing whether it had gone slack or retained its creativeness. The answer they got was a double one: from the managers and technicians the wavering evidence that they could continue their revolution of production, and from the liberals the resolve to organize this production within a system of controls which could raise living standards for all.

Thus the fragmented American radicalism, little more than a succession of spasmodic local movements of protest and passion, served to keep both the conservatives and liberals alert. Despite the low estate of radical thought during the Cold War era, an intellectual pattern so constant through American history is likely to find renewal.

The conservative intellectual tradition, while it lacked the Thoreaus, Whitmans, Debses, and Dreisers that radicalism had, exerted a stronger hold on the American mind. Unlike their European parallels, who relied upon tradition and authority, religion, state worship, family, and order, American conservatives boldly captured the citadel of the liberal enemy by taking over its high ground of individualism and natural rights. They asserted that men possess inherent natural rights but insisted that there can be no fulfillment of these rights where the state intervenes in individual economic choices. Thus they appealed to the position of the individual in an indestructible order of Nature that precedes human history. They attempted to build a solid intellectual support for property by invoking the same humanist and individualist symbols which sustained the liberals in their attacks on property. Like them, they refrained from too explosive a discussion of ends. They took for granted the same goal as the liberals—that of the "American dream"; but, in rhetoric at least, they almost appropriated the symbol as their own, and once in their hands, it has been stripped of its equalitarian emphasis and given property overtones.

But the conservatives could not maintain this position without making serious concessions on concrete issues—trade-unions, minimum wages, child labor, social insurance, public control of power sources, corporate monopoly. While retaining the catchwords of individualism and freedom, they cemented their hold on men's minds by promising a natural order presided over by neither God nor justice nor even equality of opportunity, but the brute struggle of the market. It was against this conservative tradition that the progressive reformers of the turn of the century directed their assaults. For under the guise of freedom, conservative thought built an iron trap in which there was no escape from the ruthlessness of brute struggle and survival, including the changes and chances of the business cycle. More than anything else this furnished the emotional drive behind the reformism of the New Deal, and it also explains the intellectual impact of Holmes and Brandeis, Dewey, Veblen and Beard better than any philosophical rationalization.

In another sense also the conservatives became too rigid—in their view of the human situation as a constant. ("You can't change human nature.") This pessimist determinism was at the opposite pole from the perfectionist and plastic view of the human situation which the radicals had. The conservative view was reinforced by the sense of sin in the tradition of evangelical religion. But it could not be maintained in a shifting society and an expanding economy where the individual was always re-creating his career, and where the evidences of the transformation wrought by man's will and intelligence were witness against the overrigid view of human traits.

The deepest source of the strength of conservatism has been its succession of social mystiques. The earliest was the cult of the ruling aristocracy—or (as Fisher Ames put it) the government of "the wise, the rich, and the good." This was followed by the cult of the Constitution, to which Marshall and Story so powerfully contributed. This in turn was followed by the cult of property in the natural order, of which the appeal to social Darwinism was a phase. Property came to be seen as something sanctioned at once by "Nature and Nature's God," and further fortified by being linked with the worker who was worthy of the fruits of his labor, and the businessman who had mingled his managerial skill with the products of industry. The most recent mystique for conservatives is that of an antiliberal nationalism, especially powerful in an era of war and cold war. The premise is that American power rests on its property institutions and that attacks on the sanctity of property become subversive of the nation itself.

With all this intellectual panoply, America has nevertheless no articulate conservative philosophy and no outstanding conservative thinkers who can rank with Hamilton, John Adams, and Calhoun among the earlier thinker-statesmen or with William Graham Sumner among social scientists. In political action rather than formal thought the best of the recent conservatives have been men like Chief Justice Hughes, Henry Stimson, Wendell Willkie, and Dwight Eisenhower, who held fast to what was best in the tradition but yielded generously to necessary changes. Unfortunately, in the postwar decade the center of the stage in conservatism was captured by the racist, repressive, and ultranationalist reactionaries who in every generation produce demagogic figures that strut on the political scene for a brief space and live out their transient and paranoid existence. Partly out of recoil against them and partly to fill a vacuum in American political thought, a "New Conservatism" cropped up in the 1950s to challenge the accepted creeds. I have discussed it briefly earlier;* here I want to add only that a reasoned con-

---

* See Ch. I, Sec. 6, "Tradition and the Frame of Power."

servatism is likely to have a difficult time finding a stable intellectual base amidst the tensions of the years ahead.

It is in the liberal intellectual tradition that American belief has characteristically expressed itself. "The earth belongs to the living," said Jefferson, striking the grand theme that liberalism has since followed. Its credo has been progress, its mood optimist, its view of human nature rationalist and plastic; it has used human rights rather than property rights as its ends but has concentrated on social action as its means. It has made "expedient change" an integral part of its methods and has taken from science the belief in the tools of reason and the tests of validity. It has kept its fighting edge through the emotional force of the reformist impulse. Latterly the liberal tradition has come in for drastic criticism from liberals whose new intellectual posture, especially in the academies, seems to be a strain of habitual self-deprecating irony. Much is said of the failure of liberal thought. Certainly there is a need for redefining it within the psychological realities of our time.

The weaknesses of the liberal tradition are clear enough. First, it is indebted for its individualism to the atomistic thinkers like Locke, James Mill, and Bentham, who could reduce a society to its members but could not link individuals with each other to form a society. It has had to resolve the contradiction between this atomism and the theory of strong state action with which it has allied itself. Even the Christian allegory has not repaired this weakness: its willingness to sacrifice came to mean in the American context mostly sacrifice for one's own freedom or identity and not for others, and did not issue in a sense of society. Thus liberalism built a trap for itself with an atomistic philosophy which strengthened the hold of jungle individualism on the American mind.

The second weakness flows from the alliance with pragmatic thought. The strength gained by this alliance enabled liberalism to focus on concrete situations for reform, undeflected by dogma and abstraction, but made it also vulnerable to the changes and chances of history, squeezing it dry of definite goals and standards. The "open mind" sometimes became a drafty cave of the winds, the questioning spirit became merely ironic, the revolt against past codes became an extreme relativism which left no standards by which to measure values. Eric Goldman has pointed out how this relativism, a scourge with which to lash the conservatives of the 1890s, turned into an engine of disillusionment in the 1920s. "The trouble with us reformers," said J. Allen Smith, "is that we made reform a crusade against standards. Well, we smashed them all, and now neither we nor anybody else have anything left." This was also the theme of much of Randolph Bourne's criticism of the liberalism of his day.

Finally, the liberal's view of human nature stressed the aspirations of the American dream and the supremacy of reason. The more sophisticated thinkers—notably Reinhold Niebuhr—recognized the irrationalism of the human mind and the limits of willed human action. But most liberals assume (as did the sociologist Lester Ward) that men can transform their environment and fashion their society as their own work of art. Thus one may say (leaving out thinkers like Holmes, Veblen, and Dewey) that the liberal tends to reduce everything to environment, including human nature itself, which becomes plastic material to be molded by reason, without allowing for the stubborn propensities of men.

However vulnerable, liberalism has nevertheless emerged as the central expression of the American democratic faith. It is no longer tied to the blind worship of experience, of which it was guilty in the past half century. It has proved intellectually flexible, capable of enrolling determinists like Turner and Beard, and even Darwinists like Holmes, but is more at home with the more fluid thinkers. It has absorbed both the optimism of the idealist thinkers and the cynicism of the materialists. But it could evoke from Morris Cohen equal scorn for "those who spin the world out of ideas, and those who look to earth, air, fire, and water to explain all human phenomena." Its best philosophic expression has been in thinkers like Charles H. Cooley and George H. Mead, who saw the levels of meaning in the "self" which interacts with the "group" and also saw how complex the web of causation is. It has drawn upon the currents of religious faith and at the same time based itself strongly upon the ground of scientific method. Eric Goldman's *Rendezvous with Destiny* traces the strands of thought that unite figures like Carl Schurz, Henry George, Richard T. Ely, Tom Watson, Bryan, Terence Powderly, Lincoln Steffens, Ida Tarbell, Clarence Darrow, William Allen White, Parrington, Harold Stearns, Herbert Croly, La Follette, and even H. L. Mencken. Add to these the line of statesmen-thinkers from Jefferson, Madison, and Lincoln to Wilson and the two Roosevelts, and it is apparent that liberalism has furnished the dominant political and intellectual climate of America.

Its strength lies in providing an angle of vision for viewing America and a fighting faith for the freedom of the person, higher living standards and a more spacious way of life. As Maury Maverick phrased it with a perhaps oversimplified pungency, liberalism has always meant "freedom plus groceries"—not only (one may add) for some of the people but for all, not only sometimes but all the time.

Given this angle of vision, it has developed in its concrete struggles an armory of facts and argument and a passion for battle—against the "octopus" of the big corporation, against rate discrimination by railroads, for free public education, for civil liberties, for Negro equality, for religious freedom, for land conservation, for trade-union organization, for aid to farmers at the mercy of a shifting market, for state control of public utilities, for public use of natural resources, for public development of hydroelectric power, for wage-and-hour legislation, for women's rights, for social security.

These are, of course, piecemeal reforms which do not add up to a unified program. The radicals have also expressed their disdain for liberals because of lack of toughness in fighting their big enemies. The charge strikes home. Yet the radical movements that sought to supply the long-range plans and the tough means sputtered fitfully and died, while the conservatives who scorned the liberal vision found that, without it, they had to rely mainly on social power rather than on intellectual persuasion. American liberalism is one of the few movements in history which has not been based on authority or force, yet has held its dominance in the empire of the mind. Its basic premise has been in a majority will capable of organizing itself effectively when the obstructions are blasted away by the dynamite of facts and ideas. The failures to reach the goal have been frequent and glaring, but they have been recognized and taken in stride.

This does not mean that liberalism has been free of the tensions of constant struggle. Actually one of its emotional drives is a flagellant sense of guilt over the gap between the democratic rhetoric and the social reality. With it there is a too credulous hope that all would be well if only some obstacle were removed, some enemy overcome, some reform achieved. It has been one of the illusions of liberal reformers that the only changes required to build Jerusalem on America's green and promised land are changes in social mechanisms: if only the newspapers were in the hands of the right people, if only there were a third party, if only there were currency reforms, if only the press allowed a free play of opinion, if only the schools paid their teachers enough and adopted progressive techniques, if only the movies showed fewer crime pictures and TV reduced the violence of its programs. . . . This "heart's desire" liberalism has a counterpart in the breakdown of a perspective among paranoid liberals who feel surrounded by reactionary Devil figures. Perhaps with greater maturity and a psychology that cuts deeper the liberals will manage to achieve a long view without losing their militancy.

One cannot imprison in a single mold the thought of a culture stretching over more than three centuries. What is true of American

living, however, is true also of American thought: both have characteristic patterns that mark them off from the patterns of other cultures.
This is not to deny the influence of Europe. American thought may,
in one sense, be viewed as Western thought with a distinct bent of its
own which reshaped British, French, and German influences to the
American context. Puritan thought derived from the English divines
and Calvin; the revolutionary thinking of Jefferson was the product of
his friendship with the French thinkers; the Transcendentalists borrowed from the German mystics and from Asiatic thought; and in the
era of Hitler and Stalin, America became a haven for European scholar-
refugees whose fertilizing influence proved important. Yet when this
has been said, it remains true that the foreign influences have been submerged in the main American stream, and that in the process of re-
shaping their borrowings the Americans have added more than they
have taken.

3. The Higher and Lower Learning

IN PRIMITIVE CULTURES the teacher-priests transmit the cultural tradition
in the form of ritual shrouded in mysteries. When the teaching function is separated from the priestly function, it becomes secular education.
The American school system telescoped these changes: at the start it
had strong if residual connections with the church and clergy but it
became basically secular. Except in the parochial schools it is now free
of control by the churches and is controlled by local and state governments.

The difference is important. Education always aims to some degree
at instilling beliefs in the plastic minds of the young. A secular school
system in a democracy is bound to throw its sanctions behind the existing institutions, and to that extent it may, like a religious system,
discourage skepticism and protect illusions by Platonic myths. But
since the secular tradition in the Western world is linked with free inquiry, its prime purpose (unlike the religious tradition) is to teach the
student how to use his mind for himself. The controls by government
units and by the community spokesmen may set a too-rigid fráme for
the teaching process, but within that frame there is a secular process
which does value free inquiry.

In this sense of imperfect freedom within a frame of institutional control, the school system follows the characteristic American pattern to
be found in business, the trade-union, the family, and the church denominations. Like them the school system is untidily pluralistic, with
some schools and universities privately endowed, but most of them part

of the governmental apparatus. Some of the universities are narrowly practical and technical in character, and some devote much of their energy to specialized research. Thus American education looks like a crazy quilt, with no consistent principle either of authority or philosophy. There are those who lament so sorry a patchwork, urging unity of aim and consistency of method and control. The German educational system is clearer in its lines of authority, the French more orderly in administrative terms, and any system of church-controlled schools lacks the ragged edges of educational philosophy the Americans betray. But seen historically, the growth of the American school system is the product of impulsions that have come from within instead of having been imposed from without. It is an organic expression of American life and character.

Americans have an extravagant reliance on education. It is a piously repeated truism that some concrete social problem—capital and labor, Negro-and-white relations, anti-Semitism, juvenile delinquency, war and peace—"can only be solved by education." Beyond this there is the hope for individual advancement which education holds out to the lower economic groups. It was the Workingmen's Associations that pushed free public education in the 1830s, not only on the Jeffersonian theory of creating an "aristocracy of virtue and talent" in the Republic, but even more with the practical aim of securing better income and status. Most colleges today offer scholarship aid, and rich men who were once poor boys contribute to endowments which help educate poor boys who will in turn become rich men. The significant line of relation runs between education and social mobility. Education, it is held, pays off.

Americans make a distinction, however, between the school learning which increases a man's earning power and the newfangled, dangerous ideas which unsettle his thinking. "Education spoils a good field hand" was a remark that American farmers used to make even while they celebrated the virtues of the free school system. A textile mill manager may still have the same lingering attitude toward his mill hands, or a guardian of White Supremacy toward a Negro college graduate. Many employers used to wonder whether book learning might not spoil a boy for business, preferring an exposure to the "school of hard knocks"— although the recent growth of professional schools of business administration shows this to be an archaic attitude.

All through the American experience there has been an anti-intellectualism running alongside the belief in education. Under the New Deal it expressed itself in Congressional contempt for "brain-trusters" who had "never met a pay roll." It takes the current form of a fear of ideas, ranging from the good-natured epithet of "egghead" to the unremitting hatred which some Congressmen and newspapers express for any liberal intellectuals. Actually there is a strain of anti-intellectualism inherent in the American belief in education: Americans emphasize not so much the training of the intellect as they do some marginal value such as vocational skill or "citizenship" or becoming an "interesting" person—or almost anything except creativeness. While most Americans value education as the road to "know-how" and business advance, they suspect it when carried into political action or expressed in social attitudes. The Congressional investigating committees in the mid-century climate of McCarthy, Jenner, and Velde, who made forays into the colleges to ferret out signs of Communist conspiracy, betrayed a Caliban fear of men trained for independent intellectual judgments.

Despite this anti-intellectual strain, the American belief in education has not only persisted but grown, as is shown by the influx of high-school graduates from every social level into the colleges. Between 1900 and 1950 the college enrollment increased tenfold, moving from a quarter million to two and a half million (by 1957 it was three million, and was expected to reach five to seven million by 1970), while high-school enrollment grew at the same pace, from 650,000 in 1900 to six and a half million. In 1950 there were thirty-three million young Americans enrolled in all types of schools and colleges, public, private, and parochial—which gives some notion of the burden that education has to carry in a mass democracy.

Seymour Harris has documented the trend which is saturating the "market for college graduates" and cutting the income differential between the skilled noncollege employee and the unspecialized college graduate. Yet young Americans continue to stream into the colleges. The lower-middle-class or worker's family will scrimp to give its sons, and more recently its daughters, a university training. Partly this is because it provides them with a better social standing even on the same income level, giving them the established insignia of a new kind of class rank. But it is also because they feel that education will open the door to a better and more productive life.

This makes it all the more difficult to account for the financial neglect of education in many areas of America. While new schools are continually being built, a shocking percentage of the school plant is run-down, its equipment archaic, the teachers badly underpaid when compared with the pay of skilled or even semiskilled workers, the classrooms overcrowded, the textbooks often badly out-of-date. In a typical recent year Americans spent eight billion dollars on liquor, nineteen billion on automobiles—and five billion on public education. Between 1932 and 1950—a period when the student enrollment doubled—the percentage of the national income spent on universities from both public and private sources was cut from 1 to ½ per cent. Since education is largely under local control, the public expenditures vary greatly from state to state. While New York in 1950 was spending $312 a year for each child in its school system, Mississippi was spending $73.

The Commission on Higher Education appointed by President Truman recommended a system of federally subsidized scholarships and a network of "community colleges," with local and Federal funds. The Federal government spent fourteen billion dollars over a span of seven years after World War II for the education of eight million soldiers under the GI Bill of Rights. A notable step forward was taken by the Ford Foundation when it set aside 500 million dollars to establish national competitive scholarships for American colleges and universities, and offered to match contributions from industry for the same purpose. Thus American public and philanthropic policies stand at least partially committed to educational expansion. But the hostility to Federal aid continues to be buttressed by religious differences and by a fear of its political consequences.

The continuing local control of the schools has given the big taxpayer groups a stake in holding school expenses down, and a strategic position that helps them keep the winds of dangerous doctrine out of the schoolroom. It accounts for much of the constriction of opinion, the seediness, and provincialism to be found in the school systems of many smaller American communities. It accounts also for the exodus of male teachers from the profession, since an ill-paid teacher is not a free man—hemmed in by narrow community mores and a vigilant censorship of his every move—and has little standing either with his pupils or the community.

With these trammels the American school system has had to assume one of the most massive tasks in history. It has had to take a polyglot people, thrown together from every ethnic strain and culture in the world, and give it a common body of symbols to serve both for communication and cohesion. When an Englishman remarked after the passage of the Second Reform Act, "Now we must educate our masters," he described what education must achieve in any mass democracy. Horace Mann, who devoted his life to building the public-school system of Massachusetts, had earlier put the idea in his own language: "In a Republic, ignorance is a crime." In America, with its constant stream of new immigrants, the schools had to add a second function to that of book learning. They had to take human material from many diverse cultures and teach them the whole body of what is believed, practiced,

and taken for granted in America. Considering the task of bringing cohesion into such widely different groups, the miracle is not that it was
done imperfectly but that it was done at all. Nor could any part of the
task be escaped, as in countries which have accepted a cleavage in education between the "gentleman" and the "common man." The American public schools had to accept whatever human material was offered
to them and make it part of an equalitarian society.

Two secession movements have merged to challenge the public-
school system. The children not only of the wealthy classes but even of
moderate-income professionals have increasingly been sent to private
schools, while at least five million American children are in the Catholic parochial schools, and a considerable number in Protestant and
Jewish. In James B. Conant's terms, a split is emerging between two
school-nations that is unhealthy in a democracy. The secession of the
parochial groups, who train into the student their own body of civic
premises along with their religious norms, is not likely to be healed;
the spread of the movement will probably be limited only by the financial drain it imposes on the churches. The secessionists in the private
elementary schools might possibly be won back by improved standards
in the public schools.

There is a deeper class lesion in the school system which cannot be
healed even by such reforms. There are scars of segregation and discrimination which ravage the whole premise of equal educational opportunity. Sharpening the classic question of Warner and Havighurst,
"Who gets educated?" one must ask, "Who gets educated how?" The
Negroes, not only in the South but even in the North, are still—even
after the Supreme Court school decision—largely excluded from adequate education by racist hostility and fear. Their schools are scantily
equipped, inadequately prepared. As for the Jews and Catholics, they
go to college in large numbers but their range of choice is restricted
(especially for Jews) by an operative though silent quota system in many
universities and professional schools. The fear in every university is that
if the bars are taken down they will stream in and frighten away other
groups, thus making the institution "unrepresentative." This bias, however disguised, makes a hash of the principle of equal access at the core
of an open society. It infects the atmosphere of the classroom and the
campus, and turns the college for many young people into a Heartbreak House.

It would be wrong, however, to conclude that America has a racist
or class system of education. The doors to the intellectual life are slowly
being forced open even for Negroes. On the level of class obstacles, the
Holinshed Report documents the fact that there are still large numbers

of high-school graduates equipped for college who cannot enter because they lack the means: even scholarship aid fails to solve their problem, since it rarely covers living expenses, nor does it fill the gap of their earning power in the family income. For such the free school system offers only dusty answers to their hunger for training and knowledge. Yet the big fact remains that a steadily increasing proportion of young Americans gets drawn into secondary and higher education every year. The percentage that gets to college is now something like 15 per cent. Despite the 85 per cent who don't get there, the Jacksonian ideal that every young American shall have a college education is on the way to fulfillment.*

The real issue about the Jacksonian goal is how badly it pulls down educational standards all along the line. Much of elementary and secondary schooling is little more than assembly-line processing with mechanized teaching methods and an intellectual level rarely rising above mediocrity. Since American power rests on its technology, the trend has been toward the technical and vocational, with little stress on the capacity to handle general ideas and sift irrational from rational. Given the boredom of high-school pupils and the pull of jobs and spending power, it has been found necessary in some big-city school systems to weight the high-school curriculum toward the vocational in order to keep the boys at school a few years longer. While this helps produce skilled manpower, it ignores the fact that the problems which will make or break America are no longer technological but social and cultural.

In the face of these problems the rate of contemporary illiteracy among Americans compares badly with the culture of Jeffersonian America, which had an almost complete mass literacy. Recent surveys show also that many Americans who can read have little competence or interest in the public issues on which as citizens they are supposed to reach decisions. This political illiteracy, more serious than the technical brand, is the greatest liability of American educational practices. For education has to perform a dual function in any civilization: it must transmit the cultural heritage, and it must also provide each generation with the intellectual and moral tools for assessing itself, calculating the forces that confront it, and making the necessary changes. In this sense it must be at once conservative and innovating, transmissive and unsettling.

The task is complicated by the extraordinary pace of American social change. It is hard for the teacher to step twice in the same stream. The

* I develop at greater length, later in this section, the contrast of the Jacksonian and Jeffersonian goals.

constant flux requires him to be alert to often subtle changes, capable of assessing them without becoming bewildered and lost in the maze. To add to the difficulty, the school system is only part of the constellation of educational forces. The mind of the young American is also under pressure from family, street gang, and peer group, bombarded by a clamor from all the Big Media around him—movies, radio, TV, and the comics. The hardy teacher who tries to shape the mind and character of his charges thus has access to only a small segment of their attention. He has the despairing sense of wrestling with massive demons for the child's still plastic personality, knowing that whatever brief spell he may have with him in the schoolroom, they are assaulting the child's mind everywhere else the rest of the time.*

To attack the American school system, therefore, as part of the "crowd culture" is to miss at least half the point. The strongest pressures of the crowd culture come from outside the schoolroom, which must itself combat them. To the question "How well does the school express the culture?" some critics have answered sardonically, "All too well." The schools do express one phase of the crowd culture—the spread-eagle rhetoric of nationalist pride mistaken for the democratic idea, the uncritical embrace of the life goals of success and power and prestige, the slack acceptance of questionable means alongside a hackneyed moralism. Yet there are also teachers who are the only counterforce the growing child can invoke to oppose the crassness of the crowd culture. By instilling a love of books, a hunger for experience, a critical attitude toward the prevailing idols of the tribe, a generous one toward foreign peoples and alien cultures, such teachers have a disproportionate impact on each generation. They unlock for each the treasures of history and science, literature and the arts, and place in its hands that key to whatever has been felt and created which makes every educational system potentially revolutionary and every good teacher by necessity an insurgent.

This may explain why the American school system has been under constantly increasing attack by vigilantist groups of super-patriots. Where they have not taken a lethal toll of their victims, they have succeeded in leaving timid men and women more timid than they found them.

The American school is itself a subculture, almost on a level with the family in its importance. It forms a little segregated society, with its own customs, its loyalties, its network of interpersonal relations. Its

* For the Big Media as contenders for the minds of children, see Sec. 5, "Revolution in the Big Media"; also Ch. XI.

image is that of an extended family, with most of the elementary teaching assigned to female teachers who act the role of mother for the larger brood. This female domination of the schools goes back to the village "school marm." It is also partly economic, since the men are drained off into jobs that offer better income and social standing and only the women remain—sometimes out of a sense of vocation, often because there is no alternative. In most cases they fail to act as effective authority symbols, nor can they serve as models for role-learning by the boys in their classes. It may be hard for many of them to understand the sexual and emotional urgencies of adolescent boys in their charge. Thus they often treat as instances of delinquency what is usually only evidence of normal sexual development under stress. The reverse facet is also true—that many of the teachers find in their schoolroom an outlet for long-dammed-up emotions.

The teachers themselves, along with the parents, have grounds for anxiety about the shaping of mind and personality among their charges. A 1954 study estimated that 15 per cent of the high-school enrollment in New York City was "emotionally disturbed"—a phrase that covers a wide variety of symptoms, from retarded study performance to school vandalism and sexual offenses. This is, of course, partly a reflection of similar disturbances among the adult population. What happens is that the school is made the dumping ground for tensions and problems which the family and community failed to solve. It has been found that nine out of ten of the "disturbed children" come from homes that are broken by divorce, parentless, scarred by parental conflict, or emotionally bleak because of parental neglect. Thus the schools get the harvest of family failure. The old school task of making the pupils literate has been replaced by the new task of enabling them to cope with the problems of emotional health. The principal difficulty is no longer with the three Rs and with laying a base for an effective technical culture: it is with the student's understanding of his own drives, and with his discovery of his identity, with guiding him through the curve of his emotional growth.

The growing number of cases of juvenile delinquency, both in and outside the classroom, is evidence that the schools are not succeeding where the family, the church, and the community have thus far failed. For many children from slum areas or from homes of emotional tension or deprivation, the school is the only bright spot in their lives. But for many others it remains a bleak place where their difficulties are hardly recognized, and where the necessary resources in the form of counseling and psychiatric help are available to only a minimal degree. It is true that the American school system is almost the only one which provides any psychiatric services at all, but what it does provide does not come near meeting the need. A report by a teachers' group in New York points out that "an average of three children in each class will sooner or later require institutional care because of emotional and mental breakdown, but the educational budget allows three minutes of guidance per child during an entire term." The teachers themselves try hard to fill the gap, but the burdens on them are too harassing, the classrooms are too crowded, their own economic and emotional problems too urgent to allow them to play the role of surrogates for parents and community. Somehow this task will have to be fulfilled, since the schools now occupy the strategic situation between the tensions of the family and the tensions of society.

In addition to the emotional tensions, there are class lines and cliques within the school which also mirror those of the culture. It acts as a common meeting ground for children of diverse class and ethnic origins, where each finds an increment of experience his home has not offered him, and where he feels out the personalities of his peers, measures his strength and vulnerability against them, and begins to find his identity. Important in any society, this is particularly important in a mobile one. Even as some, at the end of the educational process, find the transition to the world of social reality too abrupt, for many of them the school does offer a tolerably insulated "separate culture," with a period of eight to twelve formative years in which they can find themselves and prepare to cope with the rough ways of the culture outside. Perhaps, as some believe, Americans don't expect much more from their free elementary schools than the combating of illiteracy, the Americanizing of the children of the foreign born, the elements of literacy required for work and trade, and the preparation of technicians, laboratory research workers, inventors and scientists. Yet as a culture in miniature the school also performs a more important function.

To understand this is to see in fresh perspective the old battle of concepts that raged for a time between the "progressive education" champions and the "Essentialists." The way the issue is generally put is whether the community is best served when the children are equipped with a precisely drilled knowledge of the essential studies and tools (based on the three Rs), or whether they learn best by relating their learning to the culture and developing their capacities for growth in the context of the living problems of their day. There is nothing wrong—in fact, there is everything right—in teaching the "fundamentals" with precision, although it must be observed that even in the schools that focus on them there is a vast ignorance of geography, American history, and contemporary events. But all that a school can ever hope to do is to equip the student with tools which he can later use to become an educated man. How he will use those tools depends on the kind of person he becomes, and this in turn depends on how his plastic mind and personality are shaped within the school-as-culture.

For the schools do form a separate culture; the question is what kind it will be. A formal school, focusing rigidly on certain "essentials," is likely to carry over into its emotional tone as a culture the accents of authority and subordination: what it will fashion and graduate into the larger society may be not men but marionettes for the crowd culture. A school, in turn, which focuses on the growth of the child, which does its teaching with an eye on social reality and relates the emotional needs of the child to the inherent disciplines of the subject, is likely to develop within its own cultural frame the accents of critical inquiry and generous sympathies.

It is true that much of American education has for some time been operating in the shadow of John Dewey, and his experimental spirit has to some extent carried over into the public-school system. Progressive education, which for a time was based on a too-optimistic view of human nature, seems to have learned from its worst mistakes. It is no longer content to pose questions without offering at least tentative answers, or to underline the relativism of all standards without trying to shape operative standards. It has learned to work within a necessary frame of discipline and responsibility. John Dewey and his followers not only effected a revolution in American educational thinking but offered a characteristic American approach of trial and error and of critical inquiry which has left its mark on the world.

Where this approach seems to have the least to offer is on the level of the college and university, where the problem is not how to protect the beginnings of growth but how to help young people to maturity and shape productive thinking.

The American college did not begin to find itself until the latter decades of the nineteenth century. Founded principally by religious groups—Congregationalists, Methodists, Presbyterians, Baptists, Quakers —it was at first an instrument for turning out ministers, lawyers, and gentlemen, and remained for a time in the shadow of the denominations even after it broke away from their control. The two men who helped transform the college into a university were Daniel C. Gilman and William R. Harper. Asked to submit plans for Johns Hopkins, Gilman placed before his trustees the idea of starting not with a college program but with a graduate school and research center; he sent his faculty to train in the great universities of Germany, and they came back with their booty of European techniques in science, medicine, and historical research. Harper took what John D. Rockefeller had intended as a Baptist college at Chicago and turned it into a university by bringing to it a group of young men—Laughlin, Veblen, Dewey, Mead, Jacques Loeb—such as had never before been assembled on an American campus, and letting them follow their bent. From these sources came the two formative trends of American higher education—the pursuit of specialized research and what Robert M. Hutchins has called the "hospitality to good men pursuing unconventional work."

The danger has been the double one of idolizing the "scientific" and pursuing the specialized and the "practical." The American social thinker, hoping to be a "scientist," tries to emulate the precision methods of his colleagues in the laboratory sciences. In an earlier chapter* I have drawn the distinction between science and scientism—the latter being the belief that all reality is subject to the mathematical methods of the natural sciences, and that everything which does not fit into them can scarcely be relevant to the scholarly life. A corollary has been the cultivation of the narrowly specialized field, which can be reduced to compositable study and subjected to intense "scientific" inquiry. Still another corollary, although—like specialization—by no means a necessary one, has been the cult of the "practical." What scientism and the "practical" have in common is an impatience with whatever is elusive or subjective or in the realm of ethical values—that cannot be pinned down and measured. In pursuit of scientism and the practical, American university life has become a close ally of corporate life and the "organization man," who is dedicated to both these ideals.

Thus a new provincialism has replaced the earlier sense of inferiority that American thinkers had in the shadow of the great European intellectual tradition. It is ironic that the European thinkers themselves —Comte and Hegel, Marx, Spengler, Freud and Jung, Weber, Toynbee, Whitehead—never aped specialism or laboratory method, being philosophers who took human knowledge as their arena. At once cockier in aim and less secure at heart, the American professors seek to build faultless structures inside a narrow domain and are apologetic when they wander afield.

The American university becomes thus less an intellectual community than a collection of professional schools and graduate or research faculties, each of them a small principality. American scholars have excelled less in theory than in empirical studies, such as business fluctuations,

* See Ch. IV, Sec. 6, "The Culture of Machine Living."

personnel management, medical research and techniques, applied physics and engineering, administrative processes, attitude measurement. The tendency toward specialism and practical studies is reinforced by the availability of research funds, especially when they can be shown to "pay off." Recently there has been a drastic shift of subsidized university research to military projects, turning large segments of the universities into satellites of the Armed Services. There has also been a cry for the recruitment and training of increasing numbers of engineers to keep pace with the Russians—as if the problem were one of numbers rather than of social intelligence and humanistic training.

I do not mean to oppose the specialized forms of teaching to the generalized ones, or to imply that intensive university courses are necessarily narrowing ones or that "general education" studies are necessarily liberating ones. Charles Frankel has well pointed out how misleading it is to contrast "liberal" education with "specialized" education. Specialization may be narrow in its tendencies, but it does not follow that failure to specialize brings a humanist view in its wake: it may actually encourage a dilettantist approach to thinking and learning, with the superficiality of cocktail-party conversation. What is needed, as Frankel puts it, is a humanist and philosophical approach to whatever the subject matter may be—an approach that will emphasize the intellectual methods and the moral and aesthetic choices that govern thinking and let the student discover the setting of his particular fact in the large context of life. Seen in these terms the best kind of research may be specialized in the sense that it deals with some problem gnawing at the scholar, but it can yield fundamental results only if it moves from the special problem to broadly theoretical questions. In the ordinary sense of the term such inquiry will never be "practical," although it very often—to the delight of corporations and government agencies —ends with empirical and profitable results. It has even been possible for American physicists and other scholars, subsidized by funds from the defense services, to do fundamental theoretical work of their own choice.

As an instrument of national policy, the American university has broken with its earlier tradition. Although the great university leaders took their scholarship standards from the German institutions of their day, they did not carry over the German idea of the relation of the university to the state. Themselves the product of the state, the German universities were responsible to it, and the professors who governed them were in effect its officials. The American universities, on the other hand, followed the British tradition as voluntary associations supported by endowments. In the mid-nineteenth century this situation was changed by the "land-grant" colleges which became state universities and operated with government funds. Some of them—notably Wisconsin, Ohio State, Michigan, Illinois, Pennsylvania State, Indiana, California—have been colossi with a towering place in the education of a democracy. Yet it remains true that prestige still attaches to the older universities and smaller colleges which continue to operate under voluntary grants of individual funds. These have flowed from Maecenases who, having made their fortunes by single-mindedness and resourcefulness, feel expansive in making princely gifts to the colleges commanding the nostalgic memories and loyalties of their impressionable days. Latterly the privately endowed colleges have come upon lean years, their fixed income from investments cut in value by inflation, and the sources of their gifts being dried up by heavy taxation. Faced with dwindling funds, university heads have sometimes had to become traveling salesmen and have grown pessimistic about the future of free education. But their pessimism seems exaggerated. Even with the heavy tax system, as long as the Big Money flows freely into industry a portion of it is bound to end up in the universities.

The gloomier question is posed by the issue of control. In the growth of the universities several fateful decisions were made. One was to entrust the university to the control of laymen rather than its own faculty. The other was to choose the laymen principally from the corporate masters of business enterprise. Neither decision was inevitable. The British universities, also privately endowed, are controlled mainly by nonbusiness laymen; the German universities, creatures of the state, are controlled by their faculties. The American state universities are supervised by a committee of regents, behind whom are the legislators and the economic and political rulers of the community. The private universities are under the control of boards of trustees—a fact summed up in oversimplified terms by the title and subtitle of Veblen's book: *The Higher Learning in America: A Memorandum on the Control of Universities by Businessmen.* Generally speaking, the administrators of American universities have stood up well to the state, but not so well to the businessman armed with economic power.

But the issue is less clear-cut than Veblen saw it. Paradoxically, a body of liberal university thought developed under the control of the very men who were the targets of liberal attack. When Harold Laski, as a lecturer in history at Harvard, ran afoul of state authorities and corporate groups in the Boston police strike, President Lowell stood by him until he left for a better post at the London School of Economics. When Roscoe Pound and Felix Frankfurter of the Law School displeased the rich alumni by their views on law and (in Frankfurter's case) on the Sacco-Vanzetti case, the university again stood by them. These instances were, of course, more than matched by cases of dismissal at other institutions more intolerant than Harvard or less able to ride out storms. I cite them mainly as evidence that even within the frame of business control there are broad limits of freedom, if only the college administrators have the daring to explore them and enough mastery of men to deal creatively with their trustees. As Chancellor of the University of Chicago over a span of more than twenty years, Hutchins carried his trustees with him, appealing to their sense of innovation and their pride in the University's achievement and prestige. Harvard, under President Pusey, rode out the tide of McCarthyism with a tenacity that cried for imitation by others.

Much depends on the character of the university president. Veblen derided him as a "captain of education"—a minor captain of industry who has transferred his base of operations to the college campus. To document his indictment there are case histories of presidents who have run their faculties as they might run corporate employees, hiring and dismissing them as if they were interchangeable parts, measuring their intellectual productiveness by page of output, fearful of any heretical utterance that might slow up the flow of funds. They have displayed qualities that might have equipped them as easily to head a corporation, a newspaper, or an Army division—except that the last requires courage under fire, a rare quality among college administrators. Usually it is the pliant man, the diplomat with a good public face, who runs the university "smoothly," getting funds and staying out of trouble over "controversial" teachers.

The heads of the great universities are more than college presidents: they are the only quasi-official intellectual leaders America possesses. What is said by the president of Harvard or Columbia, Yale or Chicago, carries weight. The best presidents are trained craftsmen with an ability to handle issues on a big scale and to use judgment in crises. The successful ones often move into diplomatic posts. Sometimes, in turn, men trained in strategy (like diplomats and generals) move into a university presidency—but usually this ends in disaster for the president and the university alike.

The sharpest crisis in their history hit the American universities in mid-century—not a financial one but a crisis of freedom. For many parents education seems to threaten the religious values and the moral conditioning that the family has sought to instill. How many parents, forgetting that the college years are those of adolescent rebellion, show dismay when sons and daughters come home for the holidays with "half-baked" notions in economics and philosophy, and how many a battle has been waged to save the soul of the heretic. These traditional anxieties merged with political ones during the cold war when the colleges were attacked as "hotbeds of Communism." Test oaths for teachers, Congressional investigations, and faculty purges confronted the colleges with an unparalleled danger to free inquiry.

A few strong voices were finally raised to challenge the attack on the Republic of Learning. The more courageous ones agreed that Communist teachers, in following Party Line truth, had forfeited their intellectual integrity; but they added that test oaths and purges did a damage to American education far greater than the shabby handful of Communist teachers could have done; they insisted that the judgment of a teacher's record, character, and worth must in every case be the judgment by his peers and not only by a group of power-hungry political adventurers, or of post-card scribblers who suspect all teachers and hate all ideas.

The impulses toward social timidity, never absent among teachers and students, were strengthened by the crusade of anti-intellectualism. More than ever the teachers tended to play it safe: and the image of courage which a teacher ought to offer as an example to his students was obscured. Every educational system must learn how to present the claims of rival social systems without fear and without propaganda. But the critical sifting of competing claims became more difficult as the courses dealing, for example, with Marxist thought and the nature of Communism grew scarce. Americans had not yet developed the quiet belief in their own social system that would enable them to regard intellectual nonconformism with calmness.*

Like the public school, the American college is itself a culture, with an inner structure of authority and an internal moral and emotional climate. The professors, who have become in contemporary America the counterparts of the clergy in earlier English and American society, are allowed to arrange curriculum matters; but the worldly matters are left to a new college managerial group. It is usually the managers rather than the faculty who make the final decisions even on educational issues. In a historic case at the University of Nevada, a professor critical of the educational policies of the president was ousted after a public hearing: he found it hard to explain to the substantial citizens why the running

---

* I deal here only with academic freedom. For other aspects of freedom, see Ch. VI, Sec. 10, "The Struggle for Civil Liberties."

of a college should be different from that of a business organization by
the "boss" or a football team by the coach.

The role of college athletics has continued to be primary, conferring
prestige on the victorious universities and the hero-players even though it
is widely known that college athletics are in effect subsidized. In the
college novels, starting with the classic *Stover at Yale,* the dramatic
touchdown made by the hero at the crisis of the football game furnishes
the climax both of plot and character. The formula of these novels, with
its mingling of football games, college heroes, town-and-gown rivalries,
and caste divisions between the inner circle of social fraternities and
honor societies and the excluded pariahs, is with all its distortions a
meaningful mirror of the college culture. Scott Fitzgerald's *This Side of
Paradise,* portraying the Princeton of Amory Blaine, is, however, less an
authentic version of the undergraduate world than it is a special case
history of the flapper era of the 1920s. The more typical college culture
of today is that of the big Midwestern university, so vast and impersonal
that the student is isolated and almost forgotten in it, finding his sense
of loyalty in the totemic rivalries of athletic events and his sense of
warmth in the more compassable fraternity groups. The state universities have transformed American higher education by introducing the
type-figure of the female coed. The coed has converted the American
college culture from an all-male fellowship, with its legendry of masculine heartiness, into a society in which dating, petting, convertibles, fraternity and sorority dances, campus hairdos, and the latest campus fashions in women's clothes are themes that overshadow scholarship.

The decline in university standards, however, is not explained by the
invasion of the women. Simon Flexner made a classic attack on universities that offer courses in poultry raising, clog-dancing, and hotel administration, and every critic of mass education in America has followed
him in his indictment. It is easy to ridicule the university offerings
which reflect the utilitarian nature of American culture. If a university
wants to meet these community needs, it can segregate such courses into
extension departments, where they will not affect the more exacting intellectual work. This still leaves the destructive slackness which prevails at the core of a university. This is the twilight world where underpaid teachers, unsure of their standing and feeling themselves failures,
talk at cross-purposes to students who go listlessly through a college to
the "practical" life goals of the world outside.

In reaction against the mediocrity of college standards, some educators have insisted on rigidly high standards of specialized university
research. There are others who contend that research in itself does not

add up to education—that it may fragment the individual student and teacher, moving away from the view of an educated man as a rounded one who lives with awareness within his culture and who brings to bear on it the humanizing influence of a productive intellectual and emotional life. The "research" ideal, dependent on large grants of funds and carried through with a large-scale division of labor, reflects the values of a technological culture and can be mutilating to the personality. Caught between the poles of the vocational and research emphasis, the American university has vacillated between the slack and the sterile. Here again, as I have suggested earlier, the crucial question is not one of specialized or general education but the humanism or the narrowness with which both are carried on.

There are, as Robin Williams, Jr., suggested, two ideals in American education—the Jeffersonian goal which would make higher education accessible to all but insists on demanding standards, and the Jacksonian goal which would treat every mind as equal and open the state university to every high-school graduate regardless of capacity. It is against the Jacksonian ideal that Robert Hutchins directed his most effective attacks. The Hutchins group may be too self-consciously intellectual and has laid itself open to the charge of a nostalgic archaism. But its critics are in danger of forgetting that the transmission of the cultural heritage may itself become a radical instrument for a new approach to education in a mass democracy. By invoking the comparison of American culture with the great cultures of the past, possessed of different standards of value, it leads to a critical re-examination of the common ends which give meaning to a culture.

The teachers in contemporary America must conduct their teaching on the edge of an abyss. It is not only that many students are drafted before they have finished high school. Beyond that fact they are part of a generation that has learned something of the power of both evil and heroism, and of man's heart as the source of both potentials. The common ends of education have become those of making power responsible, insuring the survival of free inquiry, and humanizing man in a dehumanized technology. These cannot be attempted without the effort at educating the whole person-in-growth, evoking a sense of generous emotions and of the tragedy of life along with the possibilities for happiness.

This involved the fashioning of belief as well as the sharpening of knowledge. But to aim at it by turning the schools back to a religious or moralistic emphasis is to take a mechanical view of how the training of belief can be achieved. The problem is not to close off divergent views of life by the hot certainties of theology and the dusty answers of dogma but to open every possible door to productive living. Meanwhile it is important to remember that of all the techniques for creating a sense of society, education is the most effective tie for binding men together.

4. Profile of the Press

THE EAGERNESS for news is organic to American culture. "What's new?" as the American greeting puts it, conveys an avidity for fresh impressions which makes the American the largest consumer of newsprint in the world. The news thus becomes for Americans the outward garment of reality. On waking, you turn on the radio news broadcast or the TV "morning show," or run through the paper at breakfast, or scan the sports or market news while crowded in the bus or subway or commuter's train. While you have been asleep you have missed the reality and must catch up with it.

If news is the carrier of reality, it is a rapidly shifting one and must be caught on the wing. The American feels that "time is money." He also feels that each new increment of time carries with it a possibly precious freightage of new events. This passionate time sense is a natural accompaniment for the rise to power of a young people still on the make, oriented not toward an inner life but toward an outer world in which almost anything can happen to give a decisive turn to life. Since anything can happen and may affect him crucially, the American wants to know about it quickly. That is why a "news beat" is important for a wire service like the AP or UP or for the news staff of a broadcasting chain. That is also why "exclusives" are important: the urge to be on the "inside" is linked with the urge to be in on the kill first.

But it is equally true that news must give way to news. As a newspaperman put it, "What is hot stuff today is shelf paper tomorrow." No one wants to be stuck with an old piece of news. There is nothing more ridiculous to an American than to be caught reading a copy of last week's newspaper. All items in the democracy of American news are born free and equal—the trivial and the world-shaking alike. Their viability is contained within the bounds of their time unit. Like one of the species of fruit fly, each of them has its appointed span of life: it is spawned and lives for a day—sometimes only for a fraction of a day, an edition. It buzzes briefly, dies unmourned, is replaced by its successor, and the next day it is sunk in oblivion. In Waldo Frank's phrase, for the American "news is a toy." Every toy has a glittering fascination for the child—to be forgotten when the next toy appears.

Two corollaries follow from this conception of the nature of news. One is that news items are "facts," to be sharply distinguished from "opinion" or "interpretation." The second, related to the first, is that since each news event is fresh and new, it exists independently and derives its meaning from its own innards, rather than as a part of a pattern.

The truth is that the method of reporting news events does influence and mold belief. But the American hugs the illusion that he is not influenced by anything except "facts." When an editor is worried about a piece of vigorous, candid reporting, he is likely to red-pencil it as "interpretation." Very few commentators who fit the news into a pattern of meaning—the exceptions are writers like Walter Lippmann and Joseph and Stewart Alsop—have any prestige. If the pattern of interpretation is based on liberal premises, then—whether in the press or on the air—it is doubly suspect, for to the perils of distortion are added the perils of "Left-Wing slant." The most successful columnists are those who have made colorful characters of themselves, or have fed the appetite for gossip and "inside stuff" but have stayed clear of dangerous interpretation.

As a result, the American tends to be spottily informed and basically bewildered. He has had thrust on him the burden of making sense of his fragmentized world. He listens to the radio "news summaries," buys the "news magazines," which provide the background and setting to give meaning to the news—and in the process often impose their own pattern of meaning on it. They are popular partly because they pick up from the national press many items that the local press ignores, but mainly because the daily newspaper—with all its bias—offers the American few patterns of meaning.

Nietzsche's phrase about "manifold man, the most interesting chaos, perhaps, that has existed to date" describes the American. He overworks, overplays, overeats, overdrinks, drives himself too hard, reads too much newsprint, lives under an overwhelming flood of stimuli. Each news event adds another stimulus, batting him this way and that. He becomes finally only a receptacle into which the floods pour and from which they flow out in energy—a receiving and transmitting agent but not a valuing agent. He sees small and large items given the same sensational importance in the "daily disaster diet"—murders and wars and massacres, sex cases and strikes, personal incidents and revolutions. The result is a debauchery of the meaning and relation of events. The only pattern into which he can fit the unrelated items is the pattern of the stereotypes he already possesses. This is a pattern mainly of strife and combat, with the good and evil symbols taken for granted. As a result the process of history becomes for the newspaper reader a series of raging yet meaningless and impenetrable battles.

The atomized quality of the news sets the American press off from that of continental Europe, where an interpretive political slant is given to the leading news items. Not that American papers refrain from political slanting. But the distortion is implicit, rather than politically explicit, in the process of selecting and headlining the news items and assigning them space. It may be argued with considerable truth that the atomism of the American papers is healthy, since it helps guard Americans against too sharp an ideological cast of mind and prevents the clash of fanaticisms. But in the process it also retards growth toward political maturity.

Every important newspaper has its characteristic profile, which is related to the profile of its culture. A newspaper like the London *Times,* which reports the award of the honorary degrees at Oxford by giving the original Greek quotations inside the Latin citation, would be hard to imagine in America. The graceful and cultivated political essays that appear on the front page of *Figaro* could not find a parallel in the American daily press, nor could the ruthlessly rigged political propaganda of *Pravda* or *Izvestia* or *Borba,* nor the heavy economic emphasis of a German newspaper.

The profile of the American press is made up of murder and sudden death, infractions of the sexual and moral codes, conflict whether in war, diplomacy, labor troubles, politics or sports, and always—people. It is the emphasis on people that makes home-town news, gossip, and social events so important an ingredient of the formula. "One human, earthy story," says Marvin Creager, a Milwaukee newspaperman, "about something being done or happening to someone in our own city, is worth a dozen from the press association wires." It was the intense localism of the American "home-town mind" that made the war correspondents from Des Moines or Dallas papers visiting a front-line battalion in World War II pay more attention to the names and addresses of the "local boys" than to the strategy of battle.

Thus the double visage of the news in an American paper is that of the violent and the familiar. But news, whether international or local, is only one of the reader's interests to which the press ministers. It also gives advice to the lovelorn, provides hints on cooking and homemaking, runs presumably expert hints on how women can reduce and stay young, provides spelling and vocabulary-building exercises and crossword puzzles, gives tips on horse racing, sometimes serves the gambling propensity by publishing the Treasury or racing figures on which the "numbers game" is based, runs stock market quotations, provides ready-made comment on news and personalities by columnists, advises on how to bring up children, gives horoscopes, runs advertisements telling where you can buy what for how much and how to get a job and where to hire a domestic or have your Venetian blinds repaired.

Thus, news as reporting on "the glut of occurrences" (as Benjamin Harris, an early American newspaperman, put it) is only a part of the raw material of the newspaper. The American newspaper has had the same experience as the drugstore: its original purpose has been swallowed up by its accretions. So many embellishments have been added that it is hard to remember what the original function was. The emphasis has shifted away from the news itself, so that in making up a ninety-six-page or sixty-four-page tabloid or a forty-eight-page paper of conventional size, there are usually only a handful of front pages left free after the departments, features, and ads have been laid out. This is less true of papers like the *Times* and *Herald Tribune* of New York or the St. Louis *Post-Dispatch* or the *Christian Science Monitor* of Boston, which take pride in having not yet become vendors of sweets and spices. But some inroads are being made even into these fortresses by the barbarians. As in the world of drugstores, where few establishments remain pharmacies rather than emporia for miscellanies, the over-all pattern and trend are unmistakable.

At its best the American press canvasses the news of the world with an unparalleled thoroughness and competence. With their resources, their skilled man power at the shirt-sleeve and leg-man level, and their genius for organization, Americans are unexcelled at the job of news-gathering. The wire services have a world-wide staff—and use their member newspapers as part of their machinery for collecting domestic news. But what they gather at the big end of the funnel is often hardly recognizable when it emerges at the narrow end in a typical small city newspaper. A double process of selection takes place: first by the wire service editors when they decide what news to get, to hold out, to send out; by the publishers and editors when they decide what to print, given their readers and the available space. At both stages a good deal of skill and experience is invested; but at both stages also timidity, unimaginativeness, the sacred cows of the editorial office, political loves and hates, and the conscious and unconscious drives of distortion often play havoc with the final product.

A handful of newspapers, not content with the wire services alone, maintain their own foreign and Washington staffs. The foreign staffs of the New York *Times* and *Herald Tribune,* the Chicago *Daily News* (less today than earlier), the Baltimore *Sun,* the *Christian Science Monitor,* work on the assumption that the press association men will cover the chores, allowing them to concentrate on their own stories. Some of these men have made the good American foreign correspondent a world symbol of the adventurous and tenacious newspaperman, but some have been police reporters abroad. In the case of Washington coverage, the papers named above along with others like the St. Louis *Post-Dispatch*, the Chicago *Sun-Times* and *Tribune*, the Louisville *Courier-Journal*, the San Francisco *Chronicle*, the Providence *Journal*, the Milwaukee *Journal*, the Denver *Post*, maintain their own staffs. Yet it has been estimated that the combined circulation of the papers with good foreign and Washington coverage is less than the combined circulation of the two McCormick-Patterson papers, the Chicago *Tribune* and the New York *Daily News*.

Moreover, the quality of the reporting depends on the disinterestedness of the publishers in the theme being reported. The Washington staffs may take on the protective coloration that will enable them to thrive in the newspaper house built by the publisher, and some even become his political errand boys. Yet the White House correspondent can be a powerful force for political illumination, as witness the fact that the Presidential Press Conference is the only American institution which subjects the Executive to a cross fire of questioning, as in the House of Commons or the Chamber of Deputies: it has thus become informally a working part of the governmental machinery. The foreign correspondents have an independence of their own because they are further away from the scene of intense domestic, economic, and political conflict.

The product of the American press which most clearly reflects the elements of dream and reality in the culture pattern is the reporter. Like the other American power men, he is at the opposite pole from the eighteenth-century European man of sentiment as drawn by Rousseau or Laurence Sterne. His "hard-boiled" quality may be seen as a mark of the desensitizing of a competitive society in which one rarely confesses to being caught off-guard or being "played for a sucker." Under such a sun and sky the American reporter has flowered. An urban paper tends to take its stamp from him, and the good city editor or managing editor never loses the qualities that made him a good reporter. He invests the whole newspaper world with his qualities: unsentimental, brisk, shrewd, resourceful, imaginative as to means but not as to ends or sensibilities, imbued not so much with a curiosity about ideas and value as with a restless desire to know what's going on and what's new, possessed of an intrusive quality which readily disregards privacy and exploits human tragedies as sacrifices for the Moloch of the paper.

Above all the reporter is guided by two drives: never to be "scooped" and rarely to let a conviction take hold of him. To be scooped means to confess a lesser access to the "inside" and an inferior swiftness in getting to the spot first. To be seized by a conviction means a denting of the armor of insensitivity. This armor is the uncapturable part of the American mind, and nowhere in business is the uncapturable more important than on a paper. In the reminiscences of the best reporters one finds their Golden Age going back to the city room and the police court beat, with their deepest affection reserved for city editors, who are portrayed as desensitized, ruthless, and even sadistic men. The gallery of hero portraits tells a good deal about the values of the hero worshipers.

There has been a good deal of controversy about the emphasis the press gives to the sensational aspects of sex, crime, murder, war, politics, sports, and gossip. One school says the readers demand it, while another says they have been taught to like it by the editors and publishers. One may be called the demand theory of the vogue of newspaper sensationalism, the other the supply theory.

Of course, readers, publishers, and reporters alike are part of a larger culture pattern, sharing its traits, which are based on universal human traits but selected and strengthened by the climate and conditionings of the culture. That is why the most popular themes of the successful newspaper have the common elements of sex, violence, power, and—above all —trouble. In a culture at once Puritan and Babylonian, there is a widespread desire to see others implicated in some kind of web, whether of sexual waywardness, or the corruption of politics, or accidental or planned death. What the newspapers do is to whittle the tragic down to manageable (even caricatured) terms within which the popular mind can handle it.

The sensationalism of the "tabloids" has led some critics to condemn stories about sex, crime, divorce, and the foibles of Hollywood as pandering to the depraved tastes of popular culture. The more conservative newspapers that frown on using the press as a calendar of the passions no doubt deserve well of the commonwealth, but they are only a small and marginal part of an institution which can scarcely help expressing with immediacy the primary human impulses in the culture. The important issue is whether the press shall seek to stand above the culture, giving an elite view of it for the elite, or exercise its critical and creative functions from a position inside the culture, surrounded by the sweat and smell of humanity. There is rarely much criticism of the sentimental "human interest" themes: bathing-beauty-contest queens, waiters or clerks who win the Irish Sweepstakes, long lost relatives reunited with their families, "cute" snapshots of children and dogs, cops laboring to rescue a kitten caught on a dangerous ledge. Actually the taste for the sensational and the sentimental are facets of each other. The same newspaper reader who bathes in these saccharine floods also revels in the entanglements of his fellow men in the social jungle.

One other feature of the newspaper profile—the "funnies" (or "comic strip")—forms not merely another department of the paper but in some ways its crucial symbol. For in the comic strip the caricaturing of human relations, implicit but disguised in the rest of the paper, reaches its final expression in open caricature. In reading the comic strip you can let your censor slumber and surrender to unending entanglements and partial releases.

There is a high-flown theory that the comic strip derives from some "folk mind" or "folk unconscious." This is an oversubtle view of a process which—from the success stories of strip creators like Al Capp and Caniff—we know to be a matter of artful craftsmanship mixed with a hard business sense. Another theory traces the vogue of the comic strips to the illiteracy of Americans—both urban and rural—who read them as they read picture magazines, because their verbal level is childlike. This has some truth in it. But while the comic strip directs its main appeal to children and semiliterates, it has been sustained by the enthusiasm of the literates—often indeed of the intellectuals. To read the comics has become a recognized mark of belonging to the American culture.

Some of the early comic strips, like Herriman's *Krazy Kat,* had a wild satiric quality, and the tradition has been continued by Al Capp's *Li'l Abner* and Walt Kelly's *Pogo* among the recent ones. They present a take-off on contemporary characters and trends, deflating the pretentious and mocking the stuffed shirts. They do it all the more effectively because they shape an imaginary world seemingly so irrelevant to the real one that the shafts go almost unnoticed.

But most comic strips are not funny: grotesque, yes, with a kind of Gothic grotesqueness; improbable and extravagant—but not funny. One of the most widely read comic strips, *Dick Tracy,* is funny only if a Lon Chaney or Bela Lugosi movie performance is funny. It is a straight-faced record of extroverted and improbable adventure, with little humor, irony, or astringency. The comic strip offers the entanglements and extrications of a continuous cast of characters in a series of alarums and excursions linked in daily episodes. Above all, it offers recognizable virtue and derring-do on one side and recognizable villainy and skulduggery on the other. It is at once outlandish adventure and a caricatured morality play, in an imagined world in which every emotion is blocked out in stereotyped form. Thus the comics are not only the American's Gothic romance but also his Plutarch and his *Everyman.**

Through comics and crime, sex and scandal, local items, columns and features, the newspaper achieves the steady reader loyalty on which it depends for survival. It reaches the reader because it approaches him at his most expressive level, a good deal lower than the angels. James Wechsler, editor of the New York *Post,* has suggested (not wholly with tongue in cheek) that the tabloid readers were better prepared than the readers of the staider "family newspapers" for the findings of the Kinsey Report, and that "the preoccupation with sexual behavior . . . is several thousand times greater than a casual reader of the *Times* would ever guess." The valid point here is that the press, which is still the crucial big-audience medium, must try to reach the whole man within the whole culture.

In doing so, however, each newspaper must be judged by the quality of its taste and humanity. The treatment of news involving sexual entanglements or offenses can be prurient and nasty, or it can be done with honest objectivity. The news of crime can be done sadistically, carrying a love of violence for its own sake, or it can show an effort to get at motivations. A divorce scandal can be treated for the bedroom farce laughs and the Peeping Tom thrills of invading the privacy of the victims, or it can light up some of the blind alleys of American life. The trouble with the old "yellow journalism" was not that it dealt with the violence and drama of life but that it dealt with them degradingly. "Human interest stuff" need not be treated in an inhuman way, callous of human costs.

"Yellow journalism" had one trait which need never have been discarded—the editor's willingness to call a lie a lie even when uttered by a powerful public figure. The contemporary papers (with an honorable roster of exceptions that include the St. Louis *Post-Dispatch,* the Milwaukee *Journal,* the Providence *Bulletin,* the Washington *Post,* and the New York *Post*) have tended to replace crusading with an "objectivity" which often becomes timidity. This has meant in great part an abdication of the critical function inside the profession and the culture. There are still crusades left for the papers that take their craft seriously; crusades against slum housing, polluted bathing beaches, water-front crime, corrupt police and minor politicians, conditions in state welfare institutions, clogged traffic, reckless driving, inadequate or unsafe parks. It would be unfair to call these safe crusades, because usually they require

---

* I have discussed here the daily comic strip. For a discussion of comic books, which have largely broken away from their newspaper origins and become an industry and a problem in themselves, see Ch. XI, Sec. 2b, "The Reading Revolution."

courage as well as research. But most of them involve crusading in a
minor key when compared with the great newspaper tradition of the
Progressive Era. The press giants of the 1890s and the turn of the century were not loath to attack one another's politics, policies, and personalities with quill pens tipped with a searing flame. But much of their
gusto has gone, diluted by an era which fears to take any chances with
alienating either readers or advertisers. In the early 1950s most papers
were reluctant to nail down the bullying tactics and the Big Lie technique of Senator McCarthy.

Some of the reasons for the muting of the crusading note may be
found in the forms the press has taken in its organization and power.
In the era of Jefferson or Jackson the paper was shaped by the individual editor, who may have started as journeyman printer, typesetter, or
schoolteacher, who came to know his community well enough to guide
its growth and express something of its conscience. His fault was to be
too closely attached to a political party, dependent on it for funds and
political favors and inclined to turn his paper into a party organ.

The rise of the big-circulation papers gave the papers an independence of parties if they wished to exercise it: but it also linked them with
the dynastic fortunes and economic credos of men who did not need to
be the hangers-on of political machines because political machines had
become their hangers-on. These empire builders of the newspaper world
were cut of the same cloth as the empire-builders of other industries and
of finance. Men like Bennett, Dana, Pulitzer, Hearst, Medill, Scripps,
were as daring, imaginative, and ruthless as their industrial counterparts. They ushered in the era of the Barons of Opinion. After their
passing the publishing formulas they had developed and their agglom-
erates of money, plant, and circulation became entrenched in corporate
form. The Barons of Opinion gave way largely to the opinion industries.

Whitman's line—"I sound my barbaric yawp over the roofs of the
world"—might have been spoken of some newspaper Titans who were
cutting each other's throats in order to build their empires more securely on the popular passions. Some of their energy may still be found
in the newspaper battles that go on in a few big cities—in New York and
Chicago, where Colonel McCormick and Captain Patterson set
a pattern of ruthlessness almost as legendary as that of Hearst's, in San
Francisco and Denver, Atlanta and New Orleans, Washington and Boston, Milwaukee and Cleveland and Buffalo. In such cities there is competition for circulation and advertising and a calculation of what headlines will catch the eye and stir the blood: a half hour's margin of
priority or the choice of a headline theme which engages group emotions

may make a difference to the telltale graph of newspaper sales. There is also competition in building up columnists and feature writers or enticing them away from competitors. A good editor and publisher can make the rivalry infect the news pages and copy desks, and thus retain some of the haze of romance that once invested the reporter's job.

If there are a few cities left where competition is in force, the rest of the nation is becoming a desert of monopoly. Morris L. Ernst has effectively gathered, in *The First Freedom,* the figures on the growth of newspaper monopoly cities and the diminishing number of competitive cities. One of the reasons the American press does not fight against monopoly in other industries is that it has itself largely reached a monopoly position. In the case of most American cities, as is now abundantly known, there is only one newspaper; or if there are two—one for the morning field and one for the evening—they use the same presses and are controlled by the same company, though they may have separate staffs and operations. The newspaper chains, the press associations, and the feature syndicates represent concentrations of investment and economic power in no substantial respect different from concentrations in steel or autos or cigarettes, transportation or aviation, machine tools, aluminum, or the public utilities.

The important difference is in impact. As E. B. White has said, "Structurally, American business . . . tends to corner thought, hoarding it and exploiting it as it would hoard and exploit any other merchantable stuff." But the effect of a shrinkage in the steadily vanishing market place of ideas is far more serious for a democracy than the effect of a shrinkage in aluminum or rubber tires. The Hutchins Commission on Freedom of the Press gave the figures on the thinning of the pipelines of communication. In 1909 there were 2,600 daily newspapers in America; in 1945 they had been reduced to 1,750, published in about 1,300 cities. Only 117 of these cities—one out of twelve—have competing papers; which means that in eleven out of twelve cities there is only a single newspaper. In ten states there is not a single city with rival daily papers.

The technological and economic forces behind this process are clear. Since the newspaper to be popular must be kept cheap in price, the burden of keeping it going under conditions of rising labor and newsprint costs falls on advertising revenue, which in turn depends on large circulation, which in turn depends on heavy investment both in plant and features and distribution and on the capacity to bear losses until circulation can be built. This gives the competitive advantage to the big corporation. It means also that the competition becomes intolerable to the weaker papers, and they drop out or are bought out. In the Kansas

City area, serving about a million people, there is only the *Star* as a survivor of this process. In the 1840s in New York, when Greeley and Bennett and Walt Whitman were editing papers, there were sixteen dailies serving a population of 400,000. In 1950, there were seven papers for a population that had increased twentyfold to almost eight million. The New York *Sun,* which had in its lifetime resulted from the merging of five newspapers, was bought up by the *World-Telegram,* which was itself the result of the merging of three newspapers. Thus the process of newspaper cannibalism has meant that eight papers have been swallowed up in one. The facts of newspaper life—lesser competition where there had once been greater, and none where there had once been some —grew out of the strong inner currents toward bigness in all forms of American industry.

Even more than with other small business, the problem of a small newspaper is survival. "The advertisers," Max Ascoli has said, "strengthen the papers that are already strong, while the labor unions weaken those that are already weak," so that merely to stay alive becomes a form of triumph. Caught between the rising costs of newsprint and the pressure of the unions for higher wages, only the papers with growing advertising revenue can continue to publish—and they prosper and wax fat and rich, on the Biblical proposition that to them that have shall be given and from them that have not shall be taken away. In cities where the same owners run a morning and afternoon paper, they may help out the Biblical law by the "tying device," or rejecting advertisements in one unless they are also placed in the other, thus crowding out a hapless competing newspaper in one or the other field. To cut overhead costs a number of newspaper "chains" have bought up papers in city after city. The recent trend, however, has been toward the decline of the chains, since a paper cannot be run effectively by remote control, with an absentee owner or managers sitting in a tower far from the needs and tastes of the local community.

A cynic may say of the press that we have mistaken the commodity it deals in. It does not primarily sell news, features, or entertainment, but advertising space: the news and entertainment are subsidiary industries, designed to support the sale of advertising. He would be essentially right—with several crucial qualifications. One is that even the dependence between advertiser and publisher is not a one-way street but runs both ways. A powerful publisher cannot afford to alienate a large section of his advertisers, but if he can hold his circulation he can thumb his nose at any particular advertiser, no matter how big. The idea that advertisers call the tune of what goes into the newspapers is an overdrawn cliché. The newspapers that support Big Business do so not because the advertisers demand it but because the publishers are themselves Big Business and are affected by its interests and mentality. The real impact of advertising is its drive toward newspaper monopoly, not its creation of newspaper puppets.

There is another qualification: the economic motive operating with greater or lesser purity throughout the business world is not the only motive in the newspaper business. In other industries the stockholders give the managers the job of making the product and showing a profit, and pretty much leave them alone to do so. The split between ownership and management control applies far less to newspapers. Editors and staff are hired to show a big circulation, get a big advertising revenue, and bring in a profit; but the publisher reserves the final voice on the editorial and news policies to be followed. In fact, the Hearst and McCormick empires are evidence that a publisher may place profit second to partisanship, risking circulation in order to destroy an Administration which he hates. The rule of managerial independence is here sharply broken. Much depends, of course, on the regard the publisher has for the tradition of newspaper craftsmanship and on the relative strength of personality of the publisher and his top staff. Sometimes there is an internal staff struggle between the editorial and business executives.

Since the Barons of Opinion occupy the strategic approaches to the American mind, they can, like the feudal barons of old, exact their toll. The toll is not only profits but power—primarily in the effort to entrench the existing structure of economic forces and to resist programs, parties, or leaders whom they fear.

There is, of course, a strong defense for press centralization. E. B. White put it vividly: "A giant can make out a pretty good case for giantism; he has the showy muscles to flex, and he has the appearance of robust health and the air of being a benefactor in the community— which he often is. . . . The facts and figures can be turned to show that the steady tightening of the lines, by mergers and combines, actually enlarges the stream of published ideas." But one must agree with White, as also with Ernst, that this is only appearance. The reality is different.

The impact of press giantism has been a triple one. First it has led to the concentration of power in the hands of a few imperial aggregates. This power places the big publishers among the crucial "lawgivers" of America, using that term in Machiavelli's sense of power figures with a decisive influence on opinion. They might say that they care not who makes America's laws provided they can make its myths. I include in this group the publishers of big-audience papers; the heads of newspaper chains, feature syndicates, and press associations; and the heads of the magazine empires that mark a new phase in the history of the press —news magazines, picture magazines, peptonized digest magazines, along with the mixed feature magazines of the older style and the big-audience women's magazines. Anyone seeking to define the landscape of American power today would have to reckon substantially with the power aggregates contained in the Hearst, McCormick, Chandler, Cowles, Luce, DeWitt Wallace, Howard, Curtis, Knight, and Gannett publications.

This press giantism has led to the standardization of the product, whether through the syndicates that sell comic strips, columns, and other features, or through the "boiler plate" furnished to hundreds of small-town dailies and rural weeklies, providing canned editorial opinion as well as quaint items to fill out the page. Since it results in a shrinkage in the number of sources from which opinion flows and the channels which shape its flow, it brings about a tighter power relation inside the press organization. Here again E. B. White reached the heart of the matter: "The vital question . . . is not how many reporters and commentators we have, it is how many *owners* of reporters and commentators we have. . . . If you believe in private ownership, then make sure there are plenty of owners."

The relation between master and man in the structure of press power is harshly illumined by the case of Reuben Maury, who writes for the New York *Daily News* a brilliantly simple editorial page which is perhaps simpler than the truth. When John Bainbridge pointed out in a *New Yorker* profile that Maury has written "out of both sides of his mouth" on the issue of providing American money for feeding Europe, being against it in the *News* and for it when writing articles for *Collier's*, Maury clarified his plight in a letter to a newspaper craft journal: "When a hired editorial writer is writing editorials he is not writing out of either side of his mouth. . . . He is acting as mouthpiece for the publication for which he works. His job is to express the publication's policies with all the force and skill he can summon up, and without regard to his private opinions. . . . It is merely a phase of the editorial writing job."

The pathos of the craftsman-as-hireling could scarcely have been better expressed. It is a relation one finds throughout industry and government and in the arts of salesmanship and advocacy. But when it is also applied to the craftsman in ideas it turns his nature topsy-turvy. The integrity a writer owes is not to the man who pays him but to the idea. To a greater or lesser degree it is true that most newspaper writers have to stay within limits of tolerance set by those who own and control the papers. The lucky newspaperman works for an editor and publisher whose ideas coincide with his own, or who believe in expressing a diversity of viewpoint. But these are marginal, and not the rule.

It is in the political arena that the power of the press barons is most dramatically illustrated. Since the 1936 Presidential campaign, when Franklin Roosevelt battled against overwhelming press opposition, the Democrats have gibed at the "One-Party Press." They have had evidence to back up their attack. In the campaigns from 1936 to 1956, when Roosevelt, Truman, and Stevenson ran as Democrats, newpapers holding from 70 to 87 per cent of the readership of the country supported the Republican candidate. In some cases (notably the New York *Times*) the newspapers—whatever their editorial commitment—did not let it spill over into the news columns; in most cases they did, as Irving Dilliard has shown with documentation in a notable study of the 1952 elections. In the heat of campaigns the newspapers of both parties display their whole armory of weapons—distortion, suppression, unequal coverage and headlining, highly selective emphasis, the black magic of inflammatory stereotypes. Despite the American's traditional fear of propaganda, he remains vulnerable to the verbal manipulations of the press.

Ernst Cassirer pointed out that magic achieves its purposes in any culture by the dislocation of the function of language. By naming something and then putting it into the universe of magic, it takes it out of the area of communication and places it in the area of the unknowable and unarguable. Epithets like "Red," "Communist," "Marxist," "Socialist," "Fascist," "Totalitarian," "reactionary," "foreign," "subversive," "disloyal," "un-American," label the idea or measure which is attacked and cast it outside the pale of discussion. By a black magic they place a taboo on it. This is the technique of any group that refuses to share power with anyone else and will therefore not allow the competition of other ideas. It mocks Justice Holmes's words in his classic *Abrams* dissent, that the "ultimate good desired is better reached by free trade in ideas—that the best test of truth is the power of the thought to get itself accepted in the competition of the market, and that the truth is the only ground upon which men's wishes can safely be carried out."

Some observers believe that this is bound to evoke a recoil in the opposite political direction. Liberal newspapers, like the St. Louis *Post-Dispatch* and the Washington *Post,* have thrived and even managed to buy out competitive papers. The New York *Post* has also prospered with a militantly liberal policy. From 1932 to 1952 the New Deal and Fair Deal administrations held on to popular support despite almost unanimous press hostility. As Roosevelt saw it, the problem was one of opposing the "propaganda of the deed" to the "propaganda of the word": he gambled that what he did would speak more loudly to the people than what the press said. The 1948 Truman victory was similarly based. But if the Democrats hoped that they could continue to profit from this counterforce, they had their hopes deflated in the 1952 and 1956 Presidential elections, when the popular loyalties and identifications were on the same side as the big battalions of the press.

The job of publishing a newspaper has three aspects: it is a business run for profit; it is an instrument of political power and therefore part of the power structure of the society; finally, it is a craft, with a great tradition of workmanship. An example of the continuity of the tradition, even in a structure of wealth and power, is the New York *Times,* which must be reckoned one of the great newspapers of the world. It maintains a corps of correspondents in world capitals; as a "newspaper or record" it reprints important documents of contemporary history in full; it retains an austerity of view that does not veer with popular fashions or passions. Louis M. Lyons has noted that there are a handful of American cities which are today in a healthier newspaper state than they were a generation ago—among them Denver, Minneapolis, Washington, Providence, and perhaps even Chicago. The uneasy stirrings of the conscience of newspaper craftsmanship were also for a time reflected in the astringent appraisals of press performance by A. J. Liebling in the *New Yorker,* by the establishment of the Nieman Fellowships for newspapermen at Harvard, and by the Hutchins Commission. How much impact they have had is still difficult to estimate.

One of the principal recommendations of the Hutchins group was that of continuing appraisals of press performance and a self-policing system by a panel of men whose prestige would be beyond question. Another measure that has been discussed is some means for reversing the trend toward fewer papers by encouraging the launching of new ones. A one-newspaper situation in any sizable city is a disservice to everyone, including the advertisers. While it may enable them to reach their buyers more cheaply, it puts them at the mercy of a single power, leaving them without recourse to any competing advertising channel.

The problem of ways and means for achieving this goal presents obvious difficulties. The days when James Gordon Bennett could start the New York *Herald* with a capital investment of five hundred dollars are in the dim past. To launch a metropolitan newspaper effectively today would take at least ten million: even in a moderate-sized city it requires wealth. Direct government subsidies are too dangerous and would be bound to boomerang. But it should be possible to create a revolving fund, perhaps contributed by foundations and run by a disinterested group, to help competent newspapermen set up newspapers in areas where competition is most badly needed. If this be attacked as a form of indirect subsidy, one may point out that a large part of the press—and especially the big national-circulation magazines—today flourishes by virtue of indirect subsidies from taxpayers. These publications are sent through the mails at rates far below cost, which enables them to keep their circulation high and get the advertising from which their costs are paid and their profits come. These are indirect subsidies to publishers and advertisers alike. If this is in the national interest, it is even more in the national interest that the press maintain a competition of ideas.

The most dangerous prospect is the development of a cynical disbelief in most papers. In the old small-town newspaper, like William Allen White's Emporia *Gazette,* there was no gap between press and people because the town knew and loved the man who got out the paper. In the power aggregates of the modern press, the face-to-face knowledge and the love are no longer possible. Trust is still possible, and in many cases it remains; but, tragically, that too is being dissipated. In its place have come indifference and skepticism, like an armor of immunity the reader has assumed.

5. *Revolution in the Big Media*

IN SCARCELY MORE than two generations the other big-audience media went through a revolutionary change much like that of the press; in the process they transformed much of American life. Most Americans associate the magazines, movies, radio, and TV with the arts of living rather than with the molds of thinking, with entertainment and the uses of leisure rather than with attitudes and beliefs. Yet after dealing with the churches, schools, universities, and press, one cannot stop short at the newer forces that have assailed the minds and imaginations of Americans.*

Revolutionary changes took place almost simultaneously in a number of big-audience media. What made them come where and when they did, fusing them into a continuous multiple revolution, was the convergence of three important forces. One was a big audience equipped with purchasing power, not confined to one class but including all of them. The second was the emergence of leisure time needing to be filled. The third was the contrivance of inventions which filled that

* I deal here with the impact of the Big Media on opinion. For their impact on popular culture, see Ch. XI, Sec. 1, "Popular Culture in America," and Sec. 9, "Artist and Audience in a Democratic Culture."

leisure by spanning the continent, pulling the far places of America together, assaulting and capturing eye and ear—and doing it cheaply enough to make the new inventions accessible to all.

Of course this makes it sound too pat. Actually the history of the revolutions in the big media—of which the first were the big press, the big-audience magazine, the movies, and the radio, and the most recent have been paperbacks and comic books, color television, long-playing records, and three-dimensional movies—is the history of blundering struggles and experiments that often ended in blind alleys. It is also the history of pitched battles waged on the fields of business combat between giant industrial empires. The story of the radio industry alone would demand of the historian a talent for epical military description, in depicting the battles of patent pools, antitrust suits, consent decrees, and color television. The crucial fact about most of these big media, viewed as industries, is the big initial investment and the high cost of plant, transmission, and distribution. Thus the big media furnish no groves for dreamers to wander in, no secluded nooks in which individual talent can flower. As in the case of the press, their management and operation move steadily into ever fewer hands.

The impact on opinion follows from this fact. Those who control the media come to hold the strategic passes to many American minds. To be sure, the main function of the media is usually held to be not opinion but entertainment. But this only gives added weight to our concern with their effect on opinion. Reaching the mind, ear, eye, and imagination, their impact is all the greater because it eludes the inner censor that alerts the American against "highbrow stuff." Operating through the emotions, it leaves the more enduring image on the mind.

The customary phrase "mass media" implies that they are instruments aimed at targets. The target is presumably the mass of the people and the aim is to "reach" and manipulate them. Whether or not they include advertising (the movies, popular books, and records do not) the shadow of advertising hangs over all of them. Each medium must reach a big audience to provide the outlay needed for the kind of entertainment that will succeed in reaching such an audience. Thus the circle turns back on itself like a snake biting its own tail. The "masses" are the target both of the advertising and of the art, and in the process of providing the medium with an audience and a profit, they afford it also a chance to shape the furniture of the people's minds.

I make no assumption here about the docility and inertness on the part of the audience whose stereotypes are being shaped. The term "mass media" is in itself a dubious one, since it seems to imply a "mass mind" belonging to the faceless and undifferentiated crowd. It carries over the fallacies of the "crowd psychology" concept dominant at the time the new media emerged. There are "faces in the crowd"—the faces of persons who fall into many categories, depending on the handle by which you may wish to grasp their reality, yet remain individual persons.

I prefer the phrase "big-audience media," after the model of the "big-circulation magazines," or, better still, simply "big media." My point is that they have now gone beyond any limitation to a particular class or mass, or even to any particular audience. For an audience is the aggregate of individuals drawn together by a common interest and concern; when the episode that brought them together has run its course, the audience dissolves into its individual parts, only to reassemble in new clumps and aggregates around some different occasion. The editors of the big papers and magazines, the producers of movie, radio, and TV shows, the publishers of paperbacks and comic books, and of popular records, fall into the habit of abstracting some common denominator from all these audiences. I suppose they have to in order to keep from going crazy. Yet these hardheaded, sharp-featured men must know that those whom they have thus abstracted continue to be individuals with a variety of tastes. If they forget this they forget it at their peril, for an audience whose varied and changing taste is neglected will dissolve into thin air. Hence the continuous nerve-racking search for "fresh ideas," new "formulas" and "formats." If the "mass" of the "mass media" were uniform, passive, and plastic there would be no need to woo it by novelties or to watch the fever chart of the changes and chances.

Actually the editors and publishers, directors, producers, and the "idea men" on whom they draw, usually go to the other extreme of assuming that the audiences act as legislators and that their own function is merely to register the convulsions of popular taste like seismographs. Impressed by the vacillations of a curve of taste they cannot understand, they end by playing it safe. To play it safe means to exploit the easiest strata of taste in their audience, to avoid the "highbrow" and "controversial," to abdicate their own creative function by feeling the pulse of "audience response," and to rationalize the result by pretending only to furnish "what the people want." Thus the self-censorship codes of the movies, radio, and TV express a fear of alienating any section of the audience by offending its sensibilities. It is hard to reconcile the fears of these timid men who live in the shadow of the Big Audience they have made into a graven image, with the picture of them as a group of manipulators shaping the malleable material of the "masses" according to their interests and whims.

I suggest that neither of these images is wholly valid. The Big Audience is not an idol to be worshiped by its priesthood, nor is the priesthood a group of calculating knaves who use the idol as a shill. It is better to assume that while an audience retains its individual variations of taste, and while its changing styles are incalculable, it has common impulses and characteristics which do make it plastic to a degree. Put in another way: while in the long run the audience possesses a legislative power over its own tastes and ideas, there is at any time a frame of permissiveness within which the technicians of the Big-Audience media can work either creatively or destructively, either to degrade and corrupt what they find or to evoke its potential.

There is some current tendency to see these media as forms of "mass communications" but it is doubtful whether this gives much meaning to the term. As Norbert Wiener put it, communication is a dialogue between people united against the common enemy, whether we call it entropy or chaos. This implies a two-way conversation instead of a monologue with one person as performer and the other as passive target. Despite studio audiences and "reader response" surveys, it would be spurious to view the outpourings of the mass media as real dialogue. They remain, not communication that clarifies, but a technology of appeal that, for better or worse, shapes the minds and tastes of millions.

Since I treat the big media as part of the apparatus shaping belief and opinion, thought and taste, I must note another respect in which they differ from other parts of the apparatus, like church, school, and universities. However large the congregation or the class, the pastor and teacher never break the personal relation with parishioner or pupil. They too, of course, must make an abstraction of their audience, yet having made it they restore the vitality of the relation by treating each person as a person. This the directors of the big media cannot do. The abstraction remains one. The element of dialogue, which persists in the teacher-student and pastor-parishioner relation, is here broken; the creative process which depends upon the two-way circuit is to that extent truncated. It is true that experiments have been made with church sermons and classroom lectures on radio and TV, and they are likely to prove fruitful in their own way. But the distinguishing mark of the big media remains the one-way transmission. Once the audience rigidifies the habit of listening without answering back, it will become increasingly inert.

There remains the question of the role the big media play in the culture, and what ties them together. If, as W. Lloyd Warner suggests, "they function as distributors of symbols with common meanings to mass audiences," then they are shaping a new language. But every language evolves verbal symbols which convey images and overtones. What distinguishes the language of the big media from the rest of American thought and expression?

The reflective individual uses images that distinguish him from others, but a society as a whole lives by asserting the common symbols that tie it together. Language itself attempts such a function. In a complex society, where persons of disparate backgrounds fumble for a means of breaking through the walls of experience that separate them, a special social language is required. Durkheim spoke of it as "collective representations." They may take the form of religious symbolisms and rituals, or of "mysteries" embodying the religious myth, or of epics or dramas or great celebrations for the populace like the Roman games. American popular culture offers parallels to these forms, except that the "collective representations" have become secularized. Instead of the religious myths there are the myths of national uniqueness; instead of the Roman games there are baseball and football contests; instead of the Greek tragic plays there are Hollywood movies and TV horse operas; instead of the religious mysteries there are the more secular "mysteries" of the whodunits; instead of the English Morality play and the *commedia dell' arte* of the Renaissance cities there are the comic strips, comic books, and musical comedies.

The question remains as to why these particular collective forms of popular symbolism should have flowered in American culture. As one clue I have pointed to the convergence in America of a rapid pace of technological change, a multi-class audience with purchasing power and (for the first time in history) leisure available to the people as a whole rather than the monopoly of a leisure class. There may be another clue in the ethnic and class structure of American society. In his *Essay on Man,* Cassirer cited the Babylonian experience with symbolic algebra, taking it from the historian of mathematics, Otto Neugebauer. They suggest that Babylonian civilization marked a meeting and collision between the Sumerian and Akkadian races and languages, and became involved in a strong emotional effort to find common symbols that transcended these differences. Out of the climate of this straining there developed the energies from which a symbolic algebra was born.

Dare we apply a similar approach to the American case? There is no comparable record in history of the meeting and collision of so many ethnic strains and diverse experiences in a common cultural arena. Societies like the Latin American and the Asiatic, where many such strains have also met and collided, have lacked the impulse both of the free market and of democracy to move them toward a fusion: a solution of a sort has been struck in a system of caste and hierarchy, which recently has had to admit a revolutionary nationalism as a common symbol system. In the American case, out of the social climate created by the striving to break the walls of ethnic, regional, and class diversity, there has come as by-product a readiness to accept the common symbolic and emotional systems afforded by the big media.

We may lament the clichés and formulas of these media and the absence of elite standards of taste, but to do so is to lose sight of their social function. They came into existence not to break cultural molds but to form them, not to shatter a symbol language into fragments but to shape a new one. Every language standardizes its forms, and this one is no exception. But every living language also, in its growth, gives scope to great variety and richness. This has proved true of American popular speech: there is no reason why it should not prove equally true of the new symbol language of the big media which speaks so powerfully to the media audience.

The question of media control is a tangled one. The historian of American culture will note that there was a fateful moment in the history of both radio and TV when the choice was presented between control by the chains and sponsors using and playing upon media symbols, and control by the universities and state educational authorities in the interest of traditional social intelligence. The issue was not decided overnight. During the whole decade of the 1930s a little group called the National Committee on Radio strove to save a limited number of educational channels from being cut down by the commercial interests, but to no avail. A similar group was active in the TV field in the 1950s. In both cases they urged that programs conducted for profit are bound to depress intellectual levels and taste standards. They had in mind as a model the standards of the BBC in England, which has made less of a tin god out of the Big Audience. University presidents, school superintendents, teachers, parent groups, liberal industrialists, and trade-union officials joined in these movements. They caused enough stir to compel the appointment of investigating commissions in several states. But the hearings came to naught, partly because of the entrenched power of the chains and advertisers, mainly because of the prevailing conviction that radio and TV should be concerned with "entertainment," not ideas. The contempt of the "practical" men for "highbrow" tastes, and for "do-good" aims in education, gained the victory because it was a contempt shared by many Americans, some of them inside the besieged city of education. The rulers of the empire of the air pleaded their case, in effect, on the theory that the big media exist to reach the Big Audience, and that any other purpose is a dispensable luxury. They are content to let Plato and Newton and Pascal rest where they are while they create new symbolic heroes in the form of Jackie Gleason and Phil Silvers.

A primitive defense of business control, as against that of the educators and technicians, was blurted out most clearly by J. Harold Ryan, President of the National Association of Broadcasters in the 1940s. "American radio," he asserted, "is the product of American business. It is just as much that kind of product as the vacuum cleaner, the washing machine, the automobile, and the airplane. . . . If the legend still persists that a radio station is some kind of an art center, a technical museum, or a little piece of Hollywood transplanted strangely to your home town, then the first official act of the second quarter-century should be to list it along with the local dairies, laundries, banks, restaurants, and filling stations."

The more sophisticated form of the argument avoids this crudeness. It talks of "giving the people what they want" and cites the audience demand for certain programs of high entertainment and low intellectual content as proof of what Frank Stanton called a kind of "cultural democracy." To which Charles Siepmann replied that such a "theory of retailing makes as much sense as if a large department store were to clear its shelves of all commodities except the best-selling lines." It should be clear that there is no strong movement in America to displace the "American system" of private enterprise in the big media in favor of a system of public control like the British. Siepmann and others asked not for the replacement of private enterprise in entertainment and opinion but for a policy that would consider the quality and variety of the product and not only the size of the audience.

In what ways do the other big media follow or depart from the press pattern, especially on the score of the stereotypes of opinion and the struggle for power?

The case of news and picture magazines—which are also opinion magazines—is best discussed by examining the magazine empire of Henry R. Luce. *Time* is edited for the literate middle classes, helping them establish a pattern of meaning in the chaos of events. Within its own pattern-breaking mold, it avoids the more obvious press sensationalism and presents the necessary human diet of conflict, sex, gossip, and human interest indirectly through the summary of news and trends. It appeals to the same universals of human nature as do the newspapers, radio, and TV shows, but by a more decorous approach, as befits a magazine founded by two Yale men who were literary luminaries at college. Luce represents a different kind of "tycoon" of the opinion industries from Hearst, Scripps, or Pulitzer. He is the cultured, reflective man, son of a China missionary, who saw what the big media could do to shape minds in a democracy. He managed to build a circulation empire by serving as an intermediary between the classes. In *Time* and in *Life* he and his editors sought a way of interpreting the outlook and values of a business civilization to the people, while in *Fortune* they tried to interpret some liberal ideas to the managers of the corporate empires. They had more success with the first function than with the second, largely because the first is easier within the cultural frame of the freedom-property complex.

The case of *Life,* involving the first successful American use of the nonverbal symbolism of the action photograph as the heart of the big-circulation magazine, marked a revolutionary phase in the history of the big media. It was followed by *Look* and other picture magazines, each with its own variant of the basic formula. Later some cultural commentary found its way into the pages of *Life* in the form of long essays, so that the literate reader as well as the one who was tired of grappling with words could find his own intellectual level in the magazine. The number of novels and short stories which used the *Time* and *Life* editor as a symbol, much as earlier novelists had used the war correspondent, is testimony to the impact of these new forms upon the American imagination.

Henry Luce's example underscores the fact that the term "mass media" is accurate only if "mass" means big circulation rather than the underlying population. The middle classes comprise the bulk of this "mass" audience, nor does it exclude the highly educated groups. The success of the Luce power suggests that those who think of the big media as the mass-feeding of morons have been misled by old stereotypes. Luce's success lay in the fact that he made one group of his readers feel they were getting educated, and another feel they were learning about life in the raw. He gave very disparate audiences a body of symbols to hold them together in his Big Audience. His two big magazines, edited by young men who spanned the distance between the world of intellect and the world of affairs, were able to market a blend of literacy and sophistication to the Big Audience.

A similar moral is implicit in the case of the big-circulation women's magazines, of which Edward Bok's *Ladies' Home Journal* was the most successful illustration. Lloyd Morris called Bok "the grand Lama of the matrons." Certainly the formula he helped shape, continued and adapted by Bruce and Beatrice Gould, has persisted with some changes ever since—the interest in the world of the home, in fashions and child-rearing, in the dream world of fiction, and in the reform causes with which American women have identified themselves. This mingling of

home features, daydream, and uplift has ever since comprised the material of the women's media. In addition, the American woman's role
as organizer of spending and consumption made the big-circulation
women's magazines a paradise for the advertisers. Finally, the rise of
women to political importance made the women's magazine a political
instrument even when its material seemed least so: it had the power to
reach women's minds through their dreams. I should add that the current women's magazines have moved more boldly into the area of medicine, mental health, psychology and psychoanalysis, and sexual problems
than their predecessors would have dared do or thought possible.

A third development has been the radio and TV news-analyst-com-
mentator. Although liberals usually lament the murder of liberal commentators by advertisers and pressure groups, while conservatives charge
a conspiracy to keep their own champions off the air, the typical commentator is neither one nor the other but a middle-of-the-road man who
presents controversial issues guardedly. Through radio and TV news
coverage the ordinary American manages to get a more rounded view
of an issue than he can get from his single local paper. While only a
few commentators with integrity are able to reach the high audience
ratings, political influence is not a matter of counting the heads of the
audience, as if they were eggs or pins or carrots. The political literacy
generated by men like Elmer Davis, Edward Murrow, Eric Sevareid,
Howard Smith, Cecil Brown, and Martin Agronsky can in time be
diffused through the body politic. It is the national scope of the radio
that gives it the important, if small, leavening of politically literate commentators: in a single city they might be boycotted by pressure groups;
on a multi-city network they find an audience that makes them less
vulnerable.

The radio and TV discussion program, by its controversial nature,
must risk lighting little fires of hate and fanaticism among the politically
dedicated. The periods of crisis which bring such programs into demand are also periods of psychic intensity that stir the adrenalin flow
of the zealots. The popular taste for blood puts a premium on dramatic
conflict even in discussion of public issues—an instance of how the
motifs of the entertainment programs, filled with violence or senti-
mentality, have carried over into the discussion field. TV has also
brought into play the powerful medium of the documentary, whether
in the reportage of the world-crisis type presenting the background for
some important news event or the edited movie and newsreel clips that
condense a chapter of history such as the Hitler era or the American
1920s, or the filming of a child's delivery or a psychiatric interview.
The most dramatic instances have been the extended documentaries

of the Kefauver Crime Commission, the McCarthy-Army hearings, the Presidential conventions. The televising of Congressional investigations raises grave issues not only of the right of privacy but even more of the uses to which political demagoguery can put them. It would be foolish, however, to abdicate the use of an instrument whose potential for healthy political opinion is even greater than for destructiveness. The documentary is an illustration of what gives an almost incalculable power to the media which fuse an appeal to ear and eye and the imagery of both, as TV and the movies do.

A greater danger lies in the economics of the big media which, while making the Presidential conventions of both parties available under advertising sponsorship, sold time directly for the campaign speeches themselves. This throws the emotional force of the big media of radio and TV behind the political party which can better afford the steep expense—which currently means the Republicans.* Thus the economics of the big media strengthen the inherent advantage of conservative forces under a business system and add to the armory of powerful symbolic weapons they already possess in the newspapers and magazines. Frank Stanton's suggestion for free TV time to the major parties in the Presidential campaigns would remedy this inequality, but it would involve a decision to abandon the idea of giving equal facilities to fringe parties as well as major, and therefore Congressional action changing the "equal time" provision of the FCC Act.

The economic factor is, however, not always decisive in the battle of opinion, which pits one pattern of political mythology and social folklore against another. It is on the plane of competing mythologies and folklores that the big media play their more profound role. In a perceptive study of the underlying movie themes, Martha Wolfenstein stressed that of the "good-bad girl," seductive by reason of her apparent badness but turning out in the end to have been a good girl and receiving the reward for her intact virtue in marriage and happiness. In his study of the *Big Sister* radio serial, W. Lloyd Warner found a theme of contrast between the woman who has made her transition to married life by sublimating her dissatisfactions and remaining an attractive "nice person to know," and the uncontrolled woman, impatient of such restraints, who demands more direct emotional satisfaction. Using the T.A.T. projective technique, Warner found most of the program listeners identifying themselves with the first woman rather than the second. The fact that the radio daytime serial ("soap opera") thus

* See also, for the "one-party press," Sec. 4, "Profile of the Press," and for the political aspects, Ch. VI, Sec. 4, "The Party System and the Voter."

bolsters the listener's acceptance of the emotional poverty of her life points up its social meaning and function.*

The daytime serial is not like the magazine serial, an unfolding narrative with some progression in plot and character: it is a number of episodic beads on a string, with the same stereotypes repeated in each. This fact gives them an added symbolic force. Thus the big media may be as telling politically when they deal indirectly with the emotional symbols of the daytime serial as when they deal directly with political ones. In fact, their nonpolitical aspect gives them an entrance into the mind more readily than direct propaganda could achieve. The same need for a common symbolic language which gave the big media their success operates also to stress the themes of acceptance rather than rebellion and of social emulation rather than individual dissent. An audience that accepts the ambivalence of the good-bad girl will also be prepared to accept the paradox of the good-bad corporation or trade-union, which, despite its dubious practices, remains in the end a champion of public virtue; the same may apply to the good-bad government. An audience that identifies itself with the triumph of the superego in *Big Sister* will become the better target for the techniques of psychological conditioning which are looming ever larger on the political scene.

Thurman Arnold had little difficulty in showing that the "symbols of government" and the "folklore of capitalism" have scanty correspondence to the realities of the American political and economic system. The prevailing social folklore does contain some elements of truth: that American society is mobile, that great fortunes and careers have been made in it, that freedom from government controls is an important freedom. The folklore also contains elements of fiction half believed by their propagators, and some elements of doctrine which are not true but continue to be spread in the big media—just as Plato believed in the spreading of myths by the rulers for the underlying population. Whether true or untrue or partly true, such myths are the projection of the spirit of the culture as its people like to think of it. They dress themselves and their institutions in dramatic garments, as freemen capable of achieving anything in an open society, because it gives a heightened value to their lives. To call this "folklore" is an ironic literary device which should not obscure the fact that these beliefs have their roots in popular experience and are indirectly strengthened by the symbol stuff of the big-audience media.

I have tried to trace critically the profile of American belief, the gods

* For more on radio serials, see Ch. XI, Sec. 6, "Radio and TV: the World in the Home," and for more on the "content analysis" of the movies, see Ch. XI, Sec. 5, "Dream and Myth in the Movies."

Americans worship, the transmission of their heritage through education, the ideas their thinkers have evolved, and the channels through which belief and opinion have been shaped by the traditional media and the new ones. The big media present dangers to the society, but a democracy must embrace the kind of communication system which its technology has evolved, grappling with the new media as with the old, counting on being able to turn the power of camera, screen, and microphone to the uses of the culture.

I turn now to the popular culture of which these media form a part, and to the standards of taste and the quality of cultural life which it embodies.

CHAPTER XI

The Arts and Popular Culture

IN WHICH we examine the forms Americans use to express their imaginative and artistic life, and the new modes of communication and recreation that tie regions and classes together in the Big Audience of the Big Media. We ask what America has added characteristically to the great tradition of the elite arts that it inherited from Europe. But our emphasis is on "popular culture" and the folk arts—the first in the sense of the arts intended for and accepted by the Big Audience, the second in the sense of the arts that grow out of the energies of the people and are shaped most often by anonymous craftsmen (Sec. 1, "Popular Culture in America").

We first examine American literary creativeness, focusing on the novel in its relation to contemporary needs and experience, and noting the current reading revolution in America (Sec. 2, "Writers and Readers"). We move then to some of the crucial products of the folk culture, including the new types of American folk heroes, the old and new legendry and folklore, and the most impressive product of all—American speech and language (Sec. 3, "Heroes, Legends, and Speech"). Standing between the folk culture of myth-making and the popular culture of the Big Media are the spectator sports, embedded in the American passion for athletics but expressing increasingly the commercialization of that passion (Sec. 4, "Spectator and Amateur Sports"). We then examine the Big Media again—movies (Sec. 5, "Dream and Myth in the Movies"), radio and TV (Sec. 6, "Radio and TV: the World in the Home"), exploring their inner structure of power, their standards of taste and artistry, the revolutions they have brought about in American habits of thought and living, and their rivalries and interconnections. Moving away from the Big Media, we discuss American folk songs, popular music, and dance, focusing on jazz as the most expressive idiom of the mood and tempo of American living (Sec. 7, "Jazz As American Idiom"). We then analyze what the machine has done to the traditional arts, including painting, sculpture, and the theater, but we pay special attention to the contemporary forms that architecture and design have taken in an urban industrial culture (Sec. 8, "Building, Design, and the Arts").

Throughout this chapter there runs a double theme: first, the effort to trace the lines separating the elite arts from popular culture, and the vernacular style from the cultivated style; second, the question of how creative the standards of taste and achievement can be within a culture frame that stresses profit, vendibility, and the mass audience. We end with an analysis of the frustrations and productiveness that mark the dialogue between artist and audience in the American culture, asking whether America has been able to achieve a "democratic aesthetic" and what kind it is (Sec. 9, "Artist and Audience in a Democratic Culture").

The Arts and Popular Culture

1. Popular Culture in America

IS THE kind of civilization America has developed hospitable or hostile to creativeness in the arts? What has the dominance of the popular arts over the elite arts—of the low- or middlebrow over the highbrow—meant in the total pattern of artistic achievement?

Behind both questions is the assumption that what a culture does in its arts betrays its inner quality. The artist may see himself working in a self-sufficient realm, timeless and placeless. Yet what he does and the way he does it tells almost as much about his civilization as about himself. Spengler chose the statue of the Greek athlete and the Gothic spire as his symbols of the Apollonian and Faustian cultures. In every culture one gets glimpses of the inner culture style from the way its artists go about the process of creation and the way their audiences respond or do not respond to them.

For some insight into the relation of the artist to the culture style, one could do no better than turn to Walt Whitman. In the preface to *Leaves of Grass* (1855) he described with splendor the function of the poet in a great democracy. Using "poet" as abbreviation for the artist, as his masters Carlyle and Emerson had done, he sought the relation between the American artist and the cultural life of the people. Some fifteen years later, in *Democratic Vistas* (1871), after a civil war had intervened and in a bleak period in American culture, he came back to the same theme, saddened but holding to his insistence on the artistic strength a democracy required.

> Our fundamental want today in the United States [he wrote] is of a class of native authors, literateurs . . . far higher in grade than any yet known, sacerdotal, modern, fit to cope with our occasions, lands, permeating the whole mass of American mentality, taste, belief, breathing into it a new breath of life, giving it decision, affecting politics far more than the popular superficial suffrage, with results inside and underneath the selection of Presidents or Congresses—radiating, begetting appropriate teachers, schools, manners, and, as its grandest result, accomplishing (what neither the schools nor the churches and their clergy have hitherto accomplished, and without which this nation will no more stand, permanently, soundly, than a house will stand without a substratum) a re-

ligious and moral character beneath the political and productive and intellectual bases of the States. . . . The problem of humanity all over the
civilized world is social and religious, and is to be finally met and treated
by literature. The priest departs, the divine literatus comes.

Whether or not the "divine literatus" has come, there is little question that other emissaries have—the gagsters and comedians, the dramatis personae of the comic strip and comic books, the "Kings of Swat," the
super-sleuths and "shamuses," the crooners, the god and goddesses of
the movie marquee and the fan magazines whose profiles, hairdos and
kissing techniques have become the legislators of American mores.

These legislators have come to America, but regardless of whether
Whitman would have welcomed them, most of America's literary people have shrunk from them. "The proof of the poet," Whitman wrote
more hopefully than prophetically in his 1855 preface, "is that his country absorbs him as affectionately as he has absorbed it." Absorption of
this sort there has been, but not between the people and their poets and
artists. It has been, rather, between the people and their heroes of the
popular culture. From Fenimore Cooper to Van Wyck Brooks, American critics have awaited the coming of a great national art and have
lamented the failure of the culture to provide the artist with a warm
response and audience. Now the critics find the response warm enough
and the audience more than generous—but for the wrong kind of artist.

There has developed in America a double relationship between the
arts and the public. The feeling between the elite artists and the "general public" has until recently been one of neglect or even contempt; but
in recent years writers like Hemingway and Faulkner have been read
in paperback editions by millions of readers, and their books have been
turned into movies and plays, so that they have become almost popular
figures who could not maintain their isolation even if they wished to.
This is less true of painters, sculptors, and composers, where there is
still a cleavage between public and artist. Within the popular culture
itself there is, on the other hand, an uncritical hero worship.

In every civilization there is an educated culture and a popular culture—an art of the classes and an art of the masses. Matthew Arnold
defined the first (*Culture* with a capital C), as the best that has been
thought and said by the few in a civilization. The other conception
refers to the run of what is thought, felt, and liked by the many. Both
are included within the broader anthropological use of "culture" as the
total design of the life and thought of a people.*

* For a discussion of my use of the term "culture" in this book, roughly in the
anthropological sense, see Ch. II, Sec. 1, "Figure in the Carpet."

Using popular culture in the second sense above—as the culture of the many rather than the few, often deliberately differentiating itself from elite culture—there are some who claim for it the only valid elements of truth and beauty in a civilization. The cult of "folk art," like the cult of the "folk mind," goes back to the discovery of the creativeness of the innocent by the weary sophisticates of the European Enlightenment. It is true that creativeness is not the monopoly of the professional artist. An untutored talent in poetry or a "primitive" in painting may come up from the underlying population; and much of the energy of art comes from the experience of simple, anonymous people. But the "folksy" art of America, associated with the Negroes and with some of the white mountain communities, is mostly pseudo-folk. The dangers of an uncritical cult of the people are contained in Franz Boas's remark: "I should always be more inclined to accept, in regard to fundamental human problems, the judgment of the masses rather than the judgment of intellectuals. The desires of the masses are, in a wider sense, more human than those of the classes." I suggest this is the kind of sentimental thinking which is a dubious base for a theory of popular culture, although it may have some validity in the case of a cultural idiom like jazz.

The fact is that the elite arts and popular arts have different functions in a culture. Whether it be Henry James or Sargent, Virgil Thomson or Charles Griffes, Wallace Stevens or Frank Lloyd Wright, the drive of the elite artist is part of the sustained effort of individual creators to express their vision of life. The drive of popular culture (I am speaking here of the genuine folk culture and not of the synthetic and manufactured type) is mainly to find release, in performers and audience alike, for the energy, humor, and self-assertion of the people. Each is a valid form of American creativeness. The characteristic weakness of the elite arts is likely to be found in condescension of spirit, arrogance of intellect, contempt for mass culture. That of the popular arts—and, in America, what may be called the middlebrow arts as well —is found in cheapness of taste, slackness of discipline, the glossing over of real problems, a fear of depth.

The big media and the arts of reproduction have, of course, brought the high achievements of elite musicians, painters, and writers to millions who never before had access to them. But the strength of American popular culture does not consist in its spreading of elite material but in its creation of new popular material. Its relation to the elite arts is not subsidiary but imperialist: the popular arts absorb the work of even the playwrights, composers, and great novelists by a powerful suction force.

The student of the American arts must strip himself of the assumptions he is tempted to carry over from the European tradition. The Greek hero of the year was the prize-winning tragic dramatist; the Renaissance Italians turned out into the street to honor the creator of a new mural masterpiece; in Goethe's Germany the poet graced the courts of princes; in Wagner's time the composer was a national hero; but in contemporary America it is not poet, painter, composer, or tragedian who receives the accolade of the people. To move from the artistic climate of western Europe to that of New York and Hollywood is to experience a Copernican shift in values and assumptions. With the exception of some first-rate novelists who are also "best sellers," the elite arts, which have been and are still the creative categories of European civilization, are not the center of the planetary system of the arts in America.

Not that the Americans recoiled from everything European. Jefferson as architect translated Greek forms to the Monticello terrain, just as Jefferson as political thinker adapted the French Physiocrats and *philosophes* to the American revolutionary struggle. The American stonecutters carved out Greek forms with a Yankee strength and cunning of hand, just as the American shipbuilders fashioned their clipper ships with a tautness of design as economical as any design of the Greeks, yet geared to swiftness and nervous energy. Cooper and Washington Irving copied European forms even while they poured into them the content of a new continent. Emerson was a Platonist who fused the absolutism of the Greek philosopher with a Yankee astringency, and who translated the mysticism of the Eastern sages into terms of Yankee common sense. Longfellow, Whittier, Lowell, Holmes, were a bookish circle who borrowed their poetic ideas from the library stock of European memories, even when their material was native. The poetry of Poe was the inner flash of a tortured mind whose intellectual home (like his acceptance) was in European romanticism.

Yet to measure America thus by European standards is like measuring the Russians of the Czars or the commissars by the standards of the Athenian city-state. While contemporary American writers like Faulkner and Steinbeck are read in Europe as models, America is not a European civilization. Rightly or wrongly, many Americans feel that the elite arts of Europe are the products of dead-end cultures: they feel like the barbarian who, having conquered the traditional empires of power, will not bow down to the traditional empires of the spirit. This is true although contemporary American poets can compare with any in the world, and American abstract artists have created a ferment of excitement everywhere. The question is not how good the American elite art is, but what is the natural art idiom of the culture as a whole.

Despite a good deal of nonsense written by the glorifiers of the popular arts and the champions of the mucker pose, there is a genuine strain of rebellion which they express. When William Dean Howells spoke out against salon writers in the America of the 1880s he spoke as a vigorous champion of the novel but rejected whatever was prettified and derivative because it was weakening the traditional elite art. His protest was followed by the work of Frank Norris, Stephen Crane, Jack London, Ellen Glasgow, and Theodore Dreiser—the group of "rebels and ancestors" (as Maxwell Geismar called them) who ushered in the great period of the naturalistic American novel. To be sure, the creativeness of the American novel counts as part of the elite tradition: in the procession of world novelists, the Americans succeeded the Russians, as the Russians were preceded by the French, the French by the British, and the British by the Spaniards. But it may serve to underline the fact that even an elite art form neglects the popular energies at its peril. The feeling which the rebels of the American novel had, of looking at native themes and popular energies in the face of an exhausted tradition, is much the same attitude that Gilbert Seldes brilliantly expressed in his early championing of American popular culture in *The Seven Lively Arts.* In the mid-1950s, in *The Public Arts,* Seldes had to confess that the masters of the big media had betrayed many of the potentials of the lively arts; yet this does not subtract from his original insight.

It may be that the popular culture of today, for all its vulgarity and excesses, will prove to have contained the seeds of the elite arts of tomorrow. But for the present the Americans are taking the cash and letting the credit go. They devote themselves to costume-designed best sellers, mystery fiction, "true-story" pulp writing, terror comic books for those who are children in years or in mind. Their jazz has more passionate cultists than any community cult since the Dionysian mysteries. They are less concerned with casting a flawless athlete's figure in undying bronze than with action shots of sports heroes as they perform for millions of stadium, radio, TV, and newspaper followers. They care less for the epics of Roland or Don Quixote, of Aeneas or Mr. Bloom, than for the very different epics that the radio "daytime serials" bring American housewives every morning.

Thus, whatever the artistic merit of its products, American popular culture must not be viewed as a marginal aberration to be corrected as the nation's taste improves and some of its barbarisms are worn away but as part of the American cultural main stream. While much mawkish nonsense has been written about the popular arts, there is little danger that the big media will supplant the great intellectual tradition of the American elite arts. This does not mean the superiority of popular culture over the elite arts, which will continue to assert themselves even while there will be an autonomous realm for the arts of the popular culture.

That is why the student of American expression in the arts must look not only to the painters who work on rectangular strips of canvas but also to the army of amateurs carrying "candid cameras" as their passport to a photographer's Elysium. The history of building and design will fix on the webbed frame of Sullivan's skyscrapers and on Frank Lloyd Wright's poetic constructions of wood and stone, but it will also fix on the American kitchen, the American bathroom, the profile of automobiles and airplanes, and the split-level suburban house. American composers from Chadwick, Ives, and MacDowell to Aaron Copland have fashioned good symphonic music, yet the American musical idiom is probably better expressed in the haunting blend of traditional and vernacular in Gershwin's *Porgy and Bess* or in the sequence of jazz from the New Orleans brothels to Duke Ellington and Benny Goodman. The historian of the theater will trace the great tradition from O'Neill to Tennessee Williams, but he dare not neglect the musical-comedy stage which brought some of the best energies of music, lyrics, comedy, and dance into an amalgam like *Oklahoma!, South Pacific,* or *My Fair Lady.*

"There is a sub-department of American style," as Alistair Cooke has said, "which is enthusiastically saluted abroad: it is the extraordinary transformation of a bunch of hat-check girls with floppy bows on their shoes, who were formerly known as the *chorus,* into a modern ballet— a specifically American impulse which has been taken over in Sweden, France, England." This transformation could not have taken place without a disciplined treatment of the folk material of the frontier legends and the badman balladry, along with the rhythms of the popular dance hall, by choreographers and composers willing to brave the corruptions of Broadway. Similarly, the comic antics of the Keystone Cops were in themselves no great shakes, but out of them developed an element of the style of Chaplin as one of the great figures in the history of mimetic art. American "cheesecake" and the millions of publicity handouts of "pin-up" girls lack the calm beauty of the Greek Venus, but when Anatole France saw the girls in the American cheesecake art of his own day he remarked that any civilization producing them had a strength in it which could outlast the fears of its intellectuals.

American artistic expression has rarely followed the mold set by the professional arbiters of taste, who have often ignored what they were too close to see. It was Fernand Léger who made out the strongest case for American popular culture. "Thank God for the badness of American taste," he wrote after several years in the United States ". . . I always hate to see 'good taste' come to the people. . . . Still there is no need yet to worry. One only has to study the hand-painted ties on Broadway —a locomotive and four pigeons on a violet and black ground, or a buxom nude on a saffron ground—to realize there is still a vigorous survival. . . . Fourteenth Street may be ruined by the taste of Fifth Avenue, but Avenue B is still rich. And in spite of the fact that people run to good taste as soon as they discover they have bad taste, there will always be another Fourteenth Street or Avenue B while America keeps young. . . . Bad taste, strong colors—it is all here for the painter to organize and get the full use of its power. Girls in sweaters with brilliant colored skin; girls in shorts dressed more like acrobats in a circus than one would ever come across on a Paris street."

This suggests that some of the critics of American popular culture have failed to distinguish between what is in bad taste, judged by the standard of the leisure class and the Academies, and what is false and corrupted by any standard. Conversely, they fail to see that the strength of popular culture is not wholly erased even when it is corrupted by the pretentiousness of the pseudo-folk or cheapened by commercial greed. Much of American criticism of popular culture is riddled by what I should call a media fallacy, which fails to distinguish between the sins of the big media and the material of popular culture which they use and so often distort. W. H. Auden is sounder in suggesting a useful distinction between the popular culture that comes "out of the people," deriving its strength from them, and the popular culture that is merely the kind of art most people like. In the first sense it is folk art, in the second it is "lowbrow" or popular art. In both, according to Auden, it would exclude the courtly or salon art of the elites, although it would not exclude "classical" music or academic art or "serious" literature, all of which get wide popular acceptance through the new big media.

In my own definition of popular culture I should be inclined to cut across Auden's two categories. The art of Al Capp, of "Satchmo" Armstrong, "Jelly Roll" Morton, and of Chaplin, does not come "out of the people" in the sense that the great folk tales do or the Negro spirituals; yet, like them, it must be included in popular culture because it takes a vernacular form, shaped by popular taste and everyday life. Nor does everything that is "popular," in the sense of selling well and being widely accepted, fall within popular culture: when Faulkner's *Sartoris* sells in a paperback edition of a quarter million copies, it is still as much a product of elite art and the literary tradition as it was when it sold only a few thousand; when grand opera or symphony music is broadcast anew to millions, it remains part of the courtly tradition; when a historical romance jacketed with a full-bosomed heroine is adopted by a book club, it does not by that fact become a genuine part of popular culture, but is its own kind of middle-class trash. What counts is whether form and idiom are shaped by everyday American life, breaking the traditional molds of writing, music, theater, painting, architecture, and the dance.

This is not to underplay the role of the Big Audience in popular culture but only to warn against being distracted by the bigness of the audience and making it the crucial test of popular culture. The Big Audience can be drummed up by the media masters if they believe strongly enough in what they are doing and muster resourcefulness in presenting it; the Big Audience can also go by default if there is no such conviction and creative active will. The crucial fact is that the potential audience is there: the revolutionary arrival of leisure has brought such an audience into being, and the big media have made it technically possible to reach it. Like Virginia Woolf's "common reader," there is a "common listener" available. He is not the "average man," since he may range from millionaire to day laborer, from pastor to sex offender; he is not always an educated man, because American education is wayward and spotty in its expressions. It is better to say that he is the "majority man"—or woman or adolescent. The best assumption is that he is open to fresh impacts, is not manacled by tradition, is willing to give much that is new a try, provided that the sponsors and box office will expose him to it.

It is hard to find social or historical laws of general enough application to explain why a culture does well or badly in the total tradition of the world's arts, or why periods of artistic ferment or of desert stretches come when they do. The period after the French Revolution produced very little in French literature, tempting the generalization that an era of social turmoil is paralyzing to art—until one recalls (as Lewis Galantière does) that in England and Germany the same period produced some of the greatest of Europe's lyric poets. This does not mean that we must abandon the effort to find the social correlates of artistic creativeness, but only that no single formula will be adequate.

The most productive approach would see both the strength and confusion of American popular culture as flowing from the nature of the open-class system in America. In more rigidly stratified societies we are likely to find a split between elite and folk art, while in a class system as fluid as the American the boundaries between the two break down. Academic art breaks out of the academies to seek the market place; writers who start with a coterie reach a mass popularity in their lifetime; "best sellers" may turn out to be either slick or exacting; the cult of the comic strip spreads to intellectuals; symphonies find millions of listeners, while musical comedies may achieve a classic permanence almost overnight; jazz and abstract painting may develop cult proportions not only in Bohemia but among the middle classes; "little theater" groups spring up across the map; pockets of literary creativeness emerge in unlikely places in the West and South and Midwest instead of being concentrated in Eastern cities; the people become a nation of amateurs.

There are many ways of explaining this but none that can omit the ways in which Americans live. A people breaking the class mold is in a position to break also the artistic mold. In a fluid middle-class society, education of a sort becomes available to all, leisure is spread, and the dominant interest in life for many becomes access to new gradients of cultural experience. In such a society the distinction between popular and elite culture becomes murky, and the same forces which create a Big Audience for the products of the arts tend to envelope both forms.

There is also another way of seeing the same pattern. It is to see that a civilization which in many areas broke radically with the European past cannot cling to it in the arts without violating the principle of wholeness. Most of the great art forms of the Western cultures—painting, sculpture, the drama, sacred and secular architecture, the ballet, the symphony, grand opera, the epic and lyric poem—arose in largely stratified societies. They subsisted on the patronage of the rich and powerful few; and they celebrated either feudal honor and gallantry—the traits of a society of status—or the cementing power of religious belief. Only the novel as a great art form came out of a rising system of industrial capitalism and sought to meet the needs of the emerging middle classes. Except for literature, all of them assumed a tightly knit community that could assemble in a single place to see or listen, or to celebrate a collective ritual.

Americans are not tightly knit but vast and sprawling; they have not one center but a center in every city; they have a middle class with money enough to pay for new entertainments and leisure enough to be bored unless it gets them—hence the revolutionary techniques of movies, radio, sound track. They are a people with such varied ethnic origins that no one tradition could retain a hold on them for long—a people in constant motion, physically and symbolically, requiring arts that are swift, brisk, cohesive. With an economy dominated by big industry, they have naturally made their arts into big industries, through which some of the arts have found a new social support and a new economic base—but at a heavy cost in aesthetic standards which I shall consider in the sections that follow.

Unlike the material culture, the popular culture runs not in terms of what people *make* but in terms of what they *make up*—speech and rhythm and idiom, joke and plot, fable and song and dance, mimic battles of sport, movements across the stage, shadows on a screen. In what they make up they may reveal themselves more truly—because less warily—than in their more purposeful thought and action, their working or fighting, money-getting or rationalizing. It is in the more innocent and imaginative phases of their life that a people's cultural style is best revealed: for here we can catch them, so to speak, with their culture censor off-guard.

2. *Writers and Readers*

a. *The American Novel*

IN ONE OF his later books, *Faith, Reason, and Civilization,* Harold Laski paid tribute to American achievement in "its sudden creation of a literature which became, as at a bound, part of the main stream of civilized thought." But did American literature actually come into the main stream of world thought so suddenly? The historians of American thought and letters, notably Parrington and Van Wyck Brooks, give an answer involving a slower and more organic growth. What may have misled Laski was the case of the American novel, whose more notable achievements are scarcely more than a century old.

Why should it have flowered in the American soil? In its European origins the novel appealed to a middle class emerging from the Industrial Revolution and anxious to explore the reaches of a new universe. The same process happened in America on a new economic level and at a heightened pace. The varieties of experience that opened for all classes in a feverishly mobile society gave the novel at once a body of material and a reading public. The clash of old ways of thought with new ways of life found literary form in the novel of protest against emotional repression and starvation. New currents of tendency, flowing at one time from Darwin and Marx, at another from Balzac, Ibsen, Schopenhauer, and Freud, gave an impetus to fresh delineations of situation and conflict.

One can follow changes in the inner climate of the American novel by tracing that succession of its major themes. In the time of its Founding Fathers, Hawthorne and Melville, the great theme was the struggle of the individual to free himself from the burden of his original nature. Both of them master allegorists, they traced with powerful symbols the ordeal of a conscience no longer certain of Providential design. Hawthorne's obsessive sense of loss expresses itself in terms of the indelible stigma of sin and in the restless query as to whether the whole of life is not the shadow of a substance of which man has been deprived: in fact, one suspects that the Hawthorne of *The Scarlet Letter* may have been an underground believer in the forbidden sensuous joys of life, as Melville also was. In Melville's earlier period, when he writes of his voyages, there is a robust assertion and a feeling of stripped action and adventure which the Americans were to make their own. But of the later novels, one gets in *Pierre* the sense of being implicated in some crucial and inescapable guilt, in *Moby Dick* the wrestling with the Leviathan of one's inner bondage, in *Benito Cereno* the impact of violence upon innocence, in *Billy Budd* and *The Confidence Man* the betrayal of man's best energies by a lurking evil.

In the middle period of the American novel the giant figures are those of Mark Twain and Henry James. *Huckleberry Finn* and Twain's other great novels of boyhood in a Midwestern small town are the record of a lost Golden Age on the frontier, as is also his nostalgic account of *Life on the Mississippi*. When he turned from the wholeness of this remembered Eden to the adult world as he knew it, with its moral confusion and its hypocrisy, the result was a volcanic upheaval which set him to brooding over the ways of the "Mysterious Stranger" and almost shattered his sanity. In James the American novel turned on itself, exploring the nuances of sensibility in a social system being rapidly transformed. James depicted a gallery of representative Americans in a European setting (*The Ambassadors,* to use his own symbolic title) studying the American character when it was dislocated from the American scene, and dissolving it in the onrushing flood of his perceptions and insights. But the crucial aspect of James is to be found less in his insight than in the drama of the moral dilemmas his characters face and the decisions they make: this was the James of the "middle period," especially of *The Bostonians* and *The Princess Casamassima*.

In Theodore Dreiser—the most massive figure in the realistic movement that counted Howells and Jack London, Crane and Norris and perhaps Ellen Glasgow as forerunners—the realism of method seeks to come to grips with a society which Dreiser wanted to describe nakedly, without in any way prettifying it. Stumblingly he searched for some pattern of order, something other than a theological, romantic, or idealistic one, in the prevailing chaos. Himself only a rudimentary thinker (or better, a feeler) he tried to patch together a philosophy borrowed from Nietzsche, Darwin, and Marx—and from Catholic morality as well, since he was bound to it even when revolting against it. He was in essence a dramatist of ideas, casting them in a literary mold. There was a phase in his development when he felt that the man of power and genius can create his own cosmos, and another when he saw the individual caught beyond help between the tropisms of his animal nature and the pressures of his social environment. In Sherwood Anderson, the theme of alienation becomes obsessive, with most of the characters trying to find their way back to an instinctual nature that has been overlaid by the crust of business, the machine, and the small-town moral code. Farrell's *Studs Lonigan* depicts the expense of generous impulse and spirit in a waste of shame. Dos Passos's trilogy, *U.S.A.,* interweaves unfulfilled drives that have no organic relation to each other, related only because each is driven by social (not instinctual) forces of which he has little inkling and over which he has no control.

In this sense some of the important novels before the contemporary period may be seen as cultural documentaries, bearing witness to the emotions surging through the civilization and the splits rending it. They suggest why European and some American critics regard the American novel as a reflection of the grandeurs and miseries of life in America. Using the premise that the fiction stereotypes of each period are part of its social and emotional weather, Malcolm Cowley notes an interesting succession of dominant American story themes since the turn of the century. In the early 1900s the story was about man and Nature— how a Darwinian hero of the Jack London type, thinking himself a weakling, found his true stature in the frozen Arctic wastes or in the jungle or at sea. In the generation of the 1920s the story was about the conflict between artist and Philistine, as witness *Three Soldiers, The Genius, Main Street:* this theme can be traced back to the turn of the century in Henry James, Edith Wharton, and Ellen Glasgow, but it became a generalized one in the 1920s. Another theme in that decade was the American Byronic hero of Fitzgerald and the early Hemingway. In the 1930s the stereotype was that of the martyred strike hero of the proletarian novel, although a close study of the period shows that there were fewer instances of it than there appeared to be at the time. In the early 1940s it was about the American soldier finding fresh adventures abroad, or the James Jones reluctant soldier seeking to find himself through the cynicism of his army experience or the disillusionment of the brothel. In the 1950s Cowley finds a number of major fictional themes, including the artistic young men ruined by a possessive mother and the adventure story in which "the author is trying to find symbols, symbols, symbols, for the moral chaos of the modern world."

If we take the four recent novelists who have most impressed European writers—Fitzgerald, Wolfe, Hemingway, and Faulkner—we find that the prevailing mood is the sense of being ravaged and lost, yet of finding some characteristic assertion of life meaning. Fitzgerald deals with lives of individual exploits—on the margin of racketeering (*The Great Gatsby*), or in the dream world of the Hollywood power man (*The Last Tycoon*)—or with individual deterioration, as in the account of schizophrenia in *Tender Is the Night* that may be read on both a personal and cultural level. In Wolfe's case the titles of the novels (*Look Homeward, Angel* and *You Can't Go Home Again*) suggest the prevailing theme of deprivation and search that echoes in the repetitions of "Lost, lost"; the readers of Wolfe's letters know of his tortured quest for an authority principle in a world of unremitting flux. In Hemingway's work the accent on fortitude implies a world so awry that only stoicism and "grace under pressure" count enduringly. The best escape from the trauma of an overcivilized world—expressed in repeated symbols of mutilation and psychic deprivation—is found in the heroic encounters of the natural order (the big hunt, the bullfight, the struggle of the Old Man and the shark) or of revolution and war: even over these there hangs always the heavy sense of loss, for in Hemingway's world, happiness lies only in what might have been. In Faulkner the critics have traced a celebration of the bonds of soil and of family kinship with an elaborated legendry tied to a localist tradition. Faulkner is ridden by the sense that the Southern land can never get free of the curse laid on it by slavery, yet he embraces the qualities of gallantry and arrogance under a feudal order, which—for all their self-destructiveness—shine in contrast with the psychic corruption of the parvenus who have displaced them.

Vernon L. Parrington, who in his *Main Currents in American Thought* tried to place American writers in their setting of time, society, and ideas, emphasized the strain of the novel that started with Mark Twain and went through Howells, Norris, London, Dreiser, and Sinclair Lewis, coming to its fullness in the 1920s. Characteristically, in stressing this tradition, he did less than justice to the counter-strain of Hawthorne, Poe, Melville, and Henry James. Lionel Trilling refers to the Great Debate running through the history of the American novel as a dialogue between Henry James and Dreiser. Yet he rightly adds that even with the naturalists whom Dreiser represents there is a strain of individualism, a rejection of society amounting to the asocial, which marks off the American novel from the British and perhaps the French. As the 1920s and 1930s receded, taking their place in the longer historical pattern, it became clear that even Dreiser and Sinclair Lewis as naturalists worked within a frame different from that of Dickens and Thackeray in England or of Balzac and Zola in France.

The American novel has a longer and richer tradition as a vehicle of social protest and reform that is usually recognized, stretching from H. H. Breckenridge to Nelson Algren. Yet once this has been said it remains true that the stronger tradition is one I have traced in terms of alienation from the society and the lonely debate within the writer. This is the more striking because one might have expected the American novelists to reflect the pragmatic and optimistic stress in the culture, the preoccupation with the concrete, the brashness of social construction. It points up the fallacy of seeing literature only as a mirror reflection of social forces. The relation of literature to American culture is far more indirect and subtle, although the fact of relationship is clear enough since the life of the arts is not carried on in a cultural vacuum.

The climate within which American novelists wrote was one of individual dissent, deriving largely from the religious and political tradition. This dissent might have expressed itself in a drive to use the novel as a weapon for social change, yet the novelists whose primary impulse was reform, like Harriet Stowe, David Graham Phillips, and Upton Sinclair, were only marginal as craftsmen. America as an open society allowed a more direct attack on social problems, through politics and organized groups. Hence when the novelist turned to society, it was not to change it but to reject and transcend it: to do this he turned inward on himself, exploring his moral and psychological dilemmas.

By the time of Henry James, it was clear that the orderly world of the New England elite had slipped beyond their control, and that the traditional values had lost their hold. This was accompanied by a change in the social order—handicraft transformed into a machine culture, a closed order of status into a mobile one of effort and acquisition, a cohesive hierarchy into a new rampant individualism. Between the society of the Old Republic and that of contemporary mass democracy a break occurred—one which is perhaps best reflected in Howells, who sensed and acted it out in his novels. Thus the American case embodies the extremes of individualism in thought and dislocation in society: both conditions are the characteristic ones for the modern novel. The American novel flowered at a time when men saw that they had been cast out of the theological order of design into a natural order of chance and tragedy.

If the novel is the epic of the modern world, it celebrates "schism in the soul." The American novel has a continuing strain of the somber, tragic, guilt-laden. Unlike the painters, American novelists rarely go abroad as apprentices to learn their insights or techniques. They take their burden and theme directly from the Puritan and Calvinist tradition, from the marks left by slavery and civil strife, from the contrast between the American promise and the realities of a power civilization, from the gap between the vaulting idealism with which the American experiment began and the tawdry glories that now bedeck it. The novel thus contains the deposits of the psychic past of the civilization from which it derives.

In the closed societies of the ancient world or the Middle Ages the hero's tribulations and achievements express the collective experience. The hero of the epics of those periods is thus a symbol of tribal victories (the *Iliad*) or wanderings (the *Odyssey*) or of a common religious experience (*Divine Comedy*). Modern man must, however, be his own hero and carry his own burdens, and from that truth the novel takes its shape. Most novels are built around the encounters of love, the pursuit of happiness, the career of a mind, the pilgrimage of a spirit. They may be success or deterioration stories; they may end in wedding bells or be as ravaging as Faulkner's tales of guilt and incest; but always the question is what the main figure achieves or is deprived of ("What happens to him?"; "How does she come out?"). Since the novel operates on two levels—an outer one of social experience and an inner one of psychological exploration—it expresses the ambivalence of the culture. It gives a chance for the portrayal of variants from the cultural norm and is a literary form into which the novelist can pour dreams, frustrations, and obsessions.

In the Middle Ages and their world of authoritarian faith, where the individual had minimal decisions to make on major issues of morality and belief, the novel would have been a meaningless form. There is little evidence of its thriving in any authoritarian regime of today. It is the genre of a relatively open mobile society, like the eighteenth-century European society in which it emerged, where the individual must flounder on his own and find his own stability. Thus it is idle to discuss the charge that the American novel of today is "decadent" because of its pessimist theme and symbolism of method. Hawthorne and Melville were notable for their brooding bent and their inward-turning command of symbolism, yet their society was scarcely in decay—even if it was in the process of radical change. F. O. Matthiessen and Harold Laski said of both these novelists that they turned away from Emerson's easy harmonies because they sensed the night ahead. But this is scarcely adequate as an explanation. They wrote not with a prescience of the future but with a sense of their own plight in a frame where each man must make his own decisions, carry his own psychic burdens, find sympathy and identification with others not through a network of established relations of status but by exploring their common humanity. Henry James's emphasis on the individual moral decision—sometimes a startling one—was the product of a similar plight, and the impact of James was on the intellectuals and the new middle classes of a society which felt the same plight.

Thus the American novel is the product chiefly of dissidents and rebels writing in a relatively open social system where there are no authoritarian short cuts to the problems of the individual life. To be sure, not all novelists have the strength to be true dissenters and autonomous personalities. Yet every group tends to shape its own patterns: in America the young man on the margin of the culture, who rejects the life goals of his contemporaries and is thought a misfit by them, is likely to turn to fiction. In many cases he has a small but salable talent and eventually fits himself into his society. But during a phase of his life he enacts the gesture of rebellion and tussles with the Adversary through a literary exploration of his life and time.

I have said that the novel is a fluid form for a fluid society. The problems of hunger for love, of sexual bewilderment, of the struggle of personalities within a marriage, of the clash between old moral codes and new operative norms, of the search for a personal and social ethic, are questions for which American society offers no fixed solutions. Even where the majority has evolved accepted goals and standards the young novelist feels impelled to challenge them: to write about failure rather than success, the world of childhood rather than the urgencies of manhood, wayward impulses rather than power and money.

Some critics have complained, for example, that the American novelists have failed to do justice to the businessman in their portrayal of him. The complaint has a base, but it misses the main point, which is that the novel was never intended as an instrument of balanced appraisal. The novelists wrote as they did about businessmen not because they were infected with radical and Marxist heresies but because they were driven to be critical of the values of practicality and power which the culture sought to impose on them. By challenging the gods of their culture they tried to find the measure of their own personalities.

The same point is made from another direction by Trilling when he speaks of the striking difference in social attitude within the two best-known boy's books of American and English literature, Mark Twain's

Huckleberry Finn and Kipling's *Kim.* Both of them "delight in their
freedom from all familial and social ties." But where Kim carries with
him carefully the evidence of his father's identity, Huck is relieved by
his brutal father's death. Where Kim adopts surrogate fathers who are
symbols of authority, Huck has only the guidance of Jim, the Negro
slave. Trilling does not stop short at the theme of "alienation from
society": he goes on to show that in the American case this assertion
of independence is the prelude to an assumption of responsibility, and
that it underlies a social universe of difficult but open human and moral
choices.

In this sense the American novelists play the role of keepers of the
social conscience. In exploring personality and telling how people have
tried to find their bearings, they practice "philosophy teaching by example." To shopgirls and stenographers devouring the novel-of-the-
month on subways and at lunch hour, to the young wife consuming
novels while her husband is at the office, to the college student getting
an initiation into society through a paperback reprint of a fictional
classic, the novel—good or bad—is a form of popular psychology teaching
by example. The psychology it uses is not necessarily good. It reflects
the tensions and splits of the society, and too often it expresses the
poverty of philosophy and absence of depth it is meant to remedy.
Which only means that the novel is the art form of an open society at
its best and worst.

The assumption behind the novel is that answers can come only from
the natural world of experience and not from a deductive system. Without this assumption the novel could never have flowered. There are
torrents of experience pouring through the pages of American fiction.
The dust jacket of every first novel is an absorbing study in the apprentice years which the young novelist serves while "getting material" for
his novel—that is, getting the varied feel of American life. If one compares the allegorical tales of Hawthorne with the most recent best
seller, there is a striking contrast in mood and tempo. Inevitably the
big-audience media have left their mark on storytelling, putting the
emphasis on a swift pace which keeps the "story line" moving, authentic
detail, and a "clean" style—meaning one uncluttered by excesses of
phrase or difficulties of thought. For a story to be swift, authentic,
cleanly contrived, and to "pack a punch" becomes the culture form for
literary success. The characteristic American "know-how" approach is
thus applied by the fiction writer, who tailors his product either to the
sentimental or to the hard-boiled note, depending on demand, and in-
jects the proper modicum of violence and sadism for the market. At the

other extreme is the novelist who is preoccupied with anxiety-ridden psychiatric themes and with symbols that serve as a substitute for thought.

Thus while the American novel shows no signs of being "doomed," it is caught between the dangers of a slick mechanical facility and the pretentiousness of the coteries. The seductions of the big-audience media do not keep the well-heeled writer from continuing to dream of the legendary "great American novel." But the fact is that no single American novel can be the "great" one, since all of them together portray the shallows and reaches of the American spirit.

I have concentrated here on the novel because in it American achievement is most marked. I have had to omit the short story, which is probably more characteristic of the future trend in a culture where time is measured out with such precision and where there has been (in Clifton Fadiman's phrase) a "decline of attention." In lyric poetry the American record is surprising when one remembers that the main cultural impulse is toward what is useful and salable—and poetry is neither. In Poe and Emily Dickinson, in Whitman, in Hart Crane and Eliot (if he be considered an American), in Frost, MacLeish, Pound, Robinson Jeffers, and Wallace Stevens, American poetry has shown a range and lyric power which belie the usual stereotypes about the American mind.

In the nineteenth century, American poetry was to some extent a popular art and entered the popular consciousness, as witness the poems of Longfellow, Whittier, Lowell, Poe, Bryant, Eugene Field, and James Whitcomb Riley. But these poets have no standing with contemporary critics. In the twentieth century, even when it drew heavily on folk material—as in the case of Carl Sandburg and Vachel Lindsay—American poetry was largely an elite art, with an appeal only to the literate minority. America did not produce a Burns, a Wordsworth, or a Kipling who could be embraced by both audiences—unless Frost is the exception. It is as if the young American poet, searching for an idiom, could give himself individuality only by walling himself off from the rest of his society. The people, in turn, are cut off from the poet and feel something close to contempt for him. The universities find room for poet-in-residence, but as Norman Pearson put it, "The student avid to sit under him in a course on creative writing turned into a citizen who refused to buy a volume of verse after he left the university."

Even in so sketchy a survey I cannot omit a brief word about American criticism, which had a kind of flowering in the quarter century between the mid-1920s and the 1950s. It was a sign of American literary maturity that the critics could not be fitted into any one school, whether one spoke of Edmund Wilson, R. P. Blackmur, Van Wyck Brooks, Constance Rourke, Malcolm Cowley, Allen Tate, F. O. Matthiessen, Lionel Trilling, Maxwell Geismar, Kenneth Burke, Yvor Winters, or Alfred Kazin. About all of them, and a number of others as well, there was an adventurous searching for the relation of forms and meaning, and sometimes ideas and values, which expressed on another plane the restless quest within American society. If Matthew Arnold was right about the alternation of periods of critical and creative effort in a culture, the current "age of criticism" augurs a new creative flowering to come.

b. *The Reading Revolution*

IN THE LAST GENERATION something like a revolution in reading has taken place in America in the form of low-cost paper-bound books, making of Americans a nation of readers. With this has come a rise in publishing costs which makes books that are destined for a very limited audience a luxury few publishers can afford. Thus there has been simultaneously a dwindling of the Small Audience for reading and a vast growth of the Big Audience.

The "best seller" has been chronic throughout the history of American publishing. Defined by its closest student, Frank L. Mott, as any book which a decade after publication had a sale equal to 1 per cent of the population, the best seller would include in the seventeenth century Michael Wigglesworth's poem, "The Day of Doom," with the sale of a thousand copies in 1690, and Mary Rowlandson's story of her Indian captivity; in the eighteenth century *Mother Goose* and Tom Paine's *Common Sense;* in the nineteenth century Parson Weems's *A Life of Washington,* Harriet Beecher Stowe's *Uncle Tom's Cabin,* and Mrs. Southworth's novels; in the early twentieth century Gene Stratton Porter and Harold Bell Wright. In more recent decades the best sellers have been books like *Gone with the Wind, Forever Amber,* the Perry Mason mysteries, and almost any book of popular religious exhortation. To regard this list as revealing the furnishings of the American mind would be to ignore the ephemeral nature of best sellers, which the reader treats much as he treats magazine fiction or radio soap opera.

Despite the best-seller figures, "reading a book" is still felt to require a special effort and a ritual frame of mind. It is well known that President Eisenhower read few books, partly because of his crowded life, but mainly because—like other American men of action—he preferred to absorb through the ear and the eye rather than through the printed page. The estimate is that half the American adults buy no books at all, and most of the rest buy very few. The inroads of TV have threatened even the big-circulation magazines, since there is some evidence that TV viewers read less than the others. Even the college students coming from reading families are fewer than those from families where books are alien intruders.

The emergence of the paperbacks, along with the book clubs, has had a revolutionary impact on American reading habits. The clubs have served not only as large-scale distributors but also as reading counselors, and through them millions of Americans have shaped new reading tastes and habits. The book industry had been more backward than most American industries in developing large-scale merchandising through retail outlets. There are 1,400 bookstores in America, compared with 500,000 food stores, 350,000 restaurants and bars, almost 200,000 gas stations, and over 50,000 drugstores. The revolution of paperbacks has been accomplished by mass-production cuts in cost, by a shrewd editorial selection of titles suggesting sex, crime detection, and violence, along with a number of classics, and finally by a revolution in distributing techniques. This has been achieved mainly by adding drugstores, newspaper stands, and even food markets to the bookstores, thus bringing the reading habit to the ordinary American in his everyday haunts.

At mid-century Americans were buying almost a quarter billion paperbacks a year, with about a thousand titles appearing annually. Freeman Lewis calculated that the five most popular authors have been Erle Stanley Gardner, Erskine Caldwell, Thorne Smith, Ellery Queen, and Mickey Spillane. Three of the five are murder-mystery writers, and Spillane's books embody the worst fusion of violence and sexual exploitation in American writing. Yet a different kind of book, including some of the classics of social science and literature, has also found its way to a mass reading public. The long-range consequences of paperbacks are likely to include the popularization of the best in literary achievement. Whether this will counterbalance the shoddy and sadistic stuff is an unresolved question. It should also be added, for perspective, that despite their astronomic sales paperbacks are bought by something less than 10 per cent of the American population.

The most depressing part of American reading is in a category far below the paperbacks. It is what may be called the cloacal literature, with which street newsstands are filled. It falls into a number of broad divisions—the grotesques (comic books, horoscope sheets, cultist magazines), mystery and adventure (whodunits, terror stories, "Westerns"), romance (love story, "true experience" confessions, and movie magazines), the "Confidential" magazines (battening with enormous circulation success upon the "revelations" of moral lapses in the sexual behavior of movie and TV stars and other public figures), sexual exploitation (joke books, leg-and-breast cartoons, pornography), betting sheets, the how-to-do-it vade mecums (how to comb and feed your dog, how to play mah-jongg, how to improve your golf scores). Examine a newsstand thus weighted down in any American city, and it will be hard to suppress a shiver of apprehension about the American future.

It is important to understand that the corrupting principle does not lie in the machine principle—itself only a duplicative force—nor in the popular standards of taste, which are product rather than source. At the core is the apathy of people who have never been exposed to quicken-ing ideas, and the slackness of thought which makes them victims of cynical and greedy men. In this sense there is no great difference be-tween the sleaziness of the "comic books" (a hundred million copies of which flow into the American market every year) and that of the "slick" magazines produced on coated stock and selling for much higher prices. They have in common the assumption of an inert reader who will re-spond to a formula. In both cases the situation is contrived and the solutions are easy. The difference is largely that the comic books contain stronger ingredients, including violence and sadistic terror, that they take less pains at simulating plausibility, and that they mainly reach young readers.*

It is this latter fact, striking home at the conscience of Americans as parents, which has recently made them uneasy about the spectacular in-crease of the worst types of comic books. In the mid-1940s the crime-and-violence comic books formed only a tenth of the total sold; a decade later they were over a third. Part of the comic-book formula is to com-bine sex, crime, and horror, thus intertwining these themes in the fan-tasy life of growing children. The serious impact of comic books is therefore not so much on the abnormal children who become delin-quents for a variety of reasons, of which comic-book addiction is only one, but on normal children who get much of the furnishings of their mind from this source. Some students regard comic books only as an extension of the realm of make-believe, much like the classic folk tales and children's stories; while others think they leave a traumatic deposit of anxiety and terror. The difference may lie between those children who pass through the comic-book stage as a phase in their imaginative development, moving on to good romantic reading and then to the writers who deal with some of their own life problems, and those chil-dren who never move on but remain perpetual adolescents with a comic-book mentality. The experience of the Armed Forces shows that a sizable number of the young American soldiers fall into the second cate-gory, frozen at the level of comic books and whodunits.

Possibly the "reading revolution" of paperbacks may break down the

* For the newspaper comic strip, see Ch. X, Sec. 4, "Profile of the Press."

division between elite reading and moronic reading. The fruits of the experiment in popularization will not be known for several generations. But they cannot be productive unless there is a creative impulse within the reading industries which will offer the public good books to place alongside the shoddy ones.

3. Heroes, Legends, and Speech

THE MYTH-MAKING faculty is still active in contemporary America.* Its expression may be found in the folklore deposits left by the past and it is still operative in the legendry that grows up around the type-figures of popular stories and songs and in the changing forms of American speech. The common element in all of these is in the energies of the people, at once anonymous and collective, working spontaneously to produce their record.

Anyone who studies American folklore, keeping his eye not only on the past but also on the vivid facts of genuine folk interests in contemporary American life, is bound to be struck by the threads of continuity between them—but also by the extent of the break. The continuity is there in the sense that the legend-creating faculty continues active, using whatever materials are at hand. But the break is also there. The American schoolboy, whether from city or country, will know far less about Casey Jones than about Joe DiMaggio. The continuing mobility of Americans, along with the constant succession of newly arrived ethnic groups, has led to a break between the legendry of past and present. Since the traditional heroes are not readily available to tie these groups together, the need for new ones is the more urgent.

When I speak of American heroes I think of two kinds. One is the *history-book hero:* like the *heroes* of Greek civilization, he embodies the accepted culture traits and the collective achievement. A Washington, a Lincoln, a Roosevelt, a Grant, an Eisenhower, he is the man with a halo who gives Americans a satisfying sense of national stature. But he is overshadowed by the second hero type. He may be called either the *vernacular hero,* in the sense that he comes out of the everyday life of the people, or the *archetypal hero,* since he serves as a bigger-than-life figure around whom young Americans weave their wish-fulfillment fantasies.

This hero is likely to be a less imposing person than the history-book hero—probably an ordinary young-man-with-a-horn, or a crooner who

---

* For an earlier discussion of American folk myths, see Ch. VIII, Sec. 1, "The Personality in the Culture." For children's literature, see Ch. VIII, Sec. 3, "Children and Parents."

evokes exciting sounds, or a small-town girl who is no Joan of Arc and has seen no visions except her name on the movie marquees, or a King of Swat with hefty muscles and the ability to swing powerfully at a baseball. This hero's day of glory is brief and his fame is precarious and transitory, like the spurt of a lighted match, for the hero symbols of each generation seem eccentric to the next. But his hold on the popular mind, while he has it, exceeds in intensity the hold of the military and political figures. The living little hero is more important in understanding America than the dead big hero.

In some cases the hero spans both types, acting both as symbol of national achievement and projection of the individual life wish. The businessman hero will serve as an example. In earlier generations he might have been a Gates, a Drew, a Yerkes, a Vanderbilt, a Rockefeller, a Morgan—hard, acquisitive, honed to a sharp edge of predation; yet he received from the young men the final honor of imitation. It was not—as it was with the Greeks—the man of public virtue who was honored but a very imperfect man who embodied a particular strain in the social striving. A Carnegie who broke strikes or a Rockefeller who crushed his competitors was not limited in his prestige to the role of a class hero—as with Gene Debs or Big Bill Heywood—but was accepted as a national hero. Since the people identified themselves not with him as a person but with what he amassed, he did not have to be either likable or virtuous. The business Titans were accepted as almost Plutarchian models because their tenacity, resourcefulness, and single-mindedness in pursuing profits were also the traits of a power civilization. In contemporary America these picturesque pirates have been replaced by corporate managers whose names are scarcely known outside the trade journals. The new business hero is institutionalized: in an impersonalized society he has become A.T. & T. or General Motors.

It is in the archetypal heroes of movie and TV and baseball diamond that Americans seek the sense of human warmth they fail to find in their depersonalized business heroes. In Leo Lowenthal's phrase, the "idols of work" have been replaced by the "idols of leisure."

When one moves into a third hero realm—neither the public figure of politics and business nor the idol of the Big-Audience media—the processes of popular myth-making stand most clearly revealed. Here one finds the folklore hero, who may be drawn from some actual person and expanded to legendary proportions or may be a wholly fictional product of the collective imagination.

The first such folk type was the legendary Yankee who emerged from the American Revolution—slow of speech, with a high-pitched voice, homely in expression, perhaps a traveling peddler, perhaps a sailor or a farmer, full of shrewd wit and homespun resourcefulness. As the type figure around which American folklore clustered, the Yankee was succeeded by the backwoodsman of irrepressible spirits—the "gamecock of the wilderness." He might be Colonel Nimrod Wildfire, the hero of *The Lion of the West,* a play which swept the country in a number of versions, in all of which he was (in Constance Rourke's words) the "early backwoodsman, leaping, crowing, neighing, boasting, dancing breakdowns and delivering rhapsodic monologues." Or he might be Davey Crockett himself, from whom Nimrod Wildfire is believed to have been copied, or Mike Fink or Sam Slick or Sam Patch or any of the other figures, part hero, part buffoon, who were described in the tall tales that Americans spin.

Later, as the forests were felled and logging camps sprang up, as steamboats appeared on the torrential rivers, as railroads were laid and spikes driven into steel rails, new accessions of folklore were added. The heroes who had already become in great measure boasters were transformed further into giant-sized myths of miracle workers, signalizing both the pathos and the achievement of the opening of the continent— Paul Bunyan of the Big North Woods, the demigod of the shanty boys and the loggers; and Pecos Bill, who has been called the culture hero of the cowboys; and John Henry, the giant hero of the rock-tunnel gang; and the "badmen" and "rip tail roarers" of the cowboy country; and killers like Billy the Kid and Jesse James; and Joe Magarac, pourer of molten metal.

Stories were told of these men and ballads were written about them: there were tall tales and braggart lies. In time the Americans built up a body of legendry about every phase of the continent's expansion—the mountain men, the covered wagon that crossed the plains, the Mississippi steamboats and their epic trails of speed, the river gamblers, the lumberjacks and shanty boys, the Pony Express teams, the gold miners, the cowboys, the frontier-town outlaws, and even—as in the ballad of Casey Jones—the railroad men. These yarns were the literature of the bookless world. For the most part they were organic to the growing energies of the South and West, although some of them were the detritus of a kind of Lumpen-campfollower of the country's growth. At its best this folklore had a braggart quality that never took itself seriously and a humorous ferocity that stopped short of the sadistic. There are also mountainous masses of other material that consist mainly of ghastly idiocies, smart-aleck cracks and synthetic jokes. It was not all pitched to the same key. There was an astringency in the talk of the Yankee characters as against the spread-eagle, rhapsodic assertiveness of the backwoodsman, or the wild fantasy of the "strong man" legends, or the saccharine sentiment lavished on the outlaw killers. But in whatever key, American folklore was the noise an expanding culture makes as it struts and boasts, puffing its chest a little out of cocky assurance and overbrimming energies, and a little out of the insecurity that needs reassurance.

The material out of which this legendry was shaped was the everyday stuff of living; the form it took was the yarn and ballad; the setting was local, in hamlet or county, logging camp or ranch or mining town; the proportions were heroic; the mood was mock-epic; the type image was the hero who was also a bit of a charlatan and a cutter of corners, conscious of his own comic vulnerabilities; the audience was an assemblage of whoever happened to be around, but there was little dividing line between audience and performer, with the roles shifting easily and the observers becoming participants; the method was that of continual change by improvisation of the stories, ballads, and folk themes until the original text was submerged by the successive waves of change.

Since American legendry is notoriously short-lived, it is almost wholly forgotten—or, what amounts to the same thing, enshrined in scholarly books and antiquarian journals. Every so often, as happened in the 1950s with the Davey Crockett boom, one of the legendary figures of American history and mythology becomes a contemporary folk hero. When this happens, the boom takes on runaway proportions and becomes a kind of hysteria sweeping through the country, bursting into the newspapers, the movies, comic strips, and TV, inflaming the imagination of children, and spawning whole new industries, as with "Davey Crockett" hats, suits, pajamas, toys, and souvenirs. Then just as suddenly as it came, the boom subsides—and is replaced by another. In the 1950s the Davey Crockett hysteria was followed by a teen-agers' cult of James Dean, a movie star who had died in an auto crash only a few months earlier but was quickly given immortality by a young generation which formed "James Dean Clubs" and refused to believe that their hero was dead. The true nature of these booms must be left to the social psychologist who studies fads and social hysterias as well as legendry, and the clue to them must probably be sought in the psychic hunger for a compassable legendary figure in an era of the mechanical and impersonal.

Yet, quite aside from these temporary booms, American legendry has left a deposit on contemporary American character. You will recognize in Abe Lincoln's talk some of the comic bravado of the folk tales, with a new dimension of depth; and Lincoln was himself to illustrate after his tragic death the mythologizing process. The reader of Mark Twain also knows that his achievement would never have been possible unless his roots had been in the folk memory. Even in novelists as sophisticated as

Henry James, as Constance Rourke noted, there is a conscious shaping of his figures in terms of the archetypal mold of the American character, as if he meant to show triumphantly that the folk theme can permeate even a craftsman seemingly furthest removed from it. In Steinbeck, Faulkner, and Caldwell, Sherwood Anderson and Ring Lardner, the folk material is like a network of underground streams bursting through the landscaped surface.

One can see the myth-making process still going on, pouring new substances into essentially similar molds. The Western heroes and the dime novels have been replaced by the dramatis personae of the comic strip; Paul Bunyan and John Henry, who were themselves cast in the image of a frontier Hercules, are now Superman or Dick Tracy; the backwoods hero, in a modern burlesque version, has become L'il Abner; the animal tales of the Tar Baby and Br'er Rabbit have become Pogo and his companions; the yarns of the Jumping Frog have been transformed into the modern legendry of Henry Ford's Model T; the badmen of the frontier have taken more recent shape in the exploits of Dillinger and Willie Sutton; the local cracks and gibes are now radio gags or "little moron" variations; and the earlier American boy's storehouse of traditional lore has become the contemporary boy's precise knowledge of the team standing and batting averages of Big League baseball.

To say that the modern material is inferior to the earlier, or less glamorous or more synthetic, is to lose sight of the fact that the basic myth-making needs arise from the people themselves, and that they feed on whatever the culture presents them. There are figures in every era who attract the myth-making power of the people, around whom legends cluster; there are also symbolic events in every generation—inventions, wars, disasters, new media for communication. In the case of societies which have relatively stable habits of life over a long time-span, the folklore consists of traditional collective memories, as is still true in the pockets of cultural isolation that persist in the "Down East" communities of New England or the backward reaches of the Appalachians. But these are only marginal for America. In the foreground there is a process not so much of folk memory as of continually fresh hero-creation, word-coinage, stories and jokes, cults that take almost overnight possession of the people, whether in games or sport or amateur activities. A culture like the American, cutting itself off from the older mythologies, has felt freer to generate new ones. As I have suggested, the presence of so many diverse ethnic and regional groups helped the process by making a fresh start necessary in almost every generation. Yet Americans did not always cast out the importations from the foreign cultures. As in the case of Scandinavian, Jewish, or Negro myths, the myth-making process was enriched by absorbing the tributary streams of mythology that merged with the main current.

How creative have the American myths been? Have the folk heroes expressed the strength and depth of the American character? Have the stories and ballads poured into them the emotional intensity of the American experience or have they tapped only shallow springs?

It may be too early to answer these questions for a culture still young when compared with those out of which the Greek and Norse mythologies came, or the ritual celebrations of the Dionysian cult, or the great myths of the "White Goddess," or the folk material underlying the Greek tragedies, or the Homeric and Arthurian legends, or the myths clustering around a Moses or Joseph, Faustus or Siegfried. American legendry lacks the archetypal depth of these great mythical themes, nor will it offer to the imagination of individual artists the rich opportunity these themes have offered. Partly the reason lies with the nature of the American character, which has been aggressively of a debunking and deflationary turn, partly in the unwillingness to surrender to the imagination when there is so much danger of appearing merely gullible. But mainly it seems true that the tragic dimensions of the American character were contained in its religious brooding and in its great novels, and the folklore—from the impetus it got in frontier expansion—took a more expansive turn but one with less emotional richness.

The collective imagination has operated with the greatest fertility in the continuous re-creation of the inherited language. American speech is surely one of the richest products of the American experience, at the base of much else that is creative in American popular culture. Abrupt, inventive, muscular, irreverent, it expresses with striking fidelity the energies and rhythm that have gone into the making of the national experience. Rarely has a new civilization taken the mature language it has inherited and adapted it so radically to its purposes. American spelling diverged sharply from British at the end of the eighteenth century, and the efforts of men like Noah Webster gave Americans the courage to break free from their cultural colonialism and assert their independence in spelling and pronunciation. While grammar and syntax in American speech have been slow in changing, the process of vocabulary-making has been a daring one: the creation of new words and expressions in the American common speech accompanied the opening of the continent. For a parallel in linguistic inventiveness, one must go to the England of the Elizabethan Age, when the speech of the common people and that of the dramatic writers burst into a new flowering, each of them affecting the other.

With all its richness, however, American speech is strikingly uniform when compared with its mother tongue. The English developed dialects so sharply divergent from one another that a traveler from one region could scarcely understand the dialect of another: it was the Midland dialect, more progressive than the archaic Southern one but less daring than the rapidly shifting Northern dialect, which came to be established as the basis of "standard" or "general" English. The Americans had no such difficulty and no need for a standard or general American speech, since a man can travel from the Atlantic to the Pacific and encounter no difficulty in being understood. The clue lies in American mobility: with so constant a turnover of people there is no chance for the hardening of local speech peculiarities. With the big media every fresh coinage or usage or pronunciation found a vast, capturable audience with which to make its way throughout the nation. Especially through TV, where the spoken word is memorably associated with a screen image, the big media have had a standardizing effect on American speech. The uniformity of speech must not, of course, be overstressed. In his "Second Supplement" to *The American Language,* H. L. Mencken gives a state-by-state roundup of homespun terms which are so local that they sound like gibberish to the rest of the nation; but the fact that this was considered a labor of affectionate erudition is in itself proof that the local diversities are marginal rather than central.

One can also overstate the separateness of the "American language" as a whole. The structure of the language spoken in America is very much like the structure of English. The basic vocabulary is the same and there is a common freightage of literary association. The differences of pronunciation are considerable, but no greater between Americans and British than (let us say) between Americans in Mississippi and in Brooklyn. Where then do the great differences lie? They do not lie in the language seen as a structure or as an instrument of literature or ideas. There is still a common literary vehicle, in which the American of John Dewey differs little from the English of Bertrand Russell, and even the American of Sinclair Lewis differs little from the English of H. G. Wells. The chief differences lie in the idiomatic vocabulary that makes up a large part of the spoken language, especially as used in the big media. They lie in rhythms and inflections, in energy intensity, in the everyday (nonliterary) associations of everyday words. What is chiefly different between the English and American languages is the common speech in its everyday usage—American speech viewed as an expressive emotional instrument.

A people's speech is the skin of its culture. It contains the indigenous vocabulary, the inflections of meaning, the tricks of rhythm, the nuances of association, that give the members of the culture the sense of belonging together and being marked off from those who use different words, rhythms, inflections, connotations. It contains—to use a military figure— the symbolic strategies that make the "we" seem superior to the "they" —a superiority that is part of the psychology of cultural nationalism. The language of American speech is, as I have said, not separate enough from the English to be called with justice an independent language. But the whole complex bundle of intangibles, which are not so much a language as a speech, forms something as distinct from the parent English as American culture is distinct from the parent culture.

Nor is it hard to see how the separateness came about. The Americans had the English language and literature to start from, yet the heritage came from a culture to which they owed no allegiance after the Revolution. Thus American speech started off with the ingredients at once of tradition and innovation, of discipline and freedom. The political release from colonialism demanded a cultural release too. Frontier farmers and backwoodsmen, land prospectors and speculators, preachers and teachers, promoters and lawyers, peddlers and country storekeepers, forge workers and innkeepers, canal bargemen, steamboat pilots, and railroad construction gangs, country editors, newspaper reporters, shrewd young men making their fortunes in the cities, storytellers—by mid-nineteenth century all of these had built a speech with an idiom, a rhythm, a pace, an inflection, a vigor and tang of its own. It was separated by more than an ocean from the speech of the England of Anne and William and Victoria. The Americans sensed that they were shaping something with a fertility and energy of its own and treated it as a plastic instrument rather than as a classical heritage.

The homespun quality of the speech found its way into the newspapers in the late eighteenth century, into the country stores and the city streets, into Andy Jackson's talk and Abe Lincoln's anecdotes. Royal Tyler's play, *The Contrast,* depicted the gap in character and dialect between the British and the Americans. Some forty years after Tyler, Augustus Longstreet was among the first who made the spoken everyday language of Americans into a first-rate sensitive literary instrument. Lowell's *Biglow Papers* and Harriet Stowe's early short stories put New England dialect into literature. Dialect became a kind of fad in the 1880s: Mark Twain wrote the whole of *Huckleberry Finn* in dialect. But while it was amusing to the buyers and readers of books, it was not a fad for those who used it; it was their speech. Yet the writers had a function to perform. Once they had done their work, it was clear that victory had been won and that the decisive battles would never have to be fought again. There was no longer the danger that America might suffer the fate of Europe at the end of the Middle Ages, when men wrote and read in the language of the educated classes but spoke in the plebeian tongues of the new nationalities.

To be sure, some of the greatest writing by Americans was still to be done in the classical English literary tongue, and men like Henry James could make a supple literary instrument of it. Among the academic thinkers and editorial writers, political orators and literary Brahmins, the official literary language and rhythm (the "mandarin style") continued to be used without much infiltration from daily popular experience. This was more than made up by the way the popular arts embraced the new vigor of the American speech. The short story, the movie script, the vaudeville skit, the musical comedy, the newspaper column, the mystery thriller, the crime and sports reporting, the radio gagster—all came under the spell of the new idiom that had been shaped by the rhythms and mintage of American speech. Without this richness, the popular arts could not have gained their hold on Americans. Even the formal art of the novel was transformed, as witness Anderson, Lewis, Lardner, Hemingway, Farrell, Faulkner, Steinbeck, O'Hara, James Cain, Nelson Algren—to name writers widely removed in method and artistry, yet all of whom have become masters of American speech. From other genres one thinks of Hammett and Chandler, Odets and Arthur Miller and Kober, Mencken and Don Marquis, Sandburg, Broun and Damon Runyon, of Cole Porter and Hammerstein, of Ogden Nash and Perelman, and one gets a sense of a remarkably plastic language instrument that need not be cut away from the speech of the people in order to be of use to the literary craft. For American speech does not have to be split into fragments and recombined, as Joyce tried to do to the exhausted literary language of his culture in order to squeeze a desperate freshness from it. New words have cropped up out of American speech faster than they could be absorbed, so that many of them (as witness the researches of Mitford Mathews in his *Dictionary of Americanisms*) have been stuck in historical blind alleys. But every word that has survived has borne a fragment of the great hyperbolic myth of the American experience.

These accessions of richness came at first from frontier living and from the savage exaggerations and the bragging stories that grew with the opening of a continent. Then they came from the life of the growing cities, from miners, steel workers, and lumberjacks, from casual workers and stevedores, from war and the Armed Services, from the criminal rackets and from the lawless margins of business. Finally they came from big-audience sports, from the stage and the movies, and the radio, from popular music and jazz and the dance, from the stock markets and the trade-unions. The new words (and the new uses of old words) generally emerge from the routines of some pursuit, or from some sport or art which a few people follow with the devotion of *aficionados*. They may at the start form only a sort of jargon. But by an osmosis the jargon seeps through the general popular language to people who would never dream of mingling in the activities (crime, racketeering, gambling, vaudeville, burlesque, hot music, prize fighting) from which the new words or new uses first came.

The secret of the vigor of American speech is that the physical and social fluidity of American life have opened the sluices for a similar fluidity of American speech. In hierarchical societies the class strata operate to split the language of the culture into layers of language—clerical and secular, literary and vernacular, aristocratic and plebeian. But the openness of the American open-class system kept such divisions from rigidifying. Here was one creative activity in which even the humblest man could take a hand. The fashioning of American speech is the most popular of the popular arts since it admits of the widest participation, with no admission fee charged except a questing tongue, a feel for metaphor and color, and a bit of boldness in experimenting. Whatever other genius may be denied to the collective American spirit, the genius of the language surely belongs to it.

I do not mean to underestimate the conservative influences that have operated on American speech. The strongest is that of localism. Despite the great geographical mobility of Americans, the speech habits of the region and even the locality into which they move will in time shape the phrasing and pronunciation of the newcomers. A New England family settling in the South takes on the Southern dialect and intonation. It is surprising how clearly many of the contemporary American dialects can be traced back to England, and how little influence the large, non-English-speaking immigrant population has had on them. The American local dialects have been less tenacious than the English, partly because English history over a thousand years has covered a period when roads were bad and communication difficult, while American speech has been shaped for the greater part of its history in an age of rapid communication. As Donald Lloyd puts it, it has "leapfrogged" its way across the continent—yet, he adds, so great is the strength of localism in speech that one can draw lines, especially with respect to vocabulary, around California towns that are less than a half century old. Pronunciation is also largely local or regional.

The concept of American "speech communities," which Lloyd and Warfel have suggested in their *American English in Its Cultural Setting*, sheds a good deal of light on the differences within the larger structure of American speech. One can see America as a cluster of speech communities set apart from one another, each using subtle clues of language to detect and exclude outsiders and to make the insiders more cohesive and more comfortable with one another. Cutting across them, one should also distinguish professional (as on radio and TV) from conversational, and literary speech from the functional speech of people who must find a language for the material they deal with. One must reckon in addition with the conservative influence of the schools, which continue to resist innovations whenever the teacher can spot them. The "educated" American has a "correctionist" bent, both for his own speech and that of others: in the language democracy of America every man is a judge of language, yet if he pretends to an education he is a bit frightened about his judgment. As Americans move up the educational ladder, they move further away from the speech of ordinary people. Yet that speech has entered their lives nonetheless. They have no way of knowing what words that come to mind as they speak come from the literary tradition and what words from the speech community in which they move.

One clue to the strength of American speech is found in the relative absence of rigid principles of "correctness." There is an illustration of this in the animating spirit of the three great volumes of H. L. Mencken's *American Language*. Mencken had two basic principles in his work: that of studying American speech inductively, to find how it was actually spoken instead of how it ought to be spoken; and to scorn any notion of authoritative standards in language, other than the actual usage of the common speech. It was a curious paradox that the writer who had fought a crusade against popular democracy in politics and economics should have embraced in linguistics the principles of *vox populi, vox dei*. Since his time other students of American speech have followed the same emphasis, although one detects in them (as indeed in Mencken also) a certain snobbism in the ironic way in which they celebrate the victory of the barbarian mass. Most Americans have rejected authoritarianism here as elsewhere and have followed in the language wherever their daily experience, their image-making impulses, and the deep currents of their striving have led them. If they have thereby missed achieving an Alexandrian purity of speech, they have also largely avoided the film of gentility which after some centuries of history covers a language and presages linguistic and cultural stagnation.

There remains the question of the standard to be followed in appraising the validity of new coinages of speech even when academic standards are rejected. One can say that some change in grammar and syntax or some new word has met the inductive standards when it has come into general use. The final test is the naturalistic one of survival. Many new coinages never achieve currency and die from disuse. Among others that do, there are often shoddy or clumsy, pretentious or synthetic words. Mencken has some delightful passages on what he calls "scented" words

—such as, *realtor* for real-estate agent, *mortician* for undertaker, or *sanitary engineer* for plumber. Similarly, salesmanship has introduced the use of *contact* as a verb, while advertising has contributed *cost-wise* or *audience-wise*. These are the product of the streams of argot that flow into the language from every American activity. They are often adopted most quickly by those who hanker for gentility in speech or who pick up every linguistic fad in the hope of seeming sophisticated. What are usually called "vulgarisms," such as *it's me* or the use of the double negative, represent strong undercurrents of popular impulse which are bound to triumph despite the resistance of the educated classes. But the scented words and the pretentious argot of the genteel or the self-conscious (take, as a recent instance, the use of "fulsome" in the sense of "abundant") give American speech a quality of phoniness as the price it pays for opening its doors to all inventions. There are signs of the emergence of a new language of gentility, befitting an overwhelmingly middle-class society, in which workers have been replaced by salesmen and the insecurities of status make the newly successful people anxious to wear their words as badges of belonging.

We may speak of three classes of additions to the language: there are *functional words*—technical, occupational, or scientific, which make their way as effective short cuts to meaning, like "megabuck" from the new science of atomic production; there are *exuberant words,* notably in the coinage of the teen-agers and the jive and hepcat set; finally, there are *synthetic words,* the product of cerebral inventiveness rather than of life energies in the culture. The scented words and other strainings for gentility of effect belong in the last of these categories.

This raises the question of how long American speech will maintain its vigor and its principles of growth. The fact that it still has them is shown by the way the language has spread its influence to the twelve corners of the earth and attracted the imitation of young people everywhere. There is scarcely a non-English-speaking country, whether in Asia or Africa, Europe or Latin America, in which the desire to learn English has not become an urgent one: it is as if the legend of America's wealth and influence had made it a kind of *lingua franca* over a large part of the globe—a "second language" for the educated, an aspiration for young people who have not had a chance at it.

But as the big media become the principal carriers of linguistic invention, an element of falseness far more dangerous than vulgarity of taste is coming to pervade that invention. Like the eighteenth-century court ladies in France who affected the simplicity of Rousseau's milkmaids, the grandees of American cultural commercialism are trying to make a good thing of the phony posturings. They affect a nativist mucker pose or cultivate a racy extremism of jargon which often makes them unintelligible as well as synthetic. Listen to what some of the highly paid script writers dream up for the big radio comedians. Try to follow a disk jockey on the air dishing out a "hot" record with the faded remnants of the Basin Street patois. Pick up any of the "hard-boiled" mysteries, its pages larded with the effort to duplicate the staccato mouthings of a down-at-the-heels sleuth. In all these you will get a febrile jargon contrived for money, loaded with the artificiality of a literary language but without its discipline and taste.

I do not mean to overestimate the effect of the big media on American speech. To be sure, writers, announcers, actors, and commentators working in these media are deeply affected by each other. But most of their listeners are less affected by what they hear than by the usage which is rooted in their daily life and work. Isolated words and phrases are given rapid and vast currency by TV, radio, and movies, but pronunciation and idiom grow out of conversation, and you cannot converse with a TV set. The real danger is that the synthetic may be substituted for the authentic roots of popular speech. American writers are in danger of forgetting that what gave strength to Longstreet's *Georgia Scenes* or Mark Twain's *Huckleberry Finn*, George Ade's *Fables in Slang* or Ring Lardner's *You Know Me, Al* was that the language of each had been lived by millions of people before it was re-created by the individual artist. Many of the literary artifacts of latter-day America seem to have been lived by no one. Their world is of cardboard and paste, flimsy and uninhabitable; there is no smell of earth in it and no commonalty. It is contrived without ever having been experienced, and its only life is the hothouse and penthouse life of those who, in their eagerness for the sophistication of the moment, seek pathetically to imitate the imitators.

The fault does not lie in popularization. Actually the brashness, the tongue-in-cheek satire, and the quality of wild and unashamed hyperbole are exactly what gives strength to a language. What is wrong with many of the recent affectations in American speech is not that they are too much but that they are too little the speech of the people.

4. Spectator and Amateur Sports

SPORTS DO FOR the popular culture of America what "circuses" did for the Roman culture at the height of the Empire. They let the populace take part in a crucial ritual that binds them to one another and to the culture. Every people, no matter how civilized, must have a chance to yell for blood. Americans express this barbarism daily in their gladiatorial arts—in acting as spectators and psychic participants while other men fight, wrestle, and race with one another, break through human walls to make a goal in football, on ice, or in basketball arenas, hit a ball hard and race out its return.

Compared with some other historical civilizations, the ritualized violence of the American gladiatorial arts is pretty thin. There are no Carthaginian or Aztec human sacrifices to watch, no Latin bullfights, no guillotinings such as once sickened Tolstoy in Paris, no public hangings such as the British once had, no cockfights or bear fights (except on the early frontier or as survivals in the mountain areas today), no battles to the death between Roman gladiators, no mangling of men by lions. What cruelty there is in American culture is reflected less in its spectator sports than in any other of the pugnacious civilizations of history. Only wrestling, boxing, and (to some extent) football and ice hockey remain brutal, and the most ruthless of these—wrestling—has been converted into a TV buffoonery. The prize fights have had their murderousness muted since the days when frontier bullies fought catch-as-catch-can or two toughs pounded each other with bare knuckles for as many as fifty or sixty rounds. As the gladiatorial arts have become big industries, the brutal in them has been diminished and the spectacle accented.

But these spectator sports are balanced in America by a network of participant sports in which people pursue their amateur skills actively and almostly obsessively. This requires leisure, with whose development the history of American sports has been tied up. In earlier America, while work was still a life goal, fun was largely restricted to recreation at working-bees or the amenities of church socials, while on the frontier it took the form of heavy drinking and rough games. In a culture where farming exacted a round-the-clock attention to chores and factory hours were long, leisure for organized sports was rare. "Pastimes" imply that there is time to pass with them; spectator sports require purchasing power for admission—that is to say, a surplus after the necessities of life have been met. The increasing industrial productivity, by cutting down the working day and raising living standards, made both possible.

But before the big audience could find sports to watch, or the mass armies of amateurs could find sports to pursue, there had to be games carrying prestige that would furnish pyschic pleasure. This happened when the American wealthy lost their sense of guilt about "conspicuous leisure" and began to develop horse racing, polo, yachting, and golf as the sports of aristocrats. One of the early games the rich took up was baseball. But they could not keep it long as their coteried possession. By mid-nineteenth century baseball became a mania, by the 1880s a big business. The same thing happened to football, which started as the monopoly of the Eastern colleges. Fishing, hunting, bowling, lawn tennis, golf, all went through the sequence of being started by the fashionable and genteel, then becoming a diversion of the middle class, and finally a popular sport.

How far America has come away from sports as a leisure-class pursuit may be measured by the fact that Veblen's *Theory of the Leisure Class,* at the turn of the century, spoke of sports as an upper-class obsession, uncherished by the working class. His contention was that sports are a form of arrested emotional development, a survival of barbaric prowess, consisting of a "proximate workmanship and an ultimate futility." The fact is that the gladiatorial arts have become more necessary to the middle and lower classes than to the rich. The rich still have their exclusive sports—fox hunting, yachting, polo. But the elite sports of yesterday are becoming the mass sports of today: golfers swarm over municipal links, tennis is played everywhere, horse racing and greyhound racing have been taken over by the pari-mutuel betting system, and even sailing has now been opened to a large middle class. As the lower and middle classes got money and leisure they used it on entertainment to get a direct or vicarious sense of bodily prowess. What they want in a spectator game is action, excitement, speed, and power. By these standards racing, basketball, and ice hockey are the sports moving up, and even the "national game" of baseball is stodgy by comparison.

The change of scale in the mass spectator sports has brought with it also a change of phase. Much the same thing has happened to sports as to the big media: they have become adjuncts of Big Organization and the Big Money. It has proved difficult in games like football, basketball, and tennis to retain even the outward forms of amateurism. Whole industrial hierarchies have been built around the national reputation of some tennis or football star—outfitting firms, sports equipment, auxiliary children's souvenirs, the newspaper sports pages, and the new profession of sports writing. In the case of college football, what was once a contest of prowess between young players has been transformed into a struggle of strategies between highly paid coaches who instruct their players on every possible move, leaving them only the refinements of execution. In professional baseball, what the "fans" regard as the triumph of particular stars is often the result of an elaborate system of baseball "farms" and a heavy money investment that makes the assemblage of talent possible. Thus the repetitive pennant and World Series triumphs of the New York Yankees may be seen at least in part as the triumph of Big Business organization applied to the task of developing pitching and hitting power.

The fun industries (not including betting) are estimated to cost about ten billion dollars a year, and the figure may be low. The amount spent on minor sports like golf and motorboating equals the box-office receipts of the movies. On bowling alone the estimates vary from a quarter to three quarters of a billion, spent by twenty million bowlers. As for horse racing, the important figures relate to betting. The estimate is that six billion dollars a year is bet on the races, and almost an equal amount on baseball, especially on the World Series. Clearly, this is a big jump from the little groups on the frontier that gathered around the bear pit or the cock pit, or the aristocratic spectators who gathered at their watering spas or watched horse trotting. The sports themselves have become the narrow base of a top-heavy structure of the box-office and the betting industries.

The striking fact about this is that the commercialism of the spectator sports does little to trouble the American public, who take in their stride the fact that baseball, football, basketball, and boxing have become Big Business. In fact, they are the more inclined to value them for that reason and are pleasurably excited when a popular idol like DiMaggio receives a salary running into six figures. This gave him a standing in the Pantheon, just as Eddie Arcaro got it by the purses he brought in as a jockey, or Joe Louis by his winnings as a heavyweight fighter.

One of the instructive episodes in this connection is the history of the futile attempts to ban the "reserve clause" in baseball contracts as a vestige of the preindustrial peonage system on which baseball as a big business is built. In the Gardella case, which came to the U.S. Court of Appeals in 1949, Judge Jerome Frank commented wryly that "if players are regarded as quasi-peons, it is of no moment that they are well paid; only the totalitarian-minded will believe that higher pay excuses virtual slavery." But little emerged from the efforts to restrain this throwback to a feudal system under the antitrust laws—although in 1957 the Supreme Court, in a decision involving professional football, hinted that it might have second thoughts about the whole subject. The baseball fan does not seem shocked by the fact that his favorite sport rests on a system of chattel contracts by which players lose their right to bargain in a free labor market, being "bought," "sold," and "swapped." Sometimes this even cuts the deeply ingrained loyalties of the fans, as in 1956 when Jackie Robinson was sold to the New York Giants and his devoted Brooklyn Dodger followers had to contemplate either abandoning him or transferring their allegiance to a hated enemy. When Ty Cobb appeared before the Celler Congressional Committee to defend peonage in baseball, no Congressman dared challenge him, for Cobb as hero symbol embodied the whole array of sentimental loyalties—of the players, the fans, and the bettors—which give the spectator sports their mass hold.

The psychic basis of American mass sports is tribal and feudal. Baseball is a good example of the modern totem symbols (Cubs, Tigers, Indians, Pirates, Dodgers, and Braves) and of sustained tribal animosities. The spectator is not *on* the team, but he can be *for* the team; he identifies himself with one team, sometimes with one player who becomes a jousting champion wearing his colors in a medieval tournament. Hence the hero symbolism in American sports and the impassioned hero worship which makes gods of mortals mediocre in every other respect, and gives them the place among the "Immortals" that the French reserve for their Academy intellectuals.

There is a stylized relation of artist to mass audience in the sports, especially in baseball. Each player develops a style of his own—the swagger as he steps to the plate, the unique windup a pitcher has, the clean-swinging and hard-driving hits, the precision quickness and grace of infield and outfield, the sense of surplus power behind whatever is done. There is the style of the spectator also: he becomes expert in the ritual of insult, provocation, and braggadocio; he boasts of the exaggerated prowess of his team and cries down the skill and courage of the other; he develops sustained feuds, carrying on a guerilla war with the umpires and an organized badinage with the players, while he consumes mountains of ritual hot dogs and drinks oceans of ritual soda pop.

Each sport develops its own legendry, woven around the "stars" who become folk heroes. The figures in baseball's Hall of Fame have their sagas told and retold in newspapers and biographies, and the Plutarchs who recount exploits become themselves notable figures in the culture. Some of these sports writers later become political columnists, perhaps on the assumption that politics itself is only a sport riddled with greater hypocrisy and that it takes a salty and hard-hitting sports writer to expose the politicians. The sports heroes become national possessions, like the Grand Canyon and the gold in Fort Knox. It is hard for a people who in their childhood have treasured the sports legendry as a cherished illusion to surrender it when they grow up.

Each sport also forms a kind of subculture within itself, which a curious anthropologist could profitably study. The stars become life models for Americans who have played sand-lot baseball as kids and dreamed of striking out Babe Ruth or hitting like Ted Williams. This is important among the ethnic groups in slum areas where boxing and baseball give Irish, Jewish, Italian, Polish, and Negro boys a greater chance at a career, and where a boy who has made good in the ring or at Big League ball becomes the focus of the role-playing of all the neighborhood youngsters. The street-corner gangs in the tough neighborhoods serve as training and recruiting grounds for pugilists, and boxing—and to some extent baseball and football—become not only ways of getting into the big money but also of channeling the emotional tensions of lower-status groups in the society. This is especially true of

Negro players who have finally been admitted into Big League baseball and the bowling tournaments but are still kept out of golf and tennis tournaments. Negro sports figures like Joe Louis and Jackie Robinson become not only national heroes but ethnic symbols of prowess and progress.

The point at which mass sports have violated the ingrained mores of the public is on the question of bribery. Americans have long been accustomed to the crookedness of the Yahoos of wrestling and have written it off as a serious sport. In the second decade of the century there were several scandals involving the "throwing" of games by bribed baseball players which led to a rigid supervision of the morals and public relations of the teams under Judge K. M. Landis as baseball "Czar." This system of internal policing enabled Big League baseball to survive and thrive. In the 1940s similar episodes developed in big-college basketball, with evidence that players had been bribed to rig games. Actually corruption of this kind is only marginal to the betting industries, which on the whole do best financially when the games are honest. But what is not marginal is the fact that even where everything is "straight" the fun and excitement of sports have been largely crowded out by commercialism. The capital investments not only in Big League professionalism but even in the college stadiums, the clinking of gate receipts, the noise the totalizers make, have all become too insistent to be ignored.

A realistic sports writer, hearing for the thousandth time about the "clean ideals" and "manly virtues" of sports, will reflect that even in the colleges the rhetoric of amateurism has given way under the steady pressures of "big-time" spectator performances. President Hutchins made a sardonic guess that his quarter-century tenure as head of the University of Chicago would be remembered chiefly by the fact that he banned college football. A number of colleges have a structure of hidden subsidies for recruiting their football players and maintaining and tutoring them while at college. When one former college president, Dexter Keezer of Reed, ironically proposed that the college convert the hidden subsidies into open ones and hire the best football team it could get, paying the players as well as the coaches, he was taken seriously and swamped by applications. There is a logical progression from these subsidies to the game-throwing episodes: if you are furtively recruited and bribed to play well, it is only a step to being bribed to play badly. What is striking is not that so many but that so few young Americans succumb. This is a tribute to the hold that amateur sports still have on the imagination of the young. After the pattern of Ring Lardner's biting short stories, the baseball player has been depicted in fiction chiefly as a zoological specimen whose brawn exceeds his intellect. What is more impressive, however, is the degree to which the player becomes emotionally involved in his pursuit, so that a loose collection of raw-bound young men is forged into a smoothly functioning team unit.

Moralists and psychologists have made too much of the passivity of spectator sports. America has been treated by them a little like a "condemned playground," doomed as Roman culture was doomed by the mass pursuit of pleasure for its own sake and by its passive spectator role. True, the people in modern societies preferred to seek external entertainment rather than to explore their inner resources. True also, the cult of American sports may delay maturity, keeping many of its devotees frozen as eternal juveniles. But there are few parallels in history to an American culture which was presented overnight with the gift of leisure, not just to one class but to almost the entire culture. Americans have found in sports a set of loyalties that in past cultures have been linked with more destructive pursuits. They have also found in it a kind of substitute for an urban culture's loss of relation to the natural environment.

One may argue, as Plato did, that the youth of any society carries on in its civic life the modes of behavior it learns in its sports. In that sense Americans have come to view politics and war as games after the image of competitive sports. The image of the team whose players work together under a captain or quarterback has been carried over into the popular thinking. One may assert, on the other hand, with Aristotle, that the real function of sports is not emulative but purgative. It is a familiar theory that spectator sports strengthen American democracy by serving as a safety valve for tensions and emotions that might otherwise have broken into flames of violence.

Beyond these theories is the fact that American sports express the energies of the culture as a whole and the will-to-youthfulness of its people. Sometimes this takes ugly forms of expression, as with bullying and bottle-tossing fans. Sometimes it is expressed in a manic ferocity, as with Branch Rickey's description of the ideal ballplayer as one who "will break both your legs if you happen to be standing in his path to second base." Again it may take on the tinny values of the box office or the press agents. Sometimes it gets mixed up with gamblers, racketeers, and crooks, or with the fake heroics of what has been called the "grunt-and-groan business" in wrestling. Yet spectator sports are saved by a cultural vitality which both audience and players express.

The most hopeful fact about American sports is that they have reached their saturation point as passive spectacles, and that their growing point is now in the area of amateur participant sports. In sports, as also in writing, painting, photography, theater, carpentry, crafts, cooking, and dressmaking, America is becoming a nation of amateurs. The recruits for Rose Bowl football and for Big League baseball are taken from the sand-lot ball games of the kids and the skeleton football scrimmages at school and on the city streets. In the social climate of the mass sports, young Americans wrestle, race, swim, fight with their fists; in many localities high-school basketball has become a community passion. But beyond this recruiting base that the culture gives the spectator sports, there is also a new emphasis on direct participation of adults in forms of organized play and fun. The new leisure has made the beaches swarm with swimmers and sun worshipers; in winter the ski trains carry middle-class groups who never before had taken part in winter sports; golf has been largely transferred from the private links to municipal courses which make it available to almost any income group; with the automobile to transport them to formerly inaccessible streams, fishing has become possible for many new millions; in terms of the numbers engaged, bowling has become the top American national sport, reaching into the factory and offices of the corporations, each of which has bowling teams belonging to the industrial bowling leagues.

This has given sports amateurism a new meaning, broader than the earlier sense which made an amateur a steady contestant who could afford not to sell his services. Amateurism in this older meaning has been declining rather than increasing in the commercial context of big American sports. The true amateurs have become the men and women who pursue sports in their leisure because they love them and find in them new accessions of experience and a play of bodily skills which the machine culture fails to use. This may bring a psychic fulfillment more far-reaching than is involved in the theory of the spectator sports as a safety valve for tensions and frustrations. A people that finds an expressiveness at play too often denied on the job is less likely to be capturable by mass emotions. Thus the growth of sports amateurism acts as a counterforce to the more synthetic entertainments and hero worship engendered by the spectacle sports.

It is probably true that Americans will never develop in their sports the kind of ritual meaning and religious symbolism that makes the bullfight in Spanish cultures express the tragic meaning of life. The genius of American sports is a different one. It expresses exuberant energies rather than a killer instinct or a death obsession. It is suited to a people who feel that careers are open for skill and resourcefulness, and that life with its unlimited possibilities yields both the big prizes to the professional and a quieter satisfaction to the amateur.

5. *Dream and Myth in the Movies*

NEVER IN HISTORY has so great an industry as the movies been so nakedly and directly built out of the dreams of a people. Any hour of the day or the evening you can go into a darkened theater (the darkness is in itself like a dream withdrawal) and as the figures move across the wide screen you sail off on storm-tossed seas of sex, action, and violence, crime and death. The "super-colossal" is at your disposal. The loveliest girls (voluptuously feminine), the most "romantic" men (blatantly masculine), the most stylish clothes, the shapeliest legs and most prominent bosoms—these are yours with an explicitness that leaves nothing subtle to be supplied. When you come home to sleep, your dreams are woven around the symbols which themselves have been woven out of your dreams, for the movies are the stuff American dreams are made of.

New standards of living and taste have leveled up the masses and leveled down the elite into a vast movie-going audience that is more complex emotionally than the movie makers suspect, but homogeneous enough to serve as an abstract "average man" in their calculations. This audience has the thin taste of experience that marks the new American middle classes. They go to the movies not so much to get a compensation for what they have lost emotionally as to get a surrogate for what they have not yet achieved but know to be possible in their world. Thus, the movies are dreams but not necessarily "escape" dreams; they may also be ambition-and-attainment dreams. It is impossible that a people should reach for new living standards without at the same time reaching for new emotional experiences.

The trouble is that emotional richness and depth cannot be attained mechanically, especially in a civilization dominated by the practical and the pecuniary. You cannot distribute it as you might distribute Pepsi-Cola, the electric light, radio, comic books, or universal suffrage. The thirst for it is there, and when thousands of screens offer to slake the thirst the people are receptive. But they are not "escaping" from anything; they are reaching out. By their essential technique the movies make this possible: the camera picks out for the audience the elements of a scene, getting its emotional effects by selection and sequence of shots and by their pace and rhythm as they unfold a story; it can weave together past and present, annihilate time and bridge space; by varying "close-ups" with long shots, by showing the individual face and framing the total scene, it builds up tension and evokes a continuous flow of absorption; it reaches to the instinctual in man, cutting across nations and cultures; it appeals to the emotional and imaginative elements in our make-up as no other popular art has ever done.

This is what makes the movies a crucial American popular art, although in economic terms the industry is slipping. The press is stronger in shaping attitudes, the radio in reaching more people more quickly, TV in bringing a more varied world into their homes. But because they alone deal in a sustained way with dreams and fables, the movies maintain their role in America. If TV is to displace them it must first take over this dream function they possess.

The movies started as a peep show in the Edison slot machines that were housed in penny arcades. They shifted to the status of lantern slides in illustrated lectures, and finally won an independent audience in telling a connected story with the "nickel madness" of the "nickelodeons" that swept America in the first decade of the century. The Founding Fathers of the new industry were men who, by an historical accident, came mainly out of the clothing industry of the Eastern cities, largely Jews of lower-middle-class virtues and energies, intent on success and wealth. Almost at its start the new medium brought into the studio the central figure of the great directors, like D. W. Griffith, and a technical inventiveness which included the resourceful use of the camera and lighting, the crucial "close-up" bringing the actor into immediate relation with the audience, and the technique of film cutting, enabling the director to shoot his picture out of sequence and then put it together as a writer might put a novel together with structure and flow and climax.

From the start the pace of innovation in the movies was exacting. The crude early sentimental "drama" was converted into a full-length "feature," the one-reel thriller became the double-feature evening's entertainment, the slapstick comedy grew more subtle, the "star" system was introduced, with actors and actresses who became popular idols, the silent movies were revolutionized with sound, an elaborate system of distributors and exhibitors was developed, color was introduced, and under the spur of TV rivalry the movies turned to three-dimensional gadgets and the wide screen. At each stage the movie makers were obsessed with a sense of crisis, and—once successful—each step brought with it an elation which in turn gave way to another depth of despair. The movies have thus in their brief history had an almost manic-depressive succession of emotional states, feeding on the pressure of technological change and on the need to outdistance the competing big media, feeling the audience pulse, taking the temperature of an often hostile public which regards Hollywood as the seat of Satan.

What Justice Brandeis called "the curse of bigness" afflicted the movies as it afflicted the other big media. Since the industrial problem in the movies was largely one of distribution, the bigness showed itself mainly in getting control of the theater outlets. The first big "film exchange" was dissolved by the Federal courts in 1915. In the 1920s the producing companies achieved control of the theater chains and in turn became "integrated" with the manufacturers of sound equipment and the big banking houses who could find capital for the pictures which poured out inexorably at steep production costs. The Federal courts again stepped in to effect a degree of separation of the producers from the theater chains and to ban "block booking." Yet the movies differ from the press and radio industries since they do not pose primarily a problem of monopoly and its control. Although the giant producers have dominated the industry, the competitive struggle between them has been genuine, and there has always been a chance for the rise of "independents" and recently for the competition of foreign-made films.

The problem of the movies is not the power of the producers nor the silencing of competing voices, but the content and emotional level of the product. This in turn is linked with the quest for profits and the evaluation of the tastes and demands of the audience. The makers of the movies may consider them an art form, but even when they do, they think of it as an art that must be mediated through an industry that produces and sells a commodity. Whatever their origin, the movies have become one of the nation's biggest industries, with high salaries for producers, directors and stars, with experts for production, processing, distributing, selling, advertising and promotion, with a network of theater outlets reaching into city and village, and with a huge apparatus for exporting American movies to every corner of the globe.

The aim of the movie makers, as in other industries, is to make a profit on their investment. When a first-rate movie, *The Treasure of the Sierra Madre,* got an Academy Award but failed to gross even half of what a Betty Grable picture achieved, its producer said decisively, "From now on, art is out." There are undoubtedly some producers and directors who think in terms of exacting art standards. But when they do, the clinching argument they use for their view is that good art pays off. When good movies are produced—and an impressive number of them have been—the masters of the industry must be convinced that they will pay off, and enough of them must do so before the directors are allowed to attempt others. The great Hollywood problem is to integrate money-making with creativeness: where the process of integration seems silly to the greedy, or difficult to the lazy, or beyond the reach of the uncreative, money-making stands alone and unashamed as a motive.

Despite the glamour that attaches to the stars, there is a deadly assembly-line monotony about Hollywood. The qualities of the industrial process in Hollywood are the qualities of any big American industry: machine-tool technology, division of labor, mass production, bureaucracy, hierarchy. The work is infinitely subdivided, specialized and mechanized as far as one can mechanize a process where the basic material is not molten iron and rivets and sheet steel but human beings and the pantomime and inflections of human emotions. The mechanization extends even to the writing of most scripts—galling as that may seem to writers who are attracted by Hollywood prizes but outraged by the Hollywood methods that put the prizes within their reach. For the original novel or play must be "licked"—that is to say, revamped and sometimes butchered to fit it to the demands of the screen and its market. It must be reworked by many hands until it contains the exactly right formula ingredients. The scenes must be broken into manageable units, each of them acted and re-enacted until it suits the director's taste, then cut and fitted together into the final product, embellished, embossed, labeled, and packaged. This is the process that gives the Hollywood movie the qualities for which it is noted—the precision, the attention to detail, the assembly-line smoothness, the pace, the feel of collaborative effort under a central direction, the gloss, the sensuousness—and the sameness.

Given this setup, it is not surprising that the principal creativeness emerging from Hollywood is that of the director (sometimes the director-producer). He is the interweaver, manipulator, and synthesizer of everything else. I am thinking of men like Kazan, Huston, Zinnemann, Stevens, Mankiewicz, Wyler, among the directors, and among the producers men like Thalberg, Goldwyn, Schary, and Zanuck. The director, himself doing none of the specialized work, stands outside the process yet somehow at the center of it. He pulls together the strands of what others have done, keeping in mind the mood and effect he is aiming at. He makes the decisions on theme and story, scope, expense, actors, treatment, pace, mood, emotional quality. He must assess the drawing power and staying power of the "stars" and take care of their temperaments, love affairs, and marital headaches. He must tangle with the censorship, determine the strategy of promotion, watch the publicity. The producer-director is the general who, unlike Kutuzov in *War and Peace*, genuinely believes that his generalship shapes the outcome of the battle. Scott Fitzgerald saw this when he wrote his novel about Hollywood, *The Last Tycoon*, and chose as his central character Monroe Stahr, a director-producer cast in the mold of Irving Thalberg.

This line-and-staff hierarchy of Hollywood, with its pyramiding of power and its constriction of creativeness for most of the people in-

volved, represents the greatest weakness of the Hollywood system. Fitzgerald's study of Stahr is on heroic lines: he invested the movie mogul
with a Napoleonic imagination and with a half-lyrical, half-theatrical
amatory life. He had a feeling of pity for Stahr, showing him caught
between labor troubles and financial conspiracies, yet he gave him a
touch of nobility as well as the grand manner. But Fitzgerald failed to
show the curious quality of Hollywood as a way of life, built Versailles-
fashion around a set of *grands monarques,* each surrounded by cour-
tiers, jesters, parasites, and favorites—a court where men rise by predacity and live in fear, half harem and half jungle. Hollywood in
this aspect is more nakedly shown in Budd Schulberg's *What Makes
Sammy Run?* and in Nathanael West's *The Day of the Locust,* whose
George Grosz portrait was, however, meant to apply more to the movie
audience than to the movie makers.

The pictures these men make tend to run in "cycles," for Hollywood
—being attuned to shifting audience moods as sensitively as a stylish
American woman is attuned to the changes in fashion—is a place where
successes and failures are contagious. The producers are anxious to
cash in on the winds and moods of the current taste, using always the
test of what has made a killing for others. Thus there was a gangster
cycle, an anti-Nazi cycle, a G-Man cycle, a Negro and Jewish antiracist
cycle, a cycle of sophisticated "Westerns," a war action cycle, an anti-
Communist cycle, a cycle of big Biblical panoramas, a musical-comedy
cycle, a cycle of "problem" movies on juvenile delinquency and dope
addiction. The idea men tap a vein of public response, and the imitators rush in to exploit it until the ore runs thin. Recently the emphasis
has come to rest on the musical and the spectacle. Both are safe, both
nonpolitical, both appeal to the young audience that frequents the
movie houses. Girls' legs, battle scenes, catchy tunes, dream-ballet se-
quences, Samson and Delilah, and the decadent days of the Roman or
Egyptian empires are material on which it is hard to go wrong.

Recently the impact of high taxes has led to a reversal of the trend
toward concentration in movie making. A number of new producing
units have emerged, built around one or several movie stars or a talented director. But the economics of the movie industry put pressure
on reducing the number of pictures and making only the "big" ones.
A picture must now reach into small cities as well as large ones, which
means that there must be a heavy concentration on advertising and
promotion. Thus the "middle bracket" pictures are being squeezed
out, and the studios operate increasingly on the "jackpot theory"—
either you hit the jackpot or you take a loss. The low-budget pictures,
the "sleepers," and the modest experiments of the independents still

have scope—enough, at any rate, to show that a movie addressed to emotionally mature men and women may also bring in profits.

The movie industry is at its best in its technical skill. Lighting and sound, cutting and editing, the building of sets—all of these command admiration. Wherever Hollywood offers a chance to do an honest job, it can be fulfilling. Every few years some team of youngsters shows up in Hollywood with an idea of how to make good low-cost pictures and brush aside the cluttering idols. But in time the young man who came with a fire in his belly comes under the spell of the practical men and grows accustomed to astronomical figures and comfortable living. He gets cut off from the original sources of his strength and ends by offering sacrifices to the fire in the belly of the Moloch of success.

Like other forms of American popular culture, Hollywood is a little world in itself—a subculture of the larger society, but with marked mirror distortions. It has strata of prestige and power, narrowing to a small top group who sit at the peak of the pyramid. They are the studio executives in charge of production. A mass of legendry clings to each of them, and what passes for conversation in Hollywood is likely to be anecdotes, gossip, and malice about them. Their royal position casts a deep shadow on Hollywood, for independent critical judgment is impossible where the employee must also be a courtier. A Hollywood "big shot" is surrounded by yes-men whose function is to give Number One the heady sense of being right. Where one man has the power of life and death there can be none of that responsibility which must mean taking risks in order to make independent choices. No one feels secure in his tenure—not even the top executives, who fear the intrigues of their rivals and the power of the bankers, and these in turn fear the whims and hostility of the movie audience.

The final decisions that affect creativeness are made in the "front office," with an eye on picture budgets that may run into millions of dollars. Everyone connected with a picture, including the director and script writers, knows that two or three million dollars may be at stake: as a result, no one takes risks with ideas, theme, treatment. The phrase "venture capital" has an ironic meaning when applied to Hollywood: since the capital being ventured is big, nothing else can be ventured. This is the nub of Hollywood's timidity. And timidity joins with bureaucracy and the money yardstick to form Hollywood's deadly trinity.

The movie colony is always in feverish motion, always coming up with "terrific" ideas for "colossal" successes; yet for all its febrile quality, it is always in danger of becoming stagnant. It isn't a metropolis, yet it feels too important to be content with the life of a small town

—nor could it even if it wished, since it is torn away from all the normal activities of a town. Thus Hollywood is one of the loneliest places in the world. The Communists were able to exploit this loneliness in the 1930s and early 1940s by offering the young writers and actors a continuous courtship and a cause to hang their hearts on.

To create what it does Hollywood has to draw young people, often of unstable temperament, from all over the world. It plunges them into exacting work, surrounds them with a sensuous life, pays them fantastic salaries, makes them truckle to their bosses or smothers them with the flattery of their hangers-on, cuts them off from the sources of normal living. Thus the men and women who manufacture dreams for other Americans find that there are few they can snare for themselves. The Hollywood heartbreak is of two kinds: that of not getting where you want to get; and that of finding, when you have got it, that it was not worth wanting. Gilbert Seldes hit it right when he spoke of the "high potential capacity for disaster" in Hollywood.

The most publicized and glamorized figure in Hollywood is, of course, the star. Few stars have more than mediocre acting ability. They are rather heroes and heroines—men and women who by their native endowment of figure, stature, and looks, some trick of grace or radiancy of personality, or by benefit of cosmeticians and publicity "build-up," have become the dream image of movie-goers. Among the icons in Hollywood have been Pola Negri, Mary Pickford, Rudolph Valentino, Douglas Fairbanks, Jean Harlow, Carole Lombard, Clark Gable, Humphrey Bogart, Rita Hayworth, Marlon Brando, Marilyn Monroe—and, of course, the greatest of all, Chaplin and Garbo. Below them in the hierarchy are the minor stars, the temporary "rages" who last for only a few seasons, the "starlets," the hopefuls. The radiance that invests a star has come to invest the whole of Hollywood with a career dream atmosphere for millions of young Americans.

The justification sometimes made of the star system is that the movies are not theater, and that the great movie figures may know how to act but they don't have to know, since the character each creates is not something out of a script but himself: it is with him, and not with the character he portrays, that the audience identifies itself. There is truth in this, and it applies equally to the clowns and heroes of radio and TV who enter familiarly into the American home. What the movie screen adds, with its annihilation of time, its illusions of space, and its selective weaving of dreams, is an emotional identification through the star with those dreams and with the magical world spun out of them. This gives the star system its hold on the audience—and on the star too, since it is a heady wine of adulation he drinks. One must add, however, that the younger Hollywood stars are not content to be symbols: a number of them have found on the Broadway stage the kind of craft satisfaction which the studios have failed to offer them, and some have preferred miniscule salaries on or off Broadway to the fleshpots of Sunset Boulevard. A number of them have been trained in the Actors Studio, have thought a good deal about acting, and care about the suffrage of their fellows and the critics even more than they do about their popular image. The greatest of the stars, like Chaplin and Garbo, or even Muni, Fredric March, or Edward G. Robinson, have also been good actors, although Garbo carried with her always the fringes of failure and was always promising more than she achieved. An illustration of how hungry the public is for a Hollywood image to worship may be found in the curious cult that developed after his death around James Dean (as it developed once around Valentino), although Dean starred in only three pictures before he was killed in a racing car on the California roads. With a wild but still unformed talent, he was a searching, puzzled, unhappy boy: his meteoric rise and his death were a life symbol, phoenix-wise, for many young Americans who shared his frustrations as well as his dreams.

But the prizes are few and most of those who are drawn to Hollywood and do not drift home again remain to work as "extras" on the Hollywood sets, or as waitresses or soda clerks or hat-check girls—in the hope that someday the lightning may strike. However foolish their dreams may seem they are not wholly foolish, for the movie arts are among the few remaining areas of American industry where talent can reach for the big money without a heavy prior investment. Yet this fact makes the competition ruthless: nothing is more pathetic than a fading star, like a faded mistress, striving to hold attention by ingenious wile and seductiveness. The Hollywood constellation is like a crowded streetcar, and every time a new luminary pushes its way on board it pushes a declining one off.

This may explain why Hollywood, with a tiny fraction of the nation's population, supports a large percentage of the nation's psychoanalysts. The sense of personal frustration along with public success takes its toll, especially among the actors and writers. The whole atmosphere is that of demonstrative sex. Bent on careers, some of them use their looks and magnetism as a way of getting a start, while the power men are ready to offer a chance at success in return for favors. Simone de Beauvoir's *The Second Sex* uses the Hollywood actress as the prime contemporary example of the hetaira. The American people, many of whom regard the movie colony as the Jezebel of America, eagerly consume the newspaper headlines about Hollywood divorces, suicides, marijuana parties, drinking, and premarital sex relations. In his survey of the social structure of Hollywood, Leo Rosten showed that while the Hollywood divorce rate is probably higher than the American average, the gap is not great. The public-relations men, who hover over their charges like male governesses, are anxious to play them up as spotless Sunday-school characters with every private and civic virtue. They err in this effort: the attraction that the Hollywood heroes have for movie-goers is not that of small-town Catos and Brutuses but that of flesh-and-blood men and women whose lives outwardly match the glossy lives on the screen.

There is obviously a strong relation between the themes of the American movies and the psychological drives in American life. Certainly the masters of Hollywood have tried to probe into the American personality pattern, playing up whatever gets a deep response. Unfortunately, while they mirror well the life values of the culture, they present them often with only a surface fidelity and repeatedly fall into stereotypes which can appeal only to the immature. All the traits of the culture are there in the movies, but dressed up, foreshortened, softened up, made more contrived by indirections and glossiness.

To start with, of course, the movies mirror the value and power of money. "There was money in her voice," said Scott Fitzgerald, and money continues to speak through most of the Hollywood products. There is money in Hollywood's voice, in the way the camera dwells on surfaces and textures. There is money in the lavish settings, whether of estate or hotel or penthouse suite: every picture says dutifully and explicitly that money is not everything, that money (in fact) doesn't count, that love and self-respect and happiness are better than money; but every picture continues to say implicitly, by all the things it takes for granted and by its own example, that nothing really counts quite as much as money.

As for sex, what the movies express (as Gilbert Seldes documented it) is not sex or love but sexiness. In formal terms an elaborate contrivance of self-censorship, called "The Code," bans the exposure of too large a surface of the female breast, or a male and female embrace in a horizontal posture. Yet obviously there is ample leeway for blatant sexiness set against provocative backdrops, or subtle sexiness encased in the silkiest adornments. Sometimes the battle of the censorship makes the producer ingenious in suggesting more than the picture seems to say, and inventive in seeing what he can get away with. The movies rarely express the passionate attraction of mature people for each other, such as may be found in some of the foreign films. This would be difficult in a Hollywood product, extramarital liaisons being forbidden on the screen. Since movie characters cannot be caught in any strong passion, since they have babies only for humorous effect, since divorces cannot be carried through and cannot be shown as having a valid base, since marital difficulties cannot be described in the full-blooded terms of people grappling with the genuine problems of a marriage, the result is that life is presented as a series of pretend entanglements which are resolved by pretend solutions, both of them applying to people whose lives are drained of emotional meaning.

In the absence of three-dimensional figures with strong emotions, the movies must turn to action as substitute. The movies do move fast. The art of cutting sees to it that each scene slips into the next and there is never a pause for contemplation. Things must be happening all the time—threats, quarrels, dangers, traps, narrow escapes, flights, reconciliations, falling in love, misunderstandings, courtroom scenes, gun battles, mob scenes, barroom brawls, escapes from moving trains, shipwrecks, death in the skies, automobile chases, the discovery of unexpected corpses, conspiracies, skulduggery, the confusing and unmasking of identities, deathbed confessions, the triumph of virtue. Rarely do they offer an internal exploration, and then it may be the tracing out of a split personality in connection with some mystery thriller. The American conquers as a man of action, he puts his faith in action, and he expects action in his movies.

To these ingredients must be added violence. It may be that the movies reflect the strain of interior violence and tension in the culture, yet it is grotesquely inflated. When genuine love and sexuality are crowded out of any literary or dramatic production, whether by censorship or timidity, violence comes in to fill the vacuum. Where there is no mature expression of the relation between the sexes, the "battle of the sexes" is presented in a bantering way, with strong overtones of masculine dominance. The earlier movies had treated women mainly as prize and idol, as temptress and siren. A landmark in the history of the movies came in the classic episode in *Public Enemy* when James Cagney pushed a grapefruit into the face of his girl. It was greeted as the reassertion of manly power in a society beset by female values. The violence theme also finds other outlets—the tyranny of a hard parent, a sadistic jail warden or ship captain, a gangland leader.

The strain of violence is reinforced by the toughness of the detective-hero in the crime and mystery thrillers, where the girl—although spoiled and sophisticated at the start—recognizes his strength in the end. The ingredients of the murder thriller, as of the racketeer or prize-fight movie, are slickness, pace, fast dialogue, and continuous violence. The movie detective does not have to be a mastermind. His story has become that of a hard-boiled Tom Jones who is no great shakes as a detector but who shows he can take whatever punishment is in store for him. Even his ordeals are physical rather than psychological. He meets with a succession of adventures that crowd in breathlessly, he is warned but persists, he is ambushed, slugged, kicked, tortured, given up for dead, he endures all with fortitude, and in the end he gets his man and—in another sense—gets his girl. His story is a picaresque of death. In the course of his adventures he discovers or creates as many as a half dozen corpses. Every death is an unevocative event—an item rather than a tragedy. It has neither psychic roots nor psychic consequences, just as the crimes themselves have no moral roots or consequences. This pervasive violence, with its need for ever stronger stimulation to produce a "thrill," may be a portent of the desensitizing of the society itself.

Wolfenstein and Leites, in their *Movies: A Psychological Study,* did a content-analysis by searching out not the overt but the covert meanings of American movies, not what was manifest in them but what was psychologically latent. While this can be stretched to the point of burlesque, it does rest on the sound proposition that the important relation of the movies is to the daydreams and the fantasy world of Americans. The producer may guess only blunderingly at these daydreams and is severely limited by censorship and his own timidity, so that the pattern that emerges may not represent his considered judgment of what the audience is like. He may not be knowing or cynical, but only a man who wants to make a lot of movies and a lot of money, and is deeply troubled—as David Selznick was—because the movie critics approach films as an art form. To succeed, Selznick argued, a movie producer must aim not only at the "common denominator" of the people but at their "lowest common denominator."

This does not mean that the movie industry has not produced some great pictures. Actually it is the only one of the American popular arts which has thus far built up a heritage of great artistic products to leave to future generations. One may include among these classics such diverse pictures as Griffith's *The Birth of a Nation,* Chaplin's *City Lights, Monsieur Verdoux,* and *The Gold Rush,* the Westerns like *High Noon* and *Bad Day at Black Rock,* comedies like *Born Yesterday, It Happened One Night,* and *Nothing Sacred,* detective mysteries like *The Thin Man,* and *The Maltese Falcon,* murder stories like *Double Indemnity,* gangster pictures like *Public Enemy* and *Earl of Chicago,* terror movies like *Night Must Fall,* documentary pictures of urban life like *The Asphalt Jungle,* war pictures like *Hell's Angels* and *The Red*

Badge of Courage, social documentaries like *Home of the Brave, The Men, Not as a Stranger,* and *The Wild One,* movies of character and adventure like *The Treasure of Sierra Madre* and *The African Queen,* character studies like *The Informer* and *Citizen Kane.* The list could be greatly extended without lowering the quality of what it includes. And no list would be complete without the inclusion of the wonderfully inventive cartoon pictures of Walt Disney, one of the geniuses of the popular arts, who created a world of his own in his nature studies as well as his animated cartoons.

It is curious that a medium capable of such work should be confronted by the fact of a declining audience. Yet thousands of movie theaters have recently had to close up, and the audiences are heavily weighted toward those under thirty-five and especially adolescents. A number of critics put the blame on the movie products, saying that movie fare presented on a higher intellectual and emotional level would tap an unreached audience of adult minds. David Riesman feels, however, that the older people may be staying away from the movies because they don't understand them and have not yet caught up with the younger ones who do. The argument is that recent changes in American society have changed the nuances of living together, bringing in new aspects of social experience which the movies express and which the young can grasp but the old must sweat for, since their minds are turned toward the past.

I agree that young Americans go to the movies not just to be amused but (more or less consciously) to get guidance in "interpersonal relations." But this only makes more urgent the question of what kind of guidance they get. It is hard not to conclude that the worlds of feeling and thought presented to them are imaginary worlds, using that phrase in the synthetic sense. There is little feeling for growth of personality and the painful groping for identity which the best novels give, and from which young Americans do get clues to their dilemmas. I suspect that the movies stereotype not only the solutions but even the problems, and that the young people who see them get even their dilemmas from them. In time such a process could result in real emotional matching of movies and audience, but it would be one in which the audience had been first corrupted and conditioned into such a matching.

The validity of Hollywood's view of man's nature and man's fate would not be so important if it did not rule an imperial domain. What Hollywood does, and how, becomes a way of life for millions throughout the world. Hollywood produces, distributes, exports, more than pictures. People take their philosophy, their clothes style, their manners, their walk, their talk, their worldly wisdom, from the pictures they see and the Hollywood fan magazines and gossip columns they read. For the movie fan, what is called the "entertainment" value of the movies is an inextricable mixture of magic, mores, and morals. The lavishness which is meant to dazzle him remains to guide him. The action and power that are meant to thrill him remain to set his tempo. The sexual glamour that is meant to lure him remains to embellish his dreams. The violence that is meant to give him "a wallop" remains to desensitize him.

There have been great movies and movie directors, as I have noted above, who have gone against the grain and tried for different values. I hold firm to my belief that the movies as art form—despite the cynicism of some of the Hollywood businessmen—have achieved a far higher level than any of the other American big-audience media. My criticism of the movie makers is based on the gap between the reality and the potential. However great this gap is in the case of the movies, it is a good deal greater—as we shall see—in the case of the popular arts of radio and TV.

6. Radio and TV: the World in the Home

IF THE MOVIES are the art of glamour and the dream, radio and TV are the arts of the home.* They make the world accessible to almost every American. By the twisting of a dial they also make him, alas, accessible to the masters of radio and TV. While the American family is strategically trapped in its living room, they make it the victim of soap operas, horse operas, crooners, comedians, husband-and-wife breakfast shows, quiz shows, big money give-away shows, audience participation shows, variety shows, housewives' chatter, news commentators, forums, sermons, political campaigners, hot jazz and disk jockeys—and, above all, commercials. The sights and sounds that come pouring in comprise what must be the weirdest mixture history has witnessed.

There is human and social meaning in this cacophony. Radio and television are more than a potpourri of entertainment. They form one of the great tying mechanisms of American culture, bringing every part of the nation together instantaneously. They are thus the crucial arts of communication since they focus the attention of millions on the same thing at the same time. Americans are lonely people. If they cannot have a community of collective effort, they can at least form a cohesive "unseen audience." And a standardized one too: for it listens

* I deal here primarily with radio and TV as popular arts. For a discussion of their relation to the shaping of opinion and belief, see Ch. X, Sec. 5, "Revolution in the Big Media."

to the same tunes, the same gags and jokes, the same advertising slogans, the same commercial jingles, the same variations of the same stale plots, the same hackneyed arguments. This standardization drives the intellectual and taste levels downward.

Radio and TV form a single broadcasting art whose common element is that both are forms of broadcasting from a central point of origin to millions of receiving sets which pick up the material with their antennae. Both of them also make use of the electronic vacuum tube as their basic means of transmission, instead of the printed word as in the case of the press or the camera image as in the case of the movies. The differences are that TV transmits to a screen, and that its techniques of broadcasting are more elaborate and expensive. Yet the continuity was maintained: the radio broadcasters generally became the entrepreneurs of TV, and the same homes that had radio sets added TV sets. In both cases there is no intermediary public exhibition, as with movies or spectator sports. And since they do not rely on the printed word, literacy is not essential to them as it is with newspapers, magazines, and the other reading media. Radio and TV, as broadcasting arts, can reach wherever the spoken language is understood by the ear and wherever the eye can grasp a picture. They are thus the arts of sight and sound and the images raised by the spoken word. In this sense they parallel the movies.

But what they add, in the form of the electronic tube, makes it possible for the radio listeners and TV viewers to get their entertainment without ever stirring from their homes. Moreover, they get a highly diversified bill of fare, so they need never stay committed to one program or station but move as taste-shoppers and dial-turners over a number of available shows and arts, including movies, theater, musical comedy, vaudeville, dance, jazz, and sports. Thus in a sense radio and TV became the synthesizers of all the popular arts. They bring the world to the home, wrapped up in a single gleaming febrile package whose contents change magically and continuously on the quarter and half hour.

The early development of the radio belongs to the decade of the 1920s, when it was a boom industry in a boom decade. Radio first burst upon the nation when it transmitted the results of the Harding election in 1920; it reached its first climax of popular acceptance in the *Amos and Andy* show in the late 1920s. In its first phase the programs were broadcast as a public service, without advertising sponsorship and with an eye mainly to profits for the equipment companies from the sale of sets. In the next phase, the late 1920s and early 1930s, advertising came to stay as the principal source of revenue, and the same centralizing force which operated in the other media brought the big broadcasting chains into radio. Because of the limited number of available frequencies for radio and of channels for TV, this centralizing force has had a physical basis as well as an economic one. By 1934, when the Federal Communications Commission was established, the three big features of broadcasting—private enterprise, advertising sponsorship, and public regulation within broad limits—had become accepted. After that, Frequency Modulation (FM) seemed a revolutionary development that promised to give a clearer reception and make more frequencies and stations available, and was hailed as "radio's second chance." But it proved (as Trevelyan remarked about the 1848 revolution) a turning point at which history failed to turn, and it was taken over by the established networks. The two later technical revolutions, however—TV and color—proved to be genuinely revolutionary.

Unlike radio at its start, TV came into being when the principles of private ownership, advertising sponsorship, and government regulation were already accepted. Its original impulsion came from the radio broadcasters, aware that TV would cut into the radio listening audience and might even displace it, but forced to make heavy investments in their own executioner. Each chain took part in this technological race because it was anxious not to be isolated by a forced march its rival might make, and wanted to occupy the strategic high ground from which it could command the whole terrain of the popular media. The struggle between the two major networks over color television illustrated how big corporations in the big media find themselves compelled to create the obsolescence of their own plant and equipment—a compulsion through which the broadcasting media move ahead technologically to new revolutionary changes. In the process the other big media found their audience diminished, but after TV sets had their initial effect in cutting down reading, movie-going, and radio listening, the truants tended to return. The net result was the accession of a new audience to the new popular art and an increase in the total audience for all the media that TV synthesized and popularized.

There is a unique situation in broadcasting that determines who shall control the programs. One may speak of a Big Four who dominate the industry and the art: the broadcasting stations and chains, the equipment companies selling sets, the advertising sponsors, and the audience. Between them there is a chain of relation which runs somewhat as follows: when more radio and TV sets are sold, there is a profit to the equipment companies and also an increase in the audience; with a larger audience there is more for the broadcasters to sell to the advertising sponsors of the shows, which means a greater profit to both; with more money available, bigger and better programs are possible; as the offerings grow in coverage (witness the Presidential conventions or the Congressional hearings) a new audience is won, creating in turn a greater demand for radio and TV sets—and the chain reaction starts again.

This dramatizes how central the relation is between audience and advertiser. Since radio and TV are arts of the home, no admission price is charged, although in the mid-1950s the idea of a subscription radio system and of phone television was broached and debated. Business must thus levy its tax at another point. It does so through advertising. The broadcasters have chosen to take the subsidy largely on the advertiser's terms, giving him control not only over his advertising time and commercials but over the nature and even the content of the program. This was a fateful choice and an avoidable one. As a result the broadcasters not only sell advertising time but sell the audience as well —and themselves.

By that fact they have altered the axis of emphasis. In the case of the movies and press the content of picture or paper is the product of men who are themselves primarily craftsmen even while they are producing a product for sale and profit. In the case of radio and TV the content is chosen and tailored by a group of businessmen (generally advertising and sales agents) in order to *sell another product*. In their own circles their effectiveness is not judged by the artistic merit of their program. Their concern is to keep the largest audience tuned in, to lure them away from other programs advertising other products, to annoy as few as possible and outrage none, to make few experiments, to take little risk. They are judged not by the merit of the program but by its "rating." It is this "rating" that is sold to the advertiser-sponsor. In the case of a movie, the product must be entertaining enough so that the moviegoer will pay to see it. In the case of radio and TV it must catch audiences that will watch it for nothing, so that the station can sell the program to the advertiser, who buys it to sell soap, soup, razor blades, cigarettes, cosmetics, beer, refrigerators, or cars to the listener.

The listener, who is the potential buyer of these products, is not the buyer of the shows: *it is he who is being sold.* So long as he can be delivered to the advertiser, it matters little what the program does to his taste and values. This is the art of the market place brought into the living room. It is entertainment not as art but as advertising.

This gives meaning to the commercial—a sales talk, unctuous, hyperbolic, and persistent, which flanks the program and breaks into it, is usually delivered in a tense and feverish tone and is itself punctuated and capped by a slogan. When the slogan is a jingle, the result is a "singing commercial" which is turned out by highly sophisticated specialists but itself often becomes part of the musical folklore of the culture. Thus the advertiser succeeds beyond his wildest dreams in getting his product into the subconscious of his audience. There are many who are depressed by the chatty ladies selling gadgets, lotions, and household appliances in between their discourses on books and world affairs, or their interviews with famous people. But there are others for whom the agony of having to hear the commercials, as the admission price for the program, becomes a form of torture, like the drilling of a nerve. The most terrifying form of the commercial is the agency man especially detailed to do the "hard sell" or the "relaxed sell"—a long solo performance on the merits of his product, with demonstrations of its use and enjoyment. During the sales talk, there are animated cartoons on TV: as Thomas Whiteside described them, a "panorama of flying beer bottles, zooming candy bars, exploding containers of breakfast foods, singing cough drops, and animated coffee cups." The great innovation that Disney started in the movies has ended in TV advertising. If everything in the "relaxed sell" is smiling unction, everything in the accompanying cartoon seems to be bursting with an explosive purposiveness. Even ex-President Herbert Hoover, not notable for his anti-commercialism, found the commercials intolerable. To deal with this "periodic interruption of huckster chatter," Hoover proposed the invention of "a push button by which we could transmit our emotions instantly to the broadcasters."

Despite this resistance of a portion of the audience, TV has revolutionized the marketing of goods in the American economy. For the first time, you not only hear about the product but see it and almost smell and taste it. Whether it is a washing machine, a kitchen range, beer, an automobile, or a baking powder, the advertiser has seen his dream come true—the dream of being able to demonstrate his product before millions of people with the powerful aid of cartoons, jingles, and rows upon rows of shapely legs.

The broadcasters tend to regard the commercial as a necessary evil, although M. W. Loewi, director of one of the TV networks, was candid enough to say that "we are selling TV short when entertainment is allowed to dominate the schedule to the exclusion of a sales message well presented." Loewi's appeal has a certain logical consistency. Since the advertiser buys not so much the "show" as an audience for the merits of the product, the commercial which is so widely regarded as an intruder on the entertainment is actually the intrusion of reality into a system of make-believe. That indeed is why it is resented, for we are always resentful when somebody breaks into our fantasy world. The commercial awakens the listener from his belief that the resources of the entertainment world are at his command without any cost on his part. Like Dr. Faustus, bemused at having been able to call up the beautiful body of Helen, he forgets about his bargain with Mephistopheles until that personage breaks in to exact his price in the form of the commercial.

To the sponsor the commercial is not marginal to the program but the thing itself: if anything, the rest of the program is marginal to it. In this spirit he decks out the commercial in all the frumpery he can buy, lavishing his best creative energies on it. He hires the brains of young men with an expensive college preparation who have ransacked literature and philosophy, psychology, and art in order to work for an advertising agency. These young men, febrile, conscience-stricken, torn, are the "hucksters." They form a lost Foreign Legion of desperate spirits who sell themselves for a term of years into a strange country to take part in fantastic drills and meaningless adventures. The psychic cost falls first of all on the program, since the emotional tone of the whole show is set by the commercial and the men responsible for it. It is hard for either script writer or performer to slow down his pace or mute his tone when the hyperthyroidal extravagance of the advertising message permeates everything. It falls also on the whole culture, since a mass art in which everything is overvalued (as it has to be in the atmosphere of the constant radio advertising) cannot help communicating its contagion to the culture which feeds on it.

Added to this pervasive atmosphere of hyperbole there is the fact that the audience is both vulnerable and changeable. For any particular program the TV viewers are not a captive audience. There is always the chance that a competing program will lure them away by its more seductive promise of entertainment pleasure or thrills, and that the customer will flick his wrist and twist the dial to another channel. Important as it is throughout American culture, the element of time is crucial in the TV business. The researchers seem to have established that unless there is a strong counterattraction elsewhere, something like 60 per cent of the audience will stay on the same channel when the show is over, and where one "big" program follows another of the same type the legion of the loyal may be as high as 80 per cent. Hence the somewhat monotonous "back-to-back programming" of similar attractions, such as mysteries, giveaways, and comedies during the important evening hours. Along with this there is a fierce competitive effort to win away the audience from the other channels, in a wearing psychological warfare. The crucial minutes are those at the opening of a new time period: hence the tense, almost hysterical, opening gambit in any radio or TV show and the trip-hammer recurrence of intensity at crisis moments until the end.

Hence also the "rating" system which (highly unreliably) measures and remeasures on a continuing graph the size of the audience for each program. Related to this is the "research survey," where listening and viewing habits of an audience are studied in more intensive detail, and which is used to predict future trends in audience taste. The rating systems perform the function in the American media that the priests who consulted the oracles and omens performed in the Roman Empire—and by any rigorous standards of statistical technique their scientific validity is just about the same. Yet they determine whether a program shall survive or die, and a change of several points in the weekly rating may drive an agency executive to drink, ulcers, or suicide, or it may raise him to dizzying heights of joy from which the next week's drop may dash him to despair.

As for the TV programs themselves, they form a potpourri of everything the big media have developed. Here, as in the movies, there are cycles of taste that mark the birth and death of countless shows. There was a time when the discussion forum ranked high in radio, but it fell away in popular interest, and when it was transferred to TV it took on the more dramatic form of a "press conference" show, assimilating another of the big media. The news commentator is more at home on the radio than on TV, where the continued concentration on his face makes both the audience and him uneasy, and where he usually backs up his script with feverish picture clips from news photographs: easily the best of the news commentaries on TV has been *See It Now,* which relies heavily on an editing of specially prepared photographic shots around a single subject. It was on this show that Edward Murrow presented his version of McCarthyism in action—the most important single program in the history of TV thus far.

The panel of experts, which flourished on radio in the form of "quiz" programs, was transformed on TV into games where the "experts" try to unravel riddles whose solution is already known to the audience: the panels quickly hardened into a formula, usually with a moderator and four panel members, carefully distributed among glamour, wit, and celebrities. One of the ideas that swept the media for a time was the "audience participation" show, part quiz, part interview of members of the studio audience to heighten local interest and furnish a flavor of the common man. The most successful show on both media was the big "giveaway" for answering difficult factual questions:

when Louis Cowan dared to set the giveaway sum staggeringly high in his *$64,000 Question,* it broke through previous barriers and set a new level for munificence which had TV in a furor for a time—until other programs came along raising the sum even higher. Murder mysteries and crime thrillers were more successful on radio than on TV, since the concentration on the ear heightens the suspense; but TV took over the showing of mystery films as an effective ready-made substitute. Soap-opera dramas seemed equally at home in both media. The variety show, featuring an array of vaudeville talents built around the "big-name" radio comedian, came into even greater glory on TV: but in both media the comic talents of a Jerry Lewis or a Jimmy Durante, depending on rapid improvisation in the intimate atmosphere of a night club, became mechanical; and in some instances the TV comedian—at once obsessive, trivial, and epicene—proved one of the worst products of the media. Less objectionable was the female performer, sometimes chatty, usually with no particular voice or wit but with a certain conspicuously displayed sexiness. A whole separate TV realm was set aside for children, with shows which sometimes (as in the case of *Kukla, Fran and Ollie*) had a quality of fantasy and charm that "adult" shows usually lacked. Also an outgrowth of the children's audience was the vogue of the science-fiction "space" shows, which charted the imaginative worlds with such mechanical thoroughness that nothing was left to the imagination. The "crooner" shows continued their special appeal in both media, and —along with the comedians—furnished the largest number of TV idols. The broadcasting of classical and symphonic music remained an effective function of the radio even when it was overshadowed by TV. The most productive area for TV to exploit was the documentary, including not only political spectacles like the Kefauver crime investigation and the Army-McCarthy hearings, and sport spectacles like prize fights and football and baseball games, but also demonstrations of new techniques in medicine, science, and psychiatry.

This bill of fare of the media is necessarily a transient, since fads develop, fashions change, and new areas open up for exploitation. I have given it in detail to document the role of radio and TV (especially the latter) as the synthesizing arts of the popular culture. There are few things that happen in the real world of events, science, and political conflict, or in the make-believe worlds of sport and movies, theater, dance, music, that cannot be projected on a TV screen. This suggests the breath-taking potential of the broadcasting arts.

What both media have at their best is vitality, pace, timing, and an imaginativeness about technique. Without being in themselves distinctive arts, they combine a dozen different arts but are somewhat more than their passive carriers. For whatever the art may be—theater, dance, sports event, jazz, news documentary, variety show, domestic skit, mystery—it poses special problems and acquires a special tension when transferred and transformed into the new medium. It also acquires, especially on TV, a sense of immediacy. The characteristic quality that TV has is the feeling it conveys to the audience that something is happening at that very moment before their eyes. Neither medium possesses the capacity of the movies to transfer the audience back into time through the flashback nor to get inside the mind of the character by an interior monologue. Yet the capacity to bring all the arts together into one gives TV an advantage over every other communication technique thus far.

It means, however, that the men who run both media, and especially TV, have to keep their Moloch appeased by a constant stream of material—scripts, "angles," gimmicks, jokes, formats, routines, variety-show combinations. There is an insatiable cannibalism of material on TV, a constant drain on talent and ideas, on available "names," on stories and plays which can be rewritten and adapted to the new media. This does not nourish artistic creativeness. But without having in themselves much generative power, the broadcasting arts have a duplicative power such as no popular art has ever had. When well used they can insure the horizontal spread of whatever creativeness the culture develops: they can reach the subconscious of the audience, get into the crevices of their minds, hit them with an immediacy and continuity of impact denied to any other technique.

In the mid-1950s the big movie studios, which had held out against supplying TV with their storehouse of movie prints because of their fear of TV competition, finally succumbed to the lure of the big money and made almost the whole past repertoire of the movie arts available. The fear that audiences would stay away from the movie theaters was not fulfilled, and the quality of the films on TV was decisively improved. Looking ahead, we find that it is not clear whether TV will eat the movie industry, cannibalwise, or whether the movies have found a new outlet for their commercial product and their artistic creativeness, transferring from the public theater to the home. Probably both are true, and neither wholly, since each art has been enriched in the process. It is likely that TV will emerge as the dominant carrier form of the big media, combining all the rest, while the movies retain their position as the creative form.

As with the movies, there has been a continuance on TV of the system of "big name" stars, who are given long-run contracts with staggering salaries. The glamour of these heroes does not depend on the sense of distance between them and the public. Even the movie heroes and heroines are somewhat further removed. What the TV stars sell is a quality called "personality": in fact, they are usually called "TV personalities" by the same people who would never dream of calling one of the heroes or heroines of the screen a "movie personality." The difference lies in the greater familiarity of those who have become part of the domestic circle. The heroes of TV are everyday fare, entering the home weekly or even daily and becoming familiars in the household: the fact that their glamour still holds up marks the emergence of a new kind of hero-type:

> A creature not too strange or good
> For human nature's daily food . . .

and is evidence of a remarkable inner harmony between the performers and their audience. This harmony persists despite the shoddiness of much of the material the performers present and marks a triumph for their infectious personalities over the context in which they appear. Thus the big-name system not only helps sell the sponsor's product but furnishes the human continuity which makes tolerable the barrage of whirling images and exploding noises.

This may shed some light on the question of the role of laughter in the communication between star and audience. While very few of the great movies (except for the Chaplin series) have been comedies, TV would almost cease to exist without the comedians. Some of them have come from the vaudeville stage, others from the night clubs, still others from the radio. When they "arrive" on TV, they become important properties, are given teams of script writers to prepare their material, and are surrounded by pretty girls and other talent in order to keep the attention of the audience from wandering to a competing show. When the audience shows signs of growing bored with them it is not unusual for the publicity men to think up a "feud" between several of the comedians; the element of hostility seems to invest them with greater appeal, like a dark curtain against which their wit may flash the more brightly. But always they are expected to get laughs. This laughter-compulsion on TV (it spills over into the noncomedy shows as well) parallels the fun-imperative in American morality which I have discussed earlier.*

Several explanations of the demand for comedy have been suggested —one of them that since no smutty stories are allowed on the air, laughter becomes a form of emotional release, while the other stresses the sense of well-being in an America of high living standards. But other

* Ch. IX, Sec. 6, "Morals in Revolution."

explanations seem to make more sense. On the emotional level the lonely American finds in TV a sure method of getting away from the confronting of his own image, with all of its anxieties: laughter furnishes their solvent. On the social level, the fact is that most people usually watch TV not as one or two people sitting in a large audience but as a little cluster of family or friends around the set: laughter is a good way of tying this cluster together and giving it an ease of relationship. Finally, on a practical level, the advertiser who sponsors the show wants the potential purchasers of his product to associate it with something pleasant and sunny rather than with the unpleasant and the tragic. Thus TV is mainly the art of comedy because it is the social art and the advertising art.

Something of the same approach may be useful in assessing the standards of taste and intellect, courage and morality, that prevail in both radio and TV. The gap between potentials and actuality was poignantly put in a letter written to the National Association of Broadcasters by Lee De Forest, inventor of the Audion tube which was the crucial technical element of radio, on the occasion of its fortieth anniversary: "What have you gentlemen done to my child?" De Forest asked. "He was conceived as a potent instrumentality for culture, fine music, the uplifting of America's mass intelligence. You have debased this child, you have sent him out on the streets . . . to collect money from all and sundry. . . . You have made him a laughingstock of intelligence, surely a stench in the nostrils of the gods of the ionosphere. . . ." And John Crosby, a perceptive critic of broadcasting, has listed the "deadly sins of the air": among them that radio "sold its soul to the advertiser"; that it "pandered to the lowest tastes and almost ignored the highest"; that it was "avaricious and cowardly"; and that it "created an insulting picture of the American people." Most signs indicate that TV is following essentially the same road.

The way in which violence is treated on the air may illustrate these comments. There are probably at least eighty programs of horror and mystery thrillers a week on the air. Within a span of five hours on Sunday evening the three big networks during one year had nine mystery shows. On that night, in a total of perhaps twenty million homes, there were enacted a dozen violent deaths whose victims, as *Life* summed it up, were "stabbed, poisoned, shot, blown up and thrown out of windows, plus one exceptionally messy suicide."

There is little question that TV had an impact on the lives of children. A 1950 study showed pupils of junior-high-school age spending twenty-seven hours a week at it—about equal to the time they spent in the classroom; the average for children from seven to seventeen was three hours a day; in the case of five- and six-year-olds, the figure was four hours a day. Only one child out of five failed to become a regular member of the TV audience. They watched not only the children's programs, including puppet shows, circus-and-clown shows, and space shows, but many also got the nightly "adult" spell of murder, robbery, mayhem, blackmail, and kidnaping. This produced a pervasive anxiety among parents and educators who were caught between a reluctance to deprive the children of culturally accepted entertainment and a fear of the scars it might leave.

For good or ill, TV became the "unacknowledged legislator" of the minds of American children, carrying into those minds the sex and the fripperies, the silliness and stupidities and terrors of the "adult" shows. In some cases it made the children smart and cynical before their time, with the shallow smartness of those who have seen sophistication and violence but have not experienced either of them, whose imagination has been excited but not nourished. At the best it enriched the child's visual and imaginative experience faster than ever before in history. At the worst it desensitized the child while it burdened him with a heavy load of anxiety. Yet those who feared that it would produce a generation of little monsters allowed their own anxiety to overcome their good sense. Just as children have for centuries been able to absorb the terror and sadism of some of the classic fairy tales, so TV added its own contribution to the violent world of the children's imagination. An American generation brought up on comic books was able to take TV in its stride. What the children themselves get from it is much what the grownups get—a long look at the outside world, with all of its buzzing, booming confusion. Children have to visualize this world with pictorial images and not only with words. If, as some psychologists have suggested, Americans tend to keep too tight a rein on the primary impulses of their children, TV may prove a safety valve for their gathered frustrations and aggressions. A study made of children whose parents had banned their watching TV showed a disproportionate number of them ridden by the very anxiety which the ban was presumably meant to prevent.

The debate on the psychic and cultural deposit left on young and old alike by the broadcasting arts is not likely to be resolved easily. Harriet Van Horne, a TV columnist, lamented that "our people are becoming less literate by the minute. . . . As old habits decline, such as reading books and thinking thoughts, TV will absorb their time. By the twenty-first century our people doubtless will be squint-eyed, hunchbacked, and fond of the dark. Conversation will be a lost art. People will simply tell each other jokes. . . . The chances are that the grand-child of the Television Age won't know how to read this." This is bright writing, but it seems oversold on doom. The history of the big media offers proof that every new medium has been hailed as a worker of miracles and dreaded as a destroyer of the ancient virtues. Neither the salvation nor the doom has been fulfilled. The residue depends on how and for what purpose the medium is used by its masters and its audience. It also depends on the nature of the society and the culture into which it is introduced. Harold Innis, in a broad historical survey, has shown that every revolution in the techniques of communication brought with it an equal revolution in society and culture. It would be surprising if this were not proved true of the electronic revolution which has largely replaced the printed word by the visual image con-veyed over sound waves, and which is bound to transform American society—and others as well—in ways still undreamed of today.

One of the important transformations is in the area of social power. It should be obvious that those who control the images that reach into men's homes and also into their minds will have a good deal of at least indirect control over those minds as well. Hence the question of how the structure of this power shall be organized.

The issue of the control of radio and TV is no longer one between private and government ownership. Private enterprise in the big media is now established in America and is not likely to be disestablished. The British, who ran their broadcasting under a government corpora-tion, did a better job with intellectual and taste standards: yet they too found that government control narrows the choice of viewpoints pre-sented on the air, just as control by advertisers narrows it in a different way. One must doubt whether the American government is mature enough to handle this kind of power without abusing it. In the mid-1950s even the British turned to commercial sponsorship of TV, per-suaded that it provides the audience with an array of good as well as shoddy choices such as no other system had thus far offered. Yet the current British arrangement improved on the American in at least one respect: the British competition in TV is not just between one com-mercial chain and another or one advertiser and another but between a commercial and government service, between private and public.

Where the system falls down, as I have suggested, is in its sleaziness of taste standards and its pandering to greed and timidity. Raymond Rubicam, who learned to know the advertising agency from the inside, wrote that the reason for the failure of radio to serve the public inter-est lay in "the domination of radio by the advertiser . . . what amounts practically to a monopoly of radio and TV advertisers to the point where the public's choice in program is more of a theory than a fact." This challenges the usual defense of advertising control as representing a democracy of audience choice. The trouble with this defense is that the audience chooses only from what is made available, which is limited by the calculus of the advertisers. Senator Benton's suggestion for a citizens' group to appraise annually how radio and TV have served and failed to serve the public interest was never acted on—which may be just as well, since it would have meant the appointment of a group of private citizens by the Senate, and therefore the vesting of considerable power without responsibility. Another suggestion, by Frank Stanton, was the launching of a research study on the kind of anxieties and questions and answers that Americans have about TV. But this would have meant only another attitude study rather than the "dialogue" between broadcasters and public which Stanton seemed to envisage. Nor has anything been done about the suggestions for turning a TV channel over to creative people who would develop new programs without the benefit of advertising, but with public or foundation subsidy. Programs like *Omnibus,* first subsidized by the Ford Foundation and later moderately successful in finding sponsors, indicate that the commercial sponsor and the advertising agency suffer less from an anticultural bent than from a poverty of imagination, which leads them to seek the easy way to win and hold an audience. A method of subsidizing new program ventures until they could prove their appeal, a noncommercial channel for use as a yardstick, a more rigorous enforcement of the provision for "public-service programs," the use of an advisory board of technicians and laymen for a continuing reappraisal of the media—these are a few steps that might help.

This is another way of saying that the core problem is one of maturity. Just as important as the consequences of TV for American society are the consequences of the society for the art of TV. Just as serious as the question of what TV does to children is the question of what children do to TV. It is not that the programs are geared deliberately to catch them but that they are shaped so as to appeal to the child's mentality in children and adults alike. Since you can listen to radio and TV free, without budging from your living room, twisting programs on and off with the flick of a dial, this means a huge audience but also a fluid and slack one. It places a premium on the slick and the quick, the noisy, the flashy, and ephemeral. It means pampering the audience, treating it as one treats a child whose attention span is short, whose interests are sensuous and surfacy, and whose fancy is a wandering one. Perhaps nine tenths of the brains and energy in radio and TV are directed toward finding somehing gaudy to catch the attention, something wry to evoke laughter, something new and ingenious to tickle the fancy. This makes for a somewhat bizarre sprightliness and a sense of alertness and tension, but not for substance and emotional depth.

To defend this on the score of "audience choice" is to set up a new and more imperfect Benthamite calculus. In measuring the greatest happiness of the greatest number, the Calculus of Bentham sought at least to take account of pains as well as pleasure. The Calculus of TV has no clear way of determining how much pain is mixed with the pleasure of a particular program—except that the pleasure out-balances the pain enough to keep the listener tuned in. To accept this critical standard is to abdicate all others. It is as if one were to accept the suffrage of the largest number in judging the value of books, which would mean that trashy best sellers and comic books would have to be crowned with an accolade. In the world of books a number of audience taste levels are given a chance to operate, with none shut out, whether it be symbolist poetry or the dregs of the newsstand pulps. Until radio and TV find some means for providing a comparable set of choices for varying audience levels, with no significant level shut out, there can be little valid talk of a cultural democracy of audience choice.

There remains the question of the impact of TV not on the cultural level but on the social structure. Studies of the distribution of TV sets show TV to be the poor man's luxury because it has become his psycho-logical necessity. While TV flowers best in the middle-bracket income groups, its importance for the lower income groups is far out of pro-portion to their numbers and purchasing power. This can be verified by the sky line. Wandering about in the poorer quarters of the cities you will find the greatest concentration of TV antennae—exactly in the areas where people live hemmed-in lives, economically and in-tellectually. This is true of the Negro areas of Harlem and Philadelphia, Detroit and Chicago; it is true wherever ethnic groups are crammed into ghettos. In the housing developments for middle-income groups, such as the new Levittowns and Park Forests, TV sets come built in with the equipment, and have become as routine a part of the household as the phone and the refrigerator. For those who during the day are shut in-side factories or stores or offices, or for housewives who stay home with small children, TV furnishes an unparalleled release by night and day.

For those who are excluded from many forms of direct experience by the bars of discrimination, TV is a way of breaking the bars, so that they can watch the glamorous figures of make-believe and the weighty figures of the world of power. For the Negro the big fact about TV is that Jim Crow has no way of policing a man's eyes and ears as he watches the set in his home. He can turn to TV to make what is unavailable to him in the world outside available for the fleeting moment as he watches it in a world of sound and sight where everyone is equal. Another big fact is that, for the radio and TV sponsor, the purchasing power of a listener counts the same, whatever his skin. Hence the appearance of Negroes, picked for their skills on the big-prize shows like *$64,000 Question*—with far-reaching consequences in changing the earlier popular stereotypes.

If it be said that the TV audience is one of only passive watchers, the same is true of the movies and the spectator sports. Short of arranging some kind of genuine forum, accessible to thoughtful leaders of opinion and the rank and file as well, where the audience could take pot shots at some of the most revered institutions and practices of TV, the medium can do little in creating the dialogue which is the essence of communication. TV cannot transform the passive into the active, but it does bring all the spectator arts together on a single screen. It does so with a technical mastery so great that the sports promoters fear the audience will see the prize fight or football game better on the screen than from the field or arena; as a result the sale of radio and TV rights has become important in the financing of these events. From the prize fight to the movie to the Presidential convention, spectacles which were once meant for their own immediate audiences are being tailored to the TV audience.

This must have incalculable effects on the emotional cement of a democratic society. While the broadcasting media present their own internal problems of privilege and power, they will inevitably help erode the landscape of social privilege. They do not decrease the economic distance between the classes, nor can they level the walls of segregation overnight. But they can help create a common sense of belonging and provide access to the common experience for many from whom it was formerly withheld.

7. Jazz As American Idiom

THE KIND OF music, song, and dance a people generates, with their characteristic rhythm and beat, forms one of the best indexes of its cultural style. In America the national musical style is more closely related to the tom-tom than to the organ. It is not the style of church music, nor of the symphony or sonata, the madrigal or the morris dance, the ballet or opera. The dominant American musical styles are those of the "blues," "swing," and "jazz."

Every civilization finds also the musical instruments that express its idiom. In America they are brass and percussion—the trumpet and saxophone, capable of expressing both a melancholy moan and a triumphant blare like the exultant cry of an animal; the drums with their rhapsodic deafening beat; and the piano, which beat out ragtime in the 1920s and still beats out the foundation rhythm incessantly, lest tension and attention lapse. Add to these four instruments a young female voice, husky and throaty, to express the melancholy of the "blues" and the sultry sexiness of "torch songs," and you have the basic American musical unit. Around this unit there cluster the characteristic accompaniments of American musical life: the "name band," night club, blues singer, dance record, disk jockey, tinpan alley, dance hall, jam session, musical comedy, crooner, juke box, and the bobby-sox brigade of youthful music worshipers.

More than in any other popular art Americans express in their music both a mood of melancholy and the beat of Dionysian impulse. In a culture that regards sadness and pessimism almost as crimes against the Republic, the American popular songs have given expression to the plaintive along with the boisterous. The songs and ballads form one of the sources of contemporary jazz, but they are even more important in mirroring the sequence of folk experience in American history. Every aspect of the building of the country is represented in them: in the marching songs, the work and road-gang songs, the cotton-picking songs ("Oh, de boll weevil am a little brown bug"), the cowboy songs, the badman frontier songs:

> Roll me over easy, roll me over slow,
> Roll me over on my right side 'cause my left side hurts me so . . .

the trail songs, the plantation songs, the hillbilly mountain songs, the spirituals and the sinfuls:

> When dey let my baby down in de groun'
> I couldn't hear nuffin but de coffin soun' . . .

> Sometimes I'se up, sometimes I'se down,
> Sometimes I'se almos' to de groun'.
> Nobody knows the trouble I've seen,
> Nobody knows but Jesus.

In some, especially in the work songs and frontier ballads, there is an element of tongue-in-cheek exaggeration, but also a deep strain of sadness which is found wherever the Negro influence has touched American song. The work songs were intended to make the burden of manual and field labor more tolerable: Alan Lomax has called it a "spiritual speed-up." Its roots may be found in West Africa, but it developed on the American plantation system, and its call-and-response pattern is similar to the same pattern in Negro spirituals, with the work leader improvising the call and the work crew giving the chorus response. It was only a step from the cotton plantation to the railroad section gang ("I've been workin' on the railroad"), and another step to the chain gang in today's South, where forced manual labor still survives and the machine (which kills the work song) has not yet entered.

The deepest expression of the strain of sadness may be found in the "blues," born in the Negro quarters of Southern cities, drenched with the melancholy of the West African slave-serf-alien in America. It is a dithyrambic melancholy, a lament over a turn of fortune that has left the singer penniless and shorn of a lost love-object; but also an undaunted melancholy, with the quality of resilience in it. Of all the early strains in American folk songs and ballads, it alone survived as a strong shaping force in American musical culture. It alone seems to have emotional depth and an unashamed passion. The "blues" tradition reached its greatness in the genius of W. C. Handy and in the singing of Bessie Smith, Ma Rainey, Jimmy Rushing, Dinah Washington, and Billie Holliday. While it is still popular, especially in Negro night clubs, it is largely nostalgic. Its creative strain was carried on and in effect replaced by that of jazz itself.

Related to the "blues" is the spiritual, which is the most general term for the religious music of the American Negro. It goes back in its origin to the beginning of the nineteenth century but did not become known to the white community until after the Civil War. Sometimes it takes the form of gospel songs, sometimes of the closely related "jubilee," sometimes of the longer-sustained melody permeated with a sense of reverence ("Go Down Moses" and "Swing Low, Sweet Chariot" are among the best-known examples). To some extent the spiritual arises out of the church hymn, drawn from a European context and transplanted into the Negro church and revival meeting. To some extent also it comes from the African musical tradition. When the African slaves came to America they found folk hymns which had themselves been transplanted into the South from England and New England. What Negro religious life added was the "praise meeting" on the plantation and later the revival meeting, both of them using the song sermon and the "ring shout." Marshall Stearns has skillfully traced the development of these steps into the jubilee ("When the Saints Go Marching In"), with its lengthened melody, and finally into the spiritual, with its crystal-lizing of the original improvisations. However carefully we follow these steps, we must not lose sight of the relation of the spiritual as a total form to the Dionysian rhythms of jazz itself. Even today much of the new jazz takes its emotional source from the religious spirituals.

The younger and more secular cousins of the blues and the spirituals —the songs of the crooner and torch singer—have a different quality, as have most of the tin-pan alley songs and the synthetic hillbilly ballads. The emotion in them is likely to be prurient and sentimental, appeal-ing to the moon-struck: the melancholy has become a masochistic ac-companiment to teen-age. There is the cry of loneliness ("All alone on the telephone") and the confession of unworthiness ("And when I tell them how wonderful you are, They'll never believe me") and the pathos of self-pity ("I'm nobody's baby," "I'm always chasing rain-bows"). Out of jingles like these and thousands of others—Mammy songs, nonsense songs ("Yes, We Have No Bananas," "Barney Google," "Mairzy Doats"), songs of regional nostalgia (longings for the Wabash or the Sewanee or the Blue Ridge or the heart of Texas), songs of rustic love, songs of erotic innuendo, songs of sexual dream-fulfillment— a music-sheet and song-record industry has been built which seems to bring either thrill or anodyne to millions of young Americans. A diaspora of juke boxes all over the land grinds out tunes played by "big-name bands," a nickel or dime at a time, at roadhouses, saloons, restaurants, crossroads cafés. The lilt of these tunes is sweet to the taste of the youngsters, and lachrymose singers like Johnnie Ray and jaunty singers like Bing Crosby and Frank Sinatra become the objects of adoles-cent worship. The words ("lyrics") perform the same function for their imaginations that the lyric poem did for middle-class England in the century between Burns and Tennyson. They are, in fact, all the poetry that most young Americans know. Their effect on American taste makes the juke boxes a greater danger to American life than the Jukes.

The more important musical idiom of America was the "ragtime" and "hot jazz" of the twenties, the "swing" of the thirties, the "cool jazz" of the forties, and the "rock 'n roll" of the fifties. These terms im-ply complex beat and rhythm, improvisation, and musicianly teamwork. The element they have in common is a disciplined Dionysian excite-ment and a thinly sublimated eroticism. Starting among little groups of local musicians, this idiom—in more or less diluted form—reached the larger public through night clubs and concerts, radio, TV, big-name bands, and dance records. It thus became a new folk language of Ameri-can music. While very few of its creators got much income from it, many of them remaining in poverty and even obscurity until their death, their work achieved a greater popular acceptance than the language of literature.

The origins of jazz lie hidden in the folklore of lowly groups of musicians in New Orleans, St. Louis, Chicago, and other centers where American Negroes were forced to lead a segregated life but were exposed—despite the segregation—to influences from the musical traditions of every part of the world. Thus jazz had more than an African origin: there was much in it from America, and much from the Latin cultures of Europe and the Caribbean. Alan Lomax speaks of New Orleans as having "absorbed slowly over the centuries Iberian, African, Cuban, Parisian, Martiniquian, and American musical influences." The result, as he puts it, was a "musical gumbo." But the energizing force was that of the Negro musicians in the big cities, especially New Orleans. They took the syncopated ragtime developed in the honky-tonks and saloons of Sedalia and St. Louis, and turned it into the two-beat Dixieland jazz that was given shape by the "jazz professors" of the Storyville bordellos and by the marching bands that followed so many funerals through the New Orleans streets. The ragtime of the first two decades of the present century was beaten out on the piano: when the brass and wind instruments were added, it became the jazz of the 1920s.

No one has resolved the cultural mystery of how a harvest of musical talent seemed to flower in a few brief decades out of the unlikely soil of brothels and funeral rites in the Mississippi delta. With musicians like Buddy Bolden, "Jelly Roll" Morton, and Louis Armstrong, there was an authentic musicianal passion that entered the life of America and never found its like again. From the Gulf Coast the contagion spread northward to St. Louis and Chicago and eastward to New York and the other big cities there. Here it suffered a change of phase. The impoverished musicians who had improvised in the cribs and bawdy houses became the leaders of big-name bands and best-selling records; a new economic force came in which made music a nation-wide commodity and eroded the folk and regional sources of the original impulsion; the primitive music grew sophisticated, and the "hot jazz" turned into "cool jazz"—polyphonic, with an unaccented beat, and with borrowings from Hindemith and Bartók.

This summary telescopes almost a half century of jazz in America. It does scant justice to the passions and rivalries that beset the struggle of conflicting styles of musical execution. These musical wars arose not only from local rivalries but from the inherent nature of jazz. For in early jazz the composer was of little importance compared with the execution. The musicians took almost any tune, and what came out of the instruments was a miracle of transmutation—a delicate lacework of magic that intoxicated the senses and was especially tantalizing because it depended entirely upon the improvising of the moment and the interweaving of instruments caught in a common excitement. Since good jazz is evanescent, it must be captured and treasured in the memory. Hence the cult of jazz records, in which the *aficionados* feel that the accents of greatness, whether of some star performer or a "side man," have been caught forever. Hence also the lore that develops in the cult —the arguments about who played what with whom, and when and where. Jazz developed in a brief time a history and a tradition, with "great dates" and legendary figures.

The Pre-Raphaelite Brotherhood of young Americans is more likely to be found in hot and cool jazz than in the elite arts of poetry, painting, or the novel. In the 1940s, Harry James meant more to most young Americans than Henry James or William James. Negro and white trumpet players, saxophonists, and pianists were heard and appraised by the young American elite with a critical fierceness that few of them applied to poetry or philosophy. The whole structure was in some ways reminiscent of the Christian Church in its earlier phases. There were raging rivalries as to which style is orthodoxy or heresy, but there was agreement that salvation can only be found inside the musical church of jazz. There was the basic religious nostalgia for the lost Eden, the Golden Age when the church was founded amidst the apathy of surrounding heathendom. There was the rivalry between the adherents of St. Louis and the adherents of New Orleans, of Beale Street and Basin Street, for the nativity of the cult. There was the mythology growing up around the Early Fathers.

A passage in John O'Hara's novel, *Butterfield 8,* about young men in New York at the end of the 1920s, gave a taste of the hero worship:

> They . . . would have their jam sessions, and some night when they did not play they would sit and talk. The names they would talk: Bix Beiderbecke, Frankie Trumbauer, Miff Mole, Steve Brown, Bob MacDonough, Henry Busse, Mike Pingatore, Ross Gorman and Benny Goodman, Louis Armstrong and Arthur Schutt, Roy Bargy and Eddie Gilligan, Harry MacDonald and Eddie Lang and Tommy and Jimmy Dorsey and Fletcher Henderson, Rudy Wiedoeft and Isham Jones, Rube Bloom and Hoagy Carmichael, Sonny Greer and Fats Waller, Husk O'Hare and Duilie Sherbo, and other names like Mannie Kline and Louis Prima, Jenney and Morehouse, Venuti, Signorelli and Cross, Peewee Russel and Larry Binion; and some were for this one and some for that one. . . .

O'Hara, a faithful social historian of his era, caught in this reverent catalogue the right dedicated accent. One should be wary of using the analogy of the Early Church, since there is little of the Orphic element in jazz, and therefore far less of the Christian than of the Dionysian. Yet the lives, exploits, and sufferings of these men are discussed by young Americans in the same terms as those of the saints were discussed in other centuries: there is the same discovery of vocation, the same dedication to the new work, the same revelation of a special gift, the same entrance into the mystery, the same epiphanies, the same final state of grace.

In the gallery of the saints of jazz there is a central figure whom the worshipers call "Bix"—a Midwestern youth whose name was Leon Bix Beiderbecke, from Davenport, Iowa, who first heard jazz as a boy on the river boats of the Mississippi, met Louis Armstrong, and established himself quickly as the leader of the "white" jazz movement of the 1920s, dying at twenty-eight after a brief career of legendary excesses which—along with his inspired playing—became the core of a cult. Bix haunted the night spots of the Negro quarters in Chicago's South Side, where he absorbed the trumpet playing of Joe "King" Oliver and the blues singing of Bessie Smith, and took part in "jam sessions" and "cutting contests." In New York he played with Paul Whiteman's band and spent much of his time in Harlem, where he was a pioneer in the crossing of race boundaries. But mostly he was a musician's musician, the dimensions of whose power and glory are used by his worshipers as standards by which to measure everything mortal. His achievement lay neither in volume of tone nor in frenzy of playing but in a purity of note which was the product, as Wilder Hobson has put it, of "what the imagination presents to the instrument." E. M. Forster has noted that a critic's function in music is different from his function in literature: he cannot presume to tell the musician what to do or even where he is going. This suggests the overtones of fatality in the world of connoisseurs of jazz—a world of absolutes and of "can't help's" in which one either understands or does not. When Fats Waller was asked for a definition of jazz, he answered, "Man, if you don't know what it is, don't mess with it."

Obviously this forms an ideal medium for an art which is at once part of the popular culture and also of the domain of the aesthetes and intellectuals. In the era of Bach there was, to be sure, a gap between the musical language of the man on the street and of the creative artist, but in contemporary America there is more than a gap—there is an abyss. It applies less, however, to jazz and swing, where the cult has a genuine mass art as a base. In Bach's day the works by anonymous composers used the same musical language as did Bach himself. In contemporary America any "young man with a horn" who plays all day and most of the night is—even though an amateur—part of the same milieu, using the same musical language, as the virtuoso performer: and both the amateur and virtuoso are understood in a considerable segment of the culture and express its rhythms.

The "lyrics" that go with this music are often mawkish and sometimes nonsensical, but often they also embody a wild and earthy humor or (as in the case of the blues and the spirituals) a sad and tragic strain. American hot music is not written to be danced to, as distinguished from American popular tunes, which are primarily danced to. In fact, in most of the country's principal jazz clubs, like Birdland and Basin Street, there is no dance floor at all: more and more jazz is being played in concert halls, where the separation from dance is complete.

Yet there is an internal beat in jazz which relates it deeply to dance: the movements of the body interpret its intent better than words can. When there is dancing, the dances break away from a formal pattern and at their best they take on a fluid, improvised character in keeping with the improvisations of the music. Unlike the earlier American folk dances, which are collective, so-called ballroom (really dance hall) dancing is couple dancing, since to take a girl dancing is an integral part of courtship and you don't know the others well enough to join with them. But as the music mounts in the more adept swing dancing, the partners break away to execute complicated solo variations and then rejoin each other. The musicians are at the same time vying in improvisation, and as the jam session approaches one of its climaxes the dancers pay the players the tribute of gathering around to cheer them on. In the organic fusion of popular dance and music Americans reach closer to a mass exaltation and a native idiom of religious feeling than in any other aspect of their lives.

The history of the dance in America illustrates the same fusion of the elite and the popular. Unlike the religions of Asia and Africa, the Christian tradition banned dancing from its religious rituals, and as the inheritor of that tradition, Puritan America placed its dead hand on the expressive use of the body. The frontier dances broke away from this for a long time, but it was not until American students rediscovered the classical and Oriental religious dance that American dancing came into being as an elite art. Its renascence came through Isadora Duncan, Ruth St. Denis, and Martha Graham, who created an interpretive "modern" dance art. It did not reach popular audiences, however, until it was incorporated into the Broadway "musical," after being fused with the ballet and the folk dance. The turning point came with a musical like *Oklahoma*, where the dance forms of Agnes De Mille succeeded in achieving the fusion I have described.

The American "musical" is a remarkable example of how the genius of the culture forms a new entity out of scattered and seemingly discordant elements—a light opera containing a thin "story line" (sometimes taken from a play or novel) with vaudeville woven around it, a sequence of popular songs which yield the big money through dance and radio records, and a central ballet pattern created out of regional, folk, or topical material. How deeply the jazz idiom has permeated musical composition for the stage is shown in the dance and music of light opera, like *Porgy and Bess*, as well as in the musical comedies that are in a direct line of descent from *Oklahoma*. There is a strong probability that the musical direction of the new American future will lie with the popular theater and its dance, opera, and jazz forms, rather than with the "serious" composers who can write symphonies.

This is not to undervalue the receptivity of America to "serious" music. Through radio, TV, and the "hi-fi" long-playing record, the masterpieces of the classical tradition became widely known. America in the 1950s was in a Golden Age of orchestra performance, with a symphony orchestra in every big city and a large audience (mustered with brilliant business skill by experts at the job) available for first-rate traveling orchestras and musical virtuosos. This was partly due to American wealth and to the historical accident of the great European orchestra leaders who came as refugees from Fascism. But mainly it was the awakening interest of the American middle-class "middlebrows" to the treasures of the world's musical tradition which created a literate musical audience and made Americans a nation of musical amateurs. The role once played by the proud capitals of music—Milan, Munich, Dresden, Vienna, Berlin, Amsterdam, Prague—was taken over by America. Out of this receptivity came a vigorous school of contemporary American composers who felt somewhat dwarfed, however, by the historic giants who were being eagerly rediscovered. For a time there was an effort to create a school of native composers using "American themes," but it proved ineffectual, since "native" music cannot be created by will. American composers studied largely with Stravinsky, Hindemith, and Schönberg, and a number of them since the 1920s served an apprenticeship in the Paris salon of Nadia Boulanger. In the mid-1950s the names of Copland and Barber, Sessions and Schuman, Piston and Shapero, were evidence of an American composer's art that was becoming part of the great tradition. They gave themselves a freedom and a largeness of scope as did the composers in the elite societies of the past, and left the expression of popular cultural forces to the "popular" music and dance.

Like all true popular arts, jazz attracted its camp followers of pseudo-folk art. There were "Mammy writers" who tried to imitate Stephen Foster, himself a native of Pittsburgh who celebrated the Southern folkways. City youngsters who had never been south of Brooklyn wrote countless songs about "Dear Old Alabam'" or "Back Home in Tennessee" or the Sewanee River, and vowed that "nothing could be finer than to be in Carolina in the morning." What happened here was a cultural hybridism in which the ethnic accents of the Old World were grafted on to the regional traditions of the New: when Al Jolson sang his famous *Mammy,* using the black face of the American minstrel tradition, it was the Jewish mother of his own ethnic tradition he was invoking. Much more indigenous to the Southern soil were the "rocking, rolling, shouting blues" of the great blues singers.

What saved many of the tin-pan alley tunes, despite their cloying sentiment and artificial garments of a borrowed culture, was the vitality they carried over from the days of ragtime. It was this vitality that gave impetus to the Big Five among the contemporary popular song writers— Irving Berlin, Jerome Kern, George Gershwin, Cole Porter, and Richard Rodgers. Of these, Berlin was closest to the popular mind, Cole Porter was the most literate, with his combination of wit and bawdiness, while the team of Rodgers and Oscar Hammerstein II fused best the lyricism of the popular song with the virtuosity of the Broadway musical. Today the music makers, having left tin-pan alley behind, are caught between the high pressures of the radio "Hit Parade" and the timetable of Broadway and Hollywood productions. The old art of song-plugging was never quite lost but was reinforced by the microphone and movie, and became part of the "Big Time" of a mechanical culture.

This leaves jazz itself, rather than the melodies of popular music or the synthetic hillbilly ballads, as the true musical idiom of America. In fact, jazz is the most indigenous of all the American popular arts. It moved from the early New Orleans musicians, who could scarcely read a note, to the atonal "cool" jazz of a number of highly cerebral young men, each of whom had his brief spiel as the reigning divinity among the knowing. But throughout its course it was informed by a demonic response to the violent inner rhythms of the American culture. One could be wrong to attribute this wholly to the Negro influence, although that has been substantial ever since the days of the New Orleans barrel houses which Vachel Lindsay celebrated in his poem, "The Congo." Jazz has evolved from a segregated Jim Crow art into a pervasive interracial culture, which has spread over western Europe, has reached into Asia, and has penetrated even the barriers of Communist censorship in Russia. What remains primitive in it is the generic human impulses breaking through the strata of Western machine living which have threatened to overlay the instinctual life.

The breaking through of the dance beat is the triumph of the instinctual life over the institutional crust. To a foreign observer like Sartre, who described American jazz as a cultural expression, its initiates seem a new kind of possessed men, taking the place of the possessed men of the medieval religious frenzies. Not many of the young American jazz devotees are technically "hepcats," but there are few who do not yearn to be "hep"—that is, to be insiders rather than outsiders, to take part in the mysteries of abandon and possession which link them with one another. Thus jazz and swing and, more recently, "rock 'n roll"—a febrile and probably temporary variation which has its own cult and deities and does not please the true jazz men—are more than the expressions of the charged tension of American living: they are a recoil from the loneliness of an atomized culture, a not inconsiderable effort to use music to heal the psychological alienation of person from person.

The traditional elite music tends to make passive listeners out of its audiences. It is the music of the popular culture, with its widespread singing, dancing, and improvising jam sessions, that turns audiences into participants, bringing them closer to a dynamic and communal activity. This was true also of the traditional music in its origins. "Virtually up to the seventeenth century," writes Wilfrid Mellers about the English Tudor period, "all music was communal and contemporary, and either religious or domestic. It depended upon active participation between composers, performers, and audience. . . . The idea of sitting solemnly in rows and listening to music (for its own sake) would have seemed absurd to Byrd or Palestrina; either one made music oneself or listened to it as homage to God." American contemporary music and dance have captured much of this spontaneous and even devotional spirit. The hepcats and jitterbugs do not dance and sway out of devotion to any gods the churches would recognize. But they do pay homage in their own way to the Dionysian in American life.

8. Building, Design, and the Arts

IN AN INDUSTRIAL culture like the American, one would expect the great elite arts of the past—painting and sculpture, theater, architecture, and design—to be transformed in the image of what the machine can do with the materials of plastic form. For the most part, this has happened.

Sculpture is an instance of an art falling into disuse when the mode of life no longer makes it meaningful. In the civilizations of the Nile, the Euphrates, and the Mediterranean, it was a crucial art. But the carving of figures out of stone required for their display the public square, the public building, the public occasion, and a ruling class that lived by all three.

Americans once built their city life around a public square but do so less and less. They retain the park and the courthouse, and they have sculptured figures of soldiers in the one and of jurists and statesmen in the other, yet these are products of habit and nostalgia rather than of living belief. Here and there, as with the colossal seated figure of Lincoln by Daniel Chester French in the Lincoln Memorial, belief breaks through. But mostly sculptors either make their livings by getting commissions for fountains and playground figures or experiment in the new abstract international styles. Since the product of sculpture is unique, not to be reproduced in millions of copies or transmitted by the big media, it offers no jackpots. To be sure, America presents, in the grace of athletes and the beauty of women, the living material to be celebrated. But sculpture cannot compete as a mass art with photography: the sports pages are filled with action shots of athletes that make most Americans regard sculpture as static, and magazine covers and advertising pages, as well as movies and TV, are filled with the American girl in every pose of glamour and glory. The sensitive sculptor, like the painter, has to move away from the portrayal of the human body to the symbolic distortions and abstractions of it. The result needs no justifying, especially in the work of someone like Lipschitz, yet there is more of a gulf between these sculptors and the cultural experience than had been true of the sculptors of the past. An even greater departure from the general dictates of American taste was achieved successfully by Alexander Calder, whose development of abstract mobiles has become internationally known and accepted.

America has had painters of considerable talent and varied schools, but they lacked a sustaining audience and environment. They also lacked a myth to celebrate, such as the Christian myth which the Italian and Flemish painters of the Middle Ages and Renaissance had; and buildings to house that myth, like the Sistine Chapel, whose walls are there to be covered with symbolic figures. The French, Belgians, Spaniards, Italians, who produced the great schools of painting in modern times, had largely escaped the main currents of Protestant capitalist power and still had residues of the great religious tradition. The two great postreligious themes of modern times, Nature and the individual, turned painting to landscapes and portraits. Yet on the score of fidelity to the subject the arts of photography were hard to rival. To differentiate themselves from such a competitor, and also to express the confusions of contemporary life, the painters adopted a style of symbolism and expressionism which produced great work in France and Germany but was late in coming to an America that was too purposive and optimistic for it. Realism flourished with Sloan and Hopper, and it was natural in a rich economy that the painters of the rich and their women —like Sargent—should catch the burnished surface of American power and assurance. When the critics lamented the lack of an indigenous school, painters like Wood, Curry, and Benton tried to create it by using American "folk" themes. But even the talent of these men rarely dug far beneath the flat surfaces of the American character.

What was needed was a sharper probing into the inwardness of the civilization through the inwardness of the painter's own vision. This was achieved in an earlier generation by Hartley, Marin, Maurer, and Weber, and in a later one by Shahn, DeKooning, and Pollock. What took place in painting was an easing of the provincial self-consciousness which had seen Europe as the sum and source of all sensitivity: when Americans no longer felt like gawky schoolboys, when power and anxiety and the Freudian vision had moved westward across the ocean and one no longer felt guilty to be daubing a canvas with seemingly aimless shapes and splashes of gaudy color, American painting found itself. The painters broke through, discovering an idiom at once symbolic beyond place and time and yet somehow expressive of America's energy and its unceasing quest, as Melville's idiom was in literature. Since paintings could be reproduced in the era of Malraux's "Museum without Walls," they cropped up everywhere in magazines and books and were bought or rented by young couples furnishing their new homes and apartments. The new middle classes began to discover new levels of taste and enjoyment. While most of the reproductions were of the Old Masters, there was an increasing awareness by Americans of the achievements of their own painters, and contemporary American paintings began to be exhibited even in the big department stores which catered to a mass audience. American painting achieved something of an economic base.

The new art whose imperialism corroded painting and sculpture was photography, both as an obsession of amateurs and in its big-media forms of the movies and TV. Allowing light to enter an opened shutter and be inscribed on a sensitive plate, the camera as an art form was quick, faithful, fluid, mobile, infinitely reproduceable and transmittable, conquering at once time and space, and was bound to become the prime visual art of a technical civilization. Americans with cameras roamed the nation and the world. There were numberless photo clubs, photo magazines and annuals, photo contests and prizes. The art had its pioneers, like Brady, and its great prophet in Stieglitz; after him, Americans lavished on the photograph the careful and devoted artistry which other cultures had lavished on paintings and sculpture. The importance of the picture magazines like *Life* and *Look* meant that talented photographers from all over the world were drawn to New York as the arena of fame and the big prizes. In their hands photography became a form of painting, in which the material of Nature was caught in forms and designs that went beyond realism to suggest the symbolic. As a mass art form, it still expresses the main preoccupations of the culture—"human interest," dramatic action, dynamism, surface, and movement.

Many inquests have been held on the case of the "vanishing theater" in America. The premise underlying them has been that, compared with the Periclean and Elizabethan periods, or the era of Ibsen, Chekhov, Strindberg, and Shaw, in the European theater, the American experience has not proved creative for the theater. The traditional indictment is familiar enough: that the American theater has too narrow a base, being centered on Broadway, in a single area of a single city; that its economics are burdensome, involving a large capital investment, expensive contracts with the trade-unions, and the necessity of getting a "hit" in order to survive; that a tiny group of critics rules over the destiny of the play and tends to be hostile to the unfamiliar; that the theater in America is a middle-class art, written and produced for middlebrows and invested with middlebrow values; that the temptation is strong to avoid the experimental and to play it safe with a tried formula and popular stars. Finally the theater is dismissed with the remark that it depends for its material on the novel and is tributary on the other side of the movies.

However much truth there may be in any or all of these judgments, they do not reach to the heart of the matter. By the kind of logic I have traced above, the American theater *should* be a vanishing art—but it isn't. It had a remarkable upsurge of creativeness in the 1920s with Eugene O'Neill, in the 1930s with Odets, Saroyan, Lillian Hellman, and Sidney Kingsley, in the 1940s and 1950s with Tennessee Williams and Arthur Miller. Add to these the remarkably creative work of the music-and-lyrics teams in the musical comedies and dramatic operas. A record of this sort, stretching across forty years from the days of the Provincetown Theater until today, is not a mere episode but a sign that American energies have found a characteristic expression in the theater in the present century, as they have in the novel. An objective historian of theater arts would have to say that since Ibsen and Strindberg and Shaw, the focus of creativeness has tended to shift across the ocean, and that Broadway—which once depended wholly upon importations from Europe—can now hold its own with London and Paris, and even create some twinges of envy.

The fact that the theater is closely linked with TV and the movies is not in itself an element of weakness. It is true that Hollywood and Madison Avenue exploit Broadway by buying its plays and offering jackpots to the successful playwrights, hiring them much as the Roman conquerors hired the Greek intellectuals to teach them philosophy and art. But despite the swagger and brashness of the Hollywood money, one may question which is the main stream and which the tributary. There is a wholeness in a play which neither the movies nor TV offers— a wholeness of experience for playwright, actor, and audience alike.

When several arts are linked together, as is true of the theater, the movies, and TV, they may fertilize one another, and each of them may profit from the connection. The era of dramatic creativeness in America coincides curiously with the emergence of the movies and TV. I do not say that these are the only forces at work, but they help. The knowledge of a playwright that his play, while first produced on Broadway for a limited audience, may ultimately reach millions of people, must prove a stimulus to his imagination. Some of the people he ultimately reaches may lack sensibility, but this will not be true of all of them. The fact is that an Elizabethan audience showed a sense of excitement even when the crowd in the pit applauded and derided at the wrong passages. They sensed that new things were happening in their world, and the theater gave a concrete dramatic form to this awareness. The Americans too have an awareness of new things happening. And although millions of them flock to the movies and watch TV, while only the thousands go to the theater, the fact is that, for writers and actors alike, the prestige attaches to the theater and not to the big media. No great theater is possible in any culture unless the people consider it a great art—a place of great writing, poetry, and mime, and a place for the enactment of ideas and passions.

Much of the experimental work in the New York theater is done in the "off-Broadway" theaters that are smaller and more informal and therefore less subject to heavy overhead and production costs. Yet even the concentration on Broadway need not prove the hindrance that it has been portrayed. There was a similar concentration on a short radius inside London at the time of the Elizabethan tragedy, and the same applies to Athens. Broadway has become a convergence point for play-goers from every corner of the country. Replicas of the Broadway effort are to be found in "Little Theater" groups which crop up in surprisingly out-of-the-way places. And the lure of Broadway is even stronger for playwrights and actors than for playgoers—stronger, in fact, than the lure of Hollywood. The theater serves as a kind of recoil from the big media—a chance for a playwright to do some probing and exploring in depth as he may not be able to do in the other media, a form in which he does not have to express the optimism of American life or its surface values, and where he is not dependent upon big sponsors or a mass audience. Since he is writing in the first place for a relatively limited audience, he can become part of the countercyclical force, reversing old trends and creating new ones, becoming a molder who in turn will be followed by the big media.

Thus the theater has thrived in America and may continue to thrive, because it does more than serve as a supply base for the big media. Like the novel, it represents the best opportunity that America has for a dissection of motive and personality, at the same time that it expresses in heightened form the tensions and the sense of power of contemporary American life.

In the case of American domestic architecture, the product is likely to emerge from an unequal struggle between an impulse to utility and beauty on the one hand, and on the other the building codes, the high price of land, material, and labor, and the crushing of imagination by conformism. In the big income groups, the taste displayed in the showplace resorts of Newport and Saratoga Springs, and in the mansions built by New York and Chicago industrial kings at the turn of the century, is a matter of history: some of it, judged by modern standards, was garish; but the work of Hunt, McKim, Stanford White, Platt, and Halsey Wood at the turn of the century was among the most interesting in the record of American architecture. It is true that there was also display for the sake of display. Having made their money from machinery which expressed a strict fitting of means to use and was therefore beautiful, the industrial kings spent it mainly to show they had it to spend, with a resulting ostentation that violated taste because it had little relation to either use or beauty. The ostentation has been reduced in recent years, and the middle-class "homes" loom larger in the American architectural scene as in the whole life scene. There is still showiness in some of the "palatial homes" of tycoons in Florida or movie stars in Hollywood. Yet the shaping fact about domestic architecture is the large number of moderately well-to-do families who seek to express in their homes their desire for comfort and their sense of well-being. It is notable that Americans, so confident about machine tools, automobiles, bridges, and highways, are still fumbling for an architectural style—or perhaps a diversity of styles—which will express the way they feel about life and about themselves.

They have a number of styles out of their past to draw upon, each of which had meaning in its time and region. The New England colonial house had a strong and simple design which expressed the angle of vision of men and women who believed in a life ruled by orderly divine and human law: whether it was farmhouse or town house, church or school, there was a sharpness of view that the New Englander communicated to the wood he used. He showed it equally in his household furniture, and especially in the great and graceful clipper ships such as those by David McKay, which were among the best achievements of American design.

The Southerners also had their characteristic modes of building, their best early production being the Georgian style that flourished in Virginia, Maryland, and the Carolinas in the eighteenth century: its products may still be seen in the reconstruction of Williamsburg and in the great Georgian houses of Virginia, including Washington's house at Mount Vernon and Jefferson's at Monticello. The big sugar and cotton planters of the nineteenth century built their dreams into columned plantation houses in the style of the Greek Revival, made of wood and of the stuccoed brick obtained from the clay and river sand of the Mississippi. In the Southwest the settlers borrowed from the Spanish tradition, just as those on the Atlantic Coast had borrowed from Inigo Jones and Christopher Wren; and the influence of Indian and Spanish elements, along with the environmental setting of desert and vegetation, resulted in a sharply regional style which survives even among the new modern forms. The Western region has given American building the "ranch house," expressing an informal rustic theme and combining a sprawling comfort with the suggestion of outdoor simplicity.

I have omitted an interesting American contribution to home-building—the "salt box," which started in the Middle West in the 1830s and was linked with the "balloon frame." This was a new way of building the basic skeleton of a house—quick, light, inexpensive, effective even against prairie storm, and ugly. Its bareness and utility persisted into the twentieth century, dominating the lower-middle-class house in the small town and city. It is a characteristic dwelling made for people who have never known, from one generation to another, where they would be settling down to live. For such people houses are not built to last over generations or transmit a family heritage and sense of place, but for the here and now, out of available materials and skills. Americans built their houses as they built their railroad tracks and locomotives, their plows and firearms and cotton gins—for utility. When they grew wealthy, they still gave the prime job to the structural engineer and then called in the architect to add the decorative touches and the grace notes. Thus the Americans were led, by their feeling for structure, to draw a false line between the engineering and architectural phases of building. Hence the foliation of what came to be called "American baroque," and the lavish distortions both of form and function in the Brown Decades of the 1870s and 1880s.

One of the merits of what came to be known in the 1930s as the "International Style" of architecture, with the emphasis on geometrical planes and angles, on the use of steel and glass and concrete, and on the maximum access to light and openness, was that it lent itself to big public-housing projects. The members of this school, especially Le Corbusier, Gropius, and Mies Van der Rohe, stressed the close relation between form and function. Their opponents delighted in mocking Le Corbusier's epigram that houses must be "machines for living"; and it is true that the American functionalists developed a spare and cold style which made many uncomfortable, especially when separated from public housing and applied to the individual dwelling. In contrast, Frank Lloyd Wright continued with his poetic strain, calling for a close relationship between interior, exterior, and environment, using warm-colored woods and bricks and rough stone, and building houses which hug the landscape and sometimes seem to grow out of it. He professed to care less about men's daily needs than about their aspirations, less whether the house served their purposes than what living in it did to them.

The recent trend in American building has been toward a fusion of style, with some borrowings from the historical forms of Colonial, Georgian, and Southwest, with the use of whatever materials are most accessible, with a strong leaning toward regional styles: it has enough of the functional to show its impact, yet it retains the warm and informal qualities which most Americans regard as "livable." In essence, it is fluid and mobile in form, the living memorial of the fact that Americans are a composite product of many cultural strains, and that they are as little didactic in their housing as in their political ideas.

The big fact is that the battle cry of "houses for the people" which haunted the European architects at the turn of the century did find fulfillment in America, where tradesman, worker, or farmer could have a house of his own for his family. With the growth of the big city a new problem arose about housing the workers and white-collar classes in the congested areas. This seemed to leave the large mass of the population doomed to crowded and ugly living quarters. An eventual solution was indicated in the development of mass-produced housing projects in the suburbs, with the basic heating and service units prefabricated and with the arts of pouring the foundations and putting up the walls reduced to standardized procedure.* In 1910, as Peter Blake points out, an automobile and a one-family house cost about the same to build: today the house costs ten times what the automobile does, while the automobile is a good deal larger and the house a good deal smaller. This is to say that even with the new developments, the Industrial Revolution in building has not yet carried through as it has in the mass-production industries.

It has remained for the recent low-cost housing on a mechanical model to generate again the energy for town planning which American

* For a discussion of these projects, along with the whole question of American housing (as distinguished from architecture), see Ch. III, Sec. 6, "The Sinews of Welfare: Health, Food, Dwelling, Security," and Sec. 10, "The Suburban Revolution."

building once possessed, especially in Connecticut and other New England towns in the Colonial period. The planning impulse in the big American cities today comes either from the shift in dwelling patterns as the "less desirable" ethnic and income groups press against the "residential" areas, or from the problems of traffic congestion. As dwelling units grow less desirable and fall into neglect and disuse, a chance is provided for rebuilding and replanning whole sections of a city, as if it were sloughing off its old skin and growing a new one.

Great architecture is based on belief. Americans have not yet developed a way of domestic life sharply enough differentiated so that a body of belief can be built on it and in turn give rise to a distinctive architecture. But they do believe in their system of technology. To put it differently, Americans have had greater success with the arts of consumption and comfortable living than with the problem of their life purposes. Wherever they have built structures connected with production—factories, office buildings, hydroelectric dams, power generators and transmission lines, road networks—there has been a sureness about them absent from the recent fumblings with domestic architecture.

To the balloon frame for the wooden house, which I have mentioned, the Americans have added as a more lasting contribution the steel frame for the big industrial and office structure. That too emerged from Chicago, which had to be rebuilt after the Great Fire, and offered a new start for new ideas. In what may be seen as the great Renaissance period of American architecture a little group in Chicago—notably Dankmar Adler, Louis Sullivan, and William Le Baron Jenney—evolved the skeleton of the commercial skyscraper and filled the steel frame in with stone and cement.

The American skyscraper is a good illustration of John Ruskin's thesis about "The Lamp of Power" in his *Seven Lamps of Architecture*. I use skyscraper as a term for any of the tall office buildings that tower above every American city, at once an instrument and monument of American industrial genius. It may be the *Tribune* Tower in Chicago, or Rockefeller Center or the Empire State or Chrysler buildings in New York, or the *News* Building in San Francisco: almost always it is the power projection of some man, family, or institution. It is meant in theory to conserve valuable ground space in the badly congested areas of New York, Chicago, Cleveland, Detroit. But those who have seen a twenty-story office building jutting out of the flat spaces of a Texas or Oklahoma landscape, with plenty of elbow room immediately around, will understand that with these massive piles of masonry, steel, and cement built on the smallest possible plot, the congestion is not diminished but increased. There is in the skyscraper tower what Ruskin, Henry Adams, and Spengler saw in the Gothic spire—an aspiration toward stature which is as strong in an oil boom town with plenty of building space as it is in New York with little.

But even in crowded city quarters, where every foot of space counted, the problem of light persists. The new urban trend, largely influenced by the International Style, is toward buildings which use enough surrounding space so as to make their geometric designs visible. It is as if Americans had grown sure enough of themselves to afford a setting for their sense of power. Something of the same has happened with their bridges, as notably in the case of the George Washington Bridge over the Hudson: the original plan called for a "decorative" concrete sheeting around the steel towers at each end of the bridge; the structural design itself was so striking that public protest against any decorative additions left it standing "unfinished."

There is more to the skyscraper than height: there is also an economy of structure and a simplicity of line which are true of other forms of the architecture of power in America. They are true of the modern factories, bridges, parkways, auto highways, aqueducts, tunnels under rivers, railroad stations, airfields, air hangars, hospitals. Whether publicly or privately owned, these are the public buildings of America in which functions are carried on that have validity in American eyes. This cannot be said in equal degree of American colleges and schools, nor of the churches and cathedrals. Unlike the early New England village churches, which had simplicity, solidity, and harmony with the religion and the community, the current church buildings in America look hollow and derived, evidence that the true gods of America are housed elsewhere. The American state capitols tend also toward the ornate, as if their grandiose lines were a way of saying that the real power is not in the government but in the technological frame of society.

My underlying assumption here, like Ruskin's, is that it is hard to tell a lie in architecture since it will show through. The convincing buildings are those with belief behind them. The style a people develops in wood, stone, and steel is as much an expression of its inner being as the style it develops in words and music, in line and color.

Closely related to industrial building is industrial design. Americans have rediscovered the effectiveness with which the early settlers fashioned articles of daily use, giving them a simplicity later lost in the decades of the "American Provincial." Writing with a passion for what he calls the "vernacular" as against the "cultivated" tradition, John A. Kouwenhoven sang the praises of the Revolutionary rifle, the lowly manure fork, the plow, the railroad locomotive, the sewing machine, the clipper ship, the machine tool, the Model-T Ford. Certainly Americans have been at their best at industrial design when they have been least self-conscious and least "arty." Equally, as a machine culture, they would be out of character if they scorned the products of the machine process. Although skilled with their hands, their genius does not lie—as it did for the Renaissance craftsmen or for the artisans in rural and still primitive communities—in the laborious handicraft which is transmitted from generation to generation. The Americans achieve their effects by making machines which in turn produce standardized products that, at their best, have precision and cleanness of design and utility for their purpose. There is no longer any need to refute the argument that what is machine-made is inferior in either use or beauty, and what is turned out for a mass market loses the distinctiveness it would have if only one example of it were available.

The illustrations of this thesis surround American life everywhere: among the lasting contributions of American domestic architecture are the bathroom and the kitchen. Both express the American belief in sanitation and in utility. Similarly, a new profession has arisen—that of the "industrial designer," whose function is to give attractiveness of outline and packaging to the mass-produced commodities. The result has been the focusing of new attention upon cigarette packages, soap and soup wrappers, knives and forks, flatirons, automobiles, dining-room chairs, washing machines, typewriters, radio and TV sets, whisky bottles, refrigerators, electric ranges, waste baskets, perambulators.

The design of machine-made, useful American products has not always been a happy one. The case of the mass-produced automobile underscores the difficulties and compromises. Wholly in engineering terms, the automobile has many unnecessary features that the trade calls "chromium razzle-dazzle." This violates directly the principle that design which adds decoration and has no meaning for use makes little sense as design.

The American automobile industry has come a long way since the Model-T Ford, which made no concessions to gadgeteering and refused —as Ford put it in 1923—"to change designs so that old models will become obsolete and new ones will have to be bought." A self-respecting automobile owner would be terrified at the idea of holding on to a model more than two or three years old. Each year's model must seem more lustrous and dazzling than the previous year's—which in its turn was presented as the ultimate. The situation, both with respect to obsolescence and to fashion, is much as with women's clothes. Like the clothes, the automobile must set off the personality of the owner and must take not too long to wear out and be replaced. Given the conditions of city traffic and bumper-to-bumper auto roads on week ends, the swollen fenders—vulnerable to the slightest dent and abrasion—make no sense in design: they make sense only in obsolescence and show. Similarly, the size and unnecessary extra engine power of the American car are intended to nourish the feeling of magnitude rather than to serve ordinary users. These are all phases of a civilization which has a margin for waste and which has come to regard the luxurious as the necessary.

In contrast to the auto, the American airplane illustrates the best in American design. Every element of it is shaped and built for speed, engineering, reliability, and safety. There are no frills or unnecessary gadgets. Yet—or perhaps therefore—the beauty of the airplane has scarcely been surpassed in the history of industrial design. The crucial difference between the plane and the auto is that the auto is produced for a mass consumer's market while the plane is not. The pace for selling autos is set by their production. The problem in planes is to supply the demand, not to create it.

Thus the thesis that the vernacular* is always right cannot be sustained. The elements of taste that enter into design through high-pressure salesmanship and conspicuous display do not always make for simplicity, economy, and beauty. When the vernacular style wages a battle against the merely decorative elements of elite art, or against the stodginess of traditional art, it is likely to triumph through its vigor and directness. But when it becomes itself associated with the emulation of elite values, while staying in a mass-production market—as in the case of most automobiles, with the honorable exception of the "jeep" and some of the simpler station wagons—it falls foul of its own principles. Finally, the vernacular style runs into trouble when it sets up a false standard of nativism. The International Style in architecture has its own strengths and defects, but the fact that it is an importation from European experience has no relevance to its merits. American art, building, and design have throughout their history borrowed ideas from foreign cultures and have in turn had an impact upon them. America has shown a hospitality to artists and designers from abroad that has kept its indigenous elements of strength from becoming too ingrown. While there are nativist outbursts from those who resent the influence of foreign architects and designers, these are passing episodes. There is remarkably little cultural isolationism as yet among a people who can take pride in having created their own world of machine commodities with a design of their own.

* The terms "vernacular" and "cultivated" as used here need some precision of meaning. The "vernacular" style is associated with the immediate realities of democracy-and-technology; I use "cultivated" to refer to the tradition acceptable to the elites, whether of the arts, of wealth, or of birth. In Europe the vernacular tradition blended largely with the cultivated tradition; in America there has been antagonism between the two.

9. *Artist and Audience in a Democratic Culture*

PERIODICALLY, when the arts in America are in the doldrums, the blame is put on one of the new media. But it is idle to talk of any art as the enemy of the others. The theater lives in the golden shadow of Hollywood, and the novel seems at times tributary to it: but that does not make Hollywood their enemy. Nor is photography an enemy to painting, nor jazz to "serious" music, any more than night baseball is an enemy to the concert hall or the mystery to the novel. Even TV, whose shadow seems to have fallen on movies, radio, and book publishing, can scarcely be regarded as the Adversary. For to think of the arts as rivals is to think of them as flowing from a fixed fund of energy, so that a popular devotion to one of them means anemia for the others. It is true that some of the newer and lustier popular arts display an imperialistic bent in crowding their neighbors, but in its youth each of the elite arts was also arrogant in its imperialism. Actually the movies and jazz, radio and TV, the paperbacks and the spectacle arts, have reinforced one another because their vitality is contagious rather than sterilizing.

I am not talking here of the question of what medium commands a larger segment of the Big Audience. Given limited leisure, it is plausible that a revolutionary increase in the TV audience should have a drastic effect on movie attendance. But such audience rivalry is different from the rivalry in the intellectual and aesthetic standards of the media. Quite possibly American radio may be able to reach better levels of achievement by limiting itself to good music, news commentary, political discussion, and suspense shows, than it reached when it spread itself thin into areas where TV can do better. The movies may discover that TV cannot be surpassed in the histrionic display of sex and violence, or in the presentation of a documentary sense of the immediate moment: by concentrating on emotion and characterization it may perform for TV the kind of generative function that the theater over several generations performed for the movies. There is a big enough audience in America to furnish for each popular art some perceptive portion of the population that will sustain it economically, especially since another popular art may use it as a feeder for ideas and talent.

In thus dismissing the necessity of a Big Audience I do not accept the view that any art which has one is thereby cheapened. This would be to hold that the chief enemy of the arts is their popularization. One may believe that the spreading of an art wide among a mass audience necessarily brings with it a dilution of its standards: "the wider you spread it, the thinner it spreads." But to hold this view mechanically means, for example, to forget the creative achievements of an art like the movies. It implies a curious antipopulism—a fear that the wide support of an art must taint its quality or destroy its fine bloom. This is the Great Fear that one finds in American literary and art criticism; and one can match it only by the Great Contempt that one finds in turn on the part of the Big Audience—a contempt for the elite arts it cannot understand and whose aestheticism it distrusts. The contempt and the fear together split a society into a Big Audience and a Little Audience, driving a wedge between the creative people and those who are needed to nourish their creativeness.

The fear of the "horde" in art undercuts one of the cultural assumptions of a democracy—that the human personality is a bundle of potentials irrelevant to income or social or even educational rating, and that the richness of popular culture will depend on how well those potentials are fulfilled. The Elizabethan theater in Shakespeare's time, the great church music of the Middle Ages, the acting of Chaplin and Garbo in Hollywood in our own time: all have been people's arts. To be sure, the need for reaching a Big Audience has often been used to excuse the trivial and unexacting. But there is proof enough that, if greatly conceived, the popular arts can derive strength from a massive popular base and can reach the many by reducing themselves to simplest elements—that is, to their broadest humanity.

If we take American painting as an instance, we find an art that has never appealed to a wide audience. It has suffered from the twin plagues of the Expensive and the Esoteric. Having made their fortunes, the American captains of industry ransacked European galleries for their best works and brought them home at big prices. Since the dead masters were the object of their pecuniary piety, they stored them in museums; and most Americans came to think of painting as something in a museum or a rich man's house, removed from their lives—and so they ignored it. The painter, in turn, cut off from his audience except for an inner circle of means and sensibility, came to despise those whom he could not reach.

This isolation of artist and audience from each other has been attributed to the machine, which revolutionized the market for art products as for other commodities. Where the product is one of unique workmanship and is not reproducible, as in painting and sculpture, the arts have remained much as they were during the Age of Handicraft. Even in painting the revolutionary techniques of reproduction have made possible a "museum without walls." In the case of the printed and spoken word and of images and movement, the press and film and electronics have made them infinitely reproducible and infinitely accessible. The machine has made possible the widespread appreciation of music, the cheap distribution of literary classics, the enactment of dramatic performances in thousands of movie centers and millions of homes.

The problem of distribution in the arts has been effectively broken. What remains is the question of the conditions of creativeness. I have suggested that in America this problem focuses not on the fact of popularization but on the isolation of the artist. The pushing, successful people among the Americans regard him as an outsider. They do not make a hero of him, as they do of the technical or moneyed genius or the man of power, or even the successful performer in a Big-Audience medium. At best they regard him as a luxury a culture can perhaps afford. Where once the American artist had to wage the Emersonian fight for self-reliance and for freedom from a sense of provincialism, his main fight now is for acceptance in a culture that values the pecuniary. This has led him periodically to flight abroad, especially to France and Italy, where he could thrive in a social climate of acceptance. Sometimes it has led to surrender to the idols of the market, sometimes to a flight into himself. The European apprenticeship has been of value to American artists, but the surrender has been uniformly destructive, and the flight into himself has usually led to obscurity rather than depth. But the American artist has been maturing, and some have achieved the power of synthesis—of exploring their own being without cutting themselves off from the currents of their place and time.

Since the pressures to conform are strong, the artist still works in a difficult environment in America. When he fights against them he runs the danger of joining a coterie which spins out a narrowly private universe with an incommunicable language. He finds it hard to assimilate the rapid pace of cultural change and the vast human deposits of his own culture. He may retreat to the realism of describing one "slice of life" he knows, but he makes no connections between it and the universal values he has failed to grasp. The poet or painter may single out a few crucial items of experience as symbols for the whole, but he soon finds that to handle symbolism as well takes even greater grasp than to handle naturalism. He may concentrate on a locale or region which seems manageable, only to find that the problems of creativeness are not diminished by shrinking the map. Failing there, he almost always turns to the popular arts. Sometimes the Pilgrim's Progress of a writer or artist in America is a progression through all these phases.

The fatal magnetic force is that of the Big Prizes. Given the Big Audience, the prizes are big enough to engender cupidity and enforce timidity. There is no scorn in America more withering than the scorn felt for "the highbrow." The charge against him is not only that he cuts himself off from the people but also from "reality"—which is identified with making money. The easiest way to get at the Big Prizes is by pandering to the culture traits in all classes that will mean a sure-fire sale. The Midas touch which turns everything in American life to gold does not spare the energies that might otherwise go into difficult reaches of the intelligence and imagination.

If the artist decides to take the pecuniary culture in his stride, aiming at a good living without chasing the Big Prizes, he will still come up against another obstacle—the increasing bureaucratization of the arts. He will need an agent and a lawyer to take care of his contracts; or he may go on concert and lecture tours, barnstorming across the country, largely repeating himself but making money enough to let him do the work he loves the rest of the year. If he is a playwright, he must deal with Broadway producers, theater owners, stage-hand unions. If he is a musician he must pay for an initial recital and "paper the house" with free tickets. As a painter he must be *persona grata* to galleries, museums, rich customers. As an actor or radio performer, he must deal with the networks and sponsors, and with their agents and his own. If he is an architect he must tangle with building codes and city officials and the construction unions. As a novelist he must reckon with serial rights, book-club and cheap reprint rights, movie rights. For the novelist, playwright, and actor there is the guild of reviewers to reckon with, who have it in their power to damn an author or performer who has proved a literary or political heretic, slaying him either with abuse or silence. For the short-story writer there is either the poverty of a host of "little magazines" or the Big Circulation magazines that pay well but may exact in return a large measure of conventionality in art and a conformity in politics.

Even the star system, which seems at the opposite pole from bureaucracy in the arts, works in much the same way. The movie star, the boxing champion or baseball hero, the TV comic of national fame—all represent a huge investment in which many financial groups may have a stake. Highly personalized though their lives may seem, they are actually depersonalized since they must move within narrow patterns set by the bureaucracy their public image serves. It is usual for the writer, composer, or designer in the popular arts to remain anonymous while the performer is played up. It is not the creator but the executor whom the public gets to know as symbol—not the novelist or script writer or composer, but the starred actors and perhaps the director or producer; not the radio or TV writer but the gagster or crooner or the M.C. of the variety shows. The folk heroes of popular culture, as is true of all folklore, are not the creators but the protagonists—of radio serial or comic strip, baseball field or movie studio. There is thus an anonymity in the popular arts that does not exist in the elite arts—the anonymity of the creator but not of the hero. This lack of interchange between the creator and his audience may account for much of the isolation of the artist of which I have spoken. It is a tossup whether the anonymity of the creator or the stardom of the performer is more destructive to personality.

Despite these obstacles, the American artist has one advantage the European artist lacks—the sense of cultural hope and dynamism in a people reaching out for new ways of expressing itself. The American feels he has a future, while the European feels caught. Out of this sense of being caught may come a quality, at once mellow and doomed, which will not be found in the American writer, who has new media always opening for him. Thus the American artist has typically a more meteoric rise and a more abrupt collapse than the European. This has proved true of young novelists who start as sensitive recorders of what they remember, catching the characteristic tone of their generation and pinning it down as you might mount a butterfly. But the high expressive moment of the generation passes, and if the young novelist or playwright has no other resources than gaiety and vitality and the gift of transcription, he stops in his tracks as a writer and goes to pieces in his life.

If the career of the artist in America has its dangers, which I have described, it also has its strength. Popular culture has performed a great ground-clearing function by breaking the monopoly over taste that the elite arts held so long in the Western World. But to clear the ground is only a first step toward constructing a new structure of sensibility. There remains the question of by whom and for whom it will be built.

This is not a new problem in America. The split between the "vernacular" and the "cultivated," which I have discussed earlier, started with the long-barreled rifles of the frontier and the economical lines of the farmer's tools. The issues of battle have never been sharply defined: it is not always the mass-produced as against the unique product, nor the popular as against coterie art, nor the "modern" and "functional" as against the academic. Nor can one agree that when the vernacular has won out against the cultivated, as has repeatedly happened in American history, it has always been to the advantage of the product. Yet if it is possible to speak of an artistic culture predominantly phrased in the vernacular—that is to say, a popular culture—

America must be counted its most fateful experimental instance. What some of the younger art historians and critics call a "democratic aesthetic" will either be shaped in America or nowhere.

One question about it is whether it must rest on indigenous art forms alone. If this is taken to mean exclusively home-grown forms and techniques it would be absurd, since it would force each culture to cut itself off from the world and retraverse every step other cultures have taken. Throughout American history there has run a demand for a nativist art, whether in architecture or literature, music or aviation design. In part this has been a recoil from an earlier cultural provincialism, but it has maintained its self-assertiveness and been sustained long after the declaration of cultural independence. At their best the nativists have seen that an indigenous art may and must borrow widely: what makes it indigenous is how it uses the materials it finds at home and abroad, and how it weaves them into a pattern expressing the common experience.

An indigenous art in this sense need not be troubled by the question of the classes from which its material derives or by which its product is accepted. Just as Joyce could appropriate scatological language and make out of it a complex art product intelligible only to the few, so the American language has shown that it can adapt the restricted phrases of the educated classes and integrate them—often with a saving grace of irony—into its own mood and pattern. American ballet has taken traditional dance form derived from the aristocratic societies of St. Petersburg and Vienna and fused it—as in Agnes De Mille's *Fall River Legend*—with the folk material of America, giving it a tongue-in-cheek hyperbole that stamps it as American popular culture. Because these forms have been mixed with the sweat of American experience the lowly do not distrust them as highbrow, nor does the elite despise them as vulgar, but all classes can relax and accept the accents of the universal in the indigenous. These art forms are in turn accepted abroad because they bear the smell of the soil from which they came, yet break through the walls of cultural separation.

Within this frame of the universal the accents of the American vernacular often crop up in very diverse arts. Thus, there are a stridency and exaggeration running through folklore and speech as they do through the comic gag, the radio and TV program, and the spectacle sports—as if the tone of the frontier swaggerers were able to be maintained because the richness of the unbroken wilderness still persisted among the towers of the city. Thus also there is, throughout the popular arts, a blending of the rustic and urban such as will be found in few other cultures. This is illustrated by the blues songs and jazz, whose themes and overtones belong to a preindustrial people but whose beat carries the tensions of the big cities.

To a curious degree the American popular culture, unlike the "Socialist realism" of Marxian cultures, stays clear of the descriptively naturalistic. On the surface it uses the method of realism, but it achieves its characteristic effects in the abstractions from reality. It is a kind of cartoon or gargoyle art, in which everything is bigger than life. This is true of a rich vein of the comic tradition in Hollywood from the Keystone Cops and Charlie Chaplin through W. C. Fields, Harry Langdon, and the Marx Brothers, and of the radio comic tradition which Jimmy Durante expresses. It is also part of the American theater, from the early traveling minstrel shows through the masks of O'Neill's characters and the poetic expressionism of Tennessee Williams. The same abstraction from life will be found at once in movie musicals and spectacles, in jazz and in the skyscrapers (the "jazz of architecture"), as it will also be found in painting. The younger expressionist painters and sculptors who have never won popular acceptance have a quality similar to that of "cool jazz."

This makes hash of much of the "battle of the brows" in the controversies over American taste. I have mentioned in an earlier chapter the amusing discussion by Russell Lynes, in the manner of Thackeray's *Book of Snobs,* on the highbrow, lowbrow, and middlebrow in America.* The truth is that tastes of Americans, like their classes, are hopelessly intermingled. Legend has it that Justice Holmes, a Yankee Brahmin, slapped his knee while sitting at a burlesque show and muttered to his neighbor, "Thank God for our low tastes." The American who likes Jackson Pollock is likely also to delight over the travail of Li'l Abner; the enthusiast for Frank Lloyd Wright may devour cheap mystery stories and roar over the obsessive adventures of Groucho Marx. The fluidity of the class system, the sweep of common experience, and the spread of the big media have done havoc to the hierarchy of the brows, and American society never remains stable long enough for the brows to rigidify in their angle of elevation. Moreover, one can discern in contemporary American literary circles (as Riesman suggests) a separation between the Old Highbrow and the New Highbrow. The Old Highbrow has an attitude of either reserve or hostility toward popular culture, either because as an aristocrat he regards it as vulgar or because as a radical he sees it as a corrupt product of capitalist incentives. The New Highbrow, recoiling both from the genteel tradition and from Marxism, has come to embrace popular culture, finding in it—shoddi-

* Ch. IX, Sec. 3, "Manners, Taste, and Fashion."

ness and all—something of the mystique the eighteenth-century intellectual found in the Noble Savage.

There are signs, however, of a new criticism which will separate the true vernacular from the spurious mob language and combine the best of the vernacular with the best from the elite arts. Such a critic will face the fact that the big media will tend to gravitate toward whatever is flat, stale, and profitable, that the press lords will debase their product and the radio sponsors will narrow the imaginative world of the radio to the compass of their own shriveled intellectual universe. But he will not retreat in despair, but will see the growth of popular culture in perspective, just as he looks back at the history of the elite arts and sees in perspective that they too had the vigor to outgrow their excesses.

Where the Old Highbrow regards every Big Audience as a bad one and the New Highbrow sees the Big Audience as a great one, the critic I speak of will understand that the great audience is only a potential in the Big Audience, and that the potential will not be fulfilled except in an intellectual climate that affirms its possibilities even while it criticizes the actual product. He will not despise the movies and TV because mainly the young are drawn to them, but neither will he count that fact in itself an index of vitality. He will recognize that every form of popular culture has varied levels of audience appeal, and that a mature art will shape its product—as Chaplin did in the movies—to reach each audience on its own terms, yet hold them all in suspension by universals which give each a new dimension. He will respect the subtleties and richness of the American language, and the capacity of the common speech to express the common experience of Americans. He will not scorn the escapist in the arts, since imagination must create a sheath within which to feel secure before it can release its quickening energies. But he will refuse to the popular arts—as to any art—the easy, jerry-built solutions to old human dilemmas, exacting from them the emotional honesty with which a mature man cannot dispense.

This is the final test of a democratic aesthetic, whose parallel will be found in the politics and economics of a democracy. No one expects a general leveling of either income or power, but a democracy does require that the whole personality of every man be valued by giving him access to the common political and economic opportunity. Similarly, a democratic aesthetic will not level intellectual and taste standards; but it will reject the principle of a frozen elite of the arts. It will open a hospitable door to any experience which can be phrased in a universal language of art from which no one need be shut out. It will value the indigenous material not because it is "native" or "American" but be-cause—coming out of the common experience—it can be couched in this common language of emotion, so that the reader or listener is at once source and receiver of the creative process. In this sense a democratic aesthetic, like a democratic ethic, gives dignity to every personality.

The foreigner's picture of American popular culture, whether in Europe, Asia, or Latin America, is often wide of the mark. The Com-munist campaign against "degenerate" American jazz or the "corrupt" press or "degrading" movies or "Coca-Cola imperialism" sometimes im-presses many who are otherwise sympathetic to America and its demo-cratic experience. But Americans are needlessly worried about this ob-viously ephemeral phase. Foreign cultures have accepted and absorbed American movies—and in some cases gone on to produce better ones of their own; they have picked up the more colorful phrases of the Ameri-can language from soldiers, travelers, and books; they have been deeply influenced by American jazz, by American design in the items of daily use, by American novelists and playwrights. Whatever proves to be universally valid in American culture will make its way in other cultures.

The idea that movies or jazz or literature is a "weapon" in the international struggle has been overstressed in American anxieties about them. It is foolish to use this as an argument for censorship or for changing the direction of the arts themselves. Movies cannot be pretti-fied merely because they will give Communists abroad a handle for at-tacking America, nor can the historic fact that jazz originated in the brothels of Storyville be muted because it is used against America. In the domain of artistic integrity, cold wars intrude a dimension of irrelevance. The popular arts will serve American interests best when they express with depth and universality the surging impulses of the common American experience.

CHAPTER XII

America As a World Power

WE COME *finally to an over-all view of America's place in the frame of world power, asking what kind of power it embodies and how much promise or menace it holds for the world (Sec. 1, "Among the Powers of the Earth"). We examine what currents of thought, impulse, and emotion have shaped American foreign policy, what strategies of national interest it has tended to use, and what sense Americans have had of their mission in world history and their role in the world struggle (Sec. 2, "The Shaping Currents").*

Among other things we ask some of the questions that have long engaged students of American life—what are the roots of isolationism in the American mind, and to what extent it still survives, what impact the nation as a social myth has had, what has impelled America to enter the arena of world power actively, what have been the sources and forms of American expansionism, and whether America is basically an imperium—*a power mass content to let alone and be let alone, interested mainly in world order and peace—or also an* imperialism, *throwing its weight around and bent on making its own institutions and its ways of life prevail (Sec. 3, "National Interest and an Open World").*

We try to get a closer look at Americans at war and in a military posture, examining the relations of military to civilian internally and the role of the military elite in a highly technical atomic era (Sec. 4, "Landscape with Soldiers"). We then take a double exposure of the American image, asking first what image the Americans have of the world outside their national boundaries, and then what image of America is to be found in the minds of the other peoples of the world, and in both instances what leads to the distortions and stereotypes (Sec. 5, "The American World Image"; Sec. 6, "The World's Image of America"). Finally we look backward in history for parallels to the present American situation, paying special attention to the often discussed Roman parallel, and we look at the relations of the two super powers—America and Russia—in the world of today and tomorrow, and then we venture a look into the calculable future in an effort to get a glimpse of the destiny of America as a civilization (Sec. 7, "The Destiny of a Civilization").

CHAPTER XII

America As a World Power

1. Among the Powers of the Earth

THE rise of America to a position of world power focuses attention on the qualities that underlie so dramatic a rise. When the nascent Americans met in 1776 to declare their independence, they voiced the hope that they would "assume among the powers of the earth the separate and equal station to which the laws of Nature and of Nature's God entitle them." They could scarcely have suspected that these straggling colonies of small population—huddled along a strip of ocean coast, pitifully weak and disunited, with survival their most pressing problem —would assume in less than two centuries a commanding position "among the powers of the earth." To a contemporary observer so daring a perspective of the grandeurs of world power must have seemed a megalomanic fantasy of minds that had dwelt too bitterly on their weakness and grievances.

How explain this mushrooming rise to power? The important clues are less likely to be found in the history of diplomacy or the record of America's wars than in the drive within American institutions and in the intellectual and moral features of American character, helped by a cluster of favoring circumstances.

First among these circumstances was *geography,* which equipped the nation with the resources on which power always rests. It provided the timber that made it a shipbuilding people, and the sea lanes that made it a trading people while severing it by the span of oceans from the centers of world production, giving it thus the impetus to develop its own industries. It furnished the sinews first for a technology of coal, then of electricity, and now of atomic power. Geography made available also a great land mass ready to be rounded out by settlement, purchase, and conquest, giving shape to the ever-present sense of continental unity and providing a striking combination of safety and access. There have been great land empires before and great maritime empires, but it would be hard to cite an earlier land empire with its own available sea lanes, or an earlier maritime empire with so vast an expanse as its land core. The availability of land and access by sea—and later, jobs and wealth, living standards, freedom, and the legendry of America—made America the magnet that drew people from all over the world. Thus *man power* was added to *resources* and *technology*, as the sinews of the American's command over Nature.

This command made possible a high industrial *productivity*, which in turn gave weight to America's voice in peace and arms in war. It led to the repayment of the big European investments when, early in the present century, the Europeans had to call them in. It gave America a favorable trade balance, turning it into an investing nation which exported capital to the world's undeveloped regions. It was *investment* that enabled America to become a mighty engine of world finance gathering increments of power from old enterprises bolstered or new enterprises opened with American capital. It was *finance* in turn that shifted the economic center of the world westward across the Atlantic, making America the axis of power on which the non-Communist world turned.

Thus, geography, technology, man power, productivity, investment, and finance are links in the Great Chain holding American power together. America's world position is not wholly summed up in these terms of economics and geopolitics. It was a fallacy of Marxist thought to assume the inevitable collapse of world capitalism through the weight of its inner contradictions. This involved a blunder of diagnosis. It assumed that the Western World, the scene of a succession of power struggles between capitalist Great Powers, was on its deathbed. Marx and Engels announced the coming funeral, and Lenin read the funeral oration. Spengler unfolded an apocalyptic vision of what was to follow. They failed to see that the Western World, including Europe, might have a greater recuperative power than they had counted upon.

This was linked with a second blunder of diagnosis, which was concerned with America. Every great system of European thought, from Marx to Toynbee, saw America as at best an appendage of the larger "Western" system which was at the mercy of its inner laws of disintegration and decay. They did not grasp the import of this new world power—born out of straggling colonies, at the start a "have-not nation" beset by hostile "have" powers, filling out its continental expanse, sweeping away whatever obstructed it, girdling the seas with naval power, darkening the skies with air power, waxing in strength while other nations were waning, perhaps even *because* the others were waning. The Europe they saw as the center of Western power turned out to be the rim, and the America they saw as the rim turned out to be the center. Nor did they understand the capacity of this new center to extend and re-create the tradition of European power and yet remain its own entity with its own laws of being and conditions of health and unhealth.*

---

* For an earlier discussion of this failure of perspective, see Ch. II, Sec. 2.

It was not technology or economics alone that accounted for the rise of this new power, nor will they alone condition its decline and fall when the time is ripe. What is crucial about America as a world power is that very mixture of idealism and material power which has evoked many a jibe and has been the substance of almost every "exposé" of the contradictions of American foreign policy. If the Americans have been conquerors in the domain of world power they have come not as conquerors with a sword or a book, but with the machine, the dollar, and the idea of freedom. One of the difficulties with both the economic interpretation and the Machiavellian interpretation of world power is that they neglect intangibles and social myths as in themselves decisive power elements. The fact that America emerged out of a colonial revolution, the first modern symbol of liberation from imperialism, gave it an impulsion toward world power which was worth many Army divisions. It could not, of course, have risen to its present domination through this freedom symbolism alone. Yet it served as a kind of "multiplier," giving an enhanced force to every element of substantive strength derived from geography and economics.

The power factor of freedom can be spelled out on at least three scores. First, it brought some of the best human resources in the world to American shores, through a selective process of emigration by which the restless energies of each nation found an outlet in America. Second, the birth of America in colonial revolt meant that there was never any entrenched feudal class (as in France) against which continuing revolutionary action was needed: America's strength was thus not splintered by internal class struggles on the European model. Third, the legendry of America as the land of freedom has served as a dynamic weapon of political warfare on the side of every American cause, from that of the Northern States in the Civil War, through the two world wars to the present time. Marx's writings on the Civil War are testimony to the force of this legendry; in World War I the *éclat* of Wilson's Fourteen Points and the excitement produced by his appearance in Europe were additional proof of it.

Thus the "revolutionary idealism" of Wilson—and, to an extent, of Franklin Roosevelt—so bitterly attacked by champions of American "national interest," turns out to have been part of the American world strength which protects that national interest. In both world wars, America's role was to help a European coalition whose defeat America feared, just as it feared the victory of the opposing coalition. Later America became the center of a democratic coalition seeking to win and hold allies in the struggle against a Communist coalition. This change cannot be seen in Marx's terms of the weakness and inner disintegration of capitalist power, nor in Lenin's terms of the division of the world among imperialist cartels. It is more intelligible as the radiation of a strong organizing force out from the center into a vacuum left by the decline of the European power system, and into a receptive border zone of colonial countries emerging into their own in the Near East and Far East. Thus America's rise as a world power, far from being a deterioration story of the decay of an old system, marks the thrust of a strong new system into an arena where it has to meet the counterthrust of another new and expanding power.

In the process of its history and the carving out of its imperium, America shows signs of having grown conservative. It has the sense, as the Romans had, of being enveloped by the encroaching forces of the new barbarians, and it is caught within a ring of fears of "alien" and "subversive" ideas. The face it shows to the world is, however, only one aspect of its character. The other, implicit in the historical emergence I have traced, is the aspect of a continuing revolutionary energy. The nature of that energy has great bearing on the destiny and survival power of the civilization pattern I have tried to analyze. There is little question that the present age is one of world revolution, with a ferment of colonial revolt, movements of national awakening, new amalgams of economic and social power, peoples in the breaking and making. The fact that Americans shy away from the concept of revolution should not obscure the more important fact that Americans have had a revolutionary history, and that their rise to world power has itself been the product of a revolutionary era.

The present era of world power is not revolutionary in a suddenly new form: it is the extension into our own times of a long-continuing series of social transformations that have changed the profile of societies and shifted the axis of power from one capital to another. There is no single clue that will unravel the logic behind this shift, whether it be the clue of technological change, or of military vigor, or of the personality of great leaders, or of master ideas and religions. An adequate account would see world history as shaped by movements which are vaster in scope than single nations and peoples, or even continental expanses of resources and armies, but are great energy systems drawing vitality from every source, and organizing armies and ideas, economics and societies, into effective engines of action.

The American revolutionary impulse has not aimed at overthrowing a ruling class or a prevailing system of government. Once the Americans had freed themselves from England they expressed their continuing revolutionary impulse through changes in technology, which in turn have transformed the landscape of American society and culture. That is to say, it has been revolution by indirection, in the sense that the revolutionary changes have been the unintended consequences of actions taken in a matter-of-fact and nonrevolutionary spirit. For example, the demands of a warfare economy and of world power-politics have, by indirection, kept the revolutionary impulse alive in America. For the demands of international politics have in themselves a transforming effect on the internal nature of a social system; and even war is a form of revolution. The structure of heavy taxation, which seems necessary if profits are to be forcibly plowed back by governmental expenditures, was one to which the American business groups became amenable only when danger forced it upon them. The pace of capital formation was also increased by world responsibilities, for while war is one of the great destroyers of capital, the energies of a world power are heightened in the formation of new capital. Thus, far from diminishing as American power was dispersed by new demands around the ramparts of the world, it continued to grow as an energy system.

Curiously, the enlargement of the American world perspective has taken place fitfully, by a process of unwilling advances and forced retreats, almost against the will of the people and their leaders. Faced with the turmoils of a world from which they thought they had safely withdrawn themselves, and with threatening new shapes of crises and power, they reluctantly met the new challenges with new responses. First Europe, then Asia, then the Middle East and Africa were added to the map of American concern. A people that had prided itself on its isolation from foreign entanglements was forced against its will into them. A people that had scorned the wiles of diplomacy and condemned the "striped pants and Homburg boys" and the "cookie-pushers" was forced into a vigorous diplomacy and into developing its own effective type of diplomat. American soldiers, many of whom had never before left their own state, where they had gone to high school or worked at a filling station, roamed over the twelve corners of the earth, reluctant wanderers who resisted the ways of the "foreigners" but would never again be what they had been. In a world where Americans had to hold their coalition together despite the faltering economies of their allies, and where they had to keep undeveloped economies from succumbing to Communism by default, they found new political uses for reconstruction and investment capital and for the export of technical skills and the tools of war and peace.

Hostile critics called this American imperialism; certainly it was, in the sense of an American imperium—a vast structure of military, economic, and administrative power that could be used to override competing structures and achieve its power purposes. But it was also an extension of the same revolutionary process by which Americans had found tools and techniques for whatever was at hand to be done. At every stage, ideas and attitudes lagged behind the new techniques; Americans did what they had to do as a response to the challenge and then grudgingly discovered that their perspective had changed in the process. This was *homo faber,* approaching both peace and war as an engineering problem of finding the right tools. It was not the zealot with a religious idea or the thinker with an intellectual system seeking to transform the work in the image of his dream. If it now built a huge structure of power and commitments in the world, it was as a by-product of its technical drive. The British had once, in Seeley's phrase, "conquered half the world in a fit of absence of mind": the Americans did much the same thing, not absent-mindedly but like a truant school-boy who stays after hours to dispose of the lessons he should have mastered earlier.

What made the task harder was the fact that, having forgotten their own history as a revolutionary society, they confronted a world in revolution with a sullen bewilderment. The revolutionary techniques that Communists used where they came into power resulted from the welding of Marxist rationalism and predemocratic ruthlessness and were most successful in politically and economically undeveloped areas. The American revolutionary technique was that of technological change in an open-class system, assuming economic development as the prime value, and with a genuine although imperfect commitment to an open society. The question that both America and the world had now to resolve was whether this authentic revolutionary tradition could be applied fruitfully to conflicts of world power and the struggle for men's minds, or whether it had grown into a rigid mold in the process of reaching world power.

2. *The Shaping Currents*

I HAVE SPOKEN of America as the center of one of the great energy systems of history. The thrust of expansionism has been a continuous impulse in American history. Land hunger, power hunger, newness hunger, and bigness hunger, have proved wants that feed on themselves. In the earliest phase of American history it was a question of reaching from the coast far enough into the interior to tap its resources; then the felt need became one of wiping out the Indians in order to use the new resources; and of driving out or buying out the remaining outposts of the British, French, and Spanish so that America would be an exclusive preserve for Americans; then there were exploratory wars fought against Canada and Mexico, to make sure that the neighbors to the north and south were not too difficult to handle and not too imperious as rivals; then the need became that of rounding out the continental expanse and reaching the territorial limits of America's "manifest destiny."

The process was not a matter of course; it took will and imagination. With the image of a continental America in our minds, it is hard to think ourselves back into the mental atmosphere of a period when such an image must have seemed daring. Actually the radical groups of the early period—the Jeffersonians and Jacksonians—were even more eager than the conservatives of the possessing classes for this kind of expansionism. "Manifest destiny" was the rationalization that Americans gave to their expansive thrust and their hunger for land and power, for profits and bigness. Nor has this thrust ended. It would be rash to think that an energy forceful enough to push the frontiers to their continental limits would stop at the ocean's edge.

This raises again the issue of the nature of the American imperium. There can be no question that America has built one of the big empires of history. But to say this is not to carry along with it all the connotations that "imperialism" conveys as a set of drives toward aggrandizement which colors the nature of the imperium. As I have suggested, America did not set out to dominate the world as the Nazis did under Hitler, with a notion that its people were meant to be *Herrenvolk* while the rest were sub-men. There was no ideological fanaticism behind American expansion, as in the case of the Communists. The American case is not even like that of the Roman Empire, which was the product of a similar energy system but which rationalized its expansion as Rome's civilizing function in a world of outworn kingships and barbarian hordes. The Americans come much closer to the British, who had to keep the seas open for their commerce and dressed the need up as "the white man's burden." Even more sharply than the British, the Americans were moved by a drive toward economic power. The business spirit has informed American foreign policy as it has informed every other aspect of American power—the political machines, the legal system, the course of constitutional interpretation, the churches, the press, even the labor movement.

Actually, the American business spirit was for a long time isolationist rather than imperialist. It led Americans to put the development of industry ahead of the quest for territory. That was one reason why the New England shippers and manufacturers opposed the War of 1812 with Britain, while the Western farmers and frontiersmen wanted it. That was also why Americans for a long period cared more about protective tariffs for their "infant industries" than they did about foreign adventures. Once the industries had been built the stream of new immigration provided at once the labor power for exploiting the resources of the country and a vast home market for farm, mine, and factory products. The impulse which did much to shape American policy through most of the nineteenth century was the self-sufficient exploitation of resources and profits within America which Charles Beard, mocking the imperialist phrase, called "the open door at home."

This may shed light on the strain of isolationist thinking which took the form sometimes of the "hermit nation" that could shut itself off from the corruptions and subversions of the rest of the world, sometimes of the idea of defending the American "stockade" against its savage enemies in the surrounding forest, sometimes of the hard-bitten resolve of an individualist nation to "go it alone" in a world of "ungrateful" allies. I want to come back later to an analysis of the nature of the American isolationist pattern. Here I point out that it could prove strong and enduring only among a people with resources, labor power, and home markets rich enough to keep them self-sufficient, and only among a people in a position to profit from self-immersement. America could afford to turn in on itself, away from the world, partly because it was admitting within its borders as much of the world as it could digest and partly because it was already a world within itself. Hence Beard was right in calling the traditional American polity, from Jefferson on, less one of "isolationism" than of "continentalism." It was not so much a question of cutting America off from the world as it was of rounding out and fully exploiting the part of the world that was America.

One can thus trace side by side through the nineteenth century the twin impulses of expansionism and self-sufficiency. Only with the continent rounded out and the home market saturated, when the continental limits of America were bursting at the seams, did American foreign policy encounter a succession of crises. America then had to decide not whether to be a world power, which had been decided for it by events, but what form its decisions about participating in the world struggle were to take. From the 1890s there were premonitions of crisis, but it did not assume its more ominous proportions until the two world wars in the second through the fifth decades of the twentieth century.

Americans had then to reckon with the chance that another great power might not only overshadow them in the world but threaten the stability and survival of their own system at home. In 1914 the danger came from the expanding power of Imperial Germany, threatening to shut off the sea lanes that connected the American industrial system with the materials and markets outside. In 1933 it came from a new ideological force in Germany aiming to consolidate a "thousand-year empire" that would dwarf America or make it vassal. After 1945 it came from a Communist imperium using the resources of a Russian sub-continent and a whole arsenal of ideological appeals to establish Communism not "in one country" but in the frame of world power. After 1952 it came from a Moscow-Peiping axis that had consolidated a vast Eurasian land mass. In the mid-1950s it came from a set of Communist alliances that aimed to organize the slumbering energies of the under-developed countries of the Middle East, and formed a Moscow-Cairo axis. In all these cases the Americans were moved by the challenge of an opposing structure of power and by both a fear and repugnance for the image of human personality which such a threat conjured up. Through four decades America took part in power struggles whose arena was thousands of miles away, whose other contestants seemed alien and often barbaric, and which burst the continental bounds of traditional American expansion. Once the continental phase was over, the thrust outward and the thrust of concentration could no longer be compatible. In their new form these two thrusts expressed a split which was to dominate American thought and emotion. Yet even in the new form the expansionism—or, as it came to be called, "interventionism"—had little of the traditional imperialist coloring.

There have been various attempts to correlate isolationism and inter-nationalism with political attitudes on domestic issues, but it is diffi-cult to carry the parallel through American history. Actually the Jef-fersonians were expansionists as against the Federalists; the Jacksonians were apostles of Manifest Destiny as against the Whigs; at the turn of the century Bryan's liberals were the custodians of anti-imperialism and therefore of the "Little America" or isolationist position, while the conservatives were behind the Spanish-American War and the Philippine adventure. Yet there were also imperialist liberals at that time, as witness Theodore Roosevelt and Senator Beveridge, and there have been anti-imperialist conservatives like E. L. Godkin, and Senators Sumner and Hoar. In the twentieth century the political battle lines became even more confused. The liberals who had once stood with Bryan against imperialism became "internationalists" and found them-selves the apostles of a concept of internationalism which was equivalent to a Big America trend. Those who had once whooped it up for Cuba and the Philippines found themselves moving toward isolationism, for-saking the turbulent world of power politics. In most cases the forces shaping American attitudes on foreign policy had little relation to the traditional forces shaping their attitudes on the conduct of affairs at home.

One alliance was a rather striking one—the alliance between some of the big business groups (especially the Eastern ones, trained in the Ivy League colleges, with the world outlook of men of finance) with the political liberals of the persuasion of Theodore Roosevelt and Woodrow Wilson. From the time of Wilson on, each group felt it had a stake in the emergence of an active American responsibility in the world: in the case of the business groups, the stake was the maintenance of open world markets, in the case of the liberals the maintenance of a world climate hospitable to the basic freedoms; in both cases there was a belief in an open society, whether for the pursuit of profit or the life of the spirit. Basically it was this alliance against the totalitarians of both Right and Left which became ever more explicit in American policy. For a time it took the excessive and almost paranoid form of a fear of Communism. But on this score the "go-it-alone" groups were far more intense than the business and liberal groups. The same fear of Communism which led the business-liberal alliance to international commitments led in the other case to an antiforeign "go-it-alone" policy.

The question of the regional roots of isolationism is a difficult one. There has been a widespread impression that isolationism is an accident of the Midwestern mind in America—part of a glacial deposit of resentment and suspicion that has descended on that mind, and needing only some urgings of reason to be thawed out. This is too easy, yet there is a core of validity in it. Isolationism is partly a sectional fact, but it also goes beyond geography and has become a social fact. It existed long before the Populists, yet its strongest expression was linked with the Populist mind, where the suspicion both of European cunning and capitalist cupidity for war profits was most deeply rooted. As Populism hardened, these attitudes were transferred to a new social base—that of the heavy-industry reactionaries of the country's interior who feared both the Eastern financiers and the European ideas. The isolationist feeling which had started in the farm granges and among the Bryan anti-imperialists moved into the custody of Colonel McCormick and Senator Taft. Then it made another shift from the Midwestern business and farm groups to the new white-collar classes, the strata of conservative unions and unorganized labor, and the Big Money of newly rich Southwestern oil millionaires. Thus isolationism, while associated with the Midwest, was an enduring phase of the history of power struggles within America. Its base shifted in the last half century from Western Populism through Midwestern conservatism, to a widespread array of frustrated and embittered social groups. Its psychological base was also shifted from distrust for Europe's monarchies and corruptions to a panic fear of "Marxism" and "atheism" in Europe and Asia.

The isolationist forces have thus changed their class base and leadership in each generation. Most recently they were associated in military strategy with General Douglas MacArthur; in Asian policy with Senator Knowland and the "Asia First" movement; and in domestic policy with Senator McCarthy. In no case did they win a Presidential election, but—as was true of the "America First" movement of the late 1930s—they had considerable popular support and affected the foreign policy even of "internationalist" administrations.

The impact of the pressures from the "China bloc" in the 1950s may be taken as the best instance of the effects of neo-isolationism. These pressures operated both on Democratic and Republican administrations. After the success of the Chinese Revolution they prevented President Truman and Secretary Acheson from coming to terms with the new Chinese regime: it would have been political suicide, as Truman saw it, to get in the way of a force which was ready to call its opponents betrayers of America and saddle them *ex post facto* with the loss of a big segment of the world to Communism. When the Eisenhower Administration came into power in 1952, Secretary Dulles—who had previously favored the recognition of Communist China and its acceptance into the UN—was forced to retreat into a position of immobility on this issue. The devastating result in both administrations was that a small group, playing upon the fears and vulnerabilities of public opinion, was able to paralyze two internationalist regimes into a frozen isolationism with respect to Asia. Both administrations lost their power of diplomatic maneuver in this area: and with the loss of this power of maneuver, the danger of a resort to atomic politics was increased, with the constant threat of using nuclear weapons as instruments of "massive retaliation." Thus isolationist politics and atomic politics converged, and the go-it-aloners fashioned their own brand of atomic imperialism.

An illuminating clue to this phase of American impulse and opinion may be found in Josef Schumpeter's classic essays on *Imperialism and Social Classes*. Writing at the turn of the twentieth century within the context of a Europe moving toward the first World War, and wrestling with the problem presented by John A. Hobson's and Lenin's theories of imperialism as the division of the world between capitalist powers, Schumpeter rejected their approach. He saw that the business groups had far more to lose than to win from imperialist wars, and that while they often exploited and themselves succumbed to the tensions of the super-patriot they were not the driving force behind the great explosions of popular passions that led to wars. He fixed rather on the tinderbox of the formless mass, mainly outside of the trade-unions, especially the lower middle classes, which had not found a secure place in the social structure. This approach, which has never been adequately adapted to the American case, sheds considerable light on it.

The same fear of "alien" influences that caused the go-it-aloners to withdraw behind their intellectual stockade can be transformed into a war fever. As isolationism has been hard pressed by the inescapable needs and interests of America, it has not succumbed to internationalism but has moved to a militarist imperialism. Prick the skin of a go-it-aloner and you draw interventionist blood—but of an interventionism within a wholly different frame of values from that of the internationalist. For the obsessive fear of "foreign influences" leads to a hatred of many of the ethnic groups within America whom an unprincipled or slack mind can link with the sources of foreign "subversion." Thus the go-it-aloners become the allies of racist groups whose principal targets are the recent immigrant stocks. Again, the go-it-aloners are ridden by an intense hatred and contempt for the European peoples, whom they accuse of begging for American handouts. They lump the non-Communists of the labor and Socialist movements, and the neutralists of Europe and the Third Force of Asia, with the Communists. Their impulse is to destroy any broad coalition in which America might find support, and to break away also from the United Nations. But to the extent that they achieve this, their reliance must be on naked military force. That is why I link the mentality of the go-it-aloner with that of the atomic militarist. In fact, almost uniformly (as I have suggested) it is the go-it-alone group which, in recent years, has clamored most insistently for the use of atomic weapons in a preventive war.

More and more clearly these lines of thinking merged into a pattern for which Americans have found no name, as they had for the internationalists. The elements of it are clear enough: the repudiation of the UN and international action for a go-it-alone policy; the substitution of military and especially atomic weapons for negotiation and diplomatic alliances; the reliance upon the air arm, especially as a carrier of atomic weapons, rather than upon the infantry and artillery arm; the shift of orientation to Asia—to Communist China and the Arab Middle East and equally from liberal democracies as allies to the nationalist movements of the Right; the alliance at home with racist movements; the reactionary domestic programs; the use of the Congressional investigation in order to unearth "subversives" who can be linked with liberals and internationalists.

Actually this pattern adds up to a nationalist imperialism of the Right. The Communist propaganda in Europe and Asia has cynically confused this world view of the go-it-alone imperialists with that of the liberal internationalists, attributing qualities of the one to the other: thus, they find "war-mongering" aims in a program of internationalism which seeks to build a liberal coalition and work through the UN. It applies the stigma of militarism to a group which has explored the techniques of economic aid and reconstruction to a degree unparalleled in history. The pattern of Big Empire as practiced by Americans has actually been an empire unknown in the history of imperialism. For where imperial powers in the past have aimed at exploiting the colonial and economically backward areas for their own economic advantage, taking out whatever resources they could and exploiting native labor, American imperialism is the first on record to pour its resources into undeveloped areas and weak economies, exporting capital, technicians, and technical skills to them.

The motive is not altruistic. Partly there is a fear of the growth of Communist world power if such countermeasures are not taken. Partly also there is a fear, on the part of strong business and even labor groups, that the American economic machine will slow down if defense production is not kept going at full blast and if there is no way to dispose of surplus products and investment through programs of international aid. But while the motive is self-interested, the consequences are unlike those of the colonial or ideological empires of the past. This reversal of the traditional imperial pattern was possible only through a recognition—largely by American liberal thought—of the connection between economic health and unhealth and the march of ideas. This, fused with the steady accretion of America's economic power, produced what may be called a Big Empire internationalism.

This brings the analysis back to the dynamism of American world power. I have suggested that the growth of that power has been propelled by the technological impulse of the culture more than by an impulse toward conquest or domination, and that the guiding spirit informing American expansion has been not an exploiting imperialism but a Big Empire internationalism. What appeal is this view likely to have for other peoples? What they have to gain is the assurance that while all small nations are bound to live in the shadow of the big empires, the shadow cast by the American brand is likely to be that of a constitutional imperialism operating within a relatively open world constitutional structure. Americans have talked, often quite foolishly, of their own economic system as the only one that can work: in their eager confidence about its merits they have overestimated its applicability. They have on the other hand underestimated in their own economic pattern the principle of inner mobility which makes it in some degree more revolutionary than the varieties of planned systems. The real persuasiveness of the American imperium, in its world struggle for widespread allegiance, flows from this flexibly changing pattern of an open society, and from the quickening energies of the American emphasis on access to life's goods.

Thus, in terms of the revolutionary Asian situation, America failed to make effective what it had to offer to the new Asian nationalism as the image of a working society. It could offer the example of a successful colonial revolution against imperialism; it could offer the continuing effort to keep many ethnic strains living together in peace in a complex society; it could offer, finally, the image of the independent farmer and of the career still largely open to talent. If the revolutionary world ferment at mid-century was anti-imperialist, anti-landlord, and if it was assertive not only about its nationalist energies but also about ethnic equality, then the American dialogue with these peoples was not doomed to futility.

These then are some of the shaping currents in the history of American foreign policy: the thrust toward expansionism; the impulse to fill out the "manifest destiny" of the continent and at the same time retire within its self-sufficiency; the fumblings, once the old self-sufficiency was broken, to find some means by which America could use a decisive leverage power in world affairs without entering on a series of interventionist adventures; the sense of geographical and ideological encirclement that has replaced the earlier sense of security; the impulse to make America the world carrier of the democratic idea; and the pragmatic limits which the American mind sets around that impulse, keeping it from becoming a messianic idea.

3. National Interest and an Open World

AMERICA IN MID-TWENTIETH century came to recognize itself as one of the two great power aggregates of the world, the other being, of course, the Russian-Chinese Communist bloc. This has meant a revaluation of the national-interest doctrine within the frame of a world struggle for power and a world imperative of peace. The era of Wilson and Roosevelt—that is to say, of World War I and of World War II—was followed by a period of sharp disenchantment with the "idealism" and "internationalism" of both of them. Many Americans began ruefully to add up the cost, in lives and treasure, of the American adventures in the succor of other peoples. The epigram that "America always wins the war and loses the peace" came to express a widespread disillusionment whose roots reached deep in the folk mind. Since America could not secede from the world, the disenchantment led to an insistence on a realistic view of national interest rather than some vague ideal of international good will.

But the idea of national interest no longer ran in the traditional balance-of-power term. It is possible to trace a balance-of-power calculation in American diplomacy from the start. In the early days of the nation's history, when the new Republic was still weak, its leaders knew that their political independence and their ideological democracy were threats to the existing great powers. They feared these powers and made a great show of maintaining their strict neutrality amidst the European dynastic struggles. Yet this did not prevent them, when the occasion offered, from playing off each of the great powers against the others, seeking (as it were) survival in the interstices of the power struggles. In fact, they were saved from being snuffed out in their infancy by the fact that the powers of Europe were at one another's throats: no one of them alone dared crush the new American republic, yet they could not agree to do it together. Europe's distress proved America's salvation. The American leaders combined wisdom and an eye for the main chance along with their luck. They swallowed insults from British and French alike, putting survival ahead of pride. When they felt themselves strong enough in 1823 they announced the bold proposition that the European powers were to stay out of the whole American hemisphere, which was to be the special preserve of America as a great power. Only the hostility of the British and Russians toward each other, and the fact of the British fleet, which stood between America and the vengeance of Europe, saved the Monroe Doctrine from being only a ridiculous scrap of paper. Later the Americans rode out their Civil War, increased their strength and population, stretched their new territories westward and southward until the nation reached its present continental limits inside of roughly seventy-five years. The "separate and equal power" rounded out a truly imperial domain in the New World under the protecting shadow of the power conflicts and ebbing energies of the Old World.

Such a diplomatic recipe, in varying combinations of neutrality and balance-of-power politics, was the strategy of Washington, of John Adams and John Jay, of Jefferson, Monroe and John Quincy Adams, of Lincoln and Seward. When America became itself a great power, the aim of the formula shifted; it became that of preventing any other power from overshadowing America and threatening its survival. This was the logic of John Hay's "Open Door" policy, which tried to keep the Far

East from becoming the private preserve of any one European nation. It was the point of Theodore Roosevelt's balancing of Russian against Japanese power when he made himself a conciliator between the two. It was also the logic of America's entrance into the two world wars, when she joined to prevent a German world dominion.

After World War II, much of American policy continued to follow this logic. Even before America had wholly defeated Germany and Japan a brilliant American political geographer, Nicholas J. Spykman, pointed out that America would have to rebuild German power in Europe and Japanese power in Asia. This appeared cynical at the time, but it was prophetic of the policy that was actually followed. In some posthumously published letters Spykman also backed American support of a UN organization not from idealist or internationalist motives but on the ground that it would be useful as a counterweight to the Soviet network of satellites. Thus, despite the opprobrium the "power-politics" idea carries in the American mind, America has continued to practice balance-of-power politics.

The traditional policy, however, had to be pursued under drastically new world conditions. These new conditions included the emergence of a great power axis stretching west from Moscow to Berlin, east from Moscow to Peiping, south from Moscow to Cairo. Confronted by this new power reality, America had little choice except to build "positions of strength" against it. The span of oceans separating America from Europe and from Asia might have been reckoned as an insulating and isolating element, but the oceans have shrunk to the scale of rapidly traversed airways, while the new colonial revolutions—often with Marxist slogans and leadership—have given Americans a more oppressive feeling than that of geographical encirclement, namely the sense of ideological encirclement.

In meeting this challenge, the Americans had to change their policies along three main lines of direction. One was the arms race, and the testing of each phase of American policy by its impact on America's "military potential"—a phrase whose currency (along with "readiness economy" and "defense posture") attested the new mood. The traditional American fear of standing armies was broken, and American soldiers and air bases could be found in every part of the world. The second change was a new economic diplomacy which sought to strengthen the shaky economies of the areas that the Americans hoped to bring within their sphere of influence. Third, Americans accustomed themselves to think in terms of "psychological warfare"—that is, of a contest of propagandas and a war of ideas. Thus, for all its traditional idealism, the pull in American policy was toward atomic weapons, economic pressures, and political warfare. The aim was to prevent strategic areas from falling into the opposing polar pull, to consolidate their strength and make them an effective part of a structure of collective international action.

Actually the phrase "bipolar world" oversimplified the complex reality. Not only was there an American world and a Communist world; there was also a whole array of peoples in a third world who refused to commit themselves to either. Whenever one of the two "polar" powers strained too hard to hold its allies and dependents within a tight discipline, there were inner tensions which showed that there were many forces of dynamic change in the world that were too insistent to be contained within two armed camps. A number of the newer non-Communist nations of Asia, Africa, and the Middle East were especially determined to stay clear of the bipolar struggle, and the leadership of Nehru furnished them a rationale of noncommitment. It became ever clearer after mid-century that the "cold war" era had itself been only a historical phase, and that whether the world was to witness a cataclysmic war of atomic weapons or not, there was more in the Heaven and earth of world energies than were dreamed of in the philosophy of a bipolar world.

All this meant that the concept of the "national interest" would have to be defined broadly enough to include America's stake in international action and in the building of collective sanctions. In an anarchic world the drive to achieve international order became itself a form of realism. That may be why some of the chief protagonists of the national-interest concept have broken as many lances against the isolationists as against the "tender-minded" internationalists. As typified by Hans Morgenthau and George F. Kennan, what the national-interest school stresses is toughness of approach. It is in the "tough-minded" tradition of Machiavelli's state system, applied to America's situation, as against the supposedly tender-minded approach of Wilson, Roosevelt, and the "global" thinkers.

"I always consider the settlement of America with reverence and wonder," wrote John Adams in 1765, "as the opening of a grand scheme and design in Providence for the illumination and emancipation of the slavish part of mankind all over the earth." There is a literature of the "American mission," as Clinton Rossiter calls it, that stretches from the divines of the Colonial Period to the most recent newspaper editorial proposing a "liberation policy" toward the peoples enslaved by Communist power. Messianism in this sense is not restricted to the liberal internationalists. Yet what gives this weapon its strength is the

strength of world belief in the reality of American revolutionary idealism. Nothing shows more clearly the intertwining of the tough-minded
and tender-minded, the realist and idealist, in American thinking than
this paradox of "liberation." The same editorialists who called Americans "suckers" for assuming the role of world saviors saw no irony in
demanding an aggressive liberation policy which was meaningless unless
the victim people believed in the American savior mission.

The messianic element in the American tradition is more complex
than is generally understood. It is true that Americans believe in their
characteristic institutions—free elections, free worship, free discussion,
a free market. Like others who believe in an idea, they don't understand why the rest of the world does not adopt it. Yet they are pulled
back by a self-critical censor that makes them fearful of all-out causes
and disillusioned after they have succumbed to them. There was a
strong sense of revolutionary idealism in Jefferson, yet he was fearful of
allowing its logic to carry America into foreign military adventures.
He had an astringent conviction that America could best perform its
historic mission by cultivating its own continental garden. The fact that
Americans believed so deeply in the validity of their national experience meant that they rarely made it articulate but took it for granted.
One would expect such a people to be chary of ideological Holy Wars.
When a Holy War element did enter into their wars, as in 1917 and
again in 1941, the result was disillusionment.

American thinkers for a long time stayed clear of the sweep of global
problems that interested their European contemporaries and shaped
their intellectual systems. It was not until Theodore Roosevelt and his
group of intellectual intimates (John Hay, Henry Adams, his brother
Brooks Adams, Admiral Mahan) that the self-containment of American
thought was broken. None of these men, except for Brooks Adams,
was a trained social thinker. Henry Adams's letters are full of acute
political insights and a prophetic understanding of world forces which
enabled him to gauge the weakness of Great Britain as a world power
and the coming strength of Russia and America. Yet his mind was
mainly trained in the balance-of-power maneuvering of the great powers, as befitted the descendant of two Presidents and the son of an
ambassador. His theory of the coming explosion of the two concentrated energy systems of world power forecast the doom of all civilization and had little about America's own world role in the interval.
Mahan's mind, less far-ranging and more centered on naval power and
its implications, anticipated the interest of later American thinkers in
the politics of military strategy and geographical location.

Like Adams and Mahan, Theodore Roosevelt was interested in the techniques of balance-of-power politics. Declaring that "American politics is world politics," he dared to see that America's security lay not in neutrality but in helping give order to the world arena itself, and thus he burst the bounds of self-contained continentalism. His world view, like his New Nationalism, flowed from his cult of the "strenuous life." Inherently belligerent, he gave a tone of belligerence to whatever he uttered. He was contemptuous of pacifists as "molly-coddlers." He infected in this respect the thinking of Herbert Croly, who asserted in *The Promise of American Life* that "if America wants peace it must be spiritually and physically prepared to fight for it. . . . The road to any permanent international settlement will be piled high with dead bodies, and will be traveled, if at all, only after a series of abortive and costly experiments." Croly showed both the juvenile tough-guy posturing and the genuine tough-mindedness that were mingled in the thinking of the internationalist progressives.

With Woodrow Wilson, who has become the favorite target of the attack on legalist-moralist idealism, the juvenile gestures were replaced by an equally synthetic high-minded spirituality, and the tough-mindedness was diluted but not wholly dissolved by idealist doctrine. In the case of Franklin Roosevelt, who was less doctrinaire than Wilson, there was a realistic use of every American resource—economic, military, and ideological—in the interest of Wilson's ruling idea of a collective international will. How resistant Franklin Roosevelt was to the world-savior role may be seen from the fact that America waited until Pearl Harbor before formally entering World War II; but how shrewd he was as a manipulator of symbols may also be seen from the fact that he was not wholly sorry to use the Japanese aggression to resolve his dilemma as a policy-maker—the dilemma of one who understood the threat of Fascist world power but could not count on a unified American public opinion in meeting it.

Reinhold Niebuhr has written brilliantly of the "irony of American history" represented by the thinking and actions of these leaders. Given their horror of war, it was certainly ironic that both Wilson and Roosevelt were entangled by history in world wars. Yet each held fast to the central creative idea that balance-of-power politics and military force were justified only as steps toward a structure of international sanctions. Each of them thus became the symbol of vast movements of popular opinion that went far beyond the American boundaries.

Brooks Adams, who was not a statesman but a student of the materials with which statesmanship has to work, came closer than any other thinker to formulating for Americans the logic of their new power position. In his *America's Economic Supremacy,* which appeared at the turn of the century, in 1900, he saw the Spanish-American War as mark-ing a "new equilibrium of the world." In an earlier book, *The Law of Civilization and Decay,* Adams had speculated that the rise and fall of national greatness followed the shifting of the world trade routes. He added the theory that geographical imperatives shaped two great centers of economic empire—one a continental (land mass) empire and one a maritime empire. The capstone to his theoretical structure was the "law of centralization"—that in "the new struggle for life among the nations," society tends to "become organized in greater and denser masses, the more vigorous and economical mass destroying the less active and more wasteful." Like his brother Henry he saw history as an energy process in which, as in physics, there was an acceleration followed by a slowing of national energies: the world moved from one equilibrium to an-other, each interval representing a "phase" of history, each displacement of an equilibrium being marked by social convulsions, wars, revolutions, and catastrophes until a new equilibrium is achieved.

However one may quarrel with a theory of history using the meta-phors of physics as if they applied to cultural development, Adams had at least part of a truth by the tail. America's economic dominance came about at the same time as England's power decay, and America replaced England as the world's big maritime power just as Russia followed France and Germany as the big European continental land power. In both cases there was an unexampled drive toward centralized power and organizational techniques.

But it is one thing to possess an economic supremacy and another to use it maturely. Until after World War II America was the Reluctant Giant, unwilling to measure the full extent of its might. Since that time it has surprised both friends and critics by an assertive diplomacy and an almost bristling eagerness to use American power to the full. This change of policy does not register a basic transformation in American outlook or character structure. Those are unchanged: the attraction-and-recoil pattern, the fear of being "taken in" by foreign wiles, the chip-on-the-shoulder attitude, the demand for signs of affec-tion from the beneficiaries of American largess, the anxious pursuit of national "security," the belief that the American angel must always look homeward. What has happened reflects rather a reassertion of the thrust of American energy whenever it encounters a challenge from which it cannot escape.

Seen from the vantage point of the sobering problems of American power in the mid-1950s, the turn-of-the-century phase of American imperialism a half century earlier had a half-baked quality. The Spanish-American War and the protectorate thrown over the Philippines,

Hawaii, and Cuba may have seemed impressive steps toward establishing American power in the Pacific and Caribbean seas. But their very closeness to the classic pattern of colonial imperialism should have cast suspicion on how well they expressed the real drives in American life. The turn-of-the-century imperialist champions—Hay, Theodore Roosevelt, Beveridge, Mahan—were intellectuals who were moved by an image of America's Manifest Destiny across the seas. The imperialist adventure was not so much the expression of the drive of tough-minded businessmen as the high jinks of men who saw themselves as the shapers of American destiny. The great anti-imperialists of the day who opposed this pseudo-imperialism—Bryan, Mark Twain, William Vaughan Moody —took it for the real thing and fought it with passionate and generous energies. The wonderful satiric humor of Mark Twain that pilloried the missionaries and their Christian burden, and the majestic rhetoric of Moody's *On a Soldier Fallen in the Philippines,* hit home in showing how the *opéra bouffe* imperial adventure stirred the latent jingoism of Americans and made ninnies of them.

But the whole episode, with its noisy fireworks and the hoopla of Hearst journalism, was marginal to the development of American power. The amassing of American imperial power has scarcely followed the classic pattern. It has operated by the techniques of trade, investment, and profitable sales in foreign markets; it has not been averse toward using "dollar diplomacy" to remove the obstructions in the path of business profits, to start convenient revolutions or quell inconvenient ones, and it has more recently operated by economic and technical aid to underdeveloped areas.

There could be no denial that the fact of Soviet power was real and massive in the mid-1950s, and that the Communist appeal was strong, especially to the colonial peoples and the emergent nationalist movements of Asia and Africa. America found itself having to make strategic and diplomatic calculations globally, for all the continents at once. To focus on Europe, which had once seemed the widest stretch of internationalism, was no longer enough. American thought and planning underwent a drastic shift of axis from Europe to the Middle and Far East, which became the next great continental stakes for the world struggle. Since the Soviet revolutionary appeal to the Middle East and the Chinese appeal to Asia were at once economic and ideological, the Americans had to take stock of their capacity to offer a counterchallenge on both scores.

The economic problem had its setting in the fact that the underdeveloped areas would need new capital investment and technical aid.

Lenin's classic formulation put the problem as a choice between turning to the capitalist powers for investment or getting it out of the nation's own resources by a stringent program of economic planning, by austere consumer sacrifices in the early phase, and by plowing back into capital formation the whole surplus over bare subsistence. Lenin's reasoning was that to borrow from the existing powers on their terms was to become colonial to them. The Russians said in effect to the emerging nationalisms of Asia, "See, we lifted ourselves by our own economic boot straps, without becoming colonial vassals of the imperialist powers. You can do the same." As for the problem of industrial initiative and managerial efficiency, they sought to solve it by the creation of state trusts and farm collectives, by a stretch-out which went under the name of "Socialist competition," by the creation of a managerial Communist elite within industry, and by the iron "discipline" of a single party and police state. They used also the persistent propaganda of "capitalist encirclement" and the myth of an inevitable triumph of the Communist cause, which was embedded in the prophetic phase of the Marxist dogma.

America had a clear answer at its disposal. In terms of its own economic history it had achieved most of its capital formation by plowing back its surplus into railroads, factories, machines. It had at the start used British and French capital without becoming a vassal of either country. In its economic growth it had disproved the Marxist dogma of decay through the internal contradictions of capitalism. Its rich had grown richer but they let the state take the larger part of their income through taxation, and their own consumption formed only a tiny fraction of the total national product. Its poor had not, despite the Marxist dogma, grown poorer: in fact, they had grown steadily better off. As a result America had brought into being a nation which was mainly middle class, and whose middle classes had living standards previously achieved only by the wealthy of other nations. America had a surplus of capital and a command of technology which it was ready to put at the disposal of underdeveloped areas. Its greatest appeal was the example of its own living standards and its basic freedoms. It had the advantage of being able to show that both the living standards and the freedoms could be achieved without big state trusts, the rigor of farm collectives, and the barbarities of a police state.

America labored, however, under two handicaps in making this counterchallenge effective. One was its own nationalist impulse to think in military rather than economic terms, to strike alliances with authoritarian regimes provided they were anti-Communist, and dream of a *pax Americana* which would impose its own kind of order upon the world. The second and closely related handicap was the recurrence of an internal drive by a minority against civil liberties, using the fear of subversion as its chief source of popular support.

American nationalism during most of its growth had in it the self-assertiveness of a people who had won their freedom and were certain of the dimensions of their destiny. American nationalist loyalties clustered around the Constitution as a symbol, the "American mission" as an evocative myth, and American wealth and prosperity as the visible signs of Providential grace. Except for short periods of hysteria, from the Alien and Sedition Acts to the radical hunt after World War I, American patriotism was of the spread-eagle sort that was swaggering without being intolerant. For the most part it was the kind of good-natured nationalism that flourishes in a democratic society—with a strong pride of place, a we-can-do-it-better-than-anyone assertiveness, and a fierce don't-tread-on-me belligerence. "My country, may it always be right—but, right or wrong, my country" expressed the hold that the nation as a social myth had on the American mind.

The period after World War II marked a transition to a new phase of nationalist feeling. It took two main forms: a militarist emphasis in foreign policy and the increasing anxiety about "security." The two forms tended to become interlocked. The proof of "loyalty" came to be defined by the political bigots in terms of adherence to their own world view and their own political and property attitudes. For a brief interval at mid-century the symbol of this narrow nationalism, which contained elements of police-state Fascism, came to be "McCarthyism." Yet the symbol was less important than the tensions it expressed, and from which other symbols like it might draw their continuing energies. A number of foreign observers made the mistake of identifying "McCarthyism" with the main drift of American energies—a mistake welcomed by the masters of Soviet propaganda, since it distracted attention from their police state. But it was also wide of the mark to dismiss this new bigoted nationalism as irrelevant to the real America—as if there were some way of authenticating America by the standards only of its social health and discarding everything else.

The cult of the nation as social myth has run as a thread through the whole of American history. It started as the revolutionary nationalism of the War for Independence, it became the assertive nationalism of a people in industrial growth, and it reached its newest phase as the bigoted nationalism of an antidemocratic minority pretending to track down "un-Americans" and "subversives." The Marxist analysis which makes this nationalist drive the bond servant of a master class of corporate managers did not stand up historically. There were, of course, ties between the nationalist bigots and some Midwestern businessmen, some Texas oil millionaires, and some of the new economic feudal masters of the Pacific Coast. Yet the main body of American business found itself deeply disquieted by a movement of bigotry which threatened their own position ultimately because it threatened the business and constitutional fabric itself. They welcomed some of the consequences of the new tribalism, particularly in the devastation it wrought among liberals by linking them in the popular mind with "subversives." But they were aware of the final danger of the movement.

More important than its links with the corporate classes were the links the new tribalism had with the formless fears and anxieties of the middle classes and the unorganized workers. The intensity of tribal feeling was all the greater because of the insecurity of the recent immigrant groups, and the social competitiveness every group felt in a society where each man had to make and hold his own place. The chief drive was the striving for respectability, and its linkage with unquestioned "loyalty." Without being a rigidly stratified class society, America forms a kind of terraced society, with each terrace level shaped by one's income level and prestige and by the sense of security within the social group. The older and more settled Americans were less likely to become victims of nationalist bigotry than some of the more recent ones, who found it necessary to prove that they "belonged" by becoming the challengers of other people's loyalty, and who sought to outdo all others in the virulence of their attack on the "alien" element. Thus, among the new feudal rich, among the amorphous white-collar classes, among the failures and those tagging along on the margin of a failure, and among second- and third-generation immigrant groups, the nation as a social myth exerted a powerful force. While its uses were in many cases part of the defensive tactics of Big Property, the roots from which it got its popular strength were not those of class interest but of the psychic hunger to belong. Hence the tribal feeling in America was often more fanatic among those classes and groups who would prove to be its first victims if an authoritarian state were ever to be established in America.*

These inner sources upon which American tribalism fed must be correlated also with the fear of the world outside which neither the possessing nor the middle classes could grasp. Despite the revolutionary origins of America, they were fearful of a new kind of world revolutionary ferment which enveloped them. They did not see that the achievements of America had raised expectations throughout the world

* See also Ch. VI, Sec. 10, "The Struggle for Civil Liberties," and Ch. IX, Sec. 4, "Varieties of American Character."

which expressed themselves in new nationalist energies and in the demand for new living standards. The Marxist program was one phase of the Western heritage that had pre-empted the revolutionary challenge. Yet the American experience embodied a more authentic revolution, which could respond more fully to the claims of Asia and Africa as well as of Europe.

Even within the doctrine of national interest there was room for an American world view which would not deny these revolutionary claims. The conflict between the national-interest school and the internationalist was, at bottom, a clash of views about human nature. In the writings of men like Hans Morgenthau and George Kennan there is an underlying premise that in the struggle for world position the great reality is power, that international law and morality cannot be expected to displace power or even fundamentally to affect its exercise, that little can be expected of human nature except self-interest. In the internationalism of Wilson, on the other hand, there is something of the perfectionism of the eighteenth century and its belief that conflict can be resolved by the proper institutional means. The first group share a world view that goes back to Machiavelli, the second a view that goes back to Plato, who believed in the possibility of organized virtue within a frame of traditional ideas. The first view is deeply pessimistic in mood, the second optimistic. The experiences since World War I—the failure of the League of Nations, the broken balance of power, the betrayals of international agreements by both Hitler and Stalin, the tarnishing of war aims in peace settlements after both world wars—disillusioned Americans about international action and created a climate favoring a narrow version of the doctrine of national interest.

Yet there are phases of the American character that are excluded from the world view and the view of human nature implied in this doctrine. There is an inbred optimism in the American which will not let him hold too long to a pessimistic view of human nature as wholly greedy and self-seeking. Even in its Calvinist origins the American mind shaped a doctrine of what may be called practical messianism. The tradition in which Wilson worked was that of the Covenanters—a spirit translated into a doctrine of human rights as the stern imperative of history.

In spite of their tribalists and their advocates of a *pax Americana,* the Americans had the right to face the struggle for world leadership with the assurance that time was on their side, and that their philosophy contained a strong appeal. Their fault was to see this appeal in the negative terms of the dangers and evils of the Communist philosophy. Unquestionably, the Communist doctrine, when translated into action, carried with it a moral indifference to human values, the swollen arrogance of state power, and the nullifying of the individual in the impersonal drive of history. There were inner weaknesses within the Communist societies that promised in time to lead to inner breakdown, since every police state is bound to generate palace intrigues, praetorian conflict, and the murderous struggle of rivals for power, which break it from within.

But America had a more positive contribution to make in foreign policy that corresponded to its contribution in day-to-day living. It went beyond high living standards and even beyond civil liberties. One way to formulate it was to transfer the concept of the open society to the larger sphere of world action. For America has shown in its history that immense structures of economic power, a steady pace of technical and social change, and widely divergent class and ethnic groups could be contained within a society flexible enough to allow for dynamism without tyranny. The challenge was whether the rivalries of nations and the clash of power imperialism could be similarly held within the frame of an open world society.

All through the period since World War I there were fumblings toward such a world view. Since Americans are legalist and humanitarian, these efforts took the form of plans for the League of Nations and the UN, blueprints for world government, and a vague sense of responsibility toward the people in the underdeveloped areas. They were symbolized by such slogans as Wendell Willkie's "One World," the Marshall Plan, Point Four. It does not subtract from them to say that none is as deeply characteristic of the historical achievement of America as is its open society. The logic of American history has been to take one step after another, instead of attempting a broad leap to achieve an abstract idea. Thus what America could contribute in international action is the practice of an open society transferred to the broader arena of an Open World. I have noted above that the idea of a bipolar struggle does not correspond to the realities of today's world, which is too varied culturally and too diverse in the aims of the member nations and the varying phases of their development to be contained within two armed camps. The alternative to a bipolar world might conceivably be a world state, but that has difficulties that have proved insuperable thus far, and it has dangers of rigidity or tyranny. Far more feasible, as well as far more attractive, is the idea of an open world society in which national differences survive and national development is possible, but there is a core of international authority to prevent the suicidal anarchy of war.

The merit of this is that it dictates no imperialism, whether military, economic, or moral. It allows for a wide divergence of cultural forms and national traditions within a common frame of tolerance and con-stitutionalism. It involves a refusal to foreclose the future against any economic doctrine or social system—whether capitalist or Socialist, demo-cratic or authoritarian, provided it stays within the spirit and codes of an open world society. Nor does it make the mistake of pitting "West" against "East," thereby yielding to the Communists the prescriptive right not to be considered Westerners by the Asiatic peoples. The fact is that there have been fusions as well as clashes between the cultures of East and West, and each has interpenetrated the other. As the best ex-ample history offers of a mingling of all ethnic strains within a loose social frame, the Americans had a right to assert that both East and West were contained within their image of an open world society.

Thus America might put its tradition of revolutionary idealism to effective use in the interest of realistic aims, achieving a not impossible synthesis of internationalism with "national interest." Whether it can make this world view persuasive to other peoples depends, however, on the course which its own people follow internally within their own open society. The danger was that Americans might betray this image of an open world by a belligerent go-it-alone policy, by the moral arrogance of expecting other peoples to bow to their superior wealth and strength, but especially by betraying the open society from within. They found that when they had to defend themselves against the growing threat of "McCarthyism" at home, they had also to go on the defensive in the world at large. In this sense the most effective single weapon in the entire armory of American foreign policy was bound to be, in the generations ahead, the image of an open society.

4. Landscape with Soldiers

DESPITE CHARGES of "war-mongering" and the impulses toward military muscle-flexing, America can scarcely be described as a warlike civiliza-tion or a military society. Americans make pretty good fighters when they have to fight; and the statue or memorial in the public square of an American town is more likely to pay homage to a military figure than to a jurist, artist, scholar, saint, or businessman. But despite this, Americans don't glory particularly in military feats, don't like wars, don't allow their sense of bigness as a people to depend on the deeds and ordeals of their soldiers. They are combative and pugnacious; the "chip on the shoulder" (as Margaret Mead has seen) is a symbol of one of their basic character traits. But to be pugnacious as individuals is different from being aggressive as a nation or militarist as a society.

How explain the antimilitarist tradition among such a people? De

Tocqueville found a clue in the "principle of equality." In European societies there was little chance to move from one social class to another in civilian life: hence the army as a career offered the main channel for advancement. In America, however, where a man moved up rapidly in civilian life, the military offered few attractions as a permanent career: hence the passion for peace De Tocqueville found in America in the 1830s. He went on to point out, however, that while the American people abhorred war, the regular soldiers—and especially the noncommissioned officers—might be expected to desire war: their big chance for advancement comes in wartime, when the democracy has been turned into a people-in-arms, and the officers of the small standing army are jumped in rank in order to lead the expanded military forces.

But De Tocqueville was hasty in assuming that the "principle of equality" would keep Americans from military embroilments. A decade after he wrote, Americans were involved in a war with Mexico which was an imperialist adventure, aimed mainly at grabbing the rich domain of Texas. They later fought a civil war, still later a war with Spain, fought in two world wars, and then found themselves caught in military episodes in Korea and elsewhere in Asia as part of the struggle with the power of the Kremlin and Peiping. While this is not the record of a militarist people, neither is it the record of one lacking the martial impulse.

What happened was a drastic change in America's world position which forced upon it, if not militarism, then readiness for wars. The American antiwar tradition was shaped in a society which was physically separated from the rest of the world and felt itself safe between its buffer oceans, and which could therefore risk keeping its standing army small and neglect its armed strength during long stretches of peace. But when the oceans were spanned and the rise of new power structures threatened America, the antiwar tradition was drastically eroded. For a time it took the form of a neutralism which counseled America to keep itself disengaged from world struggles. Then neutralism in turn became an ever less tenable position. Three times in the course of thirty-five years, from World War I in 1917 to the Korean War in 1950, Americans found themselves plunged into major wars.

As long as they were neutral the Americans cultivated an indifference to the embroilments of other nations. But as soon as they got into a war they made a "crusade" out of its military and ideological aspects and a "campaign" out of every civilian aspect. It was under Woodrow Wilson's leadership that World War I was turned into the first of the modern ideological wars. The intensity of the original antiwar feeling seemed to be doubled as it reversed its direction. Every war becomes a total war for Americans, unless—like the Asiatic wars—it is too distant and unpopular to take the usual course. The tendency is for American war aims to be phrased in terms of total victory, and for American peace terms to be unconditional surrender. Even—or perhaps especially—the bitterest of the former isolationists become super-patriots in war, and their former apathy is turned into the loudest battle cries.

The difficulty Americans experience in their war behavior is that they cannot apply to it the logic of their peacetime society. Ordinarily they bargain and compromise, and find their goals in the step-by-step course of daily life and work. The traditional antiwar bent has been that of a people whose pursuit of profits, careers, and happiness has made them shrink from anything that might cut these short. Hence the violence of their initial reaction against war involvement. But when they are forced into a war, there is an intensity of recoil from their initial indifference. It is as if they had to overcompensate for their earlier lack of feeling by the total absorption with the war. And this in turn is reinforced by the irrational blood urge which, once set in motion, transforms the American (and especially the civilian at home) into a fire-breathing enthusiast.

The basic contradiction here is that of war itself—the most irrational of all human actions—operating in a society founded in the Age of Reason on the assumption of man's perfectibility. From this crucial contradiction most of the others flow—the almost schizoid alternation between peace-mindedness and war-mindedness, the impassioned cries, and in diplomacy a deep moralizing strain alternating with military pressures and alliances. Americans are likely to wait until the last moment before they fight, but once the blow has fallen they are caught up in enthusiasm. They start by expecting the war to be short, then settle down to a long and weary one. After the peace, the inevitable mood of disillusionment sets in, and the whole cycle is ready to be repeated.

Since they are a technological people the Americans find themselves at home in the new technology of war, which has become warfare by machines, with the soldiers functioning mainly as machine operators. I have said earlier that the American is *homo faber,* the archetypal man of the modern world. The same qualities which have given him primacy in peacetime industrial technology make him feel at home in mechanized warfare. Many of the American war novels are obsessed with the details of how the precision machinery of warfare operates. The same technical bent and engineering skills that enabled the Americans to make the start on atomic weapons also made them adept in the use of flame throwers, napalm bombs, heavy long-range jet bombers, and the range of electronic navigational and firing devices that make the warplane in a supersonic age a complex mass of machinery on which the pilot "goes along for a ride" and (as Hanson Baldwin puts it) "has become an electronics specialist and radar engineer."

This changing nature of warfare has brought about a shift in American strategic thinking. The abrupt realism that led General Nathan Forrest to sum up the whole wisdom of strategy as that of "getting there fustest with the mostest" has been translated into what is now called the science of "logistics": the problems of transporting large masses of men and material thousands of miles from the home base have taken on meaning at a time when no part of the world is outside the area of potential hostilities. But where warfare was once mainly a matter of man power, the American emphasis is now on war technology. There are few military operations which are not preceded by saturation bombing. The emphasis has been shifted from the infantry and artillery to aviation and atomic weapons, and even the naval arm has assumed importance mainly as a set of floating air bases and as a way of keeping the sea lanes open for the transportation of war material. In the infantry itself, mobile tank warfare has most dramatically captured the American imagination. The generals who emerged as heroes from World War II were either tank officers like George Patton or organizers of war administration and war diplomacy like Marshall and Eisenhower.

Arthur M. Schlesinger, Jr., has suggested traditional lines of difference on military strategy between the two major American political parties, with the Atlantic as the "Democratic ocean" and the Pacific as the "Republican ocean"; thus, too, with the branches of the Armed Services: the Army and Navy have been the Democratic branches, while the Air Force has been the Republican branch. The "New Look" in defense, as the Republicans called it in the mid-1950s, put its emphasis on atomic weapons carried by the air arm. Yet the Democrats were capable of taking over the emphasis on the air arm: the emphasis of the Symington Report, in 1957, was on the failure of a Republican Administration to keep up with the needs imposed on military aviation by war in a nuclear age.

At the core of the American attitude toward war was the hatred of using and losing American lives. It led the American leaders to use the atomic bomb in Japan in the hope—wise or otherwise—that they would thus save a million American casualties. Every American political leader knows the value of the slogan "Don't send American boys overseas." The fact that Americans were able to keep their home territory from becoming a battlefield, ever since the Civil War, has led them to think of war as a highly technical operation, fought preferably on distant shores with the minimum use of American troops and with a massive expenditure of materials and money. This may partly explain the American willingness to use massive economic aid in peacetime as a way of averting a war, and even the curious American belief that if you have money enough as a nation you can somehow buy peace. It should be added that, when the test came, Americans spent their own lives profusely in both world wars and in the Korean War. But even while they did so their sense of the sanctity of life and their reluctance to use it in battle were undiminished.

In an era when war is technology the organization of the war economy is crucial. The American tendency is to superimpose the machinery of a war economy and war state upon the peacetime pursuits, yielding reluctantly step by step to the necessity of changing from the "business as usual" pattern. This leads to a mixture of wartime and peacetime attitudes which has baffled many. Thus heavy taxation is found side by side with profiteering from war contracts, often with defective materials. There is always a cry to "mobilize" capital and labor in the war economy. Yet in every recent war the trade-unions have grown in strength and have given up none of labor's rights except that of striking in crucial war plants, while after every war the big corporate units emerge even bigger and more powerful.

Randolph Bourne, a young American radical writer during World War I, used to say ironically (quoting from a German military historian) that "war is the health of the state." Certainly state power feeds on war. The antitrust laws are suspended, and there is a machinery for controlling prices and production and allocating priorities for scarce materials that would not be possible in a peacetime America. There is full employment and a forced investment by which the high profits are skimmed off through heavy taxation and channeled into directed war uses. The businessman is caught between the bonanza of big war contracts and profits on the one hand, and a system of high taxes and military Socialism on the other. Yet the American has not lost his capacity to live with such paradoxes and make the best of both worlds.

A more baffling paradox was presented by the economy after 1945, which did not have to wage total war, yet was unable to return to peacetime standards. It was the economy of the arms race: or in somewhat gentler terms, a "readiness economy." It retained many of the features of the war economy—the danger of inflation, heavy taxes, big war contracts and profits, full employment; yet the sense of pressure which comes from the ordeal of war survival was absent and could not be supplied synthetically, although for a time it was supplied by the "Cold War" and the Communist scare.

The arms race presented America with a difficult problem of social decision. After 1938 the American economy in great measure had to use its resources for armaments, with alternations between a war economy and a readiness economy. In both cases the conditions assumed as necessary for the functioning of capitalism in peacetime did not exist. American businessmen found themselves moving steadily away from the free market for civilian goods toward a market in which the government was at once Big Customer, Big Regulator, and Big Taxer. They watched the steady transformation of private capitalism into state capitalism, with the dangers of military Socialism always present. Thus, despite the Marxist theory of war as the instrument of capitalist groups, it was the businessmen who were most worried by the revolutionary consequences of the war economy. Hence the political outlook of the business groups, typified by the career of Senator Robert A. Taft, with its demand for lower war budgets, less aid to America's allies, fewer government controls, and lower taxes. But it was the ironic destiny of American business to move steadily toward a result it dreaded. Even when the businessmen had a Republican Administration, as after 1952, they seemed powerless to reverse this trend.

American liberals were equally caught between two conflicting impulses—to use the full potential of American strength in preventing a Kremlin world domination which would mean the death of liberalism, and on the other hand to prevent the fatal militarizing of American life in the process. What troubled them most was not only the new role of American generals in decisions extending far beyond the technical aspects of warfare. Even more they were troubled by the evidence of how hard it would be to dissolve the armament economy and return it to a peacetime basis. There are economic historians who assert that the New Deal would have failed if it had not been retrieved by war contracts starting in 1938, and that postwar prosperity would have been impossible without the arms race. One need not go along with this view to recognize how many problems a democracy is absolved from meeting because a warfare economy makes it easier to avoid them. Since it is unlikely that either the arms race or the armament economy will be abolished in the calculable future, the question of what American capitalism would do without war orders is for the present an academic one. The same applies to the question of what the Communist states would do if they did not have military Communism to give force to the decisions of the governing groups and cohesion to a restless people. It is a striking fact that the American economy has survived in the artificial atmosphere of war and the arms race, and has shown an impressive flexibility in being able to move and adapt itself to the alternations of war and peace and to that twilight condition which is neither. It should be added, of course, that an armament economy is not the only solution for the problems of full employment under capitalism: as I have noted earlier* Americans have learned what is needed to keep the economy going without the artificial respiration of armaments, if only they have the will to apply their knowledge.

Even amidst the alarms of a world struggle, the American Army has not become a professional one but remains an army of civilians in uniform. The current standing army of several million men, a large number of them stationed abroad, is mainly a collection of draftees who are rotated through a term of training and service: the number of those who make a lifetime career of it is relatively small. During a period of active war, as in World War II, the larger part of America's young manhood takes part in the war experience. In this sense the American Armed Services are the "nation-in-arms" of Napoleonic times—a far-flung organization of young people who have been civilians and hope to be civilians again, and are determined to survive the strange interlude of war as best they can.

Given this civilian emphasis, it is not surprising that the American soldier judges his Army experience in civilian terms. Attitude studies of the Army, notably Samuel Stouffer's work in *The American Soldier*, found that what the soldier wanted from the Army was: status while he was a soldier, training which would help him in his job or career after he left the Army, the minimum of exposure to the dangers that would make a casualty of him, and the kind of comfort he could not get if he was stationed at a "God-forsaken place" like the Aleutians or Tasmania. These four wishes may seem the desires of men who are not serious about the business of war, but they are characteristic of a society that values the pursuits of peace and leaves them only under pressure of necessity and not from any valuing of the martial virtues.

This makes more ironic the contrast between the relative freedom of civilian life and the highly disciplined and hierarchic society of the Army. Every generation of young Americans must take the traumatic leap from the one to the other. Since many of the draftees come from relatively protected middle-class homes and a family structure that stresses individual freedom, the shock is all the greater. To be sure, there are many men for whom the drastic devaluation of the individual in Army life becomes a value in itself: they find a kind of peace in surrendering themselves to the Army collective. But for most others the transition is too abrupt, and becomes an agonizing experience. Much has been

* Ch. V, Sec. 10, "The Emerging Amalgam."

changed in the structure of the Army: it has moved from a small force
of volunteers to a vast conscript organization, and from local and state
units to a national one. But its discipline is still rigorous to the point of
being Prussian. For those who are not broken by it, the initiation into
the Army may be a valuable school of experience. For many others it is
a struggle not only for the toughening of the body but for the survival
of the spirit—a struggle through which the soldier manages to pass because his pride forces him to show his group that he "can take it." This
same group feeling underlies Army "morale," which is based less on any
personal commitment to the war or its purposes than upon an esprit de
corps.

What gives the American Army its stamp as a society is that it has
shaped its ways in relative insulation while the civilian ways were being
shaped competitively and therefore more flexibly. The Army fails to
make use of civilian society's competitive techniques, with direct rewards for merit and achievement. Instead of the high degree of mobility
in American society, there remains between the officers and the men—
the leaders and the led—a wall which cannot be overleaped. This separation and its hierarchic structure are present in every army, but they
are especially galling to the American democratic spirit. Not only must
the soldiers be broken before they can accept it, but most of the officers
must also have their earlier habits remolded. The training for officer
candidates has been described as an anxiety-ridden experience more severe than college hazing, in which the personality structure of the candidate is first broken down and then is so reconditioned that he finds a
relief in taking his repressed aggressions out on his men. Thus the Stouffer study showed that it was easier for the American Negro to adjust
himself to Army conditions than for the white, since the Negro had
already become accustomed to a situation of status.

The case of the Negro soldier illustrates the influence of levels of
expectation upon Army experience. The Negro in World War II felt
bitterly about the persisting discrimination and segregation in a struggle
whose professed aims were antiracist. Yet on the whole the Southern
Negro, with a lower level of expectation, suffered fewer psychological
scars in the Southern Army camps than the Northern Negro in his
Northern camps. Similarly the soldier who fared best in Army life was
likely to be a boy with little education, coming from a farm or a small
town. Partly because they were still strongly rural, and partly because
of their persisting authoritarian values, the Southern states have played
a role in American warfare far beyond their ratio of population. Since
the martial values are largely feudal virtues, and since Army resentments
are conditioned by the expectations with which the soldier starts and his

sense of his worth as an individual, it is the better-educated men from urban and industrial areas for whom the Army experience becomes an ordeal.

Even before warfare became thoroughly mechanized the soldier was cynical of the glory ideal. As a Union private put it in a letter from a Civil War battlefield, "Glory consisted in getting shot and having your name spelled wrong in the newspapers." To be sure, someone like young Oliver Wendell Holmes, Jr., who went through the Civil War and was several times wounded, was later to look back on this period as the most meaningful of his life. "In our youth," he wrote, "our hearts were touched with fire. It was given to us to learn at the outset that life is a profound and passionate thing." Yet even Holmes had to confess that "war, when you are at it, is horrible and dull." Only in retrospect did the passionate part emerge. "The reality was to pass a night on the ground in the rain with your bowels out of order, and after no particular breakfast to attack the enemy." In the Civil War there were more deaths from dysentery than from battle, and the problems of sanitation and diet proved more devastating than those of lead and steel. Today the American soldier is as well fed and cared for as any in history. Yet while American technical efficiency, grappling with the administrative problems of warfare, has achieved triumphs of engineering, sanitation, preventive medicine, and surgery, the American soldier has no real stomach for fighting or glory for their own sake.

What makes it worse is that war has become more destructive as the American cherishing of life and its values has grown more urgent. The old hand-to-hand combat of the Civil War has been replaced by an impersonal warfare in which destruction is wrought by remote control, as with the nuclear warfare. But the impersonality of dealing out death or of facing its chances has, if anything, increased rather than lessened its horrors. A large portion of American war casualties has proved to be that of battle shock, either in anticipation or under the stress of combat. The number of "psychoneurotic" cases has borne testimony to the gap between civilian conditioning and the conditions of war.

The remarkable fact is that the American soldier has fought well, died well, and—where he has survived—become part of civilian life again at home without being shattered. Partly it is because, with a kind of fatalism, he decides that he has a bad job on his hands which he must suffer silently and get over with. All war partakes of the nature of licensed murder, and there is a sense in which it channels impulses that have been repressed in a peaceful industrial society. But none has yet been able to assess the mutilating effect of war on the spirit of the civilian soldier. Every society demands a considerable truncating of emotion, yet the young soldier finds himself subjected to it at a time in his life when he requires elbow room for generosity.

This may offer a clue, however, to the effectiveness of America at war. The civilian premise that the individual counts for something is severely hemmed in by the Army as a society: yet it is strong enough to survive, and carries the soldier—as it carries the whole nation—through the war ordeal. American war strength is greatest just at the point at which an authoritarian society would have used up the impetus of its imposed belief and be ready for internal collapse. Here, as in other phases of American life, the conditionings of an open society reap their harvest of strength. That they should do so in something so barbarous as modern warfare serves to make the triumph more dramatic.

While it is the common soldier—Johnny Reb or Billy Yank or G.I. Joe —who is glorified by the orators and politicians, with their cult of the anonymous common man, one drastic consequence of America's new military era has been the creation of a professional military elite.* In the wartime armies many of the officers are civilians drafted for the Army, who learn the art of command and sometimes show remarkable qualities of leadership; yet the top command remains with the Army professionals.

These professionals have not been able in America, as they have in Latin America, Germany, Spain, Japan, to create a caste which would dominate the society and even challenge the powers of the civilian government. From the beginning of the national experience, Americans have feared control by the military and have insisted on control being retained by the civilian arm. Since the President functions as Commander-in-Chief of the Armed Forces it is largely through him that the control is exercised. The crucial figures in this history of military-civilian relations were Washington and Lincoln. Washington set the initial precedent, both in theory and practice. Again and again he insisted, in letters to his officers and to the Congress, that the civilian authority had to be kept paramount. As for Lincoln, since most of the military leadership talent went over to the Southern cause, he had to find promising young officers and make leaders out of them. The story of his trials, disasters, and final success in this quest is well known. But much as he valued good generals Lincoln reasserted the principle of civilian authority over the military. This does not mean an American acceptance of the principle of political commissars as in totaiitarian societies, where the soldier-technician is distrusted and his political reliability has constantly to be guarded. Where Lincoln found a good technician, as he

---

* See also Ch. VII, Sec. 2, "The Seats of the Mighty."

did in Grant, he gave him complete headway. But he never abdicated his right to appoint and dismiss, nor his right and duty to decide on the larger outlines of strategy which are bound to be as much political as military.

There have been few "political generals" and very little Bonapartism in American history: the most notable cases have been those of General McClellan, who was appointed Chief-of-Staff by Lincoln and ran for the Presidency while the Civil War was still on, and General MacArthur, who saw himself as a man of political destiny throughout his career. In the struggle between President Truman and General MacArthur during the Korean War, the issue was not the merit of the strategic ideas of the two men but the question of where the final decision lay. In this sense the episode marked a constitutional crisis. MacArthur had strong popular support, which made President Truman's challenge to him an act of courage and seemed for a time to open the possibility of civil strife. But the tradition of civilian control proved too strong to be overthrown. There is a difference (contrasting President Grant and Eisenhower) between a military man who turns after a war to the tasks of peace and one who seeks to use his military power and glamour for political ends, and seeks the supremacy of the military over the civilian. The creation of a new elite of generals has thus far been kept within the frame of civilian control, but the question of the future is more difficult.

The new American general, because he must administer an army and often act as a kind of proconsul on foreign soil, is a mixture of many men. Not only is he trained in the history and art of war; he must also be something of a diplomat, and he must know how to move and direct vast bodies of men and material, yet also how to govern occupied territory and maintain delicate relations with his allies in a coalition war. With all this he must remain a politically neutral technician, a little like an American corporate manager who runs a big plant but must take his larger directives from his board. Such requirements involve broad training, and because of this a number of the abler generals have been used in diplomatic and administrative posts. While their sympathies tend to be with business, they form one of the rare power elites in American life that is trained to keep itself free of money as an incentive.

The danger with the military group, as German history has shown, is that it will grow into a professional caste cherishing its own conception of honor, frightened at the infiltration of new ideas, cut off from the rest of the culture, and living by its sense of power. In some respects the Joint Chiefs-of-Staff have tended to parallel the development of the German General Staff, especially in the spread of its interests and the concentration of power in a single person at the top. But the inner differences between American and German society make it more likely that the American general, like the American soldier, will remain basically a civilian, and that the conditionings of democratic life will counteract the authoritarian nature of his task and training. The sharpest challenge, after the MacArthur episode, to the nonpolitical character of the Army came when Senator McCarthy tried in 1954 to use the Congressional power of investigation in order to force the generals and the civilian secretaries to take his lead in their dismissal of subordinates. The failure of this effort showed again that the nonpolitical Army is deeply ingrained in American society.

The burden rests not so much with the military as with the culture itself. Fortunately the Americans have not developed the cult of martial virtues which has paralyzed military societies since Assyria and Sparta. Such a cult is more likely to grow in a society that glorifies feudal rather than industrial qualities, despises human life instead of valuing it, and has never launched on anything like the American quest for happiness. What makes militarism suicidal is the nature of the virtues it celebrates and their deadening effect on cultural growth. The military virtues are subordination, hierarchy, loyalty, clan honor, physical prowess, and above all the habit of mind that regards all questions as settled by authority. Despite their victories and sense of power, the American soldiers have come out of their major wars with a saving distaste for such virtues and for military life. With all its pressures to conformity American society offers an unfavorable soil for militarism. The stress on mobility, on reward for effort, on creative comforts, on happiness and on individual freedom, more than counterbalances whatever glamour the military life has offered in history.

5. The American World Image

THERE IS AN episode in Thomas Jefferson's career that illumines the image which the American has of the world. As President he put through the Non-Intercourse and Embargo Acts to keep America from being drawn into the struggle between the British and French for control of the seas. "I have ever deemed it fundamental for the United States," he wrote fifteen years later, "never to take an active part in the quarrels of Europe. . . . Their mutual jealousies, their balance of power, their complicated alliances, their forms and principles of government, are all foreign to us. They are nations of eternal war. . . . On our part, never had a people so favorable a chance of trying the opposite system, of peace and fraternity with mankind and the direction of all our means and faculties to the purpose of improvement instead of destruction!"

On which Henry Adams commented in his monumental *History of the United States:*

> War, with all its horrors, could purify as well as debase; it dealt with high motives and vast interests; taught courage, discipline, and stern sense of duty. Jefferson must have asked himself what lessons of heroism or duty were taught by his system of peaceable coercion, which turned every citizen into an enemy of the laws—preaching the fear of war and self-sacrifice, making many smugglers and traitors, but not a single hero. . . . Under the shock of these discoveries Jefferson's vast popularity vanished, and the labored fabric of his reputation fell in sudden and general ruin. America began slowly to struggle, under the consciousness of pain, toward a conviction that she must bear the common burdens of humanity and fight with the weapons of other races in the same bloody arena; that she could not much longer delude herself with hopes of evading laws of Nature and instincts of life; and that her new statesmanship which made peace a passion could lead to no better results than had been reached by the barbarous system which made war a duty.

True, it was an Adams who wrote this, with the traditional Adams hostility to Jefferson; and it was written at the turn of the twentieth century about an episode a century earlier. Yet whatever their real divergence of view, it is curious that both men built their intellectual systems on the concept of the elemental principles of Nature. No less than Jefferson's, Adams's appeal was to "the laws of Nature and instincts of life." The difference was that Jefferson lived in the eighteenth-century intellectual universe which saw Nature as an initial harmony disturbed by the destructive artifices of men, while Adams lived in a post-Darwinian world which saw Nature as a cruel, unending struggle. Yet in both cases there was an appeal to a peculiar American consonance with Nature. Adams used it to justify intervention just as Jefferson had appealed to it to justify isolationism. The internationalists of today go back to the same image of America's relation to the outside world which lay at the heart of Jefferson's world view, although they derive from it a directly contrary conclusion: since America is what Jefferson felt it to be, it has the mission of setting the world aright, spreading the gospel of freedom and democracy.

This is the metaphysic of the American world image: America is the New World, while all the rest of the world that is not America is the Old World. The ruling principle of the Old World is artifice and cunning in an arena—as Charles Beard saw it—"encrusted in the blood rust of centuries." To correct this, America was founded as part of an Order of Nature, as distinguished from the Artificial Order. This gives Americans a unique relation to Nature which may justify intervention in world affairs, as it may also provide ground for its isolation from a world embroiled in hopeless quarrels. Thus the role of America as a hermit nation and its role as liberating nation are twin impulses in American history and the American mind; they are inseparable not only from the fabric of the civilization but from each other. They are the thrust and counterthrust which form the seeming paradox of the American attitude to the world.

One finds in this metaphysic a clue to some elements in the American outlook which might otherwise seem contradictory and wayward. A brilliantly acid British observer, Geoffrey Gorer, has managed in his portrait of American world attitudes (in *The American People*) to depict them as perversely juvenile and quaintly imbecilic. If this were true, it would be hard to explain why a people ridden by such idiocies could have risen to world power or could be thriving in a world which does not coddle ineptitude. There is, of course, a quality of mingled innocence and shrewdness in the American world image, as there is in the whole of the American national character. The central element of the American metaphysic is the belief that American institutions are more "natural" and therefore better than those of other peoples. This belief is part of the organic strength of America. There is a childishness in it, but this very childishness strips it of what might otherwise become a cynical imperialism. Using Spengler's symbols, the American world image is more closely related to the "springtime" of a culture than to the twilight "Caesarism" which, in its disillusioned belief in power alone, would use it to put other peoples in an inferior status.

The idols Americans worship are not primarily the idols of power but the idols of their own culture transposed upon the world scene. Since they believe in productivity within their own system, they tend to value productivity in others. The preindustrial cultures seem to them backward: they may also regard them as picturesquely quaint but they reserve their admiration for the cultures that have developed housing, sanitation, and mechanical skills. Similarly, since Americans live by machines they use them in their foreign policy, both in war and peace. Even lethal weapons are for them tools and gadgets rather than death-dealing devices. When they seek some way of aiding a friendly people, they prefer to help them achieve the same weapons and gadgets they have themselves. When President Eisenhower was confronted with the problem of accepting or refusing the method of atomic disarmament, he proposed an "atoms for peace" program to turn technology from wartime to peacetime uses and then an "open-sky" plan. They also make an idol of the dollar. Partly this is a matter of pride in their resources, partly a way of saying that there are better methods of conducting world affairs than the Old Diplomacy. As compared with diplomacy and war the use of the dollar seems to them part of a more rational New Order—saner, more logical, less destructive. They seem to have an inveterate conviction that peace is something they can buy with their dollars as readily as they can buy a house, a car, a TV set, or new clothes for their families. Again there is a degree of childishness in this view, yet it is not wayward but organic to the national character.

The American need for signs of affection from other peoples has often been noted. In part it expresses the overvaluing of love which I have already discussed.* But it also expresses a desire for a mutual generosity in relations between peoples. There is an understandable skepticism about American motives in such ventures as the Marshall Plan, NATO, and Point Four by those who note the expectation of a *quid pro quo* whenever aid is granted. But the truth is not so much that Americans believe they can buy love and affection with the dollar, as that they are bewildered when they do not find in foreign affairs the kind of reciprocity they expect between neighbors in their own towns. Gorer has remarked acutely that for Americans all international relations are interpersonal relations. Believing in their own motives, they are bewildered when—after spending some fifty or sixty billions in military and economic aid to their allies—they reap a harvest of suspicion, fear, and envy.

One of the American traits is the recoil from the unfamiliar. The trouble with the world, Salvador de Madariaga once remarked ironically, is that there are so many foreigners in it—which pretty much expresses the American attitude toward outsiders. The American traveling abroad is likely to be puzzled when he finds that others do not share his ideas on food and clothing, sanitation, work and play, manners and morals. This seems the more curious when one remembers that America is itself a "nation of nations" and contains a multitude of diverse cultural traditions. Yet this fact only serves to increase the bafflement of the American abroad: since he has seen people of foreign extraction in his own country abandoning their customs and becoming "Americanized," he cannot understand why the people of foreign countries should not do the same. There is little xenophobia, real hatred of outsiders, in this attitude. Rather does it express the American's illusion of centrality in his conviction that what he is and does and how he does it are part of the order of Nature.

This attitude turns in part on a distrust of foreign social and political

* See Ch. VIII, Sec. 5, "Courtship, Love, and Marriage."

systems. The original rejection of Europe, based on a recoil from Europe's monarchies and dynastic wars, has been transformed into a fear of Communism and a distrust even of "Socialism." Americans tend to lump under "Socialism" all economic and political forms which differ sharply from their own. Given the constant change of the American social structure, this seems a curious attitude, which can only be explained by the feeling that a "Socialist" system seems to contain not only the unfamiliar but also the subversive. Americans have not learned that they do not have to embrace Socialism in order to accept the fact that other peoples may have turned to it either out of choice or out of necessity.

I have noted in an earlier chapter the rejection of the European father which underlies much of the American attitude toward Europeans.* But something very different is involved in the American attitude toward the Asians. They seem to form a wholly different world to Americans, who speak of the struggle between Communism and democracy as one between "East" and "West." Actually, of course, Communism as a system of thought is as much a product of the Western tradition as is democracy: both flow from the science, rationalism, and industrialism of the seventeenth and eighteenth centuries. Yet by equating Communism with the East the Americans in effect give it a prescriptive claim to the whole of the Oriental world. This does not reckon with the fact that America contains within itself strands from both East and West. The American soldier in the Korean War who called the Asian soldiers "gooks" was only expressing his sense of the strangeness of finding himself fighting for or against peoples so alien to his experience. What the American finds different about the Oriental mind is its tempo, its valuing of the group rather than of the individual life, its slow continuity of tradition. Yet there are stirrings of self-questioning and self-doubt within the American mind which are making Americans readier to open themselves to influences from the Orient. This has been shown recently by an interest in the art and thought of Asia, from the Japanese dance to the temple sculptures of India and by the new understanding of Asian political leaders like Gandhi, Nehru, Magsaysay, U Nu, and by a more sympathetic approach to the foreign polities of the "uncommitted" peoples of Asia.

Americans like to think that their foreign policy is based on "the man on the street." Actually this is far truer in domestic than in foreign policy, whose direction, at least in theory, is in the President's hands. As

* See Ch. I, Sec. 3, "The Slaying of the European Father."

Alexander Hamilton put it, he is "the sole organ of foreign policy." By his power to make treaties and agreements and appoint ambassadors to represent him, by his conduct of diplomacy and his role as commander-in-chief, he can shape policy according to his own ideas. He has the power to be not a follower but a creator of public opinion since he can in large measure shape the situations to which public opinion responds.

This power of the Executive can lead to dangerous consequences. While only Congress can declare war, the Executive can by his conduct of diplomacy bring about a situation in which a declaration of war cannot be avoided. The charge that Franklin Roosevelt deliberately induced the Japanese attack on Pearl Harbor has been grossly overstated; yet the point is that it might have happened, and that it is quite possible under the American system. The action of President Truman in ordering troops to Korea immediately after the North Korean attack is another illustration. Legally it came within America's adherence to the police power of the UN and morally it was justified, yet it had the effect of plunging America into a war without any declaration by Congress. Similarly when President Eisenhower, in 1957, asked Congress for a Joint Resolution giving him a "stand-by" power to move troops to avert aggression in the Middle East, a number of Constitutional authorities argued that he had the power anyway and that the request was superfluous.

There is thus no direct relation between American popular attitudes and American policy. When the Cominform in 1948 expelled Tito, it is doubtful whether American opinion was ready to accept the break as genuine and help Communist Yugoslavia. It is also doubtful whether popular opinion supported a similar move to give aid to Franco Spain in return for military bases, or whether there was ever any popular opinion behind the Administration policy of bolstering American oil concessions in the Arab countries by military aid and alliances. In all three cases the State Department acted on grounds of high policy, and the people accepted what they may not have liked. On the other hand, when President Truman proposed the appointment of an ambassador to the Vatican he encountered a storm of protest and had to retreat. Thus public opinion sets the outer limits of tolerance for foreign-policy decisions. The policy-makers need not follow it in day-to-day decisions, but if they move too far from it on matters that seem symbolic, they must draw back or lose Congressional and popular support.

In the functioning of foreign policy the most serious question is the separation of powers between Congress and the Executive. After its honeymoon period, every administration has had to face the rise of an opposition to its foreign policy even within its own party. In time of war a skillful President can carry the country along with him from crisis to crisis, as Lincoln did in the Civil War and Roosevelt in World War II. He must balance the needs of war strategy with the requirements of military and civilian morale. In the midst of war he must think of the next election while he strives to keep the country cohesive in the face of retreats and defeats. But in one sense a crisis of peacetime diplomacy involves even greater difficulties, since the cementing force of a common danger is not present. It was the great achievement of Senator Vandenberg, after World War II, to hold the Republicans in line on a "bipartisan policy" which presented an unbroken political front to the Kremlin. But such leadership is rare and has not been duplicated since. Thus American foreign policy has had to fight constantly a two-front strategic struggle—one with America's opponents abroad, the other with the Administration's enemies in Congress. The call for party discipline, more insistent in recent years, has had scant response, and as a result both the foreign policy of successive administrations and the counterpolicy of the opposition party have been the product of haste and improvisation rather than policies planned and hammered out to represent a collective party position.

Perhaps only the abundance of American power and wealth has provided the margin of waste which has made possible the luxury of the violent expression of American attitudes on foreign affairs inside America. Commentators from countries where the press is state-controlled or where it is held "responsibly" in line with government policy cannot dissociate American press headlines from the government's position. Yet the dissociation must be made. When Colonel McCormick, the publisher of the Chicago *Tribune,* carried on his private war with the British he was engaging in this luxury. The same holds for the tenacious clan of isolationist Senators. The effect is clamorous, but it is serious only when American policy is weak enough to respond to it. If a newspaper, a Senator, or a pressure group can cow the State Department or President into a policy change, then those who forced the change emerge as the real policy-makers. The task of a wise administration is to steer its course according to its principles, but always to take soundings of public opinion in order to re-examine the wisdom of the principles. In short, foreign policy in a democracy is a two-way relation in which the decision-makers never cut themselves off from the people but never flinch from clarifying the alternatives before them and guiding the nation in the choice it makes between these alternatives.

6. The World's Image of America

WHAT THE WORLD thought of them used to be of intense concern to Americans in the days when they were making a bid for their equal place among the powers of the earth. Like every new social experiment, this one wanted to feel itself a success; like every culture coming to power, it sought a mirror to catch the reflection of its crescent might.

Americans got plenty of attention from travelers, visiting luminaries, and foreign critics. In the period before the Jacksonian era the driving curiosity of the foreigner was about the nature of this new comet, whether it would survive, and the type of new man who lived on it. Later the commentators split between Tories who recoiled from the new democracy in action, and liberals and radicals who welcomed it as the world's best hope. In the period between the Civil War and the World War, America was accepted as a successful going-concern, but anxiety fixed upon its machine culture and materialist values. In the era of the world wars and the long Armed Truce the emphasis shifted again. While Europe still sat in judgment on America it was chiefly concerned with the nature and maturity of its leadership in a world of atomic power. With these queries came a new kind of split in the world's attitude toward America.

The earlier commentators had also been split in their own way. To be sure, St. John de Crèvecoeur had the timeless accent of someone writing about Paradise in the dawn of the world. He was a European who, having discovered the charms of America, had become an American; yet he wrote in French and as part of the continental tradition. There was a naïve insight in his perceptions, an idyllic quality as in a painter of the Primitive School. "Wives and children, who before in vain demanded of him a morsel of bread, now fat and frolicsome, gladly help their father to clear those fields whence exuberant crops are to arise to feed and to clothe them all." There is, however, also an Hobbesian view of the frontiersmen "often in a perfect state of war; that of man against man . . . ; that of man against every wild inhabitant of these venerable woods, of which they have come to dispossess them. . . . These men appear to be no better than carnivorous animals of a superior rank. . . . Remote from the power of example, and check of shame, many families exhibit the most hideous parts of our society." But if De Crèvecoeur saw the early settlers of the frontier as a *Lumpenproletariat* of the forest, he felt also that they were quickly civilized by "decency of conduct, purity of morals, and respect of religion." His estimate of the salient American traits of his time (he was speaking of the Middle Colonies) could still stand: "industry, good living, selfishness, litigiousness, country polity, the pride of freemen, religious indifference, are their characteristics." Thus even in De Crèvecoeur, who is held to have presented an American idyl, one finds the beginnings of the split which was to plague the European mind in one form or another for centuries. The hopes that clustered around new American institutions fought with the fears of the untrammeled elements in American life.

De Tocqueville, the deepest of the foreign observers, also felt this split. The young banker and aristocrat, who was in his later years to play a role in French politics and write a great history of the Old Regime in France, came to America to study this new portent in the Western heavens. He was a rare mixture of student and man-of-affairs who refused to read his own preferences into history. He was himself an aristocratic liberal who hoped for enlightened policies to be carried out for the French people by a responsible elite of blood and ability. Thus the principle of "democracy" which he saw in America, and which he did more than any other writer to define as a category of modern political thought, was a sharp challenge to his own values. He sensed the danger that the political principle, "the majority will must prevail," would become the moral principle, "the majority is always right." Yet he did not let his sense of danger distort his capacity for observation. Nor was he dismayed by the fact that the stream of democracy (to use the figure in one of his famous passages) was turbulent and muddy: he saw it cutting a new channel, and he knew that the turbulence and mud were part of the process. In short, De Tocqueville still stands up because he wrote with the humility of a great political analyst.

The same cannot be said for many of the British travelers, like Basil Hall or Mrs. Trollope, who also visited America at the floodtime of Jacksonian democracy and who wrote (as Allan Nevins put it) out of a "Tory condescension" toward an America they still considered a barbaric colony. Charles Dickens, more of a radical than a Tory, who had done his share of attacking abuses in English life, blurted out in *American Notes* and *Martin Chuzzlewit* his home truths about American materialism and dollar worship with an unendearing assurance of the righteousness of his own English values. The greatest contrast to De Tocqueville's spirit was that of Macaulay, who wrote of the putative ruin of America in the future with as much finality as Gibbon wrote of the actual ruin of Rome in the past, and whose famous letter on American democracy moves with a sweep still impressive even after it has been proved dismally wrong: "It is quite plain that your government will never be able to restrain a distressed and discontented majority.

. . . There will be, I fear, spoliation. The spoliation will increase the distress. The distress will produce fresh spoliation. There is nothing to stop you. Your Constitution is all sail and no anchor. When a society has entered on this downward progress, either civilization or liberty must perish." Where Mrs. Trollope found the Americans boors, where Dickens found them money grabbers and Macaulay found them despoilers of liberty and civilization, Matthew Arnold a generation later found them only Philistines. He ushered in a whole school of criticism by asserting that America was simply neither "interesting" nor "elevating."

It was in response to such criticism that James Russell Lowell, his cultural pride goaded to a pitch of genteel anger, wrote his famous *Atlantic* essay, "On a Certain Condescension in Foreigners." Not even the urbane *American Commonwealth* of Viscount Bryce, which helped Americans to a quieter self-assurance about their institutions and their standing in the world, could quite wipe out the memory of the brash men who had come to sit in judgment on America.

There is a touch of unreality today in reading some of these traveled, sophisticated, and wise men of Europe. They came from every European culture. Some came to stay, some only to hit and run. They took inventory of the rough manners, the rich raiment, the fabled wealth of this parvenu who was knocking at the gate of world recognition with an insistence not to be denied. In the earlier phase they passed judgment on America's morals, inns, bedbugs, spitting and chewing, strong drink, factory girls, high society. Later they examined its machines, slums, political corruption, Southern lynching, Midwest isolationism, materialism, absorption in sports, yellow journalism, religious sects, crime and gangsterism, movies and TV, jazz and jive, novels, skyscrapers and bathtubs, businessmen and labor leaders, ways and failures of making love, psychoanalysis and neurotic women, booms and busts. Surely there has never been in history so full and free a concentration on a living culture over so extended a period.

In our generation a radically new phase of commentary on America has begun. Books are no longer written out of an aristocratic disdain for democracy nor out of the enthusiasm for it which was the reverse side of the shield. It is no longer America who knocks at the gate as a newcomer, peddling its wares of democracy, science, technology, high living standards, and asking the world's approval. It is not America that feels itself judged, nor Europe that sits in judgment as the acknowledged keeper of the cultural seals. The comments of the latest British novelist, arriving in New York en route to Hollywood, on American overheated houses or American clothes-horse women or any of the other standard topics, no longer draw blood. Since Americans are conscious of possessing the power, they take better to criticism of their cultural glory.

Even the myth of America, which had exerted so powerful an appeal on the minds of the European masses, has changed. Originally it was the myth of the Western Island—the legend of a bright promise amidst the surrounding darkness of the Old World. It was the place where one went to get away from the rutted stability of vested power and privilege. Many of the European novels, even as late as Lawrence's *Lady Chatterley's Lover,* had as their typical ending the hero setting off for the virile land of America. But the myth went through a number of transformations: the type-figure of the Noble Savage changed into the frontiersman, and that in turn into the commercial traveler, the Western cowboy, the Big Business tycoon, the Chicago gangster, and the devotee of the true cult of jazz. Today there is no longer a single legendary symbol for America. The immigrant's dream of streets still paved with gold is counterbalanced by the nightmare of the Congressional snooper. The "metaphysic of promise" still holds good, and young men and women the world over still long to come closer to the center of world power; but this too is counterbalanced by the image of America spread by the Kremlin propaganda lords.

There has been a double change therefore, in our time, in the world's image of America. One phase of it has been the shifting of emphasis in the appraisal of America: America is being judged no longer as a newcomer on the world scene but as a great power. The other is the civil war that rages in the hearts of those who are both drawn toward American power and dependent upon it, yet—because of the very fact of their dependence—also judge it harshly.

In this civil war raging in the mind of European and Asian man there is a danger of underestimating the pull that America still exerts on both. What attracts them is less the image of American power than of the American personality and social structure. Even many of the Russians—whatever their propagandists may teach them about American "imperialism" and "war-mongering"—are drawn toward the American personality. The case histories of Russian defectors into Germany and Austria, and of Hungarian refugees fleeing to the United States, show a residual sympathy for American society which two generations of Communist dogma have not been able to efface. This is, of course, even truer of western Europe, which shares so many of the basic American values.

But the very closeness of the European and American traditions makes the relation of dependence even more difficult. It is one thing to be conquered by an alien people—an event that can be written off as a combination of catastrophe and the Devil. But to be saved by one's kinsfolk, to be an Anchises carried out of the flames of Troy on the shoulders of Aeneas, bears the sting of humiliation. To the sensitive it implies that they are in the declining arc of their vigor—which is not an easy thing to admit, especially to oneself. They ask themselves why the Americans have been blessed with so much of material goods and they with so little. The answer cannot be American virtues and European vices, nor American merits and European defects. As they see the answer it is partly the luck of natural resources and of being cut off by oceans from the ravages of war. As much as luck it is also (as they see it) the willingness of Americans to pay a heavy human cost for what they have achieved: the willingness to be ruled by gadgets and machines, by business giants and intellectual pygmies, by political demagogues and the corruption of city bosses, by press barons, by advertising slogans and TV commercials, by spoiled women and even more spoiled children. To the European mind, with all its good will, the things that make Americans more powerful make them also more boorish, the things that make them more like giants make them also less like men. Even American aid has seemed the clinching proof that the American is the son who left home to make his fortune and now rolls in wealth while the old folk must hold out their hands for gifts to keep from going to the poorhouse.

Thus the phase of recoil is compounded of reluctant gratitude, envy for American wealth and prowess, resentful pride, and an uneasy fear of how America will use its power in world affairs. Edwin Arlington Robinson, in *Eros Tyrannos*, depicts a woman with pride of lineage drawn to a man from whom she is separated by the impassable distance between the faded aristocrat and the vigorous parvenu:

> *She fears him, and will always ask*
> *What fated her to choose him;*
> *She meets in his engaging mask*
> *All reasons to refuse him;*
> *But what she meets and what she fears*
> *Are less than are the downward years*
> *Drawn slowly to the foaming weirs*
> *Of age, were she to lose him.*

Thus Europe is caught between the need for America and the recoil from it.

This may explain the "Athens complex" which spread among the intellectuals of western Europe in the postwar years, when the shift of power to America became apparent. They were forced to compensate for their dependence by claiming for Europe the role of a cultural Greece to the American Rome—a Greece which, while conquered, takes the conqueror captive. Unquestionably the European cultures are mellower and more mature than the American. Without any overtones of provincialism the American intellectual feels that the British, French, and Scandinavians are extremely civilized people and the American artist continues to find in Italy an emotional haven he finds nowhere else.

Yet it would be wrong for the Europeans to conclude from this that the Americans have a sense of inferiority about their own culture. Except for a small number who are isolated by a cultural self-hatred and feel that nothing American can be good, the strong trend among the intellectuals is toward a critical acceptance of what was called (in a *Partisan Review* symposium) "our country and our culture." I speak of it as "critical acceptance" and not as "celebration": few of the American writers and thinkers have become apologists or have lost the skepticism which marks the craft of the thinker; nor have all of them stripped themselves of the driving impulse toward social and institutional change. But many of them have come to feel that charges born of hatred are destructive and barren and have struck a kind of pact with the basic frame of the culture within which they continue to function critically. They can absorb European criticism as well, since they value the great civilization out of which the criticisms come. If it helps the Europeans to think of themselves as Athens and of America as a less creative Rome, and to see American qualities through a glass darkly, the Americans have won enough assurance to take it in their stride.

It is natural that in the polar struggle for world position America's enemies should strive to exploit the civil war in the European and Asian mind. The Russian image of America is compounded of rivalry, fear, ideological antipathy, and cynically deliberate distortion for both home and foreign consumption. If a global war can be averted this image will in time change, as will happen also to the seriously distorted American image of Russia. In the meanwhile the Communist indictment of America has left its impact on the world's image of America.

The indictment is familiar. It charges that the American economy is riddled with "internal contradictions," that in its declining agony it turns to imperialist adventures and wars, that it is a Shylock lending money to the helpless and demanding its pound of flesh in the form of economic and political vassalage, that its prosperity has been made possible only by wars and armaments, and that as soon as it tries to stand on peacetime production alone it will collapse; that its inherent and feverish oscillation between boom and bust will be ended only by

the inner explosion of class struggle; that this explosion is being postponed through the skillful use of big armaments by a ruling class which
uses the war fever to build an increasingly Fascist police state; that its
inner savagery shows itself in barbaric methods of warfare, including
germ warfare in Korea and China and plans to use the hydrogen bomb
when the point of desperation has been reached; that its vaunted freedom does not apply to those who challenge capitalist power, and that
its façade of high living standards conceals the realities of poverty and
slum housing; that there is an inner violence in its culture which expresses itself not only in lynchings and Jim Crowing of Negroes and
in anti-Semitic hatreds, but also in literature, the arts, and the big
media; that its materialism is hoggish, its morals reckless and decadent,
its men emasculated, its women frigid, and its music and dance degenerate.

The path of this propaganda image is made easier by the widespread
fears of American power. The American policy-makers have often given
ground for such fears by reckless statements and foolish improvised
actions. The growth of America's own nationalism has led to pressures
which have cut aid abroad, put obstructions in the way of trade, or
ruffled the sensitivities of the "junior partners" in the free-world coalition. This feeds the natural feeling that Americans are immature in
the handling of their power, like children playing with toys. When
the Americans become impatient of the pain and difficulty involved in
trying to reach a consensus with their allies, the European answer is
the British quip "No annihilation without representation." The Europeans feel that, caught in a war between the two polar powers, Europe
would become an expendable continent, another lost Atlantis sunk under the dread weight of atomic destruction.

Hence the "neutralism" or "noncommitment" of many Europeans
and Asians, which helps shape—and distort—their image of America.
Hence also the rage of American policy- and opinion-makers at the
fence sitters, whom they find more exasperating than the outright enemy. It infuriates them to have an Aneurin Bevan impale them on an
epigram, a Nehru view them with a cold detachment at once anticapitalist and aristocratic, a Laski challenge the impact of the businessman upon American democracy, a Priestley depict the "new society"
as an American nightmare, a Sartre use the allegory of the respectful
prostitute to flay the conformism of American public opinion.

Many Americans who are not narrowly nationalist, and who want
America's allies to be independent, also want them to carry the responsibility of their independence. They suspect that their non-Communist
critics are able to enjoy the luxury of hurling barbs at America exactly

because it has shouldered the principal burden of democratic defense. They point out that since the Communist coup in Czechoslovakia and, even more, since the crushing of the Hungarian revolution, no one can question what happens to a European regime when Communism captures power. They see themselves not as crusaders against an ideology but as realists determined to keep the world open for a variety of social structures—provided each refrains from aggression.

The image of America current in Asia takes a somewhat different form. The Asian, newly liberated from colonialism or struggling to be liberated, finds in America a Devil symbol which serves to channel both his resentments and his newly felt sense of triumph. When Europeans take America apart, they are taking apart something they have come to regard as close to themselves. The European democrats speak and write acidly about America because they feel involved in the American venture and its destiny. In the case of Asia there is the sense neither of a shared past nor of a common destiny. The great cultural contacts of the Asian peoples have hitherto been either among themselves or with the peoples of Europe. America is viewed as the outsider, the giant who typifies what is held hostile in the Western way of life. Asia has shown a genius for religion-creating, a leaning away from activism, a distaste for materialism and the machine, a preference for refinement over raw vitality, a commitment to the family or the collective village unit as against the individual, a sense not of time but of permanence.

This may account for the fact that the Asians feel removed from the activism and machinism of both the polar powers. Thus far the Russians have managed to avoid the mistake of speaking of themselves as part of the West and thus alienating Asia. They have the advantage of facing toward both Europe and Asia, and are thus able to make an appeal to each. The Americans, who have only recently begun to face toward Asia, have made their appeal mainly as a society of freedom and abundance, of food and sanitation. They have not understood the deep Asian resentments which are further embittered by the image of America as a storehouse crammed with commodities. They have missed the fact that for the people of the Far East the American living standards seem incredible because they are incommensurable in terms of Asian experience. They fail to offer these people a compassable earthly vision, just as they fail to offer in spiritual terms a vision that will sustain the Oriental hunger for renunciation.

Thus the world's image of America is the product at once of American behavior, Communist propaganda, and the civil war that rages in the hearts of non-Communist Europeans and Asians. The result is that wherever Americans travel or wherever their official or unofficial spokesmen present America's case the questions that are asked them are a strange mixture of genuine disquiet and the unconscious echoes of political warfare. The questions are aimed at what is most vulnerable in the American reality—the surviving racist discriminations, the internal attacks on civil liberties, the strain of violence in the popular culture, the loudness with which the reactionary nationalists make their views heard, the jitters felt about "subversives," the power of a business oligarchy, the temptation to throw their weight about which American policy-makers do not always resist.

There have been distortions in the image of America all through the centuries. At the start there were the distorting lenses of hope, then the distortions of the legend of power or of wealth. For a time there were the distortions that ran in terms of gangsterism. Today there are the distortions of the violent political emotions involved in the long Armed Truce. The reality that is America gets lost in a series of fantastic mirror images.

The best answer to these questions is a candid answer. The Americans are aware that they have not struck twelve, that the struggle for an open society is by no means ended in America, that democracy is a continuing process in which every step is a compromise between opposing forces in the movement toward goals themselves in dispute. The mature American does not fear criticism of his institutions from abroad, as he does not hesitate himself to criticize them. If America is to make its qualities persuasive to world opinion, it must expect also to repair the defects of those qualities. If it reaps the advantage of such symbols as living standards, productivity, freedom for ideas, ethnic diversity, educational democracy, it must be willing to be damned for its failure to live up to them. And on a number of scores—on conformity, smugness, the overvaluing of personal security and the jitters about "national security," the resistance still offered by racist thought, and the faltering of leadership on the world scene—the failures have been real and sometimes dismal.

The problem is not one of answering the charges defensively or apologetically. It is one of finding a way of saying, through behavior as well as through words, that democratic society anywhere in the world would find it hard to survive the destruction of American democracy; that America does not seek to force conformity upon any culture; that the world it envisages is one in which diverse streams from every tradition flow into a cultural pool; and that such an open world is the fulfillment of the idea of an open society which alone gives the American experience its greatness of meaning.

7. *The Destiny of a Civilization*

"EVERY MAN," wrote Thomas Jefferson, "has two countries—his own and France." A young African writer has amended this to read "his own and America." It suggests the extent to which people far beyond the boundaries of America have had their imagination touched and their emotions engaged by the American experience. Only one other civilization in history—the Roman—can match this impact.

The comparison between Rome and America has absorbed many social thinkers. There are some striking parallels. We may, for example, sketch the lineaments common to both civilizations somewhat as follows: a world power span, by land and sea; a pride in republican institutions, with the emphasis theoretically on limited powers even while in practice the Executive is one of the most powerful offices in history; a continuing struggle between an oligarchic and a popular party, with the abler leaders gravitating toward the popular, but with the core of social power in the hands of the oligarchy; the reduction of politics to sloganeering, political recrimination, and charges of conspiracy.

Add some other parallels: a "capitalist" economy (I use "capitalist" in quotes since Rome, with land as its principal form of wealth, was not capitalist in our modern sense) growing strong in its later phases on world-wide resources and selling in far-flung markets, with cyclical swings of prosperity and depression; a distribution of wealth which arrays side by side the extremes of opulence and poverty; vast outlays on public works, an arms economy, and a network of economic controls in order to sustain the system; the piling up of a national debt, and a preoccupation with taxes and tax-gathering; the emergence of landless and toolless classes, at the mercy of fluctuations of prosperity and changes in state policy, absorbed with "bread and circuses"; the succession of ever bigger wars, enriching the nation yet draining its resources, spreading over the world the clamor of its arms; the absorption with the strategy, logistics, and technology of war; the use of military reputation as a road to high civilian office; the increasing domestic role of groups of war veterans; the creation of a remarkable system of administration and law, with armies of occupation and imperial proconsuls enveloping a turbulent world within the protective custody of border armies; the prestige and pride of citizenship in the world's greatest power structure.

To finish the portrait, add the cult of magnificence in public buildings and the growth of the gladiatorial arts at which the larger number of the people are passive spectators but emotional participants; the increasing violence within the culture; the desensitizing and depersonalizing of life; the weakening of the sense of place; the decay of rural life; the uprooting of people in a mobile culture; the concentration of a megalopolitan urbanism. In the area of personal life add the increasing split between moral standards and operative codes; the greater looseness of family ties and sexual relations, and the exploration of deviant and inverted forms of behavior; the Byzantinism of life, the refinements of luxury; the decay of formal religion, the turning toward new religious cults, the feverish search for the sources of evil; the feeling of widespread frustration, the "schism in the soul," the premonition of doom in the distant march of barbarian tribes.

It will be obvious that such a portrait of a civilization and an era might describe equally the Rome of the late Republic or early Empire and contemporary America. The parallel has been pushed hard by those who have sought in it variously a sermon against capitalism, the New Deal, or the public debt, religion or irreligion, materialism or supernaturalism, sexuality or divorce. Sermons aside, however, the question is whether the parallel is actually a deadly parallel or a mélange of striking metaphors, dramatic coincidences, and half-truths that fascinate the historical imagination while they mislead it.

The trouble with historical parallels is that they are selective and omit whole areas of unlikeness. If I may use this as a way of summing up a few of the points of emphasis of this book: there have been elements in American life crucially missing in the Roman: the steady advance of science and technology to sustain unparalleled living standards for every class; an emphasis on productivity, with an almost compulsive drive to raise living standards; a class system without the amorphous Roman proletariat; the heart of the culture in a broad middle class such as Rome lacked, and in an open-class system which dulls the sharpness of class struggle; the long-continuing survival of the constitutional tradition, the exclusion of extreme political philosophies and the minimal role played by political mobs.

Looking at it from the other direction, we find that Rome had only a narrow economic base in the skimpy and impoverished farms of an Italian peninsula not rich in resources. The treasure that gave her power came from the looting of riches in the stretch from Britain to North Africa and from Spain to India. Thus Rome as an empire was top-heavy: the superstructure of tribute and power had no self-regenerating base either in a culture of science and technology or in a fluid class system continuing to produce new talents and offer new rewards to match new hopes. It rested, rather, on the Roman legions and their mercenaries: when the imperial mold was broken, with the consequence of internal dissension and the "failure of nerve," the supports snapped and the civilization fell in ruins.

Turning to the institutions of the two societies America possesses an educational system which, for all its deficiencies, provides a constant stream of new human abilities for decision-making in industry and government. It has spread its national income widely enough to hold the allegiance of its people even in times of the most dangerous inner and world crises. It possesses a popular vigor that shows itself in the American speech, jazz, movies, and other popular arts, and offers proof that the fires of cultural strength still burn intensely. It has opened up to most of the people accessions of new experience in the big media, yet it retains a gusto for living and an earthiness of taste and style which are far from being the signs of a decadent or effeminate people. It renews its strength from institutions of freedom imbedded within the family system and the prevailing religious traditions, as well as within the economy. It has shown a resilience in bearing the shocks of war and depression, and a strength of fiber in meeting the challenges of old tyrannies and new "barbarians." Finally it evinces an inveterate optimism which restricts the prophecies of doom to small groups of moralists and intellectuals, whose experience scarcely touches the experience of the rest of the people.

I do not deny a degree of force in Spengler's contention that inner homologous structures may be "contemporary," even when they are far removed in time and place. They may face the same kind of crises, be subject to the same kind of stresses, traverse comparable life histories, run similar social and moral dangers, and (as so many civilizations have done) fall victim to the same combination of external challenge and internal weakness.

Yet I must reassert that America is not Rome but itself. The learning of all the cyclical theorists, from Vico to Toynbee, gives us no formulas that will explain the unlikely genesis of American civilization, the phenomenon of its growth, the paradox of outer slackness and inner strength, the riddle of why a power structure that by every historical parallel should have destroyed itself has retained not only its vigor but much of the unadorned directness it had in its less complex phases. This is not to say that America as a civilization is imperishable. It will perish, and it may even now be doomed by the destructive force that science has unleashed and man may not be able to control. But if so it is doomed for the ills and by the laws of development of the whole contemporary Western World, and not those of Rome or any other civilization of the past.

If America were Rome, who would be the barbarians? From America's standpoint, they would have to be the hordes of Communism, with the Russians and the Chinese as the leading tribes. The weakness in this analogy is immediately apparent. The Russians, with their tight statism, their rigid doctrinal unity, their ideological obsessiveness, their social conformism, are far from the image of amorphous barbarian bands pushing against the tottering ramparts of the empire. As for the Chinese, they combine the new steel frame of Communist doctrine with a civilization older even than that of the Russians, which in turn is older than the American, and with a highly complex structure of society and an ancient heritage of art and learning.

It is ironic for Americans to search for a "barbarian" image when they have themselves long embodied that image for Europe. Take almost any commentary on America written in the past half century by almost any culturally self-conscious European—let us say Georges Duhamel's *Scènes de la Vie Future*—and you will find in it the overpowering image of barbarians with machines coming to invade the empire of the spirit and preparing to lay waste to the ancient structures of sensibility and personality. There is also a second sense in which the concept of barbarians may be used. Spengler premised a phase of history in which politics and the state had broken down into a formless pursuit of individual greeds. He saw America as a random collection of people drifting from city to city in pursuit of the dollar, incapable of understanding politics in the Spenglerian sense of the arts of disciplined mastery. But Spengler also saw Bolshevik Russia as the same kind of barbarian horde that had "ceased to be a state," its economic man dominant over the political man, its political outlook lacking the dimension of depth. Unfortunately such a definition of the barbarian would include most of the economically developed peoples of the world, leaving only the Caesarist regimes of Fascism to sustain the idea of civilization.

The West European and the uncommitted Asiatic might regard America and Russia as expressing only alternative modes of barbarism. In both there is the abundance of energy that threatens to overwhelm the mellower or more passive civilizations, in both a high degree of organizing genius as the "practical" men seek an engineering approach through the state trusts of the commissars or the corporate trusts of capitalist Big Management. Given the polarizing pressures of the two superpowers, a large part of the world has begun to offer a growing resistance to the "either/or" choice between the two Romes. The struggle is not between a world empire and a number of barbarian outposts but between two great powers who are competing for world power while each insists it desires only its national security, and much of the rest of the world refuses to accept the terms of the struggle or to enroll as a conscript in either army.

One aspect of the struggle is the rivalry between America and Russia for the pacifying and organizing role that Rome played in the late Republic and early Empire. The period of the *pax Romana* was one of relative peace and prosperity not only in Rome but the provinces. There are few periods in world history when, over so wide an expanse, men could go about their business, arts, and pleasures in so undisturbed a way. The real disaster came out of the resulting rigidity and stagnation. Like the Americans and the Russians, the Romans were highly "practical" men who valued things more than they valued ideas: they perished by a failure of the imagination. A single world empire provides no rivalries of power and of values. Rome could destroy Carthage, but it could not overcome its own institutions of privilege and slavery which sapped its productive force and stripped its technology of dignity. It glorified the martial virtues but had not inner strength to give them meaning. When the challenge of the barbarians finally came, Rome had to pay Danegeld to buy off the marauders. The disease of war put the finishing touches to what had been left by the disease of class and underlying both was the disease of social uncreativeness.

What are these two civilizations, each of which is exerting its claim to organize the future by its own *pax Romana?* Their struggle for world influence is not an overnight phenomenon. Here is what De Tocqueville wrote of them:

> There are at the present time two great nations in the world which seem to tend toward the same end, although they started from different points; I allude to the Russians and the Americans. Both of them have grown up unnoticed; and while the attention of mankind was directed elsewhere, they have suddenly assumed a prominent place among the nations; and the world learned their existence and their greatness at almost the same time. All other nations seem to have nearly reached their natural limits . . . but these are still in the act of growth; all others are stopped, or continue to advance with extreme difficulty; these are proceeding with ease and celerity along a path to which the human eye can assign no term. The American struggles against the natural obstacles which oppose him; the adversaries of the Russian are men; the former combats the wilderness

and savage life; the latter, civilization with all its weapons and its arts;
the conquests of the one are therefore gained by the plowshare; those of
the other by the sword. The Anglo-American relies upon personal interest to accomplish his ends, and gives free scope to the unguided exer-
tions and common sense of the citizens; the Russian centers all the authority of society in a single arm: the principal instrument of the former
is freedom; of the latter, servitude. Their starting point is different, and
their courses are not the same; yet each of them seems to be marked out
by the will of Heaven to sway the destinies of half the globe.

It took a remarkable insight to discern the destinies of Russia and
America at a time when Russia was still a preindustrial despotic
monarchy and America, just beginning to look across the Mississippi,
was still a small agrarian society and had only just proclaimed the
Monroe Doctrine. But De Tocqueville sensed that there were common
elements in these two societies and comparable resources for them to
develop, which would one day make them the polarizing forces of the
world. Each had a massive continental stretch that could be exploited as
a base for empire. In the history of each the plain left its influence
on the people, as Turner saw for America and Sir John Maynard for
Russia. Each has shown an organizing capacity and a skill in amassing
power. Most of all, both have shown the capacity (which stamps a
strong civilization) to release locked-up energies.

The Russia which De Tocqueville saw was Czarist and not Communist, so that he could not have forseen the extent to which the
Communist idea would become first a religious creed for the Russians
and then a state church in which the religious fire had begun to burn
out. His eye was, then, not on the dogma but on the land and the
people. In them lay the capacity to give this or any other dogma its
strength. In the American case, on the other hand, he noted the principle of freedom that has persisted to this day—a principle available for
others as well as for Americans to develop. Thus what counted again
was the land and the people, in whom lay the capacity to give the
democratic idea its own brand of strength. What was latent in both
cultures in 1835 has been realized in the mid-twentieth century. Every
people has its high historical moments, when it feels a triumphant sense
of national energy. What marks both the Russians and the Americans is
that they moved beyond these short-lived spurts of intensity in a continuing arc of energy that they are still sustaining. This may be only a
more complex way of putting what De Tocqueville calls "the will of
Heaven" in explaining how each has come "to sway the destinies of half
the globe."

The fact that America and Russia, who are today such determined rivals and whose social systems and principles are so at variance, should share certain common traits is a fact to infuriate as well as astonish the unthinking partisans of both. Yet reflection will show that there must be common elements which have led these two civilizations to steady growth and world power. These elements are not such as can be isolated by scientists and by their rigors of scientific method. Since they have to do with the intangibles of social energy and national character, they yield more readily to the intellectual imagination. I have mentioned the prophetic insight of De Tocqueville. Curiously, Walt Whitman, poet rather than political theorist, expressed a similar insight in his famous "Letter to Russia":

> You Russians and we Americans! Our countries so distant, so unlike at first glance—such a difference in social and political conditions, and our respective methods of moral and practical development . . . and yet in certain features, and vastest ones, so resembling each other. The variety of stock elements and tongues, to be resolutely fused in a common identity and union at all hazards—the idea . . . that they both have their historic and divine mission—the fervent element of manly friendship throughout the whole people, surpass'd by no other races—the grand expanse of territorial limits and boundaries—the unform'd and nebulous state of many things, not yet permanently settled, but agreed on all hands to be the preparations of an infinitely greater future—the fact that both Peoples have their independent and leading positions to hold, keep, and . . . fight for . . . the deathless aspirations at the inmost center of each great community . . . are certainly features you Russians and we Americans possess in common.

I do not cite these common traits to argue that there are no grounds for world struggle between Russia and America. The comparable historical elements in each system may be partly what has set them in opposition to each other. Neither in the life of nations nor of individuals do somewhat parallel personality structures insure the absence of conflict. The fact is that Russia and America are also strongly unlike each other, which implies not only a basis of conflict but means that each may at some future time manage to fit into a world culture which must feed on diversities.

The crucial difference does not lie in ideologies alone, important as they are: for the hold that Communism as an ideology has on the Russians and capitalist democracy on the Americans is something that itself needs explaining. The clues are in history and national character. Russia's long history of the oppression of peasants and the muzzling of intellectuals, along with psychological factors in the life history of the individual which await closer study, produced a strain of alternating violence and submission to authority. Children of an authoritarian church and a feudal social organization, the Russians never developed free institutions. They are burdened with the oppressive weight of dynastic history, and the experience of the Communist rulers did not abolish the dynastic pattern but left it intact. It is, moreover, a history marked by a succession of sharp breaks and catastrophes. The Kiev period was followed by a shift in trade routes, the weakening of Russian economic power, and by a Tartar rule which proved to be a long history of foreign enslavement. The Moscow period was one of domestic tryanny. Then came the rule of Peter and the awakening of Russian energies from their long Asiatic sleep—the fusion of Western and Eastern elements which evoked much of Russia's later strength. The witless misrule and corruption under the later Czars led to the double disaster of the defeat by Japan and the abortive 1905 revolution. Thus the 1917 break with the *ancien régime* was part of a continuing history of breaks and new starts which conditioned the Russian people to a long patience amidst a turbulent sequence of social disturbance and violent change.

One of the deepest differences between the two cultures lies in their divergent views of human nature and history. There is a messianic strain in the Russian tradition to which the American character is less conditioned, except for the influence of Biblical sin and salvation in the nineteenth-century Communist settlements and millennial movements. Students of Russian religion have noted that its core idea has been not the individual's responsibility to his conscience but the mystical sense of the congregation as a whole. To the Russian mind, therefore, both truth and salvation are likely to lie less in the individual soul than in the collective. The 1917 Revolution gave an explosive force to the Russian mystical and messianic strain, but it added also something the Russian thinkers from Belinski to Trotsky did not foresee—the will of a disciplined party seeking to transform the society according to a dogmatic scheme. Thus the Communist era imposed upon the *mystique* of the traditional Russia a rigid frame of planning based on a wholly rationalist view of human nature.

At first sight these may seem drastically opposed, leading to the conclusion that the Communist regime, with its optimist assurance that Russia and the world can be transformed according to a plan, could not thrive in a people with strong mystical and pessimistic strains. But this is to forget the common elements in past and present: the indifference toward individual values in the pursuit of some larger collective aim, whether it be the Holy Spirit-in-the-congregation, Socialism-in-one-country, or the triumph-of-the-world proletariat. Linked with the

Byzantine rather than the Western phase of European history, the Russians skipped both the Renaissance and the Reformation—which is to say that they skipped both humanism and the individual conscience. Toynbee has pointed out the inner link between what he calls "archaism" and "futurism." The former, as in the case of the Russian church, the peasant community, and the Slavophile movement, seeks to revive ancient forms for new situations; the latter, as in the case of Communism, seeks a short cut into the future. Both are examples of a mechanical Utopianism. Swinging from one to the other, the Russians have managed to stay within the same metaphysical frame.

Another difference lies in the pace of industrial growth. In a collectively willed process of industrialization the same act of planning which creates the economic structure creates also its political counterpart in the party and the state. Thus, the willed elements become central, and by a trial-and-error process of shifting party-line policies the effort is made to fit into the same pattern the strands of war and peace, industry and agriculture, education, family life, art, and philosophy. By comparison the process of industrialization in America and indeed the whole historic growth of the culture appear almost haphazard, a product of organic unfolding rather than of collective will. Where the whole growth has been so continuous, there is no need for drastic transformations by violence. Where individual career and conscience have counted for so much, there is a strong resistance to the short cuts which would by-pass both.

It is here that the strength of America's destiny lies. To be sure, a Communist system can drive ahead with a single-minded purpose and can make and consolidate gains with a swiftness denied to the more organic civilization like the American, which must feel out all the surrounding pressures in the very act of driving ahead. Yet the more tentative process of change has the merit of being more deeply rooted in the consent and energies of a people which feels itself part of what it has shaped freely out of its own process of growth.

Seeking to pierce the obscurity of the future, one may ask what will be the destiny of these two civilizations. There is one sense in which the two destinies are linked. It is impossible for each of them to establish its own pacifying and organizing force over the world which will parallel the *pax Romana*. On the other hand, if each pushes its claims and fears to their ultimate logic, the collision will be disastrous for both. An effort to divide the world between them seems futile, since such division could hold good only between two friendly powers, and even then any rigid formula imposed on the world would be bound to break before the strong currents of change.

If the struggle is fought out to the end, with nuclear weapons and germ warfare, the only prospect is a large measure of world suicide. If this is avoided, and the divergent social systems of the world manage to live side by side, the question arises whether there will be an inner collapse within one of the two great power structures, leading to a victory for the other without war. Here too America has the advantage. Since it uses the method of freedom and has established an unquestioned machinery for the succession of power, it does not run the risk Russia and China run of having the regime fall in the struggle over the succession. The old fears of internal collapse through economic breakdown have proved exaggerated, nor is there any institutional issue like slavery which might lead again to a bitter Civil War. Nor, despite the methods of Communist penetration, is there any great danger of an overthrow of the government from within. The greatest civil danger is that of the growth of an adventurist nationalist movement which would create a police state under the guise of saving the country from totalitarianism and would ally itself with the military elite. But if this were ever to happen it would be only as a consequence of a world atomic war or as prelude to it: America has shown the capacity to survive this kind of crisis short of a nuclear war.

The chances of civil struggle within the Communist systems and their satellites are greater. Once it loses the mastery of the coercive machinery of the state, a police regime must pay the price of inner strains and doubts. The suppression of competing opinion means that every leader or movement which might otherwise be a rival of the Administration becomes an enemy of the state itself. The method of Communism, as Albert Camus pointed out, divides the community into executioners and victims—and, one may add, the politically inert who are content to accept the rule of those on top. But while a one-party state and an iron party discipline are easy ways of eliminating inconvenient dissent and establishing party truth in science and human affairs, they cannot eliminate hunger as a spur to revolt, nor praetorian conflict, nor the survival of nationalist impulses in the satellite countries. The satellites are thus always ready to use the outbreak of war as an occasion for breaking away from the Communist imperium.

Along with the danger of suicidal destruction, this adds another argument against world war which may be persuasive to the Soviet mind. The alternative for both civilizations is not merely "coexistence" but corivalry in the struggle of ideas. One finds an interesting parallel in the era of European religious wars at the time of the Reformation and counter-Reformation. If both the Protestants and Catholics had been set on establishing a universal church, and if each had controlled a segment of state power, war would have been unceasing until one or the other had been wiped out. But there was a growth of secular authorities for whom peace and national unity were more urgent than the defense of the True Faith. The religious conflict was neither forgotten nor abolished, but it was transformed into a proselytizing rivalry within the frame of a secular authority—a rivalry that was only sporadically bloody but mainly peaceful. In this corivalry Americans have the advantage of presenting to the world a political and social system which will furnish a better and freer life for the large mass of people than its rival. Yet the struggle is bound to be a bitter one. It is not too hard, however, to conceive of an international secular authority which will similarly keep the struggle of the new political religions from engulfing the world in war and hold it within the frame of nonmilitary rivalry.

In such an event America's destiny in the calculable future will be to take a hand in creating this constitutional frame while it seeks to build friendly coalitions within it and help other peoples to reach in their own way their own institutions and method of freedom. This will mean a peaceful but exacting rivalry in which America will be one of a number of spokesmen for an open society, using with greater or lesser skill its statecraft and diplomacy, its technical and economic resources and its whole armory of ideas.

It is not easy to measure the relative equipment of each of the two groups of protagonists for this rivalry in the struggle for ideas. In the Communist case there is a political orthodoxy that has become a political religion and rouses dedicated energies among numberless men and women the world over. In the American case there is a stubborn belief in individual freedom—a belief so stubborn that it generated a revolution, survived a civil war and two world wars without being snuffed out, and has kept up a continuing struggle against the centralizing forces of both governmental and corporate power. This belief lacks the flamboyancy of a political religion, yet it sustains a formidable fighting faith.

Part of the fighting faith on both sides is the conviction that while material values count in life they are not the only values. Both America and Russia are materialist. They have a common activism, a masculine strength of purpose, a drive toward results, a genius for organization, a belief in progress, an obsession with production indexes and with magnitudes of all sorts, a conviction that their way of life will yield increasing satisfactions to their people. Each system can point to considerable accomplishment in raising living standards in a brief spell of time. But when one asks toward what ends these material gains are directed, the Communists answer that society sets the ends and that in the dialectic of history they are part of a process in which men transform themselves by transforming their environment. The answer of American democracy is that the free, creative personality forms both the method and the end of the social process.

The logical extension of an open society, as I have suggested earlier, is an open world. This does not call for either the dominance or annihilation of any culture but a respect for the characteristic traits of each, just as an open society must respect the characteristic traits of its members. There is also, of course, a Communist vision of an ultimate world society. It is the vision of a world federation of Soviet states, each retaining a measure of autonomy but each also surrendering to the central body the larger decisions about world policy and perhaps a veto over any basic changes in the system of internal power. The Federal structure of the Union of Socialist Soviet Republics is itself a probable model for what a Communist world society would be like. It would go beyond the *pax Romana* of the ancient world, since it would demand the kind of ideological conformity that one finds inside a Communist society.

To the differences in the vision of a world society one must add the differences in the kind of human being the two systems envisage. The Communists have made it clear that they base their view of human nature on the psychology of conditioned behavior: that men respond rationally to rational needs; there are no primal drives in men that cannot be exploited at will, or else expunged or deflected into other channels. For them the lesson of history is mainly that human nature is plastic and that the human mind, after adapting itself over millennia to every type of social organization, still presents an open slate on which new social experience can write new records. This is an instrumental view of man's essential nature, seeing man mainly as a bundle of potentials for manipulation by an elite of social engineers. The earlier Marxist thinkers, looking ahead, saw a "new society" in which the alienation of men from one another would be ended, and new fulfillments of human values would be achieved by the release of individual and social energy. But unfortunately this humanist vision has not been translated into the current realities of Communist society.

The democrat also regards man as a bundle of potentials. But he is less brashly confident that he knows exactly what to do with those potentials. He has greater humility about his relation to the unknown forces of the Universe and more respect for the tenacity of the instinctual life of man. But he also has more belief in man's capacity to develop rich diversities of personality and find both emotional expressiveness and moral meanings in life within an open society.

Both views stress the material base of life, and both are activist: hence both may be said to have created their own types of economic man. Brooks Adams, writing about the English gentry in Cobden's day, who fought the repeal of the Corn Laws, saw them as "Nature's first attempts at creating an economic type" and noted that they were vanquished by the later and superior type of Manchester man. Writing today, one has to add that the economic man of Detroit and Stalingrad has replaced the Manchester man. What they have in common is their interest and skill in production and their use of an economic value scale for the whole range of values. But if one may draw the distinction that Peter Drucker has suggested between "economic" and "industrial" man—the latter using technology for the purposes of human life while the former cramps human life within the value scale of economics alone —then one may claim that the American vision (as vision, not as reality) is that of industrial man. In this sense it is where the material calculus ends that the conception of human personality begins. Whatever its shortcomings, the democratic vision is a humanist one. Like the Soviet view of man, it is oriented toward power and effectiveness. But where one tries to use the whole range of power and technology for the ends of the individual life, the other values the individual mainly as an instrument for the purposes of power and the state.

Another way of putting it is that one makes organization central while the other makes it instrumental. George Orwell's novel, *1984*, put into imaginative terms the logical end product of ideological or organizational man, who marks the triumph of the cerebral over the organic life processes and of automatism over personality and conscience. An American philosopher, Roderick Seidenberg, has projected this trend grimly into a future "post-historic man" who is reached when the processes of history have been wholly placed under cerebral and organizational control and when history in any meaningful sense has therefore ceased. Like his predecessors, Henry Adams and Spengler, Seidenberg interprets this trend as beyond the human will to resist.

If this tide should prove an historical reality, it may be that the differences our generation sees between the rival systems of society and views of life are only ripples on its surface. American thought has on the whole refused to accept such a determinism. On this issue the American thinkers diverge from Spengler, whose moral was that no change is possible and whose injunction to the ruling classes was to show iron resolution in repressing all challenges to their authority. There is a big gap between Spengler and Leninist thinking, but the despair over piecemeal change and the police-state methods of meeting every challenge to power are consequences of both.

The crucial question about America's destiny in the world frame brings us back to the tests of America's strength as a civilization. It is hard not to feel that while America is still on the rising arc of its world power it is on the descending arc of its inner social and moral vigor; that it has allowed itself to be switched off from the main path of its development into the futile dead ends of the fear of ideas and the tenacious cult of property. Toynbee has suggested how frequently a civilization has been weakened by its "pathological insistence upon pushing to extremes its master institution." That may be militarism or institutionalized holiness, imperial power or infallibility, but what always happens is its expansion far beyond its original meaning into a cult that becomes destructive of its utility. If the master institution of America is property, there is evidence of the beginnings of a "pathological insistence upon pushing [it] to extremes." Linked with it is a fear of subversive movements which may threaten or overthrow the institution—a fear that therefore induces a complacency about the idea-hunters and a loss of belief in the inherent efficacy of democracy. The result is a negativism of outlook which puts the stress upon the defense of the master institution rather than upon the affirmation of its linkage with democratic human values.

There is no question here of the imminent fall of America but of its long-range vitality. All that we can say for certain about the problem of the rise and fall of civilizations is that, under the conditions of modern economic and military power, a people needs the quality of creativeness for cultural survival over a long period. One may guess that America will lead the world in technology and power for at least several generations to come. But it is one thing to fill a power vacuum in the world with a transitional leadership, and quite another to offer to the world the qualities of leadership which it requires, attuned at once to the life of nature and the life of the spirit. Unfortunately American leadership in world affairs has not displayed this capacity: it has often been fumbling, hesitant, indecisive, without a clear picture of the direction in which it seeks to move or the kind of world it envisages, and with too much of a tendency to brandish its military strength and to use American wealth for purchasing things that simply cannot be bought.

America has not yet had to face many of the tests through which the other great civilizations have passed. Compared with the peoples of the European Continent, or of Russia or Asia, the history of America has been an epic continuity of almost unbroken success, with only the Civil

War as the kind of catastrophe that deepens consciousness by plowing up emotions. The French, for example, have been through a period of Roman rule, of imperial-barbarian battle, of feudal struggle, of bloody religious wars and equally bloody revolutionary upheavals; they have had the experience of invasion by the English, and of German armies sweeping three times across their country; at least twice they have had to eat the bitter bread of the conqueror's terms. Russia too has been crisscrossed many times by invading forces, steeped in a long night of Asiatic rule, torn by the bloody struggle of the Boyars, bled white by Czars and priests; it has been subjected to the battering of forces and ideas from both the East and the West, has had to meet attacks from Genghis Khan and the Tartars, from Napoleon and Hitler, has known a long history of serfdom, has been raked by revolutionary struggles and made a laboratory for the compulsive energies of a new regime.

The historic ordeals of America have been different. They have been the ordeals of endurance against a challenging frontier environment, and of having to weld a national unity out of widely divergent strains, even at the price of a terrible civil war. Its characteristic tests have, however, been technological, including the fashioning of new industrialism, and the swinging of the balance in the world wars in which it took part. Except for the Civil War, the inner crises have been those of the prosperity-depression business cycle. The typical crisis of character in an American novel is likely to turn on the endurance of economic hardship (note Norris's *McTeague,* Dreiser's *Sister Carrie,* Steinbeck's *Grapes of Wrath*), and the typical fall-from-grace situation is that of the well-to-do family which must endure a scaling down of its living standards.

As a civilization America has never had to meet the great test of apparently irretrievable failure. Except for the Civil War, its history has been without sharp breaks, and even the Civil War was (in the phrase of Allan Nevins) an "ordeal of union" rather than a break in history. Since the Revolutionary War, Americans have not as a nation had to meet the test of survival in the face of strong odds. They have never suffered decisive defeat in a war, nor the agony of internal revolutionary violence. Their history as a nation has never been cut in two by revolution, into an Old Regime followed by a New Regime. The closest they came was Franklin Roosevelt's New Deal, less a revolution than a successful attempt to forestall one.

Thus America as a civilization has been far removed from the great type-enactment of the Christian story, or the disasters of Jewish history or of the Asiatic empires: it has not suffered, died, been reborn. The weight it bears as it faces its destiny is the weight not of history but of institutions. Its great tests are still to come. One may guess that America will not meet them badly, but it would be tragic if it had to taste

disaster in order to learn the lessons of lost civilizations. One reason
why the Christian metaphysic has never struck deep psychic roots among
Americans lies in the gap between the moral experience underlying the
Christian doctrine and the moral implications of the American life
goals. Like all profound religious allegories, the Christian story pre-
supposes the capacity to face suffering, failure, and death.

The American attitude toward death, which I have touched upon
earlier,* is revealing on this score. The American today is preoccupied
with death, but not in the way that the early Calvinists were or the
later immigrants from Europe. He is interested in death in whodunit
thrillers or the sudden death of auto and plane accidents: death is an
illogical intrusion from without, or a curiosity to be taken apart like
an intricate bit of machinery, but in either case irrelevant to life. Contrast this with the almost fatalist Russian acceptance of death, which has
helped them bear the heavy burdens of a regime that regards human
life as fodder for the Time Machine. Contrast it also with the ritualistic
preoccupation with death that one finds, for example, in the literature
of Mexico. For the Hispanic peoples death is not a cul-de-sac but a fruitful act, laying bare the values of life. For Americans it is an end to the
possibilities of life, an obituary note in a newspaper signifying that a
career is closed and blankness has set in.

Related to this is the span of the American time scale. Political observers have noted that in the calculations of foreign policy and statecraft both the Russians and Chinese operate on a longer time scale
than do the Americans. This may be due to traditions stretching back
into a dim past, plus the new Communist deification of history. The
Americans are more concerned with the day-to-day and the here-and-
now. Since life offers so much and death draws a blank, the habitual calculation does not stretch much beyond the lifetime scale. This does not
mean that there is no sense of the future. But when Americans think
of the future, it is again in terms of what is compassable—providing
for the declining years of one's life and the education of one's children
until they in turn can provide for their own future.

This belief in a compassable future is part of the organic optimism
of American life. It is far removed from the mood of fatalism and renunciation which in most civilizations preceded the emergence of
modern industrial man, as it also is far removed from the tragic pessimism which the great European thinkers from Nietzsche to Malraux
have summoned in the twilight of the European experience. Because
America has this sense of tragedy only in partial degree, its capacity
to face national failure and disaster may well be questioned. It is
limited by the unwillingness of the American as an individual to con-

* See Ch. VIII, Sec. 7, "The Middle and End of the Journey."

front the Medusa head of a life experience which includes penalties as well as gains, failure as well as success, tragedy as well as happiness.

But a nation can even surmount catastrophes and be deepened by them, provided its sources of creativeness have not dried up. The great enemy of any civilization is the enemy within. Its name is not subversion or revolution or decadence but rigidity. Just as every power group tends to limit its outlook as it hardens its position, so the temptation of a successful people is to make a cult of the artifacts of its success, rather than celebrate the daring and the large outlook that made the achievements possible. In the Russian case the original revolutionary Communism has become the hard ideological mask of a state church that aims to sustain its power elite and has forgotten that the revolutionary impulse came from a tradition of Socialist humanism. There are many who feel similarly that, whether through conformism, fanaticism or rigidity, American society will succumb to the final impersonality of the Age of the Insects. The long journey we have made through these pages should lead to a different conclusion. There is still in the American potential the plastic strength that has shaped a great civilization, and it shows itself in unexpected ways, at unpredictable moments, and in disguises that require some imaginative understanding to unveil. What Emerson said a century ago I would still hold to: "We think our civilization is near its meridian, but we are yet only at the cockcrowing and the morning star."

CHAPTER XIII

Afterword:
The New America
(1957–1987)

CHAPTER XIII

Afterword:
The New America
(1957–1987)

1. Images of America

BEHIND the public exterior of every book there is always a personal memory of how the idea for it first came. It was in the early spring of 1945 that I stood in the bullet-riddled Cathedral Square at Cologne, just after its takeover by American troops. As I surveyed the debris around me—much like the ruin making of war I had seen earlier in Britain, France, and Holland—I reflected on the wrack of European civilization and the trajectory of events that had led to this moment. I found myself wondering whether a scene like this might some day come to my own country. It was then that I dared envision an overview of America and its intricate pattern of being as a civilization. When the book appeared twelve years later, in 1957, its 1,000-page spread and massiveness may not have scared the critics but it did scare me a bit.

Looking back, I was lucky in my timing. The decade from 1947–1957, when I worked intensively on the book, was a decade in American life very different from those of the Depression, the New Deal, and the war. Harry Truman and Dwight Eisenhower in the White House, both centrists, sought to contain the accelerations of postwar change and keep them from mounting too steeply. It was no "Era of Good Feelings," but there was consensus enough to contain the divisiveness of the atomic spy trials, McCarthyism, the Oppenheimer inquisition, the Communist victory in China, the Korean War.

Truman and Eisenhower didn't lack troubles, and Eisenhower's last years in office heard premonitory rumblings of the 1960s. Yet as with individual lives, there are phases of a civilization when it is in conflict with itself, and other phases when its energies are in some kind of balance. This was true of the years that followed the war, and 1957 under Eisenhower was probably the last moment when I could have found so sprawling an overview compassable, portraying a civilization in relative equilibrium. After that, with the explosive 1960s, the changes were so rapid and contradictory that they were intractable to the "patterns within patterns" (I use Gregory Bateson's phrase) essential to civilization studies.

"The dogmas of the quiet past," President Lincoln wrote to Congress in

1862, "are inadequate to the stormy present." I was not certain whether we ever had a "quiet past" but the stormy present was a reality, and a distorting one. It disarranged all figure-ground gestalt relations. During the 1960s and early 1970s, with their demonstrations, protest movements, assassinations, with the cultural revolution, the Vietnam War and Watergate, the focus was sharply on the scarring events. At one point, in 1973, I did a long overview piece in *Foreign Affairs* that I called "America Agonistes," with Miltonic overtones of America wrestling with its inner conflicts for its very soul. Behind and beyond them it was hard to see what was vulnerable, what decayed and expendable, what would take the fire and walk away wounded, what was resilient, what was strongly ingrained in the fiber of the civilization and therefore enduring.

Now in the latter 1980s we are still in a stormy present. But some decelerations of change have set in, and the figure-ground relations of the immediate and the enduring are coming back into perspective. Once again, even with deep divisions and scarring scandals, the civilization is moving toward a working equilibrium which may give its watchers a chance to view it in action as a new whole, for however long it may last.

One question should have been pretty well settled but isn't—whether America is in fact a civilization. Shortly after publication I ventured to call it one, in an exchange in Paris with Arnold Toynbee, historian of civilizations. He was polite but the idea of America as a civilization offended his grand historical sense and departed from the schema of civilizations— those spent or arrested, those still viable—which he had arrayed on the cliffs of history. Surely America was no civilization in itself but only the tag-end of Western civilization, in effect the tail of the European dog!

I persisted in my heresy. I felt that America had won its independence from Europe, not only in politics and economics but in science, technology, power, culture, religion. As a complex society and culture it had shaped a civilization style of its own. The content and sequence of the developmental phases through which it had passed were its own, not copies of others. Even as a young civilization America had already begun to cut a wide swathe in history and (this was my critical civilization test) had marked out its own trajectory in history.

Toynbee and I failed to convince one another. Yet our exchange shed light for me on how perverse the idea of an American civilization seemed to many scholars at the time, including a great one like Toynbee. With the proliferating American Studies departments in the 1960s and 1970s it became less perverse, but it is still not wholly accepted.*

---

*For the text of the exchange see *Western World*, December 1958. For another encounter between us see the symposium, *Is America a Civilization?*, organized by Marshall Fishwick in *Shenandoah* (published at Washington and Lee University), vol. X, no. 1, Autumn 1958, pp.

The reasons run deeper than what is in fashion or not. They reach to the metaphysical, even mythic underpinning of the civilization. This is what gives its history meaning in a continuum of world history that includes America in its encircling sweep.

When I decided to start this book not with an academic account of American history but with an imagist view—the images in the minds and memories of ordinary Americans—it was because I wanted the first section* to set the tone for the rest. It was a declaration that while the book was based on the research and review of hundreds of scholars, I meant to ground it in the earth of the American experience.

I had to end my imagist history in the summer of 1957 with Dwight Eisenhower as "the soldier in the White House struggling with problems of peace." It may be useful, in the present chapter, to jot down some further episodes for the imagist narrative of the intervening thirty years.

It has to include, in the latter Eisenhower years, the common man's memories of the Gary Powers U-2 incident over the Soviet Union, of Khrushchev's towering rage at the failed Paris summit, Ike's cancellation of his Tokyo visit in the face of hostile demonstrations, his warning about the "military-industrial complex" in his farewell address.

It would continue with the drama of the Nixon-Kennedy debates, the voice of a new generation in John F. Kennedy's inaugural address ("We shall pay any price, bear any burden, meet any hardship, support any friend, oppose any foe to assure the survival and the success of liberty"), the American air cover that was not supplied in the Bay of Pigs disaster, the grace and glow of Camelot, the social imagination expressed in the Peace Corps, the Berlin Wall on which Kennedy failed to act, his early Vietnam involvement, the assassination of the Diem brothers in a coup with Washington's tacit silence, the Cuban missile crisis in which the young President came to maturity, the fateful bullets at Dallas and Jackie Kennedy's blood-stained dress, the shooting of Lee Oswald by Jack Ruby on camera, the obsession of the "conspiracy theories" with the Warren Commission Report.

Picking up the thread with Lyndon Johnson as he out-Hammurabbied Hammurabi in his legislative storm of Great Society bills, the emergence of a Texan as a civil rights President, his escalating slide into the Vietnam morass, the anguish of Americans at the symbols of My Lai and the shock of the Tet Offensive, the antiwar and antidraft demonstrations, the students with guns at the takeover of a college campus, the emerging "counterculture" of rock, drugs, sex, communes, and challenger values, the surprise

3–45. Among the contributors responding to our square-off were Willard Thorp, David M. Potter, Henry Nash Smith, Louis D. Rubin, Jr., and Marcus Cunliffe.

*Ch. I, Sec. 1, "The Sense of the Past."

of Johnson's withdrawal from the 1968 presidential contest, the clash of police and protest groups at the bloody crossroads of the Chicago Democratic Convention.

With Richard Nixon's re-emergence his "secret plan" to extricate America from the Vietnam War, the "moratorium" demonstrations on American campuses, the bombings of Cambodia, the Kent State shootings, the hasty exit of Americans from the roof of their Saigon Embassy, the sickening sense of national humiliation. The secret mission of Henry Kissinger to Beijing, Mao and Nixon agreeing to reopen Chinese-American relations after the long freeze, the landslide Nixon victory over George McGovern with the Watergate burglary still in the shadows, the tapes Nixon didn't remember to destroy, the political theater of the TV Watergate hearings to uncover the cover-up, "Your President is not a crook," the "Saturday night massacre" at the Justice Department, the paralysis of government during the crisis of presidential credibility, Nixon (with Kissinger) at the White House praying to the god of history before his resignation.

Gerald Ford's succession as a President in "a time for healing," his wry admission that he was "a Ford, not a Lincoln," his pardoning of Nixon widely perceived as part of a prior understanding, the OPEC oil price shock, the bumper-to-bumper cars at gas stations, Gerald Ford stumbling over the issue of Polish freedom in his debate with Carter.

The astonishing success of "Jimmy Who?" in the campaign of a born-again Christian, Carter's *Playboy* interview remark about "lusting in my mind" after women, the earnest effort to use human rights as a diplomatic pivot, Sadat, Begin, and Carter embracing after Camp David as a turning point in Mid-East history that didn't turn, the Carter "malaise" speech and its trauma. Khomeini leading the revolution of the Ayatollahs while America debated a response, a dethroned cancer-ridden Shah roaming the world for refuge, the enraged Iranian militants at Teheran taking the American Embassy officials as hostages, the nightmare wait of a nation for their release, the rescue operation that collapsed for want of a helicopter. Ted Kennedy picking up the "fallen standard" of his two slain brothers in a damaging but futile challenge. The final cruel twist of history—the timing of the hostages' release to Carter's exit from power.

The triumphant entrance into power of aging actor and "citizen-politician" Ronald Reagan, the "Great Communicator" in a communication age, the Reagan revolution-in-reverse and its effort to undo a half-century of the welfare state, David Stockman's budget tales out of school and his trip to the Reaganomic woodshed, Reagan cracking one-liners in a Washington hospital as doctors extracted the bullet, the defense build-up against the "evil empire."

The great tides of internal change in America swirling around the early computers and their generational progeny, the videocassette, the decline of the smokestack industries, high technology and low corporate raiders and takeovers, the obsession with the Japanese as prime competitor and model, the bursting of the O-rings in the right-hand solid rocket booster that turned the *Challenger* into a streak of fiery death.

The women executives and their briefcases, the first woman on the Supreme Court and the first woman major Vice-Presidential candidate. The abortion struggle between right-to-lifers and pro-choicers over the infrared photos of fetuses, the Fundamentalist preachers pursuing Satan on nightly TV. The supply and demand aspects of cocaine addiction, the recurring fears of parents about their young in a drug culture, the publicized advances in the campaign against symbolic diseases, the heart transplants and the artificial heart, the terror and panic over AIDS.

The mushrooming of early primary contests and campaign fervors, the Gary Hart boom and the "where's the beef?" gag, Reagan's faltering recovery in the debates with Walter Mondale, his forty-seven-state sweep for his second term, but along with it the persistent image of a Teflon Presidency, Reagan's muddled decision to go to the Bitburg cemetery, Holocaust survivor Elie Wiesel at the White House "saying No to power." The monster octopus of a deficit, the sweat and grime of the budget battles, the first trillion-dollar budget, the hammering out of a historic tax reform package. The overt-covert use of the contras in a rollback effort against the Nicaraguan regime. The trauma of the Iran arms-for-hostages deal and the diversion of funds to the contras.

The continuing anxieties about "the fate of the earth," the debate over Reagan's strategic defense proposal—swiftly dubbed Star Wars by a film-oriented public, the emergence of Mikhail Gorbachev as a formidable modernizing head of the Soviet empire, two master communicators battling it out at Reykjavik and after, and out of their negotiations spinning the threads of human hopes and fears and destiny.

In this chiaroscuro of three decades I have tilted toward world events and the darker colors because they were the stuff of political theater and thus their images stuck in the public mind. The way Americans handled the more abrasive events shows something important about the civilization. This was true of the Vietnam War and its home front, with the wounds and alienations they carried with them. It was true of Watergate as a uniquely American phenomenon, which split the political culture and the national mind yet baffled the understanding of the French, Russians, Chinese. It was true of the drawn-out Iranian hostage crisis which drained the energies of Jimmy Carter and the nation.

Note that the Vietnam War brought down Lyndon Johnson as President, Watergate brought down Richard Nixon, and the hostage crisis brought down Jimmy Carter. (It remains to be seen whether Reagan's Iran arms deal would bring about a similar power shift of the ruling parties.) In all three instances the people of the greatest democratic power mass in history expressed their frustration at the impotence of their power. It was again a case of "America Agonistes"—America shorn of its vaunted strength, wrestling Samson-like with the pillars of the temple and finally with itself.

2. The Great Tides of Change

WHEN I LECTURED at Warsaw shortly after this book's publication one of Poland's young intellectuals—doubtless in exile now—asked whether there was one word to sum up American civilization. I demurred, saying I had written a 1,000-page book, but he insisted. I ransacked my memory: was it uniqueness, equality, freedom, dynamism, pluralism? Suddenly I heard myself say, "access." We know (I explained) that we are all born unequal, with unequal abilities and potentials. But we insist on equal access to life's chances, so that every youngster will be able to stretch his unequal potentials to the fullest.

In America in 1987 the access to life chances still falls short of full equality of opportunity. But the focus of attention has shifted. Americans fix their gaze on the swiftness of change, to open the portals of opportunity for all. Morally, access is a stronger goal than change. But it is the hopes and fears raised by change that better describe the latter-day American outlook. Change permeates the scientific, intellectual, and technical cultures, and the popular culture as well. Once there is change—so goes the American hope—increased access will come out of it, and everything else as well.

The continuity with the past has several times been broken. America, conceived and born in revolution, has come to specialize in multiple sociocultural revolutions. Its role as the most revolutionary society in history was resisted by the world in 1957; it is now grudgingly accepted. Increasingly America defines itself and its future by its awareness of its current revolutions, and by how it can minimize the scars they leave while exploring the life options they open.

When I originally set out the structure of the book, I did it in part from the perspective of the cultural anthropologists and their emphasis on material reality—from the bottom up, so to speak. I laid a base in the land, stock, and human needs; then built on them the layers of technology, economy, polity, and class. On those in turn, with help from the perspectives of psychology and the philosophy of history, I structured the life cycle, the high culture and popular culture, the value system and religious beliefs, with some closing reflections on America's world position and destiny.

In the interval the revolutions followed a rather different model—less from the materialist bottom up than from the subjective top down. The crucial one has been the continuing knowledge revolution, as much in brain research and the life and cognitive sciences as in the hard sciences. We imagine and think out our world and in the process we flesh it out. It is the idea that gives form and energy to the design and moves the hand that gives it reality. *Imaginatio facit casum*: the imagination creates the event.

Hence the critical levers of change, starting in the postwar years, were the information revolution and a linked revolution in communications. No less critical, although less noticed, was a selfhood revolution which placed the self concept at the very center of the changes swirling about it.

I find it useful to see a civilization as a system of systems—a knowledge and information system, a sustenance system, an ecological system, a class and ethnicity system, a power and authority system, an intimacy and relational system, a system of arts and play, a values and belief system. The problem is of course to find the connective pattern that holds the systems together, with some cohesion, in a working equilibrium.

It is hard to get at the connective pattern, whether in the individual or the society, but it is important to use the organismic model for both. It enables us to avoid the oversimplification of single causes and effects, and follow the intricate ways in which a driving complex of change ramifies from system to system through the entire civilizational organism.

In its overwrought usage the term *revolution* has suffered from a terminal case of hype. Yet it can be used more exactingly to go beyond the changes themselves to the assumptions underlying them. This kind of "structural" thinking—I use it in the sense of Thomas Kuhn's *Structure of Scientific Revolutions*—may locate areas in current American life where the term "revolution" can reasonably be applied.

I shall be discussing seven such areas. They are:

· An information and communication breakthrough within a larger knowledge revolution.

· An entrepreneurial breakthrough within a larger frame of global economic interdependence.

· A polity of pluralist cultures which defines "political" man in terms of his relation to the changes in ethnicity, class, the power and authority system, and the media.

· A set of revolutions in the individual life cycle, within a larger revolution of selfhood.

· A changed phase in intimacy relations, comprising sexuality, love, bonding, the family, and women's consciousness of their intrinsic nature and their social role.

· A heightened religious awareness and a return of the sacral, within a larger revolution of values and beliefs in the conduct of life.

· The changes (and the continuities too) in the mythic context with which the idea of America is embedded. This includes the rethinking of America's changing relation to the complex I call the Western imperium, along with its relations of rivalry and commonality with the Soviet Union. Overarching them is the question of America's civilizational health or decline, and the

mythic symbols that convey the center around which the civilization co-
heres—or doesn't—and suggests the direction in which it is moving.

3. The Enchanted Technology

REREADING Chapter IV (*The Culture of Science and the Machine*) I am struck
by how little needs changing on the basic linkage between an open science
society and the American "permanent revolution" of constantly advancing
technology. Yet although I included a section on the coming of robotry*
the strong difference the thirty years have made in the ground tone and
climate of the technological culture is now clear enough. The familiar and
the strange together—it is an effect wholly characteristic of the dynamics
of civilizational change.

In the past thirty years, Americans, whatever the changes, have continued
to see science and technology more than ever as a garden for them to work
and dream in, full of luxuriant, blossoming surprises, an enchanted garden
opening on vistas of miracle-working possibility. Even as I was working on
the book World War II and the tyrannies of Europe produced a golden
migration of refugee scientists to America, bringing their creativity in exchange for the chance to pursue their work and lives. The openness and
resources of American research laboratories served as a magnet for the best
scientific talents of the world.

There was a feedback effect on the West as a whole. Since knowledge
had been wedded to power the postwar political imperium of the West was
backed up by a republic of scientists and technologists drawn from every
continent and political system, centering in America. It became almost a
truism that the larger number of Nobel Prizes, in the hard sciences, life
sciences and medical research, would go to workers in this republic of
inquiry.

By the 1970s the emphasis had shifted from stimulus-response behaviorism to the mental and organismic disciplines. Brain research, along with
cellular structure, the genetic process, and the interconnected functioning
of the organism, became critical. So, from another direction, did information
and communication theory. Separately and together they became the focus
of a tangle of hard sciences, life sciences, mind and human sciences, along
with their technologies.

One result was the breakdown of the formerly rigid boundaries between
science and technology as they are put to the use and test of practice.
Largely the fusion came out of the urgencies of World War II and the
postwar period, although it had begun well before. The theoretical work
was in the biogenetic, information, space, and communication revolutions.

*Ch. IV, Sec. 4, "Work and the Automatic Factory."

The resulting technologies—bio-tech, computer-tech, space-tech, and communication-tech—were in time joined together in common usage under the umbrella-like "high-tech," America's abbreviation for the entire complex.

Another set of walls came tumbling down—those between the traditional disciplines. This doesn't mean that American knowledge disciplines were rooted in a community of generalists. But in the interplay among the scientific, technological, and entrepreneurial cultures, the innovative minds paid little attention to disciplinary boundaries. They roamed wherever their imagination and intuition took them, crossing over into whatever disciplines served their purposes—and they had to learn to work in teams. The gap which C. P. Snow had deplored between the "two cultures" of the sciences and the humanities didn't disappear but it narrowed.

It was a mixed bag of potentials, at once creative and destructive. The dangers of contriving new organismic forms out of genetic elements in uncontained environments hovered over the oversight committees who had to make the decisions about them. The Chernobyl disaster of the Soviets, worse than the Three Mile Island near disaster, alerted contemporaries to the limits of tolerance of industrial nuclear power. The escalation of destructive power in the nuclear weapons in both camps carried a potential that Americans had either to live with or resolve. The enchanted garden of science and technology was like the poisoned garden in Hawthorne's tale, "Rappacini's Daughter." It blended possible death with life and challenged those who tended the garden to separate the destructive from the nurturing.

In 1957, with the Holocaust in mind, I wrote about the "neutral technician" who set himself to any task without asking about its morality.* On that score the climate of the 1980s was a changed one, with a growing popular concern for bio-ethics and the moral problems involved in the life-and-death decisions at the convergence points of medicine, ecology, and technological advance.

Broadly, the great shift of emphasis that occurred was from the processing of materials and energy to the processing of information. At the height of the Industrial Revolution, America was primarily an energy society, involved with industrial products and their logistics and distribution. But the technological nerves that controlled the system became overloaded and a series of breakdowns showed the system to be under strain and presaged a basic shift, however slow.†

World War II, while diverting resources from current research, spurred the sense of urgency of scientists and inventors. It cut across conventional thinking, and acted as a catalyst for information theory, releasing not only

---

*Ch. IV, Sec. 3, "Big Technology and Neutral Technicians."

†There are good insights on this phase of technological history in James R. Beniger, *The Control Revolution* (Harvard, 1986).

technical ingenuity but also the bold leap of the imagination which made it possible.

Claude Shannon, working at Bell Laboratories, published his two classic papers on the transmission of messages, out of which emerged a concept of usable "information," clear of the "noise" and disorders of noninformation. Norbert Wiener, working during the war on the "fire control" of antiaircraft weapons, moved from there to his postwar theory of cybernetics. Alan Turing, working in wartime Britain on breaking the German "Enigma" Code, moved on to computer models and the challenge of Artificial Intelligence. A little like Columbus searching for a path to the Indies and stumbling on America, the men who sought practical ways of coping with messages, firepower, and codebreaking in the war uncovered a skein of information theory and technology out of which came in time the "universal machine."

The dynamics of war technology were of course only an episode in the far-reaching historic drift from an overladen industrial economy to the emerging information economy of the late 1950s and the 1960s, and in time to a full-blown information society.

Had I been a better science watcher I would have noted, before finishing this book in June 1957, the striking coincidence of events a few years earlier. By 1956 the earlier generation of information thinkers—Norbert Wiener, John Von Neumann, Claude Shannon, Alan Turing—had developed computers which in many ways simulated the functions of the human brain—storing information in their memory bank, programming their processing, retrieving it at hitherto unimagined speed. With the computer had come a symbolic "grammar" of its own, in effect a new information language.

In the summer of 1956 a little group of younger scholars, among them John McCarthy, Herbert Simon, Allen Newell, and Marvin Minsky, gathered at Dartmouth to explore seriously how to translate the hypothesis of the younger generation into reality, in the form of Artificial Intelligence (AI), a term they initiated. Several months later, in September, another group of the younger scientists, linguists, and psychologists met at a Symposium on Information, at M.I.T., out of which came the origins of cognitive science—a cross-disciplinary blend of mathematics, philosophy, logic, linguistics, neuroscience, and psychology that has become a new discipline of ways of knowing, thinking, and problem solving.

Thus the mid-1950s, immediately before my book appeared, saw the start of an intellectual renaissance which was recognized only later when the three major upheavals of thought and technology converged—in information, communications, and the sciences of the mind. It was a renaissance which, in the next three decades, would transform technology, economy, and society and do much to bring a new America into being. No area of life—government, management, architecture, design, engineering, music, medicine, law, education, research, and inquiry, even religion, was left unaffected by them.

Thus science, which arose originally out of magic and has gone through all the centuries, travails, and heroisms of disciplined rationality, seemed to emerge once more into the realm of magic, especially in the form of the instant global communication system and of the possible "machines who think."

Two new critical transforming environments have been created in consequence—that of telecommunications and that of the computer. Each is in its own way a symbolic environment, mediating experience for the viewer and user. Each creates a new world of representations as an enveloping sheath through which we see the larger world and its other environments.

It is a dangerous reduction to see them mainly as possible tools to be usefully employed, like the plow and the plane. Despite their differences the new environments mark a movement away from direct experience to mediated experience. TV makes the sense of place irrelevant; you can watch the enactments of the global village from wherever you may be, because what counts is that you are simultaneously at home and in Manila or South Africa. The medium was the mesmerizer that leveled space and time and all hierarchies, and made two interacting entities—the viewer and the moving and speaking screen—the center of reality.

In the computer's case, and its impact on human consciousness, there was the tantalizing question of whether it possessed "intelligence" in Turing's sense that a blind observer couldn't differentiate it from the brain it simulates. It may never be adequately answered. It seems clear that while it might be structured to thread its way through Hamlet's agonized reasoning over his "to be or not to be" decision, it could never hit upon the words that Shakespeare put into the soliloquy.

Yet this does not deny it the intelligence which moves by logical inference from syllogisms set by its programmers, and enables it to achieve results on a scale and with a speed and precision hitherto inaccessible. In an evolutionary perspective the bottom line is that the human brain has fashioned a mechanism so resourceful that it adds capacities to the brain that evolved it. To call this anything less than an evolutionary breakthrough is to miss the function that technology as an environment has played all through human history.

It will be a long time before Americans have adequately come to terms with the impact of these major environmental shifts on the neural mechanism, on consciousness, on the perception of self, on interaction with others, on the sense of time and place, on life-styles and (more important) on lifeways. The available evidence from school children involved in computer simulations of traditional problem solving suggests the most important gain—a dimension of interaction between the self and the computer as second self, with a vibrancy of relationship hitherto largely lacking.

In the decades ahead these new symbolic environments are likely to prove a watershed in defining the American and his conduct. Nothing will ever be the same for him again. While it is hard to be precise about the neural and psychological changes that will come with the internalizing of both technologies, one glimpse of the future may be ventured. When the answers given, as well as the questions posed, are mediated by both a computer screen and a TV screen, Whitman's America and Faulkner's, Truman's America and Eisenhower's, will have a quality of quaintness. The changes in the tempo and accelerations of life, in responsibility and self-reliance, in individuality, in connectedness, in identity, in work and play, in schooling, in intimacy relations, in the forms that religious faith takes, in what has been called the American "willingness of heart"—these are bound to come, even while we puzzle over the shapes they will take.

Writing this book in the mid-1950s, I tried to depict the changes in the tradition and the "modernization" of Americans as experienced in the developed industrial culture of the first half of the century. But in an era when the connective tissue of daily living is organized within an information and electronic web, one might observe a postmodern America coming into being. De Crèvecoeur's "this new man, the American" has again become the target of world attention. Friend and foe have to calculate how far to emulate, how far to resist, this contradictory creature who again lays claim to being the archetypal man of his time.

4. The Economic Culture in an Age of Interdependence

WHAT WAS THE PROFILE of the new American economic system? Too summarily, one feature was *entrepreneurial man*, emerging out of the revolution named for him—the entrepreneurial revolution. A second was a *free market* for him to operate in, largely in process of being deregulated. A third was a *new managerial style*.

A fourth was a *corporate upheaval*, with the center of gravity shifting from earlier "smokestack industries" to newer ones more oriented toward service and high technology. At the same time an upheaval in financing made corporate takeovers, mergers, and restructurings more frequent, and placed finance at the apex of the corporate power structure, leading (fifth) to a dominant *finance capitalism* as an accompaniment and consequence of an *information capitalism*. A sixth was a *global economic system* whose currency and interest fluctuations, investment and growth rates, trade policies and balances, and deficits and debts, brought its member nations into a relation at once of intense competitive rivalry and interdependence.

Taken together these formed the economic garment, as it were, of the technological corpus. To call it an "information capitalism" singles out the drive that carries the others along and gives the whole some shape. Placing that capitalism in a global setting of interdependence, among economies similarly driven, enlarges the frame and suggests its contradictions.

A fleshing out of each may be in order. The free market was an old idea but its new form stressed the free flow of intellectual and finance capital, a shift from the resource capital of heavy industry.

In a sense the stress on the free market embodies a return to the thinking of Adam Smith. But where Smith based himself on the "unseen hand" of divine guidance, whereby private greed was translated into public good, the new free market thinkers, more mundanely, relied on human intelligence and the intellectual capital of the enterpriser. The highly politicized controversies over supply-side economics would doubtless yield in later decades to new theories and semantics. But in the climate of global competitiveness the emphasis on the innovative producer was more than a passing fashion.

For the first time in a century he had a radically new technology at his command—that of information and communication. Spurred by it, the thrust was to free him from regulatory shackles, to lower inhibiting taxes, to release the pent up energies of business activity.

There was a wave of positive feeling about the entrepreneur's risk taking. Except for the initial investment most of the capital was his vision, boldness, and will. His success story was told and retold in the new "Business" and "Money" media sections and became all but mythic. After the antibusiness counterculture of the 1960s and the dour skepticism of the mid-1970s the entrepreneurs became stars, and a few even heroes.

It was a highly idealized portrait, but—true or not—an evocative one. So also were the semantics of the free-market idea—that the individual economic decisions in the impersonal market are translated into better collective judgments than the government's. The adjective *free* was what counted. The emphasis shifted from the "mixed economy" which I described in the late 1950s, with its elements of government regulation, control, and even ownership, to the idea of freedom. The power of that idea had been shown in the pantheon of American "civil religion." It was now projected into the economic sphere where it meant freedom from shackling government controls and burdensome taxes and freedom for competitive energies to express themselves.

The combined model of entrepreneurial risk taking, technological advance, competitiveness, and market freedom had much riding for it. By contrast with it, the repressive Communist regimes and outmoded Socialist ones, with their obsolescent bureaucratic planning, had lost touch with the growth principle in the economic organism.

This doctrine was zealously adopted by America's formidable partner and competitor, Japan, bidding to outstrip its original mentor. It reached the burgeoning economies of the Pacific Rim, which were striving to become Japans to Japan. It strengthened the innovative resolve of the West European regimes (France, Germany, Britain), and of Hungary in the Soviet bloc, which was exploring a market socialism with capitalist trimmings. It even reached to the Soviet Union in Mikhail Gorbachev's campaign to modernize the lagging Soviet economy by information technology and by rallying the Soviet knowledge class with promises of greater "openness" (*glasnost*).

For America in the 1980s there was a strong element of hype in the claims made for the entrepreneurial spirit, which raised as many questions as it answered.

Since an economy operates in a social setting, the free-market idea— that every man by skill and will can better his income and life—was part of a growing context of subjectivism in the society. It fed on the acceptance of the "feedback" principle of cybernetics by the "New Age" thinkers. It showed itself in political campaigning in the stress on establishing a "momentum," and in career thinking in the popular dogma that "success breeds success." It cropped up in the growing cultural conviction that a patient's belief in his recovery is at least half the story. It was part of the larger movement of self-management of the individual life. For many it came close to an economic Couéism, or (in the phrase George Bush wanted to forget) a "voodoo economics."

Such a mood encouraged the gambling impulse. The American stock market became mercurial, dominated by institutional investors who traded massive blocks of stock by preprogrammed computer-triggered decisions. It had become capitalism's gambling casino. The play was with computerized dice, in a game for which the professionals had trained for years, and at which the outsiders—steeped in a new-found investment lore—bet on a future they sought to conjure while they grappled with contingencies they could neither foresee nor control.

Despite the Great Bull Market of the mid-1980s the market crash of 1929 had not been exorcised. It was still there as a monster memory of the expulsion from Eden. Most observers knew that, once set in motion, the wave of irrationality took over, whether through herd instinct or whatever. A new genre of thriller fiction developed in which the apocalypse was not nuclear but economic, with American money men providing (in Lenin's formulation) the rope to hang capitalism by.

There was a quality of driveness in the economy as a whole, a sign that it was anything but moribund and that its dangers were those of getting explosively out of control. Over the generations Americans had learned to wrestle with the demons of the business cycle, "fine-tuning" its lesser fluctuations within the still largely unpredictable sequence of prosperities, recessions, and depressions which had taken on the character of an eternal recurrence. With the stagflation of the 1970s they had almost succumbed to the pessimism of seeing both the cycle and the economy as unmanageable. But in the upbeat climate of the mid-1980s, with the global sweep of the macroeconomists, there was a renewed sense of the possibility of managing it. What it amounted to was that, given the right policies, the economy could be helped to find and sustain some sort of equilibrium.

But even on the positive side there was a constant pressure on corporate managers to speed up business creativity to match that of technology and the demands of domestic and global competitiveness. On the negative side there was the monster deficit, and the mountain of debt owed largely by sovereign but shaky Third World nations who might never repay it. One thought of Emerson's "the world owes the world more than the world can ever repay." Watching the stock markets and money markets in feverish motion, the surges of protectionist feeling that could lead to trade wars, and the traumas in the wake of corporate takeovers, one had the feeling of a balancing act which was more like a dervish dance on a tightrope over an abyss.

It was a question of the contradictions within capitalism, as within every living and growing system. The pains, dangers, and costs were bound to be severe, just as the gains were steep. The dark side of the moon was the perception one had of an America caught in a runaway individualism, driven by a passion for riches and success, with no equal passion for the work ethic, with little concern for the responsibilities that went with success, and even less sense of genuine community.

A social organism, like a human one, needs freedom, but it also needs sheaths of protection against some of the consequences of freedom. The question raised was one of control and responsibility. In fact one of the things that makes the information-communication technology postmodern is that it also operates as a control system, yet its controls don't reach as effectively to its social consequences as to its technological ones.

This was true most seriously of corporate management and financing. The élan of venture entrepreneurs, starting new enterprises, had rubbed off on the management style of the established ones as well. The difficulty lay in the change that Berle and Means had described a half-century earlier, in the separation of corporate ownership from management. But by the 1980s there were signs of a further separation of management from control, which could be wrested from the current managers by takeover specialists on the alert for vulnerable corporate structures. The finely honed arts of making "greenmail" stock bids financed by high-yielding "junk bonds," to a scattered suffrage of stockholders, became characteristic of the decade. The struggles for control between competing investor groups became classics in corporate litigation and warfare. As in all warfare the target corporation was sometimes pressured into more muscular management, but more often the corporation—heavily debt-ridden, with worker layoffs—was itself the victim.

It was a destabilizing outcome, flowing from a changing ownership, in a corporate structure at the mercy of predators and of impersonal investors with no real concern for the company's products. Added to it was the pressure on managers to stay out of trouble by sweating for short-term quarterly earnings reports rather than long-term productivity and quality strategies. When a company with a long management tradition could be shifted from hand to hand by men with the narrowest motives of gain and power there was danger as well as pathos in an executive's cry: "There's no one out there any more who cares about our company as an institution. I am helpless as a manager."

Side by side with the slogans of entrepreneurial creativeness, a second managerial code was fashioned. Ostensibly it was that of the tough traveler through the neo-Darwinian jungle—"lean and mean," shedding his excess baggage of costs and sensibilities in the struggle of the "fittest" for survival. But behind this rhetoric the reality was often the conventional stodginess of those whom a high Treasury official, Richard Darman, called the "corpocracy."

One way or another, the ethos of human and institutional consequences often get squeezed out. A job lost in one industry and one region might be found in another, and the overall unemployment figures cancel out. But the human tragedy of the lost job, the abandoned skills, the eroded sense of personal adequacy—that remained.

Even worse, when a corporation engaged in "trimming fat" and "cutting to the bone" decided unilaterally to abandon plants around which whole communities had grown, it cut itself off from the dismissed workers as sources of innovativeness, lost the loyalty of those who remained, and destroyed local support networks that had taken decades to build.

With the postwar Bretton Woods agreement ended, and the gold standard geared to the dollar dissolved, a system of sorts for ordering the world economy struggled to emerge in their place. In the annual summit of the economic powers and the more recent periodic meetings of the Group of Five (U.S., Japan, West Germany, France, Britain), America sought to remain the first among equals, as it was with its allies in NATO against a common enemy symbol. But it was much harder to be the first among economic rivals.

Japan had adopted high tech and the entrepreneurial revolution, and was a prime instance of a nation with scarcely any resources which nevertheless knew how to assemble finance capital and use the skills of its committed people as human capital. Along with other Pacific Rim nations it was in economic terms more Calvinist than America, with a stronger work ethic, less bloated consumption habits, and more competitive wages and salaries. Japan came to haunt its economic rivals as a constant and advancing daemonic presence, moving inexorably from one "generation" of semiconductors and of inexpensive cars to another. But in its system of family bonding, its traditional continuum of company employment, its shared controls between government and business, it was better prepared than America for the competitive demands of an information economic age.

Because of the pluralist pressure groups that turn government subsidies to interest groups into entitlements, presidents were unable to cut domestic spending—and the increasing defense budgets were at once political imperatives and added entitlements. The result was the Himalayan deficit I have noted, with its interest payments as an incubus on future deficits.

With its innovations at first borrowed by its rivals and allies, America experienced what Thorstein Veblen called the "penalty of taking the lead," while Japan experienced the "merits of borrowing." Besides, both America and its allied European democracies were hobbled by the self-inflicted wounds that adhere to democratic welfare societies and pressure-group politics.

With these and other factors weakening America's competitive position, it was plagued in the 1980s by a succession of staggering unfavorable trade balances. The extent of foreign investments in America and of foreign industrial operations on American soil also raised some anxieties. It might seem a healthy thing, since it showed America as a magnet, attracting foreign assets as it attracted foreign talent. Besides, the foreign investments helped to make the massive deficit temporarily more tolerable. Yet when the U.S., in 1986, first became a debtor nation overall there was a flurry of national anxiety. Was the new American dependence on massive foreign investments and operations a sign of economic colonialism?

It was the wrong question. It made more sense to note that an interdependent global economy had been shaped by the interlinked needs of the Western economic alliance—an economy in which imperialism and colonialism were irrelevant. The important question was whether a frame of global controls could be fashioned before it was too late. The balancing act I have described, on a wire stretched across an abyss, involved not only America's economic fate but the world's.

The drama of it came with the TV territory. Never had the movement of world economic forces commanded so wide and alert an audience in the world media. Just as the political theater of the 1980s was located in global terrorism, so the economic theater was located in the volatile world finance markets and the resulting policy shifts by the Group of Five who formed the economic powers.

The public attention was caught by the buzz words of the 1980s, like productivity, competitiveness, innovation. But the hope for world controls rested on linkage—the interrelations between coordinated actions on interest rates, to influence currency values, which in turn were meant to influence exports and imports, price movements, growth rates, expansions and recessions, stock price levels, and ultimately living standards.

Each of these is a player on the world economic stage. The temptation is to watch the global dance of the interlocked players, entranced by the complexity of the moves beyond a choreographer's reach. But the realities are the well-being and living standards of whole peoples. Economic states-manship lay in the philosophy which saw the dance as not beyond cho-reography. The economic powers avoided a rigid control system, but a frame was needed, even for freedom—especially for freedom.

In September 1985 the Plaza Agreement marked the start of the frame. The Group of Five recognized that each of the powers, jealous of its sov-ereignty, had a home constituency and opposition to worry about, and that the domestic polities and societies made it harder for them to control the global forces they had set in motion. But they also knew that unless they fashioned a stronger global frame its absence could become dangerous and even intolerable.

Did Americans understand the implications of their economic experience, on the civilizational level? One thing was clear—that the highly technicized information economy might prove an organism easier to set in motion than to control later by setting limits to it. Another was that if the American economy could not sustain its inventiveness and its technological successes it could be overcome, as it were, by the ruins it had itself made.

"Economic" problems are not exclusively economic but are linked to politics, cultures, values, and morals. America was in essence an adversarial and individualist culture, whether in sports, law, or politics, while Japan was in essence a consensus culture. The values of an economic culture hold an unacknowledged sway over an entire society.

If the idea of values cycles has some validity, the 1980s witnessed a replay of the dominant economic values of the 1950s, before the cultural revolution that followed blew them away. There was an even more senseless consumer society, living beyond its means, leisure-oriented, saving little, thus drying up the sources of capital investment. Its pathologies showed themselves in an underground economy, and even more in a drug culture which disabled a sizable portion of the skilled work force.

No economy is stronger or healthier than the society which generates it and which in turn it transforms. Spurious social values matched the values of the economy. Its hyped ads clamored for attention amidst the TV frenzy. Its craftsmanship had lost its ancient pride and become sloppy. Its materials were often defective and their inspections slovenly and inadequate as in the case of the Challenger disaster. Its continuing industrial pollutants were an anachronism in an age of ecological awareness.

The American values were far from the economic virtues of the Puritan ethos. One strain of the Calvinist ethos had survived in a new form. The cry was still to "enrich yourself," not as one of the elect of God but of the Forbes 400 which boasted of twenty-six billionaires, with a cut-off point somewhere around a quarter billion. While some had inherited wealth most had started with some happy insight and run it up into a fortune.

This was America on the make, with a garish quality of will, energy and enrichment, much like that of the 1890s. The supermarket shelves were overflowing, and economic expansion was a fact of history. "Conspicuous consumption" was back again, yet "conspicuous leisure" was somewhat frowned upon since part of the new ethos, even for the monied, was to stay busy, fit and productive.

Some of the "rich and famous"—film and sports stars and best-selling authors—turned their fame into riches, and the operative epigram (revived from the Scott Fitzgerald 20s) was "Living well is the best revenge." There was an intense curiosity about how these fictional or factual gods got there and how they lived, and with it considerable emulation, rather than the envy and resentment which had once wracked the European middle classes and turned them toward political extremism. If the rich were America's ruling class (which was doubtful) it was not through their direct power but through the power of the imagery their wealth engendered, which suffused the imagination of the society.

Shakespeare might well have written *The Tempest* about America as an air-castle economy, built of gossamer dreams, removed from the grubbier realities of farm, mine, and factory. An observer might wonder whether "this unsubstantial pageant," created by the magic of Prospero's wand, could vanish by it and "leave not a wrack behind."

The representative moral philosophers of the era, whose task was to find some elevated stance on which to judge both the economy and the society, were split. John Rawls's *Theory of Justice* used the yardstick of distributive justice in a welfare society, while Robert Nozick's *Anarchy, the State and Utopia* stressed the ethic of individual effort and talent as imbedded in private property. In his *After Virtue*, a liberal Catholic philosopher, Alisdair Macintyre, reached beyond socialism and individualist capitalism to small functional communities that could give meaning to the entire pageant.

The new dimension that made the business élan different from that of earlier garish and expansionist decades—the 1890s, 1920s, 1950s—was that entrepreneurship became for many a form of secular religion. Women and minority groups had become a functioning part of the managerial force and a growing number entered the achieving class through the professions. The success of the business class as a whole carried the kick of discovering the talent of its members for affecting whatever they worked at and the time itself. The fact that they had become heroes and heroines for the next generation added to the stir of their work. This amalgam of work, achievement, and success didn't however add up to produce another Puritan ethic: they were elements of the American business style.

There was a more esoteric ingredient as well. One aspect of the counterculture of the 1960s had been the stress on personal growth through interaction with others in encounter groups. The business community had started early to incorporate that vision into its own careerism. When the teenagers of that decade became the standard-bearing "yuppies" two decades later they were returning to origins of business consciousness they could recognize. Like the scientists and technicians whom they built upon, and the rock singers they valued, they saw themselves as visionaries. The low-keyed phrase for it, less portentously meant, was "it's fun." It amounted to the same thing—involvement in depth with what was difficult but gave meaning to effort.

5. Governing, Belonging, Law

THE TESTING OF AMERICA took many forms, but mainly it was a testing of presidents and the presidency itself in the frame of a turbulent world of adversaries and allies. The centrality of the office, for good or ill, was clear in the late 1950s under Dwight Eisenhower, and even clearer in the new presidential generation that stretched from John Kennedy and Lyndon Johnson through Ronald Reagan's 1980s.

After Eisenhower there was scarcely a president under whom the prime question didn't arise: whether this complex political organism called America was in truth governable. The answer had to be reaffirmed under each, in testings that reached deep into the fiber of both the president and the people.

Whoever held the office became the world's most closely watched man. No monarch was ever followed more closely—his health and illness, his fluctuations of mood, policy and advisers, his successes and blunders, his poll standing, his stormy and peaceful times, his crises and resolutions.

He was a Prince who had strayed into a democracy. He had countless Machiavellis to instruct him in the principles of *virtù*—today's leadership principle. His face appeared upon a hundred million screens and his name was pronounced endlessly, in praise or imprecation, from the African savannahs to Russian steppes to German universities to teeming Chinese cities to some marketplace in Central America.

His own countrymen, in their efforts to define him, end by defining themselves. A recurring positive image on the screen, as the British monarchy knows, can be an antidote against fragmentation, giving the viewers a sense that they are not a congeries of discordant atoms but a society with a center. Whether the center holds is a more troublesome question I shall return to.

What about the man behind the image? After Eisenhower, who closed the Roosevelt-Truman Presidential generation, the new generation that came in with Kennedy, Johnson, and Nixon were still seen as Titans, having to carry the burden of the nation and the imperium. But they were wounded

Titans, bearing the scars their lives had left on their character and temperament. A subdiscipline called "psychohistory," with roots in Freudianism and developmental psychology, emerged in the 1960s and 1970s and had some influence. Mostly it took the presidents as its theme, reading their character into their presidential decisions, and their early life enactments into their character.

It shed some light on its subjects, after the fact, but its predictive power was slight, and there was always something unfinished about it. The psychic linkage of health or hurt with character, and that in turn with event, was too fragile to bear the implacable weight of context and history. From Franklin Roosevelt through Ronald Reagan each President offered a succession of revisionist presidential historians, a different puzzle, of mingled irony and paradox. For the changing consequences of the Presidential decisions played havoc not only with their answers but sometimes with the premises underpinning their questions.

Yet the presidents were special variants of a genus—the American as political man. The heart of their training, early or late, was in the electoral process as a prelude to the governing process. Together these formed "politics." Despite my lament in the book at its "belittling,"* Americans in time came to accept politics with a mixed skepticism and affection, and a number of them crowded into the arena, eager to take the stir and stench of battle because the prize in the end was their Grail.

The chief agents of change in the electoral system—computer and TV—transformed American politics by operating on political man. The key to the change was imagery. Where the verbal image suggested by the printed page and the disembodied voice of radio had been completed by reader and listener, TV offered its viewers the embodied image and voice. In a democracy of images everyone shared them—sound, symbols, message, emotions, fantasies, and all. By mediating the reality for their viewers the media *became* a species of reality. Hence the kernel of truth in Marshall McLuhan's "The medium is the message."

What took place on the screen was a representation of life but—especially for the young, who had it built into them early—it also became life itself. The viewer thrust his skills, dreams, hungers, purposes, all his selfhood, into the image, and together the viewer in the image and the image in the viewer fused to form the reality.

Two things have happened to the electoral process in consequence of this pervasive technology. For one, the new electoral elite embraced a corporate model, with specialized skills applied to issue demographics, and strategy brainstorming, and carefully tested TV advertising of the candidate. His role was less than heroic: he was at once the product being marketed and the ornament and beneficiary.

*See Ch. VI, pp. 356–357.

The second event is the breakthrough of media-oriented primaries as the force field in which the choice of the party's presidential candidate is all but determined. This is linked with the weakening of party authority and loyalty, the crumbling of the brokerage function of party leaders at nominating conventions, the obligatory planning over years for the primaries sweepstakes.

The metaphor of an election horse race still clings to the popular imagination, but with the new media it needs some recasting. The voters who watch it on TV are not just spectators. They are themselves at the heart of the action, identifying with a candidate as a possible winner, but also swept up in the momentum which a surprise win in early primaries gives him. The electoral process is thus opened to the acceleration effect which turns political man into a highly volatile one.

There were even larger changes centering on ethnicity and gender—how blacks (in 1957 the term still in use was "Negroes")*, Jews, Hispanics, Orientals, women, perceived themselves and were perceived. In genetic terms, early in the book ("Is There an American Stock?"), I raised the question of whether interbreeding among the entire jumble of stocks in America was moving, even distantly, toward something like an American stock, as with the case of the American character.

Thirty years later an answer is still murky. The lifting of immigration restraints and the cruel upheavals of governments and societies, by wars, terror, famines, social engineering, revolutionary overturns, brought swelling human waves to America from every continent. There was a constant rescrambling of genes and cultures. Both the civil rights and sexual revolutions of the 1960s and 1970s carried with them a breaking of earlier intimacy taboos. The cities and suburbs became even more pluralist than before. There was little stability of national character and less of stock.

Yet some symbolic events moved toward cultural homogeneity and kept the society from flying apart, even amidst the influx of political refugees and illegals. One was the operation of constitutional law in the 1950s, notably in the watershed unanimous decision of *Brown v. Board of Education.* Another was Lyndon Johnson's soaring legislative initiative in the 1960s that brought the Civil Rights Voting Acts into being.

Symbols were at work in both moves, affecting populations that had been waiting for centuries for access and hope. The blacks found a symbolic leader in Martin Luther King, who knew he was no Gandhi to overthrow the white Raj but who used the tactics of soul power ("I have a dream") to elicit the capacity of blacks to overcome their fears and act together. When King was killed, the burning inner cities became memorials of black

---

*See Ch. VII, Sec. 6, "The Negro in America," pp. 514–524. For other ethnic groups see Sec. 5, "The Minority Situation," pp. 501–514.

rage, but he left his impression. Another watershed was reached when black veterans returned with military skills from Vietnam, not to join an insurrection (as a few did) but to enter the American mainstream.

With King's passing, another legal offensive was mounted, that of "affirmative action" in government employment and contracts. This brought a national debate between those who rested on a moral base of redemptive retribution for past injustice, and many in the workplace who saw it as a form of reverse discrimination which perilously approached a quota system. It is probably best seen in the long term as a way of easing the difficult transition toward some future return to a stricter system of reward for merit and ability. Otherwise the compromised work ethic it embodied would have no built-in closure.

Within the black political culture there is a challenger intellectual movement, notably strong among political economists and psychotherapists, which focuses on the self-perception and self-reliance of the blacks as the operative reality in the mental health of the black community. It plays down long-range reliance on quotas and subsidies and the obsessive use of ethnic categories alone. It is a mainstream vision of true integration in the making. The vision is not of a conformist melting pot but of an integral organism, whose constituent parts keep their own essence but form a working, living whole.

There are residual pockets of antiblack hostility even in the late 1980s, including shabby and ugly Ku Klux Klan attempts to keep blacks out of supposedly white areas. There is also continuing anti-Jewish violence by vigilante neo-Nazi groups. There are stirrings against more recent Asian and Latin-American refugees and immigrants. No republic of reason has replaced the rancors of the past. But the triumph is that those involved are seen as lawless, are pursued by the law and overwhelmingly rejected by public opinion. There will always be those who scorn the achieved values, but they speak only for the marginal, and not for the core of common feeling and action.

A change has taken place in the earlier ethnic majority-minority assumption. America has become a nation of national minorities, as even the formerly dominant Wasps ruefully recognize. There can be no claims to membership in America as some prescriptive ethnic club.

Yet this is far from being all. What the minorities have in common, whether Hispanic, Asian, Jewish, black, Arab or whatever, is their sense of an overall America, its Constitution and its laws. They have also their hungers in common—for access, knowledge, skills, high living standards, a sense of belonging, a good life. What defines their individuality is their pride of heritage, their tight ethnic communities, their link with their countries and peoples of origin, the interweaving of their skills and traits into what they do best among the multiplicity of American cultural forms, and their satisfaction at being part of a civilization exercising the kind of world power within which their own leverage influence could have some meaning.

America is increasingly also a civilization where the ethnicities cross in courtship, bondings, intermarriage, and where a kind of *agon* flourishes as the young wrestle with their heritage and identities and the strong American component in both.

What is new in the American class system of the 1980s emerged both at the bottom and top of the mobility ladder. At the bottom is the "underclass," a term suggesting that the presumably "open-class" society was not open enough to keep its members from being poor, deprived, and alienated. Dependent on the welfare system, they are caught in a trap of adolescent joblessness, early pregnancies, and fatherless families. In adolescence and young manhood they disdain menial jobs at a minimum wage as beneath their masculinity, and miss out on the training needed for better ones in the new technologies. Their lives dangerously overlap with a streetwise drug and criminal culture. Attached to the TV world whose scenarios hawk consumer goods, violence, and direct action, they reach out to take what the whole culture celebrates and find themselves at odds with the law.

Was the entire structure of welfare dependency—and the underclass as part of it—a burden the civilization could bear without critical damage? Much of the discussion of Charles Murray's *Losing Ground* challenged his strongly argued contention that Lyndon Johnson's Great Society supportive subsidies had the unintended consequence of worsening the conditions they sought to better. Yet the free market approach, even if it could get adopted, might well be equally ineffective.

While Americans debate economic strategies and fail to face the social-cultural ones, the underclass continues somehow to live off the society with which it has a love-hate relationship and which it can neither accept nor overthrow. One thing is certain—that a permanent dependency system and a permanent underclass are incompatible with any model of a governable polity and a healthy social organism.

Does the society have a ruling class? The business cluster which I described above—in finance, entrepreneurship, management, may once have formed a ruling class but does so no longer. It is best seen not as a class but as a cluster of closely related elites. This is true as well of the clergy, lawyers, and landowners who once exercised dominance. C. Wright Mills argued in the 1950s that there was a "power elite" (in effect a ruling class) of business, finance, government, and law. But the information society played havoc with this rigidity along with others, and dissolved it into new class formations.

What is emerging is a *knowledge class* (earlier called the "new class") which is also in reality a cluster of elites (intellectual, educational, political, bureaucratic, legal, media, medical, counseling, scientific, military, planning), loosely held together by their expertise in producing and distributing symbolic information and knowledge, and their capacity to translate their skills into strategic power and influence. It is a class clearly meant for an information economy and society. Whether and when it will achieve the consciousness and cohesion of a ruling class is still in the future.

In income terms the knowledge class, except for its media and other stars, doesn't belong at the top of the class ladder but at the middle or upper-middle. The members of this class also differ in whether their skills are primary or secondary. At the upper-skill rungs of the ladder are the intellectual, scientific, and media elites that contain the primary producers of symbols; at the lower rungs are teachers, therapeutic and social workers, bureaucrats and others. As Peter Berger notes, this division has been true as well of the historical bourgeoisie, or middle class, of capitalism. He also suggests that the protracted class conflict of our time will be between the old middle class producing material goods and the new middle class producing symbolic information and knowledge.*

I prefer to think of the "upper" stratum of the knowledge class, small in number, as forming the closest approach to a ruling class in the new America, because it shapes the internal geography and climate of the minds that in turn shape other minds. That it has thus far been largely "liberal" and "left" in its angle of political vision may derive from the past glories of liberalism, or the stir of a new Enlightenment, or the consciousness of new distancing from old materialist values. It may even derive from the heady sense of human and social engineering that the symbol systems open up. Which of these will prove true, if any, is still being tested by collective experience.

The "new" middle class, at the lower strata of the knowledge class, shares strongly the politics of the upper strata. The conflict between it and the older middle class, closer to the earth of the material products that it produces and distributes, may prove to be the prime political and social conflict of the 1990s and ahead.

It will cut across the working class and the ethnicities as well, drawing them into the primary source of the conflict—the necessity for each cluster of groups to face the threat of each other's symbol system, with everything that the symbols carry with them.

Between the business and knowledge elites and the underclass are the bulk of Americans, including the middle classes and the workers. The lines between them all are even more tenuous than in the late 1950s. What gives them a class reality, especially the amorphous middle classes, is less any social ascription of roles than their sense of themselves as the "mainstream" and "heartland" of America, as the "people" and "public," as doing the hard work and carrying the harsh burdens of the society.

*See Peter L. Berger, *The Capitalist Revolution* (1986).

This is especially true of the older middle classes. They still have fears—of returning inflation, of the massive deficit, of the illegals swarming over the borders to inundate them, of crime in their streets and homes, and the drug culture, and the AIDS epidemic. More than any other class they are the defenders of the traditional ethos against the too rapid changes and the gaping discontinuities they brought.

Americans today think less strongly in class terms than ever, and more in ethnic terms, including the "white ethnics" whom Michael Novak described as "unmeltables." What counts is their self-image and hunger for belonging. Among blacks and Hispanics, and increasingly among the Asian immigrants, the thrust of leadership is to close ranks in order to achieve elective office, and to act as pressure groups for pushing and screening legislation.

The widespread attainment of political office, among blacks, Jews, Italians, Hispanics, with hopes reaching to the Supreme Court, became an important element in ethnic identity. Pride of office and clout can be almost as important as pride of cultural origin and lineage and can reinforce it. Ethnic man and political man developed not a conflict but an interplay of loyalties. Whenever ethnic groups confronted each other with real or fancied hurts, it fragmented national cohesion. But it also served as a vent for discontents and prevented what might have become explosive breaks in the national consensus.

Clearly the depth of ethnic feeling and solidarity went far beyond these hopes, prides, and strivings. The Jews and blacks, for example, both liberal-left in their leanings since their New Deal heritage, formed the great symbolic ethnic alliance and worked closely together during the 1950s and 1960s in support of civil rights. The war, the Nazis, Franklin and Eleanor Roosevelt, and the mythic Old Testament had bonded them, as well as their own objective situation as minorities. By the 1980s there were rifts between them, largely over the issue of quotas and meritocracy, but also over the symbols of the new world geopolitical forces, including the Soviet Union, the Middle East, and Africa.

Where American Jews, after Hitler, were tied to freeing the Russian Jews and supporting Israel, the blacks (especially the Black Muslims) were more oriented toward Moslem nationalism in the Middle East, the support of new African regimes, and the South African revolution. On a mythic level the basic enemy myth for the blacks was apartheid, for the Jews it was the Holocaust. It was another instance of how America as the global microcosm puts strains on its minorities. The wonder and glory are that they clash in peaceful division.

The case of the American "working class," as it used to be called, is in some ways similar. American trade unions, very early, yielded their ideology to pragmatism. But they had won their victories by having their martyrs and visionaries grapple with corporate capitalism as an enemy symbol. The problem was that in a climate hostile to labor, pragmatics could cut in either direction, for or against unionism.

The unions lost their economic clout when corporate cost cuts became the moral imperative in the economy, and there was no mystique of a labor culture or labor loyalties to counter it. In the new climate labor lost business as an enemy symbol. Long strikes were no longer viable, picket lines no longer sacrosanct, agreements for wage-cut concessions in a time of a pool of unemployed no longer unthinkable, nonunion recruiting of workers no longer taboo.

Labor risked its political clout when it ceased to be a class or a passionate movement and became only another element in election demographics— one more special interest group to be cried down, as organized labor's favored candidate, Walter Mondale, was cried down in the 1984 election.

What was active was the pull of middle-class values. It was not the least of the revolutions of the 1970s and 1980s that the corporate culture and interests became more strongly an object of middle-class emulation than the labor culture and interests. This affected the currents of ideas and reached the younger generation in the academies, which had never experienced the great labor upheavals of the 1930s through 1950s.

But it would be a mistake to write labor's future off. The same resourcefulness that labor's leaders evidenced in the past can be revived for the workers in the information society. It happened in the unionizing of the public employment and the service industries. But it will not be solved until labor rediscovers an enemy symbol, as the blacks have done with apartheid and the Jews with the Holocaust, and moves from pragmatics to a mythic dimension.

The idea of a distinct American political culture goes back to the New Deal, but the Presidential crises and the mounting media role after the early 1960s gave it sharper shape. There was substance aplenty for fervent Congressional investigation and talk-show commentators to feed on, over the quarter-century stretch from Kennedy's Bay of Pigs through Richard Nixon's Watergate, Jimmy Carter's hostage crisis and Ronald Reagan's Iran arms deal.

In terms of drama two things stand out to define the mood of the political culture. One is its relation to a succession of tempestuous presidencies in a fever-chart alternation of loves and hates, magnified by a structural media hype. The second is the bloodhound intensity of tracking down the scent of presidential malfeasance by Congress and the media.

Beyond this theater the central feature of the political culture is the dominant academic and intellectual elite that serves at once as the source of its ideas and passion, the critic of its achievements, and the validating agent of its legitimacy. There was no administration that didn't feel its sting at some point, no president who was not eager for its good will. It embraced Theodore Roosevelt, Woodrow Wilson, Franklin Roosevelt, and John F. Kennedy. It was condescending to Dwight Eisenhower, hostile to Lyndon Johnson, implacable to Richard Nixon, contemptuous of Jimmy Carter and of Ronald Reagan.

The political culture may be seen as a triangle, with the public at the base, the political elite at the tip, and the intellectual and media elites forming the two sides. Together they shape the temper and climate of the political culture within which governing takes place. The first imperative of a president, as the most visible member of the political elite, is to swim in the sea of the people. But on how well or badly he performs his governing function he is assessed for his place in history by an often adversarial intellectual establishment which has its own politics and ideology, and is often far removed from the minds and lives at the base of the larger culture.

Shelley called the poet the true "legislator of mankind." The role now devolved upon philosophers, critics, commentators, political and social theorists. During the half-century that started with the presidency of Franklin Roosevelt, the political culture became a tenaciously liberal establishment, drawing on the state-oriented energies in both parties. Roosevelt's political culture survived his disastrous policy toward Stalin and the Soviet Union.

Whether a lasting counterestablishment can emerge to challenge it is still being tested. Eisenhower and Reagan, both popular conservative presidents, could win two presidential terms and a segment of media approval. But they failed in their efforts to recruit a policy elite from the knowledge class, especially in foreign policy, and an enduring support system that could translate their popularity into viable policies.

Richard Nixon was strongly moved by an antiestablishment animus that— along with his character—was a key to Watergate. But even if he had avoided resigning he could not function as president because he had no political culture to re-establish and legitimize his authority. Ronald Reagan was able to recruit the initial makings of a political counterculture and governed for six years. But he too discovered, with the Iranian arms deal, that his vast popularity could not provide a frame for effective governing as long as mounting questions remained unanswered. It was proof again that while a president is at the core of government he cannot truly govern without a political and media culture which become the custodians of his authority.

Thus a president functions not only by his constitutional and prerogative *powers* but also by the *authority* which enables him to employ them. The powers come from the Constitution, written and unwritten. The authority comes largely from the political culture. In every instance of an imperiled presidency in the 1960s, 1970s, and 1980s it was credibility that was at stake. Without it, authority cannot be exerted, and without authority the full range of power cannot be invoked. Thus credibility and authority go with the perception of the person and character, and power goes with the office. But power cannot be released effectively without an empowerment by the people's belief both in the office and its incumbent.

It is clear now that the legitimacy of a Presidency rests in the people and the political culture. But it must constantly be retested in the fires of extreme crisis, when the authority of a president is imperiled.

Aristotle's "man as a political animal" had to be radically revised in the new America to include political woman. Her entrance into the political culture as into the economic—fought for a quarter century—was finally accepted. She also made her way into the intellectual elite, which legitimized both. Women proved formidable as activists because they were driven by an intellectual as well as political passion. That passion found expression in a cluster of "women's studies" in universities and a spate of revisionist theories in every discipline, from history and politics and psychoanalysis to theology.

Once aroused in rebellion the quest for freedom and equality (the rhetoric seemed always to come from politics) took on a daemonic liberating force of its own. It released talents in women they had considered for centuries to be a monopoly of men, including business and political skills. A woman had reached the Supreme Court and another had been nominated for vice-president. Why not a woman as president?

It would be seen as the final validation of the women's revolution. But it would take longer for women in the new America to move beyond the economic and political to the realm of relationships* and resolve some of the contradictions of their liberation.

There were contradictions as well in the perception of the role of government. Just as the political corollary of a welfare economy in FDR's day was a strong and positive government, so the political corollary of a self-sufficient entrepreneurial economy in Ronald Reagan's day had to be a nonburdensome, nonintrusive, noninterventionist "weak" government. Yet like his predecessors, Reagan found that for the foreign policy sector a high-defense interventionist "strong" government was an imperative. It was an exercise in the schizoid that is likely to haunt governments to come.

In the calculable future America will be confronting two major models in its foreign policy. In one (as in the Soviet Union and its satellites) Communist governments have almost total control and the people little. In the other (as in Iran) theocratic elites have taken over the government or (as in Lebanon) have dissolved it into a terrorist anarchy. Without either ideology or theology to inspirit the people the new America must operate in a world environment that—except for the Western imperium—is obsessed with one or the other model. Yet with all their war technologies

*See this chapter, Sec. 6, "The Pursuit of Selfhood and Belief."

America and its imperium must in the crunch fall back on consent, consensus, and the "national interest."

Whatever its attractive force, America faces the harsh reality of a world governed by the triple passions of nationalism, race, and religion. It is a world of a few great powers and of adversary imperial blocs but also of a multitude of mini-states seeking their place in the United Nations sun, a world to which law has not yet come, one without a moral community that can run beyond the writ of each nation's power elite. In the vacuum of law and community the common currency tends to be the one furnished by arms dealers and the characteristic *lingua franca*, that of terrorism.

The paradox of power in the 1970s and 1980s was the impotence of the strong, with the overkill weapons they didn't dare use, facing the resourcefulness with which the weak used their weaponry of terror—kidnapings, hijackings, the detonated car- or truck-bomb. The vulnerability of air transport, the easy access of terrorists to a global TV audience, and the sanctity that the individual human life claimed in the West combined—if only for a time—to fashion an age of terror. Looking back we see the 1960s, with all its violence, as largely a decade of principle. But we are likely to see the terror 1970s and 1980s, in the phrase W. H. Auden used about the appeasement 1930s, as "the low, dishonest decades."

Confronting the near anarchy of such a world, the American governing elite had constantly to balance the strategic imperatives and the geopolitical realities with the long and deep tradition of idealist principles. The years of bipartisan support for global policy initiatives, under Truman and Eisenhower, would be hard to restore. After the Vietnam experience and the War Powers Act, interventions of any sort had a stiff gauntlet to run. If short-range war risks were thereby diminished, the price exacted might be inaction by a soft democracy and increased war risks further down the road.

Whether strategic interest can prove a strong enough dynamic for effective action in the global arena was a question not yet decisively answered in the 1960s, 1970s, and 1980s. Could it survive the principle of checks and balances, the failures of bipartisanship, the feuding of liberals and conservatives and of Congress and the Executive? Could it, with these obstacles, sustain an enduring foreign policy? The Vietnam experience left in its wake a widespread fear, much like the isolationism of the 1930s, that strong foreign policy actions would lead to war.

It made covert action difficult because of a deep skepticism as to whether this really served "reason of state." Justice Holmes spoke much earlier of "the dirty business" of wiretapping. Unlike the older European and Asian societies, Americans were uneasy with whatever seemed dark and dirty, which violated both their open society and their national character. They wanted to bring everything into the light, to see whether rules had been defied and laws broken.

While a few covert actions succeeded, the major ones, under Eisenhower, Kennedy, Carter, and Reagan, ended badly, hurting the presidents and the nation. They raised doubts about the maturity of the covert segment of the political culture and shed light on what happens when American innocence and openness collide with the imperatives of secrecy.

The chances of shaping a reality-grounded foreign policy in a world of stratagems and fanaticisms are still incalculable. America is a young civilization, with only two centuries of existence, in a world of old civilizations steeped in history, less devoted than Americans are to the sacredness of the individual life, more adept at cunning and political survival.*

There have been few periods in American history that have better underscored Walter Bagehot's classic distinction† between the "efficient" and "dignified" aspects of a Constitution. I should call the first the "operational" Constitution bearing on how well it serves as a frame for day-to-day, year-to-year governing, in fair weather and foul. I translate Bagehot's "dignified" into our own "symbolic," and it bears on the power of document, tradition, and institutions to inspire respect and even awe, and hold the nation together by its mythic force.

If one is the *government*, vulnerable and too familiar, the other is the *state* with all its trappings, with its miseries along with its grandeurs. If one is *profane*, risking hostility and contempt thereby, the other is *sacred*, risking disillusionment and alienation.‡

As a society wedded to law grows more complex, the discontents of its discordant groups express themselves increasingly in attacks on the administration of justice, which many come to regard as an "injustice" system. The bitterest resentment in such a society is the rankling sense of injustice. The more reflective Americans understood that the roots of violence lay deep in the psyches of the uprooted and alienated, and in the absence of limits to an anything-goes morality. They resented the growth of a drug culture that fed on the crime culture and in turn fed it, and corrupted their children. Yet this didn't lessen the rage of many at a loophole-riddled justice system which seemed more efficient at the procedural protection of the rights of the accused than at guarding the victims, and which turned the home into a fortress and the streets into a jungle.

It became a familiar syndrome. In a liberal democracy which stresses civil and human rights, the legal culture takes its cast from the political

*For a discussion of the Western imperium and of nuclear weapons and deterrence, see Sec. 7 in this chapter, "Is America in Decline?"

†See his *The English Constitution* (1867).

‡I shall be dealing with the Constitution as symbol and myth in Sec. 7 in this chapter, "Is America in Decline?"

culture. The "civil religion" remained love of country and God, of freedom, equality and democracy. But in practice the state legislators and local police felt at a disadvantage because the hierarchy of judges had the final word. The popular perception was that some of the brutal crimes went unpunished, that plea bargaining flourished, deterrence languished, the jails were crowded, and a revolving-door policy put many offenders back on the streets.

The truth is that the new America, still a government of laws as its founders intended, has suffered dislocating social changes, broken institutional structures and eroded values. It has not reached a healthy equilibrium between its competing legal patterns.

The central one is the rule of law. There is an essential radicalism in it, in the best sense—that of showing (as in the classic civil rights cases) that the poorest and weakest are not without the protection of the law, and (as in the case of the Nixon tapes) that even the most powerful are not beyond the reach of the law.

Yet this carried a corollary pattern with it—that of procedural due process, even in the face of the commitment of an obvious crime and an enraged local community. The judicial decisions that threw a shield of protection around due process were the glory of the Roosevelt Court after 1937 and the Warren Court of the 1950s and 1960s, both known for their activist liberalism. They were taught at the great law schools and gave law students a cause to be passionate about.

This was inspiriting but in the long civilizational perspective it raised a haunting question: could Americans strike a balance between the substantive protections of the Bill of Rights and the perfectionist cult of procedural rigidity? Civilizations may be broken by caring too little about rights, but they have historically been broken by rigidities that cut the governing and judging group off from substantive lives in real cultures, with a real sense of injustice. Only a living constitution, interpreted in the spirit of meeting social changes flexibly but strongly, will survive the impact of those changes.

The battle over constitutional interpretation is one of the great continuing doctrinal debates, but it is not a bloodless battle of legal categories. Presidents have come to understand that their power to make judicial appointments for a life tenure may be more enduring than anything else they do. Much that happens in the tenure of every president marches to the drumbeat of federal judges who have outlived a series of Presidential terms. John Adams' choice of the "midnight judges," in spite of the Jeffersonian Revolution, has been multiplied since on every federal judicial level.

What is at stake is not patronage and power alone, but judicial principle that reaches beyond the political parties and angles of vision. The Earl Warren Court, from Eisenhower through Lyndon Johnson, embraced a liberal "judicial activism" which stretched the Constitution to keep pace with a highly modernized economy and society and in the process expanded the Supreme Court's powers. But Justices Felix Frankfurter and Robert H. Jackson, working from the Holmesian tradition of "judicial restraint," formed a counterforce. Using it as a springboard the Warren Burger Court, from Nixon to Reagan, moved away from activism to a more conservative version of restraint than the earlier one. The Senate battle over William Rehnquist's confirmation as Chief Justice suggested how high the stakes were in the struggle over the composition of the Supreme Court.

Basically it was a battle over what role the federal courts should play in mediating the power of other branches—the Presidential, Executive, Congress, and especially the state legislatures. An activist "broad construction" of the Constitution was translated into greater interventionism, with a concern for the rights of minorities. The "strict construction" of the "judicial restraint" school was translated into mediating the will of state and local majorities through the prism of legislative intent and long-range constitutional precedent.

In the end it is a polar difference, not a dualism: there is something of each school in the doctrine of the other. The differences, however, will not down. They are what make the constitutional struggles of a tangled and complicated democracy dramatic.

There were no judicial giants left in the 1980s to create new doctrinal positions as Holmes, Brandeis, Black, Frankfurter, Douglas, and Jackson had done. Nor were there constitutional crises in the 1980s to match those from the New Deal to Watergate. But in an information era and a turbulent world of power the challenges were bound to come. A new judicial doctrine might well emerge to meet them, bringing "activism" and "restraint" into a workable tension.

6. The Pursuit of Selfhood and Belief

A GREAT CHANGE in relationships occurred in the 1960s and 1970s, which set the stage for the America of the 1980s. It is in essence a tale of two polities, one within the other. The larger polity, of government, law and society, became increasingly egalitarian in the postwar years of Truman and Eisenhower. The lesser polity, that of the family, remained basically paternalistic. Something had to give, and what gave was the family polity in the cultural revolutions of the 1960s and 1970s. It opened itself—or was opened—to the liberating and democratizing forces of the larger polity and culture.

By the late 1980s the sexual revolutions were pretty much over and the women's revolution had paused to assess and consolidate its gains. But the image of the family and what happened to it remained central in American social politics and its battles. The differing perceptions of what had preceded the Great Change colored the competing political visions.

Those who had fought the prerevolution *ancien régime* saw the family polity as authoritarian, repressive, life-denying. But a sizable segment of the nation had a sense of deep loss for a vanished family constellation and a vanished era that went with it.

This group, including many social liberals, looked back with nostalgia to the Golden Age when childhood and the growing-up years were a time of enchantment, and personal bondings remained true, family ties strong, the pleasures of sex and the commitment of love authentic, the sense of manhood and womanhood confident, morals disciplined, loyalty and trust unquestioned, illness a time of trial to be met with fortitude and death with acceptance.

The prevailing principle of this family polity was the presiding presence of the patriarchal Old Testament father. In the family polity he was husband-father-provider and his authority served as cement for the whole, while the wife-mother was arbiter of family conflicts, overseer of the children's growing-up years, mistress of the domestic economy, and culture-carrier for everyone. The emphasis was on duties rather than rights, on the obligations of work rather than the uses of leisure.

The family was the arena for the unfolding of the life cycle of its members. It contained the scripts for education, sexual conduct, the rituals of childhood, adolescence, and parenting, the bittersweet interactions of love and marriage, the strengths of bondings, the nightmares of alienation, the internalizing and breakdown of values.

For some time the two polities lived in an uneasy truce, and the family constellation withstood the attacks from the larger polity outside. By the mid-1950s, when most of the present book was written, Huck Finn (in citified form) had blossomed into the male rebellion of Hugh Hefner's *Playboy* mystique, by way of Alfred Kinsey's massive sexual interview project. The women's revolution followed in the 1960s, but in my 1957 section on the many-faceted, over-burdened life of the American woman* there were already some rumblings of the thunder to come.

The big breakthrough came in the 1960s, whose protest movements (antidraft, antiwar, anticurricular, anticorporate, antigovernment, civil rights) formed the political revolutions, while the communal, ecological, sexual, antifamilial, and women's movements formed the cultural revolutions.

Of the two the impact of the cultural movements proved the more enduring. The reason may be that the political protests, as part of the American revolutionary heritage, were aimed at the shortfalls of democracy and equality. They were asking the larger society to medicine itself, using democracy to achieve a more absolute democracy, thus stretching the social organism to the breaking point. The cultural revolution, by contrast, sought to bridge the gap between the two polities, by bringing a measure of freedom

*See Ch. VIII, Sec. 6, "The Ordeal of the American Woman."

and equality into the family constellation, including its erotic and gender relationships. Nor was it one-directional. It aimed at the impersonal larger polity as well, seeking to infuse it with some of the affection and intimacy which it lacked.

The result was a striking convergence. The political and social movements took on sexual overtones, with a kind of eroticizing of their politics, while the erotic movements experienced a politicizing of eros. It was the "Great Cultural Revolution," with only marginal violence as compared with the Chinese episode of the same decade.

In its thrust it subjected every social institution to a raking, adversarial testing and rethinking, carried on under severe fire. No one was granted immunity. In the New Left parlance it was the "Long March through institutions." While a number of the institutions were battered they survived, and their survival was hailed, like the return of a wounded soldier from the wars.

Yet the form in which they survived was sometimes barely recognizable. This was true of the family, even while imbedded in its institutional matrix. Cohabitation, early out-of-wedlock childbearing, postponed marriages, single-parent households, resort to outside child-care services, shifting partners—these were not the building materials for enduring family structures. It was even truer of the entire complex of sexuality, love, gender, bondings, and the home, by which the family forms a cultural envelope for selfhood and relationships.

Going all out for freedoms the women's movement of the 1960s and early 1970s pursued the principle of equality with men in every area. Women fought their way into the marketplace of jobs and careers, relishing the economic independence that it gave them, invoking "affirmative action" to overcome the resistance. Knowing they ran the danger of becoming the men they vied with, they held on to their sexuality and their childbearing and homemaker roles, adding tensions to their already burdened lives, but also stretching themselves in the process.

What were the cultural imperatives of the late 1980s for the American woman, and what was her probable profile? A young middle-class woman born right after World War II, coming of age in the mid-1960s, reaching her mid-40s in the late 1980s, would have been through a college or technical education, would expect without question to find a job and shape a career, would intend to marry relatively late after some sexual experience and a live-in relationship with her husband-to-be. She would insist on combining her work life with children and family. She would be aware of politics, and active in church or community work. She would likely have lived in several American cities and traveled abroad for vacation. She would regard herself as the equal of the men she "dated" and the one she married, yet she would wrestle with the ways by which she could keep this sense of herself from creating tensions with them. More than any generation of women before her she would expect to live out her life balancing independence with intimacy and bondings, career and work with domestic obligations, family relations with cultural satisfactions.

It would be hard going for her, as it was for those who cleared a path before her. The leaders of the women's movement, given their time and context in the 1960s and 1970s, had to be activists in politics, business, the professions, culture, and academic life, fighting their battles with political ideals and slogans as weapons. They trusted that out of their activism everything else would flow, and that the issues of relationships, bondings, erotic engagement, childbearing and rearing would somehow be resolved.

For many they have been, for many others not. The pursuit of liberation and equality has had a largely positive outcome, the pursuit of happiness less so. For the world of intimacy and bondings is not that of power. It has its own needs and fulfillments, its own areas of strength and vulnerability, its own pleasures and joys and tragedies, its own enchantments, its own dark sacred wood. The winds of freedom and power brought upheavals in that sacred wood which didn't solve women's innermost problems but gave them another and larger context and made them problematic in a different way. Experientially that way was broader if not deeper, and opened more interesting vistas. It involved women in activities that tested (and often falsified) the older social stereotypes of gender inferiorities, and made them more confident about what the substructure of the real differences was.

One of the forms the erotic revolution took was characteristically American—the study of what Dr. William Masters termed "human sexual response" under laboratory conditions. His work shocked the humanistic and religious community, as Kinsey's interview surveys had done. Their combined effect was a new view of sexual capacity, especially of the young and of women, and a widespread release of sexual inhibitions that, among other things, transformed the attitudes toward homosexuals and their self-perceptions.

Age-old questions of the meaning of sexuality, which had engaged Western civilization for centuries, came to be couched in terms of "life-style" taste and choice. This helped tolerance but did little for serious discourse. Along with the experimental communes, growth centers and encounter groups of the 1960s and early 1970s, it turned America into a more hedonic society, less restrained by its Puritan origins and traditions than at any time before or since.

Had it happened more gradually and less explosively, within a framework of greater depth about the nature of sex, it could have been an affirmation of eros in both senses of the term—that of love and that of the life force. But this was another case where the intellectual elite failed the culture. Except for feminist writers and scholars who explored sexual history and gender theory from their own angle of vision the academics never took the erotic area seriously, as they had taken the political and economic.

As a result Americans were forced back on a seesawing alternation of sexual "revolutions" and "backlashes" in something like an erotic cycle, instead of finding some true relation to the erotic in their lives and holding to it. What started as a rebellion against a too repressive and antierotic culture came to present an image of a permissiveness so far-reaching that it struck the people at the base of the culture as anarchic.

The resulting backlash was sharp and brought divisive consequences in struggles that were fought out on the nature of family life, religion, morality, and the home. In one part of the forest there was a pitched battle on abortion between the "right-to-life" and "pro-choice" forces, in another part a revival of the old battle over "pornography" (never adequately defined) and the constitutional freedoms hemming in attempts at censorship.

Both battles offered dangers because both moved the controversial aspects of eros into the political arena. There the mixture of sexual, family, and religious passions (notably in the closing pre-Hitler years of Weimar Germany) had proved an explosive one.

Of the two sets of controversies the one about conception, contraception, and abortion was likely to change in future decades, in response to the developing life sciences and their changing bio-technologies. The pornography controversy, with deeper roots in the history of perceived sexual "aberrations," would prove more tenacious. It thrived on technologies, as witness the loosely thought out Meese Commission Report of 1986 which was aimed ostensibly at child exploitation and stressed the hard-core porn brought by cable TV and videocassettes, but also targeted traditional men's magazines. There were signs as well of an effort by the radical feminists, out of their concern with rape, to redefine the core of pornography as the masculinist attitudes toward woman as sexual object.

In the arena of changing relations the fact was that sexuality in the late 1980s no longer held the central place which it had at the height of the sexual revolution. Largely stripped of its Victorian taboos and taken more matter-of-factly, it was also largely stripped of its earlier mystery. The society continued to be pleasure-oriented but it was a pleasure experienced sexually as a staple of everyday life, much like work, recreation and "socializing." Sex therapists reported a concern with the waning of desire among their patients. Being gay or lesbian was more openly acknowledged and privately accepted, although still barely tolerated in public life.

It was not until the late 1980s that the AIDS epidemic awakened the slumbering hostility to the gay community and shook it to its depths. But it also did more. It threw a cordon of fear and danger around the sexual act, for heterosexuals as well as homosexuals. For what had been a hedonic society it undercut the celebration of Freud's "pleasure principle" which had once conquered America more completely than any other culture of the West. It played havoc with both the "modernization" and the "Americanization" of sex.*

It also became, along with cancer, the great symbolic disease of latter-day America, in part because it involved transmission by the sex act, and even more because it hit the immune system and is thus far irreversible. There was still, in the late 1980s, a continuing faith that in the end it would yield to laboratory advances. Yet it shook one of the cardinal tenets of the 1980s, the belief in the individual's self-management of his health and life. The belief implied the power of mind and will over circumstance, which the career of the AIDS virus made hard to maintain.

Faced with a tragic crisis of runaway dimensions the American response characteristically was the triad of research, sex education (in the schools and media), and reluctant controls.

The shock of the episode, however, left the basic questions still there. A healthy civilization would strive somehow to strike a balance between strongly guarded public freedoms and socially sanctioned limits in the erotic and family area. It would thus (as with religion) restore the privacy and primacy of individual decision within the frame of prevailing constitutional law and within a collective ethos which individuals could respect even as they dissented from it.

The price paid for big changes of the 1960s and 1970s was the breaking of the support system on which the battered institutions had relied. I speak of the authority of the family, and the feeling of closeness to church, school, neighborhood, and community. The traditional limits and values had served both as boundaries and safeguards for the individual ego and for its actions, passions, and fantasies. Their weakening left unexpected relational problems and vacuums of authority and commitment.

Thus the new freedoms brought new burdens with them, and evoked new forms of escape from freedom that could lighten them. As the old institutional supports were stripped away, leaving the self exposed on a parapet, the individual had to find substitutes. New socially sanctioned support systems take long to build. But the government was still there as a fallback of last resort for those on the dependency parapet—subsidies for farmers, welfare checks for dependent mothers and children, social security payments for the elderly, Medicare entitlements for health care recipients.

Reaching more deeply to the fragile self there were personal dependencies, especially on alcohol, tobacco, gambling, hard drugs. All had a long history,

---

*I am using here the titles of Paul Robinson, *The Modernization of Sex* (1976), which deals with the impact of the thinking of Havelock Ellis, Alfred Kinsey, William Masters, and Herbert W. Richardson, *The Americanization of Sex: Nun, Witch and Playmate* (1971), with a liberal theological view.

all were addictive. With past support systems weakened, all four became elements in an increasingly compulsive society. Even the contrived "anonymous" support systems of fellow drug and alcohol users became part of the compulsiveness. There had long been a role that therapies of all kinds played, that of stabilizing the frail or insecure psyche of the American as "therapeutic man." The role was now extended to the dependencies. America had always been a "willingness of heart;" it was now consumed by a compulsion of the will.

The darkest compulsion was the drug culture, which retained the chic quality it carried over from "grass" to heroin, "coke," and "crack." By the mid-1980s it crossed class and income lines, moving from the film and rock stars to the high-school youngsters of the suburbs and inner cities. There were largely futile government efforts at interdicting the "supply-side" entry of drugs across the borders, and widespread "demand-side" pleas to the young to "say No" to drugs. Yet the core problem of dependency remained— the quarter-century stripping away of the support system whose protective layers had strengthened the self.

The drug dependency had consequences for the society. It penetrated to those who were charged, as workers or controllers, with the infrastructure of planes and railroads, to key people in the delicate high-tech tasks of space and defense construction, even to the military and naval forces. The people who were entrusted with the duties (on a modern level) of the early "warders of the marches" were themselves undermining the very fortress they were guarding.

With the drug culture also came street crime to maintain the drug habit, and a violence which accompanied the drug high and was further sustained by the shrillness and tensions of the media. There were new generations which had forgotten—or never learned—the uses of limits. The "anything goes" psychology of the angry protests of the 1960s was transmuted into a similar mood of the street-smart and hep, operating in a precontract "state of nature" jungle when men live (in Hobbes' words) "without a common power to keep them all in awe."

In the generational succession on the college and career level, the latter 1970s were dubbed the "Me Generation," and with some justice. It was a put-down of the imperial ego, which wanted everything, wanted it instantly, and put itself into the center of every discourse of the decade. To the charge that Americans had turned narcissism into a cult one could find an answer from a defector from the post-Freudians, Heinz Kohut. He felt that the prevailing problem of the psyche was the loss of true selfhood, and that a restructuring of the conditions of the life history could lead to a necessary "restoration of self."

It is a paradox that the "liberation" movements, which stripped both women and men of their protective sheaths, had a double effect in the

America of the 1980s—shaping new dependencies for many, but also propelling others into increased efforts to establish selfhood. There is no single cause-and-effect sequence here but a polar one. Both drives were present, to dependence and selfhood, and often in the same person. Thus the 1980s are witnessing both a dependent and compulsive American and an America experiencing a selfhood revolution—and even the latter has compulsive elements in it.

Some of the ingredients of this change are recognizable as the staples of media discussion: jogging or running, aerobic exercise, vitamins, a shift in healthier nutritional patterns, a retreat from drinking and smoking. These may turn out in time to be fads in a culture all too fad-ridden, rather than longer-range sustained changes. Yet the growing self-awareness of the life journey goes back to the awareness movement of the 1970s. Nor is the intense assertion of will and care in its self-management likely to prove faddish. Even more sustained is the determination to make use of every medical advance and live out the life span to the fullness of the existing state-of-the-art knowledge. True, the symbolic diseases of the era—cancer, stroke, heart attack, Alzheimer's*—were still there as hard-wire facts of a deteriorating organism. Yet the change in self-perception was also there. The incidence of these diseases did not cancel out the prevailing reliance not only on medical advances but on human intelligence and will to go with them.

What needed heeding was that these were part of a perception of the nature of health as an equilibrium in the organism, of illness as a serious disturbance of it, and of healing as involving the total organism—mental as well as physical, brain and mind and will as well as soma—and the establishment of a new equilibrium. It followed from this that the patient had to be an active participant in the process, in a working collaboration with his doctors, in the search for an integral amalgam of traditional and alternative approaches.

This change of self-perception in turn was part of a subjectivism wholly different from the determinism of an earlier era, and its surrender to medical authority. There were signs of a new medical populism in the mounting protests against the long testing period by the medical establishment, which postponed the access to promising pharmaceuticals that might save the lives of terminal patients, otherwise doomed. Behind this was the proposition that an informed individual had the right to take his own risks in the management of his own health, and his own life and death.

There were signs in the 1980s of a recognition, however stumbling, that the road to selfhood could not be a solitary venture. Even while stressing self-reliance and self-management it had to involve a rediscovery of one of the decade's favorite words—"relationships." A team-written work, on

*For a discussion of AIDS as a special case see pp. 989–990.

"Habits of the Heart"* put the stress on commitment to shared community values rather than on traditional individualism. In the erotic area the earlier focus on morally indifferent "life-styles," which had become almost a matter of taste, shifted to an emphasis on bondings (whether in or outside marriage) which moved beyond the transitory to the enduring.

True, the incidence of divorce, affecting more than one out of two marriages, and its even higher incidence on second marriages, didn't speak well for the achievement of sustained bondings. Yet the experimental living-together years, the increasing lateness of marriages, and the fact of repeated trials, showed a hunger for relationships that would work.

Despite efforts to revive the old values conflict between individualism and collectivism (or social commitments) it was a pretty strained dichotomy for the decades ahead. In theory, as in the practical conduct of life in latter-day America, both selfhood and commitment were polar necessities. But the center of the moral stage was held by the necessities of decision making in a time when the knowledge advances—in gene splicing, organ transplants, in vitro insemination, life extension technology, ecological hazards, nuclear energy, laser research—involved ultimately individual decisions which depended on the priorities given to values and relationships.

There was little new clarity about either set of priorities. Mostly the choices came out of individual responses to the social environment. With a decline in voting rates and party loyalties there was also a decline in public activisms, except for spotty single-issue crusades. "Public man" and "public woman," it was widely noted, were in decline, in large measure because of the earlier overstress on activisms and the Reagan campaign against the governmental role. Some intellectuals found a substitute by moving from government and society to community, but for most people there was a flight to private man—or woman—in the setting of family (when it survived) and other bondings and relations. But mostly the drive was toward warmth, dependency, security.

In keeping with Marshall McLuhan's perception of TV as a "cool" medium, private man and woman related in a "cool" mode. There was little talk of joy and ecstasy, whether in sexuality or courtship or love, and little of passion. There was wide use of the "family" metaphor in politics, largely nostalgic, with the stress on a time when the family was central. The success of TV sit-coms on family themes rested largely on their low-key affectionate humor, with the father seeking to find a new authority in the family polity.

No new paradigm for "relations" emerged, as it had in the Puritan and Victorian era, and in the early century and the 1960s. If anything there was a borrowing of the "work" metaphor, in its double sense. The "sig-

*See Robert N. Bellah et al., *Habits of the Heart: Individualism and Commitment in American Life*, Harper and Row (1986).

nificant relations" were those that "worked," and to make them work Americans felt the need to "work at" them. In the place of the discontinuities of the 1960s there was an effort of at least minimal continuity, both with the Puritan ethos and that of pragmatism.

The idea of the family, as I have noted, persisted almost as a disembodied ideal. What enabled it to persist was the increasing hunger for it, the fear of loneliness, and the need for a home as at once symbol and means for relating. There was a shift of gravity from the nuclear family itself to the homeplace as an assemblage of technologies for consuming and living, for entertaining, for listening and watching (music, TV, videocassette, films), even for computerized working, away from the office, plant, or laboratory. At once functional in design and gadgety in equipment, relying on the new information and communication arts, the homeplace-cum-workplace operated as the center of intimacy relations, the arena of consumption, the war-room of family financing strategies. It somehow managed to combine a channel for contact with a complex, stormy world and an increasingly necessary shelter from it. For Americans whose home life was fragile and who lacked strong bondings, the workplace outside the home also took on a new urgency.

In the earlier America work had strong meaning, the workplace (field, forest, factory, mine, mill) considerably less. This was pretty much reversed in the new America: The knowledge class and the elites (political, intellectual, financial) had their own characteristic work drives on middle- and lower-management levels, while in the competitive world it was a mixed bag. Where top management stressed team-work there was a working élan, but the larger lack of corporate human responsibility evoked not energy but anxiety.

For most lower-level managers and workers—industrial, service, bureaucratic—there was a continued erosion of the work ethic, in terms of a task well done because of the satisfactions it brought. Instead of *work* there was the *job*—to give as little of yourself to it as possible, to get as much for it as possible, to retire from it as soon as possible.

Given an advancing computer technology and a stiffening world competitive market, the adversary relations between employers and unions made it harder for the job to retrieve the lineaments of satisfying work. In the machine shop and the press room the computerized work design was directed toward cutting the work force, and assigning less strategic control to the worker and more to management.

What remained with any attractiveness was less the work than the workplace, as an intersection point for human relationships. Because the work itself was increasingly depersonalized it made the humanizing encounters, interactions and rituals of the workplace all the more important. Together they formed what one regretted leaving at retirement.

The hunger for interaction showed itself also in "networking," the characteristic associational bond of an information society. The women's movement of the 1970s used it as a powerful instrument to allay loneliness and achieve a sense of belonging. The scattered outposts of "New Age" holistic thinking found reenforcement in sharing their common explorations and discoveries. In the 1980s the *aficionados* of home computers plugged into "postoffice" terminals as a way of exchanging shoptalk and touching base with each other in human terms. The essential loneliness of Americans had changed little since the days of David Riesman's "lonely crowd," but the means for coping with it were new.

I wrote my chapter *Life Cycle of the American* when the concept was just emerging with the highly important work of Erik Erikson. Since then the idea of a succession of stages in the life journey, at which the search for personal identity and life's meaning is summed up, sometimes in crisis form, and moves on to the next stage, has achieved considerable currency. Its refinement became part of American intellectual history, and of the Americanizing of developmental psychology.

By the 1980s three critical changes occurred. One was a shift from a predominantly masculine developmental schema to one that takes account of the differences in a woman's psyche, her inner life and her life experience, and therefore in her life journey. A second was a shift from a heavily determinist perception of early childhood and adolescence, in neo-Freudian psychosexual terms, to an emphasis on mental and moral development. A third was a balancing shift of interest to the later decades of the life span.

Every demographer will testify that a skew toward the aging cohorts in a society places a burden on it, of people who produce little materially, consume much, depend on subsidies, and increase medical costs exponentially. In the mid-1980s 12 percent of the Americans were over sixty-five ("young old"), 5 percent over seventy-five ("old old"), an increasing percentage over eighty, and a growing number of centenarians. Their support and their care and housing are problematic, and their voting power disproportionally strong, throwing a scare into politicians.*

Yet there may be more than demographics in the quality and destiny of a civilization. One of the prime aspects of the new America is that an aging revolution is taking place within a larger revolution—that of the social perception of the entire life journey, and its self-management in the adult stages. Together they have moved America away from the cult of youth, and the belief that creativity is its monopoly, to a mellower understanding that it is an underground stream that changes—but sustains—its flow through the closing decades. This has meant a release from the last seg-

*For my earlier discussion of "aging," see Ch. VIII, Sec. 7, "The Middle and End of the Journey."

regation and taboo, of ageism, and a humane view of the later life stages until journey's end, which can enrich the whole civilization.

I mean by "values" the priorities we assign to alternative life purposes, and the role they play in putting the prime questions to life. In that sense it was hard to find surrogates for the lost traditional family and its role in the internalizing of values. The replacement of the family as values agency by the street peer group and the hyped-up TV show and videocassette was a shoddy substitution.

Not that the values system of the 1950s was one of plain living and high thinking. In the literature of the time there was a "five-goal system"—success, prestige, money, power, security—to which I added a discussion of happiness and conformity.*

In an insightful review essay on the book† Clyde Kluckhohn, cultural anthropologist, felt that the value system I had described was already in the process of disintegration, along with much of the Puritan ethic. He saw a more tentative pattern emerging, less success-oriented and more outward-looking, although still conformist. There was a corrective emphasis in his essay that I welcomed. But at the end of the 1950s, soon after we wrote, we were both overtaken by the seismic cultural revolution from which an adversary culture emerged to challenge the largely traditional one we had both described.

The rest is history—but largely cyclical history. I have already dealt‡ with the values of the business culture and its impact on the society. But the cyclical succession of values structures is worth following, especially in the minds and life plans of students. As the avant-garde of changing values the student generation of the 1960s became even more socially conscious than the New Deal generation of the 1930s. That of the latter 1970s was career-conscious and inner-conscious, as had been the generation of the postwar 1940s. If the thirty-year cyclical return-with-a-difference is at all valid the early 1980s should resemble the success system I described for the 1950s (as indeed they do), and the later 1980s should follow Kluck-hohn's pattern of a modified success conformism. By the same cyclical logic the 1990s should show some return to a values rebellion in the image of the 1960s.**

But rigidity is the bane of all cyclical theories, however seductive. The

---

*See Ch. IX, Sec. 8, "Life Goals and the Pursuit of Happiness."

†Reprinted in Abraham S. Eisenstadt, Ed., *American History: Recent Interpretations*, Bk II (Crowell 1962, paper) 507–518.

‡See Section 4 above, on "The Economic Culture in an Age of Interdependence."

**For a provocative cycle hypothesis for American history (political rather than values cycles) see Arthur M. Schlesinger, Jr., *The Cycles of American History* (1986). Schlesinger also finds thirty-year cycles.

future never returns to the past but incorporates segments of it into its own patterns for its own purposes, whether evolutionary or revolutionary. The dynamics of values changes are more intricate and paradoxical than we give them credit for. The avant-garde student rebels of the 1960s, laying siege to college campuses, raised a banner which the rest recognized and were ready for, but their eagerness to follow the banner came from the very conformity of the 1950s against which they now rebelled. "When me they fly, I am the wings."

The point is that value systems flow mainly from economic, sexual, and religious sources in the culture, and embody their general motifs which don't always synchronize. In fact, they may at times work at cross-purposes. Each generation tends to call upon both positive and negative impulses in the preceding one—thesis and antithesis, as it were—and join them in a new synthesis. This is likely to happen also in the 1990s and beyond, but its result is still hidden.

I have contended elsewhere* that the true arena of education should be the fiery centrality of values in every classroom, picking up the battle of values formation where family, peer group, and TV screen leave off. Largely ignored earlier, this role for the schools gained strength in the 1980s, with the upsurge of support for traditional values, the return to religion, and the anxieties over what many saw as a values anarchy.

Those who care about a life-affirming civilization cannot help being concerned with values teaching. But from a different direction, there has also been a concern with the need to retrieve education from a too rigid public school bureaucracy, which has had to function as a receiver in bankruptcy for the eroded social institutions. It should be possible to give like-minded teachers and parents a more autonomous chance to follow up on the dedicated experiments, both inside and outside the public school system, that have had success with values education.

Ever since the mid-1950s the system has had to reflect the struggles over ethnic integration and more recently over sex education, abortion, contraception, the drug culture, AIDS, school prayer, and the treatment of evolution in textbooks. These formed a motley array of issues and causes, important primarily because competing groups viewed the schools as an institutional weapon for enforcing social consistency. Actually these efforts proved more socially divisive than cohesive in their impact. Worst of all, they obscured the really knotty problems of education, which cluster around modes of teaching and learning, and how they bear on life purposes and the enhancement of the spirit and imagination.

The relation of education to values can too easily be trivialized by mis-

*See *Values in Education: Notes Toward a Values Philosophy* (Phi Delta Kappa, Bloomington, Indiana, paper, 1976).

perceiving the nature of each. Values flow from personal and shared experience. Education combines the arts of structuring that experience, through teaching and learning, in ways that make it more accessible to the student. The true transmission of values doesn't come from its direct teaching, which can be particularly clumsy, simplistic, and even damaging when undertaken by a public agency. It comes rather from the student's involvement in a subject matter that counts for him, from the new experience and insights it embodies, and most of all from the teacher as role model and his skill in drawing out the values implications, whatever the subject. In fact, the school did its values work best when it came close to the way a family polity operated—with purpose and limits—to meet crises and solve problems. This is a Periclean view of education as character formation, and the remarkable fact was that Americans in the 1980s were groping for what the Greek leader knew millennia earlier.

It was a striking fact also that the upheavals in American educational circles during these thirty years came in tandem with crises in American life—with Sputnik, with Watergate, with the Challenger disaster, with the media and computer revolutions, with the "competitiveness" struggle involving Japan, with the drugs and AIDS traumas. In the era when families were true values agencies the internalizing of values by the children seemed to flow spontaneously from family crises and problem solving. Yet the models were there and were alert to their teaching opportunities. Many Americans felt that something similar could happen again, on a national level, within schools alert to their opportunities.

Can the educational venture free itself from institutional shackles and public pressures, and give some autonomy to parental choice of schools and to imaginative teachers? Historically the time was ripe for education to take advantage of the knowledge explosions which, for a half-century since the time of John Dewey, had barely touched it. There are new psychologies and moral philosophies, a new view of the stages of the life journey as itself a series of adventures in education, a new skill in cutting across the boundaries of disciplines in the life sciences and human sciences.

More concretely there is the technology of the computer that has come with the knowledge revolution and could set up a dialogue between students and teachers, and (within the child) with his "second self." After the decades of stagnation in educational thinking, something like a paradigm shift was possible, under the stimulus of the cross-disciplinary "cognitive sciences" of brain, mind, self, and the strategies of thinking.

The religious revival that swept over the New America was genuine enough: the statistical inductors leave little doubt that something important happened in American religious history. The real question is what it means and what its importance lies in.

Clearly it reconfirms the basic religiousness of Americans, which Alexis de Tocqueville and James Bryce both noted. It struck them because both belonged to nations with a state-supported church, in a European civilization which had come to take religion for granted—for its usefulness to the state and society rather than for its depth of feeling.

At no point was this as true of American religiousness. The right of a man by the First Amendment to choose and practice his particular faith gave that faith—as well as the Constitution—a special vibrancy. The continuing stream of immigrants kept the sense of providential oversight fresh. These forces still operate in the resurgent religiousness of America today.

The meaning of that resurgence must be sought centrally in the American "exceptionalism" which runs like a skein not only through my earlier discussion of religion* but through this entire book, and remains true of the new America. The gap between America and the major European nations—Britain, France, Germany, the Scandinavian countries—shows up in the annual surveys of religious attitudes. It is remarkable because the American religious culture has endured the same historic experiences as the European—the Enlightenment, the rule of science and technology, the waves of rationalism, secularism and relativism, and the impact of modernity both on the economy and on the total culture.

Elements of American religious elites have responded to these experiences in a fashion similar to their European counterparts, by leaning strongly toward a neo-isolationism in foreign policy, by applying the categories of a "just war" theology harshly, by seeing American guilt more clearly than that of an expansionist Soviet policy. This has been largely the paradigm of the leaders of the large main-line denominations. They have been challenged by the growing strength of a minority of the clergy, largely under the influence of Reinhold Niebuhr's later writing, both in its theology and its political implications.

Strikingly these theological political battles, so similar to the Western European, have been marginal in their impact on the religious consciousness of the Americans themselves. The secularizing factor in education and thought, and the modernity factor in their professional and vocational lives, have managed to co-exist with a strong upthrust of faith itself—important to them exactly because it transcends technology and economics and politics and foreign policy, giving them a sense of clarity of vision which their everyday lives would otherwise lack.

It is this element of transcendence which marks the importance of the religious revival. In the American case, as in that of the Moslem revival worldwide, it has been largely fundamentalist. Yet its scope has been broader in America, where freedom and faith are permitted to work out their dialectic in a synthesis which fuses them. It has shown great vitality among the evangelical sects. But it has gone beyond the earlier "born-again" fervor

*See Chapter X, Sec. 1, "God and the Churches."

of the 1960s and 1970s. It has not left the major mainstream denominations unaffected and has reached to Judaism as well, as note the fusion of faith and freedom in the case of the Russian-Jewish refuseniks. In fact, its strength offers an interesting vista of what may happen to religion in the Soviet Union before the century's end, if the Gorbachev initiative toward "openness" persists, and if the oppressive weight on Soviet institutions and the people themselves is lifted.

One of the forces at play in the American case has been the repudiation of the cultural nihilism and self-hatred of the 1960s and 1970s. The conviction emerged, not in the knowledge class but in the middle classes and at the base of the culture, that the long reign of secularism and modernism had resulted in a moral anarchy and a violence without end.

It was also deeply involved with the American attitudes toward death and tragedy. I noted in the 1950s* that Americans avoided acknowledging death and shrank from tragedy. This is still roughly true. But Americans learned something about both from the tragedy of the Vietnam War whose intimacy with death was too intense to be ignored and whose heroes remained too long unrecognized. The wave of national feeling that greeted the memorial to the Vietnam dead, and the inscription of their names on its wall, was evidence of new stirrings in the American consciousness.

In place of the moral relativism of past decades there was also a recognition again, as in the religiousness of the early America, of the nature of evil as well as of good. This did not mean the revival of the hell-fire imagery of America's great early theologians. Yet anyone confronting the historical fact of the Nazi regime and its Holocaust would find it hard to ignore the reality of radical evil. The debate about whether this applies equally to the Soviet regime and its Gulag will continue to rage. But there was evil enough in Soviet history, and indeed in America and the West and in human history, to support the thesis of radical evil. The potentials of nuclear destructiveness added to the dynamic of elements in the religious consciousness of the 1980s.

It would be wrong, however, to stress the political elements entering into this consciousness, just as it would be wrong to stress the political emotions clustering around constitutional issues like abortion, contraception, and school prayer.

The disestablishment of religion in America was happily beyond changing. One of its consequences in the new America was a stress on the private and personal elements of faith, in whatever theological frame, rather than on the role of religion in the public polity. People felt more secure—and more whole—in the privacy of their inner faith than in the fragmenting storms of public debate about religion. Even the contagion of the faithful who gathered in vast tabernacles to listen to the new tribe of TV revivalist

*See Ch. VIII, Sec. 7, pp. 618–620.

preachers—and the millions who followed them in their homes on TV—
didn't destroy this polarity of the private and public.

One may ask whether this resurgence of faith will continue in the phase
of postmodern man and his technology. Actually, as I have suggested, it
has less to do with modernity than with the area in human consciousness
for which the premodern and postmodern are irrelevant. It is the area
which, in a time of violence and nihilism, has evoked a return to the timeless
sacral—the sense of awe and reverence for the unresolvable but inspiriting
mysteries of life and the cosmos—the *mysterium tremendum*.

It was again an evidence of American exceptionalism that its religious
faith took this route when America's closest allies were still locked into
another, and that it persisted in using the religious sources for the renewal
of its battered values.

7. Is America in Decline?

LOOKING AT AMERICA in a long perspective, as civilization watchers, three
aspects of it must strike us. First, being organismic, it is subject to the
environments that happen to it and those that it creates. Second, it is part
of history, including its bitter and grubby realities, its imperatives and
contingencies. Third, it is mythic, living by symbols, responsive to the myths
the world attaches to it and those of its self-perception.

My use of the term "American exceptionalism"* was meant to include
at once the American's sense of the uniqueness of the American experiment,
and his conviction that it would not follow the trajectory of older civilizations
in history but would somehow carve out its own. When America was a
rising star among Western nations the emphasis was on the "two-worlds"
metaphor of a New World coming to power to shape a destiny distinct from
that of the Old. It embodied the American's sense of mission as well as of
pride. It pre-empted the ground of controversy for historical thinkers from
Frederick Turner and Charles Beard to Reinhold Niebuhr, gave the "frontier" concept an endless series of symbolic projections, and imparted a
Utopian slant to American energies.

Yet it carried with it a negative charge as well. Whenever one of the
frontiers—geographic, mental, or moral—was reached and passed, whenever America suffered a humiliating setback, there were solemn voices
proclaiming an "end" to the history of American uniqueness.

That end has not come, however volcanic some of the events since the
early 1960s have been. America remained the magnet that drew refugees
from every destroyed democracy and closed society. Whatever its own
failures it was still seen as the haven of choices, offering the freedoms of its

*See Chapter II, Sec. 2, "Is America a Civilization?"

economy, polity, and society, and the creativeness of its science and technologies.

Quite possibly, during these last decades, it is the Old World that has had to confront the end of history. Where it was once the world of dynastic monarchies it is now the world of psychologically and morally exhausted societies, largely on a Marxist and post-Marxist pattern, that have lost their energy and appeal. They are seen, along with their philosophy, as antique fortresses jutting out of a wasteland of the past. In fact their own chances of breaking out of this closure now depend largely on their success in following the new model set by America and its rivals and competitors in the Western imperium.

A more serious threat to American exceptionalism came from another direction, that of the ultimate destructive weapons which—after the H-Bomb in the early 1950s—could equate all nations, older and newer, open and closed, in the fraternity of a potentially radiated human desert.

This wrenching prospect was a watershed that moved America toward some maturity. Where it had earlier been a feisty young civilization challenging the established powers as a model of a free and egalitarian society, it now took on both a practical and symbolic role as the leader of a free-world *imperium*, extending to it the "umbrella" protection of its high technology in a common defense.

Along with an economic and social model, what America offered the imperium, on a military level, was a power base and the sinew for the exercise of deterrent power if the need should come. What the imperium offered America in turn was a way out of the end of history. With the inclusion of Alaska and Hawaii as states, America had reached its own territorial limits. Now the imperium gave it a chance, without conquest or annexation or the burden of ruling, to break out of those limits to a new geopolitical frontier.

All this had a pragmatic urgency for political elites from London and Bonn to Jerusalem to Buenos Aires to Tokyo and Seoul. The reality was a common need and a mutual dependence. Neither these peoples nor the Americans could envisage facing a formidable array of hostile forces alone. Together they had a good chance of dealing with aggression and intimidation.

What then makes the Western imperium a "myth?" It is because its impact reaches well beyond the hard power the imperium can muster. It rests on its symbolic appeal to the imagination, as well as the interests, of the world's leaders and peoples.

At its core was the idea of deterrence as the panoply of the imperium in forestalling attack and preserving a measure of safety in a destabilized world. In the strange contradictory dialectic of nuclear weapons, "peace" became an equilibrium of preventive readiness for what neither the Western nor Soviet camps needed or wanted, but what might nevertheless be some-how triggered.

The hard American thinking about weapons systems and deterrence began under Eisenhower and Kennedy with a little band of "defense in-tellectuals" (Bernard Brodie, Herman Kahn, and Albert Wohlstetter) gath-ered by the Rand Corporation as an annex to strategic policy. It was not until both camps had the H-Bomb that America and the world grasped the truth of the two-scorpions-in-a-bottle metaphor. It was a strange con-tingency of history that brought the atomic bomb and the Soviet empire into being at much the same time, and the logic of it that matched the fears and needs of each camp against the other. Out of it grew the Western imperium.

Conceivably it might have assumed the form of a territorial empire, like Russia's, with its cluster of Warsaw Pact satellites and its outer rim of compliant feudal fiefdoms. But the American experience with empire build-ing at the turn of the century was forbidding, since it violated the central two-worlds myth by assuming an Old World imperial role. It might equally have taken the form FDR aimed at, of all the Great Powers in a working alliance within a United Nations framework. But the immediate postwar experience with Stalin's Russia was too disillusioning to allow for another attempt, like the League of Nations, to measure collective heartbreak on an as yet undiscovered political Richter scale.

What actually emerged was less than empire and more than a Concert of Powers or a set of traditional alliances. Nor was it the creation of any one leader. The shaping intelligences were those of Dean Acheson and a little group of like-minded "wise men" clustered around him. Along with an interlocking group of European leaders they were (in Acheson's some-what grandiose phrase) "present at the creation"—of the Marshall Plan, the Truman Doctrine, NATO, and the will on the part of America's former major enemies—West Germany and Japan—to rebuild their democracies.

These men, whether in America or NATO (or later in Japan) were not empire builders or proconsuls. They were hard-bitten men—lawyers, busi-nessmen, soldiers, academics, career officials—who made their mark with their large view along with their tough-mindedness. Working with their Presidents, from Harry Truman on, they invested the American political elite with a deep concern for risk and security.

Over a span of forty years, they (along with the strategic elite in the Rand tradition) combined deterrence theory and the policy disciplines on a grand scale. The impressive witness to their striving was the respect accorded to deterrence despite (and because of) its perils, and to the fact of the Western imperium as a functioning organism in a fragmented and destabilized world.

At some time, in the coming decades, a more stable world structure will have to be built. Until that time the imperium, with its elements of a transnational organism, must have a bridging role. But no such organism can function without common goals and a growing structure of precedents for common action.

In that sense the imperium, constantly torn by the national interests and styles of its members, was still in the making. In an intensely competitive world its economic policies were bound to be discordant, although the interdependence of its members pushed them to practical accords. For historical reasons its defense burdens and costs were unequal. Its ruling elites came out of different political and economic cultures which often barred the path to understanding.

There were compensatory symbols—the ritual of annual economic summits of the heads of government, furnishing a public image of a working imperium. There were less frequent American-Soviet summits, of a different order, which—among other purposes—showed the American president speaking not only for his nation's interests but, as surrogate, for the imperium. The Western leaders had their own considerable stature and their own internal pressures, but by the necessity of the realities of history and the logic of the imperium the incumbent American president had to be first among equals—*primus inter pares*.

Did this mean that America had become another Rome and the Western imperium another Roman empire? In my last chapter I discussed the "America-Rome parallel" in terms both of power and decadence.* The intervening years have, if anything, accented the fault lines I pointed out in the parallel. Where Rome moved to an ever more centralized, if also feckless, empire the thrust of the Western imperium was still toward a quasi-contract which was at once political, economic, and military.

Nor were the Soviet Union and its satellites quite like the "barbarians" who infiltrated and ate away the edges of the Roman empire. The American and Russian peoples, as Tocqueville saw very early, were clearly destined to be grand opponents in the historic drama, with strong similarities as well as differences. At the time of Nikita Khruschev's reform regime in the early 1960s, and again under Mikhail Gorbachev's drive in the mid-1980s to modernize the Soviet economy and partially open the society in the Western image, there was discussion of a possible "convergence" of the two adversary systems. But the pull of the convergence was mostly one-sided, not toward the blocked societies of the East but toward the openness of the West. This was true as well of the market-driven economy of Communist China, under Deng Xiao-ping. The exceptionalism of America,

---

*See Ch. XII, Sec. 7, "The Destiny of a Civilization," pp. 927–937. See also my essay on "America Agonistes," in *Foreign Affairs*, Jan. 1974, pp. 287–300 and the criticism of it by Leighton R. Scott in a paper delivered at the International Society for the Comparative Study of Civilizations (1974), abridged in his Interfaces II, Ch. V, "Decline and Decadence in Civilizations," Appalachian State University (1979).

through some attractive force within it, had moved out into the world and achieved a measure of universalism.

In dealing with space Americans were caught between seeing it in symbolic terms, as a new dimension beyond Earth-bound effort and vision, and using it politically and technologically in the race with the Russians for military-political advantage. The Challenger disaster wrote *finis* to Tom Wolfe's "Right Stuff" mystique, while it spelled out the gap between engineers and administrators in technologies with a high political and public relations value. Americans got an education in the pathology of the governmental-industrial complex. But more would have to happen in the bitter laboratory of American experience before a clear philosophy of space and its uses could emerge.

Whether space could possibly become the habitation of peace, and in time make offensive missiles archaic, was hotly debated toward the end of the 1980s between proponents of the Strategic Defense Initiative (SDI) and those who mockingly dubbed it a too real "Star Wars." Thirty years earlier the question itself would have been seen as a surrealist fantasy. Yet the American experiment had not been built on a paradigm of limited human possibilities but on one of a new science of politics. The structure of deterrence itself, since the bomb, was made possible by a marriage of the scientific imagination and political resourcefulness.

A similar marriage applied to the SDI might well prove illusory. One thing, however, was clear. If such a breakthrough happened it would have to be based not by supplanting the deterrence balance between the two camps but by strengthening it. After the Reykjavik summit, held under the shadow of the SDI, it would have to wait for other summits and world scenarios to test.*

In an essay I wrote several years before this book was published† I saw "latter-day man" living with "an encompassing sense of doom." Still knowing the doom hangs over them Americans have lived so long with it that they no longer feel the kind of angst they did. For the European mind, however, there was a continued sense of being powerless to control their nuclear adversaries. It made the American Rome seem to some of Europe's political elites a more perilous protector than the Roman empire ever was.

It also added an edge of embitterment to Europe's feeling of cultural superiority in being the Athens to this clumsy, often arrogant, modern Rome with its blundering presidents, its overweening materialism and its high-

---

*I wrote this in the spring of 1987 when the prospect of steep future cuts in missiles in both camps seems more than a possibility. The Western imperium is bound to be affected by them, in ways still being debated.

†"The Flowering of Latter-day Man" (*American Scholar*, 1955) republished in *The American Scholar Reader*, ed. by Hiram Haydn and Betty Saunders (Atheneum, 1960).

tech gadgetry. The disconcerting fact, of course, was that America had become, in the last quarter-century, the hot crater of the sciences and disciplines in every area, and of many of the arts as well. With the help of its "golden migration" of exiles and immigrants, many from Europe itself, the new America offered the double image of Rome and Greece together.

It was another evidence of America tracing its own trajectory in history, distinct from other civilizations, making use of them as it made use of everyone and anyone, sweeping them into its capacious embrace.

Yet American thinkers mostly avoided grand civilization theory, as they avoided grand theory elsewhere in the human sciences. They tended to see the grand as grandiose, fearing that inflated ideas could become ideologies, and opting for middle-level theories in the life sciences and human sciences.*

Thus civilization theory was largely a product of the European consciousness, in the work of classicists and philosophers who were shaken by the wars and violence and crumbling dynasties of their time and turned to metahistory in search of a pattern of order. This was true of the grand theorists—Friedrich Nietzsche, Jacob Burckhardt, Oswald Spengler, and Arnold Toynbee—who all but ignored America.† Even the American historian, William McNeill, who had worked with Arnold Toynbee and whose *Rise of the West* was an answer to Spengler's *Decline of the West*, saw America in the broad frame of Western civilization. America seemed caught up in the problems and destiny, as well as the history, of the West.

Thus the essence and trajectory of America, itself a civilization—its ways of life and thought, its crises, its triumphs, its health and illnesses, its creativities—were hard to disentangle from those of its mother civilizations.

The problem was always to find a metaphor by which to compare the living, functioning realities of civilizations. Spengler's seasonal and morphological metaphors from nature, and Toynbee's from the spiritual progression, are well known. Others, like Sorokin's and Vögelin's schemas, are less known. But in one way or another all seem variations on the essential life journey, from birth through youth, maturity and middle age to decline—and death. This parallels the growing focus of the last decades, in the human sciences as in the life sciences, on the phases through which the individual organism passes with its environment and culture. The difference in studying civilizations is that it is the life history of the culture itself that is focused on—that of aggregates of individuals and their institutions, with an indeterminate ending.

---

*See Daniel Bell's review of the present book in *The New Republic*, reprinted in his *The End of Ideology* (1960, rev. 1962).

†It was also true of Pitirim Sorokin, an exile from the Soviet regime, and Eric Vögelin, an exile from Hitler's Europe, both of whom spent their later academic lives in America but were concerned with what had gone wrong in Western civilization.

My own metaphors for the civilization (as the reader may note) have become more organismic, and my stress on the symbolic and mythic has also grown. This jibes, I think, with the strong trend of the past decades in the cross-disciplinary studies that any civilization watcher must reckon with.

I take seriously the decline hypothesis, often unspoken but nevertheless present in the critical writings, that America as a civilization is in its declining—if not dying—phase.

It isn't hard, even in the 1980s, to marshal the evidence.* One need only note the persistent themes in the media and in publishers' offerings—the litany of growing crime and violence, crowded prisons, an accelerating drug culture, the breakdown of the justice system, the endangered home, the jungle atmosphere in big cities, the mounting unemployment in the underclass, the inability to control the borders, the municipal corruption, the profits made on "insider" information, the ecological crimes of omission and commission, lowered school and college standards, the extent of functional illiteracy, the decay of craft skills and of the work ethic, the litigation syndrome, the teenage pregnancies, the single-parent families, the more than residual racial hatreds and religious bigotries, the obsession with guns, the pockets of marginal vigilante groups arming for future power showdowns.

I have noted a number of these in the course of this chapter, but I bring them together here as pathologies of the civilization. I have to add the pathologies of power—the more blatant recent episodes that have produced a sense among foreigners that American leadership is erratic or blundering or both—the Bay of Pigs, the U-2 incident, Vietnam, Watergate, the Iranian arms deal—and the turmoil they have brought in their wake.

These are the pathologies of collective living. Freud called their parallels in his own day the "discontents of a civilization," noting drily that happiness is not "part of the constitution of things."† The reality principle about civilizations is that they accumulate in their life history more ailments—at least more publicly assailable ones—than the individual. If a medical model is used, as was increasingly true in the last decades, the test is which of the ailments are short-range trends, reversible by policy and leadership changes, and which become systemic, sapping the life force of the collective organism, throwing it into drastic imbalance, stifling its adaptive and recuperative powers, and ultimately dooming it to disintegration.

I would suggest that civilizations don't die of scandals and causes

---

*For my own effort to marshal it see my inaugural lecture at the University of Notre Dame, "Is American Civilization in Decline?", published by the American Studies Department, September 1982.

†See Sigmund Freud, *Civilization and its Discontents* (1920).

célèbres, of code breaking and corner cutting, of ripoffs and high jinks, or of marginal inequities. They don't even die of great tragedies, including Vietnams and Watergates. One recalls the lines in Yeats's "Crazy Jane":

> Nothing can be sole or whole
> That has not been rent.

I add Tocqueville's comment on "the self-corrective capacity" of Americans—self-corrective in the sense of learning from scarring experiences, and the increased energy that comes from the catharsis.

Civilizations are more likely to die of rigidities, of absolutisms that become divisive and tear them apart, of loss of their psychic immune and support systems, of failure of nerve in the unwillingness or inability to face collective dangers, of failures of belief (especially among the young) in the viability and promise of the whole experience. Civilizations die, above all, of the impoverishment of the imagination and will that built and sustained them.

America suffered many wounds in the decades this chapter considers. Most were self-inflicted and almost all unnecessary and reversible. The most serious was the unraveling of cohesion that came with the cross-purposes of interest groups, and with the absolutisms that worked against trade-offs. There was an erosion of the sense of limits in the imperial group egos. If the prime need of the postwar decades was for greater *access* the current prime need is for stronger *nexus*, the necessary interconnectedness between the complex of parts in any enduring organism.

It is worth going back to Finley Peter Dunne's Mr. Dooley at the turn of the century, "Don't tell me what a nation dies of. Tell me what it lives of." Latter-day America has lived of the continuing mobility of its people, the guarding of dissent amidst the efforts to achieve consensus, the understanding that no person is above the law or beneath its concern, the successive explosions of knowledge as it bursts the boundaries of the impossible, the double vision of competing and sharing, the continued self-reliance along with trust in the future, and above all the unremitting flow and use of energy.

This is again where the parallel with dying civilizations breaks down. Rome was ruled by a patrician class that had exhausted its original energies, and the "new men"—*novi homines*—never broke into the phalanx of power as America's new men and women have done, generation after generation. Thus America, whatever else it dies of, is unlikely to die of a running out either of energies or talents.

Where it is lacking is in judgment and prudence, not in vitality. Its high arts as well as its popular culture revel in obsessions and excesses. The true dangers it runs, as a collective organism, are not of a spent senility but of the turmoils of adolescence. Compared with the historic civilizations which have lasted for millenia—China, India, Russia, Europe—America is still a stripling, with almost everything ahead of it to experience and suffer, but caught—as Alexander was—between the responsibilities of power and the dreams and excesses of youth.

The forms that the sheer life force of America would take continue to be unsettling, at once to its critics and celebrators. Walt Whitman's prophecy (in his *Democratic Vistas*) was that in its continental expanse, its striking into new paths, its fragmenting, America would need a "divine literatus" (like himself) to hold it together. The fact is that the role was filled not by poets but by myths.

I spoke above of the myth of uniqueness and the two-worlds myth. Related to both, and more relevant to his everyday world, was the invincible belief of the American that his children's lot tomorrow would be better than his own yesterday. It survived the mighty testings of droughts, floods, wars, debts, depressions, as the bottom-line American myth. For what they may be worth in a documentary way, the message of the annual "happiness" poll surveys is that, whatever the course of outward events was that day, Americans continued to be expressive about their life satisfactions.

There remains the myth of the covenant, in the form of the Constitution and its Bill of Rights, and of the Supreme Court Justices as their watchful guardians. The year 1987 saw the bicentennial of that covenant and its keepers. "We live by symbols," wrote Justice Oliver Wendell Holmes. He added on another occasion that the Court was "the quiet spot at the center of a tornado"—quiet only in the sense that it deals with symbols amidst the tumult of events.

Of the entire complex of political strategies that America gave the world the Constitution as a way of ordering the society was fraught with the greatest symbolic force. In a universe of wild contingency it offered the rule of law as a fixed security point, and a set of criteria (through judicial interpretation) for adjusting to the changes.*

The political storms will continue to rage around the efforts to politicize further the extent to which Supreme Court appointments and decisions have all along been political. But what counts for the people is their sense of living under a Constitution which gives its highest appeal power to an elite that guards their rights by a zealously established and scrupulously examined tradition of interpretation. It is not values free, as Max Weber noted about all social knowledge and action. But it makes heroic efforts to replace bias by reasoned social values. Which may be why it comes as close to divine right as any democracy has allowed.

For, by the Constitution and judicial history, the nine unelected mortals have together the power that James Joyce and his hero meditated upon:

---

*For an early essay of mine on this theme see "Constitution and Court as Symbols," *Yale Law Journal* (1937) 1290–1319, reprinted in Douglas Maggs, Ed., *Selected Essays on Constitutional Law* (Chicago, 1938), also in Lerner, *Ideas for the Ice Age* (New York, 1941) 232–264.

"to forge within the smithy of my soul the uncreated conscience of the race."

Of the French social thinkers, Raymond Aron and Jean-François Revel have written with considerable sharpness of the psychological weakness of democracies that goes beyond their structural disabilities. In America a number of political thinkers, among them Samuel P. Huntington, have put a prime question to the civilization, whether it still has a center, as it once had—at least a center which (in Yeats's phrase) will "hold."

It is a question that must be addressed not only to America but to the Western imperium as a whole. We used to talk of "why democracies die," but this is no longer a situation where the structure of democracy is in question. It is one of the viability of an entire civilization complex, including the imperium.

The canvas is being lengthened by whatever painter, in the guise of history, is working at it. But whatever its fate the key to it is likely to remain the role of America and its mythmaking and myth-sustaining capacities. It may be true, as Peter Berger suggests, that capitalism as a system doesn't generate the mythopoeic power that the socialist utopias have shown. But there is more to America than capitalism: there is an entire civilization and its history and creativity. There is finally America itself as a myth, on a scale that has not thus far been rivaled in modern history.

If America's center fails to hold it will leave the world's fate to hands less gentle and more guilt-stained than the American.

Acknowledgments

OVER THE SPAN during which this book was written I owe acknowledgments to my secretaries and assistants who labored faithfully along with me: to Frances Herridge, Carol Simon, Susan Steiner Satz, Gloria Howe, Alice Lide, and especially Ruth Korzenik, to whom fell much of the burden of helping prepare the book for press; to Donald McCormick for working with me during an entire summer at Southampton while a new draft came into being; to Jules Bernstein and Martin Peretz, my students at Brandeis University, who somehow survived a stormy and protracted siege during which we prepared the "Notes for Further Reading" together. I want to add my thanks to M. Lincoln Schuster, Henry W. Simon, Justin Kaplan, and Joseph Barnes of the staff of Simon and Schuster, who went far beyond their duty as publishers in order to help lick the book into shape.

Successive drafts of the book were mimeographed and used, year after year, as basic reading for my class in American Civilization at Brandeis University. I cannot overstate how much I owe to my colleagues and my students in that course, who put it to the test of using it as a tool for understanding the complex thing we call American Civilization, and gave it their best critical and creative efforts. I want to mention especially my colleagues in the course over a number of years—Henry Steele Commager, formerly at Columbia University and now at Amherst College, Merrill Peterson, now at Princeton University, Richard Akst, Bernard Rosenberg, Jerome Himelhoch, Arno J. Mayer, John Van Doren, and (most of all) Leonard Levy and Lawrence H. Fuchs. It is their book almost as much as it is mine. I want also to express my obligation to President A. L. Sachar of Brandeis University, who supported me enthusiastically in a drastically experimental venture in teaching American Civilization by cutting across all the established boundaries between the established disciplines.

Finally, and most of all, I want to thank my colleagues in the university world, and in the professions, business, labor, and the arts, who gave generously of their time and knowledge in a task which was obviously beyond my own powers. In a work of this scope no man's scholarship, even were he to spend a lifetime on it, could adequately cover every area treated in this book. Their generosity is all the greater because of the fact that, while many of them were friends of mine, others were willing to answer a stranger's call for help in the understanding of American Civilization. I do not dare to hope that together we have eliminated all errors, both of fact and interpretation. But I was determined, so far as humanly possible, to keep them to a minimum, and I was bold enough to ask some of the best people in every field to help me to that end. Each of them read a chapter or several chapters, or sometimes portions of a chapter, that were closest to his interests, and sent me both general criticisms and detailed—sometimes line by line—corrections and suggestions. In many cases I not only accepted their ideas but even adopted some of their phrasing because I could not hope to improve on it. To a great degree this book is thus

1011

a collaborative work, and belongs not to me but to the collective of American scholarship. I hasten to add that some of my colleagues may fail to recognize or to be willing to acknowledge the book as in any way their product, and I want to make it clear that none of them is to be held responsible for my views or for my sins of omission and commission.

I want to thank especially Louis Hartz of Harvard University for reading and criticising the larger portion of the book, although I am certain that it still falls far short of his exacting standards. The others to whom I want to express my obligation and thanks are: Adam Abruzzi, Stevens Institute of Technology; Walter Adams, Michigan State University; Arthur Altmeyer, U.S. Department of Health, Education, and Welfare; Wayne Andrews, N.Y. Historical Society; Conrad Arensberg, Columbia University; Stephen Bailey, Woodrow Wilson School of Public and International Affairs, Princeton University; Read Bain, Miami University in Oxford, Ohio; Carlos Baker, Princeton University; Jacques Barzun, Columbia University; Catherine Worster Bauer, University of California in Berkeley; Daniel Bell, *Fortune;* Francis Bello, *Fortune;* Bernard Berelson, Ford Foundation; Adolf A. Berle, Jr., Columbia University; Herbert Bloch, Brooklyn College; Herbert Blumer, University of California in Berkeley; Daniel J. Boorstin, University of Chicago; Kenneth Boulding, University of Michigan; Carl Bridenbaugh, University of California in Berkeley; Robert R. R. Brooks, Williams College; Harrison Brown, California Institute of Technology; Stuart Gerry Brown, Syracuse University; Lyman Bryson, Columbia University; Gilbert Burck, *Fortune;* Roger Burlingame, New York City; and James MacGregor Burns, Williams College.

Also Richard Centers, University of California in Los Angeles; Eliot D. Chapple, E. D. Chapple Co.; Thomas I. Cook, Johns Hopkins University; Lewis Coser, Brandeis University; Avery Craven, University of Chicago; Maurice Davie, Yale University; Joseph S. Davis, Food Research Institute, Stanford University; J. Frederick Dewhurst, Twentieth Century Fund; Stanley Diamond, Brandeis University; John Dollard, Yale University; David Donald, Columbia University; Elisha P. Douglass, Princeton University; Peter F. Drucker, Montclair, N.J.; Joseph W. Eaton, Western Reserve University; Albert Ellis, New York City; Leonard W. Feather, *Down Beat;* Robert H. Ferguson, Cornell University; Donald Fleming, Brown University; Lawrence K. Frank, Belmont, Mass.; Charles Frankel, Columbia University; Lawrence Fuchs, Brandeis University; Lewis Galantiere, Free Europe Committee; Maxwell Geismar, *The Nation;* Siegfried Giedion, Harvard University; Nathan Glazer, University of California; Eric F. Goldman, Princeton University; William J. Goode, Columbia University; George W. Gray, Rockefeller Foundation; William Haber, University of Michigan; Oscar Handlin, Harvard University; Robert J. Havighurst, University of Chicago; Robert L. Heilbroner, New York City; Melville J. Herskovits, Northwestern University; Richard Hofstadter, Columbia University; Arthur N. Holcombe, Harvard University; Alfred J. Hotz, Western Reserve University; Irving Howe, Brandeis University; Cuthbert C. Hurd, International Business Machines; Stanley Hyman, Bennington College; and Howard Mumford Jones, Harvard University.

Also George Kennan, Princeton Institute for Advanced Studies; James Klee, Brandeis University; Otto Klineberg, Columbia University; Clyde Kluckhohn, Harvard University; Philip M. Klutznick, Park Forest, Illinois; Marshall Knappen, University of Michigan; Mirra Komarovsky, Barnard College; John A. Kouwenhoven, Barnard College; Oliver Larkin, Smith College; Eric Larrabee, *Harper's;* Harold D. Lasswell, Yale University; Leonard Levy, Brandeis University; Charles E. Lindblom, Yale University; Donald J. Lloyd, Wayne University; Nelson Lowry, University of Minnesota; Samuel Lubell, New York City; Robert D. Lynd, Columbia University; Fritz Machlup, Johns Hopkins University; Archibald MacLeish, Harvard University; Herbert F. Marcuse, Brandeis University; A. H. Maslow, Brandeis University; Alpheus T. Mason, Princeton University; Margaret Mead, American Museum of Natural History; Ida C. Merriam, U.S. Department of Health, Education, and Welfare; C. Wright Mills, Columbia University; B. F. Ashley Montagu, Rutgers University; Hans J. Morgenthau, University of Chicago; Samuel Eliot Morison, Harvard University; Lewis Mumford, Amenia, N.Y.; and Henry A. Murray, Harvard University.

Also Ernest Nagel, Columbia University; Theodore Newcomb, University of Michigan; James R. Newman, Washington, D.C.; Reinhold Niebuhr, Union Theological Seminary; Saul K. Padover, New School for Social Research; Talcott Parsons, Harvard University; Merrill Peterson, Princeton University; Gerard Piel, *Scientific American;* David M. Potter, Yale University; Phillip Rieff, Brandeis University; David Riesman, University of Chicago; John P. Roche, Brandeis University; Clinton Rossiter, Cornell University; George de Santillana, Massachusetts Institute of Technology; Edward N. Saveth, New York City; Meyer Schapiro, Columbia University; Arthur M. Schlesinger, Harvard University; Arthur M. Schlesinger, Jr., Harvard University; Frederick L. Schuman, Williams College; Gilbert Seldes, New York City; Jose-Luis Sert, Harvard University; Harold Shapero, Brandeis University; Edward A. Shils, University of Chicago; Edward W. Sinnott, Yale University; Henry Nash Smith, University of California in Berkeley; Herman Somers, Haverford College; Pitirim Sorokin, Harvard University; George Soule, Bennington College; Ralph Spielman, University of Kentucky; Mark Starr, International Ladies Garment Workers Union; Marshall Stearns, Institute of Jazz Studies; George Stewart, University of California in Berkeley; Cushing Strout, Yale University; Adolph Sturmthal, Roosevelt University; and G. E. Swanson, University of Michigan.

Also George Terborgh, Machinery and Allied Products Institute; Lionel Trilling, Columbia University; Christopher Tunnard, Yale University; Harry R. Warfel, University of Florida; W. Lloyd Warner, University of Chicago; Walter Prescott Webb, University of Texas; Rush Welter, Bennington College; William Wheaton, University of Pennsylvania; Leslie A. White, University of Michigan; William Foote Whyte, Cornell University; William H. Whyte, Jr., *Fortune;* Mitchell Wilson, New York City; Carl Wittke, Western Reserve University; C. Vann Woodward, Johns Hopkins University; and Dennis Wrong, University of Toronto.

Finally, I want to say how much I owe to my wife, Edna Albers Lerner, who retained her belief in what must have seemed at times a monstrously unreal venture and discussed with me every major phase of it and every draft.

June 1957   MAX LERNER
New York City

Notes for Further Reading

(These notes are arranged so as to accompany each chapter and section of the text. They give the books and articles from which I have drawn and are meant as a guide to the interested reader who may wish to pursue some particular theme further. To avoid cluttering footnotes I have also indicated here the sources of particular references in the text. The date and place of publication of each book or article referred to are given only with the first reference in the notes for each chapter. Later references give author and title only.)

Chapter I: Heritage

SEC. 1—*The Sense of the Past:* The evocation of the American past draws on many sources, most of them in the standard American histories. I have a special debt to Henry Beston, *American Memory* (New York, 1937).

SEC. 2—*Sources of the Heritage:* For the ethnic origins of America, in addition to the chapter cited in the text from De Tocqueville, see Oscar Handlin, *Race and Nationality in American Life* (Boston, 1957). For the estimate of the antiquity of Indian life in America, see recent symposia held under the Wenner-Gren Foundation; also Kenneth MacGowan, *Early Man in the New World* (New York, 1950), and Frank C. Hibben, *Treasure in the Dust* (New York, 1950). For the Indian culture as a whole, see John Collier, *The Indians of the Americas* (New York, 1948), and D'Arcy McNickle, *They Came Here First* (Philadelphia, 1949); for a history of the Hopi, see *Culture in Crisis* by Laura Thompson (New York, 1950). Of the numerous valuable volumes by Paul Radin, see particularly *The Story of the American Indian* (New York, 1927), *The Road of Life and Death, A Ritual Drama of the American Indians* (New York, 1945), and *The World of Primitive Man* (New York, 1953), which draws heavily on the American Indian experience. For the intellectual history of the image of the Indian in the American mind, see Roy H. Pearce, *The Savages of America: A Study of the Indian and the Idea of Civilization* (Baltimore, 1953), and the anthology by Richard M. Dorson, *America Begins* (New York, 1950). For the painters of Indian life, see Bernard De Voto, *Across the Wide Missouri* (Boston, 1947); Lloyd Haberly, *Pursuit of the Horizon* (New York, 1948), on George Catlin; and *The West of Alfred Jacob Miller,* edited by Marvin C. Ross (Norman, Oklahoma, 1952). Parkman's *Oregon Trail,* a classic of American history, will be found in several editions; even more valuable are *The Journals of Francis Parkman,* ed., Mason Wade, 2 vols. (New York, 1947), from which the Parkman quotation in my text is taken. See also Harvey C. Wish, *Society and Thought in America,* 2 vols. (New York, 1950-52), Vol. I, Ch. 12, "The West of Jackson and Francis Parkman." The quote from Daniel Webster will be found in *American Heritage* (VII, No. 3), April 1957, p. 3—an issue that contains also a magnificent set of reproductions from George Catlin.

For the Negroes in the American heritage, see J. Saunders Redding, *They Came in Chains: Americans from Africa* (Philadelphia, 1950); Frank Tannenbaum, *Slave and Citizen: The Negro in America* (New York, 1947); E. Franklin Frazier, *The Negro in the U.S.* (rev. ed., New York, 1957), the most comprehensive study; Eric Williams, *Capitalism and Slavery* (Chapel Hill, 1944), and John Howard Lawson, *The Hidden Heritage* (New York, 1950), both of them written from a Marxist standpoint. For slavery, see Kenneth M. Stampp, *The Peculiar Institution* (New York, 1956), and for the history of the Negro, see John Hope Franklin, *From Slavery to Freedom* (New York, 1947). For the roots of the Civil War, see Avery Craven, *The Coming of the Civil War* (2nd ed., Chicago, 1957), and for its aftermath C. Vann Woodward's researches especially *Reunion and Reaction* (Boston, 1951; new ed., New York, 1956); *Origins of the New South* (Baton Rouge, 1951).

and *The Strange Career of Jim Crow* (New York, 1955; new ed., New York, 1957). For studies in the Negro cultural tradition, see Margaret J. Butcher, *The Negro in American Culture* (New York, 1956), based on the work of Alain Locke. For the Negro religious experience in America, there is a suggestive passage in Arnold Toynbee, *A Study of History* (London, 1934), Vol. II, pp. 218-220. For the Negro tradition in music, see Marshall Stearns, *The Story of Jazz* (New York, 1956), especially Part 3. For other reading on the Negro in American society, see below the references to Ch. VII, Sec. 6 (on the Negro's place in American society), Ch. X, Sec. 1 (on his role in the churches), and Ch. XI, Sec. 7 (on his contribution to American jazz).

For the British influence, see Gerald W. Johnson, *Our English Heritage* (New York, 1949). For the Puritans and their impact on the tradition, see Perry Miller and Thomas H. Johnson, *The Puritans* (New York, 1938) for its excellent "General Introduction"; also Miller's *Orthodoxy in Massachusetts* (Cambridge, 1933); his *New England Mind: The Seventeenth Century* (New York, 1939), and *New England Mind: From Colony to Province* (Cambridge, 1953), and his *Jonathan Edwards* (New York, 1949). See also T. J. Wertenbaker, *The Puritan Oligarchy* (New York, 1947).

For the polyglot heritage, see Oscar Handlin, *Race and Nationality in American Life*. For other references, see Ch. III, Sec. 2, below, on the immigrant experience, and Ch. VII, Sec. 5 on the minority situation.

sec. 3—*The Slaying of the European Father:* For the American attitudes toward the Old World, see Geoffrey Gorer, *The American People* (New York, 1948), Ch. 1, "Europe and the Rejected Father." The quotation from Emerson is from the closing paragraph of *English Traits* (rev. ed., Boston, 1881), p. 236. The comment on the Declaration by Julian Boyd will be found in his book *The Declaration of Independence* (Princeton, 1945). For the references to Frazer, see *The Golden Bough: A Study in Magic and Religion* (1-vol. ed., New York, 1922), especially Ch. 24, "The Killing of the Divine King." The quotation from Santayana is from his *Character and Opinion in the United States* (Anchor Books ed., 1956). On the American expatriates in Europe, I have found several books suggestive: Malcolm Cowley's *Exile's Return* (new ed., New York, 1954); Matthew Josephson, *Portrait of the Artist As an American* (New York, 1930); and Fred-

erick J. Hoffman, *The Twenties: American Writing in the Postwar Decade* (New York, 1955), especially Chs. 1-3 and 5.

sec. 4—*Why Was America a Success?* On the attitude of Americans toward their own role in history I have drawn upon Edward Saveth's excellent anthology, *Understanding the American Past* (Boston, 1954); Michael Kraus, *A History of American History* (New York, 1937); and Charles and Mary Beard, *The American Spirit: A Study of the Idea of Civilization in the United States* (New York, 1942). There are some good insights into the historians of the Middle Period in A. M. Schlesinger, Jr., *The Age of Jackson* (Boston, 1945). The quote from DeWitt Clinton will be found in Beard, *op. cit.,* p. 214. On the "American mission," see Clinton Rossiter's article with that title in *American Scholar* (Jan. 1951) as well as "The Shaping of the American Tradition," *William and Mary Quarterly* (Oct. 1954). The quotation from Rush Welter is from correspondence with the author; see also Rush Welter, "The Idea of Progress in America," *Journal of the History of Ideas* (June 1955). For the cult of the American Constitution, see Schechter, "The Early History of the Tradition of the Constitution," *American Political Science Review* (1915), Vol. IX, p. 707; Thurman Arnold, *The Symbols of Government* (New Haven, 1935); Ralph H. Gabriel, *The Course of American Democratic Thought* (rev. ed., New York, 1956); E. S. Corwin, "The Constitution As Instrument and As Symbol," *American Political Science Review* (Dec. 1936); and my *Ideas for the Ice Age* (New York, 1941), Part 4, Sec. 2, "Constitution and Court as Symbols," pp. 232-264. For capitalism as an explanation of American greatness, see Louis M. Hacker, *The Triumph of American Capitalism* (New York, 1940), and also Hacker's essay, "The Anti-Capitalist Bias of American Historians," in *Capitalism and the Historians,* ed., F. A. Hayek (Chicago, 1954). For a different viewpoint, see Charles and Mary Beard, *The Rise of American Civilization,* 2 vols. (New York, 1927), and *America in Mid-Passage* (New York, 1939). For criticism of Beard's historical views, see the essays by Richard Hofstadter, Howard K. Beale, Merle Curti and myself in the collective volume *Charles A. Beard: An Appraisal* (Lexington, Ky., 1954), and two essays of mine on his historical theory: "Charles Beard's Stormy Voyage," *New Republic* (Oct. 25, 1948), and "Beard: Civilization and the Devils," *ibid.* (Nov. 1, 1948). For Veblen on American capitalism, see his *Theory of Business Enterprise*

(New York, 1904) and *Absentee Owner-ship and Business Enterprise in Recent Times* (New York, 1923); also Joseph Dorfman, "The Satire of Thorstein Veblen's *Theory of the Leisure Class*," *Political Science Quarterly* (1932), Vol. XLVII, pp. 363-409, and my essays on Veblen in *Ideas Are Weapons* (New York, 1939), pp. 117-141. See also Thurman Arnold, *The Folklore of Capitalism* (New Haven, 1937), and on Arnold, see my essay in *Ideas Are Weapons*, "The Shadow World of Thurman Arnold," pp. 198-217, and Richard Hofstadter, *The Age of Reform* (New York, 1955), "The New Opportunism," pp. 314-326. For the critique of capitalism in the whole era of Populism and social reform, see Eric F. Goldman, *Rendezvous with Destiny* (New York, 1952), and Hofstadter, *The Age of Reform*. The references in the text to Parrington are to his *Main Currents in American Thought* (3 vols., new ed., New York, 1956). The reference to Matthew Josephson is to his *Robber Barons* (New York, 1934). For Charles Beard's comments on Sumner and Turner, see his *The American Spirit*, p. 364. His quote on the theory of economic determinism is from his *Economic Interpretations of the Constitution* (New York, 1913; new ed., 1935); for criticism of this, see my *Ideas Are Weapons*, pp. 152-169; also the study by Robert E. Brown, *Charles Beard and the Constitution* (Princeton, 1956).

SEC. 5—*American History As Extended Genesis*: On Frederick Jackson Turner and the frontier theory, the classic essay is "The Significance of the Frontier in American History," written by Turner for the American Historical Association in 1893, and republished in his volume of essays, *The Frontier in American History* (New York, 1920). For a collection of critical essays on Turner's thesis, see the Amherst pamphlet series, *The Turner Thesis Concerning the Role of the Frontier in American History* (Amherst, 1949), including essays by Avery Craven, Louis M. Hacker, Carlton J. H. Hayes, George W. Pierson, Fred A. Shannon, and Benjamin F. Wright, Jr.

A key work on the whole problem, and in itself a major extension of the theory, is Walter Prescott Webb, *The Great Frontier* (Boston, 1952). Another fresh approach will be found in Henry Nash Smith, *Virgin Land: The American West As Symbol and Myth* (Cambridge, 1950). For the history of the westward movements, see Ray Allen Billington, *Westward Expansion* (New York, 1949), Bernard De Voto, *Across the Wide Missouri* and *The Year of Decision* (Boston, 1943).

For the role of Jacksonian democracy in relation to the extended American genesis, see Arthur M. Schlesinger, Jr., *The Age of Jackson*, and for what I have called the "moving democratic idea," see Parrington, *Main Currents in American Thought*, especially Vol. II, and also F. O. Matthiessen, *The American Renaissance* (New York, 1941). The reference in the text to Potter is to David M. Potter, *People of Plenty* (Chicago, 1954).

SEC. 6—*Tradition and the Frame of Power*, and SEC. 7—*American Dynamism*: On the American tradition, see Richard Hofstadter, *The American Political Tradition* (New York, 1948), and Louis Hartz, *The Liberal Tradition in America* (New York, 1955), the first emphasizing the conservative aspects and the second the "liberal" aspects (using the term in its classical Lockean sense) of the main American tradition. The comment on George Fitzhugh in the text is from Hartz's discussion (Ch. 6). See also Russell Kirk, *The Conservative Mind: From Burke to Santayana* (Chicago, 1955), which includes a discussion of the early American Federalists, the Southern conservatives, the Adamses, Irving Babbitt, Paul Elmer More, and Santayana; and see his book of essays, *A Program for Conservatives* (Chicago, 1954). A delightful little book—half commentary, half documents—is Peter Viereck, *Conservatism: From John Adams to Churchill* (Princeton, 1956), which should be read along with the same author's *Conservatism Revisited* (New York, 1949) and *The Unadjusted Man* (Boston, 1956). Clinton Rossiter's work in this vein will be found in his *Seedtime of the Republic* (New York, 1953) and his *Conservatism in America* (New York, 1955). In a somewhat similar vein, see also Daniel Boorstin, *The Genius of American Politics* (Chicago, 1953). See also Richard N. Current, *Daniel Webster and the Rise of American Conservatism* (Boston, 1955). For a critique of the extreme Right, see the valuable collection of essays, *The New American Right*, ed., Daniel Bell (New York, 1955), including essays by Bell, Hofstadter, Riesman, Glazer, Viereck, Parsons and Lipset. The quote from Morison in Sec. 6 is from his Presidential Address in 1950 to the American Historical Association. The quote from Walt Whitman in Sec. 7 will be found in the anthology edited by Louis Untermeyer, *Walt Whitman: Poetry and Prose* (New York, 1949), and is also reprinted as part of the exchange with Emerson in Edmund Wilson, ed., *The Shock of Recognition* (New York, 1943). The reference to Niebuhr's work in Sec. 7 is to Reinhold Niebuhr, *The*

Nature and Destiny of Man (1-vol. ed., New York, 1953) and to his book of essays on contemporary themes, *Christian Realism and Political Problems* (New York, 1953). The reference to Lippmann is to his *Essays in the Public Philosophy* (Boston, 1955). The quote in Sec. 7 from F. Scott Fitzgerald will be found in his novel, *The Great Gatsby* (New York, 1925).

Chapter II: The Idea of American Civilization

SEC. 1—*Figure in the Carpet*, and SEC. 2—*Is America a Civilization?* I have drawn heavily here on Beard, *The American Spirit* (New York, 1942), where the quote from Mark Twain will be found, pp. 50-51. For the American civilization pattern as De Tocqueville saw it more than a century ago, see his *Democracy in America* (2 vols., new ed., by Phillips Bradley, New York, 1954). For the culture concept as developed by the anthropologists, see E. B. Tylor, *Primitive Culture* (London, 1881) Ch. 1 from which the quote in the text is taken. See also Ruth Benedict, *Patterns of Culture* (New York, 1934); Alexander Goldenweiser, *Anthropology: An Introduction to Primitive Culture* (New York, 1937); Ralph Linton, *The Tree of Culture* (New York, 1955), with a valuable selection of essays on "Theoretical Approaches" in Part 1, pp. 29-94; see also the most recent formulation of Margaret Mead's theoretical approach to the changing nature of culture in her *New Lives for Old: Cultural Transformation—Manus, 1928-1953* (New York, 1956); see also Leslie A. White, *The Science of Culture* (New York, 1949), especially Ch. 5. The quote in Sec. 2 from Kluckhohn and Kelly is from their dialogue on "The Concept of Culture" in *The Science of Man* (New York, 1950), edited by Ralph Linton.

SEC. 3—*Archetypal Man of the West:* The quote from Robert Payne is from his *Report on America* (New York, 1949), p. 42. The quote from Wyndham Lewis is from his *America and Cosmic Man* (London, 1948).

SEC. 4—*American Exceptionalism:* For the context of American life, see Louis M. Hacker, *The Shaping of the American Tradition* (New York, 1947) and Louis Hartz, *The Liberal Tradition in America* (New York, 1955); also Ralph Barton Perry, *Characteristically American* (Boston, 1949).

My list of outstanding books on various unique aspects of the American experience refers to the following: De Tocqueville, *Democracy in America* (2 vols., New York, 1954); Charles Dickens, *American Notes* (London, 1842)—for its setting in Dickens' life and thought, see Edgar Johnson, *Charles Dickens: His Tragedy and Triumph* (2 vols., New York, 1952), Vol. I, pp. 357-448; Lord James Bryce, *The American Commonwealth* (New York, 1888; rev. ed., 1891); see also Bryce's *"American Commonwealth": 50th Anniversary*, edited by Robert C. Brooks (New York, 1939); Walt Whitman, *Democratic Vistas* (New York, 1871) reprinted in Untermeyer, *Walt Whitman: Poetry and Prose* (New York, 1949); Henry and Brooks Adams, *The Degradation of the Democratic Dogma* (New York, 1919); see also Daniel Aaron, *Men of Good Hope* (New York, 1951), Ch. 1; Thorstein Veblen, *Absentee Ownership and Business Enterprise in Recent Times* (New York, 1923); Herbert Croly, *The Promise of American Life* (New York, 1909); see Eric Goldman, *Rendezvous with Destiny* (New York, 1952), Ch. 9, pp. 188-207; Waldo Frank, *The Rediscovery of America* (New York, 1929); D. H. Lawrence, *Studies in Classical American Literature* (New York, 1923); H. L. Mencken, *The American Language* (4th rev. ed., New York, 1955); André Siegfried, *America Comes of Age* (New York, 1927)—see also his more recent formulation, *America at Mid-Century* (New York, 1955); Robert and Helen Lynd, *Middletown: A Study in Contemporary Culture* (New York, 1929) and *Middletown in Transition: A Study in Cultural Conflicts* (New York, 1937); Margaret Mead, *And Keep Your Powder Dry: An Anthropologist Looks at America* (New York, 1942), and *Male and Female: A Study of the Sexes in a Changing World* (New York, 1949), especially Part 4, "The Two Sexes in Contemporary America"; D. W. Brogan, *The American Character* (New York, 1944) and *Politics in America* (New York, 1954); Geoffrey Gorer, *The American People* (New York, 1948); Wyndham Lewis, *America and Cosmic Man;* David Riesman, *The Lonely Crowd: A Study of the Changing American Character* (New Haven, 1950; rev. ed., New York, 1953), also his *Faces in the Crowd: Individual Studies in Character and Politics* (New Haven, 1951), and his *Individualism Reconsidered* (Glencoe, 1954); David M. Potter, *People of Plenty* (Chicago, 1954); Daniel J. Boorstin, *The Genius of American Politics* (Chicago, 1953); Louis Hartz, *The Liberal Tradition in America.*

SEC. 5—*National Character and the Civilization Pattern*, and SEC. 6—*Single Key—Or Polar Pattern?* On the pattern of American civilization and national character, in addition to the books listed in the footnote to Sec. 5, see Riesman, *The Lonely Crowd;* Potter, *People of Plenty;* Lee Coleman, "What Is American: A Study of Alleged American Traits," *Social Forces* (May 1941), Vol. XIX, pp. 492-9; and H. S. Commager, *The American Mind* (New Haven, 1950). For the new approach to national character by anthropologists and psychiatrists, see as an example Ruth Benedict's on Japan, *The Chrysanthemum and the Sword* (New York, 1946). For the philosophical approach, in addition to the books by Northrop and Morris cited in the text, see Walter A. Kaufmann's study, *Nietzsche* (Princeton, 1950).

Chapter III: People and Place

SEC. 1—*Is There an American Stock?* The definition which I give to "stock" is my own, but for the discussion as a whole I have been greatly helped by Otto Klineberg, *Race Differences* (New York, 1935), although I do not make him in any sense responsible for my views. Every student of the ethnic composition of America is indebted to the pioneer book by Boas cited in the text, as also to Boas' other works, of which I have found his *Anthropology of Modern Life* (New York, 1928) most useful; see also Ch. 2, "Man the Biological Organism," in Melville J. Herskovits, *Franz Boas* (New York, 1953) and Ruth Benedict, *Race: Science and Politics* (New York, 1943) and Oscar Handlin, *Race and Nationality in American Life* (Boston, 1957), especially Ch. 8, "What Happened to Race?" I have also profited from William C. Boyd, *Genetics and the Races of Man* (Boston, 1951) and Ashley Montagu, *Statement on Race* (New York, 1951) giving the results of the UNESCO conferences on race; also Arthur M. Schlesinger's essay, "The Role of the Immigrant" in his *Paths to the Present* (New York, 1949) as well as the anthology *This Is Race,* edited by Earl W. Count, (New York, 1950). The quotation from Earnest Hooton is from a newspaper interview shortly before his death.

SEC. 2—*The Immigrant Experience:* For the immigrant experience, Handlin's *The Uprooted* (Boston, 1951) has made a permanent niche for itself in the history of American immigration, alongside Marcus Lee Hansen's *The Immigrant in American History* (Cambridge, 1940) and *The Atlantic Migration, 1860-1907* (Cambridge, 1940).

Hansen's essay on "The Third Generation in America," first delivered as a paper to The Augustana Historical Society in 1938, is reprinted in Edward N. Saveth, *Understanding the American Past* (Boston, 1954) and in *Commentary* (Nov. 1952) pp. 492-500. The quotes from De Crèvecoeur are from *Letters of an American Farmer* (London, 1782); the quote from Bryce is from *The American Commonwealth* (New York, 1888). For the reception of Israel Zangwill's book, *The Melting Pot* (New York, 1923), see Eric Goldman, *Rendezvous with Destiny* (New York, 1952), pp. 78-79. Goldman's whole Ch. 4, "A Least Common Denominator," is good on the intellectual history of the immigrant integration controversy On the same theme, see Handlin, *Race and Nationality in American Life,* especially Chs. 4-6; Barbara M. Solomon, *Ancestors and Immigrants* (Cambridge, 1956), and John Higham, *Strangers in the Land* (New Brunswick, 1955). For several good essays and bibliographies on the immigrant and his experience in America, see *Foreign Influences in American Life,* edited by David F. Bowers (Princeton, 1944). For the idea of "integration" as opposed to the "assimilation" of American foreign-born, the seminal studies are Horace M. Kallen, *Culture and Democracy in the U.S.* (New York, 1924) and Randolph Bourne's essay "Transnational America" in *A History of a Literary Radical and Other Essays* (New York, 1920); see also Nathan Glazer, "The Integration of American Immigrants," in *Law and Contemporary Problems* (Spring, 1956), pp. 256-269.

SEC. 3—*People in Motion:* On American mobility and the sense of place, Ch. 3, "We Are All Third Generation," in Margaret Mead, *And Keep Your Powder Dry* (New York, 1942), is suggestive. The reference to Stephen Benét is to his unfinished long poem, *Western Star* (New York, 1943). The reference to De Tocqueville's chapter is to *Democracy in America* (2 vols., Vintage ed.), Vol. II, Ch. 13, "Why the Americans Are So Restless in the Midst of Their Prosperity," pp. 44-147. On the migration to the western frontier, see the readings cited in the Notes to Ch. I, Sec. 5, especially Ray Allen Billington, *Westward Expansion* (New York, 1949): also Stewart H. Holbrook, *The Yankee Exodus: An Account of the Migration from New England* (New York, 1950). For the Ladies' Clubs and Literary Societies that formed in the wake of the westward migrations, see Chs. 5 and 6 of Louis B. Wright, *Culture on the Moving Frontier* (Bloomington, 1955); for the earlier westward movements that led to the finding and settling of the American continent, see Bernard De Voto, *The Course of Em-*

pire (Boston, 1952), along with his books covering the later period, *Across the Wide Missouri* (Boston, 1947), and *The Year of Decision* (Boston, 1943); see also the rousing history by an American ex-President, Theodore Roosevelt, *The Winning of the West* (3 vols., New York, 1894-1896). For the California gold rush, see the books by Oscar Lewis, especially *Silver Kings* (New York, 1947) and *Sea Routes to the Goldfields* (New York, 1949), and also *Gold Rush Album*, edited by Joseph Henry Jackson (New York, 1949). Salty volumes on the settlement of the West are J. Frank Dobie, *The Voice of the Coyote* (New York, 1949), and *The Mustangs* (Boston, 1952). For the American road system, see a series of volumes called *The American Trail Series*, published by Bobbs-Merrill & Co. (Indianapolis), especially Philip D. Jordon, *The National Road* (Indianapolis, 1948), and George R. Stewart, *U.S. 40* (Boston, 1953), a skillful synthesis of the geology, sociology, history, and literature connected with the origins of a single highway. On the automobile revolution, see David L. Cohn, *Combustion on Wheels: An Informal History of the Automobile Age* (Boston, 1944) and Frederick Lewis Allen, *The Big Change: America Transforms Itself 1900-1950* (New York, 1952), Ch. 8, "The Automobile Revolution." For opportunity migrations, see Carter Goodrich, ed., *Migration and Economic Opportunity* (Philadelphia, 1936).

SEC. 4—*Natural Resources: The American Earth:* For the American natural environment, the classic description of the look of the continent when the white settlers first came will be found in De Tocqueville, *Democracy in America*, Vol. I, Ch. 1, "Exterior Form of North America." In my own portrait of the continent I have drawn heavily on Henry Beston, *American Memory* (New York, 1937), John Bakeless, *The Eyes of Discovery* (Philadelphia, 1950), Walter Prescott Webb, *The Great Plains* (Boston, 1931), and Henry Nash Smith, *Virgin Land* (Cambridge, 1950). For the study of the relations of environmental and human patterns, see C. W. Thornthwaite in Carter Goodrich, ed., *Migration and Economic Opportunity*, pp. 202-250, and "The Living Landscape," a chapter in Paul B. Sears, *Charles Darwin* (New York, 1950); also James C. Malin, *The Grassland of North America* (Lawrence, Kansas, 1947), and Russell Lord, *Forever the Land* (New York, 1950). For waterways, see the *Rivers of America* series of volumes, published by Rinehart, with an essay by Constance Lindsay Skinner on "Rivers and Ameri-

can Folk," and especially Paul Horgan, *The Rio Grande* (New York, 1956). My reference in the text to recent studies of the Russian character emphasizing the landscape is to Sir John Maynard, *The Russian Peasant and Other Studies* (London, 1942), and Edward Crankshaw, *Russia and the Russians* (New York, 1948); for the British, see Jacquetta Hawkes, *The Land* (London, 1951); for a similar emphasis on landscape and climate in a study of American national character, see Graham Hutton, *Midwest at Noon* (Chicago, 1946). For a philosophical approach, see Alfred North Whitehead, *The Concept of Nature* (Cambridge, 1920). For American national resources in the setting of world resources, see Harrison Brown, *The Challenge of Man's Future* (New York, 1954), and Harrison Brown, James Bonner, and John Weir, *The Next Hundred Years* (New York, 1957). I have also found useful Bruce Bliven, *Preview for Tomorrow* (New York, 1953). The quote in the text from Ritchie Calder is from the *N.Y. Times Magazine* (July 9, 1950), pp. 15-17, 34-35. On erosion the best book is Paul B. Sears, *Deserts on the March* (Norman, Oklahoma, 1935). On the cattle-grazing lands in the public domain, see Wallace Stegner, "One-Fourth of a Nation—Public Lands and Itching Fingers," *Reporter* (May 12, 1953), pp. 25-29. On America's water resources, see Bernard Frank and Antony Netboy, *Water, Land, and People* (New York, 1950), and Albert N. Williams, *The Water and the Power* (New York, 1951); and on the politics of water resources, Remy Nadeau, *The Water Seekers* (New York, 1950). On hydro-electric development, the best source material is the massive *Report of the Water Resources Policy Commission*, 3 vols., (Washington, 1950-51), whose guiding spirit was Morris Llewellyn Cooke. On American forests, see Donald Culross Peattie, *A Natural History of Trees* (New York, 1950); Richard G. Lillard, *The Great Forest* (New York, 1947), and Rutherford Platt, *American Trees: A Book of Discovery* (New York, 1952); and on forest policy, see Luther H. Gulick, *American Forest Policy* (New York, 1951). For an over-all view of trends in the use of American resources and their exhaustion, see *Resources for Freedom*, the Report of the Paley Commission (the President's Materials Policy Commission, 5 vols., Washington, 1952), also the Proceedings of the *Mid-Century Conference on Resources for the Future*, Dec. 2-4, 1954 (Washington, 1954). An always valuable survey is made by the Twentieth Century Fund—*America's Needs and Re-*

sources, by J. Frederick Dewhurst and Associates (most recent ed., New York, 1956). In *Our Plundered Planet* (Boston, 1948) Fairfield Osborn gives a drastic picture of the destruction of soil and resources around the world, putting the American story in this larger setting. For a symposium on recent trends in American natural resources, see *National Policy for Economic Welfare at Home and Abroad,* edited by Robert Lekachman (New York, 1955). For regional planning as an approach to the problem of the rational use of resources, see David E. Lilienthal, *TVA: Democracy on the March* (New York, 1944; rev. ed. New York, 1953), and *Iowa Law Review* (Jan. 1947) Vol. XXXII, No. 2, devoted to river valley planning, especially the foreword by M. S. McDougal; and Alvin H. Hansen and Harvey S. Perloff, *Regional Resource Development,* No. 16 of the "Planning Pamphlets" (Oct. 1942) of the National Planning Association. For the Great Estate of the American natural environment, and an attitude of reverence for it, see Aldo Leopold, *A Sand County Almanac* (New York, 1949); also the files of *The Land,* edited by Russell Lord.

SEC. 5—*Human Resources: Population Profile:* On the American population and its trends, there is a good over-all survey, Paul H. Landis and Paul K. Hatt, *Population Problems* (New York, 1954). I have profited from a small handbook by Dennis H. Wrong, *Population* (New York, 1956); Chs. 20-21 in Kingsley Davis, *Human Society* (New York, 1949), and A. H. Hawley, *Human Ecology* (New York, 1950), pp. 104-174. The quote from De Tocqueville is from Vol. I, Ch. 18 of his *Democracy in America,* pp. 451-452. For an interesting projection of population trends into the future, see Morris L. Ernst, *Utopia, 1976* (New York, 1955), Ch. 4, "Our Population." For the doctrinal differences about American population trends, see the striking critique of the population theorists in articles by Joseph S. Davis, "Fifty Million More Americans," *Foreign Affairs* (April 1950), Vol. XXVIII, pp. 412-26; "Our Changed Population Outlook and Its Economic Significance," *American Economic Review* (1952), Vol. XLII, pp. 304-25; "The Population Upsurge and the American Economy, 1945-1980," *Journal of Political Economy* (1953), Vol. LXI, pp. 369-388, and "Economic Potentials of the U.S.," a paper read at the Columbia Bicentennial, in *National Policy for Economic Welfare at Home and Abroad,* with discussion, pp. 104-174; see also William Petersen, "The Scientific Basis of Our Immigration Pol-

icy," in *Commentary* (July 1955), pp. 77-86; for an opposing view questioning whether the current population trends are as basic as often assumed, see the technical monograph by Warren S. Thompson, "Problems of Population," in Bruce Bliven, *Twentieth Century Unlimited* (Philadelphia, 1950); also Kingsley Davis, "Ideal Size for Our Population," in *N. Y. Times Magazine* (May 1, 1955), pp. 12, 32-37. For an analysis of the human resources of America, see *Scientific American* (Sept. 1951), for a full issue devoted to that theme, especially the article on "Population" by Frank W. Notestein. See also Robert C. Cook, *Human Fertility: The Modern Dilemma* (New York, 1951). French commentators are always interested in demography; it is therefore interesting to compare the chapters on population in André Siegfried's two studies of America, separated by over a quarter-century: *America Comes of Age* (New York, 1927), and *America at Mid-Century* (New York, 1955). For a brief popular summary of changes in the American population profile, see F. L. Allen, *The Big Change,* Ch. 14, "More Americans, Living Longer." For a more somber view of these trends, see Harrison Brown, *The Challenge of Man's Future* and Paul K. Hatt, ed., *World Population and Future Resources* (New York, 1952). For an interesting theoretical approach, see Talcott Parsons, "Age and Sex in the Social Structure of the U.S.," *American Sociology Review* (1942), Vol. VII, pp. 604-616.

SEC. 6—*The Sinews of Welfare: Health, Food, Dwelling, Security:* On the criteria of American welfare, see the over-all survey in the Columbia Bicentennial volume, *National Policies for Education, Health, and Social Services,* ed. James E. Russell (New York, 1955). For the relation of diseases to a particular social structure and national character, see Henry E. Sigerist, *Civilization and Disease* (Ithaca, 1943), and for the same theme in American history, Richard H. Shryock, *Development of Modern Medicine* (rev. ed., New York, 1947), Chs. 5 and 12. Shryock also has an excellent essay exploring these relations in the case of a single disease: "The Yellow Fever Epidemics, 1793-1905," in Daniel Aaron, ed. *America in Crisis* (New York, 1952), pp. 50-70. See also John Powell, *Bring Out Your Dead* (Philadelphia, 1950). The quote from Sir William Osler will be found in Donald Fleming, *William H. Welch and the Rise of Modern Medicine* (Boston, 1954), a first-rate biographical study in the intellectual history of American medicine and public health. See also the American chapters in Paul de Kruif, *The Microbe Hunters* (New York, 1926). The quote from Laurence J. Henderson will be found in the article on "Doctors" by Alan Gregg which forms part of the number devoted to American human resources in the *Scientific American* (Sept. 1951), pp. 79-84. My figures on American diseases are mainly drawn from "Facts on the Major Killing and Crippling Diseases in the U.S. Today" compiled by the National Health Education Committee (New York, 1955); also from the Columbia Bicentennial volume; and from the 1955 *Annual Report* of Dean Willard C. Rappleye of the Columbia University College of Physicians and Surgeons, and from "Something Can Be Done About Chronic Illness," Public Affairs Pamphlet No. 176 (New York, 1951). On the Salk vaccine experience, see Len Root, "The Polio Gamble," *Reporter* (July 14, 1955), pp. 20-28, and Robert Crichton, "How Canada Handled the Salk Vaccine," *ibid*, pp. 28-32. For the new drugs currently being used in psychotherapy, see William Sargant, *Battle for the Mind* (New York, 1957), Ch. 3. For some perceptive insights into the intellectual history of medical science, see Alfred Cohn, *Minerva's Progress* (New York, 1946). For a competent layman's view of medical trends, see Bruce Bliven, *Preview for Tomorrow*, Ch. 5, "Longer and Healthier Lives." An interesting projection into the future of current trends in medicine and public health will be found in Morris L. Ernst, *Utopia, 1976*, Ch. 9, "The Healthy Body of 1976."

On social security, see the Columbia Bicentennial volume for current trends; see also the annual Proceedings of the National Conference of Social Work, published by the Columbia University Press, especially the 1955 and 1956 volumes. For the intellectual history of the social legislation which led to the Social Security Act and the welfare state, the indispensable book is Robert H. Bremner, *From the Depths: The Discovery of Poverty in the U.S.* (New York, 1956), giving the history of the rise of social work, the investigations into the condition of the poor at the turn of the century, the impact of the discovery of poverty on the literary conscience of America, the struggle for social legislation, and the role of social workers. See also Eric Goldman, *Rendezvous with Destiny*, especially Chs. 7, 10, 14, 15, and 18, and the same author's *The Crucial Decade: America 1945-1955* (New York, 1956); Ralph H. Gabriel, *The Course of American Democratic Thought*

(2d ed., New York, 1956), especially Ch. 16, "The Religion of Humanity At Work" and Ch. 17, "The Evolution of the Philosophy of the General Welfare State," and H. S. Commager, *The American Mind* (New Haven, 1950), especially Ch. 10, "Lester Ward and the Science of Society." The quote from Emerson will be found in his essay "Self-Reliance" in *The Complete Essays and Other Writings* (New York, 1940), p. 149.

For American housing and the housing revolution, I owe much to the writings of Lewis Mumford: see especially his *Culture of Cities* (New York, 1938), *Sticks and Stones* (New York, 1924), *The Human Prospect* (Boston, 1955), and especially the collection of his "Sky Line" articles from *The New Yorker*, *From the Ground Up* (New York, 1956); I have also profited from James Marston Fitch, *American Building* (New York, 1948) and Christopher Tunnard and Henry Hope Reed, *American Skyline* (Boston, 1955). For the cultural history of housing, see the remarkable Ch. 8, "Shelter," in George R. Stewart, *American Ways of Life* (New York, 1954). For the history of tenement house reform, see Robert H. Bremner, *From the Depths*, pp. 204-212. For portraits of slum living in Chicago, see Theodore Dreiser, *The Color of a Great City* (New York, 1923); Edith Abbott, *The Tenements of Chicago, 1908-1935* (Chicago, 1936), and Nelson Algren, *The Man with the Golden Arm* (New York, 1949). For the impact of American slums on a recent foreign observer, see Simone de Beauvoir, *America Day by Day* (New York, 1956). For Negro housing, see St. Clair Drake and Horace Cayton, *Black Metropolis* (New York, 1955), and Robert Weaver, *The Negro Ghetto* (New York, 1948). For the problem of continued discrimination and segregation, see Charles Abrams, *Forbidden Neighbors* (New York, 1955).

On American food habits the best discussion is in Margaret Mead, "Manual for the Study of Food Habits," Bulletin 111, National Research Council (Washington, 1955), a pioneer exploration of the history, psychology and pathology of food habits and the emotional interactions which they involve. I have also learned much from George Stewart, *American Ways of Life*, Chs. 4 and 5 on food, and Ch. 6 on drink. See also A. M. Schlesinger, *Paths to the Present*, Ch. 12.

SEC. 7—*The Way of the Farmer*: On American farming there is good historical material in Charles and Mary Beard, *The Rise of American Civilization* (1-vol. ed., New York, 1930), especially Chs. 8,

11, and 12, and Charles A. Beard, *Economic Origins of Jeffersonian Democracy* (New York, 1927), especially Ch. 12; also Harry J. Carman and Harold C. Syrett, *History of the American People* (New York, 1952), Vol. I, Chs. 15 and 16, Vol. II, Chs. 2 and 6; and F. A. Shannon, *The Farmer's Last Frontier* (New York, 1945). For the figures on the changing farm population, see Gilbert Burck, "Magnificent Decline of United States Farming," *Fortune* (June 1955), and C. Wright Mills, *White Collar* (New York, 1951), "The Rural Debacle," pp. 15-20, which discusses the farmer as a member of the "old middle classes." For the changes in farming since 1940, see also Lowry Nelson, *American Farm Life* (Cambridge, 1954), and Ronald L. Mighell, *American Agriculture* (New York, 1955). For the farmer's effort to reorient himself to an industrial economy, see Carl C. Taylor, *The Farmers' Movement, 1620-1820* (New York, 1953). For the farmer's political role, see Arthur Holcombe, *The Middle Classes in American Politics* (Cambridge, 1940), especially pp. 158-193, which is the classic discussion of the influence of middle-class agrarianism on the American political system; also Samuel Lubell, *The Future of American Politics* (New York, 1952), Ch. 8, "Battle for the Farm Vote," and his *Revolt of the Moderates* (New York, 1956), Ch. 7, "Divided We Plow"; on price supports, see Gilbert C. Fite, *George W. Peek and the Fight for Farm Parity* (Norman, Okla., 1954); on the relation of the farm economy to the economy as a whole, and Big Farming as a "countervailing power," see J. K. Galbraith, *American Capitalism* (Boston, 1952), Ch. 11, "The Case of Agriculture." For the "rural mind," see Lowry Nelson, "The American Rural Heritage," *American Quarterly* (Fall, 1949); also Thorstein Veblen, *Theory of Business Enterprise* (New York, 1904), Ch. 9, "The Discipline of the Machine," reprinted in Max Lerner, ed., *The Portable Veblen* (New York, 1948), pp. 335-348; and *Absentee Ownership* (New York, 1923), Ch. 7, Sec. 2, "The Independent Farmer," pp. 129-141, reprinted in *The Portable Veblen*, pp. 395-406. For a popular discussion of the scientists who struggled with some of the technical problems of farm crops, see Paul de Kruif, *The Hunger Fighters* (New York, 1928). For the idealization of the farmer in American history, see Henry Nash Smith, *Virgin Land*.

SEC. 8—*The Decline of the Small Town*: On the small town, the references to De Tocqueville are to the Vintage ed., Vol. I, Ch. 5, pp. 61-101. The quote about

Shannon Center is from *Time* (July 3, 1950), p. 10. Veblen's essay on "The Country Town" is from *Absentee Ownership*, Ch. 7, Sec. 3, pp. 142-165, reprinted in *The Portable Veblen*, pp. 407-430. For the movement to revive the small town, see Baker Brownell, *The Human Community* (New York, 1950), and Richard W. Poston, *Small-Town Renaissance* (New York, 1950). The references in the text to the Ladies' Clubs refer to the researches of Louis B. Wright, *Culture on the Moving Frontier*. Carol Kennicott will be found in Sinclair Lewis' novel, *Main Street* (New York, 1920). See also an article on Sauk Center today in *Life* (June 23, 1947), p. 100. The reference to T. S. Eliot is to *Notes Towards a Definition of Culture* (London, 1949); for another discussion of the face-to-face community, see Robert A. Nisbet, *The Quest for Community* (New York, 1953); *Sironia, Texas* is by Madison Cooper, 2 vols. (Boston, 1952); the reference to Maxwell Geismar is to his *Last of the Provincials* (Boston, 1947), which is one in a multi-volume history of the American novel. The reference to Homans is to George C. Homans, *The Human Group* (New York, 1950), Ch. 13, "Social Disintegration: Hilltown." In addition to the community studies of small towns mentioned in the text, see also James West, *Plainville, U.S.A.* (New York, 1945), which is about an anonymous town; Elin C. Anderson, *We Americans* (Cambridge, 1937), about Burlington, Vermont; and Townsend Scudder, *Concord: American Town* (Boston, 1947); see also Harriet L. Herring, *Passing of the Mill Village* (Chapel Hill, 1949).

SEC. 9—*City Lights and Shadows*: On the city, see Lewis Mumford, *The Culture of Cities*, sharply criticized by Meyer Schapiro in the *Partisan Reader* (New York, 1946), as well as William T. Ogburn, *Social Characteristics of Cities* (Chicago, 1937); see also Mumford's *City Development* (New York, 1945). For historical material, see Carl Bridenbaugh, *Cities in the Wilderness: The First Century of Urban Life in America 1625-1744* (New York, 1938), and also his *Cities in Revolt* (New York, 1955); also Adna F. Weber, *The Growth of Cities in the Nineteenth Century* (New York, 1899); Arthur M. Schlesinger, *The Rise of the City, 1878-1898* (New York, 1933), and the same author's *Paths to the Present*, pp. 210-223, "The City in American Civilization"; also Marshall B. Davidson, *Life in America* (2 vols., Boston, 1951), Vol. I, Ch. 7, "The Urban World," pp. 99-193—an excellent pictorial history; also John A. Kouwenhoven, *Columbia Historical Portrait of New York* (New York, 1953); also Lewis Mumford, *Sticks and Stones*. For books on particular American cities, see George Sessions Perry, *Cities of America* (New York, 1947), ranging from Portland, Maine, to Los Angeles; the June 7, 1949, issue of the *Reporter* contains articles on Gloucester, Mass., Decatur, Ill., Elmira, N.Y., Kansas City, and Los Angeles, and the issue of Dec. 20, 1940, contains several on city streets; for New York, see Lloyd Morris, *Incredible New York: High Life and Low Life in the Past 100 Years* (New York, 1951), also John Kouwenhoven, *Columbia Historical Portrait of New York,* and the special number of *Holiday* devoted to New York (April 1949), including a remarkable article by E. B. White which was reprinted in book form as *Here Is New York* (New York, 1949); also Alexander Klein, ed., *The Empire City: A Treasury of New York* (New York, 1955), and a special issue of the *N.Y. Times Magazine,* "New York City 1653-1953" (Feb. 1, 1953); for Chicago, see the special number of *Holiday* (Oct. 1951) devoted to Chicago, including an article by Nelson Algren reprinted as *Chicago, City on the Make* (New York, 1951); also A. J. Liebling, *Chicago, the Second City* (New York, 1952); Simone de Beauvoir, *America Day by Day;* Theodore Dreiser, *The Color of a Great City.* For symposia on cities, see W. A. Robson, ed., *Great Cities of the World* (New York, 1955), which includes New York, Chicago, and Los Angeles, with emphasis on government and planning; Robert S. Allen, *Our Fair City* (New York, 1947), emphasizing the darker side of urban politics in seventeen American cities; Ray B. West, ed., *Rocky Mountain Cities* (New York, 1949).

For a broad approach to the study of cities, the best book is Paul Hatt and Albert J. Reiss, *Reader in Urban Sociology* (Glencoe, Ill., 1951); see also the classic study by Robert E. Park and Ernest W. Burgess, *The City* (Chicago, 1925); another useful book of readings is T. Lynn Smith and C. H. McMahon, *The Sociology of Urban Life* (New York, 1951); see also Sven Riemer, *The Modern City* (New York, 1952). For particular phases of city life, see Harvey Zorbaugh, *The Gold Coast and the Slum* (Chicago, 1929); Robert Faris and H. W. Dunham, *Mental Disorders in Urban Areas* (Chicago, 1939); Lewis Wirth's consideration of the effects of *The Ghetto* (Chicago, 1929) on the Jewish mind; Clifford Shaw and Henry McKay, *Juvenile Delinquency in Urban Areas* (Chicago, 1942); on Italian slums,

W. F. Whyte, *Street Corner Society* (Chicago, 1943); Caroline Ware, *Greenwich Village* (Boston, 1935). For city politics, see the "muckraking" classic by Lincoln Steffens, *The Shame of the Cities* (New York, 1904), and Charles E. Merriam, *Chicago: A More Intimate View of Urban Politics* (New York, 1929); and for the role of the city vote in national politics, see Samuel Lubell, *The Future of American Politics,* Ch. 3, "Revolt of the City," Ch. 4, "The Frontier Reappears," and Ch. 5, "Civil Rights Melting Pot." On the location of American cities, see Edward C. Kirkland, *Men, Cities, and Transportation: A Study in New England History 1820-1900* (2 vols., Cambridge, 1948). On city planning, see Robert A. Walker, *The Planning Function in Urban Government* (Chicago, 1950); Christopher Tunnard, *City of Man* (New York, 1953), and Christopher Tunnard and Henry Hope Reed, *American Skyline;* also Clarence Stein, *Toward New Towns for America* (Liverpool, 1951), on the garden cities. For city renewal, see J. L. Sert, *Can Our Cities Survive?* (Cambridge, 1942). For recent problems of city administration due to decentralization and flight to the suburbs, see A. A. Berle, "How Long Will New York Wait?" in the *Reporter* of Sept. 8, 1955, pp. 14-23, and an article on Los Angeles, "A City 200 Miles Long?" in *U.S. News and World Report* (Sept. 16, 1955). On the question of the degree to which urban life still appeals to various groups, see Arthur Kornhauser, *Attitudes of Detroit People Toward Detroit: Summary of a Detailed Report* (Detroit, 1952). For an interesting view of American cities by a foreigner, see Rupert Brooke, *Letters from America* (New York, 1916), Chs. 1-4, and H. W. Nevinson, *Farewell to America* (New York, 1922)—two of many descriptions by foreign travelers. For others, see Henry S. Commager, ed., *America in Perspective* (New York, 1948), and Allan Nevins, ed., *America Through British Eyes* (New York, 1948). For the quote in the text from E. B. White, see his book, *This Is New York.* The quote from Edith Wharton on the Manhattan street plan is taken from *A Backward Glance* (New York, 1934), p. 23; I have borrowed it from Tunnard and Reed, *American Skyline.* The quote from William Wheaton is from a letter to the author. The theories of urban development cited in the text are taken from selections in Hatt and Reiss, *Reader in Urban Sociology.* The migrations that went to form Brooklyn, to which the text refers, will be found discussed in

Ralph Foster Weld, *Brooklyn Is America* (New York, 1950). The phrase from William Bolitho is from his *Cancer of Empire* (London, 1924). The quote from Alfred Roth about the St. Louis slums will be found in *Time* (March 13, 1950). The quote from Patrick Geddes is from Lewis Mumford, *From the Ground Up*.

SEC. 10—*The Suburban Revolution:* On the suburbs, see W. H. Whyte, Jr., *The Organization Man* (New York, 1956), Part 7, "The New Suburbia: Organization Man at Home"—the best discussion because it puts the suburbs in their economic and cultural setting. Some of this material first appeared in *Fortune* (June, Aug. and Nov. 1953), under the general title of "The Transients"; these articles are still worth reading. See also A. C. Spectorsky, *The Exurbanites* (Philadelphia, 1955); *The Changing American Market,* by the editors of *Fortune* (New York, 1955), including a chapter by W. H. Whyte, Jr., "The Lush Suburban Market"—interesting because it sees the whole suburban revolution in terms of a revolution in markets; Lewis Mumford, *From the Ground Up*, also Clarence Stein, *Toward New Towns for America;* see also Frederick L. Allen, "The Big Change in Suburbia" and "Crisis in the Suburbs," *Harpers Magazine* (June and July 1954); also Harry Henderson, "The Mass-Produced Suburbs," *ibid,* (Nov. and Dec. 1953); Maurice Stein, "Suburbia, A Walk on the Mild Side," *Dissent* (Summer, 1957), and Russell Lynes, *The Tastemakers* (New York, 1954), Ch. 14, "Suburbia in Excelsis." For problems of planning presented by the suburban revolution, see Walter M. Blucher, "What Are the Main Problems Which Decentralization Is Creating in Metropolitan Ideas?" in *Proceedings of First University of California Conference on City and Regional Planning* (Berkeley, 1954). For a severe criticism of American suburban life, see Erich Fromm, *The Sane Society* (New York, 1955). John R. Seeley, R. A. Sim, and E. W. Loosley, *Crestwood Heights* (New York, 1956) is a Canadian study of much relevance to the American suburban experience. The quote from Trevelyan is from G. M. Trevelyan, *Illustrated English Social History* (London, 1951), Vol. III, p. 109. The reference to "subtopia" is from *Outrage* (London, June, 1955) by I. N. Nairn and other editors of *Architectural Review.* I have been puzzled by the problem of terminology in trying to describe the new sprawling city that is emerging on the American landscape. I have had to reject Mumford's term "re-gional city" as carrying connotations of a regional culture that do not go to the heart of the new developments; the term "metropolitan area" seems to evade the problem of defining the new city by calling it an "area." I have suggested "cluster city" because it emphasizes the cluster of suburbs around the nuclear city, and includes both. The term "nuclear city" can be used to refer more strictly to the area from which the suburbs have radiated.

SEC. 11—*Regions: the Fusion of People and Place:* On regionalism there are lively and informed surveys of each of the great American regions in turn in John Gunther, *Inside U.S.A.* (2 vols., New York, 1947; Bantam ed., 1951). There are numberless descriptions by travelers: a convenient recent anthology is *A Collection of Travel in America by Various Hands,* edited by George Bradshaw (New York, 1948); a good book by a recent traveler is James Morris, *As I Saw the U.S.A.* (New York, 1956). The *American Folkways* series, ed., Erskine Caldwell (Duell, Sloan), is uneven in quality but contains some first-rate books on sub-regions. A theoretical approach will be found in Howard W. Odum, "The American Blend: Regional Diversity and National Unity," in *The Saturday Review* (Aug. 6, 1949), pp. 92-96, 169-172. The 3-volume *Report of the Water Resources Policy Commission* ed., Morris L. Cooke, contains rich material on each of the river valley regions, and a good initial statement in Vol. I, pp. 19-36. There is abundant literature on the TVA, and some of it deals with the cultural setting: see especially Robert L. Duffus, *The Valley and Its People: A Portrait of TVA* (New York, 1944) and Gordon R. Clapp, *The TVA* (Chicago, 1955), along with the original conception of river valley development by David E. Lilienthal, *TVA: Democracy on the March.* V. O. Key, Jr.'s article, "The Erosion of Sectionalism," in *Virginia Quarterly Review* (Spring, 1955), raises questions of the erosion of the whole regional concept that go beyond the South itself. On the economic problems of the older regions, see Seymour Harris, "Old-Age Security for Our Economic Areas," *N.Y. Times Magazine* (July 29, 1951), p. 17 ff.

On New England as a region, see George W. Pierson, "Obstinate Concept of New England," *New England Quarterly* (March 1955); see two books by Perry Miller, *The New England Mind: The Seventeenth Century* (New York, 1939), and *The New England Mind:*

From Colony to Province (Cambridge, 1953); also S. E. Morison, *The Puritan Pronaos* (2nd ed., New York, 1956). See also Ferris Greenslet, *The Lowells and Their Seven Worlds* (Boston, 1946); F. O. Matthiessen, *The James Family* (New York, 1947); Catherine Drinker Bowen, *Yankee from Olympus: Justice Holmes and His Family* (Boston, 1944), and the same author's *John Adams and the American Revolution* (Boston, 1950). The quote in the text from Henry Adams is from *The Education of Henry Adams* (Modern Library ed., New York, 1931), p. 7. The volume first appeared in Boston in 1918. There are a number of anthologies on Boston and other parts of New England: I have found great pleasure in June Barrows Mussey, ed., *We Were New England: Yankee Life By Those Who Lived It* (New York, 1937); Henry Beston, ed., *White Pine and Blue Water: A State of Maine Reader* (New York, 1950); Cleveland Amory, *The Proper Bostonians* (New York, 1947); and Robert N. Linscott, ed., *State of Mind: A Boston Reader* (New York, 1948).

On the Midwest the best single book, and a model of what foreign travelers do best on America, is Graham Hutton, *Midwest at Noon* (Chicago, 1946); see also the best of the Midwest anthologies, John T. Flanagan, ed., *America Is West* (Minneapolis, 1945); and for a good study of a state, John Bartlow Martin, *Indiana: An Interpretation* (New York, 1947).

On the South the best studies, unlikely to be surpassed for some time, are W. J. Cash, *The Mind of the South* (New York, 1941; Anchor reprint, 1954), and Benjamin B. Kendrick and Alex M. Arnett, *The South Looks at Its Past* (Chapel Hill, 1935). The best anthologies are Willard Thorpe, *A Southern Reader* (New York, 1955), bringing together historical, economic, political, and literary material, and the literary reader, Robert Jacobs and Louis Rubin, Jr., eds., *Southern Renascence* (Baltimore, 1953). For regional history, see a recent collection of volumes, *A History of the South*, edited by Wendell H. Stephenson and E. Merton Coulter, 6 vols. (Baton Rouge, 1947-53), including books by Coulter and C. Vann Woodward. The completed series will include ten volumes. For a 1-volume history, see Francis B. Simkins, *The South, Old and New: A History, 1820-1947* (New York, 1947). For a broad approach to Southern regionalism, see Howard W. Odum, *Southern Regions of the U.S.* (Chapel Hill, 1936), and his *The Way of the South: Toward the Regional Balance of America* (New York, 1947), which is a looser and more discursive book. On the Southern agrarians, who emerged briefly in the 1920s with an attitude and program for a revival of Southern energies, see their symposium *I'll Take My Stand, By Twelve Southerners* (New York, 1930) and their later manifesto, *Who Owns America?* (Boston, 1936), ed. by Herbert Agar and Allen Tate; see also Donald Davidson, *The Attack on Leviathan* (Chapel Hill, 1938). On the economics of the South, see Calvin B. Hoover and B. U. Ratchford, *Economic Resources and Policies of the South* (New York, 1951), and also one of the studies of the National Planning Association, *Why Industry Moves South* (Washington, 1949). For Southern politics, V. O. Key, Jr., *Southern Politics in State and Nation* (New York, 1949) is at once massive in its factual base and full of insights; see also Alexander Heard, *A Two-Party South* (Chapel Hill, 1952). For self-criticism by Southerners, the classic book is George W. Cable, *The Silent South* (New York, 1889); see also Virginius Dabney, *Liberalism in the South* (Chapel Hill, 1932); Hodding Carter, *Southern Legacy* (Baton Rouge, 1950), and *Virginia Quarterly Review*, Vol. XXXI, No. 2 (Spring, 1955), a whole issue of the magazine devoted to the New South, and including two first-rate articles, "The Erosion of Sectionalism" by V. O. Key, Jr., and "An Epitaph for Dixie" by Harry S. Ashmore. For studies of particular Southern states, Thomas Jefferson set a standard in his *Notes on the State of Virginia* (new ed., Chapel Hill, 1955), which has been hard to match since originally published; but see John Gould Fletcher, *Arkansas* (Chapel Hill, 1947), a remarkable blend of history and poetic insight; and, for Mississippi, see David L. Cohn, *Where I Was Born and Raised* (Boston, 1948), and William A. Percy, *Lanterns on the Levee* (New York, 1941). For the Negro experience in the South, see Reading Notes for Ch. I, Sec. 2, and Ch. VII, Sec. 6. But I want to mention here the series of remarkable autobiographies about Negro life in the South, including Booker T. Washington, *Up from Slavery* (New York, 1903); Richard Wright, *Black Boy* (New York, 1945), and J. Saunders Redding, *No Day of Triumph* (New York, 1942). To this should be added B. A. Botkin, *Lay My Burden Down: A Folk History of Slavery* (Chicago, 1945) and—on the life of the sharecropper, whether Negro or white—an evocative book by James Agee, *Let Us Now Praise Famous Men* (Boston, 1941).

On the Southwest there is nothing

comparable to the commentary on the South. But see J. B. Priestley, *Midnight on the Desert* (London, 1937), and J. B. Priestley and Jacquetta Hawkes, *Journey Down a Rainbow* (New York, 1955), the latter covering the whole region from Texas to California—both books go well beyond travel impressions; see also a number of recent books by Joseph Wood Krutch, writing mainly as a naturalist but with overtones that reach to an understanding of the regional life as a whole, especially *The Desert Year* (New York, 1952); also Edmund Wilson, *Red, Black, Blond, and Olive* (New York, 1956), Part 1, "Zuni," pp. 3-68, dealing mainly with the meaning of the ritual dances. On the same subject, see Erna Fergusson, *Dancing Gods* (New York, 1931); and see her *Our Southwest* (New York, 1940), and *New Mexico: A Pageant of Free Peoples* (New York, 1951), dealing with the Indians, the Spanish, and the "gringo" elements in the culture of the Southwest. For Texas there are still only fragmentary discussions, but see a series of articles on the Texas oil millionaires by Theodore White in the *Reporter* (May 25, June 8, 1954).

On the West, there is a good survey by Morris E. Garnsey, *America's New Frontier* (New York, 1950), and Ray B. West, ed., *Rocky Mountain Cities;* see also a good collection of readings, ed., Stuart H. Holbrook, *Promised Land* (New York, 1945). For California, see Robert G. Cleland, *From Wilderness to Empire* (New York, 1944), and *California in Our Time, 1900-1940* (New York, 1947). For other readings on the West, see my Notes for Further Reading, Ch. III, Sec. 3, "People in Motion," where I discuss the literature of the "Yankee exodus" and the gold rush.

Chapter IV: The Culture of Science and the Machine

SEC. 1—*The Enormous Laboratory: Science and Power:* On the history of American science and the power built upon it, the best single volume is Mitchell Wilson, *American Science and Invention* (New York, 1954), a popularized survey which has both sweep and detail; also see James P. Baxter, *Scientists Against Time* (Boston, 1946), and Bernard Jaffe, *Men of Science in America* (New York, 1944). For particular scientists and periods, see Donald Fleming, *J. W. Draper and the Religion of Science* (Philadelphia, 1950); Dirk J. Struik, *Yankee Science in the Making* (Boston, 1949); Thomas Coulson, *Joseph Henry,*

His Life and Work (Princeton, 1950); I. Bernard Cohen, *Benjamin Franklin: His Contribution to the American Tradition* (New York, 1953), and *Benjamin Franklin's Experiments*, ed., I. Bernard Cohen (Cambridge, 1941), with a long historical introduction on Franklin's work in science and electricity. The material in my text about Franklin leans heavily upon this Introduction; also, on America's greatest theoretical scientist, see Lynde P. Wheeler, *Josiah Willard Gibbs: The History of a Great Mind* (rev. ed., New Haven, 1952), and Muriel Rukeyser, *Willard Gibbs* (Garden City, 1942), an impressionistic and poetic book which will not be wholly replaced by more balanced ones. For contemporary American science, the Sept. 1950 issue of *Scientific American* is devoted to "The Age of Science, 1900-1950," and the Sept. 1952 issue deals with the principle of automatic control and the feedback, and includes an excellent essay by Ernest Nagel; see also the *Scientific American Reader* (New York, 1953) for a number of articles from the files of the magazine, written with great expository force and vividness; there is also a series of small volumes on various aspects of science, edited by the editors of the magazine, including *The Physics and Chemistry of Life, The New Astronomy,* and *Atomic Power* (published by Simon and Schuster). For studies of the meaning of science, see James B. Conant, *On Understanding Science* (London, 1947), and his *Science and Common Sense* (New Haven, 1951); also an anthology edited by James R. Newman, *What Is Science?* (New York, 1955); F. S. C. Northrop, *The Logic of the Sciences and the Humanities* (New York, 1949), and Lyman Bryson, *The Science of Freedom* (New York, 1947). A brief study which is a model of exposition is Lincoln Barnett, *The Universe and Dr. Einstein* (New York, 1948). The quote in the text from Spengler refers to his *Decline of the West* (New York, 1927-28). In the discussion of natural rights and John Locke, the reference to Walton Hamilton is to his essay, "Property—According to Locke," *Yale Law Journal* (1931-32); the reference to Merle Curti is to "The Great Mr. Locke, America's Philosopher, 1783-1861" in *Probing Our Past* (New York, 1955).

SEC. 2—*Science in an Open Society:* For further readings on the relation of science to freedom and control, see Edward Shils, *The Torment of Secrecy: The Background and Consequences of American Security Policies* (Glencoe, 1956), a forthright book which has a sense of the psychological complexities of the subject and its social implications, but is uncompromising about the values both of science and of freedom; see also Walter Gellhorn, *Security, Loyalty, and Science* (Ithaca, 1950); Charles P. Curtis gives a summary of the Oppenheimer security hearings, along with a commentary, in *The Oppenheimer Case: The Trial of a Security System* (New York, 1955); the hearings themselves have been published: "In the Matter of J. Robert Oppenheimer, Transcript of Hearing Before Personnel Security Board," U.S. Atomic Energy Commission Publications (Washington, 1954); for a perceptive commentary on the trial, see Philip Rieff, "The Case of Dr. Oppenheimer," *The Twentieth Century* (Aug.-Sept. 1954), pp. 113-24, 218-32. Oppenheimer's own Reith Lectures for the British Broadcasting Corporation have been republished as *Science and the Common Understanding* (New York, 1956). The *Fortune* study by Francis Bello, referred to in the text, will be found in the June 1954 issue of the magazine. For Russian science, see *Bulletin of Atomic Scientists*, Vol. VIII, Nos. 2 and 3, Feb. and March 1952, "The State of Russian Science Today, A Symposium"; also *Soviet Science,* a collection of essays under the auspices of the American Association for the Advancement of Science (Washington, 1952), and Barrington Moore, Jr., *Terror and Progress—USSR* (Cambridge, 1954). The quote from Jefferson in the text will be found in an Appendix to Oppenheimer, *Science and the Common Understanding.*

SEC. 3—*Big Technology and Neutral Technicians,* and SEC. 6—*The Culture of Machine Living:* On technology, a basic book is Siegfried Giedion, *Mechanization Takes Command* (New York, 1948); see also a series of books by Roger Burlingame: *The March of the Iron Men* (New York, 1938), *Engines of Democracy* (New York, 1940), and *Backgrounds of Power: The Human Story of Mass Production* (New York, 1949). I owe thanks to Ray Ginger for his comment on my Sec. 3 ("Big Technology and Neutral Technicians") when it first appeared as an article in the *American Quarterly*, Vol. IV (Summer, 1952), p. 100. Ginger's criticism was "On American Technology, 1810-1860," *ibid.,* Vol. V, (Winter, 1953), p. 357. I am also grateful to the editors of *Perspectives* for including in their French edition two articles commenting on mine, by Jean Fourastie and Jacques Ellul, *Profiles,* No. 14 (Winter, 1956), pp. 3-32. For the technological and social consequences of automation, I have used

Norbert Weiner, *The Human Use of Human Beings* (New York, 1950; rev. ed., 1954) and George Soule, *Time for Living* (New York, 1955). Peter F. Drucker, *The New Society: The Anatomy of Industrial Order* (New York, 1950) is his best book in an American setting, and I have learned from it even where I have disagreed; see also his book of collected magazine pieces, *America's Next Twenty Years* (New York, 1957), especially Chs. 1 and 2. At times in my text I carry on a friendly argument with Thorstein Veblen: the relevant book of his here is *The Instinct of Workmanship and the State of the Industrial Arts* (New York, 1914). Several excerpts from it will be found in *The Portable Veblen*, ed., Max Lerner (New York, 1948), pp. 306-34; his *Imperial Germany and the Industrial Revolution* (New York, 1915), written around the idea of the "merits of borrowing" industrial technology, is also worth reading, and a selection from it will be found in *The Portable Veblen*, pp. 349-63. On engineering, see James K. Finch, *Engineering and Western Civilization* (New York, 1951), and John Mills, *The Engineer in Society* (New York, 1946); also Richard Shelton Kirby *et al., Engineering in History* (New York, 1956). On the problems of patents and technology, see Walton Hamilton, *Patents and Free Enterprise* (Washington, 1941). The consequences of technology for the American outlook are traced with subtlety and fullness in David Potter, *People of Plenty* (Chicago, 1954). Searching questions about the future of the impact of American technology on modern man are raised by Erich Kahler, *Man the Measure* (New York, 1943); Friedrich C. Junger, *The Failure of Technology* (Chicago, 1949), and Robert Jungk, *Tomorrow Is Already Here* (New York, 1955)—the last two being portraits in almost Orwellian terms. The reference in the text to Wilbur and Orville Wright is taken from Fred C. Kelly, *The Wright Brothers* (New York, 1943); see also *Miracle at Kitty Hawk,* ed., Fred C. Kelly (New York, 1941), a selection of Wright letters, and *The Papers of Wilbur and Orville Wright,* ed., Marvin W. McFarland, 2 vols. (New York, 1953). I give these citations in some detail because the case of the Wright Brothers and the airplane is a good starting point for any study of the conditions of invention in America and the nature of technological change. The reference in the text to the "Soviet of engineers" is to Veblen's book, *The Engineers and the Price System* (New York, 1921); several excerpts from it will be found in *The Portable Veblen*, pp. 431-65. The reference in the text to the "managerial revolution" is to James A. Burnham, *The Managerial Revolution* (New York, 1941). The reference to Isis and Osiris is to a book with that title by Lawrence Hyde (London, 1947). The reference to Meier's study of the political attitudes of scientists is to Richard Z. Meier, in the *Bulletin of Atomic Scientists* (July 9, 1951).

SEC. 4—*Work and the Automatic Factory:* On the factory as a social system and the attitudes of workers toward management and toward their work, the best single book is Reinhard Bendix, *Work and Authority in Industry* (New York, 1956). For the seminal contributions of Frederick W. Taylor, see his *Scientific Management* (New York, 1947), and especially his testimony before the House Committee to Investigate the Taylor and Other Systems of Shop Management, taken in 1912 and reprinted in this book. Another pioneering study was Frank B. Gilbreth, *Motion Study* (New York, 1911). A very different approach was taken by Elton Mayo, in his *The Human Problems of an Industrial Civilization* (New York, 1933), and *The Social Problems of an Industrial Civilization* (Cambridge, 1945); Mayo's studies were the foundation of an entire new school of personnel management and "human relations." The work of other members of this school will be found in R. J. Roethlisberger and W. J. Dickson, *Management and the Worker* (Cambridge, 1940), and R. J. Roethlisberger, *Management and Morale* (Cambridge, 1941). Bendix' book, *Work and Authority in Industry*, which comprises studies of the "ideologies of management" in four cultures, contains a chapter on "the American experience" (Ch. 5) which includes suggestive criticisms of both Taylor and Mayo. See also Gordon R. Taylor, *Are Workers Human?* (Boston, 1952); Peter F. Drucker, *The New Society,* and Wilbert E. Moore, *Industrialization and Labor: Social Aspects of Economic Development* (Ithaca, 1951). For the work concept, I have leaned heavily on an all-too-brief book by Daniel Bell, *Work and Its Discontents* (Boston, 1956), and on the brilliant insights of Adam Abruzzi, *Work, Workers, and Work Measurement* (New York, 1956), especially Part 3. Mayo's pathbreaking work in the Hawthorne Experiment has led to a massive body of commentaries, some of which will be found in George C. Homans, *The Human Group* (New York, 1950), Chs. 14 and 16; in Bendix, *op. cit.;* in Abruzzi, *op. cit.;* in Bell, *op. cit.;* and in Delbert C.

Miller and W. H. Form, *Industrial Sociology* (New York, 1951); a more popular version will be found in Stuart Chase, *Men At Work* (New York, 1945), and his *Roads to Agreement* (New York, 1951). For a labor viewpoint, see William Gomberg, *A Trade Union Analysis of Time Study* (New York, 1955); see also W. Lloyd Warner and J. O. Lowe, *The Social System of the Modern Factory. The Strike: A Social Analysis* (New Haven, 1947). For the history of the doctrine of work, see Andriano Tilgher, *Work: What It Has Meant to Men Through the Ages* (New York, 1932), on which C. Wright Mills has partly based his Ch. 10, "Work," in *White Collar* (New York, 1951); see also Rexford Hersey, *Zest for Work* (New York, 1955). For De Tocqueville's view of the American gospel of work, see *Democracy in America*, Vol. II, Ch. 18. For early American factory experience, especially in the Lowell mills, see Hannah Josephson, *The Golden Threads* (New York, 1949), and the novel by Samuel Hopkins Adams, *Sunrise to Sunset* (New York, 1950). The quote in the text from Mitchell Wilson is from correspondence with the author. For the era of the sweatshops, of child labor, and of the seventy-two-hour week, see Robert H. Bremner, *From the Depths* (New York, 1956), especially Part 3. For the period of the assembly line, see Charles R. Walker and Robert H. Guest, *The Man on the Assembly Line* (Cambridge, 1952). The reference in the text to the Roper survey is to his reports in *Fortune* for May and June 1947. The reference to the almost completely automatic chemical factory will be found in "The Factory of the Future," in the April 1952 number of *Factory Management and Maintenance,* pp. 78-80.

SEC. 5—*The Wilderness of Commodities:* On the consumer and his living standard, the key work is David Potter, *People of Plenty,* and there is a good popular treatment in Frederick L. Allen, *The Big Change* (New York, 1952), Ch. 15, "The All-American Standard," pp. 209-33. See also J. S. Davis, "Standards and Content of Living," *American Economic Review* (March 1945), pp. 1-15, and the same author's paper in the Columbia Bicentennial volume, *National Policy for Economic Welfare at Home and Abroad* (New York, 1955), pp. 128-132. The concepts of "conspicuous consumption" and "conspicuous waste," which have become part of the American vocabulary of self-criticism, come from Thorstein Veblen, *Theory of the Leisure Class* (New York, 1899), especially Ch. 4,

"Conspicuous Consumption," and Ch. 5, "Pecuniary Standard of Living," reprinted in *The Portable Veblen*, pp. 111-151. Also see Paul and Percival Goodman, *Communities* (Chicago, 1947). The reference in the text to Riesman's "nylon war" is to an essay which will be found reprinted in his *Individualism Reconsidered* (Glencoe, 1954), pp. 426-34. The reference to Waldo Frank is to his *Rediscovery of America* (New York, 1929). The reference to Giedion is to his *Mechanization Takes Command*. Erich Fromm's concept of the "marketing orientation" of the personality is in his *Man for Himself* (New York, 1947), pp. 67-82—a book from which I have learned much and which seems to me the most productive of Fromm's writing. The reference to Riesman's categories of "inner-directed" and "other-directed" personalities is to his *The Lonely Crowd* (New Haven, 1950; rev. ed., New York, 1953). For the Great Market, see *The Changing American Market*, by the editors of *Fortune* (New York, 1955); also Julius Hirsch, ed., *New Horizons in Business* (New York, 1956), especially Chs. 2 and 3. The reference in the text to Motivational Research, as a bolstering to the Great Market, is to the work of Dr. Ernest Dichter of the Institute of Motivational Research, and has been analyzed by Vance Packard in *The Hidden Persuaders* (New York, 1957), Part 1, especially Ch. 16. The figures in the text from Frederick C. Mills are cited in George Soule, *Time for Living*.

For machine culture, see the Notes for Further Reading for Sec. 3.

Chapter V: Capitalist Economy and Business Civilization

SEC. 1—*American Capitalism: Trial Balance*, and SEC. 10—*The Emerging Amalgam:* For an over-all view, there is a first-rate symposium *An Examination of the American Economic System* in the "American Round Table Series," sponsored by the Advertising Council (1st part, June 23, 1952; 2nd part, Oct. 2, 1952, New York), with Lewis Galantiere as the Reporter and Henry M. Wriston as the Moderator. The give and take between businessmen, union economists, management consultants, and academic men (among them Galantiere, Elliot V. Bell, Jacob Viner, Peter Drucker, Henry S. Commager, Clinton S. Golden, Boris B. Shishkin, Allan Nevins, and Robert E. Wilson) tells more about the complexities of the economy than most textbooks. For an excellent over-all sociological view, see Robin Williams, Jr., *American Society* (New York, 1951), Ch. 6, "American Economic Institutions." For a brilliant general theory of capitalism to serve as a frame for American capitalism, see Joseph Schumpeter, *Capitalism, Socialism, and Democracy* (New York, 1950). For the theory of the Welfare State and the planned economy, see Abba P. Lerner, *The Economics of Control* (New York, 1944), and W. Arthur Lewis, *Principles of Economic Planning* (London, 1949); J. K. Galbraith, *American Capitalism: The Concept of Countervailing Power* (Boston, 1952); Adolf A. Berle, Jr., *The 20th Century Capitalist Revolution* (New York, 1954), and C. H. Hession, S. M. Miller, and C. Stoddard, *The Dynamics of the American Economy* (New York, 1956). See also Thomas C. Cochran and William Miller, *The Age of Enterprise: A Social History of Industrial America* (New York, 1942); for the emergence of the contemporary economy, and for specific periods see George Soule, *Prosperity Decade: From War to Depression 1917-1929* (New York, 1947), and Broadus Mitchell, *Depression Decade: From New Era Through New Deal 1929-1941* (New York, 1947); *Making Capitalism Work*, by Dexter Keezer and Associates (New York, 1950), is an anthology of vigorous affirmation. For a Keynesian view, see *The New Economics*, ed., Seymour Harris (New York, 1948), containing comments by a number of writers on the basic text of J. M. Keynes, *The General Theory of Employment, Interest, and Money* (New York, 1936).

For a statement of traditional theory, powerfully revised to meet the onslaught of the Keynesian school, see Henry C. Simon, *A Positive Program for Laissez-Faire* (Chicago, 1934), which should be balanced with Alvin Hansen, *Fiscal Policy and Business Cycles* (New York, 1941). A series of studies by the National Resources Planning Board have been of historic importance, especially *The Structure of the American Economy* (Washington, 1940); similarly the *TNEC Reports*, mentioned in the text, will still be found useful. For a history and critique of the TNEC inquiry, and a survey of the evidence presented to it, see David Lynch, *The Concentration of Economic Power* (New York, 1946); K. William Kapp, *The Social Costs of Private Enterprise* (Cambridge, 1950) sets forth the wasteful and irrational elements of the American economic system. The sharpest indictment of the system is Thorstein Veblen's: his most important books are *The Theory of Business Enterprise* (New York, 1904), and *Absentee Ownership and Business Enterprise in Recent Times: The Case of America* (New York, 1923). A satiric work on capitalist attitudes is Veblen's *The Theory of the Leisure Class* (New York,

1899), and it was followed by Thurman Arnold's *Folklore of Capitalism* (New York, 1935). For a contemporary Marxist critique of capitalism, particularly with an eye to the case of America, see Paul M. Sweezy, *The Theory of Capitalist Development* (new ed., New York, 1956), and *The Present As History* (New York, 1953); also Paul A. Baran, *The Political Economy of Growth* (New York, 1957), especially Chs. 3 and 4, "Standstill and Movement Under Monopoly Capitalism." For a very different analysis, see *The Triumph of American Capitalism* by Louis M. Hacker (New York, 1940); also an article addressed mainly to meet European criticisms of the American economy—Lewis Galantiere, "America Today," in *Foreign Affairs* (July 1950). For some recent trends in the thinking of American economists about capitalism, see John McDonald, "The Economists," *Fortune* (Dec. 1950), pp. 109-38; Daniel Bell, "The Prospects of American Capitalism," *Commentary* (Dec. 1952), pp. 603-12.

SEC. 2—*The Rise and Decline of the Titan:* On the businessman, see Hession, Miller, and Stoddard, *The Dynamics of the American Economy*, Ch. 5, "Age of the Moguls," and Ch. 6, "Age of the Managers," and C. Wright Mills, *The Power Elite* (New York, 1956), Ch. 6, "The Chief Executives." The phrase in the text, "The Tycoon is Dead," is taken from a *Fortune* advertisement in *Time* for Aug. 20, 1951. For a history of the Titans, see Stuart Holbrook, *The Age of the Moguls* (New York, 1950); for highly critical accounts of them and their methods, see Gustavus Myers, *History of Great American Fortunes,* 3 vols. (Chicago, 1909-10; Mod. Lib. ed., New York, 1936), and Matthew Josephson, *The Robber Barons: The Great American Capitalists 1861-1901* (New York, 1934); see also Charles and Mary Beard, *The Rise of American Civilization* (1-vol. ed., New York, 1930), Chs. 14-16, and *America in Mid-Passage* (New York, 1939), especially Chs. 1 and 2; see also Frederick Lewis Allen, *The Lords of Creation* (New York, 1935). For the dark days in the Great Depression, see Arthur M. Schlesinger, Jr., *The Crisis of the Old Order* (Boston, 1957), and the sharp and suggestive essay by Walton Hamilton, "When the Banks Closed," in Daniel Aaron, ed., *America in Crisis* (New York, 1952). The De Tocqueville passage in the text will be found in his *Democracy in America* (Vintage ed.), Vol. II, Ch. 2, p. 171; the reference to Dickens is to his *American Notes* (London, 1842). The Cowperwood Trilogy by Dreiser includes *The Financier* (New York, 1912), *The Titan* (New York, 1914), and *The Stoic*

(New York, 1947). For biographies of American businessmen, see Frederick Lewis Allen, *The Great Pierpont Morgan* (New York, 1949), Allan Nevins, *Ford: The Times, The Man, The Company* (New York, 1954), and Nevins and Frank E. Hills, *Ford: Expansion and Challenge 1915-1933* (New York, 1957) as examples of a revisionist trend. A critical but balanced view will be found in Robert L. Heilbroner's *The Quest for Wealth* (New York, 1956), especially Chs. 8-10. There is an interesting interchange between Allan Nevins and Matthew Josephson, "Should American History Be Rewritten?"—A Debate, *The Saturday Review* (Feb. 6, 1954); the paper by Nevins calling for a rethinking of the role of the Titans in the industrialization of America will be found in Edward Saveth, ed., *Understanding the American Past* (Boston, 1954). The reference in the text to John Chamberlain is to his article in *Fortune*, "The Businessman in Fiction," (Nov. 1948). For the current trends in the study of the businessman, see "The Businessman and the Social Scientist," *Clearing House Bulletin*, Vol. III. No. 3 (1955), pp. 22-24.

SEC. 3—*The Corporate Empire:* On the corporation, the best over-all view, sympathetic without being uncritical, is A. A. Berle, Jr., *20th Century Capitalist Revolution:* it ends on the hopeful note of an appeal for a "City of God" which will serve as a frame for corporate capitalism. The decisive book for the study of the corporation has been A. A. Berle and Gardiner C. Means, *The Modern Corporation and Private Property* (New York, 1933); while its figures are out of date, and Berle in his subsequent writings has come to temper the harshness of its criticism, it is still worth study for its basic analysis. It in turn followed two earlier books—Veblen's *Absentee Ownership and Business Enterprise,* and W. Z. Ripley, *Main Street and Wall Street* (Boston, 1927). A good recent study is Peter F. Drucker, *The Concept of the Corporation* (New York, 1946). The best estimate of the present degree of corporate concentration of power is M. A. Adelman, "The Measurement of Industrial Concentration," *Review of Economics and Statistics* (Nov. 1951), Vol. XXXII, No. 4. This work is the source of the statistics on business concentration used in this section, as they are quoted in Berle, *The 20th Century Capitalist Revolution,* pp. 25-26. For a theoretical approach to monopoly, see Edward Chamberlin, *The Theory of Monopolistic Competition* (Cambridge, 1933), and Arthur R. Burns, *The Decline of Competition* (New York, 1936); for the situation a generation ago, see Clair Wilcox, *Competition and Monopoly in American Industry*, Tenn. Monograph No. 21 (Washington, 1940); for the situation at mid-century, see George W. Stocking and Myron W. Watkins, *Monopoly and Free Enterprise* (New York, 1951); also Corwin D. Edwards, *Maintaining Competition* (New York, 1949); Fritz Machlup, *Political Economy of Monopoly* (Baltimore, 1952); A. D. H. Kaplan, *Big Enterprise in a Competitive System* (Washington, 1954); David E. Lilienthal, *Big Business—A New Era* (New York, 1952); T. K. Quinn, *Giant Corporations: Challenge to Freedom* (New York, 1955); Marshall E. Dimock, *Free Enterprise and the Administrative State* (University of Alabama, 1951); and Joel B. Dirlam and Alfred E. Kahn, *Fair Competition, the Law and Economics of Anti-Trust Policy* (Ithaca, 1954). On a new development in the growth of monopoly, see Walter Adams and Horace M. Gray, *Monopoly in America: The Government As Promoter* (New York, 1955), emphasizing the extent to which government action and policies, including the regulation of public utilities, the tax write-offs, defense procurement, surplus property disposal, and the atomic arms race, carry monopoly in their wake. See also, for a critique of the Galbraith thesis as applied to the problem of monopoly, Walter Adams, "Competition, Monopoly, and Countervailing Power," *Quarterly Journal of Economics* (Nov. 1953), Vol. LXVII, No. 4, pp. 469-92.

For the ethical aspects of corporate power, see Berle, *The 20th Century Capitalist Revolution*, Kenneth Boulding, *The Organizational Revolution* (New York, 1953), stressing the relation between economics and religion, and Marquis W. Childs and Douglass Cater, *Ethics in a Business Society* (New York, 1954). An excellent recent analysis is O. W. Knauth, *Business Practices, Trade Position, and Competition* (New York, 1956). A more acid view will be found in C. Wright Mills, *The Power Elite* (New York, 1956), Ch. 15, "The Higher Immorality"; also Walton Hamilton, *The Politics of Industry* (New York, 1957), especially the discussion of "Conscience and the Corporation" in Ch. 5. The whole of Hamilton's book is "institutional economics" in its best sense, bringing together history, economics, administration, law and politics, and deflating some of the more tenacious myths about the corporation and the government.

SEC. 4—*The Property Revolution:* On the concept and realities of property, there is a suggestive essay by Walton Hamilton, "Property—According to Locke," *Yale Law Journal* (1931-2). See also a special number of the *Journal of Legal and Political Sociology* devoted to the theme of "Property and Social Structure," Vol. I, Nos. 3 and 4 (April 1943); as well as my essay, "The Supreme Court and American Capitalism" in *Ideas Are Weapons* (New York, 1939); see also, for a study of the interrelations of business power, social theory, and legal action, Robert G. McCloskey, *American Conservatism in the Age of Enterprise: A Study of William Graham Sumner, Stephen J. Field, and Andrew Carnegie* (Cambridge, 1951).

SEC. 5—*Business and Its Satellites:* On the sweep of business power and influence, see Harold J. Laski, *The American Democracy* (New York, 1948), Ch. 5, and C. Wright Mills, *The Power Elite*, especially Ch. 13, "The Mass Society," and Ch. 14, "The Conservative Mood." For the stock market and its control, see W. O. Douglas, *Democracy and Finance* (New Haven, 1940); for an earlier period, see Louis D. Brandeis, *Other People's Money* (New York, 1913) on the financial intrigues uncovered by the Pujo Investigation. An account of the stock market boom and crash will be found in Frederick Lewis Allen, *Only Yesterday* (New York, 1931); see also Walton Hamilton, "When the Banks Closed," in Daniel Aaron, ed., *America in Crisis*. A basic book on stock investment is Benjamin Graham, *The Intelligent Investor* (New York, 1954), making the distinction between "security analysis" (for the "intrinsic values" of securities) and "market analysis" (for the market fluctuations); see also John B. Williams, *The Theory of Investment Value* (Cambridge, 1937). For a good exposition of the stock market, see Paul A. Samuelson, *Economics: An Introductory Analysis* (New York, 1948). See also John McDonald, "Notes on Stock Speculation," *Fortune* (June 1951), pp. 110-11, 134-42. The quote in the text from Frederick Macauley, will be found in this work. On salesmanship, see C. Wright Mills, *White Collar* (New York, 1951), Ch. 8, "The Great Salesroom"; also David Riesman, *The Lonely Crowd* (New Haven, 1950).

On advertising, see David M. Potter, *People of Plenty* (Chicago, 1954), Ch. 8, "The Institution of Abundance: Advertising"; see also Ralph M. Hower, *The History of an Advertising Agency: N. W. Ayer and Son at Work, 1869-1949* (Cambridge, 1949); Vance Packard, *The Hidden Persuaders* (New York, 1957), and Marshall McLuhen, "American Advertising," pp. 435-42 in Bernard Rosenberg and David M. White, eds., *Mass Culture: The Popular Arts in America* (Glencoe,

1957). American novelists have been attracted to the theme of the salesman's and advertiser's arts, from Herman Melville's *The Confidence Man,* edited with introduction by Elizabeth Foster (New York, 1954), and Mark Twain's *Gilded Age* (Hartford, 1873) and his *Adventures of Huckleberry Finn* (New York, 1891); to Frederic Wakeman's *The Hucksters* (New York, 1946), Al Morgan, *The Great Man* (New York, 1955), and Budd Schulberg, *A Face in the Crowd* (New York, 1957). On public relations there are books by two of the founders of the profession: Edward L. Bernays, *Propaganda* (New York, 1928), and *The Engineering of Consent* (Norman, Oklahoma, 1955), and Ivy L. Lee, *Publicity* (New York, 1925); unfortunately such brilliant current practitioners of the arts of public relations as Benjamin Sonnenberg and Carl Byoir have not as yet put on record accounts of their techniques and approaches. A good historical summary will be found in Eric F. Goldman, *Two Way Street: The Emergence of the Public Relations Counsel* (Boston, 1948); see also Norton E. Long, "Public Relations of the Bell System," *Public Opinion Quarterly* (1937), and E. S. Turner, *The Shocking History of Advertising* (New York, 1933). The best study of the public relations counsel and his impact on political life is Stanley Kelly, Jr., *Professional Public Relations and Political Power* (Baltimore, 1956). The implications of "motivational analysis" for politics are also discussed by Vance Packard in *The Hidden Persuaders,* Chs. 17-21. For an amusing but sharp view of what both advertising and publicity consciousness have done to the language and mentality of American business, see W. H. Whyte, Jr., *Is Anybody Listening?* (New York, 1952), especially Ch. 10, "The Social Engineers," and Ch. 11, "Groupthinkers."

On the corporate executive, see Chester L. Barnard, *The Functions of the Executive* (Cambridge, 1938); *The Executive Life* by the editors of *Fortune* (New York, 1956); C. Wright Mills, *The Power Elite,* Ch. 6, "The Chief Executives"; W. H. Whyte, Jr., *The Organization Man* (New York, 1956); Reinhard Bendix, *Work and Authority in Industry* (New York, 1956), especially "Managerial Conceptions of the 'Manager,'" pp. 297-308, and Warner and Abegglen, *Occupational Mobility in American Business and Industry, 1928-1952* (Minneapolis, 1955). The quote in the text from Barnard is from an article by Robert Sheehan on "Organization and Management" in *Fortune* (June 1948), pp. 188-92.

SEC. 6—*The Reach of the Business Spirit:* On the relation between business and other areas of American life, see Blaire Bolles, *How to Get Rich in Washington* (New York, 1952); Paul Douglas, *Ethics in Government* (Cambridge, 1954); H. H. Wilson, *Congress: Corruption and Compromise* (New York, 1951), and C. Wright Mills, *The Power Elite.*

SEC. 7—*Revolution in the Trade Union,* and SEC. 8—*Labor and American Society:* On labor and trade unions, the historical works of John R. Commons and associates in *The History of Labor in the U.S.* (New York, 1926-35), and of Selig Perlman, *A Theory of the Labor Movement* (New York, 1928, rev. ed., 1949) are crucial. A considerable body of commentary has developed around it. I have found especially useful two articles by Philip Taft—"A Rereading of Selig Perlman's 'Theory of the Labor Movement,'" *Industrial and Labor Relations Review* (Oct. 1950), Vol. IV, No. 1, pp. 74-77, and "Commons-Perlman Theory: A Summary," in the *Proceedings* of the Third Annual Meeting of the Industrial Relations Research Association, pp. 1-6; and an article by Adolph Sturmthal, "Comments on Selig Perlman's Theory," *Industrial and Labor Relations Review* (July 1951), Vol. IV, No. 4, pp. 483-96; the chapter on "American Labor" in H. J. Laski, *The American Democracy* is in effect a running controversy with Perlman's theory. Out of the vast number of volumes on American labor history I have found Foster Rhea Dulles, *Labor in America* (New York, 1949), useful, and also Harold U. Faulkner and Mark Starr, *Labor in America* (New York, 1944) is a compact and lucidly written survey. For the crucial leadership of Gompers, see the recent solid and balanced study by Philip Taft, *The AFL in the Time of Gompers* (New York, 1957). No comparable work has been done on the history of the CIO, but whoever does it will be indebted to Matthew Josephson, *Sidney Hillman: Statesman of American Labor* (New York, 1952); Irving Howe and B. J. Widick, *The UAW and Walter Reuther* (New York, 1949); Saul Alinsky, *John L. Lewis* (New York, 1949), and James A. Wechsler, *Labor Baron: A Portrait of John L. Lewis* (New York, 1942). For the more violent phases of American labor history, see Louis Adamic, *Dynamite: The Story of Class Violence in America* (New York, 1934). For the place of the American labor movement in the national economy, see Charles E. Lindblom, *Unions and Capitalism* (New Haven, 1949), a work of sharp reasoning from which I have learned, even while differing with it in my text; see also Frank Tannenbaum, *The Labor Movement* (New York, 1921); an uneven but provocative critique of American labor, written from the viewpoint of the anti-Communist Left, is Sidney Lens, *Left, Right, and Center: Conflicting Forces in American Labor* (Hinsdale, Illinois, 1949); also see Sumner H. Slichter, *The American Economy* (New York, 1948), analyzing it as a "laboristic economy." Much of the attention of recent scholarly work has turned to the internal structure of the trade union and its functioning as a democracy: see especially Jack Barbash, *The Practice of Unionism* (New York, 1956); Philip Taft, *The Structure and Government of Labor Unions* (Cambridge, 1955); and Lloyd Ulman, *The Rise of the National Trade Union* (Cambridge, 1955), which deals in great detail with the period from 1850 to 1900 and concentrates on the internal structure and practices of the unions during their formative era. On recent trends in the labor movement, see Daniel Bell, "The Language of Labor," and "Labor's Coming of Middle Age" in *Fortune* (Sept. and Oct. 1951). For the relation of the worker to the American class system, see Notes for Further Reading on Ch. VII, Sec. 4.

SEC. 9—*Poverty and Wealth:* On American income distribution, the history of American wealth and the contemporary situation of the "top rich" is discussed in Richard Heilbroner, *The Quest for Wealth* (New York, 1956), and in C. Wright Mills, *The Power Elite;* for an earlier book on the rich, see Gustavus Myers, *History of Great American Fortunes,* 3 vols. For the history of American poverty and its impact on the American conscience, see Robert H. Bremner, *From the Depths: The Discovery of Poverty in the U.S.* (New York, 1956). For the distribution of income, see Paul A. Samuelson, *Economics, An Introductory Analysis,* Chs. 4 and 5. For a skeptical approach to the current belief that a "people's capitalism" has drastically changed the distribution of income, see Gabriel Kolko, "America's Income Revolution," *Dissent* (Winter, 1957), pp. 35-55. See also Sumner Slichter, "The High Cost of Low Incomes" in *N.Y. Times* (March 5, 1956).

Chapter VI: The Political System

The discussion of the American political system draws particularly on two British volumes—Harold Laski, *The American Democracy* (New York, 1948), and D. W. Brogan, *Politics in America* (New York, 1954), following the pattern of Lord James Bryce, *The American Commonwealth* (New York, 1888, 1891; new ed., New York, 1950).

SEC. 1—*The Style and Genius of American Politics,* and SEC. 2—*The Democratic*

Idea: For the theoretical formulations, see De Tocqueville, *Democracy in America,* Vol. I. Ralph Barton Perry, *Puritanism and Democracy* (New York, 1944) draws the line between the secular and religious facets of the democratic spirit. Carl Becker, *The Declaration of Independence* (New York, 1922, rev. ed., 1942) is an invaluable study in the history of ideas. *The Federalist* illuminates the development of the structure of the government. The Edward M. Earle edition (Washington, 1938) of these papers is by far the best available. See also Clinton Rossiter, *Seedtime of the Republic* (New York, 1952). *The Age of Jackson* (Boston, 1945) by Arthur M. Schlesinger, Jr., is a study of the growth of democracy in the Jacksonian period. R. H. Gabriel, *The Course of American Democratic Thought* (rev. ed., New York, 1956) and Henry Steele Commager, *The American Mind* (New Haven, 1950) are first-rate studies of the development of the democratic idea, particularly in the later period. One of the rare works of fresh interpretation in American intellectual history is Louis Hartz, *The Liberal Tradition in America* (New York, 1955). Also see Walter Lippmann, *Essays in the Public Philosophy* (Boston, 1955). Edward Mims, Jr., *The Majority of the People* (New York, 1941) is an unjustly neglected book, full of theoretical insights. See also my own *Ideas for the Ice Age* (New York, 1941) and Robert A. Dahl, *A Preface to Democratic Theory* (Chicago, 1956). Vernon L. Parrington's *Main Currents in American Thought,* especially the first two volumes (New York, 1927-1930; new ed., New York, 1956), is still a basic source. Substantial studies of American critics of democracy can be found in David E. Spitz, *Patterns of Anti-Democratic Thought* (New York, 1949). For the works of some of the writers from this perspective, see Irving Babbitt, *Democracy and Leadership* (Boston, 1924); Paul Elmer More, *The Shelburne Essays,* 2 vols. (Boston, 1904-21); George Santayana, *Character and Opinion in the United States* (New York, 1920); and the brilliantly satirical *Notes on Democracy* by H. L. Mencken (New York, 1926). See also Russell Kirk, *The Conservative Mind* (Chicago, 1953).

SEC. 3—*Presidency and Demos:* Several recent volumes have aided me in my thinking on the American President. They are Clinton Rossiter, *The American Presidency* (New York, 1956), and Sidney Hyman, *The American President* (New York, 1954). Two books by E. S. Corwin are helpful: *The President: Office and Powers* (rev. ed., New York, 1948), and *The Presidency Today* (New York, 1956),

written with Louis W. Koenig. Harold
Laski, *The American Presidency* (London, 1940), written during the New Deal,
follows in the path of D. W. Brogan, *The
American Political System* (London, 1933)
in stressing the strengthening of the
Presidency. Stefan Lorant's *The Presidency* (New York, 1951) is a popularly
written, informal, illustrated history; see
also Eugene M. Roseboom, *A History of
Presidential Elections* (New York, 1957). I
have also used Wilfred E. Binkley, *The
Powers of the President* (New York, 1937);
E. Pendleton Herring, *Presidential Leadership* (New York, 1940); and George F.
Milton, *The Use of Presidential Power,
1780-1943* (New York, 1944). Richard
Hofstadter, *The American Political Tradition* (New York, 1948) includes several
incisive chapters on the underlying thinking of American presidents. Douglas
Southall Freeman, *George Washington*, 6
vols. (New York, 1948-54) is the standard
biography of the first President; among
the best biographical material on other
chief executives is Dumas Malone,
Thomas Jefferson and His Time, of which
three volumes have thus far appeared
(Boston, 1948-56); also Irving Brant,
James Madison, 5 vols. (New York, 1941-
50); Arthur M. Schlesinger, Jr., *The Age
of Jackson;* Benjamin P. Thomas, *Abraham Lincoln: A Biography* (New York,
1952); Carl Sandburg, *Abraham Lincoln
—The Prairie Years,* 2 vols. (New York,
1926) and *Abraham Lincoln—The War
Years,* 4 vols. (New York, 1934); the
essays in David Donald, *Lincoln Reconsidered* (New York, 1956); Allan Nevins, *Grover Cleveland: A Study in Courage* (New York, 1932); H. F. Pringle,
Theodore Roosevelt (New York, 1931),
and *The Politics of Woodrow Wilson*
(New York, 1956), ed., by August Heckscher. See the two studies by John M.
Blum, *The Republican Roosevelt* (Cambridge, 1954) and *Woodrow Wilson and
the Politics of Morality* (Boston, 1956). On
Franklin D. Roosevelt much has been
written, and Frank Freidel's multi-volume biography, *Franklin D. Roosevelt,* of
which three volumes have been published
(New York, 1952-1956), is bound to become the standard one. Meanwhile, the
one-volume study of FDR's leadership,
Roosevelt: The Lion and the Fox (New
York, 1956) by James MacGregor Burns, is
a brilliant political biography. Projected
on a more ambitious scale, *The Age of
Roosevelt* by Arthur M. Schlesinger, Jr.,
will be a multi-volume work; its first volume, *The Crisis of the Old Order* (Boston,
1957), presents the prelude to the New
Deal with literary skill and a feel for the
drama of ideas. See also "Roosevelt and
History" in my *Ideas Are Weapons* (New
York, 1939) and "The Presidential Office"
and "Two Presidents in War Time" in
my *Ideas for the Ice Age.* The reference to the rating of Presidents in the
text is from pp. 95-97 of *Paths to the Present* (New York, 1949) by Arthur M. Schlesinger. For the vice-presidency and the
problems of the succession, see Irving G.
Williams, *The Rise of the Vice Presidency*
(New York, 1956), and his pamphlet, *The
American Vice-Presidency: New Look*
(New York, 1954), along with *Seven by
Chance* (New York, 1948) by Peter Levin;
and E. W. Waugh, *Second Consul* (Indianapolis, 1956). See also Corwin, *The
President: Office and Powers* and Corwin
and Koenig, *The Presidency Today.*

SEC. 4—*The Party System and the Voter:*
On American parties and elections, James
Madison, Essay No. 10 in *The Federalist,*
gives an essential key to understanding
the American pattern of political parties.
I have leaned heavily on Samuel Lubell's
The Future of American Politics (New
York, 1952), and his *Revolt of the Moderates* (New York, 1956). Wilfred Binkley,
American Political Parties (New York,
1943), is a competent historical text, as is
Claude Bowers, *Party Battles of the Jackson Period* (New York, 1922). Other
sources are E. E. Schattschneider, *Party
Government* (New York, 1942); Pendleton
Herring, *The Politics of Democracy* (New
York, 1940); D. W. Brogan, *Government
of the People* (New York, 1933), and
James M. Burns, *Congress on Trial* (New
York, 1949), particularly Chs. 3 and 11.
Matthew Josephson, *The Politicos* (New
York, 1938), and *The President Makers*
(New York, 1940), have received less attention than his *The Robber Barons,* but are
likely to prove more enduring. See also
Willmoore Kendall and Austin Ranney,
Democracy and the American Party System (New York, 1956), which attempts to
synthesize in one volume the opinions of
a member of the radical right and those
of a liberal. Sigmund Neumann, ed.,
Modern Political Parties (Chicago, 1956)
is a very useful collection of essays. M. Ostrogorski, *Democracy and the Organization of Political Parties,* 2 vols. (New
York, 1908) is an excellent comparative
study of America and England. A brief
history of dissident political groups in
America is W. B. Hesseltine, *The Rise
and Decline of Small Parties* (Washington, 1948), and see Herbert Agar, *The
Price of Union* (Boston, 1950) for a discussion of the need for loose party discipline.
John Gunther provides much information on regional politics in *Inside USA*

(rev. ed., New York, 1951). An excellent and highly factual account of politics in the South is *Southern Politics in State and Nation* (New York, 1949) by V. O. Key, Jr., whose *Politics, Parties, and Pressure Groups* (New York, 1948) is equally useful, along with Dayton McKean, *Party and Pressure Politics* (Boston, 1949). Several volumes on voting behavior have appeared, particularly Paul Lazarsfeld, and associates, *The People's Choice* (New York, 1944), and Bernard Berelson, Paul F. Lazarsfeld, and William N. McPhee, *Voting* (Chicago, 1954). A. N. Holcombe, *The Middle Classes in American Politics* (Cambridge, 1940), Lawrence H. Fuchs, *The Political Behavior of American Jews* (Glencoe, 1956) and Nathan Glazer, "Immigrant Groups and Politics," in *Commentary* (July 1952) have provided information on the voting behavior of various groups within the population. Paul T. David, Malcolm Moos, and Ralph M. Goldman, ed., *The National Story* (Baltimore, 1954) is the major book in the five-volume series on *Presidential Nominating Politics in 1952*. Dean Acheson, *A Democrat Looks at His Party* (New York, 1956); Arthur Larson, *A Republican Looks at His Party* (New York, 1956), and Malcolm Moos, *The Republicans* (New York, 1956) shed much light on contemporary partisan politics. See Bernard Berelson and Morris Janowitz, eds., *Reader in Public Opinion and Communication* (Glencoe, 1950) for readings that range over the entire field of public opinion. For theoretical works, Graham Wallas, *Human Nature in Politics* (London, 1908) and Walter Lippmann, *Public Opinion* (New York, 1922) are still both readable and valuable. See also "Freedom in the Opinion Industries" in my *Ideas Are Weapons*. Gerald W. Johnson's characterization of political manipulators as "The Founding Uncles" is in one of a number of articles under that title in *The Reporter* (Jan. 17, 1950).

SEC. 5—*Power and Equilibrium:* On the power system in American life, for contemporary approaches to the nature of power, see Harold Laski, *The State in Theory and Practice* (New York, 1935) and *A Grammar of Politics* (rev. ed., New York, 1937); George Santayana, *Dominations and Powers* (New York, 1951); Bertrand de Jouvenal, *On Power: Its Nature and the History of Its Growth* (Geneva, 1945; New York, 1948), and Bertrand Russell, *Power: A New Social Analysis* (London, 1938). For power on the local scene, see Floyd Hunter, *Community Power Structure* (Chapel Hill, 1955). See also "Machiavelli and Machiavellism" in my *Ideas for the Ice Age*, and "Power Is

What You Make It" in my *It Is Later Than You Think* (rev. ed., New York, 1943). *The Federalist* lays the theoretical framework for the development of the concept of federalism in American life, which is further discussed in De Tocqueville, *Democracy in America.* See also John Calhoun's classic *Disquisition on Government*, excerpted in H. S. Commager, ed., *Living Ideas in America* (New York, 1951). For a lucid exposition of the political process, see James M. Burns and Jack W. Peltason, *Government by the People* (New York, 1952), particularly Chs. 6 and 11; and the Columbia Bicentennial volume, ed., Arthur W. MacMahon, *Federalism, Mature and Emergent* (New York, 1955), which includes valuable essays by Herbert Wechsler, Franz Neumann, Adolph A. Berle, David B. Truman, and Paul A. Freund. Of interest also is Harold Laski, "The Obsolescence of Federalism," *New Republic* (May 30, 1939). See also David Lilienthal, "Political Centralization and Administrative Decentralization" in Bishop and Hendel, eds., *Basic Issues of American Democracy* (New York, 1951). C. Wright Mills, *The Power Elite* (New York, 1956) is the sharpest recent attack on the theory of equilibrium in contemporary America; see also Arthur Kornhauser, ed., *Problems of Power in American Democracy* (Detroit, 1957), especially the essay by Robert S. Lynd, "Power in American Society As Resource and Problem." A well-documented volume on pressure groups is Karl Schriftgiesser, *The Lobbyists* (Boston, 1951), as well as V. O. Key, Jr., *Politics, Parties and Pressure Groups.* See also Ch. 10 of S. K. Bailey and H. D. Samuel, *Congress at Work* (New York, 1952). John Gunther, *Inside USA*, describes regional pressure groups and interests.

SEC. 6—*The Governmental Managers:* For the "fourth branch" of the government, see Robert K. Merton *et al.*, ed., *A Reader in Bureaucracy* (Glencoe, 1952); James M. Landis, *The Administrative Process* (New Haven, 1938), and, for contemporary changes in the power and functions of the manager, James A. Burnham, *The Managerial Revolution* (New York, 1941). See also Leonard D. White, *Introduction to the Study of Public Administration* (New York, 1938), and the same author's *The Federalists* (New York, 1948), *The Jeffersonians* (New York, 1951), and *The Jacksonians* (New York, 1954). See also John P. Roche and Murray S. Stedman, Jr., *The Dynamics of Democratic Government* (New York, 1954), Chs. 8 and 9; James M. Burns and Jack W. Peltason, *Government by the People*

Chs. 17 and 22-25; Harry K. Girvetz, *From Wealth to Welfare* (Stanford, 1950), especially Part 1, as well as John Millett, *Management in the Public Service* (New York, 1954). My essay on the government managers, "The Administrative Revolution in America," is reprinted in my *Ideas for the Ice Age;* see also a symposium, "The Limits of the Welfare State" by Louis Hacker, Charles E. Lindblom, and myself, *American Scholar* (Fall, 1950), and Robert A. Dahl and Charles Lindblom, *Politics, Economics, and Welfare* (New York, 1953). For a recent sociological approach to bureaucracy, see Peter Blau, *Bureaucracy in Modern Society* (New York, 1956), and his *Dynamics of Bureaucracy* (Chicago, 1955); also see Ordway Tead, *The Art of Administration* (New York, 1951), and Philip Selznick, "An Approach to a Theory of Bureaucracy," *American Sociological Review* (Feb. 1942), Vol. VIII, pp. 49-54. For the reference in the text to Brooks Adams, see his *Law of Civilization and Decay* (reprint, New York, 1943), with introduction by Charles A. Beard. The quote from Herbert Luethy is from his *France Against Herself* (New York, 1955), p. 40.

SEC. 7—*Tribunes of the People:* On the American Congress, the classic discussion is in Woodrow Wilson, *Congressional Government* (Baltimore, 1884; reprint, 1956, with introduction by Walter Lippmann). The legislative process is explained in Stephen K. Bailey, *Congress Makes a Law* (New York, 1949) and his *Congress at Work,* written with Howard D. Samuel. For contemporary general studies, see James M. Burns, *Congress on Trial;* Bertram M. Gross, *The Legislative Struggle* (New York, 1953), and George B. Galloway, *The Legislative Process in Congress* (New York, 1953). E. E. Schattschneider is sharply critical of the committee system in "Congress in Conflict," *Yale Review* (1951), Vol. XLI. Ernest S. Griffith, *Congress: Its Contemporary Role* (New York, 1951) is a defense of the legislature in the face of much criticism. For a comparative frame of reference, see John P. Roche and Murray S. Stedman, Jr., *Dynamics of Democratic Government,* Chs. 6 and 7. For detailed discussions, see Roland Young, *This Is Congress* (New York, 1943), and his *Congressional Politics in the Second World War* (New York, 1956); H. H. Wilson, *Congress: Corruption and Compromise* (New York, 1951) is a sharp, if now somewhat dated, discussion of corrupt pressures on the legislators. Dean Acheson, *A Citizen Looks at Congress* (New York, 1956) is excellent for the relation of Congress to the other branches of government. An important study of the

legislative role in international relations is Robert A. Dahl, *Congress and Foreign Policy* (New York, 1950). For further reading on Congressional investigations, see Sec. 10 below, on "The Struggle for Civil Liberties."

SEC. 8—*Law and Justice:* My understanding of the reception of British law draws heavily on the work of Dean Roscoe Pound, particularly *The Spirit of the Common Law* (Boston, 1921), *Interpretations of Legal History* (New York, 1923), *Law and Morals* (Chapel Hill, 1923), and his monumental *The Formative Era of American Law* (Boston, 1939). Helpful volumes dealing mainly with the history of American legal thought are Benjamin F. Wright, *American Interpretations of Natural Law* (Boston, 1942); Richard B. Morris, *Studies in the History of American Law* (New York, 1930); James Willard Hurst, *The Growth of American Law: The Lawmakers* (Boston, 1950) and *Law and the Conditions of Freedom* (Madison, 1956); William W. Crosskey, *Politics and the Constitution in the History of the United States,* 2 vols. (Chicago, 1953), and Mark A. De Wolfe Howe, *Readings in American Legal History* (Cambridge, 1949). On the growth of state law, see Leonard Levy, *The Law of the Commonwealth and Chief Justice Shaw* (Cambridge, 1957). Two of the leading Justices of the Supreme Court have contributed major theoretical works: Oliver Wendell Holmes, *The Common Law* (Boston, 1881), and Benjamin Cardozo, *The Growth of the Law* (New Haven, 1924) and *The Nature of the Judicial Process* (New Haven, 1921). I must, of course, also refer to Jerome Frank, *Law and the Modern Mind* (New York, 1930), and his *Courts on Trial* (Princeton, 1949), as well as Edmond Cahn, "Jerome Frank's Fact Skepticism and Our Future," *Yale Law Review* (May 1957) and Cahn's books, *The Sense of Injustice* (New York, 1951) and *The Moral Decision* (Bloomington, 1955). See also Morris R. Cohen, *Law and the Social Order* (New York, 1933), and Robert McCloskey, ed., *Essays in Constitutional Law* (New York, 1957). One of the best sections in Harold Laski, *The American Democracy,* is his discussion of the legal profession on pp. 571-82. The development of American jurisprudence is seen within the more general framework of our intellectual history in H. S. Commager, *The American Mind* and Morton G. White, *Social Thought in America* (New York, 1949). See also Thurman Arnold, *Symbols of Government* (New Haven, 1935) and *The Folklore of Capitalism* (New Haven, 1943). An essay on the latter work, "The Shadow World of Thurman Arnold," and a more general article, "The Jungle of Legal Thought," are found in my *Ideas Are Weapons*. The reference to Justice Holmes's comment on the Fourteenth Amendment and Spencer's *Social Statics* is found in his opinion in "Lochner vs. New York" in my *The Mind and Faith of Justice Holmes* (Boston, 1943). Many useful references are included in the Notes for Further Reading for the next section.

SEC. 9—*Keepers of the Covenant:* Several volumes on the historical development of the Supreme Court are particularly useful: Charles Warren, *The Supreme Court in United States History* (Boston, 1922); C. G. Haines, *The American Doctrine of Judicial Supremacy* (rev. ed., Berkeley, 1932); Bernard Schwartz, *The Supreme Court* (New York, 1957), and Lewis B. Boudin, *Government by Judiciary* (New York, 1932). See also E. S. Corwin, *Twilight of the Supreme Court* (New Haven, 1934); Charles Evans Hughes, *The Supreme Court of the United States* (New York, 1927); Edmond Cahn, ed., *Supreme Court and Supreme Law* (Bloomington, 1954), and Fred Rodell, *Nine Men* (New York, 1955).

Among works dealing with particular themes in Supreme Court history are Robert Jackson, *Struggle for Judicial Supremacy* (New York, 1947), and C. Herman Pritchett, *The Roosevelt Court* (New York, 1943), and his *Civil Liberties and the Vinson Court* (New York, 1954). Paul Freund, *On Understanding the Supreme Court* (Boston, 1949) and Clinton Rossiter, *The Supreme Court and the Commander in Chief* (Ithaca, 1951) are most helpful in understanding the nature of the powers of the Court. H. S. Commager, *Majority Rule and Minority Rights* (New York, 1943) is sharply critical of judicial review.

Much of the biographical material on individual Justices sheds light on the functioning of the Court itself, particularly Albert J. Beveridge, *Life of John Marshall*, 4 vols. (Boston 1916-19); C. B. Swisher, *Roger B. Taney* (New York, 1935); Charles Fairman, *Mr. Justice Miller and the Supreme Court* (Cambridge, 1938); Merlo J. Pusey, *Charles Evans Hughes*, 2 vols. (New York, 1951), and R. G. McCloskey, *American Conservatism in an Age of Enterprise* (Cambridge, 1951), which includes a discussion of Stephen J. Field.

I may cite more extensively the works on recent members of the Court: Felix Frankfurter, *Mr. Justice Holmes and the Supreme Court* (Cambridge, 1938); Felix Frankfurter, ed., *Mr. Justice Holmes* (New York, 1931), including essays by Benjamin Cardozo, Morris R. Cohen, John Dewey and Harold Laski; Felix Frankfurter, ed., *Mr. Justice Brandeis* (New Haven, 1932), including articles by Charles Evans Hughes, Oliver Wendell Holmes, and myself; Samuel J. Konefsky, *The Legacy of Holmes and Brandeis* (New York, 1956), and Alpheus Thomas Mason, *Brandeis: A Free Man's Life* (New York, 1946). The work of Mark A. De Wolfe Howe is relevant here both as editor of the revealing *Holmes-Pollock Letters*, 2 vols. (Cambridge, 1941) and the *Holmes-Laski Letters*, 2 vols. (Cambridge, 1953), and as the author of *Justice Holmes: The Shaping Years* (Cambridge, 1957), part of a projected multi-volume work. For a further understanding of recent Court trends, see Alpheus T. Mason, *Harlan Fiske Stone* (New York, 1956); John Frank, *Mr. Justice Black: The Man and His Opinions* (New York, 1948); Samuel J. Konefsky, ed., *The Constitutional World of Mr. Justice Frankfurter* (New York, 1949); John P. Roche, "The Utopian Pilgrimage of Mr. Justice Murphy," *Vanderbilt Law Review* (Spring, 1957), and John P. Frank, "Justice Murphy: The Goals Attempted," *Yale Law Journal* (Dec. 1949).

My own *Ideas Are Weapons* contains essays on John Marshall, Roger Taney, Oliver Wendell Holmes, Jr., Louis D. Brandeis, Hugo Black, "The Supreme Court and American Capitalism," and "Minority Rule and the Constitutional Tradition." "Constitution and Court as Symbols," "Notes on the Supreme Court Crisis," and "Constitutional Crisis and the Crisis State" are found in my *Ideas for the Ice Age*. See also my *The Mind and Faith of Justice Holmes* and "The Supreme Court," *Holiday* (Feb. 1950). Relevant material for this section will also be found in the Notes for Reading for Secs. 8 and 10 of this chapter. The reference to "Mr. Dooley" is from Elmer Ellis, ed., *Mr. Dooley at His Best* (New York, 1938), p. 77.

SEC. 10—*The Struggle for Civil Liberties:* The number of volumes available on the subject of civil liberties is legion and has increased with the recent assaults on individual rights. Among the most basic volumes are Zechariah Chafee, Jr., ed., *Documents on Fundamental Human Rights*, 3 vols. (Cambridge, 1951-52; *Free Speech in the United States* (Cambridge, 1941), and *Blessings of Liberty* (Philadelphia, 1956); Merle Curti, *Roots of American Loyalty* (New York, 1946); Thomas I. Emerson and David M. Haber, eds., *Political and Civil Rights in the United States* (New York, 1952), and Alan Barth, *The Loyalty of Free Men* (New York,

1951). See also H. S. Commager, *Freedom, Loyalty, and Dissent* (New York, 1954); Leo Pfeffer, *The Liberties of an American* (Boston, 1956), and Learned Hand, *The Spirit of Liberty* (New York, 1953).

Specialized studies of value are Robert K. Carr, *Federal Protection of Civil Rights: The Quest for a Sword* (Ithaca, 1947); Milton Konvitz, *The Constitution and Civil Rights* (New York, 1947), and Osmond K. Fraenkel, *The Supreme Court and Civil Liberties* (rev. ed., New York, 1955). The major works on freedom of religion in America are Leo Pfeffer, *Church, State and Freedom* (Boston, 1953); Paul Blanshard's highly controversial *American Freedom and Catholic Power* (Boston, 1949), and Joseph L. Blau, *Cornerstones of Religious Freedom in America* (Boston, 1949).

Problems of academic freedom are considered in Robert M. MacIver, *Academic Freedom in Our Time* (New York, 1955); Richard McKeon, Robert K. Merton and Walter Gellhorn, *The Freedom to Read* (New York, 1957), and Russell Kirk, *Academic Freedom* (Chicago, 1955), which conveys the position of the radical Right. The national security program is the subject of highly competent studies by Eleanor Bontecou, *The Federal Loyalty-Security Program* (Ithaca, 1953); Edward A. Shils, *The Torment of Secrecy* (Glencoe, 1956); Alan Barth, *Government by Investigation* (New York, 1955), and Harold Lasswell's earlier but most useful *National Security and Individual Freedom* (New York, 1950). See also Morton Grodzins, *Americans Betrayed* (Chicago, 1949) and *The Loyal and the Disloyal* (Chicago, 1956).

For books presenting critical reactions to the McCarthy era, see Telford Taylor, *Grand Inquest* (New York, 1955); James Wechsler, *The Age of Suspicion* (New York, 1953); Elmer Davis, *But We Were Born Free* (Indianapolis, 1953), and Norman Thomas, *The Test of Freedom* (New York, 1954). Protection from self-incrimination is considered in two strongly contrasting books: Erwin Griswold, *The Fifth Amendment Today* (Cambridge, 1955), and Sidney Hook, *Common Sense and the Fifth Amendment* (New York, 1957)—the latter's *Heresy, Yes—Conspiracy, No* (New York, 1953) was sharply reasoned and exerted considerable influence. Robert K. Carr, *The House Committee on Un-American Activities, 1945-50* (Ithaca, 1952) and Samuel A. Stouffer, *Communism, Conformity, and Civil Liberties* (New York, 1955) shed much light on recent developments. A Cornell University study includes three especially enlightening reports on civil liberties in the individual states: Edward L. Barrett, Jr., *The Tenney Committee* (Ithaca, 1951); Vern Countryman, *Un-American Activities in the State of Washington* (Ithaca, 1951), and Walter Gellhorn, *The State and Subversion* (Ithaca, 1952).

Some of the features of the national hysteria are discussed in Daniel Bell, ed., *The New American Right* (New York, 1955). The most significant books on the Alger Hiss case are Whittaker Chambers, *Witness* (New York, 1952); Alger Hiss, *In the Court of Public Opinion* (New York, 1957), and Alistair Cooke, *A Generation on Trial* (New York, 1950). Material dealing with the J. Robert Oppenheimer hearings and the relationship of science to the security program is included in the Notes for Further Reading for Ch. IV, Sec. 2. Other books on civil liberties are mentioned in the bibliographies for Secs. 1, 2, 3, 8 and 9 of this chapter.

Chapter VII: Class and Status in America

SEC. 1—*The Open-Class Society*, SEC. 7—*The Badges of Belonging*, and SEC. 8—*The Democratic Class Struggle:* For the larger picture of the class structure and social stratification, see the very useful book of readings, Reinhard Bendix and Seymour M. Lipset, *Class, Status, and Power* (Glencoe, 1953), and Bernard Barber, *Social Stratification* (New York, 1957), which also has a comprehensive bibliography. For a discussion of American status structure, see C. Wright Mills, *White Collar* (New York, 1951), Ch. 11. I have drawn heavily upon some of the classic works in American community studies: Warner *et al.*, *Democracy in Jonesville* (New York, 1949), and Robert and Helen Lynd, *Middletown* (New York, 1929), along with their later study *Middletown in Transition* (New York, 1937). I have also been helped by W. Lloyd Warner and Paul S. Lunt, *The Social Life of a Modern Community* (New Haven, 1941); Robin Williams, Jr., *American Society: A Sociological Interpretation* (New York, 1951), and W. Lloyd Warner, Marcia Meeker and Kenneth Ellis, *Social Class in America* (Chicago, 1949). Also see Frederick L. Allen, *The Big Change* (New York, 1952), Ch. 15, "The All-American Standard," pp. 209-33; and Davis, Gardner, and Gardner, *Deep South* (Chicago, 1941), "Life in the Classes," pp. 253-62. See also August B. Hollingshead, *Elmtown's Youth* (New York, 1949), and an excellent recent community study by John R. Seeley, R. A. Sim, and E. W. Loosley, *Crestwood Heights* (New York, 1956). For an analysis of the class theory of the pioneer American sociologists, see Charles H. Page, *Class and American Sociology* (New York, 1940); see also Melvin Tumin, "Some Principles of Stratification," *American Sociological Review* (Aug. 1953). A comparative study of social mobility is Pitirim Sorokin, *Social Mobility* (New York, 1927). Also see Talcott Parsons, *The Structure of Social Action* (Glencoe, 1951); Robert K. Merton, *Social Theory and Social Structure* (Glencoe, 1949), and W. Lloyd Warner, *American Life: Dream and Reality* (Chicago, 1953). Selected readings on class are to be found in *Modern American Society*, eds., Kingsley Davis, Harry C. Bredemeier, and M. J. Levy (New York, 1949), Part 4. For a brief introductory study, along with a good bibliography, see Kurt B. Mayer, *Class and Society* (New York, 1955). See also my Notes for Further Reading on Ch. III, Sec. 8.

The reference to H. Dewey Anderson and Percy E. Davidson in the text is to their study of career patterns, geographical and vertical mobility, and occupational inheritance among men in San Jose, California, *Occupational Mobility in an American Community* (Stanford, 1937). The reference to F. W. Taussig and C. S. Joslyn is to their book, *American Business Leaders* (New York, 1932). The reference to W. Lloyd Warner and James Abegglen is to *Occupational Mobility in American Business and Industry* (Minneapolis, 1955). The reference to Veblen is to his *Theory of the Leisure Class* (New York, 1899). For Mayo and Roethlisberger citations, see Notes for Further Reading on Ch. IV, Sec. 4. The reference to John Dollard is to his work *Caste and Class in a Southern Town* (New Haven, 1937; with new introduction, New York, 1957). Also see Allison Davis, Burleigh B. Gardner, and Mary R. Gardner, *Deep South*, and Hortense Powdermaker, *After Freedom* (New York, 1939), which discuss the effect of class and caste on whites and Negroes in the South. For a discussion of Warner's "six-class system," see Walter R. Goldschmidt, "America's Six Social Classes," *Commentary* (Aug. 1950).

For an analysis of voting behavior and class, see Dewey Anderson and Percy E. Davidson, *Ballots and the Democratic Class Struggle* (Stanford, 1943), especially Ch. 2, "Occupational Status and Political Behavior," and Ch. 4, "Class Consciousness and Political Behavior."

The quote from Irving Howe is from his *William Faulkner, A Critical Study* (New York, 1952). The reference to Karl Popper is to his book *The Open Society and Its Enemies* (Princeton, 1950). Rich-

ard Centers' work, *The Psychology of Social Classes* (Princeton, 1949), is an empirical cross-section study of subjective and objective class images. The quote from Russell Davenport is from his *The Dignity of Man* (New York, 1955).

SEC. 2—*The Seats of the Mighty:* On the American elites, I have drawn upon C. Wright Mills, *The Power Elite* (New York, 1956), a brilliantly conceived and written work which has left its impact on my thinking even where (as I have indicated in the text) I differ with it. In a vigorous article on Mills, Robert S. Lynd in "Power in the United States," *Nation* (May 12, 1956), argues that a dominant ruling class rather than a power elite exists in the American structure of power. For the background of much of the current discussion of American elites the reader can go back to Gaetano Mosca, *The Ruling Class* (New York, 1939), and Vilfredo Pareto, *The Mind and Society* (New York, 1939), and to my own essay, "Pareto's Republic," in *Ideas Are Weapons* (New York, 1939). José Ortega y Gasset, *The Revolt of the Masses* (new ed., New York, 1950) considers moral distinctions between mass and elite. I have also drawn upon David Riesman, *The Lonely Crowd* (rev. ed., New York, 1953), pp. 246-59, reprinted in Reinhard Bendix and Seymour Lipset, *Class, Status and Power*. In this same collection of readings, see Daniel Bell, "America's Un-Marxist Revolution"; E. Digby Baltzell, " 'Who's Who in America' and 'The Social Register': Elite and Upper Class Indexes in Metropolitan America"; Harold Kaufman, "Prestige Classes in a New Rural Community"; and Reinhard Bendix, "Social Stratification and Political Power." See also Floyd Hunter's survey, *Community Power Structure* (Chapel Hill, 1955). For a discussion of the elite tradition in America, see Gustavus Myers, *History of the Great American Fortunes* (New York, 1907; rev. ed., 1936), and Sidney Ratner, *New Lights on the History of Great American Fortunes* (New York, 1933).

SEC. 3—*The New Middle Classes:* On the middle classes, I have gained much from C. Wright Mills, *White Collar*, an outstanding book in this field. Russell Lynes, *A Surfeit of Honey* (New York, 1957) presents a fresh view of old class structures in dissolution and new ones in formation. The reference to Laski in the text is to *The American Democracy* (New York, 1948). See his *The Rise of European Liberalism* (London, 1936) for an earlier viewpoint in which middle class liberalism is interpreted as the bulwark of an emerging capitalism. In my discussion of middle class frustration I have taken Nietzsche's notion of "ressentiment" and carried it over from the proletariat (to whom Nietzsche applied it) to the middle classes. For a discussion of the same transition in the European context, see Svend Ranulf, *Moral Indignation and the Middle Class Psychology* (Copenhagen, 1938), and Max Scheler, "Das Ressentiment im Aufbau der Moralen" in *Vom Umsturz der Werte*, Vol. 1, (Leipzig, 1923; new ed., Berne, 1955). Also see Robert K. Merton, *Social Theory and Social Structure* (Glencoe, 1949). For commentary upon the relationship of wealth to social distinction in American history, see Dixon Wecter, *The Saga of American Society* (New York, 1937). For an analysis of business elites, see Robert A. Brady, *Business As a System of Power* (New York, 1943), and William Foote Whyte, ed., *Industry and Society* (New York, 1946).

SEC. 4—*Class Profile of the Worker:* On the working class as part of the American class system, see C. Wright Mills, *The New Men of Power* (New York, 1948); also Reinhard Bendix and S. N. Lipset, eds., *Class, Status, and Power*, especially Part 4, "Social Mobility in the U.S.," reprinting Katherine Archibald, "Status Orientations Among Shipyard Workers" and Herbert H. Hyman, "The Value Systems of Different Classes"; and S. M. Lipset and Joan Gordon, "Mobility and Trade Union Membership." See also Eli Chinoy, *Automobile Workers and the American Dream* (New York, 1955), and his "The Tradition of Opportunity and the Aspirations of Automobile Workers," *American Journal of Sociology* (March 1952).

SEC. 5—*The Minority Situation:* For the various minorities in American life, I have leaned upon G. E. Simpson and J. M. Yinzer, *Racial and Cultural Minorities* (New York, 1953), and Oscar Handlin, *Race and Nationality in American Life* (Boston, 1957).

On specific minorities: for the Jews see Oscar Handlin, *Adventure in Freedom* (New York, 1954) and Nathan Glazer, *American Judaism* (Chicago, 1957); on Puerto Ricans there is C. Wright Mills (in collaboration with Clarence Senior and Rose Kohn) *The Puerto Rican Journey: America's Newest Migrants* (New York, 1950); on Catholics, see John Tracy Ellis, *American Catholicism* (Chicago, 1957); on Japanese-Americans there are both Carey McWilliams, *Prejudice: Japanese-Americans, Symbol of Racial Intolerance* (Boston, 1949), and Morton Grodzins, *Americans Betrayed* (Chicago, 1949). The history of anti-Semitism in the U.S. is discussed in Oscar and Mary Handlin, *Danger in Discord: Origins of Anti-Semitism in the U.S.* (Anti-Defamation League, New York, 1948). Also see Kurt Lewin, "Self-Hatred Among Jews" in Arnold Rose, ed., *Race Prejudice and Discrimination* (New York, 1951), pp. 321-32. The chapter on "America and its Minority Problems" in Laski, *The American Democracy*, pp. 452-86, has been helpful, as well as a number of articles in Swanson, Newcomb, and Hartley, *Readings in Social Psychology* (New York, 1952). Among these are Bruno Bettelheim and Morris Janowitz, "Ethnic Tolerance: A Function of Social and Political Control," pp. 593-602; Morton Deutsch and Mary Evans Collins, "The Effect of Public Policy in Housing Projects upon Interracial Attitudes," pp. 582-92, and August Campbell, "Factors Associated with Attitudes Towards Jews," pp. 603-11. Also see J. Himelhoch, "A Personality Type Associated with Prejudice," in Arnold Rose, ed., *Race Prejudice and Discrimination*, along with other essays in that volume. Also see Will Herberg, *Protestant, Catholic, Jew* (Garden City, 1955), and Stewart G. and Mildred Wiese Cole, *Minorities and the American Promise* (New York, 1954). The reference in the text is to Carey McWilliams, *A Mask of Privilege* (Boston, 1948). The T. W. Adorno *et al.* study which is cited is *The Authoritarian Personality* (New York, 1950). The Roper poll referred to in the text was conducted in September 1948 and was reported on in a radio broadcast of *Where the People Stand* over CBS on February 27, 1949.

SEC. 6—*The Negro in America:* On the situation of the Negro, I have drawn upon the wealth of material available including several works which concern themselves with the position of Negroes in America from an over-all perspective: Gunnar Myrdal, *An American Dilemma* (New York, 1944); Maurice R. Davie, *Negroes in American Society* (New York, 1949), and E. Franklin Frazier, *The Negro in the United States* (rev. ed., New York, 1957). On the question of school desegregation, see Robin M. Williams, Jr., and Margaret W. Ryan, *Schools in Transition* (Chapel Hill, 1954); Harry S. Ashmore, *The Negro and the Schools* (Chapel Hill, 1954), and Herbert H. Hyman and Paul B. Sheatsley, "Attitudes Toward Desegregation," *Scientific American* (Dec. 1956). On Negroes as a factor in American politics and labor, see Paul Lewinson, *Race, Class and Party* (New York, 1932); Henry Lee Moon, *Balance of Power: The Negro Vote* (New York, 1948); Horace R. Cayton and George S. Mitchell, *Black Workers and the New Unions* (Chapel Hill, 1944); Herbert R. Northrup, *Organized Labor and the Negro* (New York, 1944); Sterling D. Spero and Abram L. Harris, *The Black Worker* (New York, 1931). For an analysis of Negro social adaptations to their economic gains in American society, see E. Franklin Frazier, *Black Bourgeoisie* (Glencoe, 1957), which includes a discussion of the emerging Negro middle class. An intimate view of Negro life will be found in Arnold Rose, *The Negro Morale* (Minneapolis, 1949); see also E. Franklin Frazier, *The Negro Family in the United States* (rev. ed., New York, 1951), and St. Clair Drake and Horace R. Cayton, *Black Metropolis* (New York, 1945). On race, see Franz Boas, *Race, Language, and Culture* (New York, 1940), and W. Lloyd Warner, Buford H. Junker, and Walter A. Adams, *Color and Human Nature* (Washington, 1941); see also Melville J. Herskovits, *The Myth of the Negro Past* (New York, 1941).

Other sources which I have found useful are Otto Klineberg, ed., *Characteristics of the American Negro* (New York, 1944); C. Vann Woodward, *The Strange Career of Jim Crow* (New York, 1955); Roi Ottley, *Black Odyssey: The Story of the Negro in America* (New York, 1948), and Margaret Just Butcher, *The Negro in American Culture* (New York, 1956). Of the literature which has been written by Negroes in America the following novels are noteworthy: Countee Cullen, *One Way to Heaven* (New York, 1932); Richard Wright, *Native Son* (New York, 1940); Ralph Ellison, *Invisible Man* (New York, 1952), and James Baldwin, *Go Tell It on the Mountain* (New York, 1953), as well as his *Giovanni's Room* (New York, 1956), on a homosexual theme. For poetry, see Langston Hughes, *The Weary Blues* (New York, 1926) and *Montage of a Dream Deferred* (New York, 1951).

The reference in the text is to Oliver C. Cox, *Caste, Class, and Race* (New York, 1948). The reference to Franz Boas is to *Race, Language, and Culture*. The analysis by Kardiner and Ovesey will be found in *The Mark of Oppression* (New York, 1951). The study of interracial housing mentioned in the text is M. Deutsch and M. E. Collins, "The Effect of Public Policy in Housing Projects upon Interracial Attitudes" in Swanson, Newcomb, and Hartley, eds., *Readings in Social Psychology*. The reference to Henry Lee Moon is to *Balance of Power: The Negro Vote*. The reference in the text is to John Dollard, *Caste and Class in a Southern Town*. The reference to Roi Ottley is to his *No Green Pastures* (New York, 1951).

Chapter VIII: Life Cycle of the American

SEC. 1—*The Personality in the Culture:* On the interplay of man and society, I have drawn upon several sources, among which are G. C. Homans, *The Human Group* (New York, 1950), Ch. 12, "The Individual and the Group"; Otto Klineberg, *Social Psychology* (rev. ed., New York, 1954), Chs. 12 and 13; J. J. Honigman, *Culture and Personality* (New York, 1954); James S. Plant, *The Envelope* (New York, 1950), and *Personality and the Culture Pattern* (New York, 1937), and John Dollard, *Criteria for the Life History* (New Haven, 1935). See also A. H. Maslow, *Motivation and Personality* (New York, 1954), and "Power Relationships and Patterns of Personal Development," included in Arthur Kornhauser, ed., *Patterns of Power in American Democracy* (Detroit, 1957); Ralph Linton, *The Cultural Background* (New York, 1949); David Riesman, *The Lonely Crowd* (rev. ed., New York, 1953); John Dewey, *Human Nature and Conduct* (New York, 1922); Ruth Benedict, *Patterns of Culture* (New York, 1934); Clyde Kluckhohn and Henry A. Murray, *Personality in Nature, Society, and Culture* (New York, 1948; rev. ed., 1953), and Prescott Lecky, *Self-Consistency: A Theory of Personality* (New York, 1945). An excellent discussion of the man on the periphery of his society is Bernard Rosenberg, *The Values of Veblen* (Washington, 1956), Ch. 1, "The Stranger." For something of the same problem, see Joseph Wood Krutch, *Henry David Thoreau* (New York, 1948). For a psychoanalytic discussion of the relation of society to man, see Sigmund Freud, *Civilization and Its Discontents* (New York, 1930), and Herbert Marcuse, *Eros and Civilization* (Boston, 1955).

The reference to Arnold Van Gennep is to *Les Rites des Passage* (Paris, 1909). The remark of James Klee is from correspondence with the author. The quote from John Dollard is from *Criteria for the Life History*. The reference to Ruth Benedict is to *Patterns of Culture*. Joseph Campbell's work is *The Hero with a Thousand Faces* (New York, 1949). The reference in the text to B. Malinowski is to his extensive work on the Trobriand Islands, particularly *The Sexual Life of Savages in North-West Melanesia* (New York, 1929) and *Sex and Repression in Savage Society* (new ed., New York, 1955). The reference to A. R. Radcliffe-Brown is to *The Andaman Islanders* (Cambridge, 1933). C. G. Homan's formulation will be found in *The Human Group*. The reference to Oscar Handlin is to *The Uprooted* (Boston, 1952).

SEC. 2—*The Family As Going Concern,* and SEC. 3—*Children and Parents:* On the structure and function of the family in American society and on the child-parent relationship in it, there are many good works available. On the family, see Ruth N. Anshen, ed., *The Family, Its Function and Destiny* (New York, 1949); Marvin Sussman, *Marriage and the Family* (Boston, 1955); Willard Waller, *The Family: A Dynamic Interpretation* (New York, 1938); Arthur W. Calhoun, *A Social History of the American Family* (New York, 1945); see also Meyer F. Nimkoff, *Marriage and the Family* (Cambridge, 1947); Talcott Parsons and Robert F. Bales, *Family Socialization and Interaction Processes* (Glencoe, 1955), and William Peterson, "The New American Family," *Commentary* (Jan. 1956), pp. 1-6. Further references are Howard Becker and Reuben Hill, eds., *Family, Marriage, and Parenthood* (Boston, 1948). Andrew G. Truxal and Francis E. Merrill, *The Family in American Society* (New York, 1947); Carl F. Zimmerman, *The Family of Tomorrow* (New York, 1949), and W. Allison Davis and Robert J. Havighurst, *Father of the Man* (Boston, 1947). For comparisons to the European family structure, see Max Horkheimer, ed., *Autoritaet Und Familie* (Paris, 1936), and Lewis Coser, "Some Aspects of Soviet Family Policy," *American Journal of Sociology* (March 1951). On the child-parent relationship, see Daniel R. Miller and Guy E. Swanson, *The American Parent in the Twentieth Century: A Study in the Detroit Area* (Ann Arbor, 1954); L. Joseph Stone and Joseph Church, *Childhood and Adolescence* (New York, 1957); Erik H. Erikson, *Childhood and Society* (New York, 1950) ;William E. Martin and Celia B. Stendler, *Child Development: The Process of Growing Up in Society* (New York, 1953), and Peter Blos, *The Adolescent Personality* (New York, 1941). See also J. H. S. Bossard, *The Sociology of Child Development* (New York, 1948); J. Piaget, *The Language and Thought of the Child* (New York, 1926), *The Child's Conception of the World* (New York, 1929), and *The Moral Judgment of the Child* (New York, 1932).

Of further interest will be Arnold W. Green, "The Middle Class Male Child and Neurosis," *American Sociological Review* (Feb. 1946), pp. 31-41, and Lawrence K. Frank, *Society As the Patient* (New Brunswick, 1948).

The reference in the text to Geoffrey Gorer is to *The American People* (New York, 1948). Philip Wylie's discussion of "Momism" is in his *Generation of Vipers* (New York, 1942). The reference to William J. Goode is to "Economic Factors and Marriage Stability," *American Sociological Review* (Dec. 1951). The reference to Lewis Mumford is to *The Conduct of Life* (New York, 1951). Arnold Green's discussion of "personality absorption" is in the article mentioned above.

SEC. 4—*Growing Up in America:* On the maturing process, see Dixon Wecter, *Sam Clemens of Hannibal* (Boston, 1952). For other material on the growing-up years, see the Notes for Further Reading for Sec. 3 ("Children and Parents").

SEC. 5—*Courtship, Love, and Marriage:* For the history of mating patterns, see Henri Birnbaum, *Love and Love's Philosophy* (New York, 1955), and E. S. Turner, *A History of Courting* (New York, 1955). On common problems of marriage, see Victor W. Eisenstein, ed., *Neurotic Interaction in Marriage* (New York, 1956). Also Philip Polatin and Ellen C. Phillips, *Marriage in the Modern World* (New York, 1956), and Abraham N. Franzblau, *The Road to Sexual Maturity* (New York, 1954). On divorce and its sequels, see William J. Goode, *After Divorce* (Glencoe, 1956). Other relevant material on this subject may be found in the notes for further reading for Sec. 2 of this chapter ("The Family As Going Concern"), and those on Ch. IX, Sec. 6 ("Morals in Revolution").

The reference in the text to Denis de Rougemont is to *Love in the Western World* (New York, 1939-40). The reference to Geoffrey Gorer is to *The American People* (New York, 1948). Margaret Mead's definition of a successful date will be found in *Male and Female* (New York, 1949). The reference to psychiatric views on marriage is from Victor W. Eisenstein, *Neurotic Interaction in Marriage.* The later reference in the text to Geoffrey Gorer is to *Exploring English Character* (London, 1955). William J. Goode's observations are in *After Divorce.* The reference in the text to Mirra Komarovsky is to *The Unemployed Man and His Family* (New York, 1940).

SEC. 6—*The Ordeal of the American Woman:* On women in American society, I have drawn upon a large variety of works. On the role of women in American society, see Mirra Komarovsky, *Women in the Modern World* (Boston, 1953); Ferdinand Lundberg and Marynia F. Farnham, *Modern Woman, The Lost Sex* (New York, 1947); Eric John Dingwall, *The American Woman* (New York, 1956); Elizabeth Bragdon, ed., *Women Today* (New York, 1953). On female sexuality, see Alfred Kinsey *et al., Sexual Behavior in the Human Female* (Philadelphia, 1953); Albert Ellis, ed., *Sex Life of the*

American Woman and the Kinsey Report (New York, 1954); Marie Bonaparte, *Female Sexuality* (New York, 1953), and A. M. Krich, ed., *Women: The Variety and Meaning of the Sexual Experience* (New York, 1953). A background to the study of women in American society will be found in Viola Klein, *The Feminine Character: History of an Ideology* (New York, 1949). Also see B. F. Ashley Montagu, *The Natural Superiority of Women* (New York, 1953). For a foreign view of the position of women in society, see Simone de Beauvoir, *The Second Sex* (New York, 1953). The reference in the text to Simone de Beauvoir will be found here. The remarks of Stanley Diamond are from a correspondence with the author. Diamond's views are expanded in "Kibbutz and Shtetl," *Social Problems* (Oct. 1957). The reference to Margaret Mead is to *Male and Female*. The classic studies on female sexual dissatisfaction referred to in the text are G. V. Hamilton, *A Research in Marriage* (New York, 1929), and K. B. Davis, *Factors in the Sex Life of 2200 Women* (New York, 1929). The reference in the text to Mary Wollstonecraft is to *A Vindication of the Rights of Women* (London, 1792).

SEC. 7—*The Middle and End of the Journey:* On growing old in America, I have gained much from David Riesman, "Some Clinical and Cultural Aspects of the Aging Process," in his *Individualism Reconsidered* (Glencoe, 1951), pp. 484-91, and Ruth S. Cavan, "Old Age in a City of 100,000," *Illinois Academy of Science Transactions* (1947). See also Martin Gumpert's articles: "Recharting Life for an Aging America," *New York Times Magazine* (Aug. 13, 1950); "Our 'Inca' Ideas About Retirement," *New York Times Magazine* (July 27, 1952), and "The Shock of Aging," *The American Scholar* (Jan. 1950). Research on aging and its effects has been in progress for a number of years under David Riesman and associates in Kansas City. The final results have not yet been published. However, see David Riesman, "A Career Drama in a Middle-Aged Farmer," *Bulletin of the Menninger Clinic* (Jan. 1954), pp. 1-8. See also reports of the National Conference on Aging, *Man and His Years* (Raleigh, 1951). On death, see Virginia Moore, *Ho For Heaven: Man's Changing Attitude Toward Death* (New York, 1946), and Margaret Mead and Nicholas Calas, *Primitive Heritage* (New York, 1953), Part 15, pp. 534-77. The reference in the text is to Margaret Mead, *Male and Female*. The reference to Havighurst and Albrecht is to their study, *Older People* (New York, 1953).

Chapter IX: Character and Society

SEC. 1—*The Cement of a Society:* For the cohesive factors in American society, the best discussion is in De Tocqueville, *op. cit.*, Vol. I, Ch. 17; Vol. II, Book I, Chs. 1 and 2. The best brief contemporary analysis I have found is in Robin M. Williams, Jr., *American Society* (New York, 1951), Ch. 14, "The Integration of American Society"; see also Talcott Parsons, *The Social System* (Glencoe, 1951). Among those who discuss the need for some principle of cohesion, see R. Nisbet, *The Quest for Community* (New York, 1953), Erich Fromm, *The Sane Society* (New York, 1955), and Russell W. Davenport, *The Dignity of Man* (New York, 1955). My reference to Northrop in the text is to F.S.C. Northrop, *The Meeting of East and West* (New York, 1946), Ch. 3, "The Free Culture of the U.S.," discussing Locke's ideas, and Ch. 4, "Unique Elements in British Democracy," discussing Hooker's. The reference in the text to Polanyi is to Karl Polanyi, *The Great Transformation* (New York, 1944). The movie I mention in the text is *Crossfire*. The idea of "false personalization" will be found in Riesman's *The Lonely Crowd* (rev. ed., New York, 1953). The reference to Alistair Cooke is to his book of sprightly and perceptive essays, *One Man's America* (New York, 1952). The Ferdinand Tonnies book to which I refer is his *Gemeinschaft und Gesellschaft* (Berlin, 1920). The reference to Helen Mims is to an important but still unpublished manuscript on community and society in the modern Western world. See also Max Weber, *Wirtschaft und Gesellschaft* (Tubingen, 2nd enlarged ed., 1925), Part I, Ch. 3; Part III, Chs. 7, 8 and 10.

SEC. 2—*The Joiners:* On voluntary associations and "propensity to join," the classic passage in De Tocqueville on the "principle of association" is in Vol. I (Vintage ed.), Ch. 12, especially pp. 203-5. The best brief contemporary discussion is in W. Lloyd Warner, *American Life: Dream and Reality* (Chicago, 1953), Ch. 9, "Associations in America." For an interesting theoretical approach of the anthropologists, see Eliot D. Chapple and Carleton S. Coon, *Principles of Anthropology* (New York, 1942), Ch. 17, "Associations," pp. 416-42; see also several readings in Margaret Mead and Nicolas Calas, *Primitive Heritage* (New York, 1953), especially pp. 64-6 on "Blood Brotherhood," pp. 213-21, "The Mischievous Society of Boys," and pp. 22-30, "Graded Associations and Secret Societies." For the lesser participation of the lower-income groups in clubs and associations, see Genevieve Knupfer, "Portrait of the Underdog," *Public Opinion Quarterly*, Vol. II (1947), pp. 103-14, reprinted in Bendix and Lipset, *Class, Status, and Power* (Glencoe, 1953), pp. 255-63. On the "togetherness" compulsive in middle-class suburbia, see W. H. Whyte, Jr., *The Organization Man* (New York, 1956). For the crucial place of the church in Negro organizational life, see E. Franklin Frazier, *Black Bourgeoisie* (New York, 1957), pp. 87-90, and for other Negro associations, *ibid.*, pp. 90-5. See also C. W. Ferguson, *Fifty Million Brothers* (New York, 1937). For a recent little booklet intended as a guide to joiners, see *How to Be a Member* (New York, 1956). The reference in the text to Reuel Denney is to his article, "Hail Meeters: Greeters Farewell," *Commentary* (Oct. 1951).

SEC. 3—*Manners, Taste, and Fashion:* On manners and etiquette, the theme of American manners has held a continuing fascination for foreign travelers in America. De Tocqueville, *op. cit.*, devoted the whole of Vol. II, Book III to it, "Influence of Democracy on Manners, Properly So-Called," especially Chs. 1-4 and 14; Mrs. Frances Trollope also discussed it in *Domestic Manners of the Americans*, new edition by Donald Smalley (New York, 1949), and her son, Anthony Trollope, returned to the theme in his *North America*, new edition by Donald Smalley (New York, 1951); see also David Macrae, *The Americans at Home* (Edinburgh, 1871; new ed., New York, 1952), and Warren S. Tryon, *A Mirror for Americans*, 3 vols. (Chicago, 1952), which gathers together excerpts from American travelers between 1790 and 1870. On books of etiquette, see A. M. Schlesinger, *Learning How to Behave: A Historical Study of American Etiquette Books* (New York, 1947); of the books he considers, the most famous were Lillian Eichler, *Book of Etiquette* (1st ed., Oyster Bay, New York, 1922), and Emily Post, *Etiquette* (New York, 1955), which went through many successive printings; for a good essay on Emily Post, see Edmund Wilson, "Books of Etiquette and Emily Post," *The New Yorker* (July 19, 1947); see also *Amy Vanderbilt's Complete Book of Etiquette* (New York, 1952).

On taste I have relied heavily upon Russell Lynes, *The Tastemakers* (New York, 1954), and upon Oliver W. Larkin, *Art and Life in America* (New York, 1949). The widely quoted essay by Lynes, "Highbrow, Lowbrow, Middlebrow," first published in *Harpers* (Feb. 1949), is reprinted in *The Tastemakers* as Ch. 17. There is a brilliant analysis of "Pecuniary Canons of Taste" in Veblen's *Theory of the Leisure Class* (New York, 1899), Ch. 6, which is reprinted in *The Portable Veblen* (New York, 1948), pp. 151-96; see also Louis Kronenberger, *Company Manners* (Indianapolis, 1954). The quote in the text from Cooper will be found in Lynes, *op. cit.*, p. 7.

On dress and fashion, see A. L. Kroeber, "Order in Changes of Fashion" and "Three Centuries of Women's Dress," articles reprinted in his *The Nature of Culture* (Chicago, 1952). See also Veblen's *Theory of the Leisure Class*, Ch. 7, "Dress As an Expression of the Pecuniary Culture," reprinted in *The Portable Veblen*, pp. 197-214. For a commentary on Veblen's theory of dress and fashions, see Quentin Bell, *On Human Finery* (London, 1947). See also Douglas Gorsline, *What People Wore* (New York, 1952); Winthrop Sargeant, "Fifty Years of American Women," in *Life* (Jan. 2, 1950), p. 64; Edmund Bergler, *Fashion and the Unconscious* (New York, 1953), and Wilder Hobson, "Business Suit," on the American businessman's costume, *Fortune* (July 1948). The quote about obsolescence in the fashion industry is from *Time* (July 3, 1950), p. 72.

SEC. 4—*Varieties of American Character:* On the American personality in profile, I have found David Riesman's perceptive explorations into the minds of Americans, *The Lonely Crowd* (rev. ed., New York, 1953), and *Faces in the Crowd*, in collaboration with Nathan Glazer (New Haven, 1952) of considerable use. See also David Riesman, "Psychological Types and National Character," *American Quarterly* (Winter, 1953), pp. 325-43. Of further interest will be T. W. Adorno *et al.*, *The Authoritarian Personality* (New York, 1950); Daniel Bell, ed., *The New American Right* (New York, 1955); Robert Lindner, *Prescription for Rebellion* (New York, 1952) and *Must You Conform?* (New York, 1956); Peter Viereck, *The Unadjusted Man* (Boston, 1956), and Erich Fromm, *Man for Himself* (New York, 1947). For a specific personality orientation, see Karl Mannheim, *Ideology and Utopia* (New York, 1952), Ch. 9, "The Utopian Mentality." An excellent selection of readings will be found in Guy E. Swanson, Theodore M. Newcomb and Eugene L. Hartley, *Readings in Social Psychology* (rev. ed., New York, 1952). The reference in the text to Fromm's analysis of the "marketing orientation" is to *Man for Himself*. The reference to Peter Viereck is to *The Unadjusted Man*.

SEC. 5—*The Disorders of a Society:* In my discussion of social disorganization and pathology, I have drawn heavily upon Herbert A. Bloch, *Disorganization*,

Personal and Social (New York, 1952). Other works which deal generally with criminology are E. H. Sutherland, *Principles of Criminology* (Philadelphia, rev. ed., 1955); Ruth S. Cavan, *Criminology* (New York, 1952); Walter Bromberg, *Crime and the Mind* (Philadelphia, 1948); Hans von Hentig, *Crime: Causes and Conditions* (New York, 1947), and Gresham M. Sykes, *Crime and Society* (New York, 1956). On penology, see Robert M. Lindner, *Stone Walls and Men* (New York, 1946), and Donald Clemmer, *The Prison Community* (Boston, 1940). For an analysis of the life and mind of the criminal, see Hans von Hentig, *The Criminal and His Victim* (New Haven, 1946); Jean Evans, *Three Men* (New York, 1954); Sheldon Glueck and Eleanor Glueck, *500 Criminal Careers* (New York, 1930), and *The Professional Thief* by A Professional Thief (Chicago, 1937). Recent increases in the rate of juvenile delinquency in American cities have precipitated several studies. Among them are Albert K. Cohen, *Delinquent Boys: The Culture of Gangs* (Glencoe, 1955); William and Joan McCord, *Psychopathy and Delinquency* (New York, 1956), and Herbert A. Bloch and Frank T. Flynn, *Delinquency: The Juvenile Offender in America Today* (New York, 1956). See also Benjamin Fine, *1,000,000 Delinquents* (New York, 1955); Clifford Shaw and Henry D. McKay, *Juvenile Delinquency and Urban Areas* (Chicago, 1942); William F. Whyte, *Street Corner Society* (Chicago, 1943), and Frederick M. Thrasher, *The Gang* (Chicago, 1936). On alcoholism and narcotics addiction, see Ruth Fox and Peter Lyon, *Alcoholism: Its Scope, Cause and Treatment* (New York, 1955); Marie Nyswander, *The Drug Addict As a Patient* (New York, 1956); Isador Chein and Eva Rosenfeld, "Juvenile Heroin Users in New York City," *Law and Contemporary Problems* (Winter, 1957), and Isador Chein, "Narcotics Use Among Juveniles," *Social Work* (April 1956), pp. 50-60; also my *New York Post* columns on narcotics (June 4-8, 1956). On crime among the middle and upper classes, see Edwin H. Sutherland, *White Collar Crime* (New York, 1949), and Donald R. Cressey, *Other People's Money: The Social Psychology of Embezzlement* (Glencoe, 1953). A psychiatric approach to homicide will be found in Fredric Wertham, *The Show of Violence* (New York, 1949) and *The Circle of Guilt* (New York, 1956).

On social disorders, see also Robert M. Lindner, *Must You Conform?* and *Rebel Without a Cause* (New York, 1944); Franz Alexander and Hugo Staub, *The Criminal, The Judge, and The Public* (rev. ed., Glencoe, 1956); Glanville Williams, *The Sanctity of Life and the Criminal Law* (New York, 1957); W. C. Reckless, *The Crime Problem* (New York, 1950), and C. B. Vedder, Samuel Koenig, R. E. Clark, eds., *Criminology: A Book of Readings* (New York, 1953). For an insight into gambling, see Thorstein Veblen, *The Theory of the Leisure Class* "The Belief in Luck."

The reference in the text to statistics on juvenile delinquency is to Herbert A. Bloch and Frank T. Flynn, *Delinquency: The Juvenile Offender in America Today.*

SEC. 6—*Morals in Revolution,* and SEC. 7—*Society and Sexual Expression:* On the changes in American moral codes, I have found a number of works useful. See especially Alfred C. Kinsey and Associates, *Sexual Behavior in the Human Male* (Philadelphia, 1948) and *Sexual Behavior in the Human Female* (Philadelphia, 1953). For critical and interpretive material on the Kinsey studies, see Jerome Himelhoch and Sylvia Fleis Fava, eds., *Sexual Behavior in American Society: An Appraisal of the First Two Kinsey Reports* (New York, 1955); Edmund Bergler and William S. Kroger, *Kinsey's Myth of Female Sexuality* (New York, 1954); Seward Hiltner, *Sex Ethics and the Kinsey Reports* (New York, 1953), and Albert Ellis, ed., *Sex Life of the American Woman and the Kinsey Report* (New York, 1954). Other commentaries upon sexual expression in America include Abraham N. Franzblau, *The Road to Sexual Maturity* (New York, 1954); George W. Henry, *All the Sexes* (New York, 1955); Pitirim Sorokin, *The American Sex Revolution* (Boston, 1956), and Robert E. Fitch, *The Decline and Fall of Sex* (New York, 1957). See also Sydney Ditzion, *Marriage, Morals, and Sex in America* (New York, 1953); Albert Deutsch, ed., *Sex Habits of American Men* (New York, 1948), and Clennan S. Ford and Frank A. Beach, *Patterns of Sexual Behavior* (New York, 1951). For a description of the apotheosis of sex in America, see Winthrop Sargeant, "The Cult of the Love Goddess in America," *Life* (Nov. 10, 1947). On the standards of sexual normality, see Alfred Kinsey and Associates, "Concept of Normality and Abnormality in Sexual Behavior," *Psychosexual Development in Health and Disease* (New York, 1949). On homosexuality, see two books by Donald Webster Cory, *Homosexuality: A Cross-Cultural Approach* (New York, 1956), and *The Homosexual in America* (New York, 1951); also Edmund Bergler, *Homosexuality: Disease or Way of Life?* (New York, 1956);

A. M. Krich, *The Homosexuals* (New York, 1954), and Gordon Westwood, *Society and the Homosexual* (New York, 1953). On the shifting moral basis of American life, see The American Roundtable Series on *The Moral and Religious Basis of American Society*, compiled by Lewis Galantiere and sponsored by the Advertising Council (April 14, 1952). Also see Frederick Lewis Allen, *Only Yesterday* (New York, 1931); Alexis de Tocqueville, *op. cit.*, Vol. II, Book III; Lloyd Morris, *Postscript to Yesterday* (New York, 1947); L. T. Hobhouse, *Morals in Evolution* (rev. ed., New York, 1916), and Robin Williams, Jr., *American Society*, Ch. 10, in which the formulation by James Woodward mentioned in the text will be found.

The reference in the text to Lloyd Morris is to *Postscript to Yesterday;* Max Eastman's autobiography is *Enjoyment of Living* (New York, 1943). The reference to Albert Ellis is to *The Folklore of Sex* (New York, 1951). Sorokin's discussion of American sexual freedom will be found in *The American Sex Revolution.* The reference in the text to Arthur Hirsch is to *Sexual Misbehavior of the Upper Cultured* (New York, 1955). Herbert Blumer's remarks are from correspondence with the author.

sec. 8—*Life Goals and the Pursuit of Happiness:* On the life hopes of Americans, I have drawn upon a number of pertinent and helpful works. I have found Howard Mumford Jones, *The Pursuit of Happiness* (Cambridge, 1953) most useful. See also Robin Williams, Jr., *American Society*, Ch. 11, "Value Orientations in American Society," pp. 372-442; Kenneth S. Lynn, *The Dream of Success* (Boston, 1955); David Riesman, *Individualism Reconsidered* (Glencoe, 1954), Ch. 2, "Individualism and Its Contents," pp. 15-120, and *The Lonely Crowd.* For a discussion of psychoanalysis and the psychoanalytic approach to happiness, see Karen Horney's works, including *New Ways in Psychoanalysis* (New York, 1939) and *The Neurotic Personality of Our Time* (New York, 1937); Clara Thompson, *Psychoanalysis: Evolution and Development* (New York, 1950), and Clarence P. Oberndorf, *A History of Psychoanalysis in America* (New York, 1953). See also Erich Fromm, *The Sane Society* (New York, 1955), *Man for Himself* and *Escape from Freedom* (New York, 1941); and Herbert Marcuse, *Eros and Civilization* (Boston, 1955).

The reference in the text to James Plant is to *The Envelope* (New York, 1950). The remarks of Lawrence K. Frank are from correspondence with the author.

Lloyd Warner's stratification system is discussed in *Democracy in Jonesville* (New York, 1949). The reference in the text to Howard Mumford Jones is to *The Pursuit of Happiness.* The reference to Robert Lindner is to *Prescription for Rebellion.* Erik Erikson's observations will be found in *Childhood and Society* (New York, 1950). The reference in the text to Ernest Jones is to *The Life and Work of Sigmund Freud*, Vol. I (New York, 1953), Vol. II (New York, 1955), Vol. III (New York, 1957).

Chapter X: Belief and Opinion

sec. 1—*God and the Churches:* The position and function of religion in American life were observed by Alexis de Tocqueville, *op. cit.*, Vol. II, Book I, Chs. 5-8, and Book II, Chs. 9 and 11. Ralph H. Gabriel, *The Course of American Democratic Thought* (rev. ed., New York, 1956) presents a profound understanding of the relationships between the development of Christianity and democracy in this country. See also Louis B. Wright, *Culture on the Moving Frontier* (Bloomington, 1955), for a competent discussion of English religious influences. Two European classics shed much light on the contributions of religion to the capitalist economic system: R. H. Tawney, *Religion and the Rise of Capitalism* (New York, 1926) and Max Weber, *The Protestant Ethic and the Spirit of Capitalism* (London, 1930). H. Richard Niebuhr, *Social Sources of American Democracy* (New York, 1929), and A. P. Stokes, *Church and State in the United States* (New York, 1950) contribute much toward an understanding of religion in America. The basic psychological and philosophic analysis is William James, *Varieties of Religious Experience* (New York, 1907). See also my "Christian Culture and American Democracy," *American Quarterly* (Summer, 1954). Robert Elliot Fitch, "American Presidents and Protestant Types," *Christianity and Crisis* (June 1952) is an interesting study of national policy in view of the faiths of its shapers. Also of value is the pamphlet of the American Roundtable, Lewis Galantiere, ed., *The Moral and Religious Basis of the American Society* (New York, April 14, 1952).

Charles Wright Ferguson, *Confusion of Tongues* (New York, 1928) was one of the first significant discussions of modernism. Will Herberg, *Protestant, Catholic, Jew* (New York, 1955) presents a fresh view of the subject. See also Herbert Schneider, *Religion in 20th Century America* (Cambridge, 1952). The symposium, "Religion and the Intellectuals," published by *Partisan Review* (New York, 1950), considers the conflict between secular attitudes and the growing return to religion in the English speaking countries. Other specialized volumes are Ludwig Lewisohn, *The American Jew* (New York, 1950); Elliot E. Cohen, ed., *Commentary on the American Scene: Portraits of Jewish Life in America* (New York, 1953), and *Catholicism in America* (New York, 1954), an anthology compiled by *Commonweal*. See also Simon Noveck, ed., *Judaism and Psychiatry* (New York, 1956), and Philip Rieff's critical analysis of this book and its subject in *Midstream* (Summer, 1956). The religious affiliations of the American Negro are considered in Wm. W. Sweet, *The American Churches* (New York, 1948) and Liston Pope, *Kingdom Beyond Caste* (New York, 1957).

The study by Ruby Jo Kennedy mentioned in the text is "Single or Triple Melting Pot? Intermarriage Trends in New Haven, 1870-1940," *American Journal of Sociology* (Jan. 1954). Edmund Wilson's article on Lincoln's faith is "Abraham Lincoln: The Union As Religious Mysticism," *The New Yorker* (March 14, 1953), pp. 116-36. Toynbee's view of Negro religious creativity is found in *A Study of History*, Vol. II (London, 1934), pp. 218-20.

Books on religious freedom and separation of church and state are mentioned in the Notes for Further Reading for Ch. VI, Sec. 10. Other material on religious minority groups is listed in the Notes for Ch. VII, Sec. 5. Additional references to studies of the religious roots of American thought are found in the Notes for the next section.

SEC. 2—*American Thought: The Angle of Vision:* On America's intellectual history, I have chosen for this bibliography comparatively few works from the mass of material available. The classic and indispensable work is Vernon L. Parrington, *Main Currents in American Thought*, 3 vols. (New York, 1927-30; new ed., New York, 1956), which laid the groundwork for later volumes of its kind; also Merle Curti, *The Growth of American Thought* (New York, 1943); H. S. Commager, *The American Mind* (New Haven, 1950); Louis Hartz, *The Liberal Tradition in America* (New York, 1955), and Ralph H. Gabriel, *The Course of American Democratic Thought*. See also for general surveys Charles and Mary Beard, *The American Spirit* (New York, 1942); Ralph Barton Perry, *Characteristically American* (New York, 1949); Daniel Boorstin, *The Genius of American Politics* (Chicago, 1953), and Richard Hofstadter, *The American Political Tradition* (New Nork, 1948). Hans

Kohn's penetrating *American Nationalism* (New York, 1957), expanded from Ch. 6 of his *The Idea of Nationalism* (New York, 1944), discusses one of the basic ideological strains of American development. See also Harvey Wish, *Society and Thought in America* (New York, 1950-2).

The early period in American history is discussed in T. J. Wertenbaker, *The Puritan Oligarchy* (New York, 1947), and in several books by Perry Miller: *Errand into the Wilderness* (Cambridge, 1956); *Jonathan Edwards* (New York, 1949), and *The Puritans* (Boston, 1938), edited with Thomas Johnson. The transcendentalist period is studied in F. O. Matthiessen's remarkable *The American Renaissance* (New York, 1941), and in Lewis Mumford, *The Golden Day* (New York, 1926; new ed., New York, 1957), which includes a perceptive essay on "The Pragmatic Acquiescence"; see also Perry Miller, ed., *The Transcendentalists* (Cambridge, 1950). Van Wyck Brooks's monumental multi-volume *Makers and Finders: A History of the Writers in America, 1800-1915* (New York, 1936-42) is particularly outstanding in the middle period. It is, of course, impossible to understand that period without study of such basic sources as Ralph Waldo Emerson, *Complete Essays and Other Writings* (New York, Modern Library, 1940), and Henry David Thoreau, "On Civil Disobedience," from *Collected Works* (New York, 1906).

Richard Hofstadter, *Social Darwinism in American Thought* (Philadelphia, 1944) provided essential clarification of the post-Darwinian era. The spectrum of American reactions, in terms of their social import, to the appearance of Charles Darwin, *The Origin of Species* (London, 1859), is indicated by William Graham Sumner, *Essays*, 2 vols. (New Haven, 1934) and *Folkways* with introduction by W. L. Phelps (Boston, 1940); Lester Ward, *Dynamic Sociology*, 2 vols. (New York, 1883), and John Fiske, *American Political Ideas* (New York, 1885). The social protests emerging late in the nineteenth century as responses to the Darwinian status quo are expressed in Henry George, *Progress and Poverty* (New York, 1880); Edward Bellamy, *Looking Backward* (Boston, 1889), and Walter Rauschenbusch, *Christianizing the Social Order* (New York, 1912). *The Auto-Biography of Lincoln Steffens* (New York, 1931) sheds much light on the early 20th century reform movements. The pragmatic method first formulated during this period is discussed in Morton White's distinguished volume, *Social Thought in America: Revolt Against Formalism* (New York, 1949), and Morris R. Cohen, *Amer-*

ican Thought (Glencoe, 1954). See also Perry Miller, ed., *American Thought: Civil War to World War* (New York, 1954), especially the Introduction. The major primary sources are Chauncey Wright, *Philosophical Discussions* (New York, 1877); Charles Peirce (M. R. Cohen, ed.), *Chance, Love, and Logic* (New York, 1923); Oliver Wendell Holmes, Jr., *The Common Law* (New York, 1881); William James, *Pragmatism* (New York, 1907); John Dewey (Joseph Ratner, ed.), *Intelligence in the Modern World* (New York, 1939), and Thorstein Veblen (Max Lerner, ed.), *The Portable Veblen* (New York, 1948). The revolt among historians is best expressed in James Harvey Robinson, *The New History* (New York, 1912), and Charles A. Beard, *An Economic Interpretation of the Constitution* (New York, 1913). In the meantime, Josiah Royce, *A Philosophy of Loyalty* (New York, 1908) still held to the idealist tradition. Among the prognostic works of the period are Brooks Adams, *The Law of Civilization and Decay* (New York, 1896); Herbert Croly, *The Promise of American Life* (New York, 1909), and Henry Adams, *The Education of Henry Adams* (Boston, 1918). See also Louis D. Brandeis, *The Curse of Bigness* (New York, 1934). On William James, see Ralph Barton Perry, *The Thought and Character of William James*, 2 vols. (Boston, 1935); and on Veblen, See Joseph Dorfman, *Thorstein Veblen and His America* (New York, 1934); David Riesman, *Thorstein Veblen: A Critical Interpretation* (New York, 1953); Bernard Rosenberg, *The Values of Veblen* (Washington, 1956); my introduction to *The Portable Veblen* and my essay on Veblen in *Ideas Are Weapons* (New York, 1939). See also my article on Beard in the same volume, and my "The Political Theory of Charles A. Beard," *American Quarterly* (Winter, 1950).

Randolph Bourne, *Liberalism in America* (New York, 1919) and *A History of a Literary Radical and Other Essays* (New York, 1920), as well as Harold Stearns, ed., *Civilization in the United States* (New York, 1928), are volumes that confront critically the framework of American society. On Bourne, see my essay in *Ideas Are Weapons,* and Louis Filler, *Randolph Bourne* (Washington, 1943).

Daniel Aaron, *Men of Good Hope* (New York, 1951); Charles A. Madison, *Critics and Crusaders* (New York, 1947), and Harvey Goldberg, ed., *American Radicals* (New York, 1957), written from the position of the extreme Left, consider individuals within the tradition of protest. See also Louis Filler's valuable *Crusaders for American Liberalism* (New York,

1938). By far the best histories of the recent period are Eric Goldman, *Rendezvous with Destiny* (New York, 1952), and Richard Hofstadter, *The Age of Reform* (New York, 1955). For important literary trends, see Malcolm Cowley, ed., *After the Genteel Tradition: American Writers Since 1910* (New York, 1937), and Carl Van Doren, *Contemporary American Novelists, 1900-1920* (New York, 1949). Alfred Kazin, *On Native Grounds* (New York, 1942) is an outstanding discussion of contemporary American literature, with an awareness of its social context.

David A. Shannon, *The Socialist Party of America* (New York, 1955) is a relatively short but revealing history of American socialism. Donald Drew Egbert and Stow Parsons, *Socialism and American Life*, 2 vols. (Princeton, 1952) contains Daniel Bell's perceptive and lucidly written essay on "The Background and Development of Marxian Socialism in the United States," pp. 213-394. The second volume has the most complete bibliography available on the field. Theodore Draper, *The Roots of American Communism* (New York, 1957), a scholarly study of the formative years of the Communist party, is the first of a series of Fund for the Republic volumes under the general editorship of Clinton Rossiter. Others supervising volumes in the project are Daniel Aaron, Daniel Bell, William Goldsmith, Moshe Decter, Donald Egbert, Nathan Glazer, Robert Iversen, Earl Latham, John P. Roche, Ralph L. Roy, Draper, and David A. Shannon. Another forthcoming history of the American Communist party is by Irving Howe and Lewis Coser.

Walter Lippmann, *The Good Society* (Boston, 1937) is a classic statement of conservative thought. Significant also is the enthusiastic reception accorded by American conservatives to Frederich A. Hayek, *The Road to Serfdom* (Chicago, 1944), and Ludwig Von Mises, *Human Action* (London, 1949). See also Russell Kirk, *The Conservative Mind* (Chicago, 1953), written from the position of the radical Right, which contains an excellent bibliography of this position; Peter Viereck, *Conservatism Revisited* (New York, 1949), and Clinton Rossiter, *Conservatism in America* (New York, 1955). Daniel Bell, ed., *The New American Right* (New York, 1955) analyzes sources of the reactionary movements in contemporary America.

The disintegration of liberal militancy is chronicled in Edgar Kemler, *The Deflation of American Ideals* (Washington, 1941), of which the last sections are most relevant, and Arthur Ekirch, *The Decline of American Liberalism* (New York, 1955).

Joseph Dorfman, *The Economic Mind in American Civilization,* 3 vols. (New York, 1946-49) is an exhaustive study of economic thought in the United States. Additional material on specific topics is cited in the Notes for Further Reading for the relevant sections.

SEC. 3—*The Higher and Lower Learning:* My discussion of education draws heavily on Thorstein Veblen, *The Higher Learning in America* (New York, 1918), and upon Merle Curti, *The Social Ideas of American Education* (New York, 1935). Also important here is W. Lloyd Warner and Robert J. Havighurst, *Who Shall Be Educated?* (London, 1946).

Among the most significant volumes of American educational philosophy are John Dewey, *Democracy and Education* (New York, 1916); Robert M. Hutchins, *Higher Learning in America* (New York, 1935), and *The Conflict of Education in a Democratic Society* (New York, 1953); Horace M. Kallen, *The Education of Free Men* (New York, 1949), and William H. Kilpatrick, *Philosophy of Education* (New York, 1951). See also two European works: Bertrand Russell, *Education and the Social Order* (London, 1932), and Karl Mannheim, *Freedom, Power, and Democratic Planning* (London, 1951), Ch. 10, "Education As Groundwork." Two helpful sources are the *Forty-first Yearbook* (Bloomington, Illinois, 1942), and the *Fifty-fourth Yearbook* (Bloomington, 1955) of the National Society for the Study of Education. Of relevance is Harold Rugg and Charles W. Withers, *Social Foundations of Education,* 2 vols. (New York, 1941). James Bryant Conant, *Education in a Divided World* (Cambridge, 1949) evaluates the goals of American education in the face of the Soviet challenge. David Riesman, *Constraint and Variety in American Education* (Lincoln, 1956) analyzes recent trends in the educational world. See also George Counts, *Education and American Civil Liberties* (New York, 1952).

The President's Committee on Education Beyond the High School, *Second Report to the President* (Washington, 1957) is an excellent appraisal of the current problems. See also Paul Woodring, *Let's Talk Sense About Our Schools* (New York, 1953). Arthur Bestor, *The Retreat from Learning in Our Public Schools* (Urbana, 1953) and *Restoration of Learning* (New York, 1955) are sharply critical of current educational procedures. A brief but sharp and documented attack on Hutchins, Woodring and Bestor is James C. Bay, "Our Public Schools: Are They Failing?" *Nation* (June 26, 1954). The Reconstructionist position is represented in Theodore Brameld, *Ends and Means in Education: A Mid-Century Appraisal* (New York, 1950); see also Marie Syrkin, *Your School, Your Children* (New York, 1944). See also "Education: Now and to Come," *Antioch Review* (Fall, 1955), as well as the chapter on education in Duncan Aikman, *The Turning Stream* (New York, 1948). John Walker Powell, *Learning Comes of Age* (New York, 1956) is a study of adult education. (See also C. Hartley Grattan, *In Quest of Knowledge* (New York, 1955). On teaching, see Jacques Barzun, *Teacher in America* (new ed., New York, 1956), and Gilbert Highet's work, *The Art of Teaching* (New York, 1950).

Problems of academic freedom are the subject of a Columbia University project which has produced two excellent volumes: Richard Hofstadter and Walter Metzger, *Development of Academic Freedom in the United States* (New York, 1955), and Robert MacIver, *Academic Freedom in Our Time* (New York, 1955). The Goslin case, to which there were many parallels, is the subject of David Hubbard, *This Happened in Pasadena* (New York, 1951). The "Textbook Problem" is discussed by Fred Hechinger and others in the *Saturday Review* (April 19, 1952). Other volumes on academic freedom are listed in the Notes for Further Reading for Ch. VI, Sec. 10.

SEC. 4—*Profile of the Press:* On the press, see Morris L. Ernst, *The First Freedom* (New York, 1946) for an affirmation of the principle of a free press and an attack on recent trends toward monopoly, and E. B. White, "The Vanishing Marketplace of Ideas," *The New Yorker* (March 16, 1946). The most significant discussion on press liberties and responsibility is *The Report of the Commission on a Free Press* (Chicago, 1947). I have dealt with this topic in "Freedom in the Opinion Industries," *Ideas Are Weapons,* and "Seven Deadly Press Sins," *Actions and Passions* (New York, 1949). For an excellent study of the daily press, see Alfred McClung Lee, *The Daily Newspaper in America* (New York, 1937), and Gordon W. Allport and J. Faden, "The Psychology of Newspapers," *Public Opinion Quarterly* (Dec. 1940). The role of the newspaper in American daily life is considered in Bernard Berelson, "What Missing the Newspaper Means," in Paul Lazarsfeld *et al.,* eds., *Communications Research: 1948-49* (New York, 1949), pp. 11-29.

Of interest also is Louis L. Snyder and Richard B. Morris, eds., *A Treasury of Great Reporting* (New York, 1949). I can only briefly cite the biographies of Barons of Opinion like Greeley, Bennett, Pulitzer, Hearst, and Scripps, as well as volumes on individual newspapers, but this listing would be incomplete if I did not mention Meyer Berger, *The Story of the New York Times* (New York, 1951).

The reference to Waldo Frank is from Ch. 10 of *Rediscovery of America* (New York, 1929). Marvin Craeger is quoted by Llewellyn White in "Milwaukee: A Good Paper Pays Off," *The Reporter* (Aug. 29, 1950). James Wechsler's statement comes from his discussion with August Heckscher on "Can Newspapers Survive WithoutSex?" *The Saturday Review* (July 24, 1950). The Max Ascoli citation is his article in a special issue on the press of *The Reporter* (Feb. 14, 1950). Reuben Maury is discussed by John Bainbridge in "Editorial Writer," a Profile in *The New Yorker* (May 24, 31, June 7, 1947). The Irving Dilliard citation on press coverage of the 1952 campaign comes from the Louis D. Brandeis Memorial Lecture at Brandeis University in April 1953 and in 1957 from the Wm. A. White Foundation Lecture at the University of Kansas. Justice Holmes is quoted from his opinion in *Abrams vs. U.S.*, as cited in Max Lerner, ed., *The Mind and Faith of Justice Holmes* (Boston, 1943), p. 312.

SEC. 5—*Revolution in the Big Media:* On the transformation of public communication, I have found the following helpful: W. Lloyd Warner, *American Life: Dream and Reality* (Chicago, 1953), Ch. 10, "Mass Media"; Bernard Berelson and Morris Janowitz, eds., *Reader in Public Opinion and Mass Communication* (Glencoe, 1950), including especially David Riesman and Reuel Denney, "Do the Mass Media 'Escape' from Politics?"; and Daniel Katz *et al.*, eds., *Public Opinion and Propaganda: A Book of Readings* (New York, 1954). For further references to the Big Media, see the Notes for Further Reading for Ch. XI (The Arts and Popular Culture).

The reference in the text to W. Lloyd Warner is to *American Life; Dream and Reality.* The reference to Ernst Cassirer is to *An Essay on Man* (New Haven, 1944). Martha Wolfenstein and Nathan Leites' discussion of the "good-bad girl" will be found in *Movies: A Psychological Study* (Glencoe, 1950), pp. 25-46. W. Lloyd Warner's study of "Big Sister" is in W. Lloyd Warner and William E. Henry, "The Radio Daytime Serial: A Symbolic Analysis," *Genetic Psychology Monographs* (1948), Vol. XXXVII, pp. 7-13, 55-64. The reference in the text to Thurman Arnold is to *The Folklore of Capitalism* (New Haven, 1937).

Chapter XI: The Arts and Popular Culture

SEC. 1—*Popular Culture in America:* On the public arts in America, I have found useful Bernard Rosenberg and David M. White, eds., *Mass Culture: The Popular Arts in America* (Glencoe, 1957). In that volume, see especially Walt Whitman, "From 'Democratic Vistas,'" pp. 35-40; Leo Lowenthal, "Historical Perspectives of Popular Culture," pp. 46-58; which first appeared in the *American Journal of Sociology* (1950), Vol. LV, pp. 323-32; Dwight McDonald, "A Theory of Mass Culture," pp. 59-73, which first appeared in *Diogenes* (Summer, 1953), pp. 1-17; Clement Greenberg, "Avant-Garde and Kitch," pp. 98-107, which first appeared in *The Partisan Reader* (New York, 1946), pp. 378-89. The editors of this collection have expressed opposing views on the subject in Bernard Rosenberg, "Mass Culture in America," pp. 3-12, and David M. White, "Mass Culture in America: Another Point of View," pp. 13-23. See also Ernest Van Den Haag, "Of Happiness and Despair We Have No Measure," pp. 504-36; Leslie A. Fiedler, "The Middle Against Both Ends," pp. 537-47, which originally appeared in *Encounter* (1955), Vol. V, pp. 16-23, and Melvin Tumin, "Popular Culture and the Open Society," pp. 548-56. I have also found helpful the American roundtable series on *Cultural Aspects of the American Society* (Jan. 21, 1953; Feb. 25, 1953), sponsored by the Advertising Council and compiled by Lewis Galantiere. Further discussions of popular culture will be found in Gilbert Seldes, *The Public Arts* (New York, 1956); Louis Kronenberger, *Company Manners* (Indianapolis, 1954); Marshall Davidson, *Life in America* (Boston, 1951), Vol. II, pp. 1-98; Bernard Iddings Bell, *Crowd Culture* (New York, 1952); D. W. Brogan, "The Problem of High Culture and Mass Culture," *Diogenes* (1954), No. 5, pp. 1-13; Max Horkheimer, "Art and Mass Culture," *Studies in Philosophy and Social Science* (1941), Vol. IX. See also Leo Gurko, *Heroes, Highbrows, and the Popular Mind* (Indianapolis, 1953); Foster Rhea Dulles, *America Learns to Play* (New York, 1940); David Riesman, "Some Observations on Changes in Leisure Attitudes," in his *Individualism Reconsidered* (Glencoe, 1954), pp. 202-18; G. A. Lundberg, Mirra Komarovsky, and Mary A. McIlnerny, *Leisure: A Suburban Study* (New York, 1934), and David Riesman and Reuel Denney, "Leisure in Urbanized Society," in Paul K. Hatt and Albert J. Reiss, Jr., eds., *Reader in Urban Sociology* (Glencoe, 1951), pp. 469-80.

The reference in the text to Matthew Arnold is to *Culture and Anarchy* (London, 1869). The reference to Maxwell Geismar is to *Rebels and Ancestors* (Boston, 1953). Gilbert Seldes' changing view on popular culture may be traced from *The Seven Lively Arts* (New York, 1924) to *The Public Arts* (New York, 1956). The quote from Fernand Leger will be found in Katharine Kuh, *Leger* (Chicago, 1953). The references to W. H. Auden and Lewis Galantiere are from the American roundtable series on *Cultural Aspects of the American Society,* sponsored by the Advertising Council.

SEC. 2—*Writers and Readers:* On the development of fiction in America, the essential basic reference works are V. L. Parrington, *Main Currents in American Thought,* 3 vols. (New York, 1927-30; new ed., 1956); Van Wyck Brooks's series, *Makers and Finders* (New York, 1936-52), and Alfred Kazin, *On Native Grounds* (New York, 1942). A useful reference is Robert Spiller *et al.,* eds., *A Literary History of the United States,* 3 vols. (New York, 1948). See also F. O. Matthiessen's study, *American Renaissance* (New York, 1941). Of interest here is D. H. Lawrence, *Studies in Classic American Literature* (New York, 1923); see also Robert E. Spiller, *The Cycle of American Literature* (New York, 1955). Three volumes of Maxwell Geismar's projected multi-volume history of the American novel have already appeared: *Writers in Crisis* (New York, 1942), *Last of the Provincials* (New York, 1947), and *Rebels and Ancestors* which is the most mature. Essential also is the work of Edmund Wilson, the best of the contemporary critics: *The Shock of Recognition* (New York, 1943), which he edited; *Axel's Castle* (New York, 1931); *Classics and Commercials* (New York, 1950), and *Shores of Light* (New York, 1952).

A listing of the milestones in the growth of American fiction would be less useful here than several of the works of criticism on their authors: Newton Arvin, *Hawthorne* (Boston, 1929) and *Herman Melville* (New York, 1950); F. W. Dupee, *Henry James* (New York, 1951); see also Irving Howe's essays on "Henry James: The Political Vocation" and on Hawthorne, Henry Adams, and James, "Some American Novelists: The Politics of Isolation," in his penetrating book, *Politics and the Novel* (New York, 1957). An excellent work on Dreiser is F. O. Matthiessen, *Theodore Dreiser* (New York, 1951). On Ernest Hemingway, see Carlos Baker, *The Writer As Artist* (Princeton, 1952). Among the students of Faulkner, those who have most effectively dealt with

his work are Malcolm Cowley in his introduction to *The Portable Faulkner* (New York, 1946), and Irving Howe in his *William Faulkner: A Critical Study* (New York, 1952).

Recent American writing is discussed by John Aldridge in *After the Lost Generation* (New York, 1951) and his article "America's Young Novelists: Uneasy Inheritors of a Revolution," *Saturday Review* (Feb. 12, 1949); also James T. Farrell, "The Fate of Writing in America," *New Directions 9* (New York, 1946). Of interest is Lionel Trilling's essay on "Contemporary American Literature and Its Relationship to Ideas," which first appeared in the *American Quarterly* (Fall, 1949) and was reprinted in his *The Liberal Imagination* (New York, 1950) as "The Meaning of a Literary Idea." See also my "Literature and Society" in *Ideas Are Weapons.* The reference to Harold Laski is to his *Faith, Reason, and Civilization* (New York, 1944), p. 171.

On the American literary audience, Alexis de Tocqueville wrote prophetically in *Democracy in America* of "Literary Characteristics of Democratic Times," in Vol. II, Book I, Ch. 12, pp. 58-64. Popular reading tastes in American history are studied in Frank Luther Mott, *Golden Multitudes: The Story of Best Sellers in the United States* (New York, 1947), and James D. Hart, *The Popular Book: A History of American Literary Taste* (New York, 1950). A curiously interesting work is Albert Johannsen, *The House of Beadle and Adams and Its Dime and Nickel Novels: The Story of a Vanished Literature,* 2 vols. (Norman, Oklahoma, 1950).

Contemporary publishing trends are discussed in William Miller, *The Book Industry* (New York, 1949), and Freeman Lewis' pamphlet, *Paperbound Books in America* (New York, 1952). The nature and implications of current reading habits are considered in Douglas Waples, Bernard Berelson, and F. R. Bradshaw, *What Reading Does to People* (Chicago, 1940); Bernard Berelson, "Who Reads What Books and Why?" *The Saturday Review* (May 12, 1951), and Clifton Fadiman, "The Decline of Attention," *ibid.* (Aug. 6, 1949). See also Christopher La Farge, "Mickey Spillane and His Bloody Hammer," *The Saturday Review* (Nov. 6, 1954), and Edmund Wilson, "Why Do People Read Detective Stories?" in his *Classics and Commercials* (New York, 1950). Other valuable articles and bibliographical material are included in the sections on detective fiction, comic books and magazines in Bernard Rosenberg and

David M. White, eds., *Mass Culture: The Popular Arts in America.*

SEC. 3—*Heroes, Legends, and Speech:* On folklore and language, source material on the nature of the contemporary American heroes will be found in the Notes for Further Reading for other sections of this chapter. The industrial capitalist heroes are discussed in the Notes for Ch. V, Sec. 2 ("The Rise and Decline of the Titan"). Constance Rourke, *American Humor* (New York, 1931) and *The Roots of American Culture* (New York, 1942) are valuable studies, and are discussed by Stanley Edgar Hyman, "Constance Rourke and Folk Criticism" in his *The Armed Vision* (New York, 1948).

Two excellent anthologies of American folk music are John A. Lomax and Alan Lomax, eds., *Folk Song: U.S.A.* (New York, 1948), and Margaret Bradford Boni, ed., *Fireside Book of Folk Songs* (New York, 1947). See also Clifton Fadiman, ed., *The American Treasury: 1455-1955* (New York, 1955); Ben C. Clough, ed., *The American Imagination at Work* (New York, 1947); Ben Lucien Burman, *Children of Noah* (New York, 1951), and Mody C. Boatright, *Folk Laughter on the American Frontier* (New York, 1949). Wallace Stegner's article, "Joe Hill: The Wobblies' Troubadour," *New Republic* (Jan. 5, 1948) sheds much light on radical folklore during the early years of this century. Among useful regional studies are B. A. Botkin, ed., *A Treasury of New England Folklore* (New York, 1948) and his *A Treasury of Southern Folklore* (New York, 1949); Earl Clifton Beck, *Lore of the Lumber Camps* (Ann Arbor, 1949); Vance Randolph, *Ozark Superstitions* (New York, 1947) and *We Always Lie to Strangers* (New York, 1951), and Harold Felton, ed., *The Legends of Paul Bunyan* (New York, 1947).

On language, see Margaret Schlauch, *The Gift of Language* (rev. ed., New York, 1955), and Bernard Wall, "Questions of Language," *Partisan Review* (Sept. 1948). The major study of American English is H. L. Mencken, *The American Language,* 3 vols., (New York, 1955). Other helpful volumes are Mitford M. Mathews, *A Dictionary of Americanisms* (Chicago, 1951); Donald Lloyd and Harry Warfel, *American English in Its Cultural Setting* (New York, 1956); Lester V. Berrey and Melvin Van Den Bark, *The American Thesaurus of Slang* (New York, 1947); Thomas Pules, *Words and Ways of American English* (New York, 1952); and Richard D. Mallery, *Our American Language* (New York, 1949). The reference to Leo Lowenthal is as quoted in C. Wright Mills, *White Collar* (New York, 1951), p. 236.

SEC. 4—*Spectator and Amateur Sports:* On American sports, there are regrettably few available sources. See Thorstein Veblen, *The Theory of the Leisure Class* (New York, 1899), Ch. 10, "Modern Survivals of Prowess," and Ch. 11, "The Belief in Luck"; David Riesman and Reuel Denney, "Football in America: A Study in Culture Diffusion," *American Quarterly* (Winter, 1951), pp. 309-25, and reprinted in Riesman's *Individualism Reconsidered,* pp. 242-57; S. K. Weinberg and H. Arond, "The Occupational Culture of the Boxer," *American Journal of Sociology* (March 1952), pp. 460-69. See also John R. Tunis, "Are We Sportsmen or What Are We?" *New York Times Magazine* (July 11, 1948), and the transcripts for the American Town Meeting, *How Can We Clean Up College Sports?* (March 13, 1951). An interesting discussion of baseball will be found in Jacques Barzun, *God's Country and Mine* (Boston, 1954), Ch. 8, "The Under-entertained."

SEC. 5—*Dream and Myth in the Movies:* On motion pictures in America, Hollywood and its inhabitants are discussed in Leo C. Rosten, *Hollywood* (New York, 1941) and Hortense Powdermaker, *Hollywood, the Dream Factory* (Boston, 1950). Bosley Crowther, *The Lion's Share* (New York, 1957) is a revealing study of an entertainment empire. For a content analysis of movies, see Martha Wolfenstein and Nathan Leites, *Movies, A Psychological Study* (Glencoe, 1950); also Siegfried Kracauer, "National Types As Hollywood Presents Them" in Rosenberg and White, *Mass Culture,* pp. 255-77, and "Hollywood's Terror Films," *Commentary* (1946), Vol. II, pp. 132-6. See also Frederick Elkin, "God, Radio, and the Movies," Rosenberg and White, pp. 308-14; Herbert J. Gans, "The Creator-Audience Relationship in the Mass Media: An Analysis of Movie Making," *ibid.,* pp. 315-24, and Frederick Elkin, "The Psychological Appeal of the Hollywood Western," *Journal of Educational Sociology* (1956), Vol. XXIV, pp. 72-86. On the social function of movies, see David and Evelyn T. Riesman, "Movies and Audiences," *American Quarterly* (Fall, 1952), pp. 195-202, which has also been included in his *Individualism Reconsidered,* pp. 194-201. On censorship of the movies, see Ruth A. Inglis, *Freedom of the Movies* (Chicago, 1947). Further commentaries upon Hollywood and the movies will be found in Gilbert Seldes, *The Public Arts,* pp. 1-60; Parker Tyler, *Magic and Myth of the Movies* (New York, 1957); Eric Larabee and David Riesman, "Company-Town Pastoral: The Role of Business in *Executive Suite,*" *Fortune* (1955), Vol.

LI, pp. 108-9, reprinted in Rosenberg and White, *op. cit.*, pp. 325-37, and Arnold Hauser, "Can Movies Be Profound?" *Partisan Review* (1948), pp. 69-73. Also see Henry Popkin, "Hollywood Discovers the Bible," *Midstream* (Summer, 1956), pp. 48-57 and "It Was This Way . . . See?" *Midstream* (Winter, 1957), pp. 108-11; also James Agee, "Comedy's Greatest Era," *Life* (Sept. 5, 1949), pp. 70-88. Several novels dealing with Hollywood are of permanent value: Nathanael West, *The Day of the Locust* (New York, 1939); F. Scott Fitzgerald, *The Last Tycoon* (New York, 1941), and Budd Schulberg, *The Disenchanted* (New York, 1950).

The reference in the text to Gilbert Seldes is to *The Great Audience* (New York, 1950), which also includes a good discussion of the role of sex in the movies, "Sex," pp. 68-81. The reference to Simone de Beauvoir is to her *The Second Sex* (New York, 1953). On the Hollywood divorce rate, see Leo Rosten, *Hollywood* (New York, 1941). The reference in the text is to Martha Wolfenstein and Nathan Leites, *Movies: A Psychological Study*. The reference to David Riesman is to his essay with Evelyn T. Riesman, "Movies and Audiences," *op. cit.*

SEC. 6—*Radio and TV: the World in the Home:* On radio and television, *Mass Culture, The Popular Arts in America,* edited by Bernard Rosenberg and David M. White, has been most helpful. In that volume, see especially Rolf B. Meyerson, "Social Research in Television," pp. 345-57; Gunther Anders, "The Phantom World of TV," pp. 358-67, which originally appeared in *Dissent* (1956), Vol. III, pp. 14-24; Murray Hausknecht, "The Mike in the Bosom," pp. 375-84; and T. W. Adorno, "Television and the Patterns of Mass Culture," pp. 474-88. For an over-all analysis of radio and television in American society, see Gilbert Seldes, *The Public Arts* (New York, 1956), and Charles A. Siepmann, *Radio, Television, and Society* (New York, 1950). Leo Bogart, *Age of Television* (New York, 1956), is also useful. For several studies of the content and social implications of radio broadcasts, see Herta Herzog, "On Borrowed Experience: An Analysis of Listening to Daytime Sketches," *Studies in Philosophy and Social Science* (1941), Vol. IX, pp. 65-96; Harold Lasswell, "Radio as an Instrument of Reducing Personal Insecurity," *ibid.*, pp. 49-64; W. Lloyd Warner and William E. Henry, "The Radio Daytime Serial: A Symbolic Analysis," *Genetic Psychology Monographs* (1948), Vol. XXXVII, pp. 7-13, 55-64, which also appears in Bernard Berelson and Morris Janowitz, eds., *Reader in Public Opinion and Communication* (Glencoe, 1953), and Hadley Cantril, Hazel Gaudet and Herta Hertzog, *Invasion of Mars* (Princeton, 1940). See also Paul K. Lazarsfeld and Harry Field, *The People Look at Radio* (Chapel Hill, 1946); Robert Merton, *Mass Persuasion* (New York, 1946); John Crosby, *Out of the Blue* (New York, 1952), and Thomas Whiteside, *The Relaxed Sell* (New York, 1954). The reference to Whiteside is to that volume. The reference in the text to John Crosby is to "The Seven Deadly Sins of the Air," *Life* (Nov. 6, 1950). The 1950 study on TV viewing among children is cited in Robert Shayon, *Television and Our Children* (New York, 1951), pp. 26 ff.

SEC. 7—*Jazz As American Idiom:* On native American music, much of value has been written. For a general history of jazz see Rudi Blesh, *Shining Trumpets: A History of Jazz* (New York, 1946) and Barry Ulanov, *A History of Jazz in America* (New York, 1952); also see Marshall Stearns, *The Story of Jazz* (New York, 1956), which contains an exhaustive bibliography. For biographical and autobiographical material, see Alan Lomax, *Mister Jellyroll* (New York, 1950); Louis Armstrong, *Satchmo* (New York, 1954); Robert Goffin, *Horn of Plenty: The Story of Louis Armstrong* (New York, 1947); Barry Ulanov, *Duke Ellington* (New York, 1946), and Rudi Blesh and Harriet Janis, *They All Played Ragtime* (New York, 1950).

Jazz as a subject for novelists occurs in Dorothy Baker, *Young Man with a Horn* (New York, 1938), and Duke Osborne, *Side Man* (New York, 1956). For general background on American jazz, see Melville J. Herskovits, *The Myth of the Negro Past* (New York, 1941); John A. Lomax and Alan Lomax, *Folk Song: U.S.A.,* and Howard W. Odum and Guy B. Johnson, *Negro Workaday Songs* (Chapel Hill, 1926). Also see William L. Grossman and Jack W. Farrell, *The Heart of Jazz* (New York, 1956); Leonard Feather, *Encyclopedia of Jazz* (New York, 1955); Eddie Condon and Thomas Sugrue, *We Called It Music* (New York, 1957); Billie Holliday and Bill Dufty, *Lady Sings the Blues* (New York, 1956); Milton Mezzrow and Bernard Wolfe, *Really the Blues* (New York, 1956); Wilder Hobson, *American Jazz Music* (New York, 1939); Winthrop Sargeant, *Jazz: Hot and Hybrid* (New York, 1956); and André Hodier, *L'Homme et Problèmes du Jazz* (Paris, 1954). See also T. W. Adorno, "On Popular Music," *Studies in Philosophy and Social Science* (1941), Vol. IX, No. 1, pp. 17-64. In Bernard Rosenberg and David M. White, *Mass Culture: The Popular Arts in America,* see S. I. Hayakawa, "Popular Songs Versus the Facts of Life," pp. 393-403; Monroe Berger, "The New Popularity of Jazz," pp. 404-7, and David Riesman, "Listening to Popular Music," pp. 408-17.

The reference in the text to Alan Lomax is to *Mister Jellyroll.* The reference to Wilder Hobson is to *American Jazz Music.* The reference to Wilfrid Mellers is to *Society and Music* (London, 1950).

SEC. 8—*Building, Design, and the Arts:* For American architecture and design, De Tocqueville spoke of the nature of American artistic creativity when he discussed "In What Spirit the Americans Cultivate the Arts," *Democracy in America,* Vol. II, Book I, Ch. 11, pp. 50-56. Horace Kallen's theoretical work, *Art and Freedom,* 2 vols. (New York, 1942) is a classic discussion. Also see Russell Lynes, *The Tastemakers* (New York, 1954), Ch. 15 on "The Art World."

The American art histories of importance are Oliver Larkin, *Art and Life in America* (New York, 1949); John I. H. Baur, *American Painting in the Nineteenth Century: Main Trends and Movements* (New York, 1953); Virgil Barker, *A Critical Introduction to American Painting* (New York, 1931) and *American Painting: History and Interpretation;* and E. P. Richardson, *Painting in America* (New York, 1956). Particularly on the early period, see James Thomas Flexner, *First Flowers of Our Wilderness* (New York, 1947), and *The Light of Distant Skies* (New York, 1954). Of biographical interest are Larkin's *Samuel F. B. Morse and Democratic Art* (Boston, 1954), and Francis Steegmuller, *The Two Lives of James Jackson Jarvis* (New Haven, 1951). See also *Early American Painting: The Abby Aldrich Rockefeller Collection* (New York, 1957).

The later period is studied in John I. H. Baur, *Revolution and Tradition in Modern American Art* (Cambridge, 1951); Jerome Melquist, *The Emergence of an American Art* (New York, 1942); T. B. Hess, *Abstract Painting: Background and American Phase* (New York, 1951); Andrew C. Ritchie, *Abstract Painting and Sculpture in America* (New York, 1951); and Frederick S. Wight, *Milestones of American Painting in Our Century* (New York, 1949).

The work of Lewis Mumford has added much to my understanding of American architecture. See his *The Brown Decades* (New York, 1941); *The South in Architecture* (New York, 1941); *Roots of Contemporary American Architecture* (New York, 1952), and *From the Ground Up* (New York, 1956). Other notable works are Wayne Andrews, *Architecture, Ambition, and Americans* (New York, 1955); James Marston Fitch, *American Building* (Boston, 1948), and John A. Kouwenhoven, *Made in America* (New York, 1948). Particularly on the early period, see Hugh S. Morrison, *Early American Architecture* (New York, 1952), and Anthony N. B. Garvan, *Architecture and Town Planning in Colonial Connecticut* (New Haven, 1951). Of specific interest is Carl Bridenbaugh, *Peter Harrison: First American Architect* (Chapel Hill, 1949).

On recent developments, see Talbott Hamlin, *Forms and Functions of Twentieth Century Architecture* (New York, 1952); and Carl Condit, *The Rise of the* drews, "Looking at the Latest of Frank Lloyd Wright, see the Feb. 1948 issue of *Architectural Forum;* also Wayne Andrews, "Looking at the Latest of Frank Lloyd Wright," *Perspectives, U.S.A.* (Summer, 1953), and Wright's own *The Future of Architecture* (New York, 1953). Walter Gropius, *The Scope of Total Architecture* (New York, 1955) is very valuable. See also the symposium on "What Is Happening to Modern Architecture?" in *Museum of Modern Art Bulletin* (1948).

On the American theater, an excellent analytical history of recent times is Alan S. Downer, *Fifty Years of American Drama, 1900-1950* (Chicago, 1951); other significant books on the contemporary theater in the United States are Eric Bentley, *The Dramatic Event: An American Chronicle* (New York, 1954), and Mary McCarthy, *Sights and Spectacles* (New York, 1956). John Gassner, *The Theatre in Our Times* (New York, 1954) devotes much attention to American playwrights. See also the works of our most creative dramatists: Eugene O'Neill, the anthology *Nine Plays* (New York, 1941), *Ah, Wilderness* (New York, 1933), *The Iceman Cometh* (New York, 1946), and *Long Day's Journey into Night* (New Haven, 1956); Tennessee Williams, *The Glass Menagerie* (New York, 1945), *A Streetcar Named Desire* (New York, 1947), and *Camino Real* (Norfolk, Conn., 1953); and *The Collected Plays of Arthur Miller* (New York, 1957), including *Death of a Salesman* and *A View from the Bridge.*

The reference in the text to André Malraux' "Museum Without Walls" is to his book of that title (New York, 1949), the first volume of his three-volume *The Psychology of Art* (New York, 1949-50). John Ruskin's "The Lamps of Power" is from his *Seven Lamps of Architecture* (New York, 1885).

SEC. 9—*Artist and Audience in a Democratic Culture:* On the relation of the creative artist to the public, several contributions have proved helpful. Among them are Gilbert Seldes, *The Great Audience;* Horace M. Kallen, *Art and Freedom,* 2 vols.; Kurt Lang, "Mass Appeal and Minority Taste," in Rosenberg and White, *Mass Culture,* pp. 379-84. See also the American Round Table series on *Cultural Aspects of the American Society.* Also of interest is William Phillips, ed., *Art and Psychoanalysis* (New York, 1957), which applies psychoanalytic theory to the creative process. See further André Maurois, "Art, Popular Art, and the Illusion of the Folk," *Partisan Review* (1951), Vol. XVIII, pp. 487-95; Max Horkheimer, "Art and Mass Culture," *Studies in Philosophy and Social Science* (1941), Vol. IX; and D. W. Brogan, "The Problem of High Culture and Mass Culture," *Diogenes* (1954), No. 5, pp. 1-13. On the man of letters in society, see Malcolm Cowley, *The Literary Situation* (New York, 1954); Allen Tate, *Man of Letters in the Modern World* (New York, 1955), and Edmund Wilson, *A Piece of My Mind* (New York, 1956), Ch. 10, "The Author at Sixty."

Chapter XII: America As a World Power

SEC. 1—*Among the Powers of the Earth,* SEC. 2—*The Shaping Currents,* and SEC. 3 —*National Interest and an Open World:* For the development of America in terms of her international role, among the most useful histories of American foreign policy are Samuel Flagg Bemis, *A Diplomatic History of the United States* (rev. ed., New York, 1942); S. F. Bemis and Grace Gardner Griffin, *Guide to the Diplomatic History of the United States, 1775-1921* (Washington, 1935); Thomas A. Bailey, *A Diplomatic History of the American People* (rev. ed., New York, 1950), and Julius W. Pratt, *History of U. S. Foreign Policy* (New York, 1955). An indispensable and monumental work is the 10-vol. Samuel Flagg Bemis, ed., *The American Secretaries of State and Their Diplomacy* (New York, 1929). See also Ruhl J. Bartlett, ed., *The Record of American Diplomacy: Documents and Readings in the History of American Foreign Policy* (New York, 1947). An article that sheds much light on early American diplomacy is Felix Gilbert, "The English Background of American Isolationism in the Eighteenth Century," *William and Mary Quarterly* (April 1949).

A brief but highly significant study of the twentieth century is George F. Kennan, *American Diplomacy, 1900-1950*

(Chicago, 1951); see also his *Russia Leaves the War* (Princeton, 1956), which is the first of his projected series on Russia. Trends in our relationship with Russia are studied in Thomas A. Bailey, *America Faces Russia: Russian-American Relations from Early Times to Our Day* (Ithaca, 1950). On relations with Asia, see A. Whitney Griswold, *The Far Eastern Policy of the United States* (New York, 1938), and Kenneth Scott Latourette, *The American Record in the Far East, 1945-1951* (New York, 1952). Daniel Aaron, ed., *America in Crisis* (New York, 1952) contains three excellent historical articles: Richard Hofstadter on "manifest destiny," Dexter Perkins on Woodrow Wilson, and Norman Holmes Pearson on the Nazi-Soviet pact.

The shaping of foreign policy in terms of national interest is discussed in Hans J. Morgenthau, *In Defense of the National Interest* (New York, 1951) and his *Scientific Man Versus Power Politics* (Chicago, 1947). For a comparable but not synonymous viewpoint, see George F. Kennan, *Realities of American Foreign Policy* (Princeton, 1954). For the work of Frederick L. Schuman, see *The Commonwealth of Man* (New York, 1952) and "International Ideas and the National Interest," in *Annals of the American Academy of Political and Social Science* (March 1952). Among other valuable contemporary analyses are Thomas K. Finletter, *Power and Policy* (New York, 1954); Thomas I. Cook and Malcolm Moos, *Power Through Purpose* (Baltimore, 1954); Charles B. Marshall, *The Limits of Foreign Policy* (New York, 1954), and Max Beloff, *Foreign Policy and the Democratic Process* (Baltimore, 1955). See also Richard C. Snyder and Edgar S. Furniss, *American Foreign Policy: Formulation, Principles and Programs* (New York, 1954), and Louis J. Halle, *Civilization and Foreign Policy* (New York, 1955). Brooks Adams, *America's Economic Supremacy* (new ed., New York, 1947) with commentary by Marquis Childs, contains some astute turn-of-the-century observations on America's role in the world.

On the role of the legislative branch in diplomacy, see Robert A. Dahl, *Congress and Foreign Policy* (New York, 1950), and Daniel S. Cheever and H. D. Haviland, *American Foreign Policy and the Separation of Powers* (Cambridge, 1952). On the impact of public opinion on foreign policy, Thomas A. Bailey, *The Man in the Street* (New York, 1948) is most useful. International affairs, atomic power, and limited war are discussed by Henry A. Kissinger, *Nuclear Weapons and Foreign Policy* (New York, 1957). A technical, specialized work is Richard C. Snyder, H. W. Bruck, and Burton Sapin, *Decision-Making As an Approach to the Study of International Politics* (Princeton, 1954). On the military influences, see the Snyder and Sapin pamphlet, "The Role of the Military in American Foreign Policy" (New York, 1954). For a discussion of General MacArthur's dismissal by President Truman and its meaning, see Arthur M. Schlesinger, Jr., and Richard M. Rovere, *The General and the President* (New York, 1951). On Henry L. Stimson, see Stimson and McGeorge Bundy, *On Active Service in Peace and War* (New York, 1947); on Dean Acheson, see Bundy, *The Pattern of Responsibility* (Boston, 1952), and on Arthur H. Vandenberg, see Arthur H. Vandenberg, Jr., ed., *The Private Papers of Senator Vandenberg* (Boston, 1952).

Sir John R. Seeley developed his views in *The Growth of British Policy* (Cambridge, England, 1895). The Josef Schumpeter citation is to his *Imperialism and the Social Classes* (New York, 1951). For the studies by Nicholas J. Spykman, see *American Strategy in World Politics* (New York, 1942) and *The Geography of Peace* (New York, 1944). The Herbert Croly reference is to *The Promise of American Life* (New York, 1909).

SEC. 4—*Landscape with Soldiers:* For the position of the military in America, Alexis de Tocqueville, in *Democracy in America*, discussed war and the military in Vol. II, Book III, Chs. 22-26, pp. 279-302. Thorstein Veblen gives particular attention to this area in *Imperial Germany and the Industrial Revolution* (New York, 1915) and *The Nature of Peace* (New York, 1917), both excerpted in Max Lerner, ed., *The Portable Veblen* (New York, 1948). On military conflict and the American experience, see Grayson Kirk and Richard Poate Stebbins, eds., *War and National Policy* (New York, 1942), and William F. Ogburn, *American Society in Warfare* (New York, 1944). See also Ernest W. Puttkammer, *War and the Law* (Chicago, 1944), and E. S. Corwin, *Total War and the Constitution* (New York, 1947). See also Samuel P. Huntington, *The Soldier and the State* (Cambridge, 1957).

Other works discussing the internal significance of military strength are Louis Smith, *American Democracy and Military Power* (Chicago, 1951); Hans Speier, *The Social Order and the Risks of War* (New York, 1952), and, especially, Walter Millis, *The Martial Spirit* (New York, 1931) and *Arms and Men* (New York, 1956). Particular discussions of the conflict between civilian and military power are Arthur Ekirch, *The Civilian and the Military* (New York, 1956) and Arthur M. Schlesinger, Jr., and Richard Rovere, *The General and the President* (New York, 1951), which considers the Truman-MacArthur controversy in terms of its institutional implications. On the soldier, see Samuel A. Stouffer's exhaustive study, *The American Soldier,* 2 vols. (Princeton, 1949), as well as Dixon Wecter's earlier *When Johnny Comes Marching Home* (Boston, 1944).

C. Wright Mills, *The Power Elite* (New York, 1956), in Chs. 8 and 9, considers the growth of the military elite and its relationship to other segments of the ruling group.

Vannevar Bush, *Modern Arms and Free Men* (New York, 1949), discusses the significance of "technical improvements" in modes of combat. An incisive discussion of government policies and public attitudes toward the atomic arms race is Rexford Tugwell, *A Chronicle of Jeopardy, 1945-1955* (Chicago, 1955). On the development of legislative policy on atomic energy, see Morgan Thomas, *Atomic Energy and Congress* (Ann Arbor, 1956). Of interest also is Richard A. Tybout, *Government Contracting in Atomic Energy* (Ann Arbor, 1956).

The Margaret Mead citation is to her *And Keep Your Powder Dry* (New York, 1942). The quotes from Holmes are found in Max Lerner, ed., *The Mind and Faith of Justice Holmes* (Boston, 1943), pp. 16, 23.

SEC. 5—*The American World Image,* and SEC. 6—*The World's Image of America:* On America in the community of nations, the notes for Secs. 1, 2, and 3 on American foreign policy, above, contain references to much material on America's own view of her position in the world. Several additional volumes, however, are important. Two books with great depth of understanding are Chester Bowles, *American Politics in a Revolutionary World* (Cambridge, 1956), and *Africa's Challenge to America* (Berkeley, 1956). Adlai E. Stevenson's perceptive 1954 Godkin Lectures at Harvard University, published as *A Call to Greatness* (New York, 1954), outline the pattern of American responsibility in the crisis world. Of interest also is Vera Micheles Dean, *The Nature of the Non-Western World* (New York, 1957). A three-part *Partisan Review* symposium on "Our Country and Our Culture" (May-June, July-Aug., Sept.-Oct. 1952) reveals the feelings of intellectuals on the quality of American culture in comparison to the rest of the world.

American-Asian Tensions (New York,

1956) is the subject of a helpful work edited by Robert Strausz-Hupe, Alvin J. Cottrell, and James Dougherty. Reinhold Niebuhr, *The Irony of American History* (New York, 1952) places the national experience in a world perspective. Barbara Ward, *Interplay of East and West* (New York, 1957), discusses the relative position of America in the world. See the study by Max Beloff, "The Projection of America Abroad," *American Quarterly* (Spring, 1949). For broader discussions of this topic, see Holvdahn Koht, *The American Spirit in Europe* (Philadelphia, 1949), and Lewis Galantiere, ed., *America and the Mind of Europe* (New York, 1952).

Merle Curti, "The Reputation of America Overseas, 1776-1860" in *American Quarterly* (Spring, 1949) gives excellent background material on the foreign view of America. The most significant volumes of European observation of America are Alexis de Tocqueville, *Democracy in America;* Lord James Bryce, *The American Commonwealth* (New York, 1888; rev. ed., New York, 1891; new ed., New York, 1950), and Harold J. Laski, *The American Democracy* (New York, 1948). Two particularly useful anthologies are H. S. Commager, ed., *America in Perspective* (New York, 1948), and Allan Nevins, ed., *America Through British Eyes* (New York, 1948). See also André Visson, *As Others See Us* (New York, 1948). Among the writers of individual Englishmen, see D. W. Brogan, *The American Character* (New York, 1944), and *American Themes* (London, 1947); Geoffrey Gorer, *The American People* (New York, 1948), particularly Ch. 1, "Europe and the Rejected Father," and Ch. 3, "The All-American Child"; and Wyndham Lewis, *America and Cosmic Man* (London, 1948). See also Stephen Potter, *Potter on America* (New York, 1957), and Brogan's article on "America Through British Eyes" in *Saturday Review* (Oct. 13, 1951).

Other revealing estimates are Alfonso Reyes, *The Position of America and Other Essays* (New York, 1950); Luigi Barzini, *Americans Are Alone in the World* (New York, 1953); H. J. Duteil, *The Great American Parade* (New York, 1953); and on the Russian view, Frederick C. Barghoorn, *The Soviet Image of the United States* (New York, 1950). An impressionistic but significant view is Jawaharlal Nehru, *Visit to America*

(New York, 1950). See also Daniel J. Boorstin, "America and the Image of Europe," *Perspectives, U.S.A.* (Winter, 1956) and his "American Nationalism and the Image of Europe," *The Mississippi Valley Historical Association* (April 1954).

SEC. 7—*The Destiny of a Civilization:* In preparing the Notes for Further Reading for Sec. 7, I am aware that many volumes listed above—those that see America as an Orwellian nightmare, those that see it in idyllic terms, and those that imply a mature perspective between these extremes—should be included; most of them are referred to in the notes for preceding chapters and are too numerous to repeat here. Several books, however, are uniquely relevant to this section: Lewis Mumford, *The Transformations of Man* (New York, 1956); Roderick Seidenberg, *Post-Historic Man* (Chapel Hill, 1950), and Amaury de Riencourt, *The Coming Caesars* (New York, 1957). "The Human Situation Today" in *The American Scholar* (Winter, 1955-56) contains several relevant articles, including my own "The Flowering of Latter Day Man." An excellent analysis of the American linear time perspective is Kenneth Winetrout, "What Time Is It?" *Bulletin of Atomic Scientists* (March 1953). I have previously presented my concepts of our destiny in *It Is Later Than You Think* (New York, 1938; rev. ed., 1943); *Ideas Are Weapons* (New York, 1939); *Ideas for the Ice Age* (New York, 1941); "The Human Condition" and "We Move Toward Tomorrow" from *Public Journal* (New York, 1945); and "Toward a Tragic Humanism" from *Actions and Passions* (New York, 1949). Walt Whitman's "Letter to Russia" is noted on p. 161 and quoted on p. 251 in Joseph Clifton Furness, ed., *Walt Whitman's Workshop* (Cambridge, 1928). The quote from Alexis de Tocqueville is from the conclusion of "The Three Races in the United States," *Democracy in America,* Vol. II (Vintage ed.), p. 452. The Albert Camus reference comes from *Actuelles 2: Chronicles 1948-1953* (Paris, 1953). Peter Drucker's comment is from his *The End of Economic Man* (New York, 1939), and Arnold Toynbee's statement about pushing master institutions to extremes is developed in his chapter on "The Failure of Self-Determination" in his *Study of History* as abridged by D. C. Somervell (New York, 1947).

Index

B

C

Supplementary Index